Ordnance Survey

STREET ATLAS
Greater Manchester

Contents

PHILIP'S

First colour edition published 1997
Reprinted 1997 by

Ordnance Survey®   and   George Philip Ltd
Romsey Road,   an imprint of Reed Books
Maybush,   Michelin House, 81 Fulham Road,
Southampton SO16 4GU   London SW3 6RB
                               and Auckland, Melbourne

ISBN 0-540-06485-8 (hardback)
ISBN 0-540-06486-6 (wire-o)

To the best of the Publishers' knowledge, the information in this atlas
was correct at the time of going to press. No responsibility can be
accepted for any errors or their consequences.

The representation in this atlas of a road, track or path is no evidence
of the existence of a right of way.

**The mapping between pages 1 and 171 (inclusive) in this atlas is
derived from Ordnance Survey® OSCAR® and Land-Line® data,
and Landranger® mapping.**

Ordnance Survey, OSCAR, Land-Line and Landranger are registered
trade marks of Ordnance Survey, the National Mapping Agency of
Great Britain.

Printed and bound in Spain by Cayfosa

Motorway (with junction number) 22a	
Primary route (dual carriageway and single)	
A road (dual carriageway and single)	
B road (dual carriageway and single)	
Minor road (dual carriageway and single)	
Other minor road	
Road under construction	
Railway	
Tramway, miniature railway	
Rural track, private road or narrow road in urban area	
Gate or obstruction to traffic (restrictions may not apply at all times or to all vehicles)	
Path, bridleway, byway open to all traffic, road used as a public path	

The representation in this atlas of a road, track or path is no evidence of the existence of a right of way

142 **Adjoining page indicators**
130 (The colour of the arrow indicates the scale of the adjoining page – see scales below)

141 The map area within the pink band is shown at a larger scale on the page indicated by the red block and arrow

Acad	**Academy**	Mon	**Monument**
Cemy	**Cemetery**	Mus	**Museum**
C Ctr	**Civic Centre**	Obsy	**Observatory**
CH	**Club House**	Pal	**Royal Palace**
Coll	**College**	PH	**Public House**
Ex H	**Exhibition Hall**	Resr	**Reservoir**
Ind Est	**Industrial Estate**	Ret Pk	**Retail Park**
Inst	**Institute**	Sch	**School**
Ct	**Law Court**	Sh Ctr	**Shopping Centre**
L Ctr	**Leisure Centre**	Sta	**Station**
LC	**Level Crossing**	TH	**Town Hall/House**
Liby	**Library**	Trad Est	**Trading Estate**
Mkt	**Market**	Univ	**University**
Meml	**Memorial**	YH	**Youth Hostel**

British Rail station	
Metrolink station	
Private railway station	
Bus, coach station	
Ambulance station	
Coastguard station	
Fire station	
Police station	
Casualty entrance to hospital	
Church, place of worship	
H	**Hospital**
i	**Information centre**
P	**Parking**
PO	**Post Office**
St Matthews CE Prim Sch	**Important buildings, schools, colleges, universities and hospitals**
	County boundaries
River Roch	**Water name**
	Stream
	River or canal (minor and major)
	Water
	Tidal water
	Woods
	Houses

■ The dark grey border on the inside edge of some pages indicates that the mapping does not continue onto the adjacent page

■ The small numbers around the edges of the maps identify the 1 kilometre National Grid lines

The scale of the maps on pages numbered in blue is 5.52 cm to 1 km (3½ inches to 1 mile)

0	¼	½	¾	1 mile
0	250m	500m	750m	1 kilometre

The scale of the maps on pages numbered in red is 11.04 cm to 1 km (7 inches to 1 mile)

0	220 yards	440 yards	660 yards
0	125m	250m	375m	½ kilometre

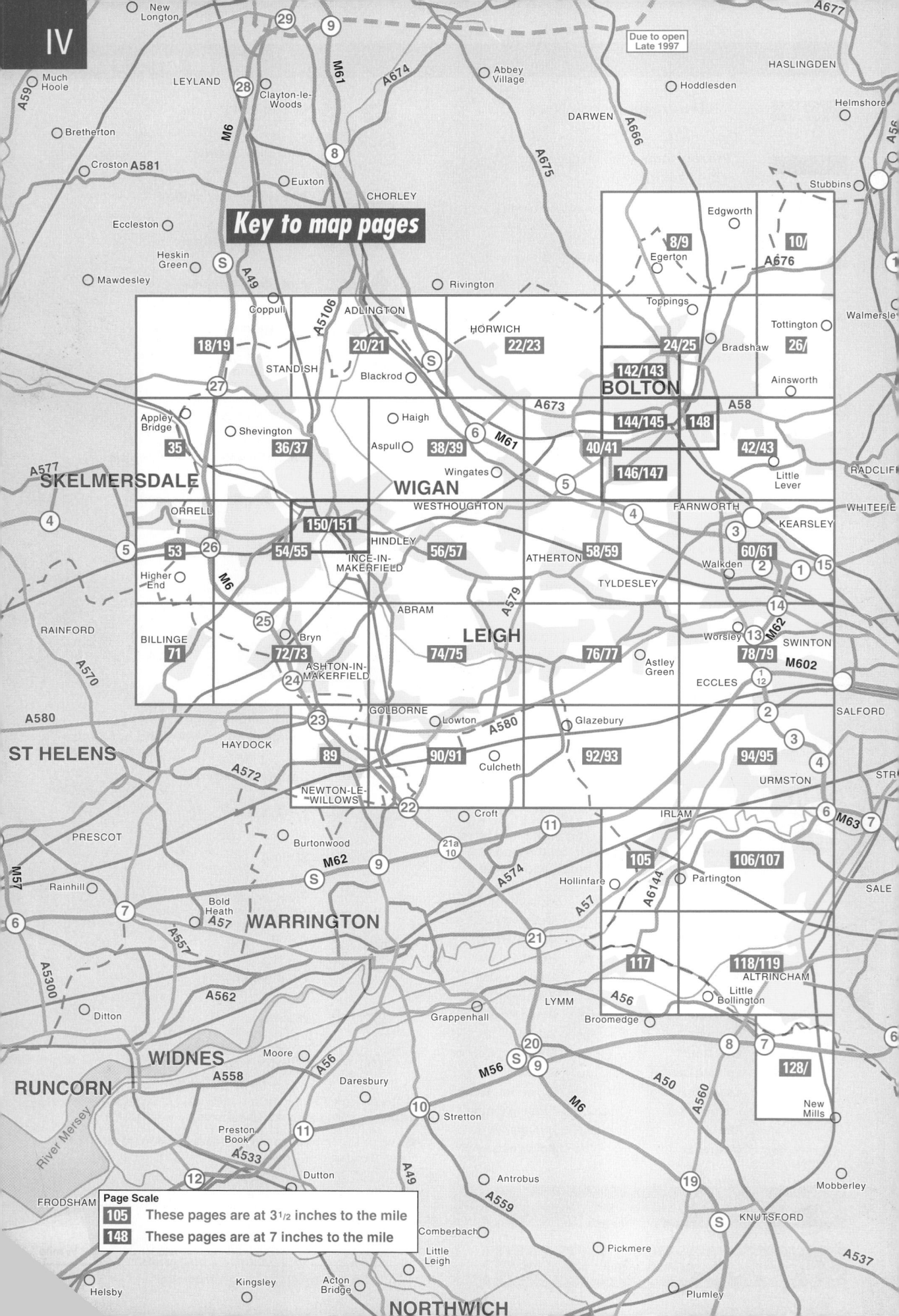

IV

Key to map pages

New Longton
Much Hoole
Bretherton
Croston **A581**
Eccleston
Mawdesley
Heskin Green
LEYLAND
Clayton-le-Woods
Euxton
CHORLEY
Rivington
Coppull
ADLINGTON
STANDISH
Blackrod
Shevington
Haigh
Aspull
Wingates
SKELMERSDALE
Appley Bridge
ORRELL
HINDLEY
INCE-IN-MAKERFIELD
WESTHOUGHTON
WIGAN
Higher End
Billinge
Bryn
ABRAM
ASHTON-IN-MAKERFIELD
LEIGH
Rainford
GOLBORNE
Lowton
Culcheth
HAYDOCK
NEWTON-LE-WILLOWS
Croft
ST HELENS
PRESCOT
Burtonwood
Rainhill
Bold Heath **A57**
WARRINGTON
Ditton
Moore
Daresbury
WIDNES
Grappenhall
RUNCORN
River Mersey
Stretton
Preston Book
Dutton
FRODSHAM
Helsby
Kingsley
Acton Bridge
NORTHWICH
Antrobus
Comberbach
Little Leigh
Pickmere
Plumley
Mobberley
KNUTSFORD

HASLINGDEN
Helmshore
Stubbins
Abbey Village
Hoddlesden
DARWEN
Edgworth
Egerton
Toppings
Bradshaw
Tottington
Walmersle
Ainsworth
BOLTON
Little Lever
RADCLIF
WHITEFIE
FARNWORTH
KEARSLEY
Walkden
Worsley
SWINTON
Astley Green
ECCLES
SALFORD
URMSTON
IRLAM
SALE
Partington
Hollinfare
Broomedge
LYMM
Little Bollington
ALTRINCHAM
New Mills

Due to open Late 1997

8/9 **10/**
18/19 **20/21** **22/23** **24/25** **26/**
142/143
144/145 **148**
35 **36/37** **38/39** **40/41** **42/43**
146/147
150/151
53 **54/55** **56/57** **58/59** **60/61**
71 **72/73** **74/75** **76/77** **78/79**
89 **90/91** **92/93** **94/95**
105 **106/107**
117 **118/119**
128/

Roads/motorways: A677, M61, A674, A675, A666, A56, A676, A58, A673, M61, A49, A577, A5106, A581, A59, A673, A579, A580, A580, A574, A572, M57, M62, A557, A5300, A562, A556, A558, A533, A49, A559, A50, A560, A537, A6144, A56, A57, A50, M56, M6, M602, M63, M62

Page Scale

105	These pages are at 3½ inches to the mile
148	These pages are at 7 inches to the mile

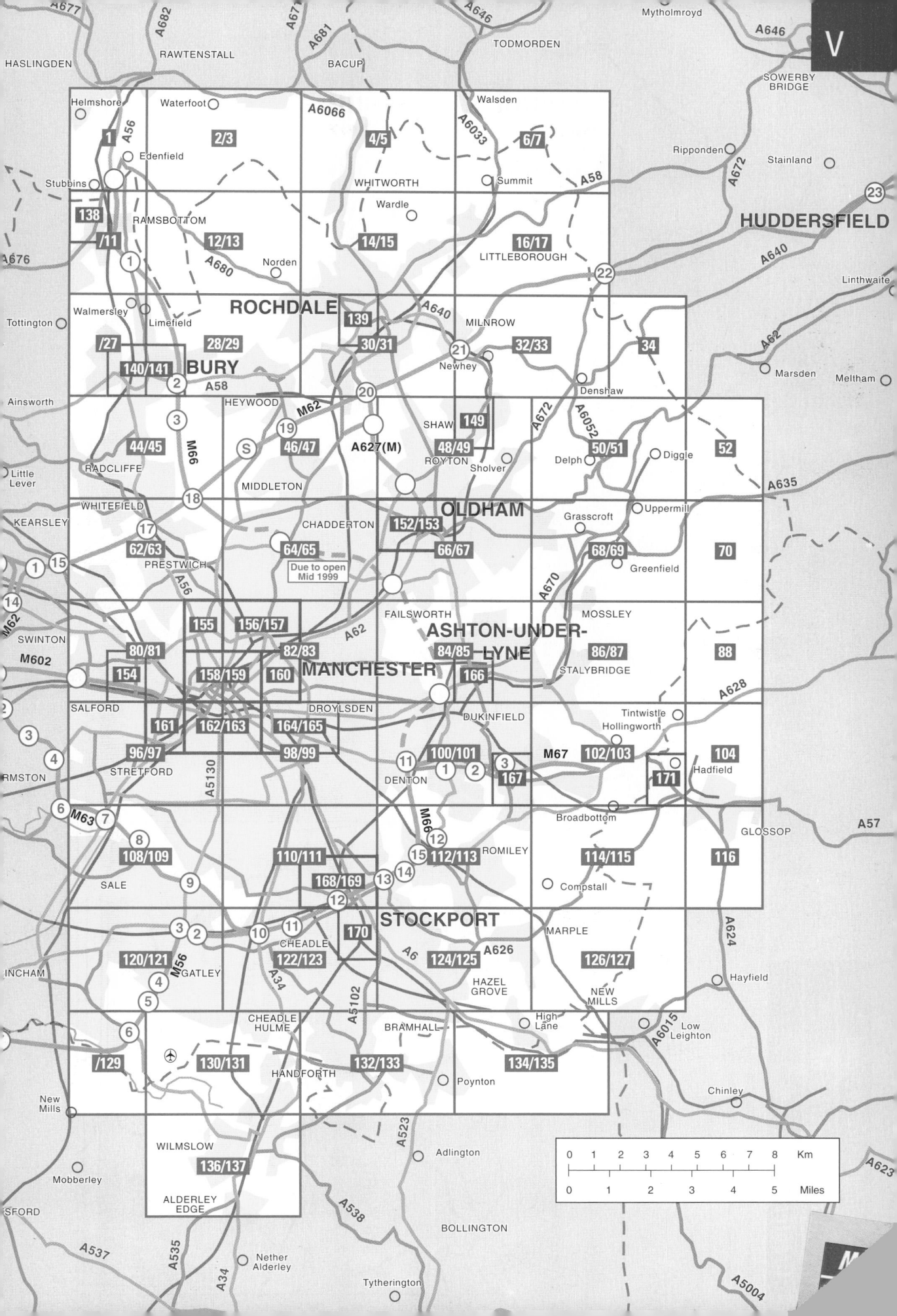

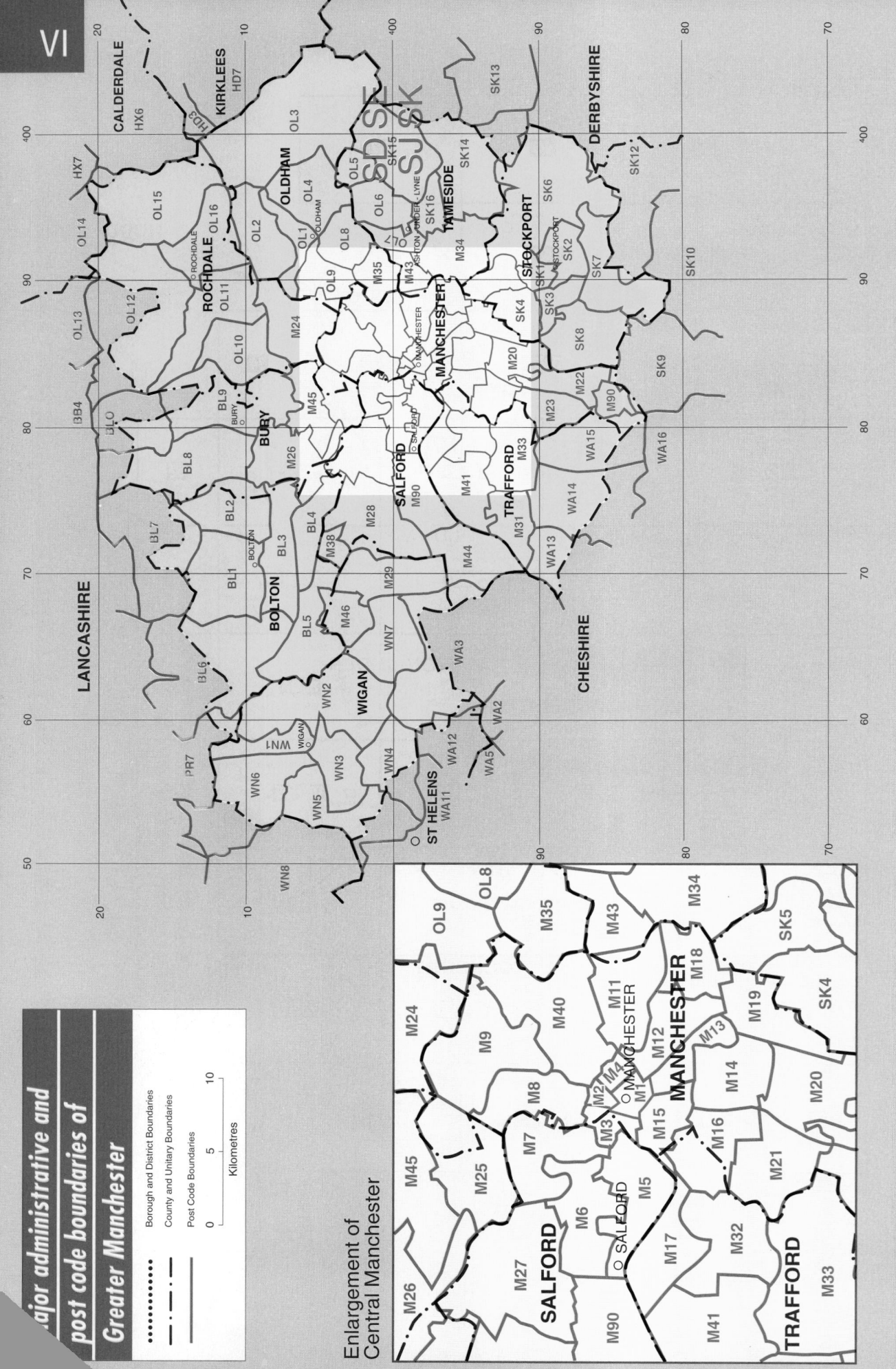

VI

ajor administrative and
post code boundaries of

Greater Manchester

.... Borough and District Boundaries

–·–· County and Unitary Boundaries

——— Post Code Boundaries

0	5	10

Kilometres

Enlargement of
Central Manchester

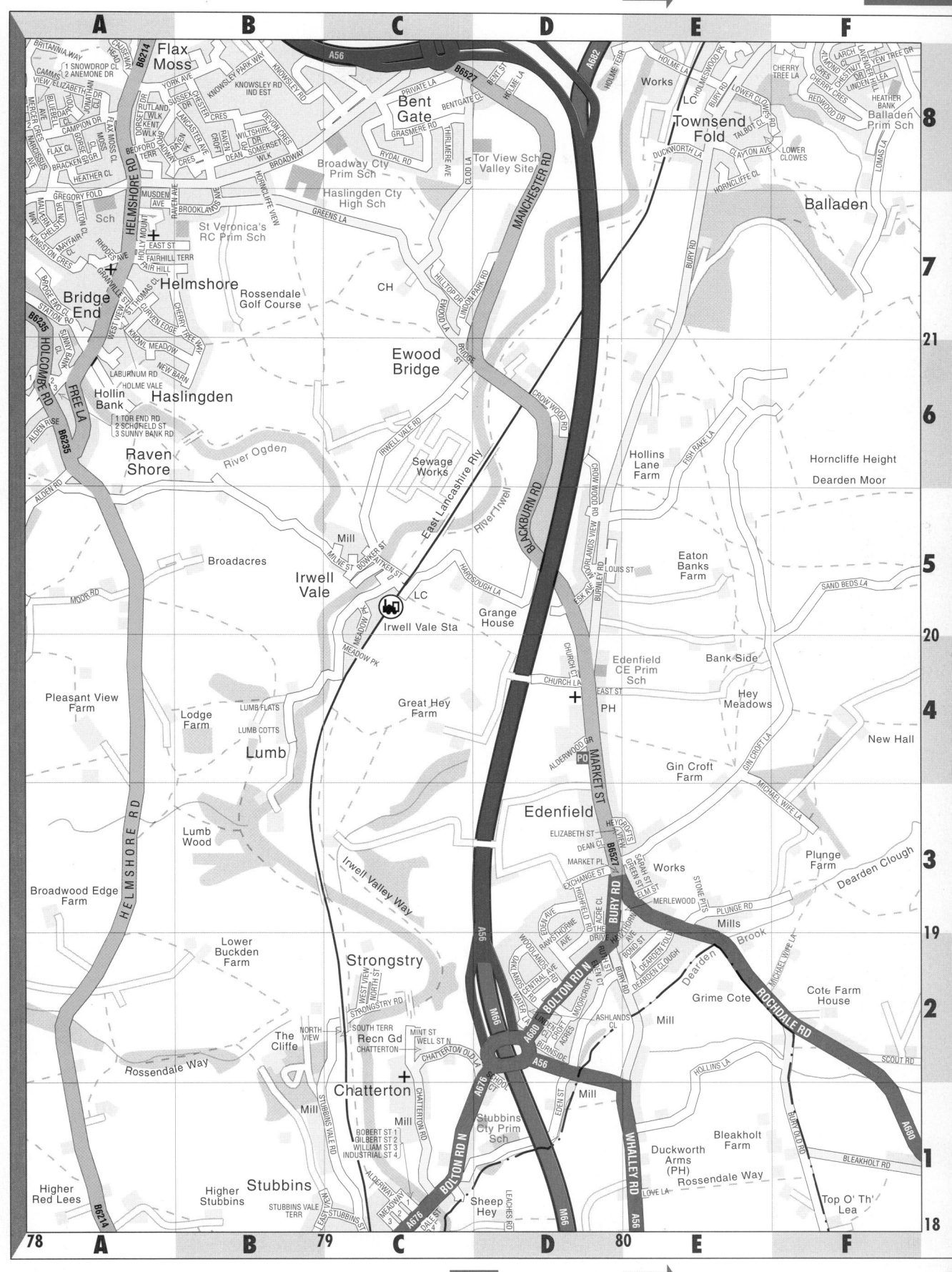

A · B · C · D · E · F

8
7
21
6
5
20
4
3
19
2
1
18

78 · A · B · 79 · C · D · 80 · E · F

Flax Moss
1 SNOWDROP CL
2 ANEMONE DR
Bent Gate
Townsend Fold
Works
LC
Balladen
Balladen Prim Sch
Heather Bank
Broadway Cty Prim Sch
Tor View Sch Valley Site
Haslingden Cty High Sch
St Veronica's RC Prim Sch
Helmshore
Rossendale Golf Course
CH
Ewood Bridge
Horncliffe Height
Dearden Moor
Bridge End
Hollin Bank
1 TOR END RD
2 SCHOFIELD ST
3 SUNNY BANK RD
Haslingden
Raven Shore
River Ogden
Sewage Works
Hollins Lane Farm
Fish Rake La
Sand Beds La
Broadacres
Mill
Irwell Vale
LC
Irwell Vale Sta
Grange House
Eaton Banks Farm
Bank Side
Pleasant View Farm
Lodge Farm
LUMB FLATS
LUMB COTTS
Lumb
Great Hey Farm
Edenfield CE Prim Sch
PH
Hey Meadows
New Hall
Lumb Wood
Irwell Valley Way
Gin Croft Farm
Plunge Farm
Dearden Clough
Broadwood Edge Farm
Lower Buckden Farm
Strongstry
ELIZABETH ST
DEAN CL
Market Pl
EXCHANGE ST
Edenfield
Works
Mills
Dearden Brook
Cote Farm House
Grime Cote
The Cliffe
NORTH VIEW
WEST VIEW
SOUTH TERR
Recn Gd
CHATTERTON
MINT ST
WELL ST N
Rossendale Way
Chatterton
Mill
Mill
Mill
Higher Red Lees
Higher Stubbins
Stubbins
ROBERT ST 1
GILBERT ST 2
WILLIAM ST 3
INDUSTRIAL ST 4
STUBBINS VALE TERR
Stubbins Cty Prim Sch
Sheep Hey
Duckworth Arms (PH)
Bleakholt Farm
Rossendale Way
Top O' Th' Lea
Grange House
Helmshore Rd
Holcombe Rd
Free La
Blackburn Rd
Manchester Rd
Bury Rd
Market St
Bolton Rd N
Whalley Rd
Rochdale Rd
A56
A680
M66
A676

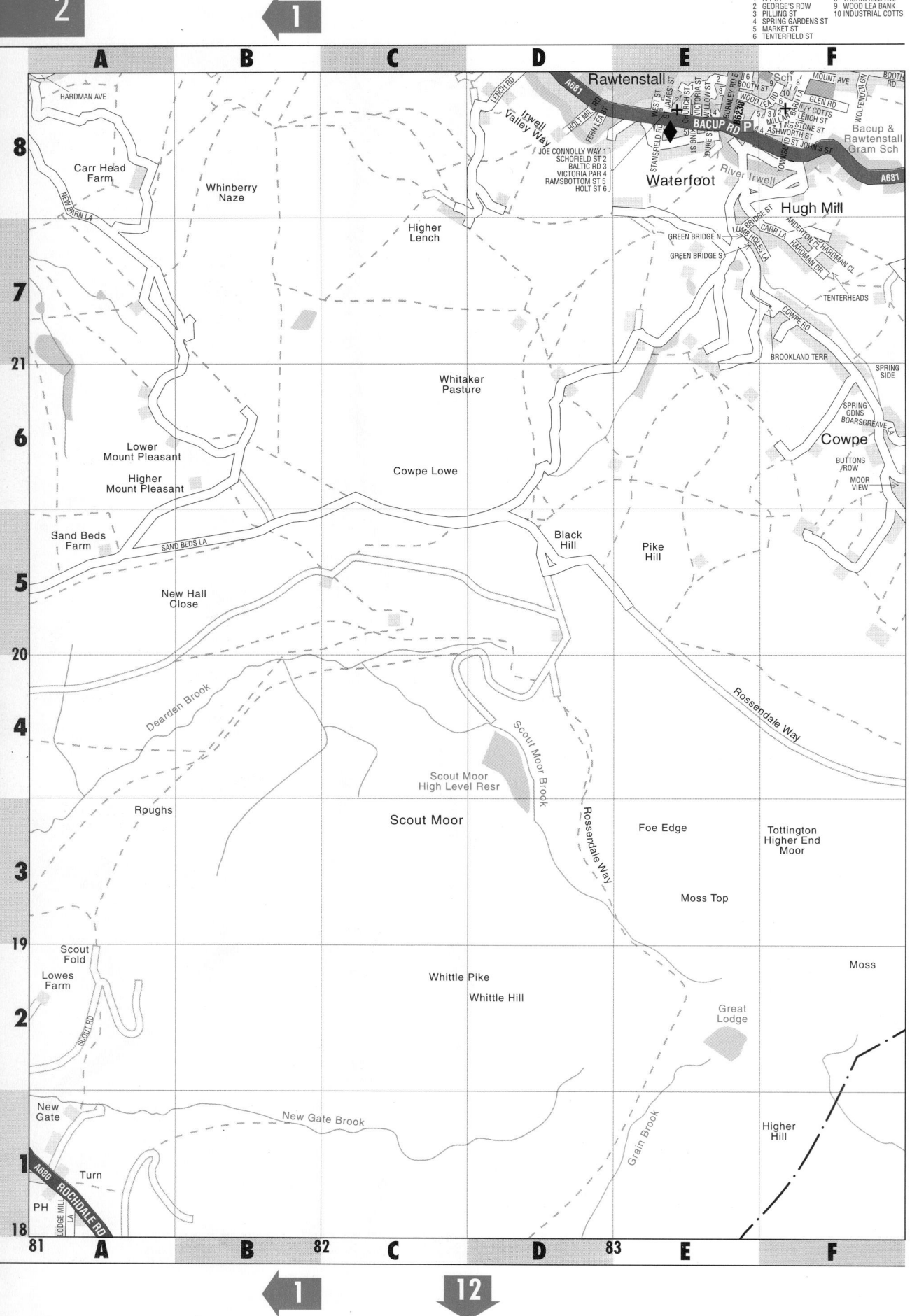

F8
1 IVY ST
2 GEORGE'S ROW
3 PILLING ST
4 SPRING GARDENS ST
5 MARKET ST
6 TENTERFIELD ST
7 YARE ST
8 THORNFIELD AVE
9 WOOD LEA BANK
10 INDUSTRIAL COTTS

A   B   C   D   E   F

HARDMAN AVE

8

Carr Head
Farm

NEW BARN LA

Whinberry
Naze

Higher
Lench

Irwell
Valley Way

LENCH RD

A681

Rawtenstall

HOLT MILL RD
FERN LEA ST
STANSFIELD RD
JAMES ST
WEST ST
CHURCH ST
VICTORIA ST
WILLOW ST
BURNLEY RD E
BOOTH ST
WOOD ST
B6238
MILL ST
ASHWORTH ST

Sch
MOUNT AVE
IVY COTTS
GLEN RD
WOLFENDEN GN
BOOTH RD

BACUP RD P

Waterfoot

River Irwell

Bacup &
Rawtenstall
Gram Sch

A681

Hugh Mill

JOE CONNOLLY WAY 1
SCHOFIELD ST 2
BALTIC RD 3
VICTORIA PAR 4
RAMSBOTTOM ST 5
HOLT ST 6

7

GREEN BRIDGE N
GREEN BRIDGE S

BRIDGE ST
LUMB HOLES LA
CARR LA
ANDERTON CL HARDMAN CL
HARDMAN DR

TENTERHEADS

21

Whitaker
Pasture

COWPE RD

BROOKLAND TERR

SPRING
SIDE

6

Lower
Mount Pleasant

Higher
Mount Pleasant

Cowpe Lowe

SPRING
GDNS
BOARSGREAVE LA

Cowpe

BUTTONS
ROW

MOOR
VIEW

Sand Beds
Farm

SAND BEDS LA

Black
Hill

Pike
Hill

5

New Hall
Close

20

Dearden Brook

Rossendale Way

4

Scout Moor Brook

Scout Moor
High Level Resr

Rossendale Way

Roughs

Scout Moor

Foe Edge

Tottington
Higher End
Moor

3

Moss Top

19

Scout
Fold

Whittle Pike

Moss

Lowes
Farm

SCOUT RD

Whittle Hill

Great
Lodge

2

New
Gate

New Gate Brook

Grain Brook

Higher
Hill

1

Turn

A680
ROCHDALE RD

PH

LODGE MILL LA

18

81   A   B   82   C   D   83   E   F

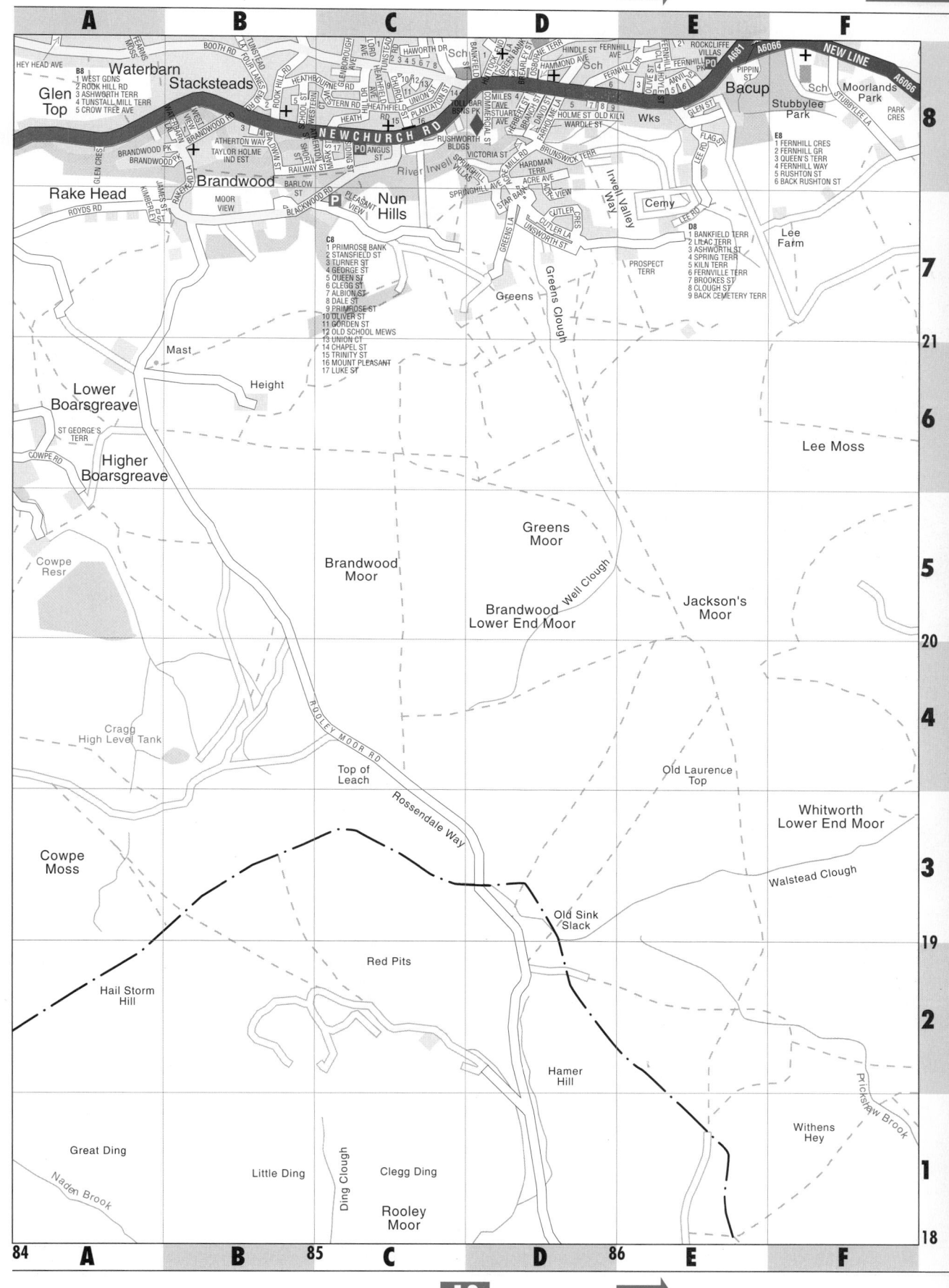

HEY HEAD AVE

Waterbarn

B8
1 WEST GDNS
2 ROOK HILL RD
3 ASHWORTH TERR
4 TUNSTALL MILL TERR
5 CROW TREE AVE

Stacksteads

Glen Top

BOOTH RD
ROOK HILL RD
TUNSTEAD
FOUR LANE ENDS

HAWORTH DR

Bacup

Moorlands Park

Stubbylee Park

PARK CRES

NEW LINE

A6066

A681

ROCKCLIFFE VILLAS

PIPPIN ST

FERNHILL AVE

Sch

NEWCHURCH RD

Brandwood

ATHERTON WAY
TAYLOR HOLME IND EST

MOOR VIEW

BARLOW ST

BLACKWOOD RD

PLEASANT VIEW

P

Nun Hills

River Irwell

RUSHWORTH BLDGS

Victoria St

HARDMAN TERR

ACRE AVE

BRUNSWICK TERR

SPRINGHILL VILLAS

STAR BANK

CUTLER ST

CUTLER CRES

CUTLER LA

UNSWORTH ST

GREENS LA

Greens

Irwell Valley Way

Cemy

PROSPECT TERR

LEE RD

E8
1 FERNHILL CRES
2 FERNHILL GR
3 QUEEN'S TERR
4 FERNHILL WAY
5 RUSHTON ST
6 BACK RUSHTON ST

Lee Farm

Lee Moss

D8
1 BANKFIELD TERR
2 LILAC TERR
3 ASHWORTH ST
4 SPRING TERR
5 KILN TERR
6 FERNVILLE TERR
7 BROOKES ST
8 CLOUGH ST
9 BACK CEMETERY TERR

Rake Head

GLEN CRES

ROYDS RD

RAKEFOLD LA

KIMBERLEY ST

JAMES ST

Mast

Height

C8
1 PRIMROSE BANK
2 STANSFIELD ST
3 TURNER ST
4 GEORGE ST
5 QUEEN ST
6 CLEGG ST
7 ALBION ST
8 DALE ST
9 PRIMROSE ST
10 OLIVER ST
11 GORDEN ST
12 OLD SCHOOL MEWS
13 UNION CT
14 CHAPEL ST
15 TRINITY ST
16 MOUNT PLEASANT
17 LUKE ST

Greens Clough

Lower Boarsgreave

ST GEORGE'S TERR

COWPE RD

Higher Boarsgreave

Cowpe Resr

Brandwood Moor

Greens Moor

Brandwood Lower End Moor

Well Clough

Jackson's Moor

Cragg High Level Tank

ROOLEY MOOR RD

Top of Leach

Rossendale Way

Old Laurence Top

Whitworth Lower End Moor

Walstead Clough

Cowpe Moss

Old Sink Slack

Red Pits

Hail Storm Hill

Hamer Hill

Withens Hey

Prickshaw Brook

Great Ding

Naden Brook

Little Ding

Ding Clough

Clegg Ding

Rooley Moor

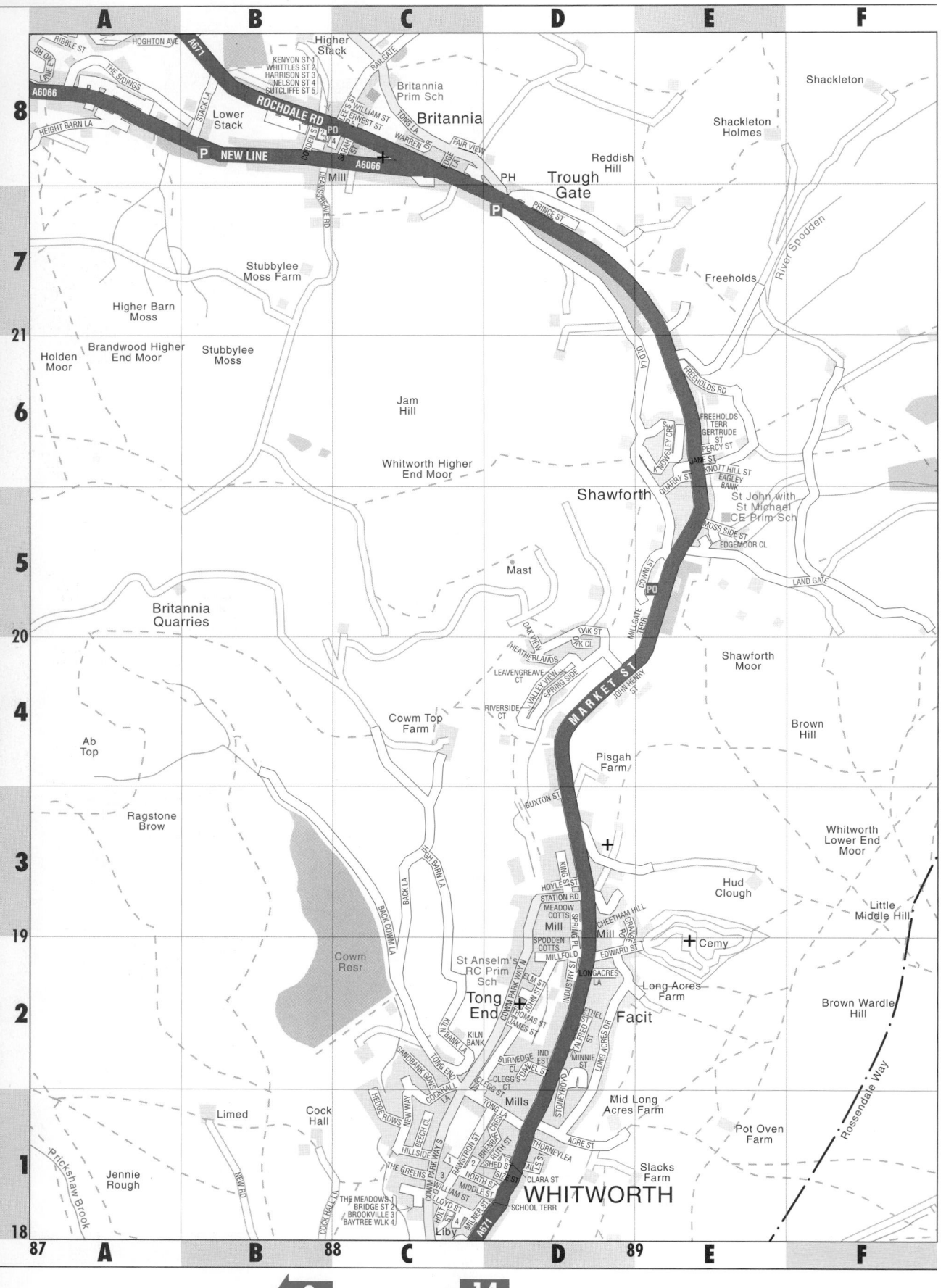

A   B   C   D   E   F

RIBBLE ST

HOGHTON AVE

THE SIDINGS

HEIGHT BARN LA

A6066

A671

STACK LA

ROCHDALE RD

Lower
Stack

NEW LINE

A6066

Mill

DEANSGREAVE RD

COBDEN ST

Higher
Stack

RAILGATE

WARREN DR

KENYON ST 1
WHITTLES ST 2
HARRISON ST 3
NELSON ST 4
SUTCLIFFE ST 5

LEE ST
WILLIAM ST
ERNEST ST
TONG LA

Britannia
Prim Sch

Britannia

FAIR VIEW

ELM ST

Britannia

PH

Trough
Gate

PRINCE ST

P

Reddish
Hill

Shackleton

Shackleton
Holmes

River Spodden

Freeholds

FREEHOLDS RD

OLD LA

FREEHOLDS
TERR
GERTRUDE
ST
PERCY ST

KNOWSLEY CRES

LANE ST

QUARRY ST

KNOTT HILL ST
EAGLEY
BANK

St John with
St Michael
CE Prim Sch

Shawforth

MOSS SIDE ST

EDGEMOOR CL

LAND GATE

COWM ST

MILLGATE TERR

PO

8

21

7

6

5

20

4

3

19

2

1

18

Height Barn La

Higher Barn
Moss

Holden
Moor

Brandwood Higher
End Moor

Stubbylee
Moss Farm

Stubbylee
Moss

Jam
Hill

Whitworth Higher
End Moor

Mast

Shawforth
Moor

Britannia
Quarries

Ab
Top

Cowm Top
Farm

HEATHERLANDS

LEAVENGREAVE
CT

RIVERSIDE
CT

OAK VIEW

PK CL

SPRING SIDE

VALLEY VIEW

OAK ST

MARKET ST

JOHN HENRY
ST

Brown
Hill

Ragstone
Brow

BACK COWM LA

BACK LA

HIGH BARN LA

Cowm Resr

Pisgah
Farm

BUXTON ST

KING ST

HOYLE ST

STATION RD

MEADOW
COTTS

SPODDEN
COTTS

MILLFOLD

SPRING PL

Mill

CHEETHAM HILL

GRANGE ST

EDWARD ST

Mill

Whitworth
Lower End
Moor

Hud
Clough

Cemy

Little
Middle Hill

St Anselm's
RC Prim
Sch

Tong
End

KILN BANK

KILN
BANK

ELM ST

THOMAS ST

JAMES ST

INDUSTRY ST

LONGACRES
LA

BETHEL ST

TALFRED ST

LONG ACRES ST

Long Acres
Farm

Facit

Brown Wardle
Hill

Rossendale Way

Jennie
Rough

Prickshaw Brook

NEW RD

Limed

Cock
Hall

SANDBANK GDNS

TONG END

NEW WAY

BEECH CL

HEDGE ROWS

HILLSIDE

COWM PARK WAY N

COWM PARK WAY

THE GREENS

FANSTON RD

RUTH ST

NORTH ST

WILLIAM ST

MIDDLE ST

LLOYD ST

BRENLEY
CRES

SHED
ST

MILLS
ST

COCKHALL LA

THE MEADOWS 1
BRIDGE ST 2
BROOKVILLE 3
BAYTREE WLK 4

CLEGG'S
CT

CLOVEL ST

BURNEDGE
CL

IND
EST

MINNIE
ST

Mills

STONEY ROYD

ACRE ST

THORNEYLEA

CLARA ST

SIZER ST

SCHOOL TERR

Mid Long
Acres Farm

Slacks
Farm

Pot Oven
Farm

WHITWORTH

Liby

A671

87   A   B   88   C   D   89   E   F

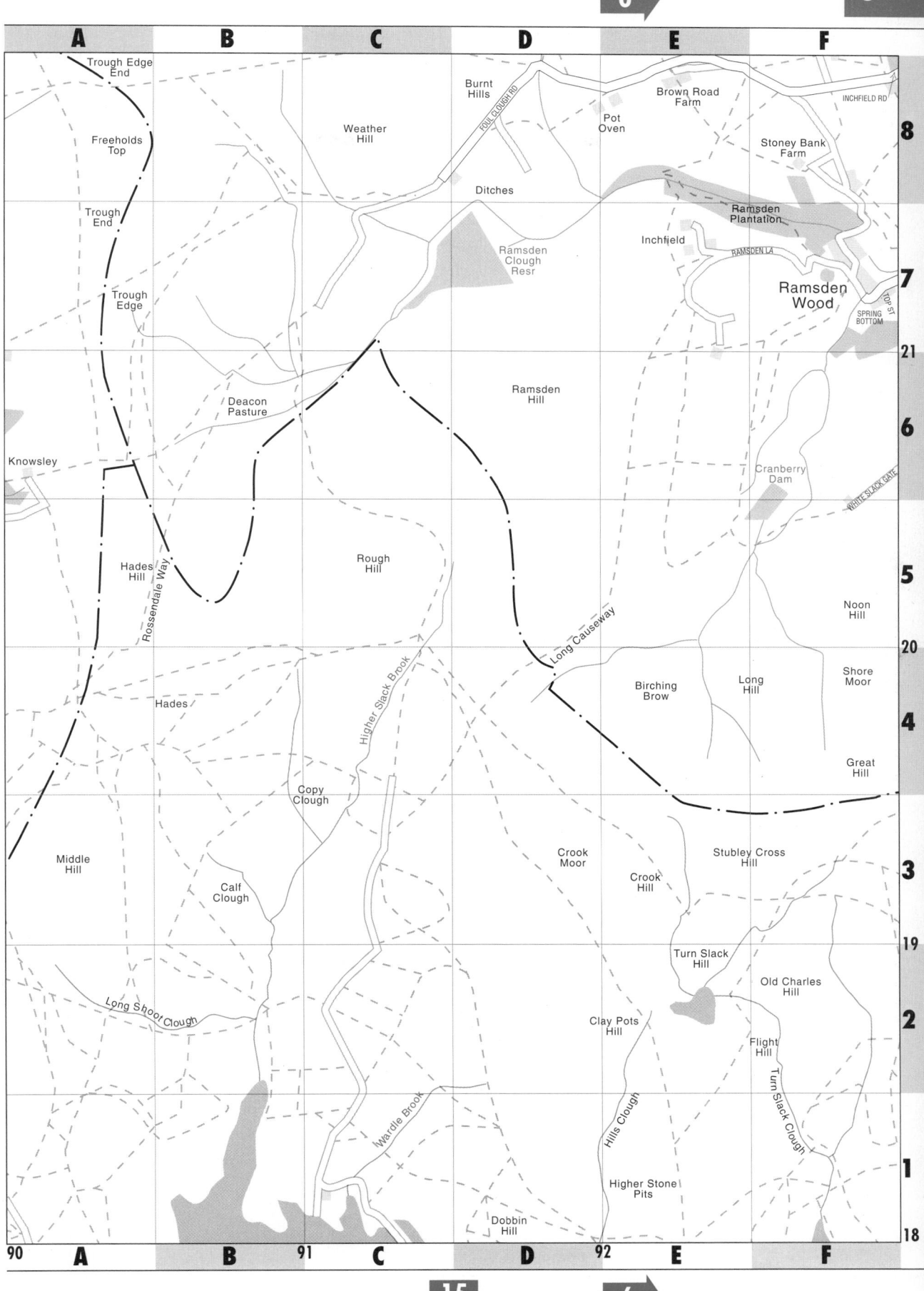

A B C D E F

Trough Edge End

Freeholds Top

Trough End

Trough Edge

Weather Hill

Burnt Hills

FOUL CLOUGH RD

Ditches

Brown Road Farm

Pot Oven

INCHFIELD RD

Stoney Bank Farm

Ramsden Plantation

Ramsden Clough Resr

Inchfield

RAMSDEN LA

Ramsden Wood

TOP ST

SPRING BOTTOM

Knowsley

Deacon Pasture

Ramsden Hill

Cranberry Dam

WHITE SLACK GATE

Hades Hill

Rossendale Way

Rough Hill

Long Causeway

Noon Hill

Shore Moor

Hades

Higher Slack Brook

Birching Brow

Long Hill

Great Hill

Copy Clough

Middle Hill

Calf Clough

Crook Moor

Crook Hill

Stubley Cross Hill

Turn Slack Hill

Old Charles Hill

Long Shoot Clough

Wardle Brook

Clay Pots Hill

Flight Hill

Turn Slack Clough

Hills Clough

Higher Stone Pits

Dobbin Hill

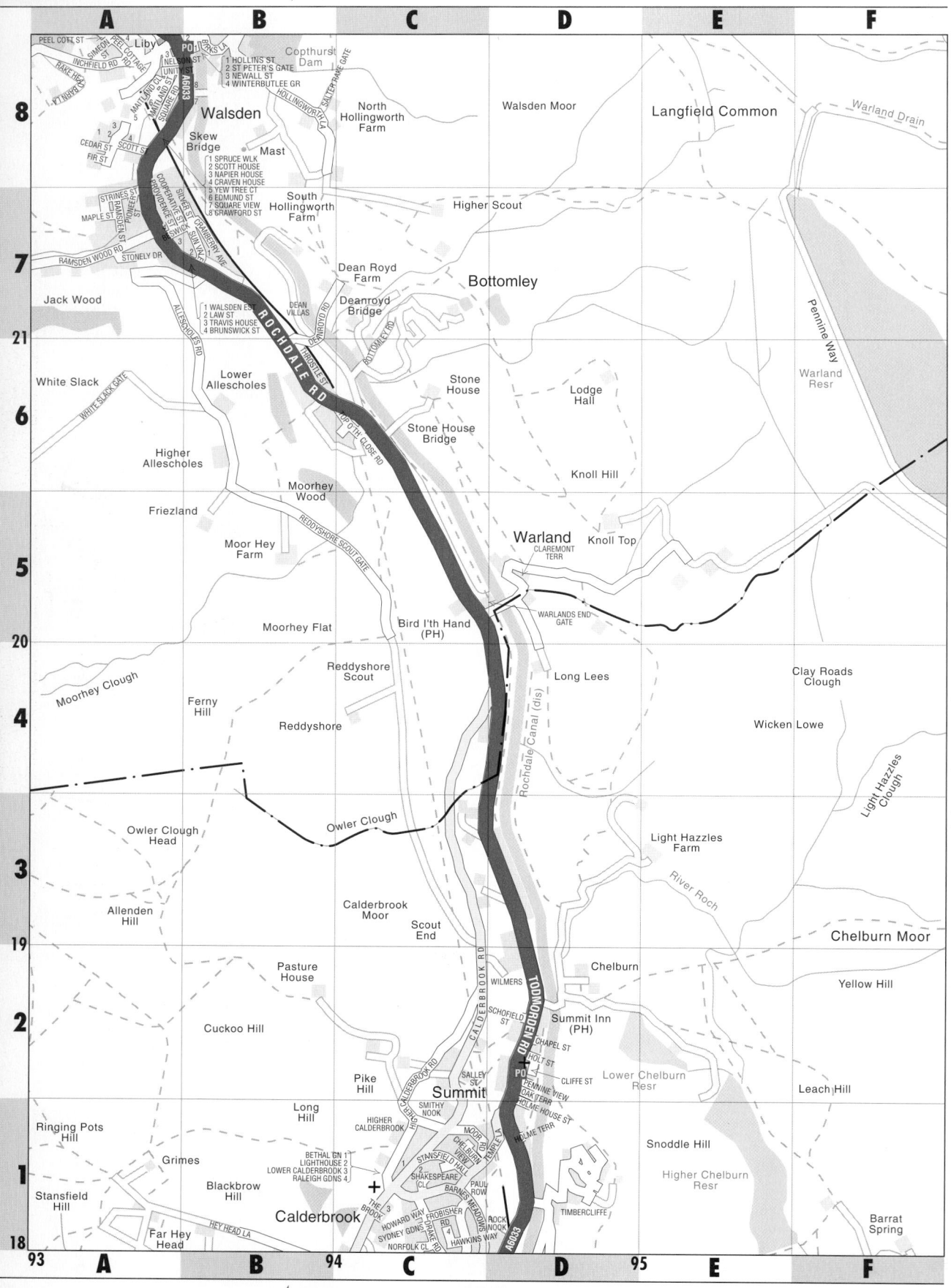

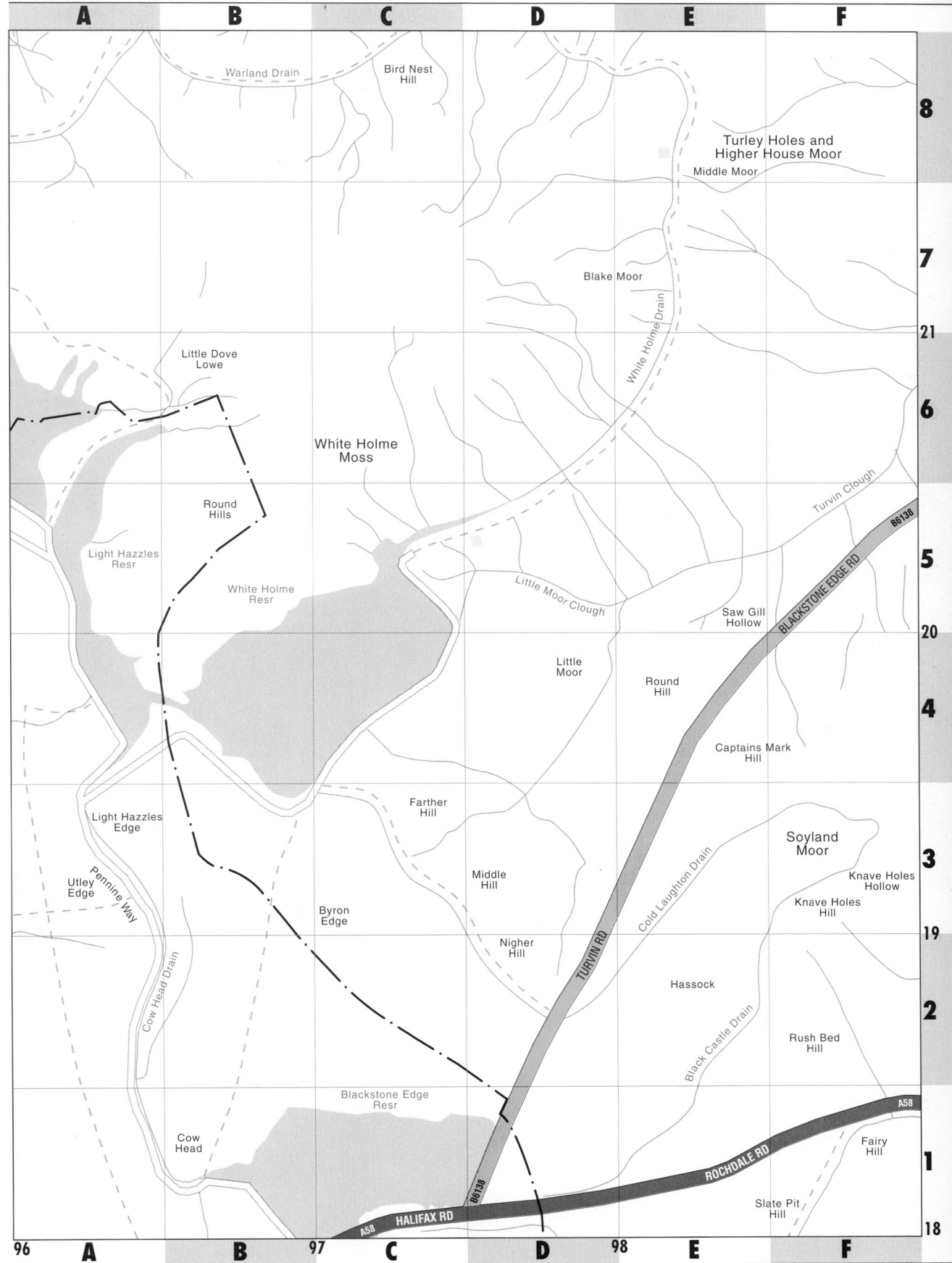

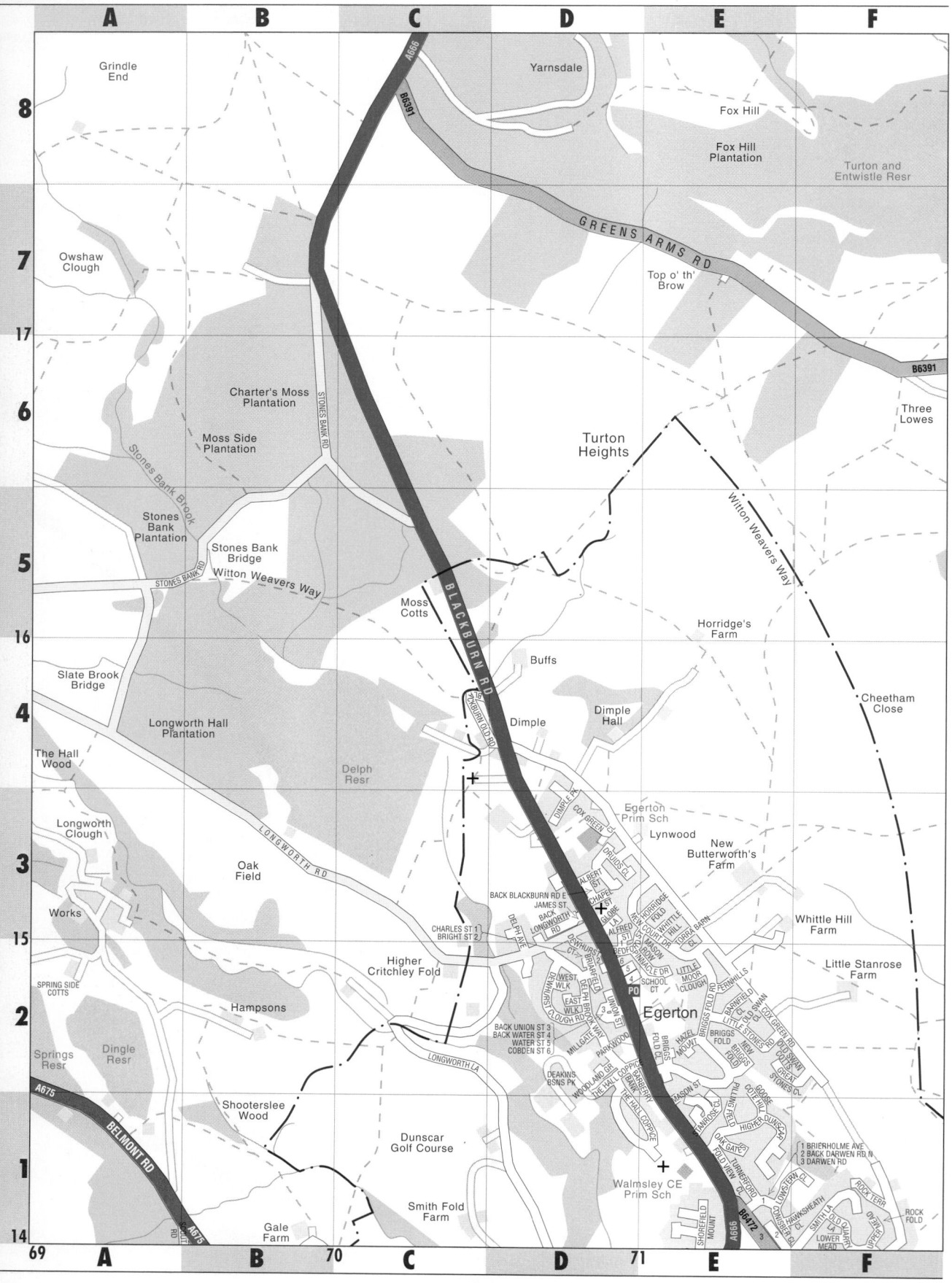

8

Grindle End

Yarnsdale

Fox Hill

Fox Hill Plantation

Turton and Entwistle Resr

A666

B6391

GREENS ARMS RD

7

Owshaw Clough

Top o' th' Brow

17

Charter's Moss Plantation

STONES BANK RD

Turton Heights

Witton Weavers Way

6

Three Lowes

Moss Side Plantation

Stones Bank Brook

5

Stones Bank Plantation

Stones Bank Bridge

STONES BANK RD

Witton Weavers Way

Moss Cotts

BLACKBURN RD

Horridge's Farm

16

Slate Brook Bridge

Buffs

Dimple Hall

Cheetham Close

4

Longworth Hall Plantation

Delph Resr

BLACKBURN OLD RD

Dimple

The Hall Wood

Egerton Prim Sch

Lynwood

New Butterworth's Farm

3

Longworth Clough

LONGWORTH RD

Oak Field

Back Blackburn Rd E
James St

ALBERT ST

CHAPEL ST

ALFRED ST

HORRIDGE FOLD

WHITTLE HILL

Whittle Hill Farm

Works

CHARLES ST 1
BRIGHT ST 2

DELPH AVE

BACK LONGWORTH RD

School Ct

LITTLE MOOR CLOUGH

Little Stanrose Farm

15

Higher Critchley Fold

WEST WLK

EAST WLK

DELPH BROOK WAY

UNION ST

PO

BARNFIELD

BRIGGS FOLD RD

FERNHILLS

2

Spring Side Cotts

Hampsons

LONGWORTH LA

BACK UNION ST 3
BACK WATER ST 4
WATER ST 5
COBDEN ST 6

MILLGATE CL

PARKWOOD

Egerton

HAZEL MOUNT

BRIGGS FOLD CL

COX GREEN RD

LITTLE STONES

STONES CL

GREAT STONES CL

Springs Resr

Dingle Resr

DEAKINS BSNS PK

WOODLAND GR

THE HALL COPPICE

THE HALL COPPICE

EASON ST

BARBER

GORSE FIELD

1

A675

BELMONT RD

Shooterslee Wood

Dunscar Golf Course

FOLD VIEW

A666

OAK GATE

TIMBERFIELD

HIGHER DUNSCAR

RANROSE CL

PITTING CL

OAKS TERN

1 BRIERHOLME AVE
2 BACK DARWEN RD N
3 DARWEN RD

ROCK TERR

ROCK FOLD

Walmsley CE Prim Sch

SHOREFIELD MOUNT

B6472

CONISBER CL

HAWKSHEATH CL

SMITH LA

OLD QUARRY LA

LOWER MEAD

UPPER MEAD

14

SCOUT RD

A675

Gale Farm

Smith Fold Farm

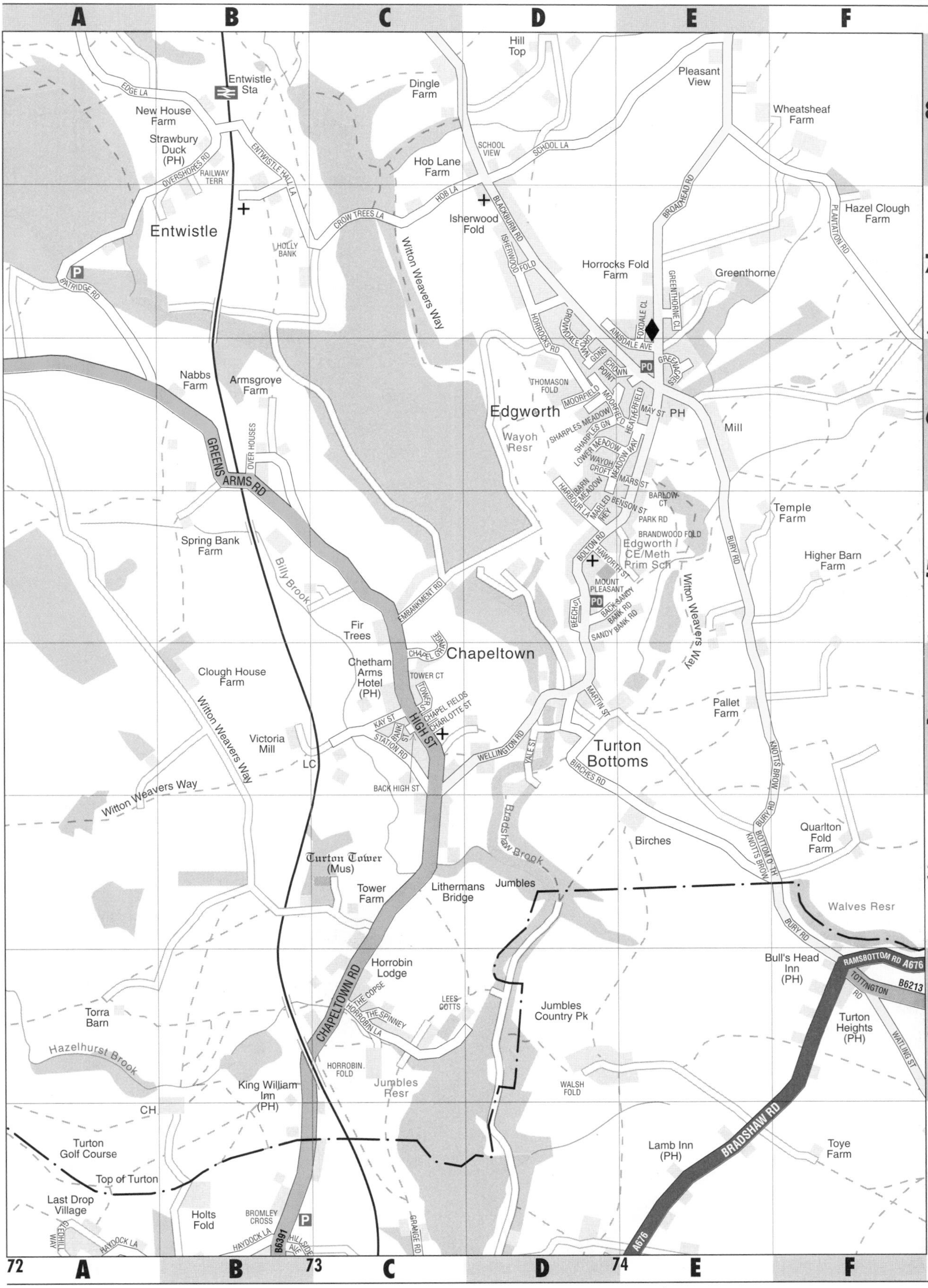

A   B   C   D   E   F

8

7

17

6

5

16

4

3

15

2

1

14

New House Farm
Strawbury Duck (PH)
EDGE LA
OVERSHORES RD
RAILWAY TERR
Entwistle Sta
Entwistle
ENTWISTLE HALL LA
HOLLY BANK
CROW TREES LA
Hill Top
Dingle Farm
SCHOOL VIEW
SCHOOL LA
Hob Lane Farm
HOB LA
Isherwood Fold
BLACKBURN RD
ISHERWOOD FOLD
Pleasant View
Wheatsheaf Farm
BROAD HEAD RD
Hazel Clough Farm
PLANTATION RD
GREENTHORNE CL
Horrocks Fold Farm
Greenthorne

PARTRIDGE RD

Nabbs Farm
Armsgroye Farm
GREENS ARMS RD
OVER HOUSES
CROWNDALE RD
HORROCKS RD
GORS
CROWN POINT
Thomason Fold
Edgworth
MOORFIELD
MOORFIELD
MAY ST
PH
Mill
Temple Farm

Wayoh Resr
SHARPLES GN
LOWER MEADOW
WAYOH CROFT
SHARPLES MEADOW
MEADOW WAY
BIRCHFIELD
MARS ST
BENSON ST
BARLOW CT
PARK RD
BRANDWOOD FOLD
Higher Barn Farm

Spring Bank Farm
BILLY BROOK
EMBANKMENT RD
Fir Trees
Chetham Arms Hotel (PH)
CHAPEL GV
TOWER CT
Chapeltown
HARBOUR LA
BOLTON RD
ELWORTH ST
BEECH
Edgworth CE/Meth Prim Sch
MOUNT PLEASANT
PO
BACK SANDY BANK RD
SANDY BANK RD
BURY RD
WITTON WEAVERS WAY

Clough House Farm
WITTON WEAVERS WAY
Victoria Mill
LC
KAY ST
KING'S ST
STATION RD
HIGH ST
TOWER ST
Chapel Fields
CHARLOTTE ST
WELLINGTON RD
MARTIN ST
TALE ST
Turton Bottoms
BIRCHES RD
Pallet Farm
KNOTTS BROW

WITTON WEAVERS WAY
BACK HIGH ST
BRADSHAW BROOK
Birches
BURY RD
BOTTOM O TH KNOTTS BROW
Quarlton Fold Farm
Walves Resr

Turton Tower (Mus)
Tower Farm
Lithermans Bridge
Jumbles

Torra Barn
HAZELHURST BROOK
CHAPELTOWN RD
Horrobin Lodge
THE COPSE
HORROBIN LA
THE SPINNEY
LEES COTTS
Jumbles Country Pk
Bull's Head Inn (PH)
RAMSBOTTOM RD A676
TOTTINGTON RD
B6213
Turton Heights (PH)
WATLING ST

King William Inn (PH)
HORROBIN FOLD
Jumbles Resr
WALSH FOLD
Lamb Inn (PH)
BRADSHAW RD
Toye Farm

CH
Turton Golf Course
Top of Turton
Last Drop Village
REDHILL WAY
HAYDOCK LA
Holts Fold
BROMLEY CROSS
HAYDOCK LA
B6391
HILLSIDE AVE
GRANGE RD
A676

72   73   74

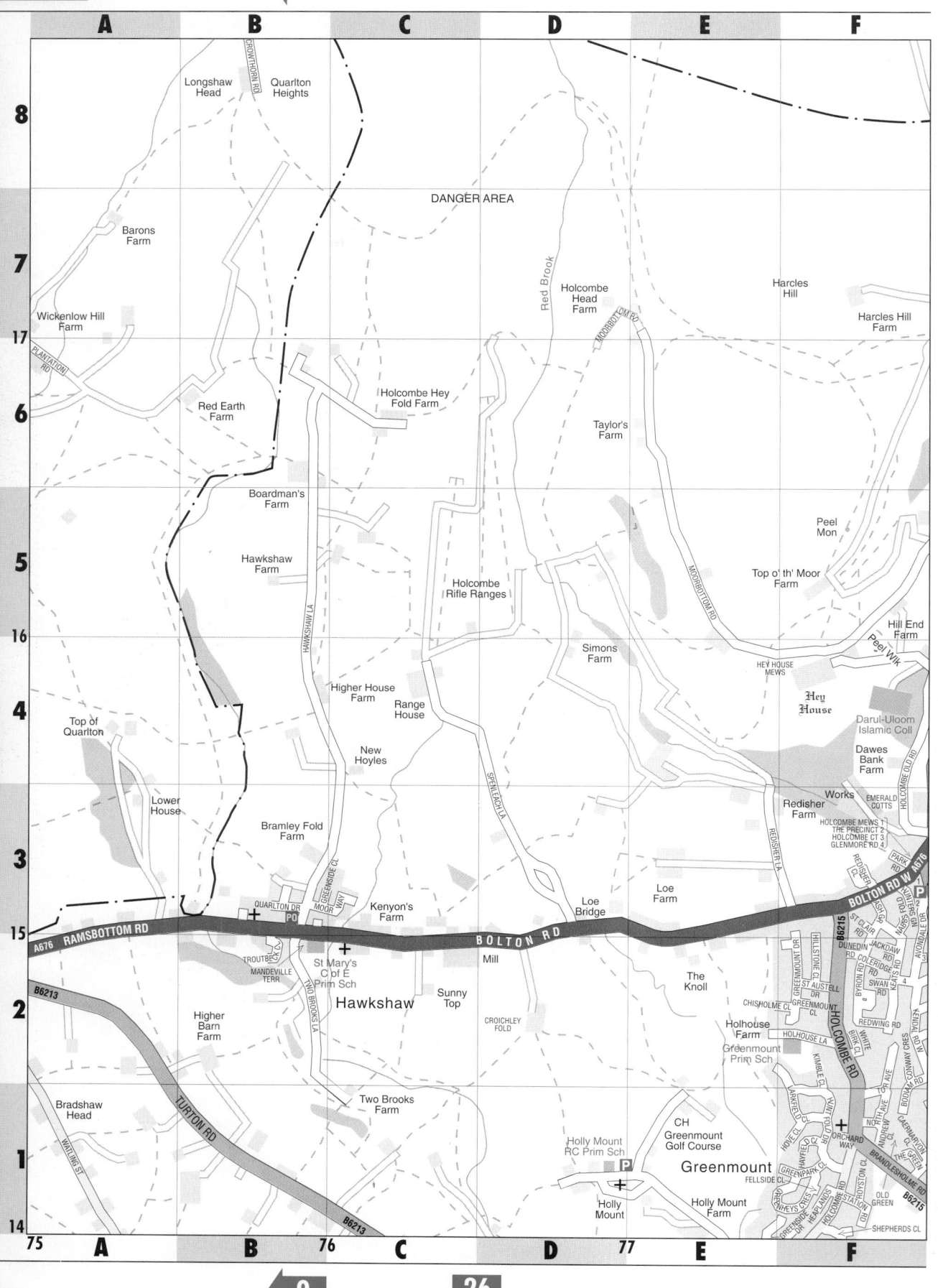

A B C D E F

8

DANGER AREA

Longshaw
Head

Quarlton
Heights

CROWTHORN RD

7

Barons
Farm

Red Brook

Holcombe
Head
Farm

MOORBOTTOM RD

Harcles
Hill

Wickenlow Hill
Farm

Harcles Hill
Farm

17

PLANTATION RD

6

Red Earth
Farm

Holcombe Hey
Fold Farm

Taylor's
Farm

Peel
Mon

Boardman's
Farm

Top o' th' Moor
Farm

5

Hawkshaw
Farm

Holcombe
Rifle Ranges

MOORBOTTOM RD

HAWKSHAW LA

Hill End
Farm

Peel Wik

16

Simons
Farm

HEY HOUSE
MEWS

Hey
House

4

Top of
Quarlton

Higher House
Farm

Range
House

Darul-Uloom
Islamic Coll

New
Hoyles

Dawes
Bank
Farm

Lower
House

Redisher
Farm

Works

EMERALD
COTTS

HOLCOMBE OLD RD

Bramley Fold
Farm

SPENLEACH LA

HOLCOMBE MEWS 1
THE PRECINCT 2
HOLCOMBE CT 3
GLENMORE RD 4

REDISHER LA

3

GREENSIDE CL

Loe
Bridge

Loe
Farm

BOLTON RD W A676

PARK RD

P

QUARLTON DR
PO

MOOR WAY

Kenyon's
Farm

15

A676

RAMSBOTTOM RD

BOLTON RD

ST CLAIR RD

Mill

DUNEDIN

JACKDAW

St Clair

The
Knoll

GREENMOUNT DR

HILLSTONE CL

ST AUSTELL
DR

BYRON CL

COLERIDGE RD

SWAN RD

REDWING RD

MARS FOLD RD

WHITE
BIRK CL

AVONDALE DR

HOLCOMBE RD

TROUTBE

MANDEVILLE
TERR

St Mary's
C of E
Prim Sch

Sunny
Top

B6213

2

Higher
Barn
Farm

TWO BROOKS LA

Hawkshaw

CROICHLEY
FOLD

Holhouse
Farm

HOLHOUSE LA

CHISHOLME CL

Greenmount
Prim Sch

GREENMOUNT CL

KIMBLE CL

CONWAY CRES

BRANDLESHOLME RD

Bradshaw
Head

WATLING ST

TURTON RD

Two Brooks
Farm

Holly Mount
RC Prim Sch

P

CH
Greenmount
Golf Course

Greenmount

HOVE CL

PARKFIELD CL

MAYFIELD CL

ANDREW LA

NORTH AVE

GREENPARK CL

FELLSIDE CL

ORCHARD
WAY

FOLD DR

KEATS RD

ROYSTON CL

HOLCOMBE CRES

HEARTONS

KENYON

OLD
GREEN

B6215

1

14

B6213

Holly
Mount

Holly Mount
Farm

GREENHEYS CRES

HEADLANDS

SHEPHERDS CL

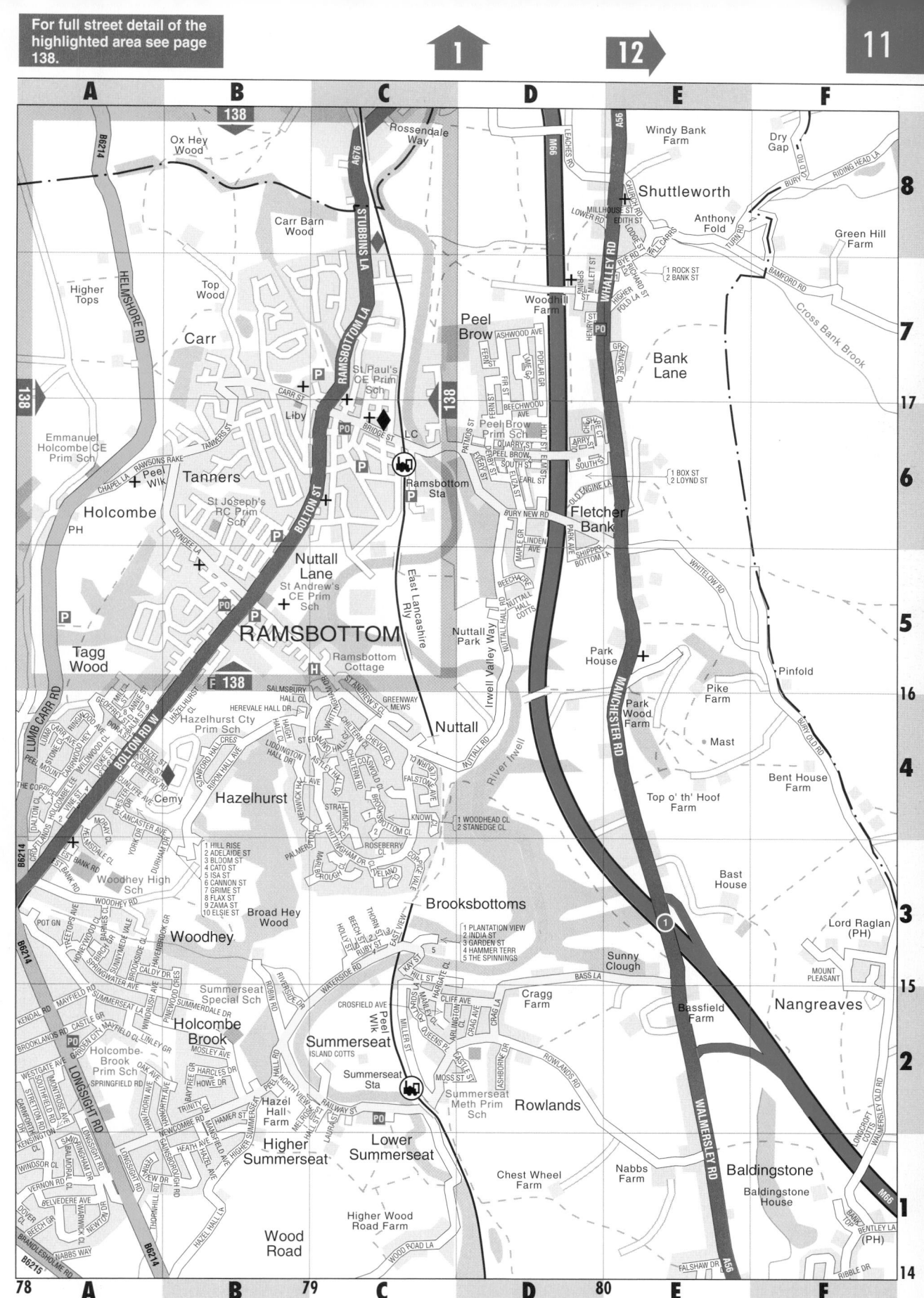

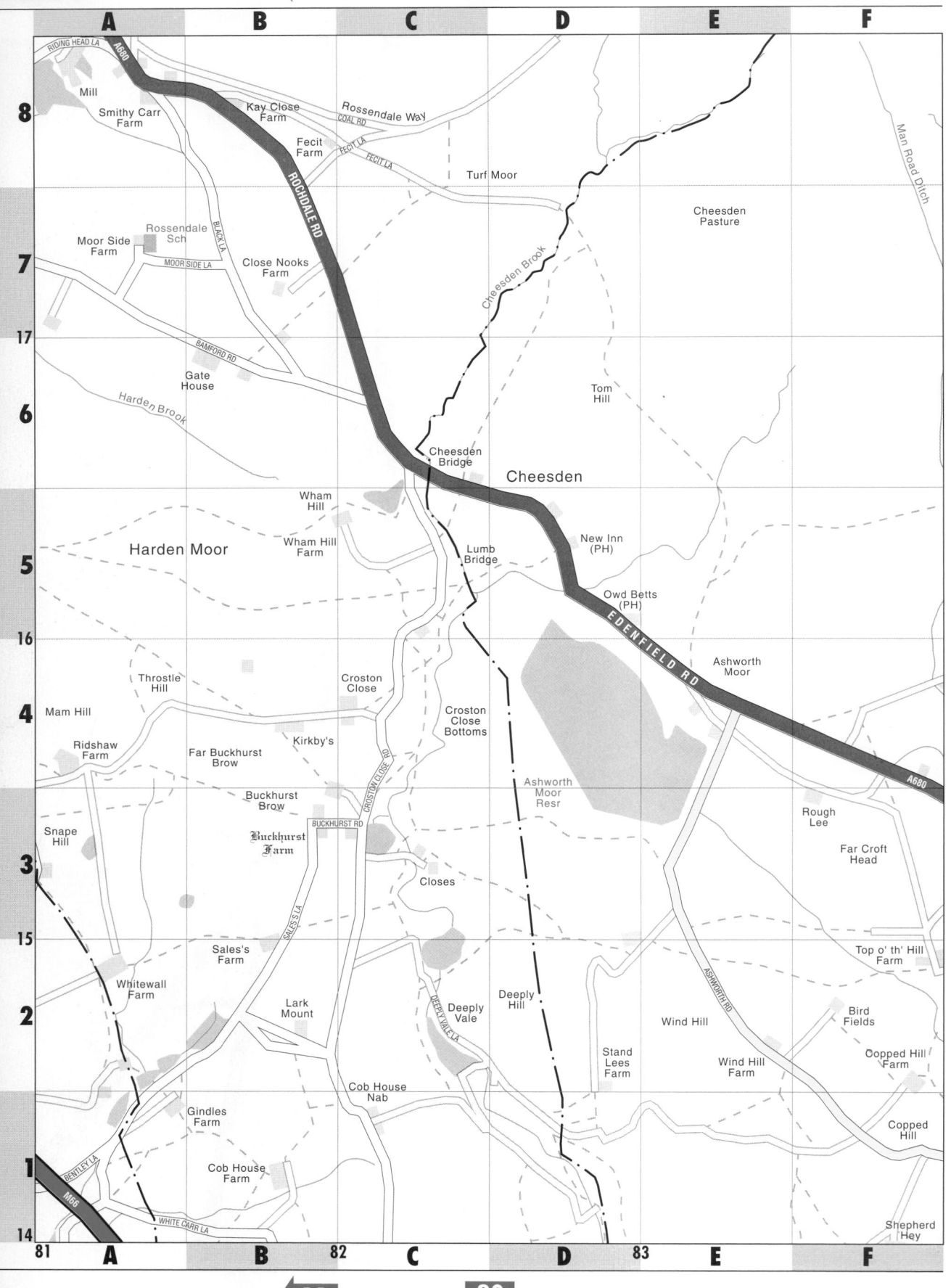

A   B   C   D   E   F

RIDING HEAD LA
A680

8
Mill
Smithy Carr Farm
Kay Close Farm
Rossendale Way
COAL RD
Fecit Farm
FECIT LA   FECIT LA
Turf Moor
Cheesden Pasture
Man Road Ditch

Moor Side Farm
Rossendale Sch
BLACK LA
ROCHDALE RD
Close Nooks Farm
7
MOOR SIDE LA
Cheesden Brook

17
BAMFORD RD
Gate House
Tom Hill

Harden Brook
6
Cheesden Bridge
Cheesden

Wham Hill
New Inn (PH)
Harden Moor
Wham Hill Farm
Lumb Bridge
5
Owd Betts (PH)
EDENFIELD RD

16
Throstle Hill
Croston Close
Ashworth Moor

4
Mam Hill
Kirkby's
Croston Close Bottoms
A680

Ridshaw Farm
Far Buckhurst Brow
Ashworth Moor Resr
Rough Lee

Buckhurst Brow
Far Croft Head

Snape Hill
CROSTON CLOSE RD
BUCKHURST RD
3
Buckhurst Farm
Closes

15
SALES'S LA
Top o' th' Hill Farm

Sales's Farm
Whitewall Farm
Deeply Vale
Deeply Hill
Wind Hill
2
Lark Mount
DEEPLY VALE LA
ASHWORTH RD
Bird Fields

Stand Lees Farm
Wind Hill Farm
Copped Hill Farm

Gindles Farm
Cob House Nab
Copped Hill

1
BENTLEY LA
Cob House Farm
M66

14
WHITE CARR LA
Shepherd Hey

81   A   82   B   C   82   D   83   E   F

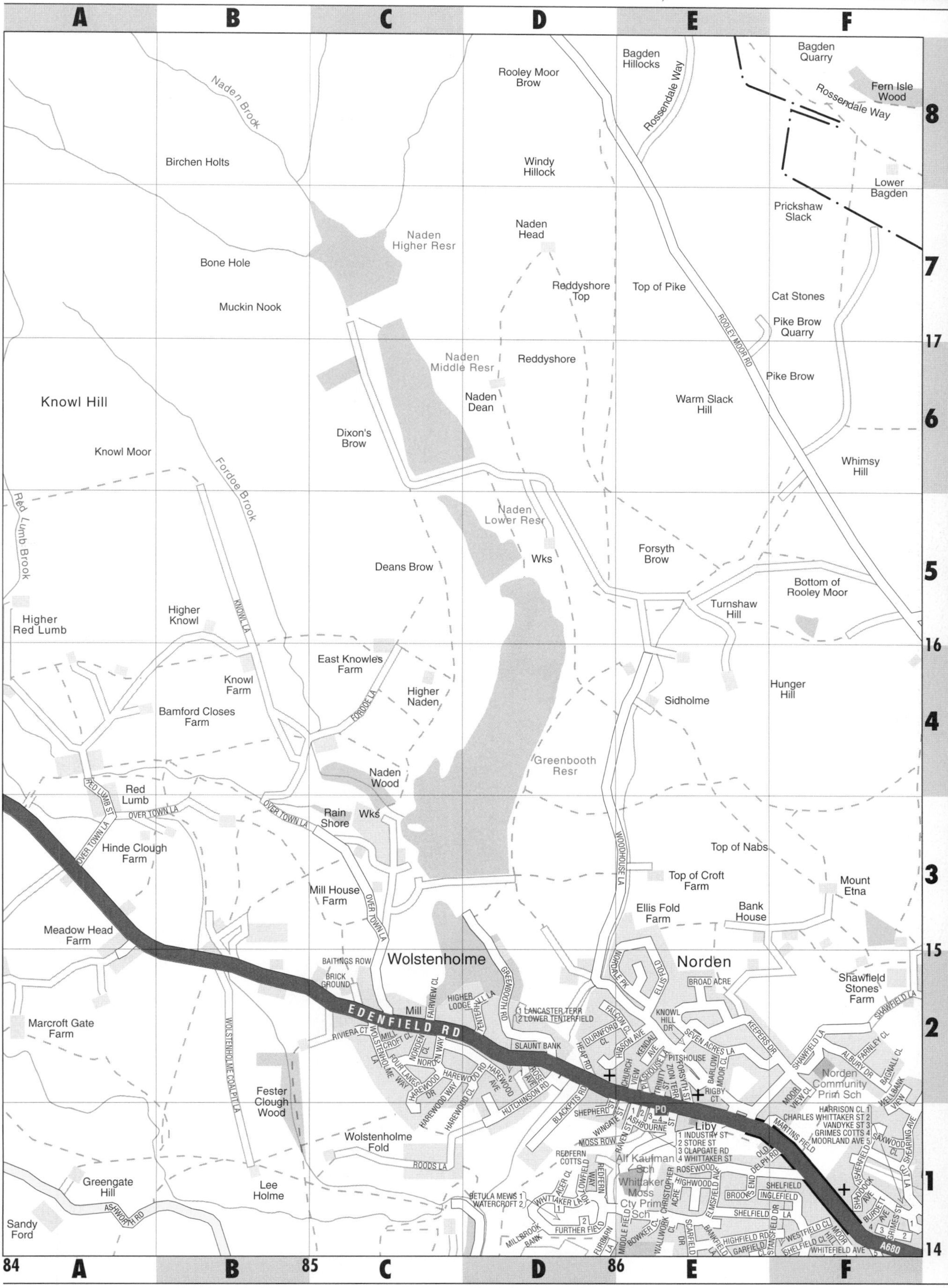

A   B   C   D   E   F

Bagden Hillocks
Bagden Quarry
Rossendale Way
Fern Isle Wood
Rossendale Way
8

Naden Brook

Birchen Holts

Windy Hillock

Prickshaw Slack
Lower Bagden

Bone Hole

Naden Higher Resr

Naden Head

Rooley Moor Brow

Reddyshore Top

Top of Pike

Cat Stones
Pike Brow Quarry
7

Muckin Nook

17

Naden Middle Resr

Reddyshore

Pike Brow

Knowl Hill

Fordoe Brook

Dixon's Brow

Naden Dean

Warm Slack Hill

Whimsy Hill

6

Knowl Moor

Naden Lower Resr

Red Lumb Brook

Knowl La

Deans Brow

Wks

Forsyth Brow

Bottom of Rooley Moor
5

Higher Red Lumb

Higher Knowl

East Knowles Farm

Turnshaw Hill

16

Knowl Farm

Higher Naden

Sidholme

Hunger Hill

4

Bamford Closes Farm

Fordoe La

Naden Wood

Greenbooth Resr

Red Lumb

Over Town La

Rain Shore

Wks

Top of Nabs

Mount Etna

3

Hinde Clough Farm

Over Town La

Mill House Farm

Woodhouse La

Top of Croft Farm

Bank House

Meadow Head Farm

EDENFIELD RD

Wolstenholme

Ellis Fold Farm

Norden

Shawfield Stones Farm
15

BAITINGS ROW
BRICK GROUND

Higher Lodge
PENTERILL CL

GREENBOOTH RD

HELP RD
DURNFORD CL

HIBSON AVE

BROAD ACRE

Knowl Hill Dr
SEVEN ACRES LA
KEEPERS DR
SHAWFIELD LA
SHAWFIELD CL

2

Marcroft Gate Farm

WOLSTENHOLME COAL PIT LA

Mill
FAIRVIEW CL
RIVIERA CT
MILLCROFT CL
FOUR LANES
WOLSTENHOLME WAY
NADEN PL

SLAUNT BANK
HAREWOOD RD
HAREWOOD CL
HARWOOD AVE
HUTCHINSON RD

FALCON CL
CHURCH VIEW
PILSWORTH
ZION TERR
TRINITY ST
BARLOW CL
MOOR LA

RIGBY CT

MOOR VIEW

ALBURY DR
MELLBANK
BAGNALL CL

FARLEY CL

HARRISON CL 1
CHARLES WHITTAKER ST 3
VANDYKE ST 3
GRIMES COTTS 4
MOORLAND AVE 5

Fester Clough Wood

Lancaster Terr 1
Lower Tenterfield 2

SHEPHERD
WINGATE

ASHBOURNE
ASHWORTH

1 INDUSTRY ST
2 STORE ST
3 CLAPGATE RD
4 WHITTAKER ST

PO

Liby

Norden Community Prim Sch

SAXWOOD AVE
SCARHILL AVE

Wolstenholme Fold

MOSS ROW
BLACKETTS RD

REDFERN COTTS

Alf Kaufman Sch

Whittaker Moss Cty Prim Sch

ROSEWOOD
HIGHWOOD
SHELFIELD INGLEFIELD

DELPH RD
OLD

SHADDOCK

1

Greengate Hill

Lee Holme

ROODS LA

BETULA MEWS 1
WATERCROFT 2

FURTHER FIELD

MILLSBROOK BANK

WHITTAKER LAND
FURBHANK
ACRE ST
COWFIELD
HAYMAKER
CHRISTOPHER DR
BOWKER CL
MIDDLE FIELD
WALLWORK DR

ROSEWOOD
HIGHWOOD
FERNSIDE
ELMSFIELD
HIGHFIELD RD
GARFIELD
STANDFIELD
WESTFIELD CL
WHITEFIELD AVE

SHELFIELD CL
MOOR

SHAWFIELD LA
BURTSETT
A680

Sandy Ford

ASHWORTH RD

84   A   85   B   C   85   D   86   E   F   14

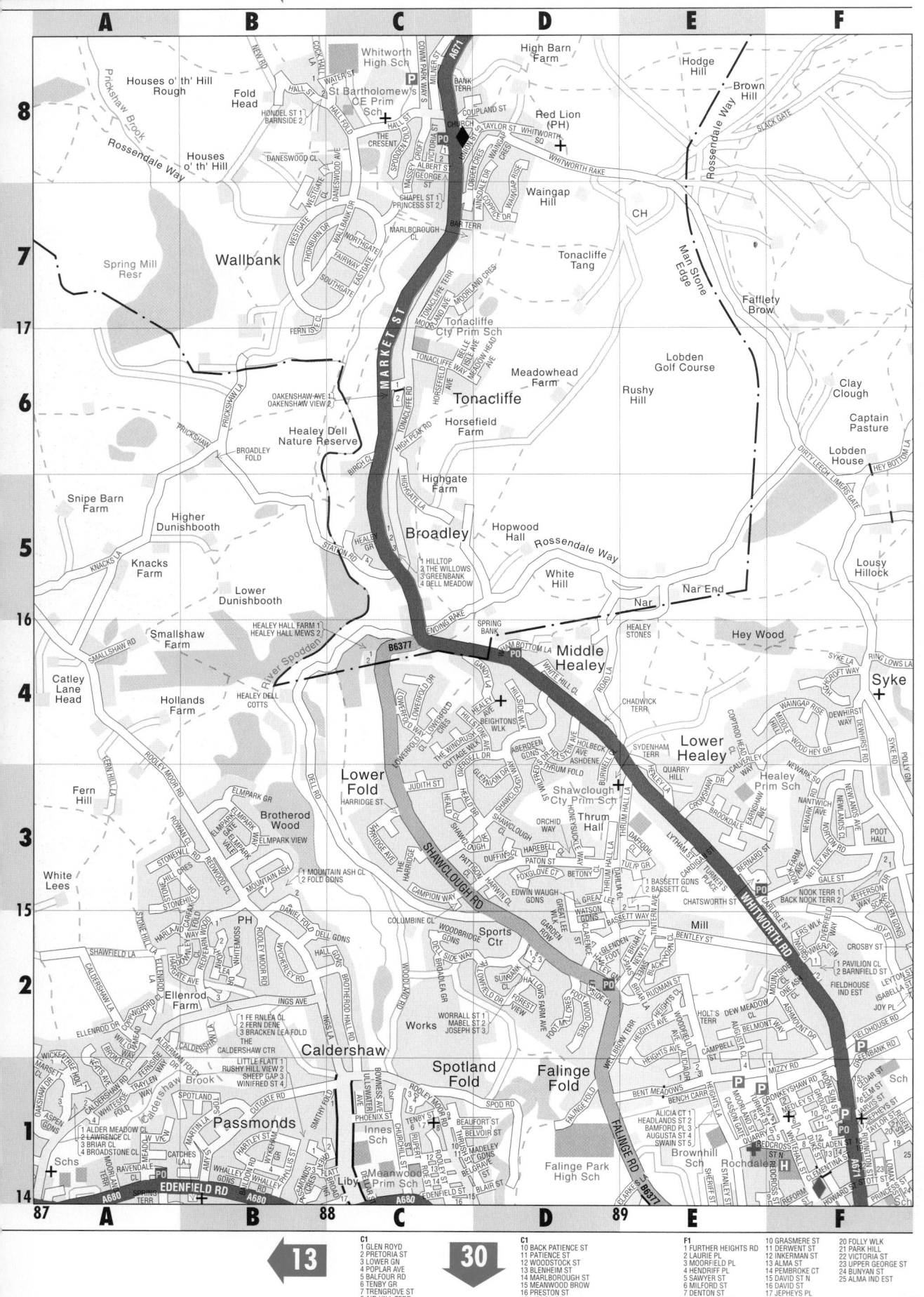

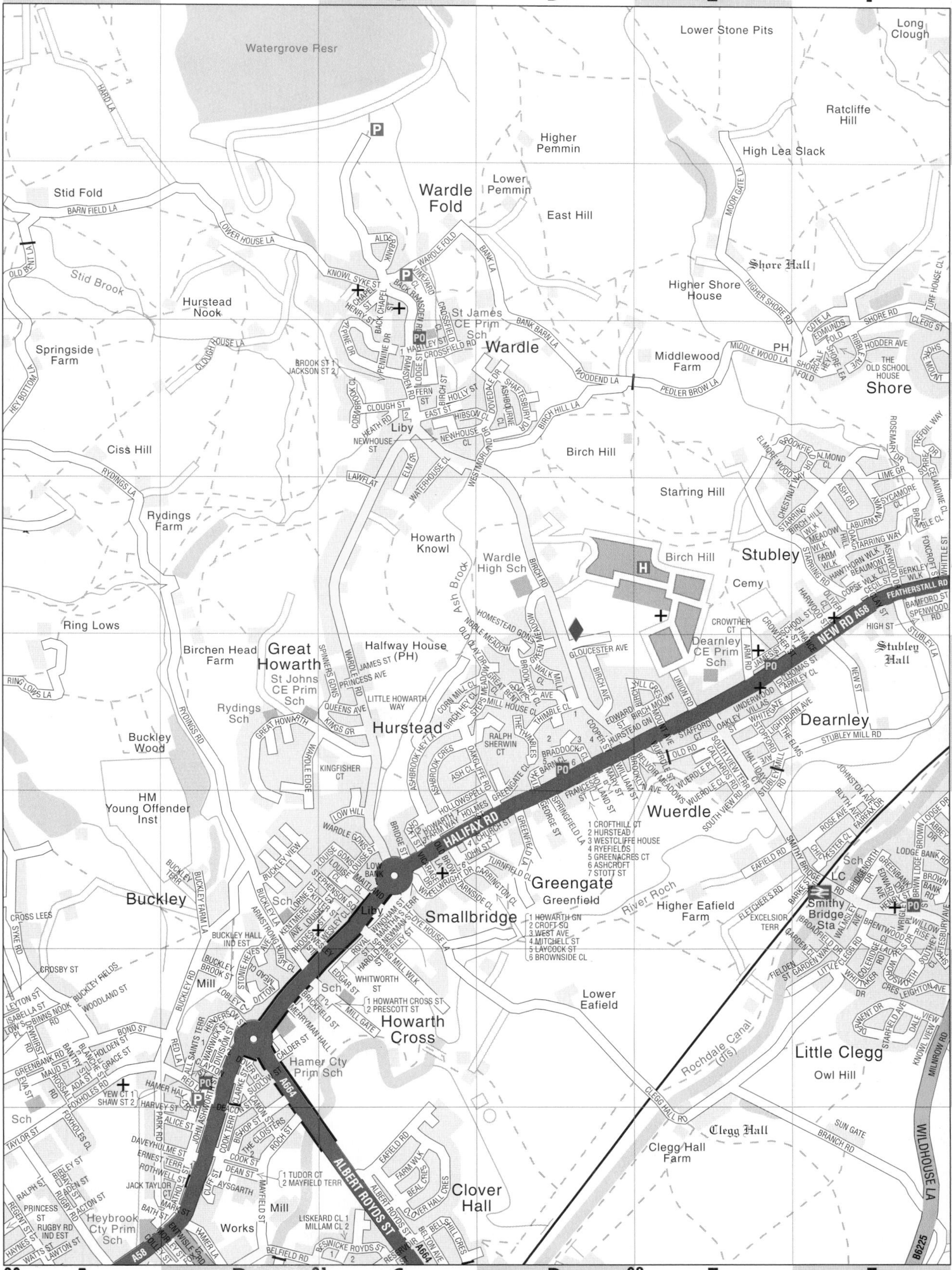

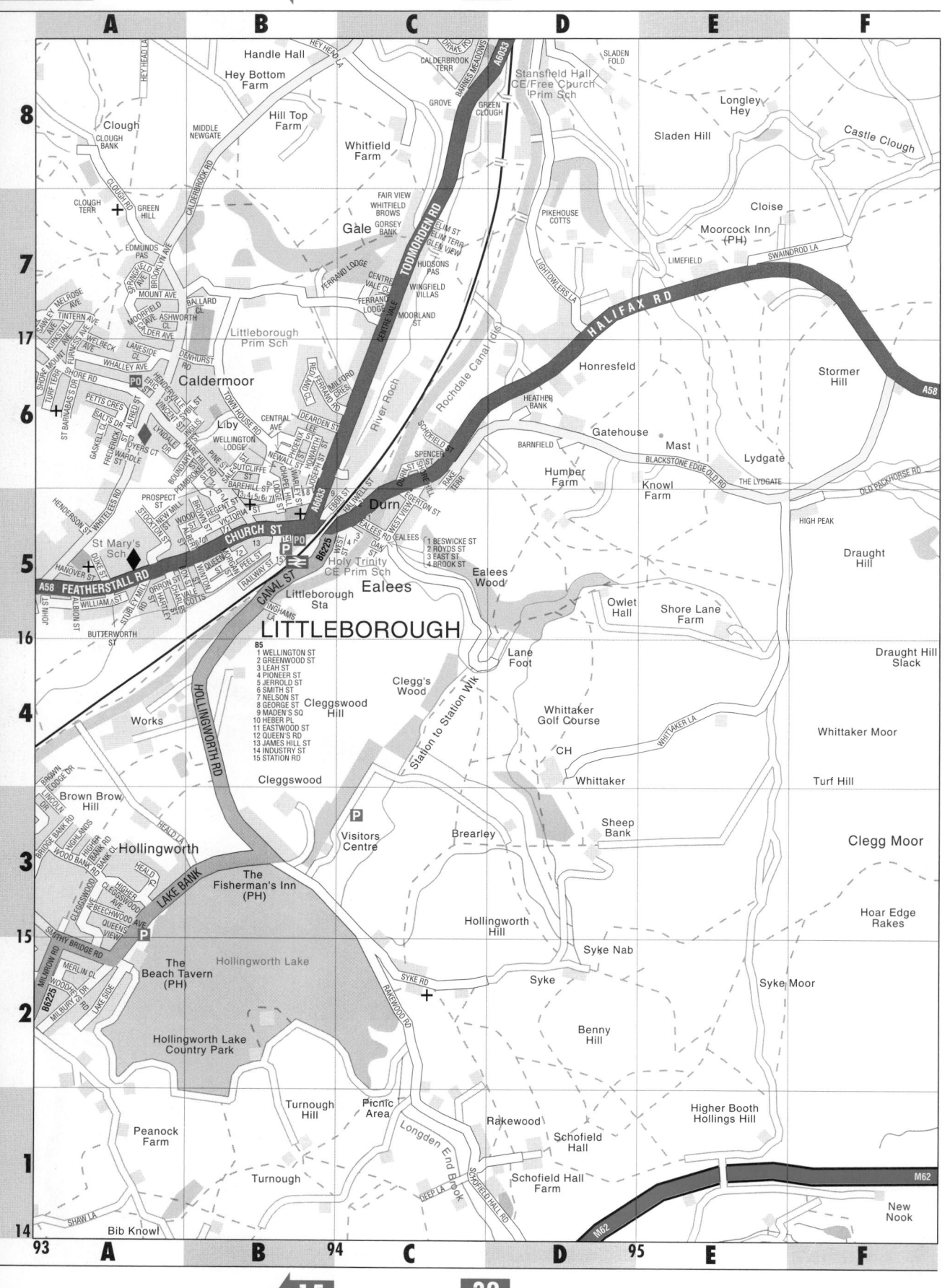

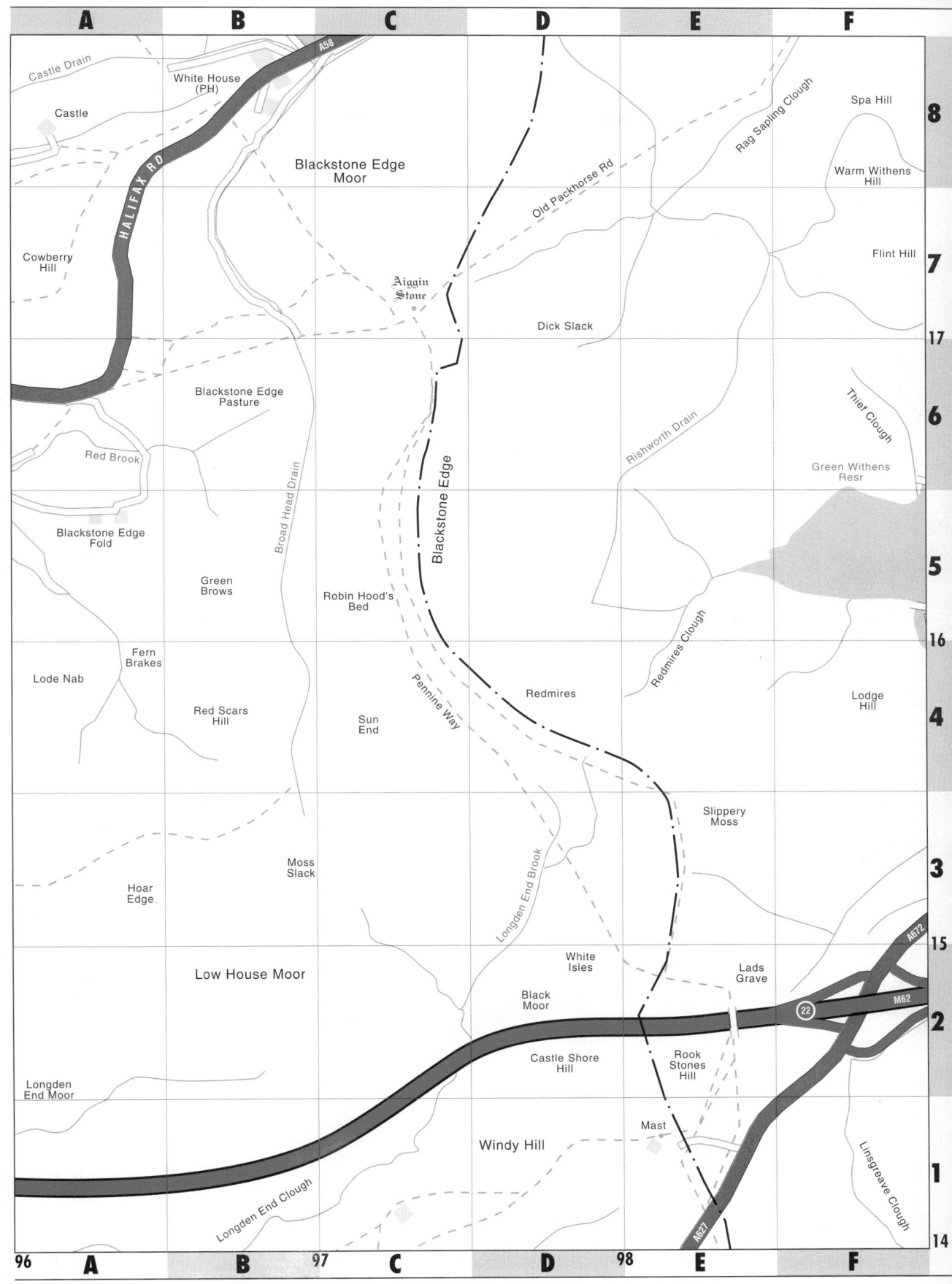

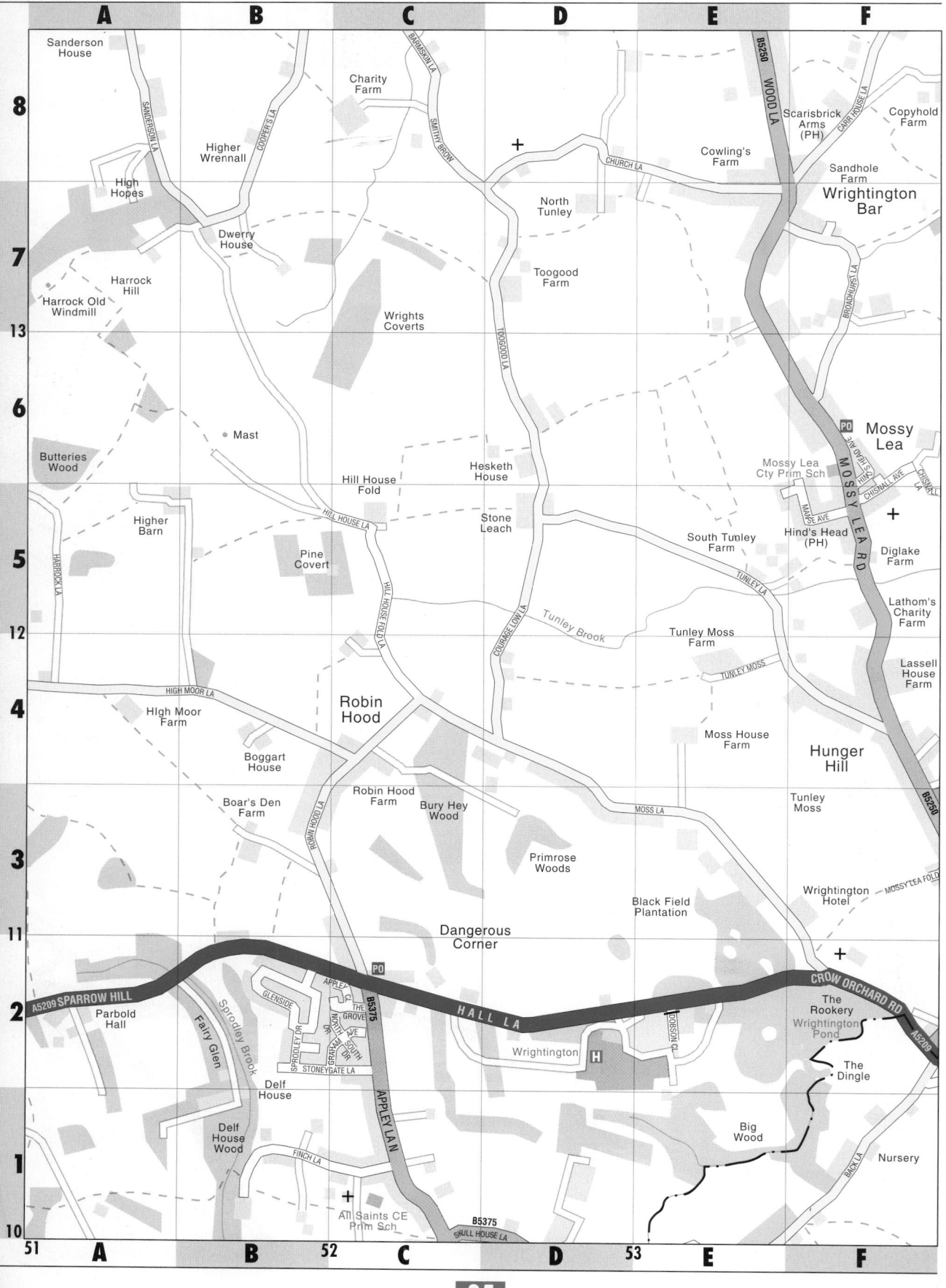

19

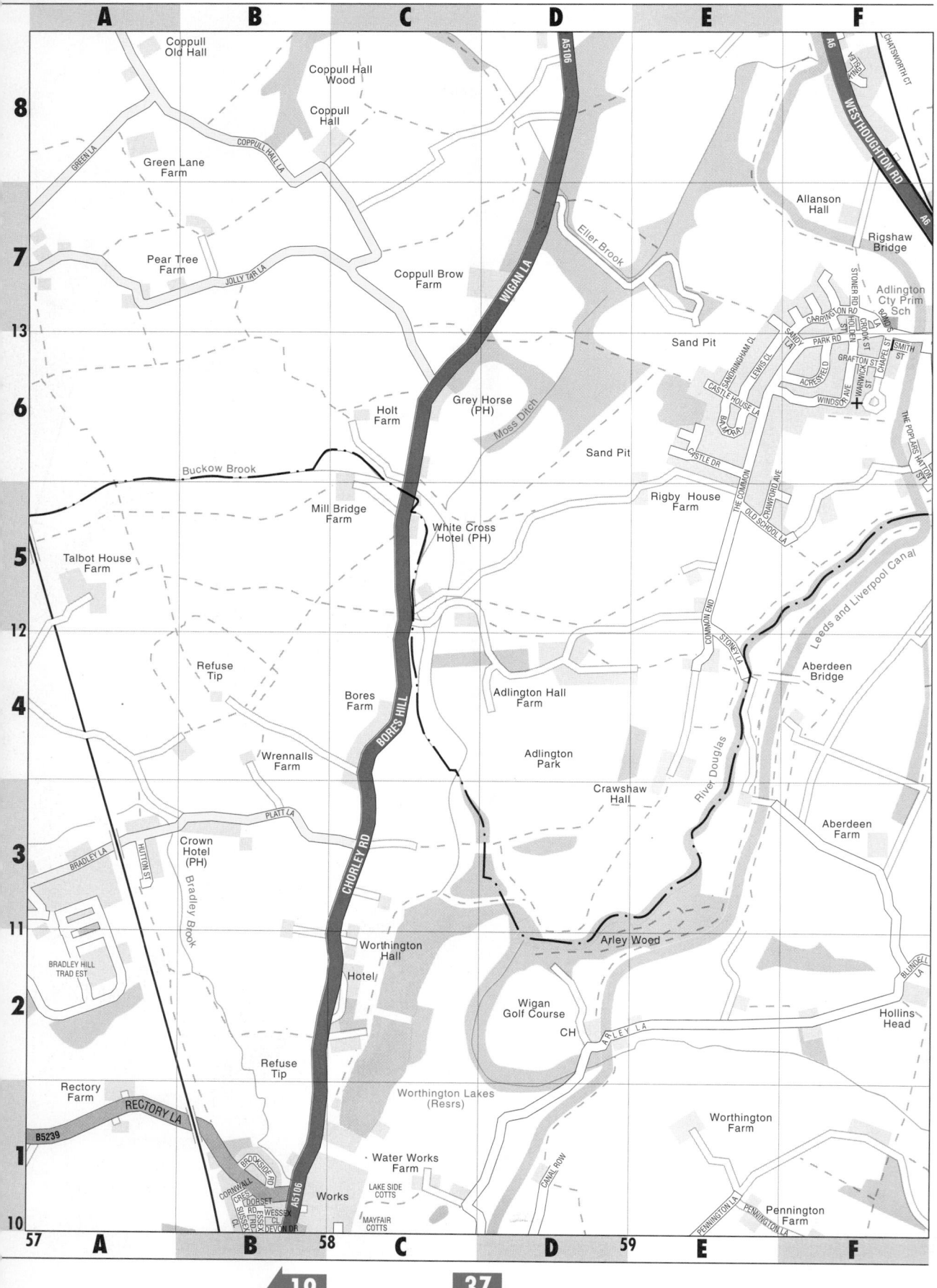

19   37

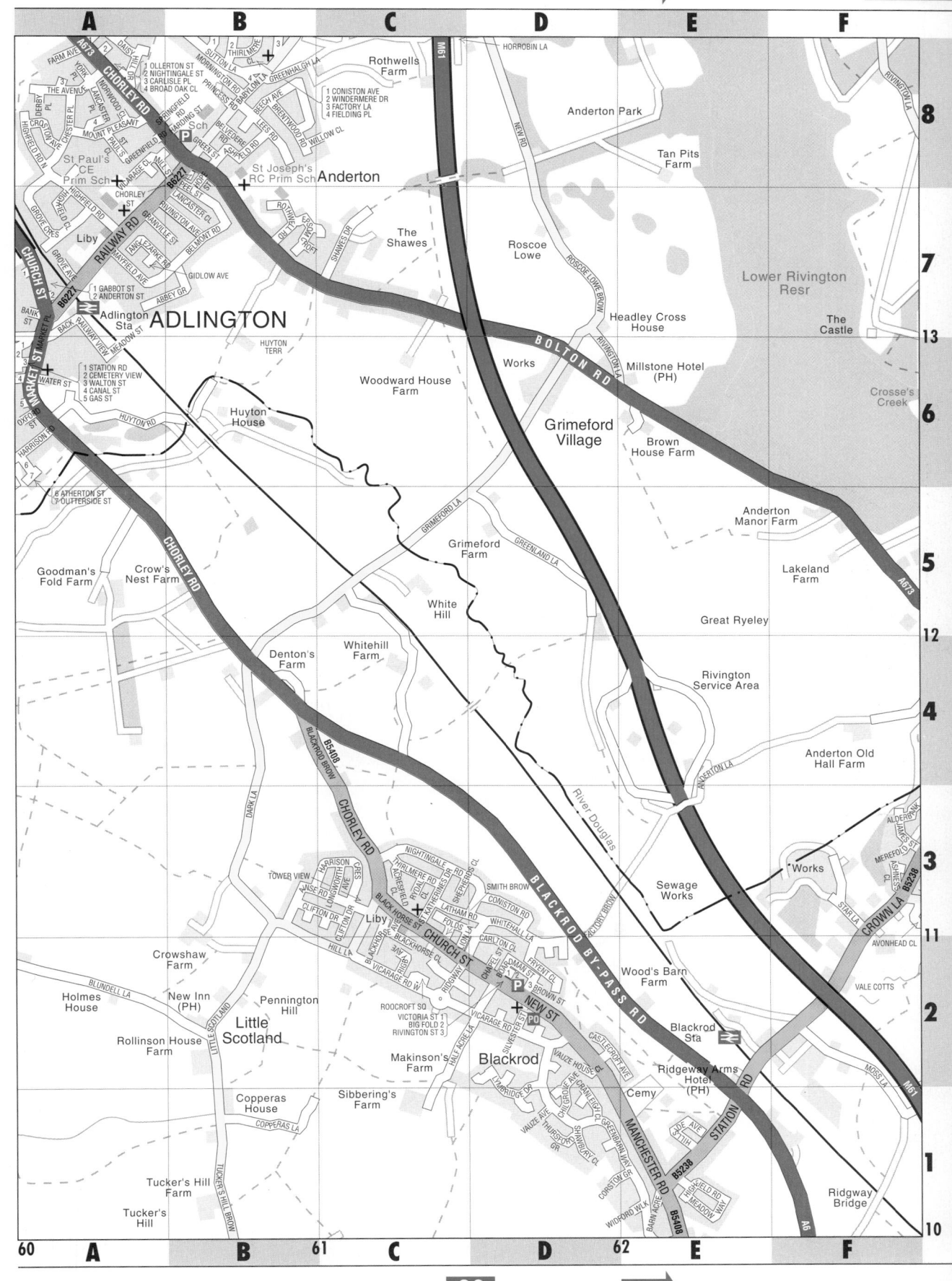

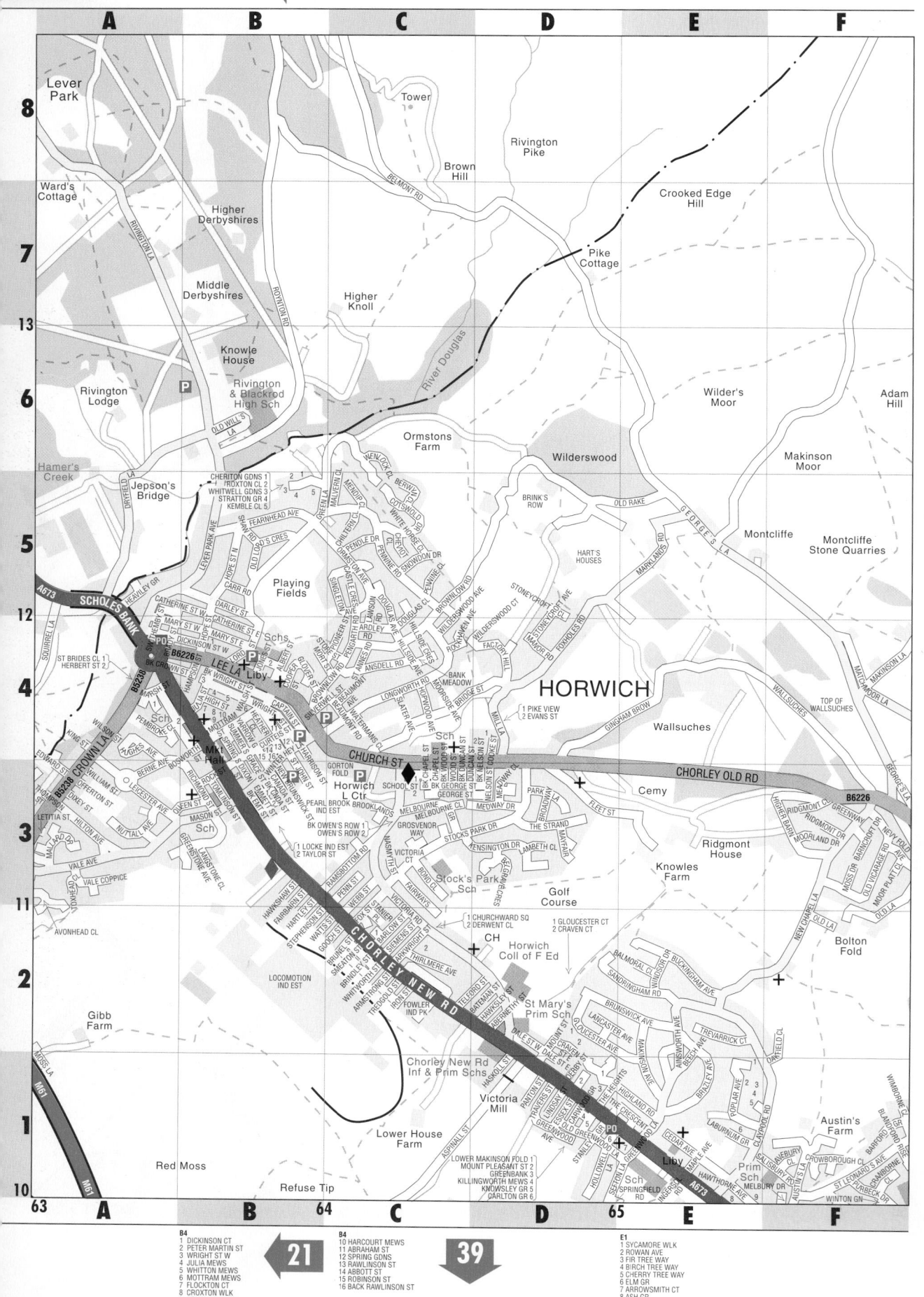

21

A B C D E F

8 Lever Park

Ward's Cottage

7 Higher Derbyshires

Middle Derbyshires

13 Knowle House

Rivington & Blackrod High Sch

6 Rivington Lodge

Hamer's Creek

Jepson's Bridge

RIVINGTON LA

ROYNTON RD

OLD WILL'S LA

DRYFIELD LA

Tower

Brown Hill

Rivington Pike

Pike Cottage

Higher Knoll

River Douglas

Ormstons Farm

Wilderswood

Brink's Row

Crooked Edge Hill

Wilder's Moor

Adam Hill

Makinson Moor

Montcliffe

Montcliffe Stone Quarries

GEORGE'S LA

BELMONT RD

OLD RAKE

HART'S HOUSES

5 CHERITON GDNS 1
ROXTON CL 2
WHITWELL GDNS 3
STRATTON GR 4
KEMBLE CL 5

FEARNHEAD AVE

LEVER PARK AVE

12 Playing Fields

SCHOLES BANK

A673

SQUIRREL LA

HEAVILEY GR

B5238

Schs

St BRIDES CL 1
HERBERT ST 2

PO

E B6226

4 LEE LA

Liby

CROWN LA

B5238

A673

KING ST

EDWARD ST

WILSON ST

CHURCH ST

HORWICH

1 PIKE VIEW
2 EVANS ST

Sch

Wallsuches

TOP OF WALLSUCHES

MATCAMOOR LA

MAKINSON LA

WALLSUCHES

GINGHAM BROW

B6226

GEORGE'S LA

Mkt Hall

Sch

LETITIA ST

HILTON AVE

VALE AVE

Vale Coppice

3 Sch

1 LOCKE IND EST
2 TAYLOR ST

CHORLEY OLD RD

Cemy

Ridgmont House

Knowles Farm

HIGHER BARN LA

RIDGMONT DR

MOORLAND DR

NEW CHAPEL LA

MOSS LA BANCROFT DR

MOOR PLATT CL

OLD LA

AVONHEAD CL

Horwich L Ctr

Brooklands

PEARL BROOK IND EST

BK OWEN'S ROW 1
OWEN'S ROW 2

Melbourne CL

GROSVENOR WAY

Victoria CT

Stocks Park Dr

KENSINGTON DR

Golf Course

Stock's Park Sch

Fairways

The Strand

BROADWAY

FLEET ST

BALMORAL CL

SANDRINGHAM RD

BUCKINGHAM AVE

2 Gibb Farm

LOCOMOTION IND EST

CHORLEY NEW RD

1 CHURCHWARD SQ
2 DERWENT CL

1 GLOUCESTER CT
2 CRAVEN CT

CH

Horwich Coll of F Ed

St Mary's Prim Sch

BRUNSWICK AVE

LANCASTER AVE

GLOUCESTER AVE

TREVARRICK CT

BRANSDALE AVE

MAKINSON AVE

POPLAR AVE

Bolton Fold

1 Red Moss

MOSS LA

M61

Chorley New Rd Inf & Prim Schs

Victoria Mill

Lower House Farm

LOWER MAKINSON FOLD 1
MOUNT PLEASANT ST 2
GREENBANK 3
KILLINGWORTH MEWS 4
KNOWSLEY GR 5
CARLTON GR 6

A673

Liby

Prim Sch

Austin's Farm

10 Refuse Tip

Red Moss

63 A 64 B C 65 D E F

B4
1 DICKINSON CT
2 PETER MARTIN ST
3 WRIGHT ST W
4 JULIA MEWS
5 WHITTON MEWS
6 MOTTRAM MEWS
7 FLOCKTON CT
8 CROXTON WLK
9 BEATRICE MEWS

B4
10 HARCOURT MEWS
11 ABRAHAM ST
12 SPRING GDNS
13 RAWLINSON ST
14 ABBOTT ST
15 ROBINSON ST
16 BACK RAWLINSON ST

E1
1 SYCAMORE WLK
2 ROWAN AVE
3 FIR TREE WAY
4 BIRCH TREE WAY
5 CHERRY TREE WAY
6 ELM GR
7 ARROWSMITH CT
8 ASH GR
9 OAK AVE

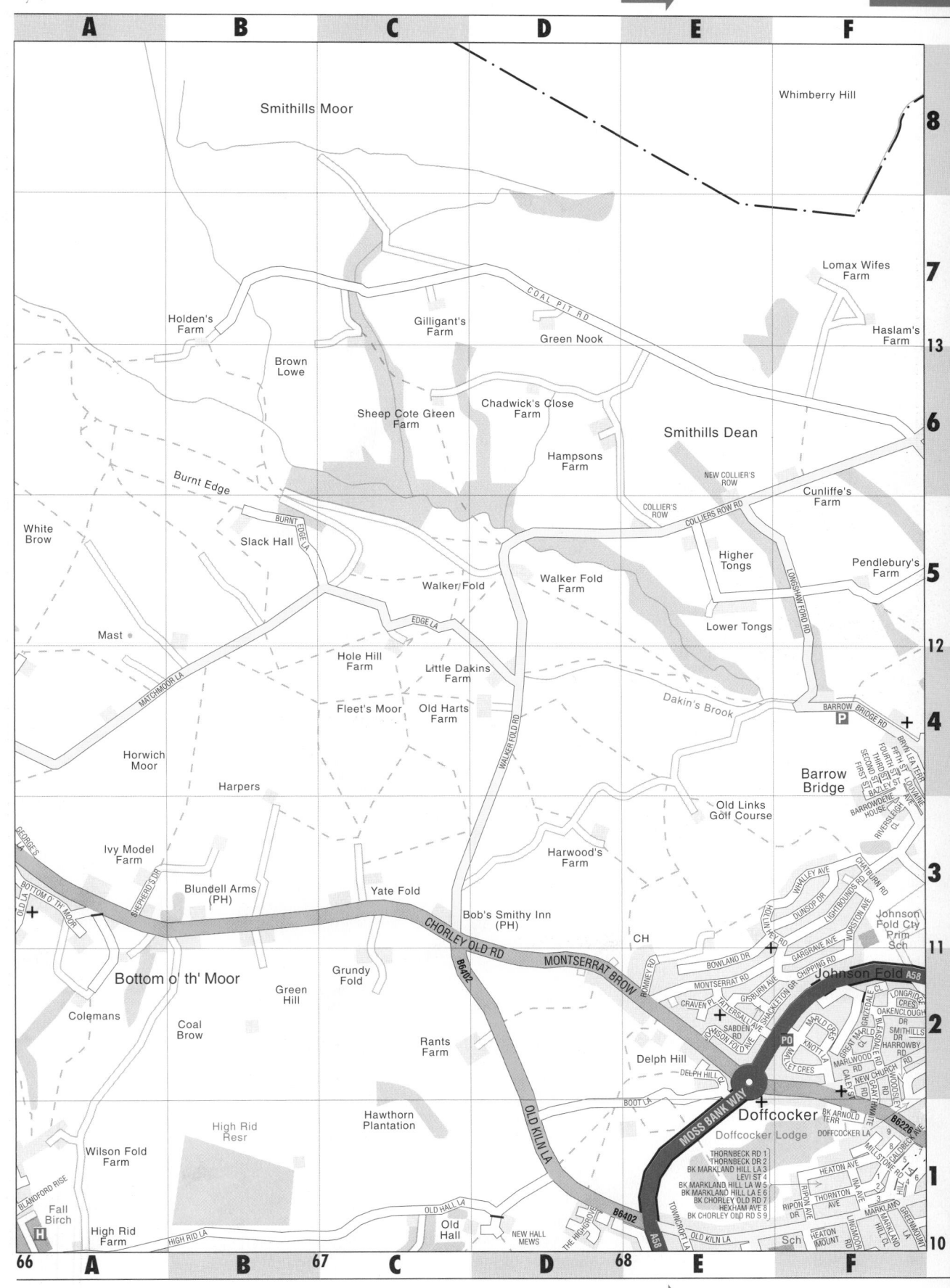

Whimberry Hill

Smithills Moor

8

Lomax Wifes
Farm

7

COAL PIT RD

Holden's
Farm

Gilligant's
Farm

Green Nook

Haslam's
Farm

13

Brown
Lowe

Sheep Cote Green
Farm

Chadwick's Close
Farm

Smithills Dean

6

Hampsons
Farm

NEW COLLIER'S
ROW

Cunliffe's
Farm

Burnt Edge

COLLIER'S
ROW

COLLIERS ROW RD

White
Brow

BURNT
EDGE LA

Slack Hall

Higher
Tongs

Pendlebury's
Farm

5

Walker Fold

Walker Fold
Farm

LONGSHAW FORD RD

EDGE LA

Lower Tongs

Mast

12

Hole Hill
Farm

Little Dakins
Farm

Dakin's Brook

BARROW BRIDGE RD

P

MATCHMOOR LA

Fleet's Moor

Old Harts
Farm

4

Horwich
Moor

Barrow
Bridge

BRYN LEA TERR
LOUVAINE
FIFTH ST
FOURTH ST
THIRD ST
SECOND ST
FIRST ST
BAZLEY ST

Harpers

Old Links
Golf Course

BARROWDENE
HOUSE
RIVERSLEIGH
CL

Ivy Model
Farm

Harwood's
Farm

3

GEORGE'S
LA

SHEPHERD'S DR

Blundell Arms
(PH)

Yate Fold

Bob's Smithy Inn
(PH)

CH

WHALLEY AVE
DUNSOP DR
LIGHTBOURNE AVE
CHATBURN RD
WORSTON AVE

Johnson
Fold Cty
Prim
Sch

OLD LA

BOTTOM O' TH' MOOR

CHORLEY OLD RD

MONTSERRAT BROW

BOWLAND DR

CHIPPING RD
GARGRAVE AVE

Johnson Fold A58

11

Bottom o' th' Moor

B6402

Grundy
Fold

Green
Hill

RUMNEY RD

MONTSERRAT RD

GISBURN AVE
SHACKLETON GR

LONGRIDGE
CRES
OAKENCLOUGH
DR
SMITHILLS
DR
HARROWBY
RD

PO

2

Colemans

Coal
Brow

Rants
Farm

CRAVEN AVE

PATTERSALL AVE

SABDEN
RD

JOHNSON FOLD AVE

GREAT MARLAND
GRIZEDALE
MARLAND

KNOTT LA

MARLWOOD
RD

MALLET CRES

NEW CHURCH
RD

WOODSEY
RD
CALEY'S

Delph Hill

DELPH HILL CL

BOOT LA

MOSS BANK WAY

B6226

High Rid
Resr

Hawthorn
Plantation

OLD KILN LA

Doffcocker

BK ARNOLD
TERR

DOFFCOCKER LA

1

Wilson Fold
Farm

Doffcocker Lodge

THORNBECK RD 1
THORNBECK DR 2
BK MARKLAND HILL LA 3
LEVI ST 4
BK MARKLAND HILL LA W 5
BK MARKLAND HILL LA E 6
BK CHORLEY OLD RD 7
HEXHAM AVE 8
BK CHORLEY OLD RD S 9

HEATON AVE

THORNTON
AVE

RIPON
DR

MILLSTONE RD
CALDBECK

MARKLAND
HILL CL
GREENMOUNT

BLANDFORD RISE

H

Fall
Birch

High Rid
Farm

HIGH RID LA

OLD HALL LA

Old
Hall

NEW HALL
MEWS

THE HEDGROVE

B6402

A58

TOWNCROFT LA

OLD KILN LA

Sch

HEATON
MOUNT

UNDERCROFT RD

10

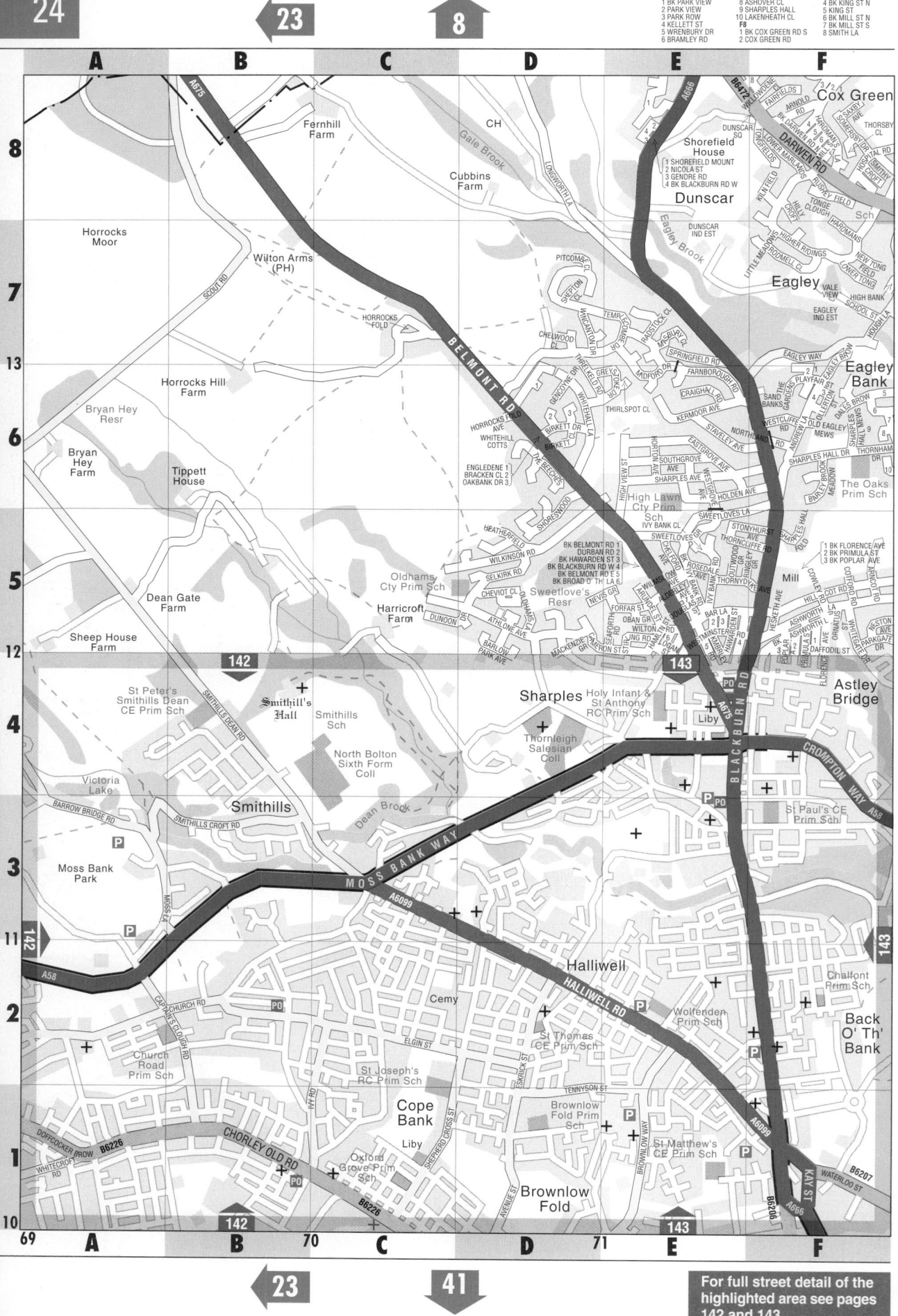

23

8

F6
1 BK PARK VIEW
2 PARK VIEW
3 PARK ROW
4 KELLETT ST
5 WRENBURY DR
6 BRAMLEY RD

7 CRUNDALE RD
8 ASHOVER CL
9 SHARPLES HALL
10 LAKENHEATH CL
F8
1 BK COX GREEN RD S
2 COX GREEN RD

3 BK COX GREEN RD N
4 BK KING ST N
5 KING ST
6 BK MILL ST N
7 BK MILL ST S
8 SMITH LA

Cox Green

Shorefield House
1 SHOREFIELD MOUNT
2 NICOLA ST
3 GENDRE RD
4 BK BLACKBURN RD W

Dunscar

Eagley

Eagley Bank

Horrocks Moor

Fernhill Farm

Cubbins Farm

Wilton Arms (PH)

Horrocks Fold

Horrocks Hill Farm

Bryan Hey Resr

Bryan Hey Farm

Tippett House

Dean Gate Farm

Sheep House Farm

Harricroft Farm

Oldhams Cty Prim Sch

Oldhams

Sweetlove's Resr

High Lawn Cty Prim Sch

BK BELMONT RD 1
DURBAN RD 2
BK HAWARDEN ST 3
BK BLACKBURN RD 4
BK BELMONT RD E 5
BK BROAD O'TH LA 6

1 BK FLORENCE AVE
2 BK PRIMULA AVE
3 BK POPLAR AVE

Mill

Astley Bridge

Sharples

Holy Infant & St Anthony RC Prim Sch

Liby

St Paul's CE Prim Sch

St Peter's Smithills Dean CE Prim Sch

Smithill's Hall

Smithills Sch

North Bolton Sixth Form Coll

Thornleigh Salesian Coll

Victoria Lake

Moss Bank Park

Smithills

Dean Brook

Chalfont Prim Sch

Halliwell

Wolfenden Prim Sch

Back O' Th' Bank

Church Road Prim Sch

Cemy

St Thomas CE Prim Sch

St Joseph's RC Prim Sch

Elgin St

Cope Bank

Liby

Oxford Grove Prim Sch

Brownlow Fold Prim Sch

St Matthew's CE Prim Sch

Brownlow Fold

For full street detail of the highlighted area see pages 142 and 143.

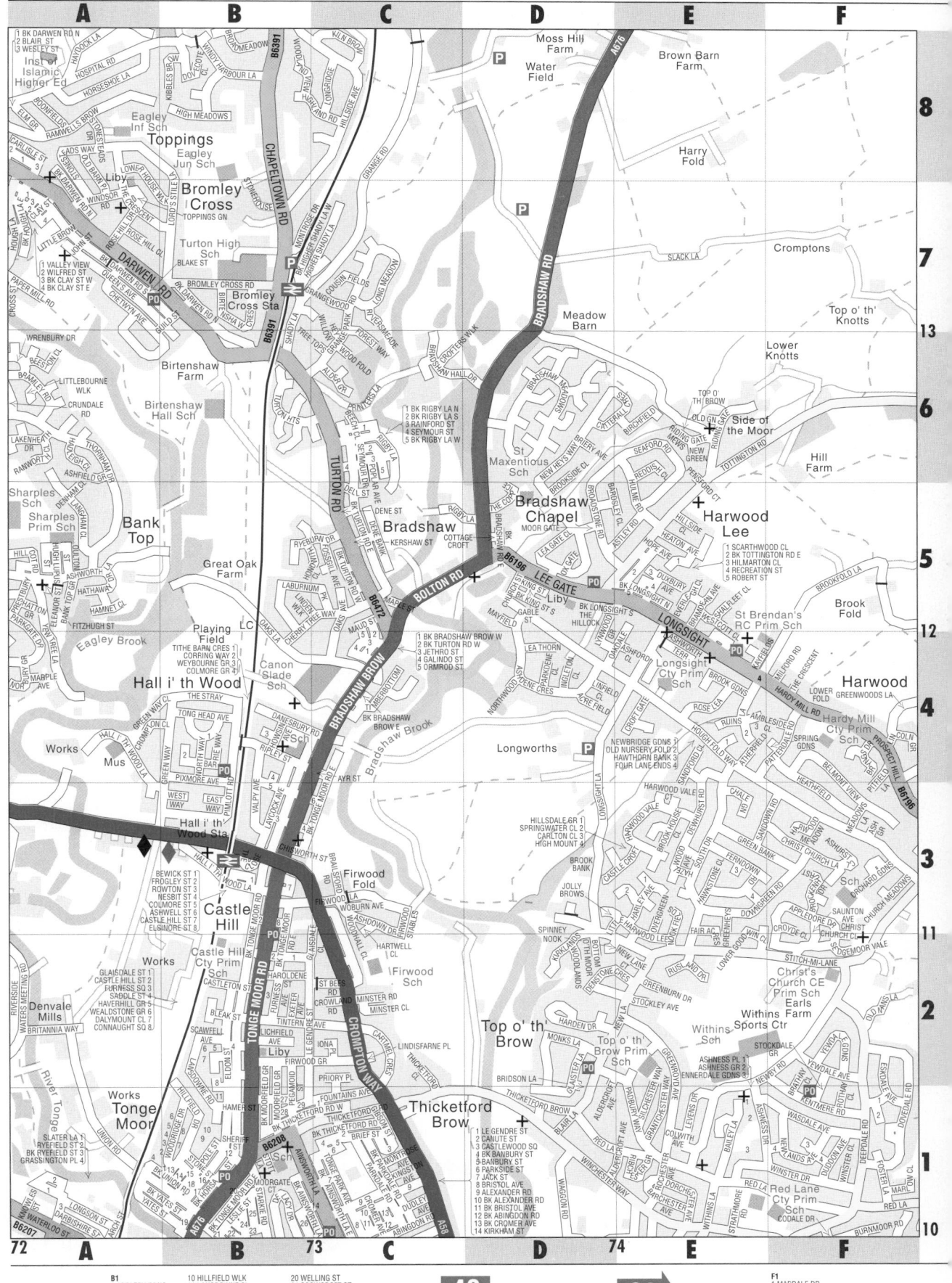

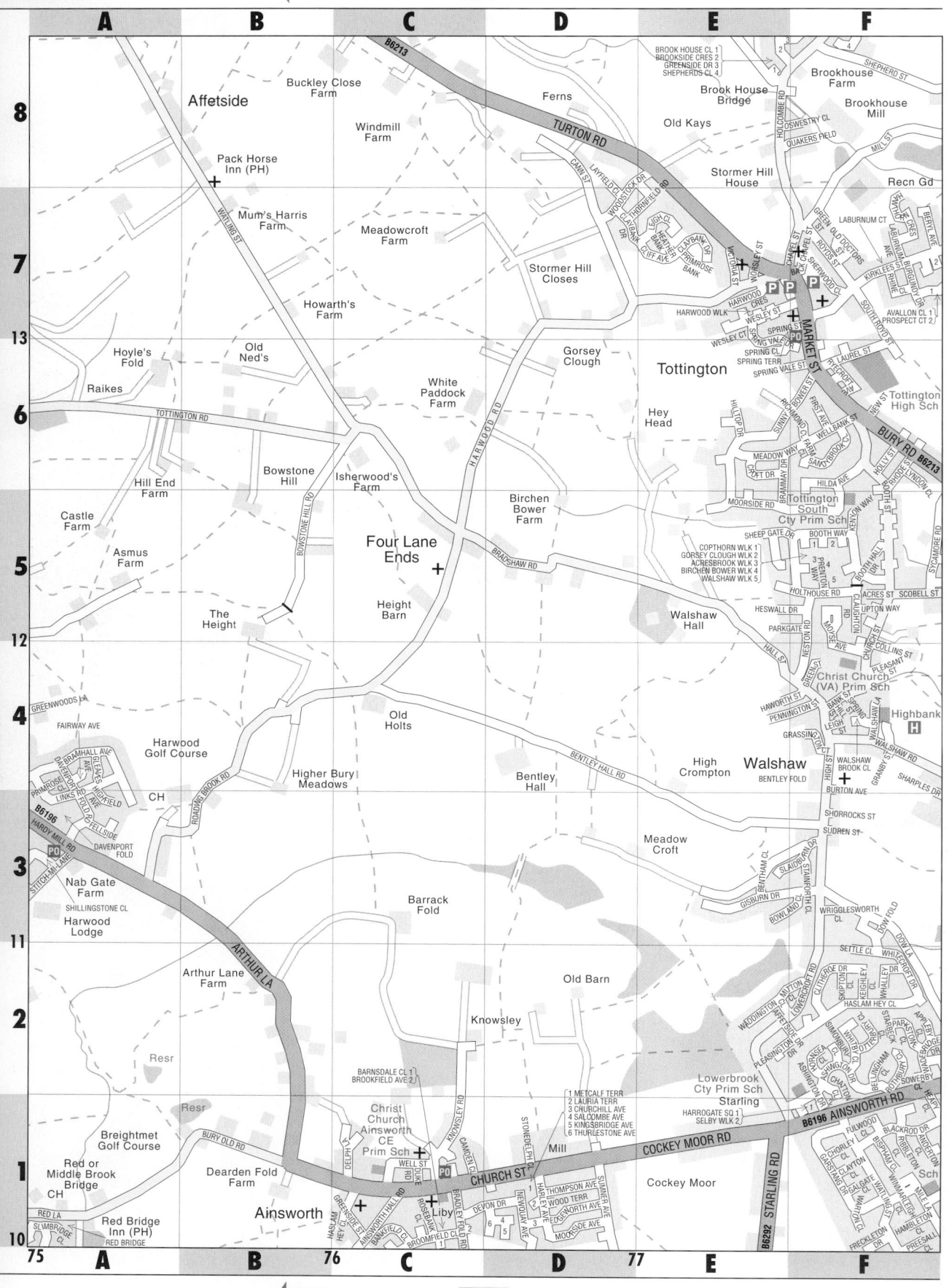

25
10

Map labels

A B C D E F

8 7 13 6 5 12 4 3 11 2 1 10

B6213

Affetside

Buckley Close Farm

Windmill Farm

Ferns

TURTON RD

BROOK HOUSE CL 1
BROOKSIDE CRES 2
GREENSIDE DR 3
SHEPHERDS CL 4

Brook House Bridge

Brookhouse Farm

SHEPHERD ST

Old Kays

Brookhouse Mill

Pack Horse Inn (PH)

Stormer Hill House

Recn Gd

Mum's Harris Farm

Meadowcroft Farm

Stormer Hill Closes

LABURNUM CT

Howarth's Farm

Hoyle's Fold

Old Ned's

White Paddock Farm

Gorsey Clough

Tottington

Hey Head

AVALLON CL 1
PROSPECT CT 2

Raikes

TOTTINGTON RD

Tottington High Sch

Hill End Farm

Bowstone Hill

Isherwood's Farm

BURY RD B6213

Castle Farm

Asmus Farm

Four Lane Ends

Birchen Bower Farm

BRADSHAW RD

HARWOOD RD

Tottington South Cty Prim Sch

COPTHORN WLK 1
GORSEY CLOUGH WLK 2
ACRESBROOK WLK 3
BIRCHEN BOWER WLK 4
WALSHAW WLK 5

The Height

Height Barn

Walshaw Hall

Christ Church (VA) Prim Sch

Highbank

Greenwoods La

Fairway Ave

Old Holts

High Crompton

Walshaw

Bentley Fold

Harwood Golf Course

Higher Bury Meadows

BENTLEY HALL RD

Bentley Hall

CH

ROADING BROOK RD

SHORROCKS ST
SUDREN ST

B6196

Meadow Croft

WRIGGLESWORTH CL

Nab Gate Farm

SHILLINGSTONE CL

Harwood Lodge

Arthur Lane Farm

ARTHUR LA

Barrack Fold

Old Barn

SETTLE CL

Resr

Knowsley

BARNSDALE CL 1
BROOKFIELD AVE 2

Lowerbrook Cty Prim Sch

Starling

Resr

Breightmet Golf Course

Bury Old Rd

Christ Church Ainsworth CE Prim Sch

Mill

COCKEY MOOR RD

1 METCALF TERR
2 LAURIA TERR
3 CHURCHILL AVE
4 SALCOMBE AVE
5 KINGSBRIDGE AVE
6 THURLESTONE AVE

HARROGATE SQ 1
SELBY WLK 2

B6196 AINSWORTH RD

Red or Middle Brook Bridge

CH

Dearden Fold Farm

Ainsworth

CHURCH ST

Liby

Cockey Moor

STARLING RD

B6292

Red Bridge Inn (PH)

RED BRIDGE

25
43

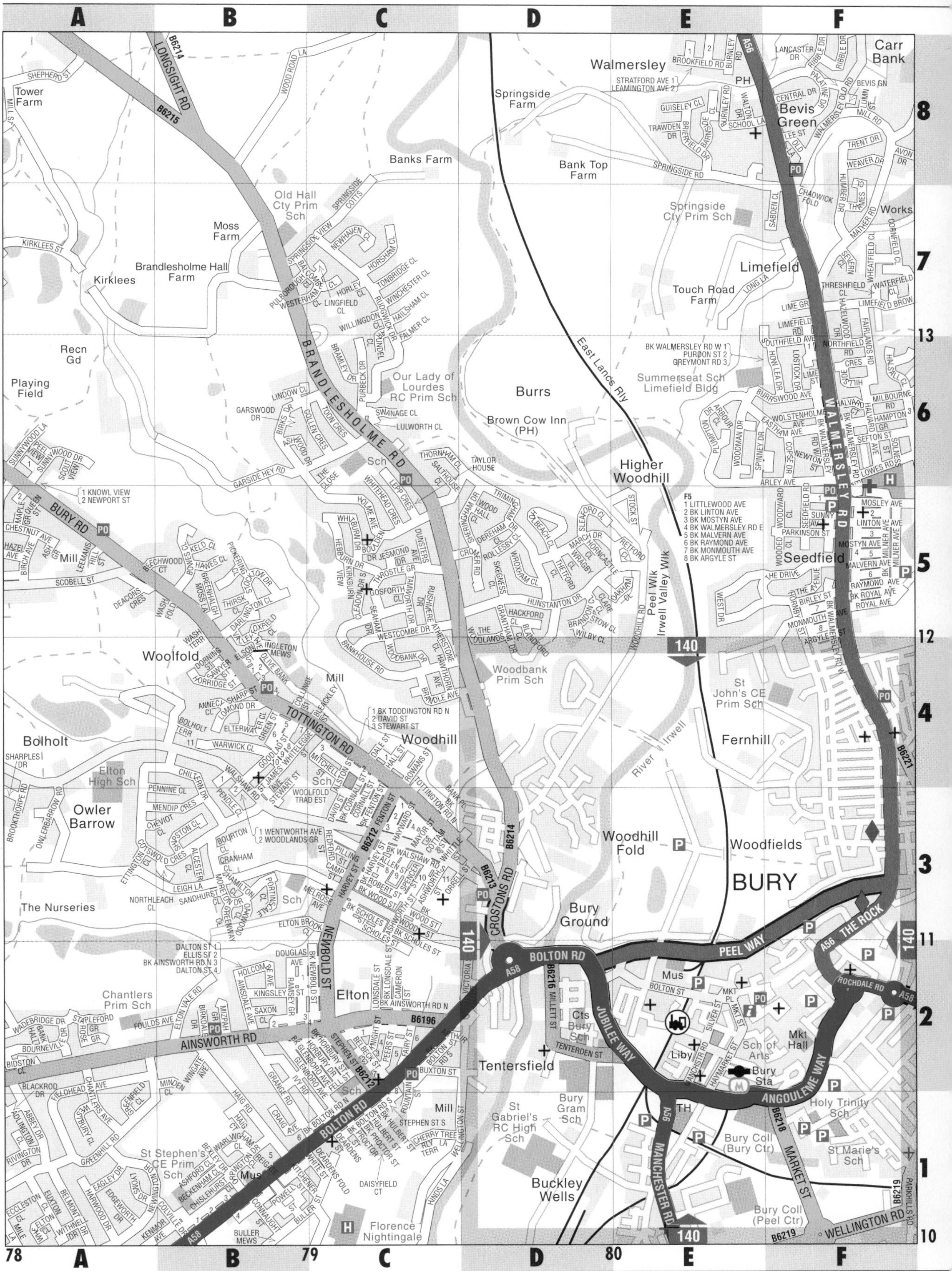

BURY

Major places / labels:

Tower Farm, Shepherd's, Kirklees, Brandlesholme Hall Farm, Moss Farm, Old Hall Cty Prim Sch, Banks Farm, Springside Farm, Bank Top Farm, Walmersley, Bevis Green, Carr Bank, Limefield, Springside Cty Prim Sch, Touch Road Farm, Summerseat Sch, Limefield Bldg, Recn Gd, Playing Field, Our Lady of Lourdes RC Prim Sch, Burrs, Brown Cow Inn (PH), Higher Woodhill, Seedfield, Mill, Woolfold, Woodbank Prim Sch, Woodhill, Bolholt, Elton High Sch, St John's CE Prim Sch, Fernhill, Owler Barrow, The Nurseries, Woodhill Fold, Woodfields, Bury Ground, Chantlers Prim Sch, Elton, Tentersfield, Bury Gram Sch, Peel Way, The Rock, Bolton Rd, Mus, MKT, Sch of Arts, Mkt Hall, Liby, Bury Sta, St Gabriel's RC High Sch, Buckley Wells, Holy Trinity Sch, Bury Coll (Bury Ctr), St Marie's Sch, St Stephen's CE Prim Sch, Florence Nightingale, Bury Coll (Peel Ctr), Jubilee Way, Manchester Rd, Angoulewe Way, Market St, Wellington Rd

Roads: LONGSIGHT RD, B6214, B6215, BRANDLESHOLME RD, BURY RD, TOTTINGTON RD, NEWBOLD ST, AINSWORTH RD, CROSTONS RD, BOLTON RD, A58, WALMERSLEY RD, A56, B6221, B6219, B6196, B6212, B6213, B6216

F5
1 LITTLEWOOD AVE
2 BK LINTON AVE
3 BK MOSTYN AVE
4 BK WALMERSLEY RD E
5 BK MALVERN AVE
6 BK RAYMOND AVE
7 BK MONMOUTH AVE
8 BK ARGYLE ST

B1
1 WOLSELEY ST
2 WARREN ST
3 LUTON ST
4 CHIRMSIDE ST
5 WELLINGTON SQ
6 WELLINGTON CT

B4
1 WALMSLEY ST
2 BK OLIVE BANK

3 HILL'S CT
4 MILL LA
5 BK TOTTINGTON RD
6 BK GOODLAD ST
7 SMETHURST ST
8 BK BYROM ST
9 BYROM ST
10 BK BYROM ST S
11 BONHOLT IND EST

C2
1 BK AINSWORTH RD S
2 BK STEPHEN ST
3 BK BELBECK ST
4 BK KNIGHT ST
5 BK PEERS ST
6 DAISY ST
7 STEPHEN CL
8 BELBECK ST S

C3
1 BK TOTTINGTON RD S
2 BK HAYWARD ST
3 BK WALSHAW RD N
4 BK MAYOR ST
5 BK COTTAM ST
6 BK WHITTLE ST
7 HILLYARD ST
8 NEW GEORGE ST
9 BK NEW GEORGE ST

10 BK ASHWORTH ST
11 BOOTHFIELD

For full street detail of the highlighted area see page 140.

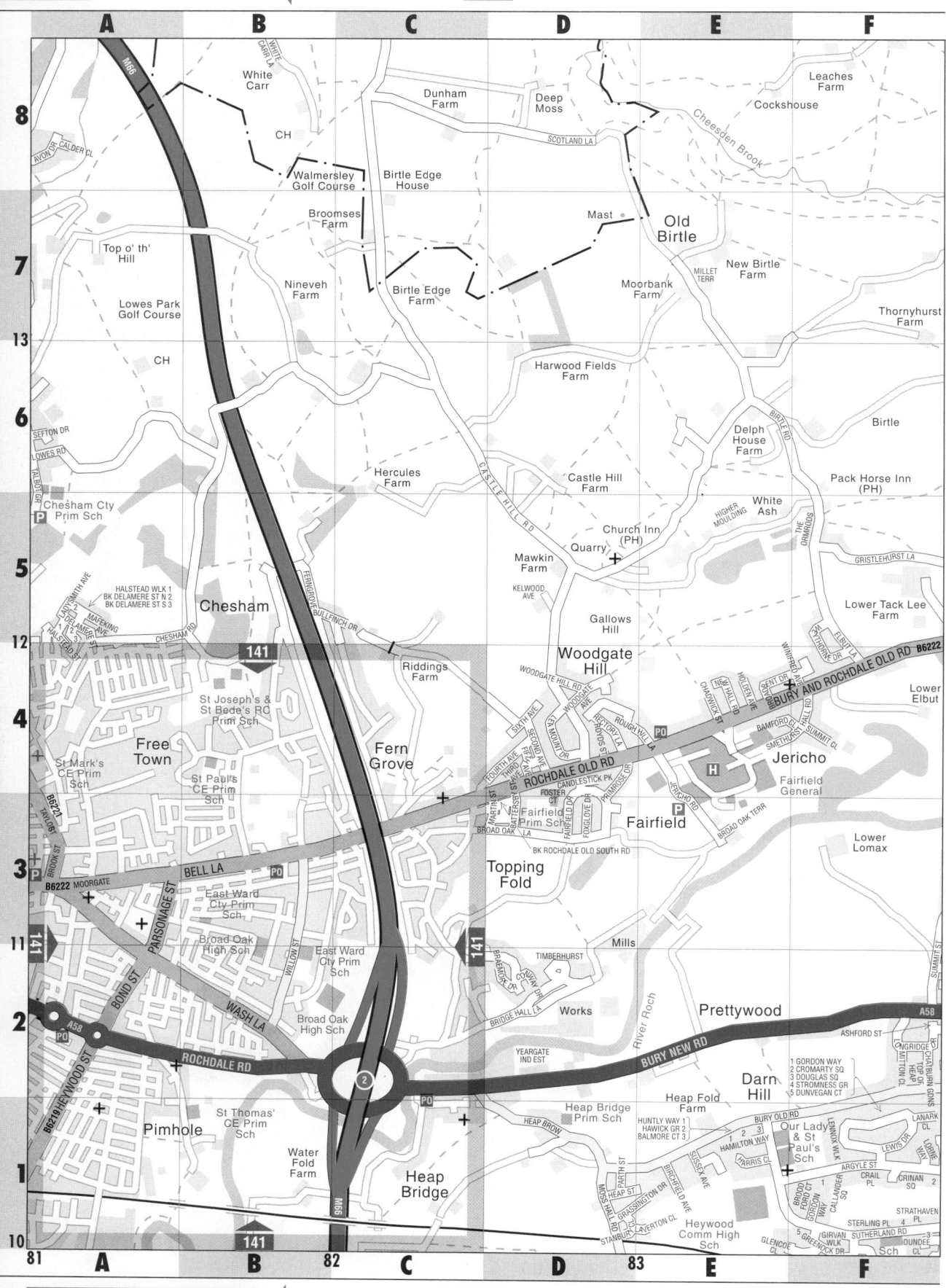

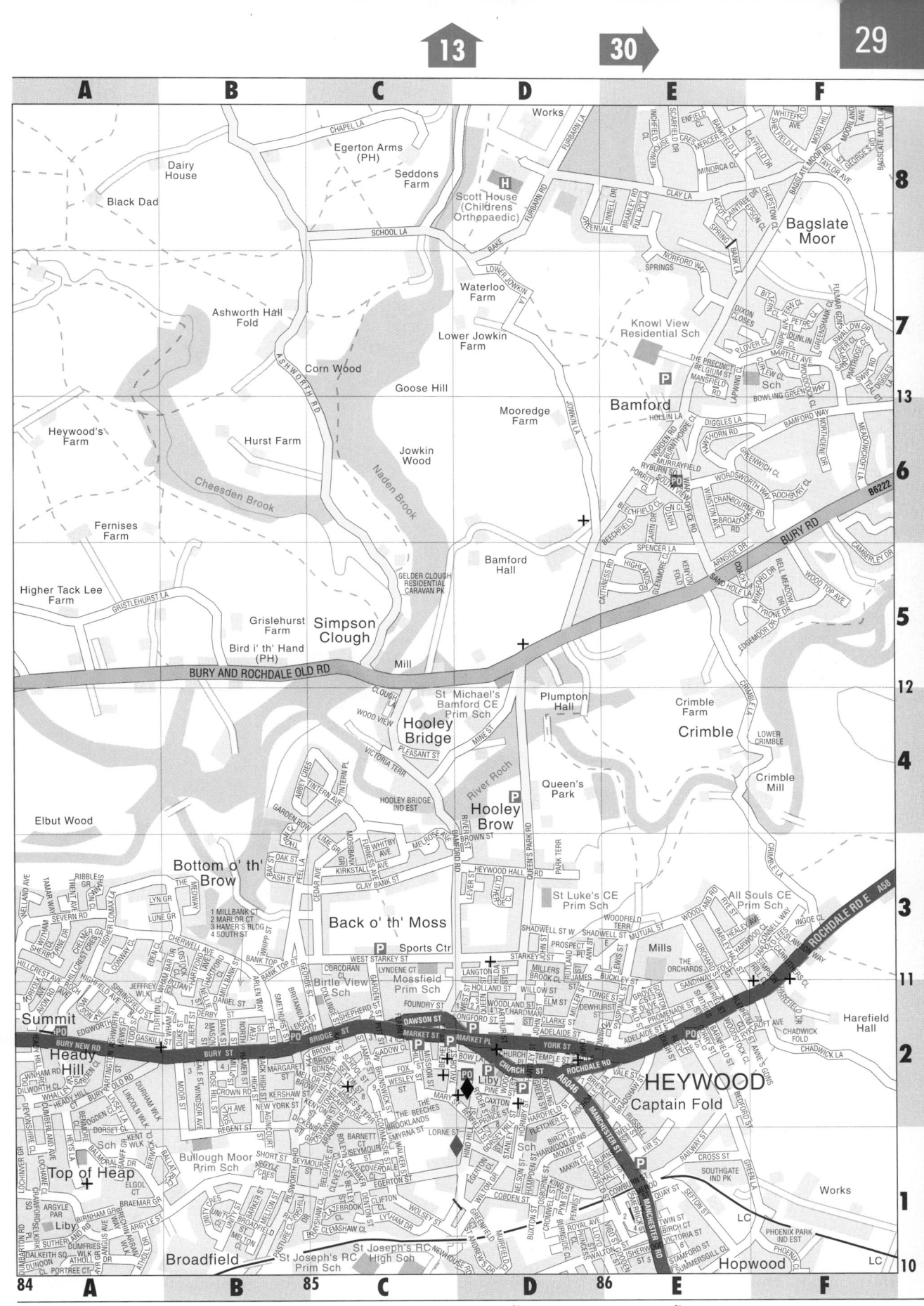

A B C D E F

8
7
13
6
5
12
4
3
11
2
1
10

84 A 85 B C 85 D 86 E F

Works
Egerton Arms (PH)
Seddons Farm
Scott House (Childrens Orthopaedic)
Bagslate Moor
Dairy House
Black Dad
Ashworth Hall Fold
Waterloo Farm
Knowl View Residential Sch
Corn Wood
Lower Jowkin Farm
Bamford
Goose Hill
Mooredge Farm
Heywood's Farm
Hurst Farm
Jowkin Wood
Bamford Hall
Cheesden Brook
Naden Brook
BURY RD B6222
Fernises Farm
Gelder Clough Residential Caravan Pk
Higher Tack Lee Farm
Grislehurst Farm
Simpson Clough
Bird i' th' Hand (PH)
Mill
Plumpton Hall
Crimble Farm
Crimble
BURY AND ROCHDALE OLD RD
St Michael's Bamford CE Prim Sch
Lower Crimble
Hooley Bridge
Wood View
Crimble Mill
Elbut Wood
Hooley Brow
Queen's Park
All Souls CE Prim Sch
Bottom o' th' Brow
Hooley Bridge Ind Est
Heywood Hall
St Luke's CE Prim Sch
ROCHDALE RD E A58
1 Millbank Ct
2 Marlor Ct
3 Hamer's Bldg
4 South St
Back o' th' Moss
Sports Ctr
Mossfield Prim Sch
Birtle View Sch
Mills
The Orchards
Harefield Hall
Summit
Heady Hill
BURY ST
Chadwick Fold
Chadwick La
HEYWOOD
Captain Fold
Top of Heap
Libry
Bullough Moor Prim Sch
A6046
MANCHESTER RD
Works
Broadfield
St Joseph's RC Prim Sch
St Joseph's RC High Sch
Phoenix Park Ind Est
Hopwood

For full street detail of the highlighted area see page 139.

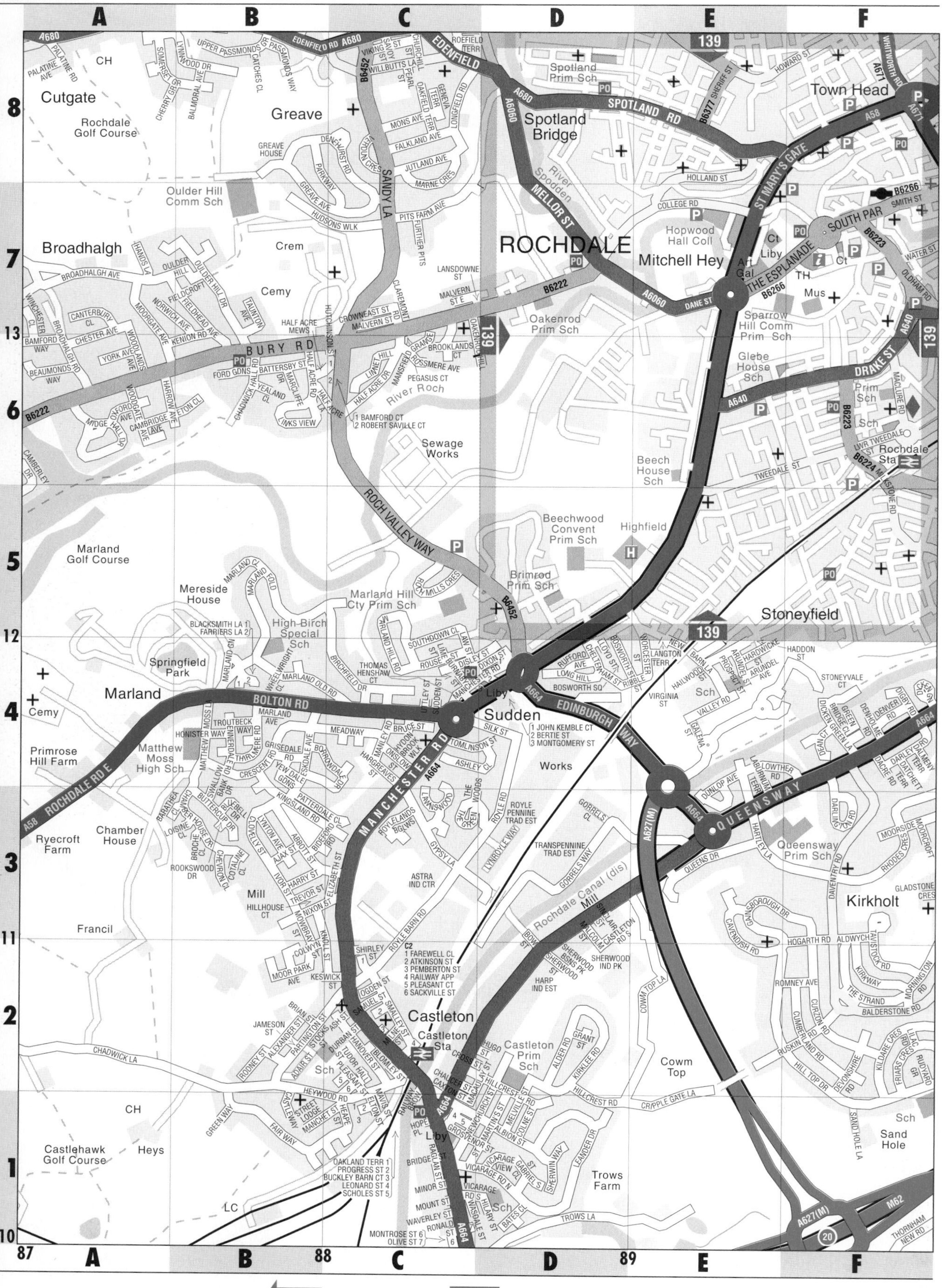

A B C D E F

8

Cutgate

Rochdale
Golf Course

Greave

Oulder Hill
Comm Sch

GREAVE
HOUSE

Spotland
Prim Sch

Spotland
Bridge

SPOTLAND RD

Town Head

139

7

Broadhalgh

Crem

Cemy

ROCHDALE

Hopwood
Hall Coll

Mitchell Hey

College Rd

St MARY'S GATE

SOUTH PAR

Ct
Liby
THE ESPLANADE

TH
Mus

i Ct

13

BURY RD

Oakenrod
Prim Sch

139

Sparrow
Hill Comm
Prim Sch

Glebe
House
Sch

DRAKE ST

139

Prim
Sch

Sch

6

B6222

River Roch

Sewage
Works

Beech
House
Sch

Rochdale
Sta

LWR TWEEDALE

B6224

TWEEDALE ST

5

Marland
Golf Course

Mereside
House

ROCH VALLEY WAY

Marland Hill
Cty Prim Sch

Beechwood
Convent
Prim Sch

Highfield

Brimrod
Prim Sch

H

Stoneyfield

12

High-Birch
Special
Sch

Springfield
Park

Thomas
Henshaw

139

4

Marland

Cemy

BOLTON RD

Matthew
Moss
High Sch

Liby

Sudden

EDINBURGH WAY

A664

1 John Kemble Ct
2 Bertie St
3 Montgomery St

Works

QUEENSWAY

Queensway
Prim Sch

3

Primrose
Hill Farm

ROCHDALE RD E

A58

Chamber
House

MANCHESTER RD

ASTRA
IND CTR

Rochdale Canal (dis)

Mill

TRANSPENNINE
TRAD EST

Queens Dr

A627(M)

A664

Kirkholt

11

Francil

HILLHOUSE
CT

Mill

SHERWOOD
IND PK

2

Ryecroft
Farm

CHADWICK LA

Castleton

Castleton
Sta

Castleton
Prim Sch

HARP
IND EST

Cowm
Top

1

Castlehawk
Golf Course

Heys

Liby

Trows
Farm

Sand
Hole

Sch

10

87 A 88 B C 88 D 89 E F

20

M62

TROWS LA

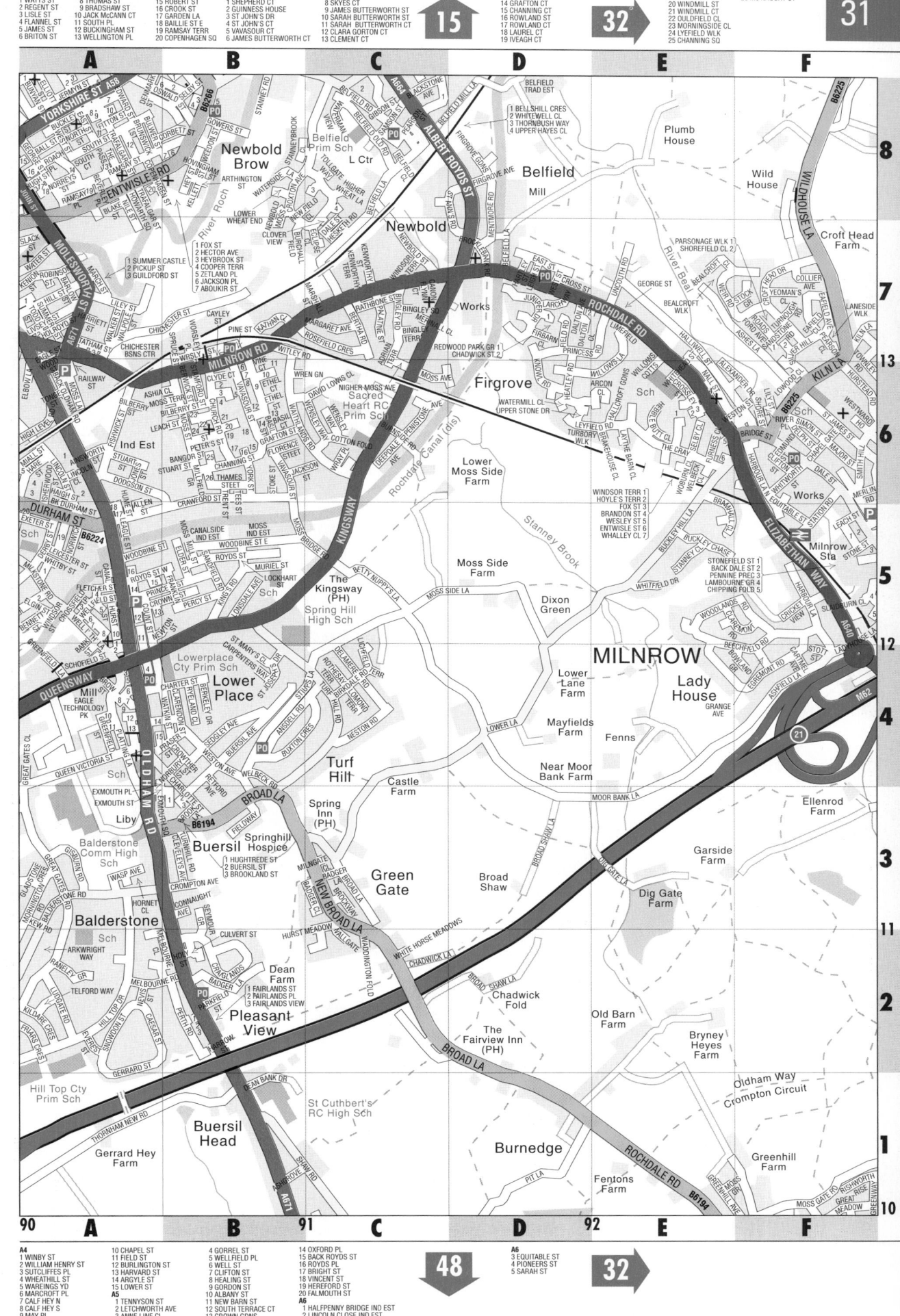

A8
1 WATTS ST
2 REGENT ST
3 LISLE ST
4 FLANNEL ST
5 JAMES ST
6 BRITON ST
7 BACK BRADSHAW ST
8 THOMAS ST
9 BRADSHAW ST
10 JACK McCANN CT
11 SOUTH PL
12 BUCKINGHAM ST
13 WELLINGTON PL
14 KITCHEN ST
15 ROBERT ST
16 CROOK ST
17 GARDEN LA
18 BAILLIE ST E
19 RAMSAY TERR
20 COPENHAGEN SQ

B6
1 SHEPHERD CT
2 GUINNESS HOUSE
3 ST JOHN'S DR
4 ST JOHN'S CT
5 VAVASOUR CT
6 JAMES BUTTERWORTH CT

7 SYKES ST
8 SKYES CT
9 JAMES BUTTERWORTH CT
10 SARAH BUTTERWORTH CT
11 SARAH BUTTERWORTH CT
12 CLARA GORTON CT
13 CLEMENT CT

B6
14 GRAFTON CT
15 CHANNING CT
16 CHANNING ST
17 ROWLAND CT
18 LAUREL CT
19 IVEAGH CT

B6
20 WINDMILL ST
21 WINDMILL CT
22 OULDFIELD CL
23 MORNINGSIDE CL
24 LYEFIELD WLK
25 CHANNING SQ

26 Mc NAUGHT ST

A4
1 WINBY ST
2 WILLIAM HENRY ST
3 SUTCLIFFES PL
4 WHEATHILL ST
5 WAREINGS YD
6 MARCROFT PL
7 CALF HEY N
8 CALF HEY S
9 MAY PL
10 CHAPEL ST
11 FIELD ST
12 BURLINGTON ST
13 HARVARD ST
14 ARGYLE ST
15 LOWER ST

A5
1 TENNYSON ST
2 LETCHWORTH AVE
3 ANNE LINE CL

4 GORREL ST
5 WELLFIELD PL
6 WELL ST
7 CLIFTON ST
8 HEALING ST
9 GORDON ST
10 ALBANY ST
11 NEW BARN ST
12 SOUTH TERRACE CT
13 CROWN GDNS

14 OXFORD PL
15 BACK ROYDS ST
16 ROYDS ST
17 BRIGHT ST
18 VINCENT ST
19 HEREFORD ST
20 FALMOUTH ST

A6
1 HALFPENNY BRIDGE IND EST
2 LINCOLN CLOSE IND EST

A6
3 EQUITABLE ST
4 PIONEERS ST
5 SARAH ST

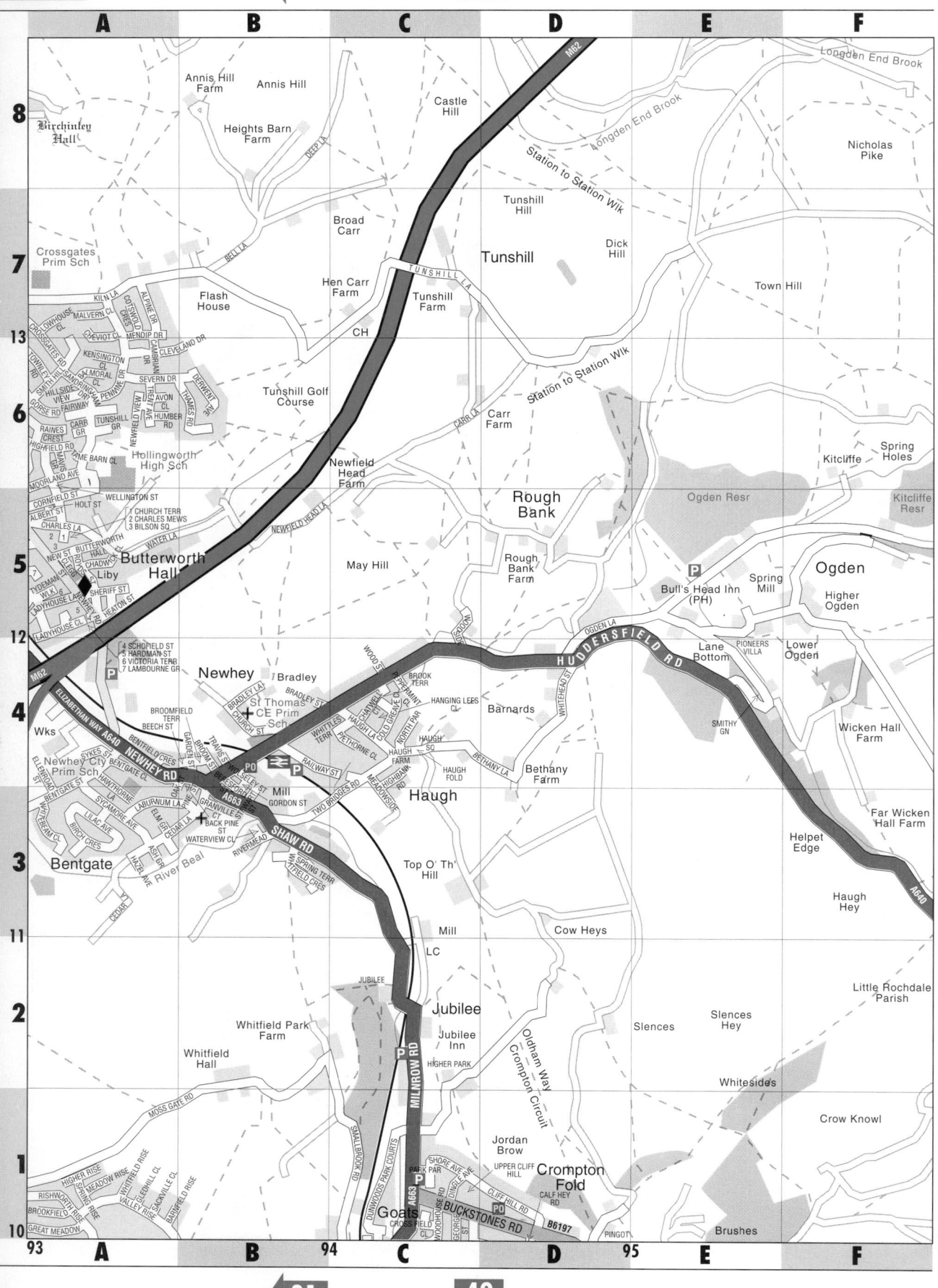

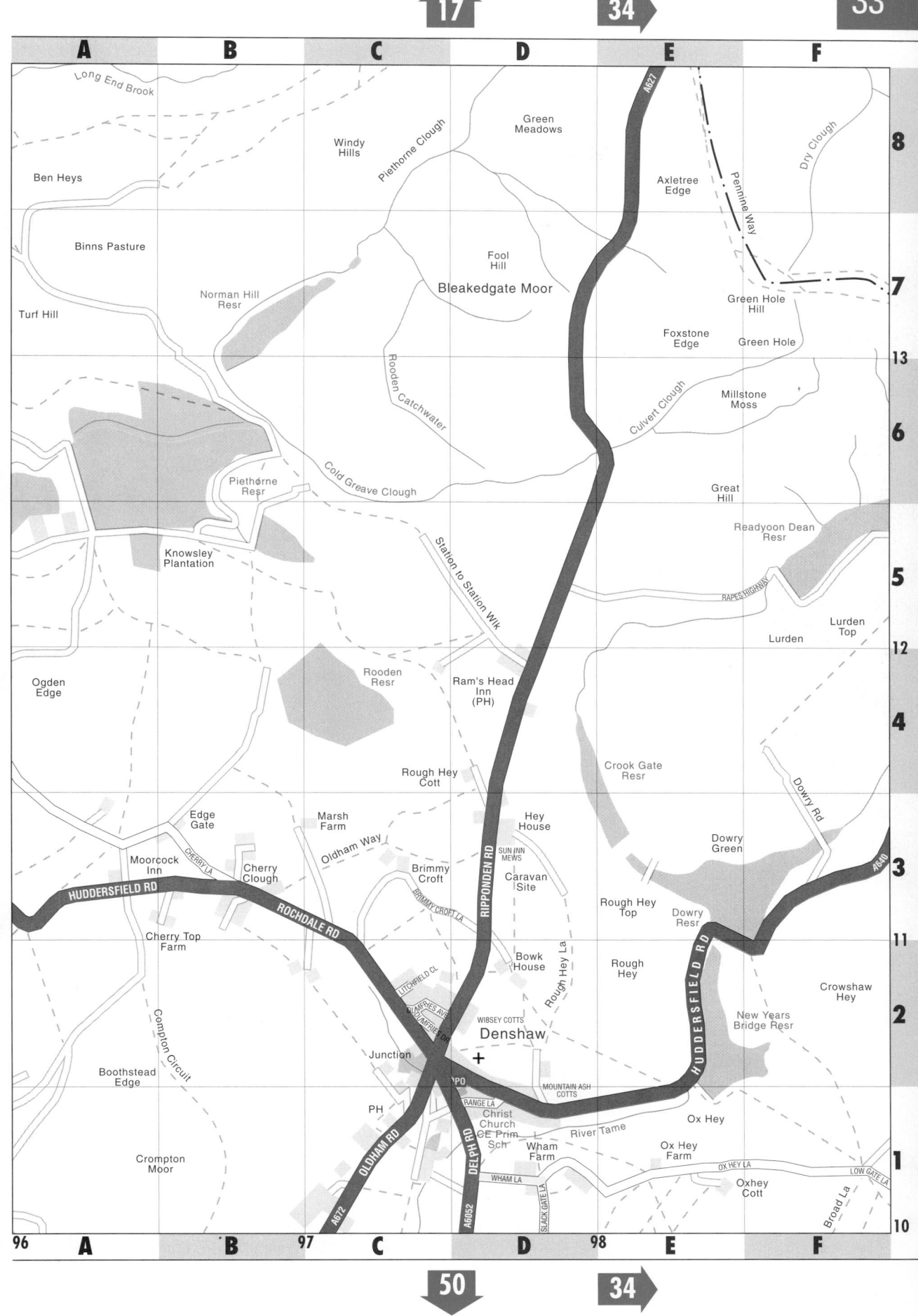

A B C D E F

8

Long End Brook

Ben Heys

Windy
Hills

Piethorne Clough

Green
Meadows

A627

Dry Clough

Axletree
Edge

Pennine Way

Binns Pasture

Norman Hill
Resr

Fool
Hill

Bleakedgate Moor

7

Green Hole
Hill

Turf Hill

Foxstone
Edge

Green Hole

13

Rooden Catchwater

Culvert Clough

Millstone
Moss

6

Piethorne Resr

Cold Greave Clough

Great
Hill

Knowsley
Plantation

Readyoon Dean
Resr

RAPES HIGHWAY

5

Ogden
Edge

Rooden
Resr

Station to Station Wlk

Ram's Head
Inn
(PH)

Lurden
Top

Lurden

12

Crook Gate
Resr

Dowry Rd

4

Rough Hey
Cott

Edge
Gate

Marsh
Farm

Oldham Way

Hey
House

CHERRY LA

Moorcock
Inn

Cherry
Clough

Brimmy
Croft

RIPPONDEN RD

SUN INN
MEWS

Caravan
Site

Dowry
Green

A640

3

BRIMMY CROFT LA

Rough Hey
Top

Dowry
Resr

HUDDERSFIELD RD

Cherry Top
Farm

HUDDERSFIELD RD

ROCHDALE RD

Bowk
House

Rough Hey La

Rough
Hey

11

LITCHFIELD CL

Crowshaw
Hey

Compton Circuit

HERDS AVE

WIBSEY COTTS

New Years
Bridge Resr

2

DITHMERE FOLD

Denshaw

Boothstead
Edge

Junction

+

MOUNTAIN ASH
COTTS

PO

GRANGE LA

Christ
Church
CE Prim
Sch

Ox Hey

PH

River Tame

Ox Hey
Farm

1

Crompton
Moor

OLDHAM RD

A672

DELPH RD

A6052

Wham
Farm

WHAM LA

SLACK GATE LA

OX HEY LA

Oxhey
Cott

LOW GATE LA

Broad La

10

96 A B 97 C D 98 E F

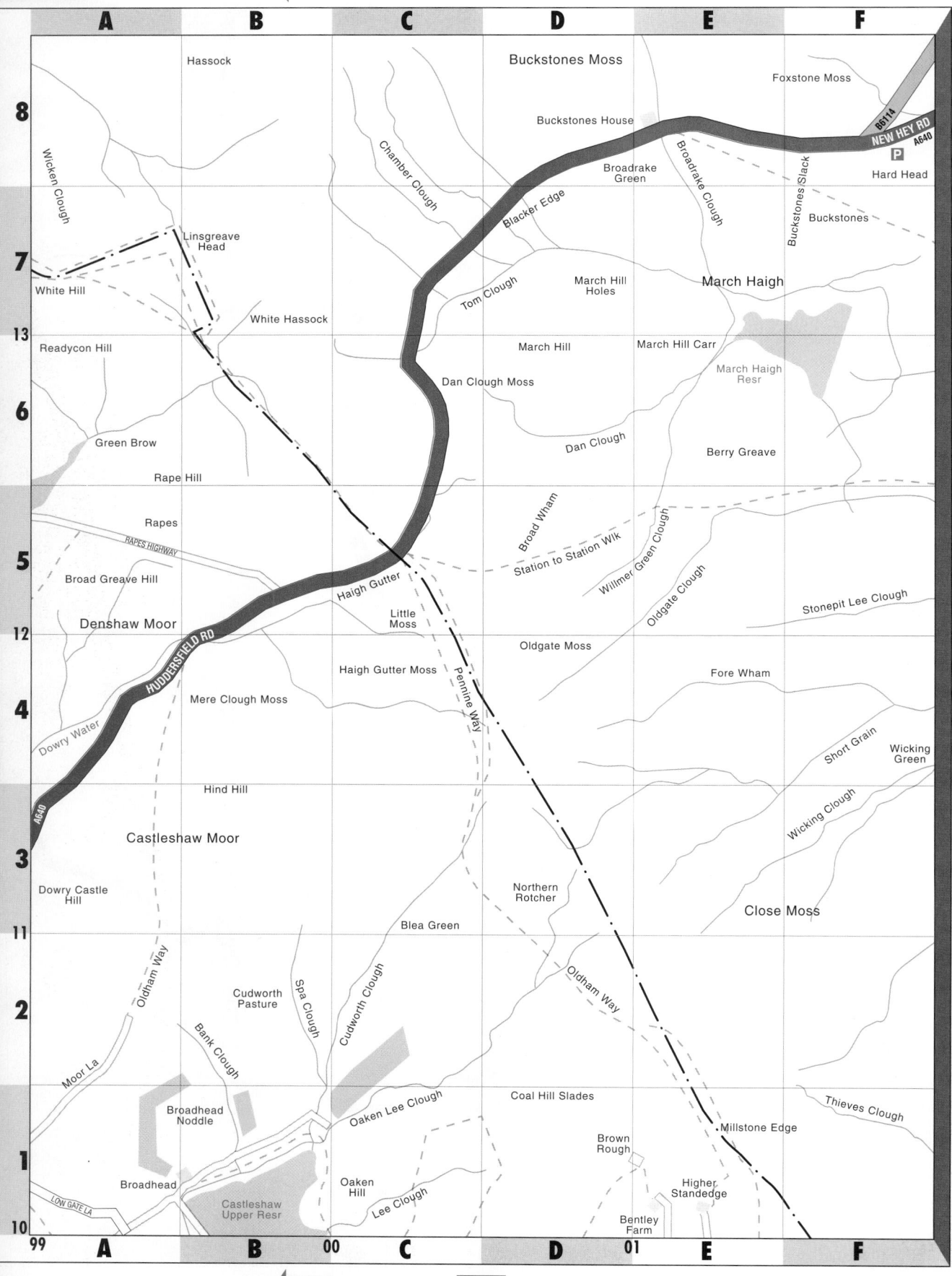

33

A　B　C　D　E　F

8

Hassock

Buckstones Moss

Foxstone Moss

Buckstones House

B6114

NEW HEY RD

A640

Wicken Clough

Chamber Clough

Broadrake Green

Broadrake Clough

Hard Head

7

Linsgreave Head

Blacker Edge

Buckstones Slack

Buckstones

White Hill

White Hassock

Tom Clough

March Hill Holes

March Haigh

13

Readycon Hill

March Hill

March Hill Carr

6

Dan Clough Moss

March Haigh Resr

Green Brow

Dan Clough

Berry Greave

Rape Hill

Rapes

RAPES HIGHWAY

Broad Wham

Station to Station Wlk

Willmer Green Clough

Oldgate Clough

Stonepit Lee Clough

5

Broad Greave Hill

Haigh Gutter

Little Moss

12

Denshaw Moor

HUDDERSFIELD RD

Oldgate Moss

Fore Wham

Mere Clough Moss

Haigh Gutter Moss

Pennine Way

4

Dowry Water

Short Grain

Wicking Green

Hind Hill

Wicking Clough

A640

Castleshaw Moor

3

Dowry Castle Hill

Northern Rotcher

Close Moss

11

Blea Green

Oldham Way

Oldham Way

2

Cudworth Pasture

Spa Clough

Cudworth Clough

Bank Clough

Coal Hill Slades

Thieves Clough

Moor La

Oaken Lee Clough

Brown Rough

Millstone Edge

1

Broadhead Noddle

Oaken Hill

Higher Standedge

Broadhead

Lee Clough

LOW GATE LA

Castleshaw Upper Resr

Bentley Farm

10

99　A　B　00　C　D　01　E　F

33

51

A   B   C   D   E   F

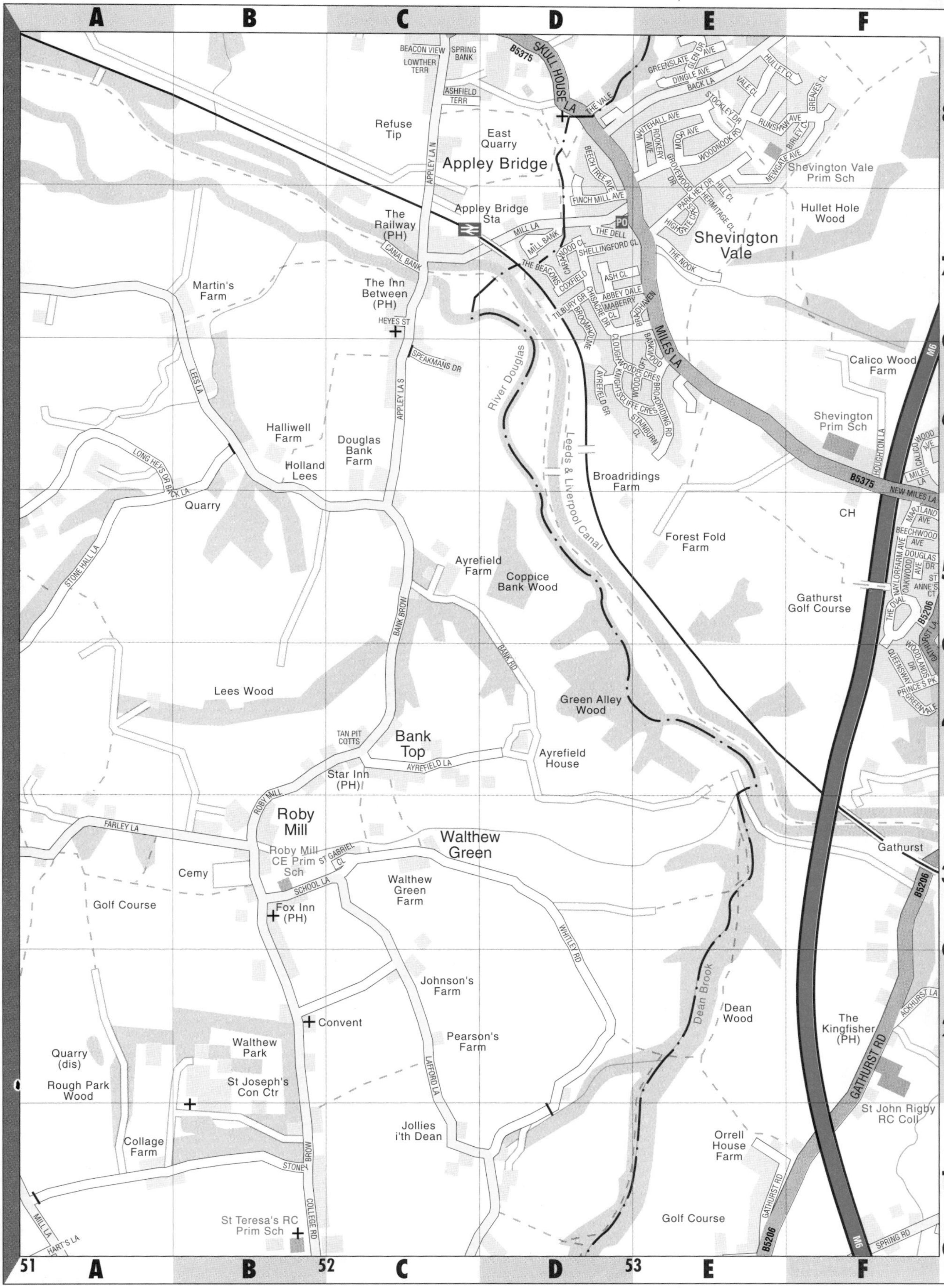

8

B5375   SKULL HOUSE LA

BEACON VIEW   SPRING BANK
LOWTHER TERR

ASHFIELD TERR

Refuse Tip

East Quarry

Appley Bridge

THE VALE
GREENSLATE CL   GLEN AVE
DINGLE AVE   HULLET CL
BACK LA   VALE CL

WHITEHALL AVE   STOCKLEY DR   RUNSHAW AVE   BIRLEY CL
ROOKERY   GROVEWOOD DR   WOQA AVE   NEWGATE AVE
GREAVES CL

FINCH MILL AVE   HILL CL
HERITAGE CL
PARK HEY DR   WOODNOOK RD

Shevington Vale Prim Sch

BEECH TREE AVE   HIGHGATE GR

Hullet Hole Wood

The Railway (PH)

Appley Bridge Sta

PO   THE DELL

MILL LA   WOOD CL
MILL BANK   SHELLINGFORD CL

CANAL BANK   THE NOOK

Shevington Vale

7

Martin's Farm

The Inn Between (PH)

HEYES ST

SPEAKMANS DR

THE BEACONS   ASH CL
COXFIELD   ABBEY DALE   MABERRY CL   KILHAVEN

TILBURY GR   CROSSDALE DR   BROXODALE
CLOUGH WOODS CRES   BROADRIDING RD   STANBURN

KNIGHTSCLIFFE CRES   AIREFIELD DR

09

MILES LA

Calico Wood Farm

6

Halliwell Farm

Douglas Bank Farm

Holland Lees

Leeds & Liverpool Canal

River Douglas

Broadridings Farm

Shevington Prim Sch

BOUGHTON LA

CH

B5375   NEW MILES LA

MILES LA
CALICO WOOD AVE

M6

LEES LA   LONG HEYS DR   BACK LA

Quarry

Ayrefield Farm

Coppice Bank Wood

Forest Fold Farm

MARTLAND AVE
BEECHWOOD AVE
HAYLOFT AVE   DOUGLAS DR
OAKWOOD AVE   DR   ANNE ST
THE OVAL

5

STONE HALL LA

BANK BROW

Lees Wood

Green Alley Wood

Gathurst Golf Course

B5206

PRINCE'S PK
GREENHILL
QUEENSWAY DR   GREENROYD DR   WOODLANDS DR

08

Bank Top

TAN PIT COTTS

AYREFIELD LA

BANK RD

Ayrefield House

4

Star Inn (PH)

ROBY MILL

FARLEY LA

Roby Mill

Walthew Green

Gathurst

B5206

3

Cemy

Roby Mill CE Prim Sch

ST GABRIEL CL   SCHOOL LA

Fox Inn (PH)

Walthew Green Farm

WHITLEY RD

07

Golf Course

Convent

Johnson's Farm

Dean Brook

Dean Wood

The Kingfisher (PH)

GATHURST RD

ACHHURST RD

2

Quarry (dis)

Rough Park Wood

Walthew Park

St Joseph's Con Ctr

LAFFORD LA

Pearson's Farm

Orrell House Farm

St John Rigby RC Coll

Collage Farm

MOOR   STONE

COLLEGE RD

Jollies i'th Dean

GATHURST RD   B5206   M6   SPRING RD

Golf Course

1

MILL LA   HART'S LA

St Teresa's RC Prim Sch

06

35
19

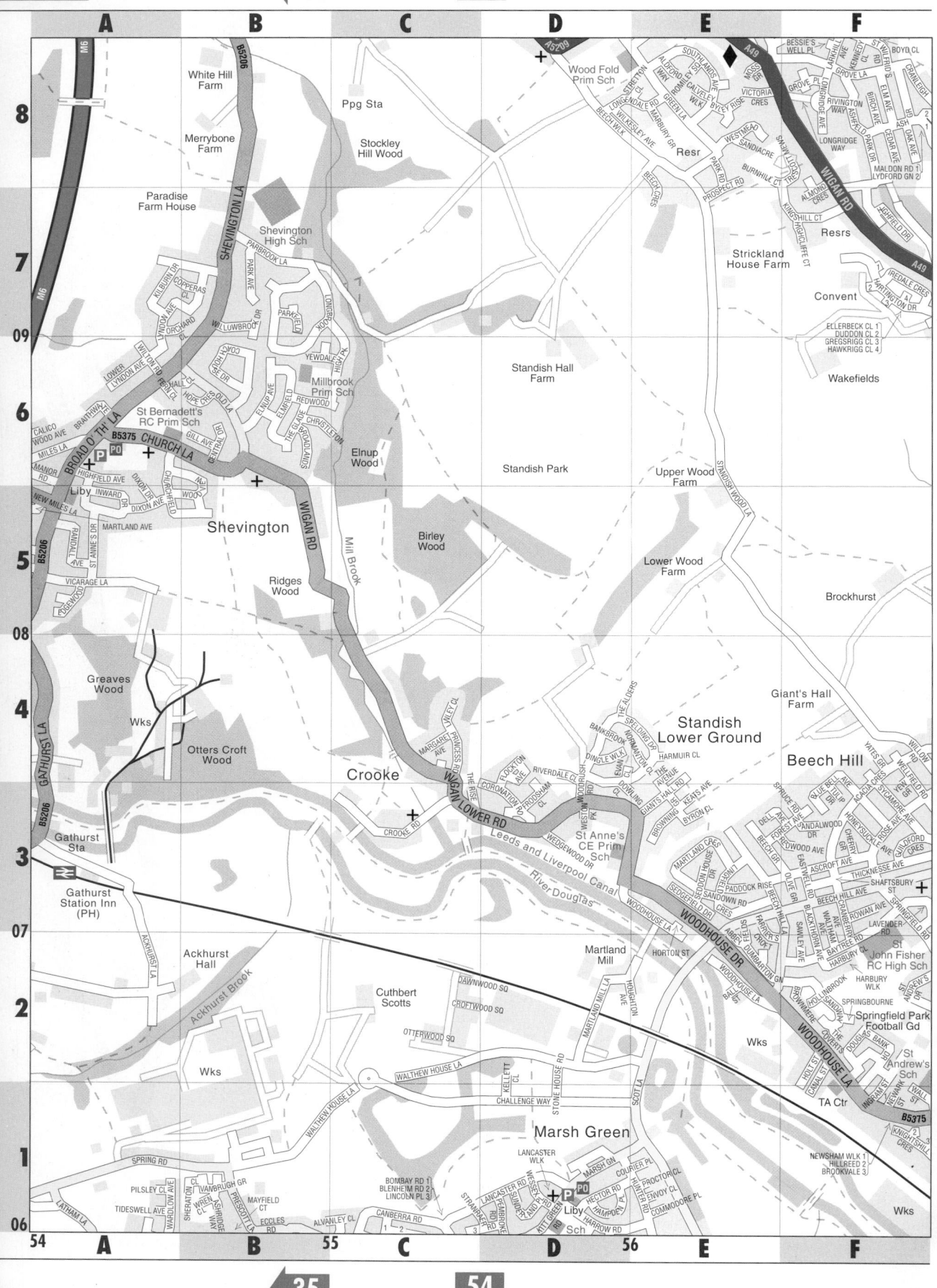

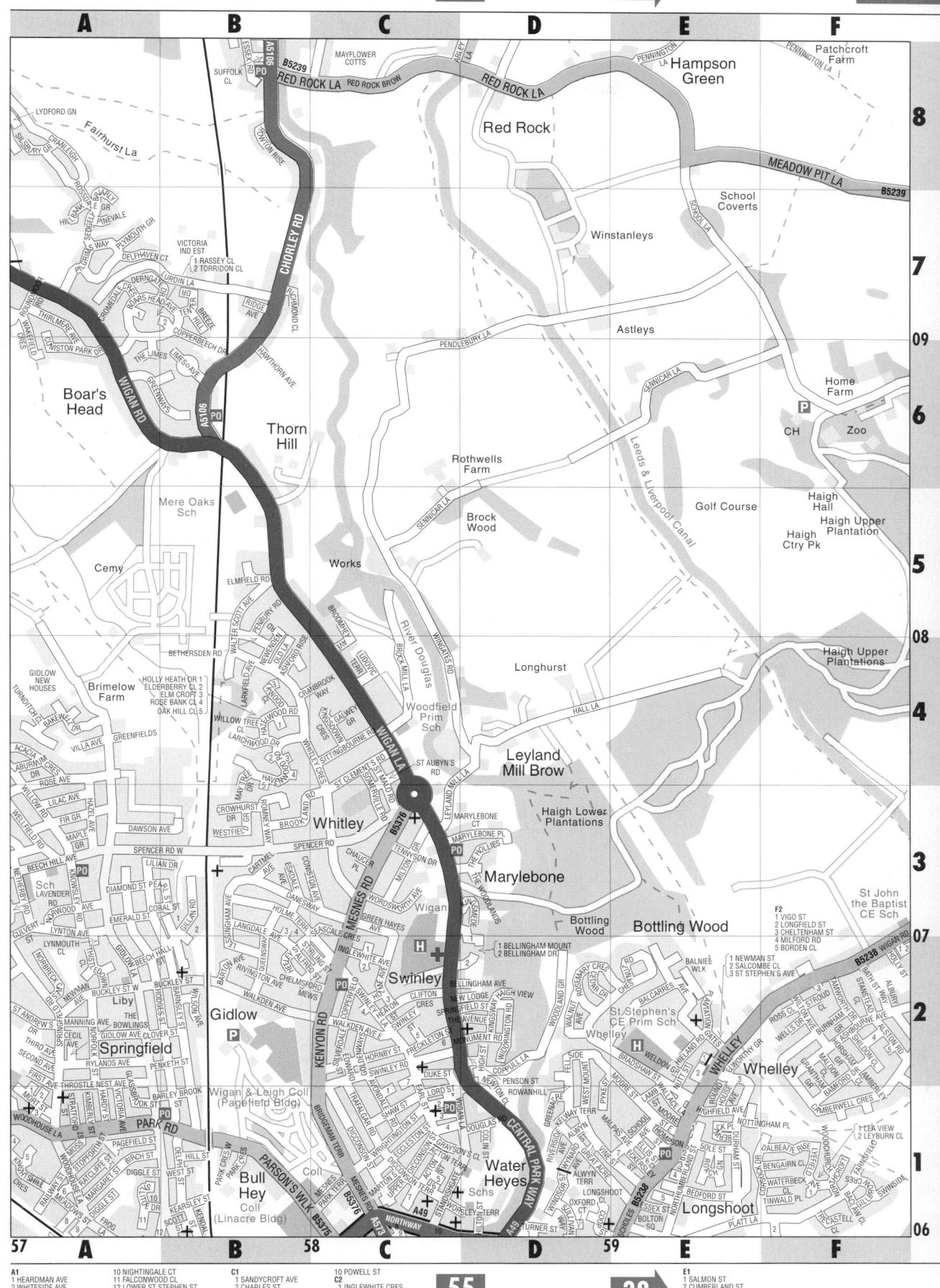

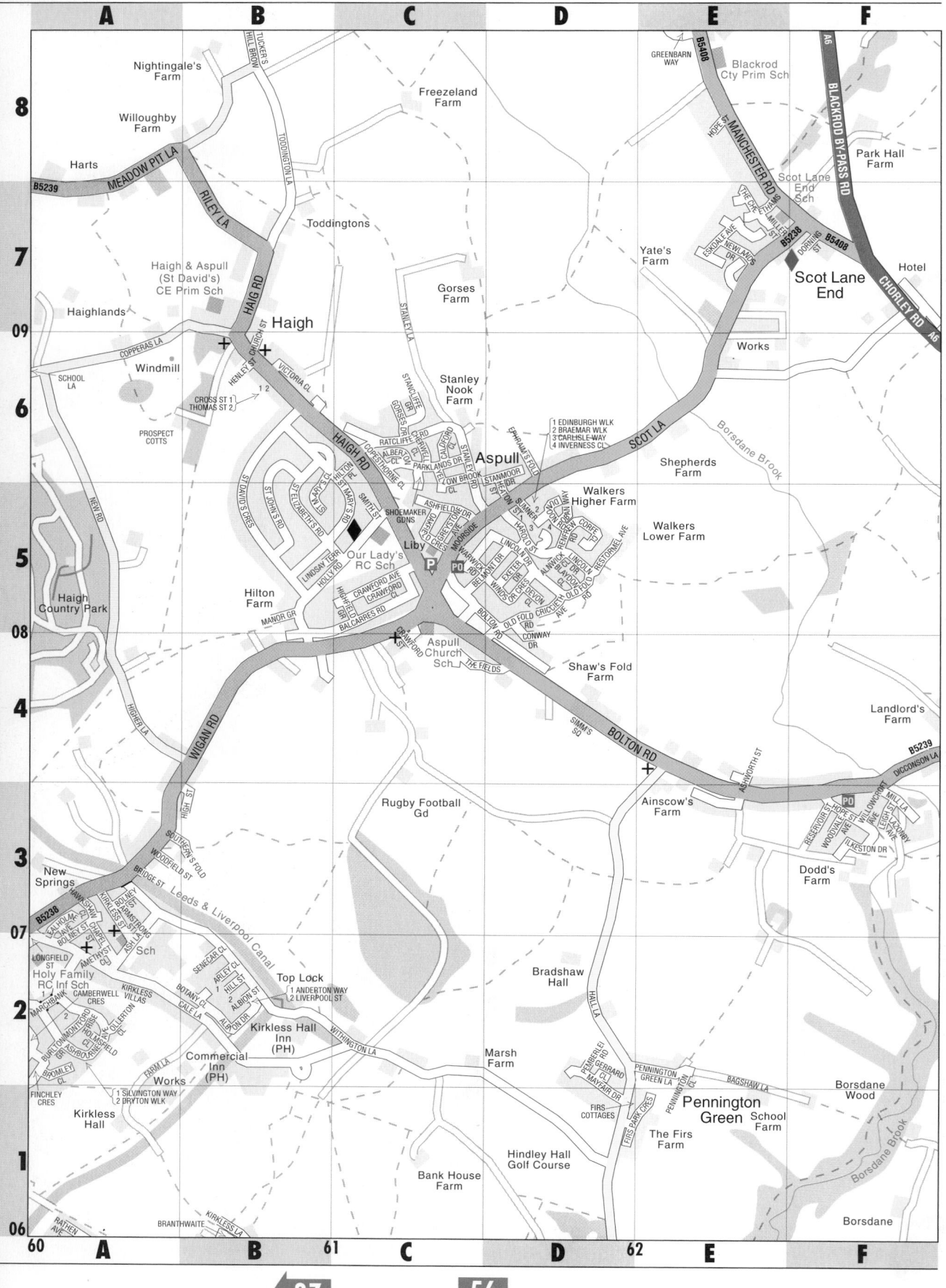

A **B** **C** **D** **E** **F**

8
7
09
6
5
08
4
3
07
2
1
06

60 61 62

Nightingale's Farm

Willoughby Farm

Harts

Haighlands

School La

Windmill

Prospect Cotts

Meadow Pit La

B5239

Riley La

Haig Rd

Toddington La

Tucker's

Hill Brow

Haigh & Aspull (St David's) CE Prim Sch

Copperas La

Cross St 1
Thomas St 2

Henley St
Church St

Victoria Cl

Haigh

Haig Rd

Freezeland Farm

Toddingtons

Gorses Farm

Stanley La

Stancliffe Gr

Gorses Dr

Ratcliffe Cl

Stanley Nook Farm

Stanmoor Dr

Aspull

Liby

Shoemaker Gdns

Our Lady's RC Sch

P

PO

Hilton Farm

St David's Cres

St John's Rd

Lindsay Terr

Holly Rd

Highfield Rd

Crawford Ave

Crawford Cl

Manor Gr

Balcarres Rd

Crawford St

Aspull Church Sch

The Fields

Scot La

Shepherds Farm

Walkers Higher Farm

Walkers Lower Farm

Shaw's Fold Farm

1 Edinburgh Wlk
2 Braemar Wlk
3 Carlisle Way
4 Inverness Cl

Borsdane Brook

Greenbarn Way

Blackrod Cty Prim Sch

Hope St

Manchester Rd

B5406

Scot Lane End Sch

B5238

B5406

Blackrod By-Pass Rd

A6

Park Hall Farm

Chorley Rd

A6

Hotel

Scot Lane End

Yate's Farm

Works

New Rd

Higher La

Haig Country Park

High St

Wigan Rd

Southern's Fold

Woodfield St

Bridge St

Leeds & Liverpool Canal

New Springs

B5238

Longfield St

Holy Family RC Inf Sch

Amethyst

Ash La

Kirkless Villas

Senecar Cl

Arley Cl

Hill St

Albion St

Botany La

Cale La

Albion St

Top Lock

1 Anderton Way
2 Liverpool St

Kirkless Hall Inn (PH)

Commercial Inn (PH)

Works

Finchley Cres

Kirkless Hall

1 Silvington Way
2 Dryton Wlk

Rathen Ave

Branthwaite

Kirkless La

Withington La

Marsh Farm

Bank House Farm

Hindley Hall Golf Course

Rugby Football Gd

Bolton Rd

Simm's Sq

Ashworth St

B5239

Ainscow's Farm

Bradshaw Hall

Hall La

Pemberton Cl

Gerrard

Mayfair Dr

Pennington Green La

Bagshaw La

Firs Cottages

Firs Park Cres

The Firs Farm

Pennington Green

School Farm

Borsdane Wood

Borsdane Brook

Borsdane

Landlord's Farm

Dicconson La

Reservoir Rd

Hope St

Woodcourt

Willowcroft

Leigh Rd

Lackmere

Mill La

Ilkeston Dr

Dodd's Farm

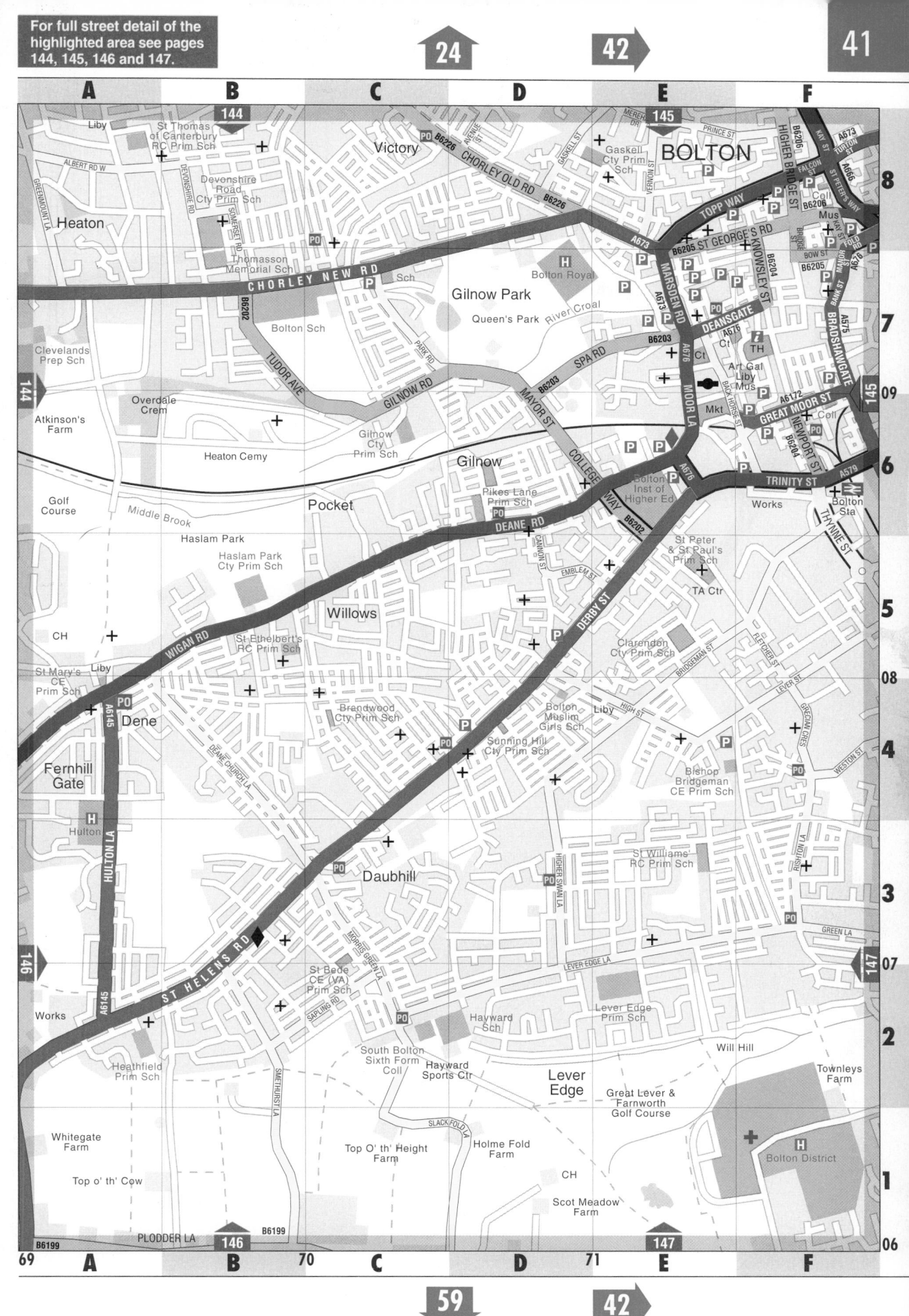

For full street detail of the highlighted area see pages 144, 145, 146 and 147.

41

24   42

A   B   C   D   E   F

144   145

8

7

09

6

5

08

4

3

07

2

1

06

Liby
St Thomas of Canterbury RC Prim Sch
Victory
Gaskell Cty Prim Sch
BOLTON
ALBERT RD W
Devonshire Road Cty Prim Sch
Heaton
CHORLEY OLD RD
B6226
Topp Way
HIGHER BRIDGE ST
Coll
Mus
Thomasson Memorial Sch
ST GEORGE S RD
CHORLEY NEW RD
Sch
Bolton Royal
Gilnow Park
Queen's Park
River Croal
DEANSGATE
Clevelands Prep Sch
TUDOR AVE
GILNOW RD
Bolton Sch
MAYOR ST
SPA RD
MOOR LA
TH
Art Gal Liby Mus
BRADSHAWGATE
Atkinson's Farm
Overdale Crem
Gilnow Cty Prim Sch
Mkt
GREAT MOOR ST
Coll
Heaton Cemy
Gilnow
NEWPORT ST
Golf Course
Middle Brook
Pocket
Pikes Lane Prim Sch
COLLEGE WAY
Bolton Inst of Higher Ed
TRINITY ST
Works
Bolton Sta
Haslam Park
DEANE RD
St Peter & St Paul's Prim Sch
THYNNE ST
Haslam Park Cty Prim Sch
EMBLEM ST
CANNON ST
TA Ctr
Willows
St Ethelbert's RC Prim Sch
DERBY ST
Clarendon Cty Prim Sch
CH
Liby
WIGAN RD
St Mary's CE Prim Sch
Dene
Brandwood Cty Prim Sch
Bolton Muslim Girls Sch
HIGH ST
Bishop Bridgeman CE Prim Sch
Fernhill Gate
Sunning Hill Cty Prim Sch
St Williams' RC Prim Sch
Hulton
DEANE CHURCH LA
HULTON LA
Daubhill
HIGHER SWAN LA
LEVER EDGE LA
Will Hill
ST HELENS RD
MORRIS GREEN LA
St Bede CE (VA) Prim Sch
Lever Edge Prim Sch
Townleys Farm
Works
SAPLING RD
Hayward Sch
Lever Edge
Great Lever & Farnworth Golf Course
Heathfield Prim Sch
SMITHURST LA
South Bolton Sixth Form Coll
Hayward Sports Ctr
Whitegate Farm
SLACK FOLD LA
Top O' th' Height Farm
Holme Fold Farm
Bolton District
Top o' th' Cow
CH
Scot Meadow Farm
PLODDER LA
B6199

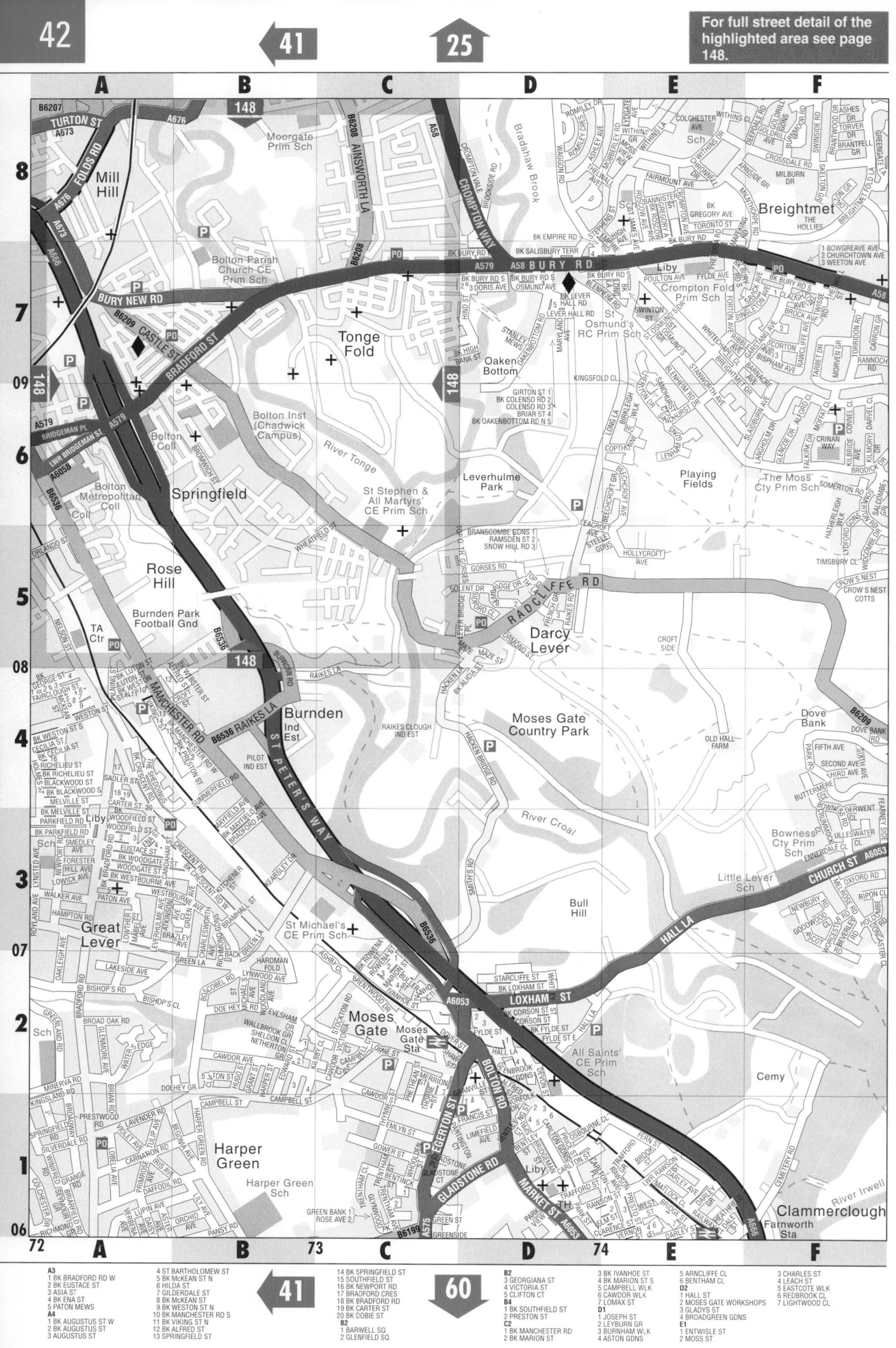

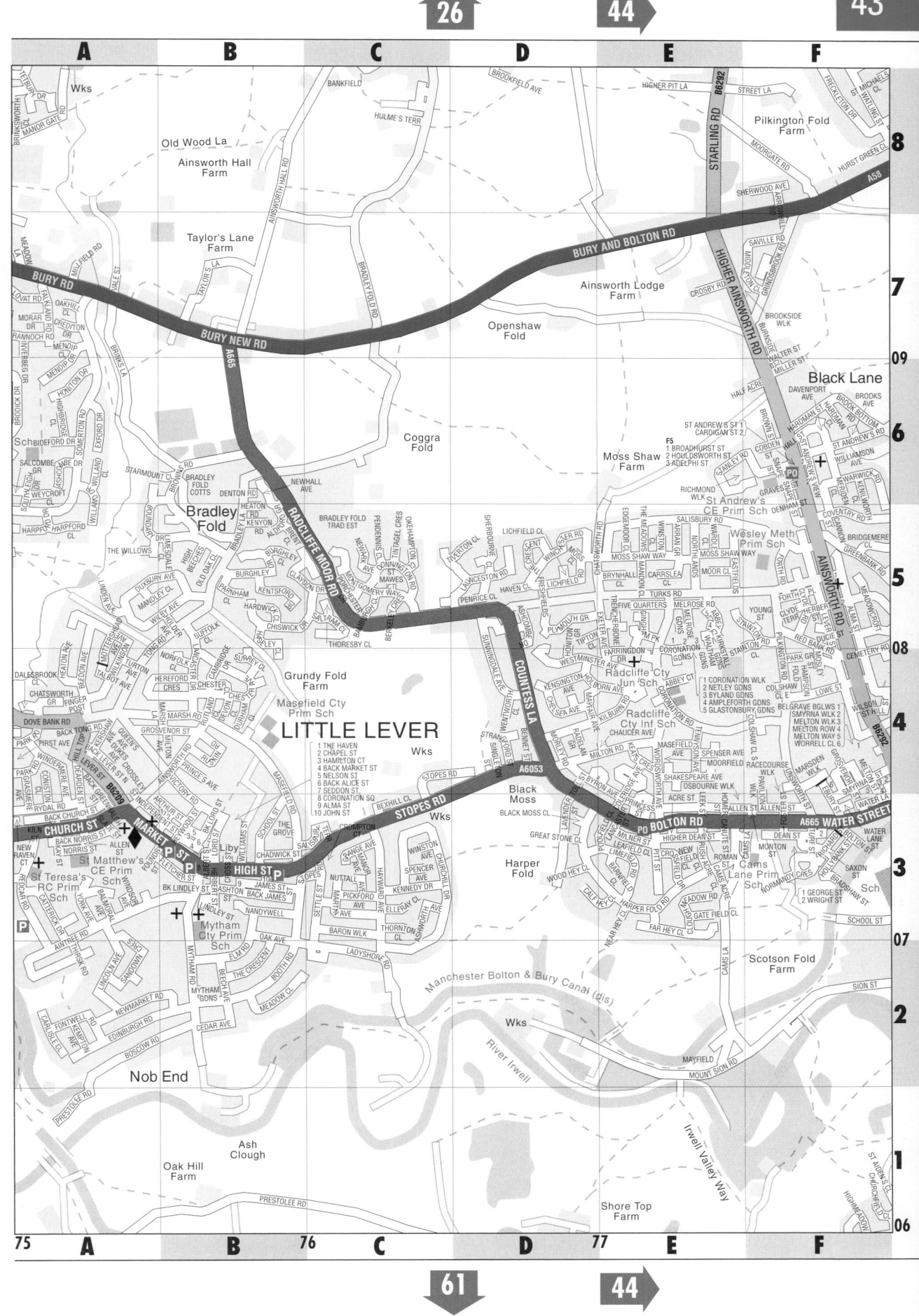

44

43 27

E8
1 BK HORNE ST N
2 BK DEVON ST N
3 WALKER ST
4 BK PARKHILLS RD S
5 MOSS PL

F8
1 BK NELSON ST S
2 BK DEVON ST S
3 BK PARKHILLS RD S
4 BK PARKHILLS RD N
5 BK NELSON ST N
6 NELSON ST

7 LINCOLN DR
8 MIDDLESEX DR

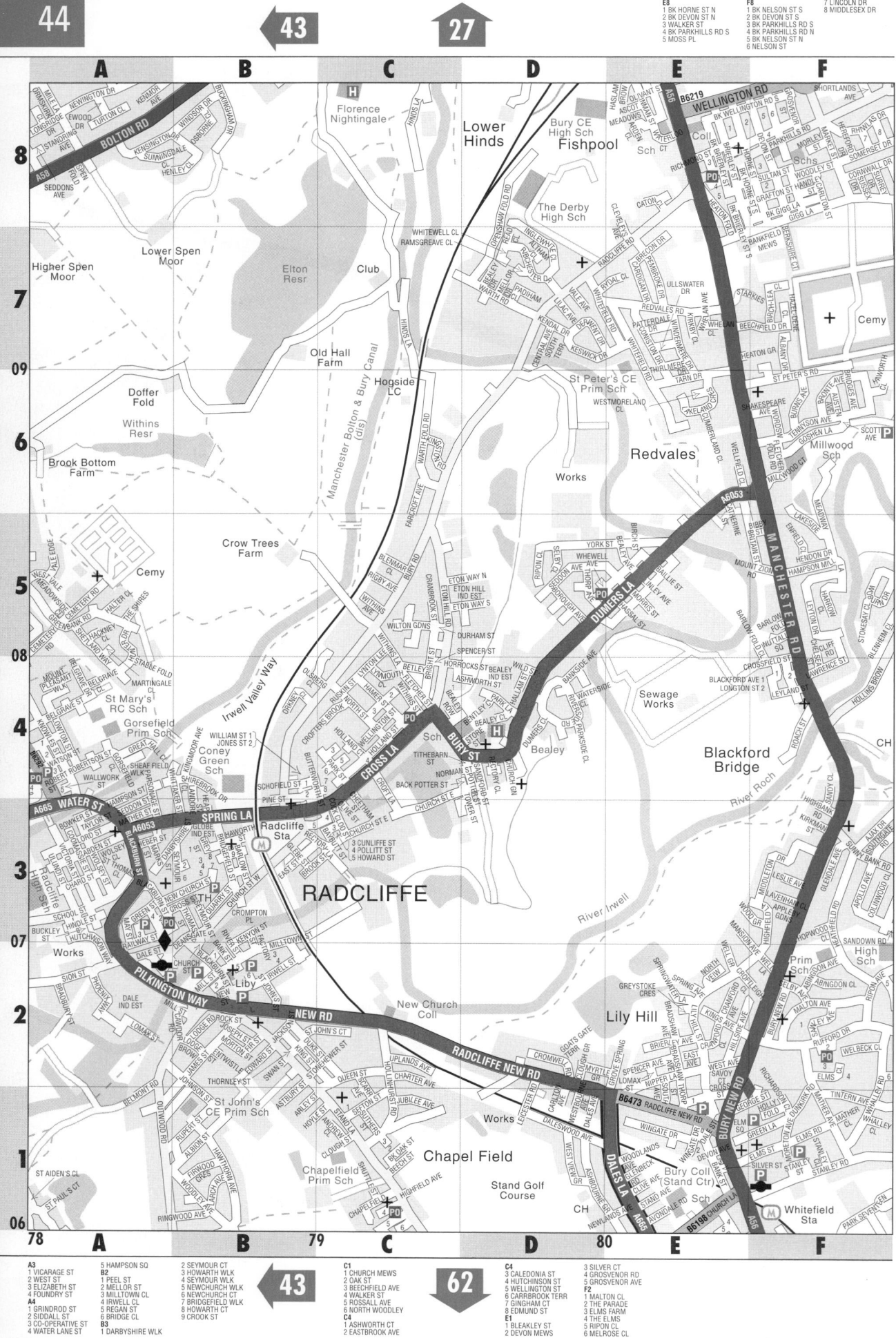

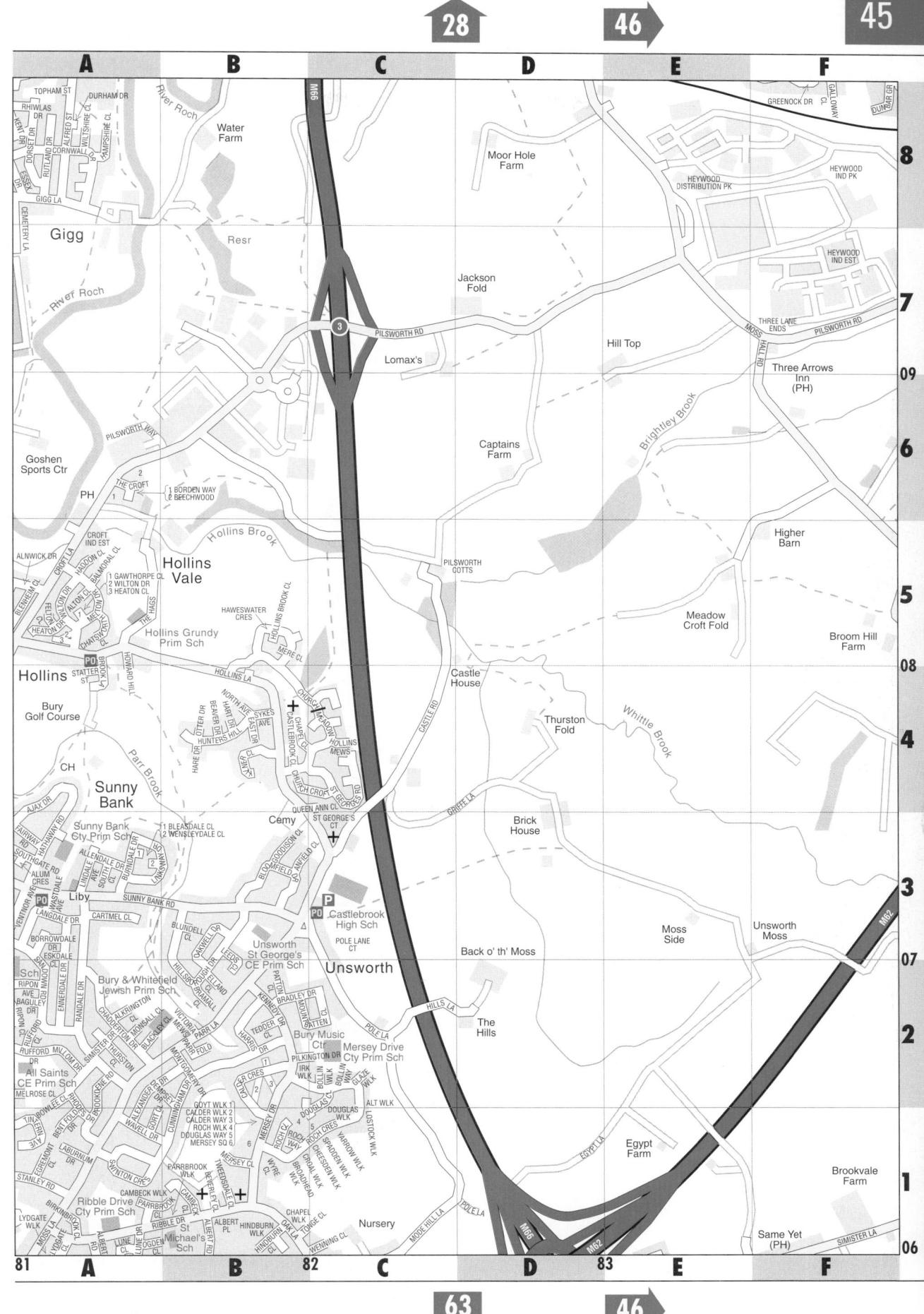

28
46
46

Heywood Distribution Pk

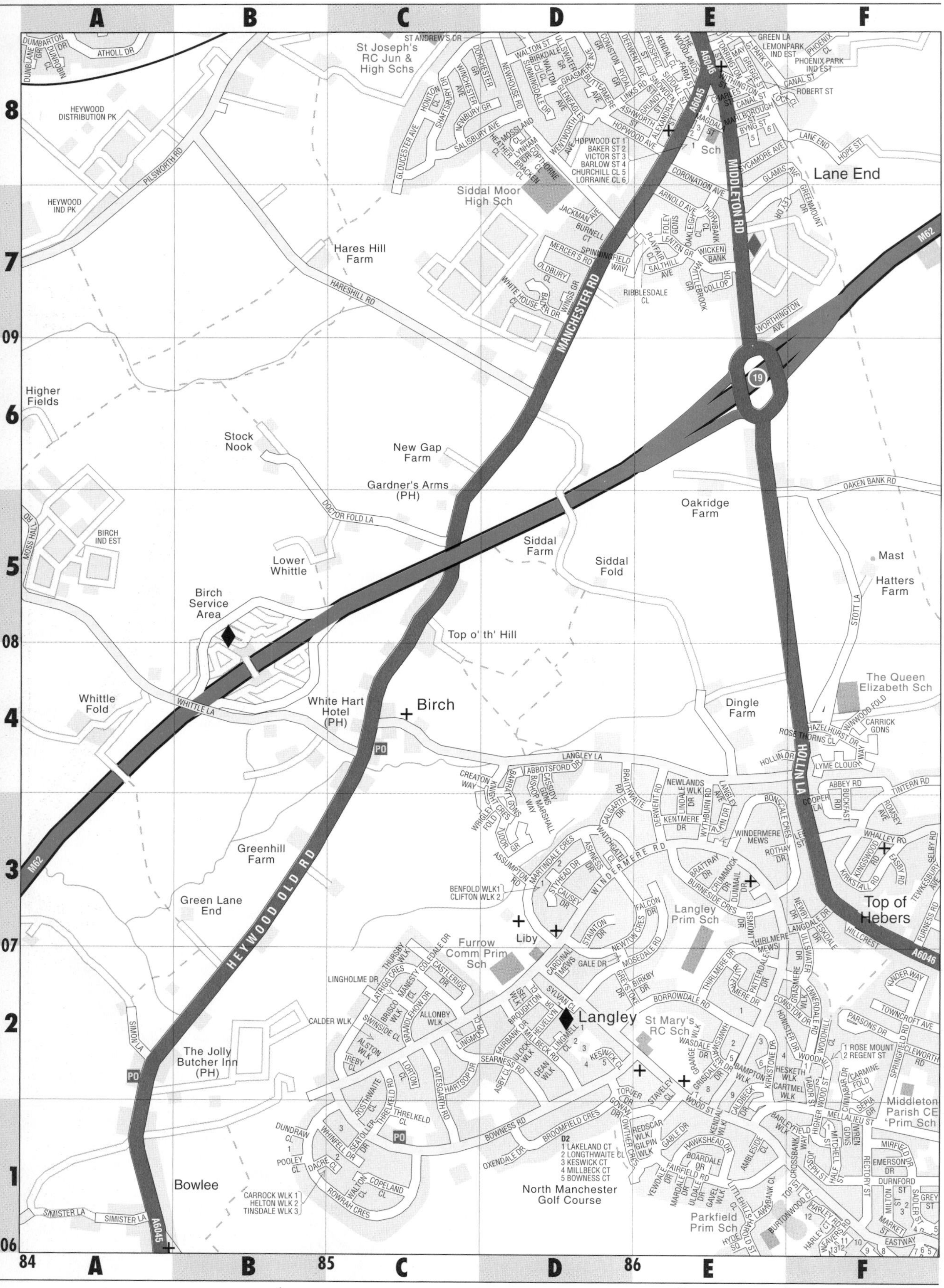

Heywood Ind Pk

Higher Fields

Birch Ind Est

Whittle Fold

St Joseph's RC Jun & High Schs

Siddal Moor High Sch

Hares Hill Farm

Stock Nook

New Gap Farm

Gardner's Arms (PH)

Lower Whittle

Birch Service Area

Top o' th' Hill

Siddal Farm

Siddal Fold

Oakridge Farm

Hatters Farm

Mast

The Queen Elizabeth Sch

White Hart Hotel (PH)

Birch

Dingle Farm

Carrick Gdns

Greenhill Farm

Green Lane End

Langley La

Langley Prim Sch

Top of Hebers

Furrow Comm Prim Sch

Liby

Langley

St Mary's RC Sch

Middleton Parish CE Prim Sch

The Jolly Butcher Inn (PH)

Bowlee

North Manchester Golf Course

Parkfield Prim Sch

MANCHESTER RD
MIDDLETON RD
HEYWOOD OLD RD
WHITTLE LA
HOLLIN LA
A6045
A6046
M62
SIMISTER LA
PILSWORTH RD

Lane End

Phoenix Park Ind Est
Lemonpark Ind Est

19

Dumbarton Dr
Atholl Dr

D2
1 LAKELAND CT
2 LONGTHWAITE CL
3 KESWICK CT
4 MILLBECK CT
5 BOWNESS CT

E2
1 DUFTON WLK
2 DUDDON WLK
3 SEASCALE WLK
4 MOWBRAY WLK
5 HAWESWATER MEWS
6 WINSTER DR
7 D'OLIVERA CT
8 DOVEDALE CT
9 ST BEES WLK

F1
1 THROSTLE HALL CT
2 NINIAN CT
3 EXETER CT
4 KID ST
5 WATER ST
6 MARKET ST
7 CHAPEL ST
8 WOOD ST
9 CROSS ST

10 CHISHOLM CT
11 WEAVERS CT
12 GREAT ARBOR WAY
13 SCHOLARS WAY

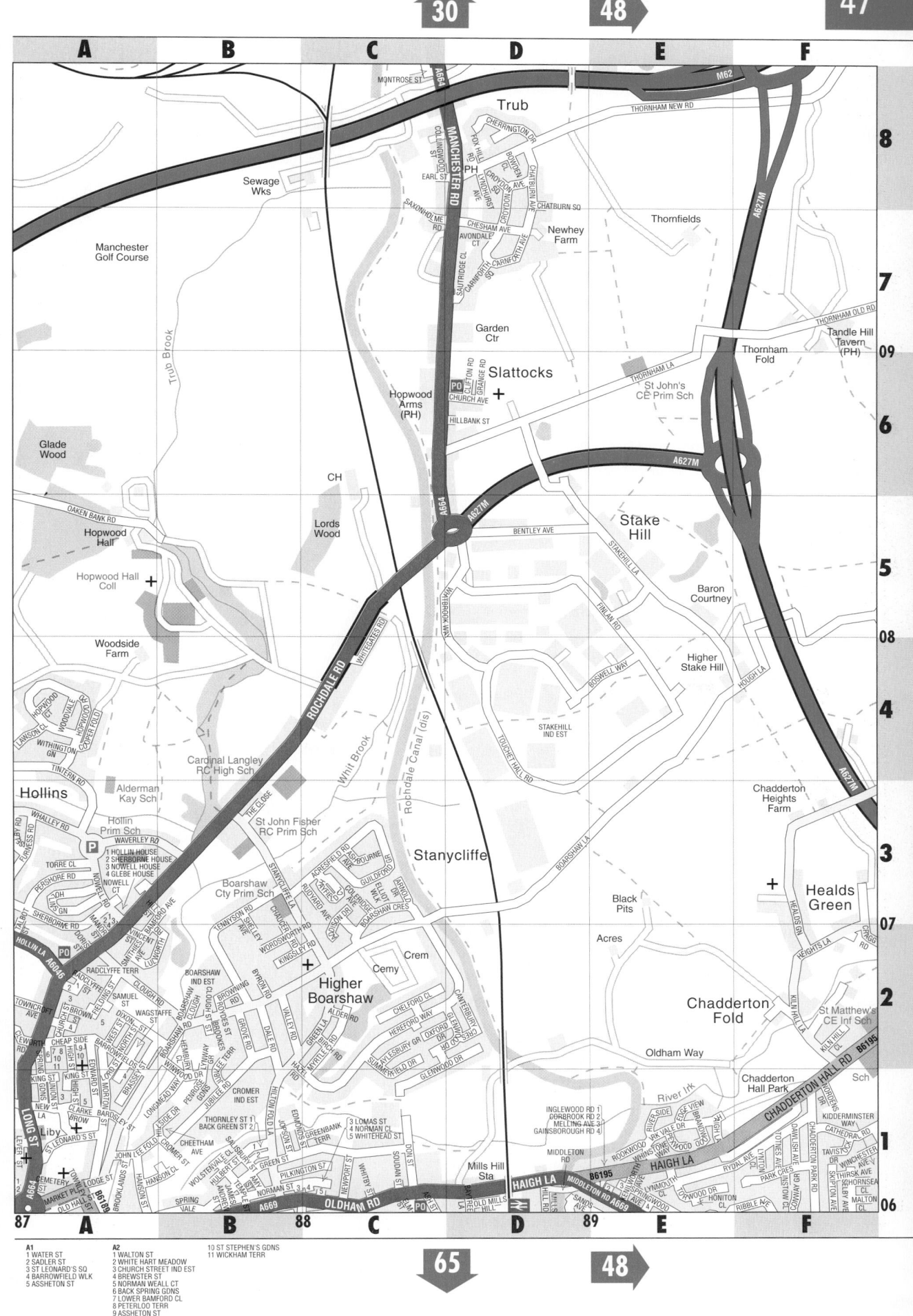

A1
1 WATER ST
2 SADLER ST
3 ST LEONARD'S SQ
4 BARROWFIELD WLK
5 ASSHETON ST

A2
1 WALTON ST
2 WHITE HART MEADOW
3 CHURCH STREET IND EST
4 BREWSTER ST
5 NORMAN WEALL CT
6 BACK SPRING GDNS
7 LOWER BAMFORD CL
8 PETERLOO TERR
9 ASSHETON ST

10 ST STEPHEN'S GDNS
11 WICKHAM TERR

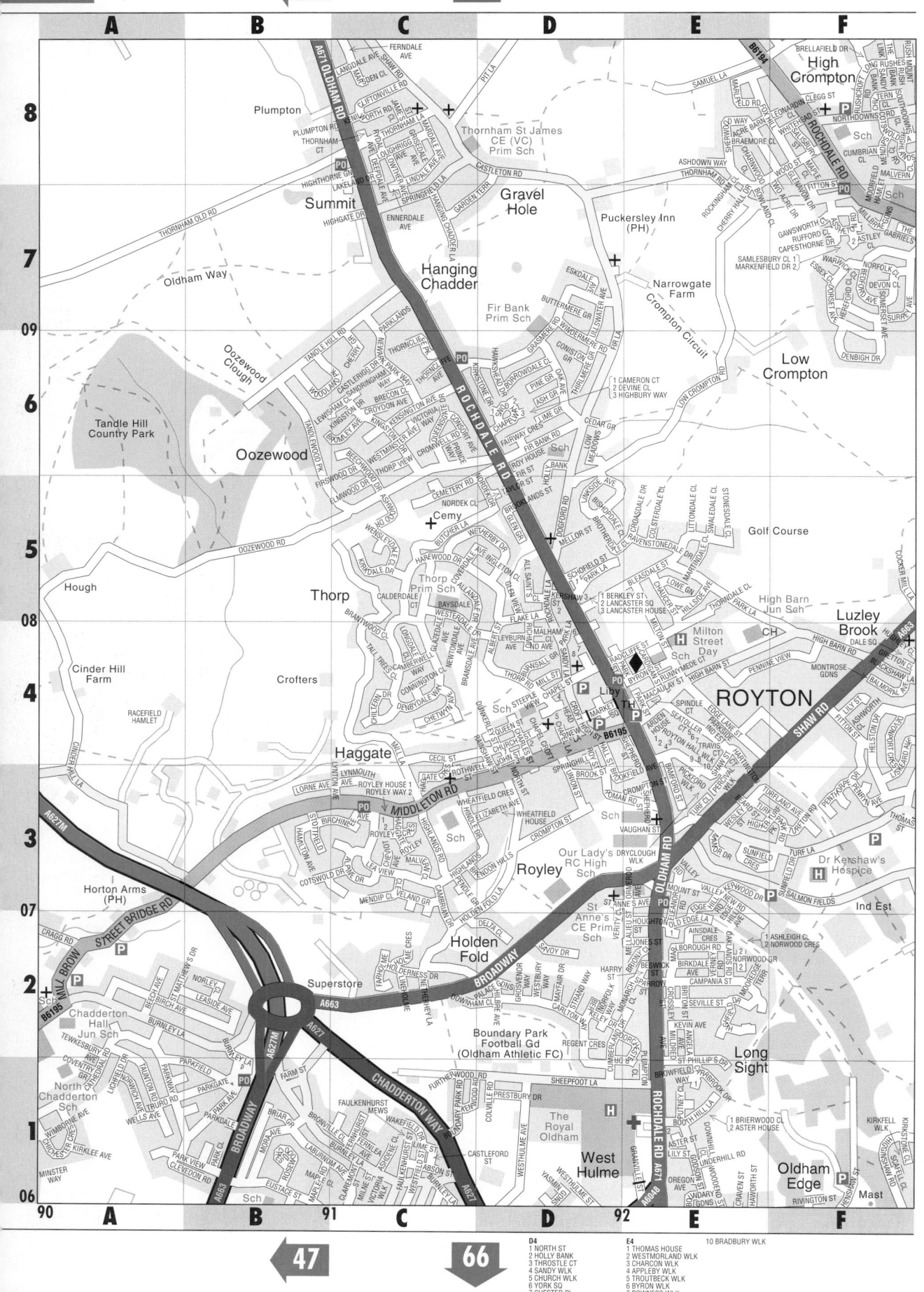

For full street detail of the highlighted area see page 149.

32

50

49

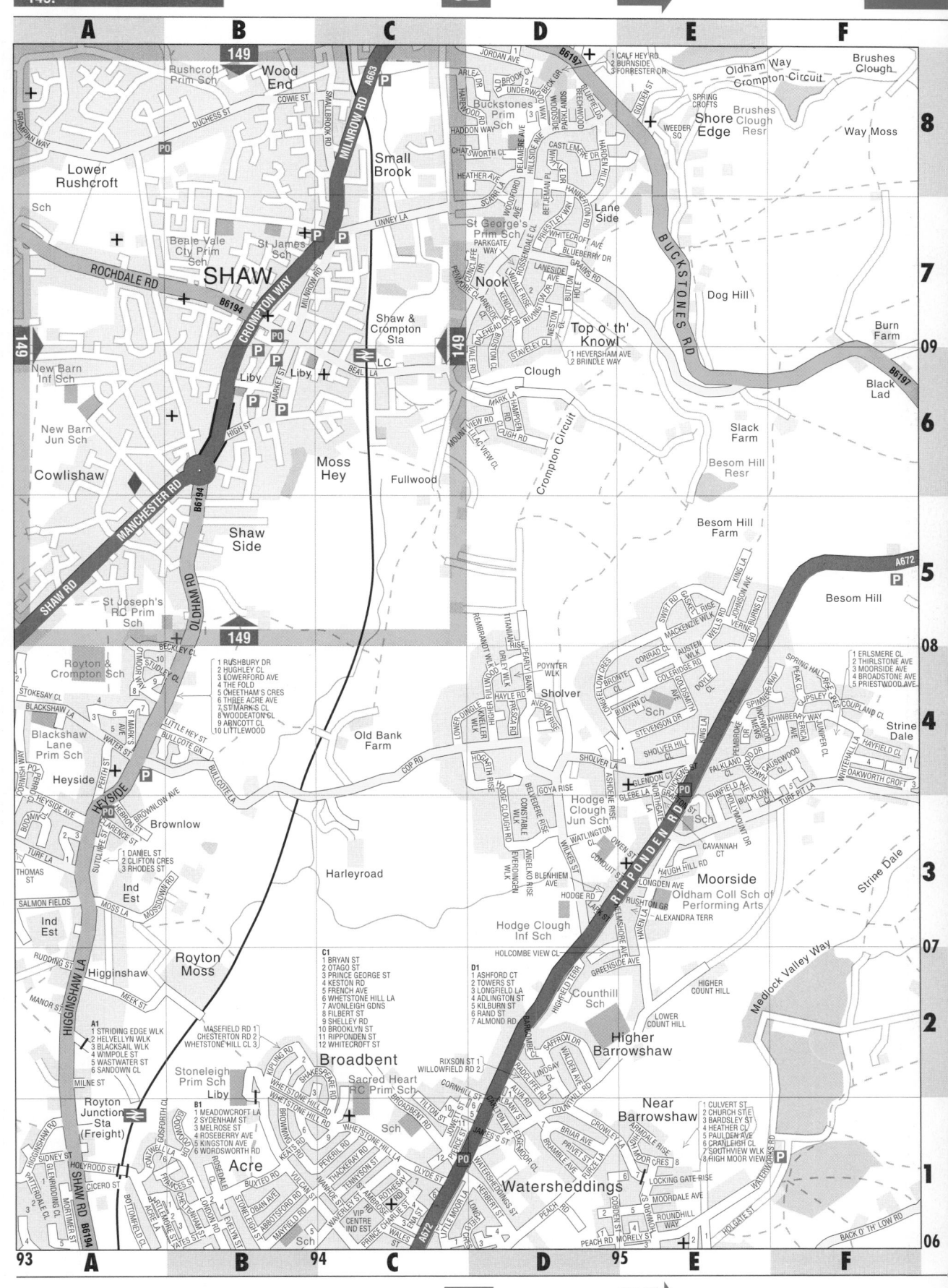

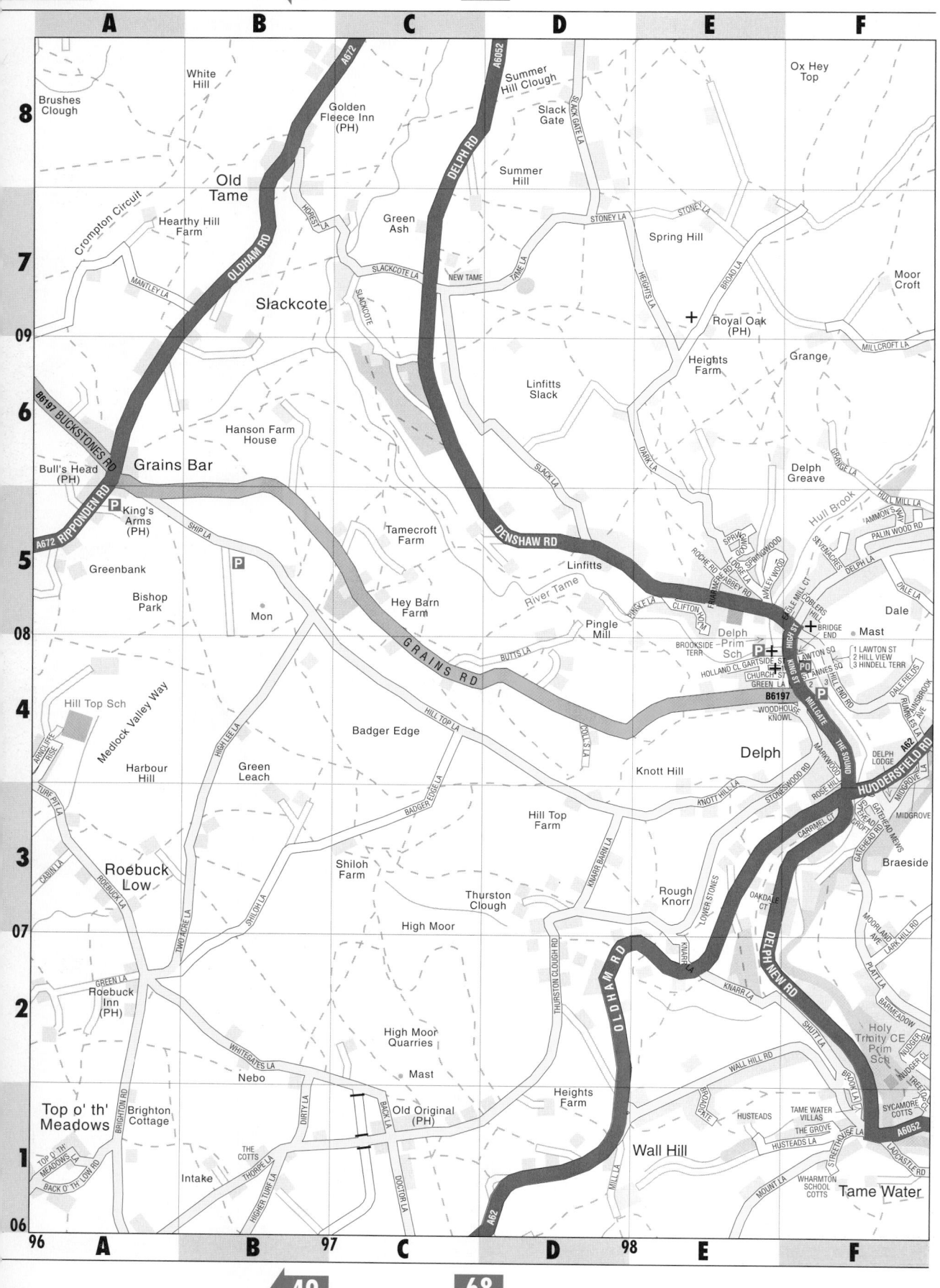

A B C D E F

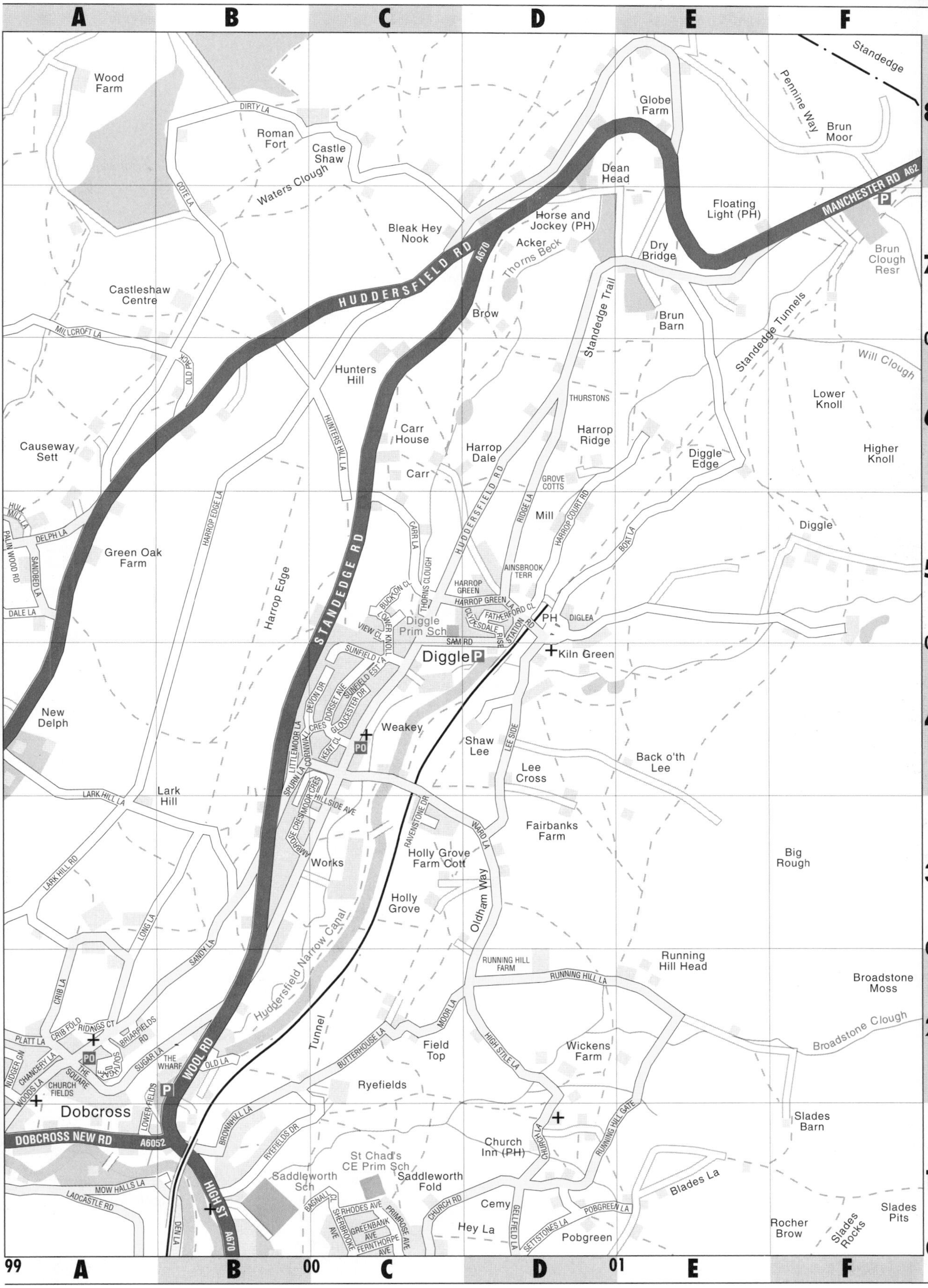

34 52

8

Wood Farm

Standedge

Pennine Way

Roman Fort

Castle Shaw

Globe Farm

Brun Moor

DIRTY LA

Waters Clough

Dean Head

Castleshaw Centre

Bleak Hey Nook

Horse and Jockey (PH)

Floating Light (PH)

MANCHESTER RD A62

7

HUDDERSFIELD RD A670

Acker

Dry Bridge

Thorns Beck

Brun Clough Resr

Standedge Tunnels

Will Clough

09

MILLCROFT LA

OTE LA

OLD PACK

Brow

Standedge Trail

Brun Barn

Causeway Sett

Hunters Hill

THURSTONS

Lower Knoll

6

Carr House

Harrop Dale

Harrop Ridge

Diggle Edge

Higher Knoll

HUNTERS HILL LA

Carr

GROVE COTTS

Diggle

HULL MILL LA

DELPH LA

PALM WOOD RD

SANDBED LA

DALE LA

Green Oak Farm

Harrop Edge

STANDEDGE RD

CARR LA

Mill

HARROP COURT RD

RIDGE LA

BOAT LA

5

Harrop Green

AINSBROOK TERR

HARROP GREEN

BUCKTON CL

LOWER KNOLL

VIEW CL

CLYDESDALE

Diggle Prim Sch

FATHERFORD CL

STATION RD

PH

DIGLEA

08

SAM RD

Diggle P

Kiln Green

New Delph

SUNFIELD EST

SUNFIELD DR

DEVON DR

LEE SIDE

4

LITTLEMOOR LA

CRES

KENT CL

SUNFIELD AVE

GLOUCESTER DR

Weakey

Shaw Lee

Back o'th Lee

SPURN LA

CORNWALL

PO

Lee Cross

HILLSIDE AVE

RAVENSTONE DR

LARK HILL LA

Lark Hill

HARROP GREEN

CRESMOOR CRES

Fairbanks Farm

Big Rough

3

LARK HILL RD

Works

Holly Grove Farm Cott

OLDHAM WAY

07

LONG LA

SANDY LA

Holly Grove

Huddersfield Narrow Canal

WARD LA

Running Hill Farm

Running Hill Head

Broadstone Moss

2

CRIB LA

RIDINGS CT

BRIARFIELDS RD

WOOL RD

OLD LA

Tunnel

BUTTERHOUSE LA

Field Top

MOOR LA

RUNNING HILL LA

Wickens Farm

HIGH STILE LA

Broadstone Clough

PLATT LA

CHANCERY LA

PO

SUGAR LA

THE WHARF

Ryefields

Slades Barn

NUDGER DN

WOODS LA

THE SQUARE

CHURCH FIELDS

P

LOWER FIELDS

BROADHILL LA

St Chad's CE Prim Sch

Saddleworth Fold

RUNNING HILL GATE

Blades La

1

Dobcross

Saddleworth Sch

Church Inn (PH)

GELLFIELD LA

DOBCROSS NEW RD A6052

RYEFIELDS DR

BAGNALL LA

PRIMROSE LA

CHURCH RD

Cemy

POBGREEN LA

Slades Pits

MOW HALLS LA

HIGH ST A670

DELPH LA

Saddleworth Fold

RHODES AVE

SHERBROOKE AVE

GREENBANK AVE

FERNTHORPE AVE

Hey La

SETTSTONES LA

Pobgreen

Rocher Brow

Slades Rocks

LADCASTLE RD

99

06

51

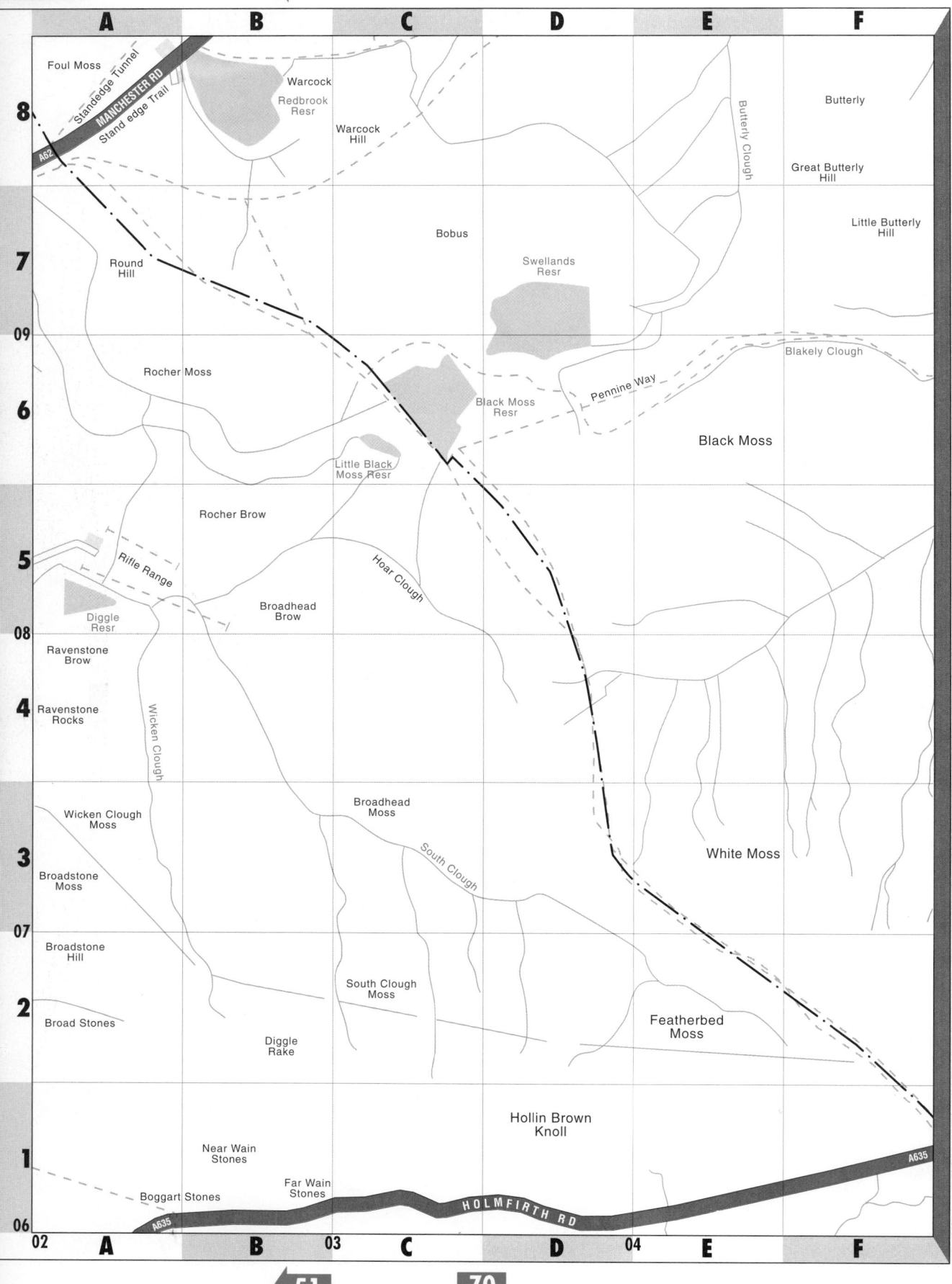

51
70

A B C D E F

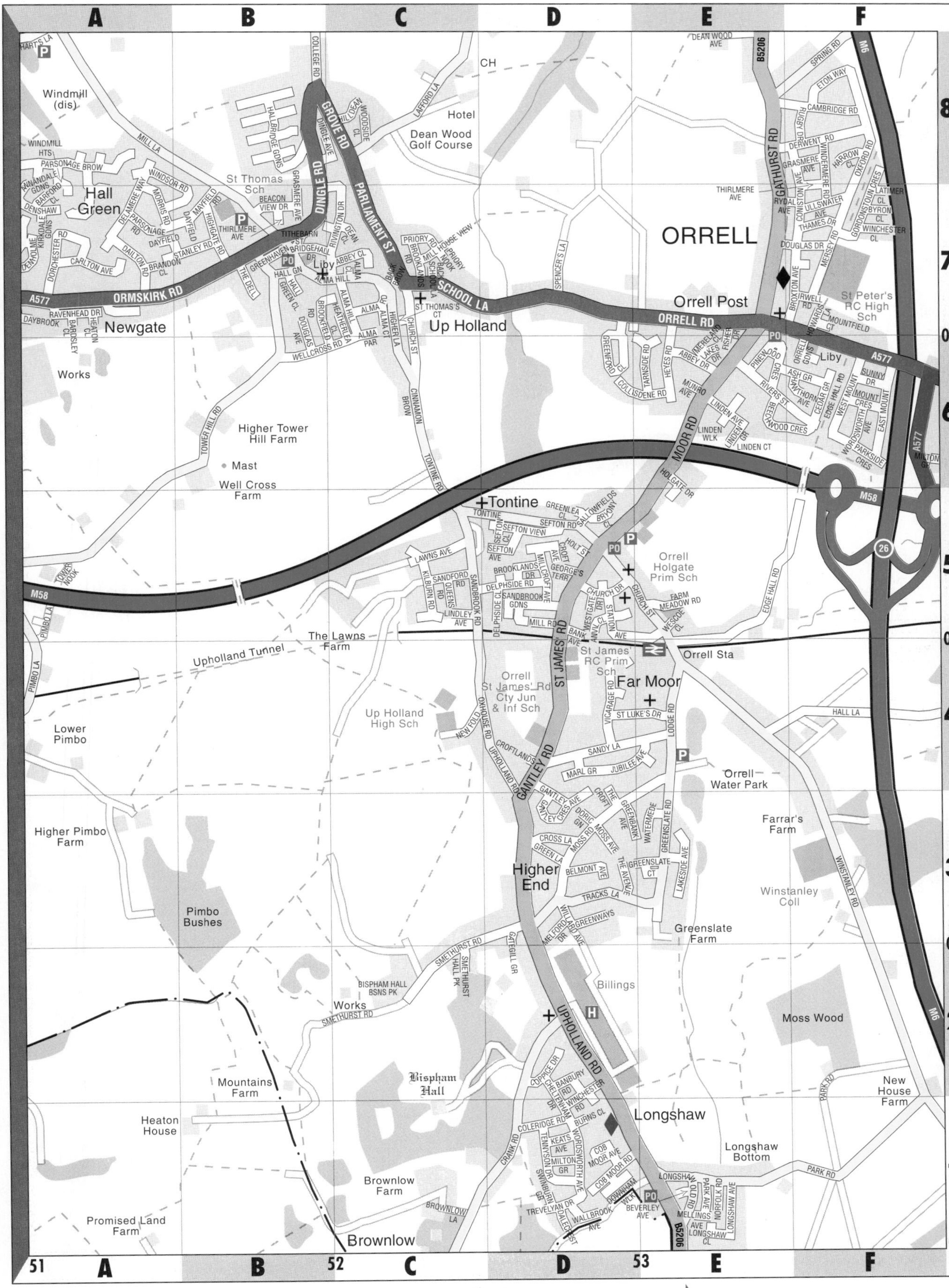

8

ORRELL

7

05

6

Windmill (dis)
Hall Green
Newgate
Up Holland
Higher Tower Hill Farm
Well Cross Farm
Mast
Orrell Post
Orrell Rd
St Peter's RC High Sch
Liby

Tontine
Orrell Holgate Prim Sch
Orrell Sta
Far Moor
St James' RC Prim Sch
Orrell St James' Rd Cty Jun & Inf Sch
Up Holland High Sch
The Lawns Farm
Upholland Tunnel
Lower Pimbo
Higher Pimbo Farm
Pimbo Bushes

5

04

03

4

3

Higher End
Orrell Water Park
Farrar's Farm
Winstanley Coll
Greenslate Farm
Moss Wood

2

Bispham Hall
Works
Bispham Hall Bsns Pk
Mountains Farm
Heaton House
Brownlow Farm
Longshaw
Longshaw Bottom
New House Farm

1

Promised Land Farm
Brownlow

02

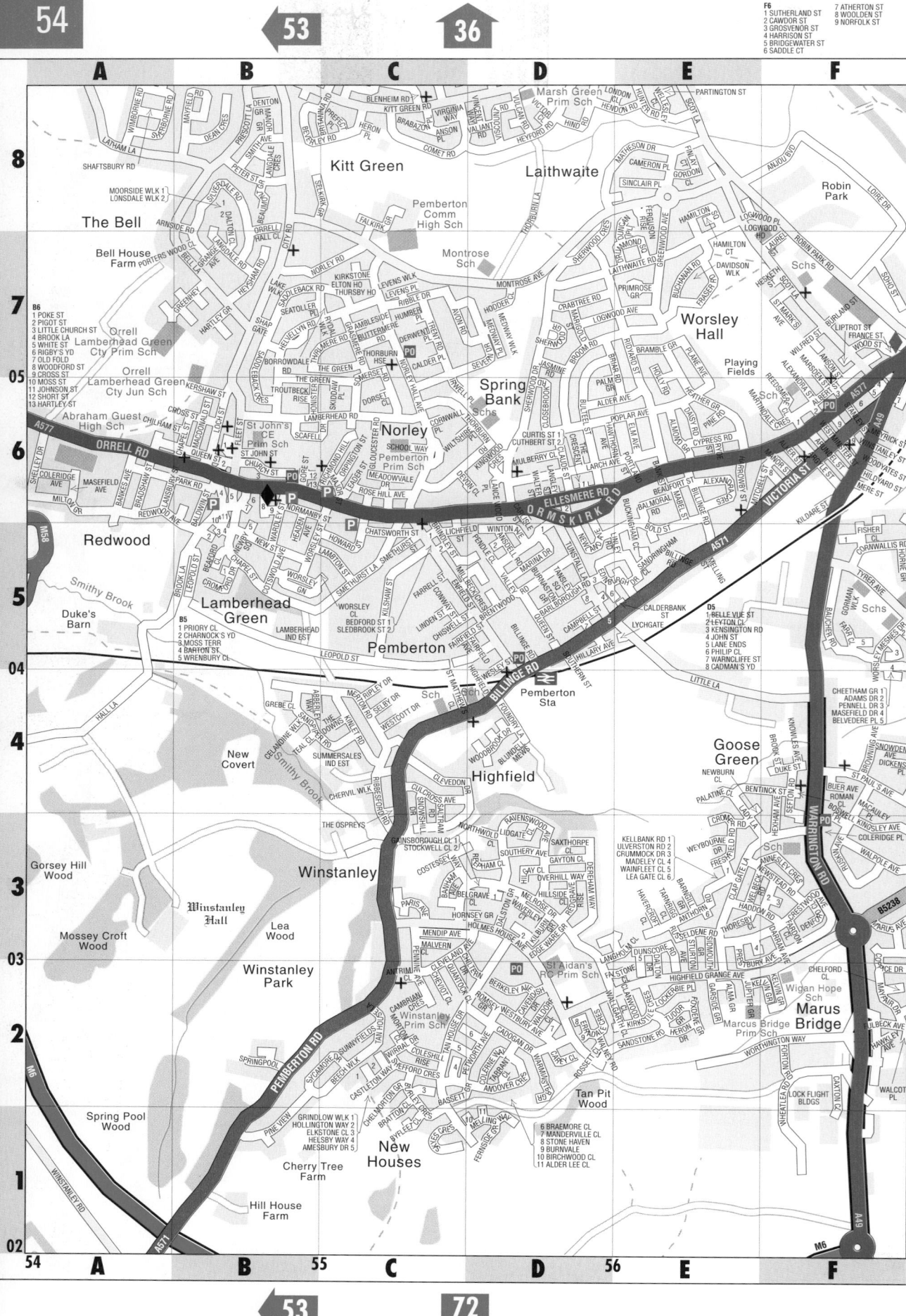

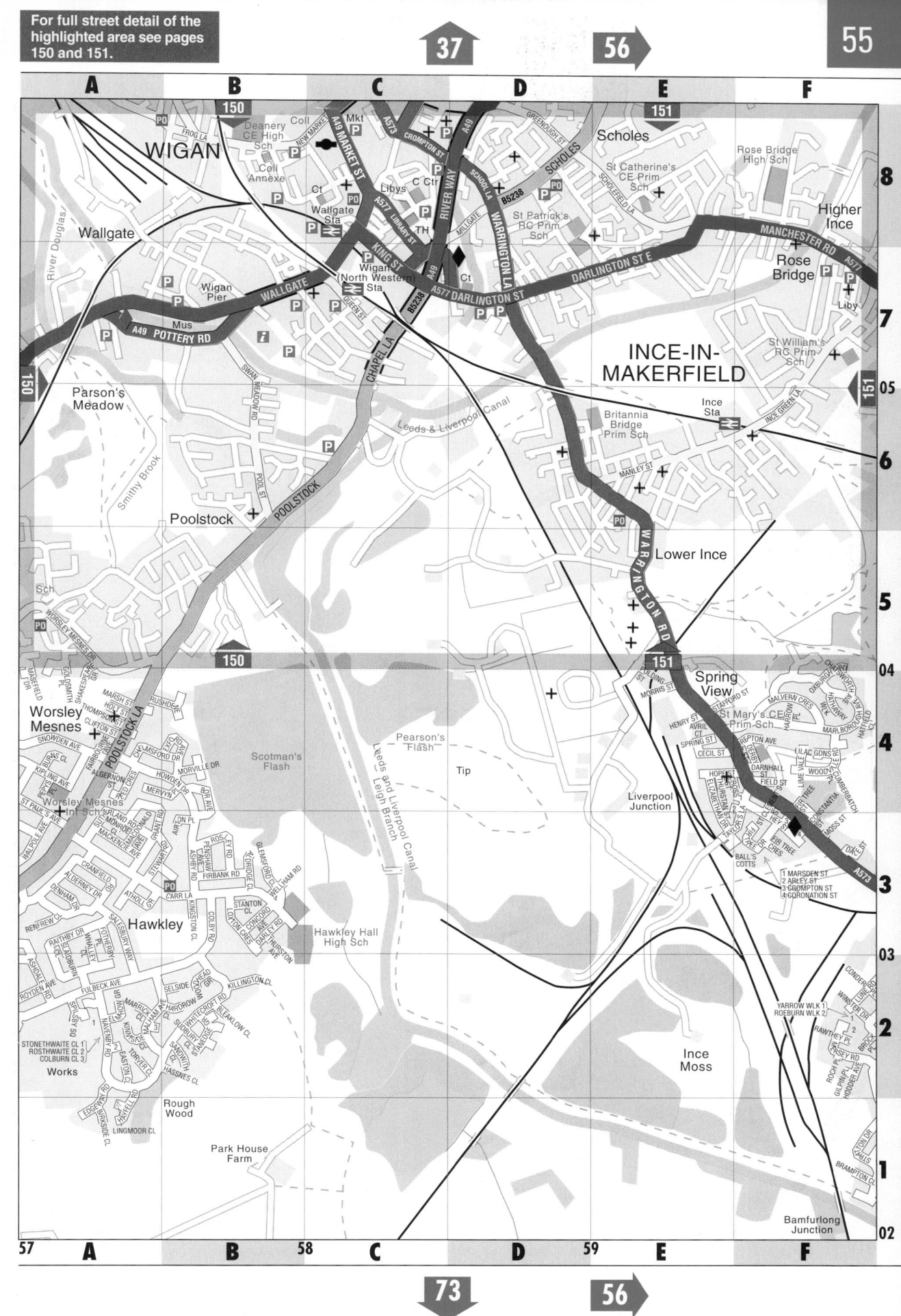

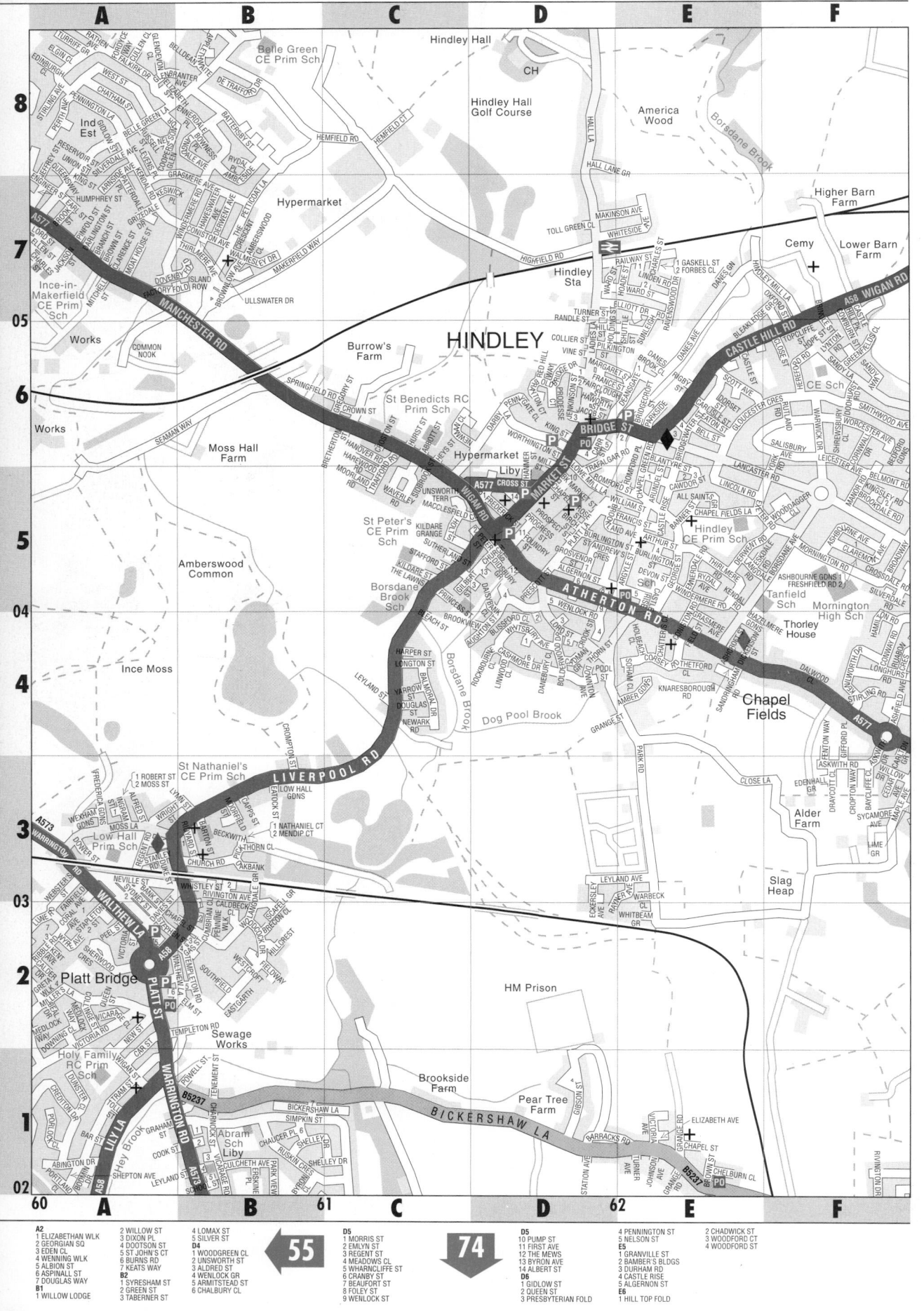

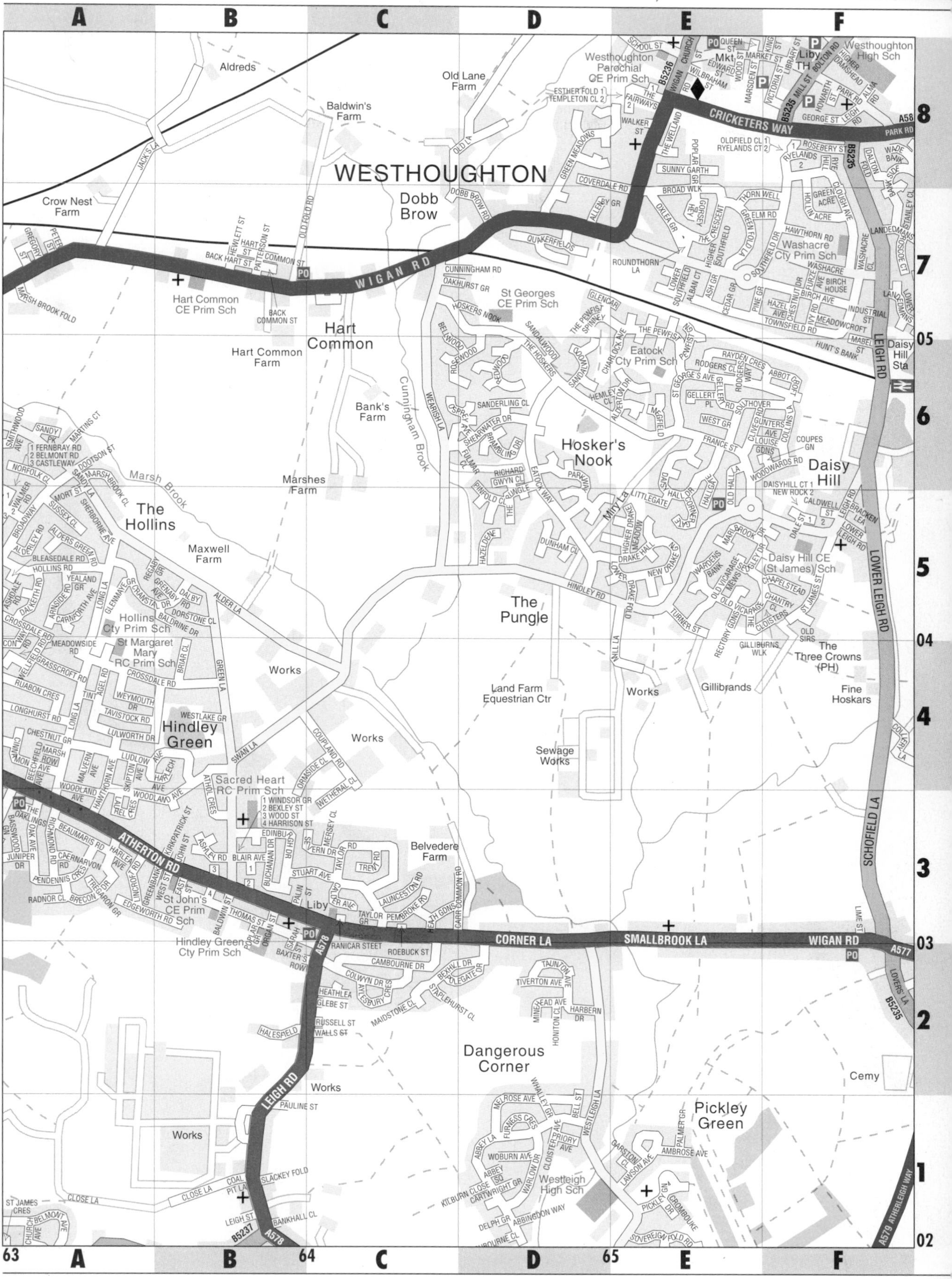

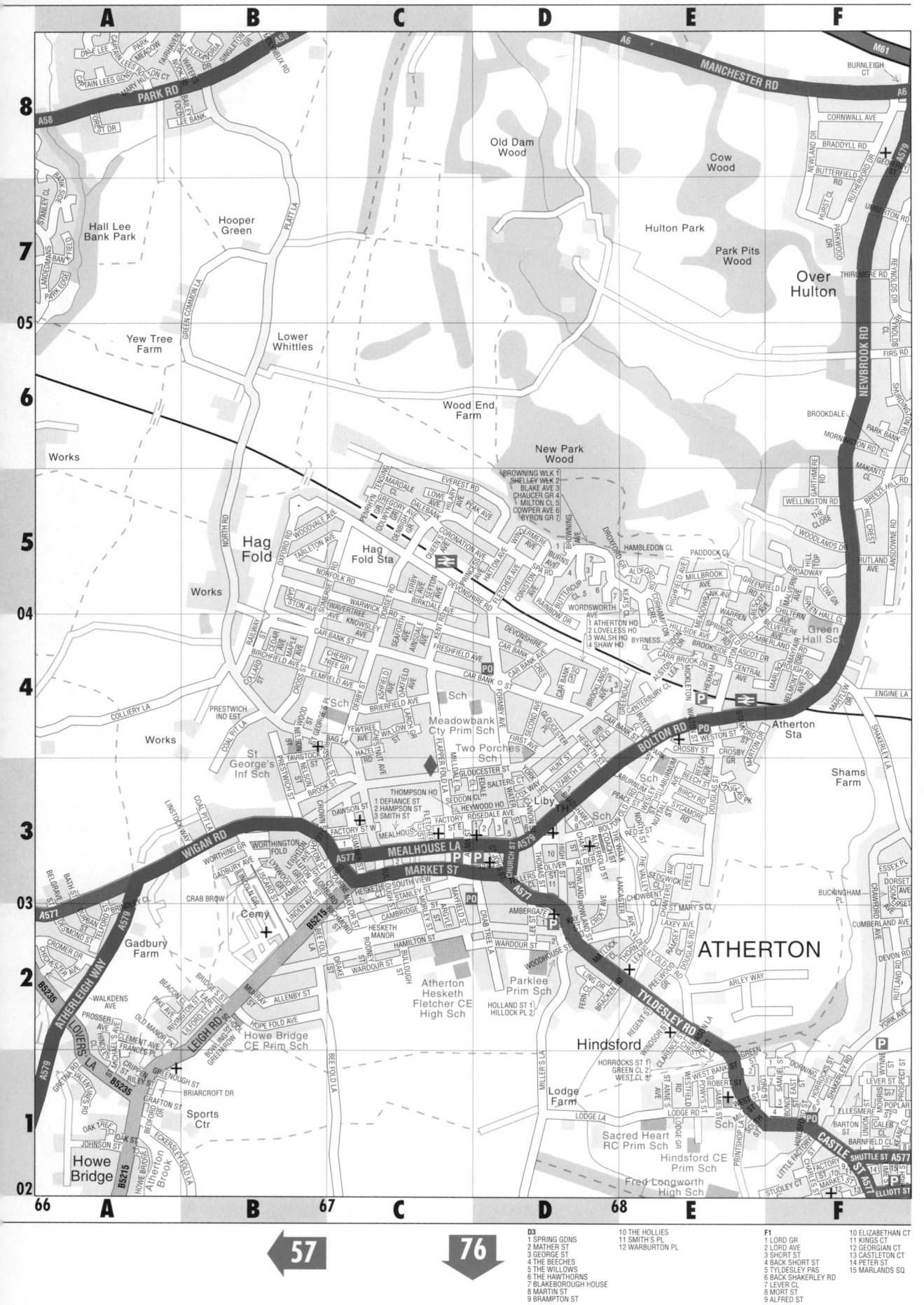

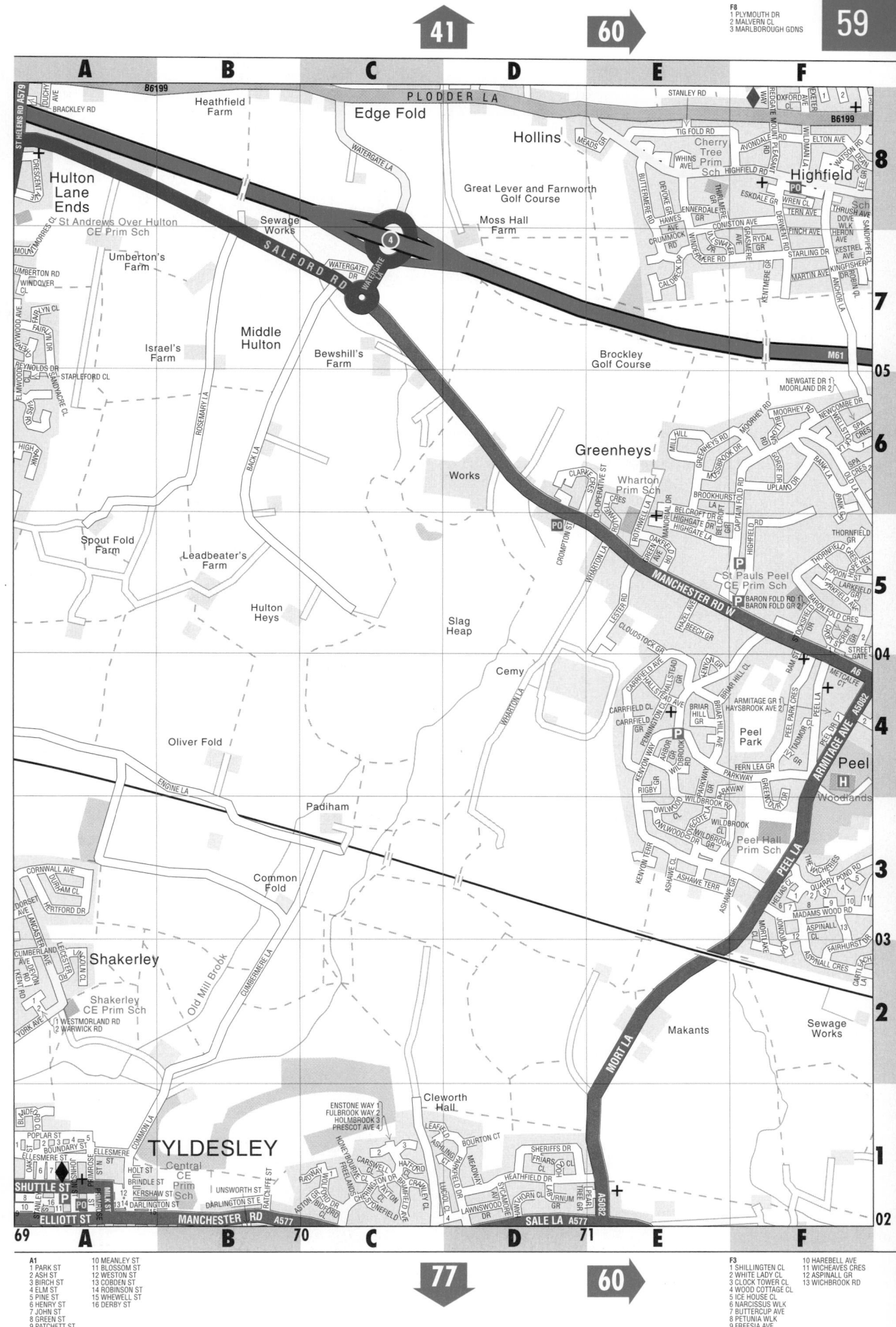

PLODDER LA

Edge Fold

Hollins

Great Lever and Farnworth
Golf Course

Moss Hall
Farm

Hulton
Lane
Ends

St Andrews Over Hulton
CE Prim Sch

Sewage
Works

SALFORD RD

WATERGATE LA

Umberton's
Farm

Cherry
Tree
Prim
Sch

Highfield

Middle
Hulton

Bewshill's
Farm

Brockley
Golf Course

M61

Israel's
Farm

Greenheys

Works

Wharton
Prim Sch

St Pauls Peel
CE Prim Sch

Spout Fold
Farm

Leadbeater's
Farm

Hulton
Heys

MANCHESTER RD W

Slag
Heap

Cemy

Oliver Fold

Peel
Park

Peel

Woodlands

Padiham

Peel Hall
Prim Sch

Common
Fold

Shakerley

Shakerley
CE Prim Sch
1 WESTMORLAND RD
2 WARWICK RD

Makants

Sewage
Works

MORT LA

Cleworth
Hall

ENSTONE WAY 1
FULBROOK WAY 2
HOLMBROOK 3
PRESCOT AVE 4

Sheriffs Dr

TYLDESLEY

Central
CE Prim
Sch

SHUTTLE ST

ELLIOTT ST

MANCHESTER RD   A577

SALE LA   A577

A1
1 PARK ST
2 ASH ST
3 BIRCH ST
4 ELM ST
5 PINE ST
6 HENRY ST
7 JOHN ST
8 GREEN ST
9 PATCHETT ST
10 MEANLEY ST
11 BLOSSOM ST
12 WESTON ST
13 COBDEN ST
14 ROBINSON ST
15 WHEWELL ST
16 DERBY ST

F3
1 SHILLINGTEN CL
2 WHITE LADY CL
3 CLOCK TOWER CL
4 WOOD COTTAGE CL
5 ICE HOUSE CL
6 NARCISSUS WLK
7 BUTTERCUP AVE
8 PETUNIA WLK
9 FREESIA AVE
10 HAREBELL AVE
11 WICHEAVES CRES
12 ASPINALL GR
13 WICHBROOK RD

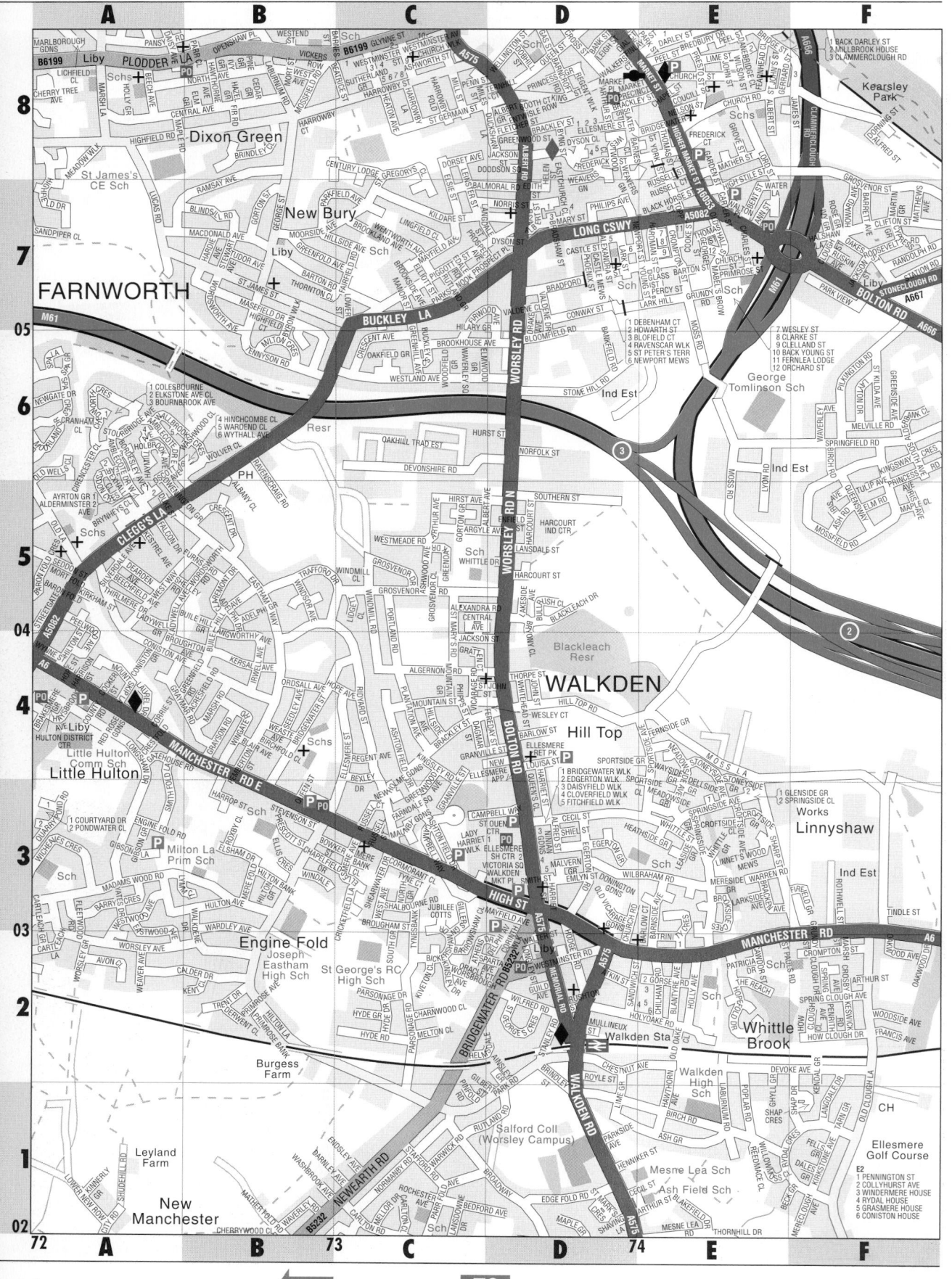

59

42

C8
1 THOMAS GARNET CT
2 PHILIP ARNOLD CT
3 SUTHERLAND ST
4 WESTMINSTER WLK
5 LONSDALE GR
6 KENTFORD GR

C8
7 LIDGATE GR
8 ASHLEY GR
9 ALMOND ST
10 ORMROD ST
D8
1 JANE BARTER HOUSE

2 BARNES HOUSE
3 ELLESMERE WLK
4 WILCOCKSON HOUSE
5 HESKETH WLK

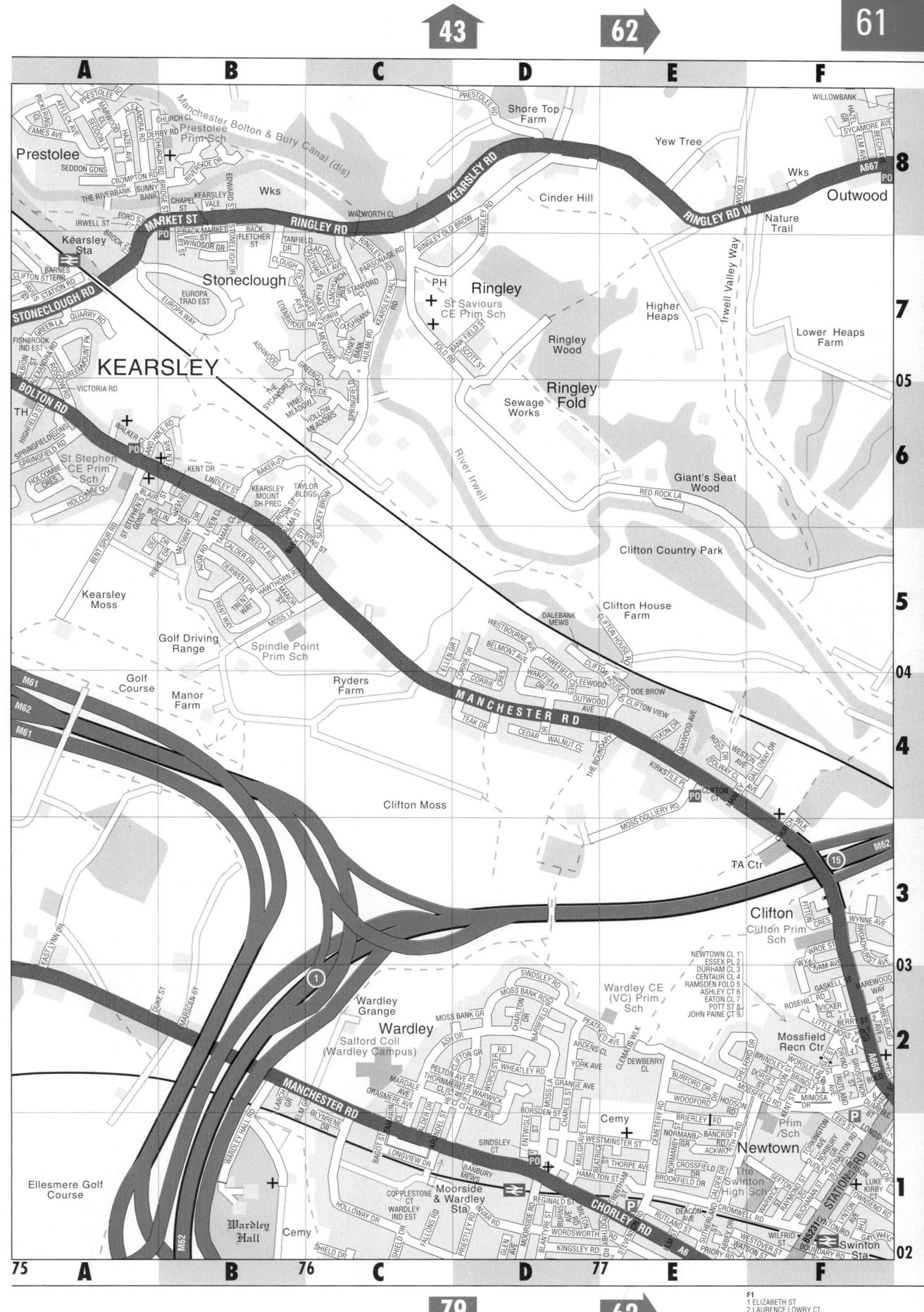

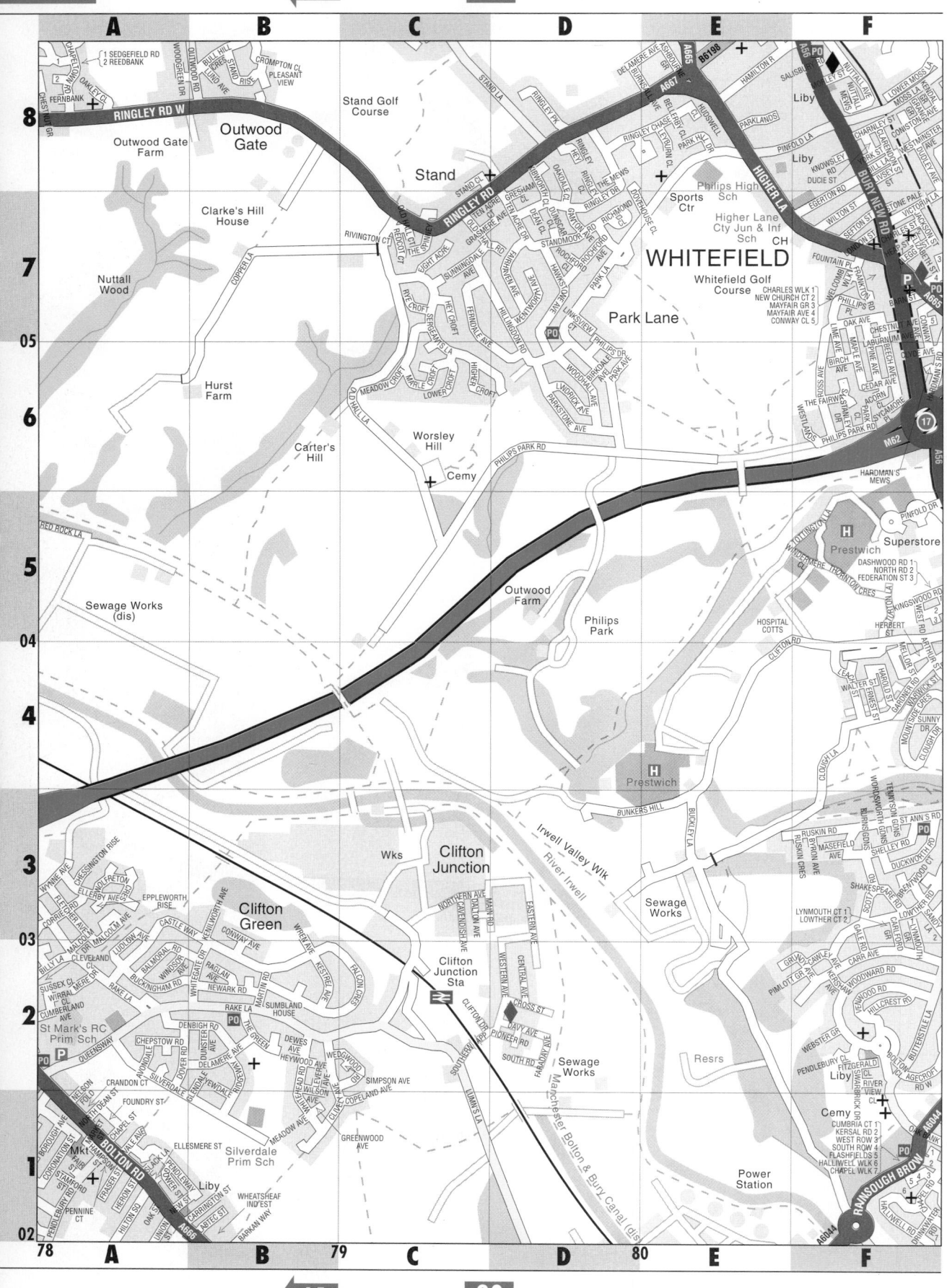

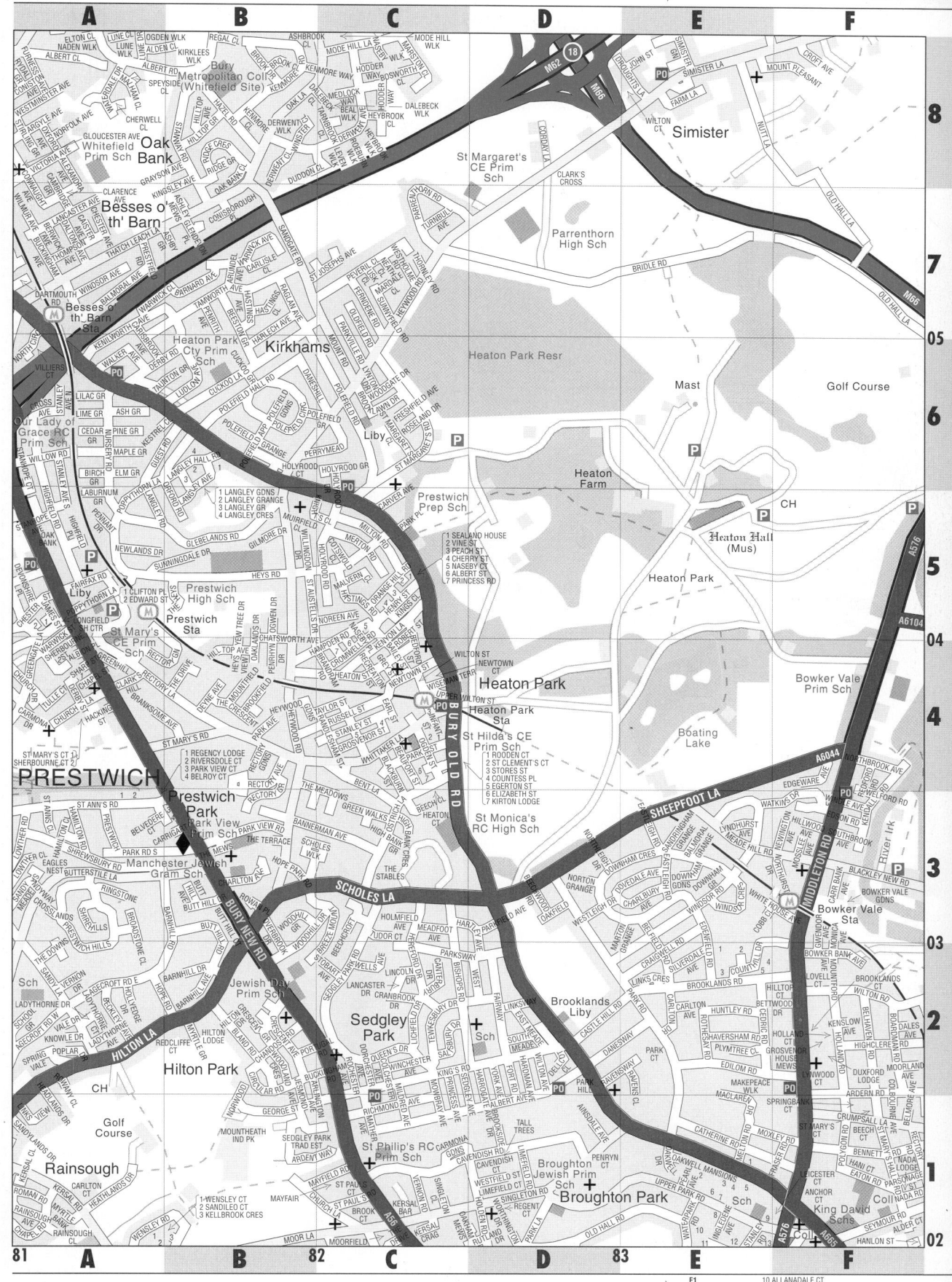

E1
1 BERKELEY CT
2 BRISTOL CT
3 NORFOLK HOUSE
4 RAVENHURST
5 MILTON CT
6 PARKLEA CT
7 CADOGAN PL
8 INGLEDENE CT
9 LANGLEY CT
10 ALLANADALE CT
11 CASTLETON RD
12 LINCOLN CT
13 GAN EDEN
E2
1 WESTHORNE FOLD
2 CLAYTHORPE WLK
3 TIXALL WLK
4 SHARBROOK WLK
5 LOWER BROOKLANDS PAR

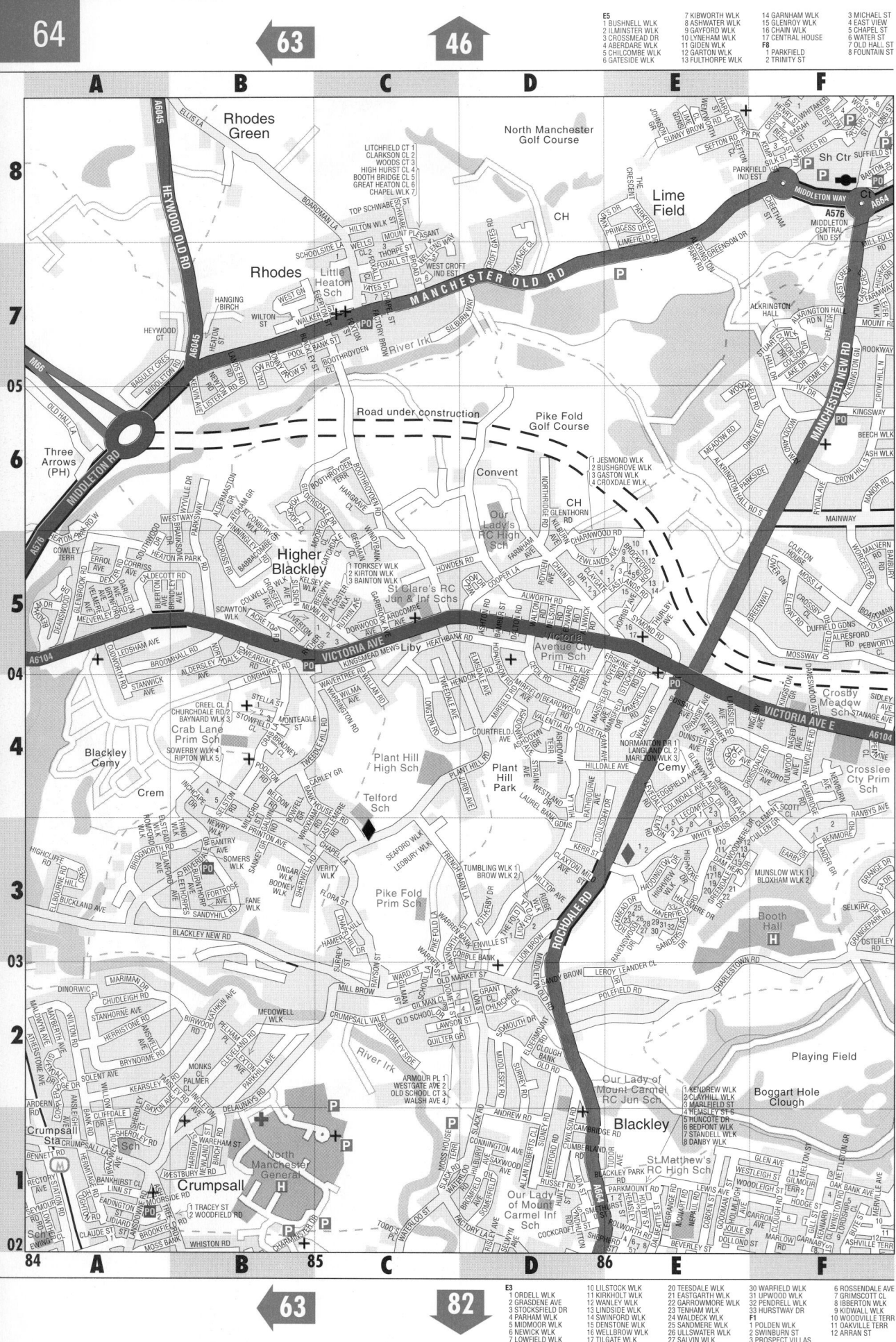

E5
1 BUSHNELL WLK
2 ILMINSTER WLK
3 CROSSMEAD DR
4 ABERDARE WLK
5 CHILCOMBE WLK
6 GATESIDE WLK

7 KIBWORTH WLK
8 ASHWATER WLK
9 GAYFORD WLK
10 LYNEHAM WLK
11 GIDEN WLK
12 GARTON WLK
13 FULTHORPE WLK

14 GARNHAM WLK
15 GLENROY WLK
16 CHAIN WLK
17 CENTRAL HOUSE
F8
1 PARKFIELD
2 TRINITY ST

3 MICHAEL WLK
4 EAST VIEW
5 CHAPEL ST
6 WATER ST
7 OLD HALL WLK
8 FOUNTAIN ST

E3
1 ORDELL WLK
2 GRASDENE AVE
3 STOCKSFIELD DR
4 PARHAM WLK
5 MIDMOOR WLK
6 NEWICK WLK
7 LOWFIELD WLK
8 PERITON WLK
9 LEAMORE WLK

10 LILSTOCK WLK
11 KIRKHOLT WLK
12 WANLEY WLK
13 LINDSIDE WLK
14 SWINFORD WLK
15 DENSTONE WLK
16 WELLBROW WLK
17 TILGATE WLK
18 MALLEY WLK
19 BRIXWORTH WLK

20 TEESDALE WLK
21 EASTGARTH WLK
22 GARROWMORE WLK
23 TENHAM WLK
24 WALDECK WLK
25 SANDMERE WLK
26 ULLSWATER WLK
27 SALVIN WLK
28 RASTELL WLK
29 MULGROVE WLK

30 WARFIELD WLK
31 UPWOOD WLK
32 PENDRELL WLK
33 HURSTWAY DR
F1
1 POLDEN WLK
2 SWINBURN ST
3 PROSPECT VILLAS
4 ROPLEY WLK
5 WESTHIDE WLK

6 ROSSENDALE AVE
7 GRIMSCOTT CL
8 IBBERTON WLK
9 KIDWALL WLK
10 WOODVILLE TERR
11 OAKVILLE TERR
12 ARRAN ST

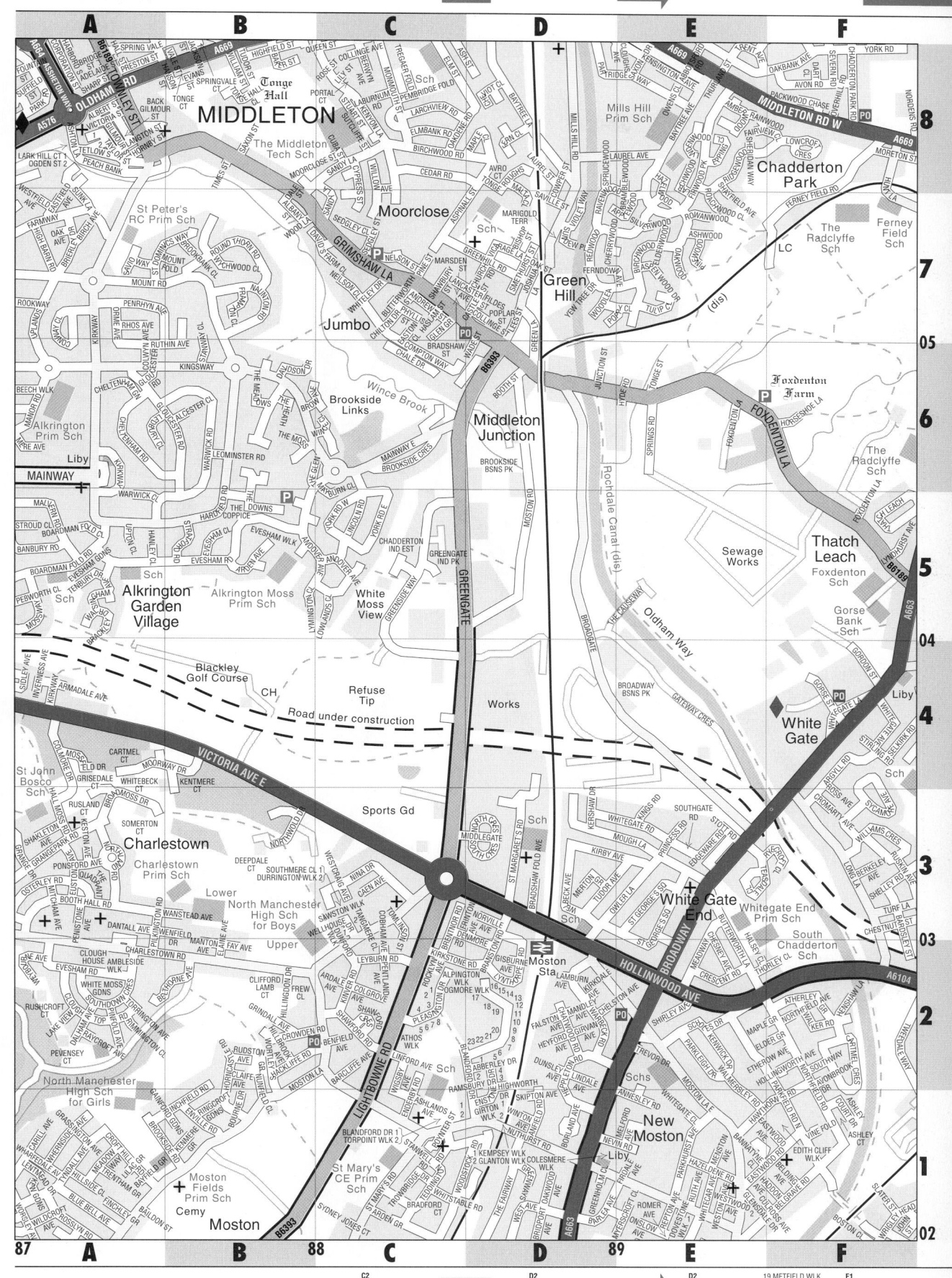

83
66

C2
1 PRESTWICK WLK
2 MILLFIELD WLK
3 WOOLTON CL
4 SNOWDEN WLK
5 ANCASTER WLK
6 ROCKLAND WLK
7 BARNWAY WLK
8 AMPORT WLK

D2
1 EDENHAM WLK
2 RAINTON WLK
3 PITMORE WLK
4 HALLKIRK WLK
5 OTTERY WLK
6 FONTWELL WLK
7 GAYTON WLK
8 GLENCAR DR
9 HENLOW WLK

D2
10 INVER WLK
11 KINLETT WLK
12 KIRKHILL WLK
13 TEDBURN WLK
14 THORNFORD WLK
15 TONGLEY WLK
16 TETSWORTH WLK
17 OXHILL WLK
18 ROXBY DR

19 METFIELD WLK
20 STANDON WLK
21 SHILTON WLK
22 SHAFTON WLK
23 SCORTON WLK

E1
1 VALIANT WLK
2 RUSTONS WLK

65
48

For full street detail of the highlighted area see pages 152 and 153.

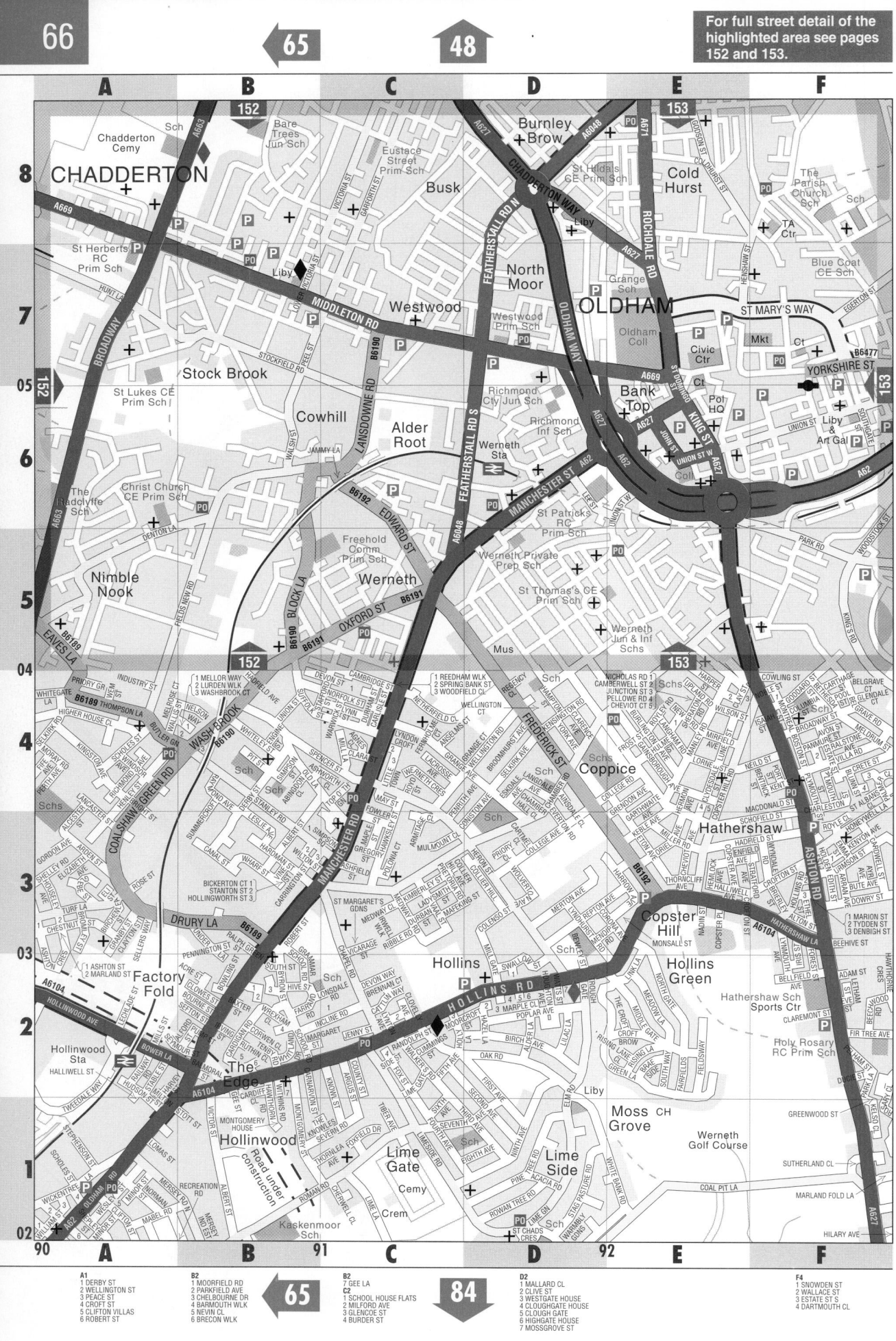

65
84

A1
1 DERBY ST
2 WELLINGTON ST
3 PEACE ST
4 CROFT ST
5 CLIFTON VILLAS
6 ROBERT ST

B2
1 MOORFIELD RD
2 PARKFIELD AVE
3 CHELBOURNE DR
4 BARMOUTH WLK
5 NEVIN CL
6 BRECON WLK

B2
7 GEE LA

C2
1 SCHOOL HOUSE FLATS
1 MILFORD AVE
3 GLENCOE ST
4 BURDER ST

D2
1 MALLARD CL
2 CLIVE ST
3 WESTGATE HOUSE
4 CLOUGHGATE HOUSE
5 CLOUGH GATE
6 HIGHGATE HOUSE
7 MOSSGROVE ST

F4
1 SNOWDEN ST
2 WALLACE ST
3 ESTATE ST S
4 DARTMOUTH CL

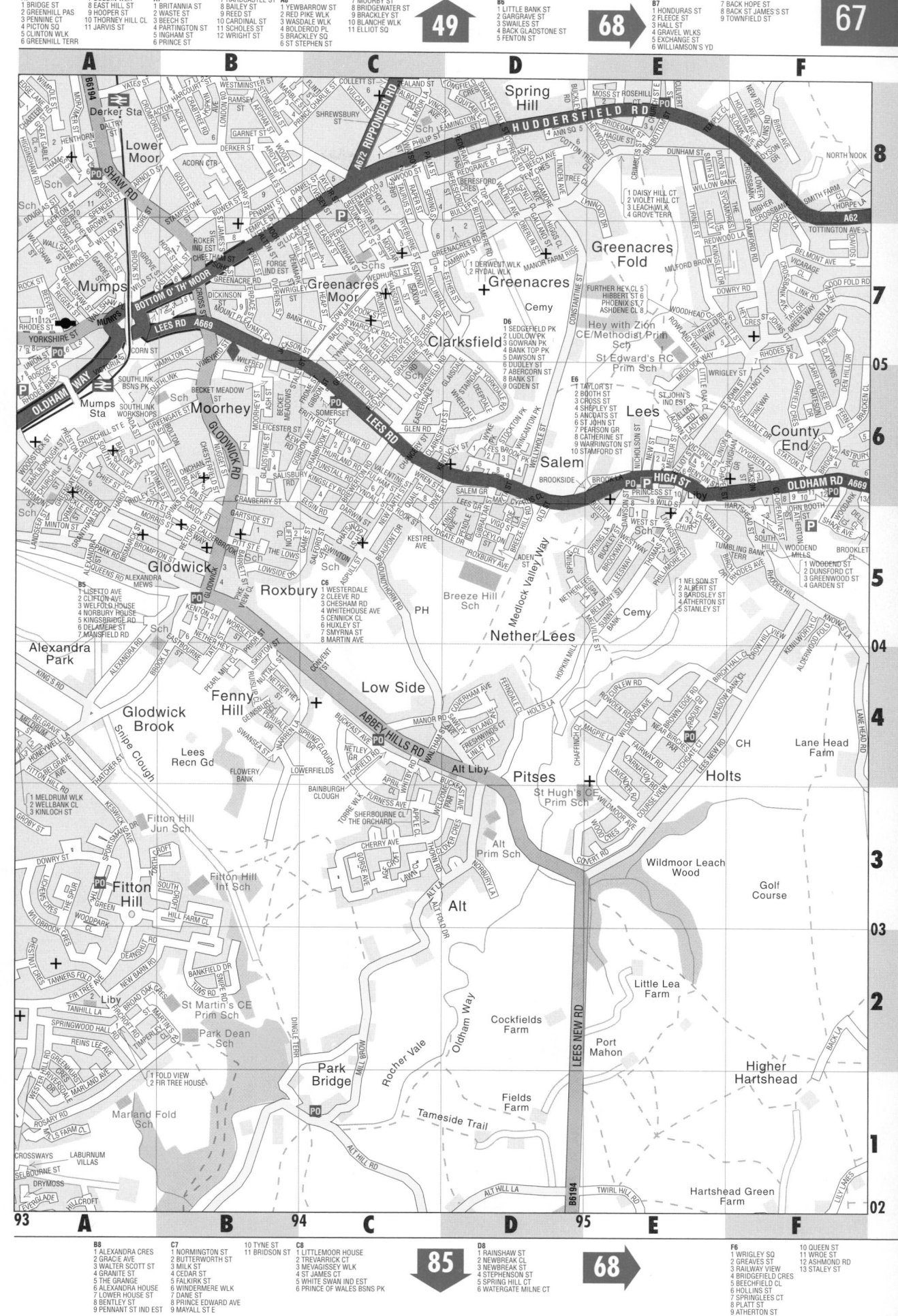

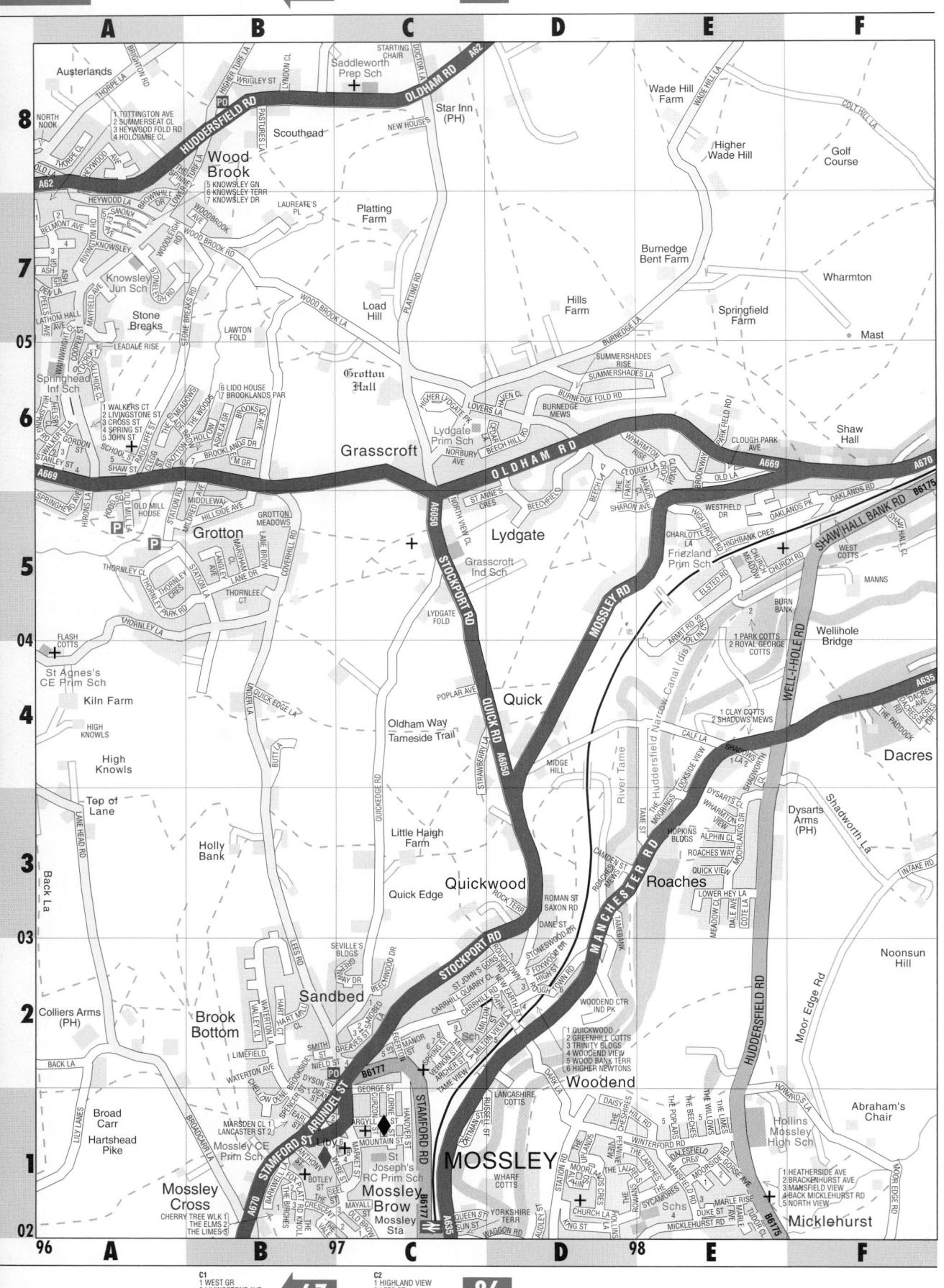

67 50

C1
1 WEST GR
2 LIVINGSTONE AVE
3 THE HIGHLANDS
4 CRADDOCK ST
5 CHAPEL CT
6 CHAPEL ST

C2
1 HIGHLAND VIEW
2 LEES ST
3 WEBSTER ST
4 CROSS ST
5 WILD'S SQ
6 SPRING COTTS
7 BACK MILL LA
8 HAWTHORN TERR
9 WOODMEADOW CT

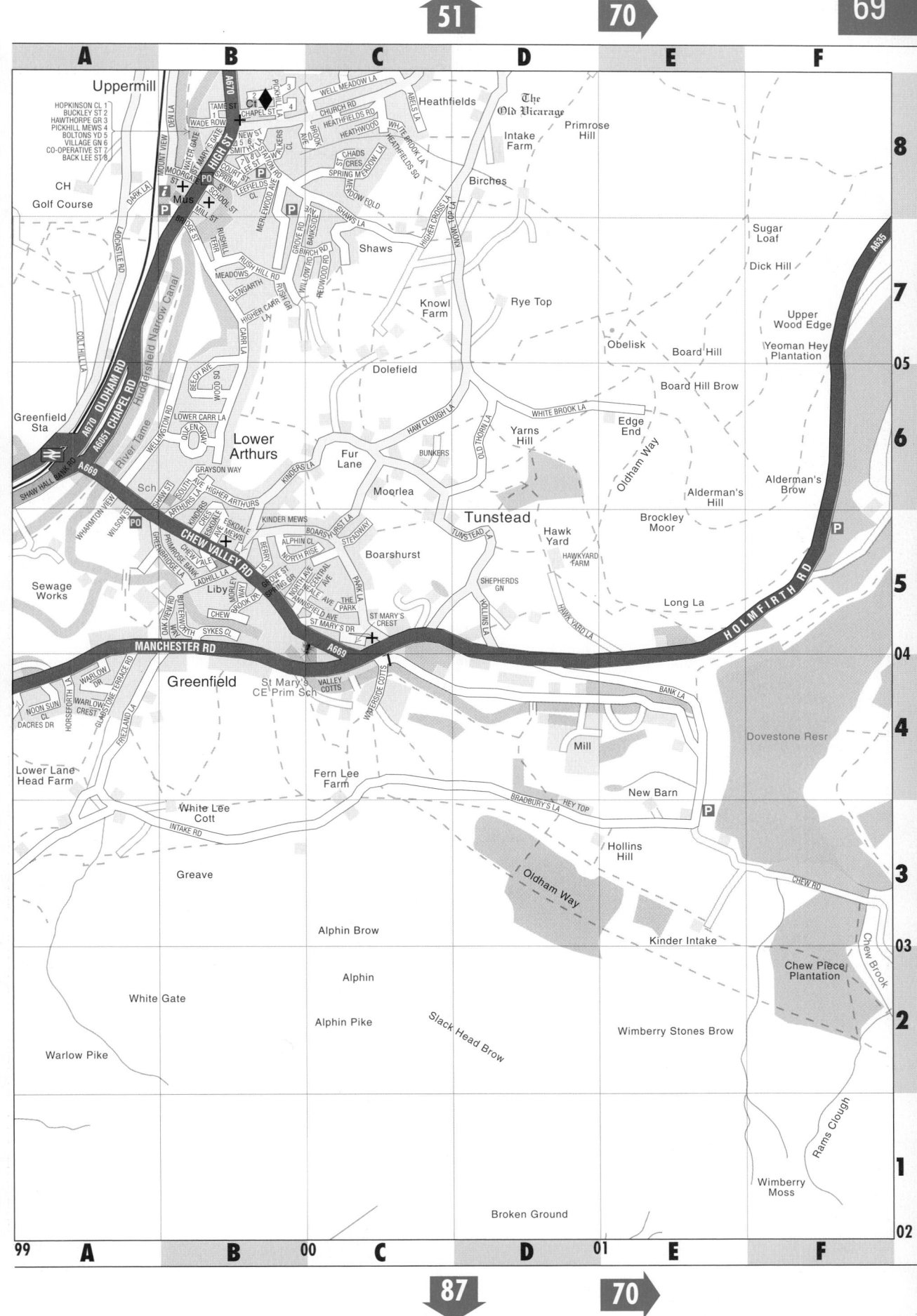

Uppermill

HOPKINSON CL 1
BUCKLEY ST 2
HAWTHORPE GR 3
PICKHILL MEWS 4
BOLTONS YD 5
VILLAGE GN 6
CO-OPERATIVE ST 7
BACK LEE ST 8

CH
Golf Course

The Old Vicarage

Heathfields

Primrose Hill

Intake Farm

Birches

Sugar Loaf

Dick Hill

Upper Wood Edge

Knowl Farm

Rye Top

Obelisk

Board Hill

Yeoman Hey Plantation

Dolefield

Board Hill Brow

Shaws

Lower Arthurs

Fur Lane

Bunkers

Haw Clough La

White Brook La

Yarns Hill

Edge End

Oldham Way

Alderman's Hill

Alderman's Brow

Greenfield Sta

Moorlea

Tunstead

Hawk Yard

Hawkyard Farm

Brockley Moor

Sewage Works

Boarshurst

Shepherds Gn

Long La

Liby

The Park

St Mary's Crest

Hollins La

Manchester Rd

Greenfield

St Mary's CE Prim Sch

Valley Cotts

Waterside Cotts

Bank La

Mill

Dovestone Resr

Lower Lane Head Farm

White Lee Cott

Fern Lee Farm

Bradbury's La

Hey Top

New Barn

Greave

Hollins Hill

Chew Rd

Oldham Way

Kinder Intake

Chew Piece Plantation

Chew Brook

Alphin Brow

Alphin

White Gate

Alphin Pike

Slack Head Brow

Wimberry Stones Brow

Warlow Pike

Rams Clough

Wimberry Moss

Broken Ground

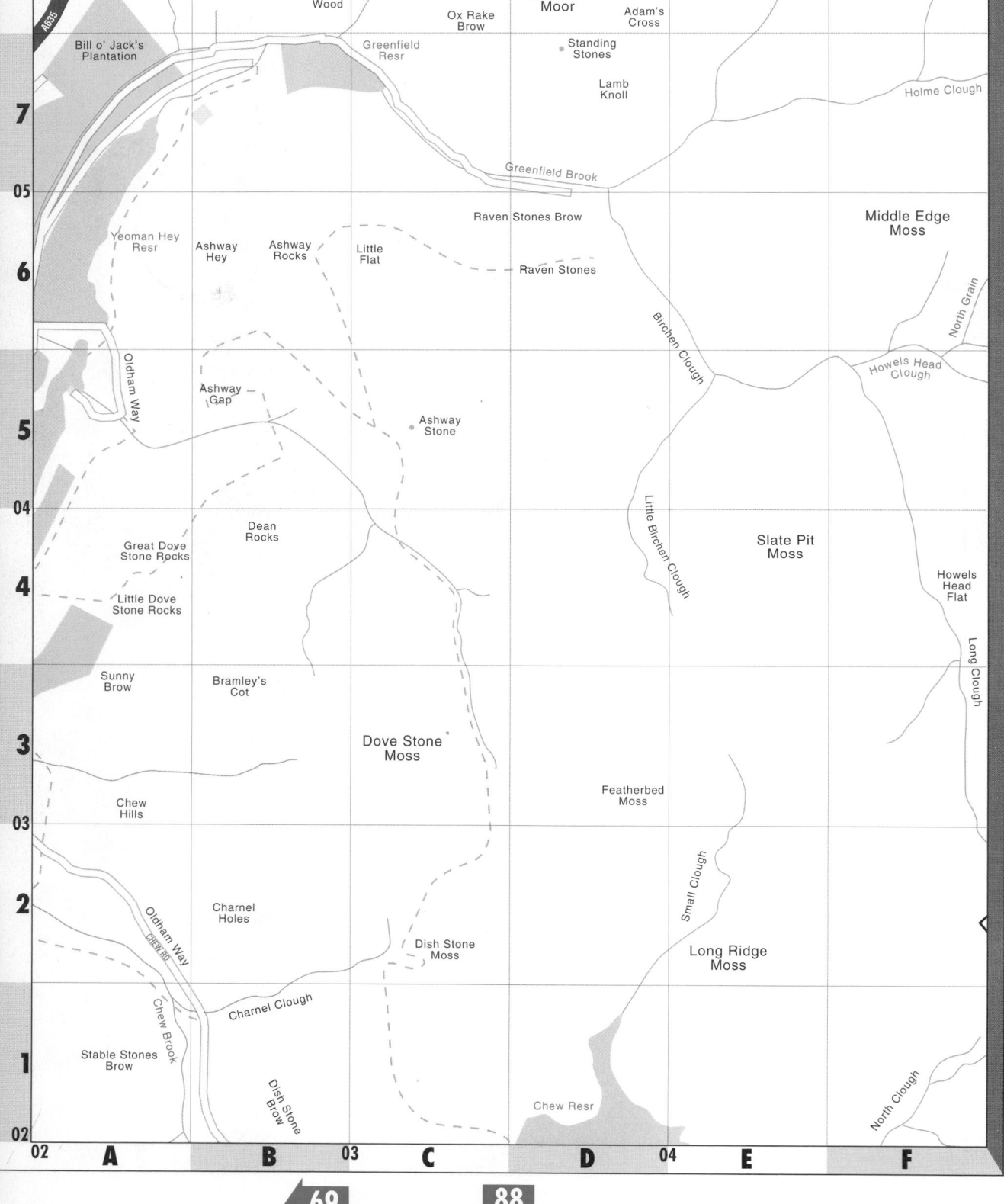

A   B   C   D   E   F

8

HOLMFIRTH RD A635

A635

Upperwood
House

Upper
Wood

Far Rough Clough

Ox Rake
Brow

Saddleworth
Moor

Sail Bark
Moss

Rimmon
Cottage

Rimmon Pit Clough

Little
Moss

Bill o' Jack's
Plantation

Greenfield
Resr

Adam's
Cross

Standing
Stones

7

Lamb
Knoll

Holme Clough

Greenfield Brook

05

Yeoman Hey
Resr

Raven Stones Brow

Middle Edge
Moss

6

Ashway
Hey

Ashway
Rocks

Little
Flat

Raven Stones

North Grain

Birchen Clough

Howels Head
Clough

Oldham Way

Ashway
Gap

5

Ashway
Stone

Little Birchen Clough

04

Dean
Rocks

Slate Pit
Moss

Howels
Head
Flat

Great Dove
Stone Rocks

Long Clough

4

Little Dove
Stone Rocks

Sunny
Brow

Bramley's
Cot

3

Dove Stone
Moss

Featherbed
Moss

Chew
Hills

03

Small Clough

2

Charnel
Holes

Oldham Way

CHEW RD

Dish Stone
Moss

Long Ridge
Moss

Charnel Clough

Chew Brook

1

Stable Stones
Brow

Dish Stone Brow

Chew Resr

North Clough

02

02   A   B   03   C   D   04   E   F

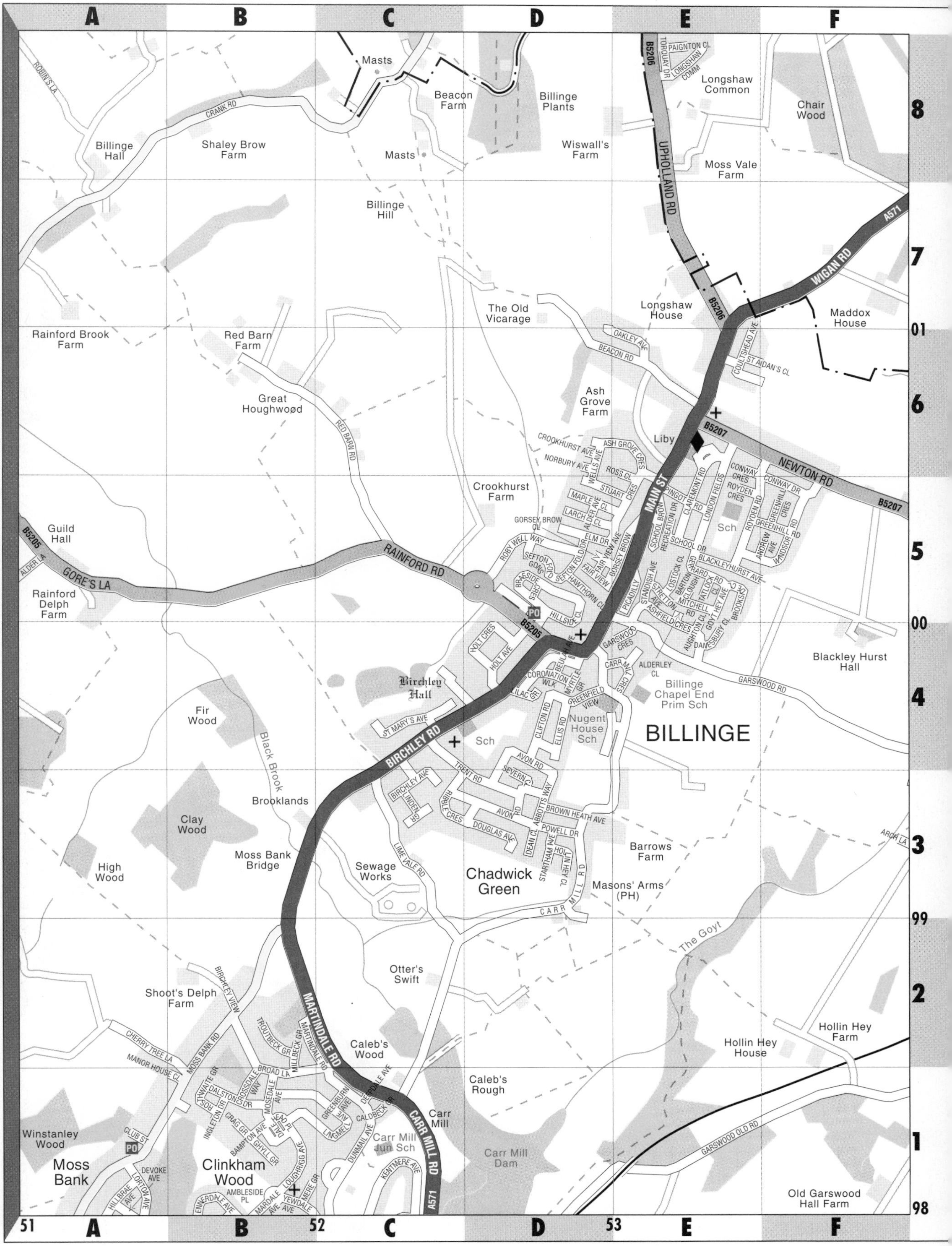

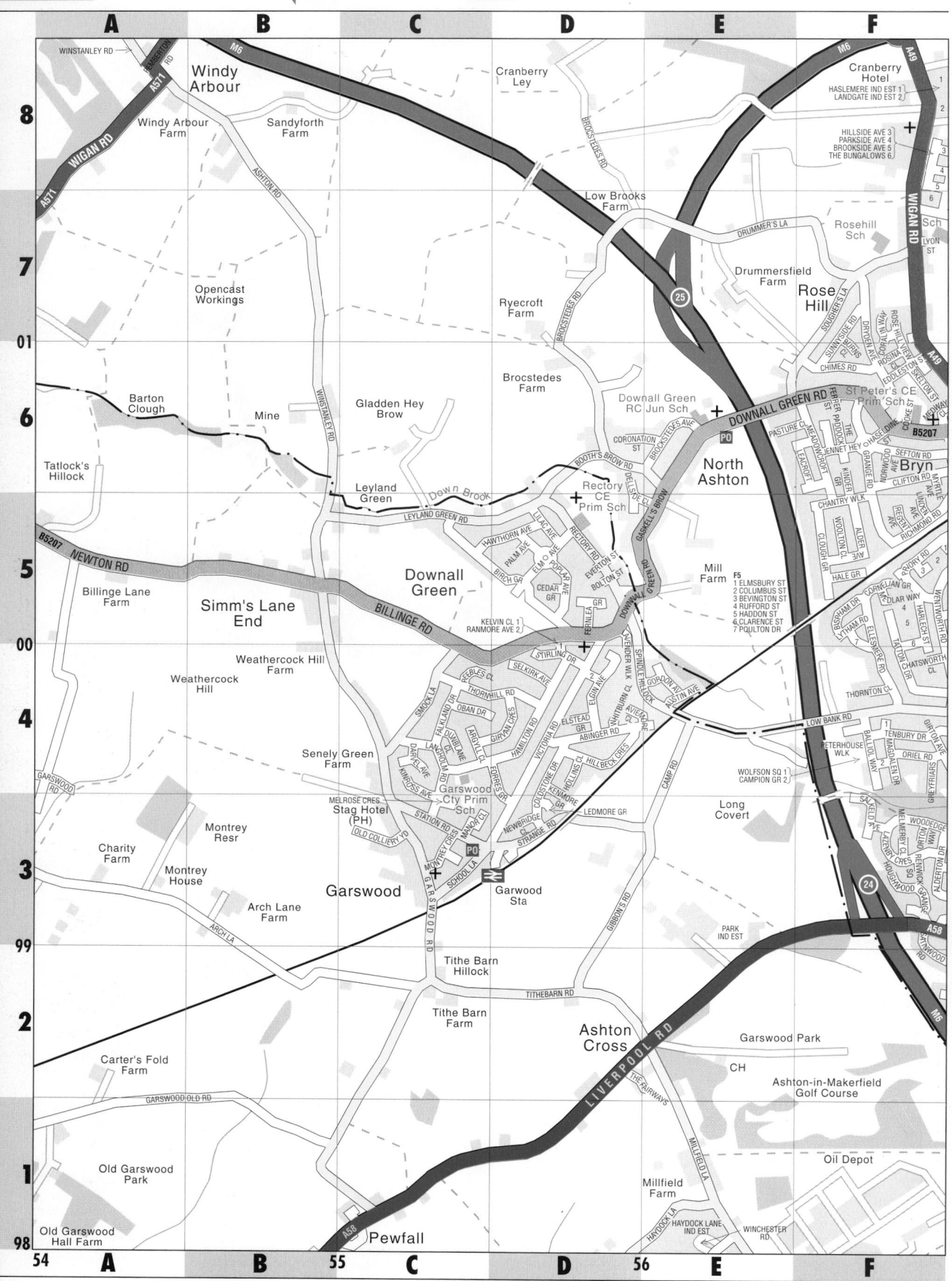

A   B   C   D   E   F

8

7

01

6

5

00

4

99

2

1

98

WINSTANLEY RD
Windy
Arbour
Windy Arbour
Farm
Sandyforth
Farm
WIGAN RD
A571
A571
M6
ASHTON RD

Cranberry
Ley
Cranberry
Hotel
HASLEMERE IND EST 1
LANDGATE IND EST 2
HILLSIDE AVE 3
PARKSIDE AVE 4
BROOKSIDE AVE 5
THE BUNGALOWS 6
Sch
LYON ST
M6
A49
WIGAN RD

Low Brooks
Farm
DRUMMER'S LA
Rosehill
Sch
Drummersfield
Farm
Rose
Hill
25

Opencast
Workings
Ryecroft
Farm
Brocstedes
Farm
BROCSTEDES RD
Downall Green
RC Jun Sch
St Peter's CE
Prim Sch
B5207
DOWNALL GREEN RD
PASTURE CL
Bryn
B5207

Barton
Clough
Mine
WINSTANLEY RD
Gladden Hey
Brow
CORONATION
ST
BROCSTEDES AVE
North
Ashton
PO

Tatlock's
Hillock
Leyland
Green
Down Brook
LEYLAND GREEN RD
Rectory
CE
Prim Sch
BOOTH'S BROW RD
DELLSIDE CL
GASKELL'S BROW
RECTORY RD
Mill
Farm
F5
1 ELMSBURY ST
2 COLUMBUS ST
3 BEVINGTON ST
4 RUFFORD ST
5 HADDON ST
6 CLARENCE ST
7 POULTON DR

B5207
NEWTON RD
Billinge Lane
Farm
Simm's Lane
End
Downall
Green
HAWTHORN AVE
PALM AVE
BIRCH GR
LILAC AVE
ELM CT
POPLAR AVE
CEDAR GR
EVERTON ST
BOLTON ST
FERN LA
FERNLEA
DOWNALL GREEN RD
BILLINGE RD
KELVIN CL 1
RANMORE AVE 2

Weathercock Hill
Farm
Weathercock
Hill
STIRLING DR
PEEBLES CT
THORNHILL RD
SELKIRK AVE
FALKLAND DR
DUNBLANE
ARGYLL CL
GIRVAN CRES
HAMILTON RD
VICTORIA RD
ELSTEAD GR
ABINGER RD
WHITBURN CL
AITREAM
GORDON CT
AUSTIN AVE
LOW BANK RD
PETERHOUSE
WLK

Senely Green
Farm
SMOCK LA
OBAN DR
LANGDON CL
DARFIELD AVE
KINROSS AVE
MELROSE CRES
Garswood
Cty Prim
Sch
FORRES GR
ELGIN AVE
HILLBECK CRES
COLLISDALE DR
KENMORE
LEDMORE GR
CAMP RD
WOLFSON SQ 1
CAMPION GR 2
Long
Covert
TENBURY DR
BALIOL WAY
ORIEL RD

Charity
Farm
Montrey Resr
Montrey
House
Stag Hotel
(PH)
OLD COLLIERY YD
STATION RD
MONTREY CRES
MANOR CT
NEWBRIDGE
STRANGE
PO
Garwood
Sta
GIBBONS RD
PARK
IND EST
A58
24

Arch Lane
Farm
ARCH LA
Garswood
GARSWOOD RD
SCHOOL LA

Tithe Barn
Hillock
TITHEBARN RD
Tithe Barn
Farm

Carter's Fold
Farm
GARSWOOD OLD RD
Ashton
Cross
LIVERPOOL RD
THE FAIRWAYS
Garswood Park
CH
Ashton-in-Makerfield
Golf Course
M6

Old Garswood
Park
Millfield
Farm
MILLFIELD LA
MILLFIELD IND EST
WINCHESTER
RD
HAYDOCK LANE
IND EST
HAYDOCK LA
Oil Depot

Old Garswood
Hall Farm
A58
Pewfall

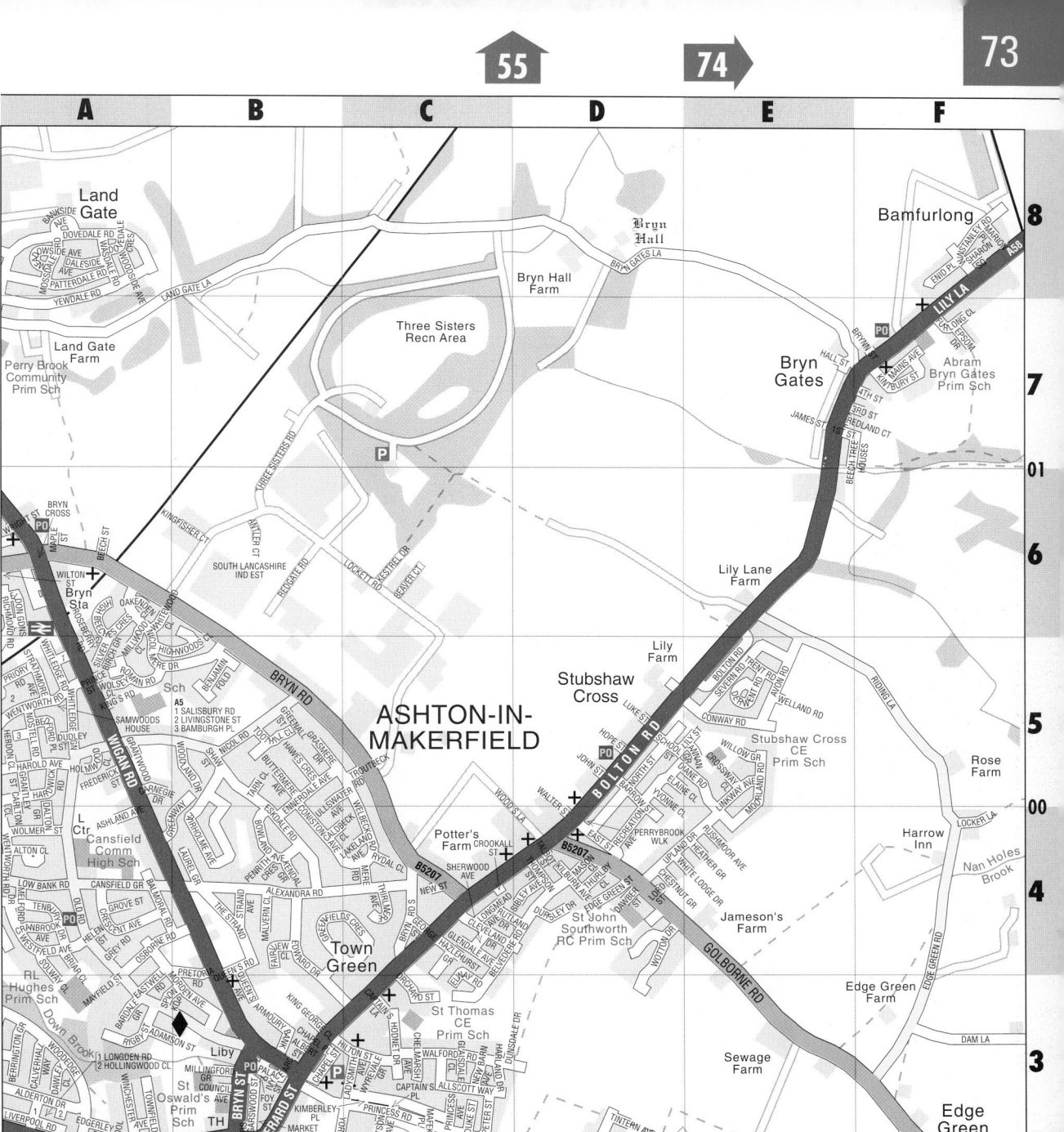

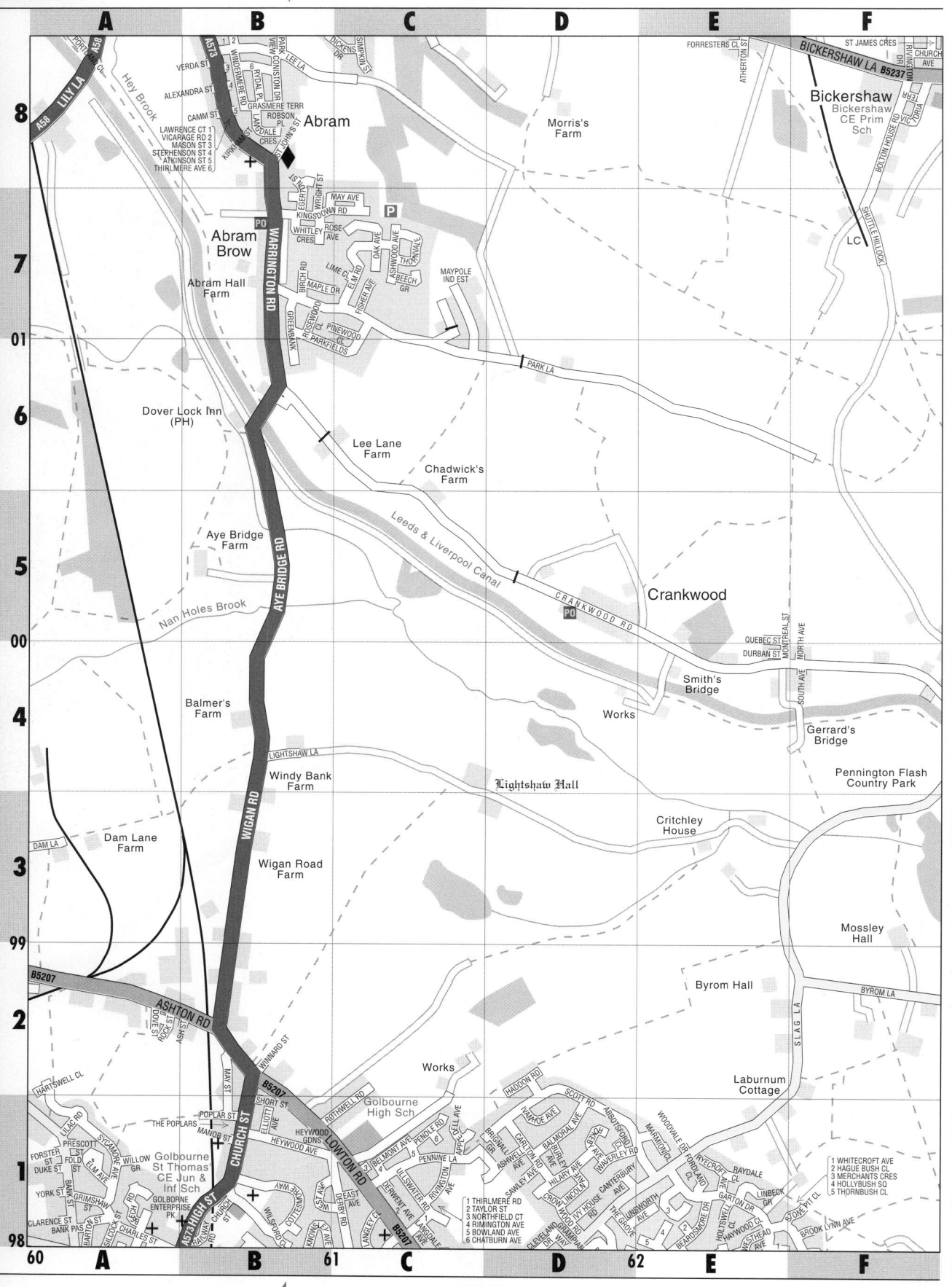
A B C D E F

8

FORRESTERS CL ST JAMES CRES
BICKERSHAW LA B5237

Bickershaw
Bickershaw CE Prim Sch

LILY LA
A58
PORTHILL CL
Hey Brook
A573
WINDERMERE RD
CONISTON RD
RYDAL AVE
PARK VIEW
LEE LA
DICKENS DR
SIMKIN ST
ATHERTON ST

VERDA ST

Alexandra St

CAMM ST
GRASMERE TERR

Abram

Morris's Farm

LAWRENCE CT 1
VICARAGE RD 2
MASON ST 3
STEPHENSON ST 4
ATKINSON ST 5
THIRLMERE AVE 6
ROBSON PL
LANGDALE CRES
KIRKHALL LA

Abram Brow

PO
WARRINGTON RD
EGERTON ST
WRIGHT ST
KINGSDOWN RD
MAY AVE
WHITLEY CRES
ROSE AVE
OAK AVE
GLENVALE
P

7

Abram Hall Farm
BIRCH RD
MAPLE DR
ELM AVE
FISHER AVE
LIME CL
ROSSWOOD
GREENBANK
PINEWOOD CL
PARKFIELDS
ASHWOOD GR
BEECH GR
THORNVALE

MAYPOLE IND EST

SHUTTLE HILLOCK

LC

01

PARK LA

6

Dover Lock Inn (PH)

Lee Lane Farm

Chadwick's Farm

AYE BRIDGE RD

Aye Bridge Farm

Leeds & Liverpool Canal

5

CRANKWOOD RD
Crankwood

PO

Nan Holes Brook

QUEBEC ST
MONTREAL ST
NORTH AVE
DURBAN ST
SOUTH AVE

00

Balmer's Farm

Smith's Bridge

Works

Gerrard's Bridge

4

DAM LA

Dam Lane Farm

LIGHTSHAW LA

Windy Bank Farm

Lightshaw Hall

Pennington Flash Country Park

WIGAN RD

Critchley House

3

Wigan Road Farm

Mossley Hall

99

B5207

Byrom Hall

BYROM LA
SLAG LA

2

ASHTON RD
B5207

Laburnum Cottage

WINMARD ST
MAY ST
DOVE ST
ROCK ST
HIGH ST

B5207

Works

HADDON RD
SCOTT RD
WOODVALE DR
BAYDALE

HARTSWELL CL
LILAC RD
THE POPLARS
POPLAR ST
SHORT ST
ELLIOTT ST
HEYWOOD GDNS
HEYWOOD AVE
ROTHWELL RD
Golbourne High Sch
LOWTON RD
BELMONT AVE
PENDLE CL
PENNINE LA
APPLE DELL AVE
BRIGHAM
BURLEY AVE
CARLTON AVE
BALMORAL AVE
ABBOTSFORD
MARSDON CL
RYECROFT CL
PORTLAND CL
LINBECK

1

FORSTER ST
PRESCOTT ST
SYCAMORE AVE
DUKE ST
WILLOW RD
Golbourne St Thomas' CE Jun & Inf Sch
MANOR ST
CHURCH ST
WILSFORD ST
THORNE WAY
ULLSWATER AVE
DERWENT AVE
LANGDALE
RIVINGTON AVE
BAWLEY AVE
HILARY AVE
WAVERLEY AVE
CROW WOOD
LINCOLN
IVY HOUSE
CANTERBURY AVE
THE GROVE
CLUNSWORTH
GARTON DR
HOLTSWELL
WESTHEAD AVE
BROOK LYNN AVE

YORK ST
CLARENCE ST
BANK PAS
BANK ST
BARTON ST
GRIMSHAW ST
SILCOCK RD
CHARLES ST
CHURCH RD
A573 HIGH ST
Golbourne Enterprise Pk
KWIK SAVE
EAST AVE
WEST
KINGS CL
LANGLEY CL
B5207

1 THIRLMERE RD
2 TAYLOR ST
3 NORTHFIELD CT
4 RIMINGTON AVE
5 BOWLAND AVE
6 CHATBURN AVE

CLEVELAND AVE
WAY
CHAPMAN
GRIMFORD
BEARDSMORE DR
STONE PIT CL
THORNBUSH CL

1 WHITECROFT AVE
2 HAGUE BUSH CL
3 MERCHANTS CRES
4 HOLLYBUSH SQ
5 THORNBUSH CL

98

60 A B 61 C D 62 E F

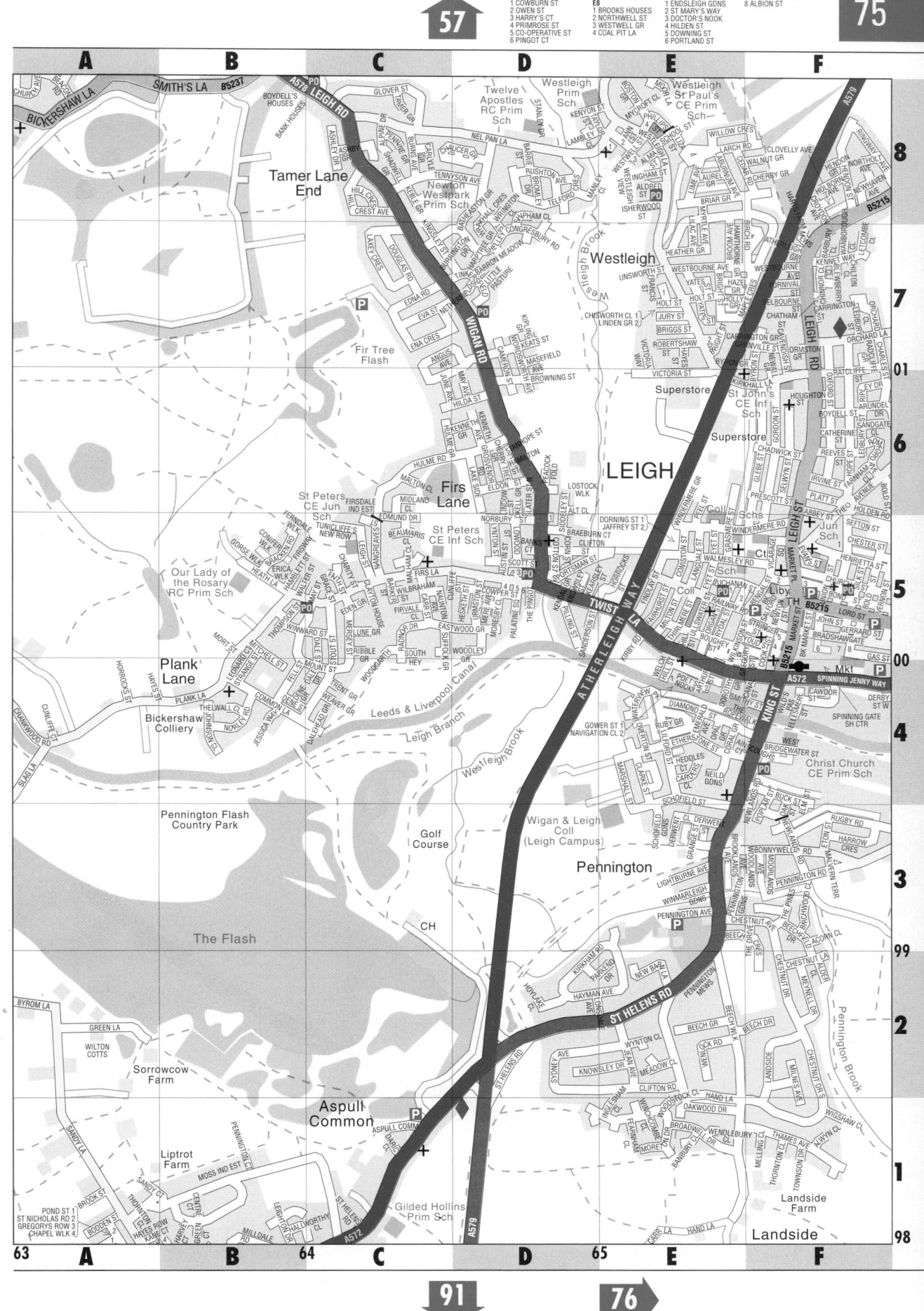

D5
1 COWBURN ST
2 OWEN ST
3 HARRY'S CT
4 PRIMROSE ST
5 CO-OPERATIVE ST
6 PINGOT CT

7 MERE ST
E8
1 BROOKS HOUSES
2 NORTHWELL ST
3 WESTWELL GR
4 COAL PIT LA

F5
1 ENDSLEIGH GDNS
2 ST MARY'S WAY
3 DOCTOR'S NOOK
4 HILDEN ST
5 DOWNING ST
6 PORTLAND ST

7 BRADSHAWGATE SH ARC
8 ALBION ST

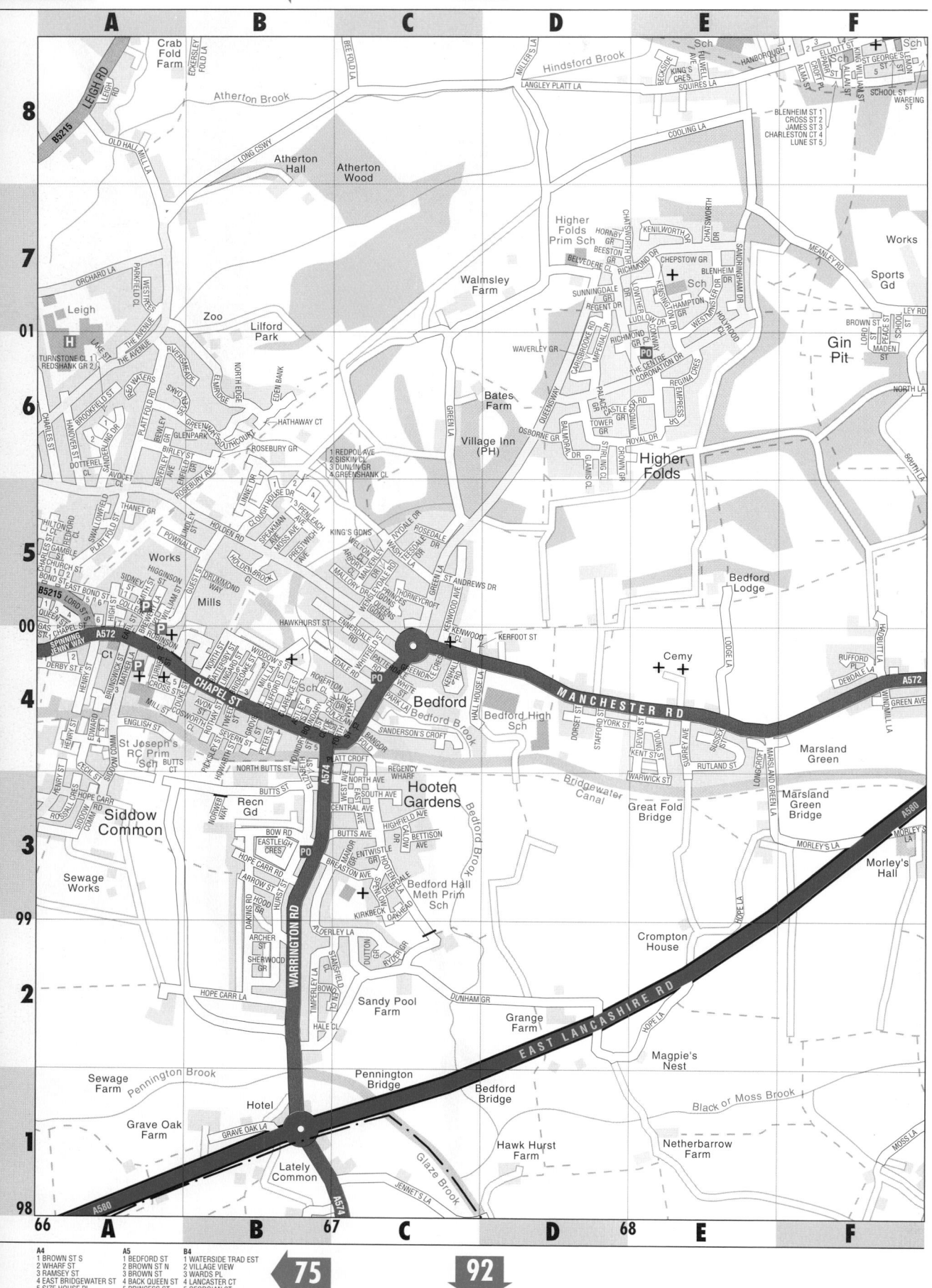

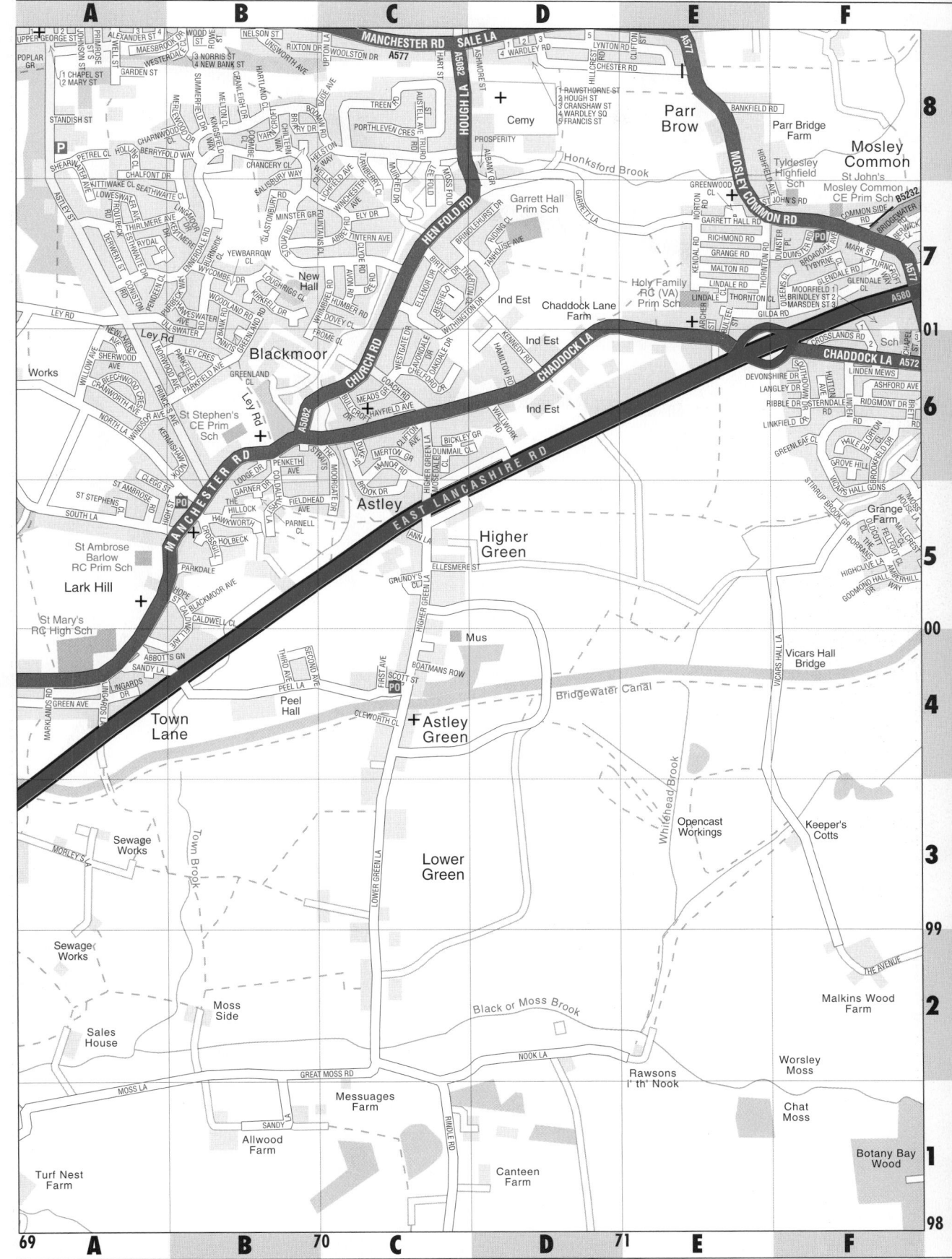

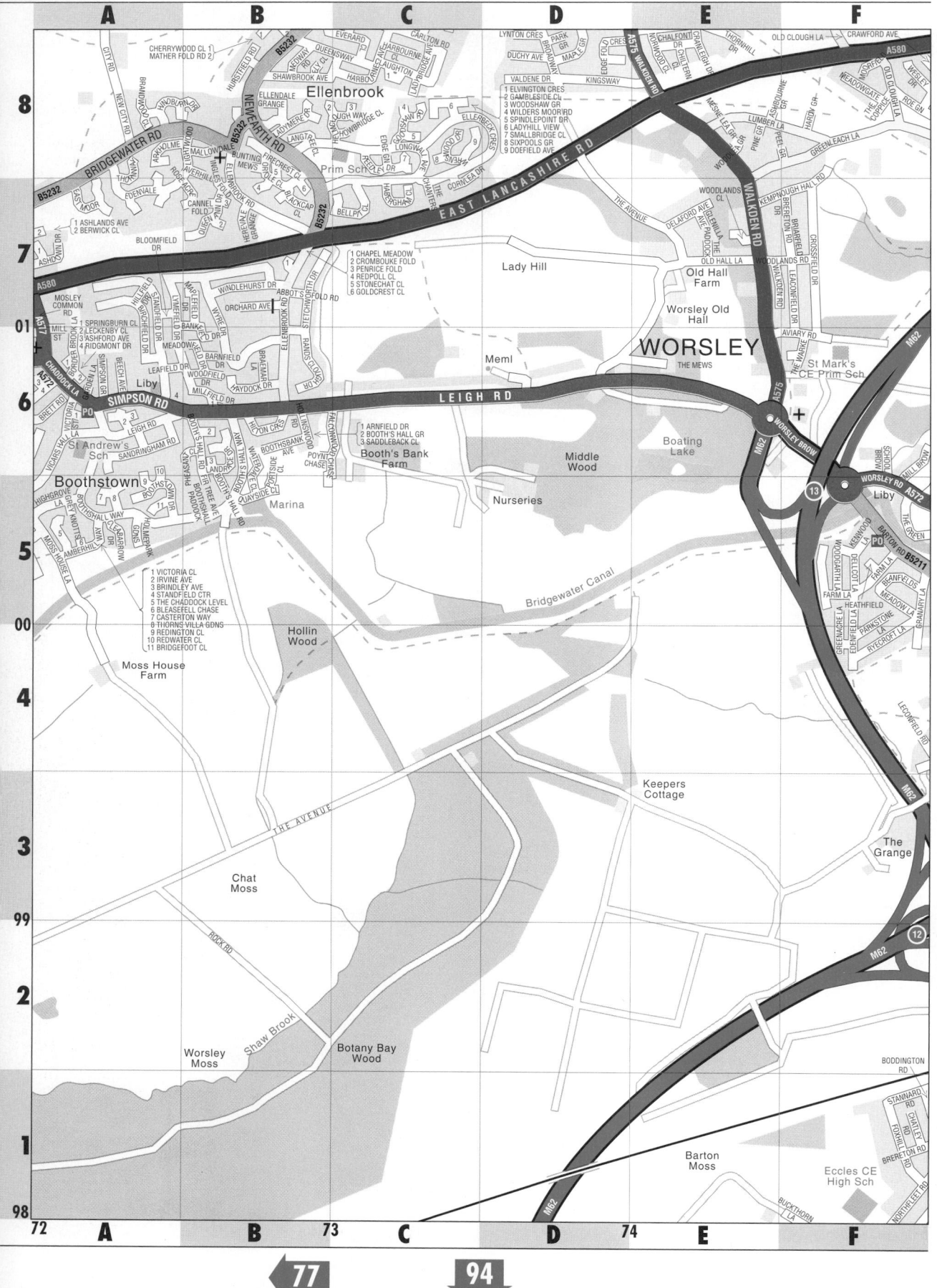

Ellenbrook

WORSLEY
THE MEWS

Boothstown

Marina

Booth's Bank Farm

Middle Wood

Nurseries

Boating Lake

Worsley Brow

Lady Hill

Old Hall Farm

Worsley Old Hall

St Mark's CE Prim Sch

St Andrew's Sch

Moss House Farm

Hollin Wood

Bridgewater Canal

Keepers Cottage

The Grange

Chat Moss

Worsley Moss

Shaw Brook

Botany Bay Wood

Barton Moss

Eccles CE High Sch

EAST LANCASHIRE RD

LEIGH RD

SIMPSON RD

BRIDGEWATER RD

NEWEARTH RD

WALKDEN RD

THE AVENUE

ROCK RD

1 CHAPEL MEADOW
2 CROMBOUKE FOLD
3 PENRICE FOLD
4 REDPOLL CL
5 STONECHAT CL
6 GOLDCREST CL

1 ELVINGTON CRES
2 GAMBLESIDE CL
3 WOODSHAW GR
4 WILDERS MOOR RD
5 SPINDLEPOINT DR
6 LADYHILL VIEW
7 SMALLBRIDGE CL
8 SIXPOOLS GR
9 DOEFIELD AVE

1 ARNFIELD DR
2 BOOTH'S HALL GR
3 SADDLEBACK CL

1 SPRINGBURN CL
2 LECKENBY CL
3 ASHFORD AVE
4 RIDGMONT DR

1 VICTORIA CL
2 IRVINE AVE
3 BRINDLEY AVE
4 STANDFIELD CTR
5 THE CHADDOCK LEVEL
6 BLEASEFELL CHASE
7 CASTERTON WAY
8 THORNS VILLA GDNS
9 REDINGTON CL
10 REDWATER CL
11 BRIDGEFOOT CL

1 CHERRYWOOD CL
2 MATHER FOLD RD

A580

M62

M62

13

12

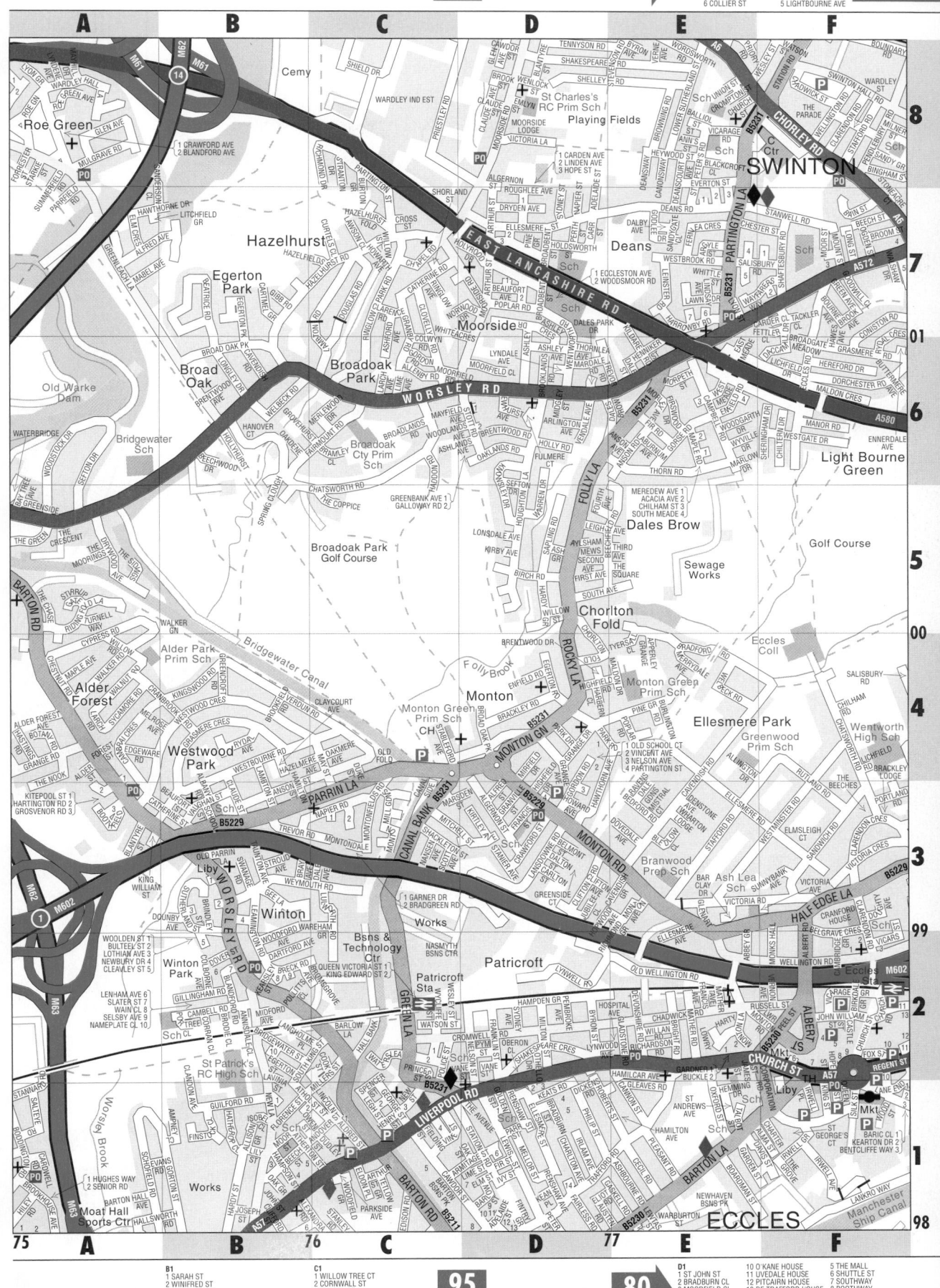

61

80

E7
1 BEDFORD AVE
2 PADDISON ST
3 STOCKTON ST
4 THORNFIELD DR
5 ALBERMARLE RD
6 COLLIER ST

7 LINCOLN RD
F7
1 GORSEFIELD DR
2 WAGGONERS CT
3 ROSETTE WLK
4 MAIDEN MEWS
5 LIGHTBOURNE AVE

B1
1 SARAH ST
2 WINIFRED ST
3 BEECH HOUSE
4 ATHERTON WAY
5 HAMPSON CL
6 GREEN ST

C1
1 WILLOW TREE CT
2 CORNWALL ST
3 CHAPEL ST
4 ELIZA ANN ST
5 SPOONER RD

D1
1 ST JOHN ST
2 BRADBURN CL
3 MOORFIELD CL
4 BRADBURN GR
5 BRADBURN ST
6 DORNING ST
7 WILHAM AVE
8 WADE HOUSE
9 WALKER HOUSE
10 O'KANE HOUSE
11 UVEDALE HOUSE
12 PITCAIRN HOUSE
13 DE TRAFFORD HOUSE
14 ELLESMERE ST
F2
1 CHAPEL WLK
2 THIRKHILL PL
3 KEMBALL
4 NORTHWAY

F3
5 THE MALL
6 SHUTTLE ST
7 SOUTHWAY
8 BOOTHWAY
9 BACK CHAPEL ST
10 COLLEGE CROFT
11 ST MARY'S RD
12 EWOOD
13 CRAUNTON

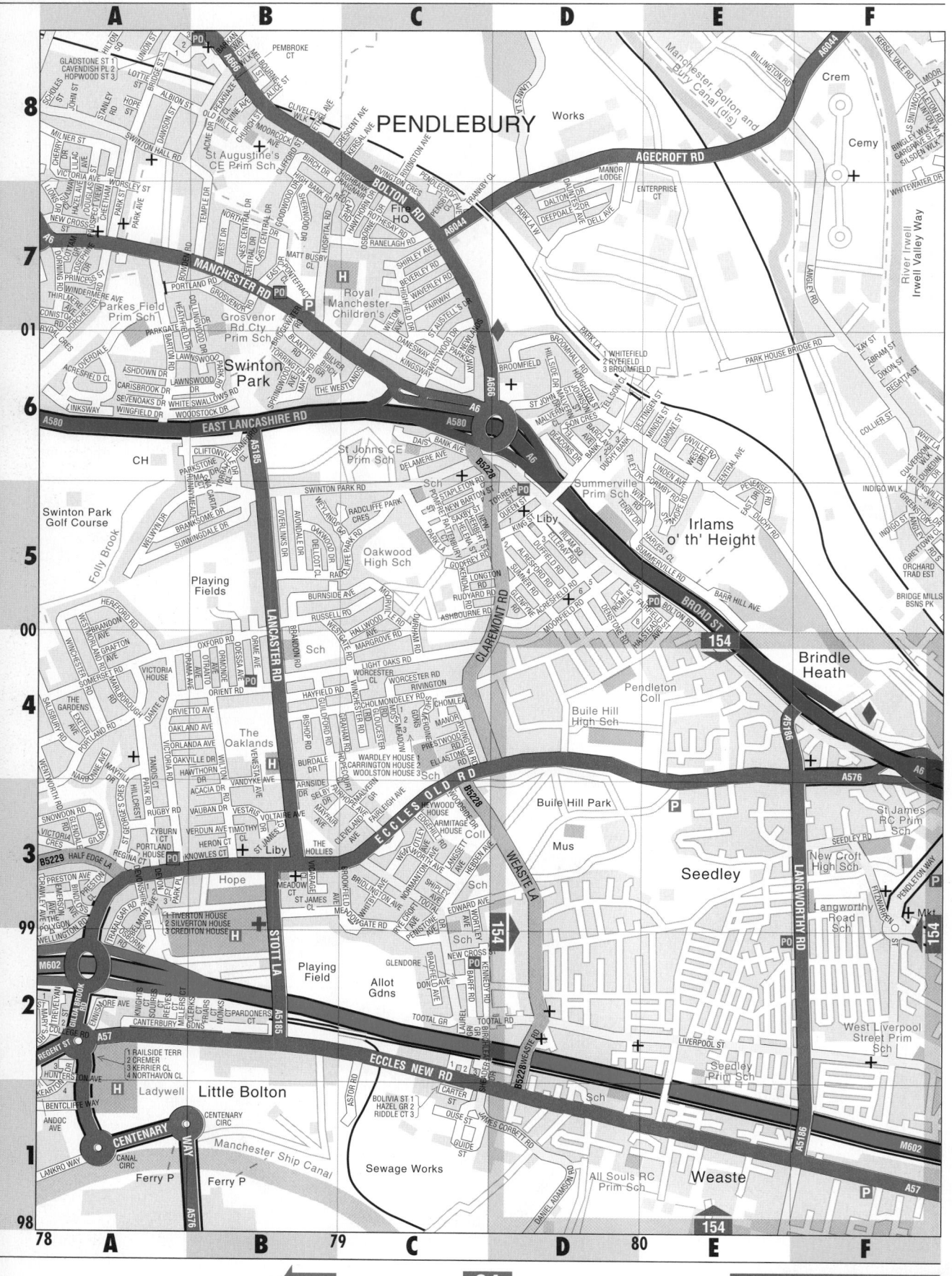

D5
1 RANULPH CT
2 HUNTS RD
3 CROSBY RD
4 PENELOPE RD
5 CHURCHFIELD RD
6 WINSTANLEY CL
7 NORBURY AVE
8 PEACOCK AVE

PENDLEBURY

Crem

Cemy

AGECROFT RD

Manchester Bolton and Bury Canal (dis)

Manor Lodge

ENTERPRISE CT

River Irwell

Irwell Valley Way

Works

Fire City HQ

Royal Manchester Children's

Park House Bridge Rd

Parkes Field Prim Sch

Grosvenor Rd City Prim Sch

Swinton Park

St John's CE Prim Sch

Summerville Prim Sch

Irlams o' th' Height

Swinton Park Golf Course

Folly Brook

Playing Fields

Oakwood High Sch

Radcliffe Park Cres

Brindle Heath

The Gardens

The Oaklands

Buile Hill High Sch

Pendleton Coll

St James RC Prim Sch

ECCLES OLD RD

Heywood House

Armitage Coll

Buile Hill Park

Mus

Seedley

New Croft High Sch

Langworthy Road Sch

Mkt

Hope

1 TIVERTON HOUSE
2 SILVERTON HOUSE
3 CREDITON HOUSE

1 MEADOW CT
St James

Playing Field

Allot Gdns

Glendore

West Liverpool Street Prim Sch

1 RAILSIDE TERR
2 CREMER
3 KERRIER CL
4 NORTHAVON CL

ECCLES NEW RD

Ladywell

Little Bolton

BOLIVIA ST 1
HAZEL GR 2
RIDDLE CT 3

Seedley Prim Sch

CENTENARY WAY

Manchester Ship Canal

Sewage Works

All Souls RC Prim Sch

Weaste

Canal Circ

Ferry P

Ferry P

For full street detail of the highlighted area see page 154.

For full street detail of the highlighted area see pages 155 and 158.

63 82 81

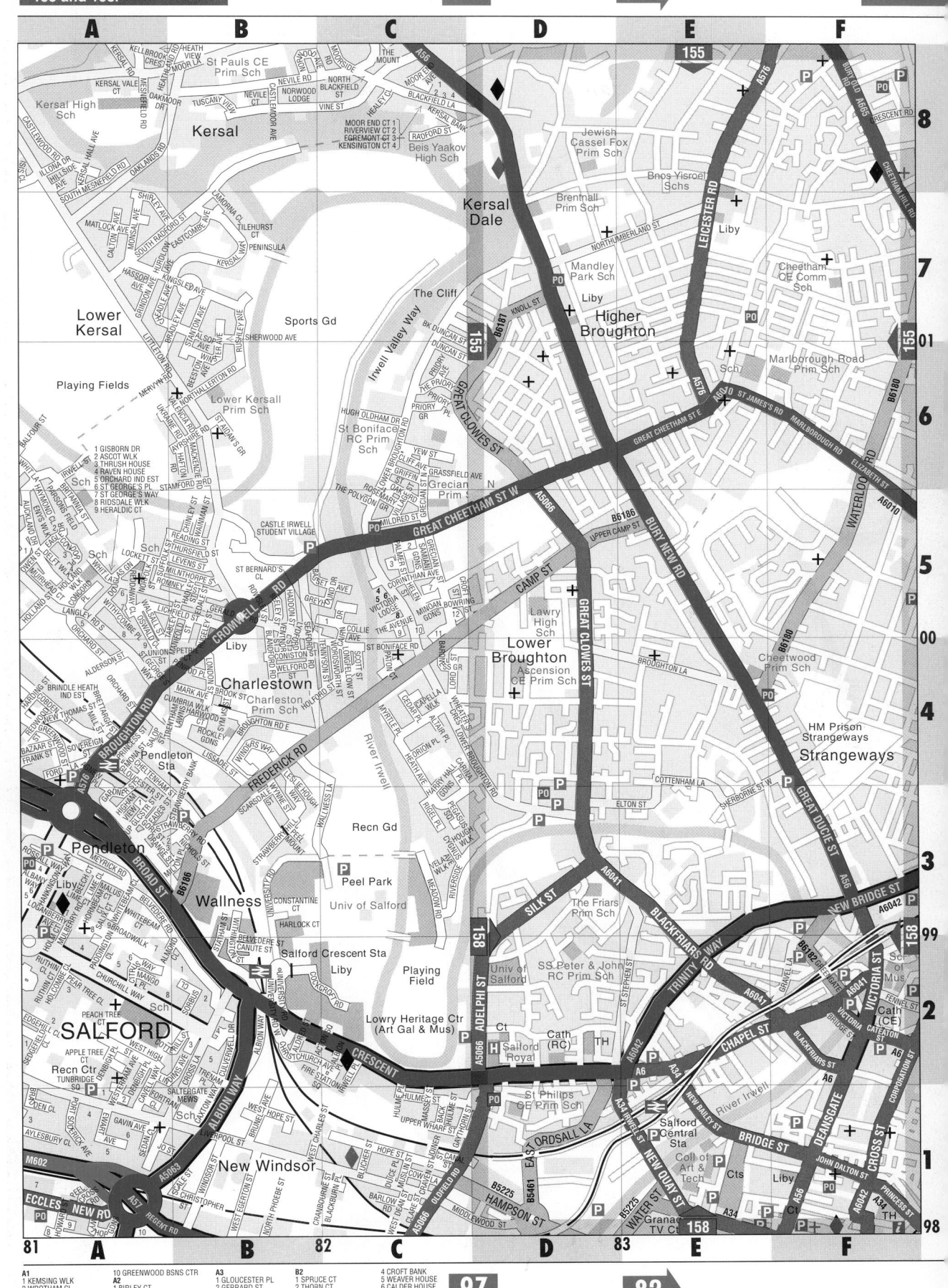

A1
1 KEMSING WLK
2 WROTHAM CL
3 SUMMERTON HOUSE
4 PETERHEAD WLK
5 GRAYTHORPE WLK
6 EDDYSTONE CL
7 REDMIRES CT
8 CHAMBERS FIELD CT
9 HAWKSHAW CT
10 GREENWOOD BSNS CTR

A2
1 BIRLEY CT
2 PLUM TREE CT
3 PEAR TREE CT
4 PLANE CT
5 LILAC CT
6 ROWAN CL
7 MAGNOLIA CT
8 CHERRY TREE CT

A3
1 GLOUCESTER PL
2 GERRARD ST
3 MANDARIN WLK
4 MATHER WAY
5 RAVEN WAY
6 BRIAR HILL WAY
7 MULBERRY CT
8 SYCAMORE CT
9 LOMBARDY CT

B2
1 SPRUCE CT
2 THORN CT
3 CHEVRON CL
4 MELKSHAM CL
5 ALBION TOWERS

C5
1 ST BERNARD'S AVE
2 IONIAN GDNS
3 AEGEAN CL

4 CROFT BANK
5 WEAVER HOUSE
6 CALDER HOUSE
7 TROJAN GDNS
8 BALLIN HOUSE
9 CROMWELL GR
10 ALBION PL
11 NEPTUNE GDNS
12 ATHENIAN GDNS

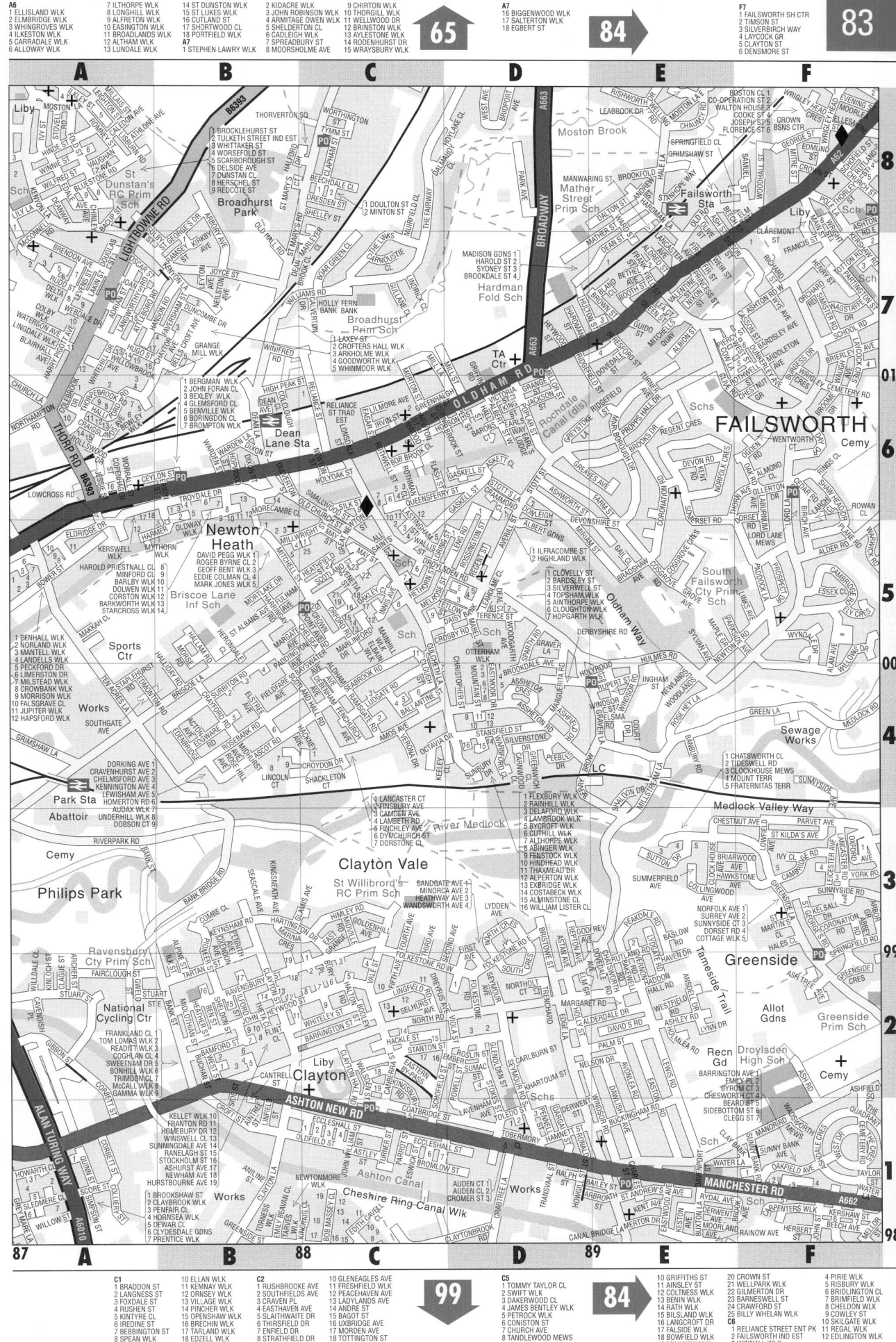

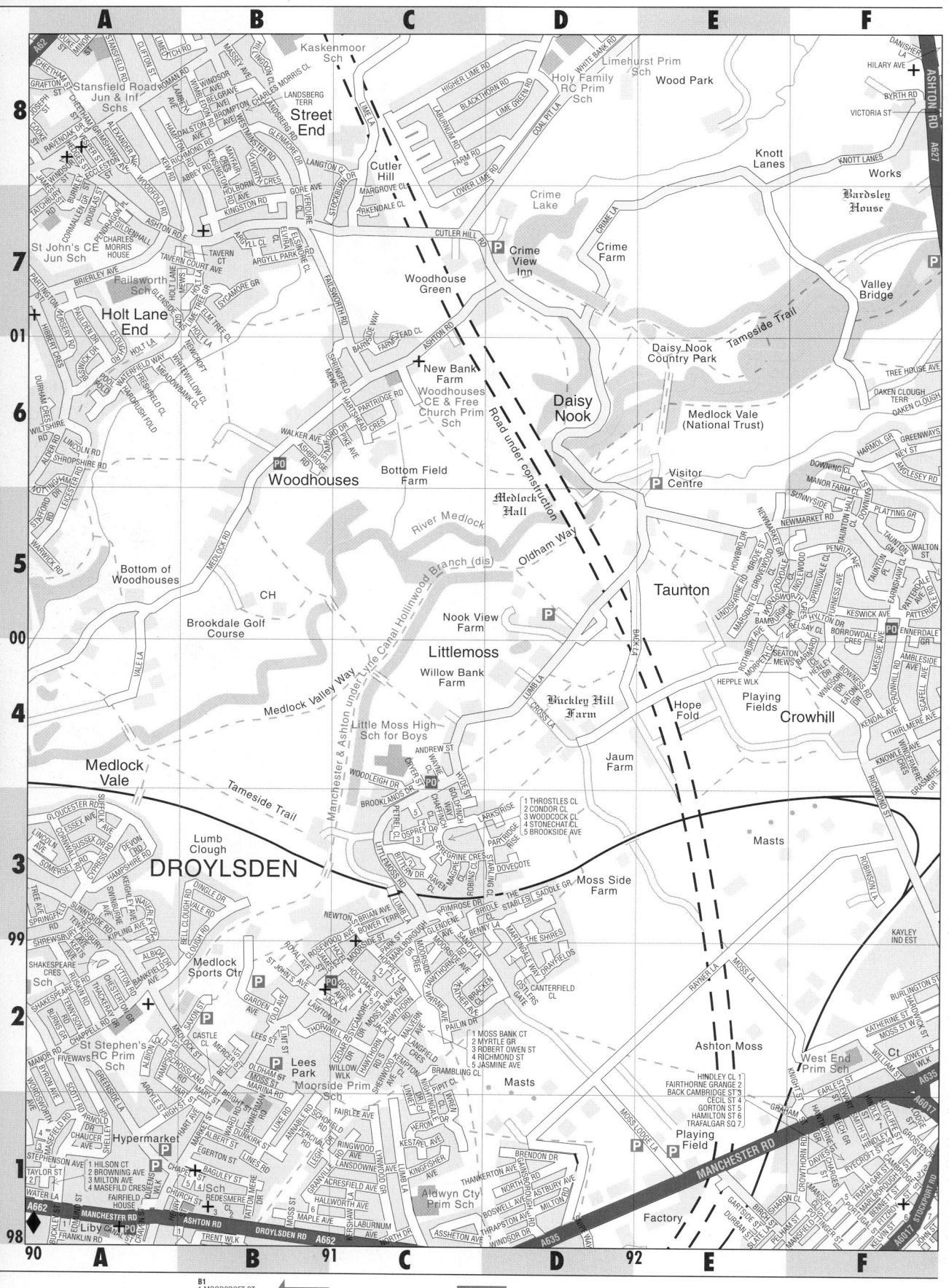

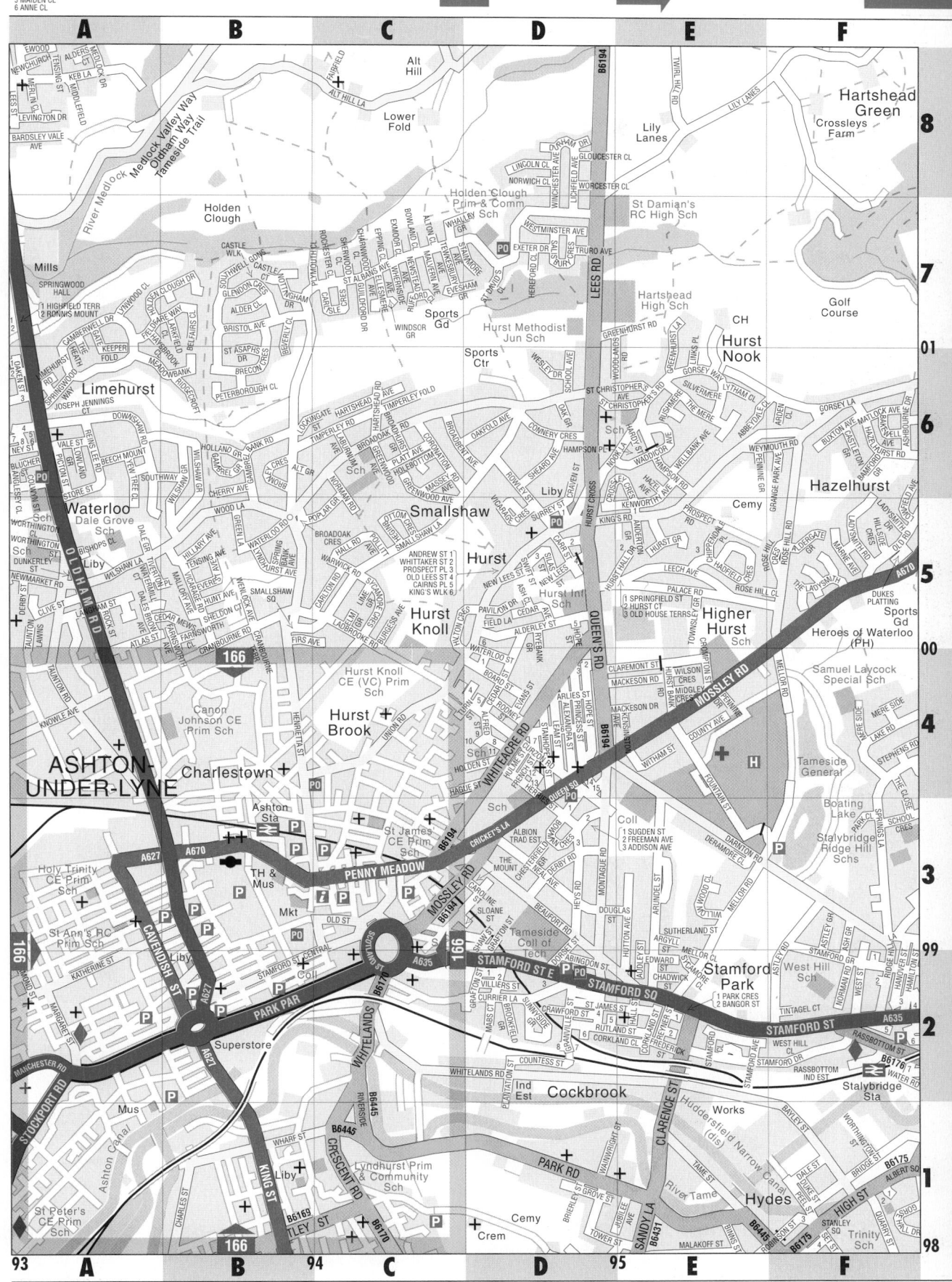

A6
1 OAKEN CLOUGH DR
2 TREE HOUSE AVE
3 OAKEN CLOUGH
4 WELLINGTON CLOUGH
5 MAIDEN CL
6 ANNE CL
7 GREENWAYS
8 LIMEHURST AVE

67

86

85

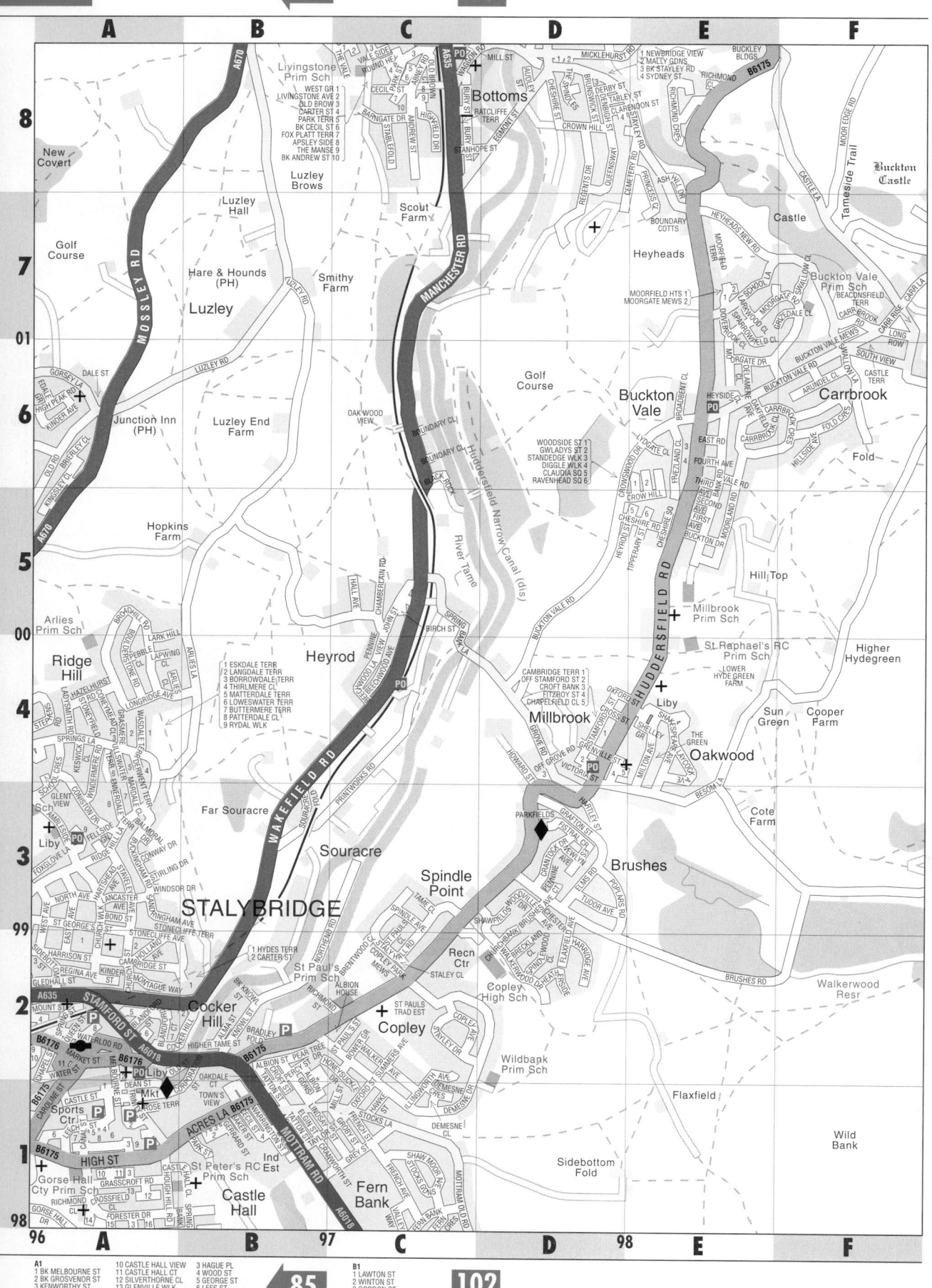

A   B   C   D   E   F

8

7

01

6

5

00

4

3

99

2

1

98

New Covert

Golf Course

Gorsey La
High Peak Ave
Kinder Ave
EDALE CL
OLD BRIERLEY CL

Junction Inn (PH)

MOSSLEY RD
A670

Hopkins Farm

Ridge Hill

Arlies Prim Sch

Liby
PO
CAMBRIDGE LA
FOXGLOVE LA

SCHOOL LA
GLENT VIEW

STEPS LA
LADYSMITH RD
HAZELHURST
COTEHILL RD

Far Souracre

Sch

Liby
PO

Sports Ctr

B6176

B6175

Mkt
ROSE TERR
DEAN ST
MELBOURNE ST
CAROLINE ST
CASTLE ST
CANAL ST
WATER ST

HIGH ST

Gorse Hall Cty Prim Sch

GORSE DR
RICHMOND
CROSSFIELD CL
FORESTER DR
HOUGH HILL RD
SPRING BANK

Luzley Hall

Hare & Hounds (PH)

Luzley

Luzley Brows

Smithy Farm

Luzley End Farm

LUZLEY RD

AUZLEY RD

Heyrod

1 ESKDALE TERR
2 LANGDALE TERR
3 BORROWDALE TERR
4 THIRLMERE CL
5 MATTERDALE TERR
6 LOWESWATER TERR
7 BUTTERMERE TERR
8 PATTERDALE CL
9 RYDAL WLK

WAKEFIELD RD

Souracre

STALYBRIDGE

Cocker Hill

STAMFORD ST
A6018

WATERLOO RD

MARKET ST

ACRES LA

MOTTRAM RD
A6018

St Peter's RC Prim Est

Castle Hall

Fern Bank

Livingstone Prim Sch

THE VALE
VALE SIDE
ROUND HEY
WEST GR 1
LIVINGSTONE AVE 2
OLD BROW 3
CARTER ST 4
PARK TERR 5
BK CECIL ST 6
FOX PLATT TERR 7
APSLEY SIDE 8
THE MANSE 9
BK ANDREW ST 10

CECIL ST
BARNGATE DR
STABLEFOLD
ANDREW ST
HIGHFIELD DR
MANCHESTER RD
A635

Scout Farm

MANCHESTER RD

BURY ST

River Tame
SPRING BANK LA
BLACK ROCK
BOUNDARY CL

Golf Course

Huddersfield Narrow Canal (dis)

BUCKTON VALE RD

HALL AVE
PENNINE VIEW
JOHN ST
CHAMBERLAIN RD
BIRCH ST
PO
BREEZE HILL RD

PRINTWORKS RD

Spindle Point

SPINDLE AVE
TAME CL
ST PAULS AVE
STALEY PARK MEWS
BRENTWOOD CL

1 HYDES TERR
2 CARTER ST

St Paul's Prim Sch

RICHMOND
ALBION HOUSE

Copley

ALBION ST
PEAR TREE DR
PERCY ST
ELBOW ST
ST PAUL'S ST

BK KNOWL
HIGHER TAME ST
BRADLEY FOLD
KNOWL ST

P

St Pauls Trad Est

COPLEY AVE
STALEY DR

Copley High Sch

Wildbank Prim Sch

Sidebottom Fold

1 NEWBRIDGE VIEW
2 MALTY GDNS
3 BK STALEY RD
4 SYDNEY ST

MICKLEHURST RD
Richmond
B6175

MILL ST

Bottoms

RATCLIFFE TERR
EGMONT ST
STANHOPE ST
CROWN HILL

Heyheads

MOORFIELD HTS 1
MOORGATE MEWS 2

Buckton Vale

WOODSIDE ST 1
GWLADYS ST 2
STANDEDGE WLK 3
DIGGLE WLK 4
CLAUDIA SQ 5
RAVENHEAD SQ 6

CROW HILL

Millbrook

CAMBRIDGE TERR 1
OFF STAMFORD ST 2
CROFT BANK 3
FITZROY ST 4
CHAPELFIELD CL 5

HUDDERSFIELD RD

Liby

OXFORD ST
CROSS ST
SHELLEY GR
SHAKESPEARE AVE
MILTON AVE

PO
VICTORIA ST

Oakwood

THE GREEN
Sun Green
Cooper Farm

Cote Farm

Brushes

PARKFIELDS

Recn Ctr

Walkerwood Resr

BRUSHES RD

Flaxfield

Wild Bank

Buckton Castle

Castle

Buckton Vale Prim Sch
BEACONSFIELD TERR
CARRBROOK
CAER LA
SOUTH VIEW
LONG ROW

CASTLE LA
MOOR EDGE RD

Tameside Trail

B6175
B6175
Richmond

Heyheads New Rd
BOUNDARY COTTS
ASH HILL RD
PRINCESS CL

Carrbrook

CARRBROOK CRES
ARUNDEL CL
Fold

Hill Top

Higher Hydegreen

LOWER HYDE GREEN FARM

St Raphael's RC Prim Sch

Millbrook Prim Sch

A1
1 BK MELBOURNE ST
2 BK GROSVENOR ST
3 KENWORTHY ST
4 BENNETT ST
5 BOROUGH ST
6 GROSVENOR ST
7 RICHMOND HOUSE
8 GROSVENOR HOUSE
9 GROSVENOR GDNS

10 CASTLE HALL VIEW
11 CASTLE HALL CT
12 SILVERTHORNE ST
13 GLENVILLE WLK
14 KENSINGTON GR
15 VAUDREY ST
16 KAY ST

A2
1 ELIZABETH AVE
2 GORDON TERR

3 HAGUE PL
4 WOOD ST
5 GEORGE ST
6 LEES ST
7 BLANDFORD HOUSE
8 KING ST
9 CROSSLEY ST
10 HARROP ST
11 SHEPLEY ST
12 DEARDEN ST

B1
1 LAWTON ST
2 WINTON ST
3 GORDON ST
4 HASSALL ST
5 COMPTON ST
6 CHEETHAM GDNS

Buckton Moor

Hare
Hill

Far Harehill Clough

Hoarstone
Edge

CARBROOK IND EST

Iron Tongue

Shire Clough
Farm

Slatepit
Moor

Irontongue
Hill

Turf
Pits

Swineshaw
Moor

Tameside Trail

Higher Swineshaw
Resr

Boar
Flat

Harridge
Pike

Harridge

Ogden Clough

Brushes

Lower Swineshaw
Resr

Lees
Hill

Ogden Brook

Brushes
Resr

Swineshaw Brook

Cock
Wood

Cock
Knarr

Middle
Bank

Arnfield
Low Moor

Pack
Saddle

Devil's
Bridge

Lower
Bank

Hollingworthhall
Moor

Arnfield
Farm

Arnfield Brook

87
70

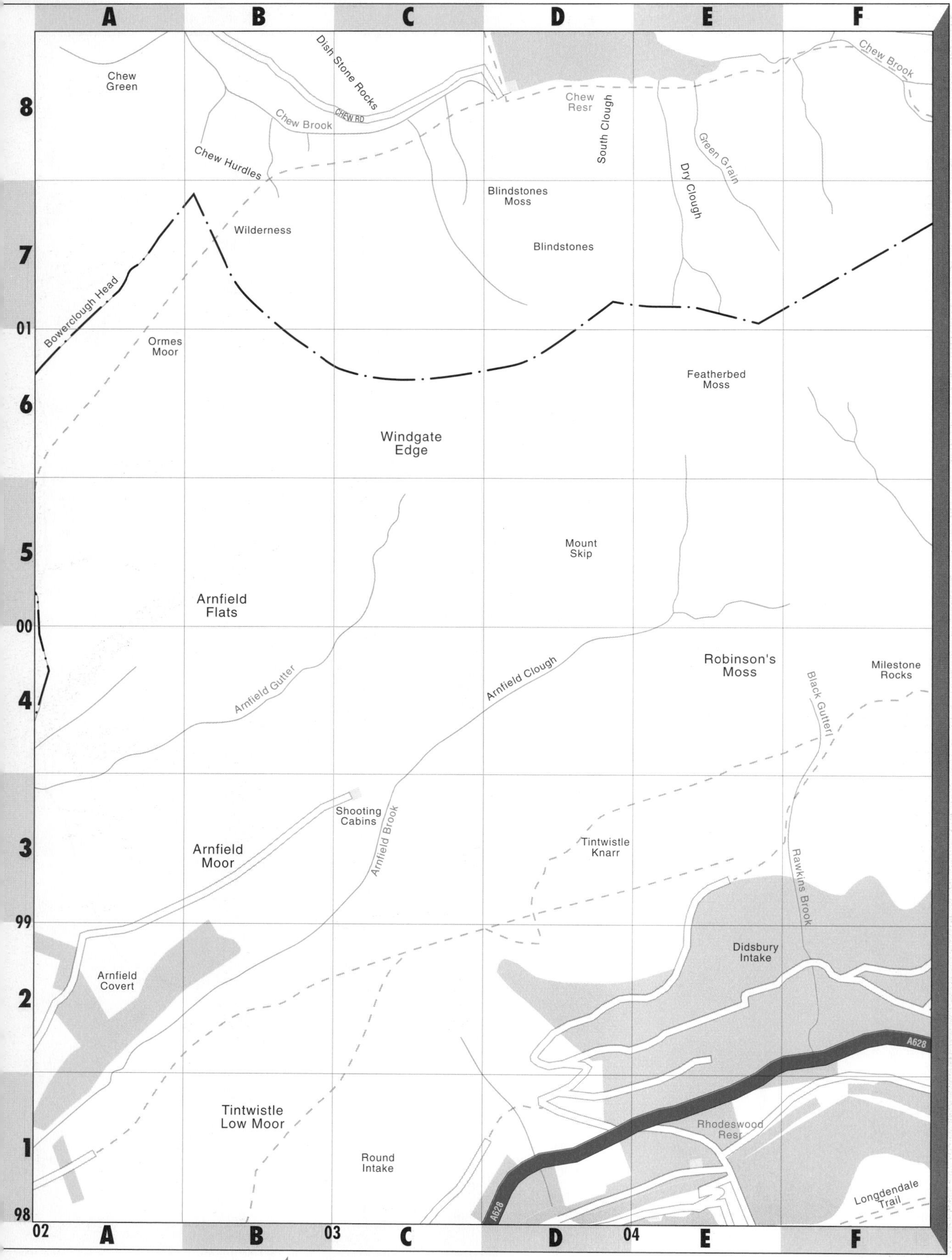

A   B   C   D   E   F

Chew
Green

Dish Stone Rocks

Chew Brook

CHEW RD

Chew
Resr

Chew Brook

8

Chew Hurdles

South Clough

Green Grain

Wilderness

Dry Clough

Blindstones
Moss

Blindstones

7

Bowerclough Head

Ormes
Moor

01

Featherbed
Moss

Windgate
Edge

6

Mount
Skip

5

Arnfield
Flats

Robinson's
Moss

Milestone
Rocks

00

Arnfield Gutter

Arnfield Clough

Black Gutter

4

Shooting
Cabins

Arnfield Brook

Tintwistle
Knarr

Rawkins Brook

Arnfield
Moor

3

Didsbury
Intake

99

Arnfield
Covert

2

A628

Tintwistle
Low Moor

Rhodeswood
Resr

1

Round
Intake

Longdendale
Trail

A628

98

02   A   B   03   C   D   04   E   F

87
104

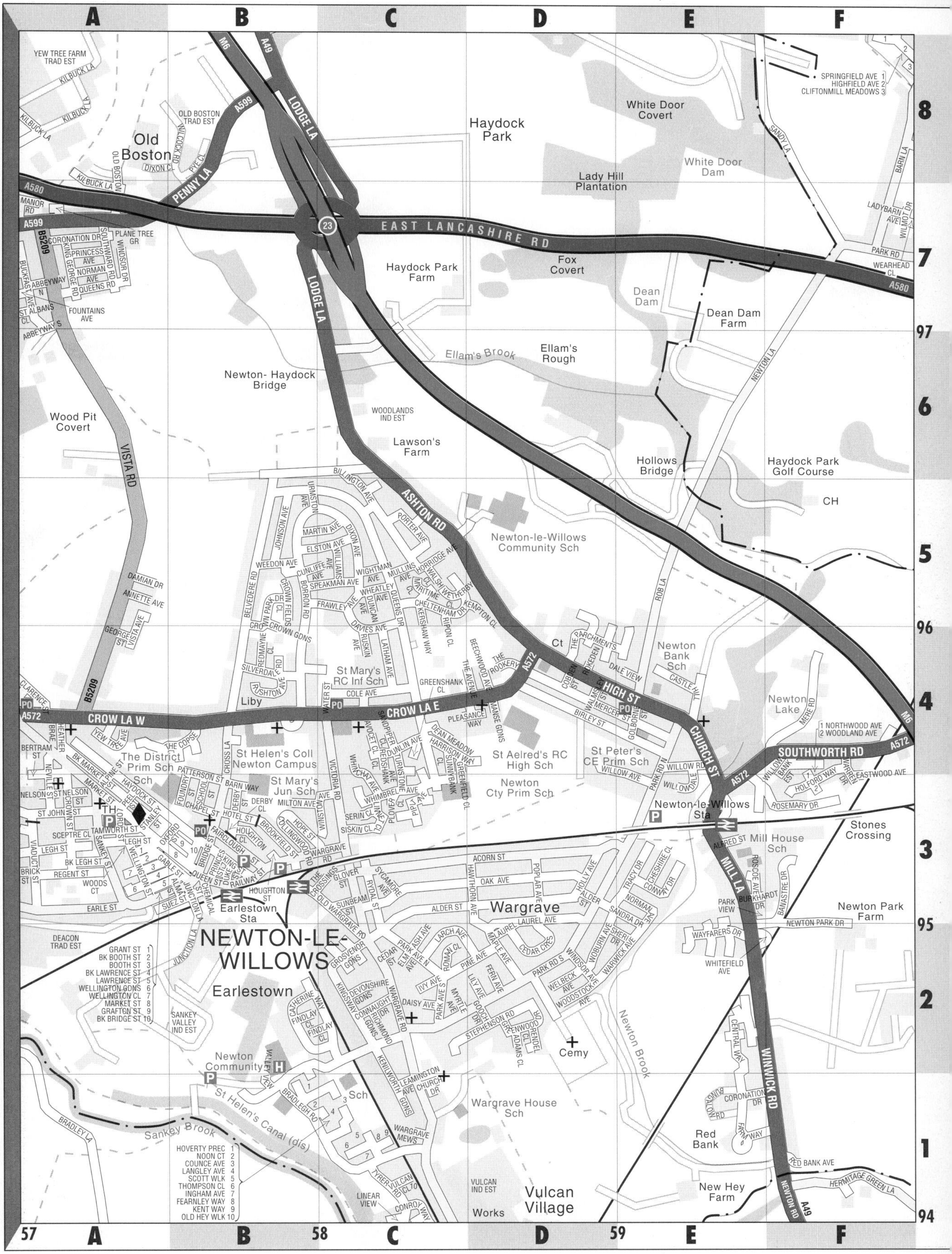

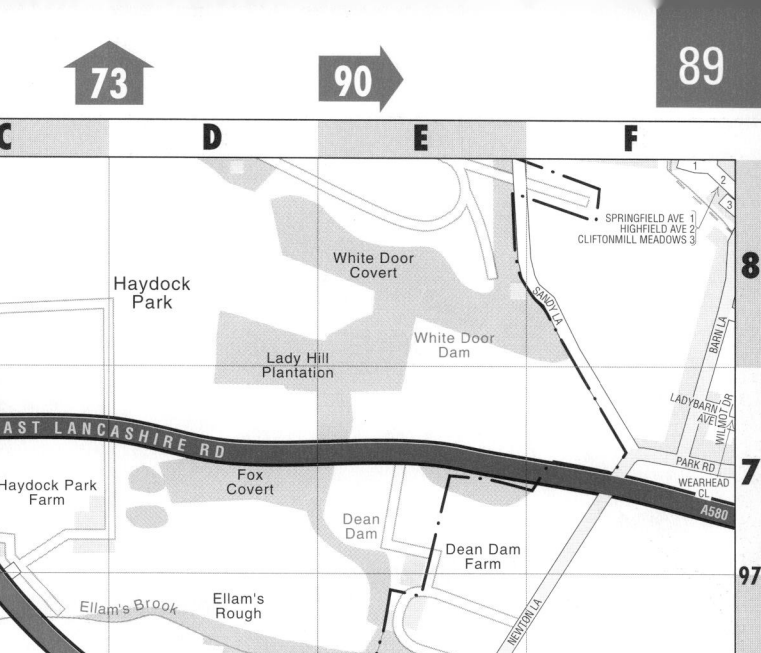

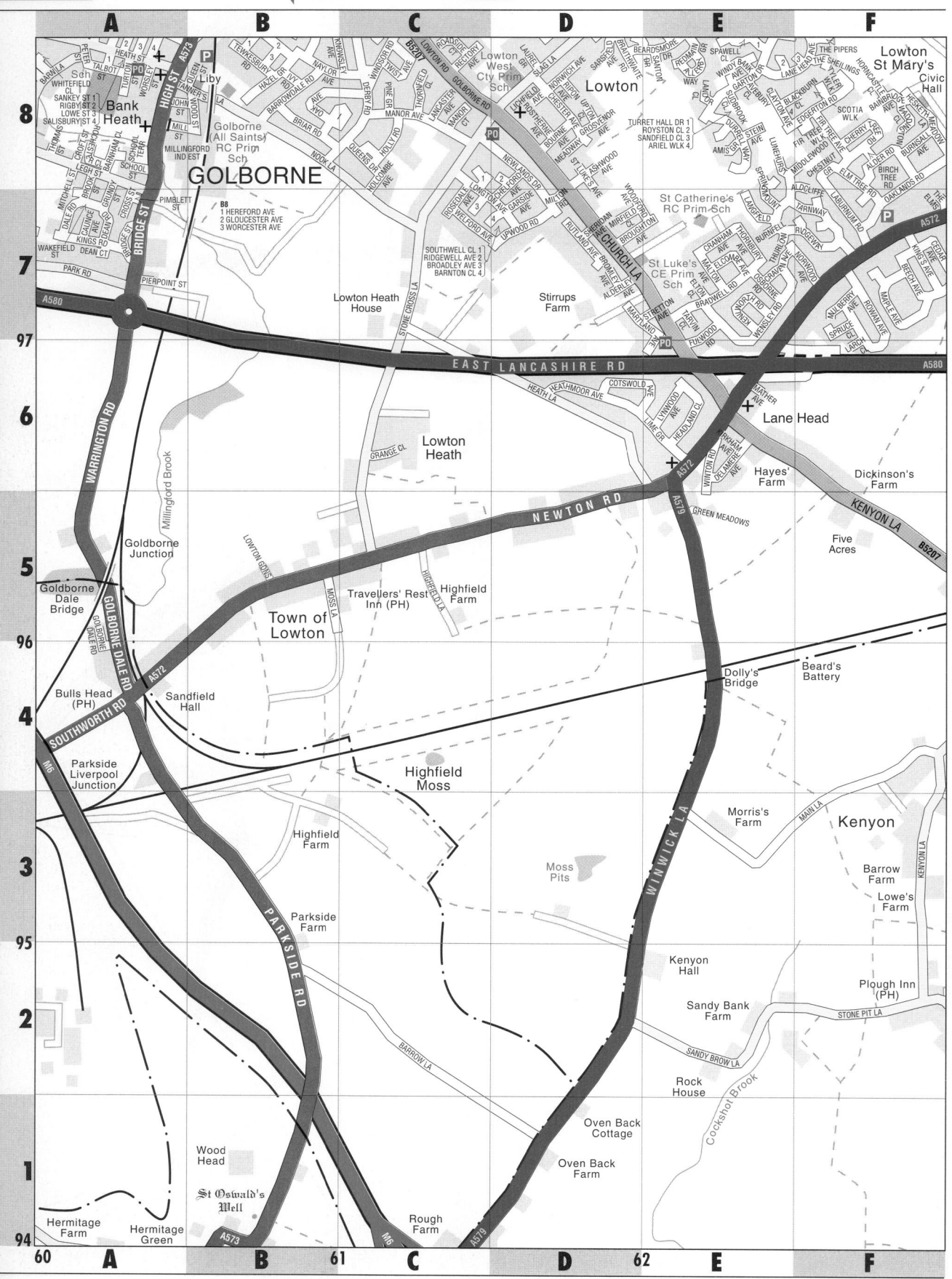

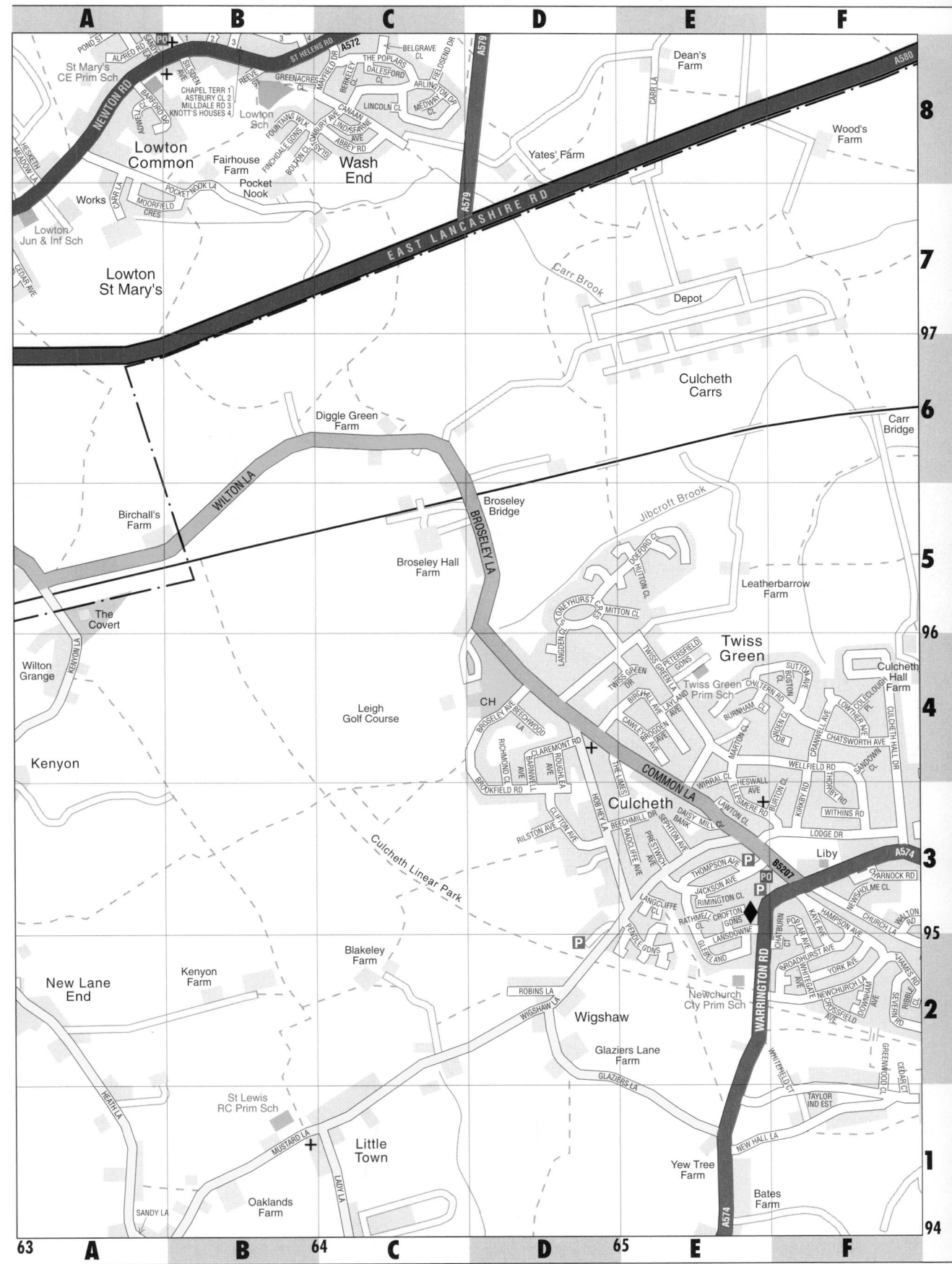

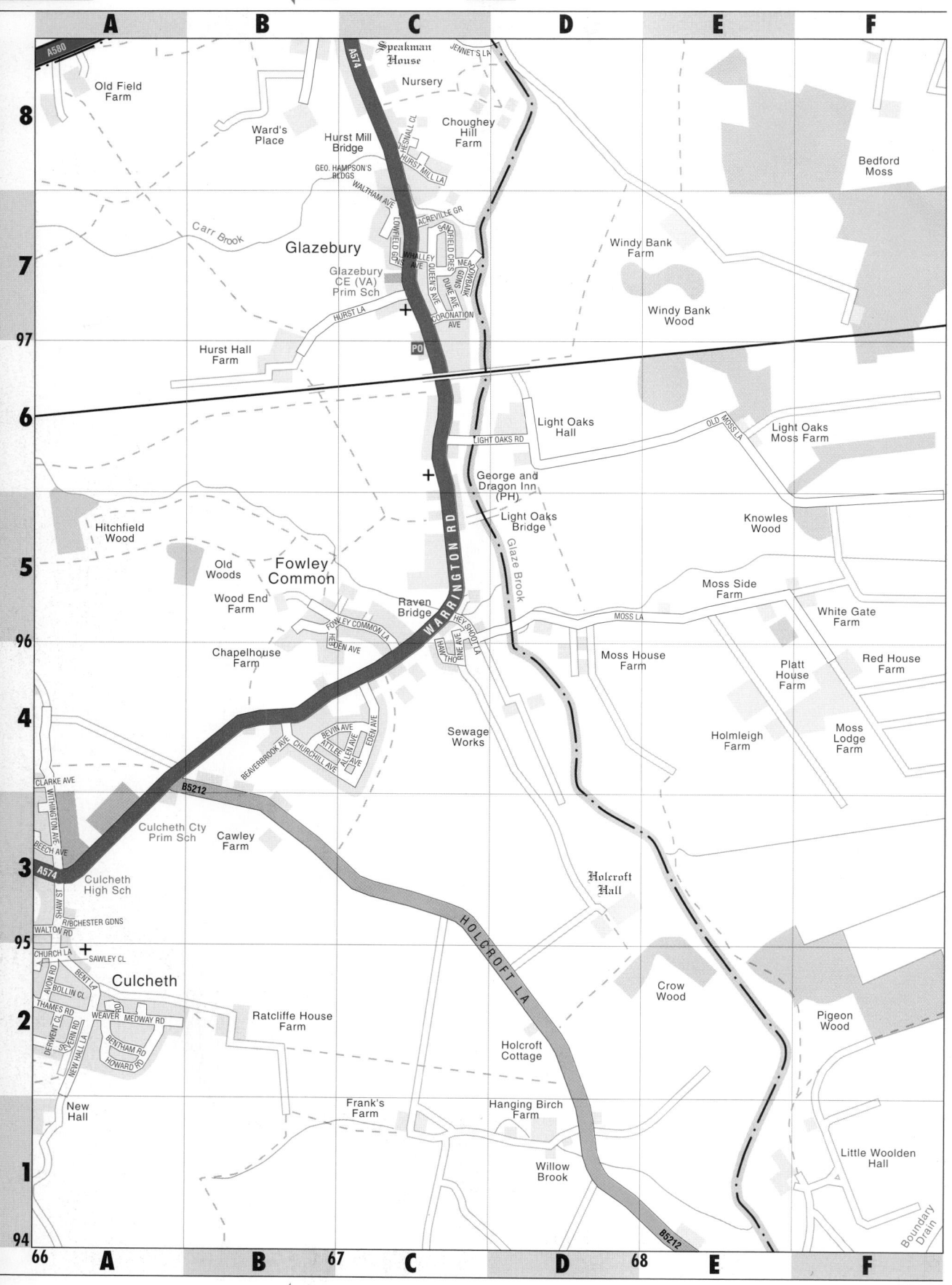

A B C D E F

8
7
97
6
5
96
4
3
95
2
1
94

69 70 71

Moss Bank
Shooter's Grove
RINDLE RD
Astley Moss
LC
Four Winds Farm
Birch Farm
Chat Moss
Olive Mount Farm
Railway View Farm
Moss Farm
CUTNOOK
RASPBERRY LA
Mosslands Farm
TWELVE YARDS RD
Woodbarn Farm
New Farm
Oakfield
Birch View Farm
Irlam Moss
ASTLEY RD
M62
Ebenezer Farm
Larkhill House
Hope Cottage Farm
Hephzibah Farm
Little Woolden Moss
Woodstock Farm
SUNNINGDALE DR
CRANFORD DR
THE CLOSES
BALSHAW CT
PARRS CT
NEWLANDS AVE
BROOKLANDS CL
Ringing Pits Farm
Plant Cottage Farm
Springfield
BALSHAW
QUEENSWAY
OLIVER AVE
Boundary Drain
Little Haven
SPRINGFIELD LA
STUART AVE
LYNDON RD
LEE CL
CALDER AVE
Birch Court
MOSS RD
ELSINORE AVE
Birch Tree Farm
Worsley View Farm
VICTORIA RD
GREENSIDE DR
GREENSIDE DR
LEADER WILLIAMS RD
HOWARTH DR
FRANCIS RD
PALATINE
Great Molden Moss
Prospect Grange
ROSCOE RD
ROSE AVE
ROSE CRES
BAINES AVE
M62
WALKER RD
B5320

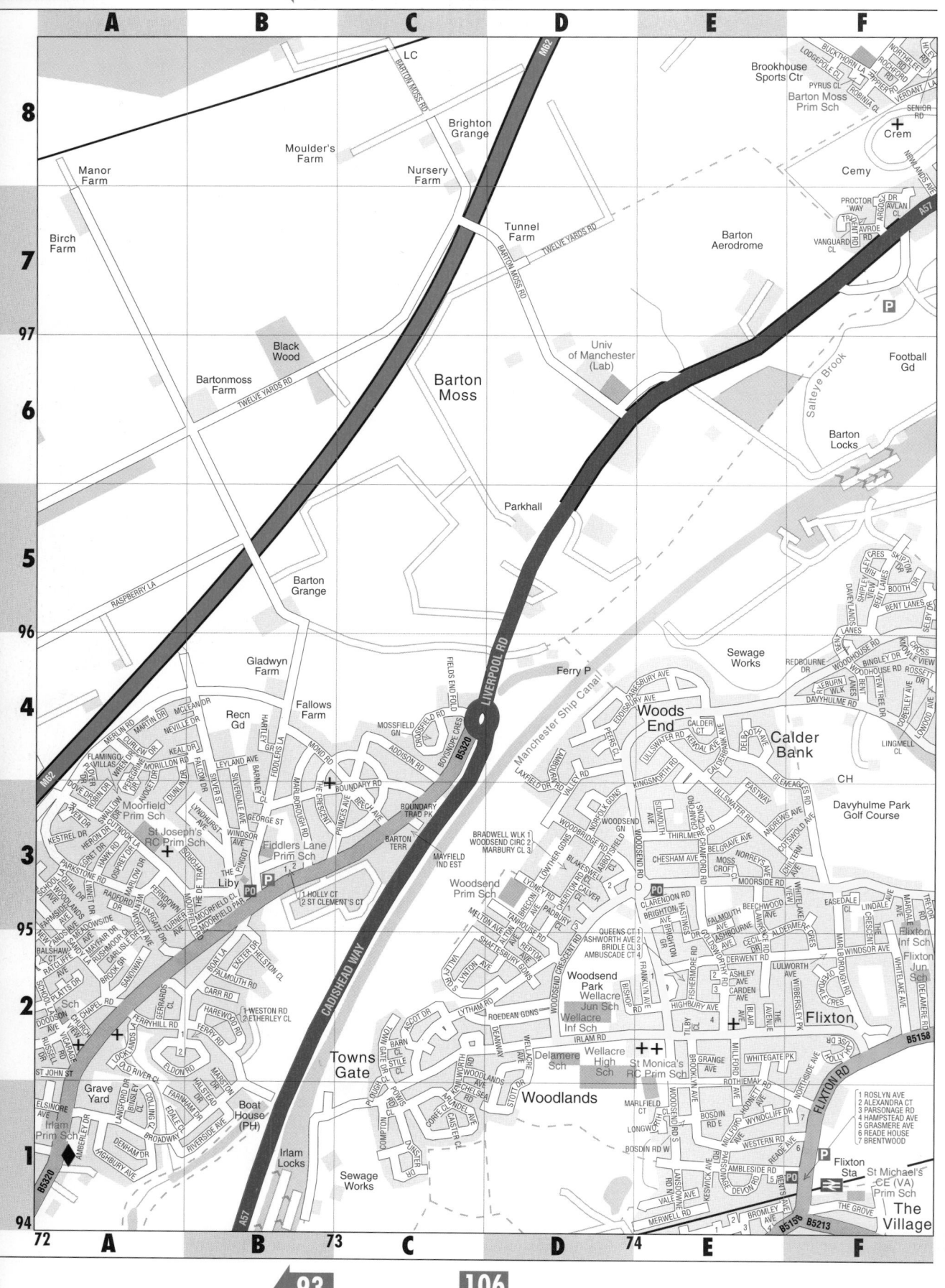

A B C D E F

8
7
97
6
5
96
4
3
95
2
1
94

Manor Farm

Birch Farm

LC

Moulder's Farm

Brighton Grange

Nursery Farm

Tunnel Farm

Twelve Yards Rd

Barton Aerodrome

Brookhouse Sports Ctr

Barton Moss Prim Sch

Crem

Cemy

PYRUS CL

PROCTOR WAY

VANGUARD CL

Black Wood

Bartonmoss Farm

Twelve Yards Rd

Barton Moss

Univ of Manchester (Lab)

Football Gd

Salteye Brook

Barton Locks

Raspberry La

Barton Grange

Parkhall

Sewage Works

Gladwyn Farm

Fallows Farm

Recn Gd

Mossfield Gn

Ferry P

Manchester Ship Canal

Woods End

Calder Bank

Davyhulme Park Golf Course

Moorfield Prim Sch

St Joseph's RC Prim Sch

Fiddlers Lane Prim Sch

Liby

Barton Terr

Boundary Trad Pk

Mayfield Ind Est

Woodsend Prim Sch

1 HOLLY CT
2 ST CLEMENT'S CT

BRADWELL WLK 1
WOODSEND CIRC 2
MARBURY CL 3

Flixton Inf Sch

Flixton Jun Sch

QUEENS CT 1
ASHWORTH AVE 2
BRIDLE CL 3
AMBUSCADE CT 4

1 WESTON RD
2 ETHERLEY CL

Woodsend Park Wellacre Jun Sch

Wellacre Inf Sch

Delamere Sch

Wellacre High Sch

St Monica's RC Prim Sch

Flixton

Towns Gate

Woodlands

1 ROSLYN AVE
2 ALEXANDRA CT
3 PARSONAGE RD
4 HAMPSTEAD AVE
5 GRASMERE AVE
6 READE HOUSE
7 BRENTWOOD

Grave Yard

Irlam Prim Sch

Boat House (PH)

Irlam Locks

Sewage Works

Flixton Sta

St Michael's CE (VA) Prim Sch

The Village

CADISHEAD WAY

LIVERPOOL RD

B5320

A57

B5158

B5213

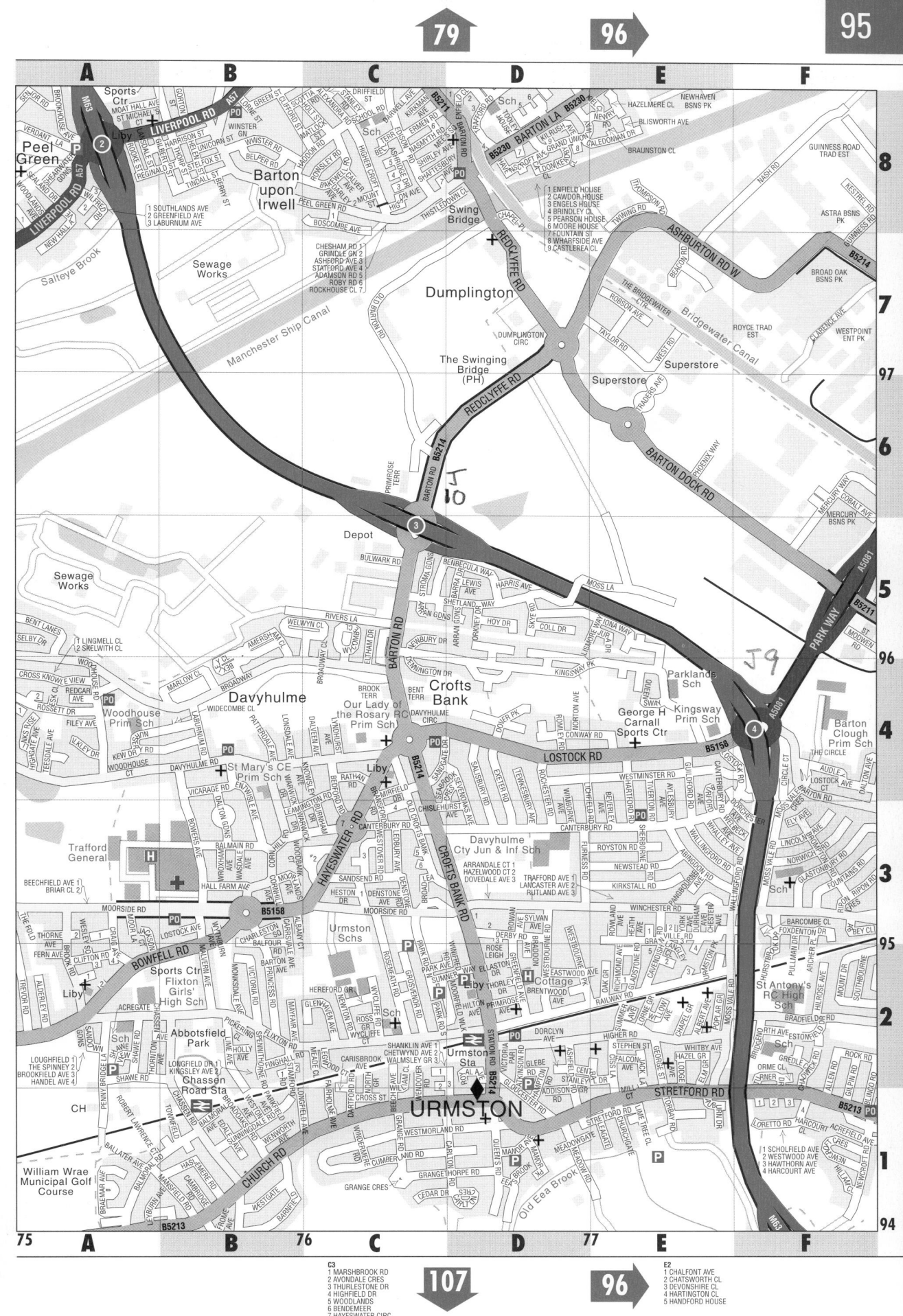

75 76 77 94

C3
1 MARSHBROOK RD
2 AVONDALE CRES
3 THURLESTONE DR
4 HIGHFIELD DR
5 WOODLANDS
6 BENDEMEER
7 HAYESWATER CIRC

107 96

E2
1 CHALFONT AVE
2 CHATSWORTH CL
3 DEVONSHIRE CL
4 HARTINGTON CL
5 HANDFORD HOUSE

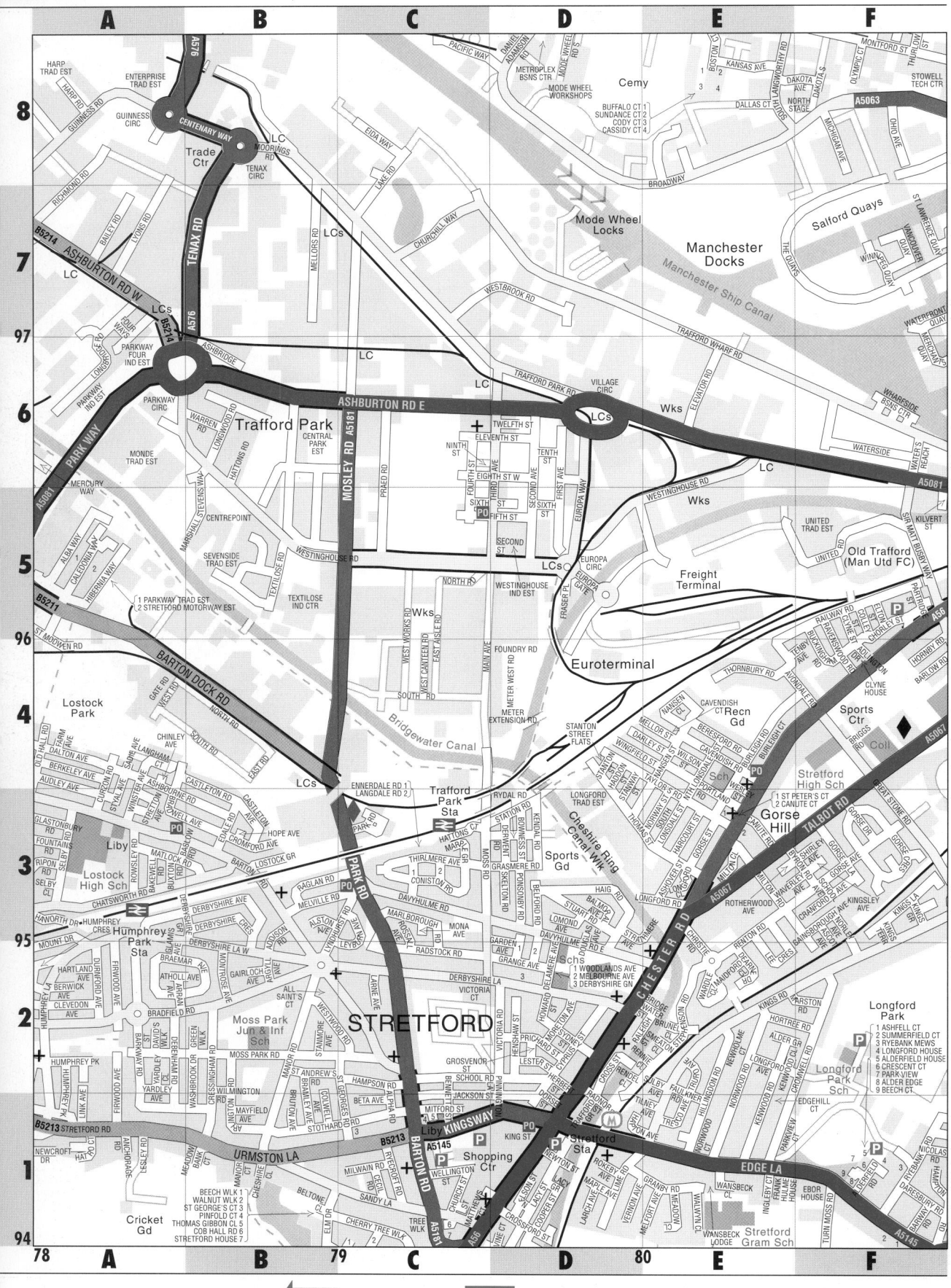

For full street detail of the highlighted area see pages 161 and 162.

97

A1
1 SUTTON MANOR
2 MAIDSTONE MEWS
3 SIBSON CT
4 SHANKLIN HOUSE

B2
1 NORTHLEIGH HOUSE
2 TRAFFORD MANSIONS
3 QUEEN'S CT
4 STRATHMORE AVE
5 RAILWAY TERR

81

98

C3
1 OAKLEA
2 CHARLTON CT
3 FONTWELL CL
4 DRYDEN RD
D3
1 WHITETHORN AVE
2 LANSBURY HOUSE
3 YEOMANRY CT
4 CARLTON MANSIONS

5 ROYSTON CT
6 WILLIAM COATES CT
7 TURNPIKE CT
8 SAXON HOUSE
9 BURLIN CT
10 DUDLEY CT
11 SYCAMORE CL
12 HAZEL CT
13 MAY CT

E3
1 THORNCOMBE CL
2 WESTERING WLK
3 TRISCOMBE WLK
4 THRUXTON CL
5 PONDWOOD CL
6 MAPPERTON WLK
7 CATHERSTON CL
8 STANWORTH CL
9 GROSVENOR CT

10 ROY GRAINGER CT
E4
1 GLENHAM CT
2 MOSS GROVE CT
3 ALMA CT
4 STOCKTON ST
5 DARSHAM WLK
6 SHAREHAM WLK
7 FROWDE WLK

8 BASSEY WLK
9 SAM REID WLK
10 BLAND WLK
11 WOODHEAD CL
12 QUANTOCK CL
13 HINCHCLIFFE WLK
14 CROWCOMBE WLK
15 CANTON WLK
16 TIMWOOD WLK
17 ADSCOMBE WLK

E4
18 EXTON WLK
19 HALLAM WLK
20 GRIERSON WLK
21 JASPER WLK
22 PORTSTONE CL
23 WESTMAN WLK
24 FROSTLANDS RD

F3
1 KERRIDGE WLK
2 KENSIDE WLK
3 GOSLING CL
4 ESCOTT WLK
5 PENTON WLK
6 PEACHEY CL
7 EXMOUTH WLK
8 ELWICK CL
9 PICTON WLK

10 YECVIL WLK
11 GABRIEL WLK
12 RADLEY WLK
13 ALISON ST
F4
1 PEPPERHILL WLK
2 CRICCIETH WAY
3 SHARCOTT WLK
4 CROSSCLIFFE CL
5 BICKLEY WLK

6 CROSSHILL CL
7 OWEN WLK
8 STAYCOTT CL
9 CRANEFIELD WLK

98

97

82

For full street detail of the highlighted area see pages 163 and 164.

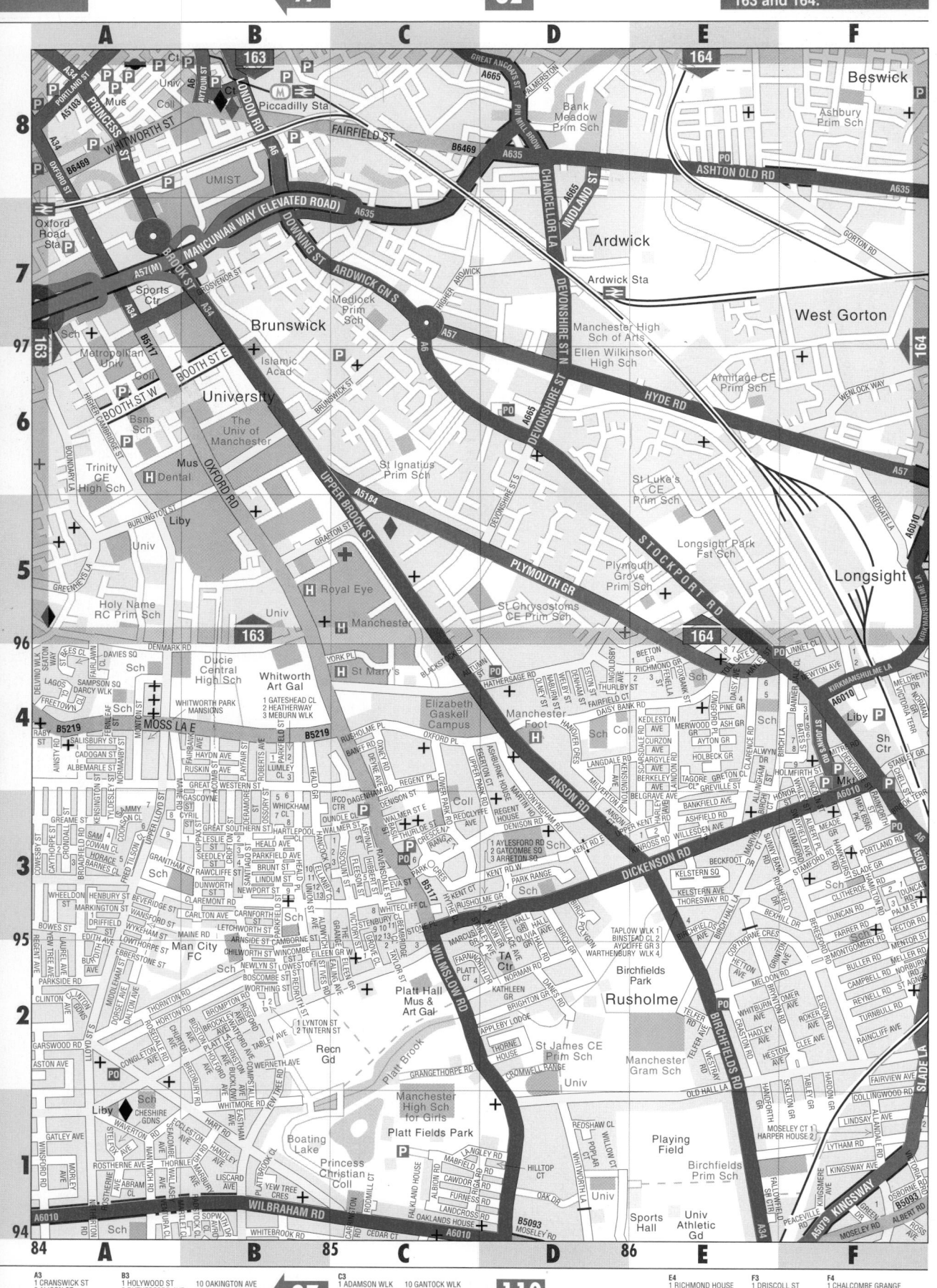

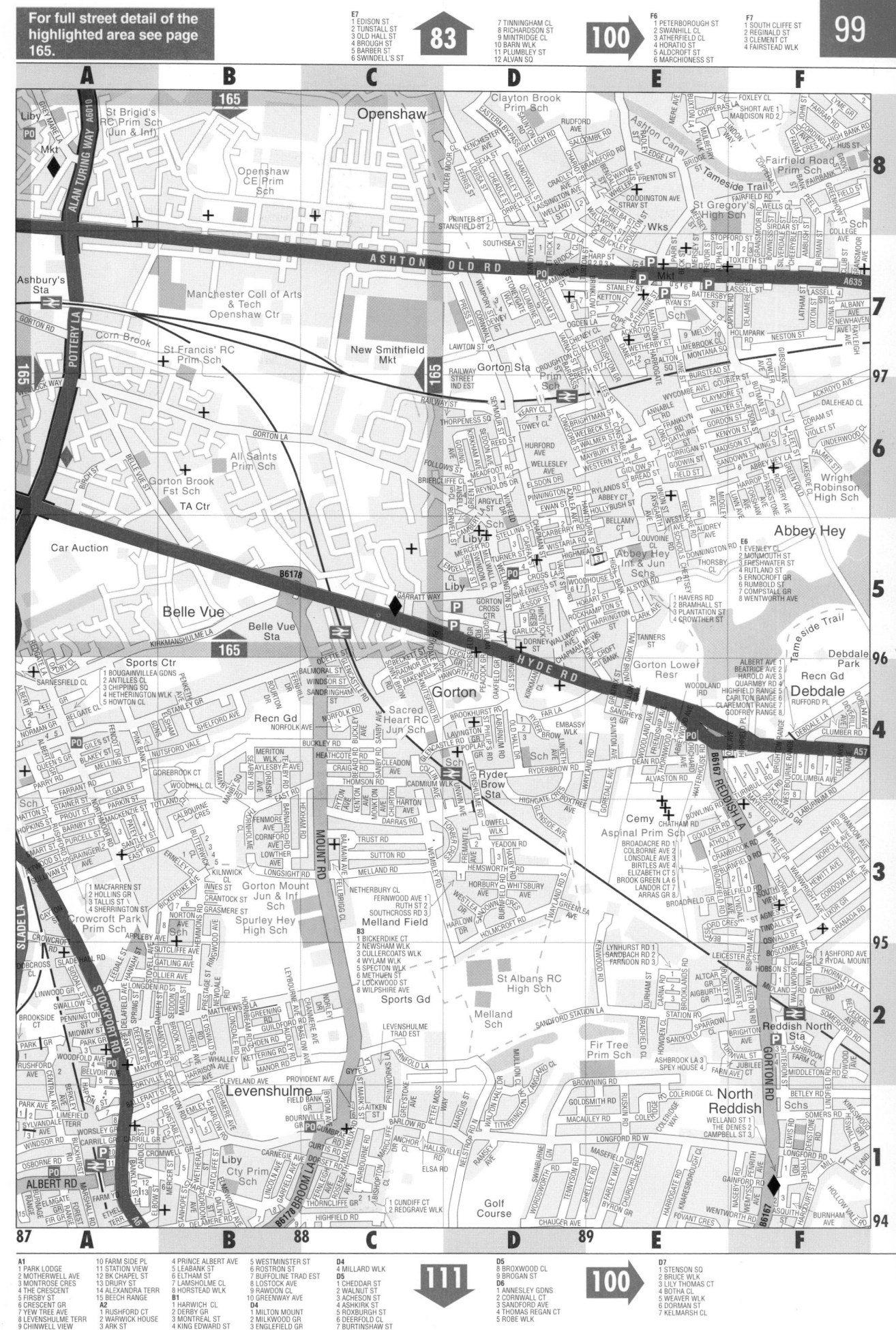

For full street detail of the highlighted area see page 165.

99

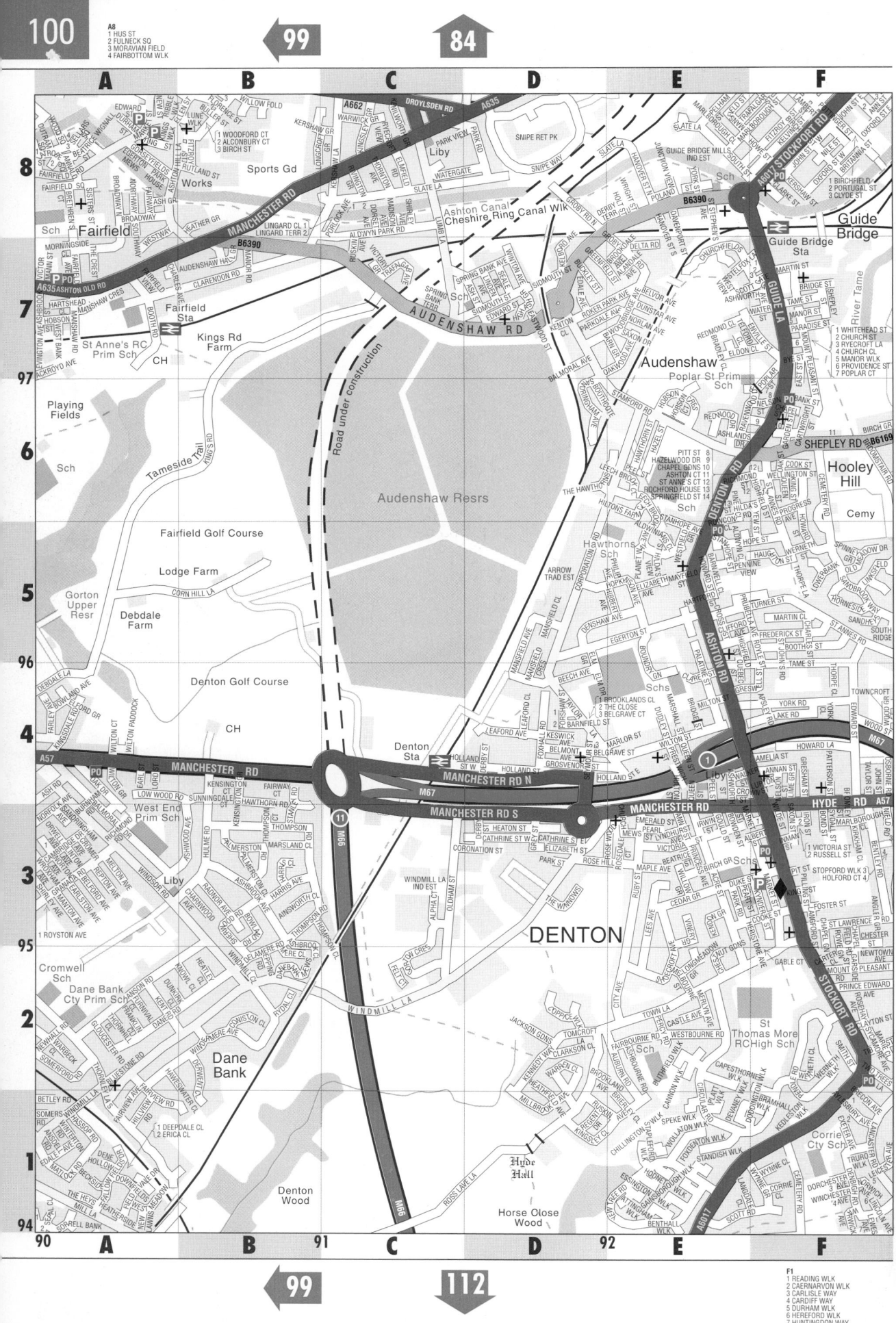

F1
1 READING WLK
2 CAERNARVON WLK
3 CARLISLE WAY
4 CARDIFF WAY
5 DURHAM WLK
6 HEREFORD WLK
7 HUNTINGDON WAY

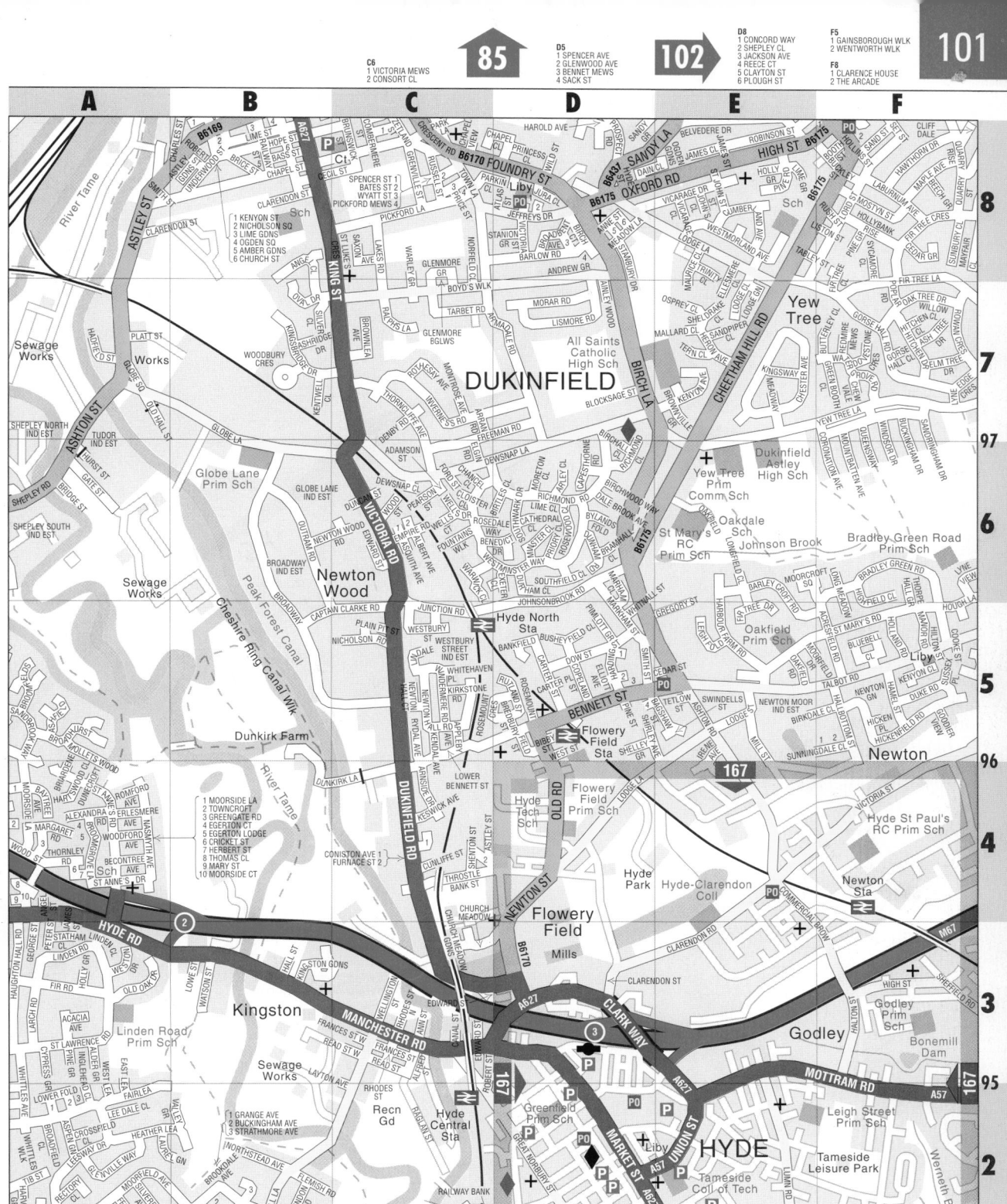

C6
1 VICTORIA MEWS
2 CONSORT CL

85

D5
1 SPENCER AVE
2 GLENWOOD AVE
3 BENNET MEWS
4 SACK ST

102

D8
1 CONCORD WAY
2 SHEPLEY CL
3 JACKSON AVE
4 REECE CT
5 CLAYTON ST
6 PLOUGH ST

F5
1 GAINSBOROUGH WLK
2 WENTWORTH WLK

F8
1 CLARENCE HOUSE
2 THE ARCADE

A1
1 NORTHAMPTON WAY
2 NEWCASTLE WAY
3 NOTTINGHAM WAY
4 OXFORD WLK
5 MAIDSTONE WLK
6 PEMBROKE WAY
7 SHREWSBURY WAY
8 BOSTON WLK
9 WELSHPOOL WAY
10 IPSWICH WAY
11 CHICHESTER WAY
12 STAFFORD WAY
13 TAUNTON WLK
14 CHELMSFORD WLK
15 GAWSWORTH WAY
16 THORSBY WAY
17 HADDON AVE
18 MORTON TERR
19 ADLINGTON WAY
20 PENSHURST WLK
21 HOLKER WAY
22 ARLEY WAY
23 HAREWOOD WLK

A2
1 WITHY TREE GR
2 WOOD HEY GR
3 GARDEN WLK

113

102

For full street detail of the highlighted area see page 167.

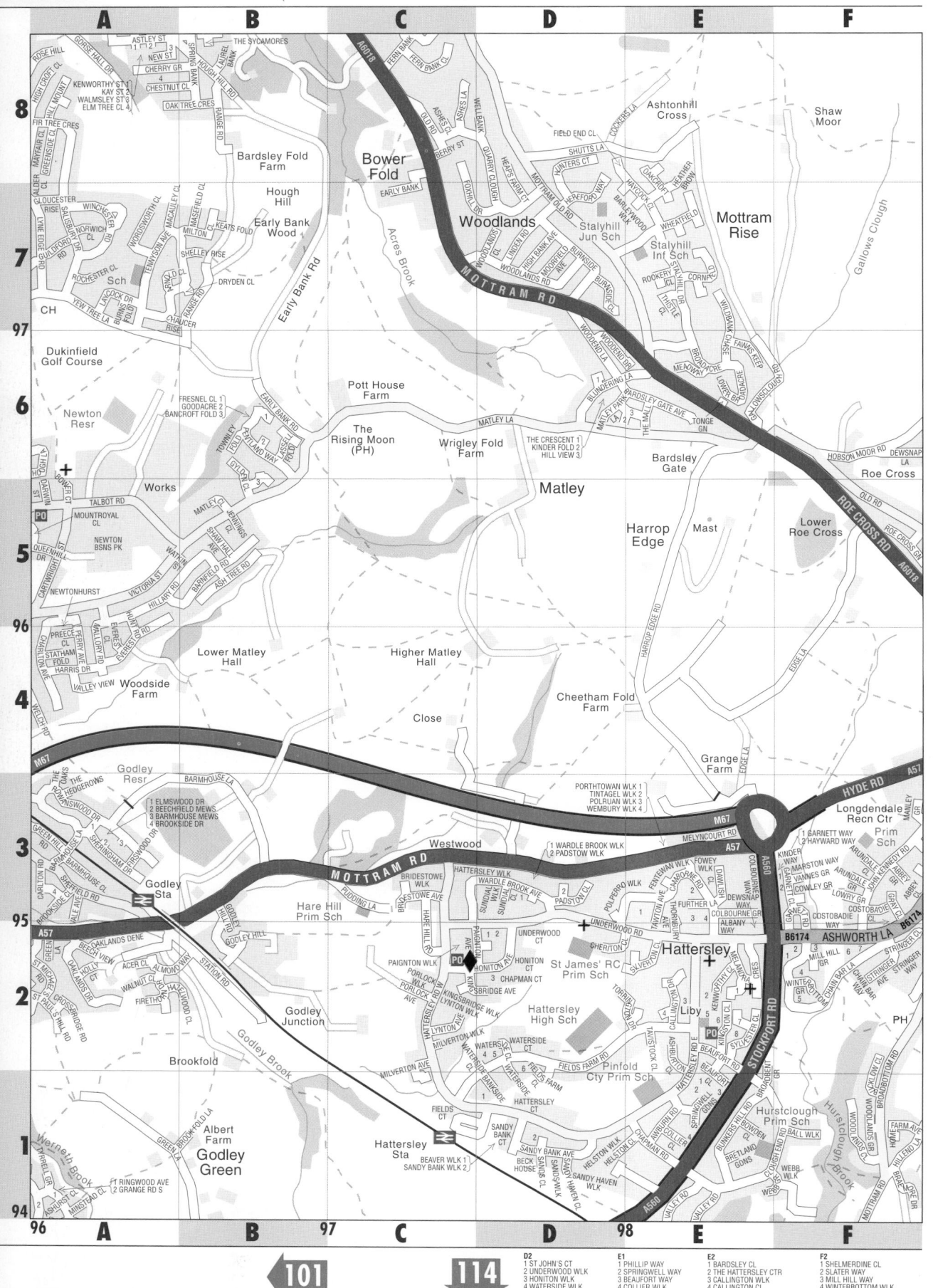

D2
1 ST JOHN'S CT
2 UNDERWOOD WLK
3 HONITON WLK
4 WATERSIDE WLK
5 BANKSIDE WLK
6 FIELDS FARM WLK

E1
1 PHILLIP WAY
2 SPRINGWELL WAY
3 BEAUFORT WAY
4 COLLIER WLK

E2
1 BARDSLEY CL
2 THE HATTERSLEY CTR
3 CALLINGTON WLK
4 CALLINGTON CL
5 TAMESIDE CT
6 KINGSTON ARC
7 WORTHINGTON CL
8 SYLVESTER WAY

F2
1 SHELMERDINE CL
2 SLATER WAY
3 MILL HILL WAY
4 WINTERBOTTOM WLK
5 KNOWLE WAY
6 GREEN WAY
7 GREEN WLK

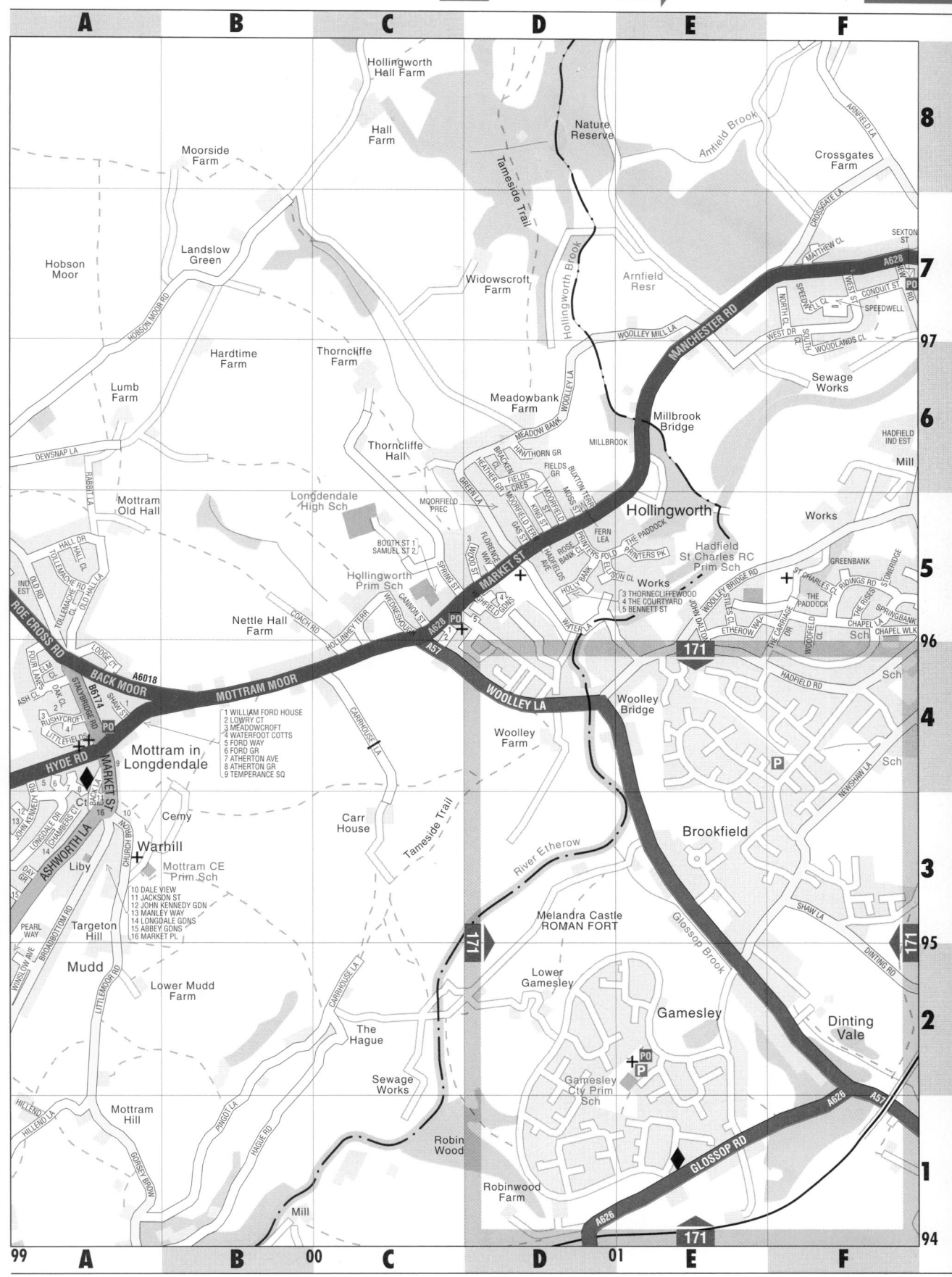

A B C D E F

8
Hollingworth Hall Farm
Hall Farm
Nature Reserve
Tameside Trail
Arnfield Brook
Crossgates Farm

Moorside Farm
Hollingworth Brook
Arnfield Resr
7
Landslow Green
Widowscroft Farm
Woolley Mill La
MANCHESTER RD
A628
SEXTON ST
MATTHEW CL
CROSSGATE LA
NORTH CL
WEST ST
CONDUIT ST
SPEEDWELL
WEST DR
SOUTH
WOODLANDS CL
97
Hobson Moor
Hardtime Farm
Thorncliffe Farm
Meadowbank Farm
Sewage Works
6
Lumb Farm
Thorncliffe Hall
Millbrook Bridge
MILLBROOK
HADFIELD IND EST
Mill
DEWSNAP LA
RABBIT LA
HOBSON MOOR RD

Mottram Old Hall
Longdendale High Sch
MEADOW BANK
HAWTHORN GR
BRACKEN
HEATHER GR
GREEN LA
FIELDS CRES
FIELDS GR
BUXTON TERR
MOSS ST
KING ST
MOORFIELD TERR
Hollingworth
Works
HADFIELD
GREENBANK
Mill
Works
5
HALL DR
TOLLEMACHE RD
OLD RD
Nettle Hall Farm
MOORFIELD PREC
BOOTH ST 1
SAMUEL ST 2
SPRING ST
WOOD ST
FLORENCE WAY
MARKET ST
GAS ST
FERN LEA
PRINTERS FOLD
PRINTERS PK
THE PADDOCK
Hadfield St Charles RC Prim Sch
ST CHARLES CL
RIDINGS RD
STONERIDGE
THE PADDOCK
THE RISGS
SPRINGBANK
CHAPEL LA
CHAPEL WLK
96
ROE CROSS RD
Hollingworth Prim Sch
HOLLINWAY TERR
WEDNESCROFT
CANNON ST
A628
PO
HADFIELDS GDNS
ROSE BANK
HOLLY BANK
WATSON CL
WATER LA
JOHN DALTON
ETHEROW
WOOLLEY BRIDGE RD
STILES CL
THE CARRIAGE DR
MOORFIELD CL
3 THORNECLIFFEWOOD
4 THE COURTYARD
5 BENNETT ST
171
Sch

4
BACK MOOR
A6018
MOTTRAM MOOR
A57
WOOLLEY LA
Woolley Bridge
HADFIELD RD
Sch
LODGE LA
FOUR LANES
STALYBRIDGE RD
SHAW ST
1 WILLIAM FORD HOUSE
2 LOWRY CT
3 MEADOWCROFT
4 WATERFOOT COTTS
5 FORD WAY
6 FORD GR
7 ATHERTON AVE
8 ATHERTON GR
9 TEMPERANCE SQ
Woolley Farm
CARRHOUSE LA
Brookfield
NEWSHAW LA
P

3
HYDE RD
Mottram in Longdendale
Cemy
Carr House
Tameside Trail
River Etherow
Glossop Brook
SHAW LA
DINTING RD
95
ELM
OAK CL
ASH
RUSHYCROFT
LITTLEFIELD
MARKET ST
BACK LA
CHAMBERS CL
JOHN KENNEDY RD
CHURCH BROW
LONGDALE DR
Warhill
Mottram CE Prim Sch
Liby
10 DALE VIEW
11 JACKSON ST
12 JOHN KENNEDY GDN
13 MANLEY WAY
14 LONGDALE GDNS
15 ABBEY GDNS
16 MARKET PL
Melandra Castle ROMAN FORT
Lower Gamesley
171
Dinting Vale
2
PEARL WAY
WINSLOW AVE
BROADBOTTOM RD
LITTLEMOOR RD
ASHWORTH LA
DAY GR
Targeton Hill
Mudd
Lower Mudd Farm
The Hague
Tameside Trail
CARRHOUSE LA
Gamesley
Gamesley Cty Prim Sch
PO
P
A626
A57
1
HILLEND
HILLEND LA
GORSEY BROW
Mottram Hill
LINGOT LA
HAGUE RD
Sewage Works
Robin Wood
Robinwood Farm
GLOSSOP RD
A626
171
94

For full street detail of the highlighted area see page 171.

103
88

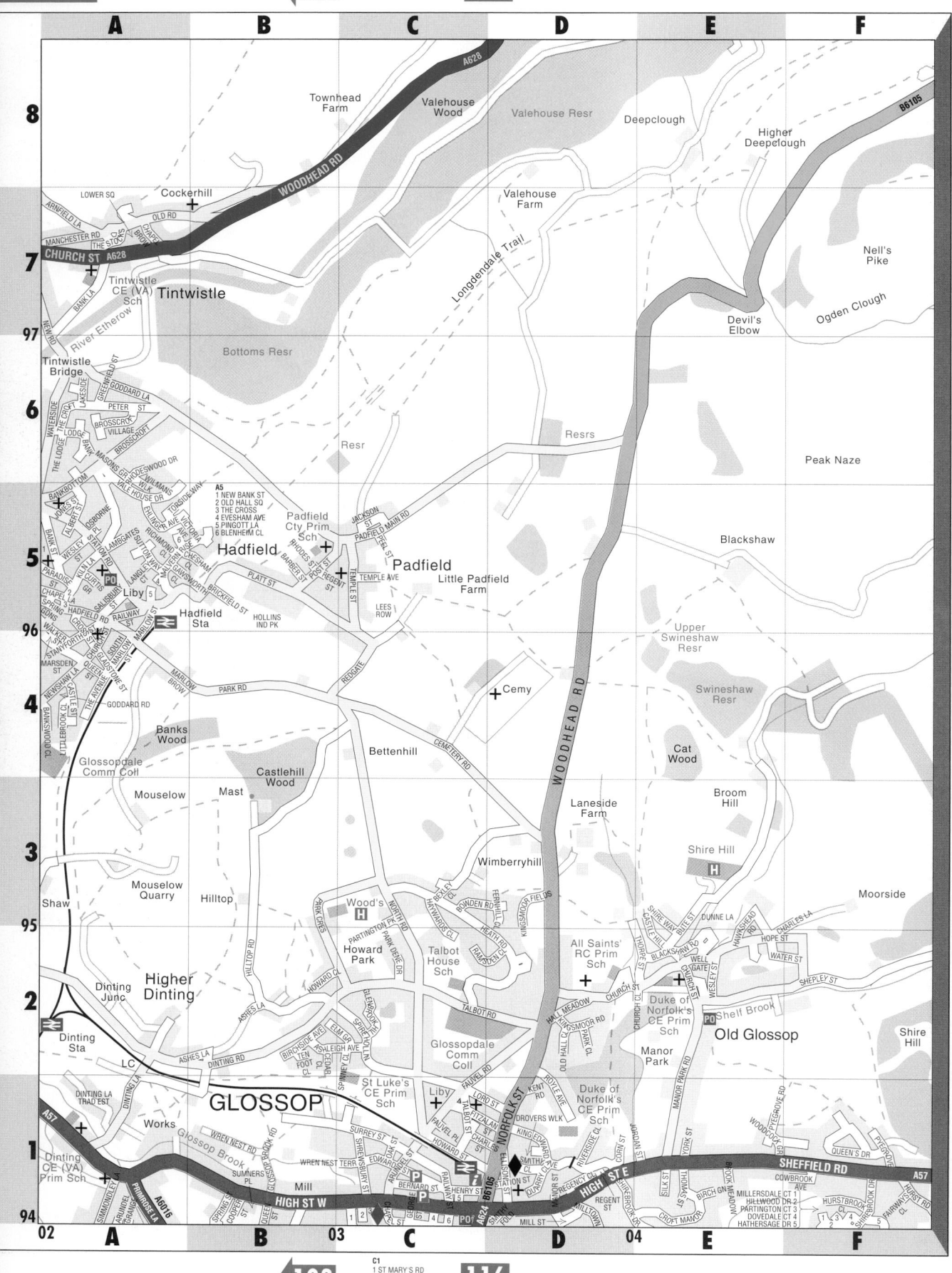

103
116

C1
1 ST MARY'S RD
2 BROOK ST
3 HALL'S CT
4 CROSS ST
5 CENTRAL STORE
6 MARKET ST

A B C D E F

8 7 93 6 5 92 4 3 91 2 1 90

Roads / Motorways
M62
B5212
B5311
FAIRHILLS RD
A57
BRINELL DR
B5320
A6144
MANCHESTER NEW RD
WARBURTON LA
LIVERPOOL RD
MANCHESTER RD
GLAZEBROOK LA
WOOLDEN RD
MOSS RD
B5212
WARBURTON BRIDGE RD
PARK RD
MOSS LA

Places
IRLAM
Cadishead
Partington
Glazebrook
Hollinfare
Hollins Green

Farms / Features
Great Woolden Hall Farm
Woolden View Farm
Rose Bank Farm
Cadishead Moss
Ryefield Farm
Ash Farm
Astley Road Farm
Brush Farm
Mount Pleasant Farm
Brook Farm
Rye Park House
Warburton Park
Heathlands Farm
Mosslane Farm
Coroners Wood
Millbank Hall
Manchester Ship Canal
Glaze Brook
Marsh Brook
Red Brook
Ortonbrook
Glazebrook Exchange Sidings
Tar Distillery
Sewage Works
Cemy
Recn Gd
Wright Tree Villas
Northbank Ind Pk
Cadishead Way
Excalibur Way
Frank Perkins Way
Thames Trad Ctr

Schools / Churches
St Teresa's RC Prim Sch
Irlam & Cadishead Comm High Sch
Cadishead Jun Sch
Cadishead Inf Sch
St Mary's CE Prim Sch
Our Lady of Lourdes RC Prim Sch
Woodlands Inf Sch
St Helens CE Prim Sch
Ortonbrook Prim Sch
Partington Prim Sch
Broadoak Comp Sch

Stations
Irlam Sta
Glazebrook Sta
Railway Cotts

Labels
Sports Ctr
Liby
Liby & Ctr
Works
PO PH

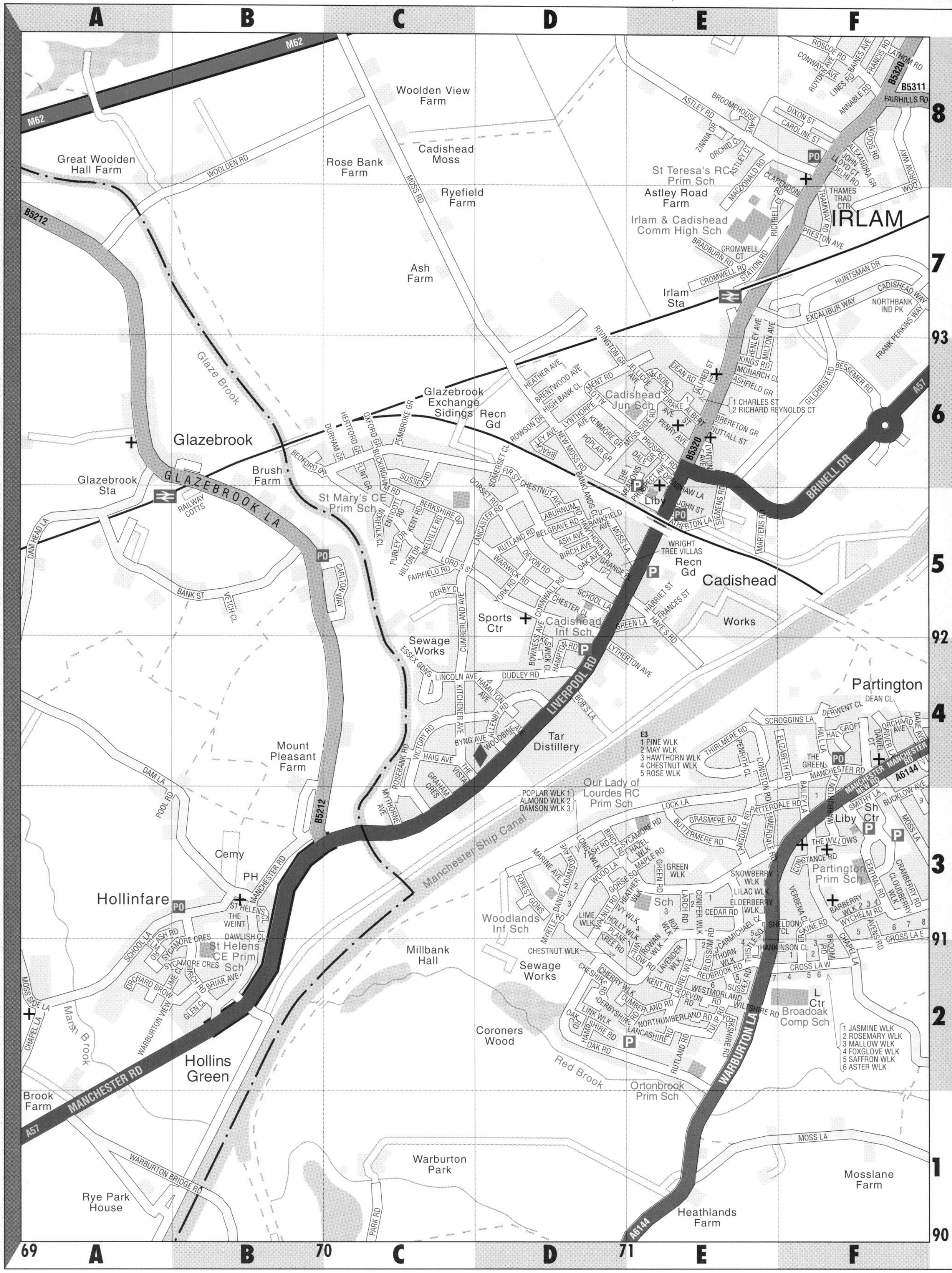

E2
1 YEW WLK
2 FORSYTHIA WLK
3 BLACKTHORN WLK
4 THISTLE WLK
5 MAGNOLIA CL
6 LOBELIA WLK
7 IRIS WLK

F3
1 STUART HAMPSON CT
2 ELM CL
3 WINTERGREEN WLK
4 BEECH CL
5 CAMOMILE WLK
6 CHARLOCK WLK
7 WOODRUFF WLK
8 COLUMBINE WLK
9 WORTHINGTON AVE

E3
1 PINE WLK
2 MAY WLK
3 HAWTHORN WLK
4 CHESTNUT WLK
5 ROSE WLK

1 POPLAR WLK 2 ALMOND WLK 3 DAMSON WLK

1 JASMINE WLK 2 ROSEMARY WLK 3 MALLOW WLK 4 FOXGLOVE WLK 5 SAFFRON WLK 6 ASTER WLK

1 CHARLES ST 2 RICHARD REYNOLDS CT

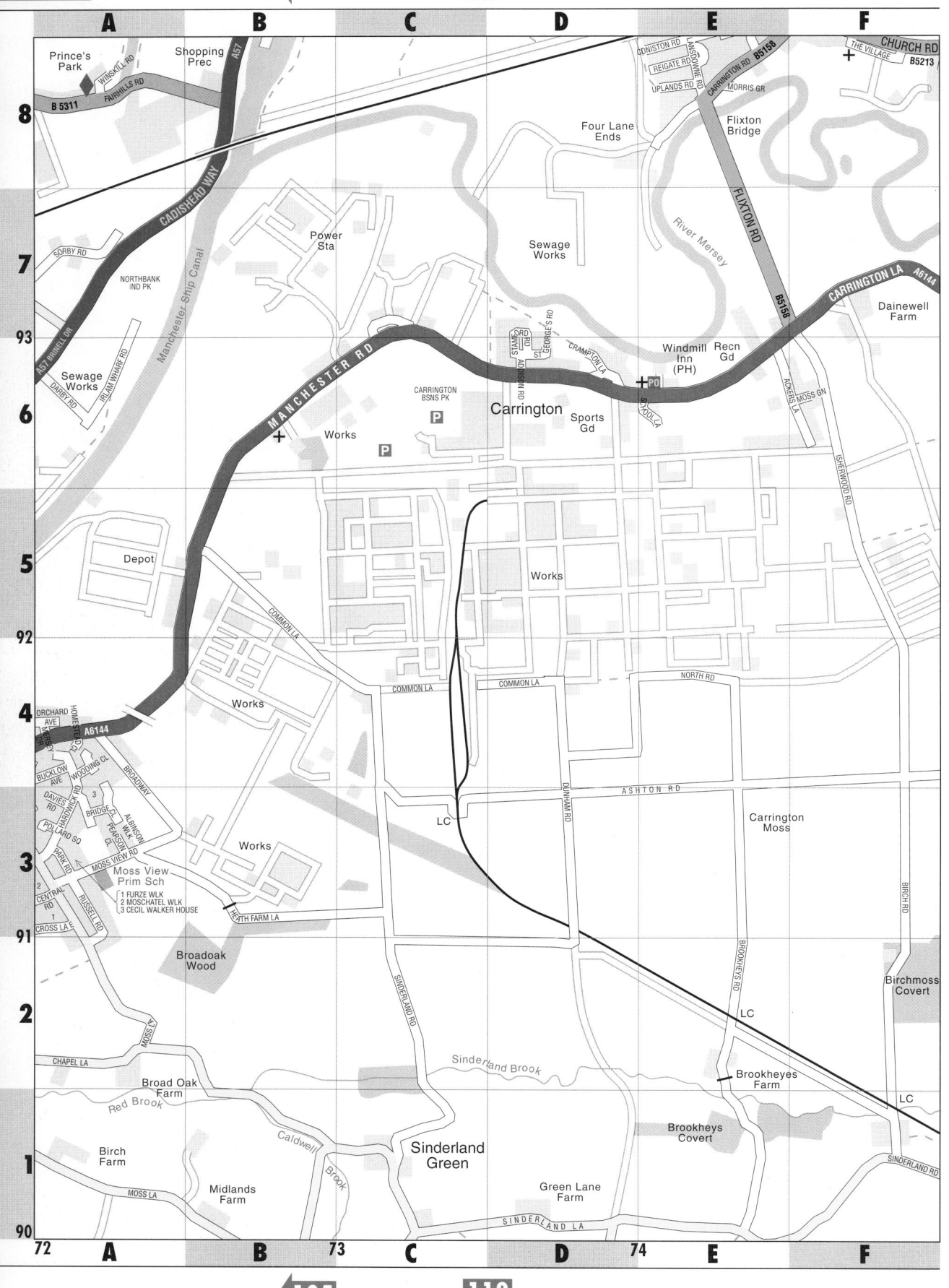

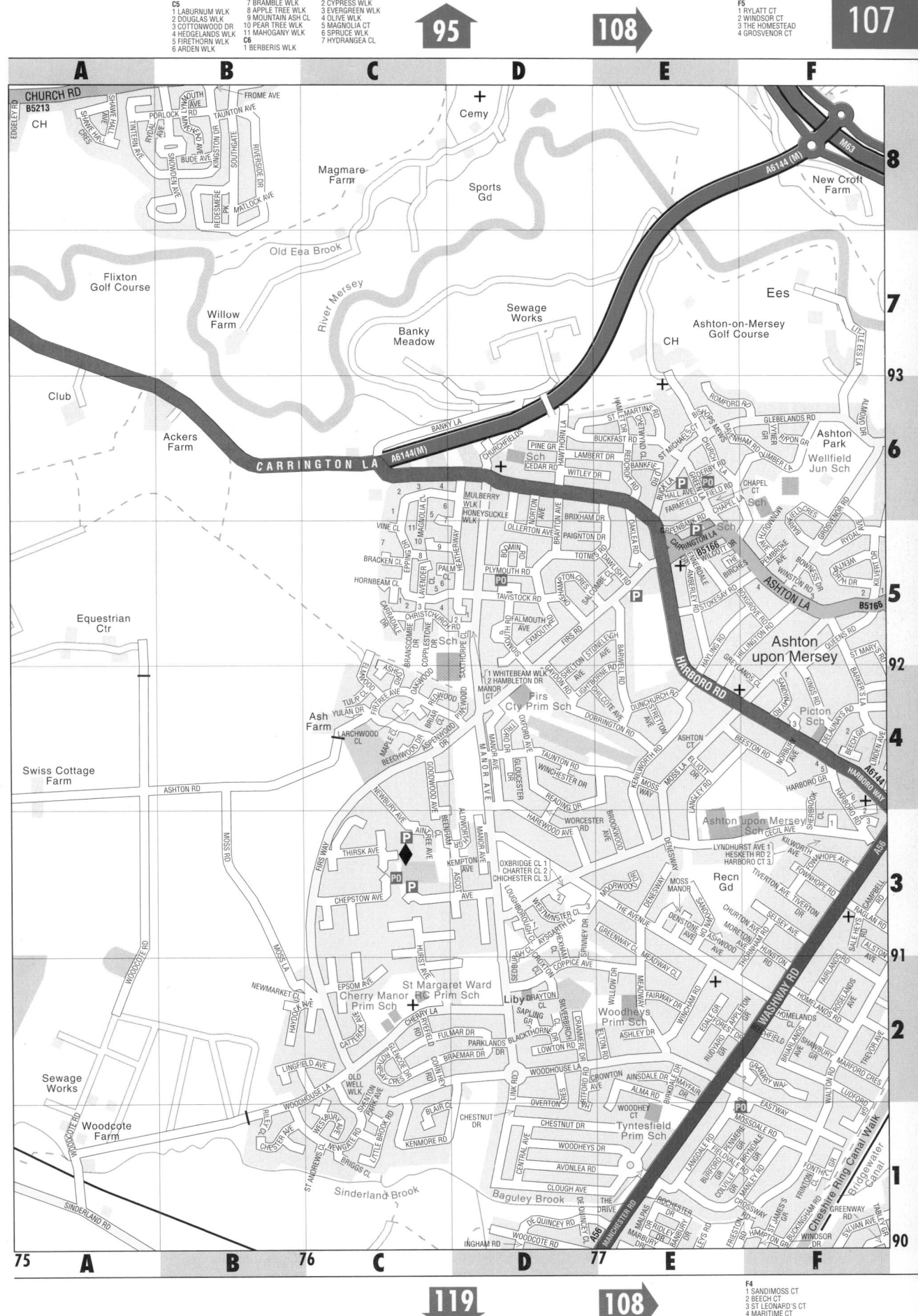

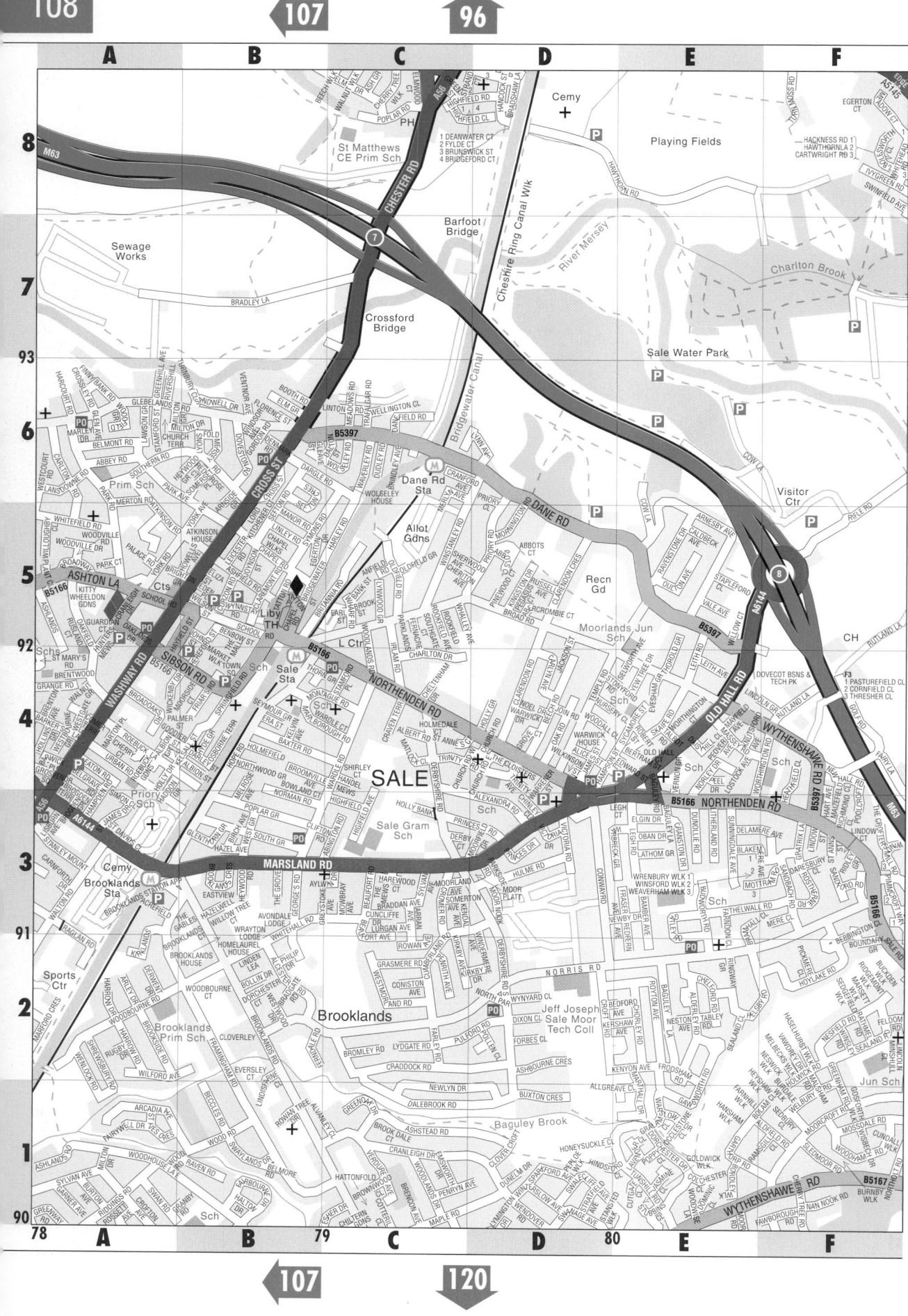

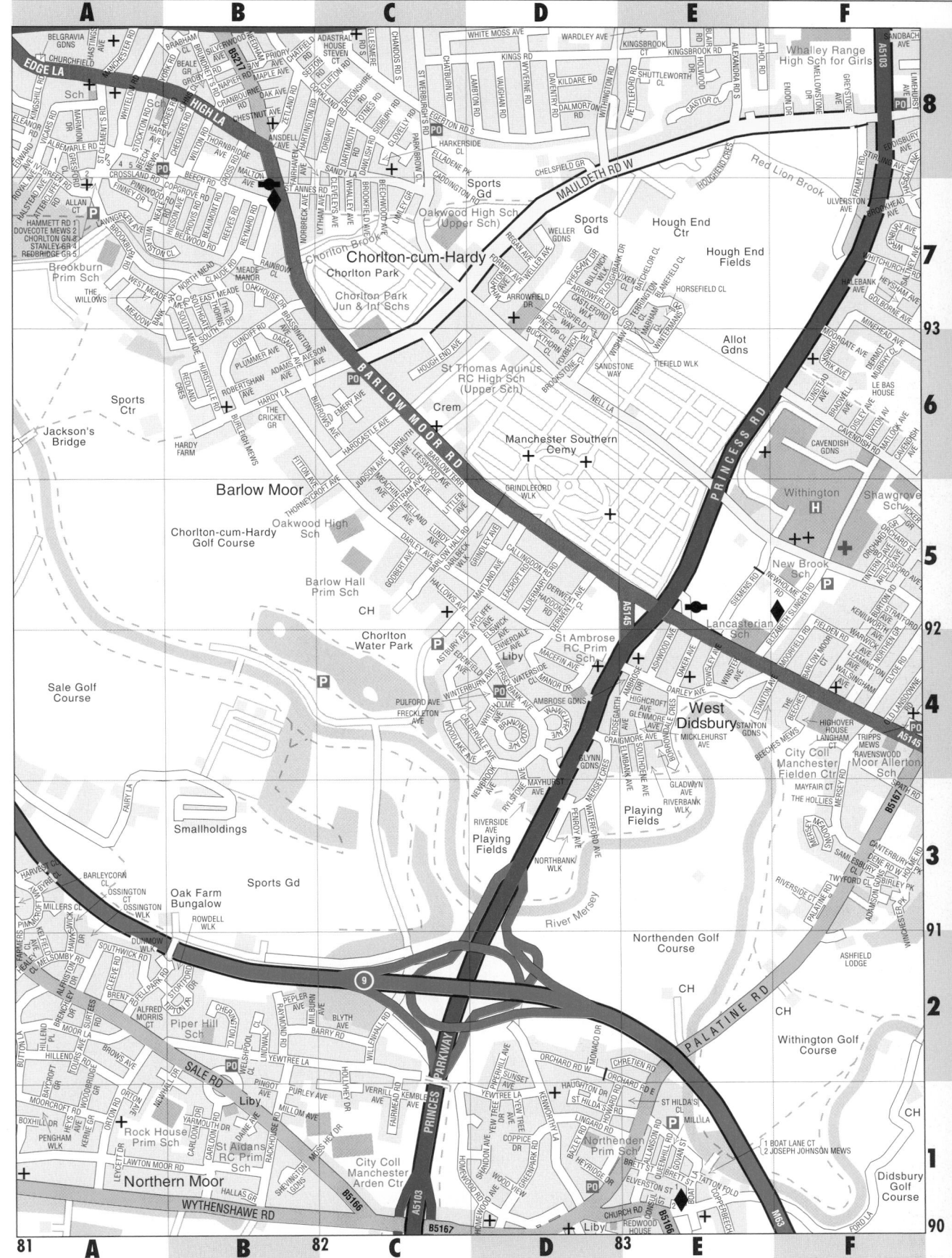

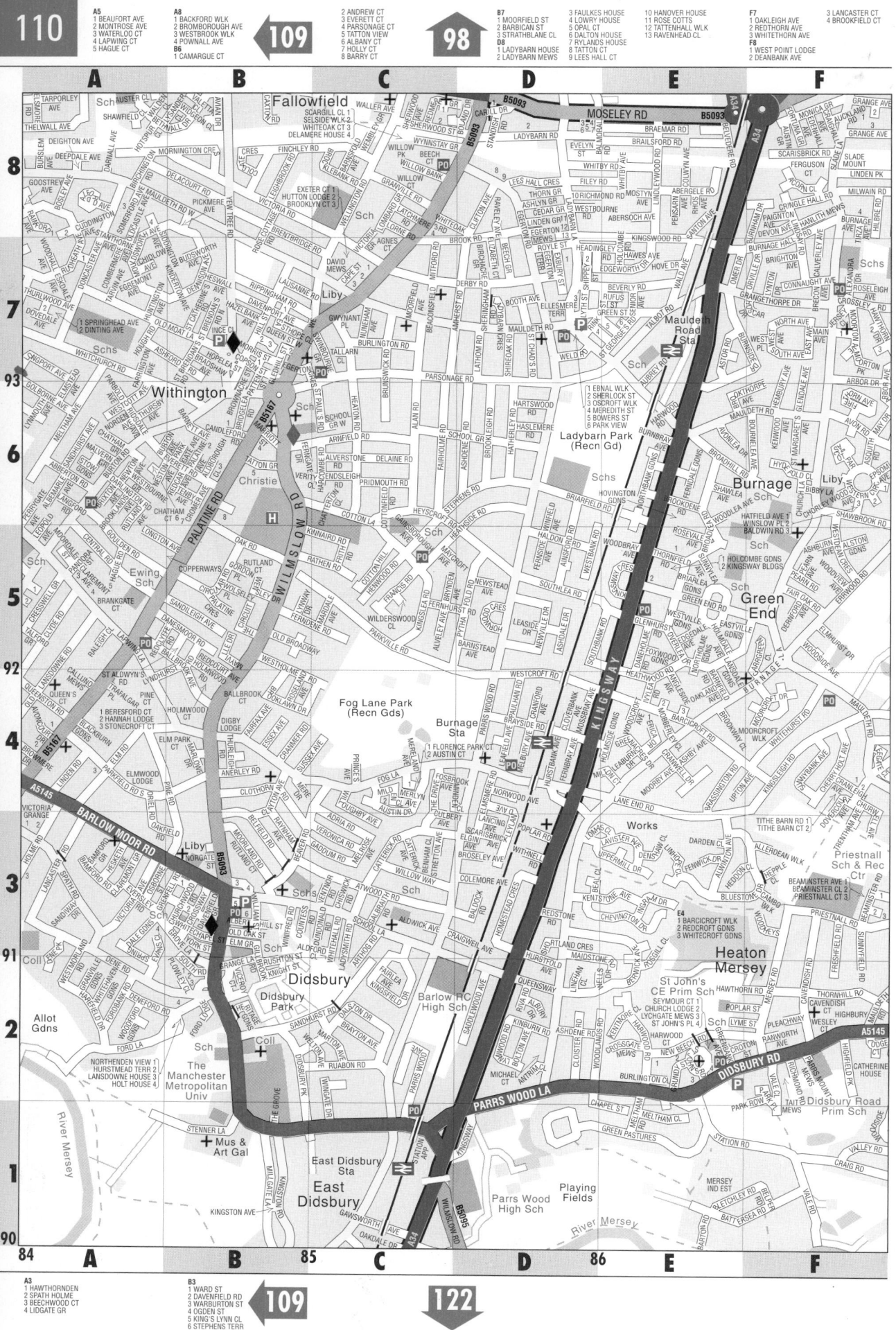

A5
1 BEAUFORT AVE
2 MONTROSE AVE
3 WATERLOO CT
4 LAPWING CT
5 HAGUE CT

A8
1 BACKFORD WLK
2 BROMBOROUGH AVE
3 WESTBROOK WLK
4 POWNALL AVE

B6
1 CAMARGUE CT

109

2 ANDREW CT
2 EVERETT CT
4 PARSONAGE CT
5 TATTON VIEW
6 ALBANY CT
7 HOLLY CT
8 BARRY ST

98

B7
1 MOORFIELD ST
2 BARBICAN ST
3 STRATHBLANE CL
D8
1 LADYBARN HOUSE
2 LADYBARN MEWS

4 FAULKES HOUSE
5 LOWRY HOUSE
6 OPAL CT
7 DALTON HOUSE
8 RYLANDS HOUSE
9 TATTON CT
9 LEES HALL CT

10 HANOVER HOUSE
11 ROSE COTTS
12 TATTENHALL WLK
13 RAVENHALL CL

F7
1 OAKLEIGH AVE
2 REDTHORN AVE
3 WHITETHORN AVE
F8
1 WEST POINT LODGE
2 DEANBANK AVE

3 LANCASTER CT
4 BROOKFIELD CT

A3
1 HAWTHORNDEN
2 SPATH HOLME
3 BEECHWOOD CT
4 LIDGATE GR

B3
1 WARD ST
2 DAVENFIELD RD
3 WARBURTON ST
4 OGDEN ST
5 KING'S LYNN CL
6 STEPHENS TERR

109

122

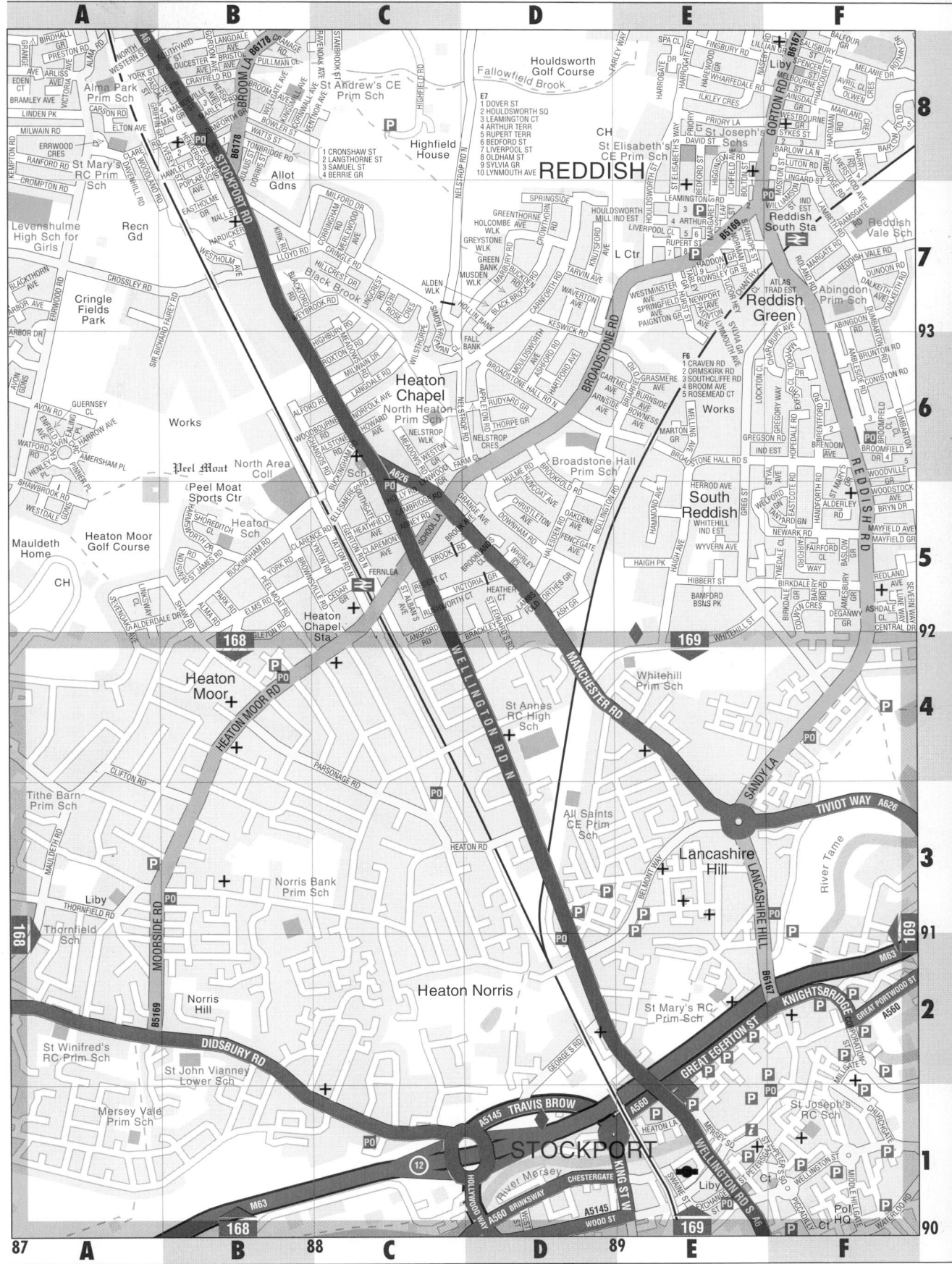

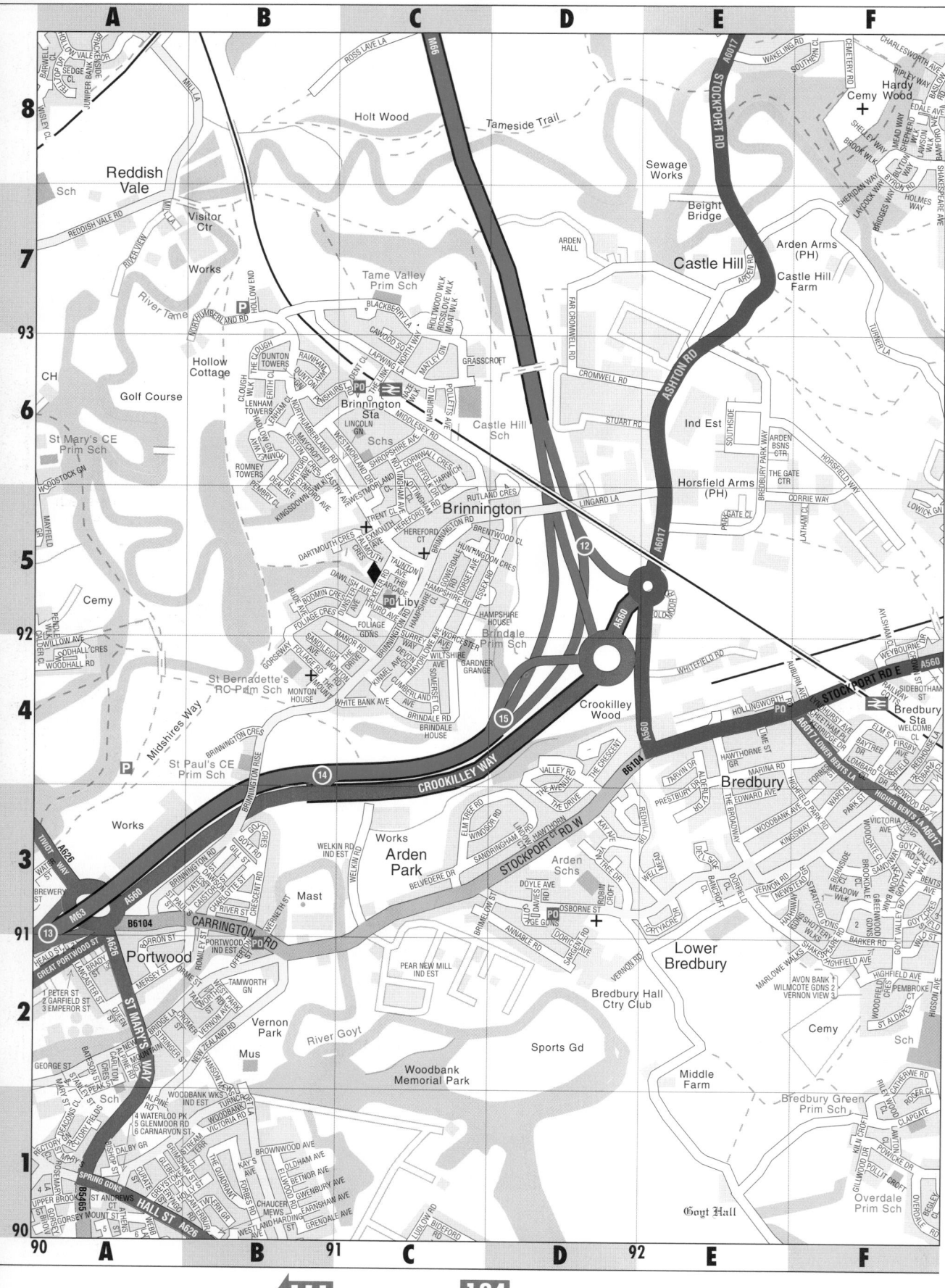

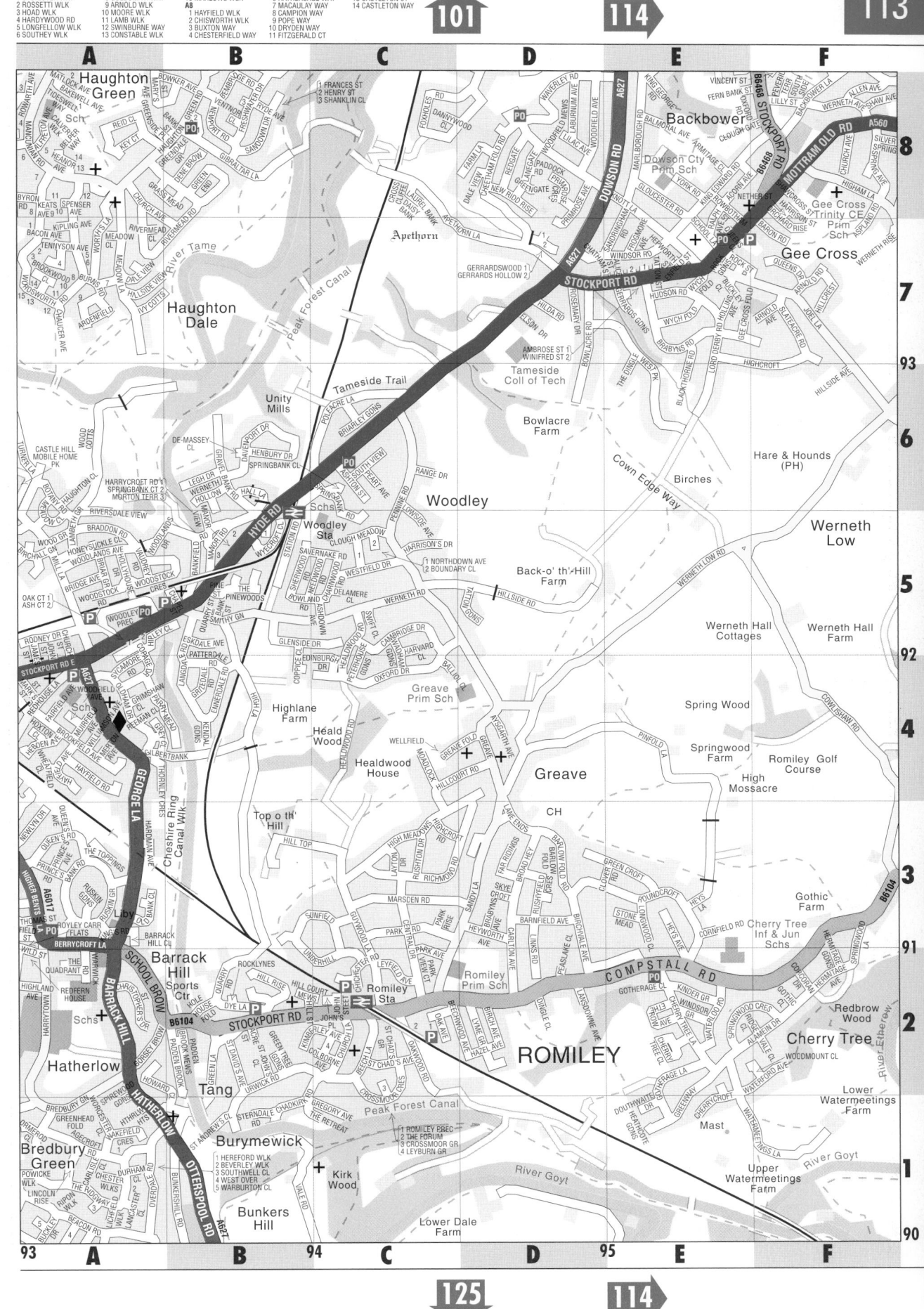

	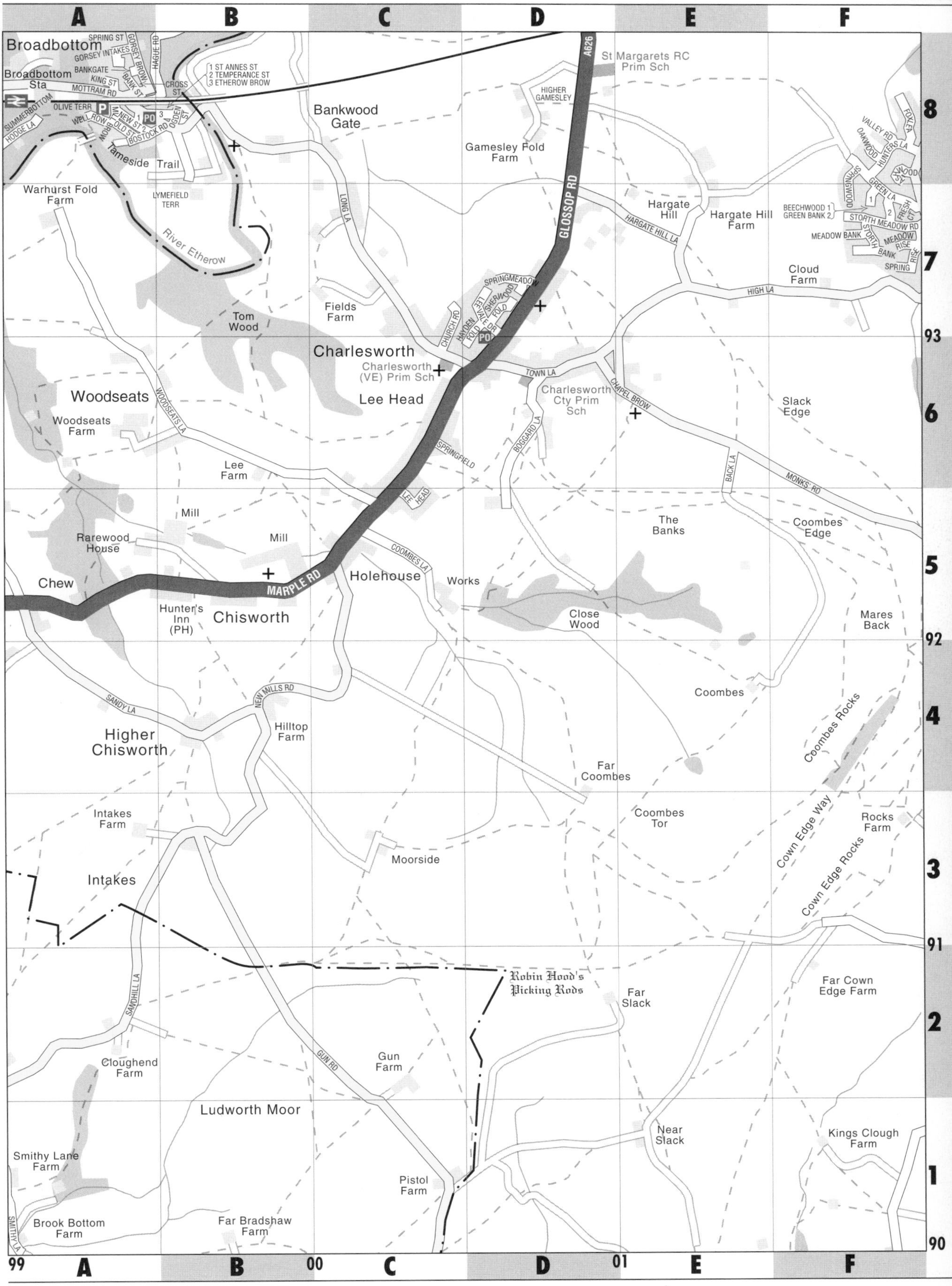 A	B	C	D	E	F	

Broadbottom
Spring St
Gorsey Brow
Hague Rd
1 ST ANNES ST
2 TEMPERANCE ST
3 ETHEROW BROW
Bankgate
King St
Bank St
Cross St
Mottram Rd
Olive Terr
Well Row
New St
Old St
Bostock Rd
Ogden
Broadbottom Sta
Summerbottom
Hodge La

8

St Margarets RC Prim Sch
HIGHER GAMESLEY
A626
GLOSSOP RD

Valley Rd
Oakwood
Springwood
Foxley La
Green La
Hunters La
Wood Rd
Beechwood 1
Green Bank 2
Storth Meadow Rd
Meadow Bank
Storth Bank
Meadow Rise
Spring

Tameside Trail
Warhurst Fold Farm
Lymefield Terr

Bankwood Gate
Long La
Gamesley Fold Farm

Hargate Hill
Hargate Hill La
Hargate Hill Farm

7

Cloud Farm
High La

River Etherow
Tom Wood
Fields Farm
Church Rd
Hayden La
Fold La
Town End Fold
Sherwood
Springmeadow
PO

Charlesworth
Charlesworth (VE) Prim Sch
Lee Head
Town La
Charlesworth Cty Prim Sch
Chapel Brow

Slack Edge

93
6

Woodseats
Woodseats Farm
Woodseats La
Lee Farm
Springfield
Lt Head
Boggaro La
The Banks
Back La
Monks Rd
Coombes Edge

Mill
Mill
Rarewood House
Coombes La
Holehouse
Works
Close Wood
Coombes
Mares Back

5

Chew
MARPLE RD
Hunter's Inn (PH)
Chisworth

92

Coombes
Coombes Rocks

Sandy La
New Mills Rd
Hilltop Farm
Far Coombes

Cown Edge Way
Rocks Farm

4

Higher Chisworth
Coombes Tor
Cown Edge Rocks

91

Intakes Farm
Moorside
Intakes

Robin Hood's Picking Rods
Far Slack
Far Cown Edge Farm

3

Sandhill La
Cloughend Farm
Gun Rd
Gun Farm

Ludworth Moor
Near Slack
Kings Clough Farm

2

Smithy Lane Farm
Pistol Farm
Brook Bottom Farm
Far Bradshaw Farm

1

Smithy

90

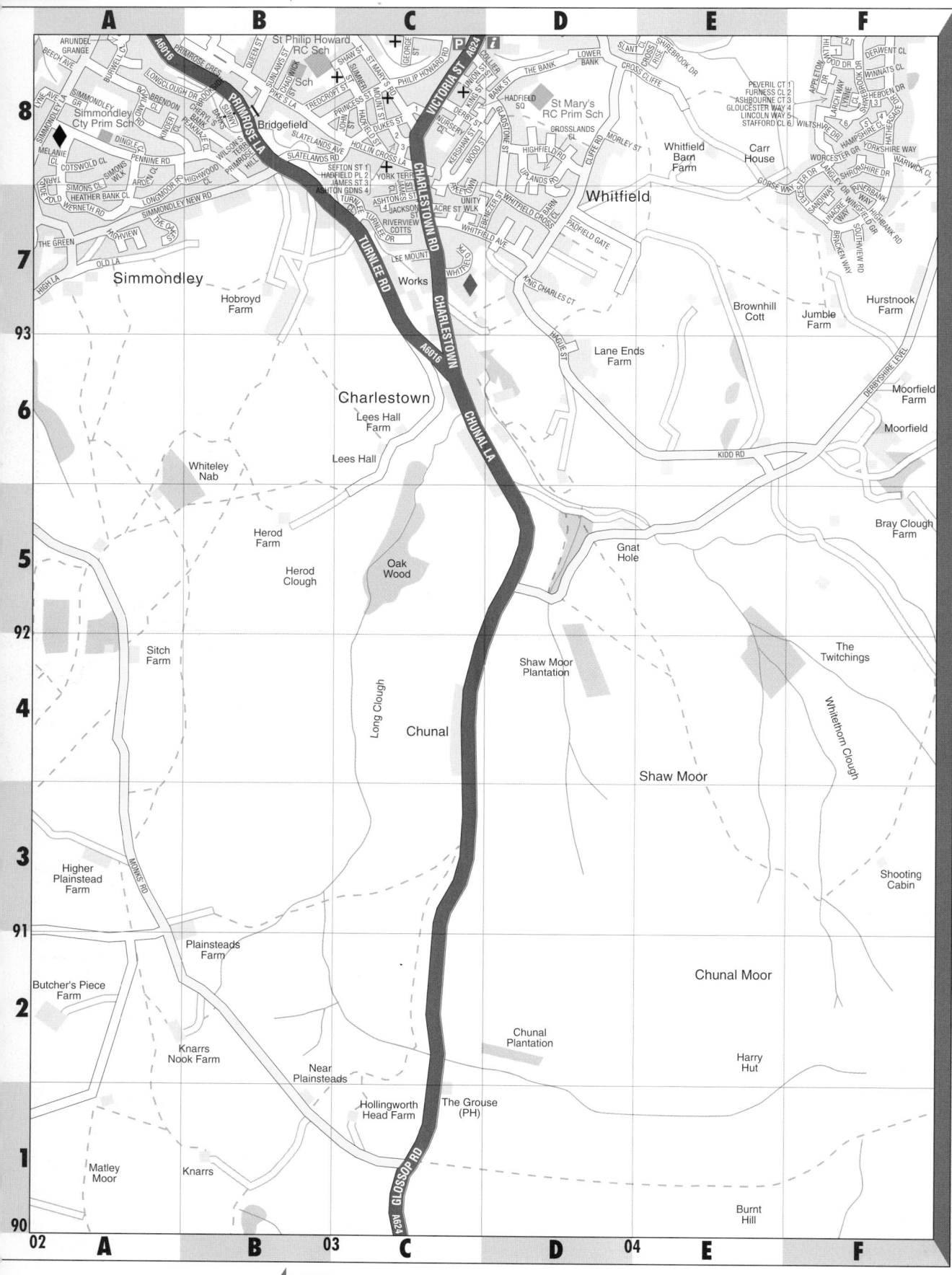

A B C D E F

8

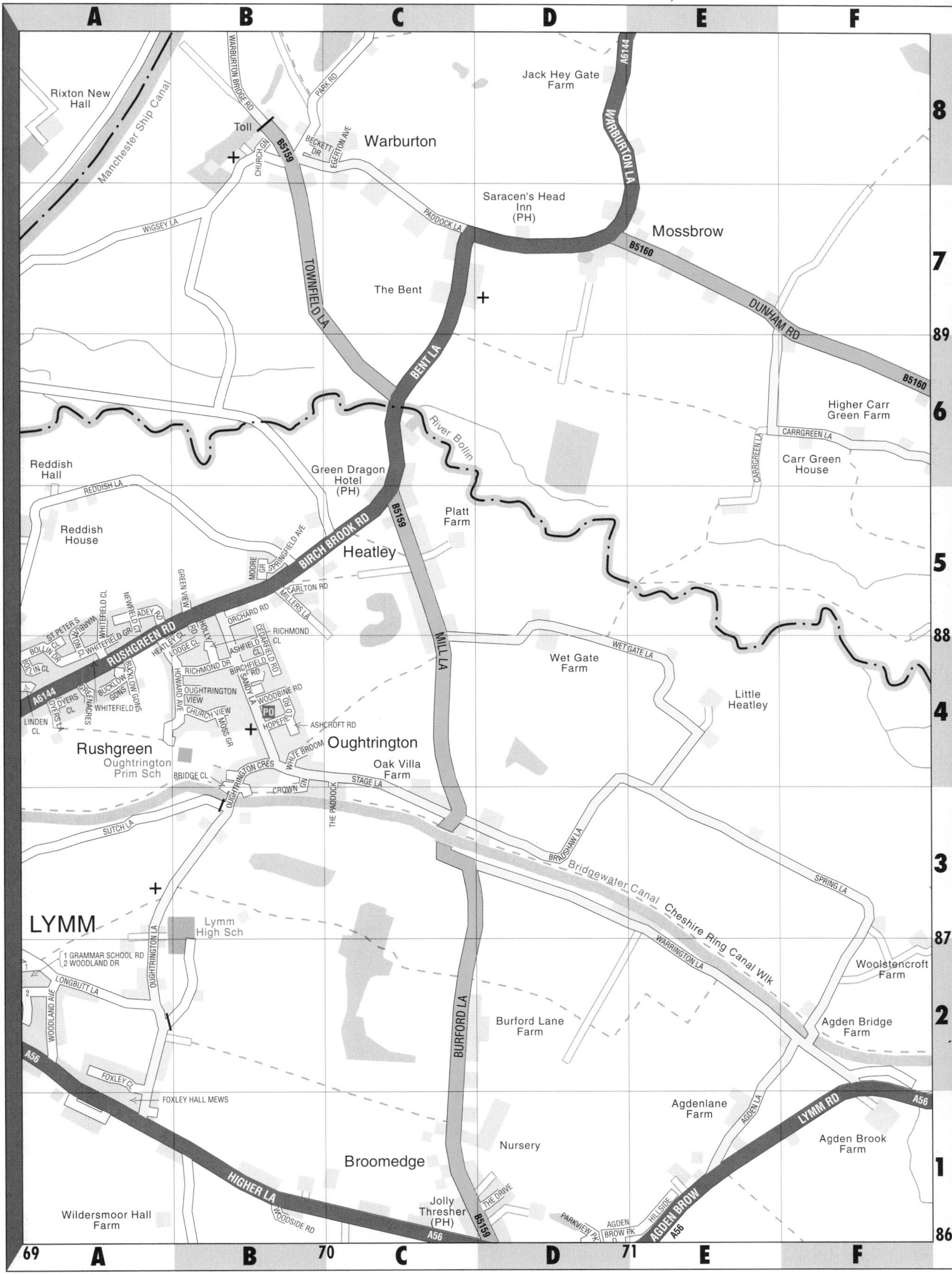

Rixton New Hall

Manchester Ship Canal

Jack Hey Gate Farm

Warburton

Toll

WARBURTON BRIDGE RD

PARK RD

BECKETT DR

EGERTON AVE

B5159

CHURCH LA

WIGSEY LA

Saracen's Head Inn (PH)

WARBURTON LA

A6144

Mossbrow

B5160

7

PADDOCK LA

The Bent

TOWNFIELD LA

DUNHAM RD

B5160

89

Higher Carr Green Farm

6

River Bollin

BENT LA

CARRGREEN LA

Carr Green House

CARRGREEN LA

Reddish Hall

REDDISH LA

Green Dragon Hotel (PH)

BIRCH BROOK RD

B5159

Platt Farm

Reddish House

SPRINGFIELD AVE

MOORE GR

Heatley

5

88

GREEN VIEW

CARLTON RD

MILLERS LA

ST PETER S

WHITEFIELD GR

WHITEFIELD CL

NEWFIELD GR

ADEY RD

HEATLEY CL

HOLLY LA

ORCHARD RD

ASHFIELD CL

CEDARFIELD RD

Richmond CL

RUSHGREEN RD

LODGE LA

RICHMOND DR

BIRCHFIELD RD

SANDY LA

Wet Gate Farm

WET GATE LA

BOLD CL

BUCKLOW GDNS

HOWARD AVE

BIRCH LA

OUGHTRINGTON VIEW

WHITEFIELD

CHURCH VIEW

WOODBINE RD

MOSS GR

PO

HOPEFIELD RD

Little Heatley

A6144

DYERS CL

LINDEN CL

ASHCROFT RD

MILL LA

4

Rushgreen

Oughtrington Prim Sch

OUGHTRINGTON CRES

BRIDGE CL

WILDE BROOM

Oughtrington

Oak Villa Farm

SUTCH LA

CROWN GN

THE PADDOCK

STAGE LA

Bridgewater Canal

Cheshire Ring Canal Wlk

SPRING LA

3

87

LYMM

OUGHTRINGTON LA

Lymm High Sch

WARRINGTON LA

Woolstencroft Farm

1 GRAMMAR SCHOOL RD
2 WOODLAND DR

LONGBUTT LA

BURFORD LA

Burford Lane Farm

Agden Bridge Farm

2

WOODLAND AVE

A56

FOXLEY CL

FOXLEY HALL MEWS

Nursery

Agdenlane Farm

AGDEN LA

LYMM RD

A56

1

Broomedge

Jolly Thresher (PH)

THE DRIVE

B5159

PARKVIEW PK

AGDEN BROW PK

HILLSIDE

AGDEN BROW

A56

Agden Brook Farm

HIGHER LA

WOODSIDE RD

A56

Wildersmoor Hall Farm

86

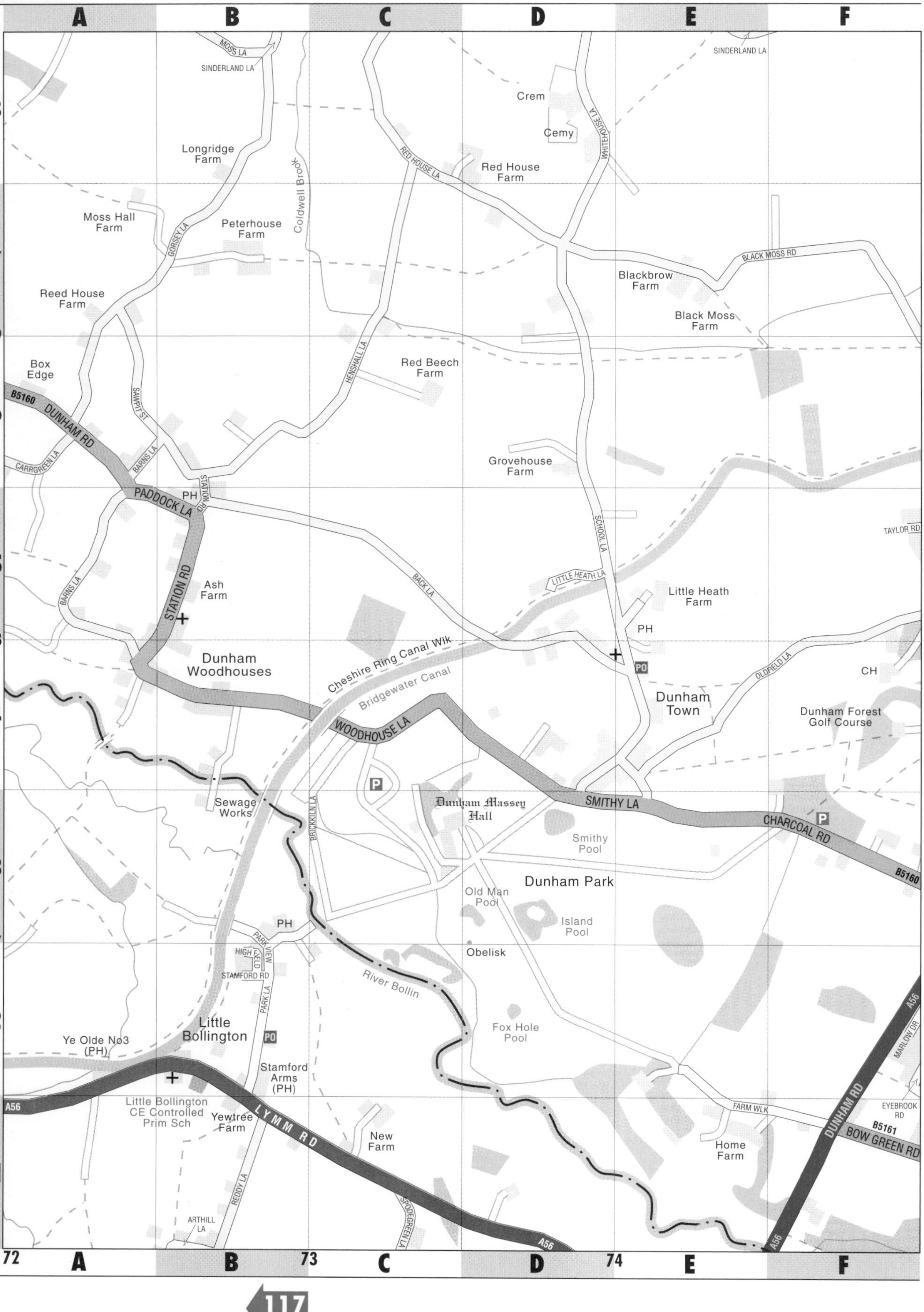

119

107
D5
1 POLICE ST
2 STAMFORD WAY
3 STAMFORD SQ

120
E6
1 LYNGARTH HOUSE
2 ASTBURY CL
3 THELWALL CL

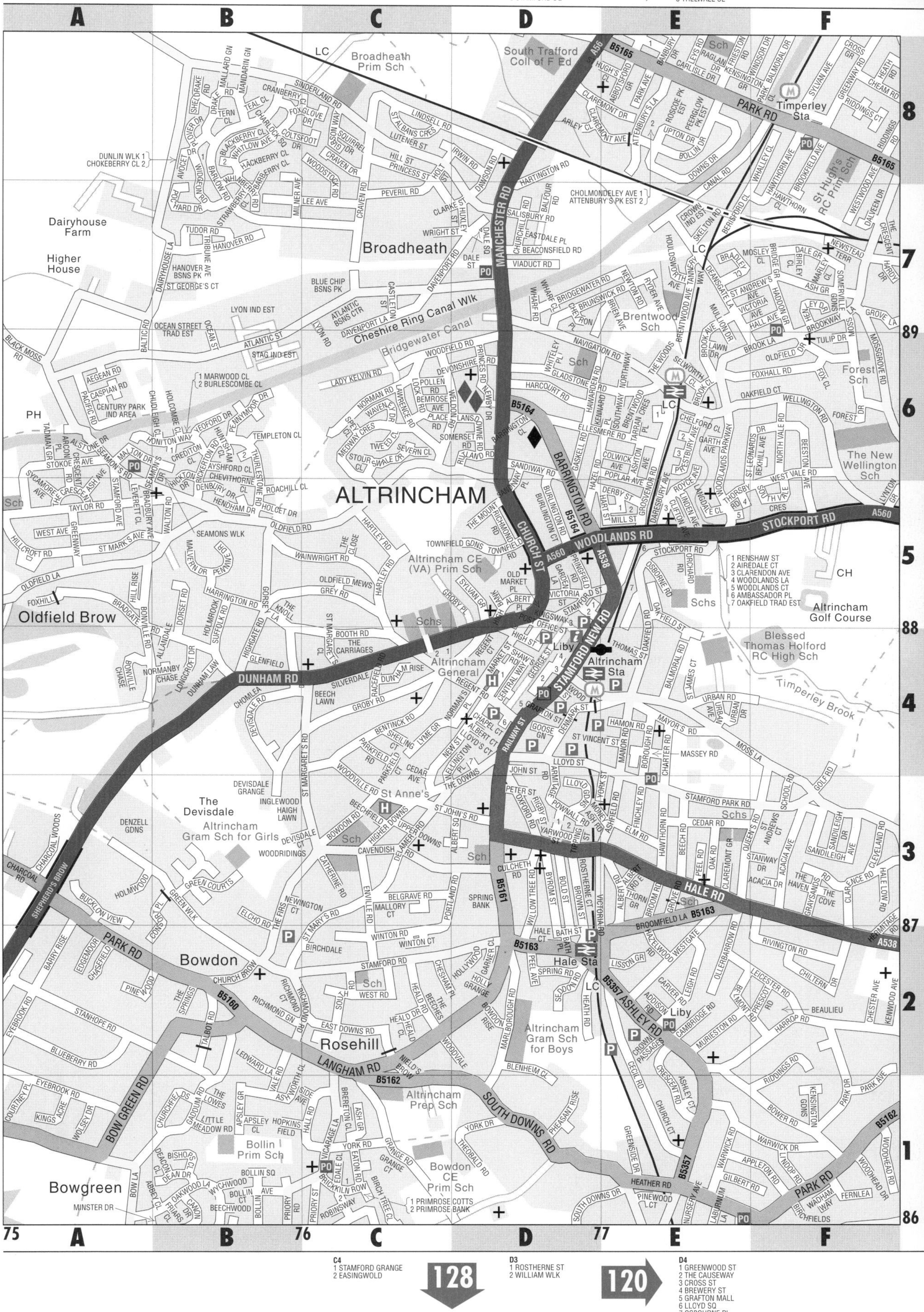

C4
1 STAMFORD GRANGE
2 EASINGWOLD

D3
1 ROSTHERNE ST
2 WILLIAM WLK

D4
1 GREENWOOD ST
2 THE CAUSEWAY
3 CROSS ST
4 BREWERY ST
5 GRAFTON MALL
6 LLOYD SQ
7 OSBOURNE PL

119
108

D7
1 THORNGROVE AVE
2 FARNCOMBE CL
3 HARLINGTON CL
4 THORNGROVE HOUSE
5 HUNGERFORD WLK

E7
1 BUSHFIELD WLK
2 CROWHURST WLK
3 STONEHOUSE WLK
4 CLAVERHAM WLK
5 ROTHERMERE WLK

F6
1 ECKERSLEY CL
2 DUNKELD GDNS
3 BARTH WLK
4 KINMEL WLK
5 DITTON WLK
6 CALCOT WLK

7 LARGS WLK
8 HOCKLEY RD
9 ROUNDTHORN WLK

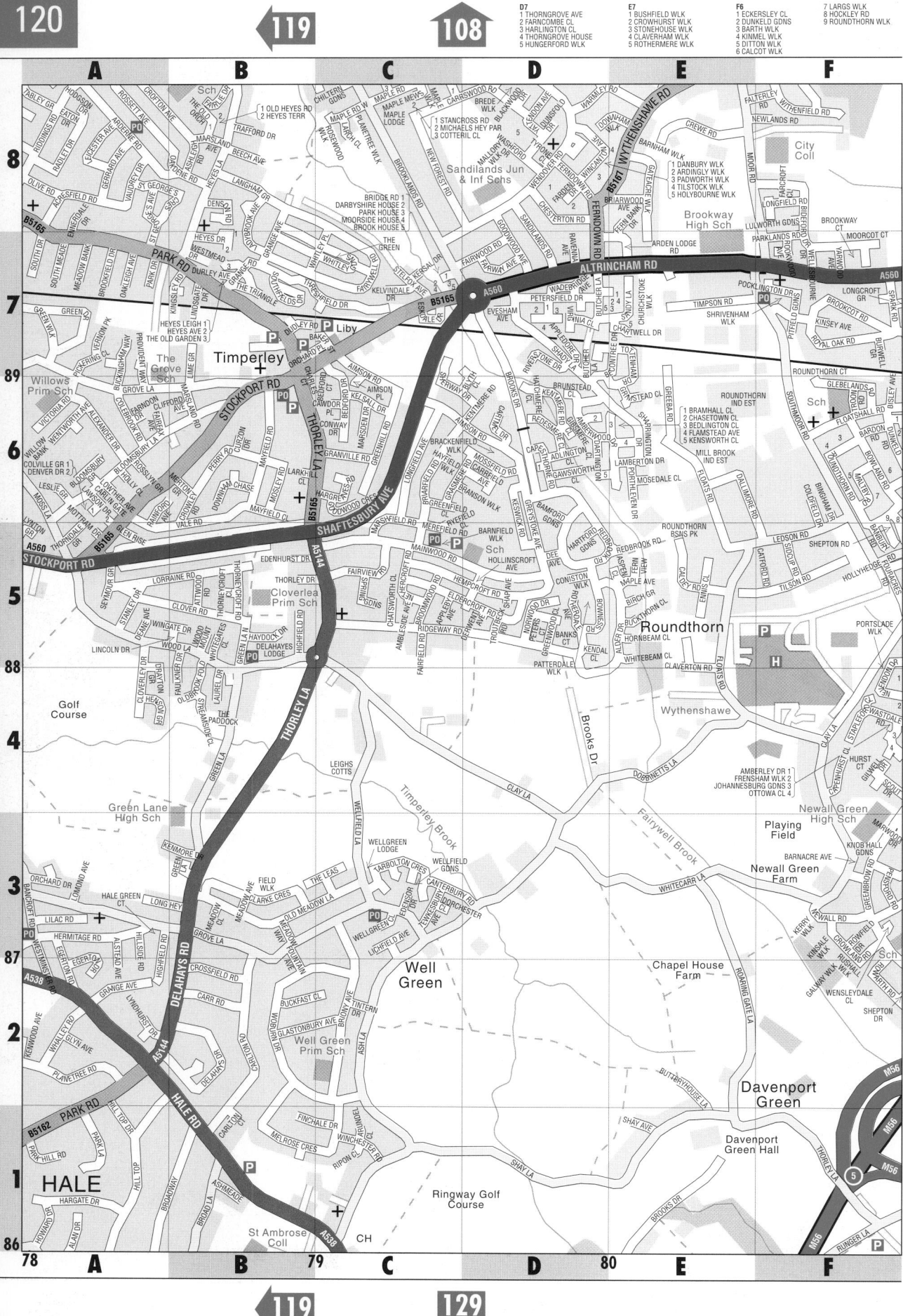

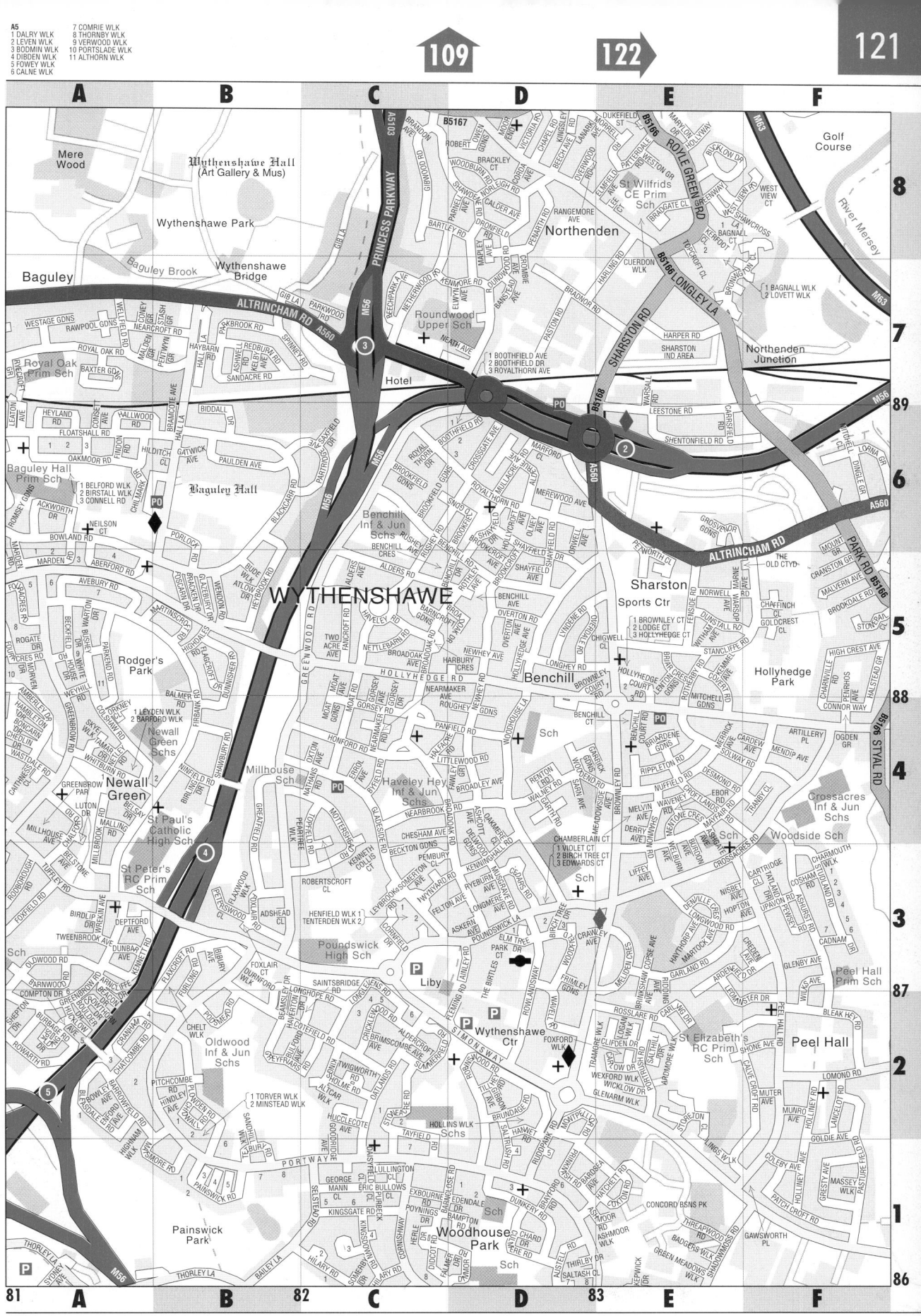

A5
1 DALRY WLK
2 LEVEN WLK
3 BODMIN WLK
4 DIBDEN WLK
5 FOWEY WLK
6 CALNE WLK

7 COMRIE WLK
8 THORNBY WLK
9 VERWOOD WLK
10 PORTSLADE WLK
11 ALTHORN WLK

109

122

121

A2
1 GARRON WLK
2 BURNSALL WLK
3 MATSON WLK
4 HURST WLK
5 FALKIRK WLK
6 FOXTON WLK

B1
1 PORTON WLK
2 FRESHFORD WLK
3 PETHERIDGE DR
4 DARNBROOK DR
5 BRIERTON DR
6 MIDBROOK WLK
7 SIBLIES WLK
8 GAMES WLK

C1
1 TORRIDON WLK
2 SALTDENE RD
3 ROTTINGDENE DR
4 RINGMER DR
5 TEYNHAM WLK
6 SIMON CT
7 GRITLEY WLK
8 BREAN WLK

C2
1 HANSEN WLK
2 TANPIT WLK
3 SAXHOLME WLK
4 BRAMBLE WLK
5 AVENING WLK
6 RUSLAND WLK

130

D1
1 SUFFIELD WLK
2 SCALBY WLK
3 BYLAND WLK
4 MOSSACK AVE
5 KNOWE AVE
6 WIGHURST WLK
7 ALTAIR AVE
8 SAFFRON WLK

122

F3
1 KETLEY WLK
2 BRETLAND WLK
3 SAXBROOK WLK
4 SANDYSHOT WLK
5 BRICKNELL WLK
6 WILLITON WLK
7 COLYTON WLK

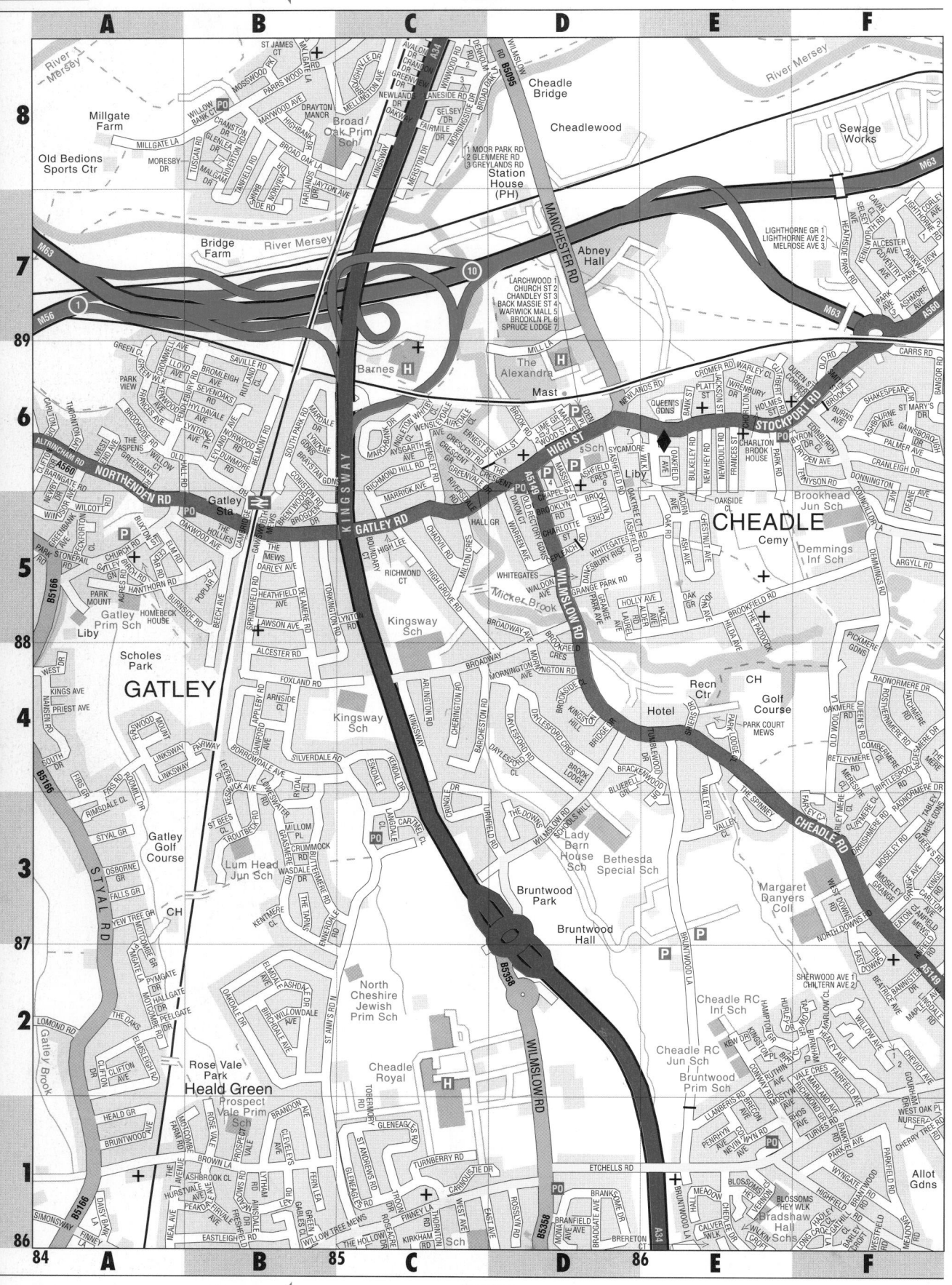

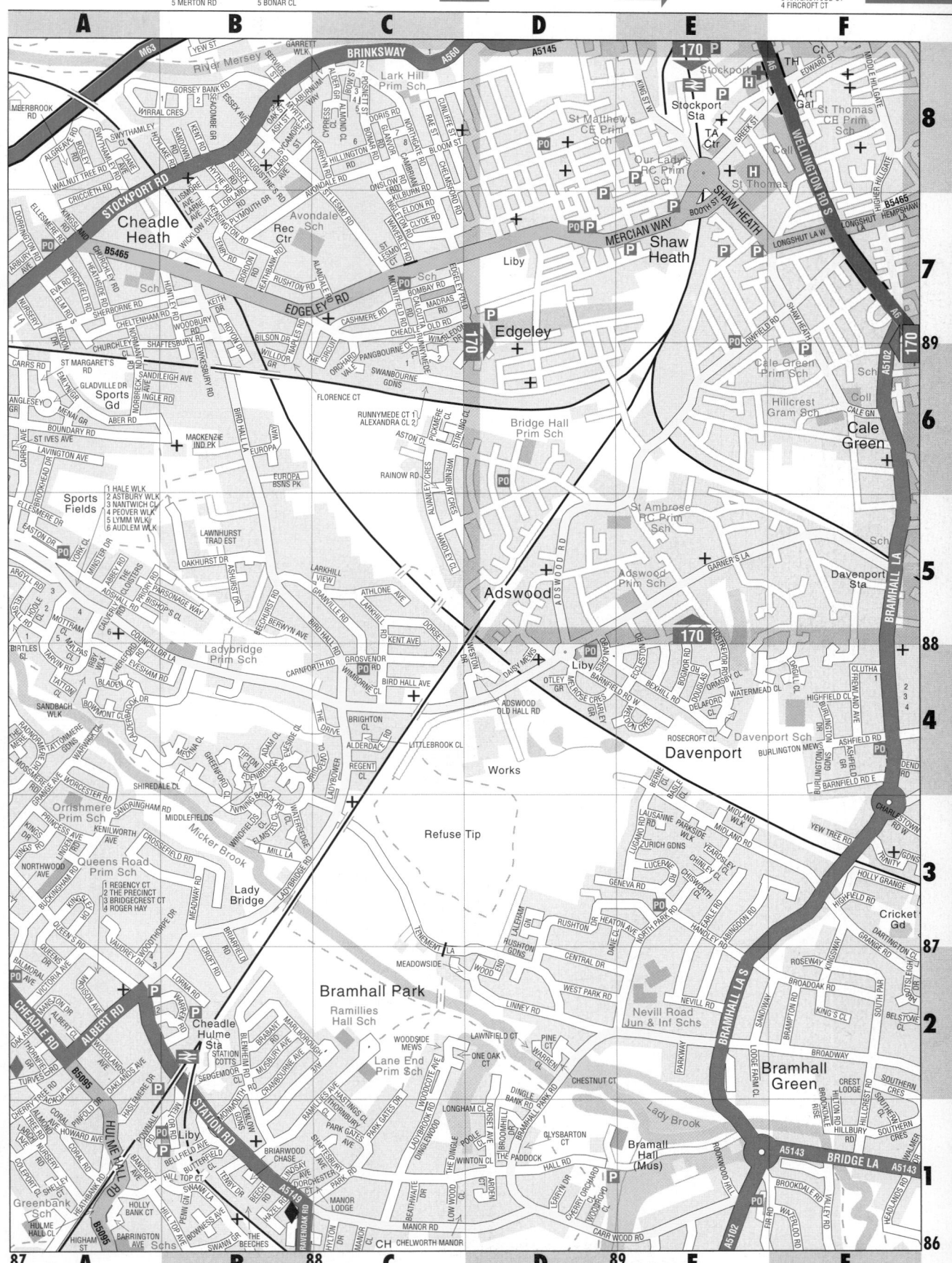

B8
1 TRANMERE RD
2 EGREMONT GR
3 ST JOHNS WLK
4 STOCKTON AVE
5 MERTON CL

C8
1 BRINKSWAY TRAD EST
2 HIGHFIELD ST
3 BENNETT ST
4 BENNETT CL
5 BONAR CL

6 CONGHAM RD
7 LLANFAIR RD
8 LAINTON CT

F4
1 HAWTHORN LODGE
2 OAKLEIGH
3 RAVENSWOOD CT
4 FIRCROFT CT

111
124
132
124

For full street detail of the highlighted area see page 170.

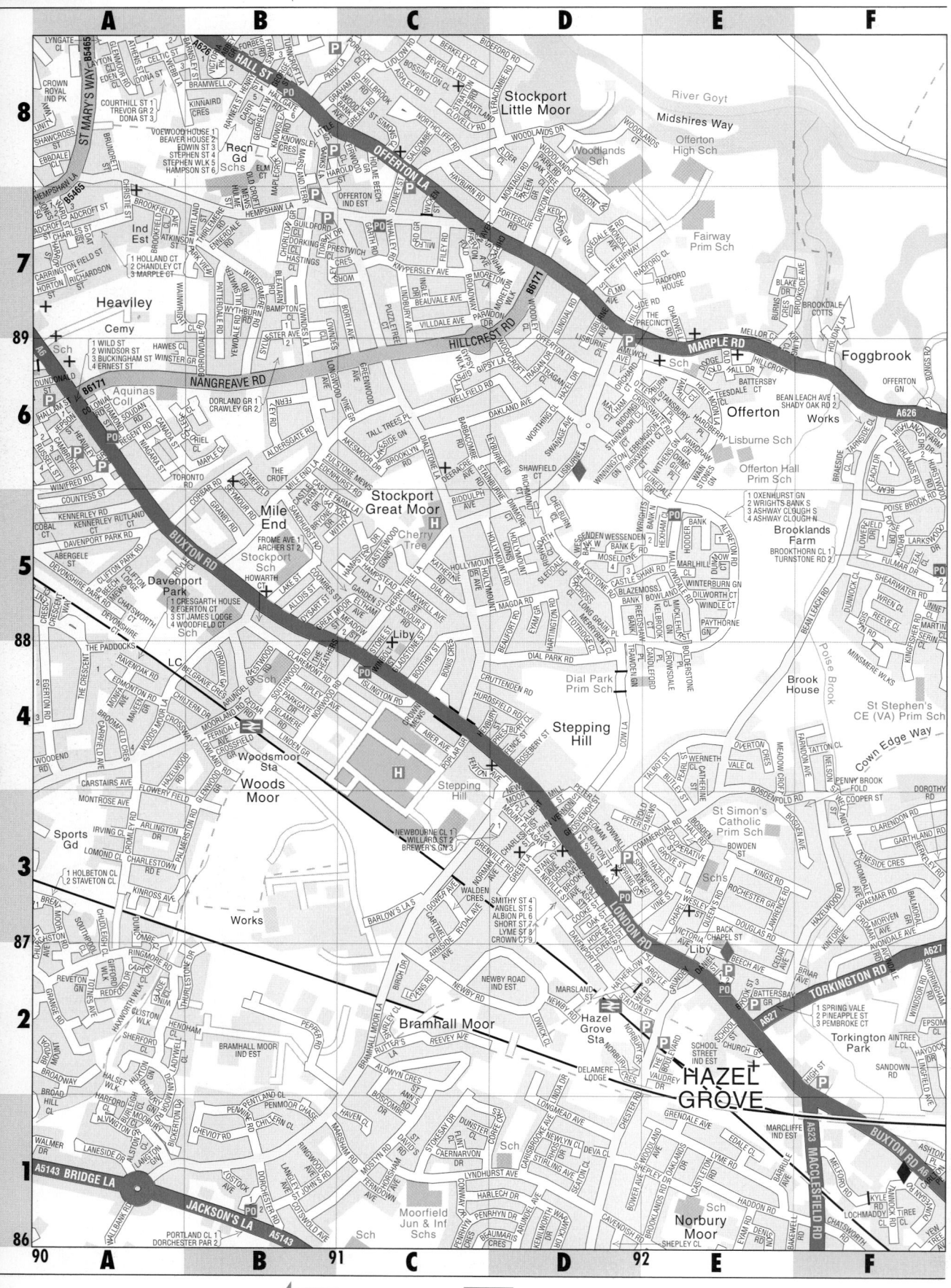

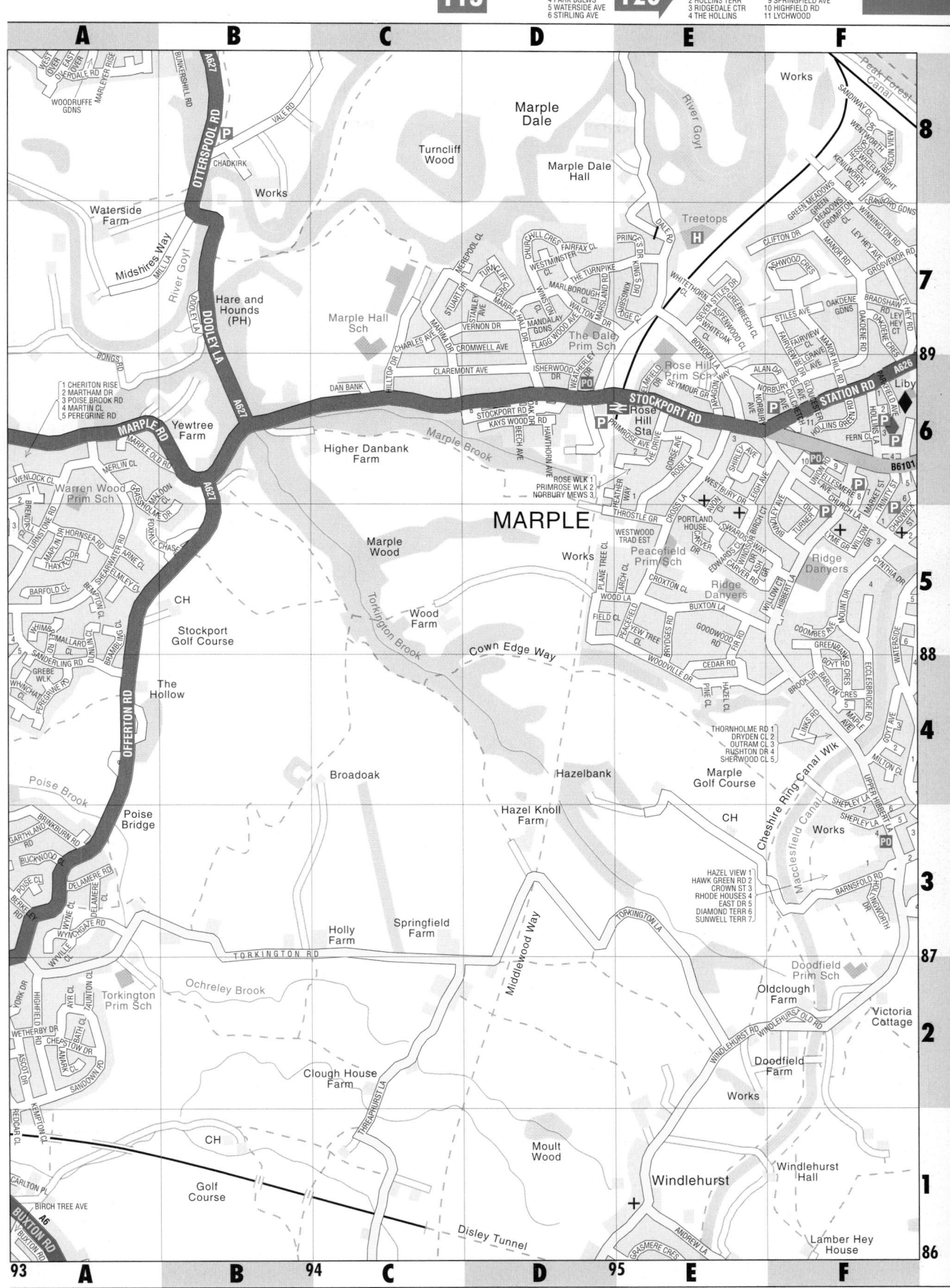

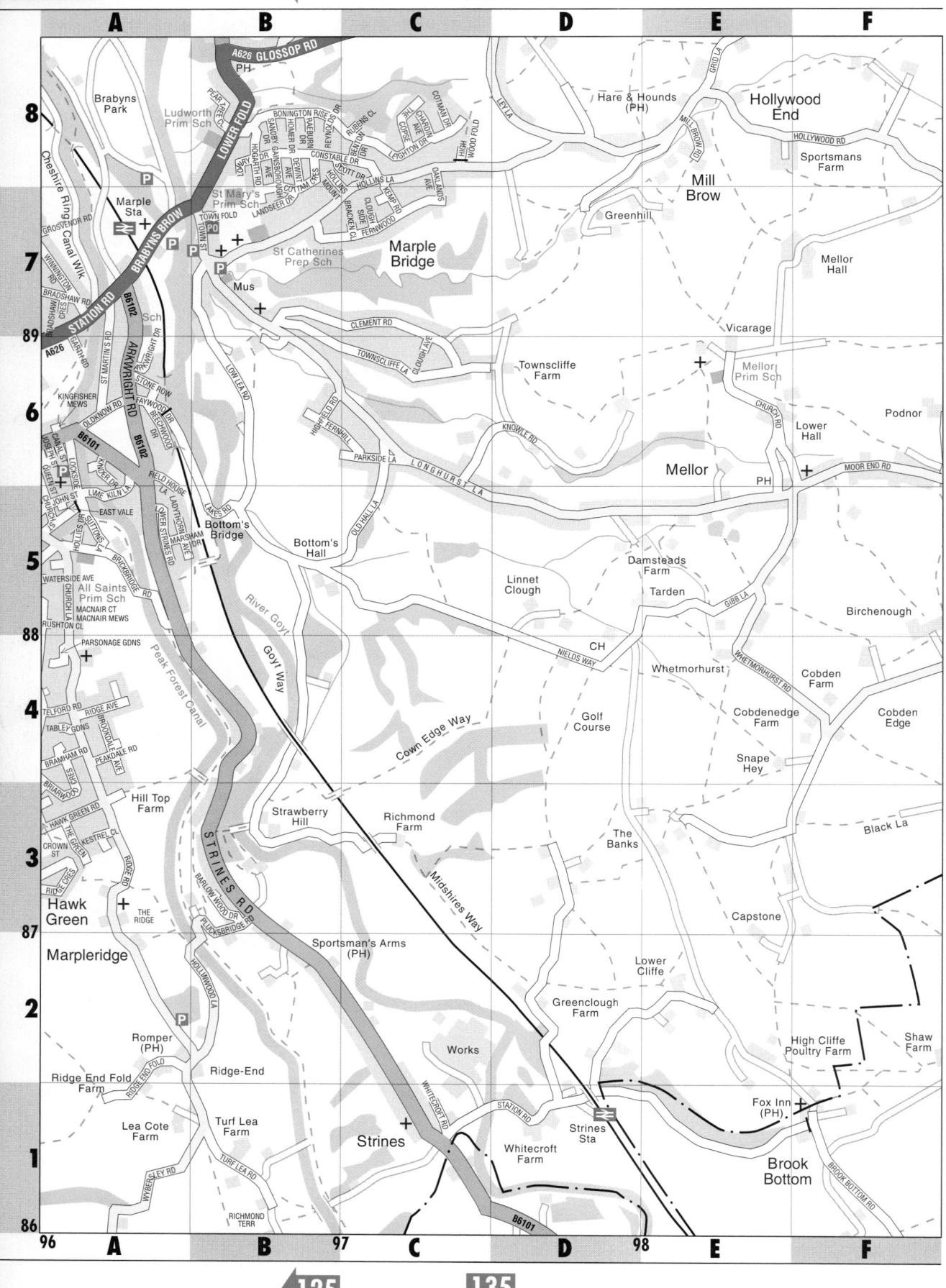

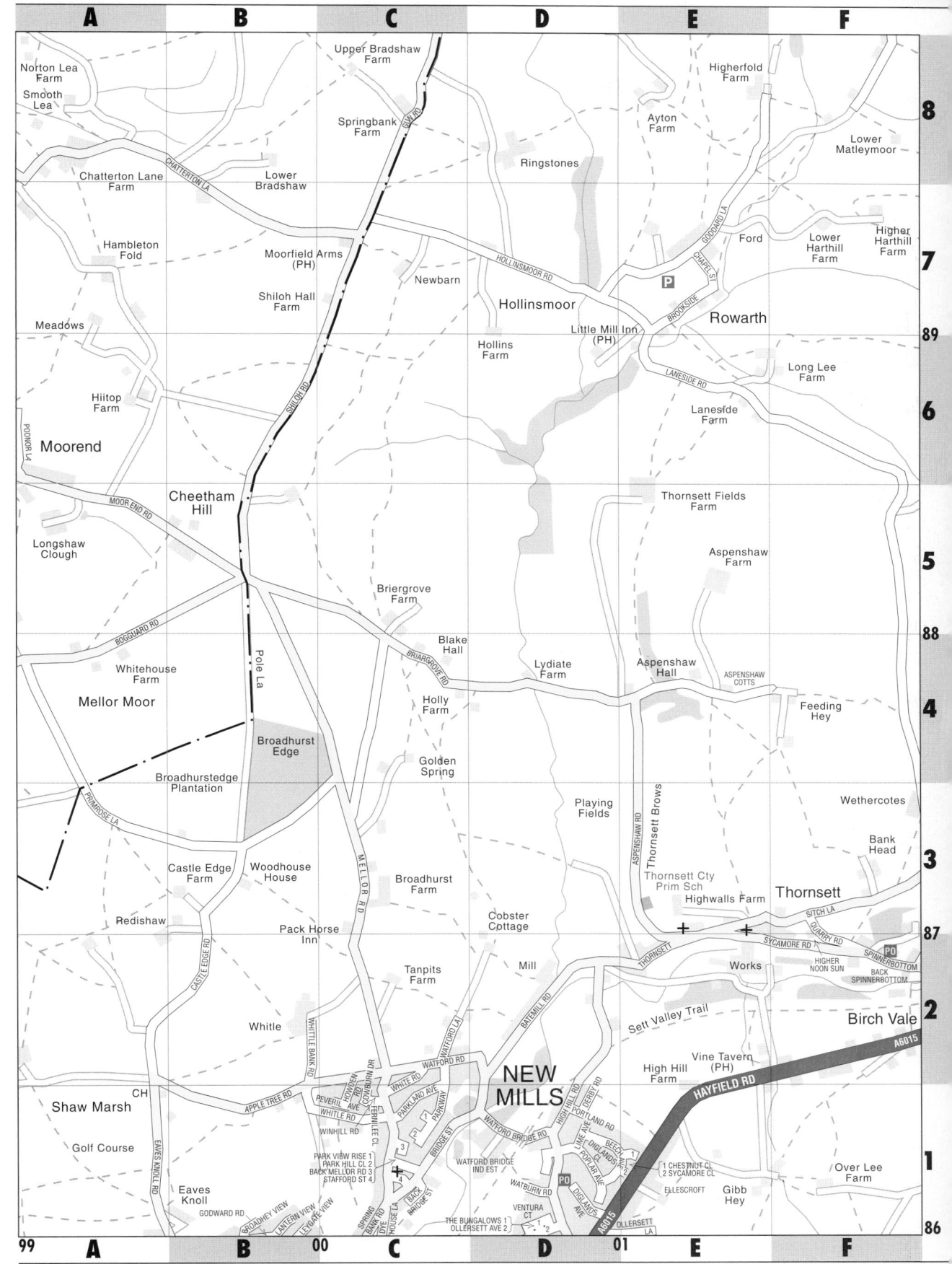

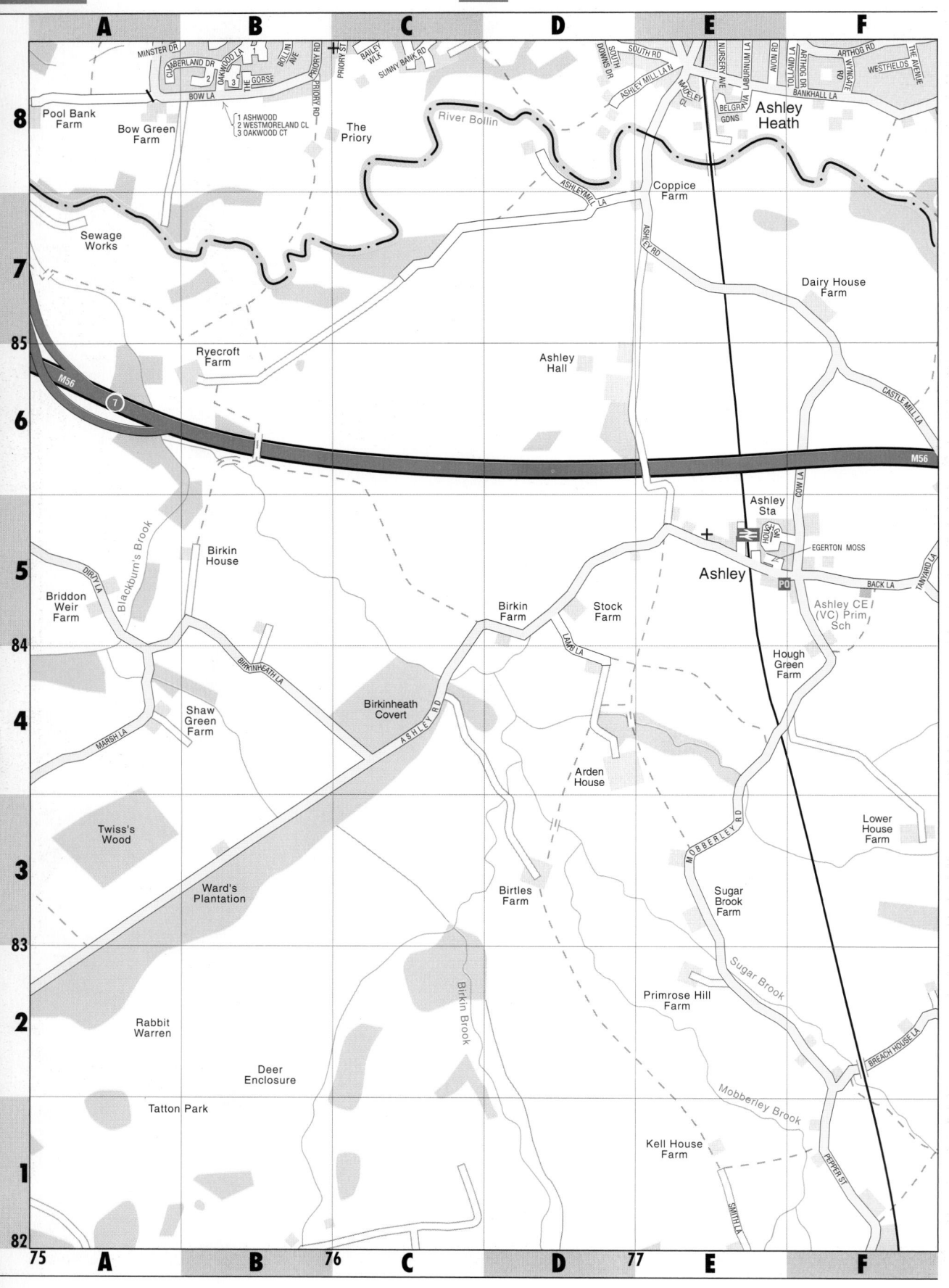

122

D5
1 TARVIN WAY
2 OVERTON WAY
3 STRETTON WAY
4 BIRTLES WAY
5 PEACOCK WAY
6 KELSALL WAY

7 CUDDINGTON WAY
8 WILLASTOR WAY
9 NORBURY WAY
10 PICKMERE CT
11 EASTHAM WAY
12 UPTON WAY
13 ASTON WAY

132

14 HOOTON WAY
15 CHRISTLETON WAY
E5
1 SUTTON WAY
2 CHELFORD CT
3 SOMERFORD WAY
4 TATTON CT

5 MARTON WAY
6 NANTWICH WAY
7 HASSALL WAY
8 MARTHALL WAY

137

D1
1 MILLBROOK GR
2 REDBROOK GR
3 SHELBROOK GR
4 WADEBROOK GR
5 DINGLEBROOK GR
6 LIME WLK
7 CROWBROOK GR

D2
1 TARBROOK GR
2 CLIFFBROOK GR
3 BENSON WLK
4 CARDENBROOK GR
5 TIMBERSBROOK GR
6 LADYBROOK GR
7 FODEN WLK
8 TAME WLK

132

D4
1 HILLBRE WAY
2 SEALAND WAY
3 ECCLESTON WAY
4 HELSBY WAY
5 HEATLEY WAY
6 ELWORTH WAY
7 PARKGATE WAY

E1
1 BUDWORTH WLK
2 EDLESTONE GR
3 WOODCOTT GR
4 KETTLESHULME WLK
5 TILSTON WLK
6 SNAPEBROOK GR
7 DAIRYBROOK GR
8 APPLETON WLK
9 MOORSBROOK GR

10 RAINOW WAY
11 PEAKFORTON WLK
12 SALTERSBROOK GR
13 PINWOOD CT

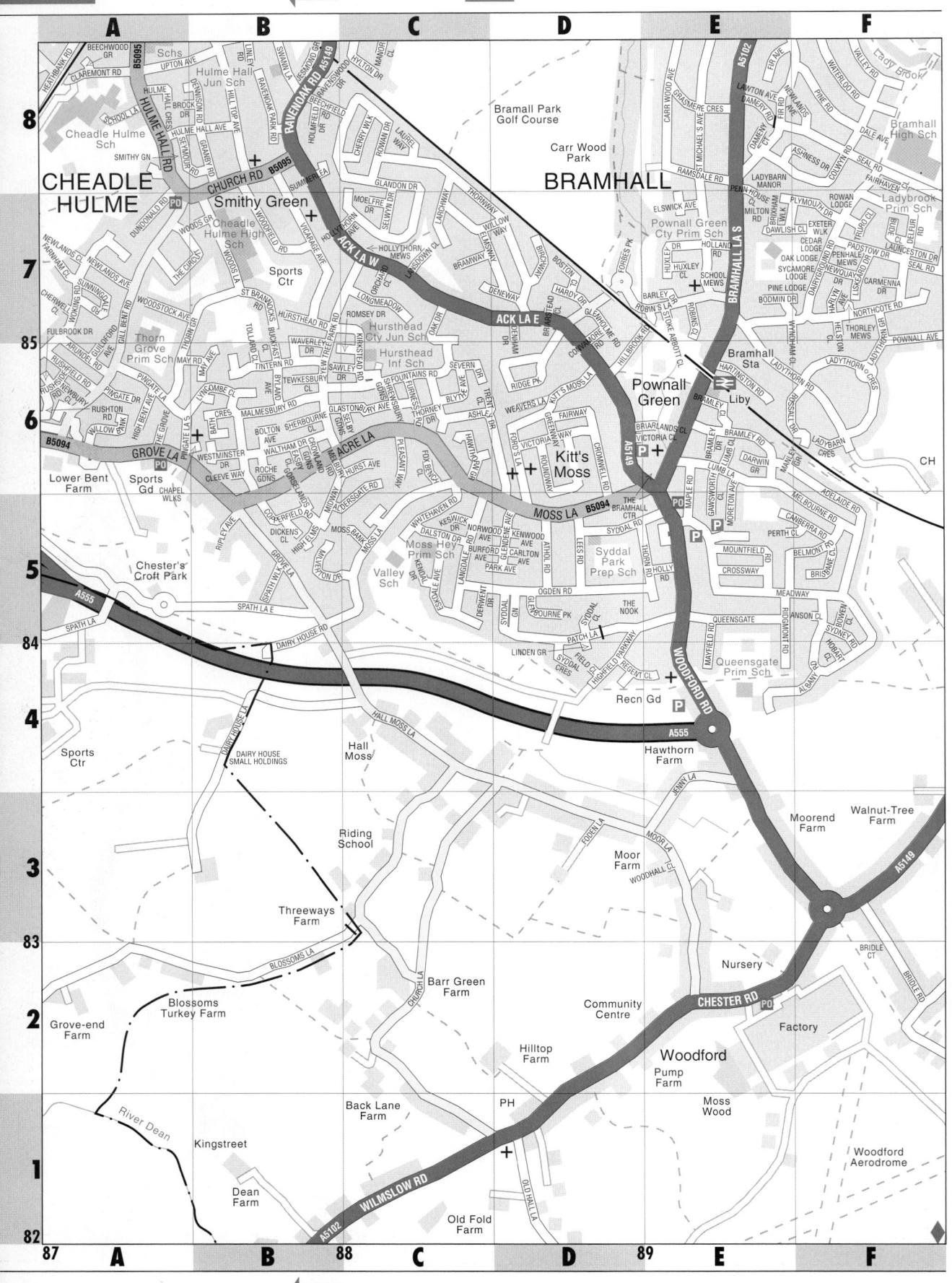

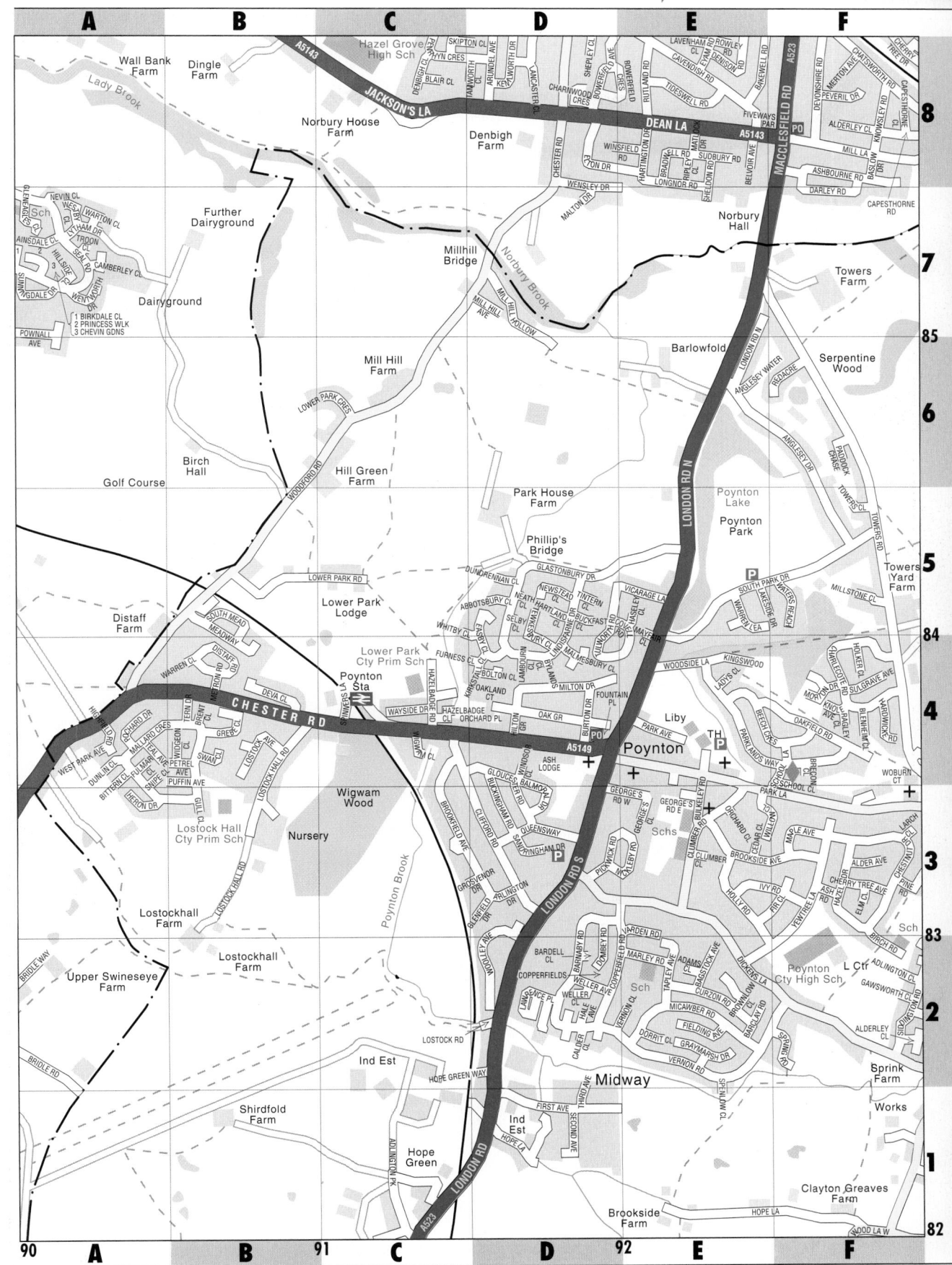

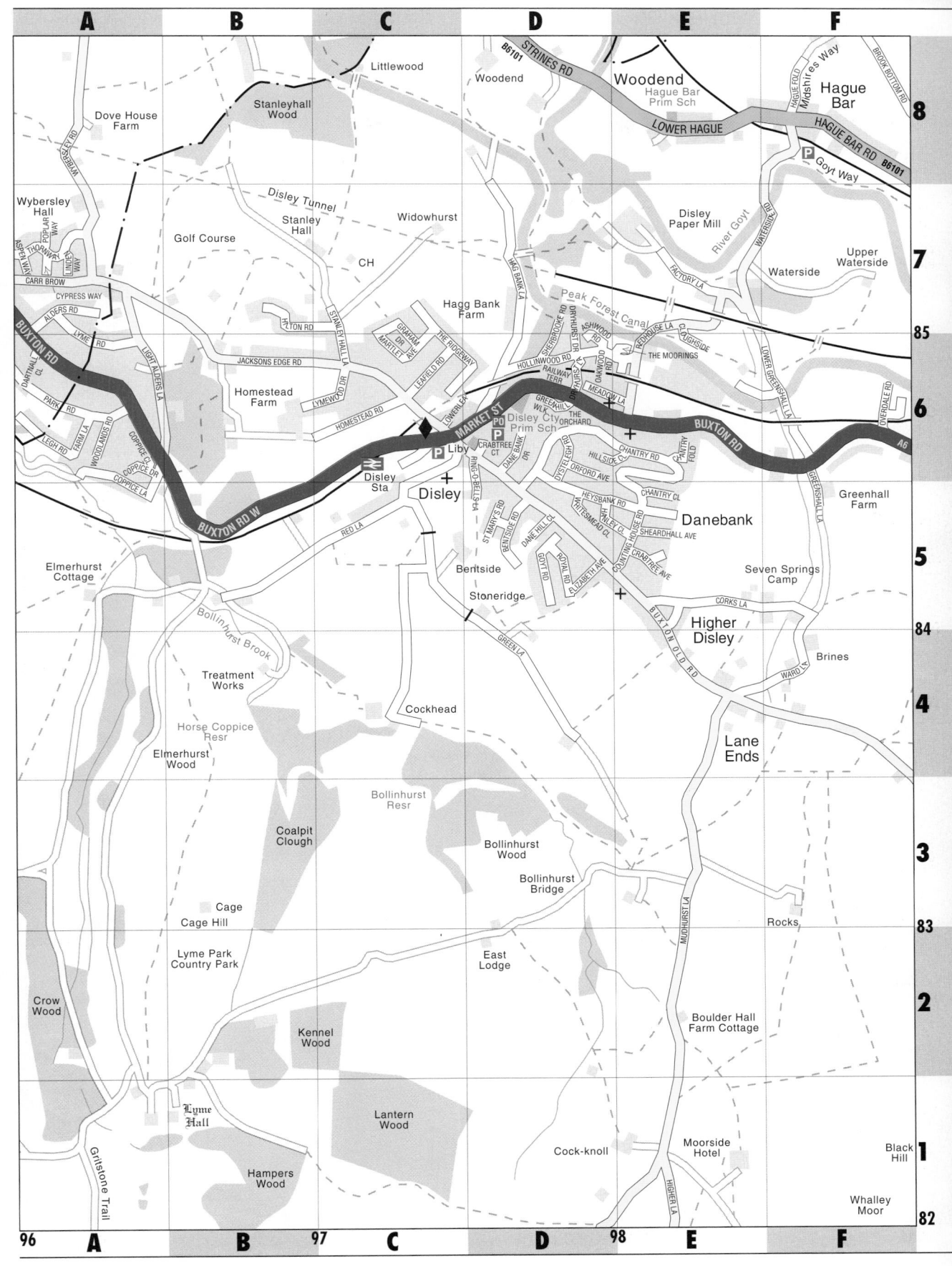

A B C D E F

8

Littlewood
Woodend
STRINES RD
B6101
Woodend
Hague Bar Prim Sch
Hague Bar
LOWER HAGUE
HAGUE BAR RD
B6101
Midshires Way
HAGUE FOLD
BROOK BOTTOM RD

Dove House Farm
Stanleyhall Wood

WYBERSLEY RD
Wybersley Hall
ASPEN WAY
THORN WAY
POPLAR WAY
LINDEN WAY

Disley Tunnel
Stanley Hall
Widowhurst
CH

Disley Paper Mill
River Goyt
Waterside
WATERSIDE RD
Upper Waterside

7

Golf Course

CARR BROW
CYPRESS WAY
ALDERS RD
LYME RD
LIGHT ALDERS LA
HYTON RD
STANLEY HALL LA
JACKSONS EDGE RD
LYMEWOOD DR

GRAHAM DR
MARTLET AVE
THE RIDGEWAY
LEAFIELD RD
HAGG BANK LA

Hagg Bank Farm
Peak Forest Canal
SHERBROOK RD
DRYHURST DR
ASHWOOD RD
OAKWOOD RD
REDHOUSE LA
CLAGHSIDE
LOWER GREENSHALL LA

85

DARNHALL CL
PARK RD
LEGH RD
FARM LA
WOODLANDS RD
COPPICE CL
COPPICE DR
COPPICE LA

Homestead Farm
HOMESTEAD RD

Hollinwood Rd
RAILWAY TERR
GREENHILL WLK
MEADOW LA
THE MOORINGS

OVERDALE RD
GREENSHALL LA

6

BUXTON RD
BUXTON RD W

Disley Sta
Disley
Liby
MARKET ST
PO
Disley Cty Prim Sch
CRABTREE CT
DANE BANK DR
RING-O-BELLS LA
ST MARY'S RD
BENTSIDE RD
DYSELEIGH RD
ORFORD AVE
THE ORCHARD
HILLSIDE CL
CHANTRY RD
CHANTRY CL
PARITY FOLD

BUXTON RD
A6
Greenhall Farm

Elmerhurst Cottage
RED LA
Bentside
Stoneridge
DANE HILL CL
GOYT RD
ROYAL RD
HEYSBANK RD
WHALEY CL
WHITESMEAD CL
SHEARDHALL AVE
ELIZABETH AVE
COUNTING HOUSE RD
CRABTREE AVE

Danebank
Seven Springs Camp

5

Bollinhurst Brook
Treatment Works
GREEN LA
CORKS LA
BUXTON OLD RD
Higher Disley
WARD LA
Brines

84

Horse Coppice Resr
Elmerhurst Wood
Cockhead
Lane Ends

4

Bollinhurst Resr
Coalpit Clough
Bollinhurst Wood
Bollinhurst Bridge
MUDHURST LA
Rocks

3

Cage
Cage Hill
East Lodge

83

Lyme Park Country Park
Boulder Hall Farm Cottage

2

Crow Wood
Kennel Wood

Lyme Hall
Lantern Wood
Cock-knoll
Moorside Hotel
HIGHER LA
Black Hill

1

Gritstone Trail
Hampers Wood
Whalley Moor

82

96 A B 97 C D 98 E F

130

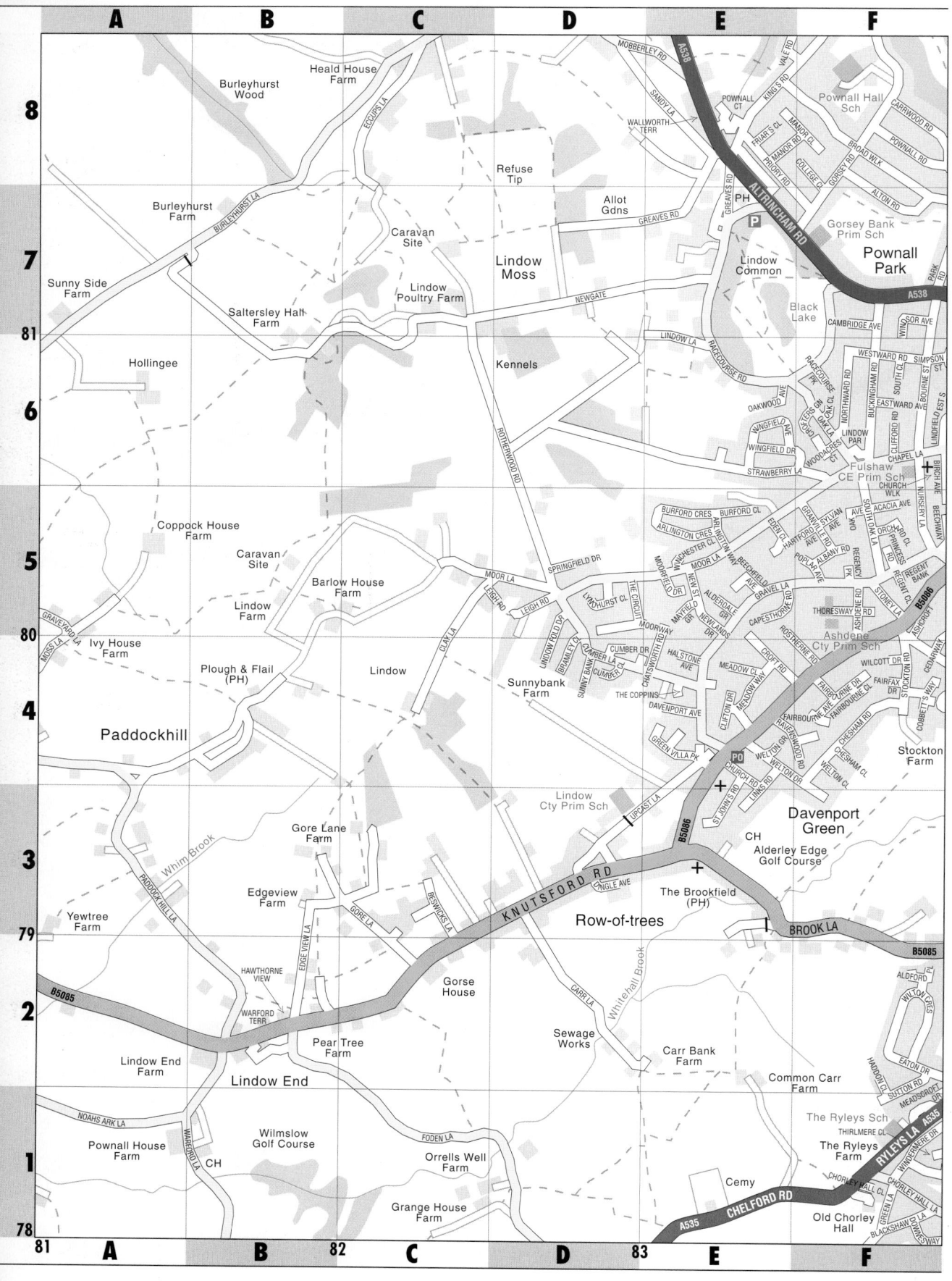

A B C D E F

8
7
81
6
5
80
4
3
79
2
1
78

81 A B 82 C D 83 E F

Burleyhurst Wood

Heald House Farm

Refuse Tip

Allot Gdns

Pownall Hall Sch

MOBBERLEY RD

ALTRINCHAM RD

Pownall Park

Gorsey Bank Prim Sch

Burleyhurst Farm

Caravan Site

Lindow Moss

Lindow Common

Black Lake

Sunny Side Farm

Saltersley Hall Farm

Lindow Poultry Farm

NEWGATE

Lindow La

Fulshaw CE Prim Sch

Hollingee

Kennels

RACECOURSE RD

ROTHERWOOD RD

Coppock House Farm

Caravan Site

Barlow House Farm

Lindow Farm

MOOR LA

LEIGH RD

SPRINGFIELD DR

Ashdene Cty Prim Sch

Ivy House Farm

CLAY LA

Lindow

Sunnybank Farm

Plough & Flail (PH)

Paddockhill

Davenport Green

Alderley Edge Golf Course

Gore Lane Farm

Lindow Cty Prim Sch

Whim Brook

PADDOCK HILL LA

Edgeview Farm

GORE LA

BESWICKS LA

KNUTSFORD RD

Row-of-trees

The Brookfield (PH)

BROOK LA

B5085

Yewtree Farm

EDGE VIEW LA

Hawthorne View

Gorse House

Warford Terr

CARR LA

Whitehall Brook

Sewage Works

Carr Bank Farm

Common Carr Farm

B5085

Pear Tree Farm

Lindow End Farm

Lindow End

NOAHS ARK LA

WARFORD LA

Pownall House Farm

CH

Wilmslow Golf Course

FODEN LA

Orrells Well Farm

Grange House Farm

Cemy

The Ryleys Sch

The Ryleys Farm

RYLEYS LA

A535

CHELFORD RD

Old Chorley Hall

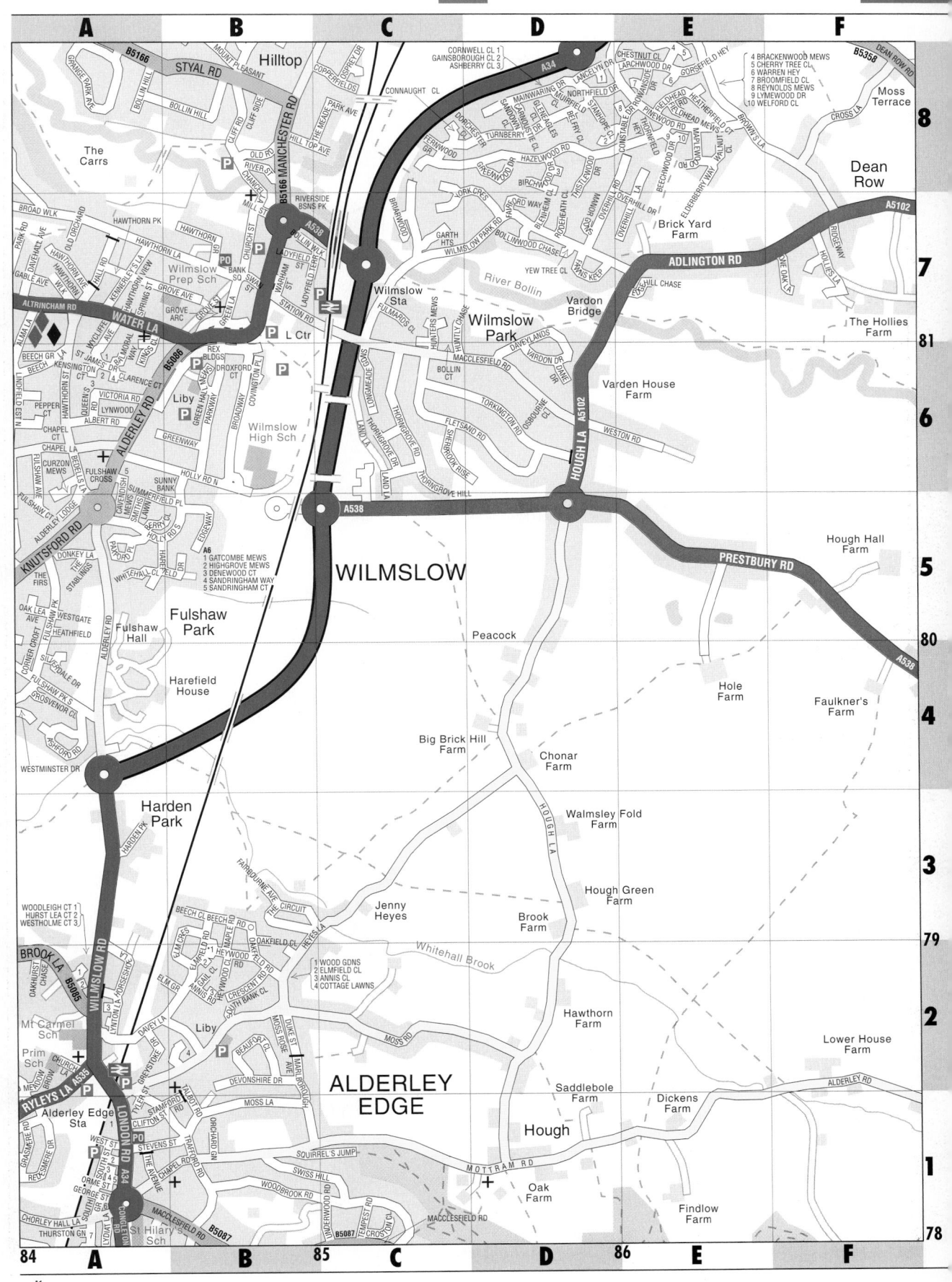

A1
1 THE PARADE
2 BROWN ST
3 GREEN ST
4 MASSEY ST
5 CHAPEL ST
6 HUBERT WORTHINGTON HOUSE
7 CARLISLE ST

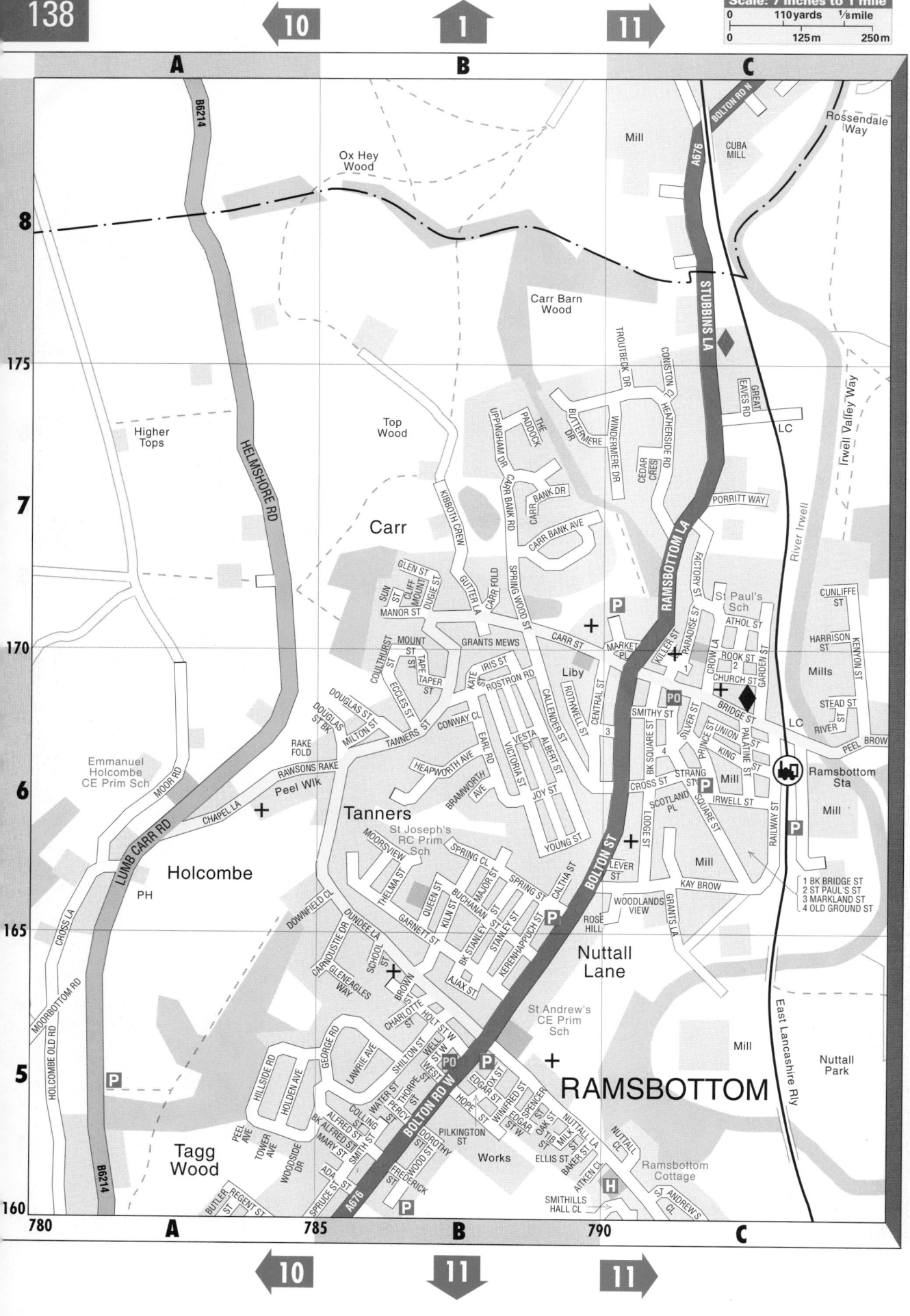

Scale: 7 inches to 1 mile
0 ... 110 yards ... ⅛ mile
0 ... 125m ... 250m

B6214

Ox Hey Wood

BOLTON RD N
A676
CUBA MILL
Rossendale Way

Mill

STUBBINS LA

Carr Barn Wood

HELMSHORE RD

GREAT EAVES RD
CONISTON CL
HETHERSIDE RD
LC
Irwell Valley Way

175

Higher Tops

Top Wood

TROUTBECK DR
BUTTERMERE DR
WINDERMERE DR
CEDAR CRES
FACTORY ST
PORRITT WAY
River Irwell

Carr

7

THE PADDOCK
UPPINGHAM DR
CARR BANK RD
CARR BANK DR
CARR BANK AVE
SPRING WOOD DR
KIBBOTH CREW
GUTTER LA
CARR FOLD

RAMSBOTTOM LA
St Paul's Sch
CUNLIFFE ST
Mills

GLEN ST
CLIFF MOUNT
DUGIE ST
SUN ST
MANOR ST
CARR ST
ATHOL ST
KENYON ST
HARRISON ST
STEAD ST

170

COULTHURST
MOUNT ST
TAPE ST
TAPER ST
KATE
IRIS ST
ROSTRON RD
GRANTS MEWS
Liby
Market PL
KILLER ST
PARADISE ST
CROW LA
ROOK
ST
2
1
GARDEN ST
Mills
LC
RIVER
PEEL BROW

DOUGLAS ST BK
ECCLES ST
MILTON ST
CONWAY CL
CALLENDER ST
ROTHWELL ST
CENTRAL ST
SMITHY ST
CHURCH ST
BRIDGE ST
SILVER ST

DOUGLAS ST
TANNERS ST
EARL RD
VESTA ST
ALBERT ST
3
PRINCE ST
UNION ST
PALATINE ST
KING ST

RAKE FOLD
HEAPWORTH AVE
VICTORIA ST
BK SQUARE ST
4
STRANG ST

RAWSONS RAKE
BRAMWORTH AVE
JOY ST
CROSS ST
SCOTLAND PL
SQUARE ST
IRWELL ST
Mill
Ramsbottom Sta

6

Peel Wlk
YOUNG ST
LODGE ST
Mill
RAILWAY ST

Emmanuel Holcombe CE Prim Sch
MOOR RD
CHAPEL LA

LUMB CARR RD

LEVER ST
KAY BROW

Tanners
St Joseph's RC Prim Sch
MOORSVIEW
SPRING CL
SPRING ST
CALTHA ST
WOODLANDS VIEW
GRANTS LA
1 BK BRIDGE ST
2 ST PAUL'S ST
3 MARKLAND ST
4 OLD GROUND ST

Holcombe
PH

THELMA ST
QUEEN ST
BUCHANAN
KILN ST
MAJOR ST

BOLTON ST
ROSE HILL

165

Nuttall Lane

CROSS LA
MOORBOTTOM RD
HOLCOMBE OLD RD

DOWNFIELD CL
DUNDEE LA
SCHOOL
GARNETT ST
BK STANLEY ST
STANLEY ST
KERENHAPPUCH ST

East Lancashire Rly

CARNOUSTIE DR
GLENEAGLES WAY
BROWN
AJAX ST

St Andrew's CE Prim Sch
Mill
Nuttall Park

HILLSIDE RD
GEORGE RD
CHARLOTTE ST
HOLT ST W
WELL ST W

RAMSBOTTOM

5

P
LAWRIE AVE
HOLDEN AVE
SHILTON ST
WATER ST
THORPE ST
WEST ST W
PO
HOPE ST
EDGAR ST W
SPENCER ST
OAK ST
NUTTALL LA
Mill

PEEL AVE
TOWER AVE
WOODSIDE DR
BK ALFRED ST
ALFRED ST
MARY ST
SMITH ST
ADA ST
DOROTHY ST
WOOD ST
WINIFRED ST
EDGAR ST W
ST
TIB
MILK
BAKER ST
ELLIS ST
AITKEN CL
NUTTALL CL
Ramsbottom Cottage

Tagg Wood
BUTLER ST
REGENT ST
SPRUCE ST
FREDERICK ST
PILKINGTON ST
Works

BOLTON RD W
A676
SMITHILLS HALL CL
H
ST ANDREW'S CL

B6214

160

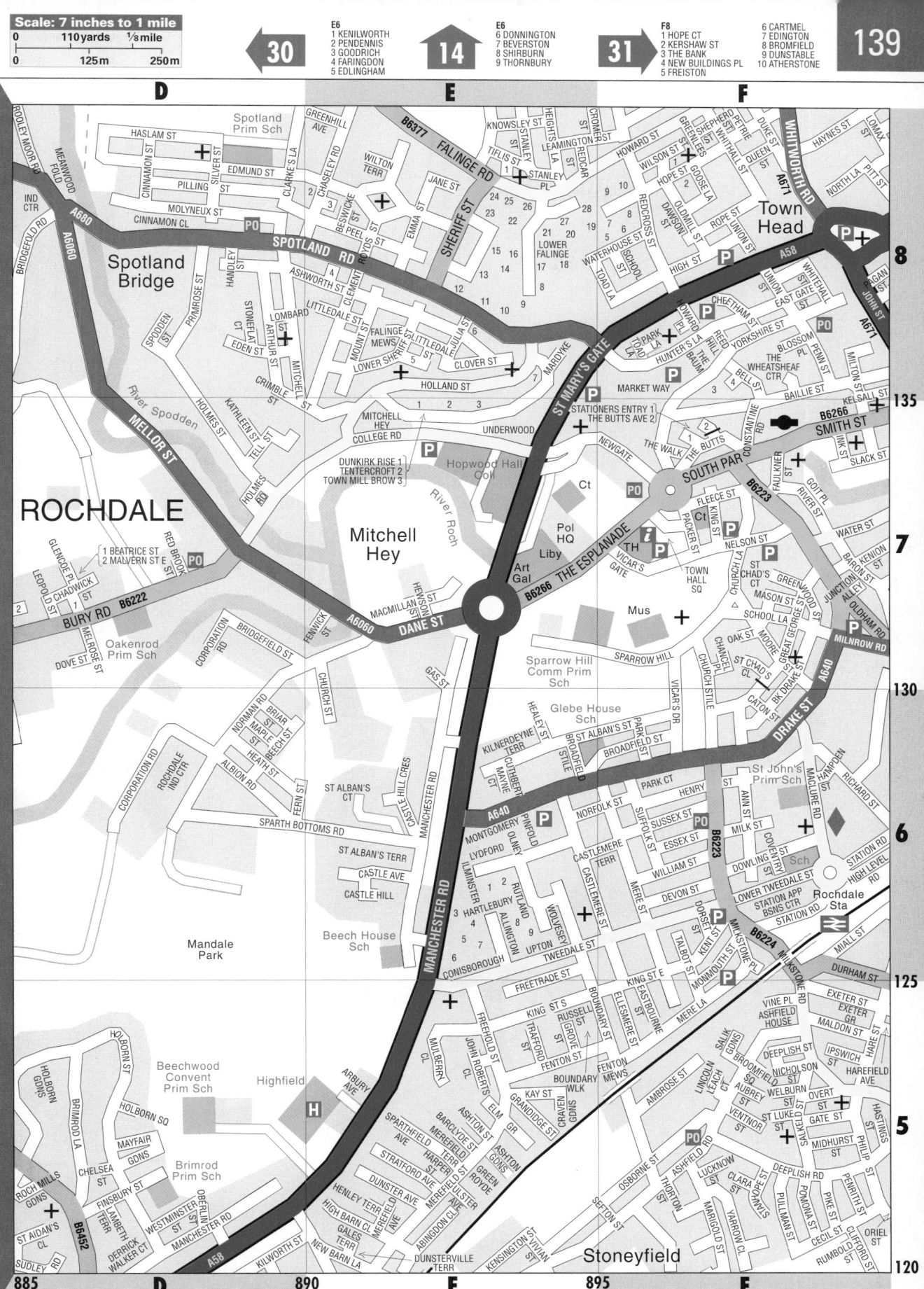

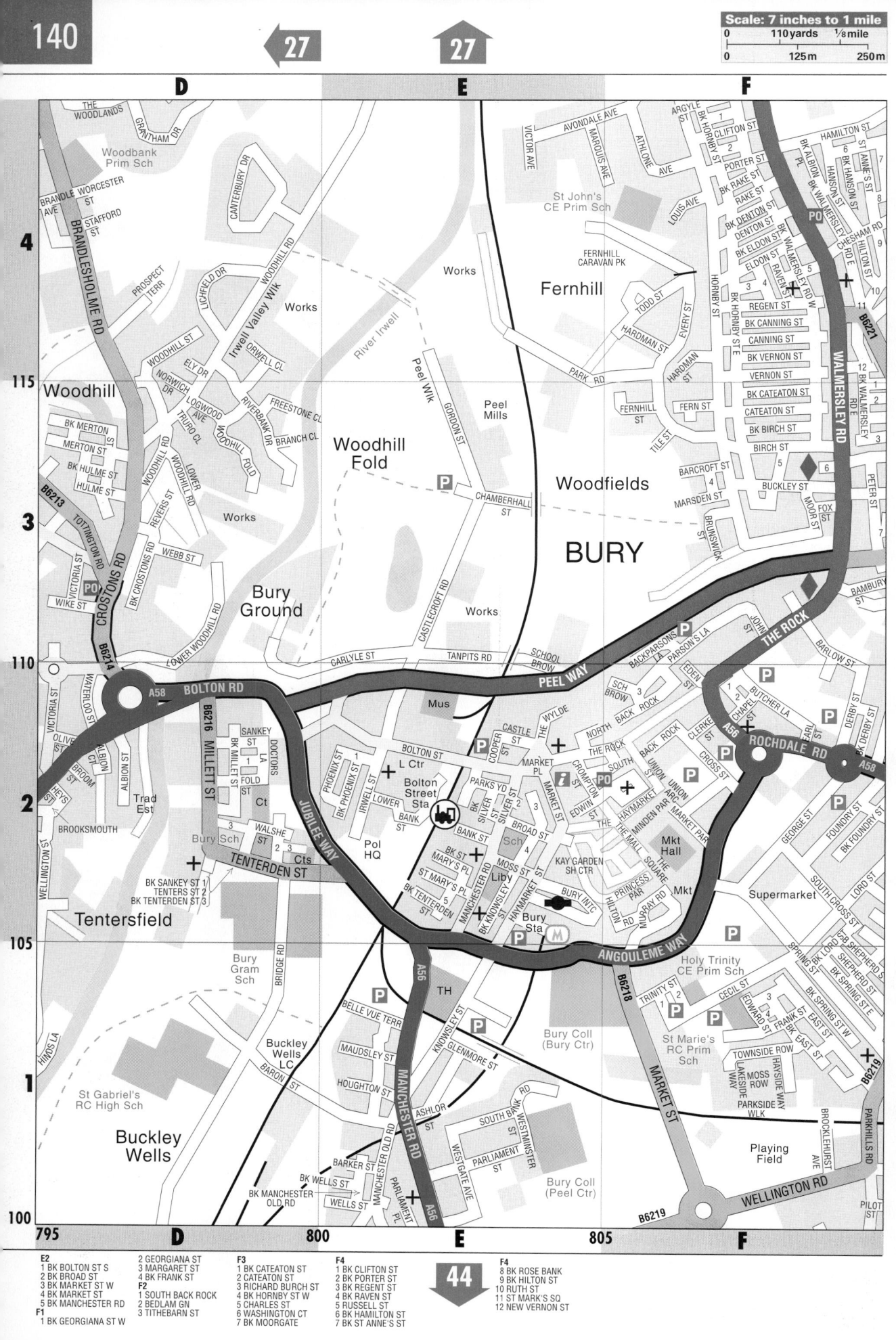

Scale: 7 inches to 1 mile

0   110 yards   ⅛ mile

0   125 m   250 m

27   27

D   E   F

4

THE WOODLANDS

GRANTHAM DR

Woodbank Prim Sch

CANTERBURY DR

BRANDLE WORCESTER AVE
STAFFORD ST
WORCESTER ST

PROSPECT TERR

LICHFIELD DR

WOODHILL RD

ORWELL CL

Irwell Valley Wlk

River Irwell

Works

Works

Works

ELY DR

WOODHILL ST

NORWICH DR

TRURO CL

RIVERBANK DR

FREESTONE CL

BRANCH CL

LOGWOOD AVE

WOODHILL FOLD

LOWER WOODHILL RD

Peel Wlk

Works

Peel Mills

GORDON ST

VICTOR AVE

AVONDALE AVE

MARQUIS AVE

ATHLONE AVE

LOUIS AVE

St John's CE Prim Sch

Fernhill

Fernhill CARAVAN PK

PARK RD

TODD ST

HARDMAN ST

EVERY ST

HORNBY ST

Works

ARGYLE ST
BK HORNBY ST
CLIFTON ST
PORTER ST
RAKE ST
BK RAKE ST

HAMILTON ST
BK ALBION ST
HANSON RD
BK WALMERSLEY RD
ANNE'S ST
BK HANSON ST

BK DENTON ST
DENTON ST
BK ELDON ST
ELDON ST
BK HORNBY ST E
BK CANNING ST
CANNING ST
BK VERNON ST
VERNON ST
BK CATEATON ST
CATEATON ST
BK BIRCH ST

REGENT ST

CHESHAM RD E
HILTON ST

WALMERSLEY RD

B6221

BK WALMERSLEY RD

PETER ST

BAMBURY

115

Woodhill

BK MERTON ST
MERTON ST
BK HULME ST
HULME ST
WOODHILL RD

WEBB ST

BK CROSTONS RD

CROSTONS RD

B6213

TOTTINGTON RD

VICTORIA ST

WIKE ST

PO

Woodhill Fold

P

CHAMBERHALL ST

CASTLECROFT RD

Works

Woodfields

TILE ST

FERNHILL ST

FERN ST

MARSDEN ST

BRUNSWICK ST

HARDMAN ST

BARCROFT ST

BIRCH ST

Buckley ST

BK BIRCH ST

MOOR ST

FOX ST

3

Bury Ground

CARLYLE ST

TANPITS RD

SCHOOL BROW

Works

BURY

THE ROCK

JOHN ST

BARLOW ST

DERBY ST

110

B6214

A58

BOLTON RD

BOLTON RD

PEEL WAY

Mus

BACKPARSONS LA
PARSON'S LA
EDEN ST
BACK ROCK
CHAPEL ST
BUTCHER LA

A56

ROCHDALE RD

A58

2

VICTORIA ST
WATERLOO ST
OLIVER ST
ALBION ST
BROOM ST
HEYS ST
WELLINGTON ST

Brooksmouth

Trad Est

MILLETT ST

B6216

SANKEY ST

BK MILLETT ST

DOCTORS
LA
FOLD
Ct

JUBILEE WAY

WALSHE ST

Bury Sch

Cts

TENTERDEN ST

BK SANKEY ST 1
TENTERS ST 2
BK TENTERDEN ST 3

Tentersfield

PHOENIX ST

BK PHOENIX ST

IRWELL ST

LOWER BANK ST

BOLTON ST

L Ctr

Bolton Street Sta

Pol HQ

BK ST MARY'S PL
ST MARY'S PL

BANK ST

BK ST

BK TENTERDEN

BK KNOWLSLEY RD

MANCHESTER RD

Liby

Sch

MOSS ST

HAYMARKET

Bury Sta

CASTLE ST

THE WYLDE

COOPER ST

MARKET PL

PARKS YD

SILVER ST

BK SILVER ST

BROAD ST

EDWIN ST

CROMPTON ST

THE ROCK

NORTH ST

SOUTH ST

HAYMARKET ST

THE MALL

UNION ARC

KAY GARDEN SH CTR

PRINCESS PARK ST

Bury INTC

BACK ROCK

UNION ST

CROSS ST

CLERKE ST

MINDEN ARC

Mkt Hall

THE SQUARE

RAY RD

Mkt

HILTON ST

M

GEORGE ST

LORD ST

BK FOUNDRY ST

FOUNDRY ST

Supermarket

SOUTH CROSS ST

105

Bury Gram Sch

BRIDGE RD

BELLE VUE TERR

P

TH

A56

KNOWSLEY ST

P

GLENMORE ST

Buckley Wells LC

MAUDSLEY ST

HOUGHTON ST

BARON ST

ANGOULEME WAY

B6218

Bury Coll (Bury Ctr)

TRINITY ST

CECIL ST

MARKET ST

P

St Marie's RC Prim Sch

Holy Trinity CE Prim Sch

EDWARD ST
FRANK ST
EAST ST
FRANK ST E

BK SPRING ST
SPRING ST E

SPRING ST W

SHEPHERD ST
BK SHEPHERD S
BK LORD ST

TOWNSIDE ROW

MOSS ROW

LAKESIDE WAY

PARKSIDE WLK

HAYSIDE WAY

B6219

1

HINDS LA

St Gabriel's RC High Sch

Buckley Wells

ASHLOR ST

MANCHESTER OLD RD

BARKER ST

BK WELLS ST

BK MANCHESTER OLD RD

WELLS ST

PARLIAMENT ST

A56

WESTGATE AVE

PARLIAMENT ST

SOUTH BANK RD

WESTMINSTER RD

Bury Coll (Peel Ctr)

MARKET ST

BROCKLEHURST RD

PARKHILLS RD

Playing Field

WELLINGTON RD

PILOT ST

B6219

100

795   D   800   E   805   F

44

E2
1 BK BOLTON ST S
2 BK BROAD ST
3 BK MARKET ST W
4 BK MARKET ST
5 BK MANCHESTER RD
F1
1 BK GEORGIANA ST W

2 GEORGIANA ST
3 MARGARET ST
4 BK FRANK ST
F2
1 SOUTH BACK ROCK
2 BEDLAM GN
3 TITHEBARN ST

F3
1 BK CATEATON ST
2 CATEATON ST
3 RICHARD BURCH ST
4 BK HORNBY ST W
5 CHARLES ST
6 WASHINGTON CT
7 BK MOORGATE

F4
1 BK CLIFTON ST
2 BK PORTER ST
3 BK REGENT ST
4 BK RAVEN ST
5 RUSSELL ST
6 BK HAMILTON ST
7 BK ST ANNE'S ST

F4
8 BK ROSE BANK
9 BK HILTON ST
10 RUTH ST
11 ST MARK'S SQ
12 NEW VERNON ST

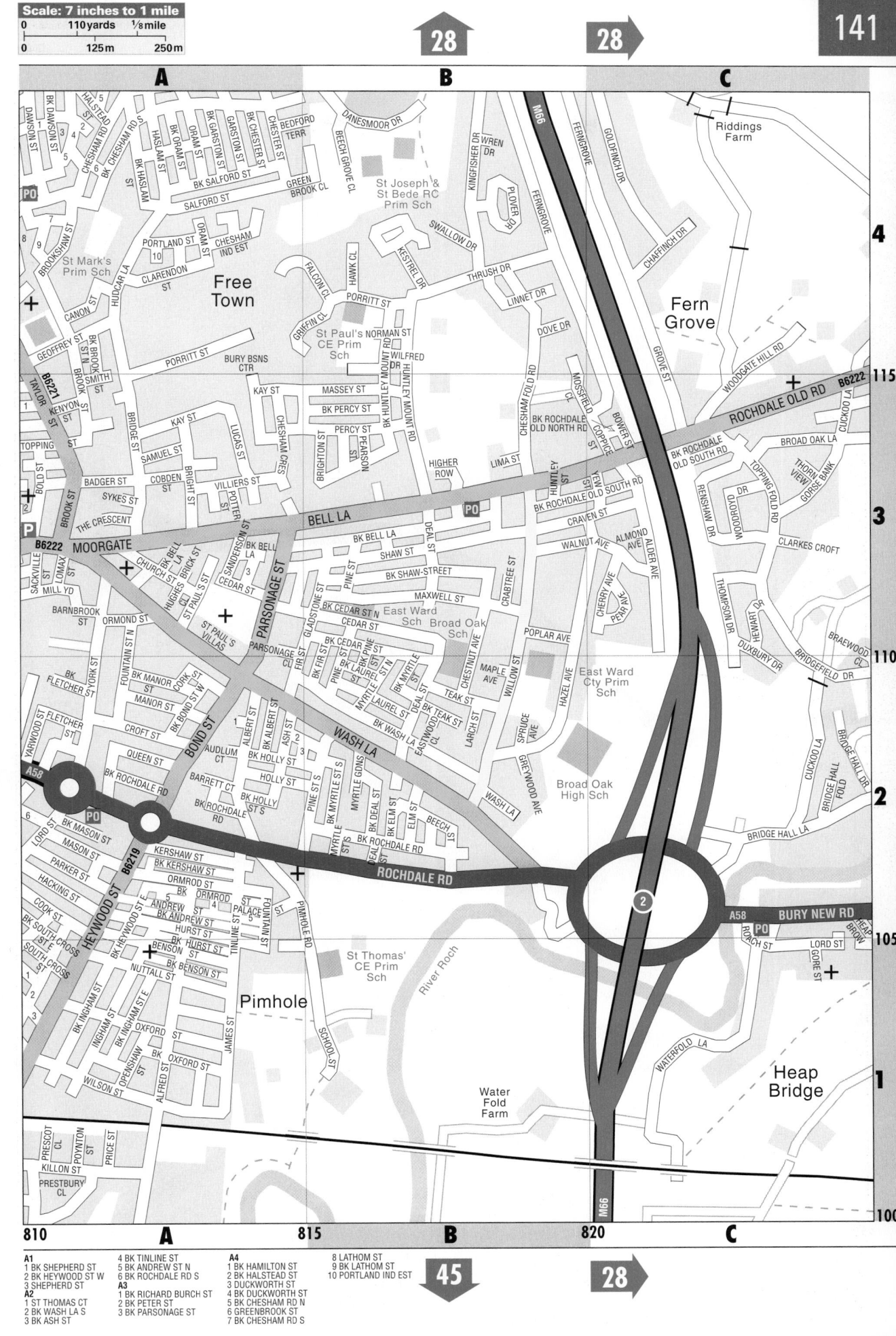

A   B   C

4

Riddings Farm

Fern Grove

115

B6222
ROCHDALE OLD RD

3

BELL LA

110

110

East Ward
Cty Prim
Sch

Broad Oak
High Sch

2

ROCHDALE RD

2

A58   BURY NEW RD   105

Pimhole

St Thomas'
CE Prim
Sch

River Roch

Heap
Bridge

1

Water
Fold
Farm

M66

100

A1
1 BK SHEPHERD ST
2 BK HEYWOOD ST W
3 SHEPHERD ST
A2
1 ST THOMAS CT
2 BK WASH LA S
3 BK ASH ST

4 BK TINLINE ST
5 BK ANDREW ST N
6 BK ROCHDALE RD S
A3
1 BK RICHARD BURCH ST
2 BK PETER ST
3 BK PARSONAGE ST

A4
1 BK HAMILTON ST
2 BK HALSTEAD ST
3 DUCKWORTH ST
4 BK DUCKWORTH ST
5 BK CHESHAM RD N
6 GREENBROOK ST
7 BK CHESHAM RD S

8 LATHOM ST
9 BK LATHOM ST
10 PORTLAND IND EST

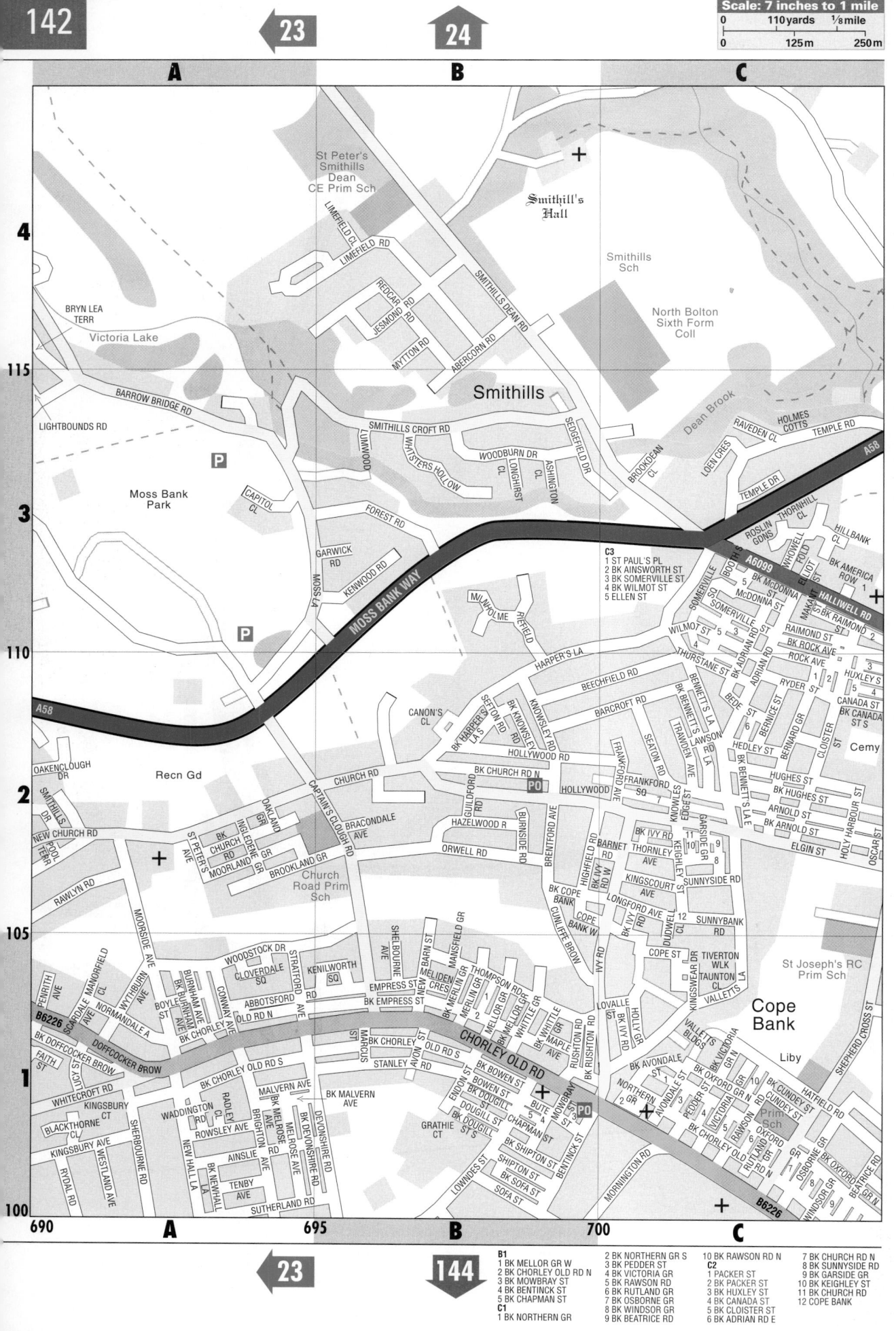

Scale: 7 inches to 1 mile

Smithills

Moss Bank Park

Cope Bank

B1
1 BK MELLOR GR W
2 BK CHORLEY OLD RD N
3 BK MOWBRAY ST
4 BK BENTICK ST
5 BK CHAPMAN ST
C1
1 BK NORTHERN GR

2 BK NORTHERN GR S
3 BK PEDDER ST
4 BK VICTORIA GR
5 BK RAWSON RD
6 BK RUTLAND GR
7 BK OSBORNE GR
8 BK WINDSOR GR
9 BK BEATRICE RD

10 BK RAWSON RD N
C2
1 PACKER ST
2 BK PACKER ST
3 BK HUXLEY ST
4 BK CANADA ST
5 BK CLOISTER ST
6 BK ADRIAN RD E

7 BK CHURCH RD N
8 BK SUNNYSIDE RD
9 BK GARSIDE GR
10 BK KEIGHLEY ST
11 BK CHURCH RD
12 COPE BANK

C3
1 ST PAUL'S PL
2 BK AINSWORTH ST
3 BK SOMERVILLE ST
4 BK WILMOT ST
5 ELLEN ST

D2
1 WORDSWORTH TRAD EST
2 BK ESKRICK ST
3 BK CHAUCER ST
4 BK LYTTON ST
5 MILES ST

6 BK GLEN BOTT ST
7 BK ESKRICK ST E
8 BK FRANCES ST
9 BK GROVE ST
10 BK ST THOMAS ST E
11 BK DARWIN ST

D2
12 ST JOSEPH ST
13 BK BOUNDARY ST
14 HALLIWELL ST
15 BK HAYDN ST
16 BK UTTLEY ST

17 BK ESKRICK ST W
18 BK ST AUGUSTINE ST
19 BK ESKRICK ST S
20 BK CARL ST
21 BK WAPPING ST
22 BK WORDSWORTH ST

23 BK VICKERMAN ST
24 RUSHEY FOLD CT
25 BK AINSWORTH ST

24

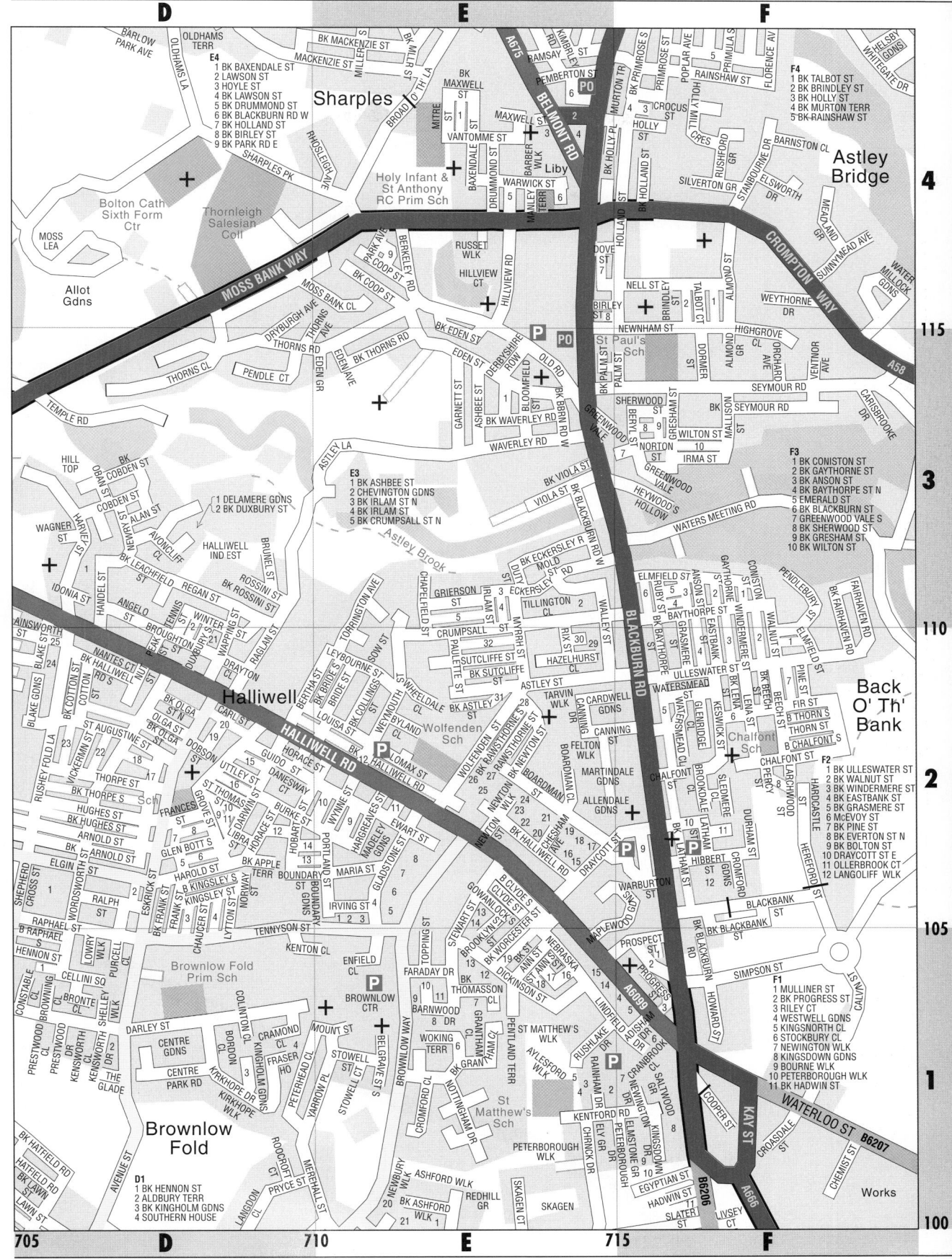

E1
1 MIDHURST CL
2 RAINHAM GR
3 WOODCHURCH CL
4 WESTMARSH CL
5 MOUNTFIELD WLK
6 BK WOKING GDNS
7 THOMASSON CL

8 ST MATTHEW'S TERR
9 FOSTER TERR
10 BARNWOOD TERR
11 BARNWOOD CL
12 DICKINSON TERR
13 DICKINSON CL
14 HIGHBROOK GR
15 FERNHURST GR

16 GLENTHORNE ST
17 BK NEVADA ST
18 NEVADA ST
19 WORCESTER ST
20 SHAFTSBURY CL
21 FARNHAM CL

E2
1 IRVING HOUSE

2 KEATS WLK
3 TENNYSON WLK
4 BELGRAVE ST
5 BELGRAVE GDNS
6 GLADSTONE CL
7 LONGTOWN GDNS
8 WHITCHURCH GDNS
9 BK HARGREAVES ST

10 BK WYNNE ST
11 BK EWART ST
12 MARSH ST
13 BK STEWART ST
14 BOSTON ST
15 WITNEY CL
16 WATFORD CL
17 WESTWICH TERR

18 BENWICK TERR
19 YORK TERR
20 CHESTER WLK
21 HUNTINGDON CL
22 LANCASTER WLK
23 NEWTON TERR
24 LANCASTER TERR
25 KEMPSTON GDNS

26 WOLFENDEN TERR
27 TANWORTH WLK
28 CHARLOTTE ST
29 HOLYHURST WLK
30 PINEWOOD CL
31 BK WOLFENDEN ST
32 BK CRUMPSALL ST

145   25

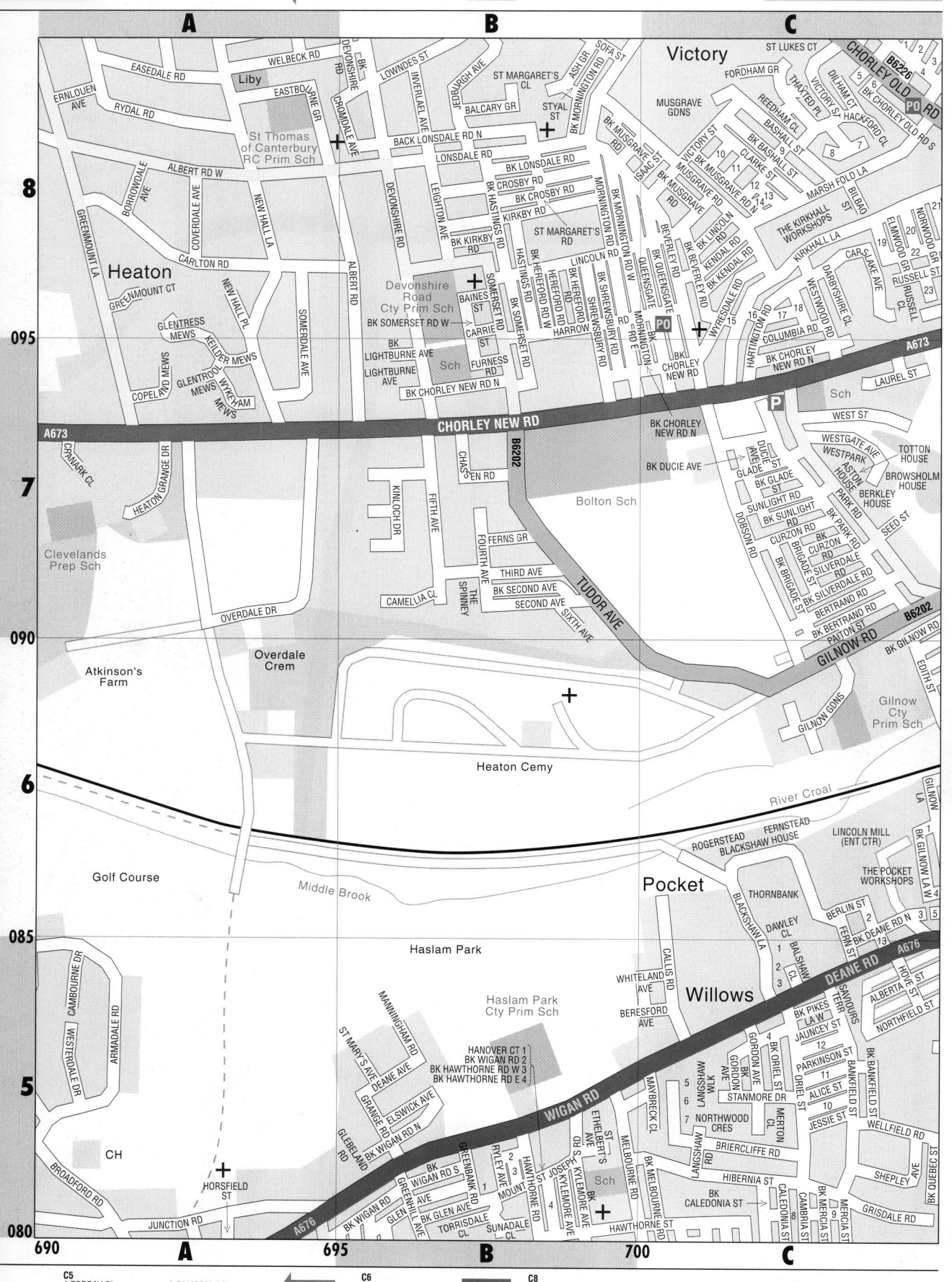

Scale: 7 inches to 1 mile

0 — 110 yards — 1/8 mile
0 — 125 m — 250 m

D5
1 SUNNINGDALE WLK
2 CHATHAM PL
3 FILTON AVE
4 BK MARY ST
5 BK VIEW ST
6 HILLSIDE ST
7 BK HILLSIDE ST

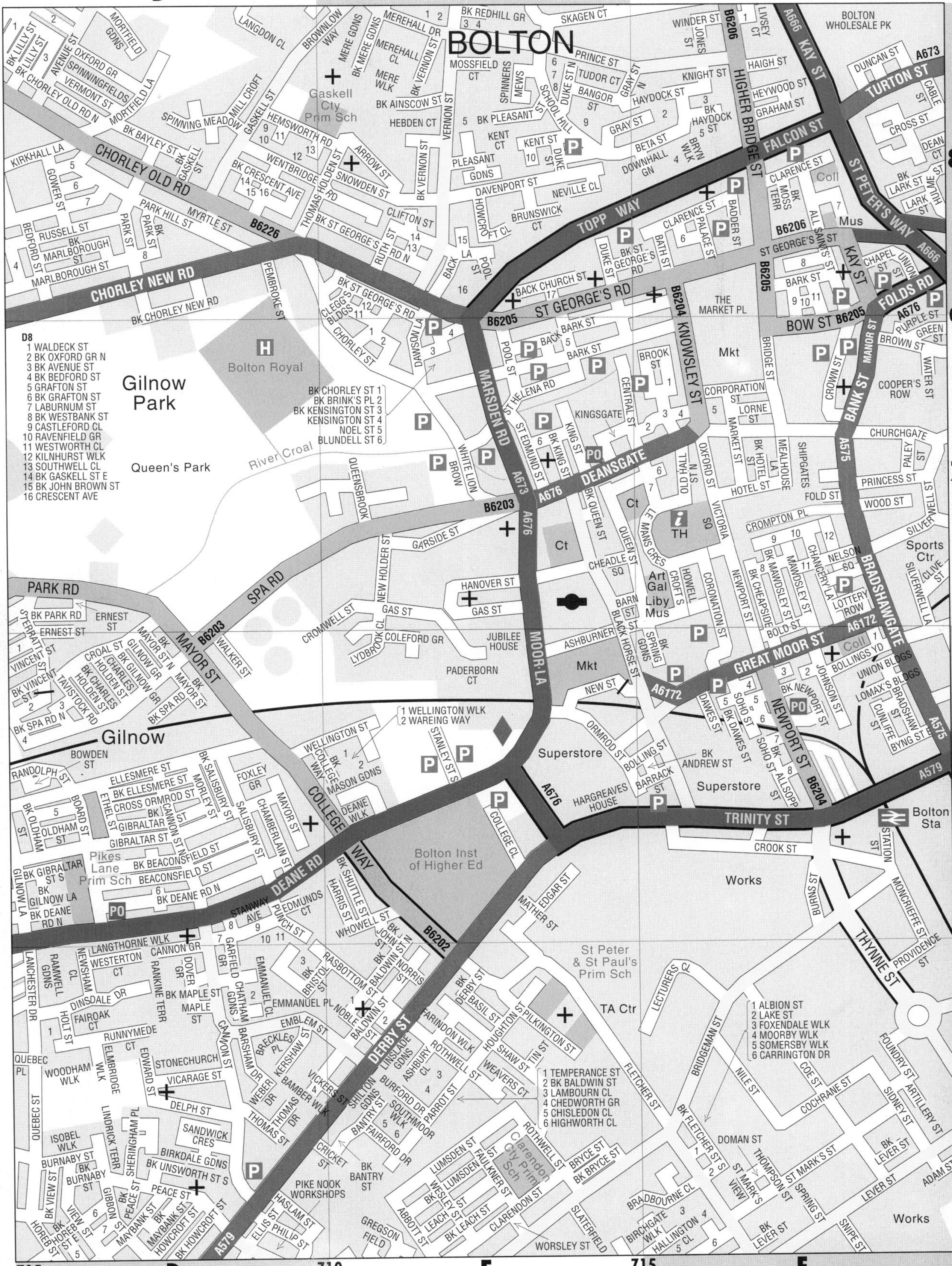

143

148

D6
1 BK ERNEST ST
2 BRIDGEWATER ST
3 BK TAVISTOCK RD
4 BK SPA RD W
5 BK ELLESMERE ST
6 BALFOUR ST
7 STANWAY CL
8 DEFENCE ST
9 BK STANWAY AVE
10 EVESHAM WLK
11 EVESHAM CL

145

BOLTON

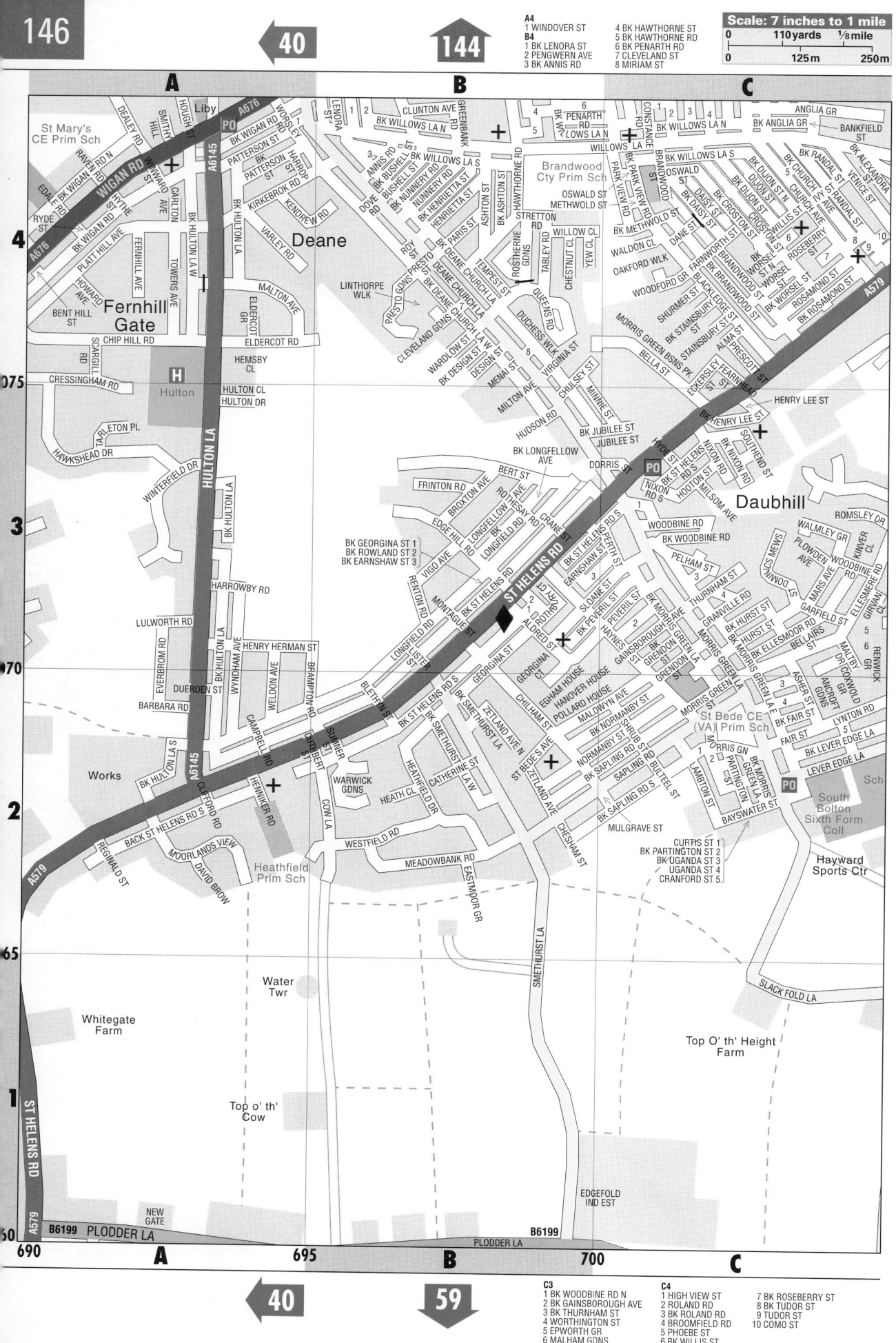

← 40

↑ 144

A4
1 WINDOVER ST
B4
1 BK LENORA ST
2 PENGWERN AVE
3 BK ANNIS RD

4 BK HAWTHORNE ST
5 BK HAWTHORNE RD
6 BK PENARTH RD
7 CLEVELAND ST
8 MIRIAM ST

Scale: 7 inches to 1 mile
0   110 yards   ⅛ mile
0   125m   250m

C3
1 BK WOODBINE RD N
2 BK GAINSBOROUGH AVE
3 BK THURNHAM ST
4 WORTHINGTON ST
5 EPWORTH GR
6 MALHAM GDNS

C4
1 HIGH VIEW ST
2 ROLAND RD
3 BK ROLAND RD
4 BROOMFIELD RD
5 PHOEBE ST
6 BK WILLIS ST
7 BK ROSEBERRY ST
8 BK TUDOR ST
9 TUDOR ST
10 COMO ST

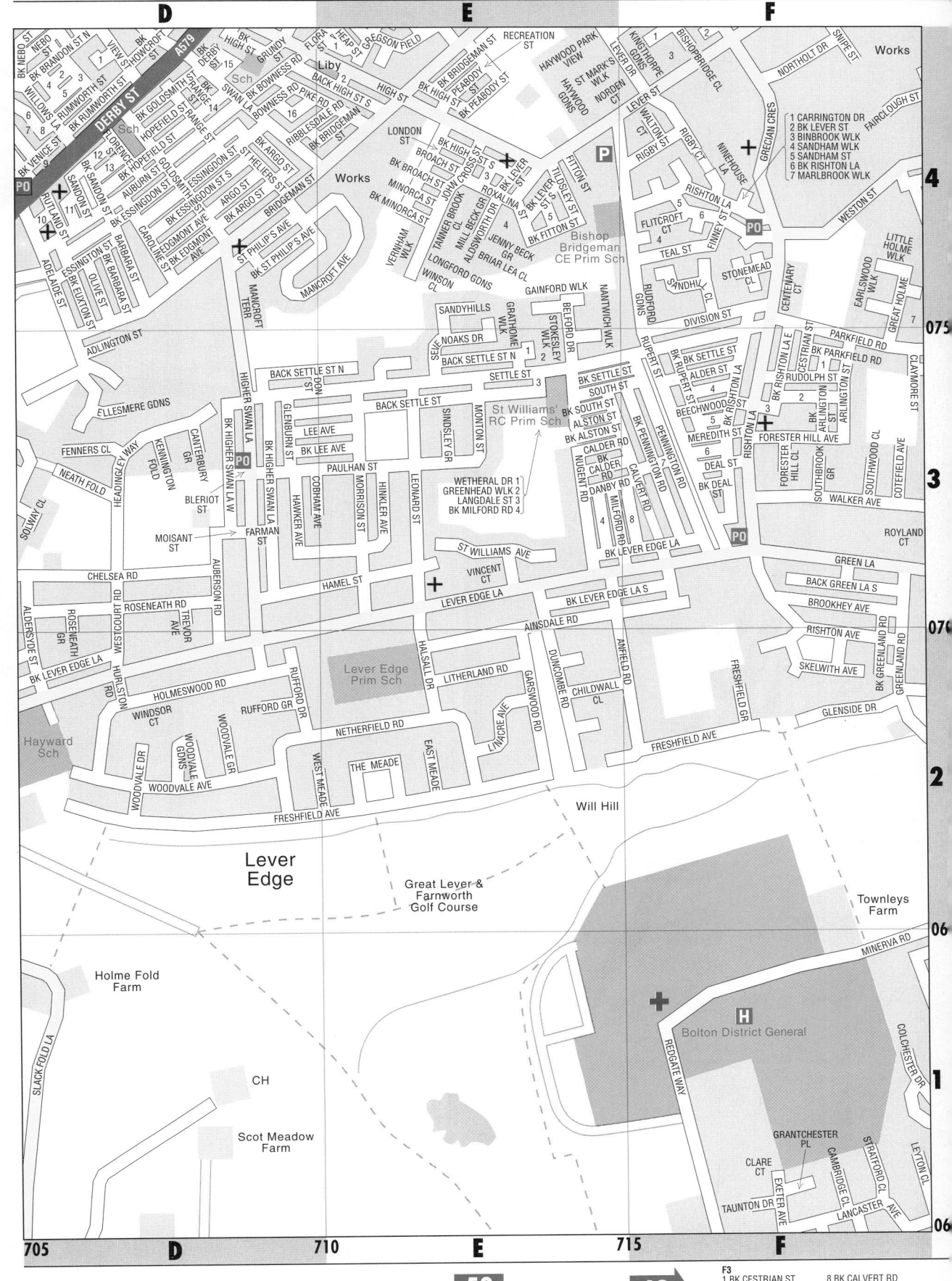

D4
1 BROADHURST CT
2 BRANDON ST
3 BROADHURST ST
4 BK BRANDON ST W
5 BK BRANDON ST

6 BK WILLOWS LA
7 MELTHAM PL
8 MARTHA ST
9 ALEXANDRA ST
10 BK ST HELENS RD
11 BK SANDON ST W

145

D4
12 BK SUNNING HILL ST
13 SUNNING HILL ST
14 BK AUBURN ST
15 BK SWAN LA
16 BK RIBBLESDALE RD

42

E4
1 BK FLORA ST
2 BK HIGH ST W
3 BK JOHN CROSS ST
4 SPRING MILL CL
5 BK ROXALINA ST

F3
1 BK CESTRIAN ST
2 BK RUDOLPH ST
3 NIGHTINGALES WLK
4 BK ALDER ST
5 BK BEECHWOOD ST
6 BK MEREDITH ST
7 WADE ST

8 BK CALVERT RD

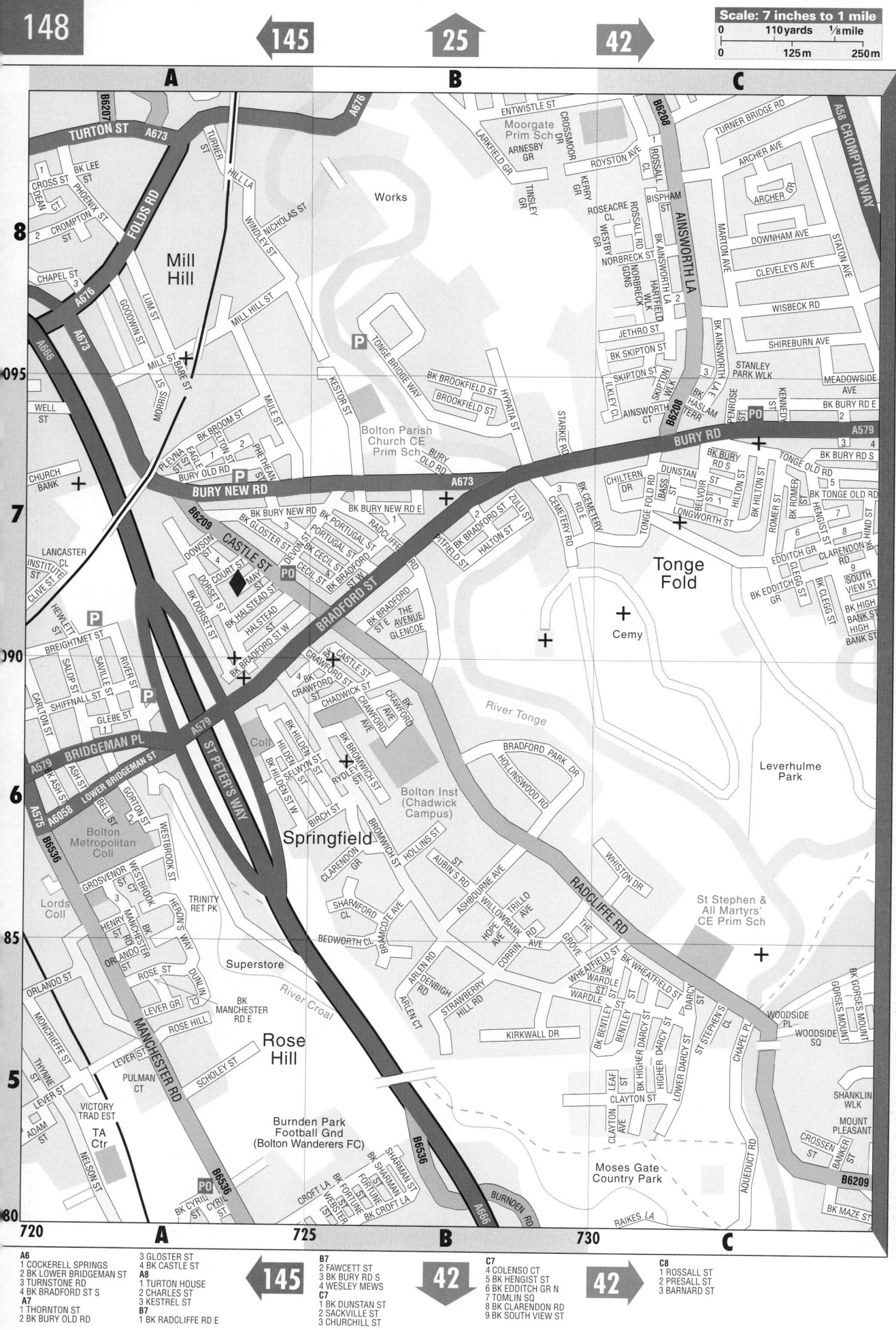

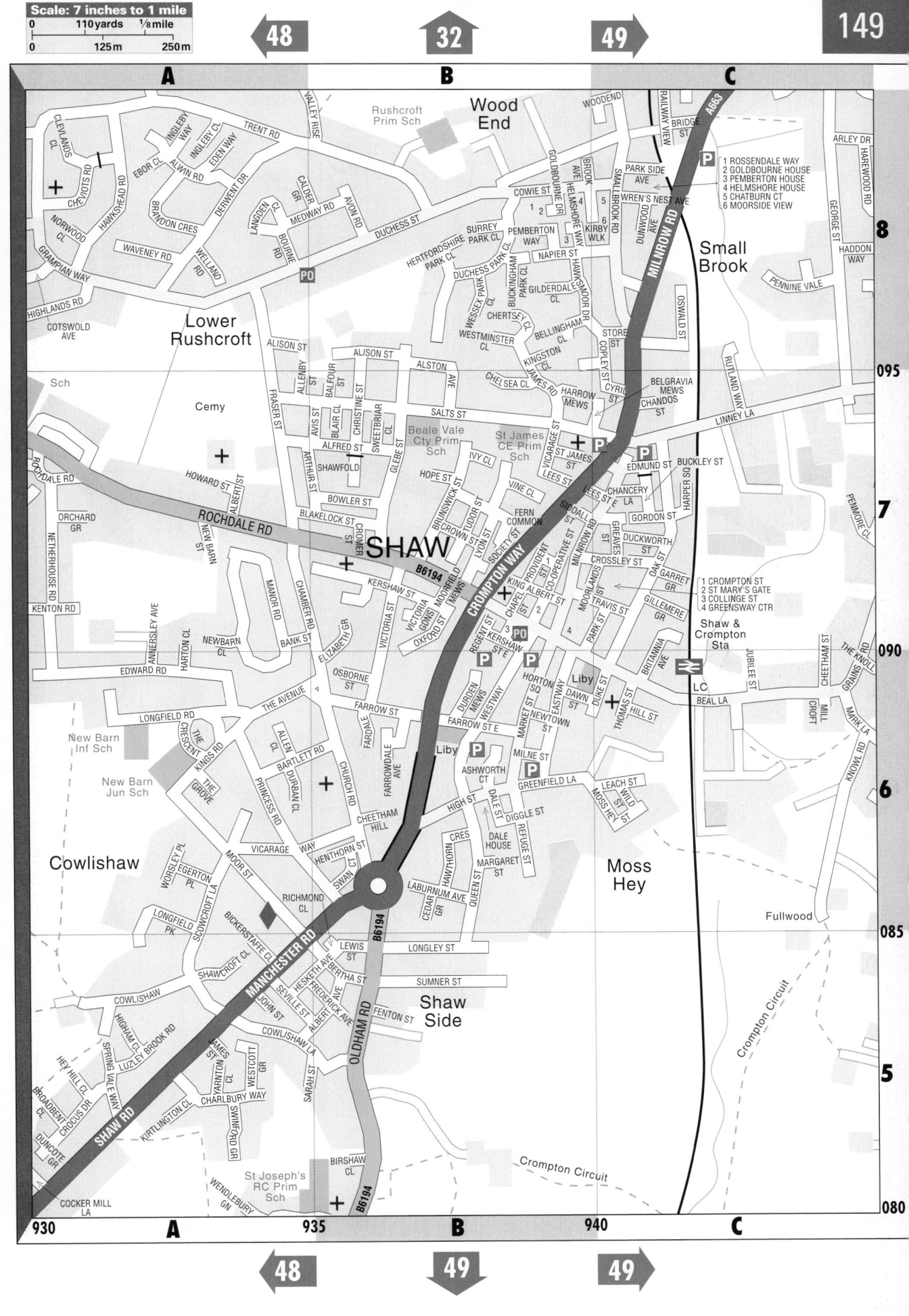

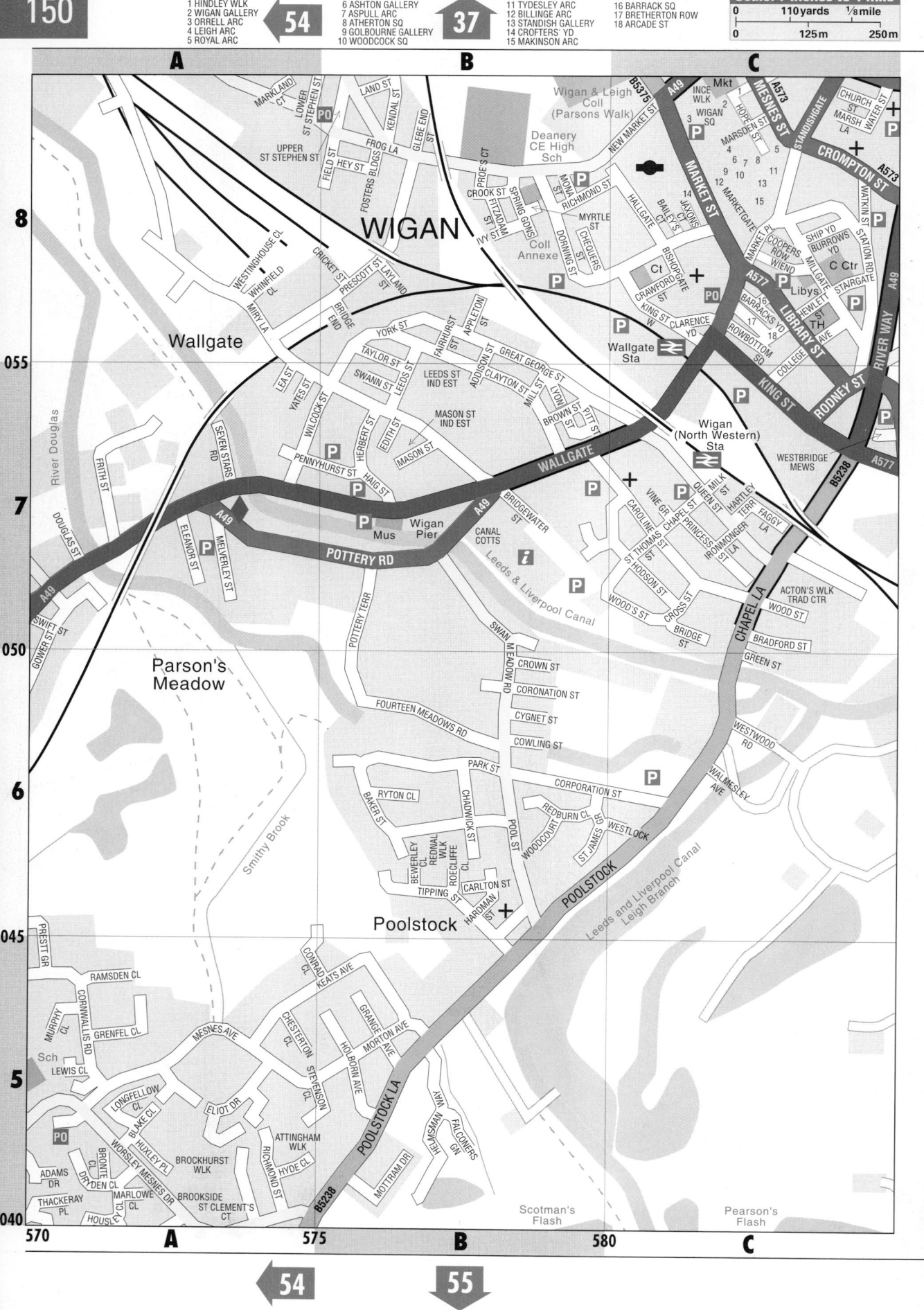

C8
1 HINDLEY WLK
2 WIGAN GALLERY
3 ORRELL ARC
4 LEIGH ARC
5 ROYAL ARC

54

6 ASHTON GALLERY
7 ASPULL ARC
8 ATHERTON SQ
9 GOLBOURNE GALLERY
10 WOODCOCK SQ

37

11 TYDESLEY ARC
12 BILLINGE ARC
13 STANDISH GALLERY
14 CROFTERS' YD
15 MAKINSON ARC

16 BARRACK SQ
17 BRETHERTON ROW
18 ARCADE ST

Scale: 7 inches to 1 mile
0   110 yards   ⅛ mile
0   125 m   250 m

WIGAN

Wallgate

Parson's
Meadow

Poolstock

54

55

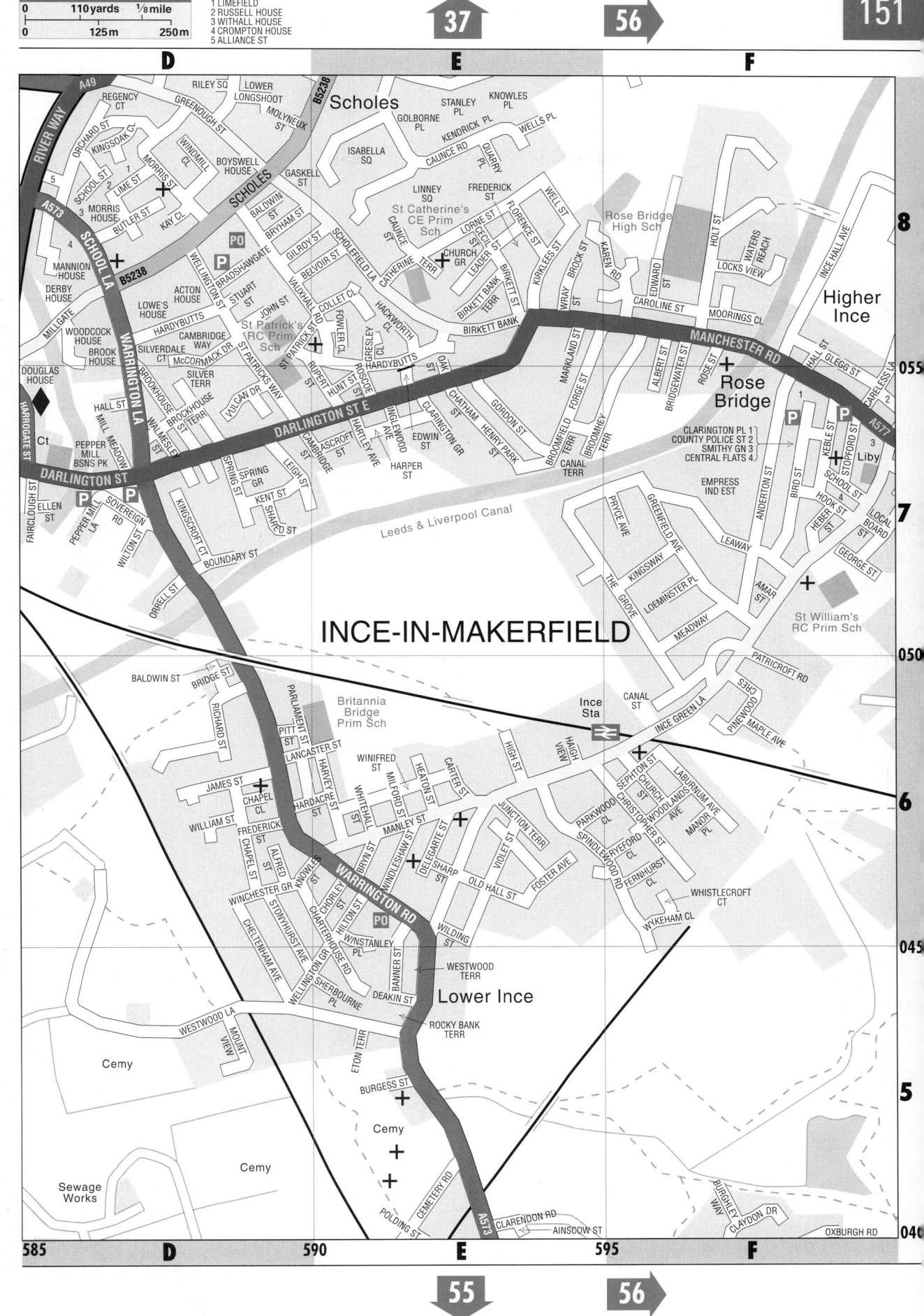

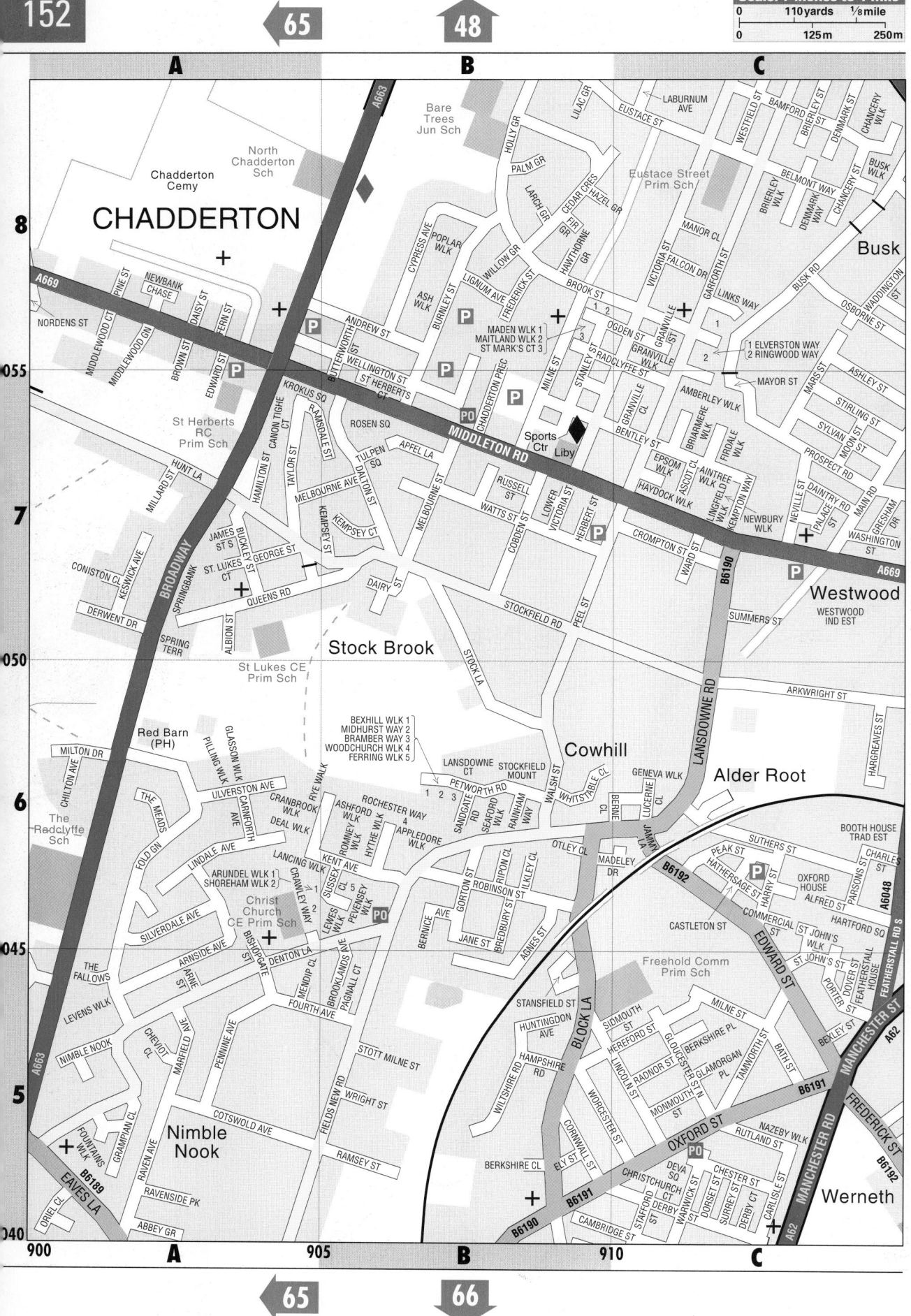

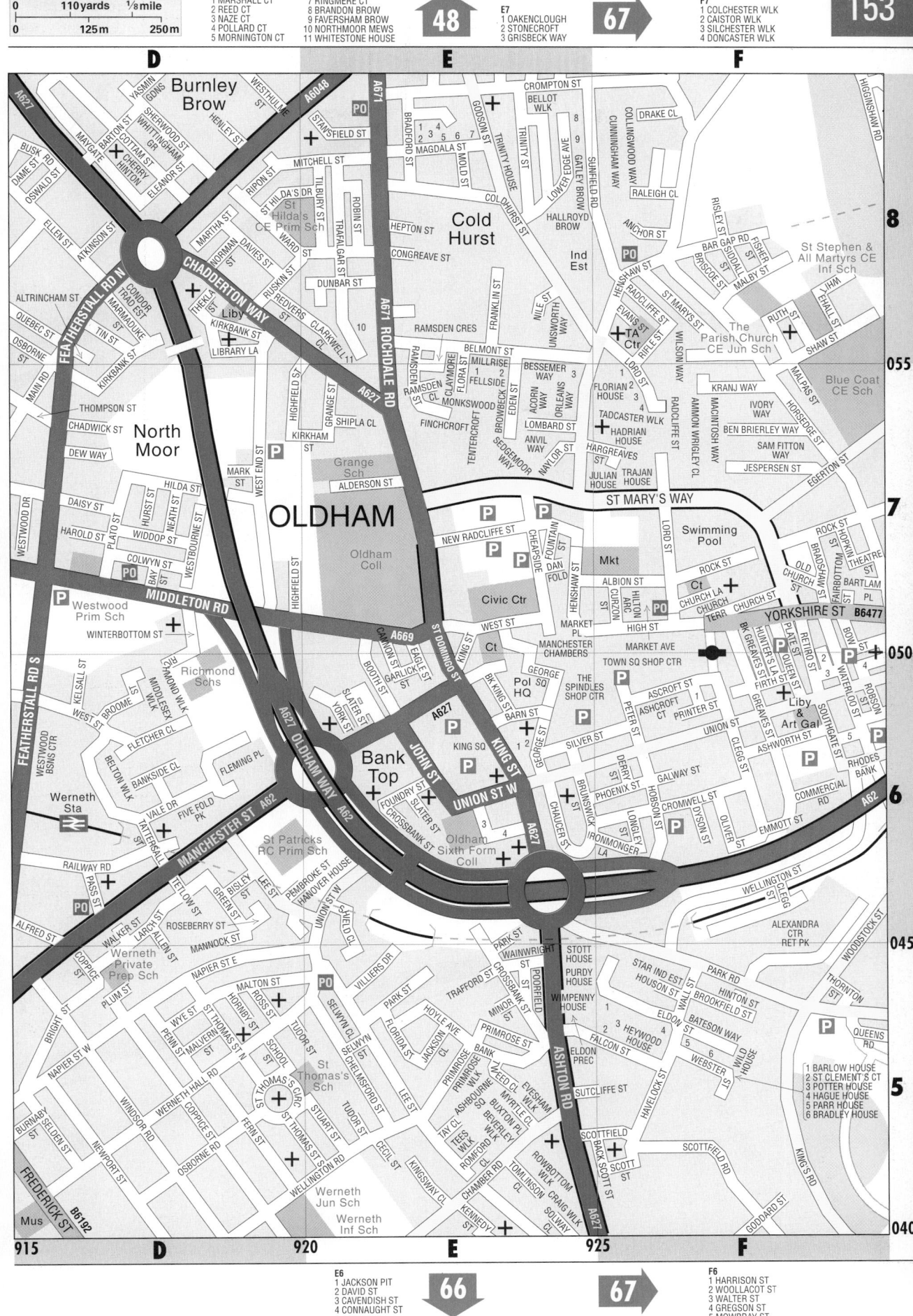

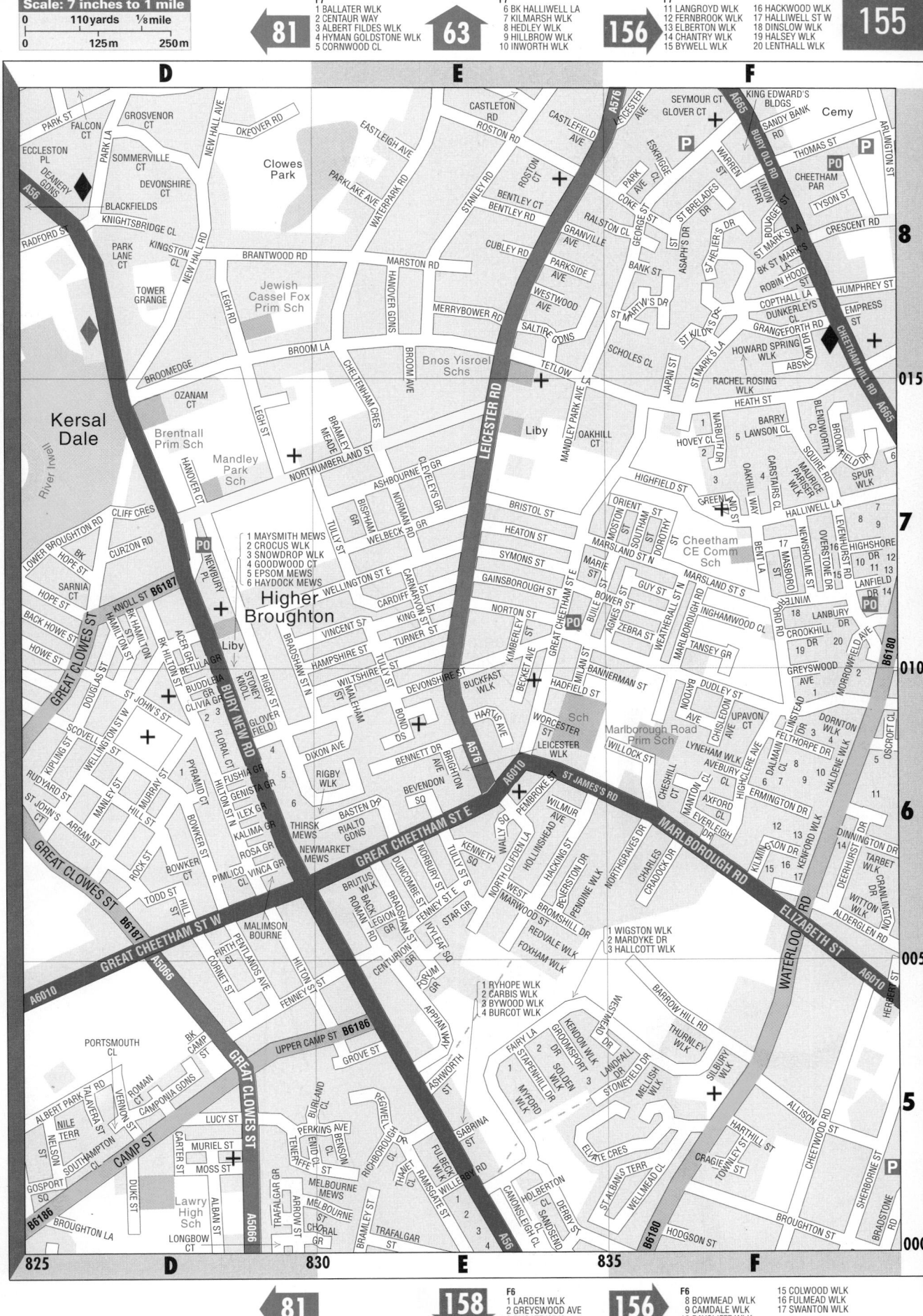

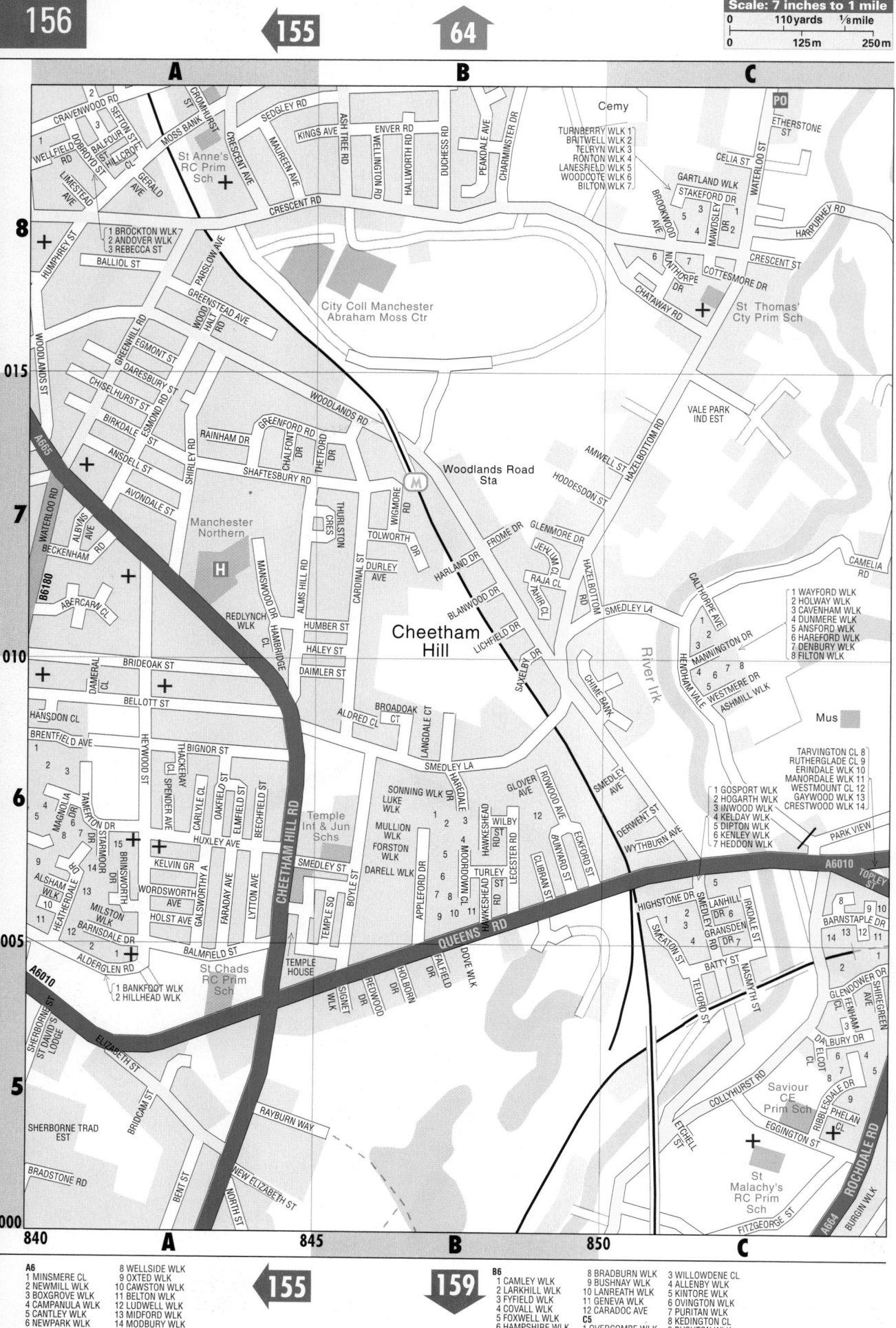

156

← 155   ↑ 64

Scale: 7 inches to 1 mile
0   110 yards   ⅛ mile
0   125m   250m

A   B   C

8

015

7

010

6

005

5

000

840   A   845   B   850   C

Cemy

PO

ETHERSTONE ST

TURNBERRY WLK 1
BRITWELL WLK 2
TELRYN WLK 3
RONTON WLK 4
LANESFIELD WLK 5
WOODCOTE WLK 6
BILTON WLK 7

CELIA ST
WATERLOO ST

GARTLAND WLK
STAKEFORD DR

MAWDSLEY

CRESCENT ST

HARPURHEY RD

BROOKWOOD AVE

NINTHORPE DR

CHATAWAY RD

COTTESMORE DR

St Thomas' Cty Prim Sch

VALE PARK IND EST

AMWELL ST

HAZELBOTTOM RD

HODDESDON ST

CRAVENWOOD RD
SEFTON ST
CROMHURST ST

MOSS BANK

SEDGLEY RD
ASH TREE RD

KINGS AVE

ENVER RD

DUCHESS RD

PEAKDALE AVE

CHARMINSTER DR

WELLFIELD RD
DOBROYD ST
BALFOUR ST
MILLCROFT CL

MAUREEN AVE

WELLINGTON RD

HALLWORTH RD

LIMESTEAD AVE
GERALD AVE

St Anne's RC Prim Sch

CRESCENT RD

1 BROCKTON WLK
2 ANDOVER WLK
3 REBECCA ST

BALLIOL ST

HUMPHREY ST

PARSLOW AVE

GREENSTEAD AVE

WOOD HALT ST

City Coll Manchester Abraham Moss Ctr

WOODLANDS RD

GREENFORD RD

EGMONT ST

DARESBURY ST

ESMOND RD

RAINHAM DR

CHALFONT DR
THETFORD DR

WOODLANDS RD

WOODLANDS RD

WOODLANDS RD

Woodlands Road Sta

GLENMORE DR

AMWELL ST

CALTHORPE AVE

1 WAYFORD WLK
2 HOLWAY WLK
3 CAVENHAM WLK
4 DUNMERE WLK
5 ANSFORD WLK
6 HAREFORD WLK
7 DENBURY WLK
8 FILTON WLK

CAMELIA RD

MANNINGTON DR

HENDHAM VALE

WESTMERE DR

ASHMILL WLK

River Irk

Mus

CHISELHURST ST

BIRKDALE ST

ANSDELL ST

SHIRLEY RD

SHAFTESBURY RD

AVONDALE ST

Manchester Northern

H

REDLYNCH WLK

MANSWOOD DR

HAMBRIDGE CL

ALMS HILL RD

THURLSTON CRES

CARDINAL ST

WIGMORE RD

DURLEY AVE

TOLWORTH DR

HARLAND DR

BLANWOOD DR

FROME DR

JEHLIM CL

RAJA CL

TAHIR CL

HAZELBOTTOM RD

SMEDLEY LA

LICHFIELD DR

Cheetham Hill

CHIME BANK

WATERLOO RD
A665

B6180

ABERCARN CL

BECKENHAM RD

ALBYNS AVE

DAMERAL CL

BRIDEOAK ST

BELLOTT ST

HUMBER ST

HALEY ST

DAIMLER ST

SMEDLEY LA

SAXELBY DR

SMEDLEY AVE

HANSDON CL

BRENTFIELD AVE

HEYWOOD ST

BIGNOR ST

THACKERAY RD

SPENCER AVE

CARLYLE CL

OAKFIELD ST

ELMFIELD ST

BEECHFIELD ST

ALDRED CL

BROADOAK CT

LANGDALE CT

SONNING WLK
LUKE WLK

MULLION WLK
FORSTON WLK
DARELL WLK

HARDALE DR

GLOVER AVE

ROWOOD AVE

DERWENT ST

WYTHBURN AVE

TARVINGTON CL 8
RUTHERGLADE CL 9
ERINDALE WLK 10
MANORDALE WLK 11
WESTMOUNT CL 12
GAYWOOD WLK 13
CRESTWOOD WLK 14

1 GOSPORT WLK
2 HOGARTH WLK
3 INWOOD WLK
4 KELDAY WLK
5 DIPTON WLK
6 KENLEY WLK
7 HEDDON WLK

PARK VIEW

A6010

TOPLEY

MAGNOLIA
TAMERTON DR
STARMOOR DR

BRINSWORTH DR

HEATHERDALE DR

ALSHAM WLK

MILSTON WLK

BARNSDALE DR

KELVIN GR

WORDSWORTH AVE

GALSWORTHY

FARADAY AVE

LYTTON AVE

HOLST AVE

BALMFIELD ST

HUXLEY AVE

SMEDLEY ST

BOYLE ST

TEMPLE SQ

Temple Inf & Jun Schs

CHEETHAM HILL RD

APPLEFORD DR

HAWKESHEAD RD

TURLEY ST

LECESTER RD

WILBY

CLIBRAN ST

BUNYARD ST

ECKFORD ST

HIGHSTONE DR

SMEDLEY RD

LANHILL

GRANSDEN DR

IRKDALE ST

SKEATON ST

BATTY ST

NASMYTH ST

TELFORD ST

BARNSTAPLE DR

ALDERGLEN RD

St Chads RC Prim Sch

Temple House

SIGNET WLK

REDWOOD DR

HOLBORN DR

FALFIELD DR

DOVE WLK

QUEENS RD

GLENDOWER DR

FENHAM CL

SHIREGREEN AVE

DALBURY DR

ELCOT CL

RIBBLESDALE DR

PHELAN CL

1 BANKFOOT WLK
2 HILLHEAD WLK

A6010

ELIZABETH ST

BRIDCAM ST

BENT ST

RAYBURN WAY

NEW ELIZABETH ST

NORTH ST

SHERBORNE TRAD EST

St David's Lodge

SHERBORNE ST

BRADSTONE RD

COLLYHURST RD

ETCHELL ST

EGGINGTON ST

FITZGEORGE ST

Saviour CE Prim Sch

St Malachy's RC Prim Sch

BURGIN WLK

ROCHDALE RD

A664

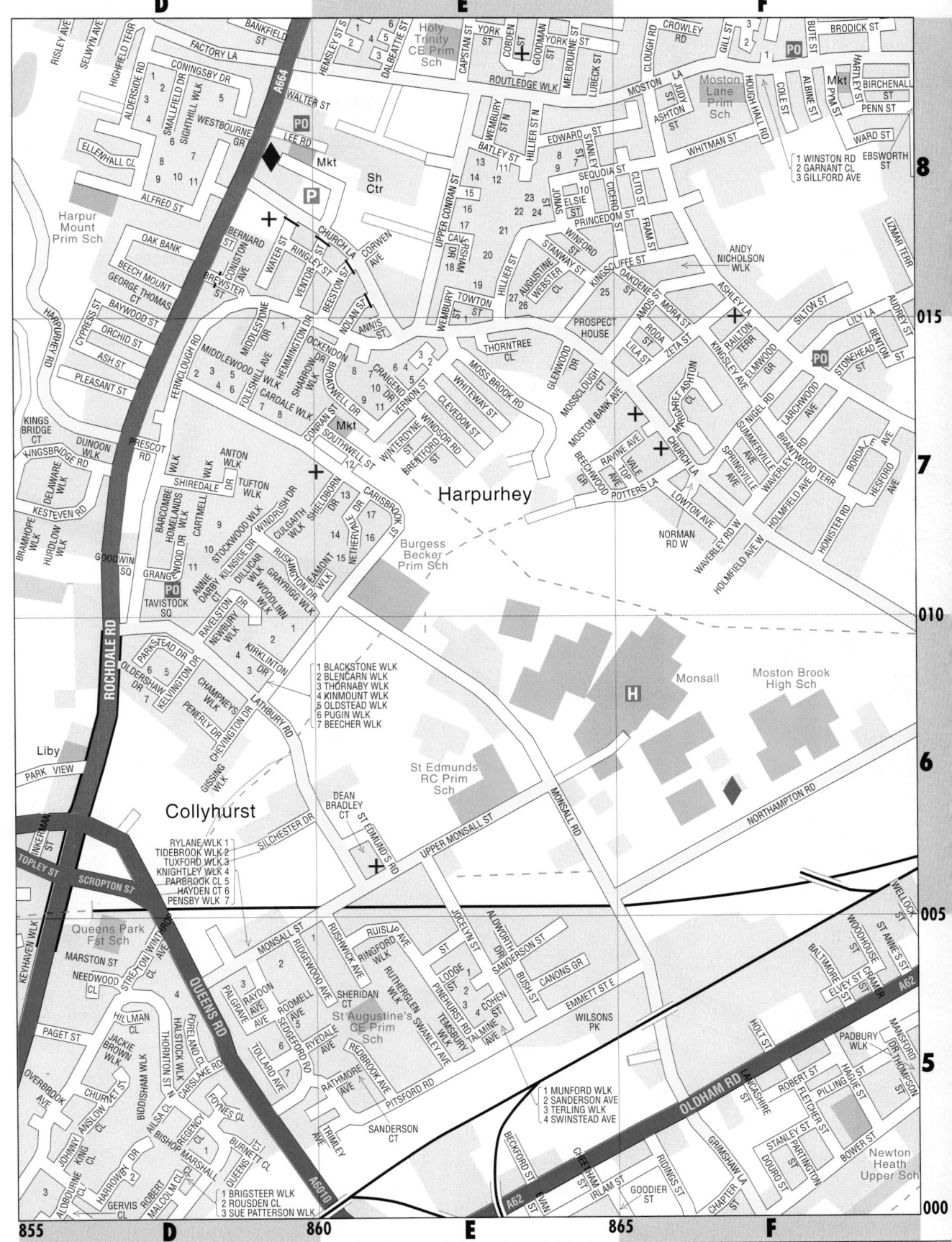

D7		7 LINSLADE WLK	2 PATHFIELD WLK	9 PORTAL WLK	4 ASHGILL WLK		11 LOWREY WLK
1 BROMWICH DR		8 SELWOOD WLK	3 MURROW WLK	10 HAYGROVE WLK	5 GLENPARK WLK		12 DURHAM ST
2 CLATFORD WLK		9 PORTWOOD WLK	4 DERVILLE WLK	11 MAYBROOK WLK	6 DRYGATE WLK		13 EVANTON WLK
3 OAKRIDGE WLK		10 TREMAIN WLK	5 SHAPWICK CL	E7	7 BELSYDE WLK		14 MERTON WLK
4 BINDON WLK		11 CALDERBROOK WLK	6 HARROWDENE WLK	1 WILLOW BANK	8 NORBET WLK		15 TRONGATE WLK
5 WATFIELD WLK		D8	7 BRENLEY WLK	2 ORPINGTON RD	9 PURTON WLK		16 VIEWFIELD WLK
6 HOLMFOOT WLK		1 MILLPOOL WLK	8 ROXWELL WLK	3 OSBORNE RD	10 BANKHALL WLK		17 FIRDON WLK

157

E8
1 HERSHAM WLK
2 RADFORD DR
3 MONKWOOD DR
4 LONGDELL WLK
5 ROCKFIELD DR
6 DENESIDE WLK
7 BROWNSON WLK

8 PRIMLEY WLK
9 DARLTON WLK
10 SIMISTER ST
11 THORNSETT CL
12 KINGCOMBE WLK
13 TIPTREE WLK
14 HANSLOPE WLK
15 SWAINSTHORPE DR

160

E8
16 BOOKHAM WLK
17 FARNDALE WLK
18 APPRENTICE CT
19 WADCROFT WLK
20 BRAXTON WLK
21 LODDEN WLK
22 BURNTWOOD WLK

83
23 SALTBURN WLK
24 NAUNTON WLK
25 CROCKER WLK
26 HIGHDOWN WLK
27 ROUNDHAM WLK

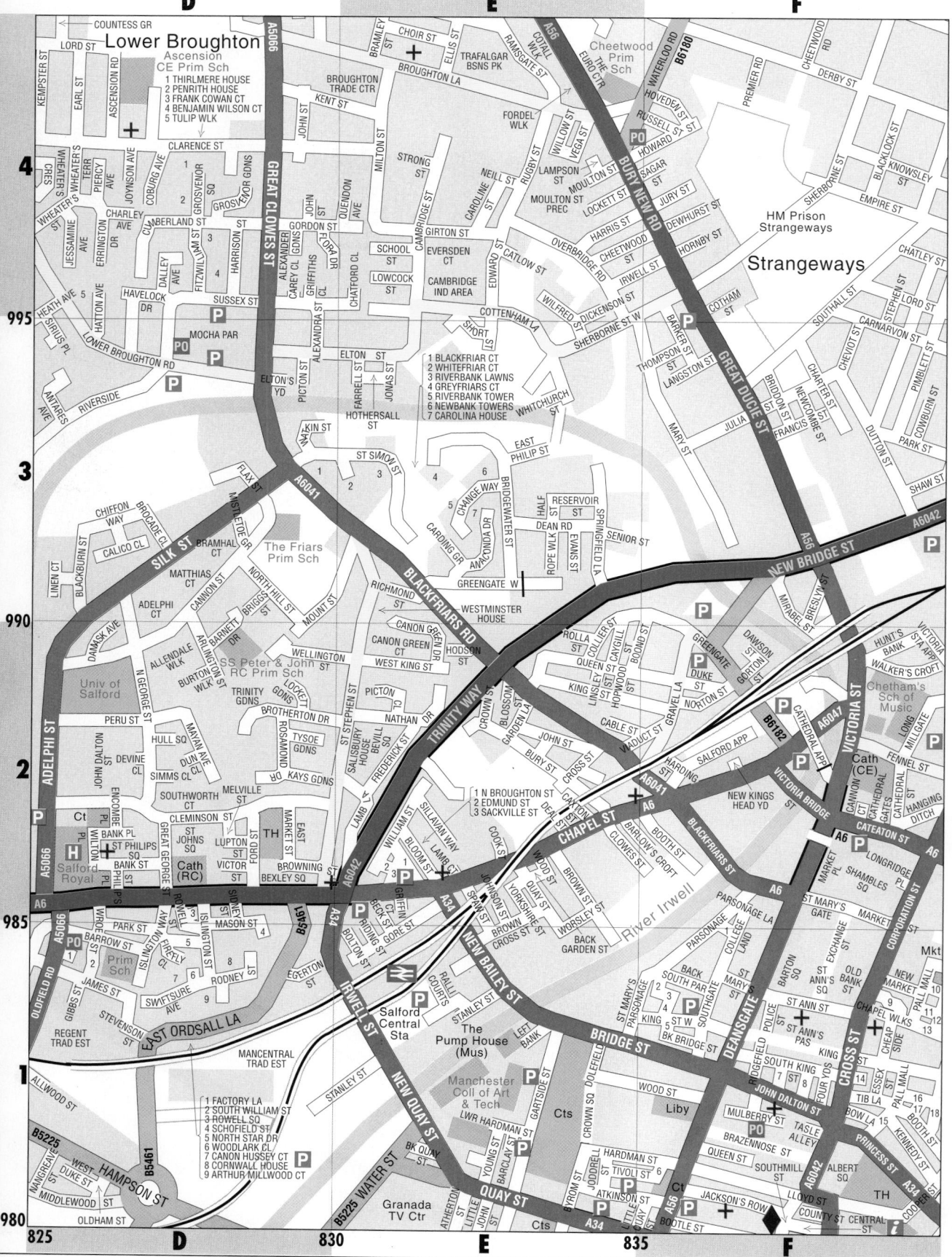

D

E

F

4

995

3

990

2

985

1

980

Lower Broughton

Ascension
CE Prim Sch
1 THIRLMERE HOUSE
2 PENRITH HOUSE
3 FRANK COWAN CT
4 BENJAMIN WILSON CT
5 TULIP WLK

Cheetwood
Prim Sch

HM Prison
Strangeways

Strangeways

1 BLACKFRIAR CT
2 WHITEFRIAR CT
3 RIVERBANK LAWNS
4 GREYFRIARS CT
5 RIVERBANK TOWER
6 NEWBANK TOWERS
7 CAROLINA HOUSE

The Friars
Prim Sch

Univ of
Salford

SS Peter & John
RC Prim Sch

1 N BROUGHTON ST
2 EDMUND ST
3 SACKVILLE ST

Salford
Royal

Cath
(RC)

Salford
Central
Sta

The
Pump House
(Mus)

Manchester
Coll of Art
& Tech

Granada
TV Ctr

River Irwell

Chetham's
Sch of
Music

Cath
(CE)

1 FACTORY LA
2 SOUTH WILLIAM ST
3 ROWELL SQ
4 SCHOFIELD ST
5 NORTH STAR DR
6 WOODLARK CL
7 CANON HUSSEY CT
8 CORNWALL HOUSE
9 ARTHUR MILLWOOD CT

F1
1 BK COLLEGE LAND
2 DUNLOP ST
3 GARDEN LA
4 SMITHY LA
5 BUTTER LA
6 SIDNEY ST
7 BOW ST

8 ST JAMES'S SQ
9 BK POOL FOLD
10 NORFOLK ST
11 KENT ST
12 SUSSEX ST
13 MARSDEN ST
14 TOWN HALL LA
15 CLARENCE ST

16 CHANCERY LA
17 CHANCERY PL
18 BROWN ST

Scale: 7 inches to 1 mile
0 110 yards 1/8 mile
0 125 m 250 m

A3
1 LITTLE NELSON ST
2 MINCING ST
3 ST MICHAEL'S SQ
4 ANGEL TRAD EST
5 NEW MOUNT ST

C3 ▶ 156
1 MORESTEAD WLK
2 WILLIAM CHADWICK CL
3 TADLOW WLK
4 KEELE WLK
5 SALCOT WLK

C3 ▶ 160
6 CALVINE WLK
7 ADSTOCK WLK
8 KIRKGATE CL
9 GLASSHOUSE ST
10 RODNEY CT

C3
11 EAST NEWTON ST
12 PORTUGAL ST
13 BUTLER CT
14 DENSMEAD WLK
15 CALVER WLK
16 BIRTLEY WLK
17 OLDHAM CT
18 LANDOS CT
19 ALFRED JAMES CL
20 GUNSON CT
21 NAYLOR CT

A2
1 BACK BALLOON ST
2 BRADSHAW ST
3 NEWBECK ST
4 HIGHER OSWALD ST
5 EAGLE ST
6 MARTLESHAM WLK
7 HARE ST
8 BK THOMAS ST
9 BRICK ST
10 EDGEHILL ST
11 CATLOW LA

B2
1 COOP ST
2 OAK ST
3 LEN COX WLK
4 SILVER JUBILEE WLK
5 BRIGHTWELL WLK
6 BK SPEAR ST
7 BRADLEY ST
8 LITTLE LEVER ST

C2
1 BARBON WLK
2 SEBASTOPOL WLK

C1 ▶ 163
3 BLACKWELL WLK
4 WILLIAM MURRAY CT
5 SPINNING JENNY WLK
6 KIRBY WLK
7 TAVERY CL
8 BASLAM WLK
9 HOLKHAM CL
10 SALTFORD CT

C1 ▶ 160
1 GREENHEIGH WLK
2 BEATSON WLK
3 WARP WLK
4 BOBBIN WLK
5 WEFT WLK
6 FINISHING WLK
7 PERCH WLK
8 DRILL WLK
9 YARN WLK
10 SLATE AVE
11 CHANCEL PL
12 JAMES BRINDLEY BASIN
13 WILLIAM JESSOP CT
14 THOMAS TELFORD BASIN
15 JOHN SMEATON CT
16 FLETCHER SQ
17 NORTON ST

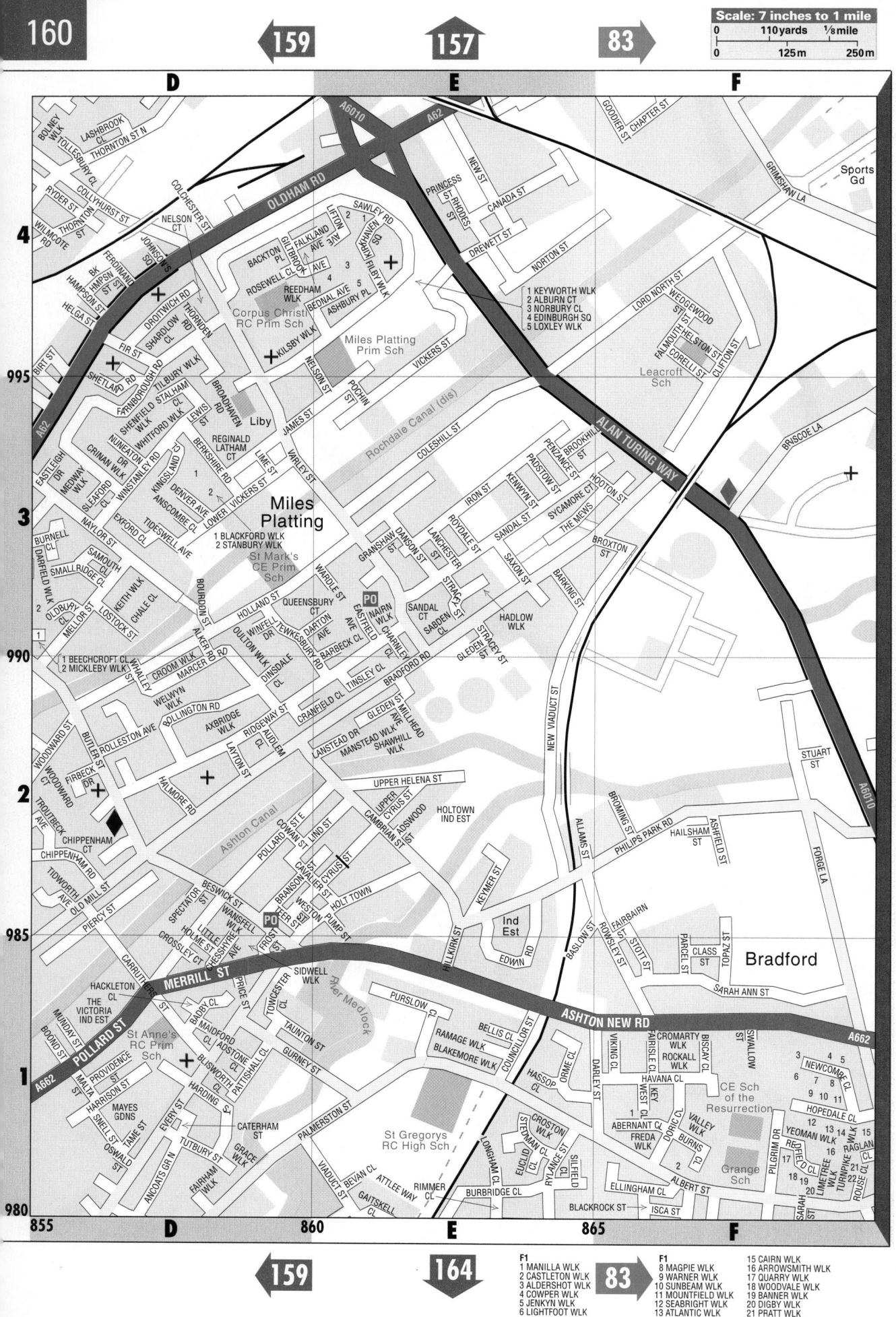

Scale: 7 inches to 1 mile

0 110 yards 1/8 mile

0 125 m 250 m

D E F

A6010

A62

OLDHAM RD

BONEY WLK
LASHBROOK
WILTON
TOLLESBURY ST
THORNTON ST N

RYDER ST
COLLYHURST ST
THORNTON ST

4

WILMCOTE RD
THORNTON
HAMPSON ST

HELGA ST

BK HMPSN ST

FERDINAND ST

JOHNSON'S

NELSON CT

COLCHESTER ST

DROITWICH RD

SHARDLOW CL

HORNDEN

FIR ST

SHETLAND RD

SHARDLOW

BACKTON WLK
GILTBROOK PL

ROSEWELL CL
REEDHAM WLK

CORPUS CHRISTI
RC PRIM SCH

KILSBY WLK

LIFTON AVE

FALKLAND AVE

REDNAL AVE

ASHBURY PL

SAWLEY RD

KIRKHAVEN SQ
FILBY WLK

3
4
5

PRINCESS ST
RHODES ST

NEW ST

CANADA ST

DREWETT ST

NORTON ST

1 KEYWORTH WLK
2 ALBURN CT
3 NORBURY CL
4 EDINBURGH SQ
5 LOXLEY WLK

GOODIER ST

CHAPTER ST

GRIMSHAW LA

Sports Gd

LORD NORTH ST

WEDGEWOOD

FALMOUTH
HELSTON CT

CORELLI ST

CLIFTON ST

Leacroft Sch

BRISCOE LA

995

BIRT ST

A62

EASTLEIGH DR
IMEDWAY WLK
CRINAN WLK

NAYLOR ST

BURNELL CL

SAMOUTH

SMALLRIDGE CL

DARFIELD WLK

OLDBURY

MELLOR CL

2

SLEAFORD

WINSTANLEY RD

SHENFIELD
WLK
WHITFORD WLK

FARNBOROUGH RD

TILBURY WLK
STALHAM CL

NUNEATON DR

KINGSLAND

DENVER AVE

ANSCOMBE CL

TIDESWELL AVE

BERKSHIRE RD

REGINALD LATHAM CT

LOWER VICKERS ST

LIME ST

VARLEY ST

JAMES ST

Liby

BROADHAVEN RD

NELSON ST

POCHIN

VICKERS ST

Miles Platting Prim Sch

Rochdale Canal (dis)

COLESHILL ST

IRON ST

KEMWYN ST

PENZANCE ST

PADSTOW ST

BROOKHILL

HOOTON ST

SYCAMORE CT

THE MEWS

ALAN TURING WAY

3

KEITH WLK

CHALE AVE

LOSTOCK ST

EXFORD CL

WHALLEY

BOURDON ST

ALKER RD

CROOM WLK

MARCER

WELWYN WLK

BOLLINGTON RD

Miles Platting

1 BLACKFORD CL
2 STANBURY WLK

St Mark's CE Prim Sch

WARDLE ST

HOLLAND ST

QUEENSBURY CT

WINFELL
TEWKESBURY RD

OULTON WLK

DINSDALE CL

PO

NAIRN WLK

EASTFIELD AVE

DARTON AVE

BARBECK CL

CHARNLEY

BRADFORD RD

GRANSHAW

DANSON ST

LANCHESTER

ROYDALE

SANDAL ST

SABDEN CL

STRACEY ST

GLEDEN ST

HADLOW WLK

SAXON ST

BARKING ST

BROXTON ST

990

1 BEECHCROFT CL
2 MICKLEBY WLK

1

1 2

WOODWARD ST

BUTLER ST

ROLLESTON AVE

AXBRIDGE WLK

RIDGEWAY RD

AUDLEM

LANSTEAD DR

MANSTEAD WLK

SHAWHILL WLK

GLEDEN ST
MILLHEAD

CRANFIELD CL

TINSLEY CL

2

WOODWARD

FIRBECK DR

HALMORE RD

LAYTON ST

NEW VIADUCT ST

ALLAMS ST

STUART ST

A6010

UPPER HELENA ST

UPPER CYRUS ST

CAMBRIAN ST

ADSWOOD

HOLTOWN IND EST

BROMING ST

PHILIPS PARK RD

HAILSHAM ST

ASHFIELD ST

FORGE LA

TROUTBECK AVE

CHIPPENHAM CT

CHIPPENHAM RD

TIDWORTH AVE

OLD MILL ST

SPECTATOR

BESWICK ST

WANSELL WLK

COWAN ST

POLLARD ST

BRANSFORD

CAVALIER ST

WESTON ST

CAVALIER CYRUS ST

LIND ST

HOLT TOWN

PUMP ST

KEYMER ST

BASLOW ST

ROWSLEY ST

STOTT ST

FAIRBAIRN

PARCEL ST

CLASS ST

TOPAZ ST

Bradford

PIERCY ST

LITTLE HOLME ST

CROSSLEY CT

CHESSHYRE

FROST

PO

SARAH ANN ST

985

HACKLETON CL

THE VICTORIA IND EST

CARRUTHERS ST

MERRILL ST

POLLARD ST

A662

PRICE ST

BADBY CL

TOWCESTER

SIDWELL WLK

River Medlock

PURSLOW WLK

ASHTON NEW RD

A662

COUNCILLOR ST

SWALLOW ST

MUNDAY ST

BOND ST

MALTA ST

HARRISON ST

PROVIDENCE ST

St Anne's RC Prim Sch

MAIDFORD CL

ADSTONE CL

BLISWORTH

PATTISHALL ST

HARDING ST

TAUNTON ST

GURNEY ST

RAMAGE WLK

BLAKEMORE WLK

BELLIS ST

HASSOP CL

ORME CL

DARLEY ST

VIKING CL

FAIRISLE CL

CROMARTY WLK

ROCKALL WLK

BISCAY ST

3
4
5

NEWCOMBE WLK

HOPEDALE CL

1

MAYES GDNS

SNELL ST

OSWALD ST

TAME ST

EVERY ST

CATERHAM ST

TUTBURY ST

GRACE WLK

FAIRHAM WLK

ANCOATS GR N

PALMERSTON ST

VIADUCT ST

BEVAN CL

GAITSKELL CL

ATTLEE WAY

RIMMER CL

St Gregorys RC High Sch

BURBRIDGE CL

LONGHAM CL

CROSTON WLK

STEDMAN CL

EUCLID CL

RYLANCE ST

SILFIELD

ALBERT ST

ELLINGHAM CL

BLACKROCK ST

ISCA ST

ABERNANT CL

FREDA WLK

BURNS

HAVANA CL

KEY WEST CL

VALLEY WLK

DORIC CL

PILGRIM DR

RDFIELD CT

Grange Sch

CE Sch of the Resurrection

LIMETREE WLK

YEOMAN CL

RAGLAN WLK

TURNPIKE WLK

ROUSE ST

ROWSE

9
10
11

12
13
14
15

16

17
18
19

20
21
22

980

855 860 865

D E F

F1
1 MANILLA WLK
2 CASTLETON WLK
3 ALDERSHOT WLK
4 COWPER WLK
5 JENKYN WLK
6 LIGHTFOOT WLK
7 ASHCOMBE WLK

F1
8 MAGPIE WLK
9 WARNER WLK
10 SUNBEAM WLK
11 MOUNTFIELD WLK
12 SEABRIGHT WLK
13 ATLANTIC WLK
14 LEGHORN WLK

15 CAIRN WLK
16 ARROWSMITH WLK
17 QUARRY WLK
18 WOODVALE WLK
19 BANNER WLK
20 DIGBY WLK
21 PRATT WLK
22 RANDALL WLK

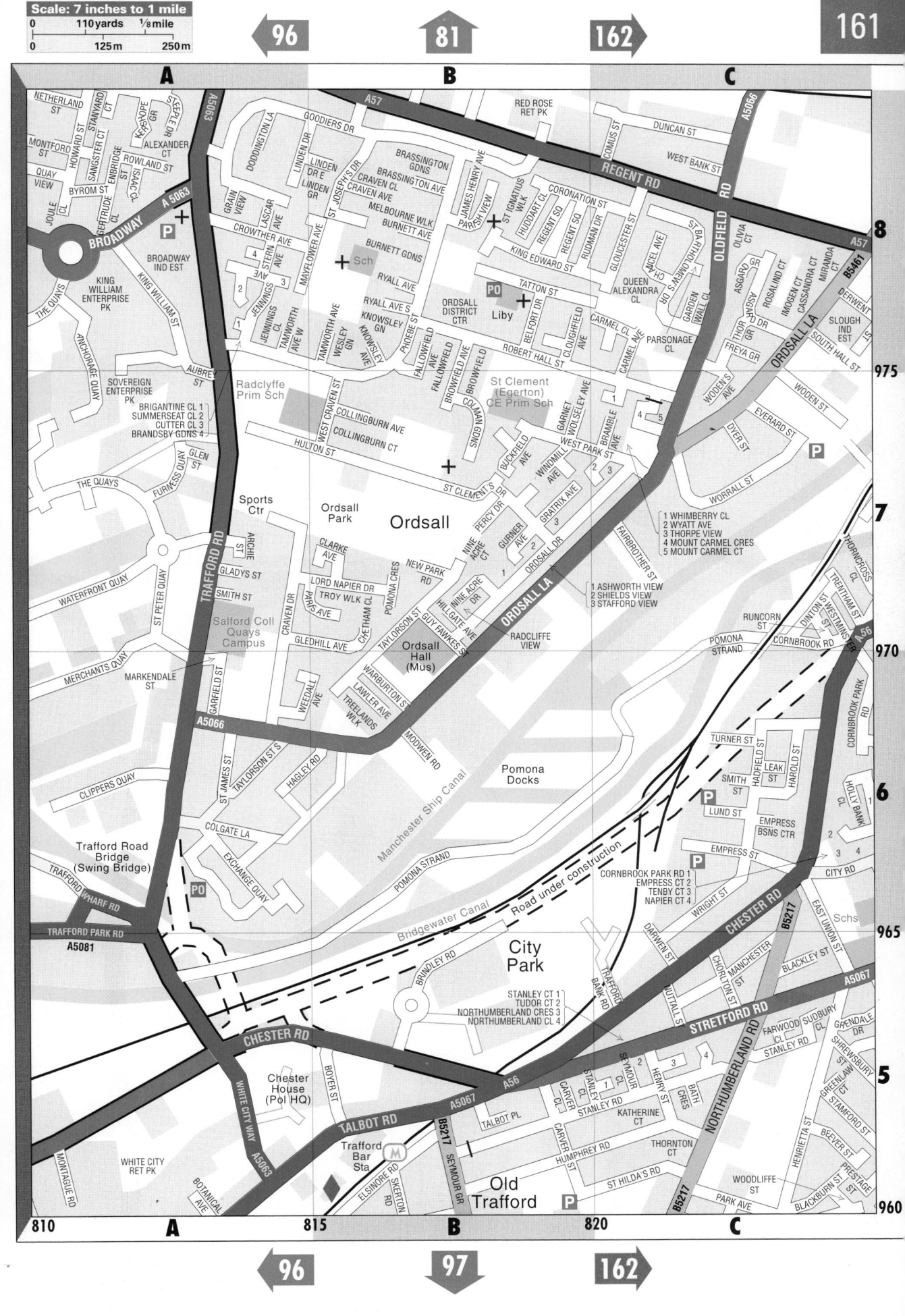

Grid references: D, E, F (top) — 825, 830, 835 (bottom); 8, 975, 7, 970, 6, 965, 5, 960

St George's

City Centre

Hulme

F7
1 GLOUCESTER ST
2 EBENEZER ST
3 NEWCASTLE ST
4 VALERIE WLK
5 CONMERE ST

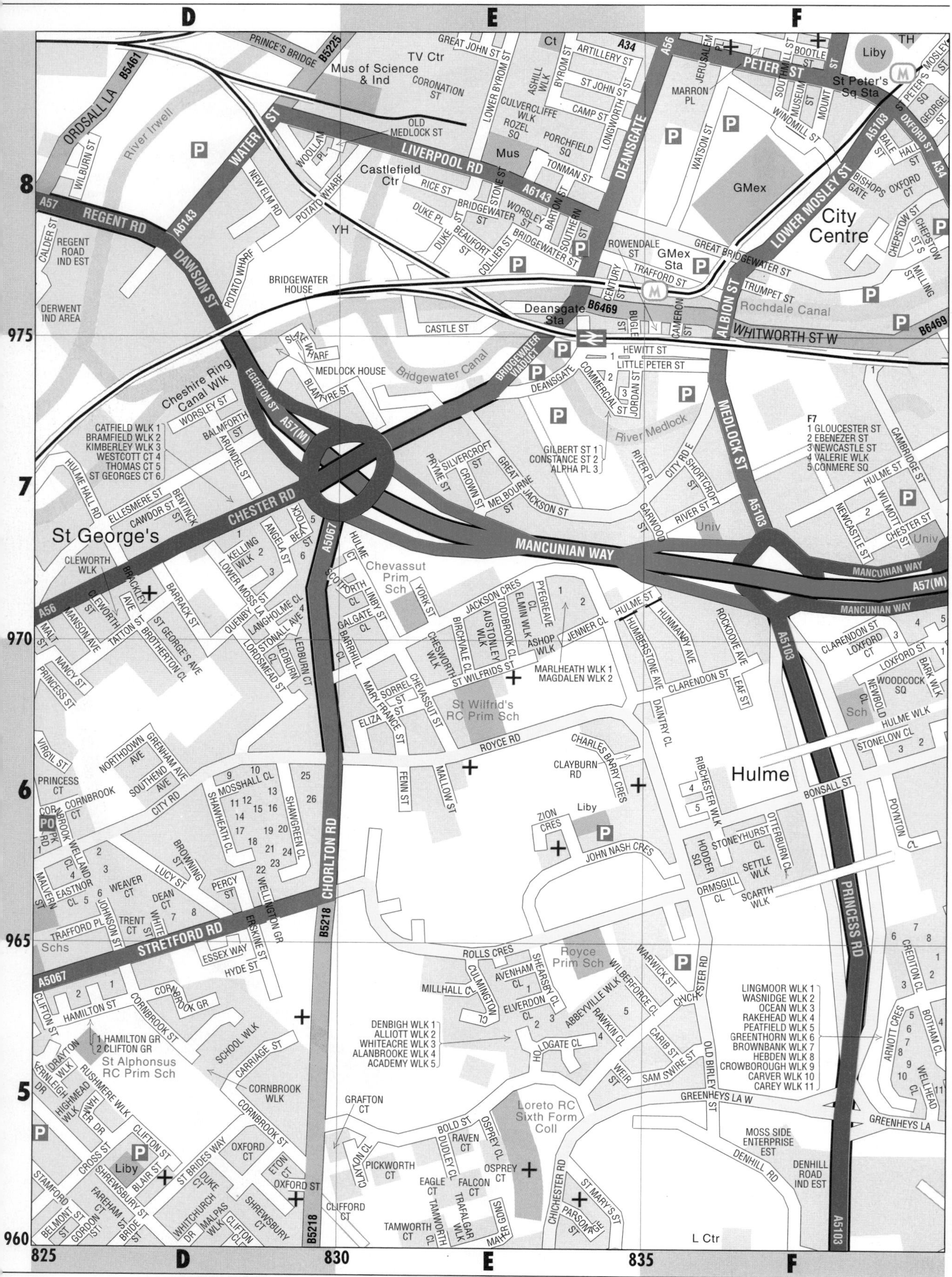

D6
1 MALVERN ROW
2 THAMES CT
3 AVON CT
4 WELLAND CT
5 TAMAR CT
6 BOLLIN CT
7 TRAFFORD CT

8 RYLANDS CT
9 MILLINGTON WLK
10 TOWNFIELD WLK
11 BOWGREEN WLK
12 MERESIDE WLK
13 WARDSEND WLK
14 HEYROSE WLK
15 NORCOT WLK

D6
16 PLATTWOOD WLK
17 OLDGATE WLK
18 TOWNCLIFFE WLK
19 DILLMASS WLK
20 STOCKLEY WLK
21 WINCHAM CL
22 ROYCE CT

D6
23 SPRINGSIDE WLK
24 DUDLOW WLK
25 HILLFOOT WLK
26 ROSSHILL WLK

F6
1 KNOWLES PL
2 HORNCHURCH CT

3 ELSTON WLK
4 DODWORTH CL
5 DARNETH CL
6 MORAN WLK
7 PINDER WLK
8 RAGLAN WLK

Hulme index (E/F region):
1 LINGMOOR WLK
2 WASNIDGE WLK
3 OCEAN WLK
4 RAKEHEAD WLK
5 PEATFIELD WLK
6 GREENTHORN WLK
7 BROWNBANK WLK
8 HEBDEN WLK
9 CROWBOROUGH WLK
10 CARVER WLK
11 CAREY WLK

1 HAMILTON GR
2 CLIFTON GR
St Alphonsus RC Prim Sch

CATFIELD WLK 1
BRAMFIELD WLK 2
KIMBERLEY WLK 3
WESTCOTT CT 4
THOMAS CT 5
ST GEORGES CT 6

MARLHEATH WLK 1
MAGDALEN WLK 2

GILBERT ST 1
CONSTANCE ST 2
ALPHA PL 3

DENBIGH WLK 1
ALLIOTT WLK 2
WHITEACRE WLK 3
ALANBROOKE WLK 4
ACADEMY WLK 5

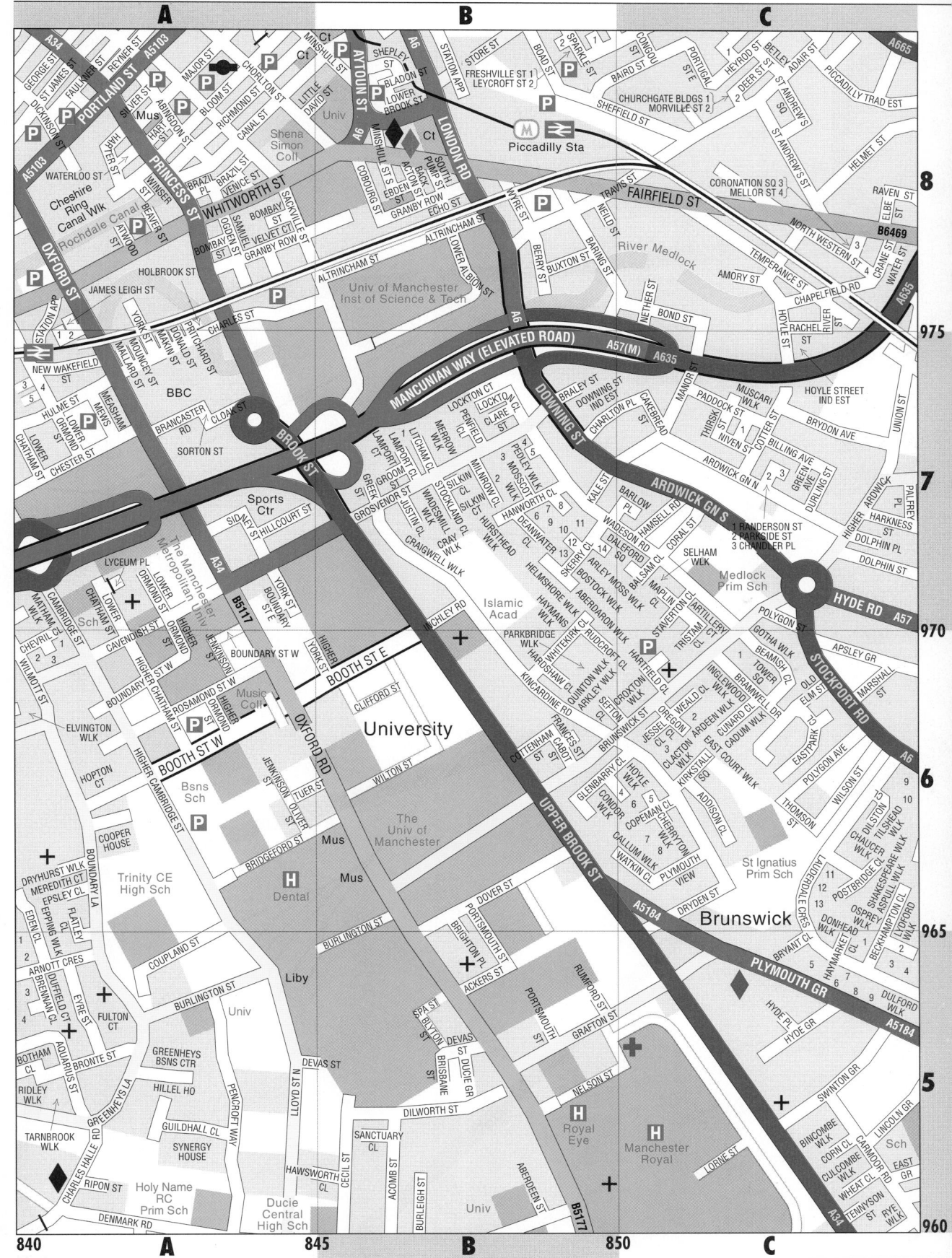

Scale: 7 inches to 1 mile
0   110 yards   ⅛ mile
0   125m   250m

A7
1 CALEY ST
2 WAKEFIELD ST
3 FRANK ST
4 GREAT MARLBOROUGH ST
5 WILLIAM ST

159

B7
1 MANCROFT WLK
2 STATHAM WLK
3 REDMOOR SQ
4 FRANDLEY WLK
5 HAREHILL CL

164

B7
6 EDGEVIEW WLK
7 FULSHAW WLK
8 BLACKHILL CL
9 ELLISBANK WLK
10 HENSHAW WLK

11 BROWNSLOW WLK
12 BANKMILL CL
13 KERFIELD WLK
14 DANEBANK WLK

A5
1 ADMEL SQ
2 HESTER WLK
3 STUDFORTH WLK
4 LONGCRAG WLK

A6
1 ELMDALE WLK
2 BROOMWOOD WLK
3 DALESMAN WLK

C5
1 HEATHCLIFFE WLK
2 TORQUAY CL
3 SEVENOAKS WLK
4 WADHURST WLK
5 NAILSWORTH WLK
6 BRIXHAM WLK
7 BEAMINSTER WLK

98

C5
8 WARSTEAD WLK
9 RADLETT WLK

164

C6
1 BELMONT WLK
2 CHAINHURST WLK
3 MALBROOK WLK
4 CUMBRIAN CL
5 LOWNDES WLK
6 ALLERTON WLK
7 HUTTON WLK

8 CRONDALE WLK
9 CONEWOOD WLK
10 JEVINGTON WLK
11 OGBOURNE WLK
12 KINETON WLK
13 MARSHFIELD WLK

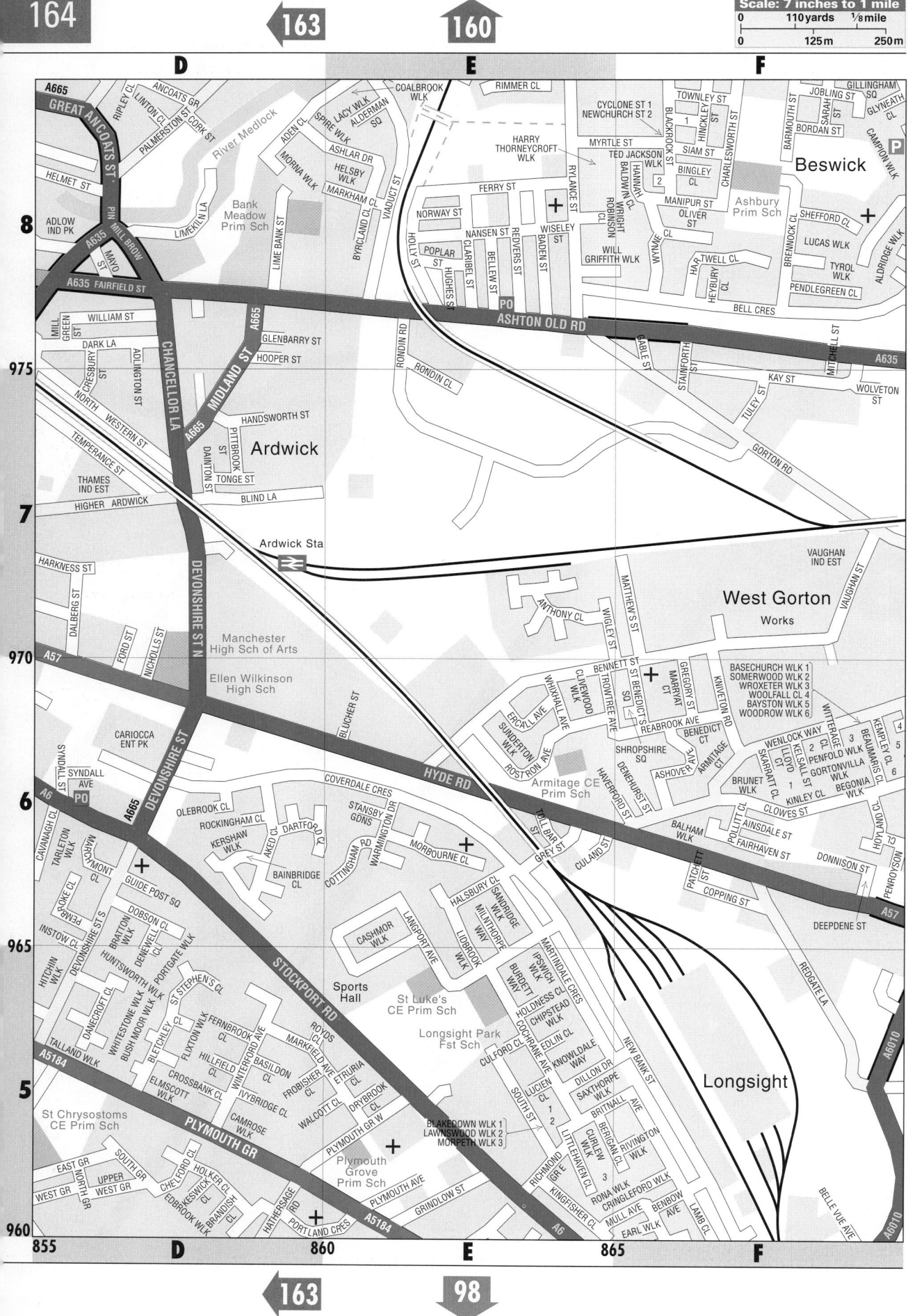

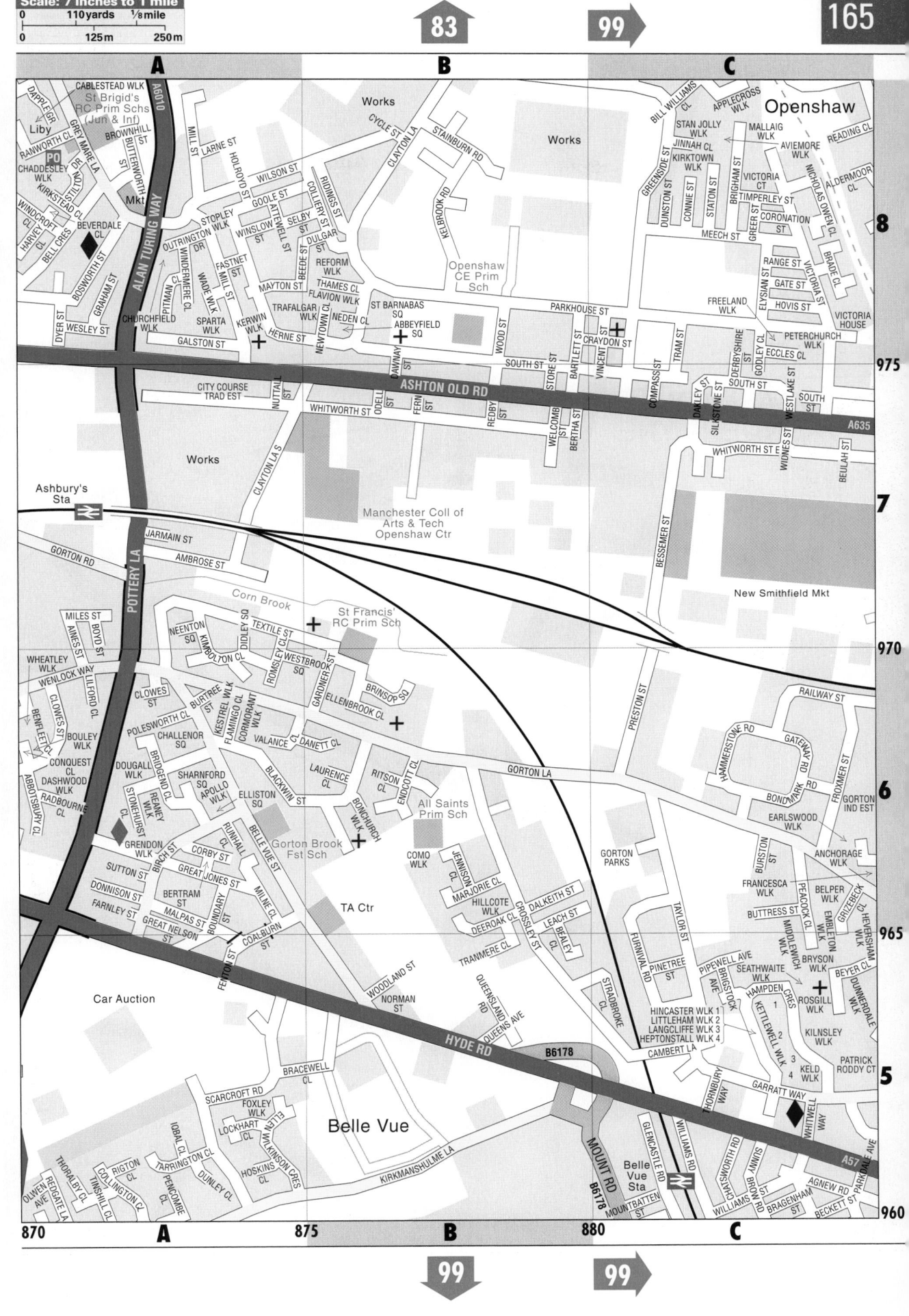

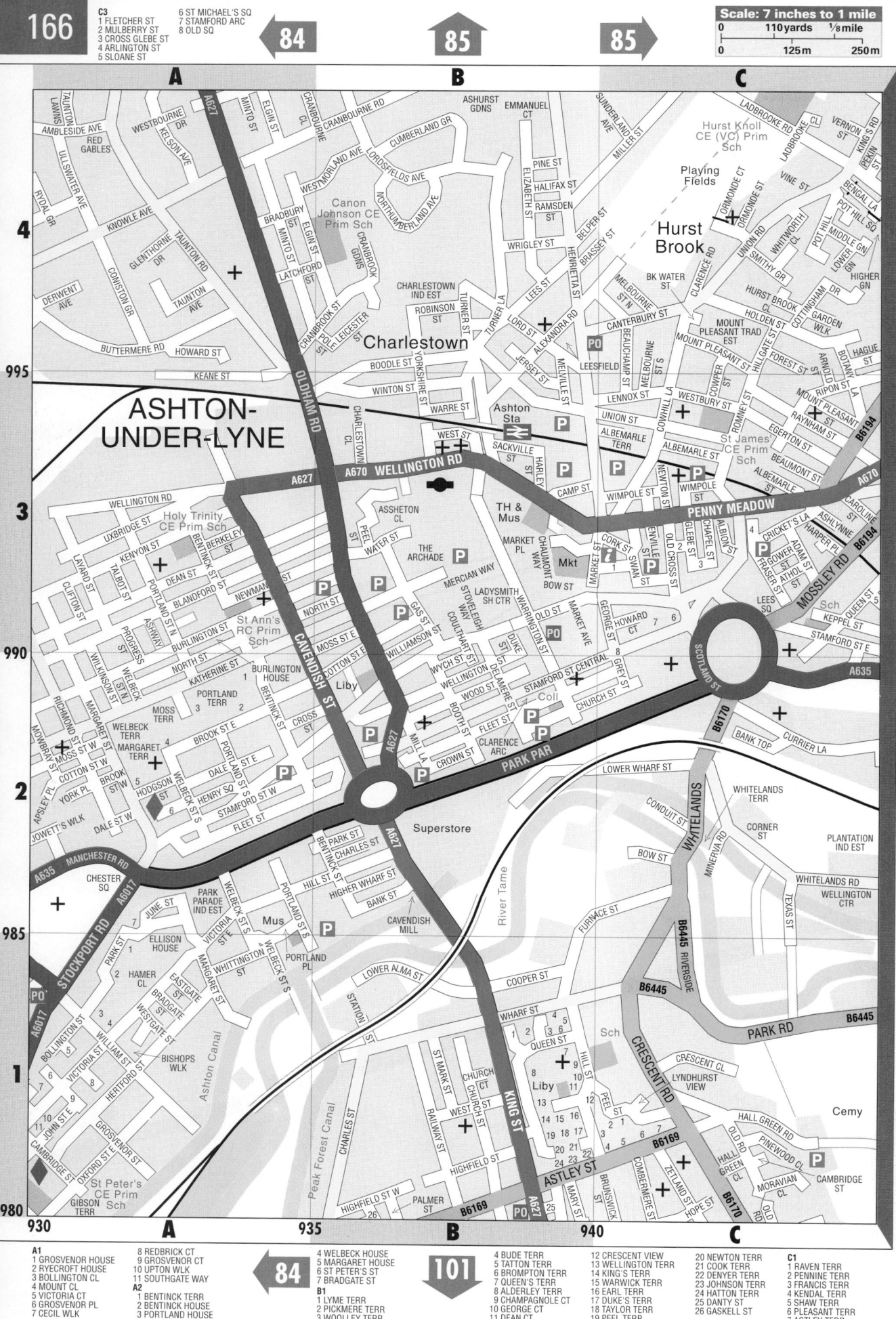

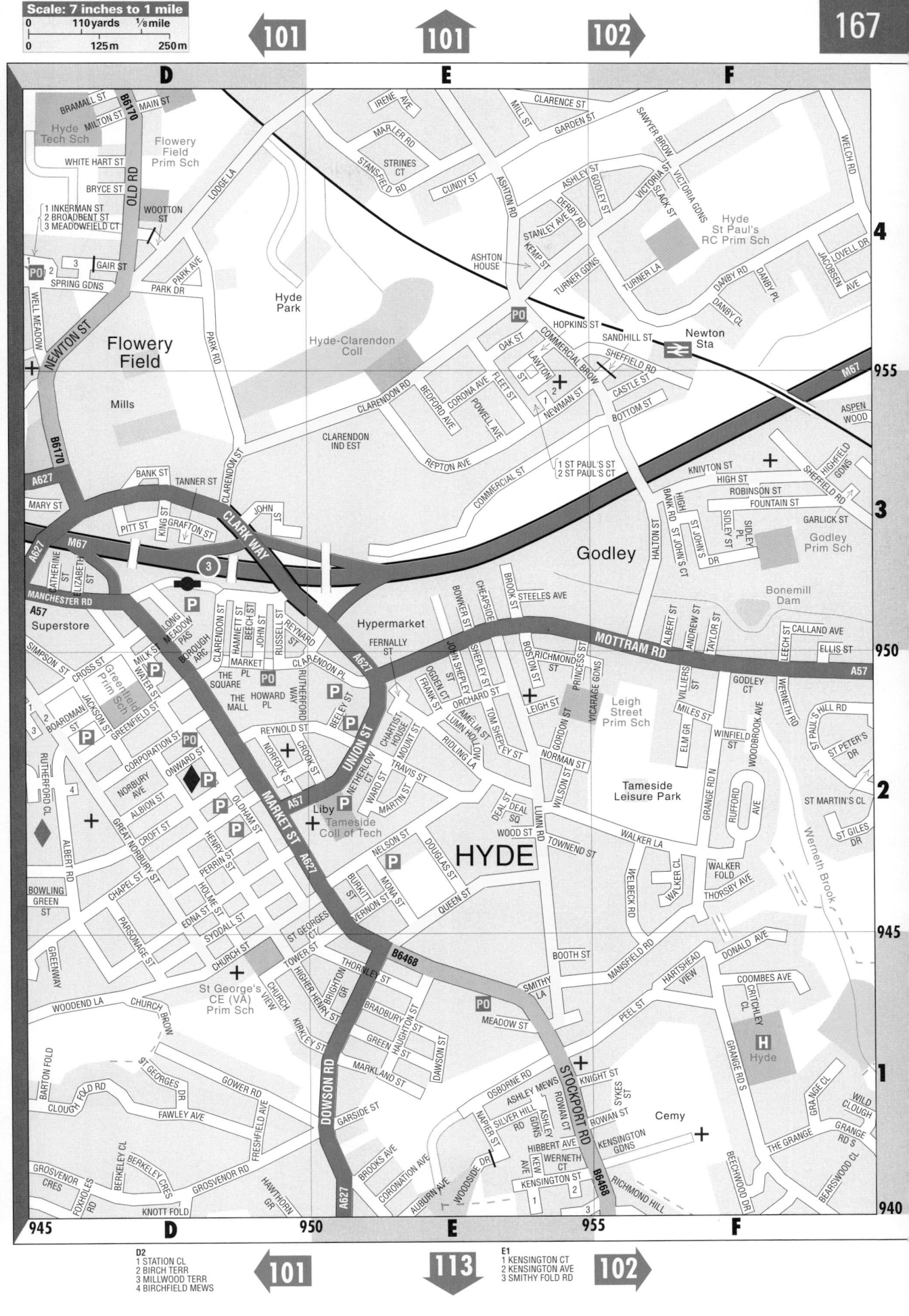

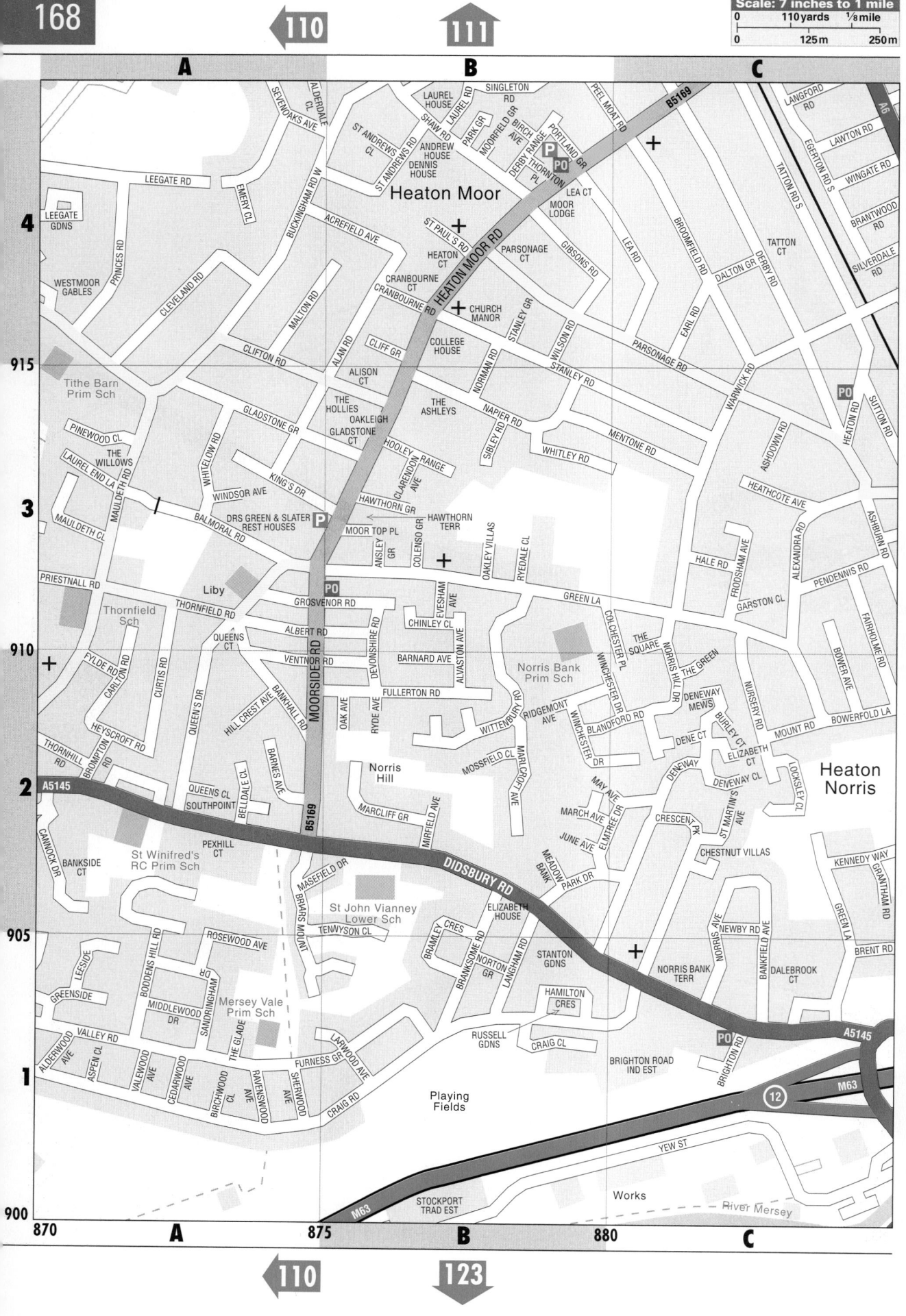

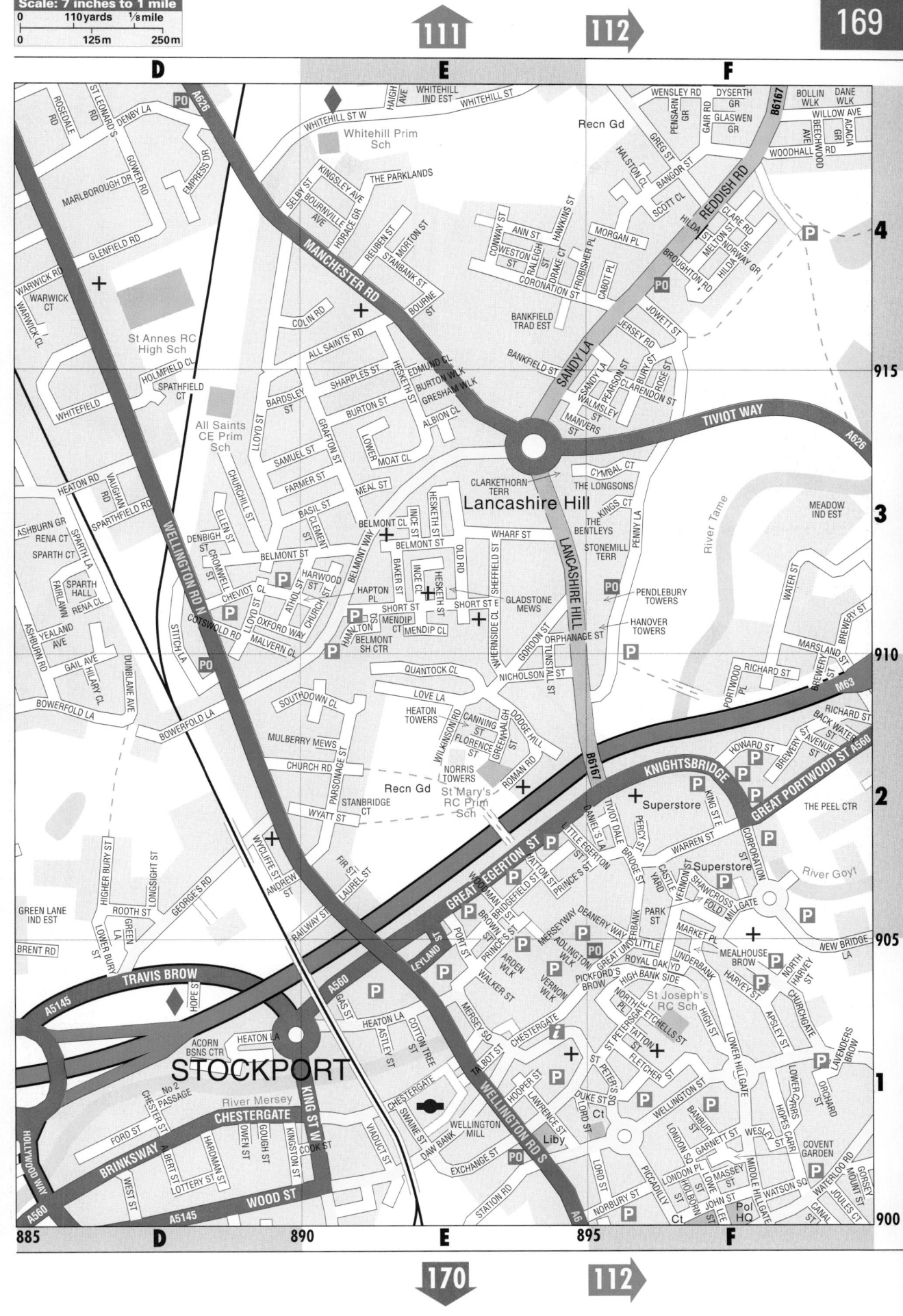

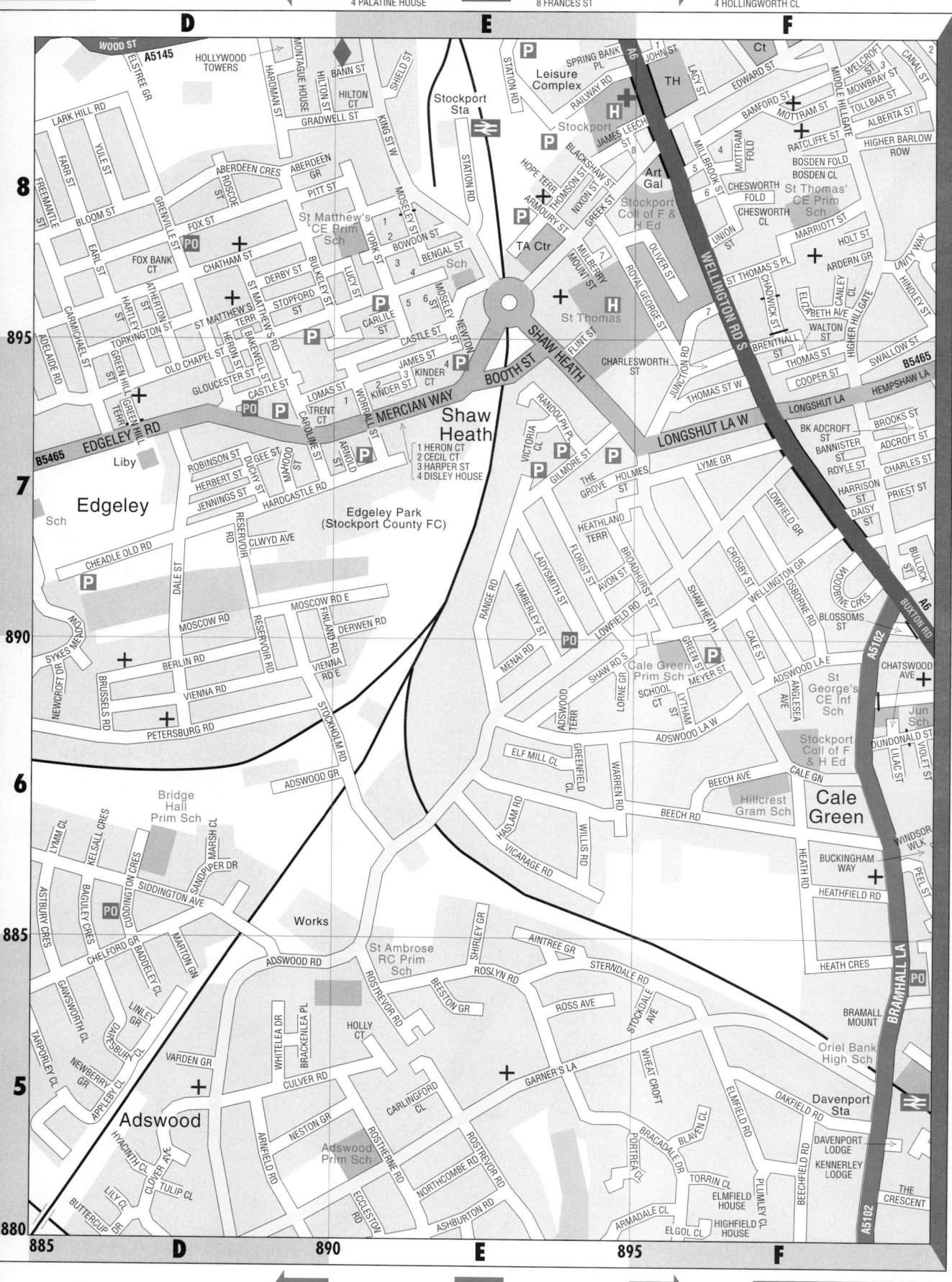

123 ← E8
1 CHATHAM HOUSE
2 BOWDON HOUSE
3 PEMBROKE HOUSE
4 PALATINE HOUSE

169 ↑ E8
5 LANCASTER HOUSE
6 DURHAM HOUSE
7 SIMPSON ST
8 FRANCES ST

124 → F8
1 LOONIES CT
2 JOULES CT
3 OLD GARDENS ST
4 HOLLINGWORTH CL
5 MOTTRAM ST
6 RATCLIFFE ST
7 GROSVENOR ST

Scale: 7 inches to 1 mile

0   110 yards   ⅛ mile
0   125 m   250 m

103 103 104

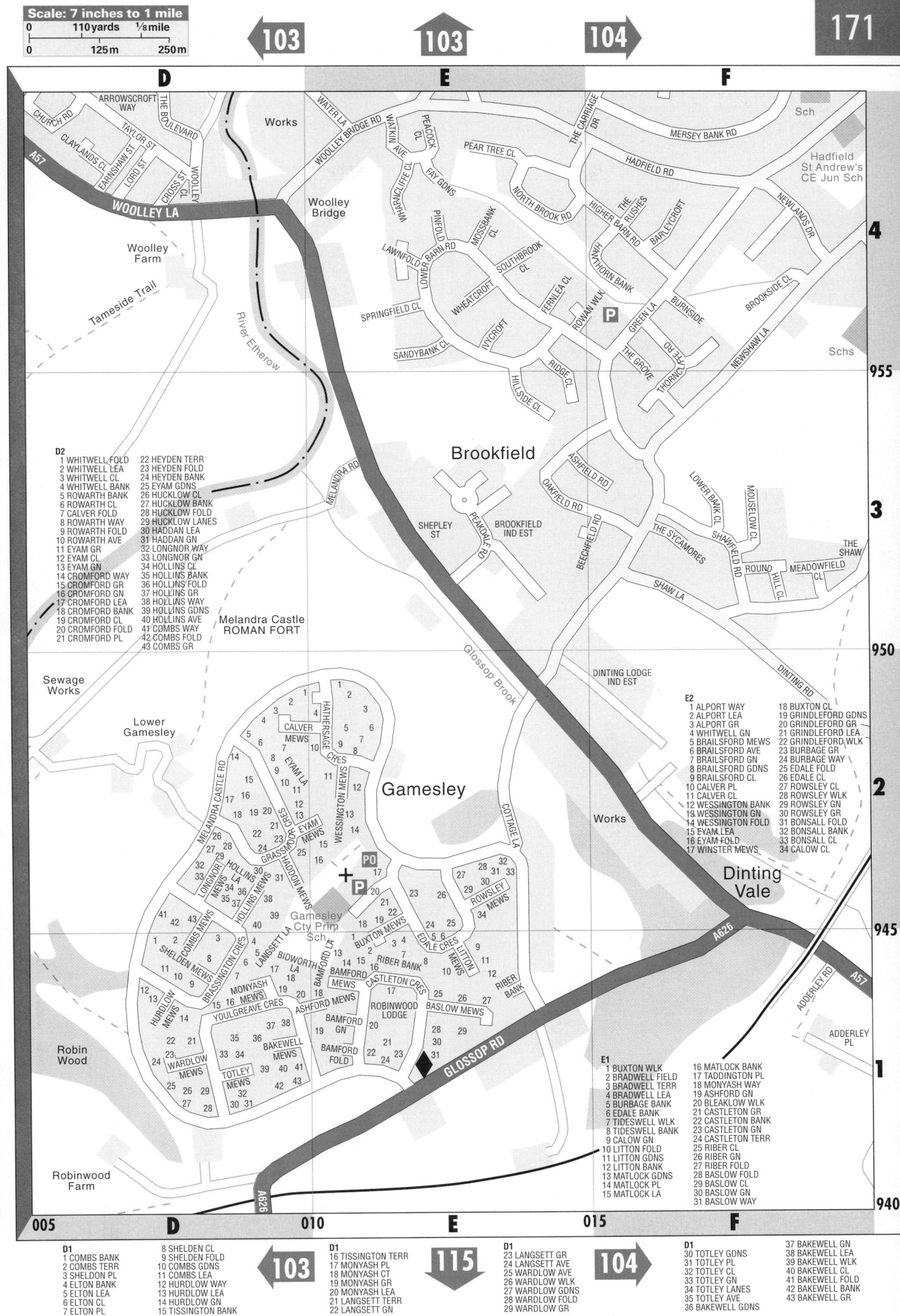

Scale: 7 inches to 1 mile

| 0 | 110 yards | 1/8 mile |
| 0 | 125m | 250m |

ARROWSCROFT WAY
THE BOULEVARD
CHURCH RD
TAYLOR ST
CLAYLANDS CL
EARNSHAW ST
LORD ST
CROSS ST
WOOLLEY
A57
WOOLLEY LA
Works
WATER LA
WOOLLEY BRIDGE RD
Woolley Bridge
WATKIN AVE
PEACOCK CL
PEAR TREE CL
WHARNCLIFFE CL
FAY GDNS
PINFOLD
NORTH BROOK RD
HIGHER BARN RD
THE CARRIAGE DR
MERSEY BANK RD
Sch
Hadfield St Andrew's CE Jun Sch
HADFIELD RD
THE RUSHES
HAWTHORN BANK
BARLEYCROFT
NEWLANDS DR
BROOKSIDE CL
4

Woolley Farm
Woolley LA
Tameside Trail
River Etherow
LAWNFOLD
LOWER BARN RD
MOSSBANK CL
WHEATCROFT
SOUTHBROOK CL
IVYCROFT
FERNLEA CL
ROMAN WLK
P
GREEN LA
THE GROVE
AYRE RD
THORNICLY
BURNSIDE
NEWSHAW LA
SPRINGFIELD CL
SANDYBANK CL
RIDGE CL
HILLSIDE CL
Schs
955

Brookfield
MELANDRA RD
SHEPLEY ST
PEAKDALE RD
Brookfield IND EST
ASHFIELD RD
OAKFIELD RD
BEECHFIELD RD
LOWER BANK CL
MOUSELOW CL
SHAWFIELD RD
THE SYCAMORES
ROUND HILL CL
MEADOWFIELD CL
THE SHAW
3

Melandra Castle
ROMAN FORT
SHAW LA
Glossop Brook
DINTING LODGE IND EST
DINTING RD
950

Sewage Works
Lower Gamesley
HATHERSAGE CRES
CALVER MEWS
EYAM LA
WESSINGTON MEWS
Gamesley
COTTAGE LA
Works
Dinting Vale
945
A626

D2
1 WHITWELL FOLD
2 WHITWELL LEA
3 WHITWELL CL
4 WHITWELL BANK
5 ROWARTH BANK
6 ROWARTH CL
7 CALVER FOLD
8 ROWARTH WAY
9 ROWARTH FOLD
10 ROWARTH AVE
11 EYAM GR
12 EYAM CL
13 EYAM GN
14 CROMFORD WAY
15 CROMFORD GR
16 CROMFORD GN
17 CROMFORD LEA
18 CROMFORD BANK
19 CROMFORD CL
20 CROMFORD GR
21 CROMFORD PL
22 HEYDEN TERR
23 HEYDEN FOLD
24 HEYDEN BANK
25 EYAM GDNS
26 HUCKLOW CL
27 HUCKLOW BANK
28 HUCKLOW FOLD
29 HUCKLOW LANES
30 HADDAN LEA
31 HADDAN GN
32 LONGNOR WAY
33 LONGNOR GN
34 HOLLINS CL
35 HOLLINS BANK
36 HOLLINS FOLD
37 HOLLINS GR
38 HOLLINS WAY
39 HOLLINS GDNS
40 HOLLINS AVE
41 COMBS WAY
42 COMBS FOLD
43 COMBS GR

E2
1 ALPORT WAY
2 ALPORT LEA
3 ALPORT GR
4 WHITWELL GN
5 BRAILSFORD MEWS
6 BRAILSFORD AVE
7 BRAILSFORD GR
8 BRAILSFORD GDNS
9 BRAILSFORD CL
10 CALVER PL
11 CALVER CL
12 WESSINGTON BANK
13 WESSINGTON GN
14 WESSINGTON FOLD
15 EYAM LEA
16 EYAM FOLD
17 WINSTER MEWS
18 BUXTON CL
19 GRINDLEFORD GDNS
20 GRINDLEFORD GR
21 GRINDLEFORD LEA
22 GRINDLEFORD WLK
23 BURBAGE GR
24 BURBAGE WAY
25 EDALE FOLD
26 EDALE CL
27 ROWSLEY CL
28 ROWSLEY WLK
29 ROWSLEY GN
30 ROWSLEY GR
31 BONSALL FOLD
32 BONSALL BANK
33 BONSALL CL
34 CALOW CL

MELANDRA CASTLE RD
LONGNOR MEWS
HOLLINS LA
GRASSMOOR CRES
HADDON MEWS
EYAM MEWS
PO
P
+
Gamesley Cty Prim Sch
BUXTON MEWS
RIBER BANK
EDALE CRES
LITTON MEWS
ROWSLEY MEWS
RIBER BANK
41 42 43
COMBS MEWS
SHELDEN MEWS
BRASSINGTON CRES
LANGSETT LA
BIDWORTH LA
BAMFORD LA
CASTLETON CRES
MONYASH MEWS
YOULGREAVE CRES
ASHFORD MEWS
BAMFORD MEWS
BAMFORD GN
BASLOW MEWS
Robinwood Lodge
Robin Wood
HURDLOW MEWS
WARDLOW MEWS
TOTLEY MEWS
BAKEWELL MEWS
BAMFORD FOLD
GLOSSOP RD
Robinwood Farm
A626
940

E1
1 BUXTON WLK
2 BRADWELL FIELD
3 BRADWELL TERR
4 BRADWELL LEA
5 BURBAGE BANK
6 EDALE BANK
7 TIDESWELL WLK
8 TIDESWELL BANK
9 CALOW GN
10 LITTON FOLD
11 LITTON GDNS
12 LITTON BANK
13 MATLOCK GDNS
14 MATLOCK PL
15 MATLOCK LA
16 MATLOCK BANK
17 TADDINGTON PL
18 MONYASH WAY
19 ASHFORD GN
20 BLEAKLOW WLK
21 CASTLETON GR
22 CASTLETON BANK
23 CASTLETON GN
24 CASTLETON TERR
25 RIBER CL
26 RIBER GN
27 RIBER FOLD
28 BASLOW FOLD
29 BASLOW CL
30 BASLOW GN
31 BASLOW WAY

ADDERLEY RD
A57
ADDERLEY PL

005 D 010 E 015 F

D1
1 COMBS BANK
2 COMBS TERR
3 SHELDON PL
4 ELTON BANK
5 ELTON LEA
6 ELTON CL
7 ELTON PL
8 SHELDEN CL
9 SHELDEN FOLD
10 COMBS GDNS
11 COMBS LEA
12 HURDLOW WAY
13 HURDLOW LEA
14 HURDLOW GN
15 TISSINGTON BANK

D1
16 TISSINGTON TERR
17 MONYASH PL
18 MONYASH CT
19 MONYASH GR
20 MONYASH LEA
21 LANGSETT TERR
22 LANGSETT GN

D1
23 LANGSETT GR
24 LANGSETT AVE
25 WARDLOW AVE
26 WARDLOW WLK
27 WARDLOW GDNS
28 WARDLOW FOLD
29 WARDLOW GR

D1
30 TOTLEY GDNS
31 TOTLEY PL
32 TOTLEY CL
33 TOTLEY GN
34 TOTLEY LANES
35 TOTLEY AVE
36 BAKEWELL GDNS
37 BAKEWELL GN
38 BAKEWELL LEA
39 BAKEWELL WLK
40 BAKEWELL CL
41 BAKEWELL FOLD
42 BAKEWELL BANK
43 BAKEWELL GR

Street names are listed alphabetically and show the locality, the Postcode District, the page number and a reference to the square in which the name falls on the map page

Coal Pit La. **4** Leigh WN7 .... **75** E8

Full street name
This may have been abbreviated on the map

Location Number
If present, this indicates the street's position on a congested area of the map instead of the name

Town, village or locality in which the street falls.

Postcode District for the street name

Page number of the map on which the street name appears

Grid square in which the centre of the street falls

Schools, hospitals, sports centres, railway stations, shopping centres, industrial estates, public amenities and other places of interest are also listed. These are highlighted in magenta

Abbreviations used in the index

Alt'ham **Altrincham**	Ctr **Centre**	Dr **Drive**	Ind Est **Industrial Estate**	Pas **Passage**
App **Approach**	Cir **Circus**	Dro **Drove**	Intc **Interchange**	Pl **Place**
Arc **Arcade**	Cl **Close**	E **East**	Junc **Junction**	Prec **Precinct**
Ave **Avenue**	Comm **Common**	Espl **Esplanade**	La **Lane**	Prom **Promenade**
Bvd **Boulevard**	Cnr **Corner**	Est **Estate**	M'ster **Manchester**	Ret Pk **Retail Park**
Bldgs **Buildings**	Cotts **Cottages**	Gdns **Gardens**	N **North**	Rd **Road**
Bsns Pk **Business Park**	Ct **Court**	Gn **Green**	Orch **Orchard**	R'dale **Rochdale**
Bsns Ctr **Business Centre**	Ctyd **Courtyard**	Gr **Grove**	Par **Parade**	Rdbt **Roundabout**
Bglws **Bungalow**	Cres **Crescent**	Hts **Heights**	Pk **Park**	S **South**

Sq **Square** · Strs **Stairs** · Stps **Steps** · St **Street, Saint** · Terr **Terrace** · Trad Est **Trading Estate** · Wlk **Walk** · W **West** · Yd **Yard**

Alb – And 173

Albany Rd. Worsley M28 79 B3
Albany Road Trad Ctr. M21 97 B1
Albany St. Middleton M24 65 B7
Albany St. Oldham OL4 49 D1
Albany St. [10] R'dale OL11 31 A5
Albany Way. Hattersley SK14 102 E2
Albany Way. Salford M6 81 A3
Albemarle Ave. M20 110 A6
Albemarle Rd. M21 109 A8
Albemarle St. Ashton-u-L OL6 166 C3
Albemarle St. M'ster M14 98 A4
Albemarle Terr. OL6 166 C3
Albermarle Rd. [5] M27 79 E7
Albert Ave. Dukinfield SK16 101 C6
Albert Ave. M'ster M25 63 D1
Albert Ave. Reddish M18 99 F4
Albert Ave. Shaw OL2 149 B5
Albert Ave. Urmston M41 95 E2
Albert Ave. Walkden M28 60 C5
Albert Cl. Cheadle SK8 123 A2
Albert Cl. Whitefield M45 63 A8
Albert Ct. WA14 119 D4
Albert Fildes Wlk. [3] M8 155 F7
Albert Gdns. M40 & M35 83 D5
Albert Gr. Farnworth BL4 60 D8
Albert Gr. M'ster M12 99 A4
Albert Hill St. M20 110 B3
Albert Park Rd. M7 155 D5
Albert Pl. Alt'ham WA14 119 D5
Albert Pl. M'ster M13 98 F3
Albert Pl. Whitefield M45 45 B1
Albert Rd. Alt'ham WA15 119 E3
Albert Rd. Cheadle SK8 123 A2
Albert Rd. Eccles M30 79 F2
Albert Rd. Farnworth BL4 60 D8
Albert Rd. Hyde SK14 167 D2
Albert Rd. M'ster M19 99 A1
Albert Rd. M'ster SK4 168 A3
Albert Rd. Sale M33 108 C4
Albert Rd. Whitefield M45 63 A8
Albert Rd. Wilmslow SK9 137 A6
Albert Rd E. WA15 119 E3
Albert Rd W. Bolton BL1 40 F8
Albert Rd W. Bolton BL1 144 A8
Albert Royds St. R'dale OL12 & OL16 15 B2
Albert Sq. Alt'ham WA14 119 D3
Albert Sq. M'ster M2 158 F1
Albert Sq. Stalybridge SK15 85 F1
Albert St. Ashton-i-M WN4 73 B3
Albert St. Bolton BL7 8 D3
Albert St. Bury BL9 141 A2
Albert St. Denton M34 100 F3
Albert St. Droylsden M43 84 B1
Albert St. Eccles M30 79 F2
Albert St. Farnworth BL4 60 D7
Albert St. Farnworth BL4 60 E8
Albert St. Hadfield SK14 104 A5
Albert St. Hazel Grove SK7 124 D3
Albert St. Heywood OL10 29 B2
Albert St. [14] Hindley WN2 56 D5
Albert St. Horwich BL6 22 B4
Albert St. Hyde SK14 167 F3
Albert St. Irlam M44 105 E6
Albert St. Little Lever BL3 43 B3
Albert St. Littleborough OL15 16 B5
Albert St. M'ster M11 160 F1
Albert St. Middleton M24 65 A8
Albert St. Milnrow OL16 32 A5
Albert St. Oldham OL8 66 B1
Albert St. Oldham OL9 66 B3
Albert St. Oldham OL4 67 E5
Albert St. Prestwich M25 63 C4
Albert St. Ramsbottom BL0 138 B6
Albert St. Royton OL2 48 D4
Albert St. Shaw OL2 149 A7
Albert St. Stockport SK3 169 D1
Albert St. Whitworth OL12 14 C8
Albert St. Wigan WN5 54 F6
Albert St. Wigan WN1 151 F8
Albert St W. M35 83 D6
Albert Webb House. [6] M6 154 E1
Alberta St. Bolton BL3 144 C5
Alberta St. Stockport SK1 170 F8
Alberton Cl. WN2 38 C6
Albine St. M40 157 F8
Albinson Wlk. M31 106 A3
Albion Cl. SK4 169 E3
Albion Ct. BL8 140 D2
Albion Dr. Droylsden M43 84 A2
Albion Dr. Wigan WN2 38 B2
Albion Fold. M43 84 A2
Albion Gdns. SK15 86 B1
Albion Gr. M33 108 A4
Albion House. SK15 86 C2
Albion Pl. Hazel Grove SK7 124 D3
Albion Pl. [10] M'ster M7 81 C5
Albion Pl. Prestwich M25 63 A4
Albion Rd. M'ster M14 98 C1
Albion Rd. R'dale OL11 139 D6
Albion St. Ashton-u-L OL6 166 C3
Albion St. [7] Bacup OL13 3 C8
Albion St. Bolton BL3 145 F5
Albion St. Bury BL8 140 D2
Albion St. Failsworth M35 83 E7
Albion St. Hyde SK14 167 D2
Albion St. Kearsley BL4 61 A7
Albion St. [8] Leigh WN7 75 F5
Albion St. Littleborough OL15 16 A5
Albion St. M'ster M16 97 D4
Albion St. M'ster M15 162 F8
Albion St. Oldham OL9 152 A7
Albion St. Oldham OL1 153 F7
Albion St [5] Platt Bridge WN2 56 A2
Albion St. R'dale OL11 30 D1
Albion St. Radcliffe M26 44 B1
Albion St. Sale M33 108 B4
Albion St. Stalybridge SK15 86 B2
Albion St. Swinton M27 80 A8
Albion St. Westhoughton BL5 39 F3
Albion St. Wigan WN2 38 B2
Albion Towers. [5] M5 81 B2
Albion Trad Est. OL6 85 D3
Albion Way. Salford M5 & M6 81 B1
Alburn Ct. M40 160 E4
Albury Dr. M'ster M19 110 D2
Albury Dr. R'dale OL12 13 F2
Albury Way. WN2 37 F2
Albyns Ave. M7 & M8 156 A7
Alcester Ave. SK3 122 F7
Alcester Cl. Bury BL8 27 B3
Alcester Cl. Middleton M24 65 B6
Alcester Rd. Gatley SK8 122 B4
Alcester Rd. Sale M33 108 B2
Alcester St. OL9 66 A3
Alcester Wlk. M9 64 C5
Alconbury Ct. M34 100 B8
Alconbury Wlk. M9 64 B6
Aldborough Cl. M20 110 B6
Aldbourne Cl. M40 157 D5
Aldbury Terr. [2] BL1 143 D1
Aldcliffe. WA3 90 F8
Aldcroft St. [5] M18 99 F6
Alden Cl. M45 63 A8
Alden Rd. BB4 1 A5
Alden Rise. BB4 1 A6
Alden Wlk. SK4 111 D7
Alder Ave. Ashton-i-M WN4 72 F5
Alder Ave. Billinge WN5 71 D5
Alder Ave. Bury BL9 141 C3
Alder Ave. Poynton SK12 133 F3
Alder Ave. Wigan WN5 54 D6
Alder Cl. Ashton-u-L OL6 85 B7
Alder Cl. Dukinfield SK16 102 A7
Alder Cl. Leigh WN7 75 F2
Alder Ct. M8 63 F1
Alder Dr. Alt'ham WA15 120 E5
Alder Dr. Swinton M27 61 C1
Alder Edge. M21 96 F1
Alder Forest Ave. M28 79 A4
Alder Gr. Bolton BL2 25 C6
Alder Gr. Denton M34 101 A3
Alder Gr. Stockport SK3 123 C8
Alder Gr. Stretford M32 96 E2
Alder La. Billinge WA11 71 A5
Alder La. Hindley WN2 57 B5
Alder La. Oldham OL8 66 D2
Alder Lee Cl. WN3 54 D1
Alder Meadow Cl. OL12 14 A1
Alder Moor Cl. M11 99 D8
Alder Park Prim Sch. M30 79 A4
Alder Rd. Cheadle SK8 122 E5
Alder Rd. Failsworth M35 83 F5
Alder Rd. Golborne WA3 90 F8
Alder Rd. Middleton M24 47 C2
Alder Rd. R'dale OL11 30 D2
Alder St. Atherton M46 58 D3
Alder St. Bolton BL3 147 F3
Alder St. Newton-l-W WA12 89 C3
Alder St. Salford M6 154 F2
Alder St. Worsley M28 79 A4
Alderbank. Horwich BL6 21 F3
Alderbank. Littleborough OL12 15 C7
Alderbank Cl. BL4 60 F6
Aldercroft Ave. Bolton BL2 25 D1
Aldercroft Ave. Wythenshawe M22 121 C2
Alderdale Cl. SK4 111 A5
Alderdale Dr. Droylsden M43 83 E2
Alderdale Dr. High Lane SK6 134 E7
Alderdale Dr. M'ster SK4 111 A5
Alderdale Gr. SK9 136 E5
Alderdale Rd. SK8 123 C4
Alderfield House. M21 96 F1
Alderfield Rd. M21 96 F1
Alderfold St. M46 58 D3
Alderford Par. [11] M8 155 F6
Aldergate Gr. OL6 85 F5
Alderglen Rd. M7 & M8 156 A5
Alderley Ave. Bolton BL1 24 E5
Alderley Ave. Golborne WA3 90 D7
Alderley Cl. Billinge WN5 71 E5
Alderley Cl. Hazel Grove SK7 133 F8
Alderley Cl. Poynton SK12 133 F2
Alderley Dr. SK6 112 E3
Alderley Edge Cty Prim Sch. SK9 137 A2
Alderley Edge Golf Course. SK9 136 E3
Alderley Edge Sta. SK9 137 A2
Alderley La. WN7 76 B2
Alderley Lodge. SK9 137 A5
Alderley Rd. Alderley Edge SK10 & SK9 137 F2
Alderley Rd. Hindley WN2 57 A5
Alderley Rd. Reddish SK5 111 F5
Alderley Rd. Sale M33 108 E2
Alderley Rd. Urmston M41 95 A2
Alderley Rd. Wilmslow SK9 137 A6
Alderley St. OL6 85 D5
Alderley Terr. [8] SK16 166 B1
Alderman Foley Dr. OL12 14 A2
Alderman Kay Sch. M24 47 A3
Alderman Smith Cty Inf Sch. BL8 27 C2
Alderman Sq. M11 164 E8
Aldermary Rd. M21 109 D5
Aldermaston Gr. M9 64 B6
Aldermere Cres. M41 94 F3
Alderminster Ave. M38 60 A5
Alderney Dr. WN3 55 A3
Alders Ave. M22 121 C5
Alders Ct. OL8 85 A8
Alders Green Rd. WN2 57 A5
Alders Rd. High Lane SK12 135 A7
Alders Rd. Wythenshawe M22 121 C5
Alders The. WN6 36 D4
Aldersgate Rd. Bramhall SK7 & SK8 132 C5
Aldersgate Rd. Stockport SK2 124 B6
Aldersgreen Ave. SK6 134 F7
Aldershot Wlk. [3] M11 160 F1
Alderside Rd. M9 157 D8
Aldersley Ave. M9 64 B5
Alderson St. Oldham OL9 153 E7
Alderson St. Salford M6 81 A4
Aldersyde St. BL3 147 D3
Alderton Dr. BL5 57 E6
Alderue Ave. M22 121 D6
Alderway. BL0 1 C1
Alderwood Ave. SK4 168 A1
Alderwood Fold. OL4 67 F5
Alderwood Gr. BL0 1 D4
Alderwood Wlk. [7] M8 155 F6
Aldfield Rd. M23 108 F1
Aldford Cl. M20 110 C3
Aldford Dr. M46 58 E5
Aldford Gr. BL3 43 B5
Aldford Pl. SK9 136 F2
Aldford Way. WN6 36 E8
Aldham Ave. M40 83 C4
Aldred Cl. M8 156 B6
Aldred St. Bolton BL3 146 B3
Aldred St. Eccles M30 79 C1
Aldred St. Failsworth M35 83 E7
Aldred St. [3] Hindley WN2 56 D4
Aldred St. Leigh WN7 75 E8
Aldred St. Salford M5 81 B2
Aldridge Cl. WN3 55 B3
Aldridge Wlk. M11 164 F8
Aldsworth Dr. BL3 147 E4
Aldwick Ave. M20 110 C3
Aldwinians Cl. M34 100 E5
Aldworth Dr. M10 & M40 157 E5
Aldworth Gr. M33 107 D3
Aldwych. OL11 30 F3
Aldwych Ave. M14 98 B2
Aldwyn Cl. M34 100 E5
Aldwyn Cres. SK7 124 C2
Aldwyn Cty Prim Sch. M34 84 C1
Aldwyn Park Rd. M34 100 C8
Alexander Ave. M35 84 A8
Alexander Ct. M5 161 A8
Alexander Dr. Alt'ham WA15 120 A6
Alexander Dr. Milnrow OL16 31 F6
Alexander Dr. Whitefield M45 45 A2
Alexander Gdns. M7 158 D4
Alexander Rd. [9] BL2 25 C1
Alexander St. R'dale OL11 30 B2
Alexander St. Salford M6 154 E2
Alexander St. Tyldesley M29 77 A8
Alexandra Ave. Hyde SK14 101 C2
Alexandra Ave. M'ster M14 97 F2
Alexandra Ave. Whitefield M45 63 A8
Alexandra Cl. SK3 123 C6
Alexandra Cres. [1] Oldham OL1 67 B8
Alexandra Cres. Wigan WN5 54 E6
Alexandra Ct. M41 94 E1
Alexandra Ctr Ret Pk. OL4 153 F6
Alexandra Dr. M19 110 F7
Alexandra Gr. M44 105 F8
Alexandra Hospl The. SK8 122 D6
Alexandra House. [6] OL1 67 B8
Alexandra Mews. OL4 67 A5
Alexandra Park Inf Sch. SK3 123 C7
Alexandra Rd. Ashton-i-M WN4 73 B4
Alexandra Rd. Ashton-u-L OL6 166 B4
Alexandra Rd. Dukinfield M34 101 A4
Alexandra Rd. Eccles M30 95 C8
Alexandra Rd. Horwich BL6 39 E8
Alexandra Rd. Kearsley BL4 61 A7
Alexandra Rd. Kearsley M26 61 A8
Alexandra Rd. M'ster M15 & M16 97 E4
Alexandra Rd. M'ster SK4 168 C3
Alexandra Rd. Oldham OL8 67 A4
Alexandra Rd. Sale M33 108 D3
Alexandra Rd. Walkden M28 60 C5
Alexandra Rd S. M16 97 E2
Alexandra St. Abram WN2 74 B8
Alexandra St. Ashton-u-L OL6 85 D4
Alexandra St. [9] Bolton BL3 147 D4
Alexandra St. Farnworth BL4 60 D7
Alexandra St. Heywood OL10 46 E8
Alexandra St. Hyde SK14 101 C1
Alexandra St. M'ster M7 158 D3
Alexandra St. Oldham OL8 67 A5
Alexandra St. Wigan WN5 54 F6
Alexandra Terr. [14] M'ster M19 99 A1
Alexandra Terr. Oldham OL4 49 E3
Alexandria Dr. BL5 58 B8
Alf Kaufman Sch. OL11 13 E1
Alford Ave. M20 110 A8
Alford Cl. BL2 42 F6
Alford Rd. SK4 111 C6
Alford St. OL9 66 B2
Alfred Ave. M28 79 A7
Alfred James Cl. [19] M10 & M40 159 C3
Alfred Morris Ct. M23 109 A2
Alfred Rd. WA3 91 A8
Alfred St. Ashton-u-L OL6 85 D4
Alfred St. Bolton BL7 8 D3
Alfred St. Bolton BL3 42 B4
Alfred St. Bury BL9 141 A1
Alfred St. Dukinfield SK14 101 C3
Alfred St. Eccles M30 79 D3
Alfred St. Farnworth BL4 42 D2
Alfred St. Ince-i-M WN3 151 D6
Alfred St. Irlam M44 105 E6
Alfred St. Kearsley BL4 60 F8
Alfred St. Littleborough OL15 16 A6
Alfred St. M'ster M9 157 D8
Alfred St. Newton-l-W WA12 89 E3
Alfred St. Oldham OL9 152 C6
Alfred St. Platt Bridge WN2 56 A3
Alfred St. Ramsbottom BL0 138 B5
Alfred St. Shaw OL2 149 B7
Alfred St. [9] Tyldesley M29 58 F1
Alfred St. Walkden M28 60 D3
Alfred St. Whitworth OL12 4 D2
Alfred St. Wigan WN1 37 B2
Alfreton Ave. M34 113 A8
Alfreton Rd. SK2 124 E5
Alfreton Wlk. [9] M40 83 A6
Alfriston Dr. M23 109 A2
Alger St. [1] OL6 85 D4
Algernon Rd. M28 60 C4
Algernon St. Eccles M30 79 D3
Algernon St. [5] Hindley WN2 56 D5
Algernon St. Swinton M27 79 D8
Algernon St. Wigan WN3 55 A4
Algreave Rd. SK3 123 A8
Alice Ingham RC Prim Sch. OL16 15 C2
Alice St. Bolton BL3 144 C5
Alice St. Hyde SK14 113 E7
Alice St. Pendlebury M27 80 B8
Alice St. R'dale OL12 15 B1
Alice St. Sale M33 108 D4
Alicia Ct. OL12 14 E1
Alicia Dr. OL12 14 E1
Alick's Fold. [9] BL5 39 E1
Alison Ct. SK4 168 B3
Alison St. [13] M'ster M14 97 F3
Alison St. [2] M'ster M14 98 A3
Alison St. Shaw OL2 149 B8
Alker Rd. M10 & M40 160 D3
Alker St. WN5 54 F6
Alkrington Cl. BL9 45 A2
Alkrington Gn. M24 64 F7
Alkrington Hall. M24 64 F7
Alkrington Hall Rd N. M24 64 F7
Alkrington Hall Rd S. M24 64 E6
Alkrington Moss Prim Sch. M24 65 B5
Alkrington Park Rd. M24 64 E7
Alkrington Prim Sch. M24 65 A6
All Saint's CE Prim Sch. M40 83 C5
All Saint's Cl. OL2 48 D5
All Saint's Ct. M32 96 B2
All Saints Catholic High Sch. SK16 101 D7
All Saints CE Prim Sch. Appley Bridge WN6 18 C1
All Saints' CE Prim Sch. Farnworth BL4 42 D2
All Saints CE Prim Sch. Marple SK6 126 A5
All Saints CE Prim Sch. R'dale OL12 15 A2
All Saints CE Prim Sch. Stockport SK4 169 D3
All Saints CE Prim Sch. Whitefield BL9 45 A2
All Saints Gr. WN2 56 E5
All Saints Prim Sch. M18 165 B6
All Saints' RC Prim Sch. Glossop SK13 104 D2
All Saints RC Prim Sch. Sale M33 107 D6
All Saints' Rd. SK4 169 E4
All Saints' St. Bolton BL1 145 F8
All Saints' St. Failsworth M40 83 C5
All Saints Terr. OL12 15 B2
All Souls CE Prim Sch. OL10 29 F3
All Souls RC Prim Sch. M5 154 D1
Allams St. M11 160 E2
Allan Ct. M21 109 A7
Allan Roberts Cl. M9 64 D1
Allan St. M29 76 F8
Allanadale Ct. [10] M7 63 E1
Allandale. WA14 119 B4
Allandale Dr. OL2 48 C5
Allandale Rd. M19 98 F1
Allanson Rd. M22 109 E1
Alldis St. SK2 124 B5
Allen Ave. Fowley Common WA3 92 C4
Allen Ave. Hyde SK14 113 F8
Allen Cl. OL2 149 A6
Allen Rd. M41 95 F2
Allen St. Bury BL8 27 C3
Allen St. Little Lever BL3 43 A3
Allen St. Oldham OL8 153 D6
Allen St. R'dale OL16 31 A5
Allen St. Radcliffe M26 43 F3
Allenby Gr. BL5 57 D7
Allenby Rd. Irlam M44 105 D4
Allenby Rd. Swinton M27 79 C6
Allenby St. Atherton M46 58 B2
Allenby St. Shaw OL2 149 A7
Allenby Wlk. [4] M40 156 C5
Allendale Dr. BL9 45 A3
Allendale Gdns. BL1 143 E2
Allendale Wlk. M3 158 D2
Allerby Way. WA3 90 E8
Allerdean Wlk. SK4 110 F3
Allerford Cl. M16 97 E4
Allerton Cl. BL5 40 A1
Allerton Ct. [7] BL1 145 E8
Allerton Wlk. [6] M13 163 C6
Allescholes Rd. OL14 6 B7
Allesley Cl. BL5 40 A1
Allgreave Cl. M33 108 E1
Alliance St. [5] WN1 151 D8
Allingham St. M13 98 E4
Allington. OL11 139 E6
Allington Dr. M30 79 E4
Alliott Wlk. M15 162 E5
Allison Gr. M30 79 B1
Allison St. M7 & M8 155 F5
Allonby Wlk. M24 46 C2
Allotment Rd. M44 105 D6
Alloway Wlk. [6] M40 83 A6
Allscott Way. WN4 73 C3
Allsopp St. BL3 145 F6
Allwood St. M3 158 D1
Alma Cl. WN8 53 C7
Alma Ct. [3] M'ster M15 97 E4
Alma Ct. Orrell WN8 53 C7
Alma Gr. WN3 54 E2
Alma Hill. WN8 53 C7
Alma Ind Est. [25] OL12 14 F1
Alma La. SK9 137 A7
Alma Par. WN8 53 C7
Alma Park Prim Sch. M19 111 A8
Alma Rd. Hazel Grove SK7 134 A8
Alma Rd. M'ster M19 111 A8
Alma Rd. M'ster SK4 111 B5
Alma Rd. Orrell WN8 53 C7
Alma Rd. Sale M33 107 E2
Alma Rd. Westhoughton BL5 57 F8
Alma St. Atherton M46 58 C3
Alma St. Bolton BL3 146 C4
Alma St. Eccles M30 79 F1
Alma St. Kearsley BL4 61 B5
Alma St. Leigh WN7 75 E8
Alma St. Little Lever BL3 43 B3
Alma St. Newton-l-W WA12 89 B3
Alma St. [13] R'dale OL12 14 F1
Alma St. Radcliffe M26 43 F5
Alma St. Stalybridge SK15 86 B2
Alma St. Tyldesley M29 76 F8
Alminstone Cl. M40 83 D4
Almond Ave. BL9 141 C3
Almond Brook Rd. WN6 19 C1
Almond Cl. Failsworth M35 83 F6
Almond Cl. Littleborough OL15 15 F6
Almond Cl. Salford M6 81 B2
Almond Cl. Stockport SK3 123 C8
Almond Cres. Rawtenstall BB4 1 F8
Almond Cres. Standish WN6 36 F7
Almond Dr. M33 107 F6
Almond Gr. Bolton BL1 143 F3
Almond Gr. Wigan WN5 54 E6
Almond Rd. [7] OL4 49 D1
Almond St. Bolton BL1 143 F4
Almond St. [9] Farnworth BL4 60 C8
Almond St. M'ster M40 159 B4
Almond Tree Rd. SK8 123 A1
Almond Way. SK14 102 A2
Almond Wlk. M31 105 D3
Alms Hill Rd. M8 156 A7
Alness Rd. M16 97 E2
Alnwick Cl. WN2 38 D5
Alnwick Dr. BL9 45 A5
Alnwick Rd. M9 64 D5
Alperton Wlk. M40 83 D4
Alpha Ct. M34 100 C3
Alpha Pl. M15 162 E7
Alpha Rd. M32 96 C1
Alpha St. M'ster M11 99 E7
Alpha St. Salford M6 154 F3
Alpha St W. M6 154 E3
Alphin Cl. Uppermill OL5 68 E3
Alphin Cl. Uppermill OL3 69 B5
Alphin Sq. OL5 68 D1
Alphonsus St. M16 97 C4
Alpine Dr. Leigh WN7 75 C8
Alpine Dr. Littleborough OL12 15 C6
Alpine Dr. Milnrow OL16 32 A7
Alpine Dr. Royton OL2 48 C3
Alpine Rd. Stockport SK1 112 A1
Alpine Rd. Stockport SK1 112 A2
Alpine St. Droylsden M11 83 B2
Alpine St. Newton-l-W WA12 89 A3
Alpington Wlk. M40 65 C2
Alport Ave. M16 97 C2
Alport Gr. [3] SK13 171 E2
Alport Lea. [2] SK13 171 E2
Alport Way. [1] SK13 171 E2
Alresford Rd. Middleton M9 64 F5
Alresford Rd. Salford M6 80 D5
Alric Wlk. M22 130 E8
Alsham Wlk. M8 156 A6
Alsop Ave. M7 81 B7
Alstead Ave. WA15 120 A3
Alston Ave. Sale M33 107 F3
Alston Ave. Shaw OL2 149 B8
Alston Ave. Stretford M32 96 B3
Alston Cl. SK7 124 A1
Alston Gdns. M19 110 F5
Alston Lea. M46 58 E4
Alston Rd. M'ster M18 99 E5
Alston Rd. Wigan WN2 37 F2
Alston St. Bolton BL3 147 E3
Alston St. Bury BL8 27 C4
Alston Wlk. M24 46 C2
Alstone Dr. WA14 119 A6
Alstone Rd. SK4 111 C6
Alt Cl. WN7 75 D6
Alt Fold Dr. OL8 67 C3
Alt Gr. OL6 85 B6
Alt Hill La. OL6 & OL7 85 C8
Alt Hill Rd. OL6 67 C1
Alt La. OL8 67 C3
Alt Liby. OL4 67 D4
Alt Prim Sch. OL8 67 D3
Alt Wlk. M45 45 C2
Altair Ave. [7] Wythenshawe M22 121 D1
Altair Pl. M7 81 C4
Altcar Gr. SK5 99 E2
Altcar Wlk. M22 121 C2
Altham Cl. BL9 44 D7
Altham Wlk. [12] M40 83 A6
Althorn Wlk. [11] M23 121 A5
Althorpe Wlk. M40 83 D4
Alton Ave. M41 94 D2
Alton Cl. Ashton-i-M WN4 73 A4
Alton Cl. Ashton-u-L OL6 85 C7
Alton Cl. Whitefield BL9 45 A5
Alton Rd. SK9 136 F7
Alton Sq. M18 99 E7
Alton St. OL8 66 F3
Alton Towers. M16 97 D1
Altrincham CE (VA) Prim Sch. WA14 119 D5
Altrincham Gen Hospl. WA14 119 D4
Altrincham Golf Course. WA15 119 F5
Altrincham Gram Sch for Boys. WA14 119 D2
Altrincham Gram Sch for Girls. Alt'ham WA14 119 B3
Altrincham Gram Sch for Girls. Alt'ham WA14 119 C3
Altrincham Prep Sch. WA14 119 C1
Altrincham Priory Hospl. WA15 129 A7
Altrincham Rd. Alt'ham M23 120 E7
Altrincham Rd. Wilmslow SK9 130 C2
Altrincham Rd. Wythenshawe M23 121 B7
Altrincham Rd. Wythenshawe M22 121 E5
Altrincham Rd. Wythenshawe SK9 130 C4
Altrincham St. M'ster M1 163 B8
Altrincham St. Oldham OL9 153 D8
Altrincham Sta. WA15 119 E4
Alum Cres. BL9 45 A3
Alva Rd. OL4 49 D2
Alvan Sq. [1] M18 99 E7
Alvanley Cl. Sale M33 108 C1
Alvanley Cl. Shevington WN5 36 C1
Alvanley Cres. SK3 123 C6
Alvaston Ave. SK4 168 B2
Alvaston Rd. M18 99 E4
Alveley Ave. M20 110 C5
Alverstone Rd. M20 110 C6
Alveston Dr. SK9 131 D1
Alvington Gr. SK7 124 A1
Alwin Rd. OL2 149 A8
Alwinton Ave. SK4 110 E3
Alworth Rd. M9 64 D5
Alwyn Cl. WN7 75 F1
Alwyn Dr. M13 98 E4
Alwyn St. WN1 37 D1
Alwyn Terr. WN1 37 D1
Amar St. WN2 151 F7
Ambassador Pl. WA15 119 E5
Amber Gdns. Dukinfield SK16 101 B8
Amber Gdns. Hindley WN2 56 E4
Amber Gr. BL5 39 F2
Amber St. M4 & M60 159 A2
Ambergate. M46 58 D2
Ambergate St. M11 160 F2
Amberhill Way. Boothstown M28 77 F5
Amberhill Way. Boothstown M28 78 A5
Amberleigh Prep Sch. M21 97 C1
Amberley Cl. Bolton BL3 40 F5
Amberley Cl. Wigan WN2 37 F2
Amberley Dr. Alt'ham WA15 129 B8
Amberley Dr. Irlam M44 94 A1
Amberley Dr. Wythenshawe M23 121 A4
Amberley Rd. M33 107 E5
Amberley Wlk. OL9 152 C7
Amberswood Cl. WN2 56 B7
Amberwood. OL9 65 E8
Amberwood Dr. M23 120 D6
Amblecote Dr E. M38 60 A6
Amblecote Dr W. M38 60 A6
Ambleside. Ince-i-M WN2 56 B7
Ambleside. Stalybridge SK15 86 A3
Ambleside. Wigan WN5 54 C7
Ambleside Ave. Alt'ham WA15 120 C5
Ambleside Ave. Ashton-u-L OL7 84 F4
Ambleside Cl. Bolton BL2 25 F4
Ambleside Cl. Middleton M24 46 E1
Ambleside Pl. WA11 71 B1
Ambleside Rd. Reddish SK5 111 F6
Ambleside Rd. Urmston M41 94 E1
Ambleside Wlk. M9 65 A2
Ambrose Ave. WN7 57 E1
Ambrose Cres. OL3 51 B3
Ambrose Dr. M20 109 E4
Ambrose Gdns. M20 109 E4
Ambrose St. Hyde SK14 113 E7
Ambrose St. M'ster M12 165 A7
Ambrose St. R'dale OL11 139 F5
Ambuscade Ct. M41 94 E2
Ambush St. M11 & M43 99 F7
Amelia St. Denton M34 100 F4
Amelia St. Hyde SK14 167 E2
Amersham Cl. M41 95 B5
Amersham Pl. M19 111 A6
Amersham St. M5 154 F1
Amesbury Dr. WN3 54 C2
Amesbury Gr. SK5 111 F5
Amesbury Rd. M9 64 E4
Amethyst Cl. WN2 38 A2
Amherst Rd. M14 & M20 110 D7
Amis Gr. WA3 90 E8
Amlwch Ave. SK2 124 D6
Ammon Wrigley Cl. OL1 153 F7
Ammon's Way. OL3 50 F5
Amory St. M12 163 C8
Amos Ave. M40 83 C4
Amos St. M'ster M9 157 F8
Amos St. Salford M6 154 E2
Ampleforth Gdns. M26 43 E5
Ampney Cl. M30 79 B1
Amport Wlk. [8] M40 65 C2
Amwell St. M8 156 C7
Amy St. Middleton M24 47 B1
Amy St. R'dale OL11 & OL12 14 B1
Anaconda Dr. M3 158 E3
Ancaster Wlk. [5] M40 65 C2
Anchor Cl. M19 99 C1
Anchor Ct. M8 63 F1
Anchor La. BL4 & M28 & M38 59 F7
Anchor St. OL1 153 F8
Anchorage Quay. M5 161 A8
Anchorage Rd. M32 96 A1
Anchorage Wlk. M18 165 C6
Ancoats Gr. M'ster M4 160 D1
Ancoats Gr. M'ster M4 164 D8
Ancoats Gr N. M4 160 D1
Ancoats Hospl. M4 159 C1
Ancoats St. [5] OL4 67 E6
Ancroft Gdns. BL3 146 C2
Anderton Cl. Bury BL8 26 F1
Anderton Cl. Rawtenstall BB4 2 F7
Anderton Gr. OL6 85 E5
Anderton La. BL6 21 E4
Anderton Prim Sch. PR6 21 B8
Anderton St. Adlington PR6 21 A7
Anderton St. Ince-i-M WN2 151 F7
Anderton Way. Handforth SK9 131 D3
Anderton Way. Wigan WN2 38 B2
Andoc Ave. M30 80 A1
Andover Ave. M24 65 C5
Andover Cres. WN3 54 D2
Andover St. M30 79 C1
Andover Wlk. M8 156 A8
Andre St. [14] M11 83 C2
Andrew Ave. WN5 71 F5
Andrew Cl. Radcliffe M26 44 C1
Andrew Cl. Ramsbottom BL8 10 F1
Andrew Ct. [2] M20 110 B6
Andrew Gr. SK16 101 D8
Andrew House. SK4 168 B4
Andrew La. Bolton BL1 & BL7 24 F6
Andrew La. High Lane SK6 134 F8
Andrew Rd. M9 64 D1
Andrew St. Ashton-u-L OL6 85 D5
Andrew St. Bury BL9 141 A2
Andrew St. Chadderton OL9 152 B8

Andrew St.
Droylsden M35 & M43 ... 84 C4
Andrew St. Failsworth M35 ... 83 E8
Andrew St. Hyde SK14 ... 167 F3
Andrew St. Middleton M24 ... 65 C7
Andrew St. Mossley OL5 ... 86 C8
Andrew St. Stockport SK4 ... 169 D2
Andrew's Terr. 3 BL5 ... 39 E1
Andrews Ave. M41 ... 94 E3
Andy Nicholson Wlk. M9 ... 157 F8
Anemone Dr. BB4 ... 1 A8
Anerley Rd. M20 ... 110 B4
Anfield Cl. BL9 ... 45 B3
Anfield Mews. SK8 ... 122 F3
Anfield Rd. Bolton BL3 ... 147 F2
Anfield Rd. Cheadle SK8 ... 122 F3
Anfield Rd. Failsworth M40 ... 65 D1
Anfield Rd. Sale M33 ... 108 C5
Angel Cl. SK16 ... 101 B8
Angel St. Dukinfield M34 ... 101 A4
Angel St. Hazel Grove SK7 ... 124 D3
Angel St. M'ster M4 ... 159 A3
Angel Trad Est. 4 M4 ... 159 A3
Angela Ave. OL1 & OL2 ... 48 E2
Angela St. M15 ... 162 D7
Angelko Rise. OL1 ... 49 D3
Angelo St. BL1 ... 143 D2
Angle St. 23 BL2 ... 25 B1
Angler Gr. M34 ... 100 F3
Anglesea Ave. SK2 ... 170 F6
Anglesey Cl. OL7 ... 85 A6
Anglesey Dr. SK12 ... 133 F6
Anglesey Gr. SK8 ... 123 A6
Anglesey Rd. OL7 ... 84 F6
Anglesey Water. SK12 ... 133 E6
Angleside Ave. M19 ... 110 A4
Anglezarke Rd. PR6 ... 21 A7
Anglia Gr. BL3 ... 146 C4
Angouleme Way. BL9 ... 140 F1
Angus Ave. Heywood OL10 ... 29 A1
Angus Ave. Leigh WN7 ... 75 C7
Angus St. OL13 ... 3 C8
Aniline St. M11 ... 83 B1
Anita St. M4 ... 159 B2
Anjou Bvd. WN5 ... 54 F8
Ann La. M29 ... 77 C5
Ann Sq. OL4 ... 67 D8
Ann St. Denton M34 ... 100 E3
Ann St. Dukinfield OL7 ... 100 F8
Ann St. Dukinfield SK14 ... 101 C3
Ann St. Farnworth BL4 ... 60 E7
Ann St. Heywood OL10 ... 29 D3
Ann St. Leigh WN7 ... 75 E8
Ann St. R'dale OL11 ... 139 F6
Ann St. Reddish SK5 ... 169 E4
Annable Rd. Bredbury SK6 ... 112 D3
Annable Rd. Droylsden M43 ... 84 B1
Annable Rd. Irlam M44 ... 105 F8
Annable Rd. M'ster M18 ... 99 E6
Annald Sq. M43 ... 100 A8
Annan Gr. WN4 ... 73 E5
Annan St. M34 ... 100 F4
Annandale Gdns. WN8 ... 53 A7
Anne Cl. 6 OL7 ... 85 A6
Anne Line Cl. 3 OL11 ... 31 A5
Anne St. SK16 ... 101 D8
Annecy Cl. BL8 ... 27 B4
Annersley Ave. OL2 ... 149 A6
Annesley Cres. WN3 ... 54 F3
Annesley Gdns. 1 M18 ... 99 D6
Annesley Rd. M40 ... 65 E1
Annette Ave. WA12 ... 89 A5
Annie Darby Ct. M9 ... 157 D7
Annie St. Ramsbottom BL0 ... 11 A4
Annie St. Salford M5 & M6 ... 154 E2
Annis Cl. SK9 ... 137 B2
Annis Rd. Alderley Edge SK9 137 B2
Annis Rd. Bolton BL3 ... 146 B4
Annis St. M9 ... 157 E7
Annisdale Cl. M30 ... 79 B2
Annisfield Ave. OL3 ... 69 C5
Anscombe Cl. M10 & M40 ... 160 D3
Ansdell Ave. M21 ... 109 C8
Ansdell Dr. M43 ... 83 E2
Ansdell Rd. Horwich BL6 ... 22 C4
Ansdell Rd. R'dale OL16 ... 31 B4
Ansdell Rd. Reddish SK5 ... 100 A1
Ansdell Rd. Wigan WN5 ... 54 D5
Ansdell St. M8 ... 156 A7
Ansell Cl. M18 ... 99 D6
Anselms Ct. OL8 ... 66 C4
Ansford Wlk. M9 ... 156 C6
Ansleigh Ave. M8 ... 64 A1
Ansley Gr. SK4 ... 168 B3
Anslow Cl. M40 ... 157 D5
Anson Ave. M27 ... 79 E6
Anson Cl. SK7 ... 132 F5
Anson Ct. M14 ... 98 D3
Anson Pl. WN5 ... 54 C8
Anson Rd. Handforth SK9 ... 131 E1
Anson Rd. M'ster M14 ... 98 D3
Anson Rd. Poynton SK12 ... 134 B3
Anson Rd.
Reddish M34 & SK5 ... 100 A2
Anson Rd. Swinton M27 ... 79 E6
Anson St. Bolton BL1 ... 143 F3
Anson St. Swinton M28 ... 79 B4
Anson St. Wigan WN5 ... 54 F7
Answell Ave. M8 ... 64 A2
Antares Ave. M7 ... 158 D3
Anthistle Ct. M5 ... 154 D2
Anthony Cl. M12 ... 164 E7
Anthony St. OL5 ... 68 B1
Anthorn Rd. WN3 ... 54 E3
Antilles Cl. M12 ... 99 A4
Antler Ct. WN4 ... 73 B6
Anton Wlk. M9 ... 157 D7
Antrim Cl. M'ster M19 ... 110 D2
Antrim Cl. Wigan WN3 ... 54 C2
Anvil Cl. WN5 ... 53 D5
Anvil St. OL13 ... 3 E8
Anvil Way. OL1 ... 153 E7
Apethorn La. SK14 ... 113 D7
Apfel La. OL9 ... 152 B7
Apollo Ave. BL9 ... 44 F3
Apollo Wlk. M12 ... 165 A6
Apperley Grange. M30 ... 79 E4
Appian Way. M7 & M8 ... 155 E5
Apple Cl. OL8 ... 67 C3
Apple Dell Ave. WA3 ... 74 C1
Apple St. SK14 ... 114 D7
Apple Tree Ct. M5 ... 81 A2
Apple Tree Rd. SK12 ... 127 B1
Apple Tree Wlk. 8 M33 ... 107 C5
Appleby Ave. Alt'ham WA15 120 C5
Appleby Ave.
Dukinfield SK14 ... 101 C5
Appleby Ave. M'ster M12 ... 99 A3
Appleby Cl. Bury BL8 ... 26 F2
Appleby Cl. Stockport SK3 ... 170 D5
Appleby Gdns. 1 Bolton BL2 25 B1
Appleby Gdns. Whitefield M45 44 F3
Appleby Lodge. M14 ... 98 D2
Appleby Rd. SK8 ... 122 B4
Appleby Wlk. 4 OL2 ... 48 E4
Applecross Wlk. M11 ... 165 C8
Appledore Dr. Alt'ham M23 120 D7
Appledore Dr. Bolton BL2 ... 25 F3
Appledore Wlk. OL9 ... 152 B6
Appleford Dr. M8 ... 156 B6
Applethwaite. WN2 ... 56 B8
Appleton Dr. SK13 ... 116 F8
Appleton Gr. M33 ... 107 E2
Appleton Rd. Alt'ham WA15 119 F1
Appleton Rd. Reddish SK4 ... 111 D6
Appleton St. WN3 ... 150 B8
Appleton Wlk. 8 SK9 ... 131 E1
Applewood. M24 ... 65 E7
Appley Bridge Sta. WN6 ... 35 C7
Appley Cl. WN6 ... 18 C2
Appley La N.
Appley Bridge WN6 ... 18 C1
Appley La S. WN6 & WN8 ... 35 C6
Apprentice Ct. 18 M9 ... 157 E8
April Cl. OL8 ... 67 C4
Apsley Cl. WA14 ... 119 B1
Apsley Gr. Alt'ham WA14 ... 119 B1
Apsley Gr. M'ster M12 ... 163 C6
Apsley Pl. OL7 ... 166 A2
Apsley Rd. M34 ... 100 F4
Apsley Side. OL5 ... 86 C8
Apsley St. SK1 ... 169 F1
Aquarius St. M15 ... 163 A5
Aqueduct Rd. BL3 ... 148 C5
Aquinas Coll. SK2 ... 124 A6
Aragon Dr. OL10 ... 29 C2
Aragon Way. SK6 ... 125 E6
Arbor Ave. M'ster M19 ... 110 F6
Arbor Dr. M19 ... 110 F7
Arbor Gr. Droylsden M43 ... 83 F3
Arbor Gr. Walkden M38 ... 59 E4
Arbory Ave. M40 ... 83 B7
Arbory Cl. WN7 ... 76 C5
Arbour Cl. Bury BL9 ... 27 E6
Arbour Cl. Salford M6 ... 154 F3
Arbour La. WN6 ... 19 B1
Arbour Rd. OL4 ... 67 E4
Arbroath St. M43 ... 83 E1
Arbury Ave. Cheadle SK3 ... 123 A7
Arbury Ave. R'dale OL11 ... 139 E5
Arcade St. 18 WN1 ... 150 C8
Arcade The. Brinnington SK5 112 C5
Arcade The. 2
Stalybridge SK15 ... 101 F8
Arcadia Ave. M33 ... 108 A1
Arch La. WN4 ... 72 B3
Arch St. Bolton BL1 ... 25 A1
Arch St. Bolton BL1 ... 148 A8
Archade The. OL6 ... 166 B3
Archer Ave. BL2 ... 148 C8
Archer Gr. BL2 ... 148 C8
Archer Pk. M24 ... 64 E8
Archer Pl. M32 ... 95 F3
Archer St. Boothstown M28 ... 77 E7
Archer St. Leigh WN7 ... 76 B2
Archer St. M'ster M11 ... 83 A2
Archer St. Mossley OL5 ... 68 C2
Archer St. Stockport SK2 ... 124 C5
Archie St. M5 ... 161 A7
Arclid Cl. SK9 ... 131 E1
Arcon Cl. OL16 ... 31 E6
Arcon Dr. M16 ... 97 E3
Arcon Pl. WA14 ... 119 A6
Ardale Ave. M40 ... 65 C2
Ardcombe Ave. M9 ... 64 C5
Ardeen Wlk. M13 ... 163 C6
Arden Ave. M24 ... 65 B5
Arden Bsns Ctr. SK6 ... 112 E6
Arden Cl. Ashton-u-L OL6 ... 85 F6
Arden Cl. Bury BL9 ... 44 E8
Arden Cl. Gatley SK8 ... 131 C7
Arden Cl. Glossop SK13 ... 116 A8
Arden Ct. SK7 ... 123 D1
Arden Gr. M40 ... 65 C1
Arden Hall. SK6 ... 112 D7
Arden House. OL2 ... 48 E4
Arden Jun Sch. SK6 ... 112 D3
Arden Lodge Rd. M23 ... 120 E7
Arden Prim Sch. SK6 ... 112 D3
Arden Rd. SK6 ... 112 E7
Arden St. OL9 ... 66 A3
Arden Wlk. 6 Sale M33 ... 107 C5
Arden Wlk. Stockport SK1 ... 169 E1
Ardenfield. M34 ... 113 A7
Ardenfield Dr. M22 ... 121 E3
Ardens Cl. M27 ... 61 D2
Ardent Way. M25 ... 63 B1
Ardern Gr. SK1 ... 169 E1
Ardern Rd. M8 ... 63 F2
Arderne Rd. WA15 ... 120 A8
Ardingly Wlk. M23 ... 120 D8
Ardley Rd. BL6 ... 22 C4
Ardmore Wlk. M22 ... 121 E2
Ardwick Gn N. M12 ... 163 C7
Ardwick Gn S. M13 ... 163 C7
Ardwick Sta. M12 ... 164 D7
Argo St. BL3 ... 147 D4
Argosy Dr.
Alt'ham M90 & WA15 ... 129 F7
Argosy Dr. Eccles M30 ... 94 F7
Argus St. OL8 ... 66 C2
Argyle Ave. M'ster M14 ... 98 E4
Argyle Ave. Walkden M28 ... 60 C5
Argyle Ave. Whitefield M45 ... 63 A8
Argyle Cres. OL10 ... 29 B1
Argyle Par. OL10 ... 29 A1
Argyle St. Atherton M46 ... 58 C2
Argyle St. Bury BL9 ... 140 F4
Argyle St. Droylsden M43 ... 84 A1
Argyle St. Hazel Grove SK7 ... 124 E2
Argyle St. Heywood OL10 ... 29 A1
Argyle St. Hindley WN2 ... 56 E5
Argyle St. M'ster M18 ... 99 D5
Argyle St. Oldham OL1 ... 67 B8
Argyle St. 14
R'dale OL11 & OL16 ... 31 A4
Argyle St. Swinton M27 ... 79 E7
Argyle St. Wigan WN5 ... 54 F6
Argyll Ave. M32 ... 96 B2
Argyll Cl. Failsworth M35 ... 84 B7
Argyll Cl. Garswood WN4 ... 72 C4
Argyll Park Rd. M35 ... 84 B7
Argyll Rd. Cheadle SK8 ... 122 F5
Argyll Rd. Oldham OL9 ... 65 F4
Argyll St. Ashton-u-L OL6 ... 85 E3
Argyll St. Mossley OL5 ... 68 C1
Ariel Wlk. WA3 ... 90 E8
Ark St. 3 M19 ... 99 A2
Arkendale Cl. M35 ... 84 C7
Arkholme. M28 ... 78 A8
Arkholme Wlk. M40 ... 83 B7
Arkle Ave. SK8 & SK9 ... 131 E4
Arkley Wlk. M13 ... 163 B6
Arkwright Dr. SK6 ... 126 A6
Arkwright Rd. SK6 ... 126 A6
Arkwright St. Horwich BL6 ... 22 C2
Arkwright St. Oldham OL9 ... 152 C6
Arkwright Way. OL11 ... 31 A2
Arlen Ct. BL2 ... 148 B5
Arlen Rd. BL2 ... 148 B5
Arlen Way. OL10 ... 29 B2
Arley Ave. Bury BL9 ... 27 F6
Arley Ave. M'ster M20 ... 109 F5
Arley Cl. Alt'ham WA14 ... 119 D8
Arley Cl. Dukinfield SK16 ... 101 D6
Arley Cl. Wigan WN2 ... 38 B2
Arley Dr. Sale M33 ... 108 A2
Arley Dr. Shaw OL2 ... 49 D8
Arley Gr. SK3 ... 123 D4
Arley La. WN1 & WN2 ... 20 D2
Arley Mere Cl. SK8 ... 122 F3
Arley Moss Wlk. M13 ... 163 B7
Arley St. Ince-i-M WN2 ... 55 F4
Arley St. Radcliffe M26 ... 44 B1
Arley Way. Atherton M46 ... 58 E2
Arley Way. 22 Denton M34 ... 101 A1
Arlies Cl. SK15 ... 86 A4
Arlies La. SK15 ... 86 B4
Arlies Prim Sch. SK15 ... 86 A4
Arlies St. OL6 ... 85 D4
Arlington Ave. Denton M34 101 A2
Arlington Ave. M'ster M25 ... 63 B2
Arlington Ave. Swinton M27 ... 79 D6
Arlington Cl. BL9 ... 11 C2
Arlington Cres. SK9 ... 136 E5
Arlington Dr.
Golborne WA3 & WN7 ... 91 C8
Arlington Dr. Poynton SK12 133 D3
Arlington Dr. Stockport SK2 124 A3
Arlington Rd. Cheadle SK8 ... 122 C4
Arlington Rd. Stretford M32 ... 96 B1
Arlington St. 4
Ashton-u-L OL6 ... 166 C3
Arlington St. Bolton BL3 ... 147 F3
Arlington St. M'ster M8 ... 155 F8
Arlington St. M'ster M3 ... 158 D2
Arlington Way. SK9 ... 136 E5
Arliss Ave. M19 ... 111 A8
Arm Rd. OL15 ... 15 E4
Armadale Ave. M9 ... 65 A4
Armadale Cl. SK3 ... 170 F5
Armadale Rd. Bolton BL3 ... 40 E5
Armadale Rd.
Dukinfield SK16 ... 101 D7
Armdale Rise. OL4 ... 49 E1
Armentieres. SK15 ... 86 A1
Armit Rd. OL4 ... 68 E5
Armitage Ave. Walkden M38 ... 59 F4
Armitage CE Prim Sch.
M12 ... 164 E6
Armitage Cl. Hyde SK14 ... 113 E8
Armitage Cl. Middleton M24 ... 64 D7
Armitage Cl. Oldham OL8 ... 66 C3
Armitage Ct. M12 ... 164 F6
Armitage Gr. M38 ... 59 F4
Armitage House. M6 ... 80 C3
Armitage Owen Wlk. 4
M40 ... 83 A7
Armitage Rd. WA14 ... 119 D3
Armitage St. M30 ... 79 D1
Armitstead St. 5 WN2 ... 56 D4
Armour Pl. M9 ... 64 C2
Armoury Bank. WN4 ... 73 B3
Armoury St. SK3 ... 170 E8
Armstrong Hurst Cl. OL12 ... 15 B2
Armstrong St. Horwich BL6 ... 22 C2
Armstrong St. Wigan WN2 ... 38 A3
Arncliffe Cl. 5 BL4 ... 42 D1
Arncliffe Dr. M23 ... 121 A3
Arncliffe Rise. OL4 ... 50 A4
Arncot Rd. BL1 ... 24 F5
Arncott Cl. OL2 ... 49 A4
Arne Cl. SK2 ... 125 A5
Arne St. OL9 ... 152 A5
Arnesby Ave. M33 ... 108 E5
Arnesby Gr. BL2 ... 148 B8
Arnfield Dr. M28 ... 78 B6
Arnfield La.
Hollingworth SK14 ... 103 F8
Arnfield Rd. M'ster M20 ... 110 C6
Arnfield Rd. Stockport SK3 ... 170 D5
Arnold Ave. Heywood OL10 ... 46 E7
Arnold Ave. Hyde SK14 ... 113 F7
Arnold Cl. SK16 ... 102 A7
Arnold Ct. M16 ... 97 E1
Arnold Dr. Droylsden M43 ... 84 A1
Arnold Dr. Middleton M24 ... 47 C3
Arnold Rd. Bolton BL7 ... 24 F8
Arnold Rd. Hyde SK14 ... 113 F7
Arnold Rd. M'ster M16 ... 97 E1
Arnold St. Ashton-u-L OL6 ... 166 C3
Arnold St. Bolton BL1 ... 142 C2
Arnold St. Oldham OL1 ... 67 A8
Arnold St. Stockport SK3 ... 170 E7
Arnold Wlk. 9 M34 ... 113 A7
Arnott Cres. M15 ... 162 F5
Arnside Ave.
Hazel Grove SK7 ... 124 C2
Arnside Ave. Ince-i-M WN2 ... 56 A7
Arnside Ave. Oldham OL9 ... 152 A5
Arnside Ave. Reddish SK4 ... 111 E6
Arnside Cl. Gatley SK8 ... 122 B4
Arnside Cl. High Lane SK6 ... 134 E8
Arnside Cl. Shaw OL2 ... 49 D7
Arnside Dr. Dukinfield SK14 101 C4
Arnside Dr. R'dale OL11 ... 29 E5
Arnside Dr. Salford M6 ... 80 B3
Arnside Gr. Bolton BL2 ... 42 E8
Arnside Gr. Sale M33 ... 108 B6
Arnside Rd. Hindley WN2 ... 57 A5
Arnside Rd. Wigan WN5 ... 54 B8
Arnside St. M14 ... 98 B2
Arran Ave. Oldham OL8 ... 66 F3
Arran Ave. Sale M33 ... 108 C3
Arran Ave. Stretford M32 ... 96 A2
Arran Cl. BL3 ... 40 E6
Arran Gdns. M41 ... 95 C5
Arran Gr. M26 ... 43 E5
Arran Rd. SK16 ... 101 C7
Arran St. 12 M'ster M40 ... 64 F1
Arran St. M'ster M7 ... 155 D6
Arran Wlk. OL10 ... 29 A1
Arrandale Ct. M41 ... 95 D3
Arras Gr. M34 ... 99 F3
Arreton Sq. M14 ... 98 D3
Arrivals Way. M90 ... 130 B7
Arrow St. Bolton BL1 ... 145 E8
Arrow St. Leigh WN7 ... 76 B3
Arrow St. M'ster M7 ... 155 D5
Arrow Trad Est. M34 ... 100 D5
Arrowfield Dr. M21 ... 109 D7
Arrowfield Rd. M21 ... 109 D7
Arrowhill Rd. BL8 ... 43 F8
Arrowscroft Way. SK14 ... 171 D4
Arrowsmith Ct. 7 BL6 ... 22 E1
Arrowsmith Wlk. 16 M11 ... 160 F1
Arthill La. WA14 ... 118 B1
Arthington St. OL16 ... 31 B8
Arthog Dr. WA15 ... 128 F8
Arthog Rd. Alt'ham WA15 ... 128 F8
Arthog Rd. M'ster M20 ... 110 C3
Arthur Ave. M28 ... 60 C5
Arthur La. BL2 ... 26 B2
Arthur Millwood Ct. M3 ... 158 D1
Arthur Rd. M16 ... 97 C3
Arthur St. Bury BL8 ... 27 C2
Arthur St. Eccles M30 ... 79 C1
Arthur St. Farnworth BL4 ... 60 D8
Arthur St. Heywood OL10 ... 29 D2
Arthur St. Hindley WN2 ... 56 E5
Arthur St. Hyde SK14 ... 101 C1
Arthur St. Leigh WN7 ... 75 E4
Arthur St. Little Lever BL3 ... 43 B3
Arthur St. Prestwich M25 ... 62 F4
Arthur St. R'dale OL12 ... 139 D8
Arthur St. Reddish SK5 ... 111 E7
Arthur St. Shaw OL2 ... 149 B7
Arthur St. Swinton M27 ... 79 D7
Arthur St. Walkden M28 ... 60 E1
Arthur St. Walkden M28 ... 60 F2
Arthur Terr. 4 SK5 ... 111 E7
Arthurs La. OL3 ... 69 B6
Artillery Ct. M13 ... 163 C7
Artillery Pl. M22 ... 121 F4
Artillery St. Bolton BL3 ... 145 F5
Artillery St. M'ster M3 ... 162 E8
Arundale. BL5 ... 39 F2
Arundale Ave. M16 & M21 ... 97 E1
Arundale Cl. SK14 ... 102 F3
Arundale Ct. M16 ... 97 E1
Arundale Gr. SK14 ... 102 F3
Arundale Prim Sch. SK14 ... 102 F3
Arundel Ave.
Hazel Grove SK7 ... 133 D8
Arundel Ave. Prestwich M45 ... 63 B7
Arundel Ave. R'dale OL11 ... 30 E4
Arundel Ave. Urmston M41 ... 94 C1
Arundel Cl. Alt'ham WA15 ... 120 C1
Arundel Cl. Bury BL8 ... 27 C6
Arundel Cl. Mossley SK15 ... 86 F6
Arundel Dr. WN7 ... 75 E6
Arundel Gr. SK2 ... 124 B4
Arundel Grange.
Glossop SK13 ... 104 A1
Arundel Rd. SK8 ... 132 A6
Arundel St. Ashton-u-L OL6 ... 85 E3
Arundel St. Bolton BL1 ... 24 E5
Arundel St. Glossop SK13 ... 104 C1
Arundel St. Hindley WN2 ... 56 E5
Arundel St. M'ster M15 ... 162 D7
Arundel St. Mossley OL5 ... 68 B1
Arundel St. Oldham OL4 ... 67 C7
Arundel St. R'dale OL11 ... 30 E4
Arundel St. Swinton M27 ... 61 C1
Arundel St. Wigan WN5 ... 54 F6
Arundel Wlk. OL9 ... 152 A6
Asby Cl. M24 ... 46 D2
Ascension CE Prim Sch.
M7 ... 158 D4
Ascension Rd. M7 ... 158 D4
Ascot Ave. Sale M33 ... 107 D3
Ascot Ave. Stretford M32 ... 96 F3
Ascot Cl. Oldham OL9 ... 152 C7
Ascot Cl. R'dale OL11 ... 29 E8
Ascot Dr. Atherton M46 ... 58 E4
Ascot Dr. Hazel Grove SK7 ... 125 A2
Ascot Dr. Urmston M41 ... 94 C2
Ascot Meadows. BL9 ... 44 E8
Ascot Par. M19 ... 110 F6
Ascot Rd. Failsworth M40 ... 83 B4
Ascot Rd. Little Lever BL3 ... 42 F3
Ascot Wlk. M6 ... 81 A5
Ascroft Ave. WN6 ... 36 F3
Ascroft St. Oldham OL1 ... 153 F6
Ascroft St. Wigan WN1 ... 151 E7
Asgard Dr. M5 ... 161 C8
Asgard Gr. M5 ... 161 C8
Ash Ave. Alt'ham WA14 ... 119 A5
Ash Ave. Cheadle SK8 ... 122 E5
Ash Ave. Irlam M44 ... 105 D5
Ash Ave. Newton-l-W WA12 ... 89 C2
Ash Cl. Appley Bridge WN6 ... 35 D7
Ash Cl. Ashton-u-L OL6 ... 85 D5
Ash Cl. Littleborough OL12 ... 15 C4
Ash Cl. Mottram-i-L SK14 ... 103 A4
Ash Ct. SK6 ... 113 A5
Ash Dr. M27 ... 61 C2
Ash Field Sch. M28 ... 60 E1
Ash Gr. Alt'ham WA14 ... 119 C1
Ash Gr. Alt'ham WA15 ... 119 F7
Ash Gr. Bolton BL2 ... 25 F3
Ash Gr. Bolton BL1 ... 144 B8
Ash Gr. Bury BL8 ... 27 A5
Ash Gr. Droylsden M34 ... 100 A8
Ash Gr. Gatley SK8 ... 131 B8
Ash Gr. 8 Horwich BL6 ... 22 E1
Ash Gr. Littleborough OL15 ... 15 F5
Ash Gr. M'ster M13 ... 98 E4
Ash Gr. Marple SK6 ... 125 E5
Ash Gr. Newhey OL16 ... 32 A3
Ash Gr. Oldham OL4 ... 68 A7
Ash Gr. Orrell WN5 ... 53 F6
Ash Gr. Prestwich M25 ... 63 A6
Ash Gr. Ramsbottom BL8 ... 10 F3
Ash Gr. Reddish SK4 ... 111 D5
Ash Gr. Royton OL2 ... 48 D6
Ash Gr. Stalybridge SK15 ... 85 F3
Ash Gr. Standish WN6 ... 36 F8
Ash Gr. Stretford M32 ... 108 C8
Ash Gr. Swinton M27 ... 79 D5
Ash Gr. Walkden M28 ... 60 E1
Ash Gr. Westhoughton BL5 ... 57 E7
Ash Grove Cres. WN5 ... 71 E6
Ash Hill Dr. OL5 ... 86 E8
Ash House. M16 ... 97 E2
Ash La. Alt'ham WA15 ... 120 C2
Ash La. Wigan WN2 ... 38 A4
Ash Lea Sch. M30 ... 79 E3
Ash Leigh Dr. BL1 ... 40 E8
Ash Lodge. SK12 ... 133 D4
Ash Rd. Coppull PR7 ... 19 E8
Ash Rd. Droylsden M43 ... 83 F2
Ash Rd. Hollinfare WA3 ... 105 A2
Ash Rd. Kearsley BL4 ... 60 F5
Ash Rd. Partington M31 ... 105 D3
Ash Rd. Poynton SK12 ... 133 F3
Ash Rd. Reddish M34 ... 99 F3
Ash Sq. OL4 ... 67 D8
Ash St. Bolton BL2 ... 148 A6
Ash St. Bury BL9 ... 141 A2
Ash St. Denton M34 ... 100 D7
Ash St. Failsworth M35 ... 83 E8
Ash St. Golborne WA3 ... 74 B2
Ash St. Hazel Grove SK7 ... 124 D3
Ash St. Heywood OL10 ... 29 B3
Ash St. M'ster M8 & M9 ... 157 D7
Ash St. Middleton M24 ... 65 C8
Ash St. Oldham OL4 ... 67 B6
Ash St. R'dale OL11 ... 30 C2
Ash St. Salford M6 ... 154 F2
Ash St. Stockport SK3 ... 123 B8
Ash St. 2 Tyldesley M29 ... 59 A1
Ash Tree Ave. M43 ... 83 F2
Ash Tree Dr. SK16 ... 101 F7
Ash Tree Rd. Hyde SK14 ... 102 B5
Ash Tree Rd. M'ster M8 ... 64 A1
Ash Wlk. Chadderton OL9 ... 152 B8
Ash Wlk. Middleton M24 ... 64 F6
Ashawe Cl. M38 ... 59 E3
Ashawe Gr. M38 ... 59 F3
Ashawe Terr. M38 ... 59 E3
Ashbank Ave. BL3 ... 40 E6
Ashbee St. BL1 ... 143 E3
Ashberry Cl. SK9 ... 137 D8
Ashborne Dr. BL9 ... 11 D2
Ashbourne Ave. Bolton BL2 148 B6
Ashbourne Ave.
Cheadle SK8 ... 122 F6
Ashbourne Ave. Hindley WN2 56 F5
Ashbourne Ave.
Middleton M24 ... 47 C3
Ashbourne Ave. Urmston M41 94 E2
Ashbourne Ave. Wigan WN2 38 A2
Ashbourne Cl. Leigh WN7 ... 57 D1
Ashbourne Cl.
Littleborough OL12 ... 15 D6
Ashbourne Cres. M33 ... 108 D2
Ashbourne Ct. SK13 ... 116 F8
Ashbourne Dr. Ashton-u-L OL6 85 F6
Ashbourne Dr.
High Lane SK6 ... 134 F6
Ashbourne Gdns. WN2 ... 56 F5
Ashbourne Gr. M'ster M7 ... 155 E7
Ashbourne Gr.
Whitefield M45 ... 44 D1
Ashbourne Gr. Worsley M28 ... 78 E8
Ashbourne Rd. Denton M34 100 E2
Ashbourne Rd. Eccles M30 ... 79 E1
Ashbourne Rd.
Hazel Grove SK7 ... 133 F8
Ashbourne Rd. Pendlebury M6 80 C5
Ashbourne Rd. Stretford M32 96 A3
Ashbourne Sq. OL8 ... 153 E5
Ashbourne St. OL11 ... 13 E1
Ashbridge. M17 ... 96 B6
Ashbridge Rd. M35 ... 84 B6
Ashbrook Ave. M34 ... 100 B3
Ashbrook Cl. Gatley SK8 ... 122 B1
Ashbrook Cl. Reddish M34 ... 100 B3
Ashbrook Cl. Whitefield M45 ... 63 B8
Ashbrook Cres. OL12 ... 15 C4
Ashbrook Farm Cl. SK5 ... 99 F2
Ashbrook Hey La.
OL12 & OL16 ... 15 C4
Ashbrook La. SK5 ... 99 F2
Ashbrook St. M11 ... 100 A7
Ashburn Ave. M19 ... 110 F5
Ashburn Gr. SK4 ... 169 D3
Ashburn Rd. SK4 ... 169 D3
Ashburne House. M14 ... 98 D4
Ashburner St. BL1 ... 145 E6
Ashburton Cl. SK14 ... 102 E2
Ashburton Rd. SK3 ... 170 E5
Ashburton Rd E. M17 ... 96 C6
Ashburton Rd W. M17, M41 ... 95 E7
Ashbury Cl. BL3 ... 145 E5
Ashbury Pl. M40 ... 160 E4
Ashbury Prim Sch. M11 ... 164 F8
Ashbury's Sta. M12 ... 165 A7
Ashby Ave. M19 ... 110 E4
Ashby Cl. BL3 ... 42 C2
Ashby Gr. Leigh WN7 ... 75 C8
Ashby Gr. Whitefield M45 ... 63 B7
Ashby Rd. WN3 ... 55 B3
Ashcombe Dr. Bolton BL2 ... 43 A6
Ashcombe Dr. Radcliffe M26 ... 43 D5
Ashcombe Wlk. 7 M11 ... 160 F1
Ashcott Ave. M22 ... 121 D4
Ashcott Cl. BL6 ... 40 E5
Ashcroft. Littleborough OL12 ... 15 D4
Ashcroft. Wilmslow SK9 ... 136 F5
Ashcroft Ave. M6 ... 154 E4
Ashcroft Ct. OL1 ... 153 F6
Ashcroft Rd. WA13 ... 117 B4
Ashcroft St. WN2 ... 56 E4
Ashdale Ave. BL3 ... 40 E5
Ashdale Cl. SK5 ... 111 F5
Ashdale Cres. M43 ... 83 F1
Ashdale Dr. Gatley SK8 ... 122 B2
Ashdale Dr. M'ster M20 ... 110 D5
Ashdale Rd. Hindley WN2 ... 57 A5
Ashdale Rd. Wigan WN3 ... 55 A2
Ashdene. OL12 ... 14 D4
Ashdene Cl.
Oldham OL1 & OL9 ... 48 C1
Ashdene Cl. Oldham OL4 ... 67 F7
Ashdene Cres. BL2 ... 25 D4
Ashdene Cty Prim Sch.
SK9 ... 136 F5
Ashdene Rd. M'ster SK4 ... 110 D2
Ashdene Rd. M'ster M20 ... 110 D6
Ashdene Rd. Wilmslow SK9 ... 136 F5
Ashdene Rise. OL1 ... 49 D4
Ashdown Ave. M'ster M9 ... 64 D4
Ashdown Ave. Romiley SK6 113 C5
Ashdown Dr. Bolton BL2 ... 25 C3
Ashdown Dr. Boothstown M28 78 A7
Ashdown Dr. Pendlebury M27 80 A6
Ashdown Gr. M9 ... 64 D4
Ashdown Rd. SK4 ... 168 C3
Ashdown Terr. M9 ... 64 D4
Ashdown Way. OL2 ... 48 E8
Asher St. BL3 ... 146 C2
Ashes Cl. SK15 ... 102 C8
Ashes Dr. BL2 ... 42 F8
Ashes La. Glossop SK13 ... 104 B2
Ashes La. Milnrow OL16 ... 31 F7
Ashes La. Oldham OL4 ... 67 F6
Ashes La. Stalybridge SK15 ... 102 C8
Ashfell Ct. M21 ... 96 F1
Ashfield. M34 ... 101 A5
Ashfield Ave. Atherton M46 ... 58 C4
Ashfield Ave. Hindley WN2 ... 56 F4
Ashfield Ave. R'dale OL11 ... 139 F5
Ashfield Cl. Lymm WA13 ... 117 B4
Ashfield Cl. Salford M6 ... 154 E3
Ashfield Cres. Billinge WN5 ... 71 E4
Ashfield Cres. Cheadle SK8 122 D6
Ashfield Cres. Oldham OL4 ... 67 F6
Ashfield Dr. Aspull WN2 ... 38 C5
Ashfield Dr. Failsworth M40 ... 83 D4
Ashfield Gr. Bolton BL1 ... 25 A6
Ashfield Gr. Irlam M44 ... 105 E6
Ashfield Gr.
Reddish M18 & M34 ... 99 F4
Ashfield Gr. Romiley SK6 ... 114 B1
Ashfield Gr. Stockport SK3 ... 123 F4
Ashfield House. OL11 ... 139 F5
Ashfield La. OL16 ... 31 F4
Ashfield Lodge. M20 ... 109 F2
Ashfield Park Dr. WN6 ... 36 F8
Ashfield Rd. Adlington PR6 ... 21 B8
Ashfield Rd. Alt'ham WA15 ... 119 E3
Ashfield Rd. Cheadle SK8 ... 122 D5
Ashfield Rd. Cheadle SK8 ... 122 D6
Ashfield Rd. Hadfield SK13 ... 171 E3
Ashfield Rd. M'ster M13 ... 98 E3
Ashfield Rd. R'dale OL11 ... 139 F5
Ashfield Rd. Sale M33 ... 108 B5
Ashfield Rd. Stockport SK3 ... 123 F4
Ashfield Rd. Urmston M41 ... 95 D2
Ashfield Sq. M43 ... 83 F2
Ashfield St. M'ster M11 ... 160 F2
Ashfield St. Oldham OL8 ... 66 C3
Ashfield Terr. WN6 ... 35 C8
Ashfield Valley Prim Sch.
OL11 ... 30 E4
Ashford. M33 ... 107 C4
Ashford Ave. Boothstown M28 77 F6
Ashford Ave. Eccles M30 ... 95 C8
Ashford Ave. Reddish SK5 ... 99 F2
Ashford Ave. Swinton M27 ... 79 C7
Ashford Cl. Bolton BL2 ... 25 E4
Ashford Cl. Bury BL8 ... 27 B1
Ashford Cl. Handforth SK9 ... 131 C4
Ashford Ct. 1 OL4 ... 49 D1
Ashford Gn. 19 SK13 ... 171 E1
Ashford Mews. SK13 ... 171 E1
Ashford Rd. M'ster M20 ... 110 B7
Ashford Rd. Reddish SK4 ... 111 D6
Ashford Rd. Wilmslow SK9 ... 137 A4
Ashford Rise. WN1 ... 37 B4
Ashford St. Heywood OL10 ... 28 F2
Ashford Wlk. Bolton BL1 ... 143 E1
Ashford Wlk. Oldham OL9 ... 152 B6
Ashgate Ave. M22 ... 121 E4
Ashgill Wlk. 4 M9 ... 157 E7
Ashgrove. OL16 ... 31 B1
Ashia Cl. OL16 ... 31 B6
Ashill Wlk. M3 ... 162 E8
Ashington Cl. BL1 ... 142 B3
Ashington Dr. BL8 ... 26 F2
Ashkirk St. 4 M18 ... 99 D5
Ashland Ave.
Ashton-i-M WN4 ... 73 A4
Ashland Ave. 5 Wigan WN1 37 C2
Ashlands. M33 ... 108 A5
Ashlands Ave.
Boothstown M28 ... 78 A7
Ashlands Ave. Failsworth M40 65 C1
Ashlands Ave. Swinton M27 ... 79 D6
Ashlands Cl. BL0 ... 1 D2
Ashlands Dr. M34 ... 100 E6
Ashlands Rd. WA15 ... 108 A1
Ashlar Dr. M12 ... 164 E8
Ashlea Gr. OL4 ... 68 B6
Ashleigh Ave. SK13 ... 104 B2
Ashleigh Cl. OL2 ... 48 E2
Ashleigh Rd. WA15 ... 120 B8
Ashley Ave. Bolton BL2 ... 42 D8
Ashley Ave. M'ster M16 ... 97 D4

Barlow Rd.
Stretford M16 & M32 96 F4
Barlow St. Bacup OL13 3 B7
Barlow St. Bury BL9 140 F3
Barlow St. Eccles M30 79 D1
Barlow St. Heywood OL10 46 E8
Barlow St. Horwich BL6 22 C2
Barlow St. Oldham OL4 67 A6
Barlow St. R'dale OL16 31 A7
Barlow St. Radcliffe M26 44 B3
Barlow St. Walkden M28 60 D4
Barlow Terr. M21 109 C6
Barlow Wlk. 3 SK5 111 F8
Barlow Wood Dr. SK6 126 B3
Barlow's Croft. M3 158 E2
Barlow's La S. SK7 124 C3
Barmeadow. OL3 50 F2
Barmhouse Cl. SK14 102 A3
Barmhouse La. SK14 102 B3
Barmhouse Mews. SK14 102 A3
Barmouth St. M11 164 F8
Barmouth Wlk. 4 OL8 66 B2
Barmskin La. WN6 18 C8
Barn Acre. BL6 21 E1
Barn Cl. Glossop SK13 116 D7
Barn Cl. Urmston M41 94 C2
Barn Field La. OL12 15 A7
Barn Fold. OL4 67 E5
Barn Gr. M34 100 E7
Barn Hill. 8 BL5 39 E1
Barn Hill Terr. 7 BL5 39 E1
Barn La. WA12 & WA3 89 F8
Barn Meadow. BL7 9 D5
Barn St. Bolton BL1 145 E7
Barn St. Oldham OL1 153 E6
Barn St. Whitefield M45 62 F7
Barn Way. WA12 89 B3
Barn Wlk. 10 M18 99 E7
Barnaby Rd. SK12 133 D2
Barnabys Rd. BL5 39 D3
Barnacre Ave. Bolton BL2 42 F7
Barnacre Ave.
Wythenshawe M23 120 F3
Barnard Ave. M'ster SK4 168 B2
Barnard Ave. Prestwich M45 63 B7
Barnard Cl. OL7 84 F4
Barnard Rd. M18 99 B3
Barnard St. 3 BL2 148 C8
Barnbrook St. BL9 141 A3
Barnby St. M12 99 A3
Barnclose Rd. M22 121 D1
Barncroft Dr. BL6 22 F3
Barncroft Gdns. M22 121 C5
Barncroft Rd. BL4 60 D8
Barnes Ave. SK4 168 A2
Barnes Cl. Farnworth BL4 60 D8
Barnes Cl. Ramsbottom BL0 11 A3
Barnes Hospl. SK8 122 C6
Barnes House. 2 BL4 60 D8
Barnes Meadows. OL15 6 C1
Barnes St. BL4 60 B8
Barnes Terr. BL4 61 A7
Barneswell St. 23 M40 83 C5
Barnet Rd. BL1 142 C2
Barnett Ave. M20 110 B6
Barnett Ct. OL10 29 C1
Barnett Dr. M3 158 D2
Barnfield. Littleborough OL15 16 D6
Barnfield. Urmston M41 95 B1
Barnfield Ave. SK6 113 D3
Barnfield Cl. Bolton BL7 8 E2
Barnfield Cl. Radcliffe M26 43 E3
Barnfield Cl. 6 Salford M6 154 F1
Barnfield Cl. Tyldesley M29 58 F1
Barnfield Cres. M33 107 F6
Barnfield Dr.
Boothstown M28 78 B6
Barnfield Dr.
Westhoughton BL5 40 A1
Barnfield Rd. Hyde SK14 102 B5
Barnfield Rd. M'ster M19 110 E4
Barnfield Rd. Swinton M27 61 D2
Barnfield Rd E. SK3 123 F4
Barnfield Rd W. SK3 123 D4
Barnfield Rise. OL2 32 A1
Barnfield St.
Denton M34 100 D4
Barnfield St. Heywood OL10 29 E2
Barnfield St. R'dale OL12 14 F2
Barnfield Wlk. WA15 120 C5
Barngate Dr. OL5 86 C8
Barngate Rd. M22 122 A6
Barngill Gr. WN3 54 E3
Barnham Cl. WA3 90 A8
Barnham Wlk. M23 120 E8
Barnhill Ave. M25 63 B2
Barnhill Dr. M25 63 B2
Barnhill Rd. M25 63 B3
Barnhill St. M14 97 F4
Barnley Cl. M44 94 B3
Barns La.
Partington WA13 & WA14 118 A5
Barns La. Partington WA13 118 A6
Barns Pl. WA15 129 C8
Barnsdale Cl. BL2 26 C1
Barnsdale Dr. M7 & M8 156 A6
Barnsfold Ave. M14 110 C8
Barnsfold Rd. SK6 125 F3
Barnside. OL12 14 B8
Barnside Ave. M28 60 E3
Barnside Cl. BL9 27 E8
Barnside Way. M35 84 C6
Barnsley St. Stockport SK1 124 B8
Barnsley St. Wigan WN6 37 B2
Barnstaple Dr. M40 156 C6
Barnstead Ave. M20 110 D5
Barnston Ave. M14 98 B2
Barnston Cl. BL1 143 F4
Barnton Cl. WA3 90 D7
Barnway Wlk. 7 M40 65 C2
Barnwell Ave. WA3 91 D4
Barnwell Cl. M34 100 E5
Barnwood Cl. 11 BL1 143 E1
Barnwood Dr. BL1 143 E1
Barnwood Rd. M23 121 A3
Barnwood Terr. 10 BL1 143 E1
Baron Fold. M38 60 A5
Baron Fold Cres. M38 59 F5
Baron Fold Gr. M38 59 F5
Baron Fold Rd. M38 59 F5
Baron Gn. SK8 131 D7
Baron Rd. SK14 113 F7
Baron St. Bury BL9 140 D1
Baron St. R'dale OL16 139 F7
Baron Wlk. BL3 43 C3
Baroness Gr. M7 81 C4
Barons Ct. M35 83 D6
Barr Hill Ave. M6 80 E5
Barra Dr. M41 95 D5
Barrack Hill. SK6 113 A2
Barrack Hill Cl. SK6 113 A3
Barrack Hill Prim Sch.
SK6 113 A2
Barrack Sq. 16 WN1 150 C8
Barrack St. Bolton BL3 145 F6
Barrack St. M'ster 162 D7
Barracks Rd. Leigh WN2 56 D1
Barracks Yd. WN1 150 C8
Barrass St. M18 99 D7
Barratt Gdns. M24 46 D4
Barrett Ave. BL4 60 F7
Barrett Ct. BL9 141 A2
Barrett St. OL4 67 B5
Barrfield Rd. M6 154 E4
Barrhill Cl. M15 162 E6
Barrie St. WN7 75 D8
Barrie Way. BL1 25 B4
Barrington Ave.
Bramhall SK8 123 A1
Barrington Ave.
Droylsden M43 83 F1
Barrington Cl. WA14 119 D6
Barrington Rd. WA14 119 D5
Barrington St. M11 83 C2
Barrington Wlk. 2 BL2 25 B1
Barrisdale Cl. BL3 40 F5
Barron Meadow. WN7 75 D7
Barrow Bridge Rd.
Bolton BL1 23 F4
Barrow Bridge Rd.
Bolton BL1 142 A3
Barrow Hill Rd. M7 & M8 155 F5
Barrow La. Alt'ham WA15 129 B7
Barrow La. Culcheth WA3 90 C2
Barrow Meadow. SK8 131 E8
Barrow St. Ashton-i-M WN4 73 D5
Barrow St. M'ster M3 158 D1
Barrowdale Rd. WA3 90 B8
Barrowdene House. BL1 23 F4
Barrowfield Rd. M22 121 A2
Barrowfield Wlk. 4 M24 47 A1
Barrowfields. M24 47 A2
Barrows Ct. 3 BL1 145 F6
Barrowshaw Cl. M28 60 C2
Barrs Fold Cl. BL5 39 D3
Barrs Fold Rd. BL5 39 D3
Barrule Ave. SK7 124 E1
Barry Cres. M28 60 A3
Barry Ct. 8 M20 110 B6
Barry Lawson Cl. M7 & M8 155 F7
Barry Rd. Reddish SK5 111 F5
Barry Rd. Wythenshawe M23 109 C2
Barry Rise. WA14 119 A2
Barry St. OL1 67 B8
Barsham Dr. BL3 145 D5
Barth Wlk. 3 M23 120 F6
Bartlam Pl. OL1 153 F7
Bartlemore St. OL1 49 B1
Bartlett Rd. OL2 149 A6
Bartlett St. M11 165 B8
Bartley Rd. M22 121 C8
Barton Ave. Urmston M41 95 B2
Barton Ave. Wigan WN1 37 B2
Barton Bsns Pk. M30 79 C1
Barton Cl. SK9 131 D2
Barton Clough. WN5 71 E5
Barton Clough Prim Sch.
M32 95 F4
Barton Dock Rd. Eccles M41 95 E6
Barton Dock Rd.
Stretford M32 96 B4
Barton Fold. SK14 167 D1
Barton Hall Ave. M30 79 A1
Barton La. Eccles M30 79 E1
Barton La. Eccles M30 95 D8
Barton Moss Prim Sch. M30 94 F8
Barton Moss Rd. M30 94 D7
Barton Rd. Eccles M30 79 C1
Barton Rd. Farnworth BL4 60 B7
Barton Rd. M'ster SK4 110 E1
Barton Rd. Middleton M24 64 F8
Barton Rd. Pendlebury M27 80 A6
Barton Rd.
Stretford M32 & M41 96 B3
Barton Rd. Stretford M32 96 C1
Barton Rd. Urmston M41 95 C5
Barton Rd. Worsley M28 78 F5
Barton Sq. M2 158 F1
Barton St. Farnworth BL4 60 E7
Barton St. Golborne WA3 74 A1
Barton St. M'ster M3 162 E8
Barton St. Oldham OL1 153 D8
Barton St. Platt Bridge WN2 56 B3
Barton St. Tyldesley M29 58 F1
Barton St. 4 Wigan WN5 54 B5
Barton Terr. M44 94 C3
Barway Rd. M21 96 F1
Barwell Cl. SK5 112 A8
Barwell Rd. M33 107 E5
Barwell Sq. 1 BL4 42 B2
Barwick Pl. M33 108 A4
Basechurch Wlk. M12 164 F6
Basford Rd. M16 97 B3
Bashall St. BL1 144 C8
Basil Ct. OL16 31 B6
Basil St. Bolton BL3 145 E5
Basil St. M'ster M14 98 C3
Basil St. M'ster SK4 169 E3
Basil St. R'dale OL16 31 B6
Basildon Cl. M13 164 D5
Baslam Wlk. 8 M4 159 C2
Basle Cl. SK7 123 E4
Baslow Ave. M19 99 C2
Baslow Cl. 29 SK13 171 E1
Baslow Dr. Gatley SK8 131 C8
Baslow Dr. Hazel Grove SK7 133 F8
Baslow Fold. 28 SK13 171 E1
Baslow Gn. 30 SK13 171 E1
Baslow Gr. SK5 111 F5
Baslow Mews. SK13 171 E1
Baslow Rd. Denton M34 112 F8
Baslow Rd. Droylsden M43 83 E3
Baslow Rd. Stretford M32 96 A3
Baslow St. M11 160 E2
Baslow Way. 31 SK13 171 E1
Bass La. BL9 11 D3
Bass St. Bolton BL2 148 C7
Bass St. Dukinfield SK16 101 B8
Basset Ave. M6 & M7 81 C5
Bassett Gr. WN3 54 C2
Bassett Way. OL12 14 E2
Bassey Wlk. 2 M16 97 E4
Basswood Gn. WN2 57 A3
Basten Dr. M7 155 E6
Batchelor Cl. M21 109 E7
Bateman St. BL6 22 D2
Batemill Rd. SK12 127 D2
Bates Cl. OL11 30 D1
Bates St. Dukinfield SK16 101 C8
Bates St. M'ster M13 98 F4
Bateson Dr. OL4 67 F6
Bateson St. SK1 112 A2
Bateson Way. OL8 153 F5
Bath Cl. SK7 125 A2
Bath Cres. Bramhall SK8 132 B6
Bath Cres. M'ster M16 161 C5
Bath Pl. WA14 119 D2
Bath St. Alt'ham WA14 119 D2
Bath St. Atherton M46 58 A3
Bath St. Bolton BL1 145 F8
Bath St. Oldham OL9 152 C5
Bath St. R'dale OL12 15 B1
Bath St. Wigan WN2 37 F2
Batheaston Gr. WN7 75 D8
Batley St. M9 157 E8
Batridge Rd. BL7 9 A7
Battenberg Rd. 2 BL1 144 C8
Battersbay Gr. SK7 124 E2
Battersby Ct. SK2 124 E6
Battersby St. Bury BL9 28 D3
Battersby St. Droylsden M11 99 E7
Battersby St. Ince-i-M WN2 56 B8
Battersby St. Leigh WN7 76 B4
Battersby St. R'dale OL11 30 B6
Battersea Rd. SK4 110 F1
Batty St. M40 & M8 156 C5
Baucher Rd. WN3 54 F5
Baum The. OL16 139 F8
Baxendale St. BL1 143 E4
Baxter Gdns. M23 121 A7
Baxter Rd. M33 108 B4
Baxter St. Oldham OL8 66 B2
Baxter St. Standish WN6 19 F1
Baxter's Row. WN2 57 C2
Bay St. Heywood OL10 29 B3
Bay St. Oldham OL9 153 D7
Bay St. R'dale OL12 15 A1
Bay Tree Ave. Worsley M28 79 A5
Baybutt St. M26 44 C3
Baycliffe Cl. WN2 56 F3
Baycliffe Wlk. 10 M8 155 F6
Baycroft Gr. M23 109 A1
Baydon Ave. M7 155 F6
Bayfield Gr. M40 65 A1
Bayley St. SK15 85 F1
Baynard Wlk. M9 64 B4
Baysdale. OL2 48 C5
Baysdale Ave. BL3 40 F4
Bayston Wlk. M12 164 F6
Bayswater Ave. M40 83 C4
Bayswater St. BL3 146 C2
Baythorpe St. BL1 143 F3
Baytree Ave.
Chadderton M24 & OL9 65 E8
Baytree Ave. Dukinfield M34 101 A4
Baytree Dr. SK6 112 F4
Baytree Gr. BL0 11 B2
Baytree La. M24 65 D8
Baytree Rd. WN6 36 F2
Baytree Wlk. OL12 4 C1
Baywood St. M9 157 D8
Bazaar St. M6 81 A4
Bazley Rd. M22 109 D1
Bazley St. BL1 23 F4
Beacomfold. SK6 114 B3
Beacon Cl. M46 58 B2
Beacon Dr. M22 & M23 121 A2
Beacon Rd. Billinge WN5 71 E6
Beacon Rd. Eccles M17 95 E7
Beacon Rd. Leigh WN2 75 A8
Beacon Rd. Romiley SK6 113 A1
Beacon Rd.
Shevington Moor WN6 19 B2
Beacon View.
Appley Bridge WN6 35 C8
Beacon View. Marple SK6 125 F8
Beacon View Dr. WN8 53 B7
Beacons The. WN6 35 D7
Beaconsfield. M14 110 C7
Beaconsfield Rd. WA14 119 D7
Beaconsfield St. BL3 145 D6
Beaconsfield Terr. SK15 86 F7
Beadham Dr. M9 64 A5
Beaford Cl. WN5 54 B5
Beaford Dr. M22 130 E8
Beagle Wlk. M22 130 E8
Beal Cl. SK4 110 D3
Beal Cres. OL16 15 C1
Beal Dr. WN2 56 A2
Beal La. OL2 149 C6
Beal Vale Cty Prim Sch.
OL2 149 B7
Beal Wlk. M45 63 C8
Bealcroft Cl. OL16 31 E7
Bealcroft Wlk. OL16 31 E7
Beale Gr. M21 109 B8
Bealey Ave. BL9 44 E5
Bealey Cl. M'ster M18 165 B5
Bealey Cl. Radcliffe M26 44 D4
Bealey Dr. BL9 44 D7
Bealey Hospl. M26 44 D4
Bealey Ind Est. M26 44 D4
Bealey Row. M26 44 C4
Beaminster Ave. SK4 110 F3
Beaminster Cl. SK4 110 F3
Beaminster Rd. SK4 110 F3
Beaminster Wlk. 7 M13 163 C5
Beamish Cl. M13 163 C6
Beamsley Dr. M22 121 B2
Bean Leach Ave. SK2 124 F6
Bean Leach Dr. SK2 124 F6
Bean Leach Rd. SK2 & SK7 124 F5
Beanfields. M28 78 F5
Beard Rd. M18 99 C4
Beard St. Droylsden M43 83 F1
Beard St. Royton OL2 48 E3
Beardsmore Dr. WA3 74 E1
Beardwood Rd. M9 64 D4
Bearswood Cl. SK14 167 F1
Beathwaite Dr. SK7 123 C1
Beattock St. M15 162 D7
Beatrice Ave. Cheadle SK8 122 F2
Beatrice Ave. Reddish M18 99 F4
Beatrice Mews. 9 BL6 22 B4
Beatrice Rd. Bolton BL1 142 C1
Beatrice Rd. Swinton M28 79 B7
Beatrice St. Denton M34 100 E3
Beatrice St. Farnworth BL4 60 C8
Beatrice St. R'dale OL11 139 D7
Beatrice St. Swinton M27 61 D1
Beatrice Wignall St. M43 100 A8
Beatson Wlk. 2 M4 159 C1
Beatty Dr. BL5 39 E1
Beauchamp St. OL6 166 C4
Beaufont Dr. OL4 67 C5
Beaufort Ave. 1 M'ster M20 110 A5
Beaufort Ave. Sale M33 108 C2
Beaufort Ave. Swinton M27 79 D7
Beaufort Chase. SK9 131 F1
Beaufort Cl.
Alderley Edge SK9 137 B2
Beaufort Cl. Hattersley SK14 102 E2
Beaufort Rd. Ashton-u-L OL6 85 D3
Beaufort Rd.
Hattersley SK14 102 E2
Beaufort Rd. Sale M33 108 C3
Beaufort Rd. Stockport SK2 124 D5
Beaufort St. 7 Hindley WN2 56 D5
Beaufort St. M'ster M3 162 E8
Beaufort St. Prestwich M25 63 C4
Beaufort St. R'dale OL12 14 C1
Beaufort St. Wigan WN5 54 E6
Beaufort St. Worsley M28 79 B3
Beaufort Way. 3 SK14 102 E1
Beaulieu. WA15 119 F2
Beaumaris Cl. Leigh WN7 75 C5
Beaumaris Cl. M'ster M12 164 F6
Beaumaris Cres. SK7 124 C1
Beaumaris Rd. WN2 57 A3
Beaumonds Way. OL11 30 A6
Beaumont Ave. BL6 22 C4
Beaumont Chase. BL3 40 F3
Beaumont Cl. OL15 15 F5
Beaumont Ct. Bolton BL1 40 D8
Beaumont Ct. Handforth SK9 131 C5
Beaumont Dr. BL3 40 E5
Beaumont Gr. WN5 54 B8
Beaumont Hospl. BL6 40 C8
Beaumont Prim Sch. BL3 40 E5
Beaumont Rd.
Bolton BL1 & BL3 & BL6 40 E5
Beaumont Rd. Horwich BL6 22 C4
Beaumont Rd. M'ster M21 109 B7
Beaumont St. OL6 166 C3
Beauvale Ave. SK2 124 C7
Beaver Ct. WN4 73 C6
Beaver Dr. BL9 45 B4
Beaver House. SK1 124 B8
Beaver Rd. M20 110 B3
Beaver Road Inf Sch. M20 110 B3
Beaver Road Jun Sch.
M20 110 B3
Beaver St. M1 163 A8
Beaver Wlk. SK14 102 D1
Beaverbrook Ave. WA3 92 B4
Bebbington Cl. M33 108 F3
Bebbington St. 7 M11 83 C1
Beccles Rd. M33 108 B1
Beck Gr. Shaw OL2 49 D8
Beck Gr. Walkden M28 60 F1
Beck House. SK14 102 D1
Beck St. Droylsden M11 99 E7
Beck St. M'ster M3 158 E1
Beckenham Cl. BL8 27 C6
Beckenham Rd. M7 & M8 156 A7
Becket Ave. M7 155 E6
Becket Meadow St. OL4 67 B6
Becket Meadows. OL4 67 B6
Beckett Dr. WA13 117 B8
Beckett St. M'ster M18 165 C5
Beckett St. Oldham OL4 67 E7
Beckfield Rd. M23 121 A5
Beckfoot Dr. M13 98 E3
Beckford St. M10 & M40 157 E5
Beckhampton Cl. M13 163 C6
Beckley Ave. M25 63 A2
Beckley Cl. OL2 49 B4
Beckside. Reddish SK5 100 A1
Beckside. Tyldesley M46 76 E8
Beckton Gdns. M22 121 C3
Beckwith. WN2 56 B3
Becontree Ave. M34 101 A4
Becontree Dr. M23 120 E7
Bede St. BL1 142 C2
Bedells La. SK9 137 A6
Bedfont Wlk. M9 64 E1
Bedford Ave. Hyde SK14 167 E3
Bedford Ave. M'ster M16 97 D2
Bedford Ave. Sale M33 108 D2
Bedford Ave. Shaw OL2 48 F7
Bedford Ave. 1 Swinton M27 79 E7
Bedford Ave. Walkden M28 60 C1
Bedford Ct. WA15 120 C6
Bedford Dr. Alt'ham WA15 120 C6
Bedford Dr. Atherton M46 58 A1
Bedford Gdns. WN2 56 F6
Bedford Gn. M44 105 B6
Bedford Hall Meth Prim
Sch. WN7 76 C3
Bedford High Sch. WN7 76 D4
Bedford Pl. WN4 73 A5
Bedford Rd. Eccles M30 79 E3
Bedford Rd. M'ster M16 97 A3
Bedford Rd. Urmston M41 95 C4
Bedford St. Bolton BL7 8 D2
Bedford St. Bolton BL1 145 D8
Bedford St. Heywood OL10 29 E2
Bedford St. 1 Leigh WN7 76 A5
Bedford St. Prestwich M25 63 C5
Bedford St. 6 Reddish SK5 111 E7
Bedford St. Reddish SK5 111 E8
Bedford St. Wigan WN1 37 E2
Bedford St. Wigan WN5 54 C5
Bedford Terr. Bury BL9 141 A4
Bedford Terr. Haslingden BB4 1 A8
Bedlam Gn. 2 BL9 140 F2
Bedlington Cl. M23 120 E6
Bednal Ave. M10 & M40 160 E4
Bedwell Cl. M16 97 F3
Bedworth Cl. BL2 148 B5
Bee Fold La. M46 58 C1
Bee Hive Ind Est. BL6 39 E8
Beech Ave. Adlington PR6 21 B8
Beech Ave. Atherton M46 58 E3
Beech Ave. Boothstown M28 78 A6
Beech Ave.
Chadderton OL1 & OL9 48 A2
Beech Ave. Culcheth WA3 92 A3
Beech Ave. Denton M34 100 D4
Beech Ave. Droylsden M43 83 E1
Beech Ave. Farnworth BL4 60 A8
Beech Ave. Gatley SK8 122 B5
Beech Ave. Glossop SK13 116 A8
Beech Ave. Golborne WA3 90 F7
Beech Ave. Hazel Grove SK7 124 E2
Beech Ave. Horwich BL6 22 E1
Beech Ave. Irlam M44 94 C3
Beech Ave. Kearsley BL4 61 B5
Beech Ave. Little Lever BL3 43 B2
Beech Ave. Marple SK6 125 D6
Beech Ave. New Mills SK12 127 D1
Beech Ave. Oldham OL4 67 D8
Beech Ave. Radcliffe M26 61 F8
Beech Ave. Sale WA15 120 B8
Beech Ave. Salford M6 154 E4
Beech Ave.
Stockport SK2 & SK3 170 F6
Beech Ave. Uppermill OL3 69 B6
Beech Ave. Urmston M41 95 C2
Beech Ave. Whitefield M45 62 F6
Beech Ave.
Wythenshawe M22 121 D8
Beech Cl. Alderley Edge SK9 137 B3
Beech Cl. Bolton BL2 25 C6
Beech Cl. 4 Partington M31 105 F3
Beech Cl. Prestwich M25 63 C3
Beech Cl. Whitworth OL12 4 C1
Beech Cres. Leigh WN7 75 F3
Beech Cres. Poynton SK12 133 E4
Beech Cres. Standish WN6 36 E8
Beech Ct. M'ster M8 63 F1
Beech Ct. M'ster M14 110 C8
Beech Ct. 2 Sale M33 107 F4
Beech Ct. Salford M6 81 A3
Beech Ct. Stretford M21 96 F1
Beech Dr. WN7 75 F2
Beech Gr. Abram WN2 74 C7
Beech Gr. Ashton-u-L OL7 84 F1
Beech Gr. Leigh WN7 75 E2
Beech Gr. M'ster M14 110 D7
Beech Gr. Ramsbottom BL8 11 A1
Beech Gr. Sale M33 107 F4
Beech Gr. Salford M6 154 E4
Beech Gr. Stalybridge SK15 101 F8
Beech Gr. Walkden M38 59 E5
Beech Gr. Wigan WN6 36 E3
Beech Gr. Wilmslow SK9 137 A6
Beech Grove Cl. BL9 141 B4
Beech Hall St. WN6 37 A2
Beech Hill Ave. WN6 36 F3
Beech Hill La. WN6 36 E3
Beech Hill Prim Sch. WN1 37 A3
Beech Hill Rd. OL4 68 D6
Beech House. 3 M30 79 B1
Beech House Sch. OL11 139 E6
Beech Hurst Cl. M16 97 D2
Beech La. Romiley SK6 113 C2
Beech La. Uppermill OL4 68 D5
Beech La. Wilmslow SK9 137 A6
Beech Lawn. WA14 119 C4
Beech Mews. M'ster M21 109 A8
Beech Mews. Stockport SK2 124 A5
Beech Mount. Ashton-u-L OL7 85 A6
Beech Mount. M'ster M9 157 D8
Beech Range. 15 M19 99 A1
Beech Rd. Alderley Edge SK9 137 B3
Beech Rd. Alt'ham WA15 119 E3
Beech Rd. Cheadle SK8 123 B1
Beech Rd. Golborne WA3 74 A1
Beech Rd. High Lane SK6 134 F7
Beech Rd. M'ster M21 109 B7
Beech Rd. Sale M33 108 D4
Beech Rd.
Stockport SK2 & SK3 170 F6
Beech St. Ashton-i-M WN4 73 A6
Beech St. Atherton M46 58 E3
Beech St. Bolton BL1 143 F2
Beech St. Bury BL9 141 B2
Beech St. Eccles M30 79 B1
Beech St. Edgworth BL7 9 D5
Beech St. Failsworth M35 83 E8
Beech St. Hyde SK14 167 D3
Beech St. Middleton M24 64 F8
Beech St. Newhey OL16 32 B4
Beech St. 3 Oldham OL1 67 A7
Beech St. R'dale OL11 139 D6
Beech St. Radcliffe M26 44 C1
Beech St. Ramsbottom BL0 11 C3
Beech St. Swinton M27 79 F7
Beech Street Cty Prim Sch.
M30 79 B1
Beech Tree Ave. WN6 35 D8
Beech Tree Houses. WN2 73 F7
Beech View. SK14 102 A2
Beech Wlk. Leigh WN7 75 E2
Beech Wlk. Middleton M24 65 A6
Beech Wlk. Standish WN6 36 D8
Beech Wlk. Stretford M32 96 C1
Beech Wlk. Wigan WN3 54 C2
Beechacre. BL0 11 D5
Beechcroft. M25 63 C3
Beechcroft Ave. BL2 42 E6
Beechcroft Cl. M10 & M40 160 D3
Beechcroft Gr. BL2 42 E6
Beechdale Cl. M40 83 C8
Beecher Wlk. M9 157 D6
Beeches Mews. M20 109 F4
Beeches The. Alt'ham WA14 119 C2
Beeches The. 4
Atherton M46 58 D3
Beeches The. Bolton BL1 24 D6
Beeches The. Cheadle SK8 123 B1
Beeches The. Eccles M30 79 F3
Beeches The. Heywood OL10 29 C2
Beeches The. M'ster M20 109 F4
Beeches The. Mossley OL5 68 E1
Beechey Sq. OL1 67 A7
Beechfield. Alt'ham WA14 119 C3
Beechfield. R'dale OL11 29 E6
Beechfield. Sale M33 107 F2
Beechfield. Uppermill OL4 68 D5
Beechfield Ave. Hindley WN2 57 A4
Beechfield Ave. 3
Radcliffe M26 44 C1
Beechfield Ave.Urmston M41 95 A3
Beechfield Ave.Walkden M38 60 A5
Beechfield Ave.
Wilmslow SK9 136 E5
Beechfield Cl. 1 Oldham OL4 67 F6
Beechfield Cl. R'dale OL11 29 E6
Beechfield Dr. Bury BL9 44 F7
Beechfield Dr. Leigh WN7 75 F3
Beechfield Mews. SK14 102 A3
Beechfield Rd. Bolton BL1 142 C2
Beechfield Rd. Cheadle SK8 132 B8
Beechfield Rd.
Hadfield SK13 171 F3
Beechfield Rd. Milnrow OL16 31 F4
Beechfield Rd.
Stockport SK3 170 F5
Beechfield Rd. Swinton M27 79 D5
Beechfield St. M7 & M8 156 A6
Beechmill Dr. WA3 91 E3
Beechpark Ave. M22 121 C7
Beechurst Rd. SK8 123 B5
Beechway. High Lane SK6 134 F7
Beechway. Wilmslow SK9 136 F5
Beechwood. Alt'ham WA14 119 B1
Beechwood. Glossop SK13 115 F7
Beechwood. Shaw OL2 49 D8
Beechwood. Whitefield BL9 45 A6
Beechwood Ave.
Ashton-i-M WN4 73 A2
Beechwood Ave.
Littleborough OL15 16 A3
Beechwood Ave.
M'ster M21 109 C7
Beechwood Ave. M'ster SK5 169 F4
Beechwood Ave.
Newton-l-W WA12 89 D4
Beechwood Ave.
Ramsbottom BL0 11 D6
Beechwood Ave.
Romiley SK6 113 D2
Beechwood Ave.
Shevington WN6 35 F5
Beechwood Ave.
Stalybridge SK15 86 C4
Beechwood Ave.
Urmston M41 94 E3
Beechwood Convent
Prim Sch. OL11 139 D5
Beechwood Cres. Orrell WN5 53 E6
Beechwood Cres.
Tyldesley M29 77 A6
Beechwood Ct. Bury BL8 27 A5
Beechwood Ct. 3
M'ster M20 110 A3
Beechwood Dr. Hyde SK14 167 F1
Beechwood Dr. Marple SK6 126 A6
Beechwood Dr. Mossley OL5 68 C2
Beechwood Dr. Royton OL2 48 C6
Beechwood Dr. Sale M33 107 C4
Beechwood Dr. Swinton M28 79 B6
Beechwood Dr.
Wilmslow SK9 137 E8
Beechwood Gr.Cheadle SK8 132 A8
Beechwood Gr.M'ster M9 157 E7
Beechwood La.Culcheth WA3 91 D4
Beechwood La.
Stalybridge SK15 86 C4
Beechwood Rd. M'ster M25 63 D3
Beechwood Rd. Oldham OL8 66 F2
Beechwood St. BL3 147 F3
Beede St. M11 165 B8
Beedon Ave. BL3 43 A4
Beehive Gn. BL5 40 B1
Beehive St. OL8 66 F3
Beeley St. Hyde SK14 167 E2
Beeley St. Salford M6 81 B5
Beenham Cl. M33 107 C3
Beeston Ave. Alt'ham WA15 119 F6
Beeston Ave. M'ster M7 81 B6
Beeston Cl. BL7 25 A6
Beeston Gr. Leigh WN7 76 D7
Beeston Gr. Prestwich M45 63 B7
Beeston Gr. Stockport SK3 170 E5
Beeston Rd. Handforth SK9 131 D5
Beeston Rd. Sale M33 107 F4
Beeston St. M9 157 E8
Beeth St. M18 99 D7
Beeton Gr. M13 98 E4
Beever Prim Sch. OL1 67 A8
Beever St. M'ster M16 161 C5
Beever St. Oldham OL1 67 A7
Begley Cl. SK6 112 F1
Begonia Ave. BL4 42 B1
Begonia Wlk. M12 164 F6
Beightons Wlk. OL12 14 D4
Beis Yaakov High Sch. M7 81 C8
Belbeck St. BL8 27 C2
Belbeck St S. 8 BL8 27 C2
Belcroft Dr. M38 59 E6
Belcroft Gr. M38 59 E5
Belding Ave. M40 65 F1
Beldon Rd. M9 64 B4
Belfairs Cl. OL6 85 B7
Belfield Cl. OL16 31 C8
Belfield La. OL16 31 C8
Belfield Mill La. OL16 31 D8
Belfield Old Rd. OL16 31 C8

Bishop's Cl. Bolton BL3 .... 42 A2
Bishop's Cl. Cheadle SK8 .... 123 A5
Bishop's Rd. BL3 .... 42 A2
Bishopbridge Cl. BL3 .... 147 F4
Bishopdale Cl. OL2 .... 48 D5
Bishopgate. WN1 .... 150 C8
Bishopgate St. OL9 .... 152 A5
Bishops Cl. Alt'ham WA14 ... 119 B1
Bishops Cl. Ashton-u-L OL7 ... 85 A5
Bishops Gate. M1 .... 162 F8
Bishops Mews. M33 .... 107 E6
Bishops Rd. M25 .... 63 C2
Bishops Wlk. OL7 .... 166 A1
Bishopton Cl. M19 .... 99 C1
Bisley Ave. M23 .... 120 F6
Bisley St. OL8 .... 153 D6
Bismarck St. OL4 & OL8 .... 67 A5
Bispham Ave. Bolton BL2 .... 42 F7
Bispham Ave. Reddish SK5 .... 99 F3
Bispham Cl. BL8 .... 26 F1
Bispham Dr. WN4 .... 72 F5
Bispham Gr. M7 .... 155 E7
Bispham Hall Bsns Pk. WN5 53 C2
Bispham St. BL2 .... 148 C8
Bittern Cl. Poynton SK12 .... 133 A4
Bittern Cl. R'dale OL11 .... 29 F7
Bittern Dr. M43 .... 84 C3
Bk Adcroft St. SK1 .... 170 F7
Bk Alfred St. BL0 .... 138 B5
Bk Andrew St. OL5 .... 86 C8
Bk Cecil St. OL5 .... 86 C8
Bk Chapel St. 12 M19 .... 99 A1
Bk Grosvenor St. 2 SK15 ... 86 A1
Bk Knowl St. SK15 .... 86 B2
Bk Melbourne St. 1 SK15 .. 86 A1
Bk Stayley Rd. OL5 .... 86 D8
Bk Water St. OL6 .... 166 C4
Black Brock Rd. SK4 .... 111 D7
Black Horse St. Blackrod BL6 21 C3
Black Horse St. Bolton BL1 145 E6
Black Horse St.
Farnworth BL4 .... 60 E7
Black La. BL0 .... 12 B7
Black Moss Cl. M26 .... 43 D3
Black Moss Rd. WA14 .... 118 F7
Blackbank St. BL1 .... 143 F2
Blackberry Cl. WA14 .... 119 B8
Blackberry La. SK5 .... 112 C7
Blackburn Cl. WA3 .... 90 E8
Blackburn Gdns. M20 .... 110 A4
Blackburn Old Rd. BL7 .... 8 C4
Blackburn Pl. M5 .... 81 C1
Blackburn Rd. Bolton BL7, BL1 8 C4
Blackburn Rd. Bolton BL1 .. 143 F2
Blackburn Rd. Edenfield BL0 ... 1 D5
Blackburn St. M'ster M3 .... 158 D3
Blackburn St. M'ster M16 .. 161 C5
Blackburn St. Prestwich M25 63 C4
Blackburn St. Radcliffe M26 .. 44 A3
Blackburn St. Radcliffe M26 .. 44 B2
Blackcap Cl. M28 .... 78 B7
Blackcarr Rd. M23 .... 121 B6
Blackcroft Cl. M27 .... 79 E8
Blackfield La. M7 .... 81 C8
Blackfields. M7 .... 155 D8
Blackford Ave. BL9 .... 44 F4
Blackford Rd. SK4 .... 111 B7
Blackford Wlk. M40 .... 160 D3
Blackfriar Ct. M3 .... 158 D3
Blackfriars Rd. M3 .... 158 E2
Blackfriars St. M3 .... 158 F2
Blackhill Cl. 8 M13 .... 163 B7
Blackhorse Ave. BL6 .... 21 C2
Blackhorse Cl. BL6 .... 21 C3
Blackleach Dr. M28 .... 60 D5
Blackledge St. BL3 .... 146 C4
Blackley Cl. BL9 .... 45 A2
Blackley Golf Course. M24 . 65 B4
Blackley New Rd. M9 & M25 64 B3
Blackley Park Rd. M9 .... 64 D1
Blackley St. M'ster M16 .... 161 C5
Blackley St. Middleton M24 ... 64 B7
Blackleyhurst Ave. WN5 .... 71 E5
Blacklock St. M8 .... 158 F4
Blackmoor Ave. M29 .... 77 B5
Blackpits Rd. OL11 .... 13 D1
Blackpool St. 19 M11 .... 83 C2
Blackrock. SK15 .... 86 C6
Blackrock St. M'ster M11 .... 164 F8
Blackrod Brow. BL6 .... 21 B4
Blackrod By-Pass Rd. BL6 .. 21 D2
Blackrod Cty Prim Sch.
WN2 .... 38 E8
Blackrod Dr. BL8 .... 26 F1
Blackrod Sta. BL6 .... 21 E2
Blacksail Wlk. 3 OL1 .... 49 A1
Blackshaw Brow. BL3 .... 144 C6
Blackshaw La.
Alderley Edge SK9 .... 136 F1
Blackshaw La. Bolton BL3 .. 144 C6
Blackshaw La. Royton OL2 .... 49 A4
Blackshaw Lane Prim Sch.
OL2 .... 49 A4
Blackshaw Prim Sch. BL2 ... 43 A6
Blackshaw Rd. SK13 .... 104 E2
Blackshaw Row. 2 BL3 .... 144 C5
Blackshaw St. SK3 .... 170 E8
Blacksmith La. OL11 .... 30 B4
Blackstock St. M13 .... 98 C4
Blackstone Ave. OL16 .... 31 C8
Blackstone Edge Old Rd.
OL15 .... 16 E6
Blackstone Edge Rd. HX6 .... 7 F5
Blackstone Rd. SK2 .... 124 D5
Blackstone Wlk. M9 .... 157 D6
Blackthorn Ave. M'ster M19 111 A7
Blackthorn Ave. Wigan WN6 36 F3
Blackthorn Cl. OL12 .... 14 E2
Blackthorn Rd. OL8 .... 84 C8
Blackthorn Wlk. 3 M31 ... 105 E2
Blackthorne Cl. BL1 .... 142 A1
Blackthorne Dr. M33 .... 107 D2
Blackthorne Rd. SK14 .... 113 E7
Blackwell Wlk. 3 M4 .... 159 C2
Blackwin St. M12 & M18 .... 165 A6
Blackwood Dr. M23 .... 120 D8
Blackwood Rd. OL13 .... 3 B7
Blackwood St. BL3 .... 42 A4
Bladen Cl. SK8 .... 123 A4
Bladon St. M1 .... 163 B8
Blainscough Rd. PR7 .... 19 E8
Blair Ave. Hindley WN2 .... 57 B3
Blair Ave. Urmston M41 .... 94 E2
Blair Ave. Walkden M38 .... 60 B4
Blair Cl. Hazel Grove SK7 .... 133 C8
Blair Cl. Sale M33 .... 107 C1
Blair Cl. Shaw OL2 .... 149 B7
Blair La. BL2 .... 25 D1
Blair Rd. M16 .... 97 E1
Blair St. Bolton BL7 .... 25 A8
Blair St. Kearsley BL4 .... 61 B6
Blair St. M'ster M16 .... 162 D5
Blair St. R'dale OL12 .... 14 D1
Blairhall Ave. M40 .... 83 A7
Blairmore Dr. BL3 .... 40 E5
Blake Ave. M46 .... 58 D5
Blake Cl. WN3 .... 150 A5
Blake Dr. SK2 .... 124 E7
Blake Gdns. BL1 .... 143 D2
Blake St. Bolton BL7 .... 25 A7
Blake St. Bolton BL1 .... 143 D2
Blake St. R'dale OL16 .... 31 A8
Blakeborough House. 7
M46 .... 58 D3
Blakedown Wlk. M12 .... 164 E5
Blakefield Dr. M28 .... 60 E1
Blakelock St. OL2 .... 149 B7
Blakemere Ave. M33 .... 108 E3
Blakemore Wlk. M11 .... 160 E1
Blakeswell Cl. M41 .... 94 D3
Blakey Cl. BL3 .... 40 F4
Blakey St. M12 & M18 .... 99 A4
Blanche St. OL12 .... 15 A2
Blanche Wlk. 10 OL1 .... 67 A8
Bland Cl. M35 .... 83 E7
Bland Rd. M25 .... 63 B2
Bland Wlk. 10 M15 .... 97 E4
Blandford Ave. M28 .... 79 A8
Blandford Cl. Bury BL8 .... 27 D5
Blandford Cl. Tyldesley M29 . 59 A1
Blandford Ct. SK15 .... 86 A2
Blandford Dr. Failsworth M40 65 D2
Blandford House. 7 SK15 .. 86 A2
Blandford Rd. Eccles M30 .... 79 B2
Blandford Rd. Salford M6 .... 81 B4
Blandford Rd.
Stockport SK4 .... 168 C2
Blandford Rise. Horwich BL6 22 F1
Blandford St.
Ashton-u-L OL6 & OL7 .... 166 A3
Blandford St.
Stalybridge SK15 .... 86 A2
Blanefield Cl. M21 .... 109 E7
Blantyre Ave. M28 .... 60 E2
Blantyre Rd. M27 .... 80 B6
Blantyre St. Hindley WN2 .... 56 E6
Blantyre St. M'ster M15 .... 162 D7
Blantyre St. Swinton M27 .... 61 D1
Blantyre St. Worsley M28 .... 79 A3
Blanwood Dr. M8 .... 156 B7
Blaven Cl. SK3 .... 170 F5
Blaydon Cl. WN2 .... 38 D5
Blazemoss Bank. SK2 .... 124 D5
Bleach St. WN2 .... 56 C4
Bleackley St. BL8 .... 27 C4
Bleak Hey Rd. M22 .... 121 F2
Bleak St. BL2 .... 25 B2
Bleakholt Rd. BL0 .... 1 F1
Bleakledge Gr. WN2 .... 56 F7
Bleakley St. 1 M45 .... 44 E1
Bleaklow Cl. WN3 .... 55 B2
Bleaklow Wlk. 20 SK13 .... 171 E1
Bleasby St. OL4 .... 67 C7
Bleasdale Cl. Horwich BL6 .... 39 F8
Bleasdale Cl. Whitefield BL9 . 45 A3
Bleasdale Rd. Bolton BL1 .... 23 F2
Bleasdale Rd.
Wythenshawe M22 .... 121 A2
Bleasdale St. OL2 .... 48 E5
Bleasedale Rd. WN2 .... 57 A5
Bleasefell Chase. M28 .... 78 A5
Bleatarn Rd. SK1 .... 124 B7
Bledlow Cl. M30 .... 79 E3
Blencarn Wlk. M9 .... 157 D6
Blendworth Cl. M8 .... 155 F7
Blenheim Ave. M16 .... 97 D2
Blenheim Cl. Alt'ham WA14 119 D2
Blenheim Cl. 6
Hadfield SK14 .... 104 A5
Blenheim Cl. Heywood OL10 . 29 E2
Blenheim Cl. Poynton SK12 . 133 F4
Blenheim Cl. Whitefield BL9 .. 45 A5
Blenheim Cl. Wilmslow SK9 137 D7
Blenheim Dr. WN7 .... 76 E7
Blenheim Rd.
Ashton-i-M WN4 .... 73 D2
Blenheim Rd. Bolton BL2 .... 42 E6
Blenheim Rd. Bramhall SK8 123 B2
Blenheim Rd. M'ster M16 .... 97 A3
Blenheim Rd. Wigan WN5 .... 54 C8
Blenheim St. 13 R'dale OL12 14 C1
Blenheim St. Tyldesley M29 .. 76 F8
Blenhiem Ave. OL1 .... 49 D3
Blenmar Cl. M26 .... 44 C5
Bleriot St. BL3 .... 147 D3
Blessed Thomas Holford
RC High Sch. WA15 .... 119 E4
Bletchley Cl. M13 .... 164 D5
Bletchley Rd. SK4 .... 111 C5
Blethyn St. BL3 .... 146 B2
Blewberry Cl. WN7 .... 75 F7
Bligh Rd. 15 BL5 .... 39 E1
Blinco Rd. M41 .... 95 A3
Blind La. M12 .... 164 D7
Blindsill Rd. BL4 .... 60 B7
Blissford Cl. WN2 .... 56 D4
Blisworth Ave. M30 .... 95 E8
Blisworth Cl. M4 .... 160 D1
Blithfield Wlk. M34 .... 100 E2
Block La. OL9 .... 152 B5
Blocksage St. SK16 .... 101 D7
Blodwell St. M5 & M6 .... 154 F2
Blofield Ct. BL4 .... 60 D7
Blomley St. OL11 .... 30 C2
Bloom St. M'ster M3 .... 158 E2
Bloom St. M'ster M1 .... 163 A8
Bloom St. Ramsbottom BL0 .... 11 A4
Bloom St. Stockport SK3 .... 170 D8
Bloomfield Dr.
Boothstown M28 .... 78 A7
Bloomfield Dr. Whitefield BL9 45 B3
Bloomfield Rd. BL4 .... 60 D6
Bloomfield St. BL1 .... 143 E3
Bloomsbury Gr. WA15 .... 120 A6
Bloomsbury La. WA15 .... 120 A6
Blossom Pl. OL16 .... 139 F8
Blossom Rd. M31 .... 105 E2
Blossom St. M'ster M3 .... 158 E2
Blossom St. M'ster M4 .... 159 B2
Blossom St. 11
Tyldesley M29 .... 59 A1
Blossoms Hey. SK8 .... 122 E1
Blossoms Hey Wlk. SK8 .... 122 E1
Blossoms La. SK7 .... 132 B2
Blossoms St. SK2 .... 170 F7
Bloxham Wlk. M9 .... 64 F3
Blucher St. Ashton-u-L OL7 .... 85 A6
Blucher St. M'ster M5 .... 81 C1
Blucher St. M'ster M12 .... 164 E6
Blue Bell Ave. M'ster M40 .... 65 A1
Blue Bell Ave. Wigan WN6 .... 36 F4
Blue Chip Bsns Pk. WA14 . 119 C7
Blue Coat CE Sch. OL1 .... 153 F7
Bluebell Ave. BB4 .... 1 A8
Bluebell Cl. SK14 .... 101 F5
Bluebell Dr. OL11 .... 30 B3
Bluebell Gr. SK8 .... 122 D4
Blueberry Dr. OL2 .... 49 D7
Blueberry Rd. WA14 .... 119 A2
Bluefields. OL2 .... 49 D8
Bluestone Dr. SK4 .... 110 E3
Bluestone Rd. M'ster M40 .... 83 A8
Bluestone Rd.
Reddish M34 & SK5 .... 100 A2
Blundell Cl. BL9 .... 45 B3
Blundell La. BL6 .... 21 A2
Blundell Mews. WN3 .... 54 D4
Blundell St. BL1 .... 145 E7
Blundering La. SK15 .... 102 D6
Blunn St. OL8 .... 66 F4
Blyborough Cl. M6 .... 154 E4
Blyth Ave. Littleborough OL15 . 15 F3
Blyth Ave. Wythenshawe M23 109 C2
Blyth Cl. WA15 .... 120 D6
Blythe Ave. SK7 .... 132 C6
Blyton St. M15 .... 163 B5
Blyton Way. M34 .... 112 F8
Bnos Yisroel Schs. M7 .... 155 E8
Boad St. M1 .... 163 B8
Boar Green Cl. M40 .... 83 C7
Board St. Ashton-u-L OL6 .... 85 D4
Board St. Bolton BL3 .... 145 D6
Boardale Dr. M24 .... 46 E1
Boardman Cl. BL1 .... 143 E2
Boardman Fold Cl. M24 .... 65 A5
Boardman Fold Rd. M24 .... 65 A5
Boardman La. M24 .... 64 C8
Boardman Rd. M8 .... 63 F2
Boardman St.
Blackrod BL6 & PR7 .... 21 D2
Boardman St. Bolton BL1 ... 143 E2
Boardman St. Eccles M30 .... 79 E1
Boardman St. Hyde SK14 ... 167 D2
Boars Head Ave. WN6 .... 37 A7
Boarsgreave La. BB4 .... 2 F6
Boarshaw Clough. M24 .... 47 B2
Boarshaw Cres. M24 .... 47 C3
Boarshaw Cty Prim Sch.
M24 .... 47 B3
Boarshaw Ind Est. M24 .... 47 B2
Boarshaw La. M24 .... 47 D3
Boarshaw Rd. M24 .... 47 B2
Boarshurst La. OL3 .... 69 C5
Boat La. Diggle OL3 .... 51 E5
Boat La. Irlam M44 .... 94 B2
Boat La. Wythenshawe M22 .. 109 E1
Boat Lane Ct. M22 .... 109 E1
Boatmans Row. M29 .... 77 C4
Bob Brook Cl. M35 & M40 .... 83 C6
Bob Massey Cl. M11 .... 83 C1
Bob's La. M44 .... 105 D4
Bobbin Wlk. 4 M'ster M4 .. 159 C1
Bobbin Wlk. 7 Oldham OL4 . 67 A6
Bodden St. WA3 .... 75 A1
Boddens Hill Rd. SK4 .... 168 A1
Boddington Rd. Eccles M30 .. 79 A1
Bodiam Rd. BL8 .... 10 F2
Bodley St. M11 .... 83 C2
Bodmin Cl. OL2 .... 49 A3
Bodmin Cres. SK5 .... 112 B5
Bodmin Dr. Bramhall SK7 .... 132 E7
Bodmin Dr. Platt Bridge WN2 56 A1
Bodmin Rd. Sale M33 .... 107 D5
Bodmin Rd. Tyldesley M29 .... 77 C8
Bodmin Wlk. 3 M23 .... 121 A5
Bodney Wlk. M9 .... 64 B3
Bogburn La. PR7 .... 19 D6
Boggard La. SK14 .... 115 D6
Bogguard Rd. SK12 & SK6 .. 127 A5
Bognor Rd. SK3 .... 123 E4
Bolam Cl. M23 .... 108 F1
Boland Dr. M14 .... 110 D8
Bold St. Alt'ham WA14 .... 119 D3
Bold St. Bolton BL1 .... 145 F6
Bold St. Bury BL9 .... 141 A3
Bold St. Leigh WN7 .... 75 F5
Bold St. Leigh WN7 .... 75 F6
Bold St. M'ster M16 .... 97 E4
Bold St. M'ster M15 .... 162 E5
Bold St. Swinton M27 .... 61 F2
Bold St. Wigan WN5 .... 54 E5
Bolderod Pl. 4 OL1 .... 67 A8
Bolderstone Pl. SK2 .... 124 E4
Bolderwood Dr. WN2 .... 56 D4
Bolesworth Cl. M21 .... 108 F8
Boleyn Ct. Handforth SK9 .... 131 B1
Boleyn Ct. Heywood OL10 .... 29 C1
Bolholt Terr. BL8 .... 27 B4
Bolivia St. M5 .... 80 C2
Bollin Ave. WA14 .... 119 B1
Bollin Cl. Culcheth WA3 .... 92 A2
Bollin Cl. Kearsley BL4 .... 61 B6
Bollin Cl. Lymm WA13 .... 117 A4
Bollin Cross Sch. SK9 .... 131 A2
Bollin Ct. Alt'ham WA14 .... 119 B1
Bollin Ct. 6 M'ster M15 .... 162 D6
Bollin Ct. Wilmslow SK9 .... 137 C6
Bollin Dr. Alt'ham WA14 .... 119 E8
Bollin Dr. Lymm WA13 .... 117 A4
Bollin Dr. Sale M33 .... 108 B2
Bollin Hill. SK9 .... 137 B8
Bollin House. M7 .... 81 C5
Bollin Prim Sch. WA14 .... 119 B1
Bollin Sq. WA14 .... 119 B1
Bollin Way. M45 .... 45 C2
Bollin Wlk. Reddish SK5 .... 169 F4
Bollin Wlk. Whitefield M45 .... 45 C2
Bollin Wlk. Wilmslow SK9 .... 137 C7
Bolling St. BL3 .... 145 F6
Bollings Yd. BL1 .... 145 F6
Bollington Cl. 3 OL7 .... 166 A1
Bollington Rd.
M'ster M10 & M40 .... 160 D2
Bollington Rd. Reddish SK4 111 D5
Bollington St. OL7 .... 166 A1
Bollinway. WA15 .... 129 A8
Bollinwood Chase. SK9 .... 137 D7
Bolney St. WN2 .... 38 A3
Bolney Wlk. M40 .... 160 D4
Bolshaw Cty Prim Sch.
SK8 .... 131 B7
Bolshaw Farm La. SK8 .... 131 C6
Bolshaw Rd. SK8 .... 131 C6
Bolton Ave. Bramhall SK8 .... 132 B6
Bolton Ave. M'ster M19 .... 110 D2
Bolton Cath Sixth
Form Ctr. BL1 .... 143 D4
Bolton Cl. Golborne WA3 .... 91 B8
Bolton Cl. Poynton SK12 .... 133 D4
Bolton Cl. Prestwich M25 .... 62 F2
Bolton Coll. BL2 .... 148 A6
Bolton District Gen Hospl.
BL4 .... 147 F1
Bolton Golf Course. BL6 .... 40 A8
Bolton House Rd. WN2 .... 74 F8
Bolton Inst (Chadwick
Campus). BL2 .... 148 B6
Bolton Inst of H Ed. BL3 ... 145 E6
Bolton Metropolitan Coll.
Bolton BL1 .... 145 F8
Bolton Metropolitan Coll.
Bolton BL2 .... 148 A6
Bolton Muslim Girls Sch.
BL3 .... 147 D4
Bolton Old Rd. M46 .... 58 E3
Bolton Parish Church
CE Prim Sch. BL2 .... 148 B7
Bolton Rd.
Adlington BL6 & PR6 .... 21 D6
Bolton Rd.
Ashton-i-M WN2 & WN4 .... 73 D5
Bolton Rd. Aspull WN2 .... 38 D4
Bolton Rd. Atherton M46 .... 58 E4
Bolton Rd. Bolton BL7 .... 9 D5
Bolton Rd. Bolton BL2 .... 25 C5
Bolton Rd. Bolton BL3 .... 40 D2
Bolton Rd. Bury BL8 .... 27 C1
Bolton Rd. Bury BL8 .... 140 D2
Bolton Rd. Farnworth BL4 .... 42 D2
Bolton Rd. Kearsley BL4 .... 60 F7
Bolton Rd. Pendlebury M27 .... 80 C7
Bolton Rd. R'dale OL11 .... 30 B4
Bolton Rd. Radcliffe M26 .... 43 E3
Bolton Rd. Ramsbottom BL8 .. 10 D2
Bolton Rd. Salford M6 .... 80 E5
Bolton Rd. Swinton M27 & BL8 62 A1
Bolton Rd. Walkden M28 .... 60 D4
Bolton Rd. Westhoughton BL5 39 F1
Bolton Rd N. BL0 .... 1 D2
Bolton Rd W. Ramsbottom BL8 10 F3
Bolton Rd W.
Ramsbottom BL0 & BL8 .... 11 A4
Bolton Royal Infmy. BL1 ... 145 D7
Bolton Sch. BL1 .... 144 B7
Bolton Sq. WN1 .... 37 E1
Bolton St. Bury BL9 .... 140 E2
Bolton St. Garswood WN4 .... 72 D5
Bolton St. M'ster M3 .... 158 E1
Bolton St. Oldham OL4 .... 67 B6
Bolton St. Radcliffe M26 .... 43 F3
Bolton St. Ramsbottom BL0 . 138 B6
Bolton St. Reddish SK5 .... 111 E7
Bolton Sta. BL3 .... 145 F6
Bolton Street Sta. BL9 .... 140 E2
Bolton Wholesale Pk. BL1 145 F8
Boltons Yd. OL3 .... 69 B8
Bombay Rd. Shevington WN5 36 C1
Bombay Rd. Stockport SK3 . 123 C7
Bombay St. 5
Ashton-u-L OL6 .... 85 D4
Bombay St. M'ster M1 .... 163 A8
Bonar Cl. SK3 .... 123 C8
Bonar Rd. 5 SK3 .... 123 C8
Boncarn Dr. M23 .... 121 A4
Bonchurch Wlk. M12 .... 165 B6
Bond Cl. BL6 .... 22 C3
Bond Sq. M7 .... 155 E6
Bond St. Bury BL9 .... 141 A2
Bond St. Denton M34 .... 100 F3
Bond St. Edenfield BL0 .... 1 E2
Bond St. Leigh WN7 .... 75 F5
Bond St. M'ster M12 .... 163 C8
Bond St. R'dale OL12 .... 15 A2
Bond St. Stalybridge SK15 .... 86 A3
Bond St. Tyldesley M46 .... 58 F1
Bond's La. PR7 .... 20 F7
Bondmark Rd. M18 .... 165 C6
Bongs Rd. SK2 & SK6 .... 125 A6
Bonhill Wlk. M11 .... 83 B2
Bonholt Ind Est. 11 BL8 .... 27 B4
Bonington Rise. SK6 .... 126 B8
Bonis Cres. SK2 .... 124 C4
Bonny Brow St. M24 .... 64 B7
Bonnywell Rd. WN7 .... 75 F3
Bonsall Bank. 32 SK13 .... 171 E2
Bonsall Cl. 33 SK13 .... 171 E2
Bonsall Fold. 31 SK13 .... 171 E2
Bonsall St. M15 .... 162 F6
Bonscale Cres. M24 .... 46 E3
Bonville Chase. WA14 .... 119 A4
Bonville Rd. WA14 .... 119 A4
Boodle St. OL6 .... 166 B4
Bookham Wlk. 16 M9 .... 157 E8
Boond St. M'ster M3 .... 158 E2
Boond St. M'ster M4 .... 160 D1
Boonfields. BL7 .... 25 A8
Boot La. BL1 .... 23 E1
Booth Ave. M14 .... 110 D7
Booth Bridge Cl. M24 .... 64 C7
Booth Cl. 4 SK15 .... 85 F1
Booth Cl. BL4 .... 60 D8
Booth Dr. M41 .... 94 F5
Booth Hall Dr. BL8 .... 26 F5
Booth Hall Hospl. M9 .... 64 F3
Booth Hall Rd. M9 .... 65 A3
Booth Hill La. OL1 .... 48 E1
Booth House Trad Est.
OL9 .... 152 C6
Booth Rd. Alt'ham WA14 .... 119 C4
Booth Rd. Bacup OL13 .... 3 B8
Booth Rd.
Droylsden M34 & M43 .... 100 A7
Booth Rd. Handforth SK9 .... 131 A1
Booth Rd. Little Lever BL3 .... 43 B2
Booth Rd. M'ster M16 .... 97 C3
Booth Rd. Sale M33 .... 108 B6
Booth St. Ashton-u-L OL6 .... 166 B2
Booth St. Bolton BL1 .... 142 C3
Booth St. Bury BL8 .... 26 F5
Booth St. Denton M34 .... 100 F5
Booth St. Failsworth M35 .... 83 E7
Booth St. Hollingworth SK14 103 C5
Booth St. Hyde SK14 .... 167 E1
Booth St. M'ster M2 .... 158 F1
Booth St. M'ster M3 .... 158 F2
Booth St. Middleton M24 .... 65 D6
Booth St. Newton-l-W WA12 .. 89 A3
Booth St. 2 Oldham OL4 .... 67 E6
Booth St. Oldham OL9 .... 153 E6
Booth St. Rawtenstall BB4 .... 2 E8
Booth St. Stalybridge SK15 .... 101 F8
Booth St. Stockport SK3 .... 170 E7
Booth St E. M13 .... 163 B6
Booth St W. M15 .... 163 A6
Booth Way. BL8 .... 26 F5
Booth's Brow Rd. WN4 .... 72 D6
Booth's Hall. M28 .... 78 B5
Booth's Hall Gr. M28 .... 78 B6
Booth's Hall Rd. M28 .... 78 B6
Booth's Hall Way. M28 .... 78 B6
Boothby Rd. M27 .... 61 E1
Boothby St. SK2 .... 124 C4
Boothcote. M34 .... 100 D6
Boothfield. 11 Bury BL8 .... 27 C3
Boothfield. Worsley M28 .... 79 A3
Boothfield Ave. M22 .... 121 D6
Boothfield Dr. M22 .... 121 D6
Boothfield Rd. M22 .... 121 D6
Boothroyden Cl. M24 .... 64 C7
Boothroyden Rd. M24 & M9 . 64 C6
Boothroyden Terr. M9 .... 64 C6
Boothsbank Ave. M28 .... 78 B6
Boothshall Paddock. M28 ... 78 B5
Boothshall Way. M28 .... 78 A5
Boothstown Dr. M28 .... 78 A5
Boothway. 8 M30 .... 79 F2
Bootle St. M2 .... 162 F8
Bor Ave. WN3 .... 55 B4
Bordale Ave. M9 .... 157 F7
Bordan St. M11 .... 164 F8
Borden Cl. 5 WN2 .... 37 F2
Borden Way. BL9 .... 45 A6
Border Brook La. M28 .... 78 A6
Bordesley Ave. M38 .... 60 A6
Bordley Wlk. M23 .... 108 E1
Bordon Cl. BL1 .... 143 D1
Bordon Rd. SK3 .... 123 B7
Bores Hill. WN1 .... 20 C4
Boringdon Cl. M40 .... 83 B6
Borland Ave. M40 .... 65 D1
Borough Arc. SK14 .... 167 D2
Borough Ave. Radcliffe BL9 ... 44 D5
Borough Ave. Swinton M27 .... 62 A1
Borough Rd. Alt'ham WA15 .... 119 E4
Borough Rd. Salford M5 .... 154 D1
Borough St. 5 SK15 .... 86 A1
Borrans The. M28 .... 77 F5
Borron Rd. WA12 .... 89 B5
Borron St. SK1 .... 112 A2
Borrowdale Ave. Bolton BL1 144 A8
Borrowdale Ave. Gatley SK8 122 B4
Borrowdale Cl. OL2 .... 48 D6
Borrowdale Cres.
Ashton-u-L OL7 .... 84 F4
Borrowdale Cres.
M'ster M20 .... 109 E4
Borrowdale Dr. R'dale OL11 . 30 C4
Borrowdale Dr.
Whitefield BL9 .... 45 A3
Borrowdale Rd.
Middleton M24 .... 46 E2
Borrowdale Rd.
Stockport SK2 .... 124 B6
Borrowdale Rd. Wigan WN5 . 54 B7
Borrowdale Terr. SK15 .... 86 A4
Borsdane Ave. WN2 .... 56 F5
Borsdane Brook Sch. WN2 . 56 C5
Borsden St. M27 .... 61 D2
Borth Ave. SK2 .... 124 C7
Borwell St. M18 .... 99 D5
Boscobel Rd. BL3 .... 42 B2
Boscombe Ave. M30 .... 95 C8
Boscombe Dr. SK7 .... 124 C1
Boscombe St. M'ster M14 .... 98 B2
Boscombe St.
Reddish M34 & SK5 .... 99 F2
Boscow Rd. BL3 .... 43 A2
Bosden Ave. SK7 .... 124 F3
Bosden Cl. Handforth SK9 .... 131 D5
Bosden Cl. Stockport SK1 .... 170 F8
Bosden Fold. SK1 .... 170 F8
Bosden Hall Rd. SK7 .... 124 E3
Bosdenfold Rd. SK7 .... 124 E3
Bosdin Rd E. M41 .... 94 E1
Bosdin Rd W. M41 .... 94 E1
Bosley Ave. M20 .... 110 A8
Bosley Cl. SK9 .... 131 D2
Bosley Dr. SK12 .... 134 A3
Bosley Rd. SK3 .... 123 B8
Bossall Ave. M9 .... 64 E4
Bossington Cl. SK2 .... 124 C8
Bostock Rd. SK14 .... 115 A8
Bostock Wlk. M13 .... 163 B7
Boston Cl. Bramhall SK7 .... 132 D7
Boston Cl. Culcheth WA3 .... 91 F4
Boston Cl. Failsworth M35 .... 83 F8
Boston Ct. M5 .... 96 E8
Boston Gr. WN7 .... 75 E8
Boston St. 14 Bolton BL1 .... 143 E2
Boston St. Hyde SK14 .... 167 E2
Boston St. Oldham OL8 .... 66 F4
Boston Wlk. 8 M34 .... 101 A1
Boswell Ave. M34 .... 84 D1
Boswell Pl. WN3 .... 54 F3
Boswell Way. M24 .... 47 E4
Bosworth Cl. M45 .... 63 C8
Bosworth Sq. OL11 .... 30 D4
Bosworth St. Horwich BL6 .... 22 B4
Bosworth St. M'ster M11 .... 165 A8
Bosworth St. R'dale OL11 .... 30 D4
Botanical Ave. M16 .... 161 A5
Botany Cl. Heywood OL10 .... 29 B2
Botany Cl. Wigan WN2 .... 38 B2
Botany La. OL6 .... 166 C3
Botany Rd. Romiley SK6 .... 113 A6
Botany Rd. Worsley M28 .... 79 A4
Botha Cl. 4 M11 .... 99 D7
Botham Cl. M'ster M15 .... 162 F5
Bothwell Rd. M10 & M40 .... 159 C3
Botley St. OL5 .... 68 B1
Bottesford Ave. M20 .... 109 F5
Bottom o' th' Knotts Brow.
BL7 .... 9 E3
Bottom o' th' Moor.
Horwich BL6 .... 23 A3
Bottom o' th' Moor.
Oldham OL1 & OL4 .... 67 B7
Bottom o'th Moor. BL2 .... 25 D2
Bottom St. SK14 .... 167 F3
Bottomfield Cl. OL1 .... 49 A1
Bottomley Rd. OL14 .... 6 C6
Bottomley Side. M9 .... 64 C2
Bougainvillea Gdns. M12 .... 99 A4
Boughey St. WN7 .... 75 E5
Boulden Dr. BL8 .... 27 C5
Boulder Dr. M23 .... 121 A2
Boulderstone Rd. SK15 .... 86 A4
Boulevard The.
Hazel Grove SK7 .... 124 E2
Boulevard The.
Hollingworth SK14 .... 171 D4
Bouley Wlk. M12 .... 165 A6
Boundary Cl. Mossley SK15 ... 86 C6
Boundary Cl. Romiley SK6 .. 113 C5
Boundary Cotts. OL5 .... 86 E7
Boundary Ct. SK8 .... 122 C5
Boundary Dr. BL2 & BL3 .... 43 A5
Boundary Gdns. Bolton BL1 143 E2
Boundary Gdns. Oldham OL1 48 E1
Boundary Gr. M33 .... 108 F2
Boundary La. M'ster M15 .... 163 A6
Boundary La.
Shevington Moor WN6 .... 19 A3
Boundary Park Football Gd
(Oldham Ath FC). OL1 .... 48 D2
Boundary Park Rd. OL1 .... 48 C1
Boundary Rd. Cheadle SK8 . 123 A6
Boundary Rd. Irlam M44 .... 94 C3
Boundary Rd. Swinton M27 ... 61 F1
Boundary St. Bolton BL1 .... 143 D2
Boundary St. Leigh WN7 .... 76 B4
Boundary St.
Littleborough OL15 .... 16 B6
Boundary St. M'ster M12 .... 165 A6
Boundary St. R'dale OL11 .... 139 F5
Boundary St. Tyldesley M29 .. 59 A1
Boundary St. Wigan WN1 .... 151 D7
Boundary St E. M13 .... 163 A7
Boundary St W. M15 .... 163 A6
Boundary Terr. SK9 .... 130 F6
Boundary The. M27 .... 61 E4
Boundary Trad Pk. M44 .... 94 C3
Boundary Wlk. OL11 .... 139 E5
Boundry Gn. M34 .... 100 E4
Bourdon St. M10 & M40 .... 160 D3
Bourget St. M7 & M8 .... 155 F8
Bournbrook Ave. M38 .... 60 A6
Bourne Ave. Golborne WA3 ... 90 D8
Bourne Ave. Swinton M27 .... 79 F7
Bourne Dr. M40 .... 65 B1
Bourne House. 1 M6 .... 154 F2
Bourne Rd. OL2 .... 149 A8
Bourne St. Oldham OL9 .... 66 B2
Bourne St. Reddish SK4 .... 169 E4
Bourne St. Wilmslow SK9 .... 136 F6
Bourne Wlk. 9 BL1 .... 143 F1
Bournelea Ave. M19 .... 110 F6
Bourneville Dr. BL8 .... 27 A2
Bournville Ave. SK4 .... 169 E4
Bournville Gr. M19 .... 99 C1
Bourton Cl. BL8 .... 27 B3
Bourton Ct. M29 .... 59 D1
Bourton Dr. M18 .... 99 B4
Bow Green Rd. WA14 .... 119 A1
Bow La. Alt'ham WA14 .... 128 B8
Bow La. Heywood OL10 .... 29 D2
Bow La. M'ster M2 .... 158 F1
Bow Rd. WN7 .... 76 B3
Bow St. Ashton-u-L OL6 .... 166 B3
Bow St. Bolton BL1 .... 145 F7
Bow St. Dukinfield SK16 .... 166 C2
Bow St. 7 M'ster M2 .... 158 F1
Bow St. Oldham OL1 .... 153 F7
Bow St. R'dale OL11 .... 30 D3
Bow St. Stockport SK3 .... 123 C8
Bowden Cl. Culcheth WA3 .... 91 F4
Bowden Cl. Leigh WN7 .... 76 C2
Bowden Cl. Middleton OL11 ... 47 D8
Bowden Cl.
Mottram-i-L SK14 .... 102 E1
Bowden La. SK6 .... 125 E6
Bowden Rd. Glossop SK13 .. 104 C3
Bowden Rd. Pendlebury M27 . 80 A7
Bowden St. Bolton BL3 .... 145 D6
Bowden St. Denton M34 .... 100 E3
Bowden St. Hazel Grove SK7 124 E3
Bowdon Ave. M14 .... 97 F1
Bowdon CE Aided Prim
Sch. WA14 .... 119 C1
Bowdon House. 2 SK3 .... 170 E8
Bowdon Prep Sch. WA14 .. 119 C2

Brookside Ave. Poynton SK2 133 E3
Brookside Ave. Stockport SK2 124 F7
Brookside Bsns Pk. M24 65 D6
Brookside Cl. Atherton M46 58 E4
Brookside Cl. Billinge WN5 71 E5
Brookside Cl. Bolton BL2 25 D5
Brookside Cl. Cheadle SK8 122 D4
Brookside Cl. Hadfield SK14 171 F4
Brookside Cl. Hyde SK14 102 A3
Brookside Cl. Ramsbottom BL0 11 A3
Brookside Cres. Bury BL8 26 E8
Brookside Cres. Middleton M24 65 C6
Brookside Cres.Walkden M28 60 E3
Brookside Ct. M19 99 A2
Brookside Dr. Hyde SK14 102 A3
Brookside Dr. M'ster M25 & M7 63 D1
Brookside La. SK6 134 E7
Brookside Prim Sch. SK6 134 E6
Brookside Rd. Bolton BL2 42 D8
Brookside Rd. Gatley SK8 122 A6
Brookside Rd. M'ster M40 65 A1
Brookside Rd. Sale M33 108 A2
Brookside Rd. Standish WN1 20 B1
Brookside Terr. OL3 50 E4
Brookside Wlk. BL8 43 F7
Brooksmouth. BL8 140 D2
Brookstone Cl. M21 109 D6
Brookthorn Cl. SK2 124 F5
Brookthorpe Ave. M19 110 E6
Brookthorpe Rd. BL8 27 A3
Brookvale. 4 Wigan WN6 37 A1
Brookview. WN2 56 D4
Brookville. OL12 4 C1
Brookway. Alt'ham WA15 119 F7
Brookway. Oldham OL4 67 E5
Brookway. Uppermill OL4 68 E6
Brookway Cl. M19 110 E4
Brookway Ct. M23 120 F7
Brookway High Sch. M23 120 D8
Brookwood Ave. M'ster M8 156 C8
Brookwood Ave. Sale M33 107 E3
Brookwood Cl. M34 113 A7
Broom Ave. Leigh WN7 75 E7
Broom Ave. M'ster M19 111 B8
Broom Ave. M'ster M7 155 E8
Broom Ave. 4 Reddish SK5 111 F6
Broom La. M'ster M19 111 B8
Broom La. M'ster M7 155 D8
Broom Rd. Alt'ham WA15 119 E3
Broom Rd. Partington M31 105 F2
Broom Rd. Wigan WN5 54 D7
Broom St. Bury BL8 140 D2
Broom St. Newhey OL16 32 B4
Broom St. Swinton M27 79 F7
Broom Way. BL5 40 A2
Broome Gr. M35 83 F6
Broome St. OL9 153 D6
Broomedge. M7 155 D8
Broomehouse Ave. M44 105 E8
Broomfield. Salford M27 80 D6
Broomfield Cl. Ainsworth BL2 26 C1
Broomfield Cl. Reddish SK5 111 F6
Broomfield Cl. Wilmslow SK9 137 E8
Broomfield Cres. Middleton M24 46 D1
Broomfield Cres. Stockport SK2 & SK3 124 A4
Broomfield Dr. M'ster M7 & M8 155 F7
Broomfield Dr. Reddish SK5 111 F6
Broomfield La. WA15 119 E3
Broomfield Pl. WN6 19 E1
Broomfield Rd. 4 Bolton BL3 146 C4
Broomfield Rd. M'ster SK4 168 C4
Broomfield Rd. Standish WN6 19 E2
Broomfield Sq. OL11 139 F5
Broomfield Terr. Newhey OL16 32 B4
Broomfield Terr. Wigan WN2 151 E7
Broomfields. M34 101 A5
Broomflat Cl. WN6 19 E1
Broomgrove La. M34 101 A4
Broomhall Rd. M'ster M9 64 B5
Broomhall Rd. Salford M27 80 D6
Broomhey Ave. WN1 37 C4
Broomhey Terr. WN1 & WN2 151 E7
Broomhill Dr. SK7 123 D1
Broomholme. WN6 35 D7
Broomhurst Ave. OL8 66 D4
Broomstair Rd. M34 100 F6
Broomville Ave. M33 108 B4
Broomwood Prim Sch. WA15 120 D5
Broomwood Rd. WA15 120 C5
Broomwood Wlk. 2 M15 163 A6
Broseley Ave. Culcheth WA3 91 D4
Broseley Ave. M'ster M20 110 D3
Broseley La. WA3 91 D5
Broseley Rd. M16 97 A2
Brosscroft. SK14 104 A6
Brosscroft Village. SK14 104 A6
Brotherdale Cl. OL2 48 D5
Brotherod Hall Rd. OL12 14 C2
Brotherton Cl. M15 162 D6
Brotherton Dr. M3 158 D2
Brough St. 4 M11 99 E7
Brougham St. 1 Stalybridge SK15 85 F1
Brougham St. Walkden M28 60 C3
Broughton Ave. Golborne WA3 90 D7
Broughton Ave.Walkden M38 60 B4
Broughton Cl. M24 46 D2
Broughton Jewish Cassel-Fox Prim Sch. M7 63 E1
Broughton Jewish Prim Sch. M7 63 D1
Broughton La. M'ster M5 & M7 155 D5
Broughton La. M'ster M7 & M8 158 E4
Broughton Rd. Reddish SK5 169 F4
Broughton Rd. Salford M6 81 A4
Broughton Rd E. M6 81 B4
Broughton St. Bolton BL1 143 D2
Broughton St. M'ster M7 & M8 159 A4
Broughton Trade Ctr. M7 158 E4
Broughville Dr. M20 122 C8
Brow Ave. M24 65 C6
Brow St. OL11 31 A4
Brow Wlk. M9 64 D3
Browbeck. OL1 153 E7
Browfield. M5 161 B8
Browfield Ave. M5 161 B8
Browfield Way. OL1 48 E1
Browmere Dr. M20 110 A4
Brown Bank Rd. OL15 15 F3
Brown Edge Rd. OL4 67 E4
Brown Heath Ave. WN5 71 D3
Brown La. SK8 122 B1
Brown Lodge Dr. OL15 15 F3
Brown Lodge St. OL15 15 F3
Brown St. Alderley Edge SK9 137 A1
Brown St. Alt'ham WA14 119 D3
Brown St. Blackrod BL6 21 D2
Brown St. Bolton BL1 145 F7
Brown St. Chadderton OL9 152 A8
Brown St. Failsworth M35 83 E7
Brown St. Heywood OL10 29 D3
Brown St. Ince-i-M WN2 56 A7
Brown St. Leigh WN2 56 E1
Brown St. 3 Leigh WN7 76 A5
Brown St. Littleborough OL15 16 B5
Brown St. M'ster M3 158 E2
Brown St. 18 M'ster M2 158 F1
Brown St. M'ster M1 & M60 159 A1
Brown St. Middleton M24 47 A2
Brown St. Oldham OL1 67 A7
Brown St. Radcliffe M26 43 F6
Brown St. Ramsbottom BL0 138 B5
Brown St. Salford M5 & M6 154 F1
Brown St. Stockport SK1 169 E2
Brown St. Tyldesley M29 76 F7
Brown St. Wigan WN3 150 B7
Brown St N. 2 WN7 76 A5
Brown St S. 1 WN7 76 A4
Brown's La. SK9 137 E8
Brownacre St. M20 110 B6
Brownbank Wlk. M15 162 F5
Browncross St. M3 158 E1
Brownhill Dr. OL4 68 A7
Brownhill La. OL3 51 B1
Brownhill Sch. OL12 14 E1
Brownhill St. M11 165 A8
Browning Ave.Atherton M46 58 D5
Browning Ave.Droylsden M43 84 A1
Browning Ave. Wigan WN3 54 F4
Browning Cl. BL1 143 D1
Browning Gr. WN6 36 E3
Browning Rd. Middleton M24 47 B2
Browning Rd. Oldham OL1 49 B1
Browning Rd. Reddish SK5 99 E2
Browning Rd. Swinton M27 79 E8
Browning St. Leigh WN7 75 D6
Browning St. M'ster M3 158 D2
Browning St. M'ster M15 162 D6
Browning Wlk. M46 58 D5
Brownlea Ave. SK16 101 C7
Brownley Court Rd. M22 121 D5
Brownley Ct. M22 121 E5
Brownley Rd. M22 121 E4
Brownlow Ave. Ince-i-M WN2 56 B7
Brownlow Ave. Royton OL2 49 A3
Brownlow Cl. SK12 133 E2
Brownlow Ctr. BL1 143 E1
Brownlow Fold Prim Sch. BL1 143 D1
Brownlow La. WN5 53 C1
Brownlow Rd. BL6 22 C5
Brownlow Way. BL1 143 E1
Brownmere. WN6 36 F2
Browns Rd. BL2 & BL3 43 B6
Brownside Cl. OL16 15 C3
Brownslow Wlk. 11 M13 163 B7
Brownson Wlk. 7 M9 157 E8
Brownsville Rd. SK4 111 C5
Brownville Gr. SK16 101 E7
Brownwood Ave. SK1 112 B1
Brownwood Cl. M33 108 C1
Brows Ave. M23 109 A2
Browsholm House. BL1 144 C7
Broxton Ave. Bolton BL3 146 B3
Broxton Ave. Orrell WN5 53 F7
Broxton St. M11 & M40 160 F3
Broxwood Cl. 8 M18 99 D5
Bruce St. OL11 30 C4
Bruce Wlk. 2 M11 99 D7
Brundage Rd. M22 121 D2
Brundrett Pl. 6 M33 107 F4
Brundrett St. SK1 124 A8
Brundrett's Rd. M21 109 B8
Brunel Ave. M5 81 B1
Brunel Cl. M32 96 E2
Brunel St. Bolton BL1 143 D3
Brunel St. Horwich BL6 22 C2
Brunet Wlk. M12 164 F6
Brunstead Cl. M23 120 D6
Brunswick Ave. BL6 22 E2
Brunswick Ct. BL1 145 E8
Brunswick Rd. Alt'ham WA14 119 D7
Brunswick Rd. M'ster M14 & M20 110 C7
Brunswick St. Bury BL9 140 F3
Brunswick St. Dukinfield SK16 101 C8
Brunswick St. 3 Heywood OL10 29 C2
Brunswick St. Leigh WN7 76 A4
Brunswick St. M'ster M13 163 B6
Brunswick St. Mossley OL5 86 D8
Brunswick St. Oldham OL1 153 E6
Brunswick St. R'dale OL16 31 A8
Brunswick St. Shaw OL2 149 B7
Brunswick St.Stretford M32 108 D8
Brunswick St. Walsden OL14 6 A7
Brunswick Terr. OL13 3 D8
Brunt St. M14 98 B3
Brunton Rd. SK5 111 F6
Bruntwood Ave. SK8 122 A1
Bruntwood La. Cheadle SK8 122 E1
Bruntwood La. Cheadle SK8 122 E2
Bruntwood Prim Sch. SK8 122 E2
Brushes Ave. SK15 86 D3
Brushes Rd. SK15 86 E2
Brussels Rd. SK3 170 D6
Bruton Ave. M32 96 B1
Brutus Wlk. M7 155 E6
Bryan Rd. M21 97 B2
Bryan St. 1 Oldham OL4 49 C1
Bryant Cl. M13 163 C5
Bryant's Acre. BL1 40 D7
Bryantsfield. BL1 40 D6
Bryce St. Bolton BL3 145 E5
Bryce St. Hyde SK14 167 D4
Brydges Rd. SK6 125 E5
Brydon Ave. M12 163 C7
Brydon Cl. Salford M6 81 A2
Brydon Cl. Salford M6 154 F2
Bryham St. WN1 151 D8
Bryn Cross. WN4 73 A6
Bryn Dr. SK5 111 F5
Bryn Gates La. WN2 & WN4 73 D8
Bryn Lea Terr. BL1 142 A4
Bryn Rd. WN4 73 B5
Bryn Rd S. WN4 73 C4
Bryn St. Ashton-i-M WN4 73 B3
Bryn St. Ince-i-M WN3 151 E6
Bryn Sta. WN4 73 A6
Bryn Wlk. BL1 145 F8
Bryndale Gr. M33 107 F1
Brynden Ave. M20 110 C5
Brynford Ave. M9 64 A5
Bryngs Dr. BL2 25 F4
Brynhall Cl. M26 43 E5
Brynheys Cl. M38 60 A5
Brynn St. WN2 73 F7
Brynorme Rd. M8 64 A2
Brynton Rd. M13 98 E2
Bryone Dr. SK2 124 B5
Bryony Cl. Orrell WN5 53 D5
Bryony Cl. Walkden M28 60 D5
Bryson Wlk. M18 165 C5
Buchan St. M11 83 B2
Buchanan Dr. WN2 57 B3
Buchanan Rd. WN5 54 E7
Buchanan St. Leigh WN7 75 E5
Buchanan St. Ramsbottom BL0 138 B5
Buchanan St. Swinton M27 61 F1
Buck La. M33 107 E6
Buck St. WN7 75 F4
Buckden Rd. SK4 111 D7
Buckden Wlk. M23 108 F2
Buckfast Ave. Newton-l-W WA11 89 A7
Buckfast Ave. Oldham OL8 67 C4
Buckfast Ave. Oldham OL8 67 D3
Buckfast Cl. Alt'ham WA15 120 B2
Buckfast Cl. Bramhall SK8 132 B6
Buckfast Cl. M'ster M21 97 B1
Buckfast Cl. Poynton SK12 133 D5
Buckfast Rd. Middleton M24 46 F3
Buckfast Rd. Sale M33 107 E6
Buckfast Wlk. M7 155 E6
Buckfield Ave. M5 161 B7
Buckhurst Rd. M'ster M19 99 A1
Buckhurst Rd. Ramsbottom BL9 12 C3
Buckingham Ave. Denton M34 101 B2
Buckingham Ave. Horwich BL6 22 E2
Buckingham Ave. Salford M5 & M6 154 D2
Buckingham Ave. Whitefield M45 63 A7
Buckingham Cl. WN5 54 E5
Buckingham Dr. Bury BL8 44 B8
Buckingham Dr. Dukinfield SK16 101 F7
Buckingham Park Cl. OL2 149 B8
Buckingham Pl. M29 58 F3
Buckingham Rd. Cheadle SK8 123 A3
Buckingham Rd. Droylsden M43 83 E1
Buckingham Rd. Irlam M44 105 C6
Buckingham Rd. M'ster M25 63 C2
Buckingham Rd. M'ster M21 97 B1
Buckingham Rd. M'ster SK4 111 B5
Buckingham Rd. Poynton SK12 133 D3
Buckingham Rd. Reddish SK4 111 C6
Buckingham Rd. Sale WA14 107 F1
Buckingham Rd. Stalybridge SK15 86 A3
Buckingham Rd. Stretford M32 96 F4
Buckingham Rd. Swinton M27 62 A2
Buckingham Rd. Wilmslow SK9 137 A6
Buckingham Rd W. SK4 168 A4
Buckingham St. 12 R'dale OL16 31 A8
Buckingham St. Salford M5 154 F1
Buckingham St. Stockport SK2 124 A6
Buckingham Way. Alt'ham WA15 120 A7
Buckingham Way. Stockport SK2 170 F6
Buckland Ave. M9 64 A3
Buckland Gr. Hyde SK14 114 A8
Buckland Rd. M6 154 D4
Buckle. M30 79 E2
Buckley Ave. M18 99 C4
Buckley Barn Ct. OL11 30 C1
Buckley Bldgs. OL5 86 E8
Buckley Brook St. OL12 15 B2
Buckley Chase. OL16 31 E5
Buckley Cl. SK14 113 E7
Buckley Dr. SK6 113 A1
Buckley Farm La. OL12 15 B3
Buckley Fields. OL12 15 A2
Buckley Hall Ind Est. OL12 15 B3
Buckley Hill La. OL16 31 E5
Buckley La. Farnworth BL4 & M38 60 C7
Buckley La. Prestwich M25 62 E3
Buckley La. R'dale OL12 & OL16 15 B3
Buckley Rd. M'ster M18 99 C4
Buckley Rd. Oldham OL4 67 D8
Buckley Rd. R'dale OL12 15 B2
Buckley Sq. BL4 60 C6
Buckley St. Bury BL9 140 F3
Buckley St. Chadderton OL9 152 A7
Buckley St. Denton M34 100 D7
Buckley St. Droylsden M43 84 A1
Buckley St. Heywood OL10 29 E3
Buckley St. M'ster M11 99 E7
Buckley St. Oldham OL4 67 E5
Buckley St. R'dale OL16 31 A8
Buckley St. Radcliffe M26 44 A3
Buckley St. Reddish SK5 99 E2
Buckley St. Shaw OL2 149 C7
Buckley St. Stalybridge SK15 101 F8
Buckley St. Uppermill OL3 69 B8
Buckley St. Wigan WN1 & WN6 37 B2
Buckley St W. WN6 37 A2
Buckley Terr. OL12 15 B3
Buckley View. OL12 15 B3
Bucklow Ave. M'ster M14 98 B1
Bucklow Ave. Partington M31 105 F4
Bucklow Cl. Mottram-i-L SK14 102 F1
Bucklow Cl. Oldham OL4 49 E4
Bucklow Dr. M22 121 E8
Bucklow Gdns. WA13 117 A4
Bucklow View. WA14 119 A3
Bucknell Ct. M40 159 C4
Buckstones Prim Sch. OL2 49 D8
Buckstones Rd. Shaw OL2 32 D1
Buckstones Rd. Shaw OL1 & OL2 49 E7
Buckstones Rd. Shaw OL1 & OL2 & OL3 50 A6
Buckthorn Cl. Alt'ham WA15 120 E5
Buckthorn Cl. M'ster M21 109 D6
Buckthorn Cl. Westhoughton BL5 39 F2
Buckthorn La. M30 94 F8
Buckton Cl. OL3 51 C5
Buckton Dr. SK15 86 E5
Buckton Vale Mews. SK15 86 F7
Buckton Vale Prim Sch. SK15 86 F7
Buckton Vale Rd. Mossley SK15 86 D5
Buckton Vale Rd. Mossley SK15 86 F6
Buckwood Cl. SK7 125 A3
Buddleia Gr. M7 155 D6
Bude Ave. Brinnington SK5 112 B5
Bude Ave. Tyldesley M29 77 C8
Bude Ave. Urmston M41 107 B8
Bude Cl. SK7 132 F7
Bude Terr. 4 SK16 166 B1
Bude Wlk. M23 121 B5
Budsworth Ave. M20 110 B7
Budworth Gdns. 2 M43 84 B1
Budworth Rd. M33 108 E3
Budworth Wlk. 1 SK9 131 E1
Buer Ave. WN3 54 F4
Buersil Ave. OL16 31 B4
Buersil St. OL16 31 B3
Buerton Ave. M9 64 A5
Buffalo Ct. M5 96 E8
Buffoline Trad Est. 7 M19 99 B1
Bugle St. M1 162 E8
Buile Hill Ave. M38 60 B5
Buile Hill Dr. M5 & M6 154 D3
Buile Hill Gr. M38 60 B5
Buile Hill High Sch. M6 154 D4
Buile St. M7 155 E7
Buille House. M6 154 E3
Bulford Ave. M22 121 B2
Bulkeley Rd. Cheadle SK8 122 E6
Bulkeley Rd. Handforth SK9 131 D3
Bulkeley Rd. Poynton SK12 133 E3
Bulkeley St. SK3 170 D8
Bull Hill Cres. M26 62 B8
Bullcote Gn. OL2 49 B4
Bullcote La. OL2 49 B4
Bullcroft Dr. M29 77 C6
Buller Mews. BL8 27 B1
Buller Rd. M13 98 F2
Buller St. Bury BL8 27 C1
Buller St. Droylsden M34 100 B8
Buller St. Farnworth BL3 42 C2
Buller St. Oldham OL4 67 D8
Bullfinch Dr. BL9 28 B5
Bullfinch Wlk. M21 109 D7
Bullock St. SK2 170 F7
Bullough Moor Prim Sch. OL10 29 B1
Bullough St. Atherton M46 58 C2
Bullough St. Atherton M46 58 C3
Bullows Rd. M38 59 F6
Bullrush Cl. M28 60 D5
Bulteel St. Bolton BL3 146 C2
Bulteel St. Boothstown M28 77 E7
Bulteel St. Eccles M30 79 B3
Bulteel St. Wigan WN5 54 D6
Bulwark Rd. M41 95 C5
Bulwer St. OL16 31 A8
Bungalow Rd. WA12 89 E1
Bungalows The. Ashton-i-M WN4 72 F7
Bungalows The. New Mills SK12 127 D1
Bunkers. OL3 69 C6
Bunkers Hill. M25 & M27 62 D3
Bunkers Hill Rd. SK14 102 E1
Bunkershill Rd. SK6 113 B1
Bunsen St. M1 159 B1
Bunting Mews. M28 78 B8
Bunyan Cl. OL1 49 E4
Bunyan St. 24 R'dale OL12 14 F1
Bunyard St. M8 156 B6
BUPA Hospl Manchester. M16 97 D3
Burbage Bank. 5 SK13 171 E1
Burbage Gr. 23 SK13 171 E2
Burbage Rd. M23 121 A2
Burbage Way. 24 SK13 171 E2
Burbridge Cl. M11 160 E1
Burchall Field. OL16 31 B7
Burcot Wlk. M8 155 E5
Burdale Dr. M6 80 B4
Burdale Wlk. M23 108 F1
Burder St. 4 OL8 66 C2
Burdett Ave. OL12 13 F1
Burdett Way. M12 164 E5
Burdith Ave. M14 98 A2
Burdon Ave. M22 121 E3
Burford Ave. Bramhall SK7 132 D5
Burford Ave. M'ster M16 97 D2
Burford Ave. Urmston M41 95 E4
Burford Cl. SK9 136 E5
Burford Cres. SK9 136 E5
Burford Dr. Bolton BL3 145 E5
Burford Dr. M'ster M16 97 D2
Burford Dr. Swinton M27 61 E2
Burford Gr. M33 107 E1
Burford La. WA13 117 C2
Burford Rd. M16 97 D2
Burford Wlk. M16 97 D2
Burgess Ave. OL6 85 C5
Burgess Becker Prim Sch. M9 157 E7
Burgess Dr. M35 83 F7
Burgess St. WN3 151 E5
Burghley Cl. BL3 43 B5
Burghley Dr. BL3 43 B5
Burghley Way. WN2 151 F5
Burgin Wlk. M40 156 C5
Burgundy Dr. BL8 26 F7
Burke St. BL1 143 D2
Burkhardt Dr. WA12 89 E3
Burkitt St. SK14 167 E2
Burland Cl. M7 155 D5
Burland St. WN5 54 F7
Burleigh Cl. SK7 124 A1
Burleigh Ct. M32 96 E4
Burleigh Mews. M21 109 B6
Burleigh Rd. M32 96 E4
Burleigh St. M15 163 B5
Burlescombe Cl. WA14 119 B6
Burley Ave. WA3 74 D1
Burley Cres. WN3 54 C2
Burley Ct. SK4 168 C2
Burleyhurst La. SK9 & WA16 136 B7
Burlin Ct. 9 M16 97 D3
Burlington Ave. OL8 66 E4
Burlington Cl. SK4 110 E2
Burlington Ct. WA14 119 D5
Burlington Dr. SK3 123 F4
Burlington Gdns. SK3 123 F4
Burlington House. OL6 166 A3
Burlington Mews. SK3 123 F4
Burlington Rd. Alt'ham WA14 119 D5
Burlington Rd. Eccles M30 79 E4
Burlington Rd. M'ster M20 110 C7
Burlington St. Ashton-u-L OL6 & OL7 166 A3
Burlington St. Hindley WN2 56 E5
Burlington St. Hindley WN2 56 E5
Burlington St. M'ster M15 163 A5
Burlington St. M'ster M15 163 B5
Burlington St. 12 R'dale OL11 31 A4
Burlton Gr. WN2 38 A2
Burman St. M11 & M43 99 F7
Burn Bank. OL3 68 F5
Burnaby St. Bolton BL3 145 D5
Burnaby St. Oldham OL8 153 D5
Burnaby St. R'dale OL11 30 C4
Burnage Ave. M19 110 F8
Burnage Hall Rd. M19 110 F7
Burnage High Sch For Boys. M'ster M20 110 D6
Burnage High Sch For Boys. M'ster M19 110 E5
Burnage La. M19 & M20 & SK4 110 F4
Burnage Range. M19 99 A1
Burnage Sta. M20 110 D4
Burnaston Gr. WN5 54 D5
Burnbray Ave. M19 110 E6
Burnby Wlk. M23 108 F1
Burndale Dr. BL9 45 A3
Burnden Park Football Gnd (Bolton W FC). BL3 148 B5
Burnden Rd. BL3 148 B5
Burnedge Cl. OL12 4 D2
Burnedge Fold Rd. OL4 68 D6
Burnedge La. OL4 68 D7
Burnedge Mews. OL4 68 D6
Burnell Cl. M10 & M40 160 D3
Burnell Ct. OL10 46 D7
Burneside Cres. M24 46 E3
Burnett Ave. M5 161 B8
Burnett Cl. M40 157 D5
Burnett Gdns. M5 161 B8
Burnfell. WA3 90 E7
Burnfield Rd. M'ster M18 99 D3
Burnfield Rd. Reddish M34 99 F3
Burnham Ave. Bolton BL1 142 A1
Burnham Ave. Reddish SK5 99 F1
Burnham Cl. Cheadle SK8 122 F2
Burnham Cl. Culcheth WA3 91 E4
Burnham Dr. M'ster M19 110 F8
Burnham Dr. Urmston M41 95 C3
Burnham Gr. WN2 37 F2
Burnham Rd. M34 100 A3
Burnham Wlk. 3 BL4 42 D1
Burnhill Ct. WN6 36 E8
Burnleigh Ct. M46 58 F8
Burnley La. Chadderton OL1 & OL9 48 A2
Burnley La. Oldham OL1 & OL9 48 C1
Burnley Rd. Bury BL9 27 E8
Burnley Rd. Edenfield BL0 1 D5
Burnley Rd E. BB4 2 E8
Burnley St. Chadderton OL9 152 B8
Burnley St. Failsworth M35 84 A8
Burnmoor Rd. Bolton BL2 42 F8
Burns Ave. Atherton M46 58 D5
Burns Ave. Bury BL9 44 F6
Burns Ave. Cheadle SK8 122 F6
Burns Ave. Leigh WN7 75 C8
Burns Ave. Swinton M27 61 D1
Burns Cl. Ashton-i-M WN4 72 F6
Burns Cl. M'ster M11 160 F1
Burns Cl. Oldham OL1 49 E5
Burns Cl. Orrell WN5 53 D1
Burns Cl. Wigan WN3 55 A4
Burns Cres. SK2 124 E7
Burns Fold. SK16 102 A7
Burns Gdns. M25 62 F3
Burns Gr. M43 84 A2
Burns Rd. 6 Abram WN2 56 B1
Burns Rd. Denton M34 113 A7
Burns Rd. Walkden M38 60 B5
Burns St. Bolton BL3 145 F6
Burns St. Heywood OL10 29 E1
Burnsall Ave. Golborne WA3 90 F8
Burnsall Ave. Whitefield M45 62 D8
Burnsall Gr. OL2 48 D4
Burnsall Wlk. 2 M22 121 A2
Burnside. Alt'ham WA15 129 D7
Burnside. Edenfield BL0 1 D2
Burnside. Hadfield SK14 171 F4
Burnside. Shaw OL2 49 D8
Burnside. Stalybridge SK15 102 D7
Burnside Ave. Pendlebury M6 80 B5
Burnside Ave. Reddish SK4 111 E6
Burnside Cl. Bredbury SK6 112 F3
Burnside Cl. Heywood OL10 29 D1
Burnside Cl. Radcliffe M26 43 F7
Burnside Cl. Stalybridge SK15 102 D7
Burnside Cl. Tyldesley M29 77 B7
Burnside Dr. M19 110 F7
Burnside Rd. Bolton BL1 142 B2
Burnside Rd. Gatley SK8 122 B5
Burnside Rd. R'dale OL16 31 C6
Burnt Edge La. BL1 23 B5
Burnthorp Ave. M9 64 B3
Burnthorpe Cl. OL11 29 E6
Burntwood Wlk. 22 M9 157 E8
Burnvale. WN3 54 D2
Burran Rd. M22 130 D8
Burrington Dr. WN7 75 D7
Burrows Ave. M21 109 C6
Burrows Yd. WN1 150 C8
Burrswood Ave. BL9 27 F6
Burslem Ave. M14 110 A8
Burstead St. M18 99 E7
Burstock St. M4 159 B3
Burston St. M18 165 C6
Burtinshaw St. 7 M18 99 D5
Burton Ave. Bury BL8 26 F4
Burton Ave. M'ster M20 110 B6
Burton Ave. Sale WA15 108 A1
Burton Cl. WA3 91 F3
Burton Dr. SK12 133 D4
Burton Gr. M28 79 C8
Burton Rd. M'ster M20 110 A6
Burton St. M'ster M40 159 B4
Burton St. M'ster SK4 169 E3
Burton St. Middleton M24 64 F8
Burton St. Oldham OL4 67 E5
Burton Wlk. M'ster M3 158 D2
Burton Wlk. M'ster SK4 169 E3
Burtonwood Ct. M24 46 F1
Burtree St. M12 165 A6
Burwell Ave. PR7 19 D8
Burwell Cl. Glossop SK13 116 A8
Burwell Cl. R'dale OL12 14 D4
Burwell Gr. M23 120 F7
Bury and Bolton Rd. BL8 43 E7
Bury Ave. M16 97 C2
Bury Bsns Ctr. BL9 141 A4
Bury Catholic Prep Sch. BL9 44 E8
Bury CE High Sch. BL9 44 D8
Bury Coll (Bury Ctr). BL9 140 E1
Bury Coll (Peel Ctr). BL9 140 E1
Bury Coll (Stand Ctr). M45 44 E1
Bury General Hospl. BL9 27 F6
Bury Golf Course. BL9 45 A4
Bury Gram Jun Sch. BL9 140 D2
Bury Gram Sch. BL9 140 D2
Bury Intc. BL9 140 E2
Bury Metropolitan Coll (Whitefield Site). M45 63 B8
Bury Music Ctr. M45 45 C2
Bury New Rd. Bolton BL2 & BL8 43 B7
Bury New Rd. Bolton BL1 & BL2 148 A7
Bury New Rd. Bury BL9 141 C2
Bury New Rd. Heywood BL9 & OL10 28 E2
Bury New Rd. M'ster M7 & M8 & M25 155 E5
Bury New Rd. Prestwich M25 63 B3
Bury New Rd. Ramsbottom BL0 11 D6
Bury New Rd. Whitefield M45 62 F7
Bury Old Rd. Ainsworth BL2 26 B1
Bury Old Rd. Bolton BL2 148 A7
Bury Old Rd. Bolton BL2 148 B7
Bury Old Rd. Edenfield BL0 1 F1
Bury Old Rd. Heywood BL9 & OL10 28 E1
Bury Old Rd. Prestwich M25,M45, M7, M8 63 C4
Bury Old Rd. Ramsbottom BL0 & BL9 11 F4
Bury Pl. M11 83 C2
Bury Rd. Bolton BL2 42 D7
Bury Rd. Bury BL8 27 A5
Bury Rd. Edenfield BL0 1 D3
Bury Rd. Edgworth BL7 9 E3
Bury Rd. R'dale OL11 & OL10 30 B6
Bury Rd. Radcliffe BL9 & M26 44 C5
Bury Rd. Rawtenstall BB4 1 E7
Bury & Rochdale Old Rd. BL9 & OL10 29 C5

Bury Sch of Arts & Crafts. BL9 140 E2
Bury St. Heywood OL10 29 B2
Bury St. M'ster M3 158 E2
Bury St. Mossley OL5 86 C8
Bury St. Radcliffe M26 44 D4
Bury St. Stockport SK5 169 F3
Bury Sta. BL9 140 E2
Bury & Whitefield Jewish Prim Sch. BL9 45 A2
Bush Moor Wlk. M13 164 D5
Bush St. M10 & M40 157 E5
Bushell St. BL3 146 B4
Bushey Dr. M23 121 A5
Busheyfield Cl. SK14 101 D5
Bushfield Wlk. 1 M23 120 E7
Bushgrove Wlk. M9 64 D5
Bushnay Wlk. 9 M8 156 B6
Bushnell Wlk. 1 M9 64 E5
Bushton Wlk. 9 M40 156 C5
Busk Rd. Oldham OL9 152 C8
Busk Wlk. OL9 152 C8
Butcher La. Alt'ham M23 120 D7
Butcher La. Bury BL9 140 F2
Butcher La. Royton OL2 48 C5
Butchers La. WN4 73 B3
Bute Ave. OL8 66 F3
Bute St. Bolton BL1 142 B1
Bute St. Glossop SK13 104 E3
Bute St. M'ster M40 64 F1
Bute St. M'ster M40 157 F8
Bute St. Salford M5 154 D1
Butler Ct. 13 M40 159 C3
Butler Gn. OL9 66 A4
Butler Green Prim Sch. OL9 66 B4
Butler La. M10 & M40 159 C3
Butler St. M'ster M10 & M40 160 D2
Butler St. Ramsbottom BL0 138 A5
Butler St. Wigan WN1 151 D8
Butley St. SK7 124 E4
Butman St. M18 99 F6
Butt Hill Ave. M25 63 B3
Butt Hill Ct. M25 63 B3
Butt Hill Dr. M25 63 B3
Butt Hill Rd. M25 63 B3
Butt La. OL4 68 B4
Butter La. 5 M3 158 F1
Buttercup Ave. 7 M28 59 F3
Buttercup Cl. M46 58 D5
Buttercup Dr. R'dale OL11 30 B3
Buttercup Dr. Stockport SK3 170 D5
Butterfield Cl. SK8 123 B1
Butterfield Rd. BL5 58 F8
Butterhouse La. OL3 51 C2
Butterley Cl. SK16 101 F7
Buttermere Ave. Ashton-i-M WN4 73 B5
Buttermere Ave. Heywood OL10 46 D8
Buttermere Ave.Swinton M27 79 F6
Buttermere Cl. BL3 42 F4
Buttermere Dr. Alt'ham WA15 129 D6
Buttermere Dr. Middleton M24 46 E2
Buttermere Dr. Ramsbottom BL0 138 B7
Buttermere Gr. OL2 48 D7
Buttermere Rd. Ashton-u-L OL7 166 A4
Buttermere Rd. Farnworth BL4 59 E8
Buttermere Rd. Gatley SK8 122 B3
Buttermere Rd. Oldham OL4 67 D8
Buttermere Rd. Partington M31 105 E3
Buttermere Rd. Wigan WN5 54 C7
Buttermere Terr. SK15 86 A3
Butterstile La. Prestwich M25 63 A3
Butterstile Prim Sch. M25 63 A2
Butterwick Cl. M18 99 B3
Butterworth Hall. OL16 32 A5
Butterworth La. M40 & OL9 65 E2
Butterworth St. Chadderton OL9 152 B8
Butterworth St. Littleborough OL15 16 A5
Butterworth St. M'ster M11 165 A8
Butterworth St. Middleton M24 65 C7
Butterworth St. 2 Oldham OL4 67 C7
Butterworth St. Radcliffe M26 44 B4
Butterworth Way. OL3 69 B5
Butteryhouse La. WA15 120 E2
Button Hole. OL2 49 D7
Button La. M23 & M33 109 A2
Button La Jun Sch. M23 108 F2
Buttons Row. BB4 2 F6
Buttress St. M18 165 C6
Butts Ave. WN7 76 C3
Butts Ave The. OL16 139 F7
Butts Ct. WN7 76 A4
Butts La. OL3 50 D4
Butts St. WN7 76 B3
Butts The. OL16 139 F7
Buxted Rd. OL1 49 B1
Buxton Ave. Ashton-u-L OL6 85 F6
Buxton Ave. M'ster M20 109 F6
Buxton Cl. Atherton M46 58 E4
Buxton Cl. 18 Gamesley SK13 171 E2
Buxton Cres. R'dale OL16 31 B4
Buxton Cres. Sale M33 108 D1
Buxton La. Droylsden M43 83 E1
Buxton La. Marple SK6 125 E5
Buxton Mews. SK13 171 E2
Buxton Old Rd. SK12 135 E4
Buxton Pl. OL8 153 E5
Buxton Rd. Disley SK12 135 E6
Buxton Rd. High Lane SK12, SK6, SK7 134 D8
Buxton Rd. Stockport SK2 124 B5
Buxton Rd. Stretford M32 96 A3
Buxton Rd W. SK12 135 B5
Buxton St. Bury BL8 27 C2
Buxton St. Gatley SK8 122 A5
Buxton St. Hazel Grove SK7 124 D3
Buxton St. Heywood OL10 29 D1
Buxton St. M'ster M1 163 B8
Buxton St. Whitworth OL12 4 D3
Buxton Terr. SK14 103 D5
Buxton Way. 3 M34 113 A8
Buxton Wlk. 1 SK13 171 E1
Bycroft Wlk. M40 83 D4
Bye Rd. BL0 11 E8
Bye St. M34 100 F7
Byfield Rd. M22 121 C4
Byfleet Cl. WN3 54 C1
Byland Ave. Bramhall SK8 132 B6
Byland Ave. Oldham OL4 67 D4
Byland Cl. BL1 143 E2
Byland Gdns. M26 43 E5
Byland Wlk. 3 M22 121 D1
Bylands Cl. SK12 133 D4
Bylands Fold. SK16 101 D6
Byley Rise. WN6 36 E8
Byng Ave. M44 105 D4
Byng St. Farnworth BL4 60 D8
Byng St. Heywood OL10 46 E8
Byng St E. BL2 145 F6
Byrchall High Sch. WN4 73 B1
Byrcland Cl. M12 164 E8
Byre Cl. M23 109 A3
Byrness Cl. M46 58 E4
Byrom Ave. M19 99 C1
Byrom Ct. M43 83 F1
Byrom La. WA3 74 F2
Byrom St. Alt'ham WA14 119 D3
Byrom St. 9 Bury BL8 27 B4
Byrom St. M'ster M16 97 D4
Byrom St. M'ster M3 162 E8
Byrom St. Salford M5 161 A8
Byron Ave. Droylsden M43 84 A2
Byron Ave. 13 Hindley WN2 56 D5
Byron Ave. Prestwich M25 62 F3
Byron Ave. Radcliffe M26 43 E4
Byron Ave. Swinton M27 79 E8
Byron Cl. Abram WN2 56 B1
Byron Cl. Orrell WN5 53 F7
Byron Cl. Wigan WN6 36 E3
Byron Cres. PR7 19 F8
Byron Dr. SK8 122 F6
Byron Gr. Atherton M46 58 D5
Byron Gr. Leigh WN7 75 F7
Byron Gr. Reddish SK5 99 E1
Byron Rd. Denton M34 112 F8
Byron Rd. Middleton M24 47 B2
Byron Rd. Ramsbottom BL8 10 F2
Byron Rd. Stretford M32 96 F3
Byron St. Eccles M30 79 D2
Byron St. Leigh WN7 75 F7
Byron St. Oldham OL8 66 B2
Byron St. Royton OL2 48 E4
Byron Street Inf Sch. OL2 48 E4
Byron Wlk. Farnworth BL4 60 B6
Byron Wlk. 6 Royton OL2 48 E4
Byrth Rd. OL8 84 F8
Bywell Wlk. 15 M8 155 F7
Bywood Wlk. M8 155 E5

'C' Ct. WN4 73 B2
Cabin La. OL4 50 A3
Cable St. Bolton BL1 145 F8
Cable St. M'ster M3 158 E2
Cable St. M'ster M4 159 B2
Cablestead Wlk. M11 165 A8
Cabot Pl. SK5 169 F4
Cabot St. M13 163 B6
Caddington Rd. M21 109 C8
Cadishead Inf Sch. M44 105 D5
Cadishead Jun Sch. M44 105 E6
Cadishead Way. Irlam M41 & M44 94 C2
Cadishead Way. Irlam M44 105 F7
Cadleigh Wlk. 6 M40 83 A7
Cadman Gr. WN2 56 D4
Cadman's Yd. 8 WN5 54 D5
Cadmium Wlk. M18 99 C4
Cadnam Dr. M22 121 F3
Cadogan Dr. WN3 54 D2
Cadogan Pl. 7 M7 63 E1
Cadogan St. M14 98 A4
Cadum Wlk. M13 163 C6
Caen Ave. M40 65 C3
Caernarvon Cl. BL8 10 F1
Caernarvon Dr. SK7 124 C1
Caernarvon Rd. WN2 57 A3
Caernarvon Way. 2 M34 100 F1
Caesar St. OL11 31 A2
Cairn Dr. R'dale OL11 29 E6
Cairn Dr. Salford M6 & M7 81 C5
Cairn Wlk. 15 M11 160 F1
Cairngorm Dr. BL3 40 E5
Cairns Pl. OL6 85 D5
Caister Ave. M45 63 A7
Caister Cl. M41 94 C1
Caistor Cl. M16 & M21 109 E8
Caistor St. SK1 112 B3
Caistor Wlk. 2 OL1 153 F7
Caithness Cl. M23 121 A4
Caithness Dr. BL3 40 E6
Caithness Rd. OL10 29 E5
Cakebread St. M12 163 C7
Calbourne Cres. M18 99 B3
Calcot Wlk. 6 M23 120 F6
Calcutta Rd. SK3 123 C7
Caldbeck Ave. Bolton BL1 23 F1
Caldbeck Ave. Sale M33 108 E5
Caldbeck Cl. Ashton-i-M WN4 73 B4
Caldbeck Cl. Platt Bridge WN2 56 B2
Caldbeck Dr. Farnworth BL4 59 E7
Caldbeck Dr. Middleton M24 46 E2
Caldbeck Gr. WA11 71 C1
Caldecott Rd. M9 64 A5
Calder Ave.Hindley WN2 57 C3
Calder Ave.Irlam M44 93 F1
Calder Ave.Littleborough OL15 16 A7
Calder Ave. Wythenshawe M22 121 D8
Calder Cl. Bury BL9 28 A8
Calder Cl. Poynton SK12 133 D2
Calder Cl. Reddish SK5 112 A4
Calder Cres. M45 45 B2
Calder Ct. M41 94 E4
Calder Dr. Kearsley BL4 61 B5
Calder Dr. Platt Bridge WN2 56 A2
Calder Dr. Swinton M27 61 E1
Calder Dr. Walkden M28 60 B2
Calder Gr. OL2 149 B8
Calder House. 6 M7 81 C5
Calder Pl. WN5 54 C7
Calder Rd. BL3 147 E3
Calder St. M'ster M5 162 D8
Calder St. R'dale OL16 15 B2
Calder Way. M45 45 B2
Calder Wlk. Middleton M24 46 C2
Calder Wlk. Whitefield M45 45 B2
Calderbank Ave. M41 94 E4
Calderbank St. WN5 54 E5
Calderbrook Dr. SK8 123 A4
Calderbrook Rd. OL14 & OL15 6 C2
Calderbrook Terr. OL15 16 C8
Calderbrook Way. OL4 67 B5
Calderbrook Wlk. 11 M9 157 D7
Calderdale Ct. OL2 48 C5
Caldershaw Ctr The. OL12 14 B2
Caldershaw La. OL12 14 A2
Caldershaw Prim Sch. OL12 14 A1
Caldershaw Rd. OL11 & OL12 14 A1
Caldervale Ave. M21 109 C4
Caldey Rd. M23 120 E5
Caldford Cl. WN2 38 C6
Caldon Cl. M30 95 D8
Caldwell Ave. M29 77 B4
Caldwell Cl. M29 77 B5
Caldwell St. BL5 57 F5
Caldy Dr. BL8 11 A3
Caldy Rd. Handforth SK9 131 D3
Caldy Rd. Salford M6 154 D4
Cale Gn. SK2 170 F6
Cale Green Prim Sch. SK3 170 F6
Cale La. WN2 38 B2
Cale St. SK2 170 F6
Caleb Cl. M29 58 F1
Caledon Ave. M40 83 A8
Caledonia St. Bolton BL3 144 C5
Caledonia St. 3 Radcliffe M26 44 C4
Caledonia Way. M32 96 A5
Caledonian Dr. M30 95 E8
Caley St. Bolton BL1 23 F2
Caley St. 1 M'ster M1 163 A7
Calf Hey. OL15 15 F6
Calf Hey Cl. M26 43 D3
Calf Hey N. 7 OL11 31 A4
Calf Hey Rd. Shaw OL2 49 D8
Calf Hey S. 8 OL11 31 A4
Calf La. OL3 & OL4 & OL5 68 E4
Calgarth Dr. M24 46 D3
Calico Cl. M3 158 D3
Calico Wood Ave. Shevington WN6 35 F6
Calland Ave. SK14 167 F3
Callander Sq. OL10 28 F1
Callender St. BL0 138 B6
Calliards Rd. OL16 15 E4
Callingdon Rd. M21 109 D5
Callington Cl. 4 SK14 102 E2
Callington Dr. SK14 102 E2
Callington Wlk. 3 SK14 102 E2
Callis Rd. BL3 144 C5
Callum Wlk. M13 163 C6
Calluno Mews. M20 110 A4
Calne Wlk. 6 M23 121 A5
Calow Cl. 34 SK13 171 E2
Calow Dr. WN7 76 C3
Calow Gn. 9 SK13 171 E1
Caltha St. BL0 138 B6
Calthorpe Ave. M8 & M9 156 C7
Calton Ave. M7 81 A7
Calve Croft Rd. M22 121 F2
Calveley Wlk. WN6 36 E8
Calver Ave. M30 95 C8
Calver Cl. 11 Gamesley SK13 171 E2
Calver Cl. Urmston M41 94 D3
Calver Fold. 7 SK13 171 D2
Calver Hey Cl. BL5 40 C2
Calver Mews. SK13 171 D2
Calver Pl. 10 SK13 171 E2
Calver Wlk. Cheadle SK8 122 E1
Calver Wlk. Denton M34 113 A8
Calver Wlk. 15 M'ster M40 159 C3
Calverhall Way. WN4 73 A3
Calverley Ave. M19 110 F7
Calverley Way. OL12 14 E4
Calverly Rd. SK8 123 A5
Calvert Rd. BL3 147 F3
Calvert St. M5 154 D2
Calverton Dr. M40 83 C7
Calvin St. BL1 143 F1
Calvine Wlk. 6 M40 159 C3
Camargue Ct. 1 M20 110 B6
Cambeck Cl. M45 45 B1
Cambeck Wlk. M45 45 A1
Cambell Rd. M30 79 B2
Camberley Cl. SK7 133 A7
Camberley Dr. OL11 29 F5
Camberly Dr. OL11 29 F6
Cambert La. M'ster M18 99 D5
Cambert La. M'ster M18 165 C5
Camberwell Cres. Wigan WN2 37 F1
Camberwell Dr. OL7 85 A7
Camberwell St. M'ster M8 159 A4
Camberwell St. Oldham OL8 66 E4
Camberwell Way. OL2 48 C4
Cambo Wlk. SK4 110 F3
Camborne Rd. SK14 102 E3
Camborne St. M14 98 B3
Cambourne Dr. Bolton BL3 144 A5
Cambourne Dr. Hindley WN2 57 C2
Cambrai Cres. M28 79 A4
Cambria Sq. 8 BL3 144 C5
Cambria St. Bolton BL3 144 C5
Cambria St. Oldham OL4 67 D7
Cambrian Cres. WN3 54 C2
Cambrian Dr. Milnrow OL16 32 A6
Cambrian Dr. Royton OL2 48 C3
Cambrian Rd. SK3 123 C8
Cambrian St. M10 & M11 & M40 160 E2
Cambridge Ave. M'ster M16 97 C2
Cambridge Ave. R'dale OL11 30 A6
Cambridge Ave. Wilmslow SK9 136 F7
Cambridge Cl. BL4 147 F1
Cambridge Dr. Little Lever BL3 43 B4
Cambridge Dr. Reddish M34 100 A3
Cambridge Dr. Romiley SK6 113 C5
Cambridge Gr. Eccles M30 79 F2
Cambridge Gr. Whitefield M45 63 A7
Cambridge Ind Area. M7 158 E4
Cambridge Rd. Alt'ham WA15 119 E2
Cambridge Rd. Droylsden M43 83 F3
Cambridge Rd. Failsworth M35 83 F5
Cambridge Rd. Gatley SK8 122 B5
Cambridge Rd. Horwich BL6 39 F8
Cambridge Rd. M'ster M9 64 D1
Cambridge Rd. Orrell WN5 53 F8
Cambridge Rd. Reddish SK4 111 C5
Cambridge Rd. Urmston M41 95 B1
Cambridge St. Ashton-u-L OL7 84 F1
Cambridge St. Atherton M46 58 C2
Cambridge St. Dukinfield SK16 166 C1
Cambridge St. M'ster M7 & M8 158 E4
Cambridge St. M'ster M15 162 F7
Cambridge St. Oldham OL9 66 C4
Cambridge St. Stalybridge SK15 86 A2
Cambridge St. Stockport SK2 124 A6
Cambridge St. Wigan WN1 151 D7
Cambridge Terr. SK15 86 D4
Cambridge Way. WN1 151 D8
Camdale Wlk. 9 M8 155 F6
Camden Ave. M40 83 C4
Camden Cl. BL2 26 C1
Camden St. OL5 68 D3
Camelia Rd. M8 & M9 156 C7
Camellia Cl. BL1 144 B7
Cameron Ct. OL2 48 D6
Cameron Pl. WN5 54 E8
Cameron St. Bolton BL1 143 D4
Cameron St. Bury BL8 27 C2
Cameron St. Leigh WN7 75 D7
Cameron St. M'ster M1 162 F8
Camley Wlk. 1 M8 156 B6
Camm St. Abram WN2 74 B8
Camms View. BB4 1 A8
Camomile Wlk. 5 M31 105 F3
Camp Rd. WN4 72 E4
Camp St. Ashton-u-L OL6 166 B3
Camp St. Bury BL8 27 C3
Camp St. M'ster M5 & M7 155 D5
Camp St. M'ster M3 162 E8
Campania St. OL2 48 E2
Campanula Wlk. 4 M8 156 A6
Campbell Ct. BL4 42 C2
Campbell Rd. Bolton BL3 146 A2
Campbell Rd. M'ster M13 98 F2
Campbell Rd. Sale M33 107 F3
Campbell Rd. Swinton M27 79 E6
Campbell St. Farnworth BL4 42 B1
Campbell St. R'dale OL12 14 E2
Campbell St. Reddish SK5 99 F1
Campbell St. Wigan WN5 54 D5
Campbell Way. M28 60 D3
Campbell Wlk. 5 BL4 42 C2
Campden Way. SK9 131 D4
Campion Dr. BB4 1 A8
Campion Gr. WN4 72 F4
Campion Way. 8 Denton M34 113 A8
Campion Way. R'dale OL12 14 C3
Campion Wlk. M11 164 F8
Camponia Gdns. M7 155 D5
Camrose Wlk. M13 164 D5
Cams Acre Cl. M26 43 E3
Cams La. M26 43 E2
Cams Lane Prim Sch. M26 43 E3
Canaan. WA3 91 C8
Canada St. Bolton BL1 142 C2
Canada St. Horwich BL6 22 B3
Canada St. M'ster M10 & M40 160 E4
Canada St. Stockport SK2 124 A6
Canal Bank. Appley Bridge WN6 35 C7
Canal Bank. Eccles M28, M30 79 C3
Canal Bridge La. M43 83 E1
Canal Circ. M30 80 A1
Canal Cotts. WN3 150 B7
Canal Rd. WA14 119 E8
Canal Row. WN2 20 D1
Canal Side. M28 79 C3
Canal St. Adlington PR7 21 A6
Canal St. Droylsden M43 84 A1
Canal St. Dukinfield SK14 101 C3
Canal St. Heywood OL10 46 F8
Canal St. Leigh WN7 75 F4
Canal St. Littleborough OL15 16 B5
Canal St. M'ster M5 81 C1
Canal St. M'ster M1 163 A8
Canal St. Marple SK6 126 A6
Canal St. Oldham OL9 66 B3
Canal St. R'dale OL11 31 A5
Canal St. Shevington WN6 36 F2
Canal St. Stalybridge SK15 86 A1
Canal St. Stockport SK1 170 F8
Canal Terr. WN2 151 F7
Canalside Ind Est. OL16 31 B5
Canberra Rd.Bramhall SK7 132 F5
Canberra Rd.Shevington WN5 36 C1
Canberra St. M11 83 C2
Candahar St. BL3 42 A3
Candleford Pl. SK2 124 E4
Candleford Rd. M20 110 B6
Candlestick Pk. BL9 28 D4
Canley Cl. SK1 170 F8
Cann St. BL8 26 D8
Cannel Fold. M28 78 B7
Canning Dr. BL1 143 E2
Canning St. Bolton BL1 143 F2
Canning St. Bury BL9 140 F4
Canning St. Stockport SK4 169 E2
Cannock Dr. SK4 168 A2
Cannon Ct. M4 158 F2
Cannon Gr. BL3 145 D5
Cannon St. Atherton M46 58 D3
Cannon St. Bolton BL3 145 D5
Cannon St. Eccles M30 79 E1
Cannon St. Hollingworth SK14 103 C5
Cannon St. M'ster M3 158 D3
Cannon St. M'ster M4 & M60 159 A2
Cannon St. Oldham OL9 153 E7
Cannon St. Radcliffe M26 43 F5
Cannon St. Ramsbottom BL0 11 A4
Cannon St N. BL3 145 D6
Cannon Wlk. M34 100 E2
Canon Burrows CE Prim Sch. OL7 85 A5
Canon Cl. WN6 19 F2
Canon Dr. WA14 119 B1
Canon Flynn Ct. OL16 31 C7
Canon Green Ct. M3 158 E2
Canon Green Dr. M3 158 E2
Canon Hussey Ct. M3 158 D1
Canon Johnson CE Prim Sch. OL7 166 B4
Canon Slade Sch. BL2 25 C4
Canon St. Bury BL9 141 A4
Canon St. R'dale OL12 & OL16 15 B2
Canon Tighe Ct. OL9 152 A7
Canon's Cl. BL1 142 B2
Canons Gr. M10 & M40 157 E5
Canonsleigh Cl. M7 & M8 155 E5
Canonsway. M27 79 E8
Cansfield Comm High Sch. WN4 73 A4
Cansfield Gr. WN4 73 A4
Canterbury Ave. WA3 74 D1
Canterbury Cl. Atherton M46 58 E4
Canterbury Cl. R'dale OL11 30 A7
Canterbury Cres. M24 47 D2
Canterbury Dr. Bury BL8 140 D4
Canterbury Dr. M'ster M25 63 C2
Canterbury Gdns. M30 & M5 80 B2
Canterbury Gr. BL3 147 D3
Canterbury Pk. M'ster M20 109 F3
Canterbury Rd. Alt'ham WA15 120 C3
Canterbury Rd. Stockport SK1 112 B1
Canterbury Rd. Urmston M41 95 D3
Canterbury St. OL6 166 C4
Canterfield Cl. M43 84 D2
Cantley Wlk. 5 M8 156 A6
Canton Wlk. 15 M16 97 E4
Cantrell St. M11 83 B2
Canute Ct. M32 96 E3
Canute Rd. M32 96 E3
Canute St. 2 Bolton BL2 25 C1
Canute St. Radcliffe M26 43 E3
Canute St. Salford M6 81 B2
Cape St. M14 110 C7
Capella Wlk. M7 81 C4
Capenhurst Cl. M23 120 F4
Capesthorne Cl. Hazel Grove SK7 133 F8
Capesthorne Dr. OL2 48 F7
Capesthorne Rd. Alt'ham WA15 120 D6
Capesthorne Rd. Dukinfield SK16 101 D6
Capesthorne Rd. Hazel Grove SK7 133 F8
Capesthorne Rd. High Lane SK6 134 E7
Capesthorne Rd. Wilmslow SK9 136 E5
Capesthorne Wlk. M34 100 E2
Capital Rd. M11 & M18 99 F7
Capitol Cl. BL1 142 A3
Capps St. WN2 56 B3
Capstan St. M9 157 E8
Captain Clarke Rd. SK14 101 C5
Captain Fold Rd. M38 59 F6
Captain Lees Gdns. BL5 58 A8
Captain Lees Rd. BL5 40 A1
Captain St. BL6 22 B4
Captain's Clough Rd. BL1 142 B2
Captain's La. WN4 73 C3
Capton Cl. SK7 124 A2
Car Bank Ave. M46 58 D4
Car Bank Cres. M46 58 D4
Car Bank Sq. M46 58 D4
Car Bank St. M46 58 D4
Car St. OL11 30 B2
Caradoc Ave. 12 M8 156 B6
Carawood Cl. WN6 35 D7
Carberry Rd. M18 99 D5
Carbis Wlk. M8 155 E5
Cardale Wlk. M9 157 D7
Carden Ave. Swinton M27 79 D7
Carden Ave. Urmston M41 94 E2
Cardenbrook Gr. 4 SK9 131 D2
Carder Cl. M27 79 F7
Carders Cl. WN7 75 E4
Cardew Ave. M22 121 F4
Cardiff Cl. OL8 66 B2
Cardiff St. M7 155 E7
Cardiff Wlk. 4 M34 100 F1
Cardigan Dr. BL9 44 E7
Cardigan Rd. OL8 66 B2
Cardigan St. R'dale OL12 14 E3
Cardigan St. Radcliffe M26 43 F6
Cardigan St. Royton OL2 48 E4
Cardigan St. 2 Salford M6 154 E1
Cardigan Terr. M14 97 F4
Cardinal Langley RC High Sch. M24 47 B4
Cardinal Mews. M24 46 D2
Cardinal St. M'ster M8 156 B7
Cardinal St. 10 Oldham OL1 67 A7
Carding Gr. M3 158 E3
Cardroom Rd. M20 & M4 159 C1
Cardus St. M19 99 A1
Cardwell Gdns. BL1 143 E2
Cardwell Rd. M30 79 A1
Cardwell St. OL8 66 F3
Careless La. WN2 151 F8
Carey Cl. M'ster M7 158 D4
Carey Cl. Wigan WN3 54 D2
Carey Wlk. M15 162 F5
Carfax Fold. OL12 14 B2
Carfax St. M18 99 D5
Cargate Wlk. 14 M8 155 F6
Carib St. M15 162 F5
Carill Ave. M40 65 A1
Carill Dr. M14 110 D8
Carina Pl. M7 81 C4
Cariocca Ent Pk. M12 164 D6
Carisbrook Ave. Prestwich M25 & M45 63 A6
Carisbrook Ave.Urmston M41 95 C2
Carisbrook Dr. M27 80 A6
Carisbrook St. M8 & M9 157 E7
Carisbrooke Ave. SK7 124 D1
Carisbrooke Dr. BL1 143 F3
Carisbrooke Rd. WN7 76 D6
Carl St. BL1 143 D2
Carlburn St. M11 83 D2
Carleton Rd. SK12 134 C4
Carley Gr. M9 64 B4
Carlford Gr. M25 62 F3
Carlile St. SK3 170 E8
Carlin Gate. WA15 120 A6
Carling Dr. M22 121 E2
Carlingford Cl. SK3 170 E5
Carlisle Cl. Little Lever BL3 43 A2
Carlisle Cl. Prestwich M45 63 B7
Carlisle Cl. Romiley SK6 113 A1
Carlisle Cres. OL6 85 C7
Carlisle Dr. Irlam M44 94 A2
Carlisle Dr. Sale WA14 119 E8
Carlisle Pl. PR6 21 A8
Carlisle St. Alderley Edge SK9 137 A1
Carlisle St. Bolton BL7 25 A8
Carlisle St. Hindley WN2 56 E6
Carlisle St. Oldham OL9 66 C4
Carlisle St. Oldham OL9 152 C5
Carlisle St. R'dale OL12 14 E3
Carlisle St. Swinton M27 61 F2
Carlisle St. Wigan WN5 54 D6
Carlisle Way. Aspull WN2 38 D5
Carlisle Way. 3 Denton M34 100 F1
Carloon Dr. M23 109 B1
Carloon Rd. M23 109 B1
Carlow Dr. M22 121 E2
Carlton Ave. Bolton BL3 146 A4
Carlton Ave. Bramhall SK7 132 D5
Carlton Ave. Cheadle SK8 122 F3
Carlton Ave. Handforth SK9 131 C2
Carlton Ave. M'ster M25 63 E2
Carlton Ave. M'ster M16 97 B4
Carlton Ave. M'ster M14 98 B3
Carlton Ave. Oldham OL4 49 D1
Carlton Ave. Orrell WN8 53 A7
Carlton Ave. Romiley SK6 113 D2
Carlton Ave. Whitefield M45 44 D1
Carlton Cl. Ashton-i-M WN4 73 A5
Carlton Cl. Blackrod BL6 21 D2
Carlton Cl. Bolton BL2 25 E3
Carlton Cl. Walkden M28 60 C1
Carlton Cres. Stockport SK1 112 A2
Carlton Cres. Urmston M41 95 D1
Carlton Ct. Alt'ham WA15 120 B1
Carlton Ct. M'ster M25 63 A1
Carlton Dr. Gatley M22 & SK8 122 A6
Carlton Dr. M'ster M25 & M8 63 E2
Carlton Gdns. BL4 42 D1
Carlton Gr. Hindley WN2 56 F4
Carlton Gr. Horwich BL6 22 D1
Carlton Mansions. 4 M16 97 D3
Carlton Pl. Farnworth BL4 42 D1
Carlton Pl. Hazel Grove SK7 125 A1
Carlton Range. M18 & M34 99 F4
Carlton Rd. Alt'ham WA15 120 B2
Carlton Rd. Ashton-u-L OL6 85 C5
Carlton Rd. Bolton BL1 144 A8
Carlton Rd. Golborne WA3 74 D1
Carlton Rd. Hyde SK14 102 A3
Carlton Rd. Lymm WA13 117 B5
Carlton Rd. M'ster M16 97 D3
Carlton Rd. M'ster SK4 168 A2
Carlton Rd. Sale M33 108 A6
Carlton Rd. Salford M6 154 E4
Carlton Rd. Urmston M41 95 D1
Carlton Rd. Walkden M28 60 C1
Carlton St. Bolton BL2 148 A6
Carlton St. Bury BL9 44 F8
Carlton St. Eccles M30 79 D3
Carlton St. Farnworth BL4 42 D1
Carlton St. M'ster M16 97 C4
Carlton St. Wigan WN5 150 B6
Carlton Way. Irlam M44 105 C5
Carlton Way. Oldham OL1 & OL2 48 D2
Carlyle Cl. M7 & M8 156 A6
Carlyle Gr. WN7 75 C8
Carlyle St. BL9 140 E3
Carlyn Ave. M33 108 D4
Carmel Ave. M5 161 C8
Carmel Cl. M5 161 C8
Carmel Mews. SK9 131 B1
Carmenna Dr. SK7 132 F7
Carmichael Cl. M31 105 E3
Carmichael St. SK3 170 D8
Carmine Fold. M24 46 F2
Carmona Dr. M25 63 A4
Carmona Gdns. M25 & M7 63 C1
Carmoor Rd. M13 163 C5
Carna Rd. SK5 99 E2
Carnaby St.M'ster M9 64 F1
Carnaby St.M'ster M40 & M9 157 F8
Carnarvon St. M'ster M7 155 E7
Carnarvon St. M'ster M3 158 F3
Carnarvon St. Oldham OL8 66 B2
Carnarvon St. Stockport SK1 112 A1
Carnation Rd. Farnworth BL4 42 A1
Carnation Rd. Oldham OL4 67 E4
Carnegie Ave. M19 99 B1
Carnegie Dr. WN4 73 A5
Carnforth Ave. Hindley WN2 57 A5
Carnforth Ave. Middleton OL11 47 D7
Carnforth Ave. Oldham OL9 152 A6
Carnforth Dr. Ramsbottom BL8 11 A2
Carnforth Dr. Sale M33 108 A3

Chapel Fields. 1 Marple SK6 125 F5
Chapel Fields La. WN2 56 E5
Chapel Gate. OL16 31 F6
Chapel Gdns. M34 100 F6
Chapel Gn. M34 100 F3
Chapel Gr. M41 95 E2
Chapel Grange. BL7 9 C4
Chapel Green Rd. WN2 56 E5
Chapel Hill. OL15 16 B5
Chapel La. Alt'ham WA15 129 C7
Chapel La. Coppull PR7 19 F8
Chapel La. Hollinfare WA3 105 A2
Chapel La. Hollingworth SK14 103 F5
Chapel La. M'ster M9 64 C3
Chapel La. Partington M31 105 F2
Chapel La. R'dale OL11 29 C8
Chapel La. Ramsbottom BL8 138 A6
Chapel La. Royton OL2 48 D4
Chapel La. Sale M33 107 E6
Chapel La. Wigan WN1 & WN3 150 C7
Chapel La. Wilmslow SK9 137 A6
Chapel Meadow. M28 78 B7
Chapel Pl. Ashton-i-M WN4 73 B3
Chapel Pl. Bolton BL2 & BL3 148 C5
Chapel Pl. Eccles M41 95 D8
Chapel Rd. Alderley Edge SK9 137 A1
Chapel Rd. Irlam M44 94 A2
Chapel Rd. M'ster M25 63 A1
Chapel Rd. Oldham OL8 66 C2
Chapel Rd. Sale M33 108 B5
Chapel Rd. Swinton M27 & M28 79 C7
Chapel Rd. Uppermill OL3 69 A6
Chapel Rd. Wythenshawe M22 121 D8
Chapel St. Adlington PR7 20 F6
Chapel St. Alderley Edge SK9 137 A1
Chapel St. Ashton-i-M WN4 73 B3
Chapel St. Ashton-u-L OL6 166 C3
Chapel St. Atherton M46 58 D3
Chapel St. 14 Bacup OL13 3 C8
Chapel St. Blackrod BL6 21 D2
Chapel St. Bolton BL7 8 D3
Chapel St. Bolton BL1 145 F8
Chapel St. Boothstown M28 77 F6
Chapel St. Bury BL8 26 F7
Chapel St. Bury BL9 140 F2
Chapel St. Cheadle SK8 122 D5
Chapel St. Denton M34 100 F6
Chapel St. Droylsden M43 84 B1
Chapel St. Dukinfield SK16 101 B8
Chapel St. 3 Eccles M30 79 C1
Chapel St. Farnworth BL4 60 E8
Chapel St. Glossop SK13 104 C1
Chapel St. Hazel Grove SK7 124 E3
Chapel St. Heywood OL10 29 D2
Chapel St. Hindley WN2 56 D5
Chapel St. Horwich BL6 22 C3
Chapel St. Hyde SK14 167 D2
Chapel St. Ince-i-M WN3 151 D6
Chapel St. Kearsley M26 61 B8
Chapel St. Leigh WN2 56 E1
Chapel St. Leigh WN7 76 B4
Chapel St. Little Lever BL3 43 B3
Chapel St. Littleborough OL15 6 D2
Chapel St. Littleborough OL12 15 C7
Chapel St. M'ster M19 99 B1
Chapel St. M'ster SK4 110 D2
Chapel St. M'ster M3 158 E2
Chapel St. 7 Middleton M24 46 F1
Chapel St. 6 Mossley OL5 68 C1
Chapel St. Newton-l-W WA12 89 B3
Chapel St. Oldham OL4 67 E6
Chapel St. Platt Bridge WN2 56 B2
Chapel St. Prestwich M25 63 A4
Chapel St. 10 R'dale OL11 31 A4
Chapel St. Romiley SK6 113 B5
Chapel St. Rowarth SK22 127 E7
Chapel St. Royton OL2 48 D4
Chapel St. Shaw OL2 149 B7
Chapel St. Stalybridge SK15 86 A2
Chapel St. Swinton M27 62 A1
Chapel St. Tyldesley M29 77 A8
Chapel St. Uppermill OL3 69 B8
Chapel St. Whitworth OL12 14 C8
Chapel St. Wigan WN2 38 A2
Chapel St. Wigan WN5 54 B5
Chapel St. Wigan WN5 54 B6
Chapel St. Wigan WN3 150 C7
Chapel Street Cty Prim Sch. M19 99 B1
Chapel Terr. WA3 91 B8
Chapel View. SK16 101 C8
Chapel Way. PR7 19 F8
Chapel Wlk. 1 Eccles M30 79 F2
Chapel Wlk. Golborne WN7 75 B1
Chapel Wlk. Hollingworth SK14 103 F5
Chapel Wlk. M'ster M25 62 F1
Chapel Wlk. Middleton M24 64 C7
Chapel Wlk. Whitefield M45 45 B1
Chapel Wlks. Bramhall SK8 132 B6
Chapel Wlks. M'ster M2 158 F1
Chapel Wlks. Sale M33 108 B5
Chapelfield. M26 44 C1
Chapelfield Cl. SK15 86 D4
Chapelfield Dr. M28 60 B3
Chapelfield Prim Sch. M26 44 C1
Chapelfield Rd. M12 163 C8
Chapelfield St. BL1 143 E3
Chapelhill Dr. M9 64 C3
Chapelstead. BL5 57 F5
Chapeltown Rd. Edgworth BL7 9 C2
Chapeltown Rd. Radcliffe M26 62 A8
Chapeltown St. M1 159 C1
Chapelway Gdns. OL2 48 D6
Chaplin Cl. M6 154 E4
Chapman Ct. SK14 102 D2
Chapman Mews. M18 99 D5
Chapman Rd. SK14 102 E1
Chapman St. Bolton BL1 142 B1
Chapman St. M'ster M18 99 D5
Chappell Rd. M43 84 A2
Chapter St. M10 & M40 160 F4
Charcoal Rd. WA14 118 F3
Charcoal Woods. WA14 119 A3
Charcon Wlk. 3 OL2 48 E4
Chard Dr. M22 121 D1
Chard St. M26 44 A3
Chardin Ave. SK6 126 C8
Charges St. OL7 84 F1
Chariot St. M11 99 D8
Charity St. WN7 75 C5
Charlbury Ave. M'ster M25 63 E3
Charlbury Ave. Reddish SK5 111 F6
Charlbury Way. OL2 149 A5
Charlecote Rd. SK12 133 F4
Charles Ave. Droylsden M34 & M43 100 A7
Charles Ave. Marple SK6 125 C7
Charles Barry Cres. M15 162 E6
Charles Cradock Dr. M7 155 F6
Charles Ct. WA15 120 B6
Charles Halle Rd. M15 163 A5
Charles Holden St. BL1 145 D6
Charles La. Glossop SK13 104 E3
Charles La. Milnrow OL16 32 A5
Charles Mews. OL16 32 A5
Charles Morris Cl. M35 84 B8
Charles Morris House. M35 84 A7
Charles St. Ashton-u-L OL7 166 B2
Charles St. Bolton BL7 8 D2
Charles St. 2 Bolton BL1 148 A8
Charles St. 5 Bury BL9 140 F3
Charles St. Denton M34 100 F5
Charles St. Droylsden M43 83 E1
Charles St. Dukinfield SK16 166 B1
Charles St. 3 Farnworth BL4 42 E1
Charles St. Farnworth BL4 60 E7
Charles St. Glossop SK13 104 C1
Charles St. Golborne WA3 74 A1
Charles St. Hazel Grove SK7 124 D3
Charles St. Heywood OL10 46 E8
Charles St. Hindley WN2 56 E7
Charles St. Ince-i-M WN2 56 A7
Charles St. Irlam M44 105 E6
Charles St. Leigh WN7 76 A5
Charles St. Leigh WN7 76 A6
Charles St. Littleborough OL15 16 A5
Charles St. M'ster M1 163 A8
Charles St. Oldham OL9 152 C6
Charles St. Royton OL2 48 D4
Charles St. Salford M6 154 F4
Charles St. Stockport SK1 124 A7
Charles St. Swinton M27 61 D2
Charles St. Tyldesley M29 58 F1
Charles St. Whitefield M45 62 F7
Charles St. 2 Wigan WN1 37 C1
Charles Whittaker St. OL12 13 F1
Charles Wlk. M45 62 F7
Charleston Cl. M29 76 F8
Charleston Prim Sch. M6 81 B4
Charleston Sq. M41 95 B3
Charleston St. OL8 66 F4
Charlestown. SK13 116 C7
Charlestown Cl. OL6 166 B3
Charlestown Ind Est. OL6 166 B4
Charlestown Prim Sch. M9 65 B3
Charlestown Rd. Glossop SK13 116 C7
Charlestown Rd. M'ster M9 64 E2
Charlestown Rd E. SK2 124 A3
Charlestown Rd W. SK3 123 F3
Charlesworth Ave. Bolton BL3 42 B3
Charlesworth Ave. Denton M34 112 F8
Charlesworth Cty Prim Sch. SK14 115 D6
Charlesworth St. M'ster M11 164 F8
Charlesworth St. Stockport SK1 170 F7
Charlesworth (VE) Prim Sch. SK14 115 C6
Charley Ave. M7 158 D4
Charlock Ave. BL5 57 E6
Charlock Sq. WA14 119 B8
Charlock Wlk. 6 M31 105 F3
Charlotte La. OL4 68 E5
Charlotte St. 28 Bolton BL1 143 E2
Charlotte St. Cheadle SK8 122 D5
Charlotte St. Edgworth BL7 9 C4
Charlotte St. M'ster M1, M60 159 A1
Charlotte St. R'dale OL11 & OL16 31 B3
Charlotte St. Ramsbottom BL0 138 B5
Charlotte St. Stockport SK1 112 B3
Charlton Ave. Eccles M30 79 D1
Charlton Ave. Hyde SK14 102 A4
Charlton Ave. Prestwich M25 63 B3
Charlton Ct. 2 M16 97 C3
Charlton Dr. Sale M33 108 C4
Charlton Dr. Swinton M27 61 D2
Charlton Pl. M12 163 B7
Charlton Rd. M19 99 B1
Charlton Sh Ctr. M21 97 B1
Charminster Dr. M8 156 B8
Charmouth Wlk. M22 121 F3
Charnley Cl. M10 & M40 160 E3
Charnley St. M45 62 F8
Charnock Dr. BL1 143 E1
Charnock Rd. WA3 91 F3
Charnock Sq. Abram WN2 56 B1
Charnock's Yd. 2 WN5 54 B5
Charnville Rd. M22 121 F5
Charnwood Ave. M34 100 B3
Charnwood Cl. Ashton-u-L OL6 85 C7
Charnwood Cl. Shaw OL2 48 E8
Charnwood Cl. Tyldesley M29 77 B8
Charnwood Cl. Walkden M28 60 C2
Charnwood Cres. SK7 133 D8
Charnwood Rd. M'ster M9 64 D5
Charnwood Rd. Romiley SK6 113 C5
Charter. M30 79 F1
Charter Ave. M26 44 C2
Charter Cl. M33 107 D3
Charter Rd. WA15 119 E4
Charter St. M'ster M3 158 F3
Charter St. Oldham OL1 67 A8
Charter St. R'dale OL11, OL16 31 B4
Charterhouse Rd. WN3 151 E6
Chartist House. SK14 167 E2
Chartwell Cl. M5 & M6 154 F2
Chartwell Dr. M23 120 E7
Chase St. M3 159 A3
Chase The. M28 79 A5
Chasefield. WA14 119 A2
Chaseley Rd. R'dale OL12 139 E8
Chaseley Rd. Salford M6 154 E4
Chasetown Cl. M23 120 D6
Chassen Ave. M41 95 B2
Chassen Rd. Bolton BL1 144 B7
Chassen Rd. Urmston M41 95 B1
Chassen Road Sta. M41 95 B1
Chataway Rd. M8 156 C8
Chatburn Ave. Golborne WA3 74 C1
Chatburn Ave. Middleton OL11 47 D8
Chatburn Ct. Culcheth WA3 91 F2
Chatburn Ct. Shaw OL2 149 C8
Chatburn Gdns. Heywood OL10 28 F2
Chatburn Rd. Bolton BL1 23 F3
Chatburn Rd. M'ster M21 109 C8
Chatburn Sq. OL11 47 D8
Chatcombe Rd. M22 121 A2
Chatfield Rd. M21 109 B8
Chatford Cl. M7 158 E4
Chatham Ct. M20 110 A6
Chatham Gdns. BL3 145 D5
Chatham Gr. M20 110 A6
Chatham House. 1 SK3 170 E8
Chatham Pl. 2 BL3 145 D5
Chatham Rd. M'ster M16 97 C3
Chatham Rd. Reddish M18 99 E3
Chatham St. Hyde SK14 113 E7
Chatham St. Ince-i-M WN2 56 A8
Chatham St. Leigh WN7 75 F7
Chatham St. M'ster M1 & M60 159 B1
Chatham St. Stockport SK3 170 D8
Chatham St. Wigan WN1 151 F7
Chatley Rd. M30 78 F1
Chatley St. M8 159 A4
Chatswood Ave. SK2 170 F6
Chatsworth Ave. Culcheth WA3 91 F4
Chatsworth Ave. Ince-i-M WN2 55 F4
Chatsworth Ave. Prestwich M25 63 B4
Chatsworth Cl. Alt'ham WA15 120 C5
Chatsworth Cl. Ashton-i-M WN4 72 F4
Chatsworth Cl. Droylsden M43 83 E3
Chatsworth Cl. Shaw OL2 49 D8
Chatsworth Cl. 2 Urmston M41 95 E2
Chatsworth Cl. Whitefield BL9 45 A5
Chatsworth Ct. Adlington PR7 20 F8
Chatsworth Ct. Stockport SK2 124 A5
Chatsworth Dr. Leigh WN7 76 D7
Chatsworth Dr. Leigh WN7 76 E7
Chatsworth Gr. Little Lever BL3 43 A4
Chatsworth Gr. M'ster M16 97 D2
Chatsworth Rd. Droylsden M43 83 E2
Chatsworth Rd. Eccles M30 79 F4
Chatsworth Rd. Hazel Grove SK7 133 F8
Chatsworth Rd. High Lane SK6 134 F6
Chatsworth Rd. M'ster M18 165 C5
Chatsworth Rd. Radcliffe M26 43 D5
Chatsworth Rd. Stretford M32 96 A3
Chatsworth Rd. Swinton M28 79 C5
Chatsworth Rd. Wilmslow SK9 136 E4
Chatsworth St. Oldham OL4 67 C5
Chatsworth St. R'dale OL12 14 E3
Chatsworth St. Wigan WN5 54 C5
Chatteris Cl. WN2 56 E4
Chatterton. BL0 1 C2
Chatterton Cl. M20 110 C6
Chatterton La. SK3 & SK6 127 B8
Chatterton Old La. BL0 1 C2
Chatterton Rd. BL0 1 C1
Chattock Cl. M16 97 E3
Chatton Cl. BL8 26 F2
Chatwell Ct. OL16 32 C4
Chatwood Rd. M40 65 D2
Chaucer Ave. Denton M34 113 A7
Chaucer Ave. Droylsden M43 84 A1
Chaucer Ave. Radcliffe M26 43 E4
Chaucer Ave. Reddish SK5 99 D1
Chaucer Gr. Atherton M46 58 D5
Chaucer Gr. Leigh WN7 75 D8
Chaucer Mews. SK1 112 B1
Chaucer Pl. Abram WN2 56 B1
Chaucer Pl. Wigan WN1 37 C3
Chaucer Rd. M24 47 B2
Chaucer Rise. SK16 102 A7
Chaucer St. Bolton BL1 143 D2
Chaucer St. Oldham OL1 153 E6
Chaucer St. R'dale OL11 30 C2
Chaucer St. Royton OL2 48 E5
Chaucer Wlk. M13 163 C6
Chaumont Way. OL6 166 B3
Chauncy Rd. M35 & M40 83 E8
Chaytor Ave. M40 83 B7
Cheadle Ave. M7 81 A7
Cheadle Heath Jun & Inf Sch. SK3 123 A7
Cheadle Hulme High Sch. SK8 132 B7
Cheadle Hulme Sch. SK8 132 A8
Cheadle Hulme Sta. SK8 123 B2
Cheadle Old Rd. SK3 123 C7
Cheadle Prep Sch. SK8 131 C7
Cheadle Prim Sch. SK8 122 D6
Cheadle RC Inf Sch. SK8 122 E2
Cheadle Rc Jun Sch. SK8 122 E2
Cheadle Rd. Cheadle SK8 122 E4
Cheadle Royal Hospl. SK8 122 C2
Cheadle Sq. BL1 145 E7
Cheadle St. M11 99 D8
Cheam Rd. WA15 119 F8
Cheap Side. M24 47 A2
Cheapside. Hyde SK14 167 E3
Cheapside. M'ster M2 158 F1
Cheapside. Oldham OL1 153 E7
Cheapside Sq. 8 BL1 145 F7
Cheddar St. 1 M18 99 D5
Chedlee Dr. SK8 131 E8
Chedlin Dr. M23 121 A4
Chedworth Cres. M38 60 A6
Chedworth Gr. BL3 145 E5
Cheeryble St. M11 & M43 99 F7
Cheesden Wlk. M45 45 C1
Cheetham Ave. M24 47 B1
Cheetham CE Comm Sch. M8 155 F7
Cheetham Fold Rd. SK14 113 D8
Cheetham Gdns. 6 SK15 86 B1
Cheetham Gr. WN3 54 F5
Cheetham Hill. Shaw OL2 149 B6
Cheetham Hill. Whitworth OL12 4 D3
Cheetham Hill Rd. Dukinfield SK14, SK15, SK16 101 E7
Cheetham Hill Rd. M'ster M3 & M7 & M8 156 A5
Cheetham Hill Rd. M'ster M3 & M4 159 A3
Cheetham Par. M8 155 F8
Cheetham Pl. SK6 112 F4
Cheetham Rd. M27 80 A7
Cheetham St. Failsworth M35 84 A8
Cheetham St. M'ster M10 & M40 157 E5
Cheetham St. Middleton M24 64 F8
Cheetham St. Oldham OL1 67 B7
Cheetham St. R'dale OL12 & OL16 139 F8
Cheetham St. Radcliffe M26 44 C4
Cheetham St. Shaw OL2 149 C6
Cheetham's Cres. OL2 49 A4
Cheethams The. BL6 38 E7
Cheetwood Prim Sch. M8 158 E4
Cheetwood Rd. M7 & M8 155 F5
Cheetwood St. M7 & M8 158 E4
Chelbourne Dr. 3 OL8 66 B2
Chelburn Cl. Leigh WN2 56 E1
Chelburn Cl. Stockport SK2 124 D5
Chelburn View. OL15 6 C1
Cheldon Wlk. 8 M40 83 C6
Chelford Ave. Bolton BL1 24 E5
Chelford Ave. Golborne WA3 90 D8
Chelford Cl. Alt'ham WA15 119 E6
Chelford Cl. M'ster M13 164 D5
Chelford Cl. Middleton M24 47 C2
Chelford Cl. Wigan WN3 54 F2
Chelford Ct. 2 SK9 131 E5
Chelford Dr. Swinton M27 61 E2
Chelford Dr. Tyldesley M29 77 C6
Chelford Gr. SK3 170 D5
Chelford Rd. Alderley Edge SK9 136 E1
Chelford Rd. Handforth SK9 131 D5
Chelford Rd. M'ster M16 97 C3
Chelford Rd. Sale M33 108 E2
Chell St. M12 98 F4
Chellow Dene. OL5 68 B1
Chelmarsh Ave. WN4 73 C3
Chelmer Cl. Westhoughton BL5 40 A1
Chelmer Gr. OL10 29 A3
Chelmorton Gr. WN3 54 C2
Chelmsford Ave. M40 83 B4
Chelmsford Dr. WN3 55 A4
Chelmsford Mews. WN1 37 C2
Chelmsford Rd. SK3 123 C8
Chelmsford St. OL8 153 E5
Chelmsford Wlk. 14 M34 101 A1
Chelsea Ave. M26 43 D4
Chelsea Cl. OL2 149 B7
Chelsea Rd. Bolton BL3 147 D3
Chelsea Rd. Failsworth M40 83 C5
Chelsea Rd. Urmston M41 94 C1
Chelsea St. Bury BL9 44 F4
Chelsea St. R'dale OL11 139 D5
Chelsfield Gr. M21 109 D8
Chelston Ave. M40 65 D2
Chelston Dr. Gatley SK8 131 C6
Chelston Dr. Haslingden BB4 1 A7
Chelt Wlk. M22 121 B2
Cheltenham Ave. WN3 151 D5
Cheltenham Cres. M7 155 F7
Cheltenham Dr. Newton-l-W WA12 89 C5
Cheltenham Dr. Orrell WN5 53 D2
Cheltenham Dr. Sale M33 108 C4
Cheltenham Gn. M24 65 A6
Cheltenham Rd. Cheadle SK3 123 A7
Cheltenham Rd. M'ster M21 97 B2
Cheltenham Rd. Middleton M24 65 A6
Cheltenham St. Oldham OL1 49 B1
Cheltenham St. R'dale OL11 30 D4
Cheltenham St. Salford M6 81 A4
Cheltenham St. 3 Wigan WN2 37 F2
Chelwood Cl. BL1 24 D7
Chelworth Manor. SK8 123 C1
Chemical St. WA12 89 B3
Chemist St. BL1 143 F1
Cheney Cl. M18 99 D7
Chepstow Ave. M33 107 C3
Chepstow Cl. OL11 29 F8
Chepstow Dr. SK7 125 A2
Chepstow Gr. WN7 76 E7
Chepstow Rd. M'ster M21 97 A1
Chepstow Rd. Swinton M27 62 A2
Chepstow St. M1 162 F8
Chepstow St S. M1 162 F8
Chequers Rd. M21 109 B8
Chequers St. WN1 150 B8
Cherington Cl. Handforth SK9 131 F3
Cherington Cl. Wythenshawe M23 109 B2
Cherington Dr. M29 59 C1
Cherington Rd. SK8 122 C4
Cheriton Ave. M33 108 C5
Cheriton Cl. SK14 102 D2
Cheriton Dr. BL2 42 E6
Cheriton Gdns. BL6 22 B5
Cheriton Rd. M41 94 D3
Cheriton Rise. SK2 125 A6
Cherrington Dr. OL11 47 D8
Cherry Ave. Ashton-u-L OL6 85 B6
Cherry Ave. Bury BL9 141 C3
Cherry Ave. Oldham OL8 67 C3
Cherry Cres. BB4 1 F8
Cherry Ct. M33 108 A4
Cherry Dr. M27 80 A8
Cherry Gr. Leigh WN7 75 F8
Cherry Gr. R'dale OL11 30 A8
Cherry Gr. Royton OL2 48 C6
Cherry Gr. Stalybridge SK15 102 A8
Cherry Gr. Wigan WN6 36 F3
Cherry Hall Dr. OL2 48 E7
Cherry Hinton. OL1 153 D8
Cherry Holt Ave. SK4 110 F4
Cherry La. Denshaw OL15 & OL3 33 B3
Cherry La. Sale M33 107 C2
Cherry Manor Prim Sch. M33 107 C2
Cherry Orchard Cl. SK7 123 D1
Cherry St. M25 63 C5
Cherry Tree Ave. Farnworth BL4 60 A8
Cherry Tree Ave. Poynton SK12 133 F3
Cherry Tree Cl. Romiley SK6 113 E2
Cherry Tree Cl. Wilmslow SK9 137 E8
Cherry Tree Ct. 8 Salford M6 81 A2
Cherry Tree Ct. Standish WN6 19 D2
Cherry Tree Dr. SK7 134 A8
Cherry Tree Gr. Atherton M46 58 C4
Cherry Tree Gr. Leigh WN7 75 D6
Cherry Tree Hospl. SK2 124 C5
Cherry Tree Inf Sch. SK6 113 E3
Cherry Tree Jun Sch. SK6 113 E2
Cherry Tree La. Billinge WA11 71 A2
Cherry Tree La. Bury BL8 27 C1
Cherry Tree La. Rawtenstall BB4 1 F8
Cherry Tree La. Romiley SK6 113 E2
Cherry Tree La. Stockport SK2 124 C5
Cherry Tree Prim Sch. BL4 59 E8
Cherry Tree Rd. Cheadle SK8 123 A1
Cherry Tree Rd. Golborne WA3 90 F8
Cherry Tree Rd. Wythenshawe M23 108 F1
Cherry Tree Way. Bolton BL2 25 C5
Cherry Tree Way. Haslingden BB4 1 B7
Cherry Tree Way. 5 Horwich BL6 22 E1
Cherry Tree Wlk. Mossley OL5 68 B1
Cherry Tree Wlk. Stretford M32 96 C1
Cherry Wlk. Cheadle SK8 132 C8
Cherry Wlk. Partington M31 105 D2
Cherrycroft. SK6 113 E1
Cherryton Wlk. M13 163 C6
Cherrywood. M24 65 D7
Cherrywood Ave. BL5 59 A7
Cherrywood Cl. Walkden M28 60 B1
Chertsey Cl. Droylsden M18 99 E5
Chertsey Cl. Shaw OL2 149 B8
Chervil Wlk. WN3 54 C4
Cherwell Ave. OL10 29 B3
Cherwell Cl. Aspull WN2 38 C6
Cherwell Cl. Cheadle SK8 132 A7
Cherwell Cl. Oldham OL8 66 C1
Cherwell Cl. Whitefield M45 63 A8
Cherwell Rd. BL5 39 F2
Cheryl's Bank. SK13 104 C1
Chesham Ave. Bolton BL1 143 E2
Chesham Ave. Middleton OL11 47 D7
Chesham Ave. Urmston M41 94 E3
Chesham Ave. Wythenshawe M22 121 C4
Chesham Cl. Hadfield SK14 104 B5
Chesham Cl. Wilmslow SK9 136 F4
Chesham Cres. BL9 141 A3
Chesham Cty Prim Sch. BL9 28 A5
Chesham Fold Rd. BL9 141 B4
Chesham House. 2 M6 154 F1
Chesham Ind Est. BL9 141 A4
Chesham Pl. WA14 119 C2
Chesham Rd. Bury BL9 28 A5
Chesham Rd. Eccles M30 95 C8
Chesham Rd. 3 Oldham OL4 67 C6
Chesham Rd. Wilmslow SK9 136 F4
Chesham St. BL3 146 B2
Cheshill Ct. M7 155 F6
Cheshire Cl. Newton-l-W WA12 89 E3
Cheshire Cl. Stretford M32 96 A5
Cheshire Ct. BL0 11 D6
Cheshire Gdns. M14 98 A1
Cheshire Rd. Mossley SK15 86 E5
Cheshire Rd. Partington M31 105 D2
Cheshire Sq. SK15 86 E5
Cheshire St. OL5 86 D8
Cheshires The. OL5 68 D1
Chesney Ave. OL9 65 E2
Chesshyre Ave. M40 160 D1
Chessington Rise. M27 62 A3
Chester Ave. Alt'ham WA15 119 F2
Chester Ave. Dukinfield SK16 101 E7
Chester Ave. Golborne WA3 90 D8
Chester Ave. Little Lever BL3 43 B4
Chester Ave. R'dale OL11 30 A6
Chester Ave. Sale M33 107 B1
Chester Ave. Stalybridge SK15 86 D3
Chester Ave. Urmston M41 95 E3
Chester Ave. Whitefield M45 63 A7
Chester Cl. Handforth SK9 131 E2
Chester Cl. Irlam M44 105 D5
Chester Cl. Little Lever BL3 43 B4
Chester Cres. BB4 1 B8
Chester Dr. Ashton-i-M WN4 73 D2
Chester Dr. Ramsbottom BL0 11 A4
Chester House (Pol HQ). M16 161 A5
Chester Pl. Adlington PR6 21 A8
Chester Pl. 7 Royton OL2 48 D4
Chester Rd. Hazel Grove SK7 & SK12 124 D1
Chester Rd. M'ster M15, M17 161 A5
Chester Rd. M'ster M15, M16 161 C6
Chester Rd. Poynton SK12 & SK7 133 B4
Chester Rd. Stretford M16 & M32 96 E3
Chester Rd. Tyldesley M29 77 D8
Chester Rd. Woodford SK7 132 E2
Chester Sq. OL7 166 A2
Chester St. Bury BL9 141 A4
Chester St. Denton M34 100 F2
Chester St. Leigh WN7 75 F5
Chester St. M'ster M1 163 A7
Chester St. Oldham OL9 152 C5
Chester St. Prestwich M25 63 A5
Chester St. Stockport SK3 169 D1
Chester St. Swinton M27 79 F7
Chester St. Tyldesley M46 58 E1
Chester Walks. SK6 113 A1
Chester Wlk. 20 BL1 143 E2
Chesterfield Gr. OL6 85 D3
Chesterfield St. OL4 67 B6
Chesterfield Way. 4 M34 113 A8
Chestergate. SK3 169 E1
Chesterton Cl. WN3 150 A5
Chesterton Dr. BL3 40 E5
Chesterton Gr. M43 84 A2
Chesterton Rd. Oldham OL1 49 B2
Chesterton Rd. Sale M23 120 D8
Chestnut Ave. Atherton M46 58 C4
Chestnut Ave. Bury BL8 27 A5
Chestnut Ave. Bury BL9 141 B2
Chestnut Ave. Cheadle SK8 122 E5
Chestnut Ave. Droylsden M43 83 F3
Chestnut Ave. Irlam M44 105 D5
Chestnut Ave. Leigh WN7 75 F3
Chestnut Ave. M'ster M21 109 B8
Chestnut Ave. Walkden M28 60 D2
Chestnut Ave. Whitefield M45 62 F7
Chestnut Cl. Bolton BL3 146 B4
Chestnut Cl. New Mills SK12 127 E1
Chestnut Cl. Oldham OL4 67 D8
Chestnut Cl. Stalybridge SK15 102 A8
Chestnut Cl. Wilmslow SK9 137 E8
Chestnut Cres. OL8 67 A2
Chestnut Ct. SK7 123 D2
Chestnut Dr. Leigh WN7 75 F2
Chestnut Dr. Poynton SK12 133 F3
Chestnut Dr. Rawtenstall BB4 1 F8
Chestnut Dr. Sale M33 107 D1
Chestnut Dr. Westhoughton BL5 57 F7
Chestnut Dr S. WN7 75 F1
Chestnut Gdns. M34 100 E2
Chestnut Gr. Ashton-i-M WN4 73 D4
Chestnut Gr. Failsworth M35 83 F6
Chestnut Gr. Golborne WA3 90 F8
Chestnut Gr. Hindley WN2 57 A4
Chestnut Gr. Radcliffe M26 62 A8
Chestnut La. WN7 75 E2
Chestnut Rd. Wigan WN1 37 E2
Chestnut Rd. Worsley M28 79 A4
Chestnut St. OL9 66 A3
Chestnut Villas. SK4 168 C2
Chestnut Way. OL15 15 F6
Chestnut Wlk. Partington M31 105 D2
Chestnut Wlk. 4 Partington M31 105 E3
Chesworth Cl. SK1 170 F8
Chesworth Ct. M43 83 F1
Chesworth Fold. SK1 170 F8
Chesworth Wlk. M15 162 D7
Chetham Cl. M5 161 B7
Chetham's Sch of Music. M4 158 F2
Chetwode Ave. WN4 73 B1
Chetwyn Ave. Bolton BL7 25 A7
Chetwyn Ave. Royton OL2 48 C4
Chetwynd Ave. M41 95 C2
Chetwynd Cres. M33 107 E6
Chevassut Prim Sch. M15 162 E7
Chevassut St. M15 162 E6
Chevin Gdns. SK7 133 A7
Chevington Dr. M'ster SK4 110 E3
Chevington Dr. M'ster M40 & M9 157 D6
Chevington Gdns. 2 BL1 143 E3
Cheviot Ave. Cheadle SK8 122 F2
Cheviot Ave. Oldham OL8 66 E3
Cheviot Ave. Royton OL2 48 C3
Cheviot Cl. Bolton BL1 24 D5
Cheviot Cl. Bury BL8 27 A3
Cheviot Cl. Horwich BL6 22 C5
Cheviot Cl. Middleton M24 65 D8
Cheviot Cl. Milnrow OL16 32 A7
Cheviot Cl. Oldham OL9 152 A5
Cheviot Cl. Ramsbottom BL0 11 C4
Cheviot Cl. Salford M6 154 E3
Cheviot Cl. Stockport SK4 169 D3
Cheviot Cl. Wigan WN3 54 C2
Cheviot Ct. OL8 66 E4
Cheviot Rd. SK7 124 B1
Cheviot St. M3 158 F3
Cheviots Rd. OL2 149 A8
Chevithorne Cl. WA14 119 B5
Chevril Cl. M15 163 A6
Chevron Cl. R'dale OL11 30 B3
Chevron Cl. 3 Salford M5 & M6 81 B2
Chevron Pl. WA14 119 D7
Chew Brook Dr. OL3 69 B5
Chew Moor La. BL5 & BL6 40 A2
Chew Rd. Uppermill OL3 70 A2
Chew Vale. Dukinfield SK16 101 F7
Chew Vale. Uppermill OL3 69 B5
Chew Valley Rd. OL3 69 B5
Chicago Ave. M90 130 B7

Cleworth Rd. M24 46 F2
Cleworth St. M15 162 D7
Cleworth Wlk. M15 162 D7
Clibran St. M8 156 B6
Clifden Dr. M22 121 E2
Cliff Ave. Bury BL8 26 E7
Cliff Ave. M'ster M7 81 C6
Cliff Ave. Ramsbottom BL9 11 C2
Cliff Cres. M7 155 D7
Cliff Dale. SK15 101 F8
Cliff Gr. SK4 168 B4
Cliff Hill Rd. OL2 32 D1
Cliff Mount. BL0 138 B7
Cliff Rd. Bury BL9 44 F5
Cliff Rd. Wilmslow SK9 137 B8
Cliff Side. SK9 137 B8
Cliff St. OL16 15 B1
Cliffbrook Gr. 2 SK9 131 D2
Cliffdale Dr. M8 64 A1
Cliffe Rd. SK13 116 D8
Cliffe St. OL15 6 D2
Cliffmere Cl. SK8 122 F3
Clifford Ave. Alt'ham WA15 120 B6
Clifford Ave. Denton M34 100 E5
Clifford Ct. M16 162 E5
Clifford Lamb Ct. M9 65 B2
Clifford Rd. Bolton BL3 146 A2
Clifford Rd. Poynton SK12 133 D3
Clifford Rd. Wilmslow SK9 136 F6
Clifford St. Eccles M30 95 B8
Clifford St. Leigh WN7 76 B4
Clifford St. M'ster M13 163 B6
Clifford St. Pendlebury M27 80 B8
Clifford St. R'dale OL11 139 F5
Clifton Ave. Alt'ham WA15 119 E5
Clifton Ave. Culcheth WA3 91 D3
Clifton Ave. Eccles M30 79 D3
Clifton Ave. Gatley SK8 122 A2
Clifton Ave. M'ster M14 110 D8
Clifton Ave. 2 Oldham OL4 67 B5
Clifton Ave. Tyldesley M29 77 C6
Clifton Cl. Heywood OL10 29 C1
Clifton Cl. M'ster M16 162 D5
Clifton Cl. Oldham OL4 67 B5
Clifton Cres. Royton OL2 49 A3
Clifton Cres. Wigan WN1 37 C2
Clifton Ct. 5 Farnworth BL4 42 B2
Clifton Ct. Swinton M27 61 F3
Clifton Ctry Pk. M27 61 E5
Clifton Dr. Blackrod BL6 21 C3
Clifton Dr. Gatley SK8 122 A2
Clifton Dr. Gatley M22 122 A6
Clifton Dr. Marple SK6 125 F7
Clifton Dr. Swinton M27 61 D2
Clifton Dr. Swinton M27 62 C2
Clifton Dr. Wilmslow SK9 136 E4
Clifton Gr. M'ster M16 162 D5
Clifton Gr. Swinton M27 61 D2
Clifton Holm. OL3 50 E5
Clifton House Rd. M27 61 E4
Clifton Junction Sta. M27 62 C2
Clifton Lodge. SK2 124 A5
Clifton Park Rd. SK2 124 A5
Clifton Pl. M25 63 A5
Clifton Prim Sch. M27 61 F3
Clifton Rd. Ashton-i-M WN4 72 F6
Clifton Rd. Billinge WN5 71 D4
Clifton Rd. Eccles M30 79 D3
Clifton Rd. Leigh WN7 75 E2
Clifton Rd. M'ster M21 109 C8
Clifton Rd. M'ster SK4 168 A4
Clifton Rd. Middleton OL11 47 D6
Clifton Rd. Prestwich M25 62 E4
Clifton Rd. Sale M33 108 B3
Clifton Rd. Urmston M41 95 A2
Clifton St. Alderley Edge SK9 137 A1
Clifton St. Ashton-u-L OL6 166 A3
Clifton St. Bolton BL1 145 E8
Clifton St. Bury BL9 140 F4
Clifton St. Failsworth M35 66 A1
Clifton St. Farnworth BL4 42 B2
Clifton St. Kearsley BL4 60 F7
Clifton St. Leigh WN7 75 D5
Clifton St. M'ster M10 & M40 160 F4
Clifton St. M'ster M16 162 D5
Clifton St. Milnrow OL16 31 F6
Clifton St. 7 R'dale OL11 31 A5
Clifton St. Tyldesley M29 77 E8
Clifton St. 4 Wigan WN1 37 C1
Clifton St. Wigan WN3 55 A4
Clifton View. M27 61 E4
Clifton Villas. 5 M35 66 A1
Clifton Wlk. OL10 46 C7
Cliftonmill Meadows. WA3 89 F8
Cliftonville Dr. M6 80 B6
Cliftonville Rd. OL16 48 C8
Clinton Ave. M14 98 A2
Clinton Gdns. M14 98 A2
Clinton House. 3 M6 154 F1
Clinton St. 7 OL6 85 D4
Clinton Wlk. 5 OL4 67 A6
Clippers Quay. M5 161 A6
Clipsley Cres. OL4 49 F4
Cliston Wlk. SK7 124 A2
Clitheroe Cl. OL10 29 D3
Clitheroe Dr. BL8 26 F2
Clitheroe Rd. M13 98 F3
Clito St. M9 157 F8
Clive Ave. M45 44 E1
Clive Rd. Failsworth M35 83 E6
Clive Rd. Westhoughton BL5 57 E6
Clive St. Ashton-u-L OL7 85 A5
Clive St. Bolton BL2 148 A7
Clive St. M'ster M4 159 B3
Clive St. 2 Oldham OL8 66 D2
Cliveley Wlk. M27 80 B8
Clively Ave. M27 62 C1
Clivewood Wlk. M12 164 E6
Clivia Gr. M7 155 D6
Cloak St. M1 163 A7
Clock House Ave. M43 83 E3
Clock Tower Cl. 3 M28 59 F3
Clockhouse Mews. M43 83 E3
Clod La. BB4 1 C8
Cloister Ave. WN7 57 D1
Cloister Cl. SK16 101 C6
Cloister Rd. SK4 110 D2
Cloister St. BL1 142 C2
Cloisters The. Cheadle SK8 123 A5
Cloisters The. R'dale OL16 15 B1
Cloisters The. Sale M33 108 D4
Cloisters The. Westhoughton BL5 57 E5
Close La. Hindley WN2 56 E3
Close La. Leigh WN2 57 A1
Close St. WN2 56 F6
Close The. Alt'ham WA14 119 C5
Close The. Atherton M46 58 F5
Close The. Bolton BL2 25 B3
Close The. Bury BL8 27 C5
Close The. Denton M34 100 D4
Close The. Middleton M24 47 B3
Close The. Romiley SK6 114 B1
Close The. Stalybridge SK15 85 F4
Closebrook Rd. WN5 54 D6
Clothorn Rd. M20 110 B4
Cloudberry Wlk. M31 105 F3
Cloudstock Gr. M38 59 E5
Clough Ave. Handforth SK9 131 B2
Clough Ave. Marple SK6 126 C6
Clough Ave. Sale M33 107 D1
Clough Ave. Westhoughton BL5 57 F7
Clough Bank. Littleborough OL15 16 A8
Clough Bank. M'ster M9 64 D2
Clough Croft. OL4 68 E6
Clough Dr. M25 62 F4
Clough End Rd. SK14 102 F1
Clough Fold. M26 61 B7
Clough Fold Rd. SK14 167 D1
Clough Gate. Hyde SK14 113 F8
Clough Gate. 5 Oldham OL8 66 D2
Clough Gr. Ashton-i-M WN4 72 F5
Clough Gr. Whitefield M45 44 D2
Clough House. M9 65 A2
Clough House Dr. WN7 76 B5
Clough House La. OL12 15 B6
Clough La. Heywood OL10 29 C4
Clough La. Prestwich M25 62 F4
Clough La. Uppermill OL4 68 E6
Clough Meadow. Bolton BL1 40 D6
Clough Meadow. Romiley SK6 113 C5
Clough Meadow Rd. M26 43 E3
Clough Park Ave. OL4 68 E6
Clough Rd. Droylsden M43 84 B2
Clough Rd. Failsworth M35 84 A6
Clough Rd. Littleborough OL15 16 A7
Clough Rd. M'ster M9 64 F1
Clough Rd. Middleton M24 47 A2
Clough Rd. Shaw OL2 49 D6
Clough Side. SK6 126 C7
Clough St. 8 Bacup OL13 3 D8
Clough St. Failsworth M40 83 C4
Clough St. Kearsley BL4 60 F7
Clough St. Littleborough OL12 15 C6
Clough St. Middleton M24 47 B2
Clough St. Radcliffe M26 44 C1
Clough Terr. OL15 16 A7
Clough The. SK5 112 B6
Clough Top Rd. M9 65 A2
Clough Wlk. SK5 112 B6
Cloughbank. M26 61 C7
Cloughfield Ave. M6 161 B8
Cloughgate House. 4 OL8 66 D2
Cloughs Ave. OL9 65 D8
Cloughside. SK12 135 E6
Cloughton Wlk. M40 83 D5
Cloughwood Cres. WN6 35 D6
Clovelly Ave. Leigh WN7 75 F8
Clovelly Ave. Oldham OL8 66 C2
Clovelly Rd. M'ster M21 109 C8
Clovelly Rd. Stockport SK2 124 C8
Clovelly Rd. Swinton M27 79 C6
Clovelly St. Failsworth M40 83 D5
Clovelly St. R'dale OL11 30 B3
Clover Ave. SK3 170 D5
Clover Cres. OL8 67 C3
Clover Croft. M33 108 D1
Clover Hall Cres. OL16 15 C1
Clover Rd. Alt'ham WA15 120 B5
Clover Rd. Romiley SK6 113 E3
Clover St. R'dale OL12 139 E8
Clover St. Wigan WN6 37 B2
Clover View. OL16 31 C7
Cloverbank Ave. M19 110 D4
Cloverdale Sq. BL1 142 A1
Cloverfield Wlk. M28 60 D3
Cloverlea Prim Sch. WA15 120 B5
Cloverley. M33 108 B2
Cloverley Dr. WA15 120 A4
Clowes St. M'ster M3 158 E2
Clowes St. M'ster M12 164 F6
Clowes St. Oldham OL9 66 B2
Club St. Billinge WA11 71 A1
Club St. Droylsden M11 99 F7
Clumber Cl. SK12 133 E3
Clumber Rd. Poynton SK12 133 E3
Clumber Rd. Reddish M18,M34 99 F4
Clunton Ave. BL3 146 B4
Clutha Rd. SK3 123 F4
Clwyd Ave. SK3 170 D7
Clyde Ave. M45 62 F6
Clyde Ct. OL16 31 B6
Clyde Rd. M'ster M20 110 A5
Clyde Rd. Radcliffe M26 43 F5
Clyde Rd. Stockport SK3 123 C7
Clyde Rd. Tyldesley M29 77 C7
Clyde St. Bolton BL1 143 E2
Clyde St. Dukinfield OL7 100 F8
Clyde St. Leigh WN7 76 B4
Clyde St. Oldham OL1 & OL4 49 C1
Clyde Terr. M26 43 F5
Clydesdale Gdns. M11 83 A1
Clydesdale Rise. OL3 51 D5
Clydesdale St. OL8 66 E4
Clyne House. M32 96 F4
Clyne St. M32 96 F5
Clysbarton Ct. SK7 123 D1
Co-operation St. M35 83 F8
Co-operative St. Hazel Grove SK7 124 E3
Co-operative St. 5 Leigh WN7 75 D5
Co-operative St. Oldham OL4 67 F5
Co-operative St. 3 Radcliffe M26 44 A4
Co-operative St. Salford M6 154 F2
Co-operative St. Shaw OL2 149 B7
Co-operative St. Uppermill OL3 69 B8
Co-operative St. Walkden M38 59 E5
Coach House Dr. WN6 36 B6
Coach La. OL11 29 E5
Coach Rd. Hollingworth SK14 103 B5
Coach Rd. Tyldesley M29 77 C6
Coach St. M46 58 D3
Coal Pit La. Atherton M46 58 B3
Coal Pit La. Atherton M46 58 B4
Coal Pit La. Leigh WN2 57 B1
Coal Pit La. 4 Leigh WN7 75 E8
Coal Pit La. Oldham OL8 66 E1
Coal Pit La. Oldham M35, OL8 84 D8
Coal Pit Rd. BL1 23 D7
Coal Rd. BL0 & OL12 12 C8
Coalbrook Wlk. M12 164 E8
Coalburn St. M12 165 A6
Coalshaw Green Rd. OL9 66 A3
Coatbridge St. M11 83 C1
Cob Hall Rd. M32 96 C1
Cob Moor Ave. WN5 53 D1
Cob Moor Rd. WN5 53 D1
Cobal Ct. SK2 124 A5
Cobalt Ave. M41 95 F6
Cobb Cl. M8 63 E3
Cobbett's Way. SK9 136 F4
Cobble Bank. M9 64 D3
Cobden Ctr The. M6 154 F1
Cobden St. 2 Ashton-u-L OL6 85 D2
Cobden St. Bacup OL13 4 B8
Cobden St. Bolton BL7 8 D2
Cobden St. Bolton BL1 143 D3
Cobden St. Bury BL9 141 A3
Cobden St. Heywood OL10 29 D1
Cobden St. M'ster M9 64 E1
Cobden St. Newton-l-W WA12 89 D4
Cobden St. Oldham OL4 49 D1
Cobden St. Oldham OL9 152 B7
Cobden St. Radcliffe M26 43 F6
Cobden St. Salford M6 81 A4
Cobden St. 13 Tyldesley M29 59 A1
Coberley Ave. M41 94 F4
Cobham Ave. Bolton BL3 147 D3
Cobham Ave. M'ster M40 65 C2
Coblers Hill. OL3 50 F5
Cobourg St. M1 163 B8
Coburg Ave. M7 158 D4
Cochrane Ave. M12 164 E5
Cochrane St. BL3 145 F5
Cock Brow. SK14 114 C7
Cock Clod St. M26 44 C3
Cock Hall La. Whitworth OL12 14 C8
Cockcroft Rd. M6 81 B2
Cockcroft St. M9 64 D1
Cocker Hill. SK15 86 B2
Cocker Mill La. Royton OL2 48 F5
Cocker Mill La. Shaw OL2 149 A5
Cocker St. M38 60 A4
Cockerell Springs. 1 BL2 148 A6
Cockers La. SK15 102 D8
Cockey Moor Rd. BL2 & BL8 26 E1
Cockhall La. OL12 4 C1
Codale Dr. BL2 25 F1
Coddington Ave. M11 99 E8
Code La. BL5 39 B4
Cody Ct. M5 96 E8
Coe St. BL3 145 F5
Coghlan Cl. M11 83 B2
Cohen St. M10 & M40 157 E5
Cojeton House. M9 64 F5
Coke St. M7 155 F8
Colborne Ave. Eccles M30 79 B2
Colborne Ave. Reddish M34 99 F3
Colborne Ave. Romiley SK6 113 C2
Colbourne Ave. M8 63 F1
Colbourne Gr. SK14 102 E3
Colbourne Way. SK14 102 E3
Colburn Cl. WN3 55 A2
Colby Rd. WN3 55 B3
Colby Wlk. M40 83 A7
Colchester Ave. Bolton BL2 42 E8
Colchester Ave. M'ster M25 63 C2
Colchester Cl. M23 108 E1
Colchester Dr. BL4 42 A1
Colchester Pl. SK4 168 C3
Colchester St. M10 & M40 160 D4
Colchester Wlk. 1 OL1 153 F7
Colclough Cl. M40 83 B6
Cold Greave Cl. OL16 32 C4
Coldalhurst La. M29 77 B5
Coldfield Dr. M23 120 F6
Coldhurst St. OL1 153 E8
Coldstone Dr. WN4 72 D4
Coldstream Ave. M9 64 D4
Cole Ave. WA12 89 C4
Cole St. M40 & M9 157 F8
Colebrook Dr. M40 83 A6
Colebrook Rd. WA15 120 A6
Coleby Ave. M'ster M16 97 C4
Coleby Ave. Wythenshawe M22 121 F1
Coleclough Pl. WA3 91 F4
Coledale Dr. M24 46 C2
Coleford Gr. BL1 145 E6
Colemore Ave. M20 110 D3
Colenso Ct. 4 BL2 148 C7
Colenso Gr. SK4 168 B3
Colenso Rd. BL2 42 D7
Colenso St. OL8 66 D3
Coleport Cl. SK8 123 A1
Coleridge Ave. Middleton M24 47 C3
Coleridge Ave.Radcliffe M26 43 E4
Coleridge Ave.Wigan WN5 54 A6
Coleridge Cl. SK5 99 E1
Coleridge Pl. WN3 54 F3
Coleridge Rd. Littleborough OL15 15 F2
Coleridge Rd. M'ster M16 97 C3
Coleridge Rd. Oldham OL1 49 E4
Coleridge Rd. Orrell WN5 53 D1
Coleridge Rd. Ramsbottom BL8 10 F2
Coleridge Rd. Reddish SK5 99 E1
Coleridge Way. SK5 99 E1
Colerne Way. WN3 54 D2
Colesbourne Cl. M38 60 A6
Coleshill Rise. WN3 54 C2
Coleshill St. M10 & M40 160 E3
Colesmere Wlk. M40 65 D1
Colgate Cres. M14 110 B8
Colgate La. M5 161 A6
Colgrove Ave. M40 65 C2
Colin Rd. SK4 169 E4
Colin St. WN1 37 D1
Colindale Ave. M9 64 E4
Colindale Cl. 7 BL3 144 C5
Colinton Cl. BL1 143 D1
Colinwood Cl. BL9 44 F3
Coll Dr. M41 95 D5
Coll's La. OL3 50 D4
Collard St. M46 58 B4
College Ave. Droylsden M43 99 F8
College Ave. Oldham OL8 66 D3
College Ave. Wigan WN1 150 C8
College Cl. Bolton BL3 145 E6
College Cl. Stockport SK2 124 A6
College Cl. Wilmslow SK9 136 F8
College Croft. 10 M30 79 F2
College Dr. M16 97 C2
College House. SK4 168 B4
College Land. M3 158 F1
College Rd. Eccles M30 80 A2
College Rd. M'ster M16 97 D2
College Rd. Oldham OL8 66 E4
College Rd. Orrell WN8 35 B1
College Rd. R'dale OL11 & OL12 139 E7
College St. WN7 76 A5
College Way. BL3 145 E6
Collen Cres. BL8 27 C6
Collet Cl. WN1 151 E8
Collett St. OL1 & OL4 67 C8
Colley St. R'dale OL16 15 B1
Colley St. Stretford M32 96 F5
Collie Ave. M6 & M7 81 C5
Collier Ave. OL16 31 F7
Collier Cl. SK14 102 E1
Collier Hill. OL8 66 D3
Collier Hill Ave. OL8 66 C3
Collier St. Glossop SK13 116 C8
Collier St. Hindley WN2 56 D6
Collier St. M'ster M3 158 E2
Collier St. M'ster M3 162 E8
Collier St. Salford M6 80 F6
Collier St. 6 Swinton M27 79 E7
Collier Wlk. 4 SK14 102 E1
Collier's Row. BL1 23 E5
Colliers Row Rd. BL1 23 E5
Colliery La. M46 58 A4
Colliery St. M'ster M11 83 A1
Colliery St. M'ster M11 165 B8
Collin Ave. M18 99 C4
Collin Cl. M44 94 A1
Colling St. BL0 138 B5
Collingburn Ave. M5 161 B7
Collingburn Ct. M5 161 B7
Collinge Ave. M24 65 C8
Collinge St. Bury BL8 27 B4
Collinge St. Heywood OL10 29 C2
Collinge St. Middleton M24 65 D7
Collinge St. Platt Bridge WN2 56 A2
Collinge St. Shaw OL2 149 B7
Collingham St. M8 159 B4
Collings St. BL1 143 E2
Collington Cl. M12 165 A5
Collingwood Ave. M43 83 E3
Collingwood Cl. SK12 134 A3
Collingwood Dr. M27 80 B7
Collingwood Rd. M'ster M19 98 F1
Collingwood Rd. Newton-l-W WA12 89 B3
Collingwood St. Middleton OL11 47 D8
Collingwood St. Standish WN6 19 E1
Collingwood Way. Oldham OL1 153 F8
Collingwood Way. Westhoughton BL5 39 E1
Collins La. BL5 57 F6
Collins St. BL8 26 F4
Collisdene Rd. WN5 53 E6
Collop Dr. OL10 46 E7
Collyhurst Ave. 2 M28 60 E2
Collyhurst Rd. M40 156 C5
Collyhurst St. M10 & M40 160 D4
Colman Gdns. M5 161 B7
Colmore Dr. M9 65 A4
Colmore Gr. BL2 25 B4
Colmore St. BL2 25 B3
Colnbrook. WN6 19 B1
Colne St. OL11 30 D1
Colonial Rd. SK2 124 A6
Colshaw Cl E. M26 43 F4
Colshaw Cl S. M26 43 F4
Colshaw Cty Prim Sch. SK9 131 D1
Colshaw Dr. SK9 131 D2
Colshaw Rd. M23 121 A4
Colshaw Wlk. SK9 131 D1
Colson Dr. M24 64 F7
Colsterdale Cl. OL2 48 E5
Colt Hill La. Uppermill OL3 68 F8
Colt Hill La. Uppermill OL3 69 A6
Coltness Wlk. 12 M40 83 C5
Coltsfoot Dr. WA14 119 B8
Columbia Ave. M18 & M34 99 F4
Columbia Rd. BL1 144 C8
Columbia St. OL8 66 F4
Columbine Cl. OL12 14 C3
Columbine St. M11 & M18 99 D7
Columbine Wlk. 8 M31 105 F3
Columbus St. 2 WN4 72 F5
Colville Dr. BL8 27 B1
Colville Gr. Alt'ham WA15 120 A6
Colville Gr. Sale M33 107 E1
Colville Rd. OL1 48 D1
Colwell Ave. M32 96 B1
Colwell Wlk. M9 64 B5
Colwick Ave. WA14 119 E6
Colwith Ave. BL2 25 E1
Colwood Wlk. 15 M8 155 F6
Colwyn Ave. M'ster M14 110 D8
Colwyn Ave. Middleton M24 65 A6
Colwyn Cres. SK5 111 F5
Colwyn Dr. WN2 57 C2
Colwyn Gr. M46 58 C5
Colwyn Rd. Bramhall SK7 132 F8
Colwyn Rd. Cheadle SK8 122 E1
Colwyn Rd. Swinton M27 79 C6
Colwyn St. Ashton-u-L OL7 85 A6
Colwyn St. Oldham OL9 153 D7
Colwyn St. R'dale OL11 30 B2
Colwyn St. Salford M6 154 F3
Colyton Wlk. 7 M22 121 F3
Combe Cl. M11 83 B3
Combermere Ave. M20 110 A7
Combermere Cl. SK8 122 F4
Combermere St. Dukinfield SK16 166 C1
Combs Bank. 1 SK13 171 D1
Combs Fold. 42 SK13 171 D2
Combs Gdns. 10 SK13 171 D1
Combs Gr. 43 SK13 171 D2
Combs Lea. 11 SK13 171 D1
Combs Mews. SK13 171 D1
Combs Terr. 2 SK13 171 D1
Combs Way. 41 SK13 171 D2
Comer Terr. M33 108 A4
Comet Rd. WN5 54 C8
Comet St. M1 159 B1
Commercial Ave. SK8 131 F5
Commercial Brow. SK14 167 E4
Commercial Rd. Hazel Grove SK7 124 E3
Commercial Rd.Oldham OL1 153 F6
Commercial St. Bacup OL13 3 D8
Commercial St. Hyde SK14 167 E3
Commercial St. M'ster M15 162 E7
Commercial St. Oldham OL9 152 C6
Commodore Pl. WN5 36 E1
Common End. PR7 20 E5
Common La. Culcheth WA3 91 E4
Common La. Leigh WN7 75 B4
Common La. Partington M31 106 B5
Common La. Partington M31 106 D4
Common La. Tyldesley M29 59 A1
Common Nook. WN2 56 A6
Common Side Rd. M28 77 F7
Common St. BL5 57 B7
Common The. PR7 20 E5
Como St. 10 BL3 146 C4
Como Wlk. M18 165 B6
Compass St. M11 165 C7
Compstall Ave. M14 98 B1
Compstall Gr. 7 M18 99 E6
Compstall Rd. SK6 113 E2
Compton Cl. M41 94 C1
Compton Dr. M23 121 A2
Compton St. 5 SK15 86 B1
Compton Way.Middleton M24 65 C6
Compton Way. Shaw OL2 149 B6
Comrie Wlk. 7 M23 121 A5
Comus St. M5 161 C8
Concert La. M60 159 A1
Concord Ave. WN3 55 B3
Concord Bsns Pk. M22 121 E1
Concord Pl. M6 81 A5
Concord Way. 1 SK16 101 D8
Conder Pl. WN2 55 F2
Condor Cl. M43 84 C3
Condor Pl. M6 81 A5
Condor Trad Est. OL9 153 D8
Condor Wlk. M13 163 B6
Conduit St. Ashton-u-L OL6 166 C2
Conduit St. Hollingworth SK14 103 F7
Conduit St. Oldham OL1 49 E3
Conewood Wlk. 9 M13 163 C6
Coney Gr. M23 121 A7
Coney Green High Sch. M26 44 B4
Coneymead. SK15 86 A4
Congham Rd. 6 SK3 123 C8
Congleton Ave. M14 98 A2
Congleton Rd. SK9 137 A1
Congou St. M'ster M1 163 C8
Congreave St. OL1 153 E8
Congresbury Rd. WN7 75 D7
Conifer Wlk. Leigh WN7 75 B5
Conifer Wlk. Partington M31 105 E3
Coningsby Dr. M9 157 D8
Conisber Cl. BL7 8 E1
Conisborough. OL11 139 E6
Conisborough Pl. M45 63 B7
Coniston Ave. Adlington PR6 21 B8
Coniston Ave. Ashton-i-M WN4 73 B4
Coniston Ave. Atherton M46 58 D5
Coniston Ave. Dukinfield SK14 101 C4
Coniston Ave. Farnworth BL4 59 F8
Coniston Ave. Ince-i-M WN2 56 B7
Coniston Ave. M'ster M9 157 D8
Coniston Ave. Oldham OL8 66 D4
Coniston Ave. Orrell WN5 53 F7
Coniston Ave. Sale M33 108 C2
Coniston Ave. Walkden M38 60 A4
Coniston Ave. Whitefield M45 62 F8
Coniston Ave. Wigan WN1 37 C3
Coniston Cl. Chadderton OL9 152 A7
Coniston Cl. Little Lever BL3 43 A4
Coniston Cl. Ramsbottom BL0 138 C7
Coniston Cl. Reddish M34 100 B2
Coniston Dr. Abram WN2 74 B8
Coniston Dr. Bury BL9 44 E7
Coniston Dr. Handforth SK9 131 C4
Coniston Dr. Middleton M24 46 F2
Coniston Dr. Stalybridge SK15 86 A3
Coniston Gr. Ashton-u-L OL7 166 A4
Coniston Gr. Heywood OL10 46 D8
Coniston Gr. Royton OL2 48 D6
Coniston Gr. Walkden M38 60 A4
Coniston House. 6 M28 60 E2
Coniston Park Dr. WN6 37 A6
Coniston Rd. Blackrod BL6 21 D3
Coniston Rd. Flixton M31 & M41 106 E8
Coniston Rd. Gatley SK8 122 B5
Coniston Rd. High Lane SK6 134 D8
Coniston Rd. Hindley WN2 56 E4
Coniston Rd. Partington M44 105 E4
Coniston Rd. Reddish SK5 111 F6
Coniston Rd. Stretford M32 96 C3
Coniston Rd. Swinton M27 79 F7
Coniston Rd. Tyldesley M29 77 A7
Coniston St. Bolton BL1 143 F3
Coniston St. 6 Failsworth M40 83 C5
Coniston St. Leigh WN7 75 E5
Coniston St. Salford M6 81 B4
Coniston Wlk. WA15 120 D5
Conmere Sq. 5 M15 162 F7
Connaught Ave. M'ster M19 110 F7
Connaught Ave. R'dale OL11 & OL16 31 B3
Connaught Ave. Whitefield M45 63 A7
Connaught Cl. SK9 137 C8
Connaught Dr. WA12 89 C2
Connaught Sq. BL2 25 B2
Connaught St. Bury BL8 27 B1
Connaught St. 4 Oldham OL9 153 E6
Connel Cl. BL2 42 F6
Connell Rd. M23 121 A6
Connell Way. OL10 29 F3
Connery Cres. OL6 85 D6
Connie St. M11 165 C8
Connington Ave. M9 64 D1
Connington Cl. OL2 48 C4
Connor Way. M22 121 F4
Conquest Cl. M'ster M12 165 A6
Conrad Cl. Oldham OL1 49 E4
Conrad Cl. Wigan WN3 150 A5
Conran St. M9 157 E7
Conroy Way. WA12 89 C1
Consett Ave. M23 121 A6
Consort Ave. OL2 48 C6
Consort Cl. 2 SK16 101 C6
Consort Pl. WA14 119 B3
Constable Cl. BL1 143 D1
Constable Dr. Marple SK6 126 B8
Constable Dr. Wilmslow SK9 137 E8
Constable St. M18 99 E6
Constable Wlk. 13 M34 113 A7
Constance Gdns. M6 154 F1
Constance Rd. Bolton BL3 146 C4
Constance Rd. Partington M31 105 F3
Constance St. M15 162 E7
Constantia St. WN2 55 F3
Constantine Ct. M6 81 B3
Constantine Rd. OL16 139 F7
Constantine St. OL4 67 D7
Consul St. M22 109 E1
Convamore Rd. SK7 132 D7
Convent St. OL8 67 C4
Conway Ave. Bolton BL1 142 A1
Conway Ave. Irlam M44 105 F8
Conway Ave. Swinton M27 62 B3
Conway Ave. Whitefield M45 62 F7
Conway Cl. Heywood OL10 29 A3
Conway Cl. Leigh WN7 76 E7
Conway Cl. M'ster M16 97 A3
Conway Cl. Middleton M24 65 A7
Conway Cl. Ramsbottom BL0 138 B6
Conway Cl. Whitefield M45 62 F7
Conway Cres. Billinge WN5 71 E6
Conway Cres. Ramsbottom BL8 10 F2
Conway Dr. Alt'ham WA15 120 C6
Conway Dr. Aspull WN2 38 D5
Conway Dr. Billinge WN5 71 F5
Conway Dr. Bury BL9 28 D2
Conway Dr. Hazel Grove SK7 124 C1
Conway Dr. Newton-l-W WA12 89 E3
Conway Dr. Stalybridge SK15 86 A3
Conway Gr. OL9 47 F1
Conway Rd. Ashton-i-M WN4 73 E5
Conway Rd. Cheadle SK8 122 E2
Conway Rd. Hindley WN2 56 F4
Conway Rd. Sale M33 108 D3
Conway Rd. Urmston M41 95 D4
Conway St. Farnworth BL4 60 D7
Conway St. Reddish SK5 169 E4
Conway St. Wigan WN5 54 C5
Conyngham Rd. M14 98 D3
Cook St. Abram WN2 56 B1
Cook St. Bury BL9 141 A2
Cook St. Denton M34 100 F6
Cook St. Eccles M30 79 C2
Cook St. Leigh WN7 75 F5
Cook St. M'ster M3 158 E2
Cook St. Oldham OL4 67 C7
Cook St. R'dale OL12 & OL16 15 B1
Cook St. Stockport SK3 169 E1
Cook Terr. 21 Dukinfield SK16 166 B1
Cook Terr. R'dale OL16 15 B1
Cooke St. Ashton-i-M WN4 72 F6
Cooke St. Denton M34 100 F3
Cooke St. Dukinfield SK14 101 F5
Cooke St. Failsworth M35 83 F8
Cooke St. Farnworth BL4 60 E7
Cooke St. Hazel Grove SK7 124 D3
Cooke St. Horwich BL6 22 D4
Cooling La. M46 & WN7 76 E8
Coomassie St. Heywood OL10 29 C1
Coomassie St. Radcliffe M26 44 A3
Coomassie St. Salford M6 154 F3
Coombe Cl. M29 77 B8
Coombes Ave. Hyde SK14 167 F1
Coombes Ave. Marple SK6 125 F5
Coombes La. SK14 115 C5
Coombes St. SK2 124 B5
Coombes View. SK14 114 F8
Coop St. Bolton BL1 143 E4
Coop St. 1 M'ster M4 159 B2
Coop St. Wigan WN1 37 D1
Cooper Fold. M24 47 A4
Cooper House. M15 163 A6
Cooper La. M'ster M9 64 D5
Cooper La. Middleton M24 46 F3
Cooper St. Bolton BL1 143 F1

Cooper St. Bury BL9 .... 140 E2
Cooper St. Dukinfield SK16 . 166 B1
Cooper St. Glossop SK13 ..... 104 B1
Cooper St. Hazel Grove SK7 . 124 F3
Cooper St. Horwich BL6 .... 22 B4
Cooper St. Littleborough OL16 15 D4
Cooper St. M'ster M2 .... 158 F1
Cooper St. Oldham OL4 .... 68 A7
Cooper St. Stockport SK1 ...... 170 F7
Cooper St. Stretford M32 ...... 96 D1
Cooper Terr. OL16 .... 31 B8
Cooper's La. PR7 .... 18 B8
Cooper's Row. BL1 .... 145 F7
Cooperative St. OL14 .... 6 A7
Coopers Glen. WN2 .... 56 A8
Coopers Row. WN1 .... 150 C8
Cop Rd. OL1 & OL2 .... 49 C4
Copage Dr. SK6 .... 113 A4
Cope Bank. 12 BL1 .... 142 C2
Cope Bank W. BL1 .... 142 B2
Cope Cl. M18 .... 99 E7
Cope St. BL1 .... 142 C1
Copeland Ave. M27 .... 62 C1
Copeland Cl. M24 .... 46 C1
Copeland Dr. WN6 .... 19 F1
Copeland Mews. BL1 .... 144 A7
Copeland St. SK14 .... 101 D5
Copeman Cl. M13 .... 163 C6
Copenhagen Sq. 20 OL16 ..... 31 A8
Copenhagen St.
Failsworth M40 .... 83 A6
Copenhagen St. R'dale OL16 31 A8
Copesthorne Cl. WN2 .... 38 C6
Copgrove Rd. M21 .... 109 B7
Copgrove Wlk. M22 .... 130 E7
Copley Ave. SK15 .... 86 C2
Copley High Sch. SK15 .... 86 D2
Copley Park Mews. SK15 ...... 86 C2
Copley Rd. M21 .... 97 A2
Copley St. OL2 .... 149 C8
Copper La. M45 .... 62 B7
Copperas Cl. WN6 .... 36 E7
Copperas La. Aspull WN2 ...... 38 A6
Copperas La. Blackrod BL6 .... 21 B1
Copperas La. Droylsden M43 99 E8
Copperas St. M4 .... 159 A2
Copperbeech. M22 .... 109 E1
Copperbeech Dr. WN6 .... 37 B7
Copperfield. WN1 .... 37 C2
Copperfield Rd.
Bramhall SK8 .... 132 B5
Copperfield Rd.
Poynton SK12 .... 133 D2
Copperfields. Bolton BL6 ...... 40 B3
Copperfields. Poynton SK12 133 D2
Copperfields. Wilmslow SK9 137 C8
Copperways. M20 .... 110 B5
Coppice Ave. M33 .... 107 D2
Coppice Cl. High Lane SK12 135 A6
Coppice Cl. Romiley SK6 ..... 113 B4
Coppice Dr. High Lane SK12 135 A6
Coppice Dr. Orrell WN5 .... 53 D2
Coppice Dr. Whitworth OL12 . 14 D7
Coppice Dr. Wigan WN3 .... 54 F2
Coppice Dr.
Wythenshawe M22 .... 109 D1
Coppice Inf Sch. OL8 .... 66 E4
Coppice Jun Sch. OL8 .... 66 E4
Coppice La. SK12 .... 135 A5
Coppice Rd. SK12 .... 134 B3
Coppice St. Bury BL9 .... 141 C3
Coppice St. Oldham OL8 ...... 153 D5
Coppice The. Alt'ham WA15 129 B8
Coppice The. Bolton BL2 ...... 25 D5
Coppice The. Middleton M24 65 B5
Coppice The.
Ramsbottom BL0 .... 11 A4
Coppice The. Swinton M28 .... 79 C5
Coppice The. Worsley M28 .... 78 F8
Coppice Vale. BL0 .... 11 C3
Coppice Way. SK9 .... 131 E3
Coppice Wlk. M34 .... 100 D2
Copping St. M12 .... 164 F6
Coppingford Cl. OL12 .... 14 A2
Coppins The. SK9 .... 136 E4
Coppleridge Dr. M8 .... 64 A2
Copplestone Ct. M27 .... 61 C1
Copplestone Dr. M33 .... 107 C5
Coppull Cross Rds. PR7 .... 19 F7
Coppull Hall La. PR7 .... 20 B8
Coppull La. WN1 .... 37 D2
Coppull Moor La. PR7 .... 19 E6
Copse Ave. M22 .... 121 E3
Copse Dr. BL9 .... 27 F6
Copse The. Alt'ham WA15 .... 129 D7
Copse The. Edgworth BL7 .... 9 C2
Copse The. Marple SK6 ...... 126 C8
Copse The.
Newton-l-W WA12 .... 89 B4
Copse Wlk. OL15 .... 15 F5
Copson St. M20 .... 110 B7
Copster Ave. OL8 .... 66 E3
Copster Hill Rd. OL8 .... 66 E4
Copster Pl. OL8 .... 66 E3
Copthall La. M7 & M8 .... 155 F8
Copthorn Wlk. BL8 .... 26 F5
Copthorne Cl. OL10 .... 46 D8
Copthorne Cres. M13 .... 98 E3
Copthorne Dr. BL2 .... 42 E6
Coptrod Head Cl. OL12 .... 14 E4
Coral Ave. Cheadle SK8 .... 123 A1
Coral Ave. Platt Bridge WN2 .. 56 A2
Coral Gr. WN7 .... 75 E4
Coral Rd. SK8 .... 123 A1
Coral St. M'ster M13 .... 163 C7
Coral St. Wigan WN6 .... 37 A3
Coralin Way. WN4 .... 72 F7
Coram St. M18 .... 99 F6
Corbar Rd. SK2 .... 124 B5
Corbett St. M'ster M11 .... 83 A1
Corbett St. R'dale OL16 .... 31 B8
Corby St. M12 .... 165 A6
Corcoran Cl. OL10 .... 29 C3
Corcoran Dr. SK6 .... 113 F2
Corda Ave. M22 .... 121 D8
Corday La. M25 .... 63 D8
Cordingley Ave. M43 .... 99 F8
Cordova Ave. M34 .... 99 F3
Corelli St. M10 & M40 .... 160 F4
Corfe Cl. Aspull WN2 .... 38 D5
Corfe Cl. Urmston M41 .... 94 C1
Corfe Cres. SK7 .... 124 D1
Corhampton Cres. M46 .... 58 E5
Corinth Wlk. M28 .... 60 D2
Corinthian Ave. M7 .... 81 C5
Cork St. Ashton-u-L OL6 ...... 166 C3
Cork St. Bury BL9 .... 141 A2
Cork St. M'ster M12 .... 164 D8
Corkland Cl. OL6 .... 85 E2
Corkland Rd. M'ster M21 ..... 109 C8
Corkland St. OL6 .... 85 E2
Corks La. SK12 .... 135 E5
Corley Ave. SK3 .... 122 F7
Cormallen Gr. M35 .... 84 A7
Cormorant Cl. M28 .... 60 C3
Cormorant Wlk. M12 .... 165 A6
Corn Cl. M13 .... 163 C5
Corn Hey Rd. M33 .... 107 C2
Corn Hill La. M34 .... 100 B5
Corn Mill Cl. OL12 .... 15 C4
Corn St. Failsworth M35 .... 83 C6
Corn St. Glossop SK13 .... 104 D1
Corn St. Leigh WN7 .... 75 D5
Corn St. Oldham OL4 .... 67 A7
Cornall St. BL8 .... 27 C3
Cornbrook Cl. OL12 .... 15 C6
Cornbrook Ct. M15 .... 162 D6
Cornbrook Gr. M16 .... 162 D5
Cornbrook Park Rd. M15 . 161 C6
Cornbrook Rd. M15 .... 161 C7
Cornbrook St. M16 .... 162 D5
Cornbrook Wlk. M16 .... 162 D5
Cornelian Gr. WN4 .... 72 F5
Cornell St. M4 .... 159 B2
Corner Croft. SK9 .... 137 A4
Corner Ct. SK8 .... 122 F6
Corner La. WN2 & WN7 .... 57 D3
Corner St. OL6 .... 166 C2
Cornergate. BL5 .... 57 E5
Cornet St. M7 .... 155 D5
Cornfield. SK15 .... 102 E7
Cornfield Cl. Bury BL9 .... 27 F7
Cornfield Cl. 2 Sale M33 .... 108 F3
Cornfield Dr. M22 .... 121 C3
Cornfield Rd. SK6 .... 113 E3
Cornfield St. OL16 .... 32 A5
Cornford Ave. M18 .... 99 B3
Cornhill Ave. M41 .... 95 B3
Cornhill Rd. M41 .... 95 B3
Cornhill St. OL1 & OL4 .... 49 D2
Cornish Way. OL2 .... 49 A4
Cornishway. M22 .... 130 D8
Cornishway Ind Est.
3 M22 .... 130 D8
Cornlea Dr. M28 .... 78 C7
Cornwall Ave. Atherton BL5 .. 58 F8
Cornwall Ave. M'ster M19 .. 111 B8
Cornwall Ave. Tyldesley M29 59 A3
Cornwall Cl. SK6 .... 134 E7
Cornwall Cres.
Brinnington SK5 .... 112 C6
Cornwall Cres. Diggle OL3 .... 51 B4
Cornwall Cres. Standish WN1 20 B1
Cornwall Ct. 2 M18 .... 99 D6
Cornwall Dr. Bury BL9 .... 45 A8
Cornwall Dr. Hindley WN2 ..... 56 F6
Cornwall House. M3 .... 158 D1
Cornwall Pl. WN5 .... 54 C6
Cornwall Rd. Droylsden M43 . 84 A3
Cornwall Rd. Gatley SK8 ..... 131 B8
Cornwall Rd. Irlam M44 .... 105 D5
Cornwall St. 2 Eccles M30 ... 79 C1
Cornwall St. M'ster M11, M18 99 D7
Cornwall St. Oldham OL9 .... 152 B5
Cornwallis Rd. WN3 .... 150 A5
Cornwell Cl. SK9 .... 137 D8
Cornwood Cl. 5 M8 .... 155 F7
Corona Ave. Hyde SK14 ...... 167 E3
Corona Ave. Oldham OL8 ...... 66 E3
Coronation Ave.
Atherton M46 .... 58 C5
Coronation Ave.
Dukinfield SK16 .... 101 F6
Coronation Ave.
Glazebury WA3 .... 92 C7
Coronation Ave.
Heywood OL10 .... 46 E8
Coronation Ave. Hyde SK14 167 E1
Coronation Dr. Leigh WN7 .... 76 E6
Coronation Dr.
Newton-l-W WA11 .... 89 A7
Coronation Dr.
Newton-l-W WA12 .... 89 E1
Coronation Gdns. M26 .... 43 E4
Coronation Rd.
Ashton-u-L OL6 .... 85 C6
Coronation Rd.
Droylsden M43 .... 83 F3
Coronation Rd.
Failsworth M35 .... 83 E6
Coronation Rd. Radcliffe M26 43 E4
Coronation Rd. Wigan WN6 .. 36 D3
Coronation Sq.
Little Lever BL3 .... 43 B3
Coronation Sq. M'ster M12 163 C8
Coronation St. Bolton BL1 ... 145 F7
Coronation St. Denton M34 100 D3
Coronation St.
Garswood WN4 .... 72 D6
Coronation St. Ince-i-M WN2 55 F3
Coronation St. M'ster M3 .. 162 E8
Coronation St. M'ster M11 165 C8
Coronation St. Reddish SK5 169 E4
Coronation St. Salford M5 . 161 B8
Coronation St. Swinton M27 . 62 A1
Coronation St. Wigan WN3 150 B6
Coronation Wlk.Billinge WN5 71 D4
Coronation Wlk.
Radcliffe M26 .... 43 E5
Coronation Rd.
Denton M34 .... 100 D5
Coronation Rd. Eccles M30 . 79 F1
Corporation Rd.
R'dale OL11 .... 139 D6
Corporation Rd.
R'dale OL11 .... 139 D7
Corporation St. Bolton BL1 . 145 F7
Corporation St. Hyde SK14 167 D2
Corporation St.
M'ster M4 & M60 .... 159 A2
Corporation St.
Middleton M24 .... 65 A8
Corporation St.
Stalybridge SK15 .... 86 A1
Corporation St.
Stockport SK1 .... 169 F2
Corporation St. Wigan WN3 150 B6
Corpus Christ RC
Inf & Jun Sch. OL9 .... 66 B4
Corpus Christi RC
Prim Sch. M40 .... 160 D4
Corran Cl. M30 .... 79 B2
Correction Brow. SK12 .... 134 C6
Corridge Wlk. 7 M8 .... 156 B6
Corrie Cl. M34 .... 100 F1
Corrie Cres. M26 & M27 .... 61 D4
Corrie Cty Sch. M34 .... 100 F1
Corrie Dr. M26 .... 61 D5
Corrie Rd. M27 .... 62 A3
Corrie St. M38 .... 60 A4
Corrie Way. SK6 .... 112 F5
Corrigan St. M18 .... 99 E6
Corrin Rd. BL2 .... 148 B5
Corring Way. BL1 .... 25 B4
Corringham Rd. M19 .... 111 C7
Corriss Ave. M9 .... 64 A5
Corry St. OL10 .... 29 E2
Corsey Rd. WN2 .... 56 E4
Corsock Dr. WN1 .... 37 E1
Corson St. BL4 .... 42 D2
Corston Gr. BL6 .... 21 D1
Corston Wlk. M40 .... 83 B6
Corwen Ave. M9 .... 157 E8
Corwen Cl. OL8 .... 66 B2
Cosgrove Cres. M35 .... 83 E5
Cosgrove Rd. M35 .... 83 E5
Cosham Rd. M22 .... 121 F3
Costabeck Wlk. M40 .... 83 D4
Costessey Way. WN3 .... 54 C3
Costobadie Cl. SK14 .... 102 F3
Costobadie Way. SK14 .... 102 F3
Cosworth Cl. WN7 .... 76 B4
Cotaline Cl. OL11 .... 30 B3
Cotall Wlk. M8 .... 158 E4
Cote Green La. SK6 .... 114 B1
Cote Green Rd. SK6 .... 114 C1
Cote La. Delph OL3 .... 51 B7
Cote La. Littleborough OL15 ... 15 F6
Cote La. Uppermill OL5 .... 68 E3
Cotefield Ave. BL3 .... 147 F3
Cotefield Cl. 7 SK6 .... 125 F5
Cotefield Rd. M22 .... 121 C2
Cotford Rd. BL1 .... 24 F5
Cotham St. M3 .... 158 F4
Cotman Dr. SK6 .... 126 C8
Cotswold Ave. Golborne WA3 90 D6
Cotswold Ave.
Hazel Grove SK7 .... 124 B1
Cotswold Ave. Oldham OL9 152 A5
Cotswold Ave. Shaw OL2 ...... 48 F8
Cotswold Ave. Shaw OL2 .... 149 A8
Cotswold Ave. Urmston M41 . 94 F3
Cotswold Ave. Wigan WN5 ... 54 B5
Cotswold Cl. Glossop SK13 . 116 A8
Cotswold Cl. Prestwich M25 .. 63 C5
Cotswold Cl. Ramsbottom BL0 11 C4
Cotswold Cres. Bury BL8 ...... 27 B3
Cotswold Cres. Milnrow OL16 32 A7
Cotswold Dr. Horwich BL6 .... 22 C5
Cotswold Dr. Royton OL2 ...... 48 B3
Cotswold Dr. Salford M6 .... 154 F3
Cotswold Rd. SK4 .... 169 D3
Cottage Croft. BL2 .... 25 D5
Cottage Gdns. SK6 .... 112 D3
Cottage Hospl. M41 .... 95 D2
Cottage La. SK13 .... 171 E2
Cottage Lawns. SK9 .... 137 B2
Cottage Wlk. Droylsden M43 . 83 F3
Cottage Wlk. R'dale OL12 ..... 14 C4
Cottam Cres. SK6 .... 126 B7
Cottam Gr. M27 .... 80 A7
Cottam St. Bury BL8 .... 27 C3
Cottam St. Oldham OL1 .... 153 D8
Cottenham La. M3 & M7 ...... 158 E4
Cottenham St. M13 .... 163 B6
Cotter St. M12 .... 163 C7
Cotterdale Cl. M16 .... 97 D2
Cotteril Cl. Sale M23 .... 120 C8
Cotterill St. M5 & M6 .... 81 B2
Cottesmore Dr. M8 .... 156 C8
Cottesmore Gdns. WA15 ..... 129 C8
Cottesmore Way. WA3 .... 74 B1
Cottingham Dr. OL6 .... 166 C4
Cottingham Rd. M12 .... 164 E6
Cotton Fold. OL16 .... 31 C6
Cotton Hill. M20 .... 110 C5
Cotton La. M20 .... 110 C6
Cotton St. Bolton BL1 .... 143 D2
Cotton St. Leigh WN7 .... 75 D5
Cotton St. M'ster M4 .... 159 B2
Cotton St E. OL6 & OL7 .... 166 B2
Cotton St W. OL7 .... 166 A2
Cotton Tree Cl. OL4 .... 67 E8
Cotton Tree St. SK3 & SK4 . 169 E1
Cottonfield Rd. M20 .... 110 C6
Cottonwood Dr. 3 M33 ...... 107 C5
Cottrell Rd. WA15 .... 129 D7
Cotts The. OL4 .... 50 B1
Coucill Sq. BL4 .... 60 E8
Coulsden Dr. M9 .... 64 D3
Coulthart St. OL6 .... 166 B3
Coulthurst St. BL0 .... 138 B6
Coultshead Ave. WN5 .... 71 E6
Counce Ave. WA12 .... 89 B1
Council Ave. WN4 .... 73 B3
Councillor La. SK8 .... 123 A4
Councillor St. M11 .... 160 E1
Count St. OL16 .... 31 A4
Countess Ave. SK8 .... 131 E5
Countess Gr. M5 & M7 .... 158 D4
Countess La. M26 .... 43 D4
Countess Pl. M25 .... 63 C4
Countess Rd. M20 .... 110 B3
Countess St. Ashton-u-L OL6 . 85 D2
Countess St. Stockport SK2 124 A5
Counthill Dr. M8 .... 63 E2
Counthill Rd. OL4 .... 49 D1
Counthill Sch. OL4 .... 49 D2
Counting House Rd. SK12 135 E5
County Ave. OL6 .... 85 E4
County Police St. WN2 .... 151 F7
County Rd. M28 .... 60 A4
County St. M'ster M2 .... 158 F1
County St. Oldham OL8 .... 66 C2
Coupes Gn. BL5 .... 57 F6
Coupland Cl. OL4 .... 49 F4
Coupland Rd. WN2 .... 57 C4
Coupland St. M'ster M15 ..... 163 A5
Coupland St. Whitworth OL12 14 C8
Courage Low La. WN6 .... 18 D5
Courier Pl. WN5 .... 36 E1
Courier St. M18 .... 99 F6
Course View. OL4 .... 67 E3
Court Dr. M40 .... 83 E4
Court House Way. 4 OL10 . 29 D2
Court St. Bolton BL2 .... 148 A7
Court St. Uppermill OL3 .... 69 B8
Courtfield Ave. M9 .... 64 D4
Courthill St. SK1 .... 124 A8
Courtney Gn. SK9 .... 131 D2
Courtney Pl. WA14 .... 119 A1
Courtyard Dr. M28 .... 60 A3
Courtyard The. SK14 .... 103 D5
Cousin Fields. BL2 .... 25 C7
Covall Wlk. 4 M8 .... 156 B6
Cove The. WA15 .... 119 F3
Covell Rd. SK12 .... 133 D5
Covent Garden. SK1 .... 169 F1
Coventry Ave. SK3 .... 122 F7
Coventry Gr. OL9 .... 48 A1
Coventry Rd. M26 .... 43 F5
Coventry St. OL11 .... 139 F6
Coverdale Ave. Bolton BL1 . 144 A8
Coverdale Ave. Royton OL2 .. 48 C5
Coverdale Cl. OL10 .... 29 C1
Coverdale Cres. M12 .... 164 E6
Coverdale Rd. BL5 .... 57 D8
Coverham Ave. OL4 .... 67 D4
Coverhill Rd. OL4 .... 68 B5
Covert Rd. Oldham OL4 .... 67 D3
Covert Rd.
Wythenshawe M22 .... 121 E5
Coverts The. WN6 .... 36 F2
Covington Pl. SK9 .... 137 B6
Cow La. Alt'ham WA15 .... 128 F6
Cow La. Bolton BL3 .... 146 B2
Cow La. Failsworth M35 .... 83 E7
Cow La. M'ster M5 .... 81 C1
Cow La. Oldham OL4 .... 67 C7
Cow La. Sale M33 .... 108 E5
Cow La. Stockport SK2 & SK7 124 D4
Cow Lees. BL5 .... 40 A1
Cowan St. M10 & M40 .... 160 D2
Cowbrook Ave. SK13 .... 104 F1
Cowburn Dr. SK12 .... 127 C1
Cowburn St. Heywood OL10 .. 29 E1
Cowburn St. Hindley WN2 ..... 56 F6
Cowburn St. 1 Leigh WN7 .... 75 D5
Cowburn St. M'ster M3 .... 158 F3
Cowdals Rd. BL6 .... 40 B4
Cowesby St. M'ster M14 .... 98 A3
Cowhill La. OL6 .... 166 C3
Cowie St. OL2 .... 149 B8
Cowley Gr. SK14 .... 102 F3
Cowley Rd. BL1 .... 24 F5
Cowley St. 9 M40 .... 83 C6
Cowley Terr. M9 .... 64 A5
Cowling St. M'ster M25 & M7 80 F8
Cowling St. Oldham OL8 .... 66 F4
Cowling St. Wigan WN3 .... 150 B6
Cowlishaw. OL2 .... 149 A5
Cowlishaw La. OL2 .... 149 A5
Cowlishaw Rd. SK14 & SK6 . 113 F4
Cowm Park Way N. OL12 .... 4 D2
Cowm Park Way S. OL12 .... 4 C1
Cowm St. OL12 .... 4 E5
Cowm Top La. OL11 .... 30 E2
Cowpe Rd. BB4 .... 2 F7
Cowper Ave. M46 .... 58 D5
Cowper St. Ashton-u-L OL6 . 166 C3
Cowper St. Leigh WN7 .... 75 D5
Cowper St. Middleton M24 .... 65 D8
Cowper Wlk. 4 M11 .... 160 F1
Cox Green Cl. BL7 .... 8 D3
Cox Green Rd. Bolton BL7 ...... 8 E2
Cox Green Rd. 2 Bolton BL7 24 F8
Coxfield. WN6 .... 35 D7
Coxton Rd. M22 .... 121 E1
Coxwold Gr. BL3 .... 146 C2
Crab Brow. M46 .... 58 B3
Crab La. M9 .... 64 B4
Crab Lane Prim Sch. M9 ...... 64 B4
Crab Tree La. M46 .... 58 D2
Crabbe St. M3 .... 159 A3
Crabtree Ave. Alt'ham WA15 129 D7
Crabtree Ave. Disley SK12 .. 135 E5
Crabtree Ct. SK12 .... 135 D6
Crabtree La. M11 .... 83 D1
Crabtree Rd. Oldham OL1 ...... 67 B8
Crabtree Rd. Wigan WN5 ...... 54 D7
Crabtree St. BL9 .... 141 B3
Craddock Rd. M33 .... 108 C2
Craddock St. 4 OL5 .... 68 C1
Cradley Ave. M11 .... 99 D8
Crag Ave. BL9 .... 11 D2
Crag Gr. WA11 .... 71 B1
Crag La. BL9 .... 11 D2
Cragg Rd. OL1 .... 48 A2
Cragie St. M7 & M8 .... 155 F5
Craig Ave. Bury BL8 .... 27 B1
Craig Ave. Urmston M41 .... 95 A3
Craig Cl. SK4 .... 168 B1
Craig Rd. M'ster M18 .... 99 C4
Craig Rd. Stockport SK4 ...... 168 B1
Craig Wlk. OL8 .... 153 E5
Craigend Dr. M9 .... 157 E7
Craighall Ave. M19 .... 110 F8
Craighall Rd. BL1 .... 24 E6
Craiglands. OL11 & OL16 .... 31 B2
Craigmore Ave. M20 .... 109 E4
Craignair Ct. M27 .... 80 C7
Craigslands Ave. M40 .... 83 A6
Craigweil Ave. M20 .... 110 D3
Craigwell Rd. M25 .... 63 E2
Craigwell Wlk. M13 .... 163 B7
Crail Pl. OL10 .... 28 F1
Cramer St. M10 & M40 .... 157 F5
Crammond Cl. M35 & M40 .... 83 D6
Cramond Cl. BL1 .... 143 D1
Crampton Dr. WA15 .... 129 C8
Crampton La. M31 .... 106 D6
Cranage Rd. M19 .... 111 B8
Cranark Cl. BL1 .... 144 A7
Cranberry Ave. Walsden OL14 . 6 B7
Cranberry Ave. Wigan WN6 .. 36 F3
Cranberry Cl. WA14 .... 119 B8
Cranberry Rd. M31 .... 105 F3
Cranberry St. OL4 .... 67 B6
Cranborne Cl. Horwich BL6 ... 22 F1
Cranborne Cl. Standish WN6 19 D1
Cranbourne Ave. SK8 .... 123 B2
Cranbourne Cl. OL7 .... 166 A4
Cranbourne Ct. SK4 .... 168 B4
Cranbourne Rd.
Ashton-u-L OL6 & OL7 .... 166 B4
Cranbourne Rd. M'ster M16 . 97 C4
Cranbourne Rd. M'ster M21 109 B8
Cranbourne Rd. M'ster SK4 168 B4
Cranbourne Rd. R'dale OL11 29 E6
Cranbourne St. M5 .... 81 C1
Cranbourne Terr. OL6 .... 85 B5
Cranbrook Ave. WN4 .... 73 A4
Cranbrook Cl. BL1 .... 143 F1
Cranbrook Dr. M25 .... 63 C2
Cranbrook Gdns. OL7 .... 166 A4
Cranbrook Rd. Reddish M34 . 99 F3
Cranbrook Rd. Swinton M28 . 79 B4
Cranbrook St.
Ashton-u-L OL7 .... 166 B4
Cranbrook St. Oldham OL4 .... 67 C6
Cranbrook St. Radcliffe M26 . 44 C5
Cranbrook Way. WN1 .... 37 B4
Cranbrook Wlk. OL9 .... 152 A6
Cranby St. 6 WN2 .... 56 D5
Crandon Ct. M27 .... 62 A1
Crandon Dr. M20 .... 122 C8
Crane St. Bolton BL3 .... 146 B3
Crane St. Coppull PR7 .... 19 D6
Crane St. M'ster M12 .... 163 C8
Cranefield Wlk. 9 M16 .... 97 F4
Cranfield Cl. M10 & M40 ..... 160 D2
Cranfield Rd. Horwich BL6 .... 39 E7
Cranfield Rd. Wigan WN3 ...... 55 A3
Cranford Ave. M'ster M20 .. 110 D4
Cranford Ave. Sale M33 .... 108 C6
Cranford Ave. Stretford M32 . 96 F3
Cranford Ave. Whitefield M45 44 E2
Cranford Cl. Pendlebury M6 .. 80 B6
Cranford Cl. Whitefield M45 .. 44 E2
Cranford Dr. M44 .... 93 F1
Cranford Gdns. Marple SK6 125 F8
Cranford Gdns. Urmston M41 94 E3
Cranford House. M30 .... 79 F3
Cranford Rd. Handforth SK9 131 A1
Cranford Rd. Urmston M41 .... 94 E3
Cranford St. BL3 .... 146 C2
Cranham Ave. WA3 .... 90 E7
Cranham Cl. Bury BL8 .... 27 B3
Cranham Cl. Walkden M38 .... 60 A6
Cranham Rd. M22 .... 121 A2
Crank Rd. WA11 & WN5 .... 71 B8
Crankwood Rd. WN2 & WN7 74 D5
Cranleigh. WN6 .... 37 A8
Cranleigh Ave. SK4 .... 110 F4
Cranleigh Cl. Blackrod BL6 ... 21 D1
Cranleigh Cl. Oldham OL4 ..... 49 E1
Cranleigh Dr. Cheadle SK8 .. 122 F6
Cranleigh Dr.
Hazel Grove SK7 .... 134 A8
Cranleigh Dr. Sale M33 .... 108 A5
Cranleigh Dr.
Sale M23 & M33 .... 108 C1
Cranleigh Dr. Tyldesley M29 . 77 B8
Cranleigh Dr. Walkden M28 .. 78 E8
Cranlington Dr. M7 & M8 ..... 155 F6
Cranmer Ct. OL10 .... 29 C1
Cranmer Rd. M20 .... 110 B4
Cranmere Ave. M18 & M19 .... 99 C2
Cranmere Dr. M33 .... 107 D2
Cranshaw St. M29 .... 77 D8
Cranstal Dr. WN2 .... 57 A5
Cranston Dr. M'ster M20 ..... 122 B8
Cranston Dr. Sale M33 .... 108 E3
Cranston Gr. M22 .... 121 F5
Cranswick St. 1 M14 .... 98 A3
Crantock Dr.Gatley SK8 ...... 131 C8
Crantock Dr.Stalybridge SK15 86 D3
Crantock St. M18 .... 99 B3
Cranwell Ave. WA3 .... 91 F4
Cranwell Dr. M19 .... 110 E4
Cranworth Ave. M29 .... 77 A6
Cranworth St. SK15 .... 86 B1
Craston Rd. M13 .... 98 E2
Craunton. 13 M30 .... 79 F2
Craven Ave. Golborne WA3 .... 90 E7
Craven Ave. Salford M5 .... 161 B8
Craven Cl. M5 .... 161 B8
Craven Ct. BL6 .... 22 D2
Craven Dr. Alt'ham WA14 ..... 119 C8
Craven Dr. Salford M5 .... 161 A7
Craven Gdns. OL11 .... 139 E5
Craven House. OL14 .... 6 A8
Craven Pl. Bolton BL1 .... 23 E2
Craven Pl. 3 Droylsden M11 83 C2
Craven Rd. Alt'ham WA14 ..... 119 C7
Craven Rd. 1 Reddish SK5 ... 111 F6
Craven St. Ashton-u-L OL6 .... 85 D5
Craven St. Bury BL9 .... 141 C3
Craven St. M'ster M5 .... 81 C1
Craven St. Oldham OL1 .... 48 E1
Craven St E. BL6 .... 22 D2
Craven Terr. M33 .... 108 C4
Cravenhurst Ave. M40 .... 83 B4
Cravenwood Prim Sch. M8 . 64 A1
Cravenwood Rd. M8 .... 156 A8
Crawford Ave. Adlington PR7 20 E5
Crawford Ave. Aspull WN2 .... 38 C5
Crawford Ave. Bolton BL2 ... 148 B6
Crawford Ave. Tyldesley M29 58 F2
Crawford Ave. Worsley M28 .. 79 A8
Crawford Cl. WN2 .... 38 C5
Crawford Sq. OL10 .... 29 A1
Crawford St. Ashton-u-L OL6 . 85 D2
Crawford St. Aspull WN2 ...... 38 C4
Crawford St. Bolton BL2 ..... 148 B6
Crawford St. Eccles M30 ...... 79 D3
Crawford St. 24
Failsworth M40 .... 83 C5
Crawford St.
R'dale OL11 & OL16 .... 31 B6
Crawford St. Walsden OL14 .... 6 B8
Crawford St. Wigan WN1 ... 150 C8
Crawley Ave. Eccles M30 ...... 80 A3
Crawley Ave.
Wythenshawe M22 .... 121 E3
Crawley Cl. M29 .... 59 C1
Crawley Gr. SK2 .... 124 B6
Crawley Way. OL9 .... 152 A6
Cray The. OL16 .... 31 E6
Cray Wlk. M13 .... 163 B7
Craydon St. M11 .... 165 C8
Crayfield Rd. M19 .... 111 B8
Crayford Rd. M40 .... 83 B4
Creaton Way. M24 .... 46 D4
Creden Ave. M22 .... 121 F3
Crediton Cl. Alt'ham WA14 . 119 B6
Crediton Cl. M'ster M15 ...... 162 F5
Crediton Dr.Bolton BL2 .... 43 A7
Crediton Dr.Platt Bridge WN2 56 A1
Crediton House. M6 .... 80 A3
Creel Cl. M9 .... 64 B4
Cremer. M30 .... 80 A2
Cresbury St. M12 .... 164 D8
Crescent. M5 .... 81 C2
Crescent Ave.
Ashton-i-M WN4 .... 73 A4
Crescent Ave. Atherton BL5 .. 59 A8
Crescent Ave. 16
Bolton BL1 .... 145 D8
Crescent Ave. Farnworth BL4 60 C6
Crescent Ave. M'ster M25 ..... 63 B2
Crescent Ave.M'ster M8 ...... 156 A8
Crescent Ave.Pendlebury M27 80 B8
Crescent Cl. Dukinfield SK16 166 C1
Crescent Cl. Stockport SK3 . 124 A5
Crescent Ct. M21 .... 96 F1
Crescent Dr. M38 .... 60 B5
Crescent Gr. Cheadle SK8 ... 122 C6
Crescent Gr. M'ster M25 ...... 63 B2
Crescent Gr. 6 M'ster M19 .. 99 A1
Crescent Pk. SK4 .... 168 C2
Crescent Range. M14 .... 98 C3
Crescent Rd.
Alderley Edge SK9 .... 137 B2
Crescent Rd. Alt'ham WA14 119 A6
Crescent Rd. Alt'ham WA15 119 E1
Crescent Rd. Bolton BL3 .... 42 B3
Crescent Rd. Cheadle SK8 .. 122 C6
Crescent Rd. Dukinfield SK16166 C1
Crescent Rd. Failsworth OL9 . 65 E2
Crescent Rd. Horwich BL6 .... 39 F8
Crescent Rd. Kearsley BL4 .... 60 F6
Crescent Rd.
M'ster M8 & M7 .... 156 A8
Crescent Rd. R'dale OL11 ...... 30 B4
Crescent Rd. Stockport SK1 112 B3
Crescent St. M8 .... 156 C8
Crescent The. Alt'ham WA14119 A5
Crescent The. Alt'ham WA15119 F7
Crescent The. Bolton BL7 ...... 25 A7
Crescent The. Bolton BL2 ...... 25 F4
Crescent The. Bredbury SK6 112 D4
Crescent The. Bury BL9 .... 141 A3
Crescent The. Cheadle SK8 122 D6
Crescent The. Droylsden M43 83 F1
Crescent The. Horwich BL6 ... 22 E1
Crescent The. Ince-i-M WN2 . 56 B7
Crescent The. Irlam M44 .... 94 B3
Crescent The. Little Lever BL3 43 B2
Crescent The. 4 M'ster M19 99 A1
Crescent The. Middleton M24 64 E8
Crescent The. Mossley OL5 ... 68 B1
Crescent The. Prestwich M25 63 B4
Crescent The. Radcliffe M26 . 43 D5
Crescent The. Shaw OL2 .... 149 A6
Crescent The.
Stalybridge SK15 .... 102 D6
Crescent The. Stockport SK3 124 A4
Crescent The. Urmston M41 . 94 F3
Crescent The.
Westhoughton BL5 .... 57 E7
Crescent The.
Whitworth OL12 .... 14 C8
Crescent The. Wigan WN5 .... 54 D6
Crescent The. Worsley M28 .. 79 A5
Crescent View. 12 SK16 .... 166 B1
Crescent Way. SK3 .... 124 A5
Cresgarth House. SK3 .... 124 A4
Cressell Pk. WN6 .... 19 B1
Cressfield Way. M21 .... 109 D7
Cressingham Rd.Bolton BL3 146 A4
Cressingham Rd.
Stretford M32 .... 96 B2
Cressington Cl. 4 M5 & M6 154 E2
Cresswell Gr. M20 .... 110 A5
Crest Lodge. SK7 .... 123 F2
Crest St. M3 .... 159 A3
Crest The. M34 & M43 .... 100 A7
Crestfold. M28 .... 60 A4
Crestwood Ave. WN3 .... 54 F3
Crestwood Wlk. M40 .... 156 C6
Crete St. OL8 .... 66 F4
Crewe Rd. M23 .... 120 E8
Crib Fold. OL3 .... 51 A2
Crib La. OL3 .... 51 A2
Criccieth Ave. WN2 .... 38 D5
Criccieth Rd. SK3 .... 123 A7
Criccieth Way. 2 M21 .... 97 F4
Cricket Gr The. M21 .... 109 B6
Cricket St. Bolton BL3 .... 145 D5
Cricket St. Dukinfield M34 ... 101 A4
Cricket St. Wigan WN6 .... 150 B8
Cricket View. OL16 .... 31 F5
Cricket's La. OL6 .... 85 D3
Cricketers Way. BL5 .... 57 F8
Cricketfield La. M28 .... 60 C3
Cricklewood Rd. M22 .... 121 C2
Crimble La. OL10 &OL11 .... 29 F3
Crimble St. OL12 .... 139 D8
Crimbles St. OL4 .... 67 E8
Crime La. M35 & OL8 .... 84 D7

Dale Rd. Golborne WA3 90 A7
Dale Rd. Marple SK6 125 E7
Dale Rd. Middleton M24 47 B2
Dale Sq. Alt'ham WA14 119 D7
Dale Sq. Royton OL2 48 F4
Dale St. Alt'ham WA14 119 D7
Dale St. Ashton-u-L OL6 86 A6
Dale St. 8 Bacup OL13 3 C8
Dale St. Bury BL8 27 C4
Dale St. Farnworth BL4 42 E1
Dale St. Ince-i-M WN2 55 F3
Dale St. Leigh WN7 75 C5
Dale St. M'ster M1, M4, M60 159 B1
Dale St. Middleton M24 65 B7
Dale St. Milnrow OL16 31 F6
Dale St. R'dale OL16 31 C7
Dale St. Ramsbottom BL0 1 C1
Dale St. Shaw OL2 149 B6
Dale St. Stalybridge SK15 85 F1
Dale St. Stockport SK3 170 D7
Dale St. Swinton M27 79 E6
Dale St. Westhoughton BL5 57 F5
Dale St. Whitefield M45 44 E1
Dale St E. Ashton-u-L OL7 166 A2
Dale St E. Horwich BL6 22 D2
Dale St W. Ashton-u-L OL7 166 A2
Dale St W. Horwich BL6 22 D2
Dale View. Denton M34 113 A7
Dale View. Hyde SK14 113 D8
Dale View. Littleborough OL15 15 F2
Dale View. Mottram-i-L SK14 103 A3
Dale View. Newton-l-W WA12 89 E4
Dalebank. M46 58 C5
Dalebank Mews. M27 61 D5
Dalebeck Cl. M45 63 C8
Dalebeck Wlk. M45 63 C8
Dalebrook Ct. SK4 168 C1
Dalebrook Rd. M33 108 C1
Dalecrest. WN5 53 D1
Daleford Sq. M13 163 C7
Dalegarth Ave. BL1 & BL6 40 C7
Dalehead Cl. M18 99 F6
Dalehead Dr. OL2 49 D7
Dalehead Gr. WN7 75 C4
Dalehead Pl. WA11 71 B1
Dales Ave. M'ster M8 63 F2
Dales Ave. Whitefield M45 44 D1
Dales Brow. Bolton BL7 24 F6
Dales Brow. Swinton M27 79 E6
Dales Brow Ave. OL7 85 A5
Dales Gr. M28 60 F1
Dales La. M45 44 E1
Dales Park Dr. M27 79 D6
Dalesbrook Cl. BL3 43 A4
Dalesfield Cres. OL5 68 E1
Dalesford Cl. WN7 91 C8
Daleside Ave. WN4 73 A8
Dalesman Wlk. 3 M15 163 A6
Daleswood Ave. M45 44 D1
Dalham Ave. M9 65 A2
Dalkeith Ave. SK5 111 F7
Dalkeith Gr. BL3 40 F5
Dalkeith Rd. Hindley WN2 57 A5
Dalkeith Rd. Reddish SK5 111 F7
Dalkeith Sq. OL10 29 A1
Dalkeith St. M18 165 B6
Dallas Ct. M5 96 E8
Dalley Ave. M7 158 D4
Dallimore Rd. M23 120 E6
Dalmahoy Cl. M40 83 C8
Dalmain Cl. M7 & M8 155 F6
Dalmeny Terr. OL11 30 F4
Dalmorton Rd. M21 109 D8
Dalny St. M19 99 B1
Dalry Wlk. 1 M23 121 A5
Dalrybrook Gr. 7 SK9 131 E1
Dalston Ave. M35 84 B8
Dalston Dr. Billinge WA11 71 B1
Dalston Dr. Bramhall SK7 132 C5
Dalston Dr. M'ster M20 110 C2
Dalston Gr. WN3 54 D3
Dalton Ave. M'ster M14 98 A2
Dalton Ave. Milnrow OL16 31 D7
Dalton Ave. Stretford M32 96 A4
Dalton Ave. Swinton M27 62 C3
Dalton Ave. Whitefield M45 63 A7
Dalton Cl. Milnrow OL16 31 D7
Dalton Cl. Ramsbottom BL0 11 A4
Dalton Cl. Wigan WN5 54 B7
Dalton Ct. M40 159 B4
Dalton Dr. Pendlebury M27 80 D7
Dalton Dr. Wigan WN3 54 E2
Dalton Fold. BL5 57 F8
Dalton Gdns. M41 95 B3
Dalton Gr. Ashton-i-M WN4 73 A4
Dalton Gr. M'ster SK4 168 C4
Dalton House. 6 M14 110 D8
Dalton Rd. M'ster M9 64 D5
Dalton Rd. Middleton M24 64 B7
Dalton St. Bury BL8 27 B2
Dalton St. Chadderton OL9 152 B7
Dalton St. Eccles M30 79 D3
Dalton St. Failsworth M35 83 E8
Dalton St. M'ster M40 159 B4
Dalton St. Oldham OL1 & OL4 67 B7
Dalton St. Sale M33 108 C6
Daltry St. OL1 67 A8
Dalveen Ave. M41 95 C4
Dalveen Dr. WA15 119 F7
Dalwood Cl. WN2 56 F4
Dalymount Cl. BL2 25 B2
Dam Head Dr. M9 64 E3
Dam Head La. WA3 105 A5
Dam La. Ashton-i-M WA3 73 F3
Dam La. Hollinfare WA3 105 A4
Damask Ave. M3 158 D2
Dame Hollow. SK8 131 D7
Dame St. OL9 153 D8
Dameny Ct. SK7 132 E8
Dameral Cl. M7 & M8 156 A6
Damery Rd. SK7 132 E8
Damian Dr. WA12 89 A5
Damien St. M12 99 B2
Dams Head Fold. BL5 39 F1
Damson Wlk. M31 105 D3
Dan Bank. SK6 125 C6
Dan Fold. OL1 153 E7
Danbury Wlk. M23 120 D8
Danby Cl. SK14 167 F4
Danby Ct. 6 OL1 153 E8
Danby Pl. SK14 167 F4
Danby Rd. Bolton BL3 147 E3
Danby Rd. Hyde SK14 167 F4
Danby Wlk. M9 64 E1
Dane Ave. Cheadle SK3 123 A8
Dane Ave. Partington M31 105 F4
Dane Bank Cty Prim Sch. M34 100 A2
Dane Bank Dr. SK12 135 D6
Dane Cl. SK7 123 D3
Dane Dr. SK9 137 D6
Dane Hill Cl. SK12 135 D5
Dane Rd. Reddish M34 100 A2
Dane Rd. Sale M33 108 D5
Dane Road Sta. M33 108 C6
Dane St. Bolton BL3 146 C4
Dane St. M'ster M18 99 E7
Dane St. Mossley OL5 68 D3
Dane St. 7 Oldham OL4 67 C7
Dane St. R'dale OL11 139 E7
Dane Wlk. SK5 169 F4
Danebank Mews. M34 100 B2
Danebank Wlk. 14 M13 163 B7
Danebridge Cl. BL4 60 E8
Danebury Cl. WN2 56 D4
Danecroft Cl. M13 164 D5
Danefield Ct. SK8 131 D8
Danefield Rd. M33 108 D5
Daneholme Rd. M19 110 E5
Danes Ave. WN2 56 E6
Danes Brook Cl. WN2 56 E6
Danes Gn. WN2 56 E7
Danes Rd. M14 98 D2
Danesbury Cl. WN5 71 E4
Danesbury Rd. BL1 & BL2 25 B4
Danesbury Rise. SK8 122 D5
Daneshill. M25 63 B6
Danesmoor Dr. BL9 141 B4
Danesmoor Rd. M20 110 B5
Danesway. M'ster M25 63 D2
Danesway. Pendlebury M27 80 C6
Danesway. Wigan WN1 37 B3
Danesway Ct. BL1 143 D2
Daneswood Ave. M'ster M9 64 F4
Daneswood Ave. Whitworth OL12 14 C8
Daneswood Cl. OL12 14 C8
Danett Cl. M12 165 B6
Danforth Gr. M19 111 B8
Daniel Adamson Ave. M31 105 D3
Daniel Adamson Rd. M5 154 D1
Daniel Ct. M31 105 F4
Daniel Fold. OL12 14 B2
Daniel St. Hazel Grove SK7 124 E2
Daniel St. Heywood OL10 29 B2
Daniel St. Oldham OL1 67 C8
Daniel St. Royton OL2 49 A3
Daniel St. Whitworth OL12 4 D2
Daniel's La. SK1 169 E2
Danisher La. OL8 84 F8
Dannywood Cl. SK14 113 C8
Danson St. M10 & M40 160 E3
Dantall Ave. M9 65 A3
Dante Cl. M6 80 A4
Danty St. 25 SK16 166 B1
Dantzic St. M4 & M60 & M8 159 A3
Danwood Cl. M34 101 B1
Dapple Gr. M11 165 A8
Darbishire St. BL1 25 A1
Darby La. WN2 56 D6
Darby Rd. M44 106 A6
Darbyshire Cl. BL1 144 C8
Darbyshire House. WA15 120 C7
Darbyshire St. M26 44 A3
Darbyshire Wlk. 1 M26 44 B3
Darcy St. BL2 148 C5
Darcy Wlk. M14 98 A4
Darden Cl. SK4 110 E3
Darell Wlk. M8 156 B6
Darenth Cl. 5 M15 162 F6
Daresbury Ave. Alt'ham WA15 119 E5
Daresbury Ave. Urmston M41 94 E4
Daresbury Cl. Sale M33 108 F3
Daresbury Cl. Stockport SK3 170 D5
Daresbury Rd. M21 96 F1
Daresbury St. M'ster M8 156 A7
Daresham Wlk. 5 M16 97 E4
Darfield Wlk. M40 160 D3
Dargai St. M11 83 D1
Dargle Rd. M33 108 B6
Darian Ave. M22 130 D8
Daric Cl. WN7 75 C1
Dark La. Blackrod BL6 21 B3
Dark La. Delph OL3 50 E6
Dark La. M'ster M12 164 D8
Dark La. Mossley OL5 68 D2
Dark La. Uppermill OL3 69 A8
Darlbeck Wlk. M21 109 C5
Darley Ave. Eccles M30 95 C8
Darley Ave. Farnworth BL4 42 E1
Darley Ave. Gatley SK8 122 B5
Darley Ave. M'ster M21 109 C5
Darley Gr. BL4 42 E1
Darley House. 5 M6 154 E1
Darley Rd. Hazel Grove SK7 133 F7
Darley Rd. M'ster M16 97 C3
Darley Rd. R'dale OL11 30 F4
Darley Rd. Wigan WN3 55 B3
Darley St. Bolton BL1 143 D1
Darley St. Farnworth BL4 60 E8
Darley St. Horwich BL6 22 B5
Darley St. M'ster M11 160 F1
Darley St. Sale M33 108 B4
Darley St. Stretford M32 96 E4
Darlington Cl. BL8 27 B5
Darlington Rd. M'ster M20 110 A6
Darlington Rd. R'dale OL11 30 F3
Darlington St. Ince-i-M WN2 56 A7
Darlington St. Tyldesley M29 59 A1
Darlington St. Wigan WN1 151 D7
Darlington St E. Tyldesley M29 59 B1
Darlington St E. Wigan WN1 151 E7
Darliston Ave. M9 64 A5
Darlton Wlk. 9 M9 157 E8
Darnall Ave. M14 110 A8
Darnbrook Dr. 4 M22 121 B1
Darncombe Cl. M16 97 F4
Darnhall St. WN2 55 F4
Darnhill Cty Prim Sch. OL10 28 F1
Darnley Ave. M28 60 C1
Darnley St. M16 97 D4
Darnton Rd. OL6 & SK15 85 E3
Darran Ave. WN3 54 F3
Darras Rd. M18 99 C3
Dart Cl. OL9 65 F8
Dartford Ave. Brinnington SK5 112 B6
Dartford Ave. Eccles M30 79 B2
Dartford Cl. M12 164 D6
Dartford Rd. M41 95 C1
Dartington Cl. Alt'ham M23 120 D6
Dartington Cl. Stockport SK7 123 F2
Dartmouth Cl. 4 OL8 66 F4
Dartmouth Cres. SK5 112 C5
Dartmouth Rd. M'ster M21 109 C8
Dartmouth Rd. Whitefield M45 63 A7
Dartnall Cl. SK12 135 A6
Darton Ave. M10 & M40 160 E3
Darul-uloom Islamic Coll. BL8 10 F4
Darvel Ave. WN4 72 C4
Darvel Cl. BL2 42 F6
Darwell Ave. M30 95 C8
Darwen Rd. Bolton BL7 25 A7
Darwen St. M16 161 C5
Darwin Gr. SK7 132 E6
Darwin St. Bolton BL1 143 D2
Darwin St. Dukinfield SK14 102 A5
Darwin St. Oldham OL4 67 C5
Dashwood Rd. M25 62 F5
Dashwood Wlk. M12 165 A6
Datchett Terr. OL11 30 F4
Dauntesy Ave. M27 80 D7
Davehall Ave. SK9 137 A7
Davenfield Gr. M20 110 B3
Davenfield Rd. 2 M20 110 B3
Davenham Rd. Handforth SK9 131 D4
Davenham Rd. Reddish SK5 99 F2
Davenham Rd. Sale M33 107 F6
Davenhill Rd. M19 111 A8
Davenport Ave. M'ster M20 110 B7
Davenport Ave. Radcliffe M26 43 F6
Davenport Ave. Wilmslow SK9 136 E4
Davenport Dr. SK6 113 B6
Davenport Fold. BL2 26 A3
Davenport Fold Rd. BL2 26 A4
Davenport Gdns. 10 BL1 145 E8
Davenport La. WA14 119 C7
Davenport Lodge. SK3 170 F5
Davenport Park Rd. SK2 124 A5
Davenport Rd. Alt'ham WA14 119 C7
Davenport Rd. Hazel Grove SK7 124 D2
Davenport Sch. SK3 123 F4
Davenport St. Bolton BL1 145 E8
Davenport St. Denton M34 100 E8
Davenport St. Droylsden M43 83 E1
Davenport Sta. SK3 170 F5
Daventry Rd. M'ster M21 109 D8
Daventry Rd. R'dale OL11 30 F3
Davey La. SK9 137 B2
Daveyhulme St. OL12 15 B1
Daveylands. Urmston M41 94 F5
Daveylands. Wilmslow SK9 137 D7
David Brow. BL3 146 A2
David Cl. M34 101 A1
David Lewis Cl. OL16 31 C6
David Mews. M14 110 C7
David Pegg Wlk. M40 83 B5
David St. Bacup OL13 3 D8
David St. Bury BL8 27 C4
David St. Denton M34 101 A2
David St. 2 Oldham OL1 153 E6
David St. 16 R'dale OL12 14 F1
David St. Reddish SK5 111 E8
David St N. 15 OL12 14 F1
David's Farm Cl. M24 65 C7
David's Rd. M43 83 E2
Davids La. OL4 67 F7
Davidson Dr. M24 65 B6
Davidson Wlk. WN5 54 E7
Davies Ave. Gatley SK8 131 B6
Davies Ave Newton-l-W WA12 89 C4
Davies Rd. Bredbury SK6 112 D3
Davies Rd. Partington M31 106 A3
Davies Sq. M14 98 A4
Davies St. Ashton-u-L OL7 84 F1
Davies St. Kearsley BL4 61 A7
Davies St. Oldham OL1 153 D8
Davies St. Platt Bridge WN2 56 A2
Davis St. M30 79 F1
Davy Ave. M27 62 D2
Davy St. M40 159 B4
Davyhulme Circ. M41 95 C4
Davyhulme Cty Jun & Inf Sch. M41 95 D3
Davyhulme Park Golf Course. M41 94 F3
Davyhulme Rd. Stretford M32 96 C3
Davyhulme Rd. Urmston M41 94 F4
Davyhulme Rd. Urmston M41 95 B4
Davyhulme Rd E. M32 96 D3
Daw Bank. SK3 169 E1
Dawber St. WN4 73 D4
Dawes St. BL3 145 F6
Dawley Cl. Ashton-i-M WN4 73 A3
Dawley Cl. Bolton BL3 144 C6
Dawlish Ave. Brinnington SK5 112 C5
Dawlish Ave. Chadderton OL9 47 F1
Dawlish Ave. Cheadle SK8 131 F7
Dawlish Ave. Droylsden M43 83 E1
Dawlish Cl. Bramhall SK7 132 E7
Dawlish Cl. Hattersley SK14 102 E3
Dawlish Cl. Hollinfare WA3 105 B3
Dawlish Rd. M'ster M21 109 C8
Dawlish Rd. Sale M33 107 E5
Dawn St. OL2 149 B6
Dawnay St. M11 165 B7
Dawnwood Sq. WN5 36 C2
Dawson Ave. WN6 37 A3
Dawson La. BL1 145 E7
Dawson Rd. Alt'ham WA14 119 D8
Dawson Rd. Gatley SK8 131 D8
Dawson St. Atherton M46 58 C3
Dawson St. Bury BL9 141 A4
Dawson St. Heywood OL10 29 C2
Dawson St. Hyde SK14 167 E1
Dawson St. M'ster M3 158 F2
Dawson St. M'ster M15 162 D8
Dawson St. 5 Oldham OL4 67 D6
Dawson St. Oldham OL4 67 E5
Dawson St. R'dale OL12 139 F8
Dawson St. Stockport SK1 112 B3
Dawson St. Swinton M27 80 A8
Day Dr. M35 83 F6
Day Gr. SK14 103 A3
Dayfield. WN8 53 B7
Daylesford Cl. SK8 122 D4
Daylesford Cres. SK8 122 D4
Daylesford Rd. SK8 122 D4
De La Salle Coll. M6 80 C3
De Lacy Dr. BL2 25 B1
De Quincey Cl. WA14 107 D1
De Quincey Rd. WA14 107 D1
De Trafford Dr. WN2 56 B8
De Trafford Ho. 13 M30 79 D1
De Traffords The. M44 94 B3
De-Massey Cl. SK6 113 B6
Deacon Ave. Swinton M27 61 E1
Deacon Cl. WA14 119 B1
Deacon St. OL16 15 B1
Deacon Trad Est. WA12 89 A2
Deacons Cl. SK1 112 A1
Deacons Cres. BL8 27 A5
Deacons Dr. M6 80 D6
Deakin St. WN3 151 E5
Deakins Bsns Pk. BL7 8 D2
Deal Ave. SK5 112 B6
Deal Cl. M40 83 D5
Deal Sq. SK14 167 E2
Deal St. Bolton BL3 147 F3
Deal St. Bury BL9 141 B2
Deal St. Hyde SK14 167 E2
Deal St. M'ster M3 158 E2
Deal Wlk. OL9 152 A6
Dealey Rd. BL3 146 A4
Dean Ave. Failsworth M40 83 B6
Dean Ave. M'ster M16 97 B3
Dean Bank Dr. OL16 31 B1
Dean Bradley Ct. M40 157 E6
Dean Brook Cl. M40 83 B7
Dean Cl. Billinge WN5 71 D3
Dean Cl. Edenfield BL0 1 D3
Dean Cl. Farnworth BL4 59 F8
Dean Cl. Handforth SK9 131 C1
Dean Cl. Orrell WN8 53 C7
Dean Cl. Partington M31 105 F4
Dean Cl. Whitefield M45 62 D7
Dean Cres. WN5 54 B8
Dean Ct. Bolton BL1 148 A8
Dean Ct. 11 Dukinfield SK16 166 B1
Dean Ct. Golborne WA3 90 A7
Dean Ct. M'ster M15 162 D6
Dean Ct. R'dale OL11 30 F4
Dean Dr. Alt'ham WA14 119 B1
Dean Dr. Handforth SK9 131 D2
Dean La. Failsworth M40 83 B6
Dean La. Hazel Grove SK7 133 E8
Dean Lane Sta. M40 83 B6
Dean Meadow. WA12 89 C4
Dean Moor Rd. SK7 124 A1
Dean Rd. Golborne WA3 90 A7
Dean Rd. Handforth SK9 131 E3
Dean Rd. Irlam M44 105 E6
Dean Rd. M'ster M3 158 E3
Dean Rd. Reddish M18 99 E4
Dean Row Cty Jun Sch. SK9 131 E1
Dean Row Rd. Wilmslow SK9 137 F8
Dean St. Ashton-u-L OL6 & OL7 166 A3
Dean St. Failsworth M35 83 E7
Dean St. M'ster M1 & M60 159 B1
Dean St. Mossley OL5 68 B1
Dean St. R'dale OL16 15 B1
Dean St. Radcliffe M26 43 F3
Dean St. Stalybridge SK15 86 A1
Dean Villas. OL14 6 B7
Dean Wlk. M24 46 D2
Dean Wood Ave. WN5 53 E8
Dean Wood Golf Crse. WN8 53 D8
Deanbank Ave. 2 M19 110 F8
Deane Ave. Alt'ham WA15 120 A5
Deane Ave. Bolton BL3 144 B5
Deane Ave. Cheadle SK8 122 F5
Deane Church La. BL3 146 B4
Deane Rd. BL3 145 D6
Deane Sch The. BL3 40 F4
Deane Wlk. BL3 145 E6
Deanery CE High Sch. WN1 150 B8
Deanery Gdns. M7 155 D8
Deanery Way. SK1 169 F2
Deanroyd Rd. OL14 6 B7
Deans Prim Sch The. M27 79 E8
Deans Rd. M27 79 E7
Deanscourt Ave. M27 79 E8
Deansgate. Bolton BL1 145 E7
Deansgate. Hindley WN2 56 E6
Deansgate. M'ster M1,M2,M3 158 F1
Deansgate. M'ster M15 162 E7
Deansgate. Radcliffe M26 44 B3
Deansgate La. WA14, WA15 119 E7
Deansgate Sta. M1 162 E7
Deansgreave Rd. OL13 4 B7
Deanshut Rd. OL8 67 A2
Deansway. M27 79 E8
Deanswood Dr. M9 64 A5
Deanwater Cl. M13 163 B7
Deanwater Ct. Gatley SK8 131 D7
Deanwater Ct. Stretford M32 108 C8
Deanway. Handforth SK9 131 C1
Deanway. M'ster M40 83 A8
Deanway. Urmston M41 94 D2
Deanway Trad Est. SK9 131 D3
Dearden Ave. M38 60 A5
Dearden Clough. BL0 1 E2
Dearden Fold. BL0 1 E2
Dearden St. Little Lever BL3 43 A4
Dearden St. Littleborough OL15 16 B6
Dearden St. 12 Stalybridge SK15 86 A2
Deardens Fold. BL8 27 C1
Deardens St. BL8 27 C1
Dearne Dr. M32 96 E2
Dearnley CE Prim Sch. OL12 15 E4
Dearnley Cl. OL15 15 E4
Debdale La. Reddish M18 & M34 99 F4
Debdale La. Tyldesley M29 76 F4
Deben Cl. WN6 19 D1
Debenham Ave. M40 83 C4
Debenham Ct. BL4 60 D7
Debenham Rd. M32 96 A2
Dee Ave. WA15 120 D5
Dee Dr. BL4 61 B5
Dee Rd. M29 77 C7
Deep La. Littleborough OL15 16 C1
Deep La. Milnrow OL15 & OL16 32 B8
Deepcar St. M12 & M19 99 A2
Deepdale. Leigh WN7 76 C3
Deepdale. Oldham OL4 67 D6
Deepdale Ave. Billinge WA11 71 C1
Deepdale Ave. M'ster M14 110 A8
Deepdale Ave. R'dale OL16 31 C6
Deepdale Ave. Royton OL2 48 C8
Deepdale Cl. SK5 100 A1
Deepdale Ct. M9 65 B3
Deepdale Dr. M27 80 D7
Deepdale Rd. BL2 25 F1
Deepdene St. M12 164 F6
Deeping Ave. M16 97 D2
Deeplish Prim Sch. OL11 31 A5
Deeplish Rd. OL11 139 F5
Deeplish St. OL11 139 F5
Deeply Vale La. BL9 12 C2
Deer St. M1 163 C8
Deeracre Ave. SK2 124 C6
Deerfold Cl. 6 M18 99 D5
Deerhurst Dr. M7 & M8 155 F6
Deeroak Cl. M18 165 B6
Deerpark Rd. M16 97 E3
Defence St. 8 BL3 145 D6
Defiance St. M46 58 C3
Deganwy Gr. SK5 111 F5
Deighton Ave. M14 110 A8
Delacourt Rd. M14 110 B8
Delafield Ave. M12 99 A2
Delaford Ave. M28 78 E7
Delaford Cl. SK3 123 E4
Delaford Wlk. M40 83 D4
Delahayes Lodge. WA15 120 B5
Delahays Dr. WA15 120 B2
Delahays Range. M18 & M34 99 F4
Delahays Rd. WA15 120 B2
Delaine Rd. M20 110 C6
Delamer Rd. WA14 119 C3
Delamere Ave. Golborne WA3 90 E6
Delamere Ave. Pendlebury M6 80 C6
Delamere Ave. Sale M33 108 E3
Delamere Ave. Shaw OL2 49 D8
Delamere Ave. Stretford M32 96 D2
Delamere Ave. Swinton M27 62 B2
Delamere Ave. Whitefield M45 62 E8
Delamere Cl. Hazel Grove SK7 125 A3
Delamere Cl. Mossley SK15 86 E6
Delamere Cl. Romiley SK6 113 C5
Delamere Gdns. BL1 143 D3
Delamere House. M14 110 C8
Delamere Lodge. SK7 124 D2
Delamere Rd. Gatley SK8 122 B5
Delamere Rd. Handforth SK9 131 E4
Delamere Rd. Hazel Grove SK7 125 A3
Delamere Rd. M'ster M19 99 B1
Delamere Rd. R'dale OL16 31 C4
Delamere Rd. Reddish M34 100 B2
Delamere Rd. Stockport SK2 124 B4
Delamere Rd. Urmston M41 94 F2
Delamere Sch. M41 94 D2
Delamere St. Ashton-u-L OL6 166 B2
Delamere St. Bury BL9 28 A5
Delamere St. Droylsden M11 & M18 99 F7
Delamere St. 6 Oldham OL8 67 B5
Delamere Way. WN8 53 A7
Delaunays Rd. M'ster M8 64 B2
Delaunays Rd. Sale M33 107 F4
Delaware Wlk. M9 157 D7
Delbooth Ave. M41 94 E4
Delegarte St. WN3 151 E6
Delfhaven Ct. WN6 37 A7
Delft Wlk. M6 81 A5
Delhi Rd. M44 105 F8
Dell Ave. Pendlebury M27 80 D7
Dell Ave. Wigan WN6 36 E3
Dell Cl. OL4 67 F5
Dell Gdns. OL12 14 B2
Dell Meadow. OL12 14 C5
Dell Rd. OL12 14 B3
Dell Side. SK6 112 E3
Dell Side Way. OL12 14 C2
Dell St. BL2 25 C5
Dell The. Appley Bridge WN6 35 D7
Dell The. Orrell WN8 53 B7
Dellar St. OL12 14 C1
Dellcot Cl. M'ster M25 63 D2
Dellcot Cl. Pendlebury M6 80 B5
Dellcot La. M28 78 F5
Dellhide Cl. OL4 68 A6
Dellside Cl. WN4 72 D5
Dellside Gr. M28 60 E3
Delph Ave. BL7 8 D3
Delph Brook Way. BL7 8 D2
Delph Gr. WN7 57 D1
Delph Hill Cl. BL1 23 E2
Delph La. Ainsworth BL2 26 C1
Delph La. Delph OL3 50 F5
Delph Lodge. OL3 50 F3
Delph New Rd. OL3 50 E2
Delph Prim Sch. OL3 50 E5
Delph Rd. OL3 50 C8
Delph St. Bolton BL3 145 D5
Delph St. Milnrow OL16 31 F6
Delph St. Wigan WN6 37 B1
Delphi Ave. M28 60 D2
Delphside Cl. WN5 53 D5
Delphside Rd. WN5 53 D5
Delside Ave. M40 83 A8
Delta Cl. OL2 48 D2
Delta Rd. M34 100 E7
Delta Wlk. M40 83 A7
Delvino Wlk. M14 98 A4
Delwood Gdns. M22 121 D3
Demesne Cl. SK15 86 C1
Demesne Cres. SK15 86 C1
Demesne Dr. SK15 86 C1
Demesne Rd. M16 97 E2
Demmings Inf Sch. SK8 122 F5
Demmings Rd. SK8 122 F5
Dempsey Dr. M45 45 B2
Den Hill Dr. OL4 67 F6
Den La. Oldham OL4 67 F7
Den La. Uppermill OL3 69 B8
Denbigh Cl. SK7 133 C8
Denbigh Dr. OL2 48 F6
Denbigh Gr. M46 58 C5
Denbigh Pl. M5 81 A2
Denbigh Rd. Bolton BL2 148 B5
Denbigh Rd. Denton M34 100 F1
Denbigh Rd. Swinton M27 62 B2
Denbigh St. Mossley OL5 86 D8
Denbigh St. Oldham OL8 66 F3
Denbigh St. Stockport SK4 169 D3
Denbigh Wlk. M15 162 E5
Denbury Dr. WA14 119 B5
Denbury Gn. SK7 124 A1
Denbury Wlk. M9 156 C6
Denby La. SK4 169 D4
Denby Rd. SK16 101 C7
Denbydale Way. OL2 48 C4
Dencombe St. M13 98 F4
Dene Bank. BL2 25 C5
Dene Brow. M34 113 B8
Dene Ct. SK4 168 C2
Dene Dr. M24 64 F7
Dene Gr. WN7 75 B4
Dene Hollow. SK5 100 A1
Dene Pk. M20 110 A3
Dene Rd. M20 110 A2
Dene Rd W. M20 109 F3
Dene St. Bolton BL2 25 C5
Dene St. Leigh WN7 75 B4
Denefield Cl. SK6 114 B1
Deneford Rd. M20 110 A2
Denehurst Rd. OL11 30 C8
Denehurst St. M12 164 F6
Denes The. SK5 99 F1
Deneside Cres. SK7 124 F3
Deneside Wlk. 6 M9 157 E8
Denesway. M33 107 E3
Deneway. Bramhall SK7 132 D7
Deneway. High Lane SK6 134 F8
Deneway. Stockport SK4 168 C2
Deneway Cl. SK4 168 C2
Deneway Mews. SK4 168 C2
Denewell Cl. M13 164 D6
Denewood Ct. SK9 137 A6
Denford Cl. WN3 54 F3
Denham Cl. BL1 25 A5
Denham Dr. Bramhall SK7 132 D7
Denham Dr. Irlam M44 94 A1
Denham Dr. Wigan WN3 55 A3
Denham St. M'ster M13 98 D4
Denham St. Radcliffe M26 43 F6
Denhill Rd. M15 162 F5
Denhill Road Ind Est. M15 162 F5
Denholm Rd. M20 122 C8
Denholme. WN8 53 A7
Denholme Rd. OL11 30 F4
Denhurst Rd. OL15 16 B6
Denis Ave. M16 97 E2
Denison Ct. 7 M14 98 C3
Denison Rd. Hazel Grove SK7 133 E8
Denison Rd. M'ster M14 98 D3
Denison St. M14 98 C3
Deniston Rd. SK4 111 B5
Denman Wlk. 12 M7 155 F6
Denmark Rd. M'ster M15 98 A4
Denmark Rd. Sale M33 108 B6
Denmark St. Alt'ham WA14 119 D4
Denmark St. Oldham OL4 67 B7
Denmark St. Oldham OL9 152 C8
Denmark St. R'dale OL16 31 A8
Denmark Way. OL9 152 C8
Denmore Rd. M40 65 D3
Dennington Dr. M41 95 C4
Dennis House. SK4 168 B4
Dennison Ave. M20 110 B7
Dennison Rd. SK8 132 B8
Denshaw. WN8 53 A7
Denshaw Ave. M34 100 D5
Denshaw Cl. M19 110 E3
Denshaw Rd. OL3 50 D5
Densmead Wlk. 14 M40 159 C3
Densmore St. 6 M35 83 F7
Denson Rd. WA15 120 B8
Denstone Ave. Eccles M30 79 E3
Denstone Ave. Sale M33 107 E3
Denstone Ave. Urmston M41 95 C3
Denstone Cres. BL2 25 D2
Denstone Rd. Reddish SK5 99 F1
Denstone Rd. Salford M6 80 D5
Denstone Rd. Urmston M41 95 C3
Denstone Wlk. 15 M9 64 E3
Dent Cl. SK5 112 C6
Dental Hospl. M15 163 A6
Dentdale Cl. BL1 40 D6
Dentdale Wlk. M22 130 C8
Denton Golf Course. M34 100 B4
Denton Gr. WN5 54 B8
Denton La. OL9 152 A5
Denton Rd. Denton M34 100 E6
Denton Rd. Little Lever BL3 43 B6
Denton St. Bury BL9 140 F4
Denton St. Heywood OL10 29 C1
Denton St. 7 R'dale OL12 14 F1
Denton Sta. M34 100 C4
Denver Ave. M10 & M40 160 D3

Denver Dr. WA15 120 A5
Denver Rd. OL11 30 F4
Denville Cres. M22 121 E3
Denyer Terr. 22 SK16 166 B1
Denzell Gdns. WA14 119 A3
Depleach Rd. SK8 122 D5
Deptford Ave. M23 121 A3
Deramore Cl. OL6 85 E3
Deramore St. M14 98 B3
Derby Ave. M5 & M6 154 E2
Derby Cl. Irlam M44 105 C5
Derby Cl. Newton-l-W WA12 89 B3
Derby Cl. Oldham OL9 152 C5
Derby Cl. Sale M33 108 C3
Derby Gr. 2 M19 99 B1
Derby High Sch The. BL9 44 D8
Derby House. WN1 151 D8
Derby Pl. PR6 21 A8
Derby Range. SK4 168 B4
Derby Rd. Ashton-u-L OL6 85 D3
Derby Rd. Golborne WA3 90 C8
Derby Rd. Hyde SK14 167 E4
Derby Rd. Kearsley M26 61 A8
Derby Rd. M'ster M14 & M20 110 D7
Derby Rd. M'ster SK4 168 C4
Derby Rd. New Mills SK12 127 D1
Derby Rd. Prestwich M25,M45 63 A6
Derby Rd. Sale M33 107 E6
Derby Rd. Salford M5 & M6 154 E2
Derby Rd. Urmston M41 95 D3
Derby St. Alt'ham WA14 119 E5
Derby St. Ashton-u-L OL7 85 A5
Derby St. Atherton M46 58 C4
Derby St. Bolton BL3 145 E5
Derby St. Bury BL9 140 F2
Derby St. Denton M34 100 D3
Derby St. Denton M34 100 D4
Derby St. 1 Failsworth M35 66 A1
Derby St. Glossop SK13 116 C8
Derby St. Heywood OL10 29 B2
Derby St. Horwich BL6 22 D1
Derby St. Ince-i-M WN2 55 F4
Derby St. M'ster M7 & M8 158 F4
Derby St. 8 Marple SK6 125 F6
Derby St. Mossley OL5 86 D8
Derby St. Newton-l-W WA12 89 B3
Derby St. Oldham OL9 66 B4
Derby St. Oldham OL9 152 C5
Derby St. Prestwich M25 63 A4
Derby St. R'dale OL11 31 A5
Derby St. Ramsbottom BL0 11 D6
Derby St. Stockport SK3 170 D8
Derby St. 16 Tyldesley M29 59 A1
Derby St. Westhoughton BL5 39 F1
Derby St E. WN7 76 A4
Derby St W. Leigh WN7 75 F4
Derby Terr. M34 100 E8
Derby Way. 7 SK6 125 F6
Derbyshire Ave. M32 96 B3
Derbyshire Cres. M32 96 B3
Derbyshire Gn. M32 96 D2
Derbyshire Gr. M32 96 B3
Derbyshire La. M32 96 C2
Derbyshire La W. M32 96 B2
Derbyshire Level. SK13 116 F6
Derbyshire Rd. Failsworth M40 83 D4
Derbyshire Rd. High Lane SK12 134 D5
Derbyshire Rd. Partington M31 105 E2
Derbyshire Rd. Sale M33 108 C4
Derbyshire Rd S. M33 108 D2
Derbyshire Row. BL1 143 E3
Derbyshire St. M11 165 C7
Dereham Cl. BL8 27 D5
Dereham Way. WN3 54 D3
Derg St. M5 & M6 154 F1
Derker St. OL1 & OL4 67 B8
Derker Sta. OL1 67 A8
Dermot Murphy Cl. M20 109 F6
Dernford Ave. M19 110 F5
Derngate Dr. WN6 37 A7
Derrick Walker Ct. OL11 139 D5
Derry Ave. M22 121 E4
Derry St. OL1 153 F6
Derville Wlk. 4 M9 157 D8
Derwen Rd. SK3 170 E7
Derwent Ave. Alt'ham WA15 120 D5
Derwent Ave. Ashton-u-L OL7 166 A4
Derwent Ave. Droylsden M43 83 E1
Derwent Ave. Golborne WA3 74 C1
Derwent Ave. Heywood OL10 46 D8
Derwent Ave. Ince-i-M WN2 56 B7
Derwent Ave. M'ster M21 109 D5
Derwent Ave. Milnrow OL16 32 B6
Derwent Ave. Whitefield M45 63 C8
Derwent Cl. Culcheth WA3 92 A2
Derwent Cl. Glossop SK13 116 F8
Derwent Cl. Horwich BL6 22 C2
Derwent Cl. Leigh WN7 75 E8
Derwent Cl. Little Lever BL3 42 F4
Derwent Cl. M'ster M21 109 D5
Derwent Cl. Partington M31 105 F4
Derwent Cl. Reddish M34 100 B2
Derwent Cl. Walkden M28 60 B2
Derwent Cl. Whitefield M45 63 B8
Derwent Dr. Bramhall SK7 132 C5
Derwent Dr. Bury BL9 44 D7
Derwent Dr. Chadderton OL9 152 A7
Derwent Dr. Handforth SK9 131 C5
Derwent Dr. Kearsley BL4 61 B5
Derwent Dr. Littleborough OL15 15 F2
Derwent Dr. Sale M33 108 A2
Derwent Dr. Shaw OL2 149 A8
Derwent Ind Area. M5 162 D8
Derwent Pl. WN5 54 C7
Derwent Rd. Ashton-i-M WN4 73 E5
Derwent Rd. Farnworth BL4 59 F7
Derwent Rd. High Lane SK6 134 E8
Derwent Rd. Hindley WN2 56 E5
Derwent Rd. Middleton M24 46 E3
Derwent Rd. Orrell WN5 53 F8
Derwent Rd. Stretford M32 96 D3
Derwent Rd. Urmston M41 94 E2
Derwent St. Droylsden M43 83 D1
Derwent St. Leigh WN7 75 E3
Derwent St. M'ster M8 156 C6
Derwent St. 11 R'dale OL12 14 F1
Derwent St. Salford M5 161 C8
Derwent St. Tyldesley M29 77 A7
Derwent Terr. SK15 86 A4
Derwent Wlk. Oldham OL4 67 D7
Derwent Wlk. Whitefield M45 63 B8
Desford Ave. M16 & M21 97 C1
Design St. BL3 146 B4
Desmond Rd. M22 121 E4
Desmond St. M46 58 A2
Dettingen St. M6 80 D6
Deva Cl. Hazel Grove SK7 124 D1
Deva Cl. Poynton SK12 133 B4
Deva Sq. OL9 152 C5
Devaney Wlk. M34 100 E1
Devas St. M15 163 B5
Deverill Ave. M18 99 F4
Devine Cl. M'ster M3 158 D2
Devine Cl. Royton OL2 48 D6
Devisdale Ct. WA14 119 C3
Devisdale Grange. WA14 119 B3
Devisdale Rd. WA14 119 B4
Devoke Ave. Billinge WA11 71 A1
Devoke Ave. Walkden M28 60 F2
Devoke Gr. BL4 59 E8
Devon Ave. M'ster M19 110 F8
Devon Ave. Whitefield M45 44 E1
Devon Cl. Aspull WN2 38 D5
Devon Cl. Brinnington SK5 112 C4
Devon Cl. Eccles M6 80 A3
Devon Cl. Little Lever BL3 43 B4
Devon Cl. Shaw OL2 48 F7
Devon Cl. Wigan WN5 54 C6
Devon Cres. BB4 1 B8
Devon Dr. Ainsworth BL2 26 D1
Devon Dr. Diggle OL3 51 C4
Devon Dr. Standish WN1 20 B1
Devon Mews. 2 M45 44 E1
Devon Rd. Droylsden M43 84 A3
Devon Rd. Failsworth M35 83 E6
Devon Rd. Irlam M44 105 D5
Devon Rd. Partington M31 105 E2
Devon Rd. Tyldesley M29 59 A2
Devon Rd. Urmston M41 94 E1
Devon St. Bolton BL2 148 A7
Devon St. Bury BL9 44 F8
Devon St. Farnworth BL4 42 D2
Devon St. Hindley WN2 56 E5
Devon St. Leigh WN7 76 E4
Devon St. Oldham OL9 66 C4
Devon St. R'dale OL11 139 F6
Devon St. Swinton M27 61 F2
Devon Way. OL8 66 C2
Devonport Cres. OL2 48 F4
Devonshire Cl.Heywood OL10 29 A1
Devonshire Cl. 3 Urmston M41 95 E2
Devonshire Cl. M'ster M7 155 D8
Devonshire Ct. Stockport SK2 124 A5
Devonshire Dr. Alderley Edge SK9 137 B2
Devonshire Dr. Boothstown M28 77 F6
Devonshire Gdns. WA12 89 C2
Devonshire Park Rd. SK2 124 A5
Devonshire Pl.Atherton M46 58 D4
Devonshire Pl.Prestwich M25 63 A5
Devonshire Rd. Alt'ham WA14 119 D6
Devonshire Rd. Atherton M46 58 C5
Devonshire Rd. Bolton BL1 144 B8
Devonshire Rd. Eccles M30 79 E2
Devonshire Rd. Eccles M6 80 A3
Devonshire Rd. Hazel Grove SK7 133 F8
Devonshire Rd. M'ster M21 109 C8
Devonshire Rd. M'ster SK4 168 B3
Devonshire Rd. R'dale OL11 30 F2
Devonshire Rd. Walkden M28 60 C6
Devonshire Road Cty Prim Sch. BL1 144 B8
Devonshire St. M'ster M7 155 E6
Devonshire St. M'ster M12 164 D6
Devonshire St E. M35 83 E5
Devonshire St N. M12 164 D7
Devonshire St S. M12 , M13 164 D5
Dew Meadow Cl. OL12 14 E2
Dew Way. OL9 153 D7
Dewar Cl. M11 83 A1
Dewberry Cl. M27 61 E2
Dewes Ave. M27 62 B2
Dewey St. M18 99 D7
Dewhirst Rd. OL12 14 F4
Dewhirst Way. OL12 14 F4
Dewhurst Clough Rd. BL7 8 D2
Dewhurst Ct. BL7 8 D3
Dewhurst Rd. BL2 25 E3
Dewhurst St. Heywood OL10 29 E2
Dewhurst St. M'ster M8 158 F4
Dewint Ave. SK6 126 B8
Dewsnap Cl. SK16 101 C6
Dewsnap La.Dukinfield SK16 101 D6
Dewsnap La. Mottram-i-L SK14 103 A6
Dewsnap Way. SK14 102 E2
Dexter Rd. M9 64 A5
Deyne Ave. M'ster M14 98 C4
Deyne Ave. Prestwich M25 63 B4
Deyne St. M5 & M6 154 E2
Dial Ct. BL4 60 D8
Dial Park Prim Sch. SK2 124 D4
Dial Park Rd. SK2 124 D4
Dial Rd. Alt'ham WA15 129 C8
Dial Rd. Stockport SK2 124 C5
Dialstone La. SK1 & SK2 124 C6
Diamond Cl. 9 OL6 85 D4
Diamond St. 8 Ashton-u-L OL6 85 D4
Diamond St. Leigh WN7 75 E4
Diamond St. Stockport SK2 124 A6
Diamond St. Wigan WN6 37 A3
Diamond Terr. SK6 125 F3
Diane Rd. WN4 73 E5
Dibden Wlk. 4 M23 121 A5
Dicconson Cres. 6 WN1 37 C1
Dicconson La. Aspull BL5 & WN2 39 A4
Dicconson La. Aspull BL5 39 B4
Dicconson St. WN1 37 C1
Dicconson Terr. WN1 37 C1
Dicken Gn. OL11 30 F4
Dicken Green La. OL11 30 F4
Dickens Cl. SK8 132 B5
Dickens Dr. Abram WN2 74 C8
Dickens La. SK12 133 E2
Dickens Pl. WN3 54 F4
Dickens Rd. Coppull PR7 19 E8
Dickens Rd. Eccles M30 79 D1
Dickens St. Heywood OL10 29 B2
Dickens St. Oldham OL1 49 E4
Dickenson Rd. M13 & M14 98 E3
Dickenson St. WN2 56 E4
Dickinson Cl. 13 BL1 143 E1
Dickinson Ct. 1 BL6 22 B4
Dickinson St. Bolton BL1 143 E1
Dickinson St. M'ster M1 163 A8
Dickinson St. Oldham OL4 67 B7
Dickinson St W. BL6 22 B4
Dickinson Terr. 12 BL1 143 E1
Dickson St W. BL6 22 A4
Didcot Rd. M22 121 C1
Didley Sq. M12 165 A7
Didsbury CE Prim Sch. M20 110 B3
Didsbury Golf Course. M22 109 F1
Didsbury Gr. WN2 56 D5
Didsbury Pk. M20 110 B2
Didsbury Rd. SK4 168 B2
Didsbury Road Prim Sch. SK4 110 F2
Dig Gate La. OL16 31 E3
Digby Lodge. M20 110 B4
Digby Rd. OL11 30 F4
Digby Wlk. 20 M11 160 F1
Diggle Prim Sch. OL3 51 C5
Diggle St. Shaw OL2 149 B6
Diggle St. Wigan WN6 37 A1
Diggle Wlk. SK15 86 E6
Diggles La. OL11 29 E6
Diglands Ave. SK12 127 D1
Diglands Cl. SK12 127 D1
Diglea. OL3 51 D5
Dijon St. BL3 146 C4
Dilham Ct. BL1 144 C8
Dillicar Wlk. M9 157 D7
Dillmass Wlk. 19 M15 162 D6
Dillon Dr. M12 164 E5
Dilston Cl. M13 163 C6
Dilworth Cl. OL10 29 A2
Dilworth Ct. SK2 124 E5
Dilworth St. M15 163 B5
Dimple Pk. BL7 8 D3
Dingle Ave. Alderley Edge SK9 136 D3
Dingle Ave. Appley Bridge WN6 35 E8
Dingle Ave. Denton M34 101 B2
Dingle Ave. Orrell WN8 53 C8
Dingle Ave. Shaw OL2 32 C1
Dingle Bank Rd. SK7 123 D1
Dingle Cl. Glossop SK13 116 A8
Dingle Cl. Romiley SK6 113 D2
Dingle Dr. M43 84 B3
Dingle Gr. M22 121 F6
Dingle Rd. Middleton M24 64 F6
Dingle Rd. Orrell WN8 53 B7
Dingle Terr. OL6 & OL8 67 B2
Dingle The. Bramhall SK7 123 C1
Dingle The. Hyde SK14 113 E7
Dingle Wlk. 4 Bolton BL1 145 F8
Dingle Wlk. Wigan WN6 36 D4
Dinglebrook Gr. 5 SK9 131 D1
Dinglewood. SK8 123 C1
Dinmor Rd. M22 121 D1
Dinmore Ct. SK2 124 D5
Dinnington Dr. M7 & M8 155 F6
Dinorwic Cl. M8 64 A2
Dinsdale Cl. M10 & M40 160 D2
Dinsdale Dr. BL3 145 D5
Dinslow Wlk. 18 M8 155 F7
Dinting Ave. M20 110 A7
Dinting CE (VA) Prim Sch. SK13 104 A1
Dinting La. SK13 104 A1
Dinting La Trad Est. SK13 104 A1
Dinting Lodge Ind Est. SK13 171 F2
Dinting Rd. SK13 104 B2
Dinting Sta. SK13 104 A2
Dinton St. M15 161 C7
Dipton Wlk. M8 156 C6
Dirty La. Alt'ham WA14 128 A5
Dirty La. Delph OL3 51 B8
Dirty La. Oldham OL4 50 B1
Dirty Leech. OL12 14 F6
Disley Ave. M20 109 F6
Disley Cty Prim Sch. SK12 135 D6
Disley House. SK3 170 E7
Disley St. OL11 30 C4
Disley Sta. SK12 135 C6
Disley Wlk. M34 101 A1
Distaff Rd. SK12 133 B4
District (VC) Prim Sch The. WA12 89 A4
Ditton Mead Cl. OL12 15 B2
Ditton Wlk. 5 M23 120 F6
Division St. Bolton BL3 147 F4
Division St. R'dale OL12 15 B2
Dixey St. BL6 22 A3
Dixon Ave. M'ster M7 155 E6
Dixon Ave. Newton-l-W WA12 89 C5
Dixon Ave. Shevington WN6 36 A5
Dixon Cl. Newton-l-W WA11 89 A8
Dixon Cl. Sale M33 108 D2
Dixon Closes. OL11 29 E7
Dixon Ct. Cheadle SK8 122 D5
Dixon Ct. Westhoughton BL5 39 E3
Dixon Dr. Kearsley M27 61 E4
Dixon Dr. Shevington WN6 36 A5
Dixon Pl. 3 Abram WN2 56 B1
Dixon Rd. M34 101 B1
Dixon St. 12 Ashton-u-L OL6 85 D4
Dixon St. Failsworth M40 83 B6
Dixon St. Horwich BL6 22 B3
Dixon St. Irlam M44 105 F8
Dixon St. Middleton M24 47 A2
Dixon St. Oldham OL4 67 E8
Dixon St. R'dale OL11 30 D4
Dixon St. Salford M6 80 F6
Dixon St. Westhoughton BL5 39 E3
Dobb Brow Rd. BL5 57 D7
Dobb Hedge Cl. WA15 129 C6
Dobbinetts La. M23 & WA15 120 E4
Dobcross Cl. M13 99 A2
Dobcross New Rd. OL3 51 A1
Dobhill St. BL4 60 D8
Dobroyd St. M8 156 A8
Dobson Cl.Appley Bridge WN6 18 E2
Dobson Cl. M'ster M13 164 D6
Dobson Ct. M40 83 B4
Dobson Rd. BL1 144 C7
Dobson St. BL1 143 D2
Doctor Fold La. OL10 46 C5
Doctor La. OL4 50 C1
Doctor's Nook. 3 WN7 75 F5
Doctors La. BL9 140 D2
Dodd La. BL5 39 B4
Dodd St. M5 154 D2
Doddington Cl. M16 97 F4
Doddington La. M5 161 A8
Doddington Wlk. M34 100 E1
Dodge Fold. SK2 124 E6
Dodge Hill. SK1 & SK4 169 E2
Dodgson St. OL11 & OL16 31 A6
Dodhurst Rd. WN2 56 F6
Dodworth Cl. 4 M15 162 F6
Doe Brow. M27 61 E4
Doe Hey Gr. BL4 42 B2
Doe Hey Rd. BL3 42 B2
Doefield Ave. M28 78 C8
Doeford Cl. WA3 91 E5
Doffcocker Brow. BL1 142 A1
Doffcocker La. BL1 23 F2
Dogford Rd. OL2 48 D5
Dolbey St. M5 & M6 154 E1
Dolefield. M3 158 E1
Dollond St. M9 64 E1
Dolman Wlk. 4 M8 155 F6
Dolphin Pl. M12 163 C7
Dolphin St. M12 163 C7
Dolwen Wlk. M40 83 B6
Doman St. BL3 145 F5
Dombey Rd. SK12 133 D2
Domestic App. M90 130 C6
Domett St. M9 64 C2
Dominic Cl. M23 108 E1
Don Ave. M5 & M6 80 C2
Don St. Bolton BL3 147 D3
Don St. Middleton M24 47 C1
Dona St. SK1 124 A8
Donald Ave. SK14 167 F1
Donald St. M1 163 A7
Doncaster Ave. M20 110 A7
Doncaster Cl. Little Lever BL3 42 F3
Doncaster Wlk. 4 OL1 153 F7
Donhead Wlk. M13 163 C6
Donington Gdns. M28 60 D3
Donkey La. SK9 137 A5
Donleigh St. M35 83 D6
Donnington. 6 OL11 139 E6
Donnington Ave. SK8 122 F6
Donnington Rd. Droylsden M18 99 E5
Donnington Rd. Little Lever M26 43 C5
Donnison St. M12 164 F6
Donovan St. M40 159 C4
Doodfield Prim Sch. SK6 125 F2
Doodson Ave. M44 94 A2
Doodson Sq. BL4 60 D8
Dooley La. SK6 125 B7
Dooley's La. SK9 130 C2
Dootson St. 4 Abram WN2 56 B1
Dootson St. Hindley WN2 57 A6
Dora St. BL0 11 A4
Dorac Ave. SK8 131 C7
Dorchester Ave.Bolton BL2 25 E1
Dorchester Ave.Denton M34 100 F1
Dorchester Ave.M'ster M25 63 C2
Dorchester Ave. Urmston M41 95 F3
Dorchester Cl. Alt'ham WA15 120 C3
Dorchester Cl. Wilmslow SK9 137 D8
Dorchester Ct. Bramhall SK8 123 B1
Dorchester Ct. Sale M33 108 B2
Dorchester Dr. Oldham OL2 48 E2
Dorchester Dr. Sale M23 & M33 108 E1
Dorchester Gr. OL10 46 D8
Dorchester Par. SK7 124 B1
Dorchester Rd. Hazel Grove SK7 124 B1
Dorchester Rd. Orrell WN8 53 A7
Dorchester Rd. Swinton M27 79 F6
Dorclyn Ave. M41 95 D2
Dorfield Cl. SK6 112 E3
Doric Ave. SK6 112 D2
Doric Cl. M11 160 F1
Doric Gn. WN5 53 D3
Doris Ave. BL2 42 D7
Doris Rd. SK3 123 C8
Doris St. M24 47 A2
Dorking Ave. M40 83 B4
Dorking Cl. SK1 & SK2 124 B7
Dorlan Ave. M18 99 F4
Dorland Gr. SK2 124 B7
Dorman St. 6 M11 99 D7
Dormer St. BL1 143 F3
Dorney St. M18 99 D5
Dorning Rd. M27 80 A7
Dorning St. Blackrod BL6 38 F7
Dorning St. Bury BL8 27 B4
Dorning St. 6 Eccles M30 79 D1
Dorning St. Kearsley BL4 60 F8
Dorning St. Leigh WN7 75 E5
Dorning St. Tyldesley M29 58 F1
Dorning St. Wigan WN1 150 B8
Dornton Wlk. M8 155 F6
Dorothy Gr. WN7 75 E4
Dorothy Rd. SK7 124 F3
Dorothy St. M'ster M7 & M8 155 F7
Dorothy St. Ramsbottom BL0 138 B5
Dorrington Rd. Cheadle SK3 123 A7
Dorrington Rd. Sale M33 107 E4
Dorris St. Bolton BL3 146 C3
Dorris St. M'ster M19 111 B8
Dorrit Cl. SK12 133 E2
Dorset Ave. Bramhall SK7 123 D1
Dorset Ave. Brinnington SK5 112 C5
Dorset Ave. Cheadle SK8 122 C5
Dorset Ave. Diggle OL3 51 C4
Dorset Ave. Droylsden M34 100 C8
Dorset Ave. Farnworth BL4 60 C8
Dorset Ave. M'ster M14 98 A2
Dorset Ave. Shaw OL2 48 F7
Dorset Ave. Tyldesley M29 59 A3
Dorset Cl. Heywood OL10 29 A1
Dorset Cl. Wigan WN5 54 C6
Dorset Dr. Bury BL9 45 A8
Dorset Dr. Haslingden BB4 1 A8
Dorset Rd. Alt'ham WA14 119 B5
Dorset Rd. Atherton M46 58 C5
Dorset Rd. Droylsden M43 83 F3
Dorset Rd. Failsworth M35 83 F6
Dorset Rd. Irlam M44 105 D5
Dorset Rd. Reddish M19 99 C1
Dorset Rd. Standish WN1 20 B1
Dorset St. Ashton-u-L OL6 85 D2
Dorset St. Bolton BL2 148 A7
Dorset St. Hindley WN2 56 E6
Dorset St. Leigh WN7 76 D4
Dorset St. Oldham OL9 152 C5
Dorset St. R'dale OL11 139 F6
Dorset St. Stretford M32 96 D1
Dorset St. Swinton M27 61 F2
Dorsey St. M4 159 B2
Dorstone Cl. Failsworth M40 83 C4
Dorstone Cl. Hindley WN2 57 B5
Dorwood Ave. M9 64 C5
Dotterel Cl. WN7 76 A6
Dougall Wlk. M12 165 A6
Doughty Ave. M30 79 F3
Dougill St. BL1 142 B1
Douglas Ave. Billinge WN5 71 D3
Douglas Ave. Bury BL8 27 B2
Douglas Ave. Horwich BL6 22 C5
Douglas Ave. Orrell WN8 53 E7
Douglas Ave. Stretford M32 96 D3
Douglas Bank Dr. WN6 36 F2
Douglas Cl. Horwich BL6 22 C5
Douglas Cl. Whitefield M45 45 C2
Douglas Dr. Orrell WN5 53 F7
Douglas Dr. Shevington WN6 35 F5
Douglas Gn. M6 81 A5
Douglas House. WN1 151 D7
Douglas Pk. M46 58 E3
Douglas Rd. Atherton M46 58 E2
Douglas Rd. Hazel Grove SK7 124 E3
Douglas Rd. Leigh WN7 75 C7
Douglas Rd. Shevington Moor WN6 19 B2
Douglas Rd. Stockport SK3 123 E4
Douglas Rd. Swinton M27 & M28 79 C7
Douglas Rd. Wigan WN1 37 D1
Douglas Sq. OL10 28 F1
Douglas St. Ashton-u-L OL6 85 D3
Douglas St. Atherton M46 58 E3
Douglas St. Bolton BL1 24 E5
Douglas St. Failsworth M35 84 A7
Douglas St. Hindley WN2 56 C4
Douglas St. Hyde SK14 167 E2
Douglas St. M'ster M40 83 A7
Douglas St. M'ster M7 155 D6
Douglas St. Oldham OL1 67 A8
Douglas St. Ramsbottom BL0 138 B6
Douglas St. Swinton M27 60 F1
Douglas St. Wigan WN5 150 A7
Douglas St Back. BL0 138 B6
Douglas Way. 7 Platt Bridge WN2 56 A2
Douglas Way. Whitefield M45 45 C1
Douglas Wlk. 2 Sale M33 107 C5
Douglas Wlk. Whitefield M45 45 C2
Doulton St. M40 83 C8
Dounby Ave. M30 79 B3
Douro St. M10 & M40 157 F5
Douthwaite Dr. SK6 113 E1
Dove Bank Rd. Little Lever BL3 43 A4
Dove Dr. Bury BL9 141 B4
Dove Dr. Irlam M44 94 A3
Dove Rd. BL3 146 B4
Dove St. Bolton BL1 143 E4
Dove St. Golborne WA3 74 A2
Dove St. Oldham OL4 67 C6
Dove St. R'dale OL11 139 D7
Dove Wlk. Farnworth BL4 59 F8
Dove Wlk. M'ster M8 156 B5
Dovebrook Cl. SK15 86 E7
Dovecot Bsns & Tech Pk. M33 108 F4
Dovecote. M43 84 D3
Dovecote Cl. BL7 25 B8
Dovecote La. Oldham OL4 67 F8
Dovecote La. Walkden M28 59 E3
Dovecote Mews. M21 109 A8
Dovedale Ave. Droylsden M43 83 E2
Dovedale Ave. Eccles M30 79 E3
Dovedale Ave. M'ster M25 63 E3
Dovedale Ave. M'ster M20 110 A7
Dovedale Ave. Urmston M41 95 D3
Dovedale Cl. SK6 134 E7
Dovedale Cres. WN4 73 A8
Dovedale Ct. Glossop SK13 104 F1
Dovedale Ct. 8 Middleton M24 46 E2
Dovedale Dr. Littleborough OL12 15 D6
Dovedale Dr. Standish WN6 19 E2
Dovedale Rd.Ashton-i-M WN4 73 A8
Dovedale Rd.Bolton BL2 25 F1
Dovedale Rd.Stockport SK2 124 D7
Dovedale St. M35 83 E6
Dovehouse Cl. M45 62 D7
Doveleys Rd. M27 & M6 154 D4
Dovenby Fold. WN2 56 B7
Dover Cl. BL8 11 A1
Dover Gr. BL3 145 D5
Dover Pk. M41 95 D4
Dover Rd. M27 62 A2
Dover St. Eccles M30 79 B2
Dover St. Farnworth BL4 42 D2
Dover St. M'ster M13 163 B6
Dover St. Oldham OL9 152 C5
Dover St. R'dale OL12 & OL16 15 B2
Dover St. 1 Reddish SK5 111 E7
Dovercourt Ave. SK4 110 F4
Doveston Rd. M33 108 B6
Dovestone Cres. SK16 101 F7
Dovestone Wlk. M40 65 E1
Dovey Cl. M29 77 C7
Dow Fold. BL8 26 F3
Dow La. BL8 26 F3
Dow St. SK14 101 D5
Dower St. WN2 56 A3
Dowling Cl. WN6 36 D3
Dowling St. OL11 139 F6
Downall Green RC Jun Sch. WN4 72 E6
Downall Green Rd. WN4 72 E6
Downesway. SK9 136 F1
Downfield Cl. BL0 138 B6
Downfields. SK5 100 A1
Downgate Wlk. 7 M8 156 A6
Downgreen Rd. BL2 25 E3
Downhall Gn. BL1 145 F8
Downham Ave. Bolton BL2 148 C8
Downham Ave. Culcheth WA3 91 F2
Downham Chase. WA15 120 B6
Downham Cl. OL1 48 D2
Downham Cres. M25 63 E3
Downham Gdns. M25 63 E3
Downham Gr. M25 63 E3
Downham Rd. Heywood OL10 29 A2
Downham Rd. Reddish SK4 111 D5
Downham Wlk. Orrell WN5 53 D1
Downham Wlk. Sale M23 120 E8
Downhill Cl. OL1 48 E1
Downing Cl. Ashton-u-L OL7 84 F6
Downing Cl. Platt Bridge WN2 56 A2
Downing St. Ashton-u-L OL7 85 A5
Downing St. 5 Leigh WN7 75 F5
Downing St. M'ster M1 163 B7
Downing Street Ind Est. M12 163 B7
Downley Cl. OL12 14 B2
Downley Dr. M4 159 C2
Downs Dr. WA14 119 E8
Downs The. Alt'ham WA14 119 D3
Downs The. Cheadle SK8 122 D3
Downs The. Middleton M24 65 B5
Downs The. Prestwich M25 63 A2
Downs The. Wigan WN3 54 C4
Downshaw Rd. OL7 85 A6
Downton Ave. WN2 56 D4
Dowry Rd. OL4 67 F7
Dowry St. OL8 67 A3
Dowson Cty Prim Sch. SK14 113 E8
Dowson Rd. SK14 113 E8
Dowson St. BL2 148 A7
Doyle Ave. SK6 112 D3
Doyle Cl. OL1 49 E4
Doyle Rd. BL3 40 E2
Dr Kershaw's Hospice. OL2 48 F3
Drake Ave. Farnworth BL4 60 D7
Drake Ave. Irlam M44 105 E6
Drake Cl. OL1 153 F8
Drake Ct. SK5 169 E4
Drake Hall. BL5 57 E5
Drake Rd. Alt'ham WA14 119 B8
Drake Rd. Littleborough OL15 6 C1
Drake St. Atherton M46 58 C2
Drake St. R'dale OL11 & OL16 139 F6
Draycott Cl. WN2 56 F3
Draycott St. BL1 143 E2
Draycott St E. 10 BL1 143 F2
Drayfields. OL7 84 D2
Drayton Ave. SK8 131 B7
Drayton Cl. Bolton BL1 143 D2
Drayton Cl. Sale M33 107 D2
Drayton Gr. WA15 120 A5
Drayton Manor. M20 122 B8
Drayton Wlk. M16 162 D5
Dresden St. M40 83 C8
Drewett St. M10 & M40 160 E4
Dreyfus Ave. M11 83 D2
Dreyfus St. M10 & M40 160 E3
Driffield St. Eccles M30 95 C8
Driffield St. M'ster M14 98 A3
Drill Wlk. 8 M4 159 C1
Drinkwater Rd. M25 62 F1
Driscoll St. 1 M13 98 F3
Drive The. Alt'ham WA15 129 D8
Drive The. Bredbury SK6 112 D3
Drive The. Brinnington SK5 112 C4
Drive The. Bury BL9 27 F5
Drive The. Cheadle SK8 123 C4
Drive The. Edenfield BL0 1 D3
Drive The. Leigh WN7 75 F3
Drive The. Lymm WA13 117 D1
Drive The. M'ster M7 63 C1
Drive The. M'ster M20 110 C4
Drive The. Marple SK6 125 E6
Drive The. Prestwich M25 63 B4
Drive The. Sale M33 107 E1
Droitwich Rd. M10 & M40 160 D4
Dronfield Rd. Salford M6 154 D4
Dronfield Rd. Wythenshawe M22 121 D8
Droughts La. M25 63 E8
Drovers Wlk. SK13 104 D1
Droxford Ct. SK9 137 B6
Droxford Gr. M46 58 E5
Droylsden High Sch. M43 83 F2
Droylsden Rd. Droylsden M34 84 C1
Droylsden Rd. Droylsden M34 100 C8
Droylsden Rd.Failsworth M40 83 D5
Drs Green & Slater Rest Houses. SK4 168 A3
Druid St. WN4 73 C2
Druids Cl. BL7 8 D3
Drummer's La. WN4 72 E7
Drummond Sq. WN5 54 E7
Drummond St. BL1 143 E4

Drummond Way. WN7 76 B5
Drury La. OL9 66 B3
Drury St. 13 M19 99 A1
Dryad Cl. M27 61 F2
Drybrook Cl. M13 164 E5
Dryburgh Ave. BL1 143 D4
Dryclough Wlk. OL2 48 E3
Dryden Ave. Ashton-i-M WN4 72 F6
Dryden Ave. Cheadle SK8 122 F6
Dryden Ave. Swinton M27 79 D7
Dryden Cl. Dukinfield SK16 102 B7
Dryden Cl. Marple SK6 125 F4
Dryden Cl. Wigan WN3 150 A5
Dryden Rd. 4 M16 97 C3
Dryden St. M13 163 C6
Dryden Way. 10 M34 113 A8
Dryfield La. BL6 22 A5
Drygate Wlk. 6 M9 157 E7
Dryhurst Dr. SK12 135 D6
Dryhurst La. SK12 135 D6
Dryhurst Wlk. M15 163 A6
Drymoss. Oldham OL8 67 A1
Dryton Wlk. WN2 38 A2
Drywood Ave. M28 79 A5
Ducal St. M40 159 B3
Duchess Park Cl. OL2 149 B8
Duchess Rd. M8 156 B8
Duchess St. OL2 149 B8
Duchess Wlk. BL3 146 B4
Duchy Ave. Atherton BL5 59 A8
Duchy Ave. Walkden M28 78 D8
Duchy Bank. M6 80 D6
Duchy Rd. M6 80 E5
Duchy St. Salford M6 154 F3
Duchy St. Stockport SK3 170 D7
Ducie Ave. BL1 144 C7
Ducie Central High Sch. M14 98 B4
Ducie Central High Sch for Boys. M14 98 D4
Ducie Gr. M15 163 B5
Ducie St. M'ster M1 & M60 159 B1
Ducie St. Oldham OL8 66 F2
Ducie St. Radcliffe M26 43 F5
Ducie St. Whitefield M45 62 F8
Duckshaw La. BL4 60 D8
Duckworth La. BB4 1 E8
Duckworth Rd. M25 62 F3
Duckworth St. 3 Bury BL9 141 A4
Duckworth St. Shaw OL2 149 C7
Duddon Ave. BL2 25 F1
Duddon Cl. Standish WN6 36 F7
Duddon Cl. Whitefield M45 63 C8
Duddon Wlk. 2 M24 46 E2
Dudley Ave. Bolton BL2 25 C1
Dudley Ave. Whitefield M45 62 F8
Dudley Cl. M15 162 E5
Dudley Ct. 10 M16 97 D3
Dudley Rd. Irlam M44 105 D4
Dudley Rd. M'ster M16 97 D3
Dudley Rd. Sale M33 108 C6
Dudley Rd. Sale WA15 120 B7
Dudley Rd. Swinton M27 61 F1
Dudley St. Ashton-i-M WN4 73 A5
Dudley St. Denton M34 100 E4
Dudley St. Eccles M30 79 C1
Dudley St. M'ster M7 & M8 155 F6
Dudley St. 6 Oldham OL4 67 D6
Dudlow Wlk. 24 M15 162 D6
Dudwell Cl. BL1 142 C2
Duerden St. BL3 146 A2
Duffield Ct. M15 163 A5
Duffield Gdns. M9 64 F5
Duffield Rd. Middleton M9 64 F5
Duffield Rd. Salford M6 80 D5
Duffins Cl. OL12 14 D3
Dufton Wlk. 1 Middleton M24 46 E2
Dufton Wlk. Wythenshawe M22 130 E8
Dugdale Ave. M9 64 E4
Dugie St. BL0 138 B7
Duice Pl. M5 81 C1
Duke Ave. Cheadle SK8 131 F6
Duke Ave. Glazebury WA3 92 C7
Duke Ct. M16 162 D5
Duke of Norfolk's CE Prim Sch. Glossop SK13 104 D1
Duke of Norfolk's CE Prim Sch. Glossop SK13 104 E2
Duke Pl. M3 162 E8
Duke Rd. Ainsworth BL2 26 C1
Duke Rd. Dukinfield SK14 101 F5
Duke St. Alderley Edge SK9 137 B2
Duke St. Ashton-i-M WN4 73 C3
Duke St. Ashton-u-L OL6 166 B3
Duke St. Bolton BL1 145 E8
Duke St. Denton M34 100 E3
Duke St. Failsworth M35 84 A8
Duke St. Golborne WA3 74 A1
Duke St. Heywood OL10 29 B2
Duke St. Leigh WN7 76 A4
Duke St. Littleborough OL15 16 A5
Duke St. M'ster M7 155 D5
Duke St. M'ster M3 158 F2
Duke St. M'ster M3 162 E8
Duke St. Mossley OL5 68 E1
Duke St. Newton-l-W WA12 89 B3
Duke St. Platt Bridge WN2 56 A3
Duke St. R'dale OL12 14 F1
Duke St. Radcliffe M26 44 B2
Duke St. Ramsbottom BL0 11 A4
Duke St. Rawtenstall BB4 2 E8
Duke St. Shaw OL2 149 C6
Duke St. Stalybridge SK15 85 F1
Duke St. Stockport SK1 169 F1
Duke St. Swinton M28 79 C4
Duke St. Tyldesley M29 77 C6
Duke St. Walkden M38 60 A5
Duke St. Walkden M27 & M28 61 A2
Duke St. Wigan WN1 37 C2
Duke St. Wigan WN3 54 F4
Duke St N. BL1 145 E8
Duke's Terr. 17 SK16 166 B1
Dukefield St. M22 121 E8
Dukes Ave. BL3 43 A4
Dukes Platting. OL6 85 F5
Dukes St. SK13 116 C8
Dukesgate Cty Prim Sch. M38 60 A5
Dukinfield Astley High Sch. SK16 101 E6
Dukinfield Golf Course. SK16 102 A6
Dukinfield Rd. SK14 101 C4
Dukinfield St. 6 WN7 76 A5
Dulford Wlk. M13 163 C5
Dulgar St. M11 165 B8
Dulverton St. M40 83 B6
Dulwich St. M40 159 B3
Dumbarton Cl. SK5 111 F6
Dumbarton Dr. OL10 46 A8
Dumbarton Gn. WN6 36 E2
Dumbarton Rd. Heywood OL10 29 A1
Dumbarton Rd. Reddish SK5 111 F6
Dumbell St. M27 61 F2
Dumber La. M33 107 F6
Dumers Cl. M26 44 D4
Dumers La. BL9 & M26 44 E5
Dumfries Ave. OL3 33 C2
Dumfries Dr. OL3 33 C2
Dumfries Wlk. OL10 29 A1
Dumplington Circ. M41 95 D7
Dun Cl. M3 158 D2
Dunbar Ave. M23 121 A3
Dunbar Gr. OL10 45 F8
Dunbar St. OL1 153 E8
Dunblane Ave. Bolton BL3 40 E5
Dunblane Ave. Stockport SK4 169 D2
Dunblane Cl. WN4 72 C4
Dunblane Gr. OL10 46 A8
Duncan Ave. WA12 89 C5
Duncan Edwards House. 13 M6 154 F3
Duncan Pl. WN5 54 E7
Duncan Rd. M13 98 F3
Duncan St. Bolton BL1 145 F8
Duncan St. Dukinfield SK16 101 C6
Duncan St. Horwich BL6 22 C3
Duncan St. M'ster M7 81 C6
Duncan St. Salford M5 161 C8
Dunchurch Cl. BL6 40 D6
Dunchurch Rd. M33 107 E4
Duncombe Cl. SK7 124 A3
Duncombe Dr. M40 83 B7
Duncombe Rd. BL3 147 E2
Duncombe St. M7 155 E6
Duncote Gr. OL2 149 A5
Dundee Cl. OL10 28 F1
Dundee La. BL0 138 B6
Dundonald Rd. Cheadle SK8 132 A7
Dundonald Rd. M'ster M20 110 C3
Dundonald St. SK2 170 F6
Dundraw Cl. M24 46 B1
Dundrennan Cl. SK12 133 D5
Dunecroft. M34 101 A4
Dunedin Dr. M6 80 F6
Dunedin Rd. BL8 10 F2
Dunelm Dr. M23 108 D1
Dunford Wlk. M40 65 C3
Dunham Ave. WA3 73 F1
Dunham Cl. BL5 57 D5
Dunham Forest Golf Course. WA14 118 F4
Dunham Gr. WA3 & WN7 76 C2
Dunham Lawn. WA14 119 B4
Dunham Pk. WA14 118 D3
Dunham Rd. Alt'ham WA14 118 F1
Dunham Rd. Alt'ham WA14 119 B4
Dunham Rd. Dukinfield SK16 101 D6
Dunham Rd. Partington M31 106 D3
Dunham Rd. Partington WA13 117 E7
Dunham Rise. WA14 119 C4
Dunham St. OL4 67 E8
Dunkeld Gdns. 2 M23 120 F6
Dunkeld Rd. M23 120 F6
Dunkerley Ave. M35 83 F7
Dunkerley St. Ashton-u-L OL7 85 A5
Dunkerley St. Oldham OL4 67 C7
Dunkerley St. Royton OL2 48 D4
Dunkerleys Cl. M8 155 F8
Dunkery Rd. M22 121 D1
Dunkirk Cl. M34 100 A2
Dunkirk La. SK14 101 B4
Dunkirk Rd. M45 44 F1
Dunkirk Rise. OL12 139 E7
Dunkirk St. M43 84 B1
Dunley Cl. M12 165 A5
Dunlin Ave. WA12 89 C4
Dunlin Cl. Bolton BL2 148 A5
Dunlin Cl. Hazel Grove SK2 125 A5
Dunlin Cl. Poynton SK12 133 A4
Dunlin Cl. R'dale OL11 29 F7
Dunlin Dr. M44 94 A3
Dunlin Wlk. WA14 119 B8
Dunlop Ave. OL11 30 E4
Dunlop St. 2 M3 158 F1
Dunmail Ave. WA11 71 C1
Dunmail Cl. M29 77 C6
Dunmail Dr. M24 46 E3
Dunmere Wlk. M9 156 C6
Dunmore Rd. SK8 122 B6
Dunmow Ct. SK2 124 E5
Dunmow Wlk. M23 109 A2
Dunne La. SK13 104 E2
Dunnerdale Wlk. M18 165 C5
Dunnisher Rd. M23 121 B5
Dunnock Cl. SK2 124 F5
Dunollie Rd. M33 108 E3
Dunoon Cl. OL10 29 A1
Dunoon Dr. BL1 24 C5
Dunoon Rd. Aspull WN2 38 D5
Dunoon Rd. Reddish SK5 111 F7
Dunoon Wlk. M9 157 D7
Dunrobin Cl. OL10 46 A8
Dunscar Cl. M45 62 D7
Dunscar Golf Course. BL7 8 C1
Dunscar Ind Est. BL7 24 E7
Dunscar Sq. BL7 24 F8
Dunscore Rd. WN3 54 E3
Dunsdale Dr. WN4 73 C3
Dunsfold Dr. M23 120 D8
Dunsford Ct. OL4 67 F5
Dunsley Ave. M40 65 D2
Dunsmore Cl. M16 97 E4
Dunsop Dr. BL1 23 F3
Dunstable. 9 OL12 139 F8
Dunstable St. M19 99 B1
Dunstall Rd. M22 121 E5
Dunstan Cl. M40 83 A8
Dunstan St. BL2 148 C7
Dunstar Ave. M34 100 E7
Dunster Ave. Brinnington SK5 112 C5
Dunster Ave. M'ster M9 64 E2
Dunster Ave. R'dale OL11 139 E5
Dunster Ave. Swinton M27 62 B2
Dunster Cl. Hazel Grove SK7 124 C1
Dunster Cl. Platt Bridge WN2 56 A1
Dunster Dr. M41 94 C1
Dunster Pl. M28 77 F7
Dunster Rd. M28 77 F7
Dunsters Ave. BL8 27 C5
Dunsterville Terr. OL11 139 E5
Dunston St. M11 165 C8
Dunton Gn. SK5 112 B6
Dunton Towers. SK5 112 B6
Dunvegan Ct. OL10 28 F1
Dunvegan Rd. SK7 124 F1
Dunwood Ave. OL2 149 C8
Dunwoods Park Cts. OL2 32 C1
Dunworth St. M14 98 B3
Durant St. M4 159 B3
Durban Cl. OL2 149 A6
Durban Rd. BL1 24 E5
Durban St. Ashton-u-L OL7 84 E1
Durban St. Atherton M46 58 A2
Durban St. Leigh WN3 & WN7 74 E4
Durban St. Oldham OL8 66 C3
Durban St. R'dale OL11 30 C2
Durden Mews. OL2 149 B6
Durham Ave. M41 95 E3
Durham Cl. Dukinfield SK16 101 D6
Durham Cl. Little Lever BL3 43 B4
Durham Cl. Romiley SK6 113 A1
Durham Cl. Swinton M27 61 F2
Durham Cl. Tyldesley M29 59 A3
Durham Cres. M35 84 A6
Durham Dr. Ashton-u-L OL6 85 D8
Durham Dr. Bury BL9 45 A8
Durham Dr. Ramsbottom BL0 11 B3
Durham Gr. M44 105 C6
Durham House. 6 SK3 170 E8
Durham Rd. Handforth SK9 131 D5
Durham Rd. 3 Hindley WN2 56 E5
Durham Rd. Pendlebury M6 80 C4
Durham St. Bolton BL1 143 F2
Durham St. Droylsden M43 100 A8
Durham St. 12 M'ster M9 157 E7
Durham St. Oldham OL9 66 C4
Durham St. R'dale OL11 31 A5
Durham St. Radcliffe M26 44 C5
Durham St. Reddish SK5 99 E2
Durham St. Wigan WN1 37 E1
Durham Wlk. 5 Denton M34 100 F1
Durham Wlk. Heywood OL10 29 A2
Durley Ave. M'ster M8 156 B7
Durley Ave. Sale WA15 120 B7
Durling St. M12 163 C7
Durn St. OL15 16 C6
Durnford Ave. M41 96 A2
Durnford Cl. OL12 13 D2
Durnford St. M24 46 F1
Durnford Wlk. M22 121 B3
Durrell Way. WA3 90 E8
Durrington Wlk. M40 65 C3
Dursley Dr. WN4 73 D4
Dutton Gr. WN7 76 C2
Dutton St. M3 158 F3
Duty St. BL1 143 E3
Duxbury Ave. Bolton BL2 25 E5
Duxbury Ave. Little Lever BL3 43 A5
Duxbury Dr. BL9 141 C2
Duxbury St. BL1 143 D2
Duxford Lodge. M8 63 F2
Dyche St. M4 159 B3
Dyche Street Trad Est. M4 159 B3
Dye House La. New Mills SK12 127 C1
Dye House La. R'dale OL12 & OL16 15 C3
Dye La. SK6 113 B2
Dyer St. Golborne WA3 73 F1
Dyer St. M'ster M11 165 A8
Dyer St. Salford M5 161 C7
Dyers Cl. WA13 117 A4
Dyers Ct. OL15 16 A6
Dyers La. WA13 117 A4
Dymchurch Ave. M26 61 C7
Dymchurch St. M40 83 C4
Dysart St. 4 Ashton-u-L OL6 85 D2
Dysart St. Stockport SK2 124 B5
Dysarts Cl. OL5 68 E3
Dyserth Gr. SK5 169 F4
Dyson Cl. BL4 60 D8
Dyson Gr. OL4 67 F8
Dyson St. Farnworth BL4 60 D7
Dyson St. Mossley OL5 68 B2
Dyson St. Oldham OL1 153 F6
Dystelegh Rd. SK12 135 D6

Eades St. M6 81 A3
Eadington St. M8 64 A1
Eafield Ave. OL16 31 F7
Eafield Cl. OL16 31 F7
Eafield Rd. Littleborough OL15 & OL16 15 E3
Eafield Rd. R'dale OL16 15 C1
Eagar St. M35 83 C6
Eagle Ct. M16 162 E5
Eagle Dr. M6 81 A5
Eagle Mill Ct. OL3 50 F5
Eagle St. Bolton BL2 148 A7
Eagle St. 5 M'ster M4 159 A2
Eagle St. Oldham OL9 153 E6
Eagle St. R'dale OL11 & OL16 31 A6
Eagle Tech Pk. OL11 31 A4
Eagles Nest. M25 63 A3
Eagley Bank. OL12 4 E6
Eagley Brow. BL7 24 F7
Eagley Dr. BL8 27 A1
Eagley Ind Est. BL7 24 F7
Eagley Inf Sch. BL7 25 A8
Eagley Jun Sch. BL7 25 B8
Eagley Way. BL1 & BL7 24 F7
Ealees. OL15 16 C5
Ealees Rd. OL15 16 C5
Ealing Ave. M14 98 C2
Ealing Pl. M19 111 A6
Eames Ave. M26 61 A8
Eamont Wlk. M9 157 D7
Earby Gr. M9 64 F3
Earl Rd. Handforth SK8 & SK9 131 E5
Earl Rd. M'ster SK4 168 C4
Earl Rd. Ramsbottom BL0 138 B6
Earl St. Atherton M46 58 B2
Earl St. Bury BL9 140 F2
Earl St. 6 Heywood OL10 29 C2
Earl St. Ince-i-M WN2 56 A7
Earl St. Leigh WN7 76 A4
Earl St. M'ster M7 158 D4
Earl St. Middleton OL11 47 D8
Earl St. Mossley OL5 68 B1
Earl St. Prestwich M25 63 C4
Earl St. Ramsbottom BL0 11 D6
Earl St. Reddish M34 100 A4
Earl St. Sale M33 108 C5
Earl St. Stockport SK3 170 D8
Earl St. Wigan WN1 37 C1
Earl Terr. 18 SK16 166 B1
Earl Wlk. M12 164 F5
Earl's Lodge. M35 83 D6
Earle Rd. SK7 123 E3
Earle St. Ashton-u-L OL7 84 F2
Earle St. Newton-l-W WA12 89 A3
Earlesdon Cres. M38 60 A5
Earlestown Dist CE Jun Sch. WA12 89 A3
Earlestown Sta. WA12 89 B3
Earls Way. M35 83 D6
Earlston Ave. M34 100 A3
Earlswood Wlk. Bolton BL1 147 F4
Earlswood Wlk. M'ster M18 165 C6
Early Bank. SK15 102 C7
Early Bank Rd. SK14 & SK16 102 B6
Earnshaw Ave. R'dale OL12 14 E3
Earnshaw Ave. Stockport SK1 112 B1
Earnshaw Cl. OL7 84 F5
Earnshaw St. Bolton BL3 146 B3
Earnshaw St. Hollingworth SK14 171 D4
Easby Cl. Bramhall SK8 132 B6
Easby Cl. Poynton SK12 133 D4
Easby Rd. M24 46 F3
Easedale Cl. M41 94 F3
Easedale Rd. BL1 144 A8
Easington Wlk. 10 M40 83 A6
Easingwold. 2 WA14 119 C4
East Aisle Rd. M17 & M32 96 C5
East Ave. Gatley SK8 131 D8
East Ave. Golborne WA3 74 C1
East Ave. Leigh WN7 76 C3
East Ave. M'ster M19 110 F7
East Ave. Stalybridge SK15 86 A3
East Ave. Whitefield M45 44 E2
East Bond St. WN7 76 A5
East Bridgewater St. 4 WN7 76 A4
East Central Dr. M27 80 B7
East Court Wlk. M13 163 C6
East Cres. M24 64 F7
East Didsbury Sta. M20 110 C1
East Downs Rd. Alt'ham WA14 119 C2
East Downs Rd. Cheadle SK8 122 F2
East Dr. Marple SK6 125 F3
East Dr. Pendlebury M27 80 B7
East Dr. Salford M6 80 E5
East Dr. Whitefield BL9 45 B4
East Gate St. OL12 & OL16 139 F8
East Gr. M13 164 D5
East Grange. M11 83 C3
East Hill St. 8 OL4 67 A6
East Lancashire Rly. BL0 138 C5
East Lancashire Rd. Ashton-i-M WA11,WA12,WA3 89 C7
East Lancashire Rd. Leigh WA3 76 B1
East Lancashire Rd. Pendlebury M27 80 B6
East Lancashire Rd. Swinton M27 & M28 79 D7
East Lancashire Rd. Tyldesley M28 & M29 & WA3 77 C5
East Lancashire Rd. Worsley M28 & M26 & M27 78 D7
East Lea. M34 101 A2
East Lynn Dr. M28 61 A3
East Market St. M3 158 D2
East Meade. Bolton BL3 147 E2
East Meade. M'ster M25 63 D2
East Meade. M'ster M21 109 B7
East Meade. Swinton M26 & M27 79 E6
East Moor. M28 78 A7
East Mount. WN5 53 F6
East Newton St. 11 M10 & M40 159 C3
East Ordsall La. M3 & M5 158 D1
East Over. SK6 125 A8
East Park Cl. M13 163 C6
East Philip St. M3 158 E3
East Rd. Eccles M41 95 F6
East Rd. M'ster M12 & M18 99 A3
East Rd. M'ster M18 99 B4
East Rd. Mossley SK15 86 E6
East Rd. Stretford M32 96 B4
East Rd. Wythenshawe M90 130 C7
East St. Ashton-i-M WN4 73 D4
East St. 3 Ashton-u-L OL6 85 D4
East St. Bury BL9 140 F1
East St. Dukinfield M34 100 F7
East St. Edenfield BL0 1 D4
East St. Haslingden BB4 1 A7
East St. Hindley WN2 57 B3
East St. Littleborough OL12 15 C6
East St. Littleborough OL15 16 C5
East St. Milnrow OL16 31 D7
East St. R'dale OL16 31 A8
East St. Radcliffe M26 44 B3
East St. Tyldesley M46 58 F1
East Union St. M16 161 C6
East Vale. SK6 126 A5
East View. 5 Middleton M24 64 F8
East View. Ramsbottom BL0 1 C1
East View. Ramsbottom BL0 11 C3
East Ward Cty Prim Sch. BL9 141 B2
East Ward Cty Prim Sch (Annexe). BL9 141 B3
East Way. BL1 25 B3
East Wlk. BL7 8 D2
Eastbank St. BL1 143 F2
Eastbourne Gr. BL1 144 A8
Eastbourne St. Oldham OL8 67 B4
Eastbourne St. R'dale OL11 139 F5
Eastbrook Ave. 2 M26 44 C4
Eastburn Ave. M10 & M40 159 C3
Eastchurch Cl. BL4 60 D7
Eastcombe Ave. M7 81 B7
Eastcote Rd. SK5 111 F5
Eastcote Wlk. 5 BL4 42 E1
Eastdale Pl. WA14 119 D7
Easterdale. OL4 67 C6
Eastern Ave. M27 62 D3
Eastern By-Pass. Droylsden M11 83 C2
Eastern By-Pass. M'ster M11 99 D8
Eastern Circ. M19 111 A6
Eastfield. M6 154 E4
Eastfield Ave. M'ster M10 & M40 160 E3
Eastfield Ave. Middleton M24 65 A7
Eastfields. M26 43 E5
Eastford Sq. M40 159 C4
Eastgarth. WN2 56 B2
Eastgarth Wlk. 21 M9 64 E3
Eastgate. OL12 14 C7
Eastgate St. OL7 166 A1
Eastgrove Ave. BL1 24 E6
Eastham Ave. Bury BL9 27 F6
Eastham Ave. M'ster M14 98 B1
Eastham Way. 11 Handforth SK9 131 D5
Eastham Way. Walkden M38 60 B5
Easthaven Ave. 4 M11 83 C2
Eastholme Dr. M19 111 B7
Easthope Cl. M20 110 B7
Eastlands Rd. M9 64 E5
Eastleigh Ave. M7 155 E8
Eastleigh Cres. WN7 76 B3
Eastleigh Dr. M10 & M40 160 D3
Eastleigh Gr. 2 BL1 145 E8
Eastleigh Rd. Gatley SK8 122 B1
Eastleigh Rd. M'ster M25 63 E3
Eastmoor Dr. M40 83 D4
Eastmoor Gr. BL3 146 B2
Eastnor Cl. M15 162 D6
Easton Cl. Middleton M24 65 C7
Easton Cl. Wigan WN3 55 A2
Easton Dr. SK8 123 A5
Easton Rd. M43 83 E1
Eastpark Cl. M13 163 C6
Eastry Ave. SK5 112 B6
Eastview. M33 108 B3
Eastville Gdns. M19 110 E5
Eastward Ave. SK9 136 F6
Eastway. Middleton M24 46 F1
Eastway. Sale M33 107 F1
Eastway. Shaw OL2 149 B6
Eastway. Urmston M41 94 E3
Eastwell Rd. Ashton-i-M WN4 73 A3
Eastwell Rd. Wigan WN6 36 F3
Eastwood Ave. Droylsden M43 83 E1
Eastwood Ave. Failsworth M40 65 F1
Eastwood Ave. Newton-l-W WA12 89 F3
Eastwood Ave. Urmston M41 95 D2
Eastwood Ave. Walkden M28 60 A2
Eastwood Cl. BL9 141 B2
Eastwood Gr. WN7 75 D5
Eastwood Rd. M40 65 E1
Eastwood St. Denton M34 100 D7
Eastwood St. 11 Littleborough OL15 16 B5
Eastwood Terr. BL1 40 E8
Eatock Cty Prim Sch. BL5 57 E6
Eatock St. WN2 56 B3
Eatock Way. BL5 57 D6
Eaton Cl. Cheadle SK8 122 F3
Eaton Cl. Poynton SK12 134 A3
Eaton Cl. Swinton M27 61 F2
Eaton Dr. Alderley Edge SK9 136 F2
Eaton Dr. Ashton-u-L OL7 84 F4
Eaton Dr. Sale WA15 120 A8
Eaton Rd. Alt'ham WA14 119 C1
Eaton Rd. M'ster M8 63 F1
Eaton Rd. Sale M33 108 A4
Eaton St. WN2 56 E6
Eaves Knoll Rd. SK12 127 A1
Eaves La. OL9 152 A5
Ebbdale Cl. SK1 124 A8
Ebberstone St. M14 98 A2
Ebden St. M1 163 B8
Ebenezer St. Glossop SK13 116 D7
Ebenezer St. 2 M'ster M15 162 F7
Ebnal Wlk. M14 110 D7
Ebor Cl. OL2 149 A8
Ebor House. M21 96 F1
Ebor Rd. M22 121 E4
Ebor St. OL15 16 B5
Ebsworth St. M'ster M40 83 A8
Ebsworth St. M'ster M40 157 F8
Ebury St. M26 43 F3
Eccles CE High Sch. M30 78 F1
Eccles Cl. M11 165 C8
Eccles Coll. M30 79 F4
Eccles New Rd. M30 & M5 & M6 80 C2
Eccles Old Rd. M30 & M6 80 C3
Eccles Rd. Swinton M27 79 F6
Eccles Rd. Wigan WN5 36 B1
Eccles St. BL0 138 B6
Eccles Sta. M30 79 F2
Ecclesbridge Rd. SK6 125 F4
Eccleshall St. M11 83 C1
Eccleston Ave. 23 Bolton BL2 25 B1
Eccleston Ave. M'ster M14 98 B1
Eccleston Ave. Swinton M27 79 D7
Eccleston Cl. BL8 27 A1
Eccleston Pl. M7 155 D8
Eccleston Rd. SK3 123 E4
Eccleston St. Failsworth M35 84 A8
Eccleston St. Wigan WN1 37 C1
Eccleston Way. 3 SK9 131 D4
Eccups La. SK9 136 C8
Echo St. M1 163 B8
Eckersley Ave. WN2 56 D3
Eckersley Cl. 1 M23 120 F6
Eckersley Fold La. M46 58 A1
Eckersley Rd. BL1 143 E3
Eckersley St. Bolton BL3 146 C4
Eckersley St. Wigan WN1 37 E1
Eckford St. M8 156 B6
Eclipse Cl. OL16 31 C7
Edale Ave. Denton M34 100 D7
Edale Ave. Denton M34 112 F8
Edale Ave. M'ster M40 83 A8
Edale Ave. Reddish SK5 100 A1
Edale Ave. Urmston M41 95 B1
Edale Bank. 6 SK13 171 E1
Edale Cl. Alt'ham WA14 119 C1
Edale Cl. Atherton M46 58 C3
Edale Cl. 26 Gamesley SK13 171 E2
Edale Cl. Gatley SK8 131 D7
Edale Cl. Hazel Grove SK7 124 E1
Edale Cl. Irlam M44 94 A1
Edale Cres. SK13 171 E1
Edale Dr. WN6 19 E2
Edale Fold. 25 SK13 171 E2
Edale Gr. Ashton-u-L OL6 86 A6
Edale Gr. Sale M33 107 E2
Edale Rd. Bolton BL3 146 A4
Edale Rd. Farnworth BL4 60 C7
Edale Rd. Leigh WN7 76 C4
Edale Rd. Stretford M32 96 B3
Edale St. M6 81 B5
Edbrook Wlk. M13 164 D5
Eddie Colman Cl. M40 83 B5
Eddisbury Ave. M'ster M20 109 F8
Eddisbury Ave. Urmston M41 94 D4
Edditch Gr. BL2 148 C7
Eddleston St. WN4 72 F6
Eddystone Cl. 6 M5 81 A1
Eden Ave. Bolton BL1 143 E3
Eden Ave. Edenfield BL0 1 D3
Eden Ave. Fowley Common WA3 92 C4
Eden Ave. High Lane SK6 134 E7
Eden Bank. WN7 76 B6
Eden Cl. Heywood OL10 29 A3
Eden Cl. M'ster M15 163 A6
Eden Cl. 3 Platt Bridge WN2 56 A2
Eden Cl. Stockport SK1 124 A8
Eden Cl. Wilmslow SK9 136 E5
Eden Ct. Edenfield BL0 1 D2
Eden Ct. M'ster M19 111 A8
Eden Gr. Bolton BL1 143 E3
Eden Gr. Leigh WN7 75 C5
Eden Pl. Cheadle SK8 122 D6
Eden Pl. Sale M33 108 B5
Eden St. Bolton BL1 143 E3
Eden St. Bury BL9 140 F2
Eden St. Edenfield BL0 1 D1
Eden St. Oldham OL1 153 E7
Eden St. R'dale OL12 139 D8
Eden Way. OL2 149 A8
Edenbridge Dr. M26 61 B7
Edenbridge Rd. Cheadle SK8 123 B4
Edenbridge Rd. Failsworth M40 83 B4
Edendale Dr. M22 121 D1
Edenfield Ave. M21 109 D4
Edenfield CE Prim Sch. BL0 1 D4
Edenfield La. M28 78 F4
Edenfield Rd. M'ster M25 & M8 63 E2
Edenfield Rd. R'dale OL11 & OL12 13 D2
Edenfield St. OL11 & OL12 14 C1
Edenhall Ave. M19 110 F8
Edenhall Gr. WN2 56 F3
Edenham Wlk. 1 M40 65 D2
Edenhurst Dr. WA15 120 B5
Edenhurst Rd. SK2 124 B6
Edensor Dr. WA15 120 C3
Edenvale. M28 78 A7
Edgar St. Bolton BL3 145 E6
Edgar St. R'dale OL16 15 C2
Edgar St. Ramsbottom BL0 138 B5
Edgar St W. BL0 138 B5
Edgbaston Dr. M16 97 A3
Edge Fold Cres. M28 78 D8
Edge Fold Rd. M28 60 D1
Edge Gn. M28 78 C8
Edge Green La. WA3 73 F2
Edge Green Rd. WA3 & WN4 73 F4
Edge Green St. WN4 73 D4
Edge Hall Rd. WN5 53 E5
Edge Hill Ave. OL2 48 E3
Edge Hill Rd. Bolton BL3 146 B3
Edge Hill Rd. Oldham OL2 48 E3
Edge La. Bacup OL13 4 C8
Edge La. Bolton BL1 23 C5
Edge La. Droylsden M43 & M11 83 D2
Edge La. Edgworth BL7 9 A8
Edge La. Stalybridge SK14 102 F4
Edge La. Stretford M21 & M32 96 E1
Edge Lane Rd. OL1 67 A8
Edge Lane St. OL2 48 E4
Edge St. M4 159 A2
Edge View. OL1 47 E1
Edge View La. WA16 136 B2
Edge Ware Gr. WN3 54 D3
Edgedale Ave. M19 110 E5
Edgefield Ave. M9 64 E4
Edgefold Ind Est. BL4 146 B1
Edgehill Chase. SK9 137 E7
Edgehill Cl. M5 & M6 154 F2
Edgehill Ct. M32 96 E1
Edgehill Rd. M6 80 C3
Edgehill St. 10 M4 159 A2
Edgeley Fold. SK3 123 C7

Fenton St. M'ster M12 165 A5
Fenton St. 5 Oldham OL4 67 B6
Fenton St. R'dale OL11 139 E5
Fenton St. Shaw OL2 149 B5
Fenton Way. WN2 56 F4
Fenwick Dr. SK4 110 E3
Fenwick St. OL11 139 E7
Ferdinand St. M10 & M40 160 D4
Fereday St. M28 60 D4
Ferguson Ct. M19 110 F8
Ferguson Rise. WN5 54 E8
Fern Ave. Newton-l-W WA12 89 D2
Fern Ave. Urmston M41 95 A2
Fern Bank. Failsworth M40 83 C7
Fern Bank. Stalybridge SK15 86 C1
Fern Bank Cl. SK15 102 C8
Fern Bank Dr. M23 120 E8
Fern Bank St. SK14 113 E8
Fern Cl. Atherton M46 58 D2
Fern Cl. Marple SK6 125 F6
Fern Cl. Middleton M24 65 D8
Fern Cl. Oldham OL4 67 F6
Fern Cl. Shevington WN6 36 A6
Fern Clough. BL1 40 F7
Fern Common. OL2 149 B7
Fern Cres. SK15 86 C1
Fern Dene. OL12 14 B2
Fern Hill La. OL12 14 A3
Fern Isle Cl. OL12 14 B6
Fern Lea. Gatley SK8 122 B1
Fern Lea. Hollingworth SK14 103 D5
Fern Lea Gr. M38 59 F4
Fern Lea St. BB4 2 D8
Fern St. Bolton BL3 144 C6
Fern St. Bury BL9 140 F3
Fern St. Chadderton OL9 152 A8
Fern St. Farnworth BL4 42 E1
Fern St. Littleborough OL12 15 C6
Fern St. M'ster M8 159 A4
Fern St. M'ster M11 165 B7
Fern St. Oldham OL8 153 D5
Fern St. R'dale OL11 139 D6
Fern St. Ramsbottom BL0 11 D7
Fern View. WA15 120 E5
Fernacre. M33 108 C5
Fernally St. SK14 167 E2
Fernbank. M26 62 A8
Fernbray Ave. M19 110 D4
Fernbray Rd. WN2 57 A5
Fernbrook Cl. M13 164 D5
Fernbrook Wlk. 12 M8 155 F7
Fernclough Rd. M9 157 D7
Ferndale Ave. Royton OL16 48 C8
Ferndale Ave. Stockport SK2 124 B4
Ferndale Ave. Whitefield M45 62 C7
Ferndale Cl. OL4 67 D4
Ferndale Gdns. M19 110 E6
Ferndale Rd. M33 108 B2
Ferndale Wlk. WN7 75 B5
Ferndene Rd. M'ster M20 110 B5
Ferndene Rd.
Prestwich M25 & M45 63 C7
Ferndown Ave.
Chadderton M24 65 E7
Ferndown Ave.
Hazel Grove SK7 124 C1
Ferndown Dr. M44 94 A3
Ferndown Rd. Bolton BL2 25 E3
Ferndown Rd. Sale M23 120 D8
Ferney Field Rd. OL9 65 F7
Ferney Field Sch. OL9 65 F7
Ferngate Dr. M20 110 B6
Ferngrove. BL9 28 B5
Fernhill. SK6 126 B6
Fernhill Ave. Bacup OL13 3 E8
Fernhill Ave. Bolton BL3 146 A4
Fernhill Caravan Pk. BL9 140 F4
Fernhill Cl. Bacup OL13 3 E8
Fernhill Cl. Glossop SK13 104 D3
Fernhill Cres. 1 OL13 3 E8
Fernhill Dr. Bacup OL13 3 E8
Fernhill Dr. M'ster M18 99 B4
Fernhill Gr. 2 OL13 3 E8
Fernhill Pk. OL13 3 E8
Fernhill St. BL9 140 F3
Fernhill Way. 4 OL13 3 E8
Fernhills. BL7 8 E2
Fernholme Ct. OL8 66 C4
Fernhurst Cl. WN3 151 F6
Fernhurst Gr. 15 BL1 143 E1
Fernhurst Rd. M20 110 C5
Fernhurst St. OL1 & OL9 48 C1
Fernie St. M4 & M8 159 A3
Fernilee Cl. SK12 127 C1
Fernlea. Alt'ham WA15 119 F1
Fernlea. M'ster SK4 111 C5
Fernlea Ave. OL1 48 C1
Fernlea Cl. Hadfield SK14 171 E4
Fernlea Cl. R'dale OL12 14 B2
Fernlea Cres. M27 79 E7
Fernlea Gr. WN4 72 D5
Fernlea Lodge. BL4 60 E7
Fernleaf St. M14 98 A4
Fernleigh Ave. M19 99 C1
Fernleigh Dr. M16 162 D5
Fernley Ave. M34 101 A2
Fernley Rd. SK2 124 B6
Fernone. SK9 131 D3
Ferns Gr. BL1 144 B7
Fernside. M26 61 C6
Fernside Ave. M20 110 D5
Fernside Gr. Walkden M28 60 E4
Fernside Gr. Wigan WN3 54 D1
Fernside Way. OL12 14 A1
Fernstead. BL3 144 C6
Fernthorpe Ave. OL3 51 C1
Fernview Dr. BL0 11 B1
Fernville Terr. 6 OL13 3 D8
Fernwood. SK6 126 C7
Fernwood Ave. M18 99 D3
Fernwood Gr. SK9 137 C8
Ferrand Lodge. OL15 16 C7
Ferrand Rd. OL15 16 B6
Ferrer St. WN4 72 F6
Ferring Wlk. OL9 152 B6
Ferris St. M11 99 D8
Ferry Rd. M44 94 B2
Ferry St. M11 164 E8
Ferryhill Rd. M44 94 A2
Fettler Cl. M27 79 F7
Fiddlers La. M44 94 B4
Fiddlers Lane Prim Sch.
M44 94 B3
Field Bank Gr. M19 99 C1
Field Cl. Bramhall SK7 132 D4
Field Cl. Marple SK6 125 D5
Field End Cl. SK15 102 D8
Field House La. SK6 126 A6
Field La. OL6 85 D5
Field Rd. Milnrow OL16 31 D7
Field Rd. Sale M33 107 E6
Field St. Droylsden M43 99 F8
Field St. Dukinfield SK14 101 D5
Field St. Failsworth M35 83 E7
Field St. Hindley WN2 56 E4
Field St. Ince-i-M WN2 55 F4
Field St. M'ster M18 99 E6
Field St. 11 R'dale OL11 31 A4
Field St. Romiley SK6 113 A3
Field St. Salford M6 154 F2
Field St. Wigan WN6 150 B8
Field Vale Dr. SK5 100 A1
Field Vale Wlk. M14 97 F2
Field Wlk. WA15 120 B3
Fieldbrook Wlk. BL5 40 A1
Fieldcroft. OL11 30 B7
Fielden Ave. M21 97 B1
Fielden Rd. M20 109 F4
Fielden St. OL15 15 E2
Fieldfare Ave. M40 83 B4
Fieldfare Way. OL6 & OL7 85 B7
Fieldhead Ave. Bury BL8 27 A2
Fieldhead Ave. R'dale OL11 30 B7
Fieldhead Ave. Tyldesley M29 77 B5
Fieldhead Mews. SK9 137 E8
Fieldhead Rd. SK9 137 E8
Fieldhouse Ind Est. OL12 14 F2
Fieldhouse Rd. OL12 14 F2
Fielding Ave. SK12 133 E2
Fielding Pl. PR6 21 B8
Fielding St. Eccles M30 79 C1
Fielding St. Middleton M24 47 A2
Fields Cres. SK14 103 D6
Fields Ct. SK14 102 C1
Fields End Fold. M30 94 C4
Fields Farm Cl. SK14 102 D1
Fields Farm Rd. SK14 102 D2
Fields Farm Wlk. 6 SK14 102 D2
Fields Gr. SK14 103 D5
Fields New Rd. OL9 152 B5
Fields The. WN2 38 C4
Fieldsend Dr. WN7 91 C8
Fieldsway. OL8 66 E2
Fieldvale Rd. M33 107 E1
Fieldway. Platt Bridge WN2 56 B2
Fieldway. R'dale OL16 31 B3
Fife Ave. OL9 66 A4
Fifth Ave. Bolton BL1 144 B7
Fifth Ave. Bury BL9 28 D4
Fifth Ave. Droylsden M11 83 C2
Fifth Ave. Little Lever BL3 42 F4
Fifth Ave. Oldham OL8 66 C2
Fifth St. Bolton BL1 23 F4
Fifth St. Stretford M17 96 D5
Filbert St. 8 OL1 49 C1
Filby Wlk. M10 & M40 160 E4
Fildes St. M24 65 D7
Filey Ave. M'ster M16 97 D2
Filey Ave. Urmston M41 95 A4
Filey Dr. M6 80 D6
Filey Rd. M'ster M14 110 D8
Filey Rd. Stockport SK2 124 C7
Filey St. OL16 15 C3
Filton Ave. 3 BL3 145 D5
Filton Wlk. M9 156 C6
Finance St. OL15 15 F4
Finborough Cl. M16 97 E4
Finch Ave. BL4 59 F7
Finch La. WN6 18 B1
Finch Mill Ave. WN6 35 D7
Finchale Dr. WA15 120 C1
Finchcroft. OL1 153 E7
Finchdale Gdns. WA3 91 B8
Finchley Ave. M40 83 C4
Finchley Cres. WN2 38 A2
Finchley Gr. M40 65 A1
Finchley Rd. Alt'ham WA15 119 E3
Finchley Rd. M'ster M14 110 B8
Findlay Cl. WA12 89 C2
Findlay St. WN7 75 E5
Findon Rd. M23 121 A6
Finger Post. BL3 43 A4
Finghall Rd. M41 95 B2
Finishing Wlk. 6 M4 159 C1
Finlan Rd. M24 47 E5
Finland Rd. SK3 170 D7
Finlay Ct. WN5 54 E8
Finlay St. BL4 60 D8
Finney Cl. SK9 131 C2
Finney Dr. Handforth SK9 131 C2
Finney Dr. M'ster M21 109 A7
Finney La. SK8 122 C1
Finney St. BL3 147 F4
Finningley Rd. M9 64 B5
Finny Bank Rd. M33 108 A6
Finsbury Ave. M40 83 C4
Finsbury Rd. SK5 111 E8
Finsbury St. OL11 139 D5
Finstock Cl. M30 79 B1
Fintry Gr. M30 79 D1
Fir Ave. SK7 132 E8
Fir Bank Prim Sch. OL2 48 D7
Fir Bank Rd. OL2 48 D6
Fir Cl. SK12 133 F3
Fir Gr. M'ster M19 99 A1
Fir Gr. Oldham OL9 152 B8
Fir Gr. Wigan WN6 37 A3
Fir La. OL2 48 D6
Fir Rd. Bramhall SK7 132 E8
Fir Rd. Denton M34 101 A3
Fir Rd. Farnworth BL4 60 B8
Fir Rd. Marple SK6 125 E5
Fir Rd. Swinton M27 79 E6
Fir St. Bolton BL1 143 F2
Fir St. Bury BL9 141 A2
Fir St. Eccles M30 79 D1
Fir St. Failsworth M35 83 E7
Fir St. Heywood OL10 29 E1
Fir St. Irlam M44 105 D6
Fir St. M'ster M16 97 C4
Fir St. M'ster M10 & M40 160 D4
Fir St. Radcliffe M26 44 B2
Fir St. Ramsbottom BL0 11 D7
Fir St. Royton OL2 48 D5
Fir St. Salford M6 154 F2
Fir St. Stockport SK4 169 E2
Fir St. Walsden OL14 6 A8
Fir Tree Ave. Boothstown M28 78 B5
Fir Tree Ave. Golborne WA3 90 F8
Fir Tree Ave. Oldham OL8 67 A2
Fir Tree Cl. SK16 101 F8
Fir Tree Cres. Ince-i-M WN2 55 F3
Fir Tree Cres.
Stalybridge SK16 101 F8
Fir Tree Dr. Dukinfield SK14 101 E5
Fir Tree Dr. Ince-i-M WN2 55 F3
Fir Tree House. OL8 67 A2
Fir Tree La. SK16 101 F8
Fir Tree Prim Sch. SK5 99 E2
Fir Tree St. WN2 55 F4
Fir Tree Way. 3 BL6 22 E1
Fir Tree Wlk. WA3 90 F8
Firbank Rd. Wigan WN3 55 B3
Firbank Rd.
Wythenshawe M23 121 B4
Firbarn Cl. OL16 31 D7
Firbeck Dr. M4 160 D2
Fircroft. WN6 19 A2
Fircroft Ct. 4 SK3 123 F4
Fircroft Rd. OL8 67 A2
Firdale Ave. M40 65 E1
Firdale Wlk. OL9 152 C7
Firdon Wlk. 17 M9 157 E7
Fire Station Sq. M5 81 C2
Firecrest Cl. M28 78 B8
Firefly Cl. M3 158 D1
Firethorn Ave. M19 110 F6
Firethorn Cl. BL5 39 F2
Firethorn Dr. SK14 102 A2
Firethorn Wlk. 5 M33 107 C5
Firfield Gr. M28 60 F3
Firgrove Ave. OL16 31 D8
Firgrove Gdns. OL16 31 D8
Firs Ave. Ashton-u-L OL6 85 B5
Firs Ave. Failsworth M35 83 E7
Firs Ave. M'ster M16 97 B2
Firs Cottages. WN2 38 D1
Firs Cty Prim Sch. M33 107 D4
Firs Gr. SK8 122 A4
Firs La. WN7 75 C5
Firs Park Cres. WN2 38 D1
Firs Rd. Atherton BL5 59 A6
Firs Rd. Gatley SK8 122 A4
Firs Rd. Sale M33 107 D5
Firs The. Alt'ham WA14 119 B3
Firs The. Wilmslow SK9 137 A5
Firs Way. M33 107 C3
Firsby Ave. SK6 112 F4
Firsby St. 5 M19 99 A1
Firsdale Ind Est. WN7 75 C6
First Ave. Atherton M46 58 D4
First Ave. Bury BL8 26 F6
First Ave. Droylsden M11 83 D2
First Ave. 11 Hindley WN2 56 D5
First Ave. Little Lever BL3 43 A4
First Ave. Mossley SK15 86 E5
First Ave. Oldham OL8 66 D2
First Ave. Poynton SK10 133 D1
First Ave. Stretford M17 96 D6
First Ave. Swinton M27 79 D5
First Ave. Tyldesley M29 77 C4
First Ave. Wigan WN6 37 A2
First St. BL1 23 F4
Firsway. WN7 75 B5
Firswood Dr. Hyde SK14 102 A3
Firswood Dr. Royton OL2 48 C6
Firswood Dr. Swinton M27 79 E6
Firswood Mount. SK8 122 A4
Firth Cl. M7 155 D6
Firth St. OL1 153 F6
Firtree Ave. M33 107 C4
Firvale Ave. SK8 122 B1
Firvale Cl. WN7 75 C5
Firwood Ave. Farnworth BL4 60 C7
Firwood Ave.
Stretford M32 & M41 96 A2
Firwood Cl. SK2 124 C8
Firwood Cres. M26 44 B1
Firwood Gr. Ashton-i-M WN4 73 A4
Firwood Gr. Bolton BL2 25 B2
Firwood La. BL2 25 C3
Firwood Pk. M24 & OL9 65 E8
Firwood Sch. BL2 25 C2
Firwood Stables. BL2 25 C3
Fish Rake La. BL0 1 E6
Fishbourne Sq. 8 M14 98 C3
Fishbrook Ind Est. BL4 61 A7
Fisher Ave. WA2 74 C7
Fisher Cl. WN3 54 F5
Fisher Dr. WN5 53 E7
Fisher St. OL1 153 F8
Fisherfield. OL12 13 F1
Fishermore Rd. M41 94 E2
Fishpool Cty Inf Sch. BL9 44 F8
Fishwick St. OL16 31 A6
Fistral Ave. SK8 131 C8
Fistral Cres. SK15 86 D3
Fitchfield Wlk. M28 60 D3
Fitton Ave. M21 109 B6
Fitton Cres. M27 61 F3
Fitton Hill Inf Sch. OL8 67 B3
Fitton Hill Jun Sch. OL8 67 A3
Fitton Hill Rd. OL8 67 A4
Fitton St. Bolton BL3 147 E4
Fitton St. R'dale OL16 31 A8
Fitton St. Royton OL2 48 F4
Fitton St. Shaw OL2 48 F7
Fitzadam St. WN1 150 B8
Fitzalan St. SK13 104 C1
Fitzgeorge St. M40 156 C5
Fitzgerald Cl. M25 62 F2
Fitzgerald Ct. 11 M34 113 A8
Fitzgerald Way. M6 154 F3
Fitzhugh St. BL1 25 A5
Fitzroy St. Ashton-u-L OL7 100 F8
Fitzroy St. Droylsden M34 100 B8
Fitzroy St. Stalybridge SK15 86 D4
Fitzwarren Ct. M6 154 F2
Fitzwarren St. M6 154 F3
Fitzwilliam St. M7 158 D4
Five Fold Pk. OL9 153 D6
Five Quarters. M26 43 E5
Fiveways. M43 84 A2
Fiveways Par. SK7 133 E8
Flag Row. M40 159 B3
Flag St. OL13 3 E8
Flagcroft Dr. M23 121 B5
Flagg Wood Ave. SK6 125 D7
Flake La. OL2 48 D5
Flamborough Wlk. 7 M14 98 B3
Flamingo Cl. M12 165 A6
Flamingo Villas. M44 94 A3
Flamstead Ave. M23 120 E6
Flannel St. 4 OL12 & OL16 31 A8
Flapper Fold La. M46 58 C3
Flash Cotts. OL4 68 A4
Flash St. M40 83 C6
Flashfields. M25 62 F1
Flatley Cl. M15 163 A5
Flavian Wlk. M11 165 B8
Flax Cl. BB4 1 A8
Flax Moss Cl. BB4 1 A8
Flax St. M'ster M3 158 D3
Flax St. Ramsbottom BL0 11 A4
Flaxcroft Rd. M22 121 B3
Flaxfield Ave. SK15 86 D2
Flaxpool Cl. M16 97 E4
Flaxwood Wlk. M22 121 B3
Fleece St. 2 Oldham OL4 67 B7
Fleece St. R'dale OL16 139 F7
Fleeson St. M14 98 C3
Fleet St. Ashton-u-L OL6 166 B2
Fleet St. Droylsden M18 99 F6
Fleet St. Horwich BL6 22 D3
Fleet St. Hyde SK14 167 E3
Fleet St. Oldham OL4 67 C7
Fleet St. Wigan WN5 54 B6
Fleetwood Rd. M28 60 A3
Fleming Pl. OL9 153 D6
Fleming Rd. M22 121 D2
Flemish Rd. M34 101 B2
Fletcher Ave. Atherton M46 58 D5
Fletcher Ave. Swinton M27 62 A3
Fletcher Cl. Heywood OL10 29 D2
Fletcher Cl. Oldham OL9 153 D6
Fletcher Dr. SK12 134 F6
Fletcher Fold Rd. BL9 44 F6
Fletcher Moss Mus
& Art Gal. M20 110 B1
Fletcher Sq. 16 M60 159 C1
Fletcher St. 1
Ashton-u-L OL6 166 C3
Fletcher St. Atherton M46 58 C3
Fletcher St. Bolton BL3 145 E5
Fletcher St. Bury BL9 141 A2
Fletcher St. Farnworth BL4 60 D8
Fletcher St. Little Lever BL3 43 B3
Fletcher St.
M'ster M10 & M40 157 F5
Fletcher St. R'dale OL11 31 A5
Fletcher St. Radcliffe M26 44 C4
Fletcher St. Stockport SK1 169 F1
Fletcher's Rd. OL16 15 E3
Fletsand Rd. SK9 137 D6
Flexbury Wlk. M40 83 D4
Flint Cl. Droylsden M11 83 B2
Flint Cl. Hazel Grove SK7 124 C1
Flint Gr. M44 105 C6
Flint St. Droylsden M43 84 B2
Flint St. Oldham OL1 67 C8
Flint St. Stockport SK3 170 F7
Flitcroft Ct. BL3 147 F4
Flixton Girls' High Sch.
M41 95 A2
Flixton Golf Course. M41 107 A7
Flixton Inf Sch. M41 94 F3
Flixton Jun Sch. M41 94 F2
Flixton Rd. Flixton M31 106 E7
Flixton Rd. Urmston M41 94 F1
Flixton Rd. Urmston M41 95 B2
Flixton Sta. M41 94 E1
Flixton Wlk. M13 164 D5
Floats Rd. Alt'ham M23 120 E4
Floats Rd. Alt'ham M23 120 E6
Floatshall Rd. M23 121 A6
Flockton Ave. WN6 36 D4
Flockton Ct. 7 BL6 22 B4
Flora Dr. M7 158 D4
Flora St. Ashton-i-M WN4 73 B2
Flora St. Bolton BL3 147 E4
Flora St. M'ster M9 64 C3
Flora St. Oldham OL1 153 E7
Floral Ct. M7 155 D6
Florence Ave. BL1 24 F5
Florence Ct. SK3 123 B6
Florence Nightingale
Hospl. BL9 27 C1
Florence Park Ct. M20 110 C4
Florence St. Bolton BL3 147 D4
Florence St. Droylsden M34 100 B8
Florence St. Eccles M30 79 B1
Florence St. Failsworth M35 83 F8
Florence St. Sale M33 108 B6
Florence St. Stockport SK4 169 E2
Florence St. Wigan WN1 151 E8
Florence Steet. OL16 31 B6
Florence Way. SK14 103 D5
Florian House. OL1 153 F7
Florida St. OL8 153 E5
Florist St. SK3 170 E7
Flowery Bank. OL8 67 B4
Flowery Field. SK2 124 A3
Flowery Field Prim Sch.
SK14 167 D4
Flowery Field Sta. SK14 101 D5
Floyd Ave. M21 109 C5
Floyer Rd. M9 64 E5
Foden La.
Alderley Edge SK9 & WA16 136 C1
Foden La. Woodford SK7 132 D3
Foden Wlk. 7 SK9 131 D2
Fog La. M19 & M20 110 C4
Fold Ave. M43 84 B2
Fold Cres. SK15 86 F6
Fold Gdns. OL12 14 B4
Fold Gn. OL9 152 A6
Fold Mews. SK7 124 E3
Fold Rd. M26 61 C7
Fold St. Bolton BL1 145 F7
Fold St. Bury BL9 140 D2
Fold St. Golborne WA3 74 A1
Fold St. Heywood OL10 29 E3
Fold St. M'ster M40 83 A8
Fold The. M'ster M9 64 D3
Fold The. Royton OL2 49 A4
Fold The. Urmston M41 95 A3
Fold View. Bolton BL7 8 E1
Fold View. Oldham OL8 67 A2
Folds. BL6 21 C3
Folds Rd. BL1 & BL2 148 A8
Foleshill Ave. M9 157 D7
Foley Gdns. OL10 46 E7
Foley St. 8 WN2 56 D5
Foley Wlk. M22 130 E8
Foliage Cres. SK5 112 B5
Foliage Gdns. SK5 112 C5
Foliage Rd. SK5 112 B4
Folkestone Rd. M11 83 D2
Folkestone Rd E. M11 & M43 83 D2
Folkestone Rd W. M11 83 D2
Follows St. M18 99 D6
Folly La. M27 79 D6
Folly Wlk. 20 OL12 14 F1
Fonthill Gr. M33 107 F1
Fontwell Cl. 3 M'ster M16 97 C3
Fontwell Cl. Standish WN6 19 F1
Fontwell La. OL1 49 A1
Fontwell Rd. BL3 43 A2
Fontwell Wlk. 6 M40 65 D2
Foot Mill Cres. OL12 14 D2
Foot Wood Cres. OL12 14 D2
Forber Cres. M18 99 D3
Forbes Cl. Sale M33 108 D2
Forbes Cl. Stockport SK1 124 B8
Forbes Pk. SK7 132 D7
Forbes Rd. SK1 112 B1
Forbes St. SK6 112 F4
Ford Gr. SK14 103 A4
Ford La. M'ster M20 110 A2
Ford La. Salford M6 81 A4
Ford La.
Wythenshawe M20 & M22 109 F1
Ford Lodge. M20 110 B2
Ford St. Dukinfield SK16 101 C6
Ford St. Kearsley M26 61 A8
Ford St. M'ster M3 158 D2
Ford St. M'ster M12 164 D7
Ford St. Stockport SK3 169 D1
Ford Way. SK14 103 A4
Ford's La. SK7 132 D6
Fordbank Rd. M20 110 A2
Fordel Wlk. M9 158 E4
Fordham Gr. BL1 144 C8
Fordland Cl. WA3 74 E1
Fordoe La. OL12 13 C4
Fordyce Way. WN2 56 A8
Foreland Cl. M40 157 D5
Forest Ave. WN6 36 F3
Forest Dr. Alt'ham WA15 119 F6
Forest Dr. Sale M33 107 E2
Forest Dr.
Shevington Moor WN6 19 A2
Forest Dr. Westhoughton BL5 58 A8
Forest Gdns. M31 105 D3
Forest Park Sch. M33 108 A4
Forest Range. M19 99 A1
Forest Rd. BL1 142 B3
Forest Sch. WA15 119 F6
Forest St. Ashton-u-L OL6 166 C4
Forest St. Oldham OL8 66 F2
Forest St. Worsley M28 79 A4
Forest View. OL12 14 D2
Forest Way. BL2 25 C6
Forester Dr. SK15 86 A1
Forester Hill Ave. Bolton BL3 42 A3
Forester Hill Ave.
Bolton BL3 147 F3
Forester Hill Cl. BL3 147 F3
Forfar St. BL1 24 E5
Forge Ind Est. OL4 67 B7
Forge La. M11 160 F2
Forge St. Oldham OL1 & OL4 67 B7
Forge St. Wigan WN1 & WN2 151 E7
Formby Ave. Atherton M46 58 D4
Formby Ave. M'ster M21 109 D7
Formby Dr. SK8 131 B8
Formby Rd. M6 80 E5
Forres Gr. WN4 72 D4
Forrest Rd. M34 101 B1
Forrester Dr. OL2 49 D8
Forrester St. M28 79 A8
Forresters Cl. WN2 74 E8
Forshaw Ave. M18 99 F6
Forshaw St. M34 100 D4
Forster St. WA3 74 A1
Forston Wlk. M8 156 B6
Forsyth St. OL12 13 E2
Forsythia Wlk. 2 M31 105 E2
Fort Rd. M25 63 D2
Fortescue Rd. SK2 124 D7
Forth Pl. M26 43 F5
Forth Rd. M26 43 F5
Forth St. WN7 76 C4
Forton Ave. BL2 42 E7
Forton Rd. WN3 54 F2
Fortran Cl. M5 81 A1
Fortrose Ave. M9 64 B3
Fortuna Gr. M19 110 F8
Fortune St. BL3 148 B5
Fortyacre Dr. SK6 112 E3
Forum Gr. M7 155 E5
Forum The. SK6 113 C2
Fosbrook Ave. M20 110 C4
Foscarn Dr. M23 121 B5
Fossgill Ave. BL2 25 C5
Foster Ave. WN3 151 E6
Foster Ct. BL9 28 D4
Foster La. BL2 25 F1
Foster St. Denton M34 100 F3
Foster St. Oldham OL4 67 C7
Foster St. Radcliffe M26 43 F3
Foster St. Salford M5 154 D1
Foster St. 6 Wigan WN6 37 A1
Foster Terr. 9 BL1 143 E1
Fosters Bldgs. WN6 150 B8
Fotherby Dr. M9 64 D3
Fotherby Pl. WN3 55 A3
Foul Clough Rd. OL14 5 D8
Foulds Ave. BL8 27 B2
Foundry La. M'ster M4 159 B2
Foundry La. Wigan WN3 54 D4
Foundry Rd. M32 96 D4
Foundry St. Bolton BL3 145 F5
Foundry St. Bury BL9 140 F2
Foundry St. Dukinfield SK16 101 D8
Foundry St. Heywood OL10 29 C2
Foundry St. Hindley WN2 56 D5
Foundry St. Leigh WN7 76 B4
Foundry St. Little Lever BL3 43 A3
Foundry St.
Newton-l-W WA12 89 B3
Foundry St. Oldham OL9 153 E6
Foundry St. 4 Radcliffe M26 44 A3
Foundry St. Swinton M27 62 A1
Fountain Ave. WA15 120 B2
Fountain Pl. Poynton SK12 133 D4
Fountain Pl. Whitefield M45 62 F7
Fountain St. Ashton-u-L OL6 85 E4
Fountain St. Bury BL8 27 C2
Fountain St. Bury BL9 141 A2
Fountain St. Eccles M30 95 D8
Fountain St. Hyde SK14 167 F3
Fountain St.
M'ster M4 & M60 159 A1
Fountain St. Middleton M24 65 A8
Fountain St. Oldham OL1 153 F7
Fountain St N. BL9 141 A3
Fountains Ave. Bolton BL2 25 C1
Fountains Ave.
Newton-l-W WA11 89 A7
Fountains Cl. M29 77 C7
Fountains Rd.
Bramhall SK7 & SK8 132 C6
Fountains Rd. Urmston M32 95 F3
Fountains Wlk.
Dukinfield SK16 101 C6
Fountains Wlk.
Golborne WA3 91 B8
Fountains Wlk. Oldham OL9 152 A5
Four Lane Ends. BL2 25 E4
Four Lanes. SK14 103 A4
Four Lanes End Rd. OL13 3 B8
Four Lanes Way. OL11 13 C2
Four Yards. M2 158 F1
Fouracres Rd. M23 121 A5
Fourgates Prim Sch. BL5 39 C4
Fourteen Meadows Rd.
WN3 150 B6
Fourth Ave. Bolton BL1 144 B7
Fourth Ave. Bury BL9 28 D4
Fourth Ave. Droylsden M11 83 C3
Fourth Ave. Mossley SK15 86 E6
Fourth Ave. Oldham OL8 66 C1
Fourth Ave. Oldham OL9 152 A5
Fourth Ave. Swinton M27 79 D5
Fourth St. Bolton BL1 23 F3
Fourth St. Stretford M17 96 C6
Fourways. M17 96 A6
Fowey Wlk. Hattersley SK14 102 E3
Fowey Wlk. 5
Wythenshawe M23 121 A5
Fowler Ave. M18 99 F7
Fowler Cl. WN1 151 E8
Fowler Ind Pk. BL6 22 C2
Fowler St. OL8 66 C3
Fowley Common La. WA3 92 C5
Fownhope Ave. M33 107 F3
Fownhope Rd. M33 107 F3
Fox Bank Ct. SK3 170 D8
Fox Bench Cl. SK7 & SK8 132 C6
Fox Cl. WA15 119 F6
Fox Hill. OL2 48 E8
Fox Hill Rd. OL11 47 D8
Fox Platt Rd. OL5 68 B1
Fox Platt Terr. OL5 86 C8
Fox St. Bury BL9 140 F3
Fox St. Eccles M30 79 F2
Fox St. Heywood OL10 29 C2
Fox St. Horwich BL6 22 C2
Fox St. Milnrow OL16 31 E6
Fox St. Oldham OL8 66 C2
Fox St. R'dale OL16 15 B1
Fox St. Stockport SK3 170 D8
Foxall Cl. M24 64 C7
Foxall St. M24 64 C7
Foxbank St. M13 98 E4
Foxbench Wlk. M21 109 D6
Foxcroft St. OL15 15 F5
Foxdale Cl. BL7 9 E7
Foxdale St. 3 M11 83 C1
Foxdene Gr. WN3 54 E2
Foxdenton Dr. M32 95 F3
Foxdenton La. M24 & OL9 65 F6
Foxdenton Sch. OL9 65 F5
Foxdenton Wlk. M34 100 E1
Foxendale Wlk. BL3 145 F5
Foxfield Cl. BL8 27 B5
Foxfield Dr. OL8 66 C1
Foxfield Rd. M23 121 A3
Foxford Wlk. M22 121 E2
Foxglove Cl. WN6 19 D2
Foxglove Ct. OL12 14 D3
Foxglove Dr. Alt'ham WA14 119 C8
Foxglove Dr. Bury BL9 28 D3
Foxglove La. SK15 86 A3
Foxglove Wlk. M31 105 F2
Foxhall Rd. Alt'ham WA15 119 F6
Foxhall Rd. Denton M34 100 D4
Foxham Wlk. M7 155 E6
Foxhill. WA14 119 A5
Foxhill Chase. SK2 125 A5
Foxhill Dr. SK15 102 C7
Foxhill Rd. M30 78 F1
Foxholes Cl. OL12 15 A1
Foxholes Rd. Horwich BL6 22 D4
Foxholes Rd. Hyde SK14 113 C8
Foxholes Rd. R'dale OL12 15 A2
Foxlair Ct. M22 121 B3
Foxlair Rd. M22 121 B3
Foxland Rd. SK8 122 B4
Foxlea. SK13 115 F8

Foxley Cl. Droylsden M43 ... 99 E8
Foxley Cl. Lymm WA13 ... 117 A2
Foxley Gr. BL3 ... 145 D6
Foxley Hall Mews. WA13 .. 117 A1
Foxley Wlk. M12 ... 165 A5
Foxton St. M24 ... 64 C7
Foxton Wlk. 6 M23 ... 121 A2
Foxwell Wlk. 5 M8 ... 156 B6
Foxwood Dr. OL5 ... 68 D2
Foxwood Gdns. M19 ... 110 E5
Foy St. WN4 ... 73 B3
Foynes Cl. M40 ... 157 D5
Fram St. M'ster M9 ... 157 F8
Fram St. Salford M6 ... 154 E2
Framingham Rd. M33 ... 108 B2
Framley Rd. M20 & M21 ... 109 F7
Frampton Cl. M24 ... 65 B7
France St. Hindley WN2 ... 56 D6
France St. Westhoughton BL5 57 E6
France St. Wigan WN5 ... 54 F7
Frances Ave. SK8 ... 122 A6
Frances Pl. M46 ... 58 A2
Frances St. Bolton BL1 ... 143 D2
Frances St. Cheadle SK8 ... 122 E6
Frances St. Denton M34 ... 113 B8
Frances St. Dukinfield SK14 101 C3
Frances St. Irlam M44 ... 105 E5
Frances St. Littleborough OL16 15 D4
Frances St. M'ster M13 ... 163 B6
Frances St. Oldham OL1 ... 49 B1
Frances St. 8
Stockport SK1 & SK3 ... 170 E8
Frances St W. SK14 ... 101 C3
Francesca Wlk. M18 ... 165 C6
Francis Ave. Eccles M30 ... 79 E2
Francis Ave. Walkden M28 ... 60 F2
Francis Rd. Irlam M44 ... 93 F1
Francis Rd. M'ster M20 ... 110 C5
Francis St. Eccles M30 ... 79 D3
Francis St. Failsworth M35 ... 83 F7
Francis St. Farnworth BL4 ... 42 D1
Francis St. Hindley WN2 ... 56 E5
Francis St. Leigh WN7 ... 75 E7
Francis St. M'ster M3 ... 158 F3
Francis St. Tyldesley M29 ... 77 D8
Francis Terr. 3 SK16 ... 166 C1
Frandley Wlk. 4 M13 ... 163 B7
Frank Cowan Ct. M7 ... 158 D4
Frank Hulme House. M32 ... 96 E1
Frank Perkins Way. M44 ... 105 F7
Frank St. Bolton BL1 ... 143 D2
Frank St. Bury BL9 ... 140 F1
Frank St. Failsworth M35 ... 83 E7
Frank St. Hyde SK14 ... 167 E2
Frank St. 3 M'ster M1 ... 163 A7
Frank St. Salford M6 ... 81 A4
Frank Swift Wlk. 5 M14 ... 98 A3
Frankby Cl. M27 ... 80 C7
Frankford Ave. BL1 ... 142 C2
Frankford Sq. BL1 ... 142 C2
Frankland Cl. M11 ... 83 B2
Franklin Cl. M34 ... 100 A2
Franklin Rd. M43 ... 84 A1
Franklin St. Eccles M30 ... 79 D2
Franklin St. Oldham OL1 ... 153 E8
Franklin St. R'dale OL16 ... 31 B5
Franklyn Ave. M41 ... 94 E2
Franklyn Rd. M18 ... 99 E6
Frankton Rd. M45 ... 62 F7
Franton Rd. M11 ... 83 B2
Fraser Ave. M33 ... 108 E3
Fraser House. BL1 ... 143 D1
Fraser Pl. M17 ... 96 D5
Fraser Rd. M'ster M8 ... 63 F1
Fraser Rd. Wigan WN5 ... 54 E7
Fraser St. Ashton-u-L OL6 ... 166 C3
Fraser St. R'dale OL11 & OL16 31 B4
Fraser St. Shaw OL2 ... 149 A7
Fraser St. Swinton M27 ... 62 A1
Fraternitas Terr. M43 ... 83 E3
Frawley Ave. WA12 ... 89 C5
Freckleton Ave. M21 ... 109 C4
Freckleton Dr. BL8 ... 43 F8
Freckleton St. WN1 ... 37 C2
Fred Longworth High Sch.
M29 ... 58 E1
Fred Tilson Cl. M14 ... 98 A3
Freda Wlk. M11 ... 160 F1
Frederica Gdns. WN2 ... 56 A3
Frederick Ave. OL2 ... 149 B5
Frederick Ct. BL4 ... 60 E8
Frederick Rd. M6 & M7 ... 81 B4
Frederick St. Ashton-i-M WN4 73 A5
Frederick St.
Ashton-u-L OL6 & SK15 ... 85 E2
Frederick St. Denton M34 ... 100 F5
Frederick St. Farnworth BL4 . 60 D8
Frederick St. Hindley WN2 ... 56 D5
Frederick St. Ince-i-M WN3 151 D6
Frederick St.
Littleborough OL15 ... 16 A6
Frederick St. M'ster M3 ... 158 E2
Frederick St. Oldham OL8 ... 66 D4
Frederick St. Oldham OL9 .. 152 B8
Frederick St.
Ramsbottom BL0 ... 138 B5
Frederick St. Wigan WN1 ... 151 E8
Free La. BB4 ... 1 A6
Freehold Comm Prim Sch.
OL9 ... 152 C5
Freehold St. OL11 ... 139 E5
Freeholds Rd. OL12 ... 4 E6
Freeholds Terr. OL12 ... 4 E6
Freeland Wlk. M11 ... 165 C8
Freelands. M29 ... 59 C1
Freeman Ave. OL6 ... 85 D3
Freeman Rd. SK16 ... 101 C7
Freemantle St. SK3 ... 170 D8
Freesia Ave. 9 M28 ... 59 F3
Freestone Cl. BL8 ... 140 D3
Freetown. SK13 ... 116 C7
Freetown Cl. M14 ... 98 A4
Freetrade St. OL11 ... 139 E6
Freiston. 5 OL12 ... 139 F8
Fremantle Ave. M18 ... 99 D5
French Ave. 5 Oldham OL1 .. 49 C1
French Ave. Stalybridge SK15 86 C1
French Barn La. M9 ... 64 C3
French Gr. BL3 ... 42 D5
French St. Ashton-u-L OL6 ... 85 D4
French St. Stalybridge SK15 ... 86 C1
Frensham Wlk. M23 ... 120 F4
Fresca Rd. OL1 ... 49 D4
Fresh Ct. SK13 ... 115 F7
Freshfield. SK8 ... 131 B8
Freshfield Ave. Atherton M46 58 C4
Freshfield Ave. Bolton BL3 . 147 D2
Freshfield Ave. Bolton BL3 .. 147 F2
Freshfield Ave. Hyde SK14 . 167 D1
Freshfield Ave.
Prestwich M25 ... 63 C6
Freshfield Cl. Failsworth M35 84 A6
Freshfield Cl. Romiley SK6 . 114 B1
Freshfield Gr. BL3 ... 147 F2
Freshfield Rd. Hindley WN2 .. 56 F5
Freshfield Rd. M'ster SK4 ... 110 F3
Freshfield Rd. Wigan WN3 ... 54 E3
Freshfield Wlk. 11 M11 ... 83 C2
Freshfields. M26 ... 43 D5
Freshford Wlk. 2 M22 ... 121 B1
Freshville St. M'ster M1 ... 163 B8
Freshwater Dr. M34 ... 113 B8
Freshwater St. 3 M18 ... 99 E6
Freshwinds Ct. OL4 ... 67 D4
Fresnel Cl. SK14 ... 102 B6
Frew Cl. M9 ... 65 B2
Frewland Ave. SK3 ... 123 F4
Freya Gr. M5 ... 161 C8
Friar's Cl. SK9 ... 136 E8
Friar's Rd. M33 ... 108 B4
Friarmere Rd. OL3 ... 50 E5
Friars Cl. Alt'ham WA14 ... 119 B1
Friars Cl. Tyldesley M29 ... 59 D1
Friars Cres. OL11 ... 30 F2
Friars Ct. M5 ... 80 B2
Friars Prim Sch The. M3 .. 158 D3
Friendship Ave. M18 ... 99 E4
Frieston Rd. WA14 ... 119 E8
Friezland Cl. SK15 ... 86 E6
Friezland La. OL3 ... 69 A4
Friezland Prim Sch. OL4 ... 68 E5
Frimley Gdns. M22 ... 121 D3
Frinton Ave. M40 ... 65 D3
Frinton Cl. M33 ... 107 F1
Frinton Rd. BL3 ... 146 B3
Frith Rd. M20 ... 110 C5
Frith St. WN5 & WN6 ... 150 A7
Frobisher Cl. M13 ... 164 D5
Frobisher Pl. SK5 ... 169 E4
Frobisher Rd. OL15 ... 6 C1
Frodsham Ave. SK4 ... 168 C3
Frodsham Cl. WN6 ... 36 D3
Frodsham Rd. M33 ... 108 E2
Frodsham St. 9 M14 ... 98 B3
Frodsham Way. SK9 ... 131 E4
Frog La. Wigan WN6 ... 37 A1
Frog La. Wigan WN1 & WN6 150 B8
Frogley St. BL2 ... 25 B3
Frogmore Ave. SK14 ... 113 E7
Frome Ave. Stockport SK2 .. 124 C5
Frome Ave. Urmston M41 ... 95 B1
Frome Cl. M29 ... 77 C6
Frome Dr. M8 ... 156 B7
Frome St. OL4 ... 67 C6
Frost St. M'ster M10 & M40 . 160 D1
Frost St. Oldham OL8 ... 66 E4
Frostlands Rd. 24 M16 ... 97 E4
Frowde Wlk. 7 M16 ... 97 E4
Froxmer St. M18 ... 165 C6
Fryent Cl. BL6 ... 21 D2
Fulbeck Ave. WN3 ... 55 A2
Fulbeck Wlk. M8 ... 155 E5
Fulbrook Dr. SK8 ... 132 A6
Fulbrook Way. M29 ... 59 C1
Fulham Ave. M40 ... 83 B5
Fulham St. OL4 ... 67 C6
Full Pot La. OL11 ... 29 E8
Fullerton Rd. SK4 ... 168 B2
Fulmar Cl. Poynton SK12 ... 133 A4
Fulmar Cl. Westhoughton BL5 57 D6
Fulmar Dr. Hazel Grove SK2 . 124 F5
Fulmar Dr. Sale M33 ... 107 C2
Fulmar Gdns. OL11 ... 29 E7
Fulmards Cl. SK9 ... 137 C7
Fulmead Wlk. 16 M7 ... 155 F6
Fulmer Dr. M40 ... 160 D2
Fulmere Ct. M27 ... 79 D6
Fulneck Sq. 2 M43 ... 100 A8
Fulshaw Ave. SK9 ... 137 A6
Fulshaw CE Prim Sch. SK9 136 F6
Fulshaw Cross. SK9 ... 137 A5
Fulshaw Ct. SK9 ... 137 A5
Fulshaw Pk. SK9 ... 137 A5
Fulshaw Pk S. SK9 ... 137 A4
Fulshaw Wlk. 7 M13 ... 163 B7
Fulstone Mews. SK2 ... 124 B6
Fulthorpe Wlk. 18 M9 ... 64 E5
Fulton Ct. M15 ... 163 A5
Fulwell Ave. M46 ... 76 E8
Fulwood Ave. M9 ... 64 F4
Fulwood Cl. BL8 ... 26 F1
Fulwood Rd. WA3 ... 90 E7
Furbarn La. OL11 ... 29 D8
Furbarn Rd. OL11 ... 29 D8
Furlong Cl. WN2 ... 73 F7
Furlong Rd. M22 ... 121 B3
Furnace St. Ashton-u-L SK16 166 B2
Furnace St. Dukinfield SK14 101 C4
Furness Ave. Ashton-u-L OL7 . 84 F5
Furness Ave. Bolton BL2 ... 25 B2
Furness Ave. Heywood OL10 . 29 C3
Furness Ave.
Littleborough OL15 ... 16 A6
Furness Ave. Oldham OL8 ... 67 C3
Furness Ave. Whitefield M45 . 63 A8
Furness Cl. Glossop SK13 ... 116 F8
Furness Cl. Milnrow OL16 ... 31 E6
Furness Cl. Poynton SK12 ... 133 D4
Furness Cres. WN7 ... 57 D1
Furness Gr. SK4 ... 168 A1
Furness Quay. M5 ... 161 A7
Furness Rd. Bolton BL1 ... 144 B7
Furness Rd. Bramhall SK8 ... 132 C6
Furness Rd. M'ster M14 ... 98 C1
Furness Rd. Middleton M24 ... 47 A3
Furness Rd. Urmston M41 ... 95 D3
Furness Sq. BL2 ... 25 B2
Furnival Cl. M34 ... 100 A2
Furnival Rd. M18 ... 165 C5
Furnival St. Leigh WN7 ... 75 F7
Furnival St. Reddish SK5 ... 99 F2
Furrow Comm Prim Sch.
M24 ... 46 D2
Further Field. OL11 ... 13 D1
Further Heights Rd. 1 OL12 14 F1
Further Hey Cl. OL4 ... 67 E7
Further La. SK14 ... 102 E3
Further Pits. OL11 ... 30 C7
Furtherwood Rd. OL1 ... 48 C1
Furze Ave. BL5 ... 57 F7
Furze La. OL4 ... 49 D1
Furze Wlk. M31 ... 106 A3
Fushia Gr. M7 ... 155 D6
Fyfield Wlk. 3 M8 ... 156 B6
Fylde Ave. Bolton BL2 ... 42 E7
Fylde Ave. Gatley SK8 ... 131 C8
Fylde Ct. M32 ... 108 C8
Fylde Rd. SK4 ... 168 A2
Fylde St. BL4 ... 42 D2
Fylde St E. BL4 ... 42 D2

Gabbot St. PR6 ... 21 A7
Gable Ave. SK9 ... 137 A7
Gable Ct. M34 ... 100 F2
Gable Dr. M24 ... 46 E1
Gable St. Bolton BL2 ... 25 D5
Gable St. M'ster M12 ... 164 F8
Gable St. Newton-l-W WA12 .. 89 B3
Gables The. M33 ... 108 B3
Gabriel Wlk. 11 M16 ... 97 F3
Gabriels The. OL2 ... 48 F7
Gadbury Ave. M46 ... 58 B3
Gaddum Rd. Alt'ham WA14 119 B1
Gaddum Rd. M'ster M20 ... 110 C3
Gail Ave. SK4 ... 169 D2
Gail Cl. Alderley Edge SK9 ... 137 B2
Gail Cl. Failsworth M35 ... 83 E5
Gainford Ave. SK8 ... 122 B4
Gainford Gdns. M40 ... 65 B1
Gainford Rd. SK5 ... 99 F1
Gainford Wlk. BL3 ... 147 E4
Gainsborough Ave.
Bolton BL3 ... 146 C3
Gainsborough Ave.
M'ster M20 ... 110 C5
Gainsborough Ave.
Marple SK6 ... 126 B8
Gainsborough Ave.
Oldham OL8 ... 66 E4
Gainsborough Ave.
Stretford M32 ... 96 F3
Gainsborough Cl.
Wigan WN3 ... 54 D3
Gainsborough Cl.
Wilmslow SK9 ... 137 D8
Gainsborough Dr.
Cheadle SK8 ... 122 F6
Gainsborough Dr.
R'dale OL11 ... 30 E3
Gainsborough Rd.
Chadderton OL9 ... 47 E1
Gainsborough Rd.
Droylsden M34 ... 84 D1
Gainsborough Rd.
Ramsbottom BL0 ... 11 B1
Gainsborough St. M7 ... 155 E7
Gainsborough Wlk.
Denton M34 ... 100 E1
Gainsborough Wlk. 1
Dukinfield SK14 ... 101 F5
Gair Rd. SK5 ... 169 F4
Gair St. SK14 ... 167 D4
Gairloch Ave. M32 ... 96 B2
Gaitskell Cl. M11 ... 160 E1
Galbraith Rd. M20 ... 110 C3
Gale Dr. M24 ... 46 D2
Gale Rd. M25 ... 62 F3
Gale St. Heywood OL10 ... 29 B2
Gale St. R'dale OL12 ... 14 F3
Galena St. OL11 ... 30 E4
Gales Terr. OL11 ... 139 E5
Galgate Cl. Bury BL8 ... 26 F1
Galgate Cl. M'ster M15 ... 162 E7
Galindo St. BL2 ... 25 C4
Galland St. OL4 ... 67 D7
Galleria The. 10 BL1 ... 145 F7
Galloway Cl. Bolton BL3 ... 40 E5
Galloway Cl. Heywood OL10 .. 45 F8
Galloway Dr. M27 ... 61 F4
Galloway Rd. M27 ... 79 D6
Gallowsclough Rd. SK15 ... 102 E6
Galston St. M11 ... 165 A8
Galsworthy Ave. M7 & M8 . 156 A6
Galvin Rd. M9 ... 64 B3
Galway St. OL1 ... 153 F6
Galway Wlk. WA15 ... 120 F2
Galwey Gr. WN1 ... 37 C4
Gamble St. WN7 ... 76 A5
Gambleside Cl. M28 ... 78 B8
Gambrel Bank Rd. OL6 ... 85 B6
Gambrel Gr. OL6 ... 85 B6
Game St. OL4 ... 67 C5
Games Wlk. 8 M22 ... 121 B1
Gamesley Cty Prim Sch.
SK13 ... 171 E2
Gamma Wlk. M11 ... 83 B2
Gan Eden. 13 M7 ... 63 E1
Gandy La. OL12 ... 14 D4
Gantley Ave. WN5 ... 53 D3
Gantley Cres. WN5 ... 53 D3
Gantley Rd. WN5 ... 53 D4
Gantock Wlk. 10 M14 ... 98 C3
Ganton Ave. M45 ... 62 D7
Garbrook Ave. M9 ... 64 C5
Garden Ave. Droylsden M43 .. 84 B2
Garden Ave. Stretford M32 ... 96 D3
Garden City. BL0 ... 11 A2
Garden Cl. OL15 ... 15 F2
Garden La. Alt'ham WA14 ... 119 D5
Garden La. Boothstown M28 .. 78 A6
Garden La. M'ster M3 ... 158 E2
Garden La. 3 M'ster M3 ... 158 F1
Garden La. 17 R'dale OL16 ... 31 A8
Garden Row. Heywood OL10 .. 29 C4
Garden Row. R'dale OL12 ... 14 D2
Garden St. Denton M34 ... 100 F6
Garden St. Eccles M30 ... 79 E1
Garden St. Farnworth BL4 ... 60 E8
Garden St. Heywood OL10 ... 29 C2
Garden St. Hyde SK14 ... 167 E4
Garden St. M'ster M4 & M60 159 A2
Garden St. Newhey OL16 ... 32 B4
Garden St. Oldham OL1 ... 67 A7
Garden St. Oldham OL4 ... 67 F5
Garden St. Ramsbottom BL0 .. 11 C3
Garden St. Ramsbottom BL0 138 C6
Garden St. Stockport SK2 ... 124 C5
Garden St. Tyldesley M29 ... 77 A8
Garden Terr. OL2 ... 48 C7
Garden Wall Cl. M5 ... 161 C8
Garden Way. OL15 ... 15 F2
Garden Wlk. Ashton-u-L OL6 166 C4
Garden Wlk. 3 Denton M34 101 A2
Gardens The. Bolton BL1, BL7 24 F6
Gardens The. Eccles M30 ... 80 A4
Gardner. M30 ... 79 E2
Gardner Grange. SK5 ... 112 C4
Gardner Rd. M25 ... 62 F4
Gardner St. M'ster M12 ... 165 B6
Gardner St. Salford M6 ... 81 A3
Garfield Ave. M19 ... 99 B1
Garfield Cl. OL11 ... 13 E1
Garfield Gr. BL3 ... 145 D5
Garfield St. Bolton BL3 ... 146 C3
Garfield St. Salford M5 ... 161 A6
Garfield St. Stockport SK1 .. 112 A2
Garforth Ave. M10 & M40 ... 159 C2
Garforth St. OL9 ... 152 C8
Gargrave Ave. BL1 ... 23 F2
Gargrave St. M'ster M7 ... 80 F8
Gargrave St. 2 Oldham OL4 . 67 B6
Garland Rd. M22 ... 121 E3
Garlick St. Hyde SK14 ... 167 F3
Garlick St. M'ster M18 ... 99 D5
Garlick St. Oldham OL9 ... 153 E6
Garnant Cl. M9 ... 157 F8
Garner Ave. WA15 ... 108 A1
Garner Cl. WA14 ... 119 D2
Garner Dr. Salford M5 & M6 154 D3
Garner Dr. Tyldesley M29 ... 77 B5
Garner Dr. Worsley M28 ... 79 C3
Garner's La. SK3 ... 170 E5
Garnet St. OL1 ... 67 B8
Garnet Wolseley Ave. M5 . 161 B7
Garnett Cl. SK14 ... 102 F3
Garnett Rd. SK14 ... 102 F3
Garnett St. Bolton BL1 ... 143 E3
Garnett St. Ramsbottom BL0 138 B5
Garnett St. Stockport SK1 ... 169 F1
Garnett Way. SK14 ... 102 F3
Garnham Wlk. 14 M9 ... 64 E5
Garratt Way. M18 ... 165 C5
Garret Gr. OL2 ... 149 C7
Garrett Hall Prim Sch. M29 77 D7
Garrett Hall Rd. M28 ... 77 E7
Garrett La. M28 & M29 ... 77 D7
Garrett Wlk. SK3 ... 123 C8
Garrick Gdns. M22 ... 121 D4
Garron Wlk. 1 M22 ... 121 A2
Garrowmore Wlk. 22 M9 ... 64 E3
Garsdale La. BL1 & BL6 ... 40 D7
Garside Ave. WA3 ... 90 D7
Garside Gr. Bolton BL1 ... 142 C2
Garside Gr. Wigan WN3 ... 54 E2
Garside Hey Rd. BL8 ... 27 B6
Garside St. Bolton BL1 ... 145 E7
Garside St. Denton M34 ... 100 F2
Garside St. Hyde SK14 ... 167 E1
Garstang Ave. BL2 ... 42 F7
Garstang Dr. BL8 ... 26 F1
Garston Ave. M46 ... 58 B5
Garston Cl. Leigh WN7 ... 57 E1
Garston Cl. M'ster SK4 ... 168 C3
Garston St. BL9 ... 141 A4
Garswood Cres. WN5 ... 71 E4
Garswood Cty Prim Sch.
WN4 ... 72 C4
Garswood Dr. BL8 ... 27 B6
Garswood Old Rd.
WA11, WN4 ... 71 E1
Garswood Rd. Billinge WN5 .. 71 F4
Garswood Rd. Bolton BL3 ... 147 E2
Garswood Rd.
Garswood WA11 ... 72 C3
Garswood Rd. M'ster M14 ... 98 A2
Garswood St. WN4 ... 73 B3
Garth Ave. WA15 ... 119 E6
Garth Hts. SK9 ... 137 C7
Garth Rd. Marple SK6 ... 126 A6
Garth Rd. Stockport SK2 ... 124 C7
Garth Rd. Wythenshawe M22 121 D4
Garth The. M5 ... 154 D2
Garthland Rd. SK7 ... 124 F3
Garthmere Rd. M46 ... 58 F5
Garthorne Cl. M16 ... 97 D4
Garthorp Rd. M23 ... 108 E1
Garthwaite Ave. OL8 ... 66 E4
Gartland Wlk. M8 ... 156 C8
Garton Dr. WA3 ... 74 E1
Garton Wlk. 12 M9 ... 64 E5
Gartside St. Ashton-u-L OL7 .. 84 F1
Gartside St. Delph OL3 ... 50 E4
Gartside St. M'ster M3 ... 158 E1
Gartside St. Oldham OL4 ... 67 B5
Garwick Rd. BL1 ... 142 B3
Garwood Sta. WN4 ... 72 D3
Garwood St. M15 ... 162 F7
Gas St. Adlington PR7 ... 21 A6
Gas St. Ashton-u-L OL6 ... 166 B3
Gas St. Bolton BL1 ... 145 E7
Gas St. Farnworth BL4 ... 60 D8
Gas St. 6 Heywood OL10 ... 29 D2
Gas St. Hollingworth SK14 ... 103 D5
Gas St. Leigh WN7 ... 75 F5
Gas St. Platt Bridge WN2 ... 56 B2
Gas St. R'dale OL11 ... 139 E7
Gas St. Stockport SK4 ... 169 E1
Gascoyne St. M14 ... 98 B3
Gaskell Cl. OL15 ... 16 A6
Gaskell Cty Prim Sch. BL1 145 E8
Gaskell Rd. Alt'ham WA14 ... 119 D6
Gaskell Rd. Eccles M30 ... 79 E1
Gaskell Rise. OL1 ... 49 E5
Gaskell St. Bolton BL1 ... 145 D8
Gaskell St. 26
Dukinfield SK16 ... 166 B1
Gaskell St. Failsworth M40 ... 83 D6
Gaskell St. Hindley WN2 ... 56 E7
Gaskell St. Swinton M27 ... 61 F2
Gaskell St. Wigan WN1 ... 151 D8
Gaskell's Brow. WN4 ... 72 E5
Gaskill St. OL10 ... 29 A2
Gaston Wlk. M9 ... 64 D5
Gatcombe Mews. SK9 ... 137 A6
Gatcombe Sq. M14 ... 98 D3
Gate Ctr The. SK6 ... 112 E6
Gate Field Cl. M26 ... 43 E3
Gate Keeper Fold. OL7 ... 85 A7
Gate Rd. M32 ... 96 A4
Gate St. Dukinfield SK16 ... 101 A6
Gate St. M'ster M11 ... 165 C8
Gate St. R'dale OL11 ... 139 F5
Gate Stirrup. M28 ... 79 A5
Gateacre Wlk. M23 ... 120 E8
Gategill Gr. WN5 ... 53 D3
Gatehead Croft. OL3 ... 50 F3
Gatehead Mews. OL3 ... 50 F3
Gatehead Rd. OL3 ... 50 F3
Gatehouse Rd. M28 ... 60 A4
Gatesgarth Rd. M24 ... 46 C2
Gateshead Cl. M14 ... 98 B4
Gateside Wlk. 6 M9 ... 64 E5
Gateway Cres. OL9 ... 65 E4
Gateway Ind Est. M1 ... 159 B1
Gateway Rd. M18 ... 165 C6
Gateways The. M27 ... 61 F1
Gathill Cl. SK8 ... 122 F1
Gathurst Golf Course. WN6 35 F5
Gathurst La. WN5 & WN6 ... 36 A4
Gathurst Rd. WN5 ... 35 F2
Gathurst St. M18 ... 99 E6
Gathurst Sta. WN5 ... 36 A3
Gatley Ave. M14 ... 98 A1
Gatley Brow. OL1 ... 153 E8
Gatley Gn. SK8 ... 122 A5
Gatley Golf Course. SK8 ... 122 A3
Gatley Prim Sch. SK8 ... 122 A5
Gatley Rd. Cheadle SK8 ... 122 C5
Gatley Rd. Sale M33 ... 108 E3
Gatley Sta. SK8 ... 122 B5
Gatling Ave. M12 ... 99 B2
Gatwick Ave. M23 ... 121 B6
Gavel Wlk. M24 ... 46 E1
Gavin Ave. M5 ... 81 A1
Gawsworth Ave. M20 ... 110 C1
Gawsworth Cl.
Alt'ham M23 & WA15 ... 120 D6
Gawsworth Cl. Bramhall SK7 132 E6
Gawsworth Cl.
Hadfield SK14 ... 104 A5
Gawsworth Cl.Poynton SK12 133 F2
Gawsworth Cl.Shaw OL2 ... 48 F7
Gawsworth Cl.
Stockport SK3 ... 170 D5
Gawsworth Mews. SK8 ... 122 B5
Gawsworth Pl. M22 ... 121 F1
Gawsworth Rd. Golborne WA3 73 F1
Gawsworth Rd. Sale M33 ... 108 E1
Gawsworth Way. 15
Denton M34 ... 101 A1
Gawsworth Way.
Handforth SK9 ... 131 E4
Gawthorpe Cl. BL9 ... 45 A5
Gaydon Rd. M33 ... 107 D4
Gayford Wlk. 9 M9 ... 64 E5
Gaythorn St. M3 & M5 ... 81 C1
Gaythorne St. BL1 ... 143 F3
Gayton Cl. WN3 ... 54 D3
Gayton Wlk. 7 M40 ... 65 D2
Gaywood Wlk. M40 ... 156 C6
Gee Cross Fold. SK14 ... 113 E7
Gee Cross Trinity CE
Prim Sch. SK14 ... 113 F8
Gee La. Eccles M30 ... 79 B3
Gee La. 7 Oldham OL8 ... 66 B2
Gee St. Oldham OL8 ... 66 B2
Gee St. Stockport SK3 ... 170 D7
Geinsbury Cl. OL8 ... 67 B4
Gelder Clough Res Cvan Pk.
OL10 ... 29 C5
Gellert Pl. BL5 ... 57 E6
Gellert Rd. BL5 ... 57 E6
Gellfield La. OL3 ... 51 D1
Gencoyne Dr. BL1 ... 24 D6
Gendre Rd. BL7 ... 24 E8
Geneva Rd. SK7 ... 123 E3
Geneva Terr. OL11 ... 30 C8
Geneva Wlk. 11 M'ster M8 . 156 B6
Geneva Wlk. Oldham OL9 ... 152 C6
Genista Gr. M7 ... 155 D6
Geo. Hampson's Bldgs.
WA3 ... 92 C8
Geoff Bent Wlk. M40 ... 83 B5
Geoffrey St. Atherton BL5 ... 58 F8
Geoffrey St. Bury BL9 ... 141 A4
Geoffrey St. Ramsbottom BL0 11 A4
George Barton St. 24 BL2 ... 25 B1
George Ct. 10 SK16 ... 166 B1
George H Carnall
Sports Ctr. M41 ... 95 E4
George La. SK6 ... 113 A4
George Leigh St. M4 ... 159 B2
George Mann Cl. M22 ... 121 C1
George Rd. BL0 ... 138 B5
George Sq. OL1 ... 153 E6
George St.Alderley Edge SK9 137 A1
George St. Alt'ham WA14 ... 119 D4
George St. Ashton-i-M WN4 ... 73 C4
George St. Ashton-u-L OL6 .. 166 C3
George St. 3 Atherton M46 .. 58 D3
George St. 4 Bacup OL13 ... 3 C8
George St. Bury BL9 ... 140 F2
George St. Chadderton OL9 . 152 A7
George St. Denton M34 ... 101 A3
George St. Eccles M30 ... 79 C1
George St. Failsworth M35 ... 83 F8
George St. Farnworth BL4 ... 60 B7
George St. Farnworth BL4 ... 60 E7
George St. Glossop SK13 ... 116 C8
George St. Heywood OL10 ... 29 C3
George St. Hindley WN2 ... 56 E5
George St. Horwich BL6 ... 22 C3
George St. Ince-i-M WN2 ... 151 F7
George St. Irlam M44 ... 94 B3
George St. Littleborough OL16 15 D3
George St. 8
Littleborough OL15 ... 16 B5
George St. M'ster M25 ... 63 B1
George St. M'ster M7 & M8 . 155 F8
George St. M'ster M1 ... 163 A8
George St. Milnrow OL16 ... 31 E7
George St. Mossley OL5 ... 68 C1
George St. Newton-l-W WA12 89 A4
George St. Oldham OL1 ... 153 E6
George St. R'dale OL12, OL16 31 A8
George St. Radcliffe M26 ... 43 F3
George St. Romiley SK6 ... 114 B2
George St. Shaw OL2 ... 149 C8
George St. 5
Stalybridge SK15 ... 86 A2
George St. Stockport SK1 ... 112 A2
George St. Urmston M41 ... 95 E2
George St. Westhoughton BL5 57 F8
George St. Whitefield M45 ... 44 E1
George St. Whitworth OL12 ... 14 C8
George St E. SK1 ... 124 B8
George St W. SK1 ... 124 B8
George Thomas Ct. M9 ... 157 D8
George Tomlinson Sch. BL4 60 E6
George's Cl. SK12 ... 133 E3
George's La. BL6 ... 22 E5
George's Rd. Sale M33 ... 108 B3
George's Rd. Stockport SK4 169 D2
George's Rd E. SK12 ... 133 E3
George's Rd W. SK12 ... 133 E3
George's Row. 2 BB4 ... 2 F8
George's Terr. WN5 ... 53 D5
Georgian Ct. 5 Leigh WN7 ... 76 B4
Georgian Ct. 12
Tyldesley M29 ... 58 F1
Georgian Sq. 2 WN2 ... 56 A2
Georgiana St. 2 Bury BL9 .. 140 F1
Georgiana St. 3
Farnworth BL4 ... 42 B2
Georgina Ct. BL3 ... 146 B3
Georgina St. BL3 ... 146 B3
Gerald Ave. M8 ... 156 A8
Gerald Rd. M6 & M7 ... 81 B5
Gerard St. WN4 ... 73 B3
Germain Cl. M9 ... 64 C5
Gerrard Ave. WA15 ... 120 A8
Gerrard Cl. WN2 ... 38 D2
Gerrard Rd. WN5 ... 71 E5
Gerrard St. Farnworth BL4 ... 60 E8
Gerrard St. Leigh WN7 ... 75 F5
Gerrard St. R'dale OL11 ... 31 A2
Gerrard St. 2 Salford M6 ... 81 A3
Gerrard St. Stalybridge SK15 . 86 B1
Gerrard St. 5
Westhoughton BL5 ... 39 E1
Gerrards Cl. M44 ... 94 A2
Gerrards Gdns. SK14 ... 113 E7
Gerrards Hollow. SK14 ... 113 D7
Gerrardswood. SK14 ... 113 D7
Gertrude Cl. M5 ... 161 A8
Gertrude St. OL12 ... 4 E6
Gervis Cl. M40 ... 157 D5
Ghyll Gr. Billinge WA11 ... 71 B1
Ghyll Gr. Walkden M28 ... 60 E2
Giants Hall Rd. WN6 ... 36 E3
Gib Fold. M46 ... 58 D4
Gib La. M23 ... 121 C8
Gibb La. SK6 ... 126 E5
Gibb Rd. M28 ... 79 B7
Gibbon Ave. M22 ... 121 D2
Gibbon St. Bolton BL3 ... 145 D5
Gibbon St. M'ster M11 ... 83 A2
Gibbon's Rd. WN4 ... 72 D3
Gibbs St. M3 ... 158 D1
Gibraltar La. M34 ... 113 B8
Gibraltar St. Bolton BL3 ... 145 D6
Gibraltar St. Oldham OL4 ... 67 D5
Gibsmere Cl. M23 ... 120 D6
Gibson Ave. M18 ... 99 F6
Gibson Gr. M28 ... 60 A3
Gibson La. M28 ... 60 A3
Gibson Pl. M3 ... 159 A3
Gibson St. Bolton BL2 ... 25 C1
Gibson St. Leigh WN2 ... 56 D1
Gibson St. Oldham OL4 ... 67 C6
Gibson St. R'dale OL16 ... 31 C8
Gibson Terr. OL7 ... 166 A1
Gibson Way. WA14 ... 119 C8
Gibsons Rd. SK4 ... 168 B4
Gibwood Rd. M22 ... 121 C8
Giden Wlk. 11 M9 ... 64 E5
Gidlow Ave. Adlington PR6 ... 21 A7
Gidlow Ave. Wigan WN6 ... 37 A2
Gidlow La. WN6 ... 37 A2
Gidlow New Houses. WN6 . 37 A4
Gidlow St. 1 Hindley WN2 ... 56 D6
Gidlow St. M'ster M18 ... 99 E6
Gifford Pl. WN2 ... 56 F4
Gifford Wlk. SK7 ... 124 A2
Gigg La. BL9 ... 44 F8
Gilbert Rd. WA15 ... 119 E1
Gilbert St. Eccles M30 ... 95 B8
Gilbert St. Hindley WN2 ... 56 D5
Gilbert St. M'ster M15 ... 162 E7
Gilbert St. Ramsbottom BL0 ... 1 C1
Gilbert St. Salford M6 ... 154 F1
Gilbert St. Walkden M28 ... 60 D1
Gilbertbank. SK6 ... 113 B4
Gilchrist Rd. M44 ... 105 F6
Gilda Brook Rd. M30 & M5 ... 80 A2
Gilda Cres. M30 ... 80 A3
Gilda Rd. M28 ... 77 F7
Gilded Hollins Prim Sch.
WN7 ... 75 C1
Gildenhall. M35 ... 84 A7
Gilderdale Cl. OL2 ... 149 B8
Gildersdale St. 7 BL3 ... 42 A4
Gildersdale Dr. M9 ... 64 C6
Gildridge Rd. M16 ... 97 E1
Giles St. M12 & M18 ... 99 A4
Gilesgate. 3 M14 ... 98 C3
Gill Ave. WN6 ... 36 B6
Gill Bent Rd. SK8 ... 132 A7
Gill St. M'ster M9 ... 64 F1
Gill St. Stockport SK1 ... 112 B3
Gillan Rd. WN6 ... 37 B3

Gillbrook Rd. M20 110 B2
Gillbrow Cres. WN1 37 F1
Gillemere Gr. OL2 149 C7
Gillers Gn. M28 60 C3
Gillford Ave. M'ster M9 64 F1
Gillford Ave. M'ster M9 157 F8
Gilliburns Wlk. BL5 57 F5
Gillingham Rd. M30 79 B2
Gillingham Sq. M11 164 F8
Gillwood Dr. SK6 112 F1
Gilman Cl. M9 64 C2
Gilman St. M9 64 C2
Gilmerton Dr. 22 M40 83 C5
Gilmore Dr. M25 63 B5
Gilmore St. SK3 170 E7
Gilmour St. M24 65 A8
Gilmour Terr. M9 64 F1
Gilnow Cty Prim Sch. BL1 144 C6
Gilnow Gdns. BL1 144 C6
Gilnow Gr. BL1 145 D6
Gilnow La. BL3 145 D6
Gilnow Rd. BL1 144 C6
Gilpin Pl. WN2 55 F2
Gilpin Rd. M41 95 F2
Gilpin Wlk. M24 46 E1
Gilroy St. WN1 151 D8
Giltbrook Ave. M10 & M40 160 D4
Gilwell Dr. M23 120 F4
Gin Croft La. BL0 1 E4
Gingham Brow. BL6 22 E4
Gingham Ct. 7 M26 44 C4
Gingham Pk. M26 43 E5
Gipsy La. Stockport SK2 124 C6
Gipsy La. Stockport SK2 124 D6
Girton Ave. WN4 72 F4
Girton St. Bolton BL2 42 D7
Girton St. M'ster M7 158 E4
Girton Wlk. M40 65 D1
Girvan Ave. M40 65 D2
Girvan Cl. BL3 146 C3
Girvan Cres. WN4 72 D4
Girvan Wlk. OL10 28 F1
Gisborn Dr. M6 81 A5
Gisburn Ave. Bolton BL1 23 E2
Gisburn Ave. Golborne WA3 73 F2
Gisburn Dr. BL8 26 E3
Gisburn Rd. OL11 31 A3
Gisburne Ave. M40 65 D2
Gissing Wlk. M40 157 D6
Givendale Dr. M8 64 A2
Glabyn Ave. BL6 39 F8
Glade Brow. OL4 68 A6
Glade St. BL1 144 C7
Glade The. Bolton BL1 143 D1
Glade The. Shevington WN6 36 B6
Glade The. Stockport SK4 168 A1
Gladeside Rd. M22 121 C4
Gladstone Cl. 6 BL1 143 E2
Gladstone Cres. OL11 31 A3
Gladstone Ct. Farnworth BL4 42 C1
Gladstone Ct.
M'ster M15 & M16 97 E4
Gladstone Ct. M'ster SK4 168 B3
Gladstone Gr. SK4 168 A3
Gladstone Mews. SK4 169 E3
Gladstone Pl. BL4 42 C1
Gladstone Rd. Alt'ham WA14 119 D6
Gladstone Rd. Eccles M30 79 E2
Gladstone Rd. Farnworth BL4 42 D1
Gladstone Rd. Urmston M41 95 E2
Gladstone St. Bolton BL1 143 E2
Gladstone St. Bury BL9 141 B3
Gladstone St. Glossop SK13 116 D8
Gladstone St. Hadfield SK14 104 A4
Gladstone St. Oldham OL4 67 B6
Gladstone St. Stockport SK2 124 C4
Gladstone St. Swinton M27 80 A8
Gladstone St.
Westhoughton BL5 39 E1
Gladstone Terrace Rd. OL3 69 A4
Gladville Dr. SK8 123 A6
Gladwyn Ave. M20 109 E4
Gladys St. 3 Farnworth BL4 42 D2
Gladys St. M'ster M16 97 C4
Gladys St. Salford M5 161 A7
Glaisdale. OL4 67 D6
Glaisdale Cl. Ashton-i-M WN4 73 C3
Glaisdale Cl. Bolton BL2 25 B2
Glaisdale St. BL2 25 B2
Glaister La. BL2 25 D1
Glamis Ave. Droylsden M11 83 B3
Glamis Ave. Heywood OL10 46 F8
Glamis Ave. Stretford M32 96 A2
Glamis Cl. WN7 76 D6
Glamorgan Pl. OL9 152 C5
Glandon Dr. SK8 132 C8
Glanford Ave. M9 64 A3
Glanton Wlk. M40 65 D1
Glanvor Rd. SK3 123 C8
Glass St. BL4 60 E7
Glassbrook St. WN6 37 A1
Glasscroft Cl. M14 97 F2
Glasshouse St. 9 M4 159 C3
Glasson Wlk. OL9 152 A6
Glastonbury. 28 OL12 139 E8
Glastonbury Ave.
Alt'ham WA15 120 B2
Glastonbury Ave.
Bramhall SK8 132 C6
Glastonbury Ave.
Golborne WA3 91 C8
Glastonbury Dr. SK12 133 D5
Glastonbury Gdns. M26 43 E5
Glastonbury Rd.
Tyldesley M29 77 B7
Glastonbury Rd. Urmston M32 95 F3
Glaswen Gr. SK5 169 F4
Glaze Wlk. M45 45 C2
Glazebrook Cl. OL10 29 C1
Glazebrook La. WA3 105 B5
Glazebrook Sta. WA3 105 B5
Glazebury CE (VA)
Prim Sch. WA3 92 C7
Glazebury Dr. M23 121 B5
Glazedale Ave. OL2 48 C5
Glaziers La. WA3 91 D2
Gleave St. 10 Bolton BL1 145 F8
Gleave St. Sale M33 108 B6
Gleaves Ave. BL2 26 A4
Gleaves Rd. M30 79 E1
Glebe Ave. WN4 73 C2
Glebe Cl. WN6 19 F1
Glebe End St. WN6 150 B8
Glebe House. M24 47 A2
Glebe House Sch. OL11 139 E6
Glebe La. OL1 49 E4
Glebe Rd. Standish WN6 19 F1
Glebe Rd. Urmston M41 95 D2
Glebe St. Ashton-u-L OL6 166 C3
Glebe St. Bolton BL2 148 A6
Glebe St. Hindley WN2 57 C2
Glebe St. Leigh WN7 75 F6
Glebe St. Oldham OL9 66 A3
Glebe St. Radcliffe M26 44 B3
Glebe St. Shaw OL2 149 B7
Glebe St. Stockport SK1 112 A1
Glebe St. Westhoughton BL5 39 E1
Glebeland. WA3 91 E2
Glebeland Rd. BL3 144 B5
Glebelands Rd.
Prestwich M25 63 B5
Glebelands Rd. Sale M33 108 A6
Glebelands Rd.
Wythenshawe M23 120 F6
Gleden St. M'ster M10, M40 160 E2
Gleden St. M'ster M10, M40 160 E3
Gledhall St. SK15 86 A2
Gledhill Ave. M5 161 B7
Gledhill Cl. OL2 32 A1
Gledhill St. M20 110 B7
Gledhill Way. BL7 9 A1
Glegg St. WN2 151 F8
Glemsford Cl. Failsworth M40 83 B6
Glemsford Cl. Wigan WN3 55 B3
Glen Ave. Bolton BL3 144 B5
Glen Ave. Kearsley BL4 61 B6
Glen Ave. M'ster M9 64 F1
Glen Ave. Sale M33 108 A6
Glen Ave. Swinton M27 79 D8
Glen Ave. Worsley M28 79 A8
Glen Bott St. BL1 143 D2
Glen Cl. WA3 105 B2
Glen Cres. OL13 3 A8
Glen Dr. WN6 35 E8
Glen Gdns. OL12 14 F2
Glen Gr. Middleton M24 65 C7
Glen Gr. Royton OL2 48 D5
Glen Rd. Oldham OL4 67 C6
Glen Rd. Rawtenstall BB4 2 F8
Glen Rise. WA15 120 A5
Glen Royd. 1 OL12 14 C1
Glen St. Bacup OL13 3 E8
Glen St. Ramsbottom BL0 138 B7
Glen St. Salford M5 161 A7
Glen The. Bolton BL1 40 E7
Glen The. Middleton M24 65 B6
Glen View. Littleborough OL15 16 C7
Glen View. Royton OL2 48 D5
Glenarm Wlk. M22 121 E2
Glenart. M30 79 E3
Glenavon Dr. R'dale OL12 14 D3
Glenavon Dr. Shaw OL2 48 F8
Glenbarry Cl. M13 163 B6
Glenbarry St. M12 164 D8
Glenbeck Rd. M45 44 E2
Glenboro Ave. BL8 27 C2
Glenborough Ave. OL13 3 C8
Glenbourne Pk. SK7 132 D5
Glenbranter Ave. WN2 56 A8
Glenbrook Gdns. BL4 42 D2
Glenbrook Hill. SK13 104 C2
Glenbrook Rd. M9 64 A5
Glenburn St. BL3 147 D3
Glenby Ave. M22 121 F3
Glencar. BL5 57 D7
Glencar Dr. 8 M40 65 D2
Glencastle Rd. M18 99 C4
Glencoe. BL2 148 B7
Glencoe Cl. OL10 28 F1
Glencoe Dr. Bolton BL2 42 F6
Glencoe Dr. Sale M33 107 C2
Glencoe Pl. OL11 139 D7
Glencoe St. 3 OL8 66 C2
Glencross Ave. M16 & M21 97 A2
Glendale. M27 62 B2
Glendale Ave.
Ashton-i-M WN4 73 C4
Glendale Ave. M'ster M19 110 F6
Glendale Ave. Whitefield BL9 44 F3
Glendale Cl. Boothstown M28 77 F7
Glendale Cl. 8
Heywood OL10 29 D2
Glendale Ct. OL8 66 F4
Glendale Dr. BL3 40 E4
Glendale Rd. Boothstown M28 77 F7
Glendale Rd. Eccles M30 80 A3
Glenden Foot. OL12 14 D2
Glendene Ave. Bramhall SK7 132 D5
Glendene Ave. Droylsden M43 84 C3
Glendevon Cl. Bolton BL3 40 F5
Glendevon Cl. Ince-i-M WN2 56 A8
Glendevon Pl. M45 63 B7
Glendinning St. M6 154 E2
Glendon Cres. OL6 85 B7
Glendon Ct. OL1 49 E4
Glendore. M5 80 C2
Glendower Dr. M40 156 C5
Gleneagles. BL3 40 F3
Gleneagles Ave. 10
Droylsden M11 83 C2
Gleneagles Ave.
Heywood OL10 46 D8
Gleneagles Cl. Bramhall SK7 133 A7
Gleneagles Cl.
Wilmslow SK9 137 D8
Gleneagles Rd. Gatley SK8 122 C1
Gleneagles Rd. Urmston M41 94 F3
Gleneagles Way. BL0 138 B5
Glenfield. WA14 119 B4
Glenfield Dr. SK12 133 D3
Glenfield Rd. SK4 169 D4
Glenfield Sq. 2 BL4 42 B2
Glenfyne Rd. M6 80 D5
Glengarth. OL3 69 B7
Glengarth Dr. BL1 & BL6 40 C6
Glenham Ct. 1 M15 97 E4
Glenhaven Ave. M41 95 C2
Glenholme Rd. SK7 132 D7
Glenhurst Rd. M19 110 E5
Glenilla Ave. M28 78 E7
Glenlea Dr. M20 122 B8
Glenluce Wlk. BL3 40 E5
Glenmaye Gr. WN2 57 A5
Glenmere Rd. M20 122 C8
Glenmoor Rd. SK1 112 A1
Glenmore Ave.
Farnworth BL3 & BL4 42 A2
Glenmore Ave. M'ster M20 109 E4
Glenmore Bglws. SK16 101 C7
Glenmore Cl. Bolton BL3 40 E5
Glenmore Cl. R'dale OL11 29 E5
Glenmore Dr. Failsworth M35 84 B8
Glenmore Dr. M'ster M8 156 B7
Glenmore Gr. SK16 101 C8
Glenmore Rd. BL8 10 F2
Glenmore St. BL9 140 E1
Glenolden St. M11 83 D2
Glenpark. WN7 76 B6
Glenpark Wlk. 5 M9 157 E7
Glenridding Cl. OL1 49 A1
Glenridge Cl. BL1 143 F2
Glenroy Wlk. 15 M9 64 E5
Glensdale Dr. M40 65 E1
Glenshee Dr. BL3 40 F5
Glenside. WN6 18 B2
Glenside Ave. M18 99 D3
Glenside Dr. Bolton BL3 147 F2
Glenside Dr. Romiley SK6 113 B5
Glenside Gdns. M35 84 B7
Glenside Gr. M28 60 E3
Glent View. SK15 86 A4
Glenthorn Gr. M33 108 B3
Glenthorn Rd. M9 64 D6
Glenthorne Dr. OL7 166 A4
Glenthorne St. 16 BL1 143 E1
Glentress Mews. BL1 144 A8
Glentrool Mews. BL1 144 A7
Glenville Way. M34 101 A2
Glenville Wlk. 13 SK15 86 A1
Glenwood Ave. 2 SK14 101 D5
Glenwood Dr. M'ster M9 157 E7
Glenwood Dr. Middleton M24 47 C1
Glenwood Gr. SK2 124 B4
Glenwyn Ave. M9 64 E4
Globe Ind Est. M26 44 B3
Globe La. Bolton BL7 8 D3
Globe La. Dukinfield SK16 101 B7
Globe Lane Ind Est. SK16 101 B6
Globe Lane Prim Sch.
SK16 101 B6
Globe Sq. SK16 101 A7
Glodwick. OL4 67 B5
Glodwick Inf Sch. OL4 67 B5
Glodwick Rd. OL4 & OL8 67 B6
Glossop Brook Rd. SK13 104 B1
Glossop Central Sta. SK13 104 C1
Glossop Rd.
Charlesworth SK13 & SK14 115 D7
Glossop Rd.
Romiley SK14 & SK6 114 D3
Glossop Rd.
Rowarth SK12 & SK13 116 C1
Glossopdale Comm Coll.
Glossop SK13 104 C2
Glossopdale Comm Coll.
Hadfield SK14 104 A4
Gloster St. 3 BL2 148 A7
Gloucester Ave. 2
Golborne WA3 90 B8
Gloucester Ave.
Heywood OL10 46 C8
Gloucester Ave. Horwich BL6 22 D2
Gloucester Ave.
Littleborough OL12 15 D4
Gloucester Ave. M'ster M19 111 B8
Gloucester Ave. Marple SK6 125 F6
Gloucester Ave.
Whitefield M45 63 A8
Gloucester Cl. OL6 85 D8
Gloucester Cres. WN2 56 E6
Gloucester Ct. BL6 22 D2
Gloucester Dr. Diggle OL3 51 C4
Gloucester Dr. Sale M33 107 D4
Gloucester Pl. Atherton M46 58 D4
Gloucester Pl. 1 Salford M6 81 A3
Gloucester Rd.
Droylsden M43 84 A3
Gloucester Rd. Gatley SK8 131 C7
Gloucester Rd. Hyde SK14 113 E8
Gloucester Rd. Middleton M24 65 B6
Gloucester Rd.
Poynton SK12 133 D4
Gloucester Rd. Reddish M34 100 A2
Gloucester Rd. Salford M6 80 C4
Gloucester Rd. Urmston M41 95 D1
Gloucester Rd. Wigan WN5 54 C6
Gloucester Rise. SK16 102 A7
Gloucester St. Atherton M46 58 D3
Gloucester St. 1
M'ster M15 162 F7
Gloucester St. Salford M6 81 A4
Gloucester St. Salford M5 161 C8
Gloucester St. Stockport SK3 170 D7
Gloucester St N. OL9 152 C5
Gloucester Way. SK13 116 F8
Glover Ave. M8 156 B6
Glover Ct. M7 155 F8
Glover Field. M7 155 D6
Glover St. Horwich BL6 22 B4
Glover St. Leigh WN7 75 C8
Glover St. Newton-l-W WA12 89 C3
Glyn Ave. WA15 120 A2
Glyneath Cl. M11 164 F8
Glynn Gdns. M20 109 D4
Glynne St. BL4 60 C8
Glynrene Dr. M27 61 C1
Glynwood Pk. BL4 42 C1
GM & BM Nat Coll The.
M16 97 D2
GMex. M2 162 F8
GMex Sta. M1 162 F8
Goadsby St. M4 159 A2
Goats Gate Terr. M45 44 D2
Godbert Ave. M21 109 C5
Goddard La. Hadfield SK14 104 A6
Goddard La. Rowarth SK12 127 F7
Goddard Rd. SK14 104 A4
Goddard St. OL8 66 F4
Godfrey Ave. M43 83 D3
Godfrey Ermen Meml
CE Prim Sch. M30 95 C8
Godfrey Range. M18 & M34 99 F4
Godfrey Rd. M6 80 C5
Godlee Dr. M27 79 E7
Godley Cl. M11 165 C8
Godley Ct. SK14 167 F2
Godley Hill. SK14 102 B2
Godley Hill Rd. SK14 102 C1
Godley Prim Sch. SK14 167 F3
Godley St. SK14 167 F4
Godley Sta. SK14 102 A3
Godmond Hall Dr. M28 77 F5
Godson St. OL1 48 E1
Godward Rd. SK12 127 B1
Godwin St. M18 99 E6
Goit Pl. OL16 139 F7
Golborne (All Saints)
RC Prim Sch. WA3 90 B8
Golborne Ave. M20 109 F7
Golborne Cty Prim Sch.
WA3 90 A8
Golborne Dale Rd. WA12 90 A5
Golborne Ent Pk. WA3 74 A1
Golborne Gallery. 9 WN1 150 C8
Golborne House. 8 BL1 145 F8
Golborne Pl. WN1 151 E8
Golborne Rd.
Ashton-i-M WA3 & WN4 73 E4
Golborne Rd. Golborne WA3 90 C8
Golborne St. WA12 89 E4
Golborne High Sch. WA3 74 C1
Golbourne St Thomas'
CE Jun & Inf Sch. WA3 74 B1
Gold St. M60 159 A1
Goldborne House. OL2 149 B8
Goldbourne Dr. OL2 149 B8
Goldbrook Cl. 2 OL10 29 E1
Goldcraft Cl. 4 OL10 29 E1
Goldcrest Cl. Boothstown M28 78 B7
Goldcrest Cl.
Wythenshawe M22 121 F5
Golden St. Eccles M30 79 D1
Golden St. Shaw OL2 49 E8
Goldenhill Ave. M11 83 C3
Goldenways. WN1 37 C2
Goldfinch Dr. BL9 141 C4
Goldfinch Way. M43 84 C3
Goldie Ave. M22 121 F2
Goldrill Ave. BL2 42 F8
Goldrill Gdns. BL2 42 F8
Goldsmith Ave. Oldham OL1 49 E4
Goldsmith Ave. Salford M5 154 D2
Goldsmith Pl. WN3 55 A4
Goldsmith Rd. SK5 99 E1
Goldsmith St. BL3 147 D4
Goldsmith Way. 8 M34 113 A7
Goldstein Rd. BL6 40 B4
Goldsworthy Rd. M41 94 E2
Goldwick Wlk. M23 108 E1
Golf Rd. Alt'ham WA15 119 F3
Golf Rd. Sale M33 108 F4
Gooch Cl. M16 97 E3
Gooch Dr. WA12 89 D2
Gooch St. BL6 22 C2
Goodacre. SK14 102 B6
Gooden St. OL10 29 E1
Goodier St. M'ster M10, M40 160 F4
Goodier St. Sale M33 108 A4
Goodier View. SK14 101 F5
Goodiers Dr. M5 161 B8
Goodison Cl. BL9 45 B3
Goodlad St. BL8 27 B4
Goodman St. M9 64 E1
Goodrich. 3 OL11 139 E6
Goodridge Ave. M22 121 C1
Goodrington Rd. SK9 131 E3
Goodshaw Rd. M28 78 C8
Goodwill Cl. M27 79 F7
Goodwin Sq. M8 & M9 157 D7
Goodwin St. BL1 148 A8
Goodwood Ave. Sale M33 107 C4
Goodwood Ave. Sale M23 120 D7
Goodwood Cl. BL3 42 F3
Goodwood Cres. WA15 120 C6
Goodwood Ct. M7 155 D6
Goodwood Dr. Oldham OL1 49 B1
Goodwood Dr.
Pendlebury M27 80 B7
Goodwood Rd. SK6 125 E5
Goodworth Wlk. M40 83 B7
Goole St. M11 165 A8
Goose Cote Hill. BL7 8 E1
Goose Gn. WA14 119 D4
Goose La. OL12 139 F8
Goosetrey Cl. SK9 131 E1
Gordon Ave. M'ster M20 110 A8
Gorden St. 11 OL13 3 C8
Gordon Ave. Bolton BL3 144 C5
Gordon Ave. Garswood WN4 72 E4
Gordon Ave. Hazel Grove SK7 124 D3
Gordon Ave. M'ster M19 111 B8
Gordon Ave. Oldham OL9 66 A3
Gordon Ave. Oldham OL4 67 C6
Gordon Cl. WN5 54 E8
Gordon Pl. M20 110 B5
Gordon Rd. Eccles M30 79 D3
Gordon Rd. Sale M33 108 B6
Gordon Rd. Swinton M27 79 C6
Gordon St. 14
Ashton-u-L OL6 85 D4
Gordon St. Bury BL9 140 E3
Gordon St. Droylsden M18 99 E6
Gordon St. Hyde SK14 167 E2
Gordon St. Leigh WN7 75 F6
Gordon St. M'ster M7 158 D4
Gordon St. M'ster M16 162 D5
Gordon St. Newhey OL16 32 B3
Gordon St. Oldham OL9 65 F4
Gordon St. Oldham OL4 68 A6
Gordon St. 9 R'dale OL11 31 A5
Gordon St. Shaw OL2 149 C7
Gordon St. 3
Stalybridge SK15 86 B1
Gordon St.
Stockport SK4 & SK5 169 E3
Gordon St. Wigan WN1 151 E7
Gordon Terr. 2 SK15 86 A2
Gordon Way. OL10 28 F1
Gordonstoun Cres. WN5 53 F7
Gore Ave. Failsworth M35 84 B7
Gore Ave. Salford M5 & M6 154 D2
Gore Cres. M5 154 D3
Gore Dr. M5 154 D3
Gore La. SK9 & WA16 136 C3
Gore St. Bury BL9 141 C1
Gore St. M'ster M3 158 E1
Gore St. M'ster M1 159 B1
Gore St. Salford M6 81 A3
Gore St. Wigan WN5 54 B6
Gore's La. WA11 71 A5
Gorebrook Ct. M18 99 A4
Goredale Ave. M18 99 E4
Gorelan Rd. M18 99 D5
Goring Ave. M18 99 D6
Gorman St. 9 WN6 37 A1
Gorman Wlk. WN3 54 F5
Gorrel St. 4 OL11 31 A5
Gorrells Way. OL11 30 D3
Gorrels Cl. OL11 30 E3
Gorrels Way. OL11 30 E3
Gorse Ave. Droylsden M43 84 C2
Gorse Ave. Marple SK6 125 E6
Gorse Ave. Mossley OL5 68 E1
Gorse Ave. Oldham OL8 67 C3
Gorse Ave. Stretford M32 96 F3
Gorse Bank. BL9 141 C3
Gorse Bank Rd. WA15 129 C7
Gorse Bank Sch. OL9 65 F5
Gorse Cres. M32 96 F3
Gorse Dr. Stretford M32 96 F3
Gorse Dr. Walkden M38 59 F6
Gorse Gr. BB4 1 A8
Gorse Hall Cl. SK16 101 F7
Gorse Hall Cty Prim Sch.
SK15 86 A1
Gorse Hall Dr. SK15 85 F1
Gorse Hall Rd. SK16 101 F7
Gorse Hill Prim Sch. M32 96 E4
Gorse La. M32 96 F3
Gorse Rd. Milnrow OL16 32 A6
Gorse Rd. Swinton M27 79 E6
Gorse Rd. Walkden M28 60 E2
Gorse Sq. M31 105 D3
Gorse St. Oldham OL9 65 F4
Gorse St. Stretford M32 96 E3
Gorse The. WA14 128 B8
Gorse Way. SK13 116 F7
Gorse Wlk. WN7 75 B5
Gorsefield Cl. M26 44 A4
Gorsefield Dr. 1 M27 79 F7
Gorsefield Hey. SK9 137 E8
Gorsefield Prim Sch. M26 44 A4
Gorselands. SK8 132 B5
Gorses Dr. WN2 38 C6
Gorses Mount. BL2 & BL3 148 C5
Gorses Rd. BL2 & BL3 42 D5
Gorseway. SK5 112 B4
Gorsey Ave. M22 121 C4
Gorsey Bank Prim Sch.
SK9 136 F7
Gorsey Bank Rd. SK3 123 B8
Gorsey Brow. Billinge WN5 71 E5
Gorsey Brow.
Mottram-i-L SK14 103 A1
Gorsey Brow. Romiley SK6 113 A2
Gorsey Brow. Stockport SK1 112 A1
Gorsey Brow Cl. WN5 71 D5
Gorsey Clough Wlk. BL8 26 F5
Gorsey Dr. M22 121 C4
Gorsey Hey. BL5 57 E7
Gorsey Hill St. OL10 29 D1
Gorsey Intakes. SK14 115 A8
Gorsey La. Alt'ham WA14 119 B5
Gorsey La. Ashton-u-L OL6 85 F6
Gorsey La. Partington WA13 118 B7
Gorsey Mount St. SK1 112 A1
Gorsey Rd. Wilmslow SK9 136 F8
Gorsey Rd.
Wythenshawe M22 121 C4
Gorsey Way. OL6 85 E6
Gorseyfields. M43 100 A8
Gorsley Bank. OL15 16 C7
Gorston Wlk. M22 130 C8
Gort Cl. M45 45 A1
Gorton Brook Fst Sch.
M12 165 A6
Gorton Cres. M34 100 C2
Gorton Cross Ctr. M18 99 D5
Gorton Fold. BL6 22 C3
Gorton Gr. M28 60 C5
Gorton Ind Est. M18 165 C6
Gorton La. M12 & M18 165 B6
Gorton Mount Inf Sch. M18 99 C3
Gorton Mount Jun Sch.
M18 99 C3
Gorton Parks. M18 165 C6
Gorton Rd. M'ster M12 164 F7
Gorton Rd. Reddish M34 & SK5 99 F2
Gorton St. Ashton-u-L OL7 84 F1
Gorton St. Bolton BL2 148 A6
Gorton St. Eccles M30 79 B1
Gorton St. Farnworth BL4 60 B7
Gorton St. Heywood OL10 29 E2
Gorton St. M'ster M3 158 F2
Gorton St. M'ster M40 159 C4
Gorton St. Oldham OL9 152 B6
Gorton Sta. M12 99 D6
Gortonvilla Wlk. M12 164 F6
Gosforth Cl. Bury BL8 27 C5
Gosforth Cl. Oldham OL1 49 A1
Gosforth Wlk. M23 108 F1
Goshen La. BL9 44 F6
Goshen Sports Ctr. BL9 45 A6
Gosling Cl. 3 M16 97 F3
Gosport Sq. M7 155 D5
Gosport Wlk. M8 156 C6
Goss Hall St. OL4 67 C6
Gotha Wlk. M13 163 C6
Gotherage Cl. SK6 113 E2
Gotherage La. SK6 113 E2
Gothic Cl. SK6 113 F2
Gough St. Heywood OL10 29 E2
Gough St. Stockport SK3 169 D1
Gould St. Denton M34 100 E3
Gould St. M'ster M4 159 B3
Gould St. Oldham OL1 67 B8
Goulden Rd. M20 110 A5
Goulden St. M'ster M4 159 B2
Goulden St. Salford M6 154 E2
Goulder Rd. M18 99 E3
Gourham Dr. SK8 122 F2
Govan St. M22 109 E1
Gowan Dr. M24 46 D1
Gowan Rd. M16 97 E1
Gowanlock's St. BL1 143 E2
Gower Ave. SK7 124 C3
Gower Rd. Hyde SK14 167 D1
Gower Rd. Reddish SK4 169 D4
Gower St. Ashton-u-L OL6 166 C3
Gower St. Bolton BL1 145 D8
Gower St. Farnworth BL4 42 C1
Gower St. Leigh WN7 75 E4
Gower St. Oldham OL1 67 A7
Gower St. Swinton M27 62 A1
Gower St. Wigan WN5 150 A7
Gowerdale Rd. SK5 112 C5
Gowers St. OL16 31 B8
Gowran Pk. 3 OL4 67 D6
Gowy Cl. SK9 131 E1
Goya Rise. OL1 49 D4
Goyt Ave. SK6 125 F4
Goyt Cres. Bredbury SK6 112 F3
Goyt Cres. Stockport SK1 112 B3
Goyt Hey Ave. WN5 71 E5
Goyt Rd. Disley SK12 135 D5
Goyt Rd. Marple SK6 125 F4
Goyt Rd. Stockport SK1 112 B3
Goyt Valley Rd. SK6 112 F3
Goyt Valley Wlk. SK6 112 F3
Goyt Wlk. M45 45 B2
Grace St. Horwich BL6 22 B3
Grace St. Leigh WN7 75 C5
Grace St. R'dale OL12 15 A2
Grace Wlk. M4 160 D1
Gracie Ave. 2 Oldham OL1 67 B8
Gradwell St. SK3 170 D8
Grafton Ave. M30 80 A4
Grafton Ct. M'ster M16 162 E5
Grafton Ct. 14 R'dale OL16 31 B6
Grafton Mall. 5 WA14 119 D4
Grafton St. Adlington PR7 20 F6
Grafton St. Alt'ham WA14 119 D4
Grafton St. Ashton-u-L OL6 85 D2
Grafton St. Atherton M46 58 A1
Grafton St. 5 Bolton BL1 145 D8
Grafton St. Bury BL9 44 F8
Grafton St. Failsworth M35 84 A8
Grafton St. Hyde SK14 167 D3
Grafton St. M'ster M13 163 B5
Grafton St. M'ster SK4 169 E3
Grafton St. Newton-l-W WA12 89 B3
Grafton St. Oldham OL1 49 E4
Grafton St. R'dale OL16 31 B6
Grafton St. Stalybridge SK15 86 D3
Graham Ave. WN6 18 C2
Graham Cres. M44 105 C3
Graham Dr. SK12 135 C6
Graham Rd. Salford M6 80 C4
Graham Rd. Stockport SK1 124 C8
Graham St. Abram WN2 56 A1
Graham St. Ashton-u-L OL7 84 F1
Graham St. Bolton BL1 145 F8
Graham St. M'ster M11 165 A8
Grain View. M5 161 A8
Grainger Ave. M12 99 A3
Grains Rd. Delph OL3 50 C4
Grains Rd. Shaw OL1 & OL2 49 D7
Gralam Cl. M33 108 E1
Grammar School Rd.
Lymm WA13 117 A2
Grammar School Rd.
Oldham OL8 66 B2
Grampian Cl. OL9 152 A5
Grampian Way.
Golborne WA3 74 D1
Grampian Way. Shaw OL2 149 A8
Granada Rd. M34 100 A3
Granada TV Ctr. M3 158 E1
Granary La. Worsley M28 78 F5
Granary Way. M33 107 F2
Granby Rd. Cheadle SK8 132 B8
Granby Rd. Sale WA15 108 A1
Granby Rd. Stockport SK2 124 B5
Granby Rd. Stretford M32 96 E1
Granby Rd. Swinton M27 79 C7
Granby Row. M1 163 A8
Granby St. Bury BL8 26 F4
Granby St. Oldham OL9 66 A3
Grand Union Way. M30 95 D8
Grandale St. 5 M14 98 C3
Grandidge St. OL11 139 E5
Grange Ave. Alt'ham WA15 120 A2
Grange Ave.
Cheadle SK8 & M19 122 F3
Grange Ave. Denton M34 101 B2
Grange Ave. Eccles M30 79 D4
Grange Ave. Little Lever BL3 43 C3
Grange Ave. Milnrow OL16 31 F4
Grange Ave. Oldham OL8 66 C4
Grange Ave. Reddish SK4 111 D5
Grange Ave. Sale WA15 120 B7
Grange Ave. Stretford M32 96 D2
Grange Ave. Swinton M27 61 D2
Grange Ave. Urmston M41 94 E2
Grange Ave. Wigan WN5 54 B7
Grange Ave. Wigan WN3 150 B5
Grange Cl. Golborne WA3 90 C6
Grange Cl. Hyde SK14 167 F1
Grange Cres. M41 95 C1
Grange Ct. Alt'ham WA14 119 C1
Grange Ct. Oldham OL8 66 D4
Grange Dr. Eccles M30 79 D4
Grange Dr. M'ster M9 64 F3
Grange Gr. M45 62 F8
Grange La. Delph OL3 50 F6
Grange La. M'ster M20 110 B2
Grange Mill Wlk. M40 83 B7
Grange Park Ave.
Ashton-u-L OL6 85 F6
Grange Park Ave.
Cheadle SK8 122 D5

Grange Park Ave.
Wilmslow SK9 ... 137 A8
Grange Park Rd. Bolton BL2 . 25 C7
Grange Park Rd.
Cheadle SK8 ... 122 D5
Grange Pl. M44 ... 105 E5
Grange Rd. Alt'ham WA14 .. 119 C1
Grange Rd. Ashton-i-M WN4 .. 72 F6
Grange Rd. Bolton BL2 & BL7 . 25 C8
Grange Rd. Bolton BL3 ... 144 B5
Grange Rd. Boothstown M28 . 77 E7
Grange Rd. Bury BL8 ... 27 B2
Grange Rd. Farnworth BL4 ... 42 A1
Grange Rd. Leigh WN2 ... 56 E1
Grange Rd. M'ster M21 ... 97 A2
Grange Rd. Middleton OL11 ... 47 D6
Grange Rd. Sale M33 ... 108 A4
Grange Rd. Sale WA15 ... 120 B7
Grange Rd. Stockport SK7 ... 123 F3
Grange Rd. Urmston M41 ... 95 C1
Grange Rd. Whitworth OL12 ... 4 D3
Grange Rd. Worsley M28 ... 79 A4
Grange Rd N. SK14 ... 167 F2
Grange Rd S. SK14 ... 102 A1
Grange Sch. M'ster M11 ... 160 F1
Grange Sch. Oldham OL9 ... 153 E7
Grange St. Failsworth M35 ... 83 D6
Grange St. Hindley WN2 ... 56 E4
Grange St. Leigh WN7 ... 75 E3
Grange St. Oldham OL9 ... 153 E7
Grange St. Salford M6 ... 154 E2
Grange The. Hyde SK14 ... 167 F1
Grange The. M'ster M14 ... 98 C2
Grange The. 5 Oldham OL1 . 67 B8
Grange Wlk. M24 ... 46 E2
Grangeforth Rd. M7 & M8 .. 155 F8
Grangepark Rd. M9 ... 65 A3
Grangethorpe Dr. M19 ... 110 F7
Grangethorpe Rd.
M'ster M14 ... 98 C2
Grangethorpe Rd.
Urmston M41 ... 95 D1
Grangeway. SK9 ... 131 D4
Grangewood. BL2 ... 25 C7
Grangewood Dr. M9 ... 157 D7
Granite St. 4 OL1 ... 67 B8
Gransden Dr. M8 ... 156 C6
Granshaw St. M10 & M40 ... 160 E3
Gransmoor Ave. M11 ... 99 F7
Gransmoor Rd. M11 & M43 .. 99 F7
Grant Cl. M9 ... 64 D2
Grant Rd. WN3 ... 55 A3
Grant St. Farnworth BL4 ... 42 B2
Grant St. Newton-l-W WA12 .. 89 A3
Grant St. R'dale OL11 ... 30 D2
Grantchester Pl. BL4 ... 147 F1
Grantchester Way. BL2 ... 25 E1
Grantham Cl. BL1 ... 143 E1
Grantham Dr. BL8 ... 140 D4
Grantham Gr. WN2 ... 37 F2
Grantham Rd. SK4 ... 168 C2
Grantham St. M'ster M14 ... 98 B3
Grantham St. Oldham OL4 ... 67 A5
Grantley St. WN4 ... 73 A5
Grants La. BL0 ... 138 C6
Grants Mews. BL0 ... 138 B7
Grantwood. WN4 ... 73 A5
Granville Ave. M'ster M16 ... 97 C2
Granville Ave. M'ster M7 ... 155 E8
Granville Cl. OL9 ... 152 C7
Granville Ct. M'ster M16 ... 97 C3
Granville Ct. Newhey OL16 ... 32 B3
Granville Gdns. M20 ... 110 A2
Granville Rd. Alt'ham WA15 120 C6
Granville Rd. Bolton BL3 ... 146 C3
Granville Rd.
Cheadle SK3 & SK8 ... 123 C5
Granville Rd. Droylsden M34 . 84 B1
Granville Rd. M'ster M14 ... 110 C8
Granville Rd. Urmston M41 ... 95 E3
Granville Rd. Wilmslow SK9 136 F5
Granville St. Adlington PR6 ... 21 A7
Granville St. Ashton-u-L OL6 .. 85 D2
Granville St. Eccles M30 ... 79 D3
Granville St. Farnworth BL4 ... 42 D2
Granville St. Haslingden BB4 ... 1 A7
Granville St. 1 Hindley WN2 56 E5
Granville St. Leigh WN7 ... 75 F7
Granville St. Oldham OL1 ... 48 E1
Granville St. Oldham OL9 ... 152 C8
Granville St. Walkden M28 ... 60 C4
Granville Wlk. OL9 ... 152 C8
Grasdene Ave. 2 M9 ... 64 E3
Grasmere Ave. Farnworth BL4 59 F7
Grasmere Ave Heywood OL10 46 D8
Grasmere Ave. Hindley WN2 . 56 E4
Grasmere Ave. Ince-i-M WN2 56 B7
Grasmere Ave.
Little Lever BL3 ... 43 A4
Grasmere Ave. Orrell WN8 ... 53 B7
Grasmere Ave. Orrell WN5 ... 53 F8
Grasmere Ave. Reddish SK4 111 E6
Grasmere Ave. Swinton M27 . 61 C2
Grasmere Ave. Urmston M41 94 E1
Grasmere Ave.
Whitefield M45 ... 62 C7
Grasmere Cl. SK15 ... 86 A4
Grasmere Cres.
Bramhall SK7 ... 132 E8
Grasmere Cres.
High Lane SK6 ... 125 E1
Grasmere Cres. Swinton M28 79 B4
Grasmere Dr. WN4 ... 73 B5
Grasmere Gr. Ashton-u-L OL7 84 F4
Grasmere Gr.
Ashton-u-L OL7 ... 166 A4
Grasmere House. 5 M28 ... 60 E2
Grasmere Rd.
Alderley Edge SK9 ... 137 A1
Grasmere Rd. Alt'ham WA15 120 C6
Grasmere Rd. Gatley SK8 ... 122 B3
Grasmere Rd. Haslingden BB4 1 C8
Grasmere Rd. Oldham OL4 ... 67 C7
Grasmere Rd.
Partington M31 ... 105 E3
Grasmere Rd. Royton OL2 ... 48 D6
Grasmere Rd. Sale M33 ... 108 C2
Grasmere Rd. Stretford M32 . 96 D3
Grasmere Rd. Swinton M27 ... 79 F6
Grasmere Rd. Wigan WN5 ... 54 C7
Grasmere St. Bolton BL1 ... 143 F2
Grasmere St. Leigh WN7 ... 75 E5
Grasmere St.
M'ster M12 & M18 ... 99 B3
Grasmere St. 10 R'dale OL12 14 F1
Grasmere Terr. Abram WN2 . 74 B8
Grasmere Wlk. M24 ... 46 F2
Grason Ave. SK9 ... 131 C1
Grass Mead. M34 ... 113 B8
Grasscroft. SK5 ... 112 C6
Grasscroft Independent Sch.
OL4 ... 68 C5
Grasscroft Rd. Hindley WN2 . 57 A4
Grasscroft Rd.
Stalybridge SK15 ... 86 A1
Grassfield Ave. M7 ... 81 C6
Grassholme Dr. SK2 ... 125 A5
Grassingham Gdns. M6 ... 154 F3
Grassington Ave. M40 ... 65 A1
Grassington Ct. BL8 ... 26 F4
Grassington Dr. OL10 ... 28 D1
Grassington Pl. BL2 ... 25 A1
Grassmoor Cres. SK13 ... 171 D2
Grathie Ct. BL1 ... 142 B1
Grathome Wlk. BL3 ... 147 E3
Gratrix Ave. M5 ... 161 B7
Gratrix La. M33 ... 108 F3
Gratrix St. M18 ... 99 E4
Gratten Ct. M28 ... 60 C4
Grave Oak La. WA3 ... 76 B1
Gravel Bank Rd. SK6 ... 113 B6
Gravel La. M'ster M3 ... 158 F2
Gravel La. Wilmslow SK9 ... 136 E5
Gravel Wlks. 4 OL4 ... 67 B7
Graver La. Failsworth M40 ... 83 D5
Graver La. Failsworth M40 ... 83 E4
Graves St. M26 ... 43 F6
Graveyard La. WA16 ... 136 A5
Gray Cl. SK14 ... 102 F3
Gray St. BL1 ... 145 E8
Gray St N. BL1 ... 145 E8
Graymar Rd. M38 ... 60 A4
Graymarsh Dr. SK12 ... 133 E2
Grayrigg Wlk. M9 ... 157 D7
Graysands Rd. WA15 ... 119 F3
Grayson Ave. M45 ... 63 B8
Grayson Rd. M38 ... 60 B4
Grayson Way. OL3 ... 69 B6
Grayson's Cl. WN1 ... 37 C1
Graythorp Wlk. 8 M14 ... 98 B3
Graythorpe Wlk. 5 M5 ... 81 A1
Graythwaite Rd. BL1 ... 23 F2
Greame St. M14 ... 98 A3
Great Acre. WN1 ... 37 D1
Great Ancoats St.
M'ster M1 & M4 & M60 ... 159 C1
Great Ancoats St. M'ster M4164 C8
Great Arbor Way. 12 M24 ... 46 F1
Great Bank Rd. BL5 ... 39 D3
Great Bent Cl. OL12 ... 15 D4
Great Bridgewater St. M1 . 162 F8
Great Cheetham St E.
M7 & M8 ... 155 E7
Great Cheetham St W.
M6 & M7 ... 81 C5
Great Clowes St. M7 ... 155 D5
Great Ducie St. M3 & M7 ... 158 F3
Great Eaves Rd. BL0 ... 138 C7
Great Egerton St. SK1, SK4 169 E2
Great Flatt. OL12 ... 14 B1
Great Gable Cl. OL1 ... 67 A8
Great Gates Cl. OL11 ... 31 A4
Great Gates Rd. OL11 ... 31 A3
Great George St. M'ster M3 158 D2
Great George St.
R'dale OL16 ... 139 F7
Great George St.
Wigan WN3 ... 150 B7
Great Hall Cl. M26 ... 44 A4
Great Heaton Cl. M24 ... 64 C7
Great Holme. BL3 ... 147 F4
Great Howarth. OL12 ... 15 B4
Great Jackson St. M15 ... 162 E7
Great John St. M3 ... 162 E8
Great Jones St. M12 ... 165 A6
Great Lee. OL12 ... 14 D3
Great Lee Wlk. OL12 ... 14 D2
Great Lever & Farnworth
Golf Course. BL4 ... 147 E2
Great Marlborough St. 4
M1 ... 163 A7
Great Marld Cl. BL1 ... 23 F2
Great Meadow. OL2 ... 31 F1
Great Moor Jun Sch. SK2 . 124 B4
Great Moor St. Bolton BL1 .. 145 F6
Great Moor St.
Stockport SK2 ... 124 B5
Great Moss Rd. M29 ... 77 C2
Great Nelson St. M12 ... 165 A6
Great Newton St. M40 ... 83 C5
Great Norbury St. SK14 ... 167 D2
Great Portwood St. SK1 ... 169 F2
Great Southern St. M14 ... 98 B3
Great Stone Cl. M26 ... 43 D3
Great Stone Rd.
M'ster M16 & M21 & M32 ... 97 A3
Great Stone Rd.
Stretford M16 & M32 ... 96 F3
Great Stones Cl. BL7 ... 8 F2
Great Underbank.
Stockport SK1 ... 169 F1
Great Western St. M14 ... 98 B4
Greatfield Rd. M22 ... 121 B4
Greave. SK6 ... 113 D4
Greave Ave. OL11 ... 30 B7
Greave Fold. SK6 ... 113 D4
Greave House. OL11 ... 30 B8
Greave Prim Sch. SK6 ... 113 D4
Greave Rd. SK1 & SK2 ... 124 C8
Greaves Ave. M35 ... 83 E6
Greaves Cl. WN6 ... 35 F8
Greaves Rd. SK9 ... 136 E7
Greaves St. Mossley OL5 ... 68 C2
Greaves St. 2 Oldham OL4 ... 67 C6
Greaves St. Oldham OL1 ... 153 F6
Greaves St. Shaw OL2 ... 149 C7
Grebe Cl. Poynton SK12 ... 133 B4
Grebe Cl. Wigan WN3 ... 54 B4
Grebe Wlk. SK2 ... 125 A4
Grecian Cres. BL3 ... 147 F4
Grecian St. M5 & M7 ... 81 C5
Grecian St N. M7 ... 81 C5
Grecian Street North
Prim Sch. M7 ... 81 C5
Gredle Cl. M41 ... 95 F2
Greeba Rd. M23 ... 120 E6
Greek St. M'ster M1 ... 163 B7
Greek St. Stockport SK1 ,SK3 170 E8
Green Acre. BL5 ... 57 F7
Green Ave. Bolton BL3 ... 42 B3
Green Ave. M'ster M12 ... 163 C7
Green Ave. Swinton M27 ... 79 F7
Green Ave. Tyldesley M29 ... 77 A4
Green Ave. Walkden M38 ... 59 E5
Green Bank. Bacup OL13 ... 3 D8
Green Bank. Bolton BL2 ... 25 E3
Green Bank. Farnworth BL4 .. 42 C1
Green Bank. Glossop SK13 .. 115 F7
Green Bank. Reddish SK4 ... 111 D7
Green Booth Cl. SK16 ... 101 D8
Green Bridge Cl. OL11 ... 30 F4
Green Bridge N. BB4 ... 2 E7
Green Bridge S. BB4 ... 2 E7
Green Brook Cl. BL9 ... 141 A4
Green Cl. Gatley SK8 ... 122 A6
Green Cl. Tyldesley M46 ... 58 E1
Green Clough. OL15 ... 16 C8
Green Common La. BL5 ... 58 B7
Green Courts. WA14 ... 119 B3
Green Croft. SK6 ... 113 E3
Green Ct. WN7 ... 75 B1
Green Dr. Alt'ham WA15 ... 120 A7
Green Dr. Bolton BL6 ... 40 C7
Green Dr. Handforth SK9 ... 131 D2
Green Dr. M'ster M19 ... 98 F1
Green End. M34 ... 113 B8
Green End Jun Sch. M19 ... 110 F5
Green End Rd. M19 ... 110 E5
Green Fold. M18 ... 99 F6
Green Fold La. BL5 ... 57 E7
Green Fold Sch. BL4 ... 59 F8
Green Gables Cl. SK8 ... 122 B1
Green Hall Cl. M46 ... 58 F5
Green Hall Mews. SK9 ... 137 B6
Green Hall Sch. M46 ... 58 F4
Green Hayes Ave. WN1 ... 37 C3
Green Hill. OL15 ... 16 A7
Green Hill Rd. SK14 ... 102 A3
Green Hill St. SK3 ... 170 D7
Green Hill Terr. SK3 ... 170 D7
Green La. Alderley Edge SK9 136 F1
Green La. Alt'ham WA15 ... 120 B4
Green La. Ashton-u-L OL6 ... 85 B5
Green La. Bolton BL3 ... 42 B2
Green La. Coppull PR7 ... 20 A8
Green La. Delph OL3 ... 50 F4
Green La. Disley SK12 ... 135 D4
Green La. Eccles M30 ... 79 C2
Green La. Failsworth M35,M40 83 F4
Green La. Glossop SK13 ... 115 F7
Green La. Golborne WA3,WN7 75 A2
Green La. Hadfield SK14 ... 171 F4
Green La. Hazel Grove SK7 .. 124 D3
Green La. Heywood OL10 ... 29 F1
Green La. High Lane SK12 ... 134 C4
Green La. Hindley WN2 ... 57 B4
Green La. Hollingworth SK14 103 D6
Green La. Horwich BL6 ... 22 B5
Green La. Hyde SK14 ... 102 A1
Green La. Hyde SK14 ... 102 A2
Green La. Irlam M44 ... 105 E5
Green La. Kearsley BL4 ... 61 A7
Green La. Leigh WN7 ... 76 C6
Green La. M'ster M18 ... 99 D6
Green La. M'ster SK4 ... 168 B3
Green La. Middleton M24 ... 47 C2
Green La. Middleton M24 ... 65 D7
Green La. Oldham OL4 ... 50 A2
Green La. Oldham OL8 ... 66 E2
Green La. 1 R'dale OL12 ... 139 E8
Green La. Romiley SK6 ... 113 B2
Green La. Sale M33 ... 107 E6
Green La. Standish WN6 ... 36 E8
Green La. Stockport SK4 ... 168 C2
Green La. Stockport SK4 ... 169 D2
Green La. Whitefield M45 ... 44 F1
Green La. Wilmslow SK9 ... 137 B7
Green La N. WA15 ... 120 B5
Green Lane High Sch.
WA15 ... 120 B3
Green Lane Ind Est. SK4 ... 169 D2
Green Meadow. OL12 ... 15 D4
Green Meadows.
Golborne WA3 ... 90 E5
Green Meadows.
Marple SK6 ... 125 F7
Green Meadows.
Westhoughton BL5 ... 57 D8
Green Meadows Dr. SK6 ... 125 F8
Green Meadows Wlk. M22 121 E1
Green Pastures.
M19 & M20 & SK4 ... 110 E1
Green Pine Rd. BL6 ... 39 D7
Green Rd. M31 ... 105 E3
Green Royde. OL11 ... 139 E5
Green St. Adlington PR6 ... 21 B8
Green St. Alderley Edge SK9 137 A1
Green St. Bolton BL1 ... 145 F7
Green St. Bury BL8 ... 26 F4
Green St. Bury BL8 ... 26 F7
Green St. Bury BL8 ... 27 B4
Green St. Eccles M30 ... 79 B1
Green St. Eccles M30 ... 95 B8
Green St. Edenfield BL0 ... 1 E3
Green St. Farnworth BL4 ... 42 C1
Green St. Hyde SK14 ... 167 E1
Green St. M'ster M14 ... 110 E7
Green St. Middleton M24 ... 47 B1
Green St. Oldham OL8 ... 153 E5
Green St. 2 Platt Bridge WN2 56 B2
Green St. Radcliffe M26 ... 44 A3
Green St. Stockport SK3 ... 170 F6
Green St. Stretford M32 ... 108 C8
Green St. Tyldesley M46 ... 58 E1
Green St. 8 Tyldesley M29 ... 59 A1
Green St. Wigan WN3 ... 150 C7
Green The. Cheadle SK8 ... 131 F8
Green The. Glossop SK13 ... 116 A7
Green The. Handforth SK9 .. 131 E3
Green The. Marple SK6 ... 126 A3
Green The. Oldham OL8 ... 67 A3
Green The. Partington M31 .. 105 F4
Green The. R'dale OL11 ... 30 C3
Green The. Ramsbottom BL8 . 10 F1
Green The. Sale WA15 ... 120 C7
Green The. Stalybridge SK15 . 86 E4
Green The. Stockport SK4 ... 168 C2
Green The. Swinton M27 ... 62 B2
Green The. Wigan WN5 ... 54 B6
Green The. Wigan WN5 ... 54 C7
Green The. Worsley M28 ... 78 F5
Green Tree Gdns. SK6 ... 113 B2
Green View. WA13 ... 117 B5
Green Villa Pk. SK9 ... 136 E4
Green Walks. M25 ... 63 C3
Green Way. Bolton BL1 ... 25 B4
Green Way. 6
Mottram-i-L SK14 ... 102 F2
Green Way. R'dale OL11 ... 30 B1
Green Way Cl. BL1 ... 25 B4
Green Wlk. Alt'ham WA14 ... 119 B3
Green Wlk. Alt'ham WA15 ... 120 A7
Green Wlk. Gatley SK8 ... 122 A6
Green Wlk. M'ster M16 ... 97 C2
Green Wlk. 7
Mottram-i-L SK14 ... 102 F2
Green Wlk. Partington M31 . 105 E3
Green Wlk. Stretford M32 ... 96 B2
Greenacre. WN1 ... 37 D1
Greenacre Cl. BL0 ... 11 E7
Greenacre La. M28 ... 78 F4
Greenacre Rd. OL1 & OL4 ... 67 B7
Greenacres. Edgworth BL7 ... 9 E6
Greenacres. Lymm WA13 ... 117 A4
Greenacres Cl. WA3 & WN7 . 91 B8
Greenacres Ct. OL12 ... 15 D4
Greenacres Dr. M19 ... 110 E4
Greenacres Prim Sch. OL4 . 67 C7
Greenacres Rd. OL4 ... 67 D7
Greenall St. WN4 ... 73 B5
Greenbank. Abram WN2 ... 74 B7
Greenbank. Hindley WN2 ... 57 B3
Greenbank.
Hollingworth SK14 ... 103 F5
Greenbank. Horwich BL6 ... 22 D1
Greenbank. Whitworth OL12 . 14 C5
Greenbank Ave. Gatley M22 122 A5
Greenbank Ave. M'ster SK4 111 C6
Greenbank Ave. Orrell WN5 . 53 D3
Greenbank Ave. Swinton M27 79 D6
Greenbank Ave.
Uppermill OL3 ... 51 C1
Greenbank Cres. SK6 ... 125 F5
Greenbank Dr. OL15 ... 15 F3
Greenbank Rd. Bolton BL3 . 144 B5
Greenbank Rd. Bolton BL3 . 146 B4
Greenbank Rd. Gatley SK8 . 122 A6
Greenbank Rd. R'dale OL12 .. 14 F2
Greenbank Rd. R'dale OL12 .. 15 A2
Greenbank Rd. Radcliffe M26 44 A5
Greenbank Rd. Romiley SK6 114 B1
Greenbank Rd. Sale M33 ... 107 E5
Greenbank Rd. Salford M6 . 154 E3
Greenbank Sch.
Cheadle SK8 ... 123 A1
Greenbank Sch. R'dale OL12 14 F1
Greenbank Sch. Royton OL2 . 48 D6
Greenbank Terr. M24 ... 47 C1
Greenbarn Way.Blackrod BL6 21 D1
Greenbeech Cl. SK6 ... 125 E7
Greenbooth Rd. OL12 ... 13 D2
Greenbridge La. OL3 ... 69 B5
Greenbrook St. 6 BL9 ... 141 A4
Greenbrow Inf Sch. M23 ... 120 F3
Greenbrow Par. M23 ... 121 A4
Greenbrow Rd. M23 ... 121 A4
Greenburn Ave. WA11 ... 71 C1
Greenburn Dr. BL2 ... 25 E2
Greencourt Dr. M38 ... 59 F3
Greencourts Bsns Pk. M22 131 A8
Greencroft Rd. M28 ... 79 B4
Greendale. M46 ... 58 E4
Greendale Cres. WN7 ... 76 C4
Greendale Dr. M9 ... 64 E3
Greendale Gr. M34 ... 113 B8
Greenfeld Cty Prim Sch.
OL3 ... 69 B6
Greenfield Ave. Eccles M30 .. 95 A8
Greenfield Ave.
Ince-i-M WN2 ... 151 F7
Greenfield Ave.Urmston M41 95 D2
Greenfield Cl.
Alt'ham WA15 ... 120 C6
Greenfield Cl. Bury BL8 ... 27 A1
Greenfield Cl.
Newton-l-W WA12 ... 89 C4
Greenfield Cl. Stockport SK3 170 E6
Greenfield Cl.
Westhoughton BL5 ... 40 A1
Greenfield Ct. OL10 ... 29 D1
Greenfield La.
Littleborough OL16 ... 15 D3
Greenfield La. R'dale OL11 ... 31 A4
Greenfield La. Shaw OL2 ... 149 B6
Greenfield Prim Sch.
SK14 ... 167 D2
Greenfield Rd. Adlington PR6 21 A8
Greenfield Rd. Atherton M46 58 E5
Greenfield Rd. Walkden M38 60 A4
Greenfield St. Denton M34 . 100 D7
Greenfield St. Hadfield SK14 104 A6
Greenfield St. Hyde SK14 ... 167 D2
Greenfield St. R'dale OL11 ... 31 A4
Greenfield Sta. OL3 ... 69 A6
Greenfield View. WN5 ... 71 D4
Greenfields. WN6 ... 37 A4
Greenfields Cl. WN2 ... 56 F6
Greenfields Cres. WN4 ... 73 B4
Greenfold Ave. BL4 ... 60 B7
Greenford Cl. Cheadle SK8 . 123 B4
Greenford Cl. Orrell WN5 ... 53 D6
Greenford Rd. M8 ... 156 A7
Greengate. Alt'ham WA15 ... 129 D7
Greengate. Hyde SK14 ... 113 D8
Greengate. M'ster M3 ... 158 F2
Greengate.
Middleton OL9, M24, M40 ... 65 C5
Greengate Cl. OL12 ... 15 D3
Greengate Ind Pk. M24 ... 65 C5
Greengate La. Bolton BL2 ... 42 F8
Greengate La. Prestwich M25 63 A4
Greengate Rd. M34 ... 101 A4
Greengate St. OL4 ... 67 B6
Greengate W. M3 ... 158 E3
Greenhalgh La. PR6 ... 21 B8
Greenhalgh Moss La. BL8 ... 27 B5
Greenhalgh St.
Failsworth M35 ... 83 C6
Greenhalgh St.
Stockport SK4 ... 169 E2
Greenham Rd. M23 ... 108 F2
Greenhaven. WN8 ... 53 B7
Greenhead Fold. SK6 ... 113 A1
Greenhead Wlk. BL3 ... 147 E3
Greenheigh Wlk. 1 M4 ... 159 C1
Greenhey. WN5 ... 54 B7
Greenheys. BL2 ... 25 E3
Greenheys Bsns Ctr. M15 . 163 A5
Greenheys Cres. BL8 ... 10 F1
Greenheys La. M'ster M15 . 163 A5
Greenheys La W. M15 ... 162 F5
Greenheys Rd. M38 ... 59 E6
Greenhill. M25 ... 63 A4
Greenhill Ave. Bolton BL3 ... 144 B5
Greenhill Ave. Farnworth BL4 60 C6
Greenhill Ave. R'dale OL12 139 E8
Greenhill Ave. Sale M33 ... 108 A6
Greenhill Ave. Shaw OL2 ... 31 E1
Greenhill Comm Sch. OL4 ... 67 A6
Greenhill Cotts. OL5 ... 68 D2
Greenhill Cres. WN5 ... 71 F5
Greenhill La. BL3 ... 40 F4
Greenhill Pas. 2 OL1 ... 67 A6
Greenhill Prim Sch. BL8 ... 26 F1
Greenhill Rd. Alt'ham WA15 120 C6
Greenhill Rd. Billinge WN5 ... 71 F5
Greenhill Rd. Bury BL8 ... 27 A1
Greenhill Rd. M'ster M7 ,M8 156 A8
Greenhill Rd. Middleton M24 . 65 D7
Greenhill Terr. 6 OL4 ... 67 A6
Greenhill Wlk. SK12 ... 135 D6
Greenholm Cl. M40 ... 65 D1
Greenhow St. M43 ... 99 F8
Greenhurst Cres. OL8 ... 67 A2
Greenhurst La. OL6 ... 85 E6
Greenhurst Rd. OL6 ... 85 D7
Greenhythe Rd. SK8 ... 131 C6
Greening Rd. M18 ... 99 B2
Greenland Ave. WN6 ... 19 E1
Greenland Cl. M29 ... 77 B6
Greenland La. PR6 ... 21 D5
Greenland Rd. Bolton BL3 ... 147 F2
Greenland Rd.
Farnworth BL3 & BL4 ... 42 A2
Greenland Rd. Tyldesley M29 77 B6
Greenland St. M'ster M7,M8 155 F7
Greenland St. 3 Salford M6 154 E2
Greenlaw Ct. M16 ... 161 C5
Greenlea Ave. M18 ... 99 D3
Greenlea Cl. WN5 ... 53 D5
Greenleach La. M28 ... 79 A7
Greenleaf Cl. M28 ... 77 F6
Greenleas. BL6 ... 40 C6
Greenlees St. OL12 ... 139 F8
Greenmount Cl. BL8 ... 10 F2
Greenmount Ct. BL1 ... 144 A8
Greenmount Dr.
Heywood OL10 ... 46 F7
Greenmount Dr.
Ramsbottom BL8 ... 10 F2
Greenmount Golf Course.
BL8 ... 10 E1
Greenmount La. BL1 ... 144 A8
Greenmount Pk. BL4 ... 61 A7
Greenmount Prim Sch. BL8 10 F2
Greenoak. M26 ... 61 C6
Greenoak Dr. Sale M33 ... 108 C1
Greenoak Dr. Walkden M28 .. 60 C5
Greenock Cl. BL3 ... 40 E5
Greenock Dr. Heywood OL10 28 F1
Greenough St. Atherton M46 58 A1
Greenough St. Wigan WN1 151 D8
Greenpark Cl. BL8 ... 10 F1
Greenpark Rd. M22 ... 109 D1
Greenpine Ind Pk. BL6 ... 39 D7
Greenroyd Ave. BL2 ... 25 E2
Greens Arms Rd. BL7 ... 8 E7
Greens La. Bacup OL13 ... 3 D7
Greens La. Haslingden BB4 ... 1 C7
Greens The. OL12 ... 4 C1
Greenshall La. SK12 ... 135 F5
Greenshank Cl.
Newton-l-W WA12 ... 89 C4
Greenshank Cl. R'dale OL11 . 29 F7
Greenside. Farnworth BL4 ... 42 C1
Greenside. Stockport SK4 ... 168 A1
Greenside. Worsley M28 ... 79 A5
Greenside Ave. Kearsley BL4 60 F6
Greenside Ave. Oldham OL4 . 49 E2
Greenside Cl.
Ramsbottom BL8 ... 10 B3
Greenside Cl.
Stalybridge SK15 & SK16 ... 102 A8
Greenside Cres. M43 ... 83 F2
Greenside Ct. M30 ... 79 D3
Greenside Dr.Alt'ham WA14 119 E1
Greenside Dr. Bury BL8 ... 26 F8
Greenside Dr. Irlam M44 ... 93 F1
Greenside La. M43 ... 83 F3
Greenside Pl. M34 ... 113 B8
Greenside Prim Sch. M43 ... 83 F2
Greenside St. Ainsworth BL2 . 26 C1
Greenside St. M'ster M11 .. 165 C8
Greenside Way. M24 ... 65 C5
Greenslate Ave. WN6 ... 35 E8
Greenslate Ct. WN5 ... 53 E3
Greenslate Rd. WN5 ... 53 E3
Greensmith Way. BL5 ... 39 E3
Greenson Dr. M24 ... 64 E7
Greenstead Ave. M8 ... 156 A8
Greenstone Ave. BL6 ... 22 B3
Greenstone Dr. M6 ... 80 F5
Greensward Cl. WN6 ... 19 B1
Greensway Ctr. OL2 ... 149 B7
Greenthorn Wlk. M15 ... 162 F5
Greenthorne Ave. SK4 ... 111 D7
Greenthorne Cl. BL7 ... 9 E7
Greenvale. R'dale OL11 ... 29 D8
Greenvale. Shevington WN6 ... 35 F4
Greenvale Dr. SK8 ... 122 C6
Greenview Dr. M20 ... 122 C8
Greenway. Alt'ham WA14 ... 119 A5
Greenway. Ashton-i-M WN4 .. 73 A4
Greenway. Bramhall SK7 ... 132 D6
Greenway. Horwich BL6 ... 22 F3
Greenway. Hyde SK14 ... 167 D1
Greenway. Middleton M9 ... 64 F5
Greenway. Romiley SK6 ... 113 E1
Greenway. Shaw OL2 ... 31 F1
Greenway. Wilmslow SK9 ... 137 B6
Greenway.
Wythenshawe M22 ... 121 E8
Greenway Ave. 10 M19 ... 99 B1
Greenway Cl. Bury BL8 ... 27 B3
Greenway Cl. Sale M33 ... 107 E3
Greenway Dr. OL5 ... 68 C2
Greenway Mews. BL0 ... 11 C4
Greenway Rd. Gatley SK8 ... 131 C6
Greenway Rd. Sale WA15 ... 119 F8
Greenways. 7 Ashton-u-L OL7 85 A4
Greenways. Failsworth M40 ... 65 D1
Greenways. Leigh WN7 ... 76 B6
Greenways. Orrell WN5 ... 53 D3
Greenways. Standish WN6 ... 37 A6
Greenwich Cl.Failsworth M40 83 D4
Greenwich Cl.R'dale OL11 ... 29 F6
Greenwood Ave.
Ashton-u-L OL6 ... 85 C6
Greenwood Ave.Horwich BL6 22 D1
Greenwood Ave.
Stockport SK2 ... 124 C6
Greenwood Ave. Swinton M2762 B1
Greenwood Ave.
Walkden M28 ... 60 C3
Greenwood Ave. Wigan WN5 54 E7
Greenwood Bsns Ctr. 10
M5 ... 81 A1
Greenwood Cl.
Alt'ham WA15 ... 120 D5
Greenwood Cl.
Boothstown M28 ... 77 E7
Greenwood Cl. Culcheth WA3 91 F1
Greenwood Dr.
Newton-l-W WA12 ... 89 D2
Greenwood Dr.
Wilmslow SK9 ... 137 D8
Greenwood Gdns. SK6 ... 112 F3
Greenwood La. BL6 ... 22 E1
Greenwood Prim Sch. M30 79 E4
Greenwood Rd.Standish WN6 19 E2
Greenwood Rd.
Wythenshawe M22 ... 121 C5
Greenwood St. 1
Alt'ham WA14 ... 119 D4
Greenwood St. Farnworth BL4 60 D8
Greenwood St. 2
Littleborough OL15 ... 16 B5
Greenwood St. Oldham OL8 .. 66 F1
Greenwood St. Oldham OL4 .. 67 C8
Greenwood St. Oldham OL4 .. 67 E6
Greenwood St. R'dale OL16 139 F7
Greenwood St. Salford M6 ... 81 A4
Greenwood St. Salford M6 .. 154 F4
Greenwood Vale. BL1 ... 143 E3
Greenwood Vale S. 7 BL1 143 F3
Greenwoods La. BL2 ... 25 F4
Greer St. M11 ... 165 C8
Greg Mews. SK9 ... 131 B2
Greg St. SK5 ... 111 E5
Gregge St. Heywood OL10 ... 29 E1
Gregge St. Heywood OL10 ... 46 E8
Gregory Ave. Atherton M46 ... 58 C5
Gregory Ave. Bolton BL2 ... 42 E8
Gregory Ave. Romiley SK6 ... 113 C1
Gregory Fold. BB4 ... 1 A7
Gregory St. Dukinfield SK14 101 E5
Gregory St. Hindley WN2 ... 56 C6
Gregory St. Leigh WN7 ... 75 E4
Gregory St. M'ster M12 ... 164 F6
Gregory St. Oldham OL8 ... 66 C3
Gregory St.
Westhoughton BL5 & WN2 ... 57 A7
Gregory Way. SK5 ... 111 F6
Gregorys Row. WA3 ... 75 A1
Gregson Field. BL3 ... 147 E4
Gregson Rd. SK5 ... 111 E6
Gregson St. 4 OL1 ... 153 F6
Gregsrigg Cl. WN6 ... 36 F7
Grelly Wlk. 2 M14 ... 98 C3
Grenaby Ave. WN2 ... 57 B5
Grendale Ave.
Hazel Grove SK7 ... 124 E1
Grendale Ave. Stockport SK1 112 B1
Grendale Dr. M16 ... 161 C5
Grendon Ave. OL8 ... 66 E4
Grendon St. BL3 ... 146 C3
Grendon Wlk. M12 ... 165 A6
Grenfel Cl. WN3 ... 150 A5
Grenfell Rd. M20 ... 110 B3
Grenham Ave. M15 ... 162 D6
Grenville Rd. SK7 ... 124 D3
Grenville St.Dukinfield SK16 101 C8
Grenville St.Stalybridge SK15 86 D4
Grenville St.Stockport SK3 .. 170 D8
Grenville Terr. 7 OL6 ... 85 D2
Gresford Cl. M21 ... 109 A8
Gresham Cl. M45 ... 62 D7
Gresham Dr. OL9 ... 152 C7
Gresham St. Bolton BL1 ... 143 F3
Gresham St. Denton M34 ... 100 F4
Gresham Wlk. SK4 ... 169 E3
Gresley Cl. WN1 ... 151 E8
Gresty Ave. M22 ... 121 F1
Greswell Prim Sch. M34 ... 100 F2
Greswell St. M34 ... 100 F4
Greta Ave. SK8 ... 131 C6
Greta Wlk. WN2 ... 56 A2
Gretna Rd. M46 ... 58 A1
Greton Cl. M13 ... 98 E4
Gretton Cl. OL2 ... 48 F4

Hannah Lodge. M20 110 A4
Hannah St. M12 99 A2
Hannerton Rd. OL2 49 D7
Hannesburg Gdns. M23 120 F4
Hannet Rd. M22 121 D2
Hanover Bsns Pk. WA14 119 B7
Hanover Cres. M14 98 D4
Hanover Ct. Bolton BL3 144 B5
Hanover Ct. M'ster M7 155 D7
Hanover Ct. Swinton M28 79 B6
Hanover Gdns. M7 155 E8
Hanover House. Bolton BL3 146 B2
Hanover House. 10 M'ster M14 110 D8
Hanover House. Oldham OL8 153 D6
Hanover Rd. Alt'ham WA14 119 B7
Hanover Rd. Hindley WN2 56 C6
Hanover St. Bolton BL1 145 E7
Hanover St. Leigh WN7 76 A6
Hanover St. Littleborough OL15 16 A5
Hanover St. M'ster M4 & M60 159 A2
Hanover St. Mossley OL5 68 C1
Hanover St. R'dale OL11 30 C2
Hanover St. Stalybridge SK15 85 F2
Hanover St N. M34 100 E8
Hanover St S. M34 100 E8
Hanover Towers. SK5 169 F3
Hansdon Cl. M8 156 A6
Hansen Wlk. 1 M22 121 C2
Hansham Wlk. M23 108 E1
Hanslope Wlk. 14 M9 157 E8
Hanson Cl. M24 47 A1
Hanson Mews. SK1 112 B2
Hanson Rd. M40 83 B7
Hanson St. Bury BL9 140 F4
Hanson St. Middleton M24 47 A1
Hanson St. Oldham OL4 67 C7
Hanworth Cl. M13 163 B7
Hapsford Wlk. M40 83 A5
Hapton Ave. M32 96 D1
Hapton Pl. SK4 169 E3
Hapton St. M19 99 A1
Harbern Cl. M30 79 D4
Harbern Dr. WN7 57 D2
Harbord St. M24 65 A8
Harboro Ct. M33 107 F3
Harboro Gr. M33 107 F4
Harboro Rd. M33 107 E4
Harboro Way. M33 107 F4
Harbour Farm Rd. SK14 101 E5
Harbour La. Edgworth BL7 9 D5
Harbour La. Milnrow OL16 31 F5
Harbour La N. OL16 31 F6
Harbourne Ave. M28 78 C8
Harbourne Cl. M28 78 C8
Harburn Wlk. M22 130 E8
Harbury Cl. WN6 36 F2
Harbury Cres. M22 121 C5
Harbury Wlk. WN6 36 F2
Harcles Dr. BL0 11 B2
Harcombe Rd. M20 110 C6
Harcourt Ave. M41 95 F1
Harcourt Cl. M41 95 F1
Harcourt Ind Ctr. M28 60 D5
Harcourt Mews. 10 BL6 22 B4
Harcourt Rd. Alt'ham WA14 119 D6
Harcourt Rd. Sale M33 108 A6
Harcourt St. Oldham OL1 67 B8
Harcourt St. Reddish SK5 111 F8
Harcourt St. Stretford M32 96 E3
Harcourt St. Walkden M28 60 D5
Hard La. OL12 15 A8
Hardacre St. WN3 151 D6
Hardberry Pl. SK2 124 E6
Hardcastle Ave. M21 109 C6
Hardcastle Rd. SK3 170 D7
Hardcastle St. Bolton BL1 143 F2
Hardcastle St. 7 Oldham OL1 67 B7
Hardcastle St. Oldham OL1 153 F7
Harden Dr. BL2 25 D2
Harden Hills. OL2 49 D8
Harden Pk. SK9 137 A3
Hardfield Rd. M24 65 B5
Hardfield St. OL10 29 D2
Hardicker St. M19 111 B7
Hardie Ave. BL4 60 B7
Harding St. Adlington PR6 21 B8
Harding St. Dukinfield SK14 101 D5
Harding St. M'ster M3 158 F2
Harding St. M'ster M4 160 D1
Harding St. Salford M6 154 A4
Harding St. Stockport SK1 112 B1
Hardman Ave. M'ster M25 63 D2
Hardman Ave. Rawtenstall BB4 2 B8
Hardman Ave. Romiley SK6 113 A3
Hardman Cl. Radcliffe M26 43 F6
Hardman Cl. Rawtenstall BB4 2 F7
Hardman Dr. BB4 2 F7
Hardman Fold. BL3 42 B2
Hardman Fold Sch. M35 83 D7
Hardman La. M35 83 E8
Hardman Rd. SK5 111 F8
Hardman St. Bury BL9 140 F4
Hardman St. Failsworth M35 83 D7
Hardman St. Farnworth BL4 60 E7
Hardman St. Heywood OL10 29 B2
Hardman St. M'ster M3 158 E1
Hardman St. Milnrow OL16 32 A5
Hardman St. Oldham OL9 66 B3
Hardman St. Radcliffe M26 43 F6
Hardman St. Stockport SK3 170 D8
Hardman St. Wigan WN3 150 B6
Hardman Terr. OL13 3 D8
Hardman's La. BL7 24 F8
Hardman's Mews. M45 62 F6
Hardman's Rd. M45 62 F6
Hardmans. BL7 24 F7
Hardon Gr. M13 98 F2
Hardrow Cl. WN3 55 B2
Hardrush Fold. M35 84 A6
Hardshaw Cl. M13 163 B6
Hardsough La. BL0 1 D5
Hardwick Cl. High Lane SK6 134 F6
Hardwick Cl. Little Lever BL3 43 B5
Hardwick Rd. Ashton-i-M WN4 73 A5
Hardwick Rd. Partington M31 106 A3
Hardwick St. OL7 84 F2
Hardwicke Rd. SK12 133 F4
Hardwicke St. OL11 30 E4
Hardy Ave. M21 109 A8
Hardy Cl. BL5 39 E3
Hardy Dr. Alt'ham WA15 119 F7
Hardy Dr. Bramhall SK7 132 D7
Hardy Farm. M21 109 B6
Hardy Gr. Swinton M27 79 D5
Hardy Gr. Worsley M28 78 F8
Hardy La. M21 109 B6
Hardy Mill Cty Prim Sch. BL2 25 F4
Hardy Mill Rd. Bolton BL2 25 F4
Hardy Mill Rd. Bolton BL2 26 A3
Hardy St. Ashton-u-L OL6 85 E6
Hardy St. Eccles M30 79 B1
Hardy St. Oldham OL4 & OL8 67 A6
Hardy St. Wigan WN6 37 A1
Hardybutts. Wigan WN1 151 D8
Hardybutts. Wigan WN1 151 E8
Hardywood Rd. 4 M34 113 A7
Hare Dr. BL9 45 B4
Hare Hill Prim Sch. SK14 102 C3
Hare Hill Rd. Hattersley SK14 102 C2
Hare Hill Rd. Littleborough OL15 16 B6
Hare St. 7 M'ster M4 159 A2
Hare St. R'dale OL11 31 A6
Hare St. R'dale OL11 139 F5
Harebell Ave. 10 M28 59 F3
Harebell Cl. OL12 14 D3
Haredale Dr. M8 156 B6
Harefield Ave. OL11 139 F5
Harefield Dr. Heywood OL10 29 F2
Harefield Dr. M'ster M20 110 F1
Harefield Dr. Wilmslow SK9 137 B5
Harefield Rd. SK9 131 E4
Hareford Wlk. M9 156 C6
Harehill Cl. 5 M13 163 B7
Hareshill Rd. OL10 46 C7
Harewood Ave. R'dale OL11 13 D2
Harewood Ave. Sale M33 107 D3
Harewood Cl. OL11 13 D2
Harewood Ct. M33 108 C3
Harewood Dr. R'dale OL11 13 C2
Harewood Dr. Royton OL2 48 C5
Harewood Gr. SK5 111 E8
Harewood Rd. Hindley WN2 56 C5
Harewood Rd. Irlam M44 94 B2
Harewood Rd. R'dale OL11 13 D2
Harewood Rd. Shaw OL2 49 D8
Harewood Way. R'dale OL11 13 C2
Harewood Way. Swinton M27 61 F2
Harewood Wlk. 23 M34 101 A1
Harford Cl. SK7 124 A1
Hargate Ave. OL12 14 A2
Hargate Cl. BL9 11 C2
Hargate Dr. Alt'ham WA15 120 A1
Hargate Dr. Irlam M44 94 A3
Hargate Hill La. SK13 115 E7
Hargrave Cl. M9 64 C6
Hargreave's St. M8 159 A3
Hargreaves House. BL3 145 E6
Hargreaves Rd. WA15 120 C6
Hargreaves St. Bolton BL1 143 E2
Hargreaves St. Oldham OL9 152 C6
Hargreaves St. Oldham OL1 153 F7
Hargreaves St. R'dale OL11 30 C4
Harkerside Cl. M21 109 C8
Harkness St. M12 164 D7
Harland Dr. Ashton-i-M WN4 73 C3
Harland Dr. M'ster M8 156 B7
Harland Way. OL12 14 B2
Harlea Ave. WN2 57 A3
Harlech Ave. Hindley WN2 57 B4
Harlech Ave. Prestwich M25 & M45 63 B7
Harlech Dr. SK7 124 D1
Harlech St. WN4 72 F5
Harleen Gr. SK2 124 D7
Harley Ave. Ainsworth BL2 26 D1
Harley Ave. Bolton BL2 25 E3
Harley Ave. M'ster M14 98 E3
Harley Ct. M24 46 F1
Harley Hall Royal Northern Coll of Music. M16 97 E1
Harley Rd. Middleton M24 46 F1
Harley Rd. Sale M33 108 C5
Harley St. Ashton-u-L OL6 166 B3
Harley St. M'ster M11 99 D8
Harling Rd. M22 121 E7
Harlington Cl. 3 M23 120 D7
Harlock Ct. M6 81 B3
Harlow Dr. M18 99 D3
Harlyn Ave. SK7 132 F7
Harmer Cl. M40 83 B5
Harmol Gr. OL7 84 F6
Harmony St. OL4 67 A6
Harmsworth Dr. SK4 111 B5
Harmsworth St. M6 154 E2
Harmuir Cl. WN6 36 E4
Harold Ave. Ashton-i-M WN4 73 A5
Harold Ave. Dukinfield SK16 101 D8
Harold Ave. Reddish M18 99 F4
Harold Lees. OL10 29 F3
Harold Priestnall Cl. M40 83 B6
Harold St. Aspull WN2 38 D5
Harold St. Bolton BL1 143 D2
Harold St. Failsworth M35 83 E7
Harold St. M'ster M15, M16 161 C6
Harold St. Middleton M24 46 E1
Harold St. Oldham OL9 153 D7
Harold St. Prestwich M25 62 F4
Harold St. R'dale OL16 15 C2
Harold St. Stockport SK ,SK2 124 B8
Haroldene St. BL2 25 B2
Harp Ind Est. OL11 30 D2
Harp Rd. M17 96 A8
Harp St. M11 99 E7
Harp Trad Est. M17 96 A8
Harper Fold Rd. M26 43 E3
Harper Green Rd. BL3 & BL4 42 B1
Harper Green Sch. BL4 42 B1
Harper House. M19 98 F1
Harper Pl. OL6 166 C3
Harper Rd. M22 121 E7
Harper Sq. OL2 149 C7
Harper St. Farnworth BL4 42 B2
Harper St. Hindley WN2 56 C4
Harper St. Oldham OL8 66 E4
Harper St. R'dale OL11 139 E5
Harper St. Stockport SK3 170 E7
Harper St. Wigan WN1 151 E7
Harper's La. BL1 142 B2
Harpford Cl. BL2 43 A5
Harpford Dr. BL2 43 A5
Harptree Gr. WN7 75 D7
Harpur Mount Prim Sch. M9 157 D8
Harpurhey Rd. M8 & M9 157 D8
Harridge Ave. R'dale OL12 14 C3
Harridge Ave. Stalybridge SK15 86 D2
Harridge St. OL12 14 C3
Harridge The. OL12 14 C3
Harriet St. Irlam M44 105 E5
Harriet St. Walkden M28 60 D3
Harriett St. M'ster M4 159 C2
Harriett St. R'dale OL16 31 A7
Harringay Rd. M40 83 B5
Harrington Rd. WA14 119 B5
Harrington St. M18 99 E5
Harris Ave. Reddish M34 100 B3
Harris Ave. Urmston M41 95 D5
Harris Cl. Heywood OL10 28 E1
Harris Cl. Reddish M34 100 B3
Harris Dr. Hyde SK14 102 A4
Harris Dr. Whitefield BL9 & M45 45 B2
Harris Rd. WN6 19 B3
Harris St. Bolton BL3 145 E6
Harris St. M'ster M7 & M8 158 E4
Harrison Ave. M19 99 B2
Harrison Cl. OL12 13 F1
Harrison Cres. BL6 21 C3
Harrison Rd. PR7 21 A6
Harrison St. Bacup OL13 4 A8
Harrison St. Eccles M30 95 B8
Harrison St. Hindley WN2 57 B3
Harrison St. Horwich BL6 22 B4
Harrison St. Hyde SK14 113 F8
Harrison St. M'ster M7 158 D4
Harrison St. M'ster M4 160 D1
Harrison St. 1 Oldham OL1 153 F6
Harrison St. Ramsbottom BL0 138 C7
Harrison St. Stalybridge SK15 86 A2
Harrison St. Stockport SK1 & SK2 170 F7
Harrison St. Walkden M38 60 A4
Harrison St. 4 Wigan WN5 54 F6
Harrison Way. WA12 89 C4
Harrison's Dr. SK6 113 C5
Harrock La. WN6 18 A5
Harrogate Ave. M25 63 D2
Harrogate Cl. M18 99 E7
Harrogate Dr. SK5 111 E8
Harrogate Rd. SK5 99 E1
Harrogate Sq. BL8 26 F1
Harrogate St. WN1 151 D7
Harrop Court Rd. OL3 51 D5
Harrop Edge La. OL3 51 B5
Harrop Edge Rd. SK14 & SK15 102 E4
Harrop Green. OL3 51 D5
Harrop Green La. OL3 51 D5
Harrop Rd. WA15 119 F2
Harrop St. Bolton BL3 146 A4
Harrop St. Droylsden M18 99 F6
Harrop St. 10 Stalybridge SK15 86 A2
Harrop St. Stockport SK1 124 A7
Harrop St. Walkden M28 60 B3
Harrow Ave. M'ster M19 111 A6
Harrow Ave. Oldham OL8 66 E3
Harrow Ave. R'dale OL11 30 A6
Harrow Cl. Bury BL9 44 F5
Harrow Cl. Orrell WN5 53 F8
Harrow Cres. WN7 75 F3
Harrow Dr. M33 108 A2
Harrow Mews. OL2 149 B7
Harrow Pl. WN2 55 F4
Harrow Rd. Bolton BL1 144 B8
Harrow Rd. Sale M33 108 A2
Harrow Rd. Shevington WN5 36 D1
Harrow St. M'ster M8 64 B1
Harrow St. R'dale OL11 31 A5
Harrowby Ct. BL4 60 B8
Harrowby Dr. M40 157 D5
Harrowby Fold. BL4 60 C8
Harrowby La. BL4 60 C8
Harrowby Rd. Bolton BL1 42 F8
Harrowby Rd. Bolton BL3 146 A3
Harrowby Rd. Swinton M27 79 E7
Harrowby St. Farnworth BL4 60 C8
Harrowby St. Wigan WN5 54 E6
Harrowdene Wlk. 6 M9 157 D8
Harry Hall Gdns. M7 81 C3
Harry Pigott Ave. M40 83 A7
Harry Rd. SK5 111 F8
Harry St. Oldham OL2 48 E2
Harry St. Oldham OL9 152 C6
Harry St. R'dale OL11 30 B3
Harry Thorneycroft Wlk. M11 164 E8
Harry's Ct. 3 WN7 75 D5
Harrycroft Rd. SK6 113 B5
Harrytown. SK6 113 A2
Harrytown RC High Sch. SK6 113 A2
Hart Ave. Droylsden M43 84 B1
Hart Ave. Sale M33 108 F3
Hart Common CE Prim Sch. BL5 57 B7
Hart Ct. OL5 68 B2
Hart Dr. BL9 45 B4
Hart Hill Dr. M5 154 D3
Hart Mill Cl. OL5 68 B2
Hart Rd. M14 98 B1
Hart St. Alt'ham WA14 119 E5
Hart St. Droylsden M43 84 B1
Hart St. M'ster M60 159 A1
Hart St. Tyldesley M29 77 C8
Hart St. Westhoughton BL5 57 B7
Hart's Houses. BL6 22 D5
Harter St. M1 163 A8
Hartfield Cl. M13 163 C6
Hartfield Wlk. BL2 148 C8
Hartford Ave. Heywood OL10 29 B3
Hartford Ave. Reddish SK4 111 D6
Hartford Ave. Wilmslow SK9 136 F5
Hartford Cl. OL10 29 B3
Hartford Gdns. WA15 120 D5
Hartford Rd. Sale M33 107 D2
Hartford Rd. Urmston M41 95 E4
Hartford Sq. OL9 152 C6
Hartford St. M34 100 E5
Harthill St. M7 & M8 155 F5
Hartington Cl. 4 M41 95 E2
Hartington Ct. OL2 48 E4
Hartington Dr. Droylsden M11 83 B3
Hartington Dr. Hazel Grove SK7 133 E8
Hartington Dr. Standish WN6 36 F7
Hartington Rd. Alt'ham WA14 119 D8
Hartington Rd. Bolton BL1 144 C8
Hartington Rd. Bramhall SK7 132 E6
Hartington Rd. Gatley SK8 131 D8
Hartington Rd. High Lane SK12 & SK6 134 F7
Hartington Rd. M'ster M21 109 B8
Hartington Rd. Stockport SK2 124 D5
Hartington Rd. Worsley M28 79 A3
Hartington St. M14 97 F3
Hartis Ave. M7 155 E6
Hartland Ave. M41 96 A2
Hartland Cl. Poynton SK12 133 D5
Hartland Cl. Stockport SK2 124 C8
Hartland Cl. Tyldesley M29 77 B8
Hartland St. OL10 29 D2
Hartlebury. OL11 139 E6
Hartlepool Cl. M14 98 B3
Hartley Ave. M'ster M25 63 D3
Hartley Ave. Wigan WN1 151 E7
Hartley Gr. Irlam M44 94 B4
Hartley Gr. Wigan WN5 54 B7
Hartley La. OL11 30 E3
Hartley Rd. Alt'ham WA14 119 C5
Hartley Rd. M'ster M21 97 A1
Hartley St. Heywood OL10 29 D2
Hartley St. Horwich BL6 22 B3
Hartley St. Littleborough OL12 15 C6
Hartley St. Littleborough OL15 16 A5
Hartley St. M'ster M40 & M9 157 F8
Hartley St. Milnrow OL16 31 D7
Hartley St. R'dale OL12 14 B1
Hartley St. Stalybridge SK15 86 D3
Hartley St. Stockport SK3 170 D8
Hartley St. 13 Wigan WN5 54 B6
Hartley Terr. WN3 150 C7
Harton Ave. M18 99 C3
Harton Cl. OL2 149 A6
Harts Farm Mews. WN7 75 F7
Harts La. WN8 53 A8
Hartshead Ave. Ashton-u-L OL6 85 C6
Hartshead Ave. Stalybridge SK15 86 A3
Hartshead Cl. M11 100 A7
Hartshead Cres. M35 84 C6
Hartshead High Sch. OL6 85 E7
Hartshead Rd. OL6 85 C6
Hartshead St. OL4 67 F5
Hartshead View. SK14 167 F1
Hartsop Dr. M24 46 C2
Hartswell Cl. WA3 74 A2
Hartswood Cl. M34 101 A4
Hartswood Rd. M20 110 D6
Hartwell Cl. Bolton BL2 25 C3
Hartwell Cl. M'ster M11 164 F8
Harty. M30 79 E2
Harvard Cl. SK6 113 C5
Harvard St. 13 OL11 31 A4
Harvest Cl. Salford M6 80 E5
Harvest Cl. Wythenshawe M33 109 A3
Harvey Cl. M11 165 A8
Harvey Ct. WN7 75 B1
Harvey La. WA3 73 F1
Harvey St. Bolton BL1 143 D3
Harvey St. Bury BL8 27 C3
Harvey St. Ince-i-M WN3 151 E6
Harvey St. Oldham OL9 66 A2
Harvey St. R'dale OL12 15 B2
Harvey St. Stockport SK1 169 F1
Harvin Gr. M34 101 A2
Harwich Cl. Brinnington SK5 112 C6
Harwich Cl. 1 M'ster M19 99 B1
Harwin Cl. OL12 14 D3
Harwood Cres. BL8 26 E7
Harwood Ct. M'ster SK4 110 E2
Harwood Ct. Salford M6 81 B4
Harwood Dr. BL8 27 A1
Harwood Gdns. OL10 29 D1
Harwood Golf Course. BL2 26 A4
Harwood Gr. 27 BL2 25 B1
Harwood Meadow. BL2 25 F3
Harwood Meadows Cty Prim Sch. BL2 25 F3
Harwood Park Prim Sch. OL10 29 D1
Harwood Rd. Bury BL2 & BL8 26 C6
Harwood Rd. M'ster SK4 110 E2
Harwood Rd. M'ster M19 110 E6
Harwood St. Littleborough OL15 15 F5
Harwood St. M'ster SK4 169 E3
Harwood Vale. BL2 25 E3
Harwood Vale Ct. BL2 25 E3
Harwood Wlk. BL8 26 E7
Haseldine St. WN4 72 F6
Haseley Cl. Little Lever BL3 43 B5
Haseley Cl. Poynton SK12 133 E5
Haselhurst Wlk. M23 108 F2
Hasguard Cl. BL1 40 F8
Haskoll St. BL6 22 D1
Haslam Brow. BL9 44 E8
Haslam Hey Cl. Ainsworth BL2 26 C1
Haslam Hey Cl. Bury BL8 26 F2
Haslam Park Cty Prim Sch. BL3 144 B5
Haslam Rd. SK3 170 E6
Haslam St. Bolton BL3 145 D5
Haslam St. Bury BL9 141 A4
Haslam St. Middleton M24 65 C7
Haslam St. R'dale OL12 139 D8
Haslemere Ave. WA15 129 C6
Haslemere Dr. SK8 123 A1
Haslemere Ind Est. WN4 72 F8
Haslemere Rd. M'ster M20 110 D6
Haslemere Rd. Urmston M41 95 B1
Haslingden Cty High Sch. BB4 1 B8
Hassal St. BL9 44 E5
Hassall Ave. M20 109 F7
Hassall St. 4 SK15 86 B1
Hassall Way. 7 SK9 131 E5
Hassnes Cl. WN3 55 B2
Hassop Ave. M7 81 A7
Hassop Cl. M11 160 E1
Hassop Rd. SK5 100 A1
Hastings Ave. M'ster M21 109 A8
Hastings Ave. Prestwich M45 63 B7
Hastings Cl. Bramhall SK8 123 C2
Hastings Cl. Prestwich M45 63 B7
Hastings Cl. Stockport SK1 & SK2 124 B7
Hastings Dr. M41 94 E3
Hastings Rd. Bolton BL1 144 B8
Hastings Rd. Prestwich M25 63 C5
Hastings Rd. Worsley M28 79 A4
Hastings St. OL11 139 F5
Hasty La. Alt'ham M90, WA15 129 F8
Hasty La. Wythenshawe M90 130 A8
Hatchett Rd. M22 121 E1
Hatchmere Cl. M23 & WA15 120 D6
Hatchmere Rd. SK8 122 F4
Hatfield Ave. M19 110 F6
Hatfield Cl. WN2 55 F4
Hatfield Rd. BL1 142 C1
Hatford Cl. M29 59 C1
Hathaway Cl. SK8 131 B7
Hathaway Ct. WN7 76 B6
Hathaway Dr. BL1 25 A5
Hathaway Gdns. SK6 112 F3
Hathaway Rd. BL9 45 A3
Hathaway Wlk. WN2 55 F4
Hatherleigh Wlk. BL2 42 F6
Hatherley Rd. M20 110 D6
Hatherlow. SK6 113 A1
Hatherlow Hts. SK6 113 A1
Hatherlow La. SK7 124 D2
Hatherop Cl. M30 79 B1
Hathersage Ave. M5 & M6 154 D3
Hathersage Cres. SK13 171 E2
Hathersage Dr. Glossop SK13 116 F8
Hathersage Rd. M13 98 D4
Hathersage St. OL9 152 C6
Hathersage Way. 6 M34 113 A8
Hathershaw La. OL8 66 F3
Hathershaw Sch. OL8 66 F2
Hatro Ct. M41 96 A1
Hatter St. M4 159 B2
Hattersley Ct. SK14 102 D1
Hattersley Ctr The. 2 SK14 102 E2
Hattersley High Sch. SK14 102 D2
Hattersley Rd E. SK14 102 E2
Hattersley Rd W. SK14 102 C2
Hattersley Sta. SK14 102 C1
Hattersley Wlk. SK14 102 C3
Hatton Ave. Atherton M46 58 D5
Hatton Ave. M'ster M7 158 D3
Hatton Gr. BL1 25 A5
Hatton St. Adlington PR7 20 F6
Hatton St. M'ster M12 99 A3
Hatton St. Stockport SK1 169 E2
Hatton Terr. 24 SK16 166 B1
Hattonfold. M33 108 C1
Hattons Ct. M32 96 C3
Hattons Rd. M17 96 B6
Haugh Farm. OL16 32 C4
Haugh Fold. OL16 32 C4
Haugh Hill Rd. OL4 49 E3
Haugh La. OL16 32 C4
Haugh Sq. OL16 32 C4
Haughton Cl. SK6 113 A6
Haughton Dr. M22 109 D1
Haughton Green Rd. M34 113 B8
Haughton Hall Rd. M34 101 A3
Haughton St. Denton M34 100 F5
Haughton St. Hyde SK14 167 E1
Havana Cl. M11 160 F1
Haveley Hey Inf Sch. M22 121 C4
Haveley Hey Jun Sch. M22 121 C4
Haveley Rd. M22 121 C5
Havelock Dr. M7 158 D4
Havelock St. OL8 153 F5
Haven Cl. Hazel Grove SK7 124 C1
Haven Cl. Radcliffe M26 43 D5
Haven Cl. Uppermill OL4 68 D6
Haven Dr. M43 83 E2
Haven La. OL4 49 E3
Haven St. M6 154 E1
Haven The. Alt'ham WA15 119 F3
Haven The. Little Lever BL3 43 B3
Havenbrook Gr. BL0 11 A3
Havenscroft Ave. M30 95 D8
Havenwood Rd. WN1 37 B4
Havercroft Cl. WN3 54 E3
Haverfield Rd. M9 64 E3
Haverford St. M12 164 F6
Haverhill Gr. BL2 25 B2
Havers Rd. M18 99 E5
Haversham Rd. M8 63 E2
Haverton Dr. M22 121 B2
Havisham Cl. BL6 40 B4
Haw Clough La. OL3 69 C6
Hawarden Ave. M16 97 C2
Hawarden Rd. WA14 119 D6
Hawarden St. BL1 24 E5
Hawdraw Gn. SK2 124 E6
Hawes Ave. Farnworth BL4 59 E8
Hawes Ave. M'ster M14 110 E7
Hawes Ave. Swinton M27 79 F6
Hawes Cl. Bury BL8 27 B5
Hawes Cl. Stockport SK2 124 A6
Hawes Cres. WN4 73 B5
Haweswater Ave. Ince-i-M WN2 56 B7
Haweswater Ave. Tyldesley M29 77 B7
Haweswater Cl. M34 100 A2
Haweswater Cres. BL9 45 B5
Haweswater Dr. M24 46 E2
Haweswater Mews. 5 M24 46 E2
Hawick Gr. OL10 28 E1
Hawk Cl. BL9 141 B4
Hawk Green Rd. SK6 126 A3
Hawk Rd. M44 94 A3
Hawk Yard La. OL3 69 D5
Hawke St. SK15 86 C1
Hawker Ave. BL3 147 D3
Hawkeshead Rd. M8 156 B6
Hawkhurst Rd. M13 98 F3
Hawkhurst St. Leigh WN7 76 B4
Hawkhurst St. Leigh WN7 76 C5
Hawkins St. SK5 169 E4
Hawkins Way. Littleborough OL15 6 C1
Hawkley Ave. WN3 54 F2
Hawkley Hall High Sch. WN3 55 B3
Hawkrigg Cl. WN6 36 F7
Hawkshaw Cl. WN2 38 A3
Hawkshaw Ct. 9 Salford M5 81 A1
Hawkshaw Ct. Salford M5 161 A8
Hawkshaw La. BL8 10 B5
Hawkshaw St. BL6 22 B3
Hawkshead Dr. Bolton BL3 146 A3
Hawkshead Dr. Middleton M24 46 E1
Hawkshead Dr. Royton OL2 48 D6
Hawkshead Rd. Glossop SK13 104 E3
Hawkshead Rd. Shaw OL2 149 A8
Hawksheath Cl. BL7 8 E1
Hawksley St. Horwich BL6 22 D2
Hawksley St. Oldham OL8 66 C3
Hawksmoor Dr. OL2 149 B8
Hawkstone Ave. Droylsden M43 83 E3
Hawkstone Ave. Whitefield M45 62 D7
Hawkstone Cl. BL2 25 E3
Hawkswick Dr. M23 109 A2
Hawkworth. M29 77 B5
Hawkyard Farm. OL3 69 D5
Hawley Dr. WA15 129 B8
Hawley Gn. OL12 14 D2
Hawley La. WA15 129 B8
Hawley St. M19 111 B8
Haworth Ave. BL0 11 A2
Haworth Cl. BL9 44 F6
Haworth Dr. Bacup OL13 3 C8
Haworth Dr. Stretford M32 96 A3
Haworth Rd. M18 99 D4
Haworth St. Bury BL8 26 F4
Haworth St. Edgworth BL7 9 D5
Haworth St. Hindley WN2 56 D6
Haworth St. Oldham OL1 48 E1
Haworth St. Radcliffe M26 44 B3
Hawsworth Cl. M15 163 B5
Hawthorn Ave. Alt'ham WA15 119 F8
Hawthorn Ave. Bury BL8 27 C4
Hawthorn Ave. Eccles M30 79 D3
Hawthorn Ave. Edenfield BL0 1 D2
Hawthorn Ave. Garswood WN4 72 D5
Hawthorn Ave. Hindley WN2 57 A4
Hawthorn Ave. Marple SK6 125 D6
Hawthorn Ave. Newton-l-W WA12 89 D3
Hawthorn Ave. Orrell WN5 53 F6
Hawthorn Ave. Radcliffe M26 44 B1
Hawthorn Ave. Ramsbottom BL0 11 A2
Hawthorn Ave. Standish WN1 37 B6
Hawthorn Ave. Urmston M41 95 F1
Hawthorn Ave. Walkden M28 60 E1
Hawthorn Ave. Wigan WN5 54 D6
Hawthorn Ave. Wilmslow SK9 137 A7
Hawthorn Bank. Bolton BL2 25 E4
Hawthorn Bank. Hadfield SK14 171 F4
Hawthorn Cl. Alt'ham WA15 119 F7
Hawthorn Cl. Billinge WN5 71 D5
Hawthorn Cl. Tyldesley M29 59 D1
Hawthorn Cres. Bury BL8 26 F7
Hawthorn Cres. Shaw OL2 149 B6
Hawthorn Ct. SK6 112 D3
Hawthorn Dr. Eccles M6 80 B4
Hawthorn Dr. Irlam M44 105 D5
Hawthorn Dr. M'ster M19 110 F7
Hawthorn Dr. Pendlebury M27 80 C7
Hawthorn Dr. Stalybridge SK15 101 F8
Hawthorn Gr. Bramhall SK7 132 C6
Hawthorn Gr. Hollingworth SK14 103 D6
Hawthorn Gr. Hyde SK14 167 D1
Hawthorn Gr. M'ster SK4 168 B3
Hawthorn Gr. Wilmslow SK9 137 B7
Hawthorn La. Sale M33 107 D6
Hawthorn La. Stretford M21 108 F8
Hawthorn La. Wilmslow SK9 137 A7
Hawthorn Lodge. 1 SK3 123 F4
Hawthorn Pk. SK9 137 A7
Hawthorn Rd. Alt'ham WA15 119 E3
Hawthorn Rd. Droylsden M43 84 C2
Hawthorn Rd. Failsworth M40 65 F1
Hawthorn Rd. Gatley SK8 122 A5
Hawthorn Rd. Kearsley BL4 61 B5
Hawthorn Rd. M'ster SK4 110 F2
Hawthorn Rd. Oldham OL8 66 B1
Hawthorn Rd. R'dale OL11 29 E6
Hawthorn Rd. Reddish M34 100 B4
Hawthorn Rd. Stretford M32 108 E8
Hawthorn Rd. Westhoughton BL5 57 F7
Hawthorn Rd S. M43 84 C2
Hawthorn St. Denton M34 100 E6
Hawthorn St. M'ster M18 99 E5
Hawthorn St. Wilmslow SK9 137 A6

Heyrose Wlk. 14 M15 ... 162 D6
Heys Ave. Romiley SK6 ... 113 E3
Heys Ave. Swinton M27 ... 61 D2
Heys Ave. Wythenshawe M23 109 A1
Heys Cl N. M27 ... 61 C2
Heys La. Heywood OL10 ... 29 A1
Heys La. Romiley SK6 ... 113 E3
Heys Prim Sch The. OL6 ... 85 D3
Heys Rd. Ashton-u-L OL6 ... 85 D3
Heys Rd. Prestwich M25 ... 63 B5
Heys St. Bury BL8 ... 140 D2
Heys St. Hindley WN2 ... 56 C6
Heys The. Prestwich M25 ... 63 B5
Heys The. Reddish SK5 ... 100 A1
Heys View. M25 ... 63 B4
Heysbank Rd. SK12 ... 135 D5
Heyscroft Rd. M'ster M20 .. 110 C6
Heyscroft Rd. M'ster SK4 ... 168 A2
Heysham Ave. M20 ... 109 F7
Heysham Rd. WN5 ... 54 B7
Heyshaw Wlk. M23 ... 108 F1
Heyside. OL2 ... 49 A3
Heyside Ave. OL2 ... 49 A3
Heyside Cl. SK15 ... 86 E6
Heywood Ave. Golborne WA3 74 B1
Heywood Ave. Oldham OL4 ... 68 A8
Heywood Ave. Swinton M27 .. 62 B2
Heywood Cl. SK9 ... 137 B2
Heywood Comm High Sch. OL10 ... 28 E1
Heywood Ct. M25 ... 64 A7
Heywood Distribution Pk. OL10 ... 46 A8
Heywood Fold Rd. OL4 ... 67 F7
Heywood Gdns. Golborne WA3 ... 74 B1
Heywood Gdns. Prestwich M25 ... 63 B4
Heywood Gr. M33 ... 108 B6
Heywood Hall Rd. OL10 ... 29 D3
Heywood House. Atherton M46 ... 58 C3
Heywood House. Oldham OL8 ... 153 F5
Heywood House. Salford M6 80 C3
Heywood Ind Est. OL10 ... 45 F7
Heywood Ind Pk. OL10 ... 45 F8
Heywood La. OL4 ... 68 A7
Heywood Old Rd. M24 & M25 & OL10 ... 46 B3
Heywood Rd. Alderley Edge SK9 ... 137 B2
Heywood Rd. Prestwich M25 63 C7
Heywood Rd. R'dale OL11 ... 30 C1
Heywood Rd. Sale M33 ... 108 B3
Heywood St. Bolton BL1 ... 145 F8
Heywood St. Bury BL9 ... 141 A2
Heywood St. Failsworth M35 . 83 D7
Heywood St. Little Lever BL3 . 43 B3
Heywood St. M'ster M7 & M8 ... 156 A6
Heywood St. Oldham OL4 ... 67 E8
Heywood St. Swinton M27 ... 79 E8
Heywood Way. M6 ... 154 F3
Heywood's Hollow. BL1 ... 143 F3
Heyworth Ave. SK6 ... 113 D3
Heyworth St. 4 M5 & M6 .. 154 E1
Hibbert Ave. Denton M34 ... 100 E5
Hibbert Ave. Hyde SK14 ... 167 E1
Hibbert Cres. M35 ... 84 A6
Hibbert La. SK6 ... 125 F5
Hibbert St. Bolton BL1 ... 143 F2
Hibbert St. M'ster M14 ... 98 C3
Hibbert St. Oldham OL4 ... 67 E7
Hibbert St. Reddish SK4 & SK5 ... 111 E5
Hibernia St. BL3 ... 144 C5
Hibernia Way. M32 ... 96 A5
Hibson Ave. OL12 ... 13 E2
Hibson Cl. OL12 ... 15 C6
Hic Bibi La. PR7 ... 19 E6
Hicken Pl. SK14 ... 101 F5
Hickenfield Rd. SK14 ... 101 F5
Hickton Dr. WA14 ... 119 B6
Hieland Rd. WN1 ... 37 E2
Higginshaw La. OL1 & OL2 .. 49 A2
Higginshaw Rd. OL1 ... 67 A8
Higginson Rd. SK5 ... 111 E8
Higginson St. WN7 ... 76 A5
Higgs Cl. OL4 ... 67 D7
High Ash Gr. M34 ... 100 D7
High Ave. BL2 ... 42 E7
High Bank. Alt'ham WA14 ... 119 D5
High Bank. Atherton BL5 ... 59 A6
High Bank. Bolton BL7 ... 24 F7
High Bank. M'ster M18 ... 99 E5
High Bank Ave. SK15 ... 102 D7
High Bank Cl. M44 ... 105 D6
High Bank Cres. M25 ... 63 C3
High Bank Gr. M25 ... 63 C3
High Bank La. BL6 ... 40 B8
High Bank Rd. Droylsden M43 99 F8
High Bank Rd. Hyde SK14 ... 167 F3
High Bank Rd. Pendlebury M27 ... 80 B7
High Bank Side. SK1 ... 169 F1
High Bank St. BL2 ... 148 C7
High Barn Cl. OL11 ... 139 E5
High Barn Jun Sch. OL2 ... 48 E4
High Barn La. OL12 ... 4 C3
High Barn Rd. Middleton M24 65 A7
High Barn Rd. Royton OL2 ... 48 F4
High Barn St. OL2 ... 48 F4
High Beeches. BL3 ... 43 B5
High Beeches Cres. WN4 ... 73 A6
High Bent Ave. SK8 ... 132 A6
High Birch Spec Sch. OL11 . 30 B4
High Brindle. M6 ... 154 F4
High Crest Ave. M22 ... 121 F5
High Croft Cl. SK15 ... 102 A8
High Elm Dr. WA15 ... 129 C8
High Elm Rd. WA15 ... 129 D7
High Elms. SK8 ... 132 B5
High Field. WA14 ... 118 B2
High Grove Rd. Cheadle SK8 122 C5
High Grove Rd. Uppermill OL4 68 E5
High Hill Rd. SK12 ... 127 D1
High Hurst Cl. M24 ... 64 C7
High Knowls. OL4 ... 68 A4
High La. Charlesworth SK13 & SK14 . 115 E7
High La. M'ster M21 ... 109 B8
High La. Romiley SK6 ... 113 B4
High Lane Prim Sch. SK6 .. 134 F8
High Lawn Cty Prim Sch. BL1 ... 24 E6
High Lee. SK8 ... 122 C5
High Lee La. OL4 ... 50 B4
High Legh Rd. M11 ... 99 D8
High Level Rd. OL11 ... 31 A6
High Meadow. SK8 ... 131 E8
High Meadows. Bolton BL7 ... 25 B8
High Meadows. Romiley SK6 113 C3
High Moor Cres. OL4 ... 49 E1
High Moor La. WN6 ... 18 B4
High Moor View. OL4 ... 49 E1
High Mount. BL2 ... 25 E3
High Peak. OL15 ... 16 F5
High Peak Rd. Ashton-u-L OL6 86 A6
High Peak Rd. Whitworth OL12 ... 14 C6
High Peak St. M40 ... 83 B6
High Pk. WN6 ... 36 C6
High Rid La. Horwich BL6 ... 23 B1
High St. Alt'ham WA14 ... 119 D4
High St. Atherton M46 ... 58 D3
High St. Bolton BL3 ... 147 E4
High St. Bury BL8 ... 26 F4
High St. Cheadle SK8 ... 122 D6
High St. Delph OL3 ... 50 F5
High St. Droylsden M43 ... 84 B1
High St. Edgworth BL7 ... 9 C4
High St. Golborne WA3 ... 90 A8
High St. Hazel Grove SK7 ... 124 F2
High St. Heywood OL10 ... 29 B2
High St. Horwich BL6 ... 22 B4
High St. Hyde SK14 ... 167 F3
High St. Ince-i-M WN3 ... 151 E6
High St. Leigh WN7 ... 76 A5
High St. Little Lever BL3 ... 43 B3
High St. Littleborough OL15 ... 15 F5
High St. M'ster M4 & M60 ... 159 A1
High St. M'ster M4 ... 159 A2
High St. Middleton M24 ... 47 A1
High St. Middleton M24 ... 47 A2
High St. Mossley OL5 ... 68 D2
High St. Newton-l-W WA12 ... 89 D4
High St. Oldham OL4 ... 67 E6
High St. Oldham OL1 ... 153 F7
High St. R'dale OL12 ... 139 F8
High St. Royton OL2 ... 48 D4
High St. Shaw OL2 ... 149 B6
High St. Stalybridge SK15 & SK16 ... 85 F1
High St. Stalybridge SK15 ... 86 A1
High St. Standish WN6 ... 19 E1
High St. Stockport SK1 ... 169 F1
High St. Tyldesley M29 ... 58 F1
High St. Tyldesley M29 ... 77 B5
High St. Uppermill OL3 ... 69 B8
High St. Walkden M28 ... 60 D3
High St. Wigan WN1 ... 37 D2
High St. Wigan WN2 ... 38 B3
High St E. SK13 ... 104 D1
High St W. SK13 ... 104 B1
High Stile La. OL3 ... 51 D2
High Stile St. BL4 ... 60 E7
High Street Sta. M1 ... 159 A1
High View St. Bolton BL1 ... 24 E6
High View St. 1 Bolton BL3 146 C4
High Wood Fold. SK6 ... 126 C8
Higham Cl. OL2 ... 149 A5
Higham La. SK14 ... 114 A7
Higham St. SK8 ... 123 A1
Higham View. M6 ... 81 A3
Highbank Cres. OL4 ... 68 E5
Highbank Dr. M20 ... 122 B8
Highbank Private Hospl. BL8 ... 26 F4
Highbank Rd. Glossop SK13 116 F7
Highbank Rd. Newhey OL16 ... 32 C4
Highbank Rd. Whitefield BL9 44 F3
Highbridge Cl. BL2 ... 43 A6
Highbrook Gr. 14 BL1 ... 143 E1
Highbury. SK4 ... 110 F2
Highbury Ave. Irlam M44 ... 94 A1
Highbury Ave. Urmston M41 . 94 E2
Highbury Rd. M'ster M16 ... 97 E1
Highbury Rd. Reddish SK4 .. 111 C6
Highbury Way. OL2 ... 48 D6
Highclere Ave. M7 & M8 ... 155 F6
Highclere Rd. M8 ... 63 F2
Highcliffe Ct. WN6 ... 36 F7
Highcliffe Rd. M9 ... 64 A3
Highclove La. M28 ... 77 F5
Highcroft. SK14 ... 113 F6
Highcroft Ave. M20 ... 109 E4
Highcroft Rd. SK6 ... 113 C3
Highcroft Way. OL12 ... 14 F4
Highdales Rd. M23 ... 121 B5
Highdown Wlk. 26 M9 ... 157 E8
Higher Ainsworth Rd. BL8 & M26 ... 43 E7
Higher Ardwick. M12 ... 163 C7
Higher Arthurs. OL3 ... 69 B6
Higher Bank Rd. OL15 ... 16 A3
Higher Barlow Row. SK1 ... 170 F8
Higher Barn. BL6 ... 22 F3
Higher Barn Rd. SK13 ... 171 F4
Higher Bents La. SK6 ... 113 A3
Higher Blue Bell Cotts. BL5 39 C4
Higher Bridge St. BL1 ... 145 F8
Higher Bury St. SK4 ... 169 D2
Higher Calderbrook Rd. OL15 ... 6 C2
Higher Cambridge St. M15 ... 163 A6
Higher Carr La. OL3 ... 69 B7
Higher Chatham St. M15 .. 163 A6
Higher Cleggswood Ave. OL15 ... 16 A3
Higher Count Hill. OL4 ... 49 E2
Higher Croft. Eccles M30 ... 95 C8
Higher Croft. Whitefield M45 62 D4
Higher Cross La. OL3 ... 69 C8
Higher Crossbank. OL4 ... 67 F8
Higher Damshead. BL5 ... 57 F8
Higher Darcy St. BL2 ... 148 C5
Higher Dean St. M26 ... 43 E3
Higher Downs. WA14 ... 119 C3
Higher Drake Meadow. BL5 57 E5
Higher Dunscar. BL7 ... 8 E1
Higher Fold La. BL0 ... 11 E7
Higher Folds Prim Sch. WN7 ... 76 D7
Higher Fullwood. OL1 ... 49 D4
Higher Gamesley. SK14 ... 115 D8
Higher Gn. Ashton-u-L OL6 .. 166 C4
Higher Gn. Salford M6 ... 154 F4
Higher Green La. M29 ... 77 C6
Higher Henry St. SK14 ... 167 E1
Higher Hillgate. SK1 & SK2 170 F8
Higher House Cl. OL9 ... 66 A4
Higher La. Aspull WN2 ... 38 A4
Higher La. Disley SK12 ... 135 E1
Higher La. Lymm WA13 ... 117 B1
Higher La. Orrell WN8 ... 53 C7
Higher La. Whitefield M45 ... 62 E8
Higher Lane Cty Jun & Inf Sch. M45 ... 62 F7
Higher Lime Rd. OL8 ... 84 C8
Higher Lodge. OL12 ... 13 D2
Higher Lomax La. OL10 ... 29 A3
Higher Lydgate Pk. OL4 ... 68 C6
Higher Market St. BL4 ... 60 E8
Higher Moulding. BL9 ... 28 E5
Higher Newtons. OL5 ... 68 D2
Higher Noon Sun. SK12 ... 127 F2
Higher Ormond St. M15 ... 163 A6
Higher Oswald St. 4 M4 . 159 A2
Higher Park. OL2 ... 32 C2
Higher Pit La. BL8 ... 43 E8
Higher Rd. M41 ... 95 E2
Higher Ridings. BL7 ... 24 F7
Higher Rise. OL2 ... 32 A1
Higher Row. BL9 ... 141 B3
Higher Shady La. BL7 ... 25 C7
Higher Shore Rd. OL12, OL15 15 E7
Higher Southfield. BL5 ... 57 E7
Higher Summerseat. BL0 ... 11 B2
Higher Swan La. BL3 ... 147 D3
Higher Tame St. SK15 ... 86 B2
Higher Turf La. OL4 ... 50 B1
Higher Turf Pk. OL2 ... 48 E3
Higher Wharf St. OL6 & OL7 ... 166 B2
Higher Wheat La. OL16 ... 31 C8
Higher Wood St. M24 ... 46 F1
Higher York St. M13 ... 163 B6
Highfield. Sale M33 ... 108 C3
Highfield. Wigan WN3 ... 54 D4
Highfield Ave. Atherton M46 . 58 E5
Highfield Ave. Bolton BL2 ... 26 A3
Highfield Ave. Boothstown M28 & M29 ... 77 F7
Highfield Ave. Bredbury SK6 112 F2
Highfield Ave. Golborne WA3 89 F8
Highfield Ave. Heywood OL10 29 A2
Highfield Ave. Leigh WN7 ... 76 C3
Highfield Ave. Radcliffe M26 . 44 C1
Highfield Ave. Shevington WN6 ... 36 A6
Highfield Ave. Wigan WN1 ... 37 E1
Highfield CE Prim Sch. WN3 ... 54 D4
Highfield Cl. Adlington PR6 ... 21 A7
Highfield Cl. Dukinfield SK14 101 F6
Highfield Cl. Stockport SK3 . 123 F4
Highfield Cl. Stretford M32 108 C8
Highfield Cres. SK9 ... 131 C1
Highfield Ct. BL4 ... 60 B7
Highfield Dr. Eccles M30 ... 95 C8
Highfield Dr. Farnworth BL4 . 60 A7
Highfield Dr. Middleton M24 . 64 F7
Highfield Dr. Mossley OL5 ... 86 C8
Highfield Dr. Oldham OL2 ... 48 E2
Highfield Dr. Pendlebury M27 80 C7
Highfield Dr. Standish WN6 .. 36 F7
Highfield Dr. 4 Urmston M41 95 C3
Highfield Est. SK9 ... 131 C1
Highfield Gdns. Hollingworth SK14 ... 103 D5
Highfield Gdns. Hyde SK14 . 167 F3
Highfield Gr. WN2 ... 38 C5
Highfield Grange Ave. WN3 54 D2
Highfield House. SK3 ... 170 F5
Highfield La. Golborne WA3 .. 90 C5
Highfield La. Whitefield M45 . 44 F3
Highfield Park Rd. SK6 ... 112 F3
Highfield Parkway. SK7 ... 132 D4
Highfield Pk. SK4 ... 110 F2
Highfield Pl. Prestwich M25 .. 63 A5
Highfield Pl. Reddish M18 ... 99 F4
Highfield Prim Sch. M41 ... 95 F2
Highfield Private Hospl. OL11 ... 139 E5
Highfield Range. M18 ... 99 F4
Highfield Rd. Adlington PR6 ... 21 A7
Highfield Rd. Alt'ham WA15 120 A3
Highfield Rd. Alt'ham WA15 120 B5
Highfield Rd. Blackrod BL6 ... 21 E1
Highfield Rd. Bolton BL1 ... 142 B2
Highfield Rd. Cheadle SK8 .. 122 F1
Highfield Rd. Eccles M30 ... 79 D4
Highfield Rd. Edenfield BL0 ... 1 D3
Highfield Rd. Farnworth BL4 . 60 A8
Highfield Rd. Glossop SK13 116 D8
Highfield Rd. Hazel Grove SK7 ... 125 A2
Highfield Rd. Hindley WN2 ... 56 D7
Highfield Rd. Marple SK6 ... 125 F6
Highfield Rd. Marple SK6 ... 126 B6
Highfield Rd. Milnrow OL16 .. 32 A6
Highfield Rd. Poynton SK12 133 A4
Highfield Rd. Prestwich M25 . 63 A5
Highfield Rd. R'dale OL11 ... 31 A6
Highfield Rd. Reddish M19 ... 99 C1
Highfield Rd. Salford M5 & M6 ... 154 F2
Highfield Rd. Stockport SK7 123 F3
Highfield Rd. Stretford M32 108 C8
Highfield Rd. Walkden M38 ... 59 F5
Highfield Rd N. PR6 ... 21 A8
Highfield St. Denton M34 ... 100 E5
Highfield St. Denton M34 ... 100 F6
Highfield St. Dukinfield SK16 166 B1
Highfield St. Kearsley BL4 ... 61 A6
Highfield St. M'ster M7, M8 155 F7
Highfield St. Middleton M24 .. 65 B8
Highfield St. Oldham OL9 ... 153 D7
Highfield St. 2 Stockport SK3 ... 123 C8
Highfield St W. SK16 ... 166 B1
Highfield Terr. Ashton-u-L OL7 ... 85 A7
Highfield Terr. M'ster M9 .. 157 D8
Highfield Terr. Oldham OL1 & OL4 ... 49 D2
Highfields Cty Prim Sch. BL4 ... 60 A8
Highgate. BL3 ... 40 C2
Highgate Ave. M41 ... 95 A4
Highgate Cres. Appley Bridge WN6 ... 35 E7
Highgate Cres. M'ster M18 ... 99 D3
Highgate Dr. Royton OL2 ... 48 C7
Highgate Dr. Walkden M38 ... 59 E5
Highgate House. 6 OL8 ... 66 D2
Highgate La. Walkden M38 ... 59 E5
Highgate La. Whitworth OL12 14 C5
Highgate Rd. Alt'ham WA14 119 B4
Highgate Rd. Orrell WN8 ... 53 B7
Highgrove Cl. BL1 ... 143 F3
Highgrove La. M28 ... 78 A5
Highgrove Mews. SK9 ... 137 A6
Highgrove The. BL1 ... 23 D1
Highland Ave. SK6 ... 113 A2
Highland Rd. Bolton BL7 ... 25 C8
Highland Rd. Horwich BL6 ... 22 E1
Highland View. 1 OL5 ... 68 C2
Highland Wlk. M35 ... 83 D6
Highlands. Littleborough OL15 16 A3
Highlands. Royton OL2 ... 48 C3
Highlands Dr. SK2 ... 124 F6
Highlands Rd. Hazel Grove SK2 ... 124 F6
Highlands Rd. R'dale OL10 ... 29 E5
Highlands Rd. Royton OL2 ... 48 C3
Highlands Rd. Shaw OL2 ... 149 A8
Highlands The. 3 OL5 ... 68 C1
Highmead St. M18 ... 99 D5
Highmead Wlk. M16 ... 162 D5
Highmeadow. M26 ... 43 F1
Highmore Dr. M9 ... 64 E3
Highnam Wlk. M22 ... 121 A1
Highover House. M20 ... 109 F4
Highshore Dr. M7 & M8 ... 155 F7
Highstone Dr. M8 ... 156 C6
Highthorne Gn. OL2 ... 48 C8
Highview. SK13 ... 116 A7
Highview Wlk. M9 ... 64 E3
Highwood. OL11 ... 13 E1
Highwood Cl. 3 Bolton BL2 . 25 F1
Highwood Cl. Glossop SK13 116 B8
Highwoods Cl. WN4 ... 73 B5
Highworth Cl. BL3 ... 145 E5
Highworth Dr. M40 ... 65 D2
Higifield Ave. M33 ... 108 C3
Higson Ave. Bredbury SK6 ... 112 F2
Higson Ave. Eccles M30 ... 95 C8
Higson Ave. M'ster M21 ... 109 B7
Hilary Ave. Atherton M46 ... 58 C5
Hilary Ave. Gatley SK8 ... 131 D8
Hilary Ave. Golborne WA3 ... 74 D1
Hilary Ave. Oldham OL8 ... 84 F8
Hilary Cl. SK4 ... 169 D2
Hilary Gr. BL4 ... 60 D7
Hilary Rd. M22 ... 121 C1
Hilary St. OL11 ... 30 D1
Hilbre Ave. OL1 ... 48 D2
Hilbre Rd. M19 ... 110 F8
Hilbury Ave. M9 ... 64 D1
Hilda Ave. Bury BL8 ... 26 F6
Hilda Ave. Cheadle SK8 ... 122 E5
Hilda Gr. SK5 ... 169 F4
Hilda Rd. SK14 ... 113 D7
Hilda St. 6 Bolton BL3 ... 42 A4
Hilda St. Heywood OL10 ... 29 D3
Hilda St. Leigh WN7 ... 75 D6
Hilda St. Oldham OL9 ... 153 D7
Hilda St. Reddish SK5 ... 169 F4
Hilden Ct. M16 ... 97 D4
Hilden St. Bolton BL2 ... 148 A6
Hilden St. 4 Leigh WN7 ... 75 F5
Hilditch Cl. M23 ... 121 B6
Hildyard St. WN5 ... 54 F6
Hiley Rd. Eccles M30 ... 79 A1
Hilgay Cl. WN3 ... 54 D3
Hill Cl. WN6 ... 35 E8
Hill Cot Rd. BL1 ... 24 F5
Hill Court Mews. SK6 ... 113 B2
Hill Cres. Leigh WN7 ... 75 C8
Hill Cres. M'ster M9 ... 64 A3
Hill Crest. M46 ... 58 F5
Hill Crest Ave. Leigh WN7 ... 75 C8
Hill Crest Ave. M'ster SK4 .. 168 A2
Hill Dr. SK9 ... 131 E3
Hill End Rd. OL3 ... 50 F4
Hill Farm Cl. OL8 ... 67 B3
Hill House Fold La. WN6 ... 18 C5
Hill House La. WN6 ... 18 C5
Hill La. Blackrod BL6 ... 21 C2
Hill La. Bolton BL2 ... 148 A8
Hill La. M'ster M9 ... 64 D4
Hill Mount. SK15 ... 102 A8
Hill Rise. Alt'ham WA14 ... 119 A5
Hill Rise. Ramsbottom BL0 ... 11 A4
Hill Rise. Romiley SK6 ... 113 B2
Hill Side. BL1 ... 40 F7
Hill St. Alt'ham WA14 ... 119 C8
Hill St. Ashton-u-L OL6 & OL7 166 B2
Hill St. Bury BL8 ... 26 F4
Hill St. Dukinfield SK16 ... 166 B1
Hill St. Heywood OL10 ... 29 C2
Hill St. Hindley WN2 ... 56 D6
Hill St. Leigh WN7 ... 75 E5
Hill St. M'ster M20 ... 110 B7
Hill St. M'ster M7 ... 155 D6
Hill St. Middleton M24 ... 47 A3
Hill St. Oldham OL4 ... 67 B7
Hill St. R'dale OL16 ... 31 A7
Hill St. Radcliffe M26 ... 43 F4
Hill St. Ramsbottom BL9 ... 11 C3
Hill St. Romiley SK6 ... 113 B2
Hill St. Shaw OL2 ... 149 C6
Hill St. Wigan WN6 ... 37 B1
Hill St. Wigan WN2 ... 38 B2
Hill Top. Alt'ham WA14 ... 120 A1
Hill Top. Atherton M46 ... 58 F5
Hill Top. Bolton BL2 ... 143 D3
Hill Top. Little Lever BL3 ... 43 A4
Hill Top. Romiley SK6 ... 113 B3
Hill Top Ave. Cheadle SK8 .. 132 B8
Hill Top Ave. Prestwich M25 . 63 B4
Hill Top Ave. Wilmslow SK9 137 B8
Hill Top Ct. SK8 ... 123 B1
Hill Top Cty Prim Sch. OL11 31 A1
Hill Top Dr. Alt'ham WA15 .. 120 A1
Hill Top Dr. R'dale OL11 ... 30 F2
Hill Top Fold. 1 WN2 ... 56 E6
Hill Top La. OL3 & OL4 ... 50 C4
Hill Top Rd. M28 ... 60 D4
Hill View. Delph OL3 ... 50 F4
Hill View. Stalybridge SK15 . 102 E6
Hill View Dr. PR7 ... 19 D8
Hill's Ct. 3 BL8 ... 27 B4
Hillam Cl. M41 ... 95 F1
Hillary Ave. Ashton-u-L OL6 & OL7 ... 85 B5
Hillary Ave. Wigan WN5 ... 54 D5
Hillary Rd. SK14 ... 102 A5
Hillbank. WN6 ... 37 A7
Hillbank Cl. BL1 ... 142 C3
Hillbank St. OL11 ... 47 D6
Hillbeck Cres. WN4 ... 72 D4
Hillbrae Ave. WA11 ... 71 A1
Hillbre Way. 1 SK9 ... 131 D4
Hillbrook Ave. M40 ... 65 B2
Hillbrook Rd. Bramhall SK7 132 D6
Hillbrook Rd. Stockport SK1 & SK2 ... 124 C8
Hillbrow Wlk. 9 M8 ... 155 F7
Hillbury Rd. SK7 ... 123 F1
Hillcote Wlk. M18 ... 165 B6
Hillcourt Rd. High Lane SK6 134 F7
Hillcourt Rd. Romiley SK6 ... 113 C4
Hillcourt St. M1 ... 163 A7
Hillcrest. Eccles M6 ... 80 A3
Hillcrest. Hyde SK14 ... 113 F7
Hillcrest. Middleton M24 ... 46 F3
Hillcrest. Platt Bridge WN2 ... 56 B2
Hillcrest Ave. OL10 ... 29 A3
Hillcrest Cres. OL10 ... 29 A3
Hillcrest Dr. Denton M34 ... 101 B1
Hillcrest Dr. Reddish M19 ... 111 C7
Hillcrest Gram Sch. SK3 ... 170 F6
Hillcrest Rd. Prestwich M25 .. 62 F2
Hillcrest Rd. R'dale OL11 ... 30 D1
Hillcrest Rd. Stockport SK7 .. 123 F1
Hillcrest Rd. Stockport SK2 . 124 C7
Hillcrest Rd. Tyldesley M29 ... 77 D8
Hillcroft. Oldham OL8 ... 67 A1
Hillcroft. Stockport SK2 ... 124 E6
Hillcroft Cl. M8 ... 156 A8
Hillcroft House. 6 M6 ... 154 F3
Hillcroft Rd. WA14 ... 119 A5
Hilldale Ave. M9 ... 64 E4
Hilldean. WN8 ... 53 C8
Hillel House. M15 ... 163 A5
Hillend. SK14 ... 103 A1
Hillend La. SK14 ... 103 A1
Hillend Pl. M23 ... 109 A2
Hillend Rd. M23 & M33 ... 109 A2
Hillfield. M5 ... 154 D2
Hillfield Cl. M13 ... 164 D5
Hillfield Dr. Bolton BL2 ... 25 B1
Hillfield Dr. Boothstown M28 78 A7
Hillfield Wlk. 10 BL2 ... 25 B1
Hillfoot Wlk. 25 M15 ... 162 D6
Hillgate Ave. M5 ... 161 B7
Hillgate St. OL6 ... 166 C4
Hillhead Wlk. M8 ... 156 A5
Hillhouse Ct. OL12 ... 30 B3
Hillier St. M9 ... 157 E8
Hillier St N. M9 ... 157 E8
Hillingdon Cl. M35 ... 84 B8
Hillingdon Dr. M9 ... 65 B2
Hillingdon Rd. Stretford M32 . 96 E2
Hillingdon Rd. Whitefield M45 62 D7
Hillington Rd. Sale M33 ... 107 F5
Hillington Rd. Stockport SK3 123 C8
Hillkirk St. M11 ... 160 E1
Hillman Cl. M40 ... 157 D5
Hillock The. Bolton BL2 ... 25 D5
Hillock The. Tyldesley M29 ... 77 B5
Hillreed. WN6 ... 36 F1
Hills La. BL9 ... 45 C2
Hillsborough Dr. BL9 ... 45 B2
Hillsdale Gr. BL2 ... 25 E3
Hillside. WA13 ... 117 E1
Hillside Ave. Ashton-i-M WN4 72 F8
Hillside Ave. Atherton M46 ... 58 E4
Hillside Ave. Blackrod BL6 ... 21 E1
Hillside Ave. Bolton BL7 ... 25 C8
Hillside Ave. Diggle OL3 ... 51 C3
Hillside Ave. Farnworth BL4 .. 60 C7
Hillside Ave. Horwich BL6 ... 22 C4
Hillside Ave. M'ster M7 ... 81 A8
Hillside Ave. Mossley SK15 ... 86 F6
Hillside Ave. Oldham OL4 ... 67 C7
Hillside Ave. Oldham OL4 ... 68 B5
Hillside Ave. Romiley SK14 .. 113 F6
Hillside Ave. Royton OL2 ... 48 E5
Hillside Ave. Shaw OL2 ... 49 D8
Hillside Ave. Walkden M28 ... 60 C4
Hillside Ave. Whitefield M45 . 44 F2
Hillside Cl. Billinge WN5 ... 71 D5
Hillside Cl. Bolton BL2 ... 25 E5
Hillside Cl. Bolton BL3 ... 40 D2
Hillside Cl. Bramhall SK7 ... 133 A7
Hillside Cl. Disley SK12 ... 135 E6
Hillside Cl. Hadfield SK14 ... 171 E3
Hillside Cl. M'ster M40 ... 65 A1
Hillside Cl. Wigan WN3 ... 54 D3
Hillside Cres. Ashton-u-L OL6 85 F5
Hillside Cres. Bury BL9 ... 27 A4
Hillside Cres. Horwich BL6 ... 22 C4
Hillside Ct. BL1 ... 40 F7
Hillside Dr. Middleton M24 ... 47 A2
Hillside Dr. Salford M27 ... 80 D6
Hillside Gr. SK6 ... 114 B1
Hillside Rd. Alt'ham WA15 .. 120 A3
Hillside Rd. Ramsbottom BL0 138 A5
Hillside Rd. Romiley SK14 & SK6 ... 113 D5
Hillside Rd. Stockport SK2 .. 124 D7
Hillside St. 6 BL3 ... 145 D5
Hillside View. Denton M34 . 113 A7
Hillside View. Milnrow OL16 . 32 A6
Hillside Way. OL12 ... 4 C1
Hillside Wlk. OL12 ... 14 D4
Hillspring Rd. OL4 ... 68 A6
Hillstone Ave. OL12 ... 14 D4
Hillstone Cl. BL8 ... 10 F2
Hilltop. OL12 ... 14 C5
Hilltop Ave. M'ster M9 ... 64 D3
Hilltop Ave. Whitefield M45 ... 63 B8
Hilltop Ct. M'ster M8 ... 63 F2
Hilltop Ct. M'ster M14 ... 98 D1
Hilltop Dr. Bury BL8 ... 26 E6
Hilltop Dr. Haslingden BB4 ... 1 C7
Hilltop Dr. Marple SK6 ... 125 C7
Hilltop Gr. M45 ... 63 B8
Hilltop Rd. SK13 ... 104 B2
Hillview Ct. BL1 ... 143 E4
Hillview Rd. Bolton BL1 ... 143 E4
Hillview Rd. Reddish M34 & SK5 ... 100 A1
Hillwood Ave. M8 ... 63 F3
Hillwood Dr. Glossop SK13 .. 116 F8
Hilly Croft. BL7 ... 24 F8
Hillyard St. 7 BL8 ... 27 C3
Hilmarton Cl. BL2 ... 25 E5
Hilrose Ave. M41 ... 95 F2
Hilson Ct. M43 ... 84 A1
Hilton Arc. OL1 ... 153 F7
Hilton Ave. Horwich BL6 ... 22 A3
Hilton Ave. Urmston M41 ... 95 D2
Hilton Bank. M28 ... 60 B3
Hilton Cl. WN7 ... 76 A5
Hilton Cres. Ashton-u-L OL6 .. 85 C5
Hilton Cres. Boothstown M28 78 B6
Hilton Ct. SK3 ... 170 E8
Hilton Dr. Irlam M44 ... 105 C5
Hilton Dr. M'ster M25 ... 63 B2
Hilton Fold La. M24 ... 47 B1
Hilton Gr. Poynton SK12 ... 133 D4
Hilton Gr. Walkden M28 ... 60 B3
Hilton La. Prestwich M25 ... 63 A2
Hilton La. Walkden M28 ... 60 B2
Hilton Lodge. M25 ... 63 B2
Hilton Pl. WN2 ... 38 C6
Hilton Rd. Bury BL9 ... 140 F2
Hilton Rd. Disley SK12 ... 135 B7
Hilton Rd. High Lane SK12 ... 134 C5
Hilton Rd. Stockport SK7 ... 123 F1
Hilton Sq. M27 ... 62 A1
Hilton St. Ashton-i-M WN4 ... 73 C3
Hilton St. Bolton BL2 ... 148 C7
Hilton St. Bury BL9 ... 140 F4
Hilton St. Dukinfield SK14 ... 101 F5
Hilton St. M'ster M7 ... 155 D5
Hilton St. M'ster M1 ... 159 B1
Hilton St. M'ster M4 & M60 . 159 B2
Hilton St. Stockport SK3 ... 170 D8
Hilton St. Walkden M38 ... 60 A4
Hilton St. Wigan WN1 ... 37 D1
Hilton St N. M7 ... 155 D6
Hilton Wlk. M24 ... 64 C8
Hiltons Farm Cl. M34 ... 100 E6
Himley Rd. M11 ... 83 C3
Hincaster Wlk. M18 ... 165 C5
Hinchcliffe Wlk. 13 M16 ... 97 E4
Hinchcombe Cl. M38 ... 60 A6
Hinckley St. M11 ... 164 F8
Hind Hill St. OL10 ... 29 D1
Hind Rd. WN5 ... 54 D8
Hind St. BL2 ... 148 C7
Hind's Head Ave. WN6 ... 18 F6
Hindburn Cl. M45 ... 45 B1
Hindburn Dr. M28 ... 78 A8
Hindburn Wlk. M45 ... 45 B1
Hinde St. M40 ... 83 A8
Hindell Terr. OL3 ... 50 F4
Hindhead Wlk. M40 ... 83 D4
Hindle Dr. OL2 ... 48 C3
Hindle St. Bacup OL13 ... 3 D8
Hindle St. Radcliffe M26 ... 44 A3
Hindles Cl. M46 ... 58 A1
Hindley (All Saints) CE Prim Sch. WN2 ... 56 E5
Hindley Ave. M22 ... 121 B2
Hindley Castle Hill St Philips CE Sch. WN2 ... 56 F6
Hindley Cl. OL7 ... 84 F1
Hindley Cty Prim Sch. WN2 56 E5
Hindley Green Cty Prim Sch. WN2 ... 57 B3
Hindley Hall Golf Course. Hindley WN2 ... 56 D8
Hindley Mill La. WN2 ... 56 F7
Hindley Rd. BL5 & WN2 ... 57 D5
Hindley St. Ashton-u-L OL7 ... 84 F1
Hindley St. Stockport SK1 ... 170 F8
Hindley Sta. WN2 ... 56 D7
Hindley Wlk. 1 WN1 ... 150 C8
Hinds La. Bury BL8 ... 27 C1
Hinds La. Bury BL8 & BL9 ... 44 C7
Hindsford CE Prim Sch. M46 ... 58 E1
Hindsford Cl. M23 & M33 ... 108 E1
Hindsford St. M46 ... 58 F1
Hinkler Ave. BL3 ... 147 E3
Hinstock Cres. M18 ... 99 D5
Hinton. 19 OL12 ... 139 E8
Hinton Cl. OL11 ... 29 E6
Hinton Gr. Hyde SK14 ... 114 A8
Hinton St. M'ster M4 ... 159 B3
Hinton St. Oldham OL8 ... 153 F5
Hipley Cl. SK6 ... 113 A5
Hirons La. OL4 ... 68 A5
Hirst Ave. M28 ... 60 C5
Hitchen Cl. SK16 ... 101 F7
Hitchen Dr. SK16 ... 101 F7
Hitchin Wlk. M13 ... 164 D5
Hive St. OL8 ... 66 B2
HM Prison Strangeways. M3 ... 158 F4
Hoad Wlk. 3 M34 ... 113 A7
Hoade St. WN2 ... 56 E7
Hob Hey La. WA3 ... 91 D3

Houghton Rd. M8 ... 64 A1
Houghton St. Bolton BL3 ... 145 E5
Houghton St. Bury BL9 ... 140 E1
Houghton St. Leigh WN7 ... 75 F6
Houghton St.
Newton-l-W WA12 ... 89 B3
Houghton St. Oldham OL2 ... 48 E2
Houghton St. Salford M27 ... 80 D6
Houghwood Grange. WN4 ... 72 F3
Houldsworth Ave. WA14 ... 119 E7
Houldsworth Golf Course.
SK5 ... 111 D8
Houldsworth Mill Ind Est.
SK5 ... 111 E7
Houldsworth Sq. 2 SK5 ... 111 E7
Houldsworth St.
M'ster M1 & M60 ... 159 B2
Houldsworth St. 2
Radcliffe M26 ... 43 F5
Houldsworth St.
Reddish SK5 ... 111 E7
Houseley Ave. OL9 ... 66 A3
Housley Cl. WN3 ... 150 A5
Houson St. OL8 ... 153 F5
Houston Pk. M5 ... 154 F1
Hove Cl. BL8 ... 10 F1
Hove Dr. M14 ... 110 E7
Hove St. BL3 ... 144 C5
Hove St N. 13 BL3 ... 144 C5
Hoveden St. M8 ... 158 F4
Hoverty Prec. WA12 ... 89 B1
Hovey Cl. M7 & M8 ... 155 F7
Hovingham St. OL16 ... 31 B8
Hovington Gdns. M19 ... 110 E6
Hovis St. M11 ... 165 C8
How Clough Cl. M28 ... 60 F2
How Clough Dr. M28 ... 60 F2
How Lea Dr. BL9 ... 27 F6
Howard Ave. Bolton BL3 ... 146 A4
Howard Ave. Cheadle SK8 ... 123 A1
Howard Ave. Eccles M30 ... 79 D3
Howard Ave. Kearsley BL4 ... 60 F7
Howard Ave. Lymm WA13 ... 117 B4
Howard Ave. Reddish SK4 ... 111 C6
Howard Cl. Glossop SK13 ... 104 B2
Howard Cl. Romiley SK6 ... 113 A2
Howard Ct. OL6 ... 166 C3
Howard Dr. WA15 ... 120 A1
Howard Hill. BL9 ... 45 A5
Howard La. M34 ... 100 F4
Howard Pl. Hyde SK14 ... 167 D2
Howard Pl.
R'dale OL12 & OL16 ... 139 F8
Howard Rd. Culcheth WA3 ... 92 A2
Howard Rd.
Wythenshawe M22 ... 109 D1
Howard Spring Wlk. M8 ... 155 F8
Howard St. Ashton-u-L OL7 ... 166 A4
Howard St. Denton M34 ... 100 E5
Howard St. Glossop SK13 ... 104 C1
Howard St. M'ster M8 ... 158 F4
Howard St. Oldham OL4 ... 49 E1
Howard St. R'dale OL12 ... 139 F8
Howard St. Radcliffe M26 ... 43 E4
Howard St. Salford M5 ... 161 A8
Howard St. Shaw OL2 ... 149 A7
Howard St. Stalybridge SK15 ... 86 D4
Howard St. Stockport SK1 ... 169 F2
Howard St. Stretford M32 ... 96 D2
Howard St. Wigan WN5 ... 54 C5
Howard Way. OL15 ... 6 C1
Howard's La. OL5 ... 68 F1
Howarths La. WN5 ... 53 F7
Howarth Ave. M28 ... 79 C7
Howarth Cl. M11 ... 83 A1
Howarth Cross St. OL16 ... 15 B2
Howarth Ct. 8 Radcliffe M26 ... 44 B3
Howarth Ct. Stockport SK2 ... 124 B5
Howarth Dr. M44 ... 93 F1
Howarth Farm Way. OL12 ... 15 C3
Howarth Gn. OL12 ... 15 C3
Howarth Sq. OL16 ... 31 A8
Howarth St. Farnworth BL4 ... 60 D7
Howarth St. Leigh WN7 ... 76 B4
Howarth St.
Littleborough OL15 ... 16 B6
Howarth St. M'ster M16 ... 97 C4
Howarth St.
Westhoughton BL5 ... 57 F8
Howarth Wlk. 3 M26 ... 44 B3
Howbridge Cl. M28 ... 78 C8
Howbro Dr. OL7 ... 84 F5
Howcroft Cl. BL1 ... 145 E8
Howcroft St. BL3 ... 145 D5
Howden Cl. SK5 ... 99 E2
Howden Dr. WN3 ... 55 B4
Howden Rd. M'ster M9 ... 64 C5
Howden Rd. New Mills SK12 ... 127 C1
Howe Bridge CE Prim Sch.
M46 ... 58 B2
Howe Bridge Cl. WN7 ... 58 A1
Howe Dr. BL0 ... 11 B2
Howe St. Ashton-u-L OL7 ... 100 F8
Howe St. M'ster M7 ... 155 D7
Howell Croft N. 7 BL1 ... 145 F7
Howell Croft S. BL1 ... 145 F7
Howell's Yd. 6 BL1 ... 145 F7
Howells Ave. M33 ... 108 B5
Howgill St. M11 & M43 ... 83 D1
Howsin Ave. BL2 ... 25 B4
Howton Cl. M12 ... 99 A4
Howty Cl. SK9 ... 131 D1
Hoxton Cl. SK6 ... 113 A4
Hoy Dr. M41 ... 95 D5
Hoylake Cl. Failsworth M40 ... 83 D8
Hoylake Cl. Leigh WN7 ... 75 D2
Hoylake Rd. Stockport SK3 ... 123 B8
Hoylake Rd.
Wythenshawe M33 ... 108 F2
Hoyland Cl. M12 ... 164 F6
Hoyle Ave. OL8 ... 153 E5
Hoyle St. Bacup OL13 ... 3 E8
Hoyle St. 3 Bolton BL1 ... 143 E4
Hoyle St. M'ster M12 ... 163 C8
Hoyle St. Radcliffe M26 ... 44 C1
Hoyle St. Whitworth OL12 ... 4 D3
Hoyle Street Ind Est. M12 ... 163 C7
Hoyle Wlk. M13 ... 163 C6
Hoyle's Terr. OL16 ... 31 E6
Hqward St. BL1 ... 143 F1
Hubert Worthington House.
SK9 ... 137 A1
Hucclecote Ave. M22 ... 121 C2
Hucklow Ave. M23 ... 121 A2
Hucklow Bank. 27 SK13 ... 171 D2
Hucklow Cl. 26 SK13 ... 171 D2
Hucklow Fold. 28 SK13 ... 171 D2
Hucklow Lanes. 29 SK13 ... 171 D2
Hudcar La. BL9 ... 141 A4
Huddart Cl. M5 ... 161 B8
Huddersfield Rd. Diggle OL3 ... 51 C7
Huddersfield Rd. Diggle OL3 ... 51 D5
Huddersfield Rd.
Newhey OL16 & OL2 & OL3 ... 32 D5
Huddersfield Rd.
Oldham OL1 & OL4 ... 67 D8
Huddersfield Rd.
Stalybridge OL5 & SK15 ... 86 E4
Hudson Rd. Bolton BL3 ... 146 B3
Hudson Rd. Hyde SK14 ... 113 E7
Hudson St. OL9 ... 66 A2
Hudsons Pas. OL15 ... 16 C7
Hudsons Wlk. OL11 ... 30 C7
Hudswell Cl. M45 ... 62 E8
Hugh Lupus St. BL1 ... 25 A5
Hugh Oldham Dr. M7 ... 81 C6
Hugh St. OL16 ... 31 A8
Hughes Ave. BL6 ... 22 A4
Hughes Cl. BL9 ... 141 A3
Hughes St. Bolton BL1 ... 142 C2
Hughes St. Bolton BL1 ... 143 D2
Hughes St. M'ster M11 ... 164 E8
Hughes Way. M30 ... 79 A1
Hughley Cl. Royton OL2 ... 49 A4
Hughtrede St. OL11 ... 31 B3
Hugo St. Failsworth M40 ... 83 A7
Hugo St. Farnworth BL4 ... 42 B2
Hugo St. R'dale OL11 ... 30 D2
Hulbert St. Bury BL8 ... 27 C1
Hulbert St. Middleton M24 ... 47 B1
Hull Mill La. OL3 ... 50 F5
Hull Sq. M3 ... 158 D2
Hullet Cl. WN6 ... 35 E8
Hully St. 7 SK15 ... 85 F2
Hulme Ct. M15 ... 162 E7
Hulme Gr. WN7 ... 75 C6
Hulme Gram Sch
for Girls The. OL8 ... 66 D4
Hulme Gram Sch The. OL8 ... 66 D4
Hulme Hall Ave. SK8 ... 132 B8
Hulme Hall Cl. SK8 ... 123 A1
Hulme Hall Cres. SK8 ... 132 A8
Hulme Hall Jun Sch. SK8 ... 132 B8
Hulme Hall Rd. Cheadle SK8 ... 123 A1
Hulme Hall Rd. M'ster M15 ... 162 D7
Hulme Hall Schs. SK8 ... 123 A1
Hulme Pl. M5 ... 81 C2
Hulme Rd. Bolton BL2 ... 25 E5
Hulme Rd. Kearsley BL4 & M26 ... 61 C7
Hulme Rd. Leigh WN7 ... 75 C6
Hulme Rd. Reddish M34 ... 100 B3
Hulme Rd. Reddish SK4 ... 111 D6
Hulme Rd. Sale M33 ... 108 D3
Hulme St. Ashton-u-L OL6 ... 85 D4
Hulme St. Bolton BL1 ... 145 F8
Hulme St. Bury BL8 ... 140 D3
Hulme St. M'ster M3 & M5 ... 81 C1
Hulme St. M'ster M15 ... 162 D7
Hulme St. M'ster M15 ... 162 E7
Hulme St. Oldham OL8 ... 66 E4
Hulme St. Stockport SK1 ... 124 B7
Hulme Wlk. M15 ... 162 F6
Hulme's Terr. BL2 ... 43 C8
Hulmes Rd. M35 & M40 ... 83 E5
Hulton Ave. M28 ... 60 B3
Hulton Cl. BL3 ... 146 A3
Hulton District Ctr. M28 ... 60 A4
Hulton Dr. Bolton BL3 ... 146 A3
Hulton Dr. M'ster M16 ... 97 E4
Hulton Hospl. BL3 ... 146 A3
Hulton La. BL3 ... 146 A3
Hulton St. Denton M34 ... 100 E4
Hulton St. Failsworth M35 ... 83 E7
Hulton St. Salford M5 ... 161 A7
Humber Dr. BL9 ... 27 F7
Humber Pl. WN5 ... 54 C7
Humber Rd. Milnrow OL16 ... 32 A6
Humber Rd. Tyldesley M29 ... 77 C7
Humber St. M'ster M8 ... 156 B7
Humber St. Salford M5 ... 154 D1
Humberstone Ave. M15 ... 162 F6
Hume St. M'ster M19 ... 111 B8
Hume St. R'dale OL16 ... 31 A5
Humphrey Booth Gdns.
M6 ... 154 E3
Humphrey Cres. M41 ... 96 A2
Humphrey La. M32 & M41 ... 96 A2
Humphrey Park Sta. M32 ... 96 A3
Humphrey Pk. M41 ... 96 A2
Humphrey Rd. M16 ... 161 B5
Humphrey St. Ince-i-M WN2 ... 56 A7
Humphrey St.
M'ster M7 & M8 ... 155 F8
Humphries Ct. M40 ... 159 C4
Huncoat Ave. SK4 ... 111 D5
Huncote Dr. M9 ... 64 E1
Hunger Hill Ave. BL3 ... 40 E2
Hungerford Wlk. 5 M23 ... 120 D7
Hunmanby Ave. M15 ... 162 F7
Hunstanton Dr. BL8 ... 27 D5
Hunston Rd. M33 ... 107 F2
Hunt Ave. OL6 & OL7 ... 85 B5
Hunt Fold Dr. BL8 ... 10 F1
Hunt La. OL9 ... 152 A7
Hunt Rd. SK14 ... 102 A5
Hunt St. Atherton M46 ... 58 D3
Hunt St. M'ster M9 ... 64 D1
Hunt St. Wigan WN1 ... 151 E7
Hunt's Bank. M'ster M3 ... 158 F2
Hunt's Bank.
Westhoughton BL5 ... 57 F6
Hunter Dr. M26 ... 44 A5
Hunter Rd. WN5 ... 36 E1
Hunter's La. Oldham OL1 ... 153 F7
Hunter's La.
R'dale OL12 & OL16 ... 139 F8
Hunter's View. SK9 ... 131 C3
Hunters Cl. SK9 ... 131 F1
Hunters Ct. SK15 ... 102 D8
Hunters Gn. BL8 ... 10 F3
Hunters Hill. BL9 ... 45 B4
Hunters Hill La. OL3 ... 51 C6
Hunters La. Glossop SK13 ... 115 F8
Hunters La. R'dale OL16 ... 139 F8
Hunters Mews. Sale M33 ... 108 A5
Hunters Mews.
Wilmslow SK9 ... 137 C7
Hunterston Ave. M30 ... 80 A2
Huntingdon Ave. OL9 ... 152 B5
Huntingdon Cres. SK5 ... 112 C5
Huntingdon Way. 7 M34 ... 100 F1
Huntingdon Wlk. 21 BL1 ... 143 E2
Huntington Ave. M20 ... 110 A7
Huntley Mount Rd. BL9 ... 141 B3
Huntley Rd. Cheadle SK3 ... 123 B7
Huntley Rd. M'ster M8 ... 63 E2
Huntley St. BL9 ... 141 B3
Huntly Chase. SK9 ... 137 C7
Huntly Way. OL10 ... 28 E1
Huntroyde Ave. 26 BL2 ... 25 C1
Hunts Rd. 2 M6 ... 80 D5
Huntsham Cl. WA14 ... 119 B6
Huntsman Dr. M44 ... 105 F7
Huntsworth Wlk. M13 ... 164 D5
Hurdlow Ave. M7 ... 81 A7
Hurdlow Gn. 14 SK13 ... 171 D1
Hurdlow Lea. 13 SK13 ... 171 D1
Hurdlow Mews. SK13 ... 171 D1
Hurdlow Way. 12 SK13 ... 171 D1
Hurdlow Wlk. M9 ... 157 D7
Hurdsfield Rd. SK2 ... 124 D4
Hurford Ave. M18 ... 99 D6
Hurlbote Cl. SK9 ... 131 D5
Hurley Dr. SK8 ... 122 E2
Hurlston Rd. BL3 ... 147 D2
Hurst Ave. Bramhall SK8 ... 132 C6
Hurst Ave. Sale M33 ... 107 C2
Hurst Bank Rd. OL6 ... 85 E4
Hurst Brook Cl. OL6 ... 166 C4
Hurst Cl. BL5 ... 58 F7
Hurst Cross. OL6 ... 85 D5
Hurst Ct. Ashton-u-L OL6 ... 85 E5
Hurst Ct. Wythenshawe M23 ... 120 F4
Hurst Gr. OL6 ... 85 E5
Hurst Green Cl. BL8 ... 43 F8
Hurst Hall Dr. OL6 ... 85 E5
Hurst Inf Sch. OL6 ... 85 D5
Hurst Knoll CE (VC)
Prim Sch. OL6 ... 166 C4
Hurst La. WA3 ... 92 C7
Hurst Lea Ct. SK9 ... 137 A2
Hurst Meadow. OL16 ... 31 C3
Hurst Methodist Jun Sch.
OL6 ... 85 D7
Hurst Mill La. WA3 ... 92 C8
Hurst Rd. SK13 ... 104 F1
Hurst St. Bolton BL3 ... 146 C3
Hurst St. Bury BL9 ... 141 A2
Hurst St. Dukinfield SK16 ... 101 A6
Hurst St. Hindley WN2 ... 56 E5
Hurst St. Leigh WN7 ... 76 B3
Hurst St. Oldham OL9 ... 153 D7
Hurst St. R'dale OL11 ... 31 A5
Hurst St. Reddish SK5 ... 111 E7
Hurst St. Walkden M28 ... 60 D6
Hurst Wlk. 4 M22 ... 121 A2
Hurstbank Ave. M19 ... 110 D4
Hurstbourne Ave. M11 ... 83 B2
Hurstbrook Cl. SK13 ... 104 F1
Hurstclough Prim Sch.
SK14 ... 102 E1
Hurstead. OL12 ... 15 D4
Hurstead Gn. OL16 ... 15 D4
Hurstead Rd. OL16 ... 31 F6
Hursted Rd. OL16 ... 31 F6
Hurstfield Rd. M28 ... 78 B8
Hurstfold Ave. M19 ... 110 D3
Hursthead Cty Jun Sch.
SK8 ... 132 C7
Hursthead Inf Sch. SK8 ... 132 C6
Hursthead Rd. SK8 ... 132 B7
Hursthead Wlk. M13 ... 163 B7
Hurstmead Terr. M20 ... 110 B2
Hurstvale Ave. SK8 ... 122 B1
Hurstville Rd. M21 ... 109 B6
Hurstway Dr. 33 M9 ... 64 E3
Hurstwood Rd. SK2 ... 124 F6
Hus St. 1 Droylsden M43 ... 100 A8
Husteads. OL3 ... 50 E1
Husteads La. OL3 ... 50 F1
Hutchinson Rd. OL11 & OL12 ... 13 D2
Hutchinson St. R'dale OL11 ... 30 C6
Hutchinson St. 4
Radcliffe M26 ... 44 C4
Hutchinson Way. M26 ... 44 A3
Huttock End La. OL13 ... 3 D8
Hutton Ave. Ashton-u-L OL6 ... 85 E3
Hutton Ave. Boothstown M28 ... 77 F6
Hutton Cl. WA3 ... 91 E5
Hutton Lodge. M14 ... 110 C7
Hutton St. WN1 ... 20 A3
Hutton Wlk. 7 M13 ... 163 C6
Huxley Ave. M7 & M8 ... 156 A6
Huxley Cl. SK7 ... 132 E7
Huxley Dr. SK7 ... 132 E7
Huxley Pl. WN3 ... 150 A5
Huxley St. Alt'ham WA14 ... 119 D7
Huxley St. Bolton BL1 ... 142 C2
Huxley St. 6 Oldham OL4 ... 67 C6
Huxton Gn. SK7 ... 124 A2
Huyton Rd. PR6 ... 21 A6
Huyton Terr. PR6 ... 21 B6
Hyacinth Cl. SK3 ... 170 D5
Hyatt Cres. WN6 ... 19 C3
Hyde Central Sta. SK14 ... 101 C2
Hyde Cl. WN3 ... 150 A5
Hyde Dr. M28 ... 60 C3
Hyde Fold Cl. M19 ... 110 F6
Hyde Gr. M'ster M13 ... 163 C5
Hyde Gr. Sale M33 ... 108 B4
Hyde Gr. Walkden M28 ... 60 C2
Hyde Hospl. SK14 ... 167 F1
Hyde North Sta. SK14 ... 101 C5
Hyde Pl. M13 ... 163 C5
Hyde Rd. Denton
M34 & SK14 ... 101 A3
Hyde Rd.
M'ster M12 & M18 & M34 ... 99 D4
Hyde Rd. M'ster M12 ... 164 E6
Hyde Rd. Oldham M24 ... 65 E6
Hyde Rd. Romiley SK14 & SK6 ... 113 B5
Hyde Rd. Walkden M28 ... 60 C2
Hyde Sq. M24 ... 46 E1
Hyde St. Bolton BL3 ... 146 C3
Hyde St. Droylsden M35 & M43 ... 84 C4
Hyde St. Dukinfield SK16 ... 101 D8
Hyde St. M'ster M15 ... 162 D5
Hyde St Paul's RC
Prim Sch. SK14 ... 167 F4
Hyde Tech Sch. SK14 ... 167 D4
Hyde's Cross. M4 ... 159 A2
Hyde-Clarendon Coll. SK14 ... 167 E4
Hydes Terr. SK15 ... 86 B2
Hydon Brook Wlk. OL11 ... 30 C4
Hydrangea Cl. 7 M33 ... 107 C6
Hyldavale Ave. SK8 ... 122 B6
Hylton Dr. Ashton-u-L OL7 ... 84 F5
Hylton Dr. Cheadle SK8 ... 132 C8
Hyman Goldstone Wlk. 4
M8 ... 155 F7
Hyndman Ct. M5 ... 154 D2
Hypatia St. BL2 ... 148 B7
Hythe Cl. M14 ... 98 C3
Hythe Rd. SK3 ... 123 B8
Hythe St. BL3 ... 146 A4
Hythe Wlk. OL9 ... 152 B6

Ibbert on Wlk. 8 M9 ... 64 F1
Ibsley. 20 OL12 ... 139 E8
Ice House Cl. 5 M28 ... 59 F3
Iceland St. M6 ... 154 F2
Idonia St. BL1 ... 143 D3
Ifco Ctr. M14 ... 98 C3
Ilex Gr. M7 ... 155 D6
Ilford St. M11 ... 83 B2
Ilfracombe Rd. SK2 ... 124 D8
Ilfracombe St. M40 ... 83 D6
Ilk St. M11 ... 83 B2
Ilkeston Dr. WN2 ... 38 F3
Ilkeston Wlk. 5 Denton M34 ... 113 A8
Ilkeston Wlk. 4
Failsworth M40 ... 83 A6
Ilkley Cl. Bolton BL2 ... 148 C7
Ilkley Cl. Oldham OL9 ... 152 B6
Ilkley Cres. SK5 ... 111 E8
Ilkley Dr. M41 ... 95 A4
Ilkley St. M'ster M40 ... 83 A8
Illingworth Ave. SK15 ... 86 C2
Illona Dr. M7 ... 81 A8
Ilminster. OL11 ... 139 E6
Ilminster Wlk. 2 M9 ... 64 E5
Ilthorpe Wlk. 7 M40 ... 83 A6
Imex Bsns Pk. M13 ... 98 F3
Imogen Ct. M5 ... 161 C8
Imperial Dr. WN7 ... 76 D6
Ina Ave. BL1 ... 23 F1
Ince Cl. M'ster M20 ... 110 B7
Ince Cl. M'ster SK4 ... 169 E3
Ince Green La.
Ince-i-M WN2 & WN3 ... 151 F6
Ince Hall Ave.
Ince-i-M WN2 & WN3 ... 56 A8
Ince Hall Ave. Wigan WN2 ... 151 F8
Ince St. SK4 ... 169 E3
Ince Sta. WN2 ... 151 F6
Ince Wlk. WN1 ... 150 C8
Ince-in-Makerfield CE
Prim Sch. WN2 ... 56 A7
Inchcape Dr. M9 ... 64 B4
Inchfield Cl. OL11 ... 29 E8
Inchfield Rd. M'ster M40 ... 65 B1
Inchfield Rd. Walsden OL14 ... 6 A8
Inchley Rd. M13 ... 163 B7
Inchwood Mews. OL4 ... 49 E4
Incline Rd. OL8 ... 66 C2
Independent St. BL3 ... 43 A3
India St. BL0 ... 11 C3
Indigo St. M6 ... 80 F5
Indigo Wlk. M6 ... 80 F5
Industrial Cotts. 10 BB4 ... 2 F8
Industrial St. Ramsbottom BL0 ... 1 C1
Industrial St.
Westhoughton BL5 ... 57 F7
Industry Rd. 8 OL12 ... 14 F1
Industry St. 14
Littleborough OL15 ... 16 B5
Industry St. Oldham OL9 ... 66 A4
Industry St. R'dale OL11 ... 13 E1
Industry St. Whitworth OL12 ... 4 D2
Infant St. M25 ... 63 C4
Infirmary St. 11 BL1 ... 145 F7
Ingersol Rd. BL6 ... 22 E1
Ingham Ave. WA12 ... 89 B1
Ingham Brow. BL6 ... 22 F4
Ingham Rd. Sale WA14 ... 107 D1
Ingham St. Bury BL9 ... 141 A1
Ingham St. Failsworth M40 ... 83 E4
Ingham St. Leigh WN7 ... 75 E8
Ingham St. 5 Oldham OL1 ... 67 A7
Inghams La. OL15 ... 16 B5
Inghamwood Cl. M7 & M8 ... 155 F7
Ingle Dr. SK2 ... 124 C7
Ingle Rd. SK8 ... 123 A6
Ingleby Ave. M9 ... 64 F4
Ingleby Cl. Shaw OL2 ... 149 A8
Ingleby Cl. Standish WN6 ... 19 D2
Ingleby Ct. M32 ... 96 E1
Ingleby Way. OL2 ... 149 A8
Ingledene Ave. M7 ... 63 E1
Ingledene Ct. 8 M7 ... 63 E1
Ingledene Gr. BL1 ... 142 A2
Inglefield. OL11 ... 13 F1
Inglehead Cl. M34 ... 101 A2
Ingles Fold. M28 ... 78 B7
Inglesham Cl. WN7 ... 75 E1
Ingleton Ave. M8 ... 64 B2
Ingleton Cl. Bolton BL2 ... 25 D4
Ingleton Cl. Cheadle SK8 ... 122 C6
Ingleton Cl. Royton OL2 ... 48 D5
Ingleton Dr. WA11 ... 71 B1
Ingleton Mews. BL8 ... 27 B4
Ingleton Rd. SK3 ... 123 C7
Inglewhite Ave. WN1 ... 37 C2
Inglewhite Cl. BL9 ... 44 D7
Inglewhite Cres. 1 WN1 ... 37 C2
Inglewhite Pl. 2 WN1 ... 37 C2
Inglewood. WA14 ... 119 B3
Inglewood Ave. WN1 ... 151 E7
Inglewood Cl. OL7 ... 84 F5
Inglewood Rd. M24 ... 47 E1
Inglewood Wlk. M13 ... 163 C6
Inglis St. OL15 ... 16 B6
Ingoe Cl. OL10 ... 29 F3
Ingoldsby Ave. M13 ... 98 D4
Ingram Dr. SK4 ... 110 E3
Ingram St. Platt Bridge WN2 ... 56 A3
Ingram St. Shevington WN6 ... 36 F2
Ings Ave. OL12 ... 14 B2
Ings La. OL12 ... 14 C2
Ink St. OL16 ... 139 F7
Inkerman St. Hyde SK14 ... 167 D4
Inkerman St. M'ster M40 ... 157 D6
Inkerman St. 12 R'dale OL12 ... 14 F1
Inman St. Bury BL9 ... 44 E8
Inman St. Denton M34 ... 100 F3
Innes Sch. OL12 ... 14 C1
Innes St. M18 ... 99 B3
Innis Ave. M40 ... 83 C5
Inst of Islamic H Ed. BL7 ... 25 A8
Institute St. BL1 & BL2 ... 148 A7
Instow Cl. Chadderton OL9 ... 47 F1
Instow Cl. M'ster M13 ... 164 D6
Intake Rd. OL3 ... 69 B3
International App. M90 ... 130 C7
Invar Rd. M27 ... 61 D1
Inver Wlk. 10 M40 ... 65 D2
Inverbeg Dr. Bolton BL2 ... 43 A7
Invergarry Wlk. 19 M11 ... 83 C1
Inverlael Ave. BL1 ... 144 B8
Inverness Ave. M9 ... 65 A4
Inverness Cl. WN2 ... 38 D5
Inverness Rd. SK16 ... 101 C7
Inward Dr. WN6 ... 36 A5
Inwood Wlk. M8 ... 156 C6
Inworth Wlk. 10 M8 ... 155 F7
Iona Pl. BL2 ... 25 C2
Iona Way. M41 ... 95 E5
Ionian Gdns. 2 M7 ... 81 C5
Ipswich St. OL11 ... 139 F5
Ipswich Way. 10 M34 ... 101 A1
Ipswich Wlk. M12 ... 164 E5
Iqbal Cl. M12 ... 165 A5
Irby Wlk. SK8 ... 123 A4
Ireby Cl. M24 ... 46 C2
Iredale Cres. WN6 ... 36 F7
Iredine St. 6 M11 ... 83 C1
Irene Ave. SK14 ... 101 E5
Iris Ave. Farnworth BL4 ... 42 A1
Iris Ave. Kearsley BL4 ... 60 F5
Iris St. Oldham OL8 ... 66 F3
Iris St. Ramsbottom BL0 ... 138 B6
Iris Wlk. 7 M31 ... 105 E2
Irk St. M4 ... 159 A3
Irk Vale Dr. OL1 & OL9 ... 47 E1
Irk Wlk. M45 ... 45 B2
Irkdale St. M40 & M8 ... 156 C6
Irlam Ave. M30 ... 79 D1
Irlam & Cadishead
Comm High Sch. M44 ... 105 E7
Irlam Endowed Prim Sch.
M44 ... 94 A2
Irlam Prim Sch. M44 ... 94 A1
Irlam Rd. Sale M33 ... 108 C4
Irlam Rd. Urmston M41 ... 94 D2
Irlam Sq. M6 ... 80 D5
Irlam St. Bolton BL1 ... 143 E3
Irlam St. M'ster M10 & M40 ... 157 E5
Irlam Sta. M44 ... 105 E7
Irlam Wharf Rd. M44 ... 106 A6
Irma St. BL1 ... 143 F3
Iron St. Denton M34 ... 100 F3
Iron St. Horwich BL6 ... 22 C2
Iron St. M'ster M10 & M40 ... 160 E3
Ironmonger La. Oldham OL1 ... 153 F6
Ironmonger La. Wigan WN3 ... 150 C7
Irvin Dr. M22 & SK8 ... 131 A8
Irvin St. M35 ... 83 C6
Irvine Ave. M28 ... 78 A6
Irvine St. WN7 ... 75 F6
Irving Cl. SK2 ... 124 A3
Irving House. 1 BL1 ... 143 E2
Irving St. Bolton BL1 ... 143 E2
Irving St. Oldham OL8 ... 66 B2
Irwell Ave. Eccles M30 ... 79 F1
Irwell Ave. Walkden M38 ... 60 B4
Irwell Cl. 4 M26 ... 44 B2
Irwell Gr. M30 ... 79 F1
Irwell Pl. Eccles M30 ... 79 F1
Irwell Pl. Salford M5 ... 81 C2
Irwell Pl. Wigan WN5 ... 54 C6
Irwell Rd. WN5 ... 53 F7
Irwell St. Bury BL9 ... 140 E2
Irwell St. Kearsley M26 ... 61 A8
Irwell St. M'ster M3 ... 158 E1
Irwell St. M'ster M7 & M8 ... 158 E4
Irwell St. Radcliffe M26 ... 44 B2
Irwell St. Ramsbottom BL0 ... 138 C6
Irwell St. Salford M6 ... 81 A6
Irwell Vale Rd. BB4 ... 1 C6
Irwell Vale Sta. BL0 ... 1 C5
Irwell Wlk. OL8 ... 66 C3
Irwin Dr. SK9 ... 131 C5
Irwin Rd. WA14 ... 119 D8
Irwin St. M34 ... 100 E3
Isa St. BL0 ... 11 A4
Isaac Cl. M5 ... 161 A8
Isaac St. BL1 ... 144 C8
Isabella Cl. M16 ... 97 C4
Isabella Sq. WN1 ... 151 E8
Isabella St. OL12 ... 15 A2
Isaiah St. OL8 ... 66 F4
Isca St. M11 ... 160 F1
Isel Wlk. M24 ... 46 D2
Isherwood Dr. SK6 ... 125 D6
Isherwood Fold. BL7 ... 9 D7
Isherwood Rd. M31 ... 106 F6
Isherwood St. Heywood OL10 ... 29 E1
Isherwood St. Leigh WN7 ... 75 E8
Isherwood St. R'dale OL11 ... 31 A6
Isis Cl. M7 ... 81 A8
Islamic Acad. M13 ... 163 B6
Islamic High Sch for Girls.
M21 ... 109 A8
Island Cotts. BL9 ... 11 C2
Island Row. WN2 ... 56 B7
Islington Rd. SK2 ... 124 C4
Islington St. M3 ... 158 D2
Islington Way. M3 ... 158 D1
Isobel Cl. M30 ... 79 B1
Isobel Wlk. Bolton BL1 ... 145 D5
Isobel Wlk. M'ster M16 ... 97 F4
Ivanhoe Ave. WA3 ... 74 D1
Ivanhoe Ct. BL3 & BL4 ... 42 C2
Ivanhoe St.
Farnworth BL3 & BL4 ... 42 C2
Ivanhoe St. Oldham OL1 ... 49 C1
Iveagh Ct. 19 OL16 ... 31 B6
Ivor St. OL11 ... 30 B3
Ivory Way. OL1 ... 153 F7
Ivy Ave. WA12 ... 89 C2
Ivy Bank Cl. BL1 ... 24 E5
Ivy Bank Rd. BL1 ... 24 E5
Ivy Cl. Droylsden M43 ... 83 F3
Ivy Cl. Shaw OL2 ... 149 B7
Ivy Cotts. Denton M34 ... 113 A7
Ivy Cotts. Rawtenstall BB4 ... 2 F8
Ivy Dr. M24 ... 64 F6
Ivy Gr. Farnworth BL4 ... 60 B8
Ivy Gr. Kearsley BL4 ... 60 F7
Ivy Gr. Walkden M38 ... 59 F4
Ivy House Rd. WA3 ... 74 D1
Ivy Rd. Bolton BL1 ... 142 B1
Ivy Rd. Bury BL8 ... 27 B2
Ivy Rd. Golborne WA3 ... 90 B8
Ivy Rd. Poynton SK12 ... 133 E3
Ivy Rd. Westhoughton BL5 ... 57 F7
Ivy St. Ashton-i-M WN4 ... 73 B3
Ivy St. Bolton BL3 ... 146 C4
Ivy St. Eccles M30 ... 79 D1
Ivy St. M'ster M40 ... 83 A8
Ivy St. 1 Rawtenstall BB4 ... 2 F8
Ivy St. Wigan WN1 & WN6 ... 150 B8
Ivy Wlk. M31 ... 105 D3
Ivybridge Cl. M13 ... 164 D5
Ivycroft. SK14 ... 171 E4
Ivydale Dr. WN7 ... 76 C5
Ivygreen Dr. OL4 ... 67 F6
Ivygreen Rd. M'ster M21 ... 109 A8
Ivylea Rd. M19 ... 110 E4
Ivyleaf Sq. M7 ... 155 E6

Jack La. Droylsden M43 ... 84 C2
Jack La. Urmston M41 ... 95 E2
Jack McCann Ct. 10 OL16 ... 31 A8
Jack St. 7 BL2 ... 25 C1
Jack Taylor Ct. OL12 ... 15 B1
Jack's La. BL5 ... 57 A8
Jackdaw Rd. BL8 ... 10 F2
Jackie Brown Wlk. M40 ... 157 D5
Jackman Ave. OL10 ... 46 D7
Jackroom Dr. M4 ... 159 C1
Jackson Ave. Culcheth WA3 ... 91 E3
Jackson Ave. 3
Dukinfield SK16 ... 101 D8
Jackson Cl. OL8 ... 153 E5
Jackson Cres. M15 ... 162 E7
Jackson Ct. M41 ... 95 A3
Jackson Gdns. M34 ... 100 D2
Jackson Pit. 1 OL1 ... 153 E6
Jackson Pl. OL16 ... 31 B8
Jackson St. Cheadle SK8 ... 122 E6
Jackson St. Failsworth M35 ... 83 D6
Jackson St. Farnworth BL4 ... 60 D8
Jackson St. Glossop SK14 ... 104 C5
Jackson St. Glossop SK13 ... 116 C7
Jackson St. Hyde SK14 ... 167 D2
Jackson St. Ince-i-M WN2 ... 56 A7
Jackson St. Kearsley BL4 ... 60 F7
Jackson St. Littleborough OL12 ... 15 C6
Jackson St. Middleton M24 ... 65 B8
Jackson St.
Mottram-i-L SK14 ... 103 A3
Jackson St. Oldham OL4 ... 67 B7
Jackson St. Oldham OL4 ... 67 F6
Jackson St. R'dale OL16 ... 31 B6
Jackson St. Radcliffe M26 ... 44 B2
Jackson St. Sale M33 ... 108 D5
Jackson St. Stretford M32 ... 96 C1
Jackson St. Walkden M28 ... 60 C4
Jackson St. Whitefield M45 ... 62 F7
Jackson's La.
Hazel Grove SK7 ... 133 C8
Jackson's Row. M2 ... 158 F1
Jacksons Edge Rd.
SK12 & SK6 ... 135 B6
Jacob St. WN2 ... 56 D6
Jacobsen Ave. SK14 ... 167 F4
Jaffrey St. WN7 ... 75 E5
James Andrew St. M24 ... 47 B1
James Bentley Wlk. 4 M40 ... 83 C5
James Brindley Basin. 12
M1 ... 159 C1
James Brindley Prim Sch.
M28 ... 60 C1
James Butterworth Ct. 6
OL16 ... 31 B6
James Butterworth St. 9
OL16 ... 31 B6
James Cl. SK16 ... 101 E8
James Corbett Rd. M5 ... 154 D1
James Henry Ave. M5 ... 161 B8
James Hill St. 13 OL15 ... 16 B5
James Leech St. SK1 & SK3 ... 170 E8
James Leigh St. M1 ... 163 A8
James Pl. Coppull PR7 ... 19 E8
James Pl. Standish WN6 ... 19 D2
James Rd. OL2 ... 149 B7
James Sq. WN6 ... 19 D2
James St. Ashton-i-M WN2 ... 73 E7
James St. Bacup OL13 ... 3 B7
James St. Bolton BL7 ... 8 D3
James St. Bury BL9 ... 141 A1
James St. Droylsden M43 ... 84 B2
James St. Dukinfield M34 ... 101 A4
James St. Dukinfield SK16 ... 101 E8
James St. Failsworth M35 ... 84 A7
James St. Glossop SK13 ... 116 C8
James St. Heywood OL10 ... 29 D2
James St. Horwich BL6 ... 21 F3
James St. Ince-i-M WN3 ... 151 D6

Kershaw St. Bolton BL2 25 C5
Kershaw St. Bolton BL3 145 D5
Kershaw St. Bury BL9 141 A2
Kershaw St. Droylsden M43 83 F1
Kershaw St. Dukinfield OL7 100 F8
Kershaw St. Glossop SK13 116 C8
Kershaw St. Heywood OL10 29 B2
Kershaw St. 2 R'dale OL12 139 F8
Kershaw St. Royton OL2 48 D5
Kershaw St. Shaw OL2 149 B7
Kershaw St. Tyldesley M29 59 A1
Kershaw St. Wigan WN5 54 B6
Kershaw St E. OL2 149 B7
Kershaw Way. WA12 89 C5
Kershaw Wlk. M12 164 D6
Kershope Gr. M5 161 A8
Kersley St. OL4 67 B6
Kerswell Wlk. M40 83 A6
Kerwin Wlk. M11 165 A8
Kerwood Dr. OL2 48 E3
Kesteven Rd. M8 & M9 157 D7
Keston Ave. Droylsden M43 83 E1
Keston Ave. M'ster M9 65 A3
Keston Cres. SK5 112 B6
Keston Rd. 4 OL1 49 C1
Kestor St. BL2 148 B7
Kestrel Ave. Droylsden M34 84 C1
Kestrel Ave. Farnworth BL4 59 F7
Kestrel Ave. Oldham OL4 67 C5
Kestrel Ave. Swinton M27 62 B2
Kestrel Ave. Walkden M38 60 A5
Kestrel Cl. Marple SK6 126 A3
Kestrel Cl. Prestwich M25 63 B6
Kestrel Dr. Ashton-i-M WN4 73 C6
Kestrel Dr. Bury BL9 141 B4
Kestrel Dr. Irlam M44 94 A3
Kestrel Rd. M17 95 F8
Kestrel St. 3 BL1 148 A8
Kestrel Wlk. M12 165 A6
Keswick Ave. Ashton-u-L OL7 84 F5
Keswick Ave. Chadderton OL9 152 A7
Keswick Ave. Denton M34 100 D4
Keswick Ave. Dukinfield SK14 101 C4
Keswick Ave. Gatley SK8 122 B4
Keswick Ave. Oldham OL8 67 A3
Keswick Ave. Urmston M41 94 E1
Keswick Cl. Irlam M44 105 D4
Keswick Cl. M'ster M13 164 D5
Keswick Cl. Middleton M24 46 D2
Keswick Cl. Stalybridge SK15 86 A4
Keswick Ct. 3 M24 46 D2
Keswick Dr. Bramhall SK7 132 C5
Keswick Dr. Bury BL9 44 D7
Keswick Gr. M6 154 F2
Keswick Pl. WN2 56 A7
Keswick Rd. Alt'ham WA15 120 D6
Keswick Rd. High Lane SK6 134 E8
Keswick Rd. Reddish SK4 111 D7
Keswick Rd. Walkden M28 60 F2
Keswick St. Bolton BL1 143 F2
Keswick St. R'dale OL11 30 C2
Ketley Wlk. 1 M22 121 F3
Kettering Rd. M19 99 B2
Kettleshulme Way. SK12 134 A3
Kettleshulme Wlk. 4 SK9 131 E1
Kettlewell Wlk. M18 165 C5
Ketton Cl. M11 99 E7
Kevin Ave. OL2 48 E2
Kevin St. M19 111 B8
Kew Ave. SK14 167 E1
Kew Dr. Cheadle SK8 122 E2
Kew Dr. Urmston M41 95 A4
Kew Gdns. M40 65 A1
Kew Rd. Failsworth M35 84 A8
Kew Rd. Oldham OL4 67 C6
Kew Rd. R'dale OL11 31 A3
Key Ct. M34 113 A8
Key West Cl. M11 160 F1
Keyhaven Wlk. M40 157 D6
Keymer St. M11 160 E2
Keynsham Rd. M11 83 B3
Keystone Cl. M6 154 E4
Keyworth Wlk. M40 160 E4
Khartoum St. Droylsden M11 83 D2
Khartoum St. M'ster M16 97 D4
Kibbles Brow. BL7 25 B8
Kibboth Crew. BL0 138 B7
Kibworth Cl. M45 62 D8
Kibworth Wlk. 7 M9 64 E5
Kid St. 4 M24 46 F1
Kidacre Wlk. 2 M40 83 A7
Kidd Rd. SK13 116 E6
Kidderminster Way. OL9 47 F1
Kidwall Wlk. 9 M9 64 F1
Kiel Cl. M30 95 E8
Kilbride Ave. BL2 42 F6
Kilbuck La. WA11 89 A8
Kilburn Ave. Ashton-i-M WN4 73 D4
Kilburn Ave. M'ster M9 64 D5
Kilburn Cl. SK8 131 B7
Kilburn Ct. WN7 57 D1
Kilburn Dr. WN6 36 A7
Kilburn Gr. WN3 54 D3
Kilburn Rd.Orrell WN5 & WN8 53 C5
Kilburn Rd. Radcliffe M26 43 E4
Kilburn Rd. Stockport SK3 123 C7
Kilburn St. 5 OL1 & OL4 49 D1
Kildale Cl. BL3 40 E4
Kildare Cres. OL11 30 F2
Kildare Grange. WN2 56 C5
Kildare Rd. M'ster M21 109 D8
Kildare Rd. Swinton M27 79 E6
Kildare St. Farnworth BL4 60 C7
Kildare St. Hindley WN2 56 C5
Kildare St. Wigan WN5 54 F6
Kildonan Dr. BL3 40 F6
Killer St. BL0 138 C6
Killington Cl. WN3 55 B2
Killingworth Mews. BL6 22 D1
Killon St. BL9 141 A1
Kilmaine Dr. BL3 40 E5
Kilmarsh Wlk. 7 M8 155 F7
Kilmington Dr. M7 & M8 155 F6
Kilmory Dr. BL2 42 F6
Kiln Bank. OL12 4 C2
Kiln Bank La. OL12 4 C2
Kiln Brow. BL7 25 C8
Kiln Croft. SK6 112 F1
Kiln Croft La. SK9 131 E4
Kiln Field. BL7 24 F8
Kiln Hill Cl. OL1 47 F2
Kiln Hill La. OL1 47 F2
Kiln La. Hadfield SK14 104 A5
Kiln La. Milnrow OL16 31 F6
Kiln St. Little Lever BL3 43 A3
Kiln St. Ramsbottom BL0 138 B5
Kiln Terr. 5 OL13 3 D8
Kilner Cl. BL9 45 B4
Kilner Wlk. M40 159 C4
Kilnerdeyne Terr. OL16 139 E6
Kilnhurst Wlk. 12 BL1 145 D8
Kilnside Dr. M9 157 D7
Kilnsley Wlk. M18 165 C5
Kilnwick Cl. M18 99 B3
Kilphin The. BL6 40 B8
Kilrush Ave. M30 95 D8
Kilsby Cl. Bolton BL6 40 D6
Kilsby Cl. Farnworth BL4 42 C2
Kilsby Wlk. M40 160 D4
Kilshaw St. WN5 54 C5
Kilton Wlk. M40 159 C4
Kilvert Dr. M33 107 F5
Kilvert St. Stretford M17 96 F5
Kilworth Ave. M33 107 F3
Kilworth Dr. BL6 40 D6
Kilworth St. OL11 139 D5
Kimberley Ave. SK6 113 C2
Kimberley Pl. WN4 73 B3
Kimberley Rd. BL1 24 E5
Kimberley St. Bacup OL13 3 A7
Kimberley St. M'ster M7 155 F7
Kimberley St. Oldham OL8 66 C3
Kimberley St. Stockport SK3 170 E7
Kimberley Wlk. M15 162 D7
Kimberly St. WN6 37 A1
Kimble Cl. BL8 10 F2
Kimbolton Cl. M12 165 A6
Kinburn Rd. M19 & SK4 110 D2
Kinbury Wlk. M40 159 C4
Kincardine Rd. M13 163 B6
Kincraig Cl. Bolton BL3 40 E4
Kincraig Cl. M'ster M11 83 C1
Kinder Ave. Ashton-u-L OL6 86 A6
Kinder Ave. Oldham OL4 67 D5
Kinder Cl. SK13 116 A8
Kinder Ct. SK3 170 E7
Kinder Dr. SK6 126 A6
Kinder Fold. SK15 102 D6
Kinder Gr. Ashton-i-M WN4 72 F6
Kinder Gr. Romiley SK6 113 E2
Kinder House. M5 154 D3
Kinder Mews. OL3 69 B5
Kinder St. Stalybridge SK15 86 A2
Kinder St. Stockport SK3 170 E7
Kinder Way. Middleton M24 46 F2
Kinder Way. Mottram-i-L SK14 102 F3
Kinders Cres. OL3 69 B5
Kinders La. OL3 69 B6
Kinderton Ave. M20 110 B7
Kineton Wlk. 12 M13 163 C6
King Albert St. OL2 149 B7
King Charles Ct. SK13 116 D7
King David High Sch. M8 63 F1
King David Jun & Inf Schs. M8 63 F1
King Edward Ave. SK13 104 D1
King Edward Rd. SK14 113 E8
King Edward St. Eccles M30 79 C2
King Edward St. 4 M'ster M19 99 B1
King Edward St. Salford M5 161 B8
King Edward's Bldgs. M7 155 F8
King George Cl. WN4 73 B3
King George Rd. Hyde SK14 113 E8
King George Rd. Newton-l-W WA11 89 A7
King La. Oldham OL1 49 E4
King La. Oldham OL1 49 E5
King Sq. OL9 153 E6
King St. 5 Bolton BL7 24 F8
King St. Bolton BL2 25 D5
King St. Bolton BL1 145 E7
King St. Delph OL3 50 F4
King St. Denton M34 100 F3
King St. Denton M34 100 E3
King St. Droylsden M43 100 A8
King St. Dukinfield SK16 101 C7
King St. Eccles M30 79 F3
King St. Failsworth M35 83 D6
King St. Farnworth BL4 60 D8
King St. Glossop SK13 116 C8
King St. Heywood OL10 29 D1
King St. Hindley WN2 56 D6
King St. Hollingworth SK14 103 D5
King St. Horwich BL6 22 A4
King St. Hyde SK14 167 D3
King St. Ince-i-M WN2 56 A7
King St. Leigh WN7 75 F4
King St. M'ster M7 155 E7
King St. M'ster M3 158 E2
King St. M'ster M2 158 F1
King St. Middleton M24 47 A1
King St. Mossley OL5 68 C1
King St. Mottram-i-L SK14 115 A8
King St. Newton-l-W WA12 89 B3
King St. Oldham OL9 153 E6
King St. R'dale OL16 139 F7
King St. Radcliffe M26 44 B2
King St. Ramsbottom BL0 138 C6
King St. Rawtenstall BB4 2 E8
King St. Salford M6 80 D5
King St. 8 Stalybridge SK15 86 A2
King St. Stretford M32 96 D1
King St. Westhoughton BL5 39 F1
King St. Whitworth OL12 4 D3
King St. Wigan WN1 150 C7
King St E. R'dale OL11 139 F6
King St E. Stockport SK1 169 F2
King St S. OL11 139 E5
King St W. M'ster M3 158 F1
King St W. Wigan WN1 150 C8
King William Ent Pk. M5 161 A8
King William St. Salford M5 161 A8
King William St. Tyldesley M29 76 F8
King William St.Worsley M28 79 A3
King's Ave. WA3 90 F7
King's Cl. Droylsden M18 99 F6
King's Cl. Stockport SK7 123 F2
King's Cres. M46 76 E8
King's Dr. M'ster SK4 168 A3
King's Dr. Marple SK6 125 E7
King's Dr. Middleton M24 64 D8
King's Gdns. WN7 76 C5
King's Lynn Cl. 5 M20 110 B3
King's Rd. Ashton-i-M WN4 73 A5
King's Rd. Ashton-u-L OL6 85 E5
King's Rd. M'ster M25 63 C2
King's Rd. Oldham OL8 153 F5
King's Rd. R'dale OL16 31 B5
King's Rd. Reddish M34 100 B6
King's Rd. Romiley SK6 113 A3
King's Rd. Wilmslow SK9 136 E8
King's Terr. 14 SK16 166 B1
King's Wlk. OL6 85 D5
Kingcombe Wlk. 12 M9 157 E8
Kingfisher Ave. M34 84 C1
Kingfisher Cl. M12 164 E5
Kingfisher Ct. Ashton-i-M WN4 73 B6
Kingfisher Ct. R'dale OL12 15 C4
Kingfisher Dr. Bury BL9 141 B4
Kingfisher Dr. Farnworth BL4 59 F7
Kingfisher Mews. SK6 126 A6
Kingfisher Rd. SK2 124 F5
Kingham Dr. M4 159 C2
Kingholm Gdns. BL1 143 D1
Kingmoor Ave. M26 44 B4
Kings Acre. WA14 119 A1
Kings Ave. Gatley SK8 122 A4
Kings Ave. M'ster M8 156 B8
Kings Ave. Whitefield M45 44 E2
Kings Cl. Prestwich M25 63 C5
Kings Cl. Wilmslow SK9 137 A6
Kings Cres. M16 97 B3
Kings Ct. Stockport SK5 169 F3
Kings Ct. 11 Tyldesley M29 58 F1
Kings Dr. SK8 123 A3
Kings Gr. R'dale OL12 15 C4
Kings Gr. Stretford M32 96 F3
Kings La. M16 & M32 96 F3
Kings Rd. Cheadle SK8 123 A3
Kings Rd. Failsworth OL9 65 E3
Kings Rd. Golborne WA3 90 A7
Kings Rd. Hazel Grove SK7 124 E3
Kings Rd. Irlam M44 105 E6
Kings Rd. M'ster M16 & M32 97 B3
Kings Rd. M'ster M16 & M21 109 D8
Kings Rd. Sale M33 107 F4
Kings Rd. Shaw OL2 149 A6
Kings Rd. Stretford M32 96 E2
Kings Road Prim Sch. M16 97 A3
Kings Terr. M32 96 F3
Kings Wlk. M43 100 A8
Kingsbridge Ave. Ainsworth BL2 26 D1
Kingsbridge Ave. Hattersley SK14 102 C2
Kingsbridge Cl. SK6 125 E7
Kingsbridge Ct. M9 157 D7
Kingsbridge Dr. SK16 101 B7
Kingsbridge Rd. M'ster M8 & M9 157 D7
Kingsbridge Rd. 5 Oldham OL8 67 B5
Kingsbridge Wlk. SK14 102 C2
Kingsbrook Ct. M21 109 E8
Kingsbrook Rd. M16 & M21 109 E8
Kingsbury Ave. BL1 142 A1
Kingsbury Ct. BL1 142 A1
Kingsbury Rd. M11 83 C2
Kingscliffe St. M9 157 E8
Kingscourt Ave. BL1 142 C2
Kingscroft Ct. WN1 151 D7
Kingsdale Rd. M18 & M34 100 A4
Kingsdown Cres. WN1 37 C4
Kingsdown Dr. BL1 143 F1
Kingsdown Gdns. 8 BL1 143 F1
Kingsdown Rd. Abram WN2 74 B7
Kingsdown Rd. Wythenshawe M22 121 C1
Kingsdown Wlk. SK5 112 B5
Kingsfield Dr. M20 110 C2
Kingsfield Way. M29 77 B8
Kingsfold Ave. M40 159 C4
Kingsfold Cl. BL2 42 E6
Kingsford St. M5 154 D2
Kingsgate. BL1 145 E7
Kingsgate Rd. M22 121 C1
Kingshill Ct. WN6 36 F7
Kingshill Rd. M21 109 A8
Kingsholme Rd. M22 121 C2
Kingsland Cl. M10 & M40 160 D3
Kingsland Rd. Cheadle SK3 123 A8
Kingsland Rd. Farnworth BL4 42 A1
Kingsland Rd. R'dale OL11 30 B3
Kingslea. PR7 20 F8
Kingslea Rd. M20 110 C5
Kingsleigh Rd. SK4 110 F4
Kingsley Ave. Handforth SK9 131 C2
Kingsley Ave. M'ster M7 81 B7
Kingsley Ave. M'ster M9 157 F7
Kingsley Ave. Reddish SK4 169 E4
Kingsley Ave. Stretford M32 96 F3
Kingsley Ave. Urmston M41 95 B2
Kingsley Ave. Whitefield M45 63 B8
Kingsley Ave. Wigan WN3 54 F3
Kingsley Cl. Ashton-u-L OL6 86 A5
Kingsley Cl. Denton M34 100 D1
Kingsley Dr. Cheadle SK8 123 A3
Kingsley Dr. Oldham OL4 67 E7
Kingsley Gr. M34 100 C8
Kingsley Rd. Alt'ham WA15 120 B7
Kingsley Rd. Hindley WN2 56 F5
Kingsley Rd. Middleton M24 47 B2
Kingsley Rd. Oldham OL4 67 C6
Kingsley Rd. Swinton M27 61 D1
Kingsley Rd. Walkden M28 60 C4
Kingsley Rd. Wythenshawe M22 121 D8
Kingsley St. Bolton BL1 143 D2
Kingsley St. Bury BL8 27 B2
Kingsley St. Leigh WN7 75 C7
Kingsmead Mews. M9 64 C5
Kingsmede. WN1 37 D3
Kingsmere Ave. M19 98 F1
Kingsmill Ave. M19 111 B8
Kingsmoor Fields. SK13 104 D3
Kingsmoor Rd. SK13 104 D2
Kingsneath Ave. M11 83 B3
Kingsnorth Cl. 5 BL1 143 F1
Kingsnorth Rd. M41 94 E4
Kingsoak Cl. WN1 151 D8
Kingston Arc. 6 SK14 102 E2
Kingston Ave. Bolton BL2 25 C1
Kingston Ave. M'ster M20 110 B1
Kingston Ave. 5 Oldham OL1 49 B1
Kingston Ave. Oldham OL9 66 A4
Kingston Cl. Hattersley SK14 102 E2
Kingston Cl. M'ster M7 155 D8
Kingston Cl. Shaw OL2 149 B8
Kingston Cl. Wigan WN3 55 B3
Kingston Cres. BB4 1 A7
Kingston Dr. Royton OL2 48 C6
Kingston Dr. Sale M33 108 D5
Kingston Dr. Urmston M41 107 B8
Kingston Gdns. SK14 101 B3
Kingston Gr. M9 64 F4
Kingston Hill. SK8 122 D4
Kingston Pl. SK8 123 A2
Kingston Rd. Failsworth M35 84 B7
Kingston Rd. Handforth SK9 131 D5
Kingston Rd. M'ster M20 110 B1
Kingston Rd. Radcliffe BL9 44 C6
Kingston St. SK3 169 D1
Kingsway. Alt'ham WA14 119 D5
Kingsway. Bredbury SK6 112 E3
Kingsway. Cheadle M20 & SK8 122 C6
Kingsway. Dukinfield SK16 101 E7
Kingsway. Ince-i-M WN2 151 F7
Kingsway. Kearsley BL4 60 F6
Kingsway. M'ster M19 98 F1
Kingsway. M'ster M19 110 D4
Kingsway. Middleton M24 65 B6
Kingsway. Newton-l-W WA12 89 C2
Kingsway. Pendlebury M27 80 C6
Kingsway. R'dale OL11 & OL16 31 C5
Kingsway. Stockport SK7 123 F2
Kingsway. Stretford M32 96 C1
Kingsway. Walkden M28 78 D8
Kingsway. Wigan WN1 37 D2
Kingsway Ave. M19 98 F1
Kingsway Bldgs. M19 110 E5
Kingsway Cl. OL8 153 E5
Kingsway Cres. M19 110 E5
Kingsway Pk. M41 95 D4
Kingsway Prim Sch. M41 95 E4
Kingsway Sch. SK8 122 C4
Kingswear Dr. BL1 142 C1
Kingswood. SK12 133 E4
Kingswood Gr. SK5 99 F1
Kingswood Rd. M'ster M14 & M19 110 E8
Kingswood Rd.Middleton M24 46 F3
Kingswood Rd. Prestwich M25 62 F5
Kingswood Rd. Swinton M28 79 B4
Kingthorpe Gdns. BL1 147 F4
Kingwood Ave. BL1 40 F8
Kingwood Cres. WN5 54 D6
Kinlet Rd. WN3 54 C4
Kinlett Wlk. 11 M40 65 D2
Kinley Cl. M12 164 F6
Kinloch Dr. BL1 144 B7
Kinloch St. M'ster M11 83 A2
Kinloch St. Oldham OL8 67 A4
Kinmel Ave. SK5 112 C4
Kinmel Wlk. 4 M23 120 F6
Kinmount Wlk. M9 157 D6
Kinnaird Cres. SK1 124 B8
Kinnaird Rd. M20 110 C5
Kinnerly Gr. M29 60 A1
Kinniside Cl. WN3 55 A2
Kinross Ave. Garswood WN4 72 C4
Kinross Ave. Stockport SK2 & SK7 124 A3
Kinross Dr. BL3 40 F5
Kinross Rd. M14 98 E3
Kinsale Wlk. M23 120 F3
Kinsey Ave. M23 120 F7
Kinsley Dr. M28 60 C2
Kintbury St. M4 73 F7
Kintore Ave. SK7 124 F3
Kintore Wlk. 5 M40 156 C5
Kintyre Ave. M5 154 E1
Kintyre Cl. 5 M11 83 C1
Kintyre Dr. BL3 40 E5
Kinver Cl. BL3 146 C3
Kinver Rd. M40 65 C2
Kipling Ave. Denton M34 113 A7
Kipling Ave. Droylsden M43 84 A3
Kipling Ave. Wigan WN3 55 A4
Kipling Cl. SK2 124 E7
Kipling Gr. WN7 75 D7
Kipling Rd. OL1 49 B2
Kipling St. M7 155 D6
Kippax St. M14 98 B3
Kirby Ave. Atherton M46 58 C5
Kirby Ave. Failsworth OL9 65 D3
Kirby Ave. Swinton M27 79 D5
Kirby Rd. WN7 75 E5
Kirby Wlk. 6 M'ster M4 159 C2
Kirby Wlk. Shaw OL2 149 B8
Kirk Rd. M19 111 B7
Kirk St. M18 99 D5
Kirkbank St. Oldham OL9 153 D7
Kirkbank St. Oldham OL9 153 D8
Kirkbeck. WN7 76 C3
Kirkburn View. BL8 27 C5
Kirkby Ave. Failsworth M40 83 B7
Kirkby Ave. Sale M33 108 C2
Kirkby Cl. BL9 44 E7
Kirkby Dr. M33 108 D2
Kirkby Rd. Bolton BL1 144 B8
Kirkby Rd. Culcheth WA3 91 F3
Kirkdale Ave. M40 65 D2
Kirkdale Dr. OL2 48 C5
Kirkdale Gdns. WN8 53 A7
Kirkebrok Rd. BL3 146 A4
Kirkfell Dr. High Lane SK6 134 E8
Kirkfell Dr. Tyldesley M29 77 B7
Kirkfell Wlk. OL1 48 F1
Kirkgate Cl. 8 M10 & M40 159 C3
Kirkhall La. Bolton BL1 144 C8
Kirkhall La. Leigh WN7 75 F6
Kirkhall Wkshp The. BL1 144 C8
Kirkham Ave. Golborne WA3 90 E6
Kirkham Ave. M'ster M18 99 D6
Kirkham Cl. M34 100 F3
Kirkham Rd. Gatley SK8 131 C8
Kirkham Rd. Leigh WN7 75 D2
Kirkham St. Abram WN2 74 B8
Kirkham St. Bolton BL2 25 C1
Kirkham St. Oldham OL9 153 E7
Kirkham St. Salford M5 154 E1
Kirkham St. Walkden M38 60 A5
Kirkhaven Sq. M10 & M40 160 E4
Kirkhill Wlk. 12 M40 65 D2
Kirkholt Wlk. 11 M9 64 E3
Kirkhope Dr. BL1 143 D1
Kirkhope Wlk. BL1 143 D1
Kirklands. Bolton BL2 25 D2
Kirklands. Sale M33 108 A2
Kirklee Ave. OL9 48 A1
Kirklee Rd. OL11 30 D2
Kirklees St. Bury BL8 26 F7
Kirklees St. Wigan WN1 151 E8
Kirklees Wlk. M45 63 B8
Kirkless La. WN2 38 B1
Kirkless St. WN2 38 A3
Kirkless Villas. WN2 38 A2
Kirkley St. SK14 167 E1
Kirklinton Dr. M9 157 D6
Kirkman Ave. M30 95 C8
Kirkman Cl. M18 99 D4
Kirkman St. BL9 44 F3
Kirkmanshulme La. M'ster M12 164 F4
Kirkmanshulme La. M'ster M12 & M18 165 B5
Kirkpatrick St. WN2 57 B3
Kirkstall. 27 OL12 139 E8
Kirkstall Ave. Heywood OL10 29 C3
Kirkstall Ave. Littleborough OL15 16 A7
Kirkstall Cl. SK12 133 D4
Kirkstall Gdns. M26 43 E5
Kirkstall Rd. Middleton M24 46 F3
Kirkstall Rd. Urmston M41 95 E3
Kirkstall Sq. M13 163 C6
Kirkstead Cl. M11 165 A8
Kirkstead Rd. SK8 132 C6
Kirkstile Cres. WN3 54 E2
Kirkstile Pl. M27 61 E4
Kirkstone. WN5 54 C7
Kirkstone Ave. M28 60 F1
Kirkstone Cl. OL1 48 F1
Kirkstone Dr. Middleton M24 46 E2
Kirkstone Dr. Royton OL2 48 D6
Kirkstone Rd. Dukinfield SK14 101 C5
Kirkstone Rd. Failsworth M40 65 C2
Kirktown Wlk. M11 165 C8
Kirkwall Dr. BL2 148 B5
Kirkway. M'ster M9 65 A4
Kirkway. Middleton M24 65 A7
Kirkway. R'dale OL11 30 F2
Kirkwood Dr. M40 159 C4
Kirtley Ave. M30 79 D3
Kirtlington Cl. OL2 149 A5
Kirton Lodge. M25 63 C4
Kirton Wlk. M9 64 C5
Kitchen St. 14 OL16 31 A8
Kitchener Ave. M44 105 C4
Kitchener St. Bolton BL3 42 B3
Kitchener St. Bury BL8 27 B1
Kitepool St. M28 79 A4
Kitt Green Rd. WN5 54 C8
Kitt's Moss La. SK7 132 D6
Kitter St. OL12 15 C3
Kittiwake Cl. M29 77 A7
Kitty Wheeldon Gdns. M33 108 A5
Kiveton Cl. M28 60 C2
Kiveton Dr. WN4 73 C2
Knacks La. OL12 14 A5
Knaresborough Cl. SK5 99 E1
Knaresborough Rd. WN2 56 E4
Knarr Barn La. OL3 50 D3
Knarr La. OL3 50 E2
Kneller Wlk. OL1 49 D4
Knight Cres. M24 46 D4
Knight St. Ashton-u-L OL7 84 F2
Knight St. Bolton BL1 145 F8
Knight St. Bury BL8 27 C2
Knight St. Hyde SK14 167 E1
Knight St. M'ster M20 110 B2
Knight's Cl. M25 63 B5
Knightley Wlk. M40 157 D5
Knights Ct. M30 80 A2
Knightsbridge. SK1 169 F2
Knightsbridge Cl. M7 155 D8
Knightscliffe Cres. WN6 35 D6
Knightshill Cres. WN6 37 A1
Kniveton Rd. M12 164 F6
Knivton St. SK14 167 F3
Knob Hall Gdns. M23 120 F3
Knole Ave. SK12 133 F4
Knoll St. M'ster M7 155 D7
Knoll St. R'dale OL11 30 C2
Knoll The. Alt'ham WA14 119 B5
Knoll The. Mossley OL5 68 B1
Knoll The. Shaw OL2 149 C6
Knott Fold. SK14 167 D1
Knott Hill La. OL3 50 E3
Knott Hill St. OL12 4 E6
Knott La. Bolton BL1 23 F2
Knott La. Hyde SK14 113 E8
Knott Lanes. OL8 84 F8
Knott St. M5 154 D1
Knott's Houses. WN7 91 C8
Knotts Brow. BL7 9 F4
Knowe Ave. 5 M22 121 D1
Knowl Cl. Ramsbottom BL0 11 C4
Knowl Cl. Reddish M34 100 B2
Knowl Hill Dr. OL12 13 E2
Knowl La. OL12 13 B5
Knowl Meadow. BB4 1 A6
Knowl Rd. Milnrow OL16 31 D6
Knowl Rd. Shaw OL2 149 C6
Knowl St. Oldham OL8 66 C2
Knowl St. Stalybridge SK15 86 B2
Knowl Syke St. OL12 15 C7
Knowl Top La. OL3 69 D7
Knowl View. Bury BL8 27 A6
Knowl View. Littleborough OL15 15 F2
Knowl View Res Sch. OL11 29 E7
Knowldale Way. M12 164 E5
Knowle Ave. OL7 166 A4
Knowle Dr. M25 63 A2
Knowle Gn. SK9 131 C3
Knowle Pk. SK9 131 C3
Knowle Rd. SK6 126 D6
Knowle Way. 5 SK14 102 F2
Knowles Ave. WN3 54 F4
Knowles Ct. M6 80 B3
Knowles Edge St. BL1 142 C2
Knowles Pl. 1 M'ster M15 162 F6
Knowles Pl. Wigan WN1 151 E8
Knowles St. Bolton BL1 25 A1
Knowles St. Ince-i-M WN3 151 D6
Knowles St. Radcliffe M26 44 A4
Knowles The. OL8 66 C1
Knowls La. OL4 67 F5
Knowlsley Grange. BL1 40 D7
Knowsley. OL4 68 A7
Knowsley Ave. Atherton M46 58 C4
Knowsley Ave. Golborne WA3 74 B1
Knowsley Ave. Oldham OL4 68 A7
Knowsley Ave. Salford M5 161 B8
Knowsley Ave. Urmston M41 95 C4
Knowsley Cres. Stockport SK1 124 B8
Knowsley Cres. Whitworth OL12 4 E6
Knowsley Dr. Leigh WN7 75 E2
Knowsley Dr. Oldham OL4 68 A7
Knowsley Dr. Swinton M27 79 D5
Knowsley Gn. Oldham OL4 68 A7
Knowsley Gn. Salford M5 161 B8
Knowsley Gr. BL6 22 D1
Knowsley Jun Sch. OL4 68 A7
Knowsley Park Way. BB4 1 B8
Knowsley Rd. Ainsworth BL2 26 C1
Knowsley Rd. Bolton BL1 142 B2
Knowsley Rd. Haslingden BB4 1 B8
Knowsley Rd. Hazel Grove SK7 133 F8
Knowsley Rd. Stockport SK1 124 B8
Knowsley Rd. Whitefield M45 62 F8
Knowsley Rd. Wigan WN6 37 A3
Knowsley Rd Ind Est. BB4 1 B8
Knowsley St. Bolton BL1 145 F7
Knowsley St. Bury BL9 140 E1
Knowsley St. Leigh WN7 75 D5
Knowsley St. M'ster M8 159 A4
Knowsley St. R'dale OL12 139 E8
Knowsley Terr. OL4 68 A7
Knutsford Ave. M'ster M16 97 D3
Knutsford Ave. Reddish SK4 111 D7
Knutsford Ave. Sale M33 108 E4
Knutsford Rd. M'ster M18 99 C4
Knutsford Rd. Wilmslow SK9 & WA16 136 D3
Knutsford St. M6 154 E2
Knutsford View. WA15 129 C8
Knutshaw Cres. BL3 40 E2
Knypersley Ave. SK2 124 C7
Kranj Way. OL1 153 F7
Krokus Sq. OL9 152 A7
Kyle Rd. SK7 124 F1
Kylemore Ave. BL3 144 B5
Kynder St. M34 100 F3

Labtec St. M27 62 B1
Laburnum Ave. Ashton-u-L OL6 85 C6
Laburnum Ave. Atherton M46 58 E3
Laburnum Ave. Bury BL8 26 F7
Laburnum Ave. Droylsden M34 84 C1
Laburnum Ave. Eccles M30 95 A8
Laburnum Ave. Failsworth M35 83 F6
Laburnum Ave. Hyde SK14 113 D8
Laburnum Ave. Ince-i-M WN3 151 F6
Laburnum Ave. Leigh WN7 75 E8
Laburnum Ave. Oldham OL9 48 C1
Laburnum Ave. Shaw OL2 149 B6
Laburnum Ave. Stalybridge SK15 101 F8
Laburnum Ave. Swinton M27 79 E6
Laburnum Ave. Whitefield M45 62 F7
Laburnum Ct. BL8 26 F7
Laburnum Dr. Whitefield M45 & BL9 45 A1
Laburnum Dr. Wigan WN6 37 A4
Laburnum Gr. Horwich BL6 22 E1
Laburnum Gr. Prestwich M25 63 A5
Laburnum Gr. Tyldesley M29 59 D1
Laburnum La. Alt'ham WA15 128 E8
Laburnum La. Newhey OL16 32 A3
Laburnum Pk. BL2 25 B5
Laburnum Rd. Farnworth BL4 60 B8
Laburnum Rd. Golborne WA3 90 F7
Laburnum Rd. Haslingden BB4 1 A7
Laburnum Rd. Irlam M44 105 D5
Laburnum Rd. M'ster M18 99 D4
Laburnum Rd. Middleton M24 65 C8
Laburnum Rd. Oldham OL8 84 C8
Laburnum Rd. Reddish M34 99 F3
Laburnum Rd. Urmston M41 95 B4
Laburnum Rd. Walkden M28 60 E1
Laburnum St.Ashton-i-M WN4 73 B2
Laburnum St. Atherton M46 58 E3
Laburnum St. 7 Bolton BL1 145 D8
Laburnum St. Salford M6 154 F2
Laburnum Terr. OL11 30 E4
Laburnum Villas. OL8 67 A1
Laburnum Way. Littleborough OL15 15 F5
Laburnum Way. Stockport SK3 123 B8
Laburnum Wlk. 1 M33 107 C5
Lacey Ave. SK9 131 B1

Lower Wheat End. OL16 31 B8
Lower Woodhill Rd. BL8 140 D3
Lowerbank. M34 100 F5
Lowerbrook Cty Prim Sch. BL8 26 F2
Lowercroft Rd. BL8 26 F2
Lowerfield Dr. SK2 124 F5
Lowerfields. OL8 67 B4
Lowerfold Cl. OL12 14 C4
Lowerfold Cres. OL12 14 C4
Lowerfold Dr. OL12 14 C4
Lowerfold Way. OL12 14 C4
Lowerford Ave. OL2 49 A4
Lowerlea. SK12 135 C6
Lowerplace Cty Prim Sch. OL16 31 B4
Lowerwood La. 12 BL2 25 B1
Lowes Park Golf Cse. BL9 28 A7
Lowes Rd. BL9 28 A6
Lowes The. WA14 119 B1
Lowestead Rd. 9 M11 83 C2
Lowestoft St. M14 98 B2
Loweswater Ave. M29 77 A7
Loweswater Rd. SK8 122 B3
Loweswater Terr. SK15 86 A4
Lowfell Wlk. M18 99 D3
Lowfield Ave. Ashton-u-L OL6 85 F5
Lowfield Ave. Droylsden M43 83 F3
Lowfield Gdns. WA3 92 C7
Lowfield Gr. SK2 170 F7
Lowfield Rd. SK2 & SK3 170 E7
Lowfield Wlk. 7 M9 64 E3
Lowhouse Cl. OL16 32 A7
Lowick Ave. BL3 42 A3
Lowick Cl. SK7 124 D2
Lowick Gn. SK6 112 F5
Lowland Gr. OL7 85 A6
Lowland Rd. SK2 124 B4
Lowlands Cl. M24 65 C5
Lowndes Cl. SK2 124 B7
Lowndes La. SK1 & SK2 124 B7
Lowndes St. BL1 142 B1
Lowndes Wlk. 5 M13 163 C6
Lownorth Rd. M22 130 E8
Lowood Ave. M41 94 F4
Lowood Cl. OL16 31 F6
Lowood St. WN7 75 D5
Lowrey Wlk. 11 M9 157 E7
Lowry. M30 79 E2
Lowry Ct. SK14 103 A4
Lowry Dr. Marple SK6 126 B8
Lowry Dr. Swinton M27 61 F1
Lowry Gr. SK14 102 F3
Lowry Heritage Ctr (Art Gal & Mus). M6 81 C2
Lowry House. 4 M14 110 D8
Lowry Wlk. BL1 143 D1
Lows The. OL4 67 B5
Lowside Ave. Bolton BL1 & BL6 40 C6
Lowside Ave. Romiley SK6 113 C5
Lowside Dr. OL4 67 B5
Lowstern Cl. BL7 8 E1
Lowther Ave. Alt'ham WA15 120 A6
Lowther Ave. Culcheth WA3 91 F4
Lowther Ave. M'ster M18 99 B3
Lowther Ave. Royton OL2 48 C8
Lowther Cl. M25 63 A3
Lowther Cres. M24 46 D1
Lowther Ct. M25 62 F3
Lowther Dr. WN7 76 E7
Lowther Gdns. M41 94 D3
Lowther Rd. M'ster M8 64 A1
Lowther Rd. Prestwich M25 62 F3
Lowther Rd. R'dale OL11 30 E4
Lowther St. BL3 42 A3
Lowther Terr. WN6 35 C8
Lowthorpe St. M14 98 A2
Lowton Ave. M9 157 F7
Lowton Comm High Sch. WA3 91 B8
Lowton Gdns. WA3 90 B5
Lowton Jun & Inf Sch. WA3 91 A7
Lowton Rd. Golborne WA3 74 C1
Lowton Rd. Sale M33 107 D2
Lowton St. M26 44 A4
Lowton West Cty Prim Sch. WA3 90 D8
Loxford Ct. M15 162 F6
Loxford St. M15 162 F6
Loxham St. BL4 42 D2
Loxley Wlk. M40 160 E4
Loxton Cres. WN3 55 B3
Loynd St. BL0 11 D6
Lubeck St. M9 157 E8
Lucas Rd. BL4 60 A7
Lucas St. Bury BL9 141 A3
Lucas St. Oldham OL4 67 B7
Lucas Wlk. M11 164 F8
Lucerne Cl. OL9 152 C6
Lucerne Rd. SK7 123 E3
Lucien Cl. M12 164 E5
Luciol Cl. M29 59 D1
Lucknow St. OL11 139 F5
Lucy St. Bolton BL1 142 A1
Lucy St. M'ster M7 155 D5
Lucy St. M'ster M15 162 D6
Lucy St. Stockport SK3 170 E8
Ludford Gr. M33 107 F1
Ludgate Hill. M4 159 B3
Ludgate Rd. Failsworth M40 83 C4
Ludgate Rd. R'dale OL11 31 A2
Ludgate St. M4 159 A3
Ludlow Ave. Hindley WN2 57 A4
Ludlow Ave. Prestwich M25 & M45 63 B6
Ludlow Ave. Swinton M27 62 A2
Ludlow Dr. WN7 76 E7
Ludlow Pk. 2 OL4 67 D6
Ludlow Rd. SK1 & SK2 124 C8
Ludlow St. WN6 19 D3
Ludovic Terr. WN1 37 C4
Ludwell Wlk. 12 M8 156 A6
Ludworth Prim Sch. SK6 126 B8
Lugano Rd. SK7 123 E3
Luke Kirby Ct. M27 61 F1
Luke Rd. M43 84 B1
Luke St. Ashton-i-M WN4 73 D5
Luke St. 17 Bacup OL13 3 C8
Luke Wlk. M8 156 B6
Lullington Cl. M22 121 C1
Lullington Rd. M6 154 D4
Lulworth Ave. M41 94 F2
Lulworth Cl. BL8 27 C6
Lulworth Cres. M35 84 B8
Lulworth Dr. WN2 57 A4
Lulworth Gdns. M23 120 F8
Lulworth Rd. Bolton BL3 146 A3
Lulworth Rd. Eccles M30 79 C3
Lulworth Rd. Middleton M24 47 A2
Lum Head Jun Sch. SK8 122 B3
Lum St. BL1 148 A8
Lumb Carr Ave. BL0 & BL8 11 A4
Lumb Carr Rd. BL0 & BL8 11 A4
Lumb Cl. SK7 132 E6
Lumb Cotts. BL0 1 A4
Lumb Flats. BL0 1 A4
Lumb Holes La. BB4 2 E7
Lumb La. Bramhall SK7 132 E6
Lumb La. Droylsden M34,M43 84 C1
Lumb La. Droylsden M43 84 C3
Lumb La. Droylsden M35, M43, OL7 84 D4
Lumb La. Droylsden M34 100 C8
Lumber La. M28 78 E8
Lumley Cl. M14 98 B4
Lumn Hollow. SK14 167 E2
Lumn Rd. SK14 167 E2
Lumn St. BL9 27 F8
Lumn's La. M27 62 C1
Lumsden St. BL3 145 E5
Lumwood. BL1 142 B3
Luna St. M4 159 B2
Lund Ave. M26 62 B8
Lundale Wlk. 13 M40 83 A6
Lundy Ave. M21 109 C5
Lune Cl. Whitefield M45 45 A1
Lune Dr. M45 63 A8
Lune Gr. Heywood OL10 29 B3
Lune Gr. Leigh WN7 75 C5
Lune Rd. WN2 56 A2
Lune St. Oldham OL8 66 E4
Lune St. Tyldesley M29 76 F8
Lune Way. SK5 111 F5
Lune Wlk. Droylsden M43 100 B8
Lune Wlk. Whitefield M45 63 A8
Lunedale Gn. SK2 124 E6
Lunehurst. WA3 90 E8
Lunn Ave. M18 99 F6
Lupin Ave. BL4 42 A1
Lupton St. Denton M34 100 F4
Lupton St. M'ster M3 158 D2
Lurden Wlk. OL9 66 B4
Lurdin La. WN1 & WN6 37 B7
Lurgan Ave. M33 108 C3
Lutener St. WA14 119 C8
Luton Dr. M23 121 A4
Luton Gr. M46 58 B3
Luton Rd. SK5 111 F8
Luton St. Bolton BL3 42 A4
Luton St. 3 Bury BL8 27 B1
Luxor Gr. M34 99 F3
Luzley Brook Rd. OL2 149 A5
Luzley Rd. OL5 & OL6 & SK15 86 B7
Lyceum Pl. M15 163 A7
Lychgate. WN5 54 E5
Lychgate Ct. OL4 67 E4
Lychgate Mews. SK4 110 E2
Lychwood. 11 SK6 125 F6
Lydbrook Cl. BL1 145 E6
Lydden Ave. M11 83 D3
Lydford. OL11 139 E6
Lydford Gdns. BL2 42 F6
Lydford Gn. Standish WN6 36 F8
Lydford St. M6 81 B4
Lydford Wlk. M13 163 C6
Lydgate Ave. BL2 42 E8
Lydgate Cl. Denton M34 101 B1
Lydgate Cl. Mossley SK15 86 E6
Lydgate Cl. Whitefield M45 45 A1
Lydgate Dr. OL4 67 D5
Lydgate Fold. OL4 68 C5
Lydgate Prim Sch. OL4 68 C6
Lydgate Rd. Droylsden M43 83 E2
Lydgate Rd. Sale M33 108 C2
Lydgate The. OL15 16 E6
Lydgate Wlk. M45 45 A1
Lydiat La. SK9 137 A1
Lydney Ave. SK8 131 C7
Lydney Rd. M41 94 D3
Lyefield Ave. WN1 37 F1
Lyefield Wlk. 24 OL16 31 B6
Lymbridge Dr. BL6 21 D1
Lyme Ave. SK9 131 B1
Lyme Clough Way. M24 46 F4
Lyme Gr. Alt'ham WA14 119 C4
Lyme Gr. Droylsden M43 99 F8
Lyme Gr. Marple SK6 125 F5
Lyme Gr. Romiley SK6 113 D2
Lyme Gr. Stockport SK2, SK3 170 F7
Lyme Park Ctry Pk. SK12 135 B2
Lyme Rd. Disley SK12 134 C3
Lyme Rd. Hazel Grove SK7 124 E1
Lyme Rd. High Lane SK12 135 A6
Lyme St. Hazel Grove SK7 124 D3
Lyme St. M'ster SK4 110 F2
Lyme Terr. 1 SK16 166 B1
Lymefield Dr. M28 78 A7
Lymefield Gr. SK2 124 B6
Lymefield Terr. SK14 115 B6
Lymewood Dr. Disley SK12 135 C6
Lymewood Dr. Wilmslow SK9 137 E8
Lymington Cl. M24 65 B5
Lymington Dr. M23 108 D1
Lymm Cl. Stockport SK3 170 D6
Lymm Cl. Walkden M28 60 A3
Lymm High Sch. WA13 117 B3
Lymm Rd. WA13 & WA14 118 B1
Lymm Wlk. SK8 123 A5
Lymn St. WN2 56 B3
Lyn Gr. OL10 29 A3
Lyncombe Cl. SK8 132 B6
Lyndale Ave. Reddish M34,SK5 99 F3
Lyndale Ave. Swinton M27 79 D6
Lyndale Dr. OL15 16 A6
Lyndene Ave. M28 79 A8
Lyndene Ct. OL10 29 C3
Lyndene Gdns. SK8 122 B6
Lyndene Rd. M22 121 D5
Lyndhurst Av.Ashton-u-L OL6 85 B5
Lyndhurst Av. Bredbury SK6 112 F4
Lyndhurst Ave. Denton M34 100 E3
Lyndhurst Ave. Hazel Grove SK7 124 C1
Lyndhurst Ave. Irlam M44 94 B3
Lyndhurst Ave. M'ster M25 63 E3
Lyndhurst Ave. Middleton OL11 47 D8
Lyndhurst Ave. Oldham OL9 65 F5
Lyndhurst Ave. Sale M33 107 F3
Lyndhurst Ave. Urmston M41 95 C4
Lyndhurst Cl. SK9 136 D5
Lyndhurst Dr. WA15 120 A2
Lyndhurst Prim & Comm Sch. SK16 166 C1
Lyndhurst Prim Sch. OL8 66 D3
Lyndhurst Rd. M'ster M20 110 B5
Lyndhurst Rd. Oldham OL8 66 D3
Lyndhurst Rd. Reddish SK5 99 E2
Lyndhurst Rd. Stretford M32 96 B3
Lyndhurst St. M5 154 E2
Lyndhurst View. SK16 166 C1
Lyndon Ave. WN6 36 A7
Lyndon Cl. Bury BL8 26 F6
Lyndon Cl. Oldham OL4 68 B8
Lyndon Croft. OL8 66 C4
Lyndon Rd. M44 93 F2
Lyne Ave. SK13 116 A8
Lyne Edge Cres. SK16 101 F7
Lyne Edge Rd. SK16 102 A7
Lyne View. SK14 101 F6
Lyneham Wlk. 10 M'ster M9 64 E5
Lyneham Wlk. M'ster M8 155 F6
Lyngard Cl. SK9 131 E1
Lyngarth House. 1 WA14 119 E6
Lyngate Cl. SK1 124 A8
Lynham Dr. OL10 46 D8
Lynmouth Ave. M'ster M20 110 A6
Lynmouth Ave. Oldham OL8 66 F3
Lynmouth Ave. 10 Reddish SK5 111 E7
Lynmouth Ave. Royton OL2 48 C3
Lynmouth Ave. Urmston M41 107 B8
Lynmouth Cl.Chadderton OL9 47 E1
Lynmouth Cl. Radcliffe M26 44 C4
Lynmouth Cl. Wigan WN6 37 A2
Lynmouth Ct. M25 62 F3
Lynmouth Gr. M25 62 F3
Lynn Ave. M33 108 D6
Lynn Dr. M43 83 E2
Lynn St. OL9 66 C4
Lynne Cl. SK13 116 F8
Lynnwood Dr. OL11 30 B8
Lynnwood Rd. M19 110 D2
Lynroyle Way. OL11 30 D3
Lynside Wlk. M22 130 E8
Lynsted Ave. BL3 42 A3
Lynstock Way. BL6 39 E6
Lynthorpe Ave. M44 105 D6
Lynthorpe Rd. M40 65 D2
Lynton Ave. Hattersley SK14 102 C2
Lynton Ave. Irlam M44 105 E6
Lynton Ave. Oldham OL8 66 C2
Lynton Ave. R'dale OL11 30 B3
Lynton Ave. Royton OL2 48 C3
Lynton Ave. Swinton M27 61 F1
Lynton Ave. Urmston M41 94 C2
Lynton Ave. Wigan WN6 37 A3
Lynton Cl. OL9 47 F1
Lynton Cres. M28 78 D8
Lynton Dr. High Lane SK6 134 E8
Lynton Dr. M'ster M19 110 F7
Lynton Dr. Prestwich M25 63 C6
Lynton Gr. Alt'ham WA15 119 F5
Lynton La. SK9 137 A2
Lynton Lea. M26 44 C4
Lynton Park Rd. SK8 131 F8
Lynton Rd. Bolton BL3 146 C2
Lynton Rd. Cheadle SK8 122 C5
Lynton Rd. Hindley WN2 56 F6
Lynton Rd. M'ster M21 97 A1
Lynton Rd. M'ster SK4 111 C5
Lynton Rd. Swinton M27 61 F1
Lynton Rd. Tyldesley M29 77 D8
Lynton St. Leigh WN7 75 D5
Lynton St. M'ster M14 98 B2
Lynton Wlk. SK14 102 C2
Lyntonvale Ave. SK8 122 B6
Lynway Dr. M20 110 B5
Lynway Gr. M24 47 B2
Lynwell Rd. M30 79 D2
Lynwood. Alt'ham WA15 129 A8
Lynwood. Wilmslow SK9 137 A6
Lynwood Ave. Bolton BL3 42 B2
Lynwood Ave. Eccles M30 79 D2
Lynwood Ave. Golborne WA3 90 E6
Lynwood Ave. M'ster M16 97 C2
Lynwood Cl. OL7 85 A7
Lynwood Ct. M8 63 F2
Lynwood Dr. OL4 67 E8
Lynwood Gr. Atherton M46 58 B3
Lynwood Gr. Bolton BL2 25 D4
Lynwood Gr. Droylsden M34 84 C1
Lynwood Gr. Reddish SK4 111 C6
Lynwood Gr. Sale M33 108 C5
Lyon Gr. M28 79 A8
Lyon Ind Est. WA14 119 B7
Lyon Rd. Alt'ham WA14 119 C7
Lyon Rd. Kearsley BL4 60 E6
Lyon St. Ashton-i-M WN4 72 F7
Lyon St. Shaw OL2 149 B7
Lyon St. Swinton M27 & M28 79 E7
Lyon St. Wigan WN3 150 B7
Lyons Dr. BL8 27 A1
Lyons Fold. M33 108 B6
Lyons Rd. M17 96 A7
Lysander Cl. M14 110 B8
Lyth St. M14 110 D7
Lytham Ave. M21 109 C7
Lytham Cl. OL6 85 E6
Lytham Dr. Bramhall SK7 133 A7
Lytham Dr. Heywood OL10 29 C1
Lytham Rd. Ashton-i-M WN4 72 F5
Lytham Rd. Gatley SK8 122 B1
Lytham Rd. M'ster M14, M19 98 F1
Lytham Rd. Urmston M41 94 C2
Lytham St. R'dale OL12 14 E3
Lytham St. Stockport SK3 170 F6
Lytherton Ave. M44 105 D4
Lytton Ave. M7 & M8 156 A6
Lytton Rd. M43 84 A2
Lytton St. BL1 143 D2

Mab's Cross Prim Sch. WN1 37 D1
Mabel Ave. Bolton BL3 42 A3
Mabel Ave. Swinton M28 79 A7
Mabel Rd. M35 66 A1
Mabel St. 9 Bolton BL1 144 C8
Mabel St. Failsworth M40 83 D5
Mabel St. R'dale OL12 14 D2
Mabel St. Westhoughton BL5 57 F6
Mabel St. Wigan WN5 54 E6
Mabel's Brow. BL4 60 E7
Maberry Cl. WN6 35 D7
Mabfield Rd. M14 98 C1
Mableden Cl. SK8 131 D8
Mabs Ct. OL6 85 D2
Macaulay St. R'dale OL11 30 D2
Macaulay St. Royton OL2 48 E4
Macaulay Way. 7 M34 113 A8
Macauley Cl. SK16 102 A7
Macauley Pl. WN3 54 F4
Macauley Rd. M'ster M16 97 B2
Macauley Rd. Reddish SK5 99 E1
Macclesfield Cl. WN2 56 C5
Macclesfield Rd. Alderley Edge SK9 137 B1
Macclesfield Rd. Hazel Grove SK7 133 F8
Macclesfield Rd. Wilmslow SK9 137 D6
Macdonald Ave. Farnworth BL4 60 B7
Macdonald Ave. Wigan WN3 55 A3
Macdonald Rd. M44 105 E8
Macdonald St. Oldham OL8 66 F4
Macdonald St. Wigan WN5 54 B6
Macefin Ave. M21 109 D4
Macfarren St. M12 99 A3
Macintosh Way. OL1 153 F7
Mackenzie Ave. WN3 55 A3
Mackenzie Gr. BL1 24 D5
Mackenzie Ind Pk.SK3,SK8 123 B6
Mackenzie Rd. M7 81 B6
Mackenzie St. Bolton BL1 143 D4
Mackenzie St. M'ster M12 & M18 99 A3
Mackenzie Wlk. OL1 49 E5
Mackeson Dr. OL6 85 E4
Mackeson Rd. OL6 85 E4
Maclaren Dr. M8 63 E1
Maclaren House. 11 M6 154 F3
Maclure Cl. M16 97 E3
Maclure Rd. OL11 139 F6
Macmillan St. OL11 & OL12 139 E7
Macnair Ct. SK6 126 A5
Macnair Mews. SK6 126 A5
Madams Wood Rd. M28 60 A3
Maddison Rd. M43 99 F8
Madeley Cl. Alt'ham WA14 128 E8
Madeley Cl. Wigan WN3 54 E3
Madeley Dr. OL9 152 B6
Madeley Gdns. Bolton BL1 143 E2
Madeley Gdns. R'dale OL12 14 C1
Maden St. M29 76 F6
Maden Wlk. OL9 152 B8
Maden's Sq. 9 OL15 16 B5
Madison Ave. Cheadle SK8 123 A3
Madison Av. Droylsden M34 100 C8
Madison Gdns. M35 83 E7
Madison St. M18 99 F6
Madras Rd. SK3 123 C7
Maesbrook Dr. M29 77 A8
Mafeking Ave. BL9 28 A5
Mafeking Pl. WN4 73 C3
Mafeking Rd. BL2 42 E7
Mafeking St. OL8 66 C3
Magda Rd. SK2 124 D5
Magdala St. Heywood OL10 46 E8
Magdala St. Oldham OL1 153 E8
Magdalen Dr. WN4 72 F4
Magdalen Wlk. M15 162 E7
Magna Carta Ct. M6 80 B6
Magnolia Cl. 5 Partington M31 105 E2
Magnolia Cl. Sale M33 107 C6
Magnolia Ct. 5 Sale M33 107 C6
Magnolia Ct. 7 Salford M6 81 A2
Magnolia Dr. M7 & M8 156 A6
Magpie Cl. M43 84 C3
Magpie La. OL4 67 E4
Magpie Wlk. 8 M11 160 F1
Maher Gdns. M15 97 E4
Mahogany Wlk. 11 M33 107 C5
Mahood St. SK3 170 D7
Maida St. M12 99 B2
Maiden Cl. 5 OL7 85 A6
Maiden Mews. 4 M27 79 F7
Maidford Cl. M'ster M4 160 D1
Maidford Cl. Stretford M32 96 E2
Maidstone Ave. M21 97 A1
Maidstone Cl. WN2 57 C2
Maidstone Mews. 2 M21 97 A1
Maidstone Rd. M19 & SK4 110 D3
Maidstone Wlk. M34 101 A1
Main Ave. M'ster M19 110 F7
Main Ave. Stretford M17,M32 96 C4
Main La. WA3 90 F3
Main Rd. Oldham OL9 152 C7
Main Rd. Swinton M27 62 C3
Main St. Billinge WN5 71 E5
Main St. Failsworth M35 83 F8
Main St. Hyde SK14 167 D4
Maine Rd. M14 98 A3
Maine Rd (Manchester City FC). M14 98 A2
Mainhill Wlk. M40 83 C5
Mainprice Cl. M6 154 F4
Mains Ave. WN2 73 F7
Mainwaring Dr. SK9 137 D8
Mainway. M24 64 F6
Mainway E. M24 65 C6
Mainwood Rd. WA15 120 C5
Maismore Rd. M22 121 B1
Maitland Ave. M21 109 D5
Maitland Cl. R'dale OL12 15 C3
Maitland Cl. Walsden OL14 6 A8
Maitland St. Stockport SK1 124 B7
Maitland St. Walsden OL14 6 A8
Maitland Wlk. OL9 152 B8
Maizefield Cl. M33 108 F4
Major St. M'ster M1 163 A8
Major St. Milnrow OL16 31 F6
Major St. Ramsbottom BL0 138 B6
Major St. Wigan WN5 54 C6
Makants Cl. M46 58 F5
Makepeace Wlk. M8 63 E2
Makerfield Way. WN2 56 B7
Makin Ct. OL10 29 D1
Makin St. M1 163 A7
Makinson Arc. 15 WN1 150 C8
Makinson Ave. Hindley WN2 56 E7
Makinson Ave. Horwich BL6 22 E1
Makinson La. BL6 22 F4
Makkah Cl. M40 83 A5
Malaga Ave. M90 130 B7
Malakoff St. SK15 85 E1
Malbrook Wlk. 3 M13 163 C6
Malby St. OL1 153 F8
Malcolm Ave. M27 62 A3
Malcolm Dr. M27 62 A2
Malcolm St. OL11 30 D3
Malden Gr. M23 121 A7
Maldon Cl. Hazel Grove SK2 125 A6
Maldon Cl. Wigan WN2 37 F2
Maldon Cres. M27 79 F6
Maldon Dr. M30 79 E4
Maldon Rd. WN6 36 F8
Maldon St. OL11 139 F5
Maldwyn Ave. Bolton BL3 146 C2
Maldwyn Ave. M'ster M8 64 A2
Maleham St. M7 155 E6
Malgam Dr. M20 122 B8
Malham Ave. WN3 55 A2
Malham Cl. Leigh WN7 75 C5
Malham Cl. Royton OL2 48 D4
Malham Cl. Whitefield M45 45 A3
Malham Ct. SK2 124 D6
Malham Gdns. 6 BL3 146 C3
Malimson Bourne. M7 155 D6
Mall The. Bury BL9 140 F2
Mall The. 5 Eccles M30 79 F2
Mall The. Hyde SK14 167 D2
Mall The. Sale M33 108 B5
Mall The. Stalybridge SK15 102 E6
Mallaig Wlk. M11 165 C8
Mallard Cl. Dukinfield SK16 101 E7
Mallard Cl. Hazel Grove SK2 125 A5
Mallard Cl. 1 Oldham OL8 66 D2
Mallard Cres. SK12 133 A4
Mallard Ct. SK8 131 B8
Mallard Dr. BL6 22 A3
Mallard Gn. WA14 119 B8
Mallard St. M1 163 A7
Mallet Cres. BL1 23 F2
Malley Wlk. 18 M9 64 E3
Malling Rd. M23 121 A4
Mallison St. BL1 143 F3
Mallory Ave. OL7 85 A6
Mallory Ct. WA14 119 C3
Mallory Dr. WN7 76 C5
Mallory Rd. SK14 102 D2
Mallory Wlk. M23 120 D8
Mallow St. M15 162 E6
Mallow Wlk. M31 105 F2
Mallowdale. M28 78 B8
Mallowdale Cl. BL1 40 D7
Mallowdale Rd. SK2 124 E5
Mally Gdns. OL5 86 D8
Malmesbury Cl. SK12 133 D4
Malmesbury Rd. SK8 132 B6
Malpas Ave. WN1 37 E1
Malpas Cl. Cheadle SK8 123 A4
Malpas Cl. Handforth SK9 131 E1
Malpas Dr. WA14 107 E1
Malpas St. M'ster M12 165 A6
Malpas St. Oldham OL1 153 F7
Malpas Wlk. M16 162 D5
Malsham Rd. M23 108 F2
Malt St. M15 162 D7
Malta Cl. M24 65 D8
Malta St. M'ster M4 160 D1
Malta St. Oldham OL4 67 D6
Maltby Dr. BL3 146 C3
Maltby Rd. M23 120 F6
Malton Ave. Bolton BL3 146 A4
Malton Ave. Golborne WA3 90 E7
Malton Ave. M'ster M21 109 B8
Malton Ave. Whitefield M45 44 F2
Malton Cl. Chadderton OL9 47 F1
Malton Cl. Leigh WN7 75 C6
Malton Cl. 1 Whitefield M45 44 F2
Malton Dr. Alt'ham WA14 119 A6
Malton Dr. Hazel Grove SK7 133 D7
Malton Rd. Boothstown M28 77 E7
Malton Rd. M'ster SK4 168 A4
Malton St. OL8 153 D5
Malus Ct. M6 81 A3
Malverley Dr. WN7 76 C5
Malvern Ave. Ashton-u-L OL6 85 C7
Malvern Ave. Atherton M46 58 F5
Malvern Ave. Bolton BL1 142 A1
Malvern Ave. Bury BL9 27 F5
Malvern Ave. Droylsden M43 84 C2
Malvern Ave. Hindley WN2 57 A4
Malvern Ave. Urmston M41 95 B2
Malvern Ave. Wythenshawe M22 121 F5
Malvern Cl. Ashton-i-M WN4 73 B4
Malvern Cl. 2 Farnworth BL4 59 F8
Malvern Cl. Horwich BL6 22 C5
Malvern Cl. Milnrow OL16 32 A7
Malvern Cl. Prestwich M25 63 C5
Malvern Cl. Royton OL2 48 C3
Malvern Cl. Salford M27 80 D6
Malvern Cl. Shaw OL2 48 F8
Malvern Cl. Stockport SK4 169 D3
Malvern Cl. Wigan WN3 54 C3
Malvern Cres. WN2 55 F4
Malvern Dr. Alt'ham WA14 119 B5
Malvern Dr. Salford M27 80 D6
Malvern Gr. M'ster M20 110 A6
Malvern Gr. Salford M6 80 C3
Malvern Gr. Walkden M28 60 D3
Malvern Rd. M24 65 A5
Malvern Rise. SK14 104 A5
Malvern Row. 1 M15 162 D6
Malvern St. M'ster M15 162 D6
Malvern St. Oldham OL8 153 D5
Malvern St. Standish WN6 19 D3
Malvern St E. OL11 30 C7
Malvern St W. OL11 30 C7
Malvern Terr. WN7 75 F3
Malvern Way. BB4 1 A7
Manby Rd. M18 99 B4
Manby Sq. M18 99 B4
Mancentral Trad Est. M3 158 D1
Manchester Airport. M90 130 A7
Manchester Airport Sta. M90 130 B7
Manchester Bsns Sch. M15 163 A6
Manchester Cath (CE). M4 158 F2
Manchester Cath (RC).M3 158 D2
Manchester Chambers. OL1 153 E7
Manchester Coll of Art & Tech. M3 158 E1
Manchester Coll of A & T (Openshaw Ctr). M11 165 B7
Manchester Foot Hospl. M14 98 D4
Manchester Golf Cse. OL11 47 A7
Manchester Gram Sch. M13 98 E2
Manchester High Sch for Girls. M14 98 C1
Manchester High Sch of Arts. M12 164 D7
Manchester Jewish Gram Sch. M25 63 B3
Manchester Met Univ The (Gaythorn House). M15 162 F7
Manchester Met Univ The (Fine Arts Ctr). M15 162 F7
Manchester Metropolitan Prep Sch. M41 95 A2
Manchester Met Univ Hollings Building. M14 98 D2
Manchester Met Univ The. M20 110 B2
Manchester Met Univ The. M1 & M15 163 A7
Manchester New Rd. Middleton M24 & M9 64 F6
Manchester New Rd. Partington M31 105 F3
Manchester Northern Hospl. M8 156 A7
Manchester Old Rd. Bury BL9 140 E1
Manchester Old Rd. Middleton M24 64 D7
Manchester Rd. Alt'ham WA14 119 D7
Manchester Rd. Ashton-u-L M34, M43, OL7 84 E1
Manchester Rd. Blackrod BL6 38 E8
Manchester Rd. Bolton BL3 42 B4
Manchester Rd.Bury BL9,M45 44 F5
Manchester Rd. Bury BL9 140 E1
Manchester Rd. Bury BL9 140 E2
Manchester Rd. Carrington M31 106 B6
Manchester Rd. Cheadle M20 & SK8 122 D7
Manchester Rd.Denton M34 100 E3
Manchester Rd. Diggle HD7 & OL3 52 A8
Manchester Rd. Droylsden M34 100 B8
Manchester Rd. Dukinfield SK14 101 C3
Manchester Rd. Handforth SK9 131 C2
Manchester Rd. Haslingden BB4 1 D7
Manchester Rd. Heywood OL10 46 D7
Manchester Rd. Hollinfare WA3 105 A2
Manchester Rd. Hollinfare WA3 105 B3
Manchester Rd. Hollingworth SK14 103 E7
Manchester Rd. Ince-i-M WN2 & WN1 56 A7
Manchester Rd. Kearsley BL4, M26, M27 61 D4
Manchester Rd. Leigh M46, WN7, BL5 76 D4
Manchester Rd. M'ster M16 & M21 97 B1
Manchester Rd. M'ster M21 109 A8
Manchester Rd. Mossley OL3, OL5, SK15 68 D3
Manchester Rd. Oldham OL8 66 C3
Manchester Rd. Pendlebury M27 80 B7
Manchester Rd. R'dale OL11 & OL10 30 C4
Manchester Rd. Ramsbottom BL0 & BL9 11 E4
Manchester Rd. Reddish M34 100 B4
Manchester Rd. Reddish SK4 169 E4
Manchester Rd. Shaw OL2 149 A5
Manchester Rd. Swinton M27 & M28 61 C2
Manchester Rd. Tintwistle SK14 104 A7
Manchester Rd. Tyldesley M29 77 C8
Manchester Rd Walkden M28 60 D3
Manchester Rd. Westhoughton BL5 40 B1
Manchester Rd E. M38 60 B4
Manchester Rd N. M34 100 D4

Massey Ave. Ashton-u-L OL6 85 C6
Massey Ave. Failsworth M35 84 B8
Massey Croft. OL12 14 C8
Massey Rd. Alt'ham WA15 119 E4
Massey Rd. Sale M33 108 E4
Massey St. Alderley Edge SK9 137 A1
Massey St. Bury BL9 141 B3
Massey St. M'ster M5 81 C1
Massey St. Stockport SK1 169 F1
Massey Wlk. M22 121 F1
Massie St. SK8 122 D6
Matchmoor La. BL1 & BL6 23 A4
Matham Wlk. M15 163 A7
Mather Ave. Eccles M30 79 E2
Mather Ave. Golborne WA3 90 E6
Mather Ave. M'ster M25 63 C1
Mather Ave. Whitefield M45 44 F1
Mather Cl. M45 44 F1
Mather Fold Rd. M28 60 B1
Mather La. WN7 76 A4
Mather Rd. Bury BL9 27 F7
Mather Rd. Eccles M30 79 E2
Mather St. 2 Atherton M46 58 D3
Mather St. Bolton BL3 145 E6
Mather St. Failsworth M35 83 E7
Mather St. Farnworth BL4 60 E8
Mather St. Radcliffe M26 44 A3
Mather Street Prim Sch. M35 83 D7
Mather Way. 4 M6 81 A3
Matheson Dr. WN5 54 E8
Matley Cl. SK14 102 B5
Matley Gn. SK5 112 C6
Matley La. SK14 & SK15 102 D6
Matley Park La. SK15 102 D6
Matlock Ave. Ashton-u-L OL6 85 F6
Matlock Ave. Denton M34 113 A8
Matlock Ave. M'ster M7 81 A7
Matlock Ave. M'ster M20 109 F6
Matlock Ave. Urmston M41 107 B8
Matlock Bank. 16 SK13 171 E1
Matlock Cl. Atherton M46 58 D2
Matlock Cl. Farnworth BL4 42 E1
Matlock Cl. Sale M33 108 C4
Matlock Dr. SK7 133 E8
Matlock Gdns. 13 SK13 171 E1
Matlock La. 15 SK13 171 E1
Matlock Pl. 14 SK13 171 E1
Matlock Rd. Gatley SK8 131 C7
Matlock Rd. Reddish SK5 100 A1
Matlock Rd. Stretford M32 96 A3
Matlock St. M30 95 C8
Matson Wlk. 3 M22 121 A2
Matt Busby Cl. M27 80 B7
Matterdale Terr. SK15 86 A4
Matthew Cl. SK14 103 F7
Matthew Moss High Sch. OL11 30 B4
Matthew Moss La. OL11 30 B4
Matthew's St. M12 164 F7
Matthews Ave. BL4 60 F7
Matthews La. M12,M18,M19 99 B2
Matthias Ct. M3 158 D3
Mattison St. M11 & M18 99 E7
Maud St. Bolton BL2 25 C5
Maud St. R'dale OL12 15 A2
Maudsley St. BL9 140 E1
Mauldeth Cl. SK4 168 A3
Mauldeth Rd. M'ster M14, M19, M20 110 D7
Mauldeth Rd. M'ster M19 110 F6
Mauldeth Rd. M'ster SK4 & M19 168 A3
Mauldeth Rd W. M'ster M20 & M21 109 D8
Mauldeth Rd W. M'ster M20 110 B8
Mauldeth Road Prim Sch. M20 110 E7
Mauldeth Road Sta. M20 110 E7
Maunby Gdns. M38 60 C3
Maureen Ave. M8 156 A8
Maurice Cl. SK16 101 E8
Maurice Dr. M27 & M6 154 F4
Maurice Pariser Wlk. M8 155 F7
Maurice St. M6 154 F4
Maveen Gr. SK2 124 A4
Mavis Gr. OL16 32 A6
Mavis St. OL11 30 C1
Mawdsley Dr. M8 156 C8
Mawdsley St. BL1 145 F7
Max Woosnam Wlk. 3 M14 98 A3
Maxwell Ave. SK2 124 C5
Maxwell St. Bolton BL1 143 E4
Maxwell St. Bury BL9 141 B3
May Ave. Abram WN2 74 C7
May Ave. Bramhall SK8 132 B6
May Ave. Leigh WN7 75 D6
May Ave. Stockport SK4 168 C2
May Ct. 13 M16 97 D3
May Dr. M19 110 F4
May Gr. M19 111 B8
May Pl. 9 OL11 31 A4
May Rd. Bramhall SK8 132 B6
May Rd. M'ster M16 97 D3
May Rd. Pendlebury M27 80 B8
May St. Bolton BL2 148 A7
May St. Edgworth BL7 9 E6
May St. Failsworth M40 83 B5
May St. Golborne WA3 74 B2
May St. Heywood OL10 46 E8
May St. Leigh WN7 75 C5
May St. Oldham OL8 66 C4
May St. Radcliffe M26 44 A3
May St. Swinton M28 79 C4
May Tree Dr. WN1 37 B4
May Wlk. 2 M31 105 E3
Mayall St. OL5 68 C1
Mayall St E. 9 OL4 67 C7
Mayan Ave. M3 158 D2
Maybank St. BL3 145 D5
Mayberth Ave. M8 64 A2
Maybreck Cl. BL3 144 C5
Maybrook Wlk. 11 M9 157 D8
Mayburn Cl. M24 65 C5
Maybury St. M18 99 E6
Maycroft. SK5 112 B6
Maycroft Ave. M20 110 C5
Maycroft Inf Sch. SK5 112 C6
Maycroft Prim Sch. SK5 112 C6
Mayer St. SK2 124 C7
Mayes Gdns. M4 160 D1
Mayes St. M4 159 A2
Mayfair. Horwich BL6 22 D3
Mayfair. M'ster M7 63 C1
Mayfair Ave. Radcliffe M26 43 D4
Mayfair Ave. Salford M6 80 B3
Mayfair Ave. Urmston M41 95 B2
Mayfair Ave. Whitefield M45 62 F7
Mayfair Cl. Haslingden BB4 1 A7
Mayfair Cl. Poynton SK12 133 E4
Mayfair Cl. Stalybridge SK16 101 F8
Mayfair Cl. Stalybridge SK15 & SK16 102 A8
Mayfair Cotts. WN1 20 C1
Mayfair Cres. M35 84 B8
Mayfair Ct. M20 109 F3
Mayfair Dr. Atherton M46 58 F4
Mayfair Dr. Irlam M44 94 A2
Mayfair Dr. Oldham OL2 48 D2
Mayfair Dr. Pennington Green WN2 38 D2
Mayfair Dr. Sale M33 107 E2
Mayfair Dr. Wigan WN3 54 F2
Mayfair Gdns. OL11 139 D5
Mayfair Gr. M45 62 F7
Mayfair Rd. M22 121 E4
Mayfield. Bolton BL2 25 D5
Mayfield. Radcliffe M26 43 E4
Mayfield Ave. Adlington PR6 21 A7
Mayfield Ave. Bolton BL3 42 B3
Mayfield Ave. 7 Denton M34 113 A7
Mayfield Ave. Farnworth BL4 60 C7
Mayfield Ave. Oldham OL4 68 A7
Mayfield Ave. Reddish SK5 111 F5
Mayfield Ave. Sale M33 108 E4
Mayfield Ave. Stretford M32 96 B1
Mayfield Ave. Swinton M27 79 C6
Mayfield Ave. Walkden M28 60 D3
Mayfield Cl. Alt'ham WA15 120 B6
Mayfield Cl. Ramsbottom BL0 11 A2
Mayfield Ct. WN5 36 B1
Mayfield Dr. WA3 & WN7 91 C8
Mayfield Gr. Reddish M18,M34 99 F3
Mayfield Gr. Reddish SK5 111 F5
Mayfield Gr. Wilmslow SK9 136 E5
Mayfield Ind Est. M44 94 C3
Mayfield Mansions. M16 97 E3
Mayfield Prim Sch. OL1 49 B1
Mayfield Rd. Alt'ham WA15 120 B6
Mayfield Rd. Bramhall SK7 132 E4
Mayfield Rd. M'ster M25 63 C1
Mayfield Rd. M'ster M16 97 E3
Mayfield Rd. Oldham OL1 49 B1
Mayfield Rd. Orrell WN8 53 B7
Mayfield Rd. Ramsbottom BL0 11 A2
Mayfield Rd. Romiley SK6 114 B1
Mayfield Rd. Wigan WN5 40 C7
Mayfield St. Ashton-i-M WN4 73 A3
Mayfield St. Atherton M46 58 C2
Mayfield St. Denton M34 100 E5
Mayfield St. R'dale OL16 15 B1
Mayfield Terr. OL16 15 B1
Mayflower Ave. M5 161 B8
Mayflower Cotts. WN6 37 C8
Mayford Rd. M19 99 B2
Maygate. OL1 153 D8
Mayhill Dr. Eccles M30 80 A4
Mayhill Dr. Worsley M28 79 A8
Mayhurst Ave. M21 109 D3
Mayo St. M12 164 D8
Mayor St. Bolton BL1 145 D6
Mayor St. Bury BL8 27 C3
Mayor St. Oldham OL9 152 C7
Mayor's Rd. WA15 119 E4
Mayorlowe Ave. SK5 112 C4
Maypole Ind Est. Abram WN2 74 C7
Maypool Dr. SK5 111 F6
Maysmith Mews. M7 155 D6
Mayton St. M11 165 A8
Mayville Dr. M20 110 B5
Maywood Ave. M20 122 B8
Maze St. BL3 42 D5
Mc Naught St. 28 OL16 31 B6
McCall Wlk. M11 83 B2
McConnell Rd. M40 83 A7
McCormack Dr. WN1 151 D8
McDonna St. BL1 142 C3
McEvoy St. 6 BL1 143 F2
McKean St. BL3 42 A4
McLaren Ct. M21 97 A1
McLean Dr. M44 94 B4
Meachin Ave. M21 109 C5
Mead The. M'ster M21 109 B7
Mead The. Salford M5 154 D2
Mead Way. M34 112 F8
Meade Cl. M41 95 C2
Meade Gr. M13 98 F3
Meade Hill Rd. M25 & M8 63 E3
Meade Manor. M21 109 B7
Meade The. Bolton BL3 147 E2
Meade The. Wilmslow SK9 137 C8
Meadfoot Ave. M25 63 C3
Meadfoot Rd. M18 99 D6
Meadland Gr. BL1 143 F4
Meadow Ave. Alt'ham WA15 120 B3
Meadow Ave. Swinton M27 62 B1
Meadow Bank. Alt'ham WA15 120 A7
Meadow Bank. Bredbury SK6 112 F3
Meadow Bank. Glossop SK13 115 F7
Meadow Bank. Hollingworth SK14 103 D6
Meadow Bank. M'ster M21 109 A7
Meadow Bank. Stockport SK4 168 B2
Meadow Bank Cl. OL4 67 E4
Meadow Bank Ct. M32 96 B1
Meadow Brow. SK9 137 A2
Meadow Cl. Alt'ham WA15 120 B3
Meadow Cl. Denton M34 113 A7
Meadow Cl. Heywood OL10 29 C2
Meadow Cl. High Lane SK6 134 F8
Meadow Cl. Leigh WN7 75 E2
Meadow Cl. Little Lever BL3 43 B2
Meadow Cl. Romiley SK6 113 A5
Meadow Cl. Stretford M32 96 E1
Meadow Cl. Uppermill OL5 68 E3
Meadow Cl. Wilmslow SK9 136 E4
Meadow Cotts. OL12 4 D3
Meadow Croft. Hazel Grove SK7 124 E4
Meadow Croft. Whitefield M45 62 C6
Meadow Ct. Salford M6 80 C5
Meadow Ct. Stretford M21 108 F8
Meadow Fold. OL3 69 C8
Meadow Head Ave. OL12 14 D6
Meadow Ind Est. SK5 169 F3
Meadow La. Bolton BL2 43 A7
Meadow La. Denton M34 113 A7
Meadow La. Disley SK12 135 D6
Meadow La. Dukinfield SK16 101 D8
Meadow La. Oldham OL8 66 E2
Meadow La. Worsley M28 78 F5
Meadow Pit La. Aspull WN2 37 F8
Meadow Pk. BL0 1 C4
Meadow Rd. M'ster M24 64 E6
Meadow Rd. M'ster M7 81 C3
Meadow Rd. Urmston M41 95 D1
Meadow Rise. Glossop SK13 115 F7
Meadow Rise. Shaw OL2 32 A1
Meadow St. Adlington PR6 21 A6
Meadow St. Hyde SK14 167 E1
Meadow St. Stockport SK2 124 C5
Meadow The. BL6 40 C7
Meadow View. OL12 14 A1
Meadow Way. Alt'ham WA15 120 B3
Meadow Way. Blackrod BL6 21 E1
Meadow Way. Bury BL8 26 E6
Meadow Way. Coppull PR7 19 D8
Meadow Way. Edgworth BL7 9 E6
Meadow Way. M'ster M40 65 A1
Meadow Way. Wilmslow SK9 136 E4
Meadow Wlk. Bredbury SK6 112 F3
Meadow Wlk. Farnworth BL4 60 A8
Meadow Wlk. Littleborough OL15 15 F5
Meadowbank. OL6 & OL7 85 B6
Meadowbank Ave. M46 58 E5
Meadowbank Cl. M35 84 A6
Meadowbank Cty Prim Sch. M46 58 D4
Meadowbank Gdns. WA3 92 C7
Meadowbank Rd. BL3 146 B2
Meadowbrook Cl. BL6 40 B3
Meadowcroft. Ashton-i-M WN4 72 F6
Meadowcroft. Mottram-i-L SK14 103 A4
Meadowcroft. Radcliffe M26 43 F5
Meadowcroft. Westhoughton BL5 57 F7
Meadowcroft La. 1 Oldham OL1 49 B1
Meadowcroft La. R'dale OL11 29 F6
Meadowfield. BL6 40 C7
Meadowfield Cl. SK13 171 F3
Meadowfield Ct. SK14 167 D4
Meadowfield Dr. M28 78 B6
Meadowgate. Urmston M41 95 D1
Meadowgate. Worsley M28 78 F4
Meadowgate Rd. M30 & M6 80 C3
Meadows. OL3 69 B7
Meadows Cl. 4 WN2 56 D5
Meadows La. BL2 25 F3
Meadows Rd. Cheadle SK8 131 F8
Meadows Rd. Gatley SK8 122 B1
Meadows Rd. Reddish SK4 111 C6
Meadows Rd. Sale M33 108 C6
Meadows St. WN6 37 A1
Meadows The. Irlam M44 105 E6
Meadows The. Middleton M24 65 B6
Meadows The. Oldham OL4 68 A6
Meadows The. Prestwich M25 63 C3
Meadows The. Radcliffe M26 43 E5
Meadows The. Whitworth OL12 4 C1
Meadowside. Bramhall SK7 123 C2
Meadowside. Newhey OL16 32 C3
Meadowside Ave. Ashton-i-M WN4 73 A8
Meadowside Ave. Bolton BL2 148 C7
Meadowside Ave. Irlam M44 94 A2
Meadowside Ave. Walkden M28 60 E4
Meadowside Ave. Wythenshawe M22 121 E4
Meadowside Cl. M26 44 A5
Meadowside Gr. M28 60 E3
Meadowside Rd. WN2 57 A4
Meadowvale Dr. WN5 54 C6
Meads Gr. Farnworth BL4 59 E8
Meads Gr. Tyldesley M29 77 C6
Meads The. OL9 152 A6
Meadscroft Dr. SK9 136 F1
Meadway. Bramhall SK7 132 E5
Meadway. Bury BL9 44 F6
Meadway. Dukinfield SK16 101 E7
Meadway. Failsworth OL9 65 E2
Meadway. Golborne WA3 90 D8
Meadway. High Lane SK6 134 F8
Meadway. Ince-i-M WN2 151 F7
Meadway. Poynton SK12 133 B4
Meadway. R'dale OL11 30 C4
Meadway. Ramsbottom BL0 1 C1
Meadway. Sale M33 107 E2
Meadway. Stalybridge SK15 102 E6
Meadway. Tyldesley M29 59 D1
Meadway Cl. Horwich BL6 22 D3
Meadway Cl. Sale M33 107 E2
Meadway Rd. SK8 123 B3
Meal St. SK4 169 E3
Mealhouse Brow. SK1 169 F1
Mealhouse Ct. M46 58 C3
Mealhouse La. Atherton M46 58 C3
Mealhouse La. Bolton BL1 145 F7
Meanley Rd. M29 & WN7 76 F7
Meanley St. 10 M29 59 A1
Meanwood Brow. 15 OL12 14 C1
Meanwood Fold. OL12 139 D8
Meanwood Prim Sch. OL12 14 C1
Measham Mews. M1 163 A7
Meburn Wlk. M14 98 B4
Meddings Cl. SK9 136 F1
Medina Cl. SK8 123 B4
Medlar Way. WN4 72 F5
Medley St. OL12 14 F1
Medlock Dr. OL8 85 A8
Medlock House. M15 162 D7
Medlock Prim Sch. M13 163 C7
Medlock Rd. M35 84 B5
Medlock Sports Ctr. M43 84 B2
Medlock St. Droylsden M43 84 B2
Medlock St. M'ster M15 162 F7
Medlock Vale. OL7 84 E6
Medlock Way. Oldham OL4 67 E6
Medlock Way. Platt Bridge WN2 56 A2
Medlock Way. Whitefield M45 63 C8
Medowell Wlk. M8 64 B2
Medway Cl. Ashton-i-M WN4 72 F6
Medway Cl. Golborne WN7 91 C8
Medway Cl. Oldham OL8 66 C3
Medway Cl. Salford M5 154 D3
Medway Cres. WA14 119 C6
Medway Dr. Horwich BL6 22 D3
Medway Dr. Kearsley BL4 61 B5
Medway Pl. WN5 54 D7
Medway Rd. Culcheth WA3 92 A2
Medway Rd. Oldham OL8 66 C3
Medway Rd. Shaw OL2 149 B8
Medway Rd. Walkden M28 78 B8
Medway The. OL10 29 B3
Medway Wlk. M'ster M40 160 D3
Medway Wlk. Wigan WN5 54 D7
Mee's Sq. M30 95 D8
Meech St. M11 165 C8
Meek St. OL1 49 A2
Meerbrook Rd. SK3 123 A8
Megfield. BL5 57 E6
Melandra Castle Rd. SK13 171 D2
Melandra Cres. SK14 102 E2
Melandra Rd. SK13 171 E3
Melanie Cl. SK13 116 A8
Melanie Dr. SK5 111 F8
Melba St. M11 99 E8
Melbecks Wlk. M23 108 F2
Melbourne Ave. Oldham OL9 152 B7
Melbourne Ave. Stretford M32 96 D2
Melbourne Ave. Wythenshawe M90 130 A8
Melbourne Cl. Horwich BL6 22 C3
Melbourne Cl. R'dale OL11 31 B2
Melbourne Gr. BL6 22 C3
Melbourne Mews. M7 155 E5
Melbourne Rd. Bolton BL3 144 B5
Melbourne Rd. Bramhall SK7 132 F5
Melbourne Rd. R'dale OL11 31 A2
Melbourne St. Denton M34 100 E2
Melbourne St. M'ster M7 155 E5
Melbourne St. M'ster M9 157 E8
Melbourne St. M'ster M15 162 E7
Melbourne St. Oldham OL9 152 B7
Melbourne St. Pendlebury M27 80 B8
Melbourne St. Reddish SK5 111 F8
Melbourne St. Stalybridge SK15 86 A1
Melbourne St N. OL6 166 C4
Melbourne St S. OL6 166 C3
Melbourne Wlk. M5 161 B8
Melbury Ave. M20 110 D4
Melbury Dr. Horwich BL6 39 F8
Melbury Rd. SK8 132 B6
Meldon Rd. M13 98 E2
Meldreth Dr. M12 98 F4
Meldrum St. OL8 66 F4
Meldrum Wlk. OL8 67 A4
Melford Ave. M40 65 E1
Melford Dr. Ashton-i-M WN4 73 A4
Melford Dr. Orrell WN5 53 D3
Melford Rd. SK7 124 F1
Melfort Ave. M32 96 E1
Meliden Cres. Bolton BL1 142 B1
Meliden Cres. Wythenshawe M22 121 E3
Melksham Cl. 4 M5 & M6 81 B2
Mellalieu St. Middleton M24 46 F1
Mellalieu St. Oldham OL2 48 E2
Melland Ave. M21 109 C5
Melland Rd. M18 99 C3
Melland Sch. M18 99 D2
Meller Rd. M13 98 F2
Melling Ave. Chadderton OL9 47 E1
Melling Ave. Reddish SK4 111 E6
Melling Cl. WN7 75 F1
Melling Rd. OL4 67 C6
Melling St. M'ster M12 & M18 99 A4
Melling St. Wigan WN5 54 E5
Melling Way. WN3 54 D1
Mellings Ave. WN5 53 E1
Mellington Ave. M20 122 C8
Mellish Wlk. M8 155 F5
Mellor Brow. OL10 29 C2
Mellor Cl. OL6 85 E2
Mellor Ct. SK2 124 E6
Mellor Dr. Bury BL9 44 D7
Mellor Dr. Walkden M28 60 C1
Mellor Gr. BL1 142 B1
Mellor Prim Sch. SK6 126 E6
Mellor Rd. Ashton-u-L OL6 85 E3
Mellor Rd. Ashton-u-L OL6 85 E4
Mellor Rd. Cheadle SK8 123 B1
Mellor Rd. New Mills SK12 127 C3
Mellor St. Droylsden M43 83 F1
Mellor St. Eccles M30 79 D1
Mellor St. Failsworth M35 83 D6
Mellor St. M'ster M10 & M40 160 D3
Mellor St. M'ster M12 163 C8
Mellor St. Oldham OL4 67 E6
Mellor St. Prestwich M25 62 F4
Mellor St. R'dale OL11 & OL12 139 D7
Mellor St. 2 Radcliffe M26 44 B2
Mellor St. Royton OL2 48 D5
Mellor St. Stretford M32 96 E4
Mellor Way. OL9 66 B4
Mellors Rd. M17 96 B7
Mellowstone Dr. M21 109 F8
Melloy Pl. M8 159 A4
Melmerby Cl. WN4 72 F3
Melmerby Ct. M5 154 F1
Melrose. 18 OL12 139 E8
Melrose Ave. Bolton BL1 142 A1
Melrose Ave. Bury BL8 27 C3
Melrose Ave. Cheadle SK3 122 F7
Melrose Ave. Heywood OL10 29 C3
Melrose Ave. Leigh WN7 57 D1
Melrose Ave. Littleborough OL15 16 A7
Melrose Ave. M'ster M20 110 C3
Melrose Ave. Sale M33 108 B4
Melrose Ave. Swinton M28 79 B4
Melrose Cl. 6 M45 44 F2
Melrose Cres. Alt'ham WA15 120 B1
Melrose Cres. Garswood WN4 72 C3
Melrose Cres. High Lane SK12 134 D5
Melrose Cres. Stockport SK3 123 D4
Melrose Ct. OL9 66 A4
Melrose Dr. WN3 54 D3
Melrose Gdns. M26 43 E5
Melrose Rd. Little Lever BL3 42 F3
Melrose Rd. Radcliffe M26 43 E5
Melrose St. Failsworth M40 83 C5
Melrose St. 3 Oldham OL1 49 B1
Melrose St. R'dale OL11 139 D7
Melrose St. Ramsbottom BL0 11 B2
Melsomby Rd. M23 109 A2
Meltham Ave. M20 110 A6
Meltham Cl. SK4 110 E1
Meltham Pl. 7 BL3 147 D4
Meltham Rd. SK4 110 E1
Melton Ave. Reddish M34 100 A3
Melton Ave. Urmston M41 94 D3
Melton Cl. Heywood OL10 29 A1
Melton Cl. Tyldesley M29 77 B8
Melton Cl. Walkden M28 60 C2
Melton Dr. BL9 45 A5
Melton Rd. M8 63 E1
Melton Row. M26 43 F4
Melton St. Heywood OL10 29 B1
Melton St. M'ster M9 64 F1
Melton St. Radcliffe M26 43 F4
Melton St. Reddish SK5 169 F4
Melton Way. M26 43 F4
Melton Wlk. M26 43 F4
Melverley Rd. M9 64 A5
Melverley St. WN3 150 A7
Melville Cl. M18 99 E7
Melville Rd. Irlam M44 105 C5
Melville Rd. Kearsley BL4 60 F6
Melville Rd. Stretford M32 96 C4
Melville St. Ashton-u-L OL6 166 B3
Melville St. Bolton BL3 42 A4
Melville St. M'ster M3 158 D2
Melville St. Oldham OL4 67 E5
Melville St. R'dale OL11 30 D1
Melvin Ave. M22 121 E4
Melyncourt Rd. SK14 102 E3
Memorial Rd. M28 60 D2
Menai Gr. SK8 123 A6
Menai Rd. SK3 170 E6
Menai St. BL3 146 B4
Mendip Ave. Wigan WN3 54 C3
Mendip Ave. Wythenshawe M22 121 F4
Mendip Cl. Bolton BL2 43 A7
Mendip Cl. Gatley SK8 131 B7
Mendip Cl. Horwich BL6 22 C5
Mendip Cl. Oldham OL9 152 A5
Mendip Cl. Royton OL2 48 C3
Mendip Cl. Stockport SK4 169 E3
Mendip Cres. BL8 27 B3
Mendip Ct. Platt Bridge WN2 56 B3
Mendip Ct. Stockport SK4 169 E3
Mendip Dr. Bolton BL2 43 A6
Mendip Dr. Milnrow OL16 32 A7
Mendip Rd. OL8 66 D3
Mendips Cl. OL2 48 F8
Menston Ave. M40 65 E1
Mentmore Rd. OL16 31 D8
Mentone Cres. M22 121 E4
Mentone Rd. SK4 168 C3
Mentor St. M13 98 F3
Menzies Ct. M21 97 B1
Mercer Ct. BB4 1 A8
Mercer La. OL11 29 E8
Mercer Rd. M18 99 D5
Mercer St. Droylsden M43 84 B2
Mercer St. M'ster M19 99 B1
Mercer St. Newton-l-W WA12 89 D4
Mercer's Rd. OL10 46 D7
Merchants Cres. WA3 74 E1
Merchants Quay. M5 161 A6
Mercia St. BL3 144 C5
Mercian Way. Ashton-u-L OL6 166 B3
Mercian Way. Stockport SK3 170 E7
Mercury Bsns Pk. M41 95 F6
Mercury Way. M41 95 F6
Mere Ave. Droylsden M43 99 E8
Mere Ave. Leigh WN7 75 D5
Mere Ave. Middleton M24 65 A6
Mere Ave. Salford M6 154 E2
Mere Bank Cl. M28 60 C3
Mere Cl. Reddish M34 100 B2
Mere Cl. Sale M33 108 F3
Mere Cl. Whitefield BL9 45 B5
Mere Dr. M'ster M20 110 B4
Mere Dr. Swinton M27 62 A2
Mere Fold. M28 60 B3
Mere Gdns. BL1 145 E8
Mere Gr. WA11 71 B1
Mere La. OL11 139 F5
Mere Oaks Sch. WN6 37 B5
Mere Rd. Ashton-i-M WN4 73 C4
Mere Rd. Newton-l-W WA12 89 F4
Mere Side. SK15 85 F4
Mere St. 7 Leigh WN7 75 D5
Mere St. R'dale OL11 & OL16 139 F6
Mere St. Wigan WN5 54 F6
Mere The. Ashton-u-L OL6 85 E6
Mere The. Cheadle SK8 123 A4
Mere Wlk. BL1 145 E8
Mereclough Ave. M28 60 F1
Meredew Ave. M27 79 E6
Meredith Ct. M15 163 A6
Meredith St. Bolton BL3 43 A3
Meredith St. M'ster M14 110 D7
Merefield Ave. OL11 139 E5
Merefield Rd. WA15 120 C5
Merefield St. OL11 139 E5
Merefield Terr. OL11 139 E5
Merefold. BL6 21 F3
Merehall Cl. BL1 145 E8
Merehall Dr. Bolton BL1 145 E8
Merehall St. BL1 143 E1
Mereland Ave. M20 110 C4
Mereland Cl. WN5 53 E6
Merepool Cl. SK6 125 C7
Mereside Cl. SK8 122 F4
Mereside Gr. M28 60 E3
Mereside Wlk. 12 M15 162 D6
Merewood Ave. M22 121 D6
Meriden Cl. M26 43 F6
Meriden Gr. BL6 40 D6
Merinall Cl. OL16 31 C7
Meriton Rd. SK9 131 D4
Meriton Wlk. M18 99 B4
Merlewood. BL0 1 E3
Merlewood Ave. 6 Droylsden M34 84 B1
Merlewood Ave. Reddish M19 111 C7
Merlewood Ave. Uppermill OL3 69 B8
Merlewood Dr. Swinton M27 & M28 79 C6
Merlewood Dr. Tyldesley M29 77 B8
Merlin Cl. Hazel Grove SK2 125 A6
Merlin Cl. Littleborough OL15 16 A2
Merlin Cl. Oldham OL8 85 A8
Merlin Gr. BL1 142 B1
Merlin Rd. Irlam M44 94 A4
Merlin Rd. Milnrow OL16 31 F6
Merlyn Ave. Denton M34 100 E2
Merlyn Ave. M'ster M20 110 C4
Merlyn Ave. Sale M33 108 C6
Merrick Ave. M22 121 E4
Merrick St. OL10 29 E1
Merridale The. Alt'ham WA15 129 A8
Merridge Wlk. 5 M8 155 F6
Merrill St. M11 & M40 160 D1
Merriman Cl. M16 97 E4
Merrion St. BL4 42 C2
Merrow Wlk. M1 163 B7
Merrybent Cl. SK2 124 D4
Merrybower Rd. M7 155 E8
Merrydale Ave. M30 79 E4
Merryman Hall. OL16 15 B2
Mersey Bank Rd. SK14 171 F4
Mersey Cl. Hindley WN2 57 C3
Mersey Cl. Whitefield M45 45 B1
Mersey Cres. M20 & M21 109 D3
Mersey Dr. Partington M31 106 A4
Mersey Dr. Whitefield M45 45 B1
Mersey Drive Cty Prim Sch. M45 45 C2
Mersey Ind Est. M'ster M19, M20, SK4 110 E1
Mersey Ind Est. Oldham M35 66 B1
Mersey Meadows. M20 109 F3
Mersey Rd. M'ster M20 109 F3
Mersey Rd. M'ster SK4 110 F2
Mersey Rd. Orrell WN5 53 F7
Mersey Rd. Platt Bridge WN2 55 F2
Mersey Rd. Sale M33 108 B6
Mersey Rd N. M35 66 B1
Mersey Sq. Stockport SK1 & SK4 169 E1
Mersey Sq. Whitefield M45 45 B1
Mersey St. Droylsden M11 99 E7
Mersey St. Leigh WN7 75 C5
Mersey St. Stockport SK1 112 A2
Mersey Vale Prim Sch. SK4 168 A1
Merseybank Ave. M21 109 D4
Merseyway. SK1 169 F2
Merston Dr. M20 122 C8
Merton Ave. Hazel Grove SK7 133 F8
Merton Ave. Oldham OL8 66 D3
Merton Ave. Romiley SK6 113 A4
Merton Cl. BL3 144 C5
Merton Dr. M43 83 E1
Merton Gr. Alt'ham WA15 120 B6
Merton Gr. Failsworth OL9 65 D3
Merton Gr. Tyldesley M29 77 C6
Merton Rd. Prestwich M25 63 C5
Merton Rd. Sale M33 108 A6
Merton Rd. 5 Stockport SK3 123 B8
Merton Rd. Wigan WN3, WN5 54 C4
Merton St. BL8 140 D3
Merton Wlk. 14 M9 157 E7
Merville Ave. M40 64 F1
Mervyn Pl. WN3 55 B4
Mervyn Rd. M7 81 B6
Merwell Rd. M41 94 E1
Merwood Ave. SK8 131 D8
Merwood Gr. M13 98 E4
Mesne Lea Gr. M28 78 E8
Mesne Lea Rd. M28 60 E1
Mesne Lea Sch. M28 60 E1
Mesnefield Rd. M7 81 A8
Mesnes Ave. WN3 150 A5
Mesnes Park Terr. 9 WN1 37 C1
Mesnes Rd. Wigan WN1 37 C3
Mesnes Rd. Wigan WN1 150 C8
Mesnes Terr. WN1 37 C1
Metal Box Way. Westhoughton BL5 40 A2
Metcalf Terr. BL2 26 D1
Metcalfe Ct. M38 59 F4
Meter Extension Rd. M32 96 D4
Meter West Rd. M32 96 D4
Metfield Pl. 8 BL1 144 C8
Metfield Wlk. 19 M40 65 D2
Methodist Cotts. BL5 39 D3
Methuen St. 6 M12 & M18 99 B3
Methwold St. BL3 146 C4
Metron Rd. SK12 133 B4
Metroplex Bsns Ctr. M5 96 D8
Mevagissey Wlk. 3 OL4 67 C8
Mews The. Gatley SK8 122 B5
Mews The. 12 Hindley WN2 56 D5
Mews The. M'ster M10, M40 160 E3
Mews The. Prestwich M25 63 B3
Mews The. Sale M33 108 C3

Mews The. Whitefield M45 62 D8
Mews The. Wilmslow SK9 130 D4
Mews The. Worsley M28 78 E6
Meyer St. SK2 & SK3 170 F6
Meynell Dr. WN7 75 F2
Meyrick Rd. M6 81 A3
Meyrick St. WN5 54 F6
Miall St. OL11 139 F6
Micawber Rd. SK12 133 E2
Michael Ct. M19 110 D2
Michael St. 3 M24 64 F8
Michael Wife La. Edenfield BL0 1 F2
Michael Wife La. Edenfield BL0 1 F3
Michaels Hey Par. M23 120 C8
Michigan Ave. M5 96 F8
Mickleby Wlk. M40 160 D3
Micklehurst All Saints' CE Prim Sch. OL5 68 E1
Micklehurst Ave. M20 109 E4
Micklehurst Gn. SK2 124 E5
Micklehurst Jun Comm Sch. OL5 68 E1
Micklehurst Rd. Mossley OL5 68 E1
Mickleton. M46 58 E4
Midbrook Wlk. 6 M22 121 B1
Middle Field. OL11 13 E1
Middle Gate. OL8 66 E2
Middle Gn. OL6 166 C4
Middle Hill. OL12 14 F4
Middle Hillgate. SK1 170 F8
Middle Newgate. OL15 16 B8
Middle Rd. M41 95 F6
Middle St. OL12 4 D1
Middle Wood La. OL12, OL15 15 E6
Middlebourne St. M6 154 E2
Middlebrook Dr. BL6 40 D6
Middlefield. OL8 85 A8
Middlefields. SK8 123 B4
Middlegate. M40 65 D3
Middleham St. M14 98 A2
Middlesex Dr. 8 BL9 44 F8
Middlesex Rd. Brinnington SK5 112 C6
Middlesex Rd. M'ster M9 64 D2
Middlesex Wlk. OL9 153 D6
Middlestone Dr. M9 157 D7
Middleton Ave. M35 83 F7
Middleton Central Ind Est. M24 64 F8
Middleton Cl. BL8 43 F7
Middleton Dr. BL9 & M45 44 F3
Middleton Old Rd. M9 64 D2
Middleton Parish CE Prim Sch. M24 46 F2
Middleton Rd. Chadderton M24 & OL9 47 E1
Middleton Rd. Heywood OL10 46 E7
Middleton Rd. M'ster M7, M8, M9 63 F3
Middleton Rd. Middleton M24 64 A6
Middleton Rd. Oldham OL9 152 B7
Middleton Rd. Reddish SK5 99 F2
Middleton Rd. Royton OL2 48 C3
Middleton Rd W. OL9 65 F8
Middleton Tech Sch The. M24 65 C8
Middleton Way. M24 64 F8
Middleway. OL4 68 B5
Middlewich Wlk. M18 165 C5
Middlewood. WA3 90 E8
Middlewood Ct. OL9 152 A8
Middlewood Dr. SK4 168 A1
Middlewood Gn. OL9 152 A8
Middlewood Rd. High Lane SK12 & SK7 134 C7
Middlewood Rd. High Lane SK6 134 D7
Middlewood Rd. Poynton SK12 134 B4
Middlewood St. M5 158 D1
Middlewood Sta (lower). SK6 134 D6
Middlewood Wlk. M9 157 D7
Midford Ave. M30 79 B2
Midford Dr. BL1 24 E7
Midford Wlk. 13 M8 156 A6
Midge Hall Dr. OL11 30 A6
Midge Hill. OL5 68 D4
Midgley Ave. M18 99 E6
Midgley Cres. OL6 85 E4
Midgley St. M27 79 D6
Midgrove. OL3 50 F3
Midgrove La. OL3 50 F4
Midhurst Ave. M40 83 B4
Midhurst Cl. 1 Bolton BL1 143 E1
Midhurst Cl. Cheadle SK8 131 F8
Midhurst St. OL11 139 F5
Midhurst Way. OL9 152 B6
Midland Cl. WN7 75 C6
Midland Rd. Reddish SK5 99 F2
Midland Rd. Stockport SK7 123 E3
Midland St. M12 164 D7
Midland Wlk. SK7 123 E3
Midlothian St. M11 83 B2
Midmoor Wlk. 5 M9 64 E3
Midville Rd. M11 83 C3
Midway. SK8 132 B5
Midway St. M12 & M19 99 A2
Milan St. M7 155 E7
Milbourne Rd. BL9 27 F6
Milburn Ave. M23 109 B2
Milburn Dr. BL2 42 F8
Milbury Dr. OL15 16 A2
Milden Cl. M20 110 C4
Mildred Ave. M'ster M25 63 C1
Mildred Ave. Oldham OL2 48 E2
Mildred Ave. Oldham OL4 68 B5
Mildred St. M7 81 C5
Mile End La. SK2 124 B6
Mile La. BL8 26 F1
Miles Ave. OL13 3 D8
Miles La. Appley Bridge WN6 35 E6
Miles La. Shevington WN6 36 A6
Miles Platting Prim Sch. M40 160 E4
Miles St. 5 Bolton BL1 143 D2
Miles St. Farnworth BL4 60 C8
Miles St. Hyde SK14 167 F2
Miles St. M'ster M12 165 A7
Miles St. Oldham OL1 & OL4 67 B8
Milford Ave. 2 OL8 66 C2
Milford Brow. OL4 67 F7
Milford Cres. OL15 16 B6
Milford Dr. M19 111 C7
Milford Gr. SK2 124 C7
Milford Rd. Bolton BL2 25 F4
Milford Rd. Bolton BL3 147 E3
Milford Rd. 4 Wigan WN2 37 F2
Milford St. Ince-i-M WN3 151 E6
Milford St. M'ster M9 64 B4
Milford St. 6 R'dale OL12 14 F1
Milford St. Salford M6 154 E2
Milk St. Hyde SK14 167 D2
Milk St. M'ster M60 159 A1
Milk St. 3 Oldham OL4 67 C7
Milk St. R'dale OL11 139 F6
Milk St. Ramsbottom BL0 138 B5
Milk St. Tyldesley M29 59 A1
Milk St. Wigan WN3 150 C7
Milkstone Pl. OL11 139 F6
Milkstone Rd. OL11 139 F6
Milkwood Gr. 2 M18 99 D4
Mill Bank. WN6 35 D7
Mill Beck Gr. BL3 147 E4
Mill Brook Ind Est. M23 120 E6
Mill Brow. Chadderton OL1 48 A2
Mill Brow. M'ster M9 64 C2
Mill Brow. Mottram-i-L SK14 115 A8
Mill Brow. Oldham OL6 & OL8 67 C2
Mill Brow. Worsley M28 78 F6
Mill Brow Rd. SK6 126 E8
Mill Brow Rd. Marple SK6 126 E8
Mill Cl. WA3 91 E3
Mill Croft. Bolton BL1 145 D8
Mill Croft. Shaw OL2 149 C6
Mill Croft Cl. OL11 13 C2
Mill Ct. M41 95 E1
Mill Fold Rd. M24 64 F8
Mill Gate. Oldham OL8 66 D2
Mill Gate. R'dale OL16 15 C2
Mill Green St. M12 164 D8
Mill Hill. M38 59 E6
Mill Hill Ave. SK12 133 D7
Mill Hill Gr. SK14 102 F2
Mill Hill Hollow. SK12 133 D7
Mill Hill St. BL2 148 A8
Mill Hill Way. 3 SK14 102 F2
Mill House Cl. OL12 15 D4
Mill House Sch. WA12 89 F3
Mill House View. WN8 53 C7
Mill La. Appley Bridge WN6 35 D7
Mill La. Ashton-u-L OL6 166 B2
Mill La. Aspull WN2 38 F3
Mill La. 4 Bury BL8 27 B4
Mill La. Cheadle SK8 122 D6
Mill La. Cheadle SK8 123 B3
Mill La. Denton M34 & SK14 101 B2
Mill La. Droylsden SK5 99 F1
Mill La. Failsworth M35 83 C7
Mill La. Hazel Grove SK6 125 B7
Mill La. Hazel Grove SK7 133 F8
Mill La. Horwich BL6 22 D4
Mill La. Leigh WN7 76 B4
Mill La. Lymm WA13 117 C4
Mill La. Mobberley WA15 129 E4
Mill La. Mossley OL5 68 C2
Mill La. Newton-l-W WA12 89 E3
Mill La. Oldham OL9 66 C4
Mill La. Orrell WN8 53 A8
Mill La. Reddish SK5 112 B8
Mill La. Romiley SK6 113 A5
Mill La. Royton OL2 48 C4
Mill La. Uppermill OL4 50 D1
Mill La. Westhoughton BL5 57 E5
Mill La. Wythenshawe M22 109 E1
Mill Meadow. WN1 151 D7
Mill Rd. Bury BL9 27 F8
Mill Rd. Orrell WN5 53 D5
Mill St. Adlington PR6 21 B8
Mill St. Alt'ham WA14, WA15 119 E5
Mill St. Ashton-i-M WN4 73 C2
Mill St. Bolton BL7 24 F8
Mill St. Bolton BL1 & BL2 148 A8
Mill St. Boothstown M28 78 A6
Mill St. Bury BL8 26 F8
Mill St. Dukinfield SK14 101 E5
Mill St. Failsworth M35 83 D7
Mill St. Farnworth BL4 60 C8
Mill St. Glossop SK13 104 D1
Mill St. Golborne WA3 90 A8
Mill St. Hazel Grove SK7 124 D3
Mill St. Hindley WN2 56 D5
Mill St. Leigh WN7 76 A4
Mill St. M'ster M11 165 A8
Mill St. Mossley OL5 86 C8
Mill St. Radcliffe M26 44 B2
Mill St. Ramsbottom BL0 11 A4
Mill St. Royton OL2 48 D4
Mill St. Salford M6 81 A4
Mill St. Stalybridge SK15 86 C1
Mill St. Tyldesley M46 58 E1
Mill St. Uppermill OL3 69 B8
Mill St. Westhoughton BL5 57 F8
Mill St. Wigan WN3 150 B7
Mill St. Wilmslow SK9 137 B7
Mill Yd. BL9 141 A3
Millais St. M40 83 A8
Millam Cl. OL16 15 C1
Millar Barn La. BB4 2 F8
Millard St. OL9 152 A7
Millard Wlk. 4 M18 99 D4
Millbank Ct. OL10 29 B2
Millbank Jun Sch. M31 105 E3
Millbank St. Heywood OL10 29 B2
Millbank St. M'ster M1 159 C1
Millbeck Cres. WN5 54 D5
Millbeck Ct. 4 M24 46 D2
Millbeck Gr. WA11 71 B2
Millbeck Rd. M24 46 D2
Millbrae Gdns. OL2 48 F7
Millbrook. SK14 103 E6
Millbrook Ave. Atherton M46 58 E5
Millbrook Ave. Denton M34 100 D1
Millbrook Bank. OL11 13 D1
Millbrook Gr. 1 SK9 131 D1
Millbrook House. BL4 60 E8
Millbrook Prim Sch. Mossley SK15 86 E5
Millbrook Prim Sch. Shevington WN6 36 B6
Millbrook Rd. M23 121 A4
Millbrook St. SK1 170 F8
Millcrest Cl. M28 77 F5
Millcroft Ave. WN5 53 D5
Millcroft La. OL3 51 A7
Milldale Cl. M46 58 C5
Milldale Rd. WN7 75 B1
Miller Rd. OL8 66 E3
Miller St. Ashton-u-L OL6 166 C4
Miller St. Blackrod WN2 38 F7
Miller St. Bolton BL1 143 E4
Miller St. Heywood OL10 29 D2
Miller St. M'ster M4 159 A2
Miller St. Radcliffe M26 43 F6
Miller St. Ramsbottom BL9 11 C2
Miller's La. Atherton M46 58 D1
Miller's La. Platt Bridge WN2 56 A2
Millers Brook Cl. OL10 29 D3
Millers Cl. M23 109 A3
Millers Ct. M5 80 A2
Millers La. WA13 117 B5
Millers St. M30 79 C2
Millersdale Ct. SK13 104 F1
Millet Terr. BL9 28 E7
Millett St. Bury BL9 140 D2
Millett St. Ramsbottom BL0 11 D7
Millfield Dr. M28 78 B6
Millfield Gr. OL16 31 B6
Millfield La. WN4 72 E1
Millfield Rd. BL2 43 A7
Millfield Wlk. 2 M40 65 C2
Millfold. OL12 4 D2
Millford Ave. M41 94 E2
Millgate. Bolton BL7 8 D2
Millgate. Delph OL3 50 F4
Millgate. Stockport SK1 169 F2
Millgate. Wigan WN1 150 C8
Millgate La. M20 110 B1
Millgate Terr. OL12 4 E5
Millhall Cl. M15 162 E5
Millhead Ave. M10 & M40 160 E2
Millhouse Ave. M23 121 A4
Millhouse Sch. M22 121 C4
Millhouse St. BL0 11 E8
Milling St. M1 162 F8
Millingford Ave. WA3 73 F2
Millingford Gr. WN4 73 B3
Millingford Ind Est. WA3 90 A8
Millington Wlk. 9 M15 162 D6
Millom Ave. M23 109 B1
Millom Dr. BL9 45 A2
Millom Pl. SK8 122 B3
Millow St. M4 159 A3
Millpool Wlk. 1 M9 157 D8
Millrise. OL1 153 E8
Mills Farm Cl. OL8 67 A1
Mills Hill Prim Sch. OL9 65 E8
Mills Hill Rd. M24 65 D8
Mills Hill Sta. M24 47 D1
Mills St. Heywood OL10 29 B2
Mills St. Oldham OL9 66 A2
Mills St. Whitworth OL12 4 D1
Millstone Cl. SK12 133 F5
Millstone Rd. BL1 23 F1
Millstream La. M40 & M43 83 E4
Milltown. SK13 104 D1
Milltown Cl. 3 M26 44 B2
Milltown St. M26 44 B3
Millwall Cl. M18 99 D5
Millway. WA15 129 C7
Millway Wlk. 19 M40 83 C5
Millwell La. 5 BL1 145 F7
Millwood Cl. WN4 73 A5
Millwood Cl. BL9 44 F6
Millwood Sch. BL9 44 F6
Millwood Terr. 3 SK14 167 D2
Millwright St. M40 83 C5
Milne Cl. M12 165 A6
Milne St. Haslingden BB4 1 C5
Milne St. Oldham OL9 48 C1
Milne St. Oldham OL1 49 A2
Milne St. Oldham OL9 152 B7
Milne St. Oldham OL9 152 C5
Milne St. R'dale OL11 30 C2
Milne St. Shaw OL2 149 B6
Milner Ave. Alt'ham WA14 119 B7
Milner Ave. Bury BL9 27 F5
Milner St. M'ster M16 97 D4
Milner St. Radcliffe M26 43 E3
Milner St. Swinton M27 80 A8
Milner St. Whitworth OL12 4 C1
Milner St. Whitworth OL12 14 C8
Milnes Ave. WN7 75 F2
Milngate Cl. OL16 31 C3
Milnholme. BL1 142 B3
Milnrow Cl. M13 163 B7
Milnrow Parish CE Prim Sch. OL16 31 F6
Milnrow Rd. Littleborough OL15 16 A2
Milnrow Rd. R'dale OL11 & OL16 31 B7
Milnrow Rd. Shaw OL16, OL2 32 C2
Milnrow Rd. Shaw OL2 149 B7
Milnrow Rd. Shaw OL2 149 C8
Milnrow Sta. OL16 31 F5
Milnthorpe Rd. BL2 42 F8
Milnthorpe St. M6 81 B5
Milnthorpe Way. M12 164 E6
Milo St. M9 64 D3
Milsom Ave. BL3 146 C3
Milstead Wlk. M40 83 A5
Milston Wlk. M8 156 A6
Milton Ave. Bolton BL3 146 B4
Milton Ave. Droylsden M43 84 A1
Milton Ave. Irlam M44 105 E6
Milton Ave. Little Lever BL3 43 B4
Milton Ave. Newton-l-W WA12 89 B3
Milton Ave. Salford M5 154 D2
Milton Ave. Stalybridge SK15 86 E4
Milton Cl. Atherton M46 58 D5
Milton Cl. Dukinfield SK16 102 B7
Milton Cl. Haslingden BB4 1 A7
Milton Cl. Marple SK6 125 F4
Milton Cl. Stretford M32 96 E3
Milton Cres. Cheadle SK8 122 C5
Milton Cres. Farnworth BL4 60 B6
Milton Ct. 5 M'ster M7 63 E1
Milton Ct. M'ster M19 110 E4
Milton Dr. Oldham OL9 152 A6
Milton Dr. Poynton SK12 133 D4
Milton Dr. Sale M33 & WA15 108 A1
Milton Dr. Sale M33 108 B6
Milton Gr. M'ster M16 97 C2
Milton Gr. Sale M33 108 A6
Milton Gr. Wigan WN1 37 C3
Milton Gr. Wigan WN5 54 A6
Milton La Prim Sch. M28 60 B3
Milton Lodge. M16 97 C2
Milton Mount. 1 M18 99 D4
Milton Pl. M6 81 B3
Milton Rd. Bramhall SK7 132 E7
Milton Rd. Coppull PR7 19 E8
Milton Rd. Droylsden M34 84 D1
Milton Rd. Golborne WA3 90 D7
Milton Rd. Prestwich M25 63 C5
Milton Rd. Radcliffe M26 43 E4
Milton Rd. Stretford M32 96 E3
Milton Rd. Swinton M27 61 D1
Milton St. Denton M34 100 E4
Milton St. Eccles M30 79 D2
Milton St. Failsworth OL9 66 A1
Milton St. Hyde SK14 167 D4
Milton St. Leigh WN7 75 E5
Milton St. M'ster M7 158 E4
Milton St. Middleton M24 46 F1
Milton St. Mossley OL5 68 C2
Milton St. R'dale OL16 139 F7
Milton St. Ramsbottom BL0 138 B6
Milton St. Royton OL2 48 E4
Milton St John's CE Prim Sch. OL5 68 C2
Milton St Day Hospl. OL2 48 E4
Milton View. OL5 68 D2
Milverton Ave. SK14 102 C2
Milverton Cl. BL6 40 D5
Milverton Dr. SK7 & SK8 132 B5
Milverton Rd. M14 98 D3
Milverton Wlk. SK14 102 C2
Milwain Dr. SK4 111 C6
Milwain Rd. M'ster M19 111 A8
Milwain Rd. Stretford M32 96 C1
Mimosa Dr. M27 61 F2
Mincing St. 2 M4 159 A3
Minden Cl. Bury BL8 27 B2
Minden Cl. M'ster M20 110 D4
Minden Par. BL9 140 F2
Minden St. M6 80 E6
Mine St. OL10 29 D4
Minehead Ave. Hindley WN7 57 D2
Minehead Ave. M'ster M20 109 F6
Minehead Ave. Urmston M41 107 B8
Minerva Rd. Ashton-u-L OL6 & SK16 166 C2
Minerva Rd. Farnworth BL4 42 A2
Minford Cl. M40 83 B6
Minnie St. Bolton BL3 146 B3
Minnie St. Whitworth OL12 4 D2
Minoan Gdns. M7 81 C5
Minor St. Failsworth M35 66 A1
Minor St. Oldham OL8 153 E5
Minor St. R'dale OL11 30 C1
Minorca Ave. M11 83 D2
Minorca Cl. OL11 29 E8
Minorca St. BL3 147 E4
Minshull St. M1 & M60 159 A1
Minshull St S. M1 163 B8
Minsmere Cl. 1 M8 156 A6
Minsmere Wlks. SK2 124 F4
Minstead Cl. SK14 102 A1
Minster Cl. Bolton BL2 25 C2
Minster Cl. Dukinfield SK16 101 D6
Minster Dr. Alt'ham WA14 128 A8
Minster Dr. Cheadle SK8 123 A5
Minster Gr. M29 77 B7
Minster Rd. BL2 25 C2
Minster Way. OL9 48 A1
Mint St. BL0 1 C2
Minto St. OL7 166 A4
Minton St. Failsworth M40 83 C8
Minton St. Oldham OL4 67 A5
Mintridge Cl. 9 M18 99 E7
Mirabel St. M3 158 F3
Miranda Ct. M5 161 C8
Mirfield Ave. M'ster M9 64 D4
Mirfield Ave. Oldham OL8 66 E4
Mirfield Ave. Stockport SK4 168 B2
Mirfield Cl. WA3 90 D7
Mirfield Dr. Eccles M30 79 D4
Mirfield Dr. Middleton M24 46 F1
Mirfield Dr. Urmston M41 95 C4
Mirfield Rd. M9 64 D4
Miriam St. 8 Bolton BL3 146 B4
Miriam St. Failsworth M35 83 D5
Miry La. WN3 & WN6 150 A8
Mission St. OL10 29 C2
Missouri Ave. M5 154 E1
Mistletoe Gr. M3 158 D3
Mistral Ct. M30 79 E3
Mitcham Ave. M9 65 A3
Mitchell Cl. M22 121 F6
Mitchell Gdns. M22 121 E4
Mitchell Hey. OL12 139 E7
Mitchell Rd. WN5 71 E5
Mitchell St. Ashton-i-M WN4 73 C2
Mitchell St. Bury BL8 27 C4
Mitchell St. Failsworth M40 83 B5
Mitchell St. Golborne WA3 90 A8
Mitchell St. Ince-i-M WN2 56 A7
Mitchell St. Leigh WN7 75 B5
Mitchell St. Littleborough OL16 15 C3
Mitchell St. M'ster M12 164 F8
Mitchell St. Middleton M24 46 F1
Mitchell St. Oldham OL1 153 E8
Mitchell St. R'dale OL12 139 D8
Mitchell St. Wigan WN5 54 E6
Mitchell St. Worsley M28,M30 79 C3
Mitchells Quay. M35 83 E7
Mitcheson Gdns. M27 & M6 154 F3
Mitford Rd. M14 110 C7
Mitford St. M32 96 C1
Mitre Rd. M13 98 F4
Mitre St. Bolton BL1 143 E4
Mitre St. Failsworth M35 83 F8
Mitton Cl. Bury BL8 26 F2
Mitton Cl. Culcheth WA3 91 E5
Mitton Cl. Heywood OL10 28 F2
Mizpah Gr. BL8 27 B2
Mizzy Rd. OL12 14 F1
Moadlock. SK6 113 C4
Moat Ave. M22 121 C5
Moat Gdns. M22 121 C4
Moat Hall Ave. M30 95 A8
Moat Hall Sports Ctr. M30 79 A1
Moat House St. WN2 56 A7
Moat Rd. M22 121 C4
Moat Wlk. SK5 112 C7
Mobberley Cl. M19 110 E4
Mobberley Rd. Bolton BL2 42 E8
Mobberley Rd. Mob'ley WA14, WA15, WA16 128 E3
Mobberley Rd. Wilmslow SK9 130 D1
Mocha Par. M7 158 D3
Modbury Cl. SK7 124 A1
Modbury Wlk. 14 M8 156 A6
Mode Hill La. M45 45 C1
Mode Hill Wlk. M45 63 C8
Mode Wheel Rd. M5 154 D1
Mode Wheel Rd S. M5 154 D1
Mode Wheel Wkshp. M5 96 D8
Modwen Rd. M5 161 B6
Moelfre Dr. SK8 132 C7
Moffat Cl. BL2 42 F6
Moisant St. BL3 147 D3
Mold St. Bolton BL1 143 E3
Mold St. Oldham OL1 153 E8
Molesworth St. OL16 31 A7
Mollets Wood. M34 101 A5
Mollington Rd. M22 130 E8
Molyneux Rd. Reddish M19 99 C1
Molyneux Rd. Westhoughton BL5 40 B1
Molyneux St. R'dale OL12 139 D8
Molyneux St. Wigan WN1 151 D8
Mona Ave. Cheadle SK8 122 D1
Mona Ave. Stretford M32 96 C3
Mona St. Hyde SK14 167 E2
Mona St. Salford M6 81 A4
Mona St. Wigan WN1 150 B8
Monaco Dr. M22 109 D2
Monarch Cl. Irlam M44 105 E6
Monarch Cl. Oldham OL2 48 E5
Monart Rd. M9 64 E1
Moncrieffe St. Bolton BL3 145 F6
Moncrieffe St. Bolton BL4 148 A5
Mond Rd. M44 94 B4
Monde Trad Est. M17 96 A6
Money Ash Rd. WA15 119 E3
Monfa Ave. SK2 & SK3 124 A4
Monica Ave. M8 & M9 63 F2
Monica Gr. M19 110 F8
Monica Terr. WN4 73 B2
Monks Cl. M8 64 B2
Monks Ct. M5 80 B2
Monks Hall Gr. M30 79 F2
Monks La. BL2 25 D2
Monks' Rd. SK13 & SK14 116 A3
Monksdale Ave. M41 95 B2
Monkswood. OL1 153 E7
Monkton Ave. M18 99 C3
Monkwood Dr. 3 M9 157 E8
Monmouth Ave. Bury BL9 27 F5
Monmouth Ave. Sale M33 107 F5
Monmouth Cres. WN4 73 D2
Monmouth Rd. SK8 123 B1
Monmouth St. 2 M'ster M18 99 E6
Monmouth St. Middleton M24 65 C8
Monmouth St. Oldham OL8 152 C5
Monmouth St. R'dale OL11 139 F6
Monroe Cl. Salford M6 154 E4
Monroe Cl. Wigan WN3 55 A3
Mons Ave. OL11 30 C8
Monsal Ave. M'ster M7 81 A7
Monsal Ave. Stockport SK2 124 D7
Monsall Cl. BL9 45 A2
Monsall Hospl. M40 157 F6
Monsall Rd. M10 & M40 & M9 157 E6
Monsall St. M'ster M40, M9 157 D5
Monsall St. Oldham OL8 66 E3
Montagu Rd. SK2 124 D8
Montagu St. SK6 114 B2
Montague House. SK3 170 D8
Montague Rd. Ashton-u-L OL6 85 D3
Montague Rd. M'ster M16 & M17 161 A5
Montague Rd. Sale M33 108 B4
Montague St. BL3 146 B3
Montague Way. SK15 86 A5
Montana Sq. M18 99 E7
Montcliffe Cres. M14 & M16 97 F2
Monteagle St. M9 64 B4
Montford Rise. WN2 38 A2
Montford St. M5 96 F8
Montgomery. OL11 139 E6
Montgomery Dr. M45 & BL9 45 B2
Montgomery House. OL8 66 B1
Montgomery Rd. M13 98 F2
Montgomery St. Oldham OL8 66 B1
Montgomery St. R'dale OL11 30 C4
Montgomery Way. BL, M26 43 C5
Monton Ave. M30 79 E3
Monton Gn. M30 79 D4
Monton Green Prim Sch. Eccles M30 79 C4
Monton Green Prim Sch. Eccles M30 79 E4
Monton House. SK5 112 B4
Monton La. M30 79 E2
Monton Mews. 4 WN1 37 B3
Monton Mill Gdns. M28 79 C3
Monton Prep Sch. M30 79 D3
Monton Rd. Brinnington SK5 112 C4
Monton Rd. Eccles M30 79 D3
Monton St. Bolton BL3 147 E3
Monton St. M'ster M14 98 A4
Monton St. Radcliffe M26 43 E3
Montondale. M28 79 C3
Montonfields Rd. M28 79 C3
Montpellior Rd. M22 121 D2
Montreal St. Leigh WN7 74 E4
Montreal St. 3 M'ster M19 99 B1
Montreal St. Oldham OL8 66 F4
Montrey Cres. WN4 72 C3
Montrose Ave. Bolton BL2 25 C1
Montrose Ave. Dukinfield SK16 101 C7
Montrose Ave. 2 M'ster M20 110 A5
Montrose Ave. Ramsbottom BL0 11 A2
Montrose Ave. Stockport SK2 124 A3
Montrose Ave. Stretford M32 96 B2
Montrose Ave. Wigan WN5 54 D7
Montrose Cres. 3 M19 99 A1
Montrose Dr. BL7 25 B7
Montrose Gdns. OL2 48 F4
Montrose Sch. WN5 54 D7
Montrose St. R'dale OL11 30 C1
Montserrat Brow. BL1 23 D2
Montserrat Rd. BL1 23 E2
Monument Mansions. 6 WN1 37 C2
Monument Rd. WN1 37 D2
Monyash Ct. 18 SK13 171 D1
Monyash Gr. 19 SK13 171 D1
Monyash Lea. 20 SK13 171 D1
Monyash Mews. SK13 171 D1
Monyash Pl. 17 SK13 171 D1
Monyash Way. 18 SK13 171 E1
Moody St. WN6 19 E1
Moon Gr. M14 98 D3
Moon St. OL9 152 C7
Moor Allerton Sch. M20 109 F4
Moor Ave. WN6 35 E8
Moor Bank La. OL16 31 E3
Moor Cl. M26 43 E5
Moor Cres. OL3 51 B3
Moor Edge Rd. SK15 & OL5 86 F8
Moor End. M22 121 D8
Moor End Ave. M7 81 C8
Moor End Ct. M7 81 C8
Moor End Rd. SK12 & SK6 127 A5
Moor Gate. BL2 25 D5
Moor Gate La. OL12 & OL15 15 E7
Moor Hill. R'dale OL11 29 F8
Moor La. Bolton BL1 & BL3 145 E6
Moor La. Leigh WN7 75 E8
Moor La. M'ster M7 63 C1
Moor La. M'ster M25 & M7 81 B8
Moor La. Uppermill OL3 51 C2
Moor La. Urmston M41 95 A3
Moor La. Wilmslow SK9 136 D5
Moor La. Wilmslow SK9 136 E5
Moor La. Woodford SK7 132 E3
Moor La. Wythenshawe M23 109 A2
Moor Lodge. SK4 168 B4
Moor Nook. M33 108 D3
Moor Park Ave. OL11 30 B2
Moor Park Rd. M20 122 C8
Moor Platt. M33 108 D3
Moor Platt Cl. BL6 22 F3
Moor Rd. Haslingden BB4 1 A5
Moor Rd. Littleborough OL15 6 C1
Moor Rd. Orrell WN5 53 E6
Moor Rd. Ramsbottom BL8 138 A6
Moor Rd. Wythenshawe M23 120 E8
Moor Side La. BL0 12 A7
Moor St. Bury BL9 140 F3
Moor St. Eccles M30 79 B1
Moor St. Heywood OL10 29 B2
Moor St. Oldham OL1 & OL4 67 B7
Moor St. Shaw OL2 149 A6
Moor St. Swinton M27 79 F7
Moor Top Pl. SK4 168 B3
Moor View. Bacup OL13 3 B7
Moor View. Rawtenstall BB4 2 F6
Moor View Cl. OL12 13 F2
Moor Way. BL8 10 C3
Moorbottom Rd. BL8 10 E5
Moorby Ave. M19 110 E4
Moorby St. 7 OL1 67 A8
Moorby Wlk. BL3 145 F5
Moorclose St. M24 65 C8
Moorcock Ave. M27 80 B8
Moorcot Ct. M23 120 F7
Moorcroft. Edenfield BL0 1 D2
Moorcroft. R'dale OL11 30 F3
Moorcroft Dr. M19 110 F4
Moorcroft Rd. M23 & M33 108 F1
Moorcroft Sq. SK14 101 E6
Moorcroft St. 1 Droylsden M43 84 B1
Moorcroft St. Oldham OL8 66 C2
Moorcroft Wlk. M19 110 F4
Moordale Ave. OL4 49 E1
Moordale St. M20 110 A5
Moordown Cl. M8 156 B6
Moore Gr. WA13 117 B5
Moore House. M30 95 D8
Moore St. R'dale OL16 139 F7
Moore St. Wigan WN1 37 E1
Moore St E. WN1 37 E1
Moore Wlk. 10 M34 113 A7
Moore's Ct. 5 BL1 144 C8
Mooredge Terr. OL2 48 E2
Moores La. WN6 19 D2
Moorfield. Boothstown M28 77 F6
Moorfield. Edgworth BL7 9 D6
Moorfield. M'ster M7 63 C1
Moorfield. Radcliffe M26 43 E4
Moorfield. Worsley M28 78 F6
Moorfield Ave. Denton M34 101 A2
Moorfield Ave. Littleborough OL15 16 A7
Moorfield Ave. M'ster M14 110 C7
Moorfield Ave. Stalybridge SK15 102 D7
Moorfield Cl. 3 Eccles M30 79 D1
Moorfield Cl. Irlam M44 94 B3
Moorfield Cl. Swinton M27 79 D6
Moorfield Cres. WA3 91 A7
Moorfield Dr. Dukinfield SK14 101 E5
Moorfield Dr. Wilmslow SK9 136 E5
Moorfield Gr. Bolton BL2 25 B1
Moorfield Gr. M'ster SK4 168 B4
Moorfield Gr. Sale M33 108 D3
Moorfield Hamlet. OL2 48 F7

Napier St E. OL8 153 D5
Napier St W. OL8 153 D5
Naples Rd. SK3 123 B7
Naples St. M4 159 A3
Narbonne Ave. M30 80 A4
Narbuth Dr. M7 & M8 155 F7
Narcissus Ave. BB4 1 A8
Narcissus Wlk. 6 M28 59 F3
Narrow La. SK10 134 A1
Naseby Ave. M9 64 F4
Naseby Ct. M25 63 C5
Naseby Pl. M25 63 C5
Naseby Rd. SK5 99 F1
Naseby Wlk. M45 63 C8
Nash Rd. M17 95 F8
Nasmyth Ave. M34 101 A4
Nasmyth Bsns Ctr. M30 79 C2
Nasmyth Rd. M30 95 C8
Nasmyth St. Horwich BL6 22 C3
Nasmyth St. M'ster M40 & M8 156 C5
Nately Rd. M16 97 A2
Nathan Dr. M3 158 E2
Nathaniel Ct. WN2 56 B3
Nathans Rd. M22 121 C4
National Cycling Ctr. M11 83 A2
Naunton Ave. WN7 75 C5
Naunton Rd. M24 65 B7
Naunton Wlk. 24 M9 157 E8
Naval St. M4 159 C2
Navenby Ave. M16 97 C4
Navenby Rd. WN3 55 A2
Navigation Cl. WN7 75 E4
Navigation Prim Sch. WA14 119 D6
Navigation Rd.WA14, WA15 119 D6
Navigation Road Sta.WA14 119 E6
Naylor Ave. WA3 90 B8
Naylor Ct. 21 M40 159 C3
Naylor St. Atherton M46 58 C2
Naylor St. M'ster M10 & M40 160 D3
Naylor St. Oldham OL1 153 E7
Naylorfarm Ave. WN6 35 F5
Nazarene Theological Coll The. M20 110 A3
Naze Ct. 3 OL1 153 E8
Naze Wlk. SK5 112 C6
Nazeby Wlk. OL9 152 E5
Neal Ave. Ashton-u-L OL6 85 D3
Neal Ave. Gatley SK8 122 A1
Neale Ave. OL3 69 B5
Neale Rd. M21 109 B7
Near Birches Par. OL4 67 E4
Near Hey Cl. M26 43 E3
Nearbrook Rd. M22 121 C4
Nearcroft Rd. M23 121 B7
Nearmaker Ave. M22 121 C4
Nearmaker Rd. M22 121 C4
Neasden Gr. 6 BL3 144 C5
Neath Ave. M22 121 D7
Neath Cl. Poynton SK12 133 D5
Neath Cl. Prestwich M45 63 C7
Neath Fold. BL3 147 D3
Neath St. OL9 153 D7
Nebo St. BL3 147 D4
Nebraska St. BL1 143 E1
Neden Cl. M11 165 B8
Needham Ave. M21 109 B8
Needwood Cl. M40 157 D5
Needwood Rd. SK6 113 C5
Neenton Sq. M12 165 A7
Neild Gdns. WN7 75 E4
Neild St. M'ster M1 163 B8
Neild St. Oldham OL8 66 F4
Neill St. M7 158 E4
Neilson Cl. M24 65 C7
Neilson Ct. M23 121 A6
Neilston Ave. M40 83 B7
Nel Pan La. WN7 75 D8
Nell Carrs. BL0 11 E8
Nell La. M20 & M21 109 D6
Nell St. BL1 143 F4
Nellie St. OL10 29 B2
Nelson Ave. Eccles M30 79 D3
Nelson Ave. Poynton SK12 134 A3
Nelson Cl. SK12 134 A3
Nelson Ct. M'ster M15 97 E4
Nelson Ct. M'ster M40 160 D4
Nelson Dr. Droylsden M43 83 E2
Nelson Dr. Ince-i-M WN2 56 A8
Nelson Dr. Irlam M44 105 E6
Nelson Fold. M27 62 A1
Nelson Mandela Ct. 11 M16 97 E3
Nelson Rd. M9 64 D5
Nelson Sq. BL1 145 F7
Nelson St. Atherton M46 58 B3
Nelson St. Atherton M46 58 B4
Nelson St. Bacup OL13 4 C8
Nelson St. Bolton BL3 148 A5
Nelson St. 6 Bury BL9 44 F8
Nelson St. Denton M34 100 F4
Nelson St. Denton M34 100 F6
Nelson St. Eccles M30 79 D2
Nelson St. Farnworth BL4 60 E8
Nelson St. Hazel Grove SK7 124 F4
Nelson St. Heywood OL10 29 D1
Nelson St. 5 Hindley WN2 56 D6
Nelson St. Horwich BL6 22 D3
Nelson St. Hyde SK14 167 E2
Nelson St. Little Lever BL3 43 B3
Nelson St. 7 Littleborough OL15 16 B5
Nelson St. M'ster M7 155 D5
Nelson St. M'ster M10, M40 160 E4
Nelson St. M'ster M13 163 B5
Nelson St. Middleton M24 65 C7
Nelson St. Newton-l-W WA12 89 A3
Nelson St. Oldham OL4 67 E5
Nelson St. R'dale OL16 139 F7
Nelson St. Salford M5 154 E1
Nelson St. Stretford M32 96 D1
Nelson St. Tyldesley M29 77 B8
Nelson St. Walsden OL14 6 A8
Nelson Way. OL9 66 B4
Nelstrop Cres. SK4 111 D6
Nelstrop Rd. SK4 111 D6
Nelstrop Rd N.M19,SK4,SK5 111 C8
Nelstrop Wlk. SK4 111 C6
Nepaul Rd. M9 64 E1
Neptune Gdns. 11 M7 81 C5
Nesbit St. BL2 25 B3
Nesfield Rd. M23 108 F2
Neston Ave. Bolton BL1 24 F5
Neston Ave. M'ster M20 110 A6
Neston Ave. Sale M33 108 E2
Neston Cl. OL2 49 D7
Neston Gr. SK3 170 D5
Neston Rd. Bury BL8 26 F5
Neston Rd. R'dale OL16 31 C4
Neston St. M18 99 F7
Neston Way. SK9 131 D3
Neswick Wlk. M23 108 F2
Nether Hey St. OL8 67 B4
Nether St. Hyde SK14 113 F8
Nether St. M'ster M12 163 C8
Netherbury Cl. M18 99 C3
Netherby Rd. WN6 37 A3
Nethercroft Rd. WA15 120 C5
Netherfield Cl. OL8 66 C4
Netherfield Rd. BL3 147 E2
Netherfields. WN7 75 D7
Netherhey La. OL1 48 C2
Netherhouse Rd. OL2 149 A7
Netherland St. M5 161 A8
Netherlees. OL4 67 D5
Netherley Rd. PR7 19 E8
Netherlow Ct. SK14 167 E2
Netherton Gr. BL4 42 B2
Netherton Rd. M14 98 A1
Nethervale Dr. M9 157 E7
Netherwood Rd. M22 121 C7
Netley Ave. OL12 14 F3
Netley Gdns. M26 43 E5
Netley Gr. OL8 67 C4
Netley Rd. M23 121 A4
Nettlebarn Rd. M22 121 C5
Nettleford Rd. M16 & M21 109 E8
Nettleton Gr. M9 64 F1
Nevada St. 18 BL1 143 E1
Nevendon Dr. M23 120 F4
Nevile Ct. M7 81 B8
Nevile Rd. M7 81 B8
Nevill Rd. SK7 123 E2
Nevill Road Inf Sch. SK7 123 E2
Nevill Road Jun Sch. SK7 123 E2
Neville Cardus Wlk. 12 M14 98 C3
Neville Cl. BL1 145 E8
Neville Dr. M44 94 A4
Neville St. Hazel Grove SK7 124 D3
Neville St. Newton-l-W WA12 89 A3
Neville St. Oldham OL9 152 C7
Neville St. Platt Bridge WN2 56 A3
Nevin Ave. SK8 122 E1
Nevin Cl. Bramhall SK7 133 A7
Nevin Cl. 5 Oldham OL8 66 B2
Nevin Rd. M40 65 D1
Nevis Gr. BL1 24 D5
Nevis St. OL11 31 A2
Nevy Fold Ave. BL6 22 F3
New Allen St. M10 & M40 159 C3
New Bailey St. M3 158 E1
New Bank St. Hadfield SK14 104 A5
New Bank St. M'ster M12 164 F5
New Bank St. Tyldesley M29 77 A8
New Barn. BB4 1 B6
New Barn Ave. WN4 73 C3
New Barn Inf Sch. OL2 149 A6
New Barn Jun Sch. OL2 149 A6
New Barn La. Leigh WN7 75 E2
New Barn La. R'dale OL11 30 E4
New Barn La. Rawtenstall BB4 2 A8
New Barn Rd. OL8 67 A2
New Barn St. Bolton BL1 142 B1
New Barn St. 11 R'dale OL11 31 A5
New Barn St. Shaw OL2 149 A7
New Barton St. M6 80 C5
New Beech Rd. SK4 110 E2
New Bridge La. SK1 112 A2
New Bridge St. M3 158 F3
New Briggs Fold. BL7 8 E2
New Broad La. OL16 31 C3
New Broadcasting House (BBC). M1 163 A7
New Brook Sch. M20 109 F5
New Brunswick St. BL6 22 B3
New Buildings Pl. 4 OL16 139 F8
New Chapel La. BL6 22 F2
New Church Coll. M26 44 C2
New Church Ct. M45 62 F7
New Church Rd. BL1 23 F2
New Church St. M26 44 B3
New City Rd. M28 78 A8
New Collier's Row. BL1 23 E6
New Court Dr. BL7 8 E3
New Croft High Sch. M6 154 F3
New Cross. M4 159 B2
New Cross St.Salford M5, M6 80 C2
New Cross St. Swinton M27 80 A7
New Drake Gn. BL5 57 E5
New Earth St. Mossley OL5 68 D2
New Earth St. Oldham OL4 67 C5
New Elizabeth St. M8 156 A5
New Ellesmere App. M28 60 D4
New Elm Rd. M3 162 D8
New Field Cl. R'dale OL16 31 B8
New Field Cl. Radcliffe M26 43 E3
New Fold. WN5 53 C4
New Forest Rd. M23 120 C8
New Gate. BL5 146 A1
New George St. 8 BL8 27 C3
New Green. BL2 25 E6
New Hall Ave. Eccles M30 95 A8
New Hall Ave. Gatley SK8 131 B7
New Hall Ave. M'ster M7 155 D8
New Hall La. Bolton BL1 144 A8
New Hall La. Culcheth WA3 91 E1
New Hall La. Culcheth WA3 92 A2
New Hall Mews. BL6 23 D1
New Hall Pl. BL1 144 A8
New Hall Rd. Bury BL9 28 E4
New Hall Rd. M'ster M7 155 D8
New Hall Rd. Sale M33 108 F4
New Herbert St. M6 80 C5
New Hey Rd. Cheadle SK8 122 E6
New Hey Rd. Denshaw HD3 34 F8
New Heys Way. BL2 25 D6
New Holder St. BL1 145 E7
New Houses. OL4 68 C8
New Islington. M20 & M4 159 C2
New Kings Head Yd. M3 158 F2
New La. Bolton BL2 25 E2
New La. Eccles M30 79 B1
New La. Middleton M24 47 A1
New La. Royton OL2 48 D4
New Lane Ct. BL2 25 E2
New Lawns. SK5 100 A1
New Lees St. OL6 85 D5
New Line. OL13 4 B8
New Lodge. WN1 37 D2
New Market. M2 158 F1
New Market La. M1 159 A1
New Market St. WN1 150 C8
New Meadow. BL6 40 C7
New Miles La. WN6 35 F5
New Mill St. OL15 16 A5
New Mills Rd. SK14 & SK6 115 B4
New Moor La. SK7 124 D3
New Moss Rd. M44 105 D6
New Moston Inf Sch. M40 65 E2
New Moston Jun Sch. M40 65 E2
New Mount St. 5 M4 159 A3
New Park Rd. M5 161 B7
New Quay St. M3 158 E1
New Radcliffe St. OL1 153 E7
New Raven Ct. BL3 43 A3
New Rd. Adlington PR6 21 D8
New Rd. Aspull WN2 38 A5
New Rd. Littleborough OL15 15 F5
New Rd. Oldham OL8 66 E4
New Rd. Radcliffe M26 44 B2
New Rd. Tintwistle SK14 104 A7
New Rd. Whitworth OL12 4 B1
New Ridd Rise. SK14 113 D8
New Rock. BL5 57 F5
New Royd Ave. OL4 67 E8
New Smithfield Mkt. M18 165 C7
New St. Alt'ham WA14 119 D4
New St. Ashton-i-M WN4 73 C4
New St. Blackrod BL6 21 D2
New St. Bolton BL1 145 E6
New St. Bury BL8 26 F6
New St. Droylsden M43 100 A8
New St. Eccles M30 79 C1
New St. Littleborough OL15 15 F4
New St. M'ster M10 & M40 160 E4
New St. Milnrow OL16 32 A5
New St. Mottram-i-L SK14 115 A8
New St. Oldham OL4 67 E6
New St. Platt Bridge WN2 56 A2
New St. R'dale OL12 14 E2
New St. Radcliffe M26 44 B2
New St. Stalybridge SK15 102 A8
New St. Swinton M27 62 A1
New St. Uppermill OL3 69 B8
New St. Wigan WN5 54 B5
New St. Wilmslow SK9 136 E5
New Tame. OL3 50 C7
New Tempest Rd. BL6 40 C4
New Thomas St. M6 81 A4
New Tong Field. BL7 24 F7
New Union St. M20 & M4 159 C2
New Vernon St. 12 BL9 140 F4
New Viaduct St. M12 160 E2
New Wakefield St. M1 163 A7
New Way. OL12 4 C1
New Wellington Sch The. WA15 119 F6
New York. BL3 40 F5
New York Ave. M90 130 B7
New York St. OL10 29 B2
New Zealand Rd. SK1 112 B2
Newall Gr. WN7 75 F6
Newall Green High Sch. M23 120 F3
Newall Green Inf Sch. M22 121 B4
Newall Green Jun Sch. M22 121 A4
Newall Rd. M23 120 F3
Newall St. Littleborough OL15 16 B6
Newall St. Walsden OL14 6 A8
Newark Ave. Little Lever M26 43 C5
Newark Ave. 3 M'ster M14 98 B3
Newark Park Way. OL2 48 C6
Newark Rd. Hindley WN2 56 C4
Newark Rd. R'dale OL12 14 F3
Newark Rd. Reddish SK5 111 F5
Newark Rd. Swinton M27 62 B2
Newark Sq. OL12 14 F3
Newark St. WN6 36 F1
Newbank Chase. OL9 152 A8
Newbank Towers. M3 158 E3
Newbarn Cl. OL2 149 A7
Newbeck St. 3 M4 159 A2
Newberry Gr. SK3 170 D5
Newbold Cl. M15 162 F6
Newbold Moss. OL16 31 B8
Newbold St. Bury BL8 27 C2
Newbold St. R'dale OL16 31 C7
Newboult Rd. SK8 122 E6
Newbourne Cl. SK7 124 D3
Newbreak Cl. 2 OL4 67 D8
Newbreak St. 3 OL4 67 D8
Newbridge. OL5 86 D8
Newbridge Cl. WN4 72 D3
Newbridge Gdns. BL2 25 E4
Newbrook Ave. M21 109 D4
Newbrook Rd. BL5 & M46 58 F6
Newburn Ave. M9 64 F4
Newburn Cl. WN3 54 E4
Newbury Ave. M33 107 C4
Newbury Cl. SK8 132 A6
Newbury Dr. Eccles M30 79 B3
Newbury Dr. Urmston M41 95 C8
Newbury Gr. OL10 46 C8
Newbury Pl. M7 155 D7
Newbury Rd. Gatley SK8 131 C7
Newbury Rd. Little Lever BL3 42 F3
Newbury Wlk. Bolton BL1 143 E1
Newbury Wlk. M'ster M9 157 D6
Newbury Wlk. Oldham OL9 152 C7
Newby Dr. Alt'ham WA14 119 D6
Newby Dr. Gatley M22 122 A6
Newby Dr. Middleton M24 46 F3
Newby Dr. Sale M33 108 E3
Newby Rd. Bolton BL2 25 F2
Newby Rd. Hazel Grove SK7 124 D2
Newby Rd. Stockport SK4 168 C2
Newby Road Ind Est. SK7 124 D2
Newby Sq. WN5 54 B5
Newcastle St. M15 162 F7
Newcastle St. 3 M15 162 F7
Newcastle Way. 2 M34 101 A1
Newchurch. OL8 85 A8
Newchurch Ct. 6 M26 44 B3
Newchurch Cty Prim Sch. WA3 91 E2
Newchurch La. WA3 91 F2
Newchurch Rd. OL13 3 C8
Newchurch St. M'ster M11 164 F8
Newchurch St. R'dale OL11 30 D1
Newchurch Wlk. 5 M26 44 B3
Newcliffe Rd. M9 64 F4
Newcombe Cl. M11 160 F1
Newcombe Dr. M38 59 F6
Newcombe Rd. BL0 11 B2
Newcombe St. M3 158 F3
Newcroft. M35 84 B6
Newcroft Cres. M41 95 F1
Newcroft Dr. Stockport SK3 170 D6
Newcroft Dr. Stretford M41 96 A1
Newcroft Rd. M41 95 F1
Newdale Rd. M18 99 B2
Newearth Rd. M28 78 B8
Newenden Rd. WN1 37 B4
Newfield Ct. WA13 117 A5
Newfield Head La. OL16 32 B5
Newfield View. OL16 32 A6
Newgate. R'dale OL12, OL16 139 F7
Newgate. Wilmslow SK9 136 D7
Newgate Ave. WN6 35 E8
Newgate Dr. M38 60 A6
Newgate Rd. M33 107 C1
Newgate St. M4 & M60 159 A2
Newhall Ave. BL3 43 B6
Newhall Dr. M23 109 B2
Newhall Rd. SK5 100 A2
Newham Ave. M11 83 B2
Newhaven Ave. Droylsden M18 99 F7
Newhaven Ave. Leigh WN7 75 F8
Newhaven Bsns Pk. M30 79 E1
Newhaven Cl. BL8 27 C7
Newhaven Wlk. 4 BL2 25 B1
Newhey Ave. M22 121 D5
Newhey Cty Prim Sch. OL16 32 A4
Newhey Rd. Milnrow OL16 32 A5
Newhey Rd. Wythenshawe M22 121 D5
Newholme Ct. M32 96 E2
Newholme Gdns. M38 60 C3
Newholme Rd. M20 109 F5
Newhouse Cl. OL12 15 C6
Newhouse Cres. OL11 29 E8
Newhouse Rd. OL10 46 D8
Newhouse St. OL12 15 C6
Newick Wlk. 6 M9 64 E3
Newington Ave. M8 63 F3
Newington Ct. WA14 119 B3
Newington Dr. Bolton BL1 143 F1
Newington Dr. Bury BL8 27 A1
Newington Wlk. 7 BL1 143 F1
Newland Ave. WN5 54 D5
Newland Dr. BL5 58 F8
Newland St. M8 64 B1
Newlands. M35 83 E4
Newlands Ave. Bolton BL2 25 F1
Newlands Ave.Bramhall SK7 132 F7
Newlands Ave. Cheadle SK8 132 A7
Newlands Ave. Eccles M30 94 F7
Newlands Ave. Irlam M44 94 A2
Newlands Ave. R'dale OL12 14 F3
Newlands Ave. Tyldesley M29 77 A6
Newlands Ave.Whitefield M45 44 E1
Newlands Cl. Cheadle SK8 132 A7
Newlands Cl. R'dale OL12 14 F3
Newlands Dr. Blackrod BL6 38 E7
Newlands Dr. Golborne WA3 90 D8
Newlands Dr. Hadfield SK14 171 F4
Newlands Dr. M'ster M20 122 C8
Newlands Dr.Pendlebury M27 80 C6
Newlands Dr. Prestwich M25 63 A5
Newlands Dr. Wilmslow SK9 136 E5
Newlands Rd. Cheadle SK8 132 A7
Newlands Rd. Leigh WN7 75 F3
Newlands Rd. Wythenshawe M23 120 F8
Newlands Wlk. M24 46 E3
Newlyn Ave. SK15 86 D3
Newlyn Cl. SK7 124 D1
Newlyn Dr. Ashton-i-M WN4 73 B1
Newlyn Dr. Romiley SK6 113 A3
Newlyn Dr. Sale M33 108 C1
Newlyn St. M14 98 B2
Newman Ave. WN6 37 A2
Newman Cl. WN2 56 C6
Newman St. Ashton-u-L OL6 166 A3
Newman St. Hyde SK14 167 E3
Newman St. R'dale OL16 15 C3
Newman St. Wigan WN1 37 E2
Newmarket Cl. M33 107 B2
Newmarket Gr. OL7 84 E5
Newmarket Mews. M7 155 D6
Newmarket Rd. Ashton-u-L OL7 84 F5
Newmarket Rd. Little Lever BL3 43 A2
Newmill Wlk. 2 M8 156 A6
Newnham St. BL1 143 F4
Newpark Wlk. 6 M8 156 A6
Newport Ave. SK5 111 E7
Newport Mews. BL4 60 D7
Newport Rd. Bolton BL3 42 A3
Newport Rd. Denton M34 113 B8
Newport Rd. M'ster M21 97 A1
Newport St. Bolton BL1, BL3 145 F6
Newport St. Bury BL8 27 A5
Newport St. Farnworth BL4 60 D7
Newport St. M'ster M14 98 B3
Newport St. Middleton M24 47 C1
Newport St. Oldham OL8 153 D5
Newport St. Salford M6 154 E2
Newquay Ave. BL2 26 D1
Newquay Dr. SK7 132 F7
Newry Rd. M30 95 E8
Newry St. BL1 143 D3
Newry Wlk. M9 64 B3
Newsham Cl. BL3 145 D5
Newsham Wlk. 2 M'ster M18 99 B3
Newsham Wlk. Shevington WN6 36 F1
Newshaw La. SK13 171 F4
Newsholme Cl. WA3 91 F3
Newsholme St. M7 & M8 155 F7
Newstead. 14 OL12 139 E8
Newstead Ave. Ashton-u-L OL6 85 C7
Newstead Ave. M'ster M20 110 D5
Newstead Cl. SK12 133 D5
Newstead Gr. SK6 112 F3
Newstead Rd. Urmston M41 95 E3
Newstead Rd. Wigan WN3 54 F3
Newstead Terr. WA15 119 F7
Newton Ave. M'ster M12 98 F4
Newton Ave. M'ster M20 110 A6
Newton Bank Sch. WA12 89 E4
Newton Bsns Pk. SK14 102 A5
Newton Cl. WN1 37 D2
Newton Comm Hospl.WA12 89 B2
Newton Cres. M24 46 D3
Newton Cty Prim Sch.WA12 89 D3
Newton Dr. BL8 11 A1
Newton Gn. SK14 101 F5
Newton Hall Ct. SK14 101 C5
Newton Hall Rd. SK14 101 C5
Newton Heath Upper Sch. M40 157 F5
Newton La. WA12 89 E6
Newton Moor Ind Est.SK14 101 E5
Newton Park Dr. WA12 89 F3
Newton Rd. Alt'ham WA14 119 E7
Newton Rd. Billinge WN5, WA9, WN4 71 F6
Newton Rd. Failsworth M35 83 F5
Newton Rd. Golborne WA12 90 D5
Newton Rd. Golborne WA3 & WN7 91 A8
Newton Rd. Handforth SK9 131 A1
Newton Rd. M'ster M24 64 B6
Newton Rd.Newton-l-W WA12 89 F1
Newton Rd. Urmston M41 95 C2
Newton St. Ashton-u-L OL6 166 C3
Newton St. Bolton BL1 143 E2
Newton St. Bury BL9 27 F6
Newton St. Droylsden M43 84 C3
Newton St. Failsworth M40 83 C6
Newton St. Hyde SK14 167 D4
Newton St. Leigh WN7 75 F5
Newton St. M'ster M1, M4, M60 159 B1
Newton St. R'dale OL16 31 A5
Newton St. 4 Stalybridge SK15 85 F2
Newton St. Stockport SK3 170 E8
Newton St. Stretford M32 96 D1
Newton Sta. SK14 167 F4
Newton Terr. 23 Bolton BL1 143 E2
Newton Terr. 20 Dukinfield SK16 166 B1
Newton Westpark Prim Sch. WN7 75 C8
Newton Wlk. BL1 143 E2
Newton Wood Rd. SK16 101 B6
Newton-le-Willows Comm Sch. WA12 89 D5
Newton-le-Willows Sta. WA12 89 E3
Newtondale Ave. OL2 48 C4
Newtonhurst. SK14 102 A5
Newtonmore Wlk. M11 83 B1
Newtown Ave. M34 100 F2
Newtown Cl. M'ster M11 165 B8
Newtown Cl. Swinton M27 61 F2
Newtown Ct. M'ster M40 159 C4
Newtown Ct. Prestwich M25 63 C4
Newtown St. Prestwich M25 63 C4
Newtown St. Shaw OL2 149 B6
Newville Dr. M20 110 D5
Ney St. OL7 84 F6
Neyland Cl. BL1 40 F7
Niagara St. SK2 124 A6
Nicholas Croft. M4 159 A2
Nicholas Owen Cl. M11 165 C8
Nicholas Rd. OL8 66 E4
Nicholas St. Bolton BL2 148 A8
Nicholas St. M'ster M1 & M60 159 A1
Nicholls St. M12 164 D7
Nichols St. M6 81 B3
Nicholson Rd. SK14 101 C5
Nicholson Sq. SK16 101 B8
Nicholson St. Oldham OL4 67 E6
Nicholson St. R'dale OL11 139 F5
Nicholson St. Stockport SK4 & SK5 169 E2
Nickleby Rd. SK12 133 E3
Nicol Mere Cty Prim Sch. WN4 73 B5
Nicol Mere Dr. WN4 73 A5
Nicol Rd. WN4 73 B5
Nicola St. BL7 24 E8
Nicolas Rd. M21 97 A1
Nield Rd. M34 100 F3
Nield St. OL5 68 B2
Nield's Brow. WA14 119 C2
Nields Way. SK6 126 D4
Nigel Rd. M9 157 F7
Nigher Moss Ave. OL16 31 C6
Nightingale Cl. SK9 131 B1
Nightingale Ct. 10 WN1 37 A1
Nightingale Dr. M34 & M43 84 C1
Nightingale Rd. BL6 21 C3
Nightingale St. PR6 21 A8
Nightingales Wlk. 3 BL3 147 F4
Nile St. Bolton BL3 145 F5
Nile St. Dukinfield OL7 100 F8
Nile St. Oldham OL1 153 E8
Nile St. R'dale OL16 31 A8
Nile Terr. M7 155 D5
Nimble Nook. OL9 152 A5
Nina Dr. M40 65 C3
Nine Acre Ct. M5 161 B7
Nine Acre Dr. M5 161 B7
Ninehouse La. BL3 147 F4
Ninfield Rd. M22 & M23 121 B4
Ninian Ct. 2 M24 46 F1
Ninian Gdns. M28 60 D3
Ninth Ave. OL8 66 D1
Ninth St. M17 96 C6
Nipper La. M45 44 E2
Nisbet Ave. M22 121 E3
Niven St. M12 163 C7
Nixon Rd. BL3 146 C3
Nixon Rd S. BL3 146 C3
Nixon St. Failsworth M35 83 F7
Nixon St. R'dale OL11 30 B3
Nixon St. Stockport SK3 170 E8
No 2 Passage. SK3 169 D1
Noahs Ark La. WA16 136 A1
Noble Meadow. OL12 15 D4
Noble St. Bolton BL3 145 E5
Noble St. 7 Leigh WN7 76 A5
Noble St. Oldham OL8 66 F4
Noel Dr. M33 108 D4
Noel St. BL1 145 E7
Nolan St. M9 157 E8
Nona St. M6 154 E3
Nook Farm Ave. OL12 14 F3
Nook Fields. BL2 25 E3
Nook La. Ashton-u-L OL6 85 E6
Nook La. Golborne WA3 90 B8
Nook La. Tyldesley M29 77 D2
Nook Terr. OL12 14 F3
Nook The. Appley Bridge WN6 35 E7
Nook The. Bramhall SK7 132 D5
Nook The. Worsley M28 79 A4
Noon Ct. WA12 89 B1
Noon Sun Cl. OL3 69 A4
Noon Sun St. OL12 14 F1
Norbet Wlk. 8 M9 157 E7
Norbreck Ave. Cheadle SK8 123 A6
Norbreck Ave. M'ster M21 109 B7
Norbreck Cres. WN6 37 A2
Norbreck Gdns. BL2 148 C8
Norbreck St. BL2 148 C8
Norburn Rd. M13 98 F2
Norbury Ave. Billinge WN5 71 D6
Norbury Ave. Hyde SK14 167 D2
Norbury Ave. Marple SK6 125 E6
Norbury Ave. Sale M33 107 F4
Norbury Ave. 7 Salford M6 80 D5
Norbury Ave. Uppermill OL4 68 C6
Norbury Cl. M40 160 E4
Norbury Cres. SK7 124 D2
Norbury Dr. SK6 125 F6
Norbury Gr. Bolton BL1 25 A4
Norbury Gr.Hazel Grove SK7 124 E2
Norbury Gr. Swinton M27 61 F1
Norbury Hall Prim Sch. SK7 124 E1
Norbury Hollow Rd. SK7 134 B8
Norbury House. 4 OL4 67 B5
Norbury La. OL8 67 D3
Norbury Mews. SK6 125 E6
Norbury St. Leigh WN7 75 D5
Norbury St. M'ster M7 155 E6
Norbury St. R'dale OL16 31 B4
Norbury St. Stockport SK1 169 F1
Norbury Way. 9 SK9 131 D5
Norcot Wlk. 15 M15 162 D6
Norcross Cl. SK2 124 D5
Nordale Pk. OL12 13 D2
Nordek Cl. OL2 48 D5
Nordek Dr. OL2 48 D5
Norden Ave. M20 110 A6
Norden Cl. OL11 13 C2
Norden Comm Prim Sch. OL12 13 F2
Norden Ct. BL3 147 E4
Norden Rd. OL10 & OL11 29 E6
Norden Way. OL11 13 C2
Nordens Dr. OL9 47 F1
Nordens Rd. OL9 65 F8
Nordens St. OL9 152 A8
Noreen Ave. M25 63 C5
Norfield Cl. SK16 101 C8
Norfolk Ave. Droylsden M43 83 F3
Norfolk Ave. Heywood OL10 29 A2
Norfolk Ave. M'ster M18 99 C4
Norfolk Ave. Reddish M34 99 F3
Norfolk Ave. Reddish SK4 111 C6
Norfolk Ave. Whitefield M45 63 A8
Norfolk Cl. Hindley WN2 57 A6
Norfolk Cl. Irlam M44 105 C5
Norfolk Cl. Little Lever BL3 43 B4
Norfolk Cl. Littleborough OL15 6 C1
Norfolk Cl. Shaw OL2 48 F7
Norfolk Cres. M35 83 E6
Norfolk Dr. BL4 42 D1
Norfolk Gdns. M41 94 D3
Norfolk House. 3 M7 63 E1
Norfolk Rd. Atherton M46 58 C5
Norfolk Rd. M'ster M18 99 C4
Norfolk Rd. Orrell WN5 53 E1
Norfolk St. Glossop SK13 104 D1
Norfolk St. Hyde SK14 167 D2
Norfolk St. 10 M'ster M2 158 F1
Norfolk St. M'ster M1 159 A1
Norfolk St. Oldham OL9 66 C4
Norfolk St. R'dale OL11 139 F6
Norfolk St. Salford M6 81 A5
Norfolk St. Walkden M28 60 D6
Norfolk St. Wigan WN6 37 A2
Norfolk St. 9 Wigan WN5 54 F6
Norfolk Way. OL2 48 D2
Norford Way. OL11 29 E7
Norgate St. M20 110 B3
Norlan Ave. M34 100 E7
Norland Wlk. M40 83 A5
Norleigh Rd. M22 121 D8
Norley Ave. M32 96 F3
Norley Cl. OL1 48 B2
Norley Dr. M'ster M19 99 C2
Norley Dr. Sale M33 108 E4
Norley Hall Ave. WN5 54 C6
Norley Rd. Leigh WN7 75 B4
Norley Rd. Wigan WN5 54 C7
Norman Ave. Hazel Grove SK7 124 C3

Norman Ave. Newton-l-W WA11 ... 89 A7
Norman Ave. Newton-l-W WA12 ... 89 E3
Norman Cl. M24 ... 47 C1
Norman Gr. M'ster M12 ... 98 F4
Norman Gr. M'ster M12, M18 99 A4
Norman Gr. Reddish SK5 ... 111 E7
Norman House Prep Sch. M40 ... 65 D3
Norman Rd. Alt'ham WA14 . 119 C6
Norman Rd. Ashton-u-L OL6 .. 85 C6
Norman Rd. M'ster M14 ... 98 D2
Norman Rd. M'ster M7 ... 155 E7
Norman Rd. M'ster SK4 ... 168 B3
Norman Rd. R'dale OL11 ... 139 D6
Norman Rd. Sale M33 ... 108 B3
Norman Rd. Stalybridge SK15 85 F2
Norman Rd W. M9 ... 157 F7
Norman St. Bury BL9 ... 141 B4
Norman St. Failsworth M35 ... 66 A1
Norman St. Hyde SK14 ... 167 E2
Norman St. M'ster M12 ... 165 B5
Norman St. Middleton M24 ... 47 B1
Norman St. Oldham OL1 ... 153 D8
Norman St. Radcliffe M26 ... 44 D4
Norman Weall Ct. 5 M24 ... 47 A2
Norman's Pl. WA14 ... 119 D4
Normanby Chase. WA14 ... 119 B4
Normanby Gr. M27 ... 61 E1
Normanby Rd. M28 ... 60 C1
Normanby St. Bolton BL3 ... 146 C2
Normanby St. M'ster M14 ... 98 A4
Normanby St. Swinton M27 ... 61 E1
Normanby St. Wigan WN5 ... 54 B6
Normandale Ave. BL1 ... 142 A1
Normandy Cres. M26 ... 43 F3
Normanton Ave. M6 ... 80 C3
Normanton Cl. WN6 ... 36 E4
Normanton Dr. M9 ... 64 E4
Normanton Rd. SK3 & SK8 . 123 A6
Normington St. 1 OL4 ... 67 C7
Norreys Ave. M41 ... 94 E3
Norreys St. OL16 ... 31 A8
Norris Ave. SK4 ... 168 C2
Norris Bank Prim Sch. SK4 ... 168 B3
Norris Bank Terr. SK4 ... 168 C1
Norris Hill Dr. SK4 ... 168 B3
Norris Rd. M33 ... 108 D2
Norris St. Bolton BL3 ... 145 E5
Norris St. Farnworth BL4 ... 60 D7
Norris St. Little Lever BL3 ... 43 A3
Norris St. Tyldesley M29 ... 77 A8
Norris Towers. SK4 ... 169 E2
North Area Coll. SK4 ... 111 B5
North Ave. Eccles M41 ... 95 E6
North Ave. Farnworth BL4 ... 60 B8
North Ave. Leigh WN7 ... 74 F4
North Ave. Leigh WN7 ... 76 C3
North Ave. M'ster M19 ... 110 F7
North Ave. Ramsbottom BL8 .. 10 F1
North Ave. Stalybridge SK15 .. 86 A3
North Ave. Uppermill OL3 ... 69 B5
North Ave. Whitefield BL9 ... 45 B4
North Back Rock. Bury BL9 140 F2
North Blackfield La. M7 ... 81 C8
North Bolton Sixth Form Coll. BL1 ... 142 C4
North Brook Rd. SK14 ... 171 E4
North Broughton St. M3 ... 158 E2
North Butts St. WN7 ... 76 B3
North Cestrian Gram Sch. WA14 ... 119 C5
North Chadderton Sch. Chadderton OL9 ... 48 A2
North Chadderton Sch. Chadderton OL9 ... 152 A8
North Cheshire Jewish Prim Sch. SK8 ... 122 C2
North Circ. M45 ... 63 A6
North Cl. SK14 ... 103 F7
North Clifden La. M7 ... 155 E6
North Cres. Droylsden M11 & M43 ... 83 D3
North Cres. Failsworth M40 ... 65 D3
North Croft. OL8 ... 67 A3
North Dean St. M27 ... 62 A1
North Downs Rd. SK8 ... 122 F3
North Dr. Appley Bridge WN6 . 18 C2
North Dr. Droylsden M34 ... 84 C1
North Dr. Pendlebury M27 ... 80 B7
North Edge. WN7 ... 76 B6
North Gate. OL8 ... 66 E2
North George St. M3 ... 158 D2
North Gr. M'ster M13 ... 164 D5
North Gr. Urmston M41 ... 95 C2
North Gr. Walkden M28 ... 60 C3
North Harvey St. SK1 ... 169 F1
North Heaton Prim Sch. SK4 ... 111 C6
North Hill St. M3 ... 158 D3
North La. R'dale OL12 ... 139 F8
North La. Tyldesley M29 ... 77 A6
North Lonsdale St. M32 ... 96 E4
North Manchester General Hospl. M8 ... 64 B1
North Manchester Golf Course. M24 ... 64 D8
North Manchester High Sch for Boys. M9 ... 65 B3
North Manchester High Sch for Girls. M40 ... 65 A1
North Mead. M21 ... 109 B7
North Nook. OL4 ... 67 F8
North Par. Newhey OL16 ... 32 C4
North Par. Sale M33 ... 108 D2
North Park Rd. SK7 ... 123 E3
North Phoebe St. M5 ... 161 B8
North Pl. SK1 ... 169 F1
North Rd. Alt'ham WA15 ... 129 A8
North Rd. Atherton M46 ... 58 B5
North Rd. Carrington M31 ... 106 E4
North Rd. Droylsden M11, M43 ... 83 C2
North Rd. Droylsden M34 ... 84 D1
North Rd. Glossop SK13 ... 104 C3
North Rd. Prestwich M25 ... 62 F5
North Rd. Stretford M32 ... 96 B4
North Rd. Stretford M17 ... 96 C5
North Rd. Wythenshawe M90 130 C6
North Reddish Inf Sch. SK5 99 F1
North Reddish Jun Sch. SK5 99 F1
North Rise. OL3 ... 69 B5
North St. Ashton-i-M WN4 ... 73 D5
North St. Ashton-u-L OL6 ... 166 A2
North St. Atherton M46 ... 58 E3
North St. Heywood OL10 ... 29 B2
North St. Leigh WN7 ... 76 B4
North St. M'ster M8 ... 159 A4
North St. Middleton M24 ... 47 A2
North St. R'dale OL16 ... 31 A8
North St. Radcliffe M26 ... 44 C4
North St. Ramsbottom BL0 ... 1 C2
North St. Royton OL2 ... 48 D3
North St. 1 Royton OL2 ... 48 D4
North St. Whitworth OL12 ... 4 C1
North Stage. M5 ... 96 F8
North Star Dr. M3 ... 158 D1
North Trafford Coll of F Ed. M32 ... 96 F4
North Vale Rd. WA15 ... 119 F6
North Veiw. M45 ... 44 E2
North View. Mossley OL5 ... 68 E1
North View. Ramsbottom BL0 .. 1 C2
North View. Ramsbottom BL0 11 B2
North View Cl. OL4 ... 68 C5
North Walkden Prim Sch. M28 ... 60 C5
North Way. Bolton BL1 ... 25 B4
North Way. Brinnington SK5 112 C6
North Western St. M'ster M19 ... 111 A8
North Western St. M'ster M1 & M2 ... 163 C8
North Western St. M'ster M12 ... 164 D7
North Woodley. 6 M26 ... 44 C1
Northallerton Rd. M7 ... 81 B6
Northampton Rd. M10 & M40 & M9 ... 157 F6
Northampton Way. 1 M34 101 A1
Northavon Cl. M30 ... 80 A1
Northbank Gdns. M19 ... 110 E6
Northbank Ind Pk. M44 ... 105 F7
Northbank Wlk. M20 ... 109 D3
Northbourne St. M6 ... 154 E2
Northbrook Ave. M9 ... 63 F4
Northcliffe Rd. SK2 ... 124 C8
Northcombe Rd. SK3 ... 170 E5
Northcote Rd. SK7 ... 132 F7
Northcroft. WN1 ... 37 F1
Northdale Rd. M9 ... 64 B5
Northdene Dr. OL11 ... 29 F6
Northdown Ave. M'ster M15 162 D6
Northdown Av. Romiley SK6 113 C5
Northdowns Rd. OL2 ... 48 F8
Northen Gr. M20 ... 109 F4
Northend Rd. SK15 ... 86 B2
Northenden Golf Cse. M22 109 E2
Northenden Prim Sch. M22 ... 109 D1
Northenden Rd. Gatley M22 & SK8 ... 122 A6
Northenden Rd. Sale M33 . 108 C4
Northenden Rd. Sale M33 . 108 E3
Northenden View. M20 ... 110 B2
Northern Ave. M27 ... 62 C3
Northern Gr. BL1 ... 142 C1
Northfield Ave. M40 & OL9 ... 65 F2
Northfield Ct. WN3 ... 74 C1
Northfield Dr. SK9 ... 137 D8
Northfield Rd. Bury BL9 ... 27 F6
Northfield Rd. Failsworth M40 65 F2
Northfield St. BL3 ... 144 C5
Northfleet Rd. Eccles M30 ... 94 F8
Northgate. OL12 ... 14 C7
Northgate La. OL1 ... 49 E3
Northgate Rd. SK3 ... 123 C8
Northgraves Dr. M7 ... 155 F6
Northland Rd. Bolton BL1 ... 24 F6
Northland Rd. M'ster M9 ... 65 A3
Northlands. M26 ... 43 E5
Northleach Cl. BL8 ... 27 B3
Northleigh Dr. M25 ... 63 D3
Northleigh House. 1 M16 .. 97 B2
Northleigh Rd. M16 ... 97 B3
Northmoor Mews. 10 OL1 153 E8
Northmoor Rd. M12 & M18 ... 99 A3
Northolme Gdns. M19 ... 110 E5
Northolt Ave. WN7 ... 75 F8
Northolt Ct. M11 ... 83 D2
Northolt Dr. BL3 ... 147 F4
Northolt Rd. Wythenshawe M23 ... 108 F1
Northridge Rd. M9 ... 64 D6
Northside Ave. M41 ... 94 F1
Northstead Ave. M34 ... 101 B2
Northumberland Ave. OL6 & OL7 ... 166 B4
Northumberland Cl. M16 . 161 C5
Northumberland Cres. M16 ... 161 C5
Northumberland Rd. Brinnington SK5 ... 112 B6
Northumberland Rd. M'ster M16 ... 161 C5
Northumberland Rd. Partington M31 ... 105 E2
Northumberland St. M'ster M7 ... 155 E7
Northumberland St. Wigan WN1 ... 37 E1
Northumbria St. 9 BL3 ... 144 C5
Northurst Dr. M8 ... 63 F3
Northward Rd. SK9 ... 136 F6
Northway. Alt'ham WA14 ... 119 E6
Northway. Droylsden M43 ... 100 A8
Northway. 4 Eccles M30 ... 79 F2
Northway. Wigan WN1 ... 37 C1
Northways. WN6 ... 19 D2
Northwell St. 2 WN7 ... 75 E8
Northwold Cl. WN3 ... 54 D3
Northwold Dr. Bolton BL1 ... 40 E8
Northwold Dr. M'ster M9 ... 65 B3
Northwood. BL2 ... 25 D4
Northwood Ave. Cheadle SK8 ... 123 A3
Northwood Ave. Newton-l-W WA12 ... 89 F3
Northwood Cres. BL3 ... 144 C5
Northwood Gr. M33 ... 108 B4
Norton Ave. M'ster M12 ... 99 B3
Norton Ave. Reddish M34 ... 100 A3
Norton Ave. Sale M33 ... 107 D6
Norton Ave. Urmston M41 ... 95 D4
Norton Gr. SK4 ... 168 B1
Norton Grange. M25 ... 63 D3
Norton Rd. Boothstown M28 .. 77 E7
Norton Rd. R'dale OL12 ... 14 F3
Norton St. Bolton BL1 ... 143 F3
Norton St. M'ster M16 ... 97 D4
Norton St. M'ster M7 ... 155 E7
Norton St. 1 M'ster M3 ... 158 F2
Norton St. 17 M'ster M60 ... 159 C1
Norton St. M'ster M10, M40 160 E4
Norview Dr. M20 ... 122 B8
Norville Ave. M40 & M9 ... 65 D3
Norway Gr. SK5 ... 169 F4
Norway St. Bolton BL1 ... 143 D2
Norway St. M'ster M11 ... 164 E8
Norway St. Salford M6 ... 154 E2
Norway St. Stretford M32 ... 96 E3
Norweb Way. WN7 ... 76 B3
Norwell Rd. M22 ... 121 E5
Norwich Ave. Ashton-i-M WN4 73 D3
Norwich Ave. Chadderton OL9 48 A1
Norwich Ave. Denton M34 ... 100 F1
Norwich Ave. Golborne WA3 . 90 D8
Norwich Ave. R'dale OL11 ... 30 B7
Norwich Cl. Ashton-u-L OL6 ... 85 D8
Norwich Cl. Dukinfield SK16 102 A7
Norwich Dr. BL8 ... 140 D3
Norwich Rd. M32 ... 95 F3
Norwich St. OL11 ... 31 A5
Norwick Cl. BL3 ... 40 E4
Norwood. M25 ... 63 B2
Norwood Ave. Ashton-i-M WN4 ... 72 F6
Norwood Ave. Bramhall SK7 132 D5
Norwood Ave. Golborne WA3 90 F7
Norwood Ave. High Lane SK6 ... 134 D7
Norwood Ave. M'ster M7 ... 81 B8
Norwood Ave. M'ster M20 . 110 D4
Norwood Ave. Tyldesley M29 77 B6
Norwood Ave. Wigan WN6 ... 37 A3
Norwood Cl. Adlington PR6 ... 21 A8
Norwood Cl. Shaw OL2 ... 149 A8
Norwood Cl. Walkden M28 ... 78 E8
Norwood Cres. OL2 ... 48 E2
Norwood Ct. M32 ... 96 E1
Norwood Dr. Alt'ham WA15 120 D5
Norwood Dr. Swinton M27 ... 79 D7
Norwood Gr. Bolton BL1 ... 144 C8
Norwood Gr. Oldham OL2 ... 48 E2
Norwood Lodge. M7 ... 81 B8
Norwood Rd. Gatley SK8 ... 122 B6
Norwood Rd. Stockport SK2 124 B4
Norwood Rd. Stretford M32 .. 96 E2
Noseby Ct. M25 ... 63 C5
Nostell Rd. WN4 ... 73 A5
Nottingham Ave. SK5 ... 112 C5
Nottingham Cl. SK5 ... 112 C6
Nottingham Dr. Ashton-u-L OL6 ... 85 B7
Nottingham Dr. Bolton BL1 143 E1
Nottingham Dr. Brinnington SK5 ... 112 C6
Nottingham Dr. Failsworth M35 ... 84 A6
Nottingham Pl. WN1 ... 37 E1
Nottingham Way. 3 M34 . 101 A1
Nowell Ct. M24 ... 47 A3
Nowell House. M24 ... 47 A3
Nowell Rd. M24 ... 47 A3
Nudger Cl. OL3 ... 50 F2
Nudger Gn. OL3 ... 51 A2
Nuffield Rd. M22 ... 121 E4
Nugent House Sch. WN5 ... 71 D4
Nugent Rd. BL3 ... 147 E3
Nugget St. OL4 ... 67 B6
Nuneaton Dr. M10 & M40 ... 160 D3
Nuneham Ave. M20 ... 110 C7
Nunfield Cl. M40 ... 65 B2
Nunnery Rd. BL3 ... 146 B4
Nunthorpe Dr. M8 ... 156 C8
Nursery Ave. WA15 ... 128 E8
Nursery Cl. Glossop SK13 ... 116 C8
Nursery Cl. Sale M33 ... 108 D4
Nursery La. Cheadle SK3 ... 123 A7
Nursery La. Wilmslow SK9 ... 136 F5
Nursery Rd. Cheadle SK8 ... 123 A1
Nursery Rd. Failsworth M35 ... 84 A7
Nursery Rd. Prestwich M25 ... 63 A6
Nursery Rd. Stockport SK4 ... 168 C2
Nursery Rd. Urmston M41 ... 95 A4
Nursery St. M'ster M16 ... 97 F3
Nursery St. Salford M6 ... 154 F3
Nuthurst Rd. M40 ... 65 D1
Nutsford Vale. M18 ... 99 B4
Nutt La. M25 ... 63 E8
Nutt St. WN1 ... 37 E2
Nuttal Ave. M45 ... 62 F8
Nuttal Mews. M45 ... 62 F8
Nuttall Ave. Horwich BL6 ... 22 A3
Nuttall Ave. Little Lever BL3 ... 43 C3
Nuttall Ave. Whitefield M45 ... 62 F8
Nuttall Cl. BL0 ... 138 C5
Nuttall Hall Cott s. BL0 ... 11 D5
Nuttall Hall Rd. BL0 ... 11 D5
Nuttall La. BL0 ... 138 B5
Nuttall Mews. M45 ... 62 F8
Nuttall Rd. BL0 ... 11 D4
Nuttall Sq. BL9 ... 44 F5
Nuttall St. Atherton M46 ... 58 E3
Nuttall St. Bury BL9 ... 141 A1
Nuttall St. Irlam M44 ... 105 E6
Nuttall St. M'ster M16 ... 161 C5
Nuttall St. M'ster M11 ... 165 A7
Nuttall St. Oldham OL8 ... 67 B4

O'Kane House. 10 M30 ... 79 D1
Oadby Cl. M12 ... 99 A4
Oak Ave. Abram WN2 ... 74 C7
Oak Ave. Cheadle SK8 ... 123 A2
Oak Ave. Golborne WA3 ... 90 B8
Oak Ave. Hindley WN2 ... 57 A3
Oak Ave. 9 Horwich BL6 ... 22 E1
Oak Ave. Irlam M44 ... 105 D5
Oak Ave. Little Lever BL3 ... 43 B3
Oak Ave. M'ster M21 ... 109 B8
Oak Ave. M'ster SK4 ... 168 B2
Oak Ave. Middleton M24 ... 65 A7
Oak Ave. Newton-l-W WA12 ... 89 D3
Oak Ave. Ramsbottom BL0 ... 11 A2
Oak Ave. Reddish M18 ... 99 F4
Oak Ave. Romiley SK6 ... 113 C2
Oak Ave. Royton OL2 ... 48 D6
Oak Ave. Standish WN6 ... 36 F8
Oak Ave. Whitefield M45 ... 62 F7
Oak Ave. Wilmslow SK9 ... 136 F5
Oak Bank. M'ster M9 ... 157 D8
Oak Bank. Prestwich M25 ... 62 F1
Oak Bank. Prestwich M25 ... 63 C5
Oak Bank Ave. M9 ... 64 F1
Oak Bank Cl. M45 ... 63 B8
Oak Brow Cotts. SK9 ... 130 E4
Oak Cl. Mottram-i-L SK14 ... 103 A4
Oak Cl. Whitworth OL12 ... 4 D4
Oak Cl. Wilmslow SK9 ... 136 F6
Oak Cotts. SK9 ... 130 E4
Oak Ct. SK6 ... 113 A5
Oak Dr. Bramhall SK7 ... 132 C7
Oak Dr. M'ster M14 ... 98 D1
Oak Dr. Marple SK6 ... 125 D6
Oak Dr. Reddish M34 ... 100 A4
Oak Gates. BL7 ... 8 E1
Oak Gr. Ashton-u-L OL6 ... 85 D6
Oak Gr. Cheadle SK8 ... 122 E5
Oak Gr. Eccles M30 ... 79 B1
Oak Gr. Poynton SK12 ... 133 D4
Oak Gr. Urmston M41 ... 95 E2
Oak Hill. OL15 ... 15 F5
Oak Hill Cl. WN1 ... 37 B4
Oak La. Whitefield M45 ... 63 B8
Oak La. Wilmslow SK9 ... 136 F6
Oak Lea Ave. SK9 ... 137 A5
Oak Lodge. SK7 ... 132 F7
Oak Mews. SK9 ... 131 C1
Oak Rd. Alt'ham WA15 ... 119 E3
Oak Rd. Cheadle SK8 ... 122 E5
Oak Rd. Failsworth M35 ... 83 F6
Oak Rd. M'ster M7 ... 81 C5
Oak Rd. M'ster M20 ... 110 B5
Oak Rd. Oldham OL8 ... 66 D2
Oak Rd. Partington M31 ... 105 D2
Oak Rd. Sale M33 ... 108 D4
Oak St. Atherton WN7 ... 58 A1
Oak St. Denton M34 ... 100 F6
Oak St. Eccles M30 ... 79 D1
Oak St. Glossop SK13 ... 104 C1
Oak St. Hazel Grove SK7 ... 124 D3
Oak St. Heywood OL10 ... 29 B3
Oak St. Hyde SK14 ... 167 E4
Oak St. Leigh WN7 ... 75 F3
Oak St. Littleborough OL15 ... 16 C5
Oak St. M'ster M4 ... 159 A2
Oak St. 2 M'ster M4 ... 159 B2
Oak St. Middleton M24 ... 65 D7
Oak St. Newhey OL16 ... 32 B4
Oak St. R'dale OL16 ... 139 F7
Oak St. 2 Radcliffe M26 ... 44 C1
Oak St. Ramsbottom BL0 ... 138 B5
Oak St. Shaw OL2 ... 149 C7
Oak St. Stockport SK3 ... 123 B8
Oak St. Swinton M27 ... 62 A1
Oak St. Tyldesley M29 ... 59 A1
Oak St. Whitworth OL12 ... 4 D5
Oak St. Wigan WN1 ... 151 E7
Oak Terr. OL15 ... 6 D2
Oak Tree Cl. Atherton WN7 ... 58 A1
Oak Tree Cl. Stockport SK2 . 124 D8
Oak Tree Cres. SK15 ... 102 B8
Oak Tree Dr. SK16 ... 101 F7
Oak View. OL12 ... 4 D4
Oak View Rd. OL3 ... 69 B5
Oak Wood View. SK15 ... 86 C6
Oakbank. WN2 ... 56 B3
Oakbank Ave. OL9 ... 65 F8
Oakbank Dr. BL1 ... 24 D6
Oakcliffe Rd. OL12 & OL16 ... 15 D4
Oakcroft. SK15 ... 102 E8
Oakdale. BL2 ... 25 E4
Oakdale Cl. M45 ... 62 D8
Oakdale Ct. Delph OL3 ... 50 E3
Oakdale Ct. Stalybridge SK15 86 B2
Oakdale Dr. Gatley SK8 ... 122 B2
Oakdale Dr. M'ster M20 ... 110 C1
Oakdale Dr. Tyldesley M29 ... 77 C6
Oakdale Sch. SK16 ... 101 E6
Oakdene. M27 & M28 ... 79 B6
Oakdene Ave. Gatley SK8 ... 131 C7
Oakdene Ave. Reddish SK4 111 D5
Oakdene Cres. SK6 ... 125 F7
Oakdene Gdns. SK6 ... 125 F7
Oakdene Rd. Marple SK6 ... 125 F7
Oakdene Rd. Middleton M24 . 65 C8
Oakdene Rd. Sale WA15 ... 120 B8
Oakdene St. M9 ... 157 F8
Oaken Bank Rd. OL10 ... 47 A5
Oaken Clough. 3 OL7 ... 85 A6
Oaken Clough Dr. 1 OL7 ... 85 A6
Oaken Clough Terr. OL7 ... 84 F6
Oaken St. OL7 ... 85 A6
Oakenbottom Rd. BL2 ... 42 D7
Oakenclough. 1 OL1 ... 153 E7
Oakenclough Cl. SK9 ... 131 D2
Oakenclough Dr. BL1 ... 23 F2
Oakenden Cl. WN4 ... 73 A6
Oakengates. WN6 ... 19 F1
Oakenrod Hill. OL11 ... 30 C6
Oakenrod Prim Sch. OL11 139 D7
Oakenshaw Ave. OL12 ... 14 C6
Oakenshaw View. OL12 ... 14 C6
Oaker Ave. M20 ... 109 E4
Oakes St. BL4 ... 60 F7
Oakes The. SK13 ... 116 A7
Oakfield. Dukinfield SK16 ... 101 E6
Oakfield. M'ster M25 ... 63 D3
Oakfield. Sale M33 ... 108 A5
Oakfield Ave. Atherton M46 .. 58 C4
Oakfield Ave. Cheadle SK8 . 122 E6
Oakfield Ave. Droylsden M43 83 F1
Oakfield Ave. Golborne WA3 . 73 F1
Oakfield Ave. M'ster M16 ... 97 A3
Oakfield Ave. M'ster M16 ... 97 D3
Oakfield Ave. Mossley SK15 .. 86 E6
Oakfield Cl. Alderley Edge SK9 ... 137 B3
Oakfield Cl. Horwich BL6 ... 22 F2
Oakfield Cres. WN2 ... 38 C5
Oakfield Ct. WA15 ... 119 F6
Oakfield Dr. M38 ... 59 E5
Oakfield Gr. Farnworth BL4 ... 60 C6
Oakfield Gr. M'ster M18 ... 99 D4
Oakfield Prim Sch. SK14 ... 101 E5
Oakfield Rd. Alderley Edge SK9 ... 137 B2
Oakfield Rd. Alt'ham WA15 119 E4
Oakfield Rd. Dukinfield SK14 101 E5
Oakfield Rd. Hadfield SK13 . 171 E3
Oakfield Rd. M'ster M20 ... 110 A3
Oakfield Rd. Poynton SK12 ... 133 F4
Oakfield Rd. Stockport SK3 .. 170 F5
Oakfield St. Alt'ham WA15 . 119 E5
Oakfield St. M'ster M7 & M8 156 A6
Oakfield Terr. OL11 ... 30 C8
Oakfield Trad Est. WA15 ... 119 E5
Oakfold Ave. OL6 ... 85 D6
Oakford Ave. M10 & M40 ... 159 C3
Oakford Wlk. BL3 ... 146 C4
Oakham Cl. BL8 ... 27 D5
Oakham Mews. M7 ... 63 D1
Oakham Rd. M34 ... 101 A1
Oakhead. WN7 ... 76 C3
Oakhill Cl. BL2 ... 43 A7
Oakhill Ct. M7 ... 155 E7
Oakhill Trad Est. M28 ... 60 C6
Oakhill Way. M8 ... 155 F7
Oakhouse Dr. M21 ... 109 B7
Oakhurst Chase. SK9 ... 137 A2
Oakhurst Dr. SK3 & SK8 ... 123 B5
Oakhurst Gr. BL5 ... 57 C7
Oakington Ave. 10 M14 ... 98 B3
Oakland Ave. Eccles M6 ... 80 B4
Oakland Ave. M'ster M19 ... 110 E4
Oakland Ave. Stockport SK2 124 D6
Oakland Ct. SK12 ... 133 D4
Oakland Gr. BL1 ... 142 A2
Oakland Terr. OL11 ... 30 C1
Oaklands. BL1 ... 40 F7
Oaklands Ave. Cheadle SK8 123 A2
Oaklands Ave. Marple SK6 . 126 C8
Oaklands Cl. SK9 ... 131 E1
Oaklands Cty Inf Sch. SK9 131 E1
Oaklands Dene. SK14 ... 102 A2
Oaklands Dr. Hazel Grove SK7 ... 124 E1
Oaklands Dr. Hyde SK14 ... 102 A2
Oaklands Dr. Prestwich M25 . 63 B4
Oaklands Dr. Sale M33 ... 108 A5
Oaklands Hospl The. M6 ... 80 B4
Oaklands House. M14 ... 98 C1
Oaklands Pk. OL4 ... 68 F5
Oaklands Rd. Edenfield BL0 ... 1 D2
Oaklands Rd. Golborne WA3 . 90 F7
Oaklands Rd. M'ster M7 ... 81 A8
Oaklands Rd. Oldham OL2 ... 48 E2
Oaklands Rd. Swinton M27 ... 79 D6
Oaklands Rd. Uppermill OL4 .. 68 F5
Oaklea. 1 M'ster M16 ... 97 C3
Oaklea. Shevington Moor WN6 19 A2
Oaklea Rd. M33 ... 107 E5
Oakleigh. M'ster SK4 ... 168 B3
Oakleigh. 2 Stockport SK3 . 123 F4
Oakleigh Ave. Alt'ham WA15 120 A7
Oakleigh Ave. Bolton BL3 ... 42 A2
Oakleigh Ave. 1 M'ster M19 110 F7
Oakleigh Cl. OL10 ... 46 E7
Oakley Ave. WN5 ... 71 E6
Oakley Cl. Failsworth M40 ... 83 C5
Oakley Cl. Radcliffe M26 ... 62 A8
Oakley Pk. BL1 ... 40 F7
Oakley St. Littleborough OL15 15 E4
Oakley St. Salford M5 ... 154 D1
Oakley Villas. SK4 ... 168 B3
Oaklings The. WN2 ... 57 A3
Oakmere Ave. M28 ... 79 C4
Oakmere Cl. M22 ... 121 D4
Oakmere Rd. Cheadle SK8 ... 122 F4
Oakmere Rd. Handforth SK9 131 D5
Oakmoor Dr. M7 ... 81 B8
Oakmoor Rd. M23 ... 121 A6
Oakridge Wlk. 3 M9 ... 157 D7
Oaks Ave. BL2 ... 25 C5
Oaks La. BL1 & BL2 ... 25 B5
Oaks Prim Sch The. BL1 ... 24 F6
Oaks The. Gatley SK8 ... 122 A2
Oaks The. Hyde SK14 ... 102 A3
Oakshaw Dr. OL12 ... 14 A1
Oakside Cl. SK8 ... 122 E6
Oaktree Ct. SK8 ... 122 D5
Oakville Dr. M30 ... 80 A4
Oakville Terr. 11 M40 ... 64 F1
Oakway. M20 ... 122 C8
Oakwell Dr. M'ster M7 & M8 . 63 E1
Oakwell Dr. Whitefield BL9 ... 45 B3
Oakwell Mansions. M7 ... 63 E1
Oakwood. Chadderton M24 ... 65 E7
Oakwood. Glossop SK13 ... 115 F8
Oakwood. Sale M33 ... 107 C4
Oakwood Ave. Ashton-i-M WN4 ... 73 A2
Oakwood Ave. Denton M34 100 E7
Oakwood Ave. Failsworth M40 ... 65 D1
Oakwood Ave. Gatley SK8 .. 122 B5
Oakwood Ave. Kearsley M27 61 E4
Oakwood Ave. Shevington WN6 ... 35 F5
Oakwood Ave. Walkden M28 60 F2
Oakwood Ave. Wilmslow SK9 ... 136 E6
Oakwood Cl. BL8 ... 27 B3
Oakwood Ct. WA14 ... 128 B8
Oakwood Dr. Bolton BL1 ... 40 F8
Oakwood Dr. Leigh WN7 ... 75 E1
Oakwood Dr. Pendlebury M6 . 80 B5
Oakwood Dr. Walkden M28 ... 60 F2
Oakwood Est. M5 ... 154 D1
Oakwood High Sch. M'ster M21 ... 109 C5
Oakwood High Sch. Pendlebury M6 ... 80 C5
Oakwood High Sch (Upper Sch). M21 ... 109 C7
Oakwood La. WA14 ... 119 B1
Oakwood Rd. Disley SK12 .. 135 D6
Oakwood Rd. Romiley SK6 . 113 C2
Oakworth Croft. OL4 ... 49 F4
Oakworth St. M9 ... 64 C3
Oat St. SK1 ... 124 A7
Oatlands Rd. M22 ... 121 C2
Oban Ave. OL1 ... 49 B1
Oban Cres. SK3 ... 123 D4
Oban Dr. Garswood WN4 ... 72 C4
Oban Dr. Sale M33 ... 108 E3
Oban Gr. BL1 ... 24 E5
Oban St. BL1 ... 143 D3
Oban Way. WN2 ... 38 D5
Oberlin St. Oldham OL4 ... 67 D7
Oberlin St. R'dale OL11 ... 139 D5
Oberon Cl. M30 ... 79 D2
Occlestone Cl. M33 ... 108 E1
Ocean St. WA14 ... 119 B6
Ocean Street Trad Est. WA14 ... 119 B7
Ocean Wlk. M15 ... 162 F5
Ockendon Dr. M9 ... 157 E7
Octavia Dr. M40 ... 83 C4
Octavia House. 7 M6 ... 154 F3
Odell St. M11 ... 165 B7
Odessa Ave. M6 ... 80 B4
Odette St. M18 ... 99 C4
Off Grove Rd. SK15 ... 86 D4
Off Ridge Hill La. 2 SK15 ... 85 F2
Off Stamford St. SK15 ... 86 D4
Offerton Dr. SK2 ... 124 D6
Offerton Fold. SK2 ... 124 C7
Offerton Gn. SK2 ... 124 F6
Offerton Hall Prim Sch. SK2 ... 124 E6
Offerton High Sch. SK2 ... 124 E8
Offerton Ind Est. SK2 ... 124 C7
Offerton La. SK1 & SK2 ... 124 C8
Offerton Rd. SK2 & SK7 ... 125 A4
Offerton St. Horwich BL6 ... 22 D4
Offerton St. Stockport SK1 .. 112 B2
Ogbourne Wlk. 11 M13 ... 163 C6
Ogden Cl. Heywood OL10 ... 29 A2
Ogden Cl. Whitefield M45 ... 45 A1
Ogden Ct. SK14 ... 167 E2
Ogden Gdns. SK16 ... 101 E8
Ogden Gr. M22 ... 121 F4
Ogden La. M'ster M11 & M18 99 D7
Ogden La. Newhey OL16 ... 32 D5
Ogden Rd. Bramhall SK7 ... 132 D5
Ogden Rd. Failsworth M35 ... 83 F6
Ogden Sq. SK16 ... 101 B8
Ogden St. 4 M'ster M20 ... 110 B3
Ogden St. Middleton M24 ... 65 A8
Ogden St. Mottram-i-L SK14 115 B8
Ogden St. 9 Oldham OL4 ... 67 D6
Ogden St. Oldham OL9 ... 152 C8
Ogden St. Prestwich M25 ... 63 C4
Ogden St. R'dale OL11 ... 30 C2
Ogden St. Swinton M27 ... 79 F7
Ogden Wlk. M45 ... 63 A8
Ogmore Wlk. M40 ... 65 C2
Ogwen Dr. M25 ... 63 B5
Ohio Ave. M5 ... 96 F8
Okehampton Cl. M26 ... 43 C5
Okehampton Cres. M33 ... 107 D5
Okell Gr. WN7 ... 75 D6
Okeover Rd. M7 ... 155 D8
Olaf St. 13 BL2 ... 25 B1
Old Bank Cl. SK6 ... 113 A3
Old Bank St. M2 ... 158 F1
Old Barn Pl. BL7 ... 25 A8
Old Barton Rd. M41 ... 95 C7
Old Bedions Spts Ctr. M20 122 A8
Old Bent La. OL12 ... 15 A7
Old Birley St. M15 ... 162 F5
Old Boston. WA11 ... 89 A7
Old Boston Trad Est. WA11 89 B8
Old Broadway. M20 ... 110 B5
Old Brook Cl. OL2 ... 49 D8
Old Brow. Mossley OL5 ... 68 C1
Old Brow La. OL16 ... 15 C3
Old Brown Ct. OL15 ... 86 C8
Old Chapel St. SK3 ... 170 D7
Old Church St. Failsworth M40 ... 83 C6
Old Church St. Oldham OL1 153 F7
Old Clay Dr. OL12 ... 15 D4
Old Clough La. Walkden M28 60 F1
Old Clough La. Worsley M28 78 F8
Old Colliery Yd. WN4 ... 72 C3
Old Croft Mews. SK1 ... 124 B7
Old Crofts Bank. M41 ... 95 C3
Old Cross St. OL6 ... 166 C3
Old Ctyd The. M22 ... 121 F5
Old Delph Rd. OL11 ... 13 F1
Old Doctors St. BL8 ... 26 F7
Old Eagley Mews. BL1 ... 24 F6
Old Edge La. OL2 ... 48 E2
Old Elm St. M13 ... 163 C6
Old Engine La. BL0 ... 11 D6
Old Farm Cres. M43 ... 99 F8
Old Farm Dr. SK2 ... 124 F6
Old Fold. Swinton M30 ... 79 C4
Old Fold. 7 Wigan WN5 ... 54 B6
Old Fold Rd. Aspull WN2 ... 38 D5
Old Fold Rd. Westhoughton BL5 ... 57 C7
Old Garden The. WA15 ... 120 B7
Old Gardens St. 3 SK1 ... 170 F8
Old Gn. BL2 ... 25 E6
Old Green. BL8 ... 10 F1
Old Greenwood La. BL6 ... 22 D1
Old Ground St. BL0 ... 138 C6
Old Hall Cl. SK13 ... 104 D2
Old Hall Clough. BL6 ... 40 C7
Old Hall Cres. SK9 ... 131 E3
Old Hall Ct. Sale M33 ... 108 E4
Old Hall Ct. Whitefield M45 ... 62 C7
Old Hall Cty Prim Sch. BL8 . 27 B7
Old Hall Dr. Ashton-i-M WN4 . 73 A2
Old Hall Dr. M'ster M18 ... 99 D4
Old Hall Dr. Stockport SK2 .. 124 E6

218 Old – Pal

Old Hall Drive Prim Sch. M18 99 D4
Old Hall Farm. BL3 42 E4
Old Hall La. Bolton BL1 & BL6 23 C1
Old Hall La. M'ster M25 64 A6
Old Hall La. M'ster M13, M14, M19 98 E2
Old Hall La. Marple SK6 126 C5
Old Hall La. Mottram-i-L SK14 103 A5
Old Hall La. Westhoughton BL5 57 E6
Old Hall La. Whitefield M45 & M26 62 C6
Old Hall La. Woodford SK7 132 D1
Old Hall La. Worsley M28 78 E7
Old Hall Mill La. M46 & WN7 76 A8
Old Hall Rd. Failsworth M40 83 B7
Old Hall Rd. Gatley SK8 122 A6
Old Hall Rd. M'ster M7 63 D1
Old Hall Rd. Sale M33 108 E4
Old Hall Rd. Stretford M32 96 A4
Old Hall Rd. Whitefield M45 62 C7
Old Hall Sq. 2 SK14 104 A5
Old Hall St. Dukinfield SK16 101 A7
Old Hall St. Farnworth BL4 60 E7
Old Hall St. Ince-i-M WN3 151 E6
Old Hall St. 3 M'ster M11 99 E7
Old Hall St. Middleton M24 47 A1
Old Hall St N. BL1 145 F7
Old Hey Wlk. WA12 89 B1
Old Heyes Rd. WA15 120 B8
Old House Terrs. OL6 85 E5
Old Kiln. OL13 3 D8
Old Kiln La. BL1 23 D1
Old La. Bury BL9 27 F8
Old La. Glossop SK13 116 A7
Old La. Horwich BL6 22 F2
Old La. M'ster M11 99 D7
Old La. Oldham OL9 66 B4
Old La. Oldham OL4 68 A8
Old La. Shevington WN6 36 B6
Old La. Uppermill OL3 51 B2
Old La. Uppermill OL4 68 E6
Old La. Walkden M38 59 F6
Old La. Westhoughton BL5 57 D8
Old La. Whitworth OL12 & OL13 4 E6
Old La. Wigan WN1 37 B4
Old Lansdowne Rd. M20 110 A4
Old Lees St. OL6 85 D5
Old Links Golf Course. BL1 23 E3
Old Lord's Cres. BL6 22 B5
Old Manor Pk. M46 58 A2
Old Market Pl. WA14 119 D5
Old Market St. M9 64 D2
Old Meadow Dr. M34 100 F5
Old Meadow La. WA15 120 B3
Old Medlock St. M3 162 E8
Old Mill Cl. M27 80 B8
Old Mill House. OL4 68 B5
Old Mill La. Hazel Grove SK7 134 A8
Old Mill La. Oldham OL4 68 A5
Old Mill St. M40 159 C1
Old Mills Hill. M24 47 D1
Old Moat Inf Sch. M20 110 A7
Old Moat Jun Sch. M20 110 A7
Old Moat La. M20 110 B7
Old Moss La. WA3 92 E6
Old Mount St. M4 159 B3
Old Nans La. BL2 25 F2
Old Nursery Fold. BL2 25 E4
Old Oak Cl. BL3 43 B5
Old Oak Dr. M34 101 A3
Old Oak St. M20 110 B3
Old Oake Cl. M28 60 E2
Old Orch The. WA15 120 B8
Old Orchard. SK9 137 A7
Old Pack Horse Rd. OL3 51 B6
Old Packhorse Rd. OL15 16 F6
Old Parrin La. M30 79 B3
Old Pepper La. WN6 19 B2
Old Quarry La. BL7 8 F1
Old Rake. BL6 22 E5
Old Rd. Ashton-i-M WN4 73 A4
Old Rd. Ashton-u-L OL6 86 A6
Old Rd. Bolton BL1 143 E3
Old Rd. Cheadle SK8 122 F6
Old Rd. Dukinfield SK16 166 C1
Old Rd. Failsworth M35 83 E8
Old Rd. Handforth SK9 131 D3
Old Rd. Hyde SK14 167 D4
Old Rd. Littleborough OL15 & OL16 15 E4
Old Rd. M'ster M9 64 D2
Old Rd. Stalybridge SK15 102 C8
Old Rd. Stalybridge SK14 102 F5
Old Rd. Stockport SK4 169 E3
Old Rd. Tintwistle SK14 104 A7
Old Rd. Wilmslow SK9 137 B8
Old Rectory Gdns. SK8 122 D5
Old River Cl. M44 94 A2
Old School Ct. Eccles M30 79 D4
Old School Ct. M'ster M9 64 C2
Old School Dr. M9 64 C2
Old School House The. OL15 15 F6
Old School La. PR7 20 E5
Old School Mews. 12 OL13 3 C8
Old School Pl. WN4 73 A2
Old Sirs. BL5 57 F5
Old Sq. 8 OL6 166 C3
Old St. Ashton-u-L OL6 & OL7 166 B3
Old St. Mottram-i-L SK14 115 A8
Old St. Oldham OL4 67 D5
Old St. Stalybridge SK15 86 A2
Old Swan Cl. BL7 8 E2
Old Swan Cotts. BL7 8 E2
Old Thorn La. OL3 69 D8
Old Trafford Jun Sch. M16 161 C5
Old Trafford (Man Utd FC). M17 96 F5
Old Trafford Prim Sch. M16 161 C6
Old Trafford Sta. M16 97 A4
Old Vicarage. BL5 57 E5
Old Vicarage Gdns. M28 60 D3
Old Vicarage Mews. BL5 57 E5
Old Vicarage Rd. BL6 22 F3
Old Wargrave Rd. WA12 89 C3
Old Well Wlk. M33 107 C2
Old Wellington Rd. M30 79 E2
Old Wells Cl. M38 60 A6
Old Will's La. BL6 22 B6
Old Wool La. SK8 122 F4
Oldbridge Dr. WN2 56 D6
Oldbrook Fold. WA15 120 B4
Oldbury Cl. Heywood OL10 46 D7
Oldbury Cl. M'ster M10,M40 160 D3
Oldcastle Ave. M20 110 A8
Oldcott Cl. M28 77 F5
Oldcroft. OL4 68 A6
Oldershaw Dr. M9 157 D6
Oldfield Brow Prim Sch. WA14 119 A5
Oldfield Cl. BL5 57 F8
Oldfield Dr. WA15 119 F6
Oldfield Gr. M33 108 C5
Oldfield La. WA14 118 F4
Oldfield Mews. WA14 119 C5
Oldfield Rd. Alt'ham WA14 119 B5
Oldfield Rd. M'ster M30 81 C1
Oldfield Rd. Prestwich M25 63 C7
Oldfield Rd. Sale M33 108 C5
Oldfield Rd. Salford M5 161 C8
Oldfield St. M11 83 C1
Oldgate Wlk. 17 M15 162 D6
Oldham Ave. SK1 112 B1
Oldham Coll. OL9 153 E7
Oldham Coll Sch of Performing Arts. OL4 49 E3
Oldham Ct. 17 M40 159 C3
Oldham Dr. SK6 113 A4
Oldham Rd. Ashton-u-L OL6 & OL7 85 A5
Oldham Rd. Delph OL3 & OL4 50 D2
Oldham Rd. Failsworth M35 & M40 83 D6
Oldham Rd. M'ster M10,M40 160 D4
Oldham Rd. Middleton M24 65 A8
Oldham Rd. R'dale OL11, OL16, OL2 31 A3
Oldham Rd. Royton OL1 & OL2 48 E3
Oldham Rd. Shaw OL3 & OL4 50 B7
Oldham Rd. Shaw OL2 149 B5
Oldham Rd. Uppermill OL4 & OL3 68 D6
Oldham Sixth Form Coll. OL8 153 E6
Oldham St. Bolton BL3 145 D6
Oldham St. Denton M34 100 C3
Oldham St. Droylsden M43 84 B2
Oldham St. Hyde SK14 167 D2
Oldham St. M'ster M5 158 D1
Oldham St. M'ster M1, M4, M60 159 B2
Oldham St. 8 Reddish SK5 111 E7
Oldham Study Ctr & Nat History Mus. OL8 153 D5
Oldham Way. OL1, OL4, OL8, OL9 153 E6
Oldhams Cty Prim Sch. BL1 24 C5
Oldhams La. BL1 143 D4
Oldhams Terr. BL1 143 D4
Oldknow Rd. SK6 126 A6
Oldmill St. OL12 139 F8
Oldmoor Rd. SK6 112 E5
Oldstead Gr. BL3 40 F3
Oldstead Wlk. M9 157 D6
Oldway Wlk. M40 83 B5
Oldwood Inf Sch. M22 121 B2
Oldwood Jun Sch. M22 121 B2
Oldwood Rd. M23 121 A3
Olebrook Cl. M12 164 D6
Olga St. BL1 143 D2
Olivant St. Bury BL9 44 E8
Olivant St. Bury BL9 140 E1
Olive Bank. BL8 27 B4
Olive Gr. WN6 36 F3
Olive Rd. WA15 120 A8
Olive St. Bacup OL13 3 E8
Olive St. Bolton BL3 147 D4
Olive St. Bury BL8 140 D2
Olive St. Failsworth M35 83 E8
Olive St. Heywood OL10 29 E2
Olive St. R'dale OL11 30 C1
Olive St. Radcliffe M26 44 C3
Olive Terr. SK14 115 A8
Olive Wlk. 4 M33 107 C6
Oliver Cl. OL15 15 F5
Oliver St. Atherton M46 58 D3
Oliver St. 10 Bacup OL13 3 C8
Oliver St. M'ster M15 163 A6
Oliver St. M'ster M11 164 F8
Oliver St. Oldham OL1 153 F6
Oliver St. Stockport SK1, SK3 170 F8
Olivia Ct. M5 161 C8
Olivia Gr. M14 98 D3
Ollerbarrow Rd. WA15 119 E2
Ollerbrook Ct. 11 BL1 143 F2
Ollersett Ave. SK12 127 D1
Ollersett La. SK12 127 E1
Ollerton. 16 OL12 139 E8
Ollerton Ave. M'ster M16 97 C3
Ollerton Ave. Sale M33 107 D5
Ollerton Cl. WN2 38 A2
Ollerton Dr. M35 83 F6
Ollerton Rd. SK9 131 E5
Ollerton St. Adlington PR6 21 A8
Ollerton St. Bolton BL1 & BL7 24 F6
Ollier Ave. M12 & M18 99 B2
Olney. OL11 139 E6
Olney Ave. M22 121 D6
Olney St. M13 98 D4
Olsberg Cl. M26 44 C4
Olwen Ave. M12 165 A5
Olwen Cres. SK5 111 F8
Olympic Ct. M5 96 F8
Omer Ave. M13 98 F2
Omer Dr. M19 110 E7
Onchan Ave. OL4 67 B6
One Ash Cl. OL12 14 F2
One Oak Ct. SK7 123 C2
One Oak La. SK9 137 F7
Ongar Wlk. M9 64 B3
Onslow Ave. M40 65 E1
Onslow Rd. SK3 123 C8
Onslow St. OL11 30 C4
Onward St. SK14 167 D2
Oozewood Rd. M24 & OL2 48 B5
Opal Ct. 5 M14 110 D8
Opal Gr. WN7 75 E4
Opal St. M19 111 B8
Open Coll The. M20 110 B2
Openshaw CE Prim Sch. M11 165 B8
Openshaw Fold Rd. BL9 44 D8
Openshaw La. M44 105 E6
Openshaw Pl. BL4 60 B8
Openshaw St. BL9 141 A1
Openshaw Wlk. 15 M11 83 C1
Oracle Ct. M28 60 D2
Oram St. BL9 141 A4
Orama Ave. M30 80 A4
Orange Hill Rd. M25 63 C5
Orange St. M6 81 A3
Orchard Ave. Bolton BL1 143 F3
Orchard Ave. Boothstown M28 78 B7
Orchard Ave. Partington M31 105 F4
Orchard Ave. Reddish M18 99 E4
Orchard Brow. WA3 105 A2
Orchard Cl. Bramhall SK8 132 C7
Orchard Cl. Leigh WN7 75 F7
Orchard Cl. Poynton SK12 133 E3
Orchard Cl. Shevington WN6 36 A7
Orchard Cl. Wilmslow SK9 136 F5
Orchard Ct. SK2 124 D6
Orchard Dr. Alt'ham WA15 120 A3
Orchard Dr. Handforth SK9 131 E2
Orchard Gdns. BL2 25 F3
Orchard Gn. SK9 137 B1
Orchard Gr. M'ster M20 109 F5
Orchard Gr. Shaw OL2 149 A7
Orchard Ind Est. M6 81 A5
Orchard La. M46 & WN7 76 A7
Orchard Pl. Poynton SK12 133 D4
Orchard Pl. Sale WA15 120 B7
Orchard Rd. Alt'ham WA15 119 E5
Orchard Rd. Failsworth M35 83 F7
Orchard Rd. Lymm WA13 117 B5
Orchard Rd. Romiley SK6 114 B2
Orchard Rd E. M20 & M22 109 E2
Orchard Rd W. M22 109 D2
Orchard Rise. SK14 113 F7
Orchard St. Ashton-i-M WN4 73 C3
Orchard St. Farnworth BL4 60 E7
Orchard St. Heywood OL10 29 E3
Orchard St. Hyde SK14 167 E2
Orchard St. M'ster M20 109 F5
Orchard St. Salford M6 81 A4
Orchard St. Stockport SK1 169 F1
Orchard St. Wigan WN1 151 D8
Orchard The. Disley SK12 135 D6
Orchard The. Oldham OL4 67 C3
Orchard The. 4 Westhoughton BL5 39 E1
Orchard Trad Est. M6 80 F5
Orchard Vale. SK3 123 C6
Orchards The. OL10 29 E2
Orchid Ave. BL4 42 B1
Orchid Cl. M44 105 E8
Orchid St. M8 & M9 157 D7
Orchid Way. OL12 14 D3
Ordell Wlk. 1 M9 64 E3
Ordsall Ave. M38 60 B4
Ordsall District Ctr. M5 161 B8
Ordsall Dr. M5 161 B7
Ordsall Hall (Mus). M5 161 B7
Ordsall La. Salford M5 161 B7
Oregon Ave. OL1 48 E1
Oregon Cl. M13 163 C6
Orford Ave. SK12 135 D6
Orford Cl. SK6 134 E7
Orford Rd. Failsworth M40 83 C5
Orford Rd. Prestwich M25 63 B5
Organ St. Hindley WN2 57 B3
Organ St. Leigh WN7 75 E5
Oriel Ave. OL8 66 E3
Oriel Bank High Sch. SK3 170 F5
Oriel Cl. Oldham OL9 152 A5
Oriel Cl. Stockport SK2 124 B6
Oriel Rd. Ashton-i-M WN4 72 F4
Oriel Rd. M'ster M20 110 A4
Oriel St. Bolton BL3 144 C5
Oriel St. R'dale OL11 139 F5
Orient Rd. M6 80 B4
Orient St. M7 & M8 155 F7
Oriole Cl. M28 78 B8
Orion Pl. M7 81 C4
Orkney Cl. Radcliffe M26 44 B4
Orkney Cl. Wythenshawe M23 121 A4
Orkney Dr. M41 95 D5
Orlanda Ave. M6 80 B4
Orlando St. BL3 148 A5
Orleans Way. OL1 153 E7
Orley Wlk. OL1 49 D4
Orme Ave. Eccles M6 80 B4
Orme Ave. Middleton M24 65 A7
Orme Cl. M'ster M11 160 E1
Orme Cl. Urmston M41 95 F2
Orme St. Alderley Edge SK9 137 A1
Orme St. Oldham OL4 & OL8 67 A5
Orme St. Stockport SK1 112 B2
Ormerod Ave. OL2 48 E3
Ormerod Cl. SK6 113 A1
Ormerod St. OL10 29 E1
Ormond St. Bolton BL3 42 D5
Ormond St. Bury BL9 141 A3
Ormonde Ave. M6 80 B4
Ormonde Ct. OL6 166 C4
Ormonde St. OL6 166 C4
Ormrod St. Bolton BL2 25 C4
Ormrod St. Bolton BL3 145 E6
Ormrod St. Bury BL9 141 A2
Ormrod St. 10 Farnworth BL4 60 C8
Ormrods The. BL9 28 F5
Orms Gill Pl. SK2 124 E6
Ormsby Ave. M18 99 B4
Ormsby Cl. Standish WN6 19 E2
Ormsby Cl. Stockport SK3 123 E4
Ormsgill Cl. M15 162 F6
Ormside Cl. WN2 57 C4
Ormskirk Ave. M20 109 F6
Ormskirk Cl. BL8 44 A8
Ormskirk Rd. Orrell WN8 53 A7
Ormskirk Rd. 2 Reddish SK5 111 F6
Ormskirk Rd. Wigan WN5 54 D6
Ormston Ave. BL6 22 C5
Ormston Gr. WN7 75 F7
Ornatus St. BL1 24 F5
Ornsey Wlk. 12 M11 83 C1
Oronsay Gr. M5 154 E1
Orphanage St. SK4 & SK5 169 E3
Orpington Dr. BL8 27 B1
Orpington Rd. 2 M9 157 E7
Orpington St. WN5 54 C6
Orrel St. M5 & M6 154 E2
Orrell Arc. 3 WN1 150 C8
Orrell Gdns. WN5 53 F6
Orrell Hall Cl. WN5 54 B8
Orrell Holgate Prim Sch. WN5 53 E5
Orrell Lamberhead Green Cty Jun Sch. WN5 54 B6
Orrell Lamberhead Green Cty Prim Sch. WN5 54 A7
Orrell Rd. Orrell WN5 53 E7
Orrell St. Bury BL8 140 D3
Orrell St. M'ster M11 99 D8
Orrell St. Wigan WN1 151 D7
Orrell St James' Road Cty Jun & Inf Sch. WN5 53 D4
Orrell Sta. WN5 53 E4
Orrell Water Pk. WN5 53 E4
Orrishmere Prim Sch. SK8 123 A3
Orrishmere Rd. SK8 122 F3
Orron St. OL15 16 A5
Orsett Cl. M10 & M40 159 C3
Orthes Gr. SK4 111 D5
Orton Ave. M23 109 A1
Orton Rd. M23 109 A1
Orton Way. WN4 72 F3
Ortonbrook Prim Sch. M31 105 E2
Orvietto Ave. M6 80 B4
Orville Dr. M19 110 F7
Orwell Ave. Reddish M34 100 A3
Orwell Ave. Wythenshawe M22 121 D6
Orwell Cl. BL8 140 D4
Orwell Rd. BL1 142 B2
Osborne Cl. BL8 44 B8
Osborne Dr. M27 80 C7
Osborne Gr. Bolton BL1 142 C1
Osborne Gr. Gatley SK8 122 A3
Osborne Gr. Leigh WN7 76 D6
Osborne Pl. SK14 104 A5
Osborne Rd. Alt'ham WA15 119 E5
Osborne Rd. Ashton-i-M WN4 73 A4
Osborne Rd. Denton M34 100 F4
Osborne Rd. Eccles M6 80 A2
Osborne Rd. Golborne WA3 90 E7
Osborne Rd. Hyde SK14 167 E1
Osborne Rd. M'ster M19 99 A1
Osborne Rd. 3 M'ster M9 157 E7
Osborne Rd. Oldham OL8 153 D5
Osborne Rd. Stockport SK2 170 F7
Osborne St. Bredbury SK6 112 D3
Osborne St. Heywood OL10 29 D1
Osborne St. M'ster M20 110 A3
Osborne St. M'ster M10, M40 159 C4
Osborne St. Oldham OL9 152 C8
Osborne St. R'dale OL11 139 F5
Osborne St. Salford M6 154 F2
Osborne St. Shaw OL2 149 B6
Osborne Terr. Bacup OL13 3 D8
Osborne Terr. Sale M33 108 B4
Osbourne Cl. Farnworth BL4 42 D1
Osbourne Cl. Wilmslow SK9 137 D6
Osbourne Ct. M46 58 C3
Osbourne Pl. 7 WA14 119 D4
Osbourne Wlk. M26 43 E3
Oscar St. Bolton BL1 142 C2
Oscar St. Failsworth M40 83 A7
Oscott Ave. M38 60 A6
Oscroft Cl. M7 & M8 155 F6
Oscroft Wlk. M14 110 D7
Osmond St. OL4 67 C7
Osmund Ave. BL2 42 D7
Osprey Ave. BL5 57 D6
Osprey Cl. Dukinfield SK16 101 E7
Osprey Cl. M'ster M15 162 E5
Osprey Ct. M16 162 E5
Osprey Dr. Droylsden M43 84 C3
Osprey Dr. Irlam M44 94 A3
Osprey Dr. Wilmslow SK9 137 C8
Osprey Wlk. M13 163 C6
Ospreys The. WN3 54 C4
Ossington Ct. M23 109 A3
Ossington Wlk. M23 109 A2
Ossory St. M14 98 B3
Osterley Rd. M'ster M9 65 A3
Ostlers Gate. OL7 84 D2
Ostrich La. M25 63 C3
Oswald Cl. M6 81 A5
Oswald La. M21 97 B1
Oswald Rd. M16 & M21 97 A1
Oswald Road Prim Sch. M21 97 A1
Oswald St. Bolton BL3 146 C4
Oswald St. M'ster M4 159 A3
Oswald St. M'ster M4 160 D1
Oswald St. Oldham OL9 153 D8
Oswald St. R'dale OL16 31 B8
Oswald St. Reddish M34 & SK5 99 F3
Oswald St. Shaw OL2 149 C8
Oswestry Cl. BL8 26 F8
Otago St. 2 OL4 49 C1
Othello Dr. M30 79 D2
Otley Ave. M6 80 C3
Otley Cl. OL9 152 B6
Otley Gr. SK3 123 D4
Otmoor Way. OL2 49 A4
Otranto Ave. M6 80 B4
Otter Dr. BL9 45 B4
Otterburn Cl. M15 162 F6
Otterburn Pl. SK2 124 E6
Otterbury Cl. BL8 26 F2
Otterham Wlk. M40 83 D5
Otterspool Rd. SK6 125 B8
Otterwood Sq. WN5 36 C2
Ottery Wlk. 5 M40 65 D2
Ottowa Cl. M23 120 F4
Oughtrington Cres. WA13 117 B4
Oughtrington La. WA13 117 A2
Oughtrington Prim Sch. WA13 117 B4
Oughtrington View. WA13 117 B4
Oulder Hill. OL11 30 B7
Oulder Hill Comm Sch. OL11 30 B7
Oulder Hill Dr. OL11 30 B7
Ouldfield Cl. 22 OL16 31 B6
Oulton Ave. M33 108 E5
Oulton St. BL1 25 A5
Oulton Wlk. M40 160 D3
Oundle Cl. M14 98 C3
Our Lady Mount Carmel RC High Sch. M6 80 C3
Our Lady of Grace RC Prim Sch. M25 63 A6
Our Lady of Lourdes RC Prim Sch. Bury BL8 27 C6
Our Lady of Lourdes RC Prim Sch. Farnworth BL4 60 A8
Our Lady of Lourdes RC Prim Sch. Partington M31 105 E3
Our Lady of Mount Carmel Inf Sch. M9 64 D1
Our Lady of Mount Carmel RC Jun Sch. M9 64 D2
Our Lady of the Rosary RC Prim Sch. Leigh WN7 75 B5
Our Lady of the Rosary RC Prim Sch. Urmston M41 95 C4
Our Lady & St Paul's RC Prim Sch. OL10 28 F1
Our Lady & the Lancs Martyrs RC Prim Sch. M28 60 A3
Our Lady's RC High Sch. M'ster M9 64 D5
Our Lady's RC High Sch. Royton OL2 48 D3
Our Lady's RC Prim Sch. Aspull WN2 38 C5
Our Lady's RC Prim Sch. M'ster M16 97 D3
Our Lady's RC Prim Sch. Oldham OL4 49 E3
Our Lady's RC Prim Sch. Stockport SK3 170 E8
Ouse St. M5 80 C1
Outram Cl. SK6 125 F4
Outram Rd. SK14 & SK16 101 D6
Outram Sq. M43 100 A8
Outrington Dr. M11 165 A8
Outterside St. PR7 21 A6
Outwood Ave. M27 61 D4
Outwood Dr. SK8 131 A8
Outwood Gr. BL1 24 E5
Outwood La. M90 130 C7
Outwood La W. M90 130 B8
Outwood Prim Sch. SK8 131 D7
Outwood Rd. Cheadle SK8 131 B7
Outwood Rd. Radcliffe M26 44 A1
Oval Dr. SK16 101 B7
Oval The. Gatley SK8 131 B8
Oval The. Shevington WN6 35 F5
Over Houses. BL7 9 B6
Over Town La. R'dale OL12 13 A5
Over Town La. R'dale OL11 & OL12 13 C3
Overbridge Rd. M7 & M8 158 E4
Overbrook Ave. M40 157 D5
Overbrook Dr. M25 63 B3
Overcombe Wlk. 1 M40 156 C5
Overdale. 1 Marple SK6 125 F6
Overdale. Pendlebury M27 80 A6
Overdale Cres. M41 94 F2
Overdale Dr. BL1 144 A7
Overdale Prim Sch. SK6 112 F1
Overdale Rd. New Mills SK12 135 F6
Overdale Rd. Romiley SK6 125 A8
Overdale Rd. Wythenshawe M22 121 D5
Overdell Dr. OL12 14 C4
Overdene Cl. BL6 40 C6
Overens St. OL4 67 B7
Overfield Way. OL12 14 F2
Overgreen. BL2 25 E3
Overhill Dr. SK9 137 E7
Overhill La. SK9 137 E7
Overhill Rd. Chadderton OL9 65 F8
Overhill Rd. Wilmslow SK9 137 D7
Overhill Way. WN3 54 D3
Overlea Dr. M19 110 E5
Overlinks Dr. M6 80 B5
Overshores Rd. BL7 9 B8
Overstone Dr. M7 & M8 155 F7
Overt St. OL11 139 F5
Overton Ave. M22 121 D5
Overton Cres. Hazel Grove SK7 124 E4
Overton Cres. Sale M33 107 D1
Overton Rd. M22 121 D5
Overton St. WN7 75 E4
Overton Way. 2 SK9 131 D5
Overwood Rd. M22 121 D8
Ovington Wlk. 6 M40 156 C5
Owen St. Eccles M30 79 B1
Owen St. 2 Leigh WN7 75 D5
Owen St. Oldham OL1 49 E3
Owen St. Salford M6 81 A5
Owen St. Stockport SK3 169 D1
Owen Wlk. 7 M16 97 F4
Owen's Row. BL6 22 C3
Owenington Gr. M38 60 A5
Owens Cl. OL9 65 E8
Owler La. OL9 65 E3
Owlerbarrow Rd. BL8 27 A3
Owlwood Cl. M38 59 E3
Owlwood Dr. M38 59 E3
Ox Gate. BL2 25 D5
Ox Hey Cl. BL6 39 E8
Ox Hey La. Denshaw OL3 33 E1
Ox Hey La. Horwich BL6 39 F7
Ox St. BL0 138 B5
Oxbridge Cl. M33 107 D3
Oxburgh Rd. WN2 55 F4
Oxendale Dr. M24 46 D1
Oxendon Ave. M11 83 B3
Oxenhurst Gn. SK2 124 E5
Oxford Ave. Droylsden M43 83 F3
Oxford Ave. R'dale OL11 30 A6
Oxford Ave. Sale M33 107 D4
Oxford Ave. Whitefield M45 63 A8
Oxford Cl. BL4 59 F8
Oxford Ct. M'ster M16 162 D5
Oxford Ct. M'ster M1 162 F8
Oxford Ct. Wigan WN1 37 D1
Oxford Dr. Middleton M24 47 C2
Oxford Dr. Romiley SK6 113 C4
Oxford Gr. Bolton BL1 142 C1
Oxford Gr. Irlam M44 105 C6
Oxford Grove Prim Sch. BL1 142 C1
Oxford House. OL9 152 C6
Oxford Pl. M'ster M14 98 C4
Oxford Pl. 14 R'dale OL11 31 A5
Oxford Rd. Alt'ham WA14 119 D3
Oxford Rd. Atherton M46 58 B5
Oxford Rd. Dukinfield SK16 101 D8
Oxford Rd. Eccles M6 80 B4
Oxford Rd. Horwich BL6 39 F8
Oxford Rd. Hyde SK14 113 E8
Oxford Rd. Little Lever BL3 42 F3
Oxford Rd. M'ster M1 & M13 163 B6
Oxford Rd. Orrell WN5 53 F8
Oxford Road Sta. M1 163 A7
Oxford St. Adlington PR7 21 A6
Oxford St. Bolton BL1 145 F7
Oxford St. Bury BL9 141 A1
Oxford St. Eccles M30 79 E1
Oxford St. Hindley WN2 56 F7
Oxford St. Leigh WN7 75 F6
Oxford St. M'ster M16 162 D5
Oxford St. M'ster M1,M60,M2 163 A8
Oxford St. Newton-i-W WA12 89 B3
Oxford St. Oldham OL9 152 C5
Oxford St. Shaw OL2 149 B7
Oxford St. Stalybridge SK15 86 C1
Oxford St. Stalybridge SK15 86 D4
Oxford St E. OL7 166 A1
Oxford St W. OL7 100 F8
Oxford Way. SK4 169 D3
Oxford Wlk. 2 M34 101 A1
Oxhill Wlk. 17 M40 65 D2
Oxhouse Rd. WN5 53 D4
Oxlea Gr. BL5 57 E7
Oxney Rd. M14 98 C4
Oxted Wlk. 9 M8 156 A6
Oxton Ave. M22 121 C4
Oxton St. M11 & M18 99 F7
Ozanam Ct. M7 155 D7

Pacific Rd. WA14 119 A6
Pacific Way. M5 96 C8
Packer St. 1 Bolton BL1 142 C2
Packer St. R'dale OL16 139 F7
Packwood Chase. OL9 65 F8
Padbury Cl. M41 94 D3
Padbury House. 7 M6 154 F1
Padbury Way. BL2 25 E1
Padbury Wlk. M40 157 F5
Padden Brook. SK6 113 B2
Padden Brook Mews. SK6 113 B2
Paddington Ave. M40 83 B5
Paddington Cl. M6 81 A2
Paddison St. 2 M27 79 E7
Paddock Chase. SK12 133 F6
Paddock Cl. M46 58 E5
Paddock Hill La. WA16 136 A3
Paddock La. Failsworth M35 83 F5
Paddock La. Lymm WA13 117 C7
Paddock La. Partington WA13 & WA14 118 B5
Paddock Rd. SK14 113 D8
Paddock Rise. WN6 36 E3
Paddock St. M12 163 C7
Paddock The. Alt'ham WA15 120 B4
Paddock The. Ashton-i-M WN4 72 F6
Paddock The. Bramhall SK7 123 D1
Paddock The. Cheadle SK8 122 E5
Paddock The. Handforth SK9 131 D4
Paddock The. Hollingworth SK14 103 F5
Paddock The. Lymm WA13 117 C4
Paddock The. Ramsbottom BL0 138 B7
Paddock The. Uppermill OL3 68 F4
Paddock The. Worsley M28 78 E7
Paddocks The. SK3 124 A4
Paderborn Ct. BL1 145 E6
Padfield Cty Prim Sch. SK14 104 B5
Padfield Gate. SK13 116 D7
Padfield Main Rd. SK14 104 C5
Padiham Cl. BL9 44 D7
Padstow Cl. SK14 102 D3
Padstow Dr. SK7 132 F7
Padstow St. M10 & M40 160 E3
Padstow Wlk. SK14 102 D3
Padworth Wlk. M23 120 D8
Pagan St. OL16 139 F8
Pagefield Cl. 7 WN6 37 A1
Pagefield St. WN6 37 A1
Paget St. M40 157 D5
Pagnall Ct. OL9 152 B5
Paignton Ave. Hattersley SK14 102 D2
Paignton Ave. M'ster M19 110 F8
Paignton Ave. Reddish SK5 111 E7
Paignton Cl. WN5 71 E8
Paignton Dr. M33 107 D5
Paignton Gr. SK5 111 E7
Paignton Wlk. SK14 102 C2
Pailin Dr. OL7 84 C2
Pailton Cl. BL6 40 D6
Painswick Rd. M22 121 B1
Paiton St. BL1 144 C7
Palace Arc. WN4 73 B3
Palace Gdns. OL1 48 D2
Palace Gr. WN7 76 D6
Palace Rd. Ashton-u-L OL6 85 E5
Palace Rd. Sale M33 108 A5
Palace St. Bolton BL1 145 F8
Palace St. Bury BL9 141 A2
Palace St. Oldham OL9 152 C7
Palatine Ave. M'ster M20 110 B6
Palatine Ave. R'dale OL11 30 A8
Palatine Cl. Irlam M44 93 F1
Palatine Cl. Wigan WN3 54 E4

Pal – Pem 219

Palatine Cres. M20 110 B5
Palatine Dr. BL9 27 F8
Palatine House. 4 SK3 170 E8
Palatine Rd. M'ster M20 110 B6
Palatine Rd. R'dale OL11 30 A8
Palatine Rd.
Wythenshawe M20 & M22 109 E2
Palatine Sq. WN7 75 D5
Palatine St. 4 Bolton BL1 145 F7
Palatine St. Denton M34 100 E4
Palatine St. R'dale OL16 31 C7
Palatine St. Ramsbottom BL0 138 C6
Paley St. BL1 145 F7
Palfrey Pl. M12 163 C7
Palgrave Ave. M10 & M40 157 D5
Palin St. WN2 57 B3
Palin Wood Rd. Delph OL3 50 F5
Pall Mall. M'ster M2 158 F1
Pall Mall. M'ster M1,M2,M60 159 A1
Palm Ave. WN4 72 D5
Palm Cl. M33 107 D5
Palm Gr. Oldham OL9 152 B8
Palm Gr. Wigan WN5 54 D6
Palm St. Bolton BL1 143 F3
Palm St. Droylsden M43 83 E2
Palm St. M'ster M13 98 F3
Palm St. Oldham OL4 67 C8
Palma Ave. M90 130 B8
Palmer Ave. SK8 122 F6
Palmer Cl. M'ster M8 64 B2
Palmer Cl. Oldham OL8 66 F4
Palmer Gr. WN7 57 E1
Palmer St. Dukinfield SK16 166 B1
Palmer St. M'ster M7 81 C5
Palmer St. Sale M33 108 A4
Palmerston Ave. M16 97 D2
Palmerston Cl.
Ramsbottom BL0 11 C4
Palmerston Cl.
Reddish M34 100 B3
Palmerston Rd.
Reddish M34 100 B3
Palmerston Rd.
Stockport SK2 124 B3
Palmerston St. M'ster M12 160 E1
Pandora St. M20 110 A5
Panfield Rd. M22 121 D4
Pangbourne Ave. M41 95 E3
Pangbourne Cl. SK3 123 C6
Pankhurst Wlk. 11 M14 98 B3
Panmure St. OL8 66 F4
Pansy Rd. BL4 60 A8
Panton St. BL6 22 D1
Paper Mill Rd. BL7 25 A7
Parade Rd. M90 130 C7
Parade The.
Alderley Edge SK9 137 A1
Parade The. Swinton M27 79 F8
Parade The. 2
Whitefield M45 44 F2
Paradise St. Dukinfield M34 100 F7
Paradise St. Hadfield SK14 104 A5
Paradise St.
Ramsbottom BL0 138 C7
Parbold Ave. M20 110 A6
Parbrook Cl. M40 157 D5
Parbrook La. WN6 36 B7
Parcel St. M11 160 F1
Parchments The. WA12 89 D4
Pardoners Ct. M30 & M5 80 B2
Parham Wlk. 4 M9 64 E3
Paris Ave. Salford M5 161 B7
Paris Ave. Wigan WN3 54 C3
Paris St. BL3 146 B4
Parish Church CE Jun
Sch The. OL1 153 F8
Parish View. M5 161 B8
Park Ave. Alt'ham WA14 119 E8
Park Ave. Alt'ham WA15 119 F1
Park Ave. Bolton BL1 143 E4
Park Ave. Bramhall SK7 132 D5
Park Ave. Chadderton OL9 48 B1
Park Ave. Cheadle SK8 122 F1
Park Ave. Cheadle SK3 122 F7
Park Ave. Failsworth M35 83 D8
Park Ave. Golborne WA3 73 F2
Park Ave. Hyde SK14 167 D4
Park Ave. M'ster M19 99 A1
Park Ave. M'ster M7 155 F8
Park Ave. M'ster M16 161 C5
Park Ave. Orrell WN5 53 E1
Park Ave. Poynton SK12 133 E4
Park Ave. Prestwich M25 63 B4
Park Ave. Ramsbottom BL0 11 D6
Park Ave. Romiley SK6 113 C2
Park Ave. Sale M33 108 A6
Park Ave. Shevington WN6 36 B7
Park Ave. Swinton M27 80 A7
Park Ave. Urmston M41 95 C2
Park Ave. Whitefield M45 62 D6
Park Ave. Wilmslow SK9 137 C8
Park Ave N. WA12 89 C2
Park Ave S. WA12 89 C2
Park Bank. M46 58 F6
Park Bglws. 4 SK6 125 F5
Park Brow Cl. M21 109 C7
Park Cl. Chadderton OL9 48 B1
Park Cl. Glossop SK13 104 D2
Park Cl. Sale WA14 119 F8
Park Cl. Stalybridge SK15 85 F3
Park Cl. Whitefield M45 62 F6
Park Cotts. OL4 68 E5
Park Court Mews. SK8 122 E4
Park Cres. Ashton-u-L OL6 85 E2
Park Cres. Bacup OL13 3 F8
Park Cres. Chadderton OL9 47 F1
Park Cres. Glossop SK13 104 B3
Park Cres. Handforth SK9 131 B1
Park Cres. M'ster M14 98 C3
Park Cres. Wigan WN1 37 B1
Park Cres W. WN1 37 B1
Park Ct. M'ster M25 63 E2
Park Ct. R'dale OL11 139 F6
Park Ct. Sale M33 108 A5
Park Ct. Wythenshawe M22 121 D3
Park Dean Sch. OL8 67 B2
Park Dene Dr. SK13 104 C2
Park Dr. Alt'ham WA15 119 F1
Park Dr. Alt'ham WA15 120 A7
Park Dr. Eccles M30 79 D4
Park Dr. Hyde SK14 167 D4
Park Dr. M'ster M16 97 C2
Park Dr. Stockport SK4 168 B2
Park Edge. BL5 58 A7
Park Field Rd. OL4 68 E6
Park Gate Ave. M20 110 B6
Park Gates Ave. SK8 123 C1
Park Gates Dr. SK7 & SK8 123 C1
Park Gr. M'ster M19 99 A2
Park Gr. M'ster SK4 168 B4
Park Gr. Radcliffe M26 43 F4
Park Gr. Walkden M28 78 D8
Park Hey Dr. WN6 35 E7
Park Hill. M'ster M25 63 D2
Park Hill. 21 R'dale OL12 14 F1
Park Hill Cl. SK12 127 C1
Park Hill Dr. M45 62 E8
Park Hill Rd. WA15 120 A1
Park Hill St. BL1 145 D8
Park House. Droylsden M43 100 A8
Park House. Sale WA15 120 C7
Park House Bridge Rd. M6 80 E6
Park Ind Est. WN4 72 E3
Park La. Abram WN2 & WN7 74 D6
Park La. Alt'ham WA15 120 A1
Park La. Dukinfield SK16 101 C8
Park La. Horwich BL6 22 D3
Park La. Leigh WN7 76 C4
Park La. Lymm WA14 118 B2
Park La. M'ster M7 155 D8
Park La. Oldham OL8 66 F2
Park La. Pendlebury M6 80 C5
Park La. Poynton SK12 133 F3
Park La. R'dale OL16 139 F8
Park La. Radcliffe M26 44 D4
Park La. Royton OL2 48 D4
Park La. Royton OL2 48 D5
Park La. Royton OL2 48 E5
Park La. Salford M27 80 D6
Park La. Stockport SK1 124 B8
Park La. Uppermill OL3 69 C5
Park La. Whitefield M45 62 D7
Park La W. M27 80 D7
Park Lane Ct. M7 155 D8
Park Lane Inf Sch. WN4 72 F7
Park Lodge. 1 M19 99 A1
Park Lodge Cl. SK8 122 E4
Park Meadow. BL5 58 A8
Park Mews. M16 97 C2
Park Mount. SK8 122 A5
Park Par. Ashton-u-L OL6 166 B2
Park Par. Shaw OL2 32 C1
Park Par Ind Est. OL7 166 A2
Park Pl. Eccles M6 80 A3
Park Pl. M'ster SK4 110 F2
Park Pl. M'ster M3 159 A3
Park Pl. Prestwich M25 63 C5
Park Range. M14 98 D3
Park Rd. Adlington PR7 20 F6
Park Rd. Alt'ham WA14 119 A2
Park Rd. Alt'ham WA15 119 F1
Park Rd. Bolton BL1 144 C7
Park Rd. Bramhall SK8 123 C1
Park Rd. Bury BL9 140 E4
Park Rd. Cheadle SK8 122 E6
Park Rd. Denton M34 100 E3
Park Rd. Droylsden M34 100 D8
Park Rd. Eccles M30 79 D4
Park Rd. Eccles M6 80 A3
Park Rd. Edgworth BL7 9 E5
Park Rd. Glossop SK14 104 B4
Park Rd. Golborne WA12 90 A7
Park Rd. High Lane SK12 134 F6
Park Rd. Hindley WN2 56 E3
Park Rd. Hyde SK14 167 D4
Park Rd. Little Lever BL3 42 F4
Park Rd. M'ster M25, M7, M8 63 E2
Park Rd. M'ster SK4 111 B5
Park Rd. Middleton M24 65 A8
Park Rd. Oldham OL8 67 A5
Park Rd. Oldham OL8 153 F5
Park Rd. Orrell WN5 53 F1
Park Rd. Partington M31 106 A3
Park Rd. Partington WA13 117 C8
Park Rd. R'dale OL12 15 A1
Park Rd. Ramsbottom BL8 10 F3
Park Rd. Romiley SK6 113 C3
Park Rd. Sale WA14 107 E1
Park Rd. Sale M33 108 A6
Park Rd. Sale WA15 & WA14 120 B7
Park Rd.
Stalybridge SK15 & SK16 85 D1
Park Rd. Standish WN6 36 E8
Park Rd. Stretford M17 & M32 96 C3
Park Rd. Walkden M28 60 D1
Park Rd. Westhoughton BL5 58 A8
Park Rd. Wigan WN1 & WN6 37 A1
Park Rd. Wigan WN5 54 B6
Park Rd. Wilmslow SK9 136 F7
Park Rd. Wythenshawe M22 121 F5
Park Rd N. Newton-l-W WA12 89 E4
Park Rd N. Urmston M41 95 C2
Park Rd S. Newton-l-W WA12 89 D2
Park Rd S. Urmston M41 95 C2
Park Rise. SK6 113 C3
Park Road Prim Sch.
Sale M33 108 A6
Park Road Prim Sch.
Sale WA14 119 E8
Park Row. 3 Bolton BL7 24 F6
Park Row. M'ster SK4 110 F2
Park Seventeen. M45 44 F1
Park Side Ave. OL2 149 C8
Park Sq. M16 97 A2
Park St. Ashton-u-L OL7 166 A1
Park St. Ashton-u-L OL7 166 B2
Park St. Atherton M46 58 E4
Park St. Bolton BL1 145 D8
Park St. Bredbury SK6 112 F3
Park St. Denton M34 100 D3
Park St. Droylsden M43 84 C2
Park St. Farnworth BL4 42 D1
Park St. Heywood OL10 46 E8
Park St. M'ster M7 155 D8
Park St. M'ster M3 158 D1
Park St. M'ster M3 158 F3
Park St. Mossley OL5 86 C8
Park St. Oldham OL8 153 E5
Park St. Oldham OL8 153 E6
Park St. Prestwich M25 63 C4
Park St. R'dale OL11 & OL16 139 F6
Park St. Radcliffe M26 44 C4
Park St. Royton OL2 48 E4
Park St. Shaw OL2 149 C7
Park St. Stalybridge SK15 86 B1
Park St. Stockport SK1 169 F2
Park St. Swinton M27 80 A7
Park St. 1 Tyldesley M29 59 A1
Park St. Wigan WN3 150 B6
Park Sta. M40 83 A4
Park Terr. Heywood OL10 29 D3
Park Terr. Mossley OL5 86 C8
Park Terr. Westhoughton BL5 39 F1
Park The. Uppermill OL4 68 D6
Park The. Uppermill OL3 69 C5
Park View. Abram WN2 56 B1
Park View. Ashton-i-M WN4 73 B2
Park View. 2 Bolton BL7 24 F6
Park View. Chadderton OL9 48 B1
Park View. Cheadle SK3 122 F7
Park View. Droylsden M34 100 D8
Park View. Farnworth BL4 42 D1
Park View. Gatley SK8 122 A6
Park View. High Lane SK7 134 B8
Park View. Kearsley BL4 60 F7
Park View. Lymm WA14 118 B2
Park View. M'ster M14 110 E7
Park View.
M'ster M40, M8, M9 156 C6
Park View. Newton-l-W WA12 89 E3
Park View. Stockport SK1 124 B7
Park View. Stretford M21 96 F1
Park View Ct. Prestwich M25 63 B3
Park View Ct. Romiley SK6 113 C2
Park View Prim Sch. M25 63 B3
Park View Rd. Bolton BL3 146 C4
Park View Rd. Prestwich M25 63 B3
Park View Rise. SK12 127 C1
Park Way. Eccles M32 & M41 95 F5
Park Way. Eccles M17 & M41 96 A6
Parkbridge Wlk. M13 163 B6
Parkbrook Rd. M23 121 B7
Parkdale. Chadderton OL9 48 B1
Parkdale. Tyldesley M29 77 B5
Parkdale Ave. Denton M34 100 D7
Parkdale Ave. M'ster M18 165 C5
Parkdale Rd. BL2 25 C1
Parkdene Cl. BL2 25 D4
Parkend Dr. WN7 75 D2
Parkend Rd. M23 121 A5
Parker St. Bury BL9 141 A2
Parker St. M'ster M1 & M60 159 A1
Parkes Field Prim Sch. M27 80 A7
Parkfield. Chadderton OL9 48 B1
Parkfield. 1 Middleton M24 64 F8
Parkfield. Salford M5 154 D2
Parkfield. Shevington WN6 36 B7
Parkfield Ave. Farnworth BL4 60 C7
Parkfield Ave. M'ster M25 63 D3
Parkfield Ave. M'ster M14 98 B3
Parkfield Ave. Marple SK6 125 F6
Parkfield Ave. 2 Oldham OL8 66 B2
Parkfield Ave. Tyldesley M29 77 B6
Parkfield Ave. Urmston M41 95 B1
Parkfield Cl. Leigh WN7 76 A7
Parkfield Cl. Tyldesley M29 77 B6
Parkfield Ct. WA14 119 C4
Parkfield Dr. Middleton M24 64 E8
Parkfield Dr. Tyldesley M29 59 D1
Parkfield Ind Est. M24 64 F8
Parkfield Prim Sch. M24 46 E1
Parkfield Rd. Alt'ham WA14 119 C4
Parkfield Rd. Bolton BL3 147 F3
Parkfield Rd. Cheadle SK8 122 F1
Parkfield Rd N. M40 65 F1
Parkfield Rd S. M20 110 A4
Parkfield St. M'ster M14 98 B3
Parkfield St. M'ster M14 98 B4
Parkfield St.
R'dale OL11 & OL16 31 B2
Parkfields. Abram WN2 74 C6
Parkfields. Stalybridge SK15 86 D3
Parkgate. Bury BL8 26 F5
Parkgate. Chadderton OL9 48 B1
Parkgate Cl. SK6 112 E5
Parkgate Dr. Bolton BL1 25 A5
Parkgate Dr. Stockport SK2 124 B4
Parkgate Dr. Swinton M27 80 A7
Parkgate Way. 7
Handforth SK9 131 D4
Parkgate Way. Shaw OL2 49 D7
Parkhill Ave. M8 64 B2
Parkhills Rd. BL9 44 F8
Parkhouse St. M11 & M40 165 B8
Parkhurst Ave. M40 65 E1
Parkin Cl. SK16 101 C8
Parkin St. M12 & M18 99 A3
Parkinson St. Bolton BL3 144 C5
Parkinson St. Bury BL9 27 F5
Parklake Ave. M7 155 F8
Parkland Ave. SK12 127 C1
Parklands. Royton OL2 48 C7
Parklands. Sale M33 108 C5
Parklands. Shaw OL2 49 D8
Parklands. Whitefield M45 62 E8
Parklands Dr. Aspull WN2 38 C6
Parklands Dr. Sale M33 107 D2
Parklands Rd. M23 120 F7
Parklands Sch. M41 95 E4
Parklands The. SK4 169 E4
Parklands Way. SK12 133 E4
Parklea Ct. 6 M7 63 E1
Parklee Prim Sch. M46 58 D2
Parkleigh Dr. M40 65 E2
Parkmount Rd. M9 64 E1
Parks Nook. BL4 60 C7
Parks The. WA12 73 B1
Parks Yd. BL9 140 E2
Parkside. Hindley WN2 56 E6
Parkside. Middleton M24 64 F6
Parkside Ave.
Ashton-i-M WN4 72 F8
Parkside Ave. Eccles M30 79 C1
Parkside Ave. Failsworth M35 83 F5
Parkside Ave. M'ster M7 155 E8
Parkside Ave. Walkden M28 60 D1
Parkside Cl. High Lane SK6 134 D8
Parkside Cl. Radcliffe M26 44 D4
Parkside Cres. WN5 53 F6
Parkside Ind Est. OL2 48 E4
Parkside La. SK6 126 C6
Parkside Rd.
Culcheth WA12 & WA3 90 B2
Parkside Rd. M'ster M14 98 A2
Parkside Rd. Sale M33 108 D3
Parkside St. 6 Bolton BL2 25 C1
Parkside St. M'ster M12 163 C7
Parkside Wlk. Bury BL9 140 F1
Parkside Wlk. Stockport SK7 123 E3
Parkstead Dr. M9 157 D6
Parkstone Ave.
Droylsden M18 99 F6
Parkstone Ave.
Whitefield M45 62 D6
Parkstone Cl. BL8 26 F2
Parkstone Dr. M6 80 B6
Parkstone La. M28 78 F4
Parkstone Rd. M44 94 A3
Parksway. M'ster M25 63 C2
Parksway. M'ster M9 64 B6
Parksway. Pendlebury M27 80 C6
Parkview Ct. M32 96 E1
Parkview Pk. WA13 117 D1
Parkville Rd. M'ster M20 110 C5
Parkville Rd. Prestwich M25 63 C6
Parkway. Chadderton OL9 48 A1
Parkway. Cheadle SK3 122 F7
Parkway. New Mills SK12 127 C1
Parkway. R'dale OL11 30 B8
Parkway.
Shevington Moor WN6 19 A2
Parkway. Stockport SK7 123 E2
Parkway. Walkden M38 59 F4
Parkway. Westhoughton BL5 57 D6
Parkway. Wilmslow SK9 137 B6
Parkway Bsns Ctr. M14 97 F2
Parkway Circ. M17 96 A6
Parkway Four Ind Est. M17 96 A6
Parkway Gr. M38 59 E4
Parkway Ind Est. M17 96 A6
Parkway Trad Est. M32 96 A5
Parkwood. BL7 8 D2
Parkwood Cl. WN3 151 E6
Parkwood Dr. BL5 58 F7
Parkwood Rd. M22 & M23 121 C7
Parlane St. M4 159 B3
Parliament Pl. BL9 140 E1
Parliament St. Bury BL9 140 E1
Parliament St.
Ince-i-M WN3 151 D6
Parliament St. Orrell WN8 53 C7
Parndon Dr. SK2 124 C7
Parnell Ave. M22 121 D8
Parnell Cl. M29 77 B5
Parnham Cl. BL3 43 B5
Parochial CE Prim Sch.
OL6 166 C3
Parr Cl. BL4 60 B8
Parr Fold. M45 45 B2
Parr Fold Ave. M28 60 C1
Parr House. OL8 153 F5
Parr La. BL9 & M45 45 B2
Parr St. Droylsden M11 99 E7
Parr St. Eccles M30 79 D1
Parr St. Tyldesley M29 76 F8
Parrbrook Cl. M45 45 A1
Parrbrook Wlk. M45 45 B1
Parrenthorn High Sch. M25 63 D7
Parrenthorn Rd. M25 63 C7
Parrfield Rd. M28 79 A7
Parrin La. M28 79 C3
Parrot St. Bolton BL3 145 E5
Parrot St. Droylsden M11 83 C1
Parrs Ct. M44 93 F2
Parrs Mount Mews. SK4 110 F2
Parrs Wood Ave. M20 110 C2
Parrs Wood High Sch.
M20 110 D1
Parrs Wood La.
M19 & M20 & SK4 110 D2
Parrs Wood Rd. M'ster M20 110 D4
Parrs Wood Rd. M'ster M20 122 B8
Parry Mead. SK6 113 A4
Parry Rd. M12 99 A4
Parry Wlk. 11 OL6 85 D4
Parslow Ave. M8 156 A8
Parson's La. BL9 140 F3
Parson's Wlk. WN1 37 B1
Parsonage. M3 158 F1
Parsonage Brow. WN8 53 A8
Parsonage Cl. Bury BL9 141 A3
Parsonage Cl. Salford M5 161 C8
Parsonage Ct. 4
M'ster M20 110 B6
Parsonage Ct. M'ster SK4 168 B4
Parsonage Dr. M28 60 C2
Parsonage Gdns. SK6 126 A4
Parsonage La. M3 158 F2
Parsonage Rd.
Flixton M31 & M41 106 E8
Parsonage Rd. Kearsley M26 61 C7
Parsonage Rd. M'ster M20 110 C7
Parsonage Rd. M'ster SK4 168 C4
Parsonage Rd. Urmston M41 95 D2
Parsonage Rd. Walkden M28 60 C2
Parsonage St. Bury BL9 141 A3
Parsonage St. Hyde SK14 167 D1
Parsonage St. M'ster M8 63 F1
Parsonage St. M'ster M15 162 E5
Parsonage St. Radcliffe M26 44 A3
Parsonage St. Stockport SK4 169 E2
Parsonage Way. SK8 123 B5
Parsonage Wlk. OL16 31 F7
Parsons Dr. M24 46 F2
Parsons Field. M27 81 A5
Parsons St. OL9 152 C6
Part St. BL5 39 E2
Parth St. OL10 28 D1
Partington Ct. Farnworth BL4 42 C1
Partington Ct. Glossop SK13 104 F1
Partington La. M26 & M27 79 E7
Partington Pk. SK13 104 C3
Partington Prim Sch. M31 105 F3
Partington St. Bolton BL3 146 C2
Partington St. Eccles M30 79 D3
Partington St. Failsworth M35 83 F7
Partington St. Heywood OL10 29 A2
Partington St.
M'ster M10 & M40 157 F5
Partington St. 4 Oldham OL1 67 A7
Partington St. R'dale OL11 30 B2
Partington St. Swinton M28 79 C8
Partington St. Wigan WN5 54 E8
Partridge Ave. M23 121 C6
Partridge Cl. OL11 29 F7
Partridge Rd. M35 84 C6
Partridge Rise. M43 84 D3
Partridge St. M16, M17, M32 96 F5
Partridge Way. M24 & OL9 65 E8
Parvet Ave. M43 83 F3
Pascal St. M19 111 A8
Pass St. OL9 153 D6
Pass The. OL16 31 A8
Passmonds Cres. OL11, OL12 14 B1
Passmonds Way. OL11 30 B8
Paston Rd. M22 121 D7
Pasture Cl. Ashton-i-M WN4 72 E6
Pasture Cl. Heywood OL10 29 B1
Pasture Field Rd. M22 121 F1
Pasturefield Cl. 1 M33 108 F3
Pastures La. OL4 68 B8
Patch Croft Rd. M22 121 F1
Patch La. SK7 132 D5
Patchett St. M'ster M12 164 F6
Patchett St. 9 Tyldesley M29 59 A1
Patey Sq. 2 WN6 37 B3
Patey St. M18 99 A3
Pathfield Wlk. 2 M9 157 D8
Patience St. 11 OL12 14 C1
Patmos St. BL0 11 D6
Paton Ave. BL3 42 A3
Paton Ct. M7 81 C4
Paton Mews. 5 BL3 42 A3
Paton St. M'ster M1 & M60 159 B1
Paton St. R'dale OL12 14 D3
Patricia Dr. M28 60 E2
Patrick Roddy Ct. M18 165 C5
Patricroft Rd. WN2 151 F6
Patricroft Sta. M30 79 C2
Patten St. M20 110 B6
Patterdale Ave.
Ashton-u-L OL7 84 F5
Patterdale Ave. Urmston M41 95 B4
Patterdale Cl. Oldham OL1 49 A1
Patterdale Cl. R'dale OL11 30 B3
Patterdale Cl.
Stalybridge SK15 86 A3
Patterdale Dr. Bury BL9 44 E7
Patterdale Dr. Middleton M24 46 E2
Patterdale Pl. WN2 56 A7
Patterdale Rd.
Ashton-i-M WN4 73 A8
Patterdale Rd.
Ashton-u-L OL7 84 F5
Patterdale Rd. Bolton BL2 25 F4
Patterdale Rd. Leigh WN7 76 C4
Patterdale Rd.
Partington M31 105 E3
Patterdale Rd. Romiley SK6 113 B4
Patterdale Rd.
Stockport SK1 & SK2 124 B7
Patterdale Rd.
Wythenshawe M22 121 E8
Patterdale Wlk. WA15 120 D5
Patterson Ave. M21 97 A1
Patterson St. Bolton BL3 146 A4
Patterson St. Denton M34 100 F4
Patterson St.
Newton-l-W WA12 89 B3
Patterson St.
Westhoughton BL5 57 B7
Pattishall Cl. M4 160 D1
Pattison Cl. OL12 14 D3
Patton Cl. BL9 45 B2
Paul Row. OL15 6 C1
Paulden Ave. Oldham OL4 49 E1
Paulden Ave.
Wythenshawe M23 121 B6
Paulden Dr. M35 84 A7
Paulette St. BL1 143 E2
Paulhan Rd. M20 110 D4
Paulhan St. BL3 147 E3
Pauline St. WN2 57 B1
Pavilion Cl. OL12 14 F2
Pavilion Dr. OL6 85 D5
Pavilion Wlk. M26 43 F3
Paxford Pl. SK9 137 A5
Paythorne Gn. SK2 124 E5
Peabody St. BL3 147 E4
Peace St. Atherton M46 58 E3
Peace St. Bolton BL3 145 D5
Peace St. 3 Failsworth M35 66 A1
Peace St. Tyldesley M29 76 F7
Peacefield. SK6 125 E5
Peacefield Prim Sch. SK6 125 E5
Peacehaven Ave. 12 M11 83 C2
Peaceville Rd. M19 98 F1
Peach Bank. M24 65 A8
Peach Rd. OL4 49 D1
Peach St. M25 63 C5
Peach Tree Ct. M6 81 A2
Peachey Cl. 6 M16 97 F3
Peacock Ave. Gatley SK8 131 B6
Peacock Ave. 8 Salford M6 80 D5
Peacock Cl. Hadfield SK14 171 E4
Peacock Cl. M'ster M18 165 C6
Peacock Fold. WN7 75 D6
Peacock Gr. M18 99 D4
Peacock Way. 5 SK9 131 D5
Peak Ave. M46 58 D5
Peak Cl. OL4 49 F4
Peak St. Bolton BL1 143 D2
Peak St. M'ster M1 159 B1
Peak St. Oldham OL9 152 C6
Peak St. Stockport SK1 112 A2
Peakdale Ave. Gatley SK8 122 B1
Peakdale Ave. M'ster M8 156 B8
Peakdale Rd. Droylsden M43 83 E3
Peakdale Rd. Hadfield SK13 171 E3
Peakdale Rd. Marple SK6 126 A4
Peakforton Wlk. 11 SK9 131 E1
Peaknaze Cl. Glossop SK13 116 B8
Peaknaze Cl. Pendlebury M27 80 B8
Pear Ave. BL9 141 C3
Pear New Mill Ind Est. SK6 112 C2
Pear Tree Cl. Hadfield SK14 171 E4
Pear Tree Cl. Marple SK6 126 B8
Pear Tree Cl. Salford M6 81 A2
Pear Tree Ct. 3 M6 81 A2
Pear Tree Dr. SK15 86 B2
Pear Tree Gr. M29 59 E1
Pear Tree Wlk. 10 M33 107 C5
Pearl Ave. M7 63 E1
Pearl Brook Ind Est. BL6 22 B3
Pearl Mill Cl. OL8 67 B4
Pearl St. Denton M34 100 E3
Pearl St. Hazel Grove SK7 124 E4
Pearl St. R'dale OL11 30 C8
Pearl St. Wigan WN6 37 B3
Pearl Way. SK14 103 A2
Pearly Bank. OL1 49 D4
Pearn Ave. M19 110 F5
Pearn Rd. M19 110 F5
Pearson Cl. Milnrow OL16 31 F7
Pearson Cl. Partington M31 106 A3
Pearson Gr. 7 OL4 67 E6
Pearson House. M30 95 D8
Pearson St. Bury BL9 141 B3
Pearson St. Dukinfield SK16 101 C6
Pearson St. R'dale OL16 31 C8
Pearson St. Stockport SK5 169 F3
Peart Ave. SK6 113 C6
Peart St. M34 100 E3
Peartree Wlk. M22 121 B4
Peary St. M4 159 B3
Peaslake Cl. SK6 113 D2
Peatfield Ave. M27 61 E2
Peatfield Wlk. M15 162 F5
Pebble Cl. SK15 86 A4
Pebworth Cl. M24 & M9 64 F5
Peckford Dr. M40 83 A5
Peckforton Cl. M22 122 A5
Peckmill Cl. SK9 131 E2
Pedder St. BL1 142 C1
Pedler Brow La. OL12 15 E6
Pedley Wlk. M13 163 B7
Peebles Cl. WN4 72 C4
Peebles Dr. M40 83 D4
Peel Ave. Alt'ham WA14 119 D2
Peel Ave. Ramsbottom BL0 138 A5
Peel Brow. BL0 11 D6
Peel Brow Prim Sch. BL0 11 D6
Peel Cl. M46 58 E3
Peel Cott St. OL14 6 A8
Peel Cottage Rd. OL14 6 A8
Peel Cross Rd. M5 81 A1
Peel Ctr The. SK1 169 F2
Peel Dr. Sale M33 108 E4
Peel Dr. Walkden M38 59 F4
Peel Gr. M'ster M12 & M18 99 A4
Peel Gr. Worsley M28 78 F8
Peel Green Rd. M30 95 C8
Peel Hall Prim Sch.
Walkden M38 59 F3
Peel Hall Prim Sch.
Wythenshawe M22 121 F3
Peel Hall Rd. Ramsbottom BL0 11 B2
Peel Hall Rd.
Wythenshawe M22 121 F2
Peel La. Heywood OL10 29 B3
Peel La. M'ster M8 159 B4
Peel La. Tyldesley M29 77 B4
Peel La. Walkden M28 & M38 59 F3
Peel Moat Rd. SK4 111 B5
Peel Moat Sports Ctr. SK4 111 B5
Peel Mount. Ramsbottom BL0 11 A4
Peel Mount. Salford M6 81 B3
Peel Park Cres. M38 59 F4
Peel Rd. WA15 119 E3
Peel St. Adlington PR6 21 B8
Peel St. Ashton-u-L OL6 166 B3
Peel St. Denton M34 100 E4
Peel St. Denton M34 100 E6
Peel St. Droylsden M11, M43 99 F8
Peel St. Dukinfield SK16 166 C1
Peel St. Eccles M30 79 F2
Peel St. Failsworth M35 83 D6
Peel St. Farnworth BL4 60 E8
Peel St. Glossop SK14 104 C5
Peel St. Heywood OL10 29 B2
Peel St. Hyde SK14 167 F1
Peel St. Leigh WN7 75 E5
Peel St. Littleborough OL15 16 B5
Peel St. Newton-l-W WA12 89 A3
Peel St. Oldham OL9 152 B7
Peel St. Platt Bridge WN2 56 A2
Peel St. R'dale OL12 139 E8
Peel St. 1 Radcliffe M26 44 B2
Peel St. Stalybridge SK15 85 F1
Peel St. Stockport SK2 170 F6
Peel St. Westhoughton BL5 39 E1
Peel Terr. 19 SK16 166 B1
Peel View. BL8 27 A6
Peel Way. BL9 140 E2
Peelgate Dr. SK8 122 A2
Peels Ave. OL4 68 A7
Peelwood Ave. M38 60 A4
Peelwood Gr. M46 58 E2
Peerglow Pk Est. WA14 119 E8
Peers Cl. M41 94 D4
Peers St. BL8 27 C2
Pegamoid St. BL2 25 B1
Pegasus Ct. R'dale OL11 30 C6
Pegasus Ct. Sale M33 108 D5
Pegasus Sq. M7 81 C3
Pegwell Dr. M7 & M8 155 E5
Pekin St. OL6 166 C4
Pelham Pl. M8 64 B2
Pelham St. Ashton-u-L OL7 84 E1
Pelham St. Bolton BL3 146 C3
Pelham St. Oldham OL8 66 F2
Pellowe Rd. OL8 66 E4
Pelton Ave. M27 61 D2
Pemberlei Rd. WN2 38 D2
Pemberton Comm
High Sch. WN5 54 C7
Pemberton House. OL2 149 B8
Pemberton Prim Sch. WN5 54 C6
Pemberton Rd.
Wigan WN3 & WN5 54 B2
Pemberton St. Bolton BL1 143 E4

Pemberton St. M'ster M16 .... 97 C4
Pemberton St. 3 R'dale OL11 30 C2
Pemberton St. Walkden M38 60 B4
Pemberton Sta. WN3 .... 54 D4
Pemberton Way. OL2 .... 149 B8
Pembridge Fold. M24 .... 65 C8
Pembridge Rd. M9 .... 64 F4
Pembroke Ave. Eccles M30 .. 79 D2
Pembroke Ave. Sale M33 .... 107 F5
Pembroke Cl. Horwich BL6 .... 22 A4
Pembroke Cl. M'ster M13 .. 164 D6
Pembroke Ct. Bredbury SK6 112 F2
Pembroke Ct.
Hazel Grove SK7 .... 124 E2
Pembroke Ct. Pendlebury M27 80 B8
Pembroke Ct. 14 R'dale OL12 14 F1
Pembroke Dr. Bury BL9 .... 44 E7
Pembroke Dr. Oldham OL4 .... 49 E4
Pembroke Gr. M44 .... 105 C6
Pembroke House. 3 SK3 . 170 E8
Pembroke Rd. Hindley WN2 .. 57 C3
Pembroke Rd.
Shevington WN5 .... 36 D1
Pembroke St. Bolton BL1 ... 145 D8
Pembroke St.
Littleborough OL15 .... 16 B6
Pembroke St. M'ster M7 ..... 155 E6
Pembroke St. Oldham OL8 . 153 D6
Pembroke St. 3 Salford M6 154 E1
Pembroke Way. 6 M34 .... 101 A1
Pembry Cl. SK5 .... 112 B5
Pembury Cl. M22 .... 121 C3
Penarth Rd. Bolton BL3 ...... 146 B4
Penarth Rd.
Wythenshawe M22 .... 121 D8
Penbury Rd. WN1 .... 37 B5
Pencombe Cl. M12 .... 165 A5
Pencroft Way. M15 .... 163 A5
Pendeen Cl. M29 .... 77 A7
Pendennis. 2 OL11 .... 139 E6
Pendennis Ave. BL6 .... 40 D5
Pendennis Cl. M26 .... 43 C5
Pendennis Cres. WN2 .... 57 A3
Pendennis Rd. SK4 .... 168 C3
Pendine Wlk. M7 .... 155 E6
Pendle Cl. Bury BL8 .... 27 B3
Pendle Cl. Oldham OL4 .... 67 D5
Pendle Cl. Wigan WN5 .... 54 D5
Pendle Ct. BL1 .... 143 D3
Pendle Dr. BL6 .... 22 C5
Pendle Gdns. WA3 .... 91 E2
Pendle Gr. OL2 .... 48 C3
Pendle Rd. Denton M34 ...... 100 F2
Pendle Rd. Golborne WA3 ..... 74 C1
Pendle Wlk. SK5 .... 112 A4
Pendlebury Cl. M25 .... 62 F2
Pendlebury Fold. BL3 .... 40 D2
Pendlebury La. WN1 & WN2 . 37 D6
Pendlebury Rd. Gatley SK8 122 B6
Pendlebury Rd. Swinton M27 79 F8
Pendlebury St. BL1 .... 143 F3
Pendlebury Towers. SK5 ... 169 F3
Pendlecroft Ave. M27 .... 80 C7
Pendlegreen Cl. M11 .... 164 F8
Pendleton Coll. M6 .... 154 D4
Pendleton Gn. 14 M6 .... 154 F3
Pendleton Sta. M6 .... 81 A4
Pendleton Way. M6 .... 154 F3
Pendleway. M27 .... 62 A1
Pendragon Pl. M35 .... 84 A7
Pendrell Wlk. 23 M9 .... 64 E3
Penelope Rd. 4 M6 .... 80 D5
Penerly Dr. M40 & M9 .... 157 D6
Penfair Cl. M11 .... 83 A1
Penfield Cl. M1 .... 163 B7
Penfold Wlk. M12 .... 164 F6
Pengarth Rd. BL6 .... 22 C4
Pengham Wlk. M23 .... 109 A1
Pengwern Ave. 2 BL3 .... 146 B4
Penhale Mews. SK7 .... 132 F7
Penhall Wlk. M40 .... 83 A5
Peninsula. M7 .... 81 B7
Penistone Ave. M'ster M9 .... 65 A3
Penistone Ave. R'dale OL16 .. 31 C6
Penistone Ave. Salford M6 .... 80 C3
Penketh Ave. M'ster M18 ..... 99 B4
Penketh Ave. Tyldesley M29 . 77 B6
Penketh St. WN6 .... 37 B2
Penleach Ave. WN7 .... 76 B5
Penmere Gr. M33 .... 107 E1
Penmoor Chase. SK7 .... 124 B1
Penmore Cl. OL2 .... 49 D7
Penn Gn. SK8 .... 123 B1
Penn House Cl. SK7 .... 132 E8
Penn St. Farnworth BL4 .... 60 C8
Penn St. Heywood OL10 .... 29 D1
Penn St. Horwich BL6 .... 22 C3
Penn St. M'ster M40 .... 157 F8
Penn St. Oldham OL8 .... 153 D5
Penn St. R'dale OL16 .... 139 F8
Pennant Dr. M25 .... 63 A5
Pennant St. OL1 .... 67 B8
Pennant St Ind Est. 9 OL1 . 67 B8
Pennell Dr. WN3 .... 54 F5
Pennell St. M11 .... 83 D1
Pennine Ave. Oldham OL9 ... 152 A5
Pennine Ave. Wigan WN3 ..... 54 C2
Pennine Cl. Bury BL8 .... 27 B3
Pennine Cl. Horwich BL6 ...... 22 B3
Pennine Cl. M'ster M9 .... 64 F4
Pennine Ct. 3 Oldham OL4 .. 67 A6
Pennine Ct. Stalybridge SK15 86 D3
Pennine Ct. Swinton M27 ...... 62 A1
Pennine Dr. Alt'ham WA14 ... 119 B5
Pennine Dr. Ashton-u-L OL6 .. 85 E4
Pennine Dr.
Littleborough OL12 .... 15 C6
Pennine Dr. Milnrow OL16 .... 32 A6
Pennine Gr. Ashton-u-L OL6 .. 85 E6
Pennine Gr. Leigh WN7 .... 75 C8
Pennine La. WA3 .... 74 C1
Pennine Prec. OL16 .... 31 F5
Pennine Rd. Glossop SK13 .. 116 A8
Pennine Rd. Horwich BL6 ...... 22 C5
Pennine Rd. Romiley SK6 .... 113 C6
Pennine Rd. Stockport SK7 . 124 B1
Pennine Terr. 2 SK16 .... 166 C1
Pennine Vale. OL2 .... 149 C8
Pennine View. Denton M34 100 E5
Pennine View.
Littleborough OL15 .... 6 D2
Pennine View. Mossley OL5 .. 68 D1
Pennine View. Royton OL2 .... 48 E4
Pennine View.
Stalybridge SK15 .... 86 C4
Pennine Wlk. WN2 .... 56 B2
Pennington Ave. WN7 .... 75 E3
Pennington Cl.
Pennington Green WN2 .... 38 E2
Pennington Cl. Walkden M38 59 E4
Pennington Ct. WN7 .... 75 B1
Pennington Flash Ctry Pk.
WN7 .... 75 B3
Pennington Gdns. WN7 .... 75 E3
Pennington Green La. WN2 38 E2
Pennington La. Ince-i-M WN2 56 A8
Pennington La. Standish WN2 37 E8
Pennington Mews. WN7 ...... 75 E2
Pennington Rd. Bolton BL3 . 147 F3
Pennington Rd. Leigh WN7 .. 75 F3
Pennington St. Bury BL8 ...... 26 F4
Pennington St. 4
Hindley WN2 .... 56 D6
Pennington St.
M'ster M12 & M19 .... 99 A2
Pennington St. Oldham OL9 .. 66 B3
Pennington St. 1
Walkden M28 .... 60 E2
Penny Bridge La. M41 .... 95 A2
Penny Brook Fold. SK7 ...... 124 F3
Penny La.
Newton-l-W WA11 & WA12 .... 89 A7
Penny La. Stockport SK5 ..... 169 F3
Penny Meadow. OL6 .... 166 C3
Pennygate Cl. WN2 .... 56 D6
Pennyhurst St. WN3 .... 150 B7
Pennymoor Dr. WA14 .... 119 B6
Penrhos Ave. M22 .... 121 F4
Penrhyn Ave. Cheadle SK8 . 122 E1
Penrhyn Ave. Middleton M24 65 A7
Penrhyn Cres. SK7 .... 133 C8
Penrhyn Dr. Hazel Grove SK7 124 D1
Penrhyn Dr. Prestwich M25 ... 63 B4
Penrhyn Gr. M46 .... 58 C5
Penrhyn Rd. SK3 .... 123 C8
Penrice Cl. M26 .... 43 D5
Penrice Fold. M28 .... 78 B7
Penrith Ave. Ashton-u-L OL7 .. 84 F5
Penrith Ave. Bolton BL1 ...... 142 A1
Penrith Ave. Droylsden M11 .. 83 B3
Penrith Ave. Oldham OL8 ...... 66 C4
Penrith Ave. Prestwich M45 .. 63 B7
Penrith Ave. Reddish SK5 ..... 99 F1
Penrith Ave. Sale M33 .... 108 C2
Penrith Ave. Walkden M28 ..... 60 F2
Penrith Cl. M44 .... 105 E4
Penrith Cres. WN4 .... 73 B4
Penrith House. M7 .... 158 D4
Penrith St. OL11 .... 139 F5
Penrod Pl. M6 .... 81 B4
Penrose Gdns. M24 .... 47 B1
Penrose St. BL2 .... 148 C7
Penroy Ave. M20 .... 109 D3
Penroyson Cl. M12 .... 164 F6
Penruddock Wlk. 4 M13 ...... 98 F4
Penry Ave. M44 .... 105 E6
Penryn Ave. Royton OL2 ...... 48 F3
Penryn Ave. Sale M33 .... 108 C1
Penryn Ct. M7 .... 63 D1
Pensarn Ave. M14 .... 110 E8
Pensarn Gr. SK5 .... 169 F4
Pensby Cl. M27 .... 80 C7
Pensby Wlk. M40 .... 157 D5
Pensford Ct. BL2 .... 25 E6
Pensford Rd. M23 .... 120 F3
Penshaw Ave. WN3 .... 55 B3
Penshurst Rd. SK5 .... 112 B6
Penshurst Wlk. 20 M34 ..... 101 A1
Penson St. WN1 .... 37 D2
Penthorpe Dr. OL2 .... 48 F3
Pentland Ave. M40 .... 65 C2
Pentland Cl. SK7 .... 124 B1
Pentland Terr. BL1 .... 143 E1
Pentland Way. SK14 .... 102 B6
Pentlands Ave. M7 .... 155 D5
Penton Wlk. 5 M16 .... 97 F3
Pentwyn Gr. M23 .... 121 B7
Penzance St. M10 & M40 .... 160 E3
Peover Ave. M33 .... 108 E4
Peover Rd. SK9 .... 131 E5
Peover Wlk. SK8 .... 123 A5
Pepler Ave. M23 .... 109 B2
Peploe Wlk. M23 .... 108 D1
Pepper Ct. SK9 .... 137 A6
Pepper La. WN6 .... 19 B3
Pepper Mill Bsns Pk. WN1 151 D7
Pepper Mill La. WN1 .... 151 D7
Pepper Rd. SK7 .... 124 B2
Pepper St. WA16 .... 128 F1
Pepperhill Wlk. 1 M21 .... 97 F4
Peppermint Cl. OL16 .... 32 C4
Pepys Pl. WN3 .... 55 A4
Perch St. 4 WN1 .... 37 E1
Perch Wlk. 7 M4 .... 159 C1
Percival Rd. M43 .... 84 B1
Percival Wlk. OL2 .... 48 E3
Percy Dr. M5 .... 161 B7
Percy Rd. M34 .... 100 E2
Percy St. Bolton BL1 .... 143 F2
Percy St. Bury BL9 .... 141 B3
Percy St. Farnworth BL4 .... 60 E7
Percy St. M'ster M15 .... 162 D6
Percy St. Oldham OL4 .... 67 C7
Percy St. R'dale OL16 .... 31 B5
Percy St. Ramsbottom BL0 .. 138 B5
Percy St. Stalybridge SK15 ... 86 B2
Percy St. Stockport SK1 ...... 169 F2
Percy St. Whitworth OL12 .... 4 E6
Peregrine Cres. M43 .... 84 C3
Peregrine Dr. M44 .... 94 A3
Peregrine Rd. SK2 .... 125 A4
Periton Wlk. 8 M9 .... 64 E3
Perivale Dr. OL8 .... 67 B4
Perkins Ave. M7 .... 155 E5
Pernham St. OL4 .... 67 C7
Perrin St. SK14 .... 167 D2
Perry Ave. SK14 .... 102 A4
Perry Brook Comm Prim
Sch. WN4 .... 73 A7
Perry Rd. WA15 .... 120 B6
Perrybrook Wlk. WN4 .... 73 D4
Perrygate Ave. M20 .... 110 A6
Perrymead. M25 .... 63 C6
Perryn Pl. WN6 .... 19 F1
Pershore. 8 OL12 .... 139 E8
Pershore Rd. M24 .... 47 A3
Perth Ave. Ince-i-M WN2 ...... 56 A8
Perth Ave. Oldham OL9 .... 66 A4
Perth Cl. SK7 .... 132 F5
Perth Rd. OL11 .... 31 B2
Perth St. Bolton BL3 .... 146 C3
Perth St. Royton OL2 .... 49 A4
Perth St. Swinton M27 .... 79 D7
Peru St. M3 .... 158 D2
Peter Martin St. 2 BL6 .... 22 B4
Peter Moss Way. M19 .... 99 C1
Peter St. Alt'ham WA14 ...... 119 D3
Peter St. Ashton-i-M WN4 ..... 73 C3
Peter St. Bury BL9 .... 140 F3
Peter St. Denton M34 .... 101 A3
Peter St. Eccles M30 .... 79 D1
Peter St. Golborne WA3 .... 90 A8
Peter St. Hadfield SK14 ...... 104 A6
Peter St. Hazel Grove SK7 ... 124 D3
Peter St. Hindley WN2 .... 56 D5
Peter St. Leigh WN7 .... 76 B4
Peter St. M'ster M2 .... 162 F8
Peter St. Oldham OL1 .... 153 F6
Peter St. Stockport SK1 ...... 112 A2
Peter St. 14 Tyldesley M29 ..... 58 F1
Peter St. Westhoughton BL5 ... 57 A7
Peter St. Wigan WN5 .... 54 B8
Peterborough Cl. OL6 .... 85 B6
Peterborough Dr. 10 BL1 .. 143 F1
Peterborough St. 1 M18 .... 99 F6
Peterborough Wlk. BL1 ...... 143 E1
Peterchurch Wlk. M11 .... 165 C8
Peterhead Cl. BL1 .... 143 D1
Peterhead Wlk. 4 M5 .... 81 A1
Peterhouse Gdns. SK6 .... 113 C4
Peterhouse Wlk. WN4 .... 72 F3
Peterloo Ct. 5 M5 .... 154 E2
Peterloo Terr. 8 M24 .... 47 A2
Peters Ct. WA15 .... 120 D5
Petersburg Rd. SK3 .... 170 D6
Petersfield Dr. M23 .... 120 D7
Petersfield Gdns. WA3 .... 91 F3
Petersfield Wlk. 1 BL1 ..... 145 E8
Peterswood Cl. M22 .... 121 B3
Petheridge Dr. 3 M22 .... 121 B1
Petrel Ave. SK12 .... 133 B4
Petrel Cl. Droylsden M43 ...... 84 C3
Petrel Cl. R'dale OL11 .... 29 F7
Petrel Cl. Tyldesley M29 ...... 77 A8
Petrie Ct. M6 .... 81 B4
Petrie St. OL12 .... 139 F8
Petrock Wlk. 5 M40 .... 83 C5
Petticoat La. WN2 .... 56 B7
Petts Cres. OL15 .... 16 A6
Petunia Wlk. 8 M28 .... 59 F3
Petworth Ave. WN3 .... 54 D2
Petworth Cl. M22 .... 121 C2
Petworth Rd. OL9 .... 152 B6
Pevensey Ct. M9 .... 64 E5
Pevensey Rd. M6 .... 80 E5
Pevensey Wlk. OL9 .... 152 B6
Peveril Ave. SK12 .... 127 C1
Peveril Cl. M25 & M45 .... 63 C7
Peveril Cres. M21 .... 97 A2
Peveril Ct. SK13 .... 116 F8
Peveril Dr. SK7 .... 133 F8
Peveril Rd. Alt'ham WA14 ... 119 C7
Peveril Rd. Oldham OL1 .... 49 C1
Peveril Rd. Salford M5 .... 154 D2
Peveril St. BL3 .... 146 C3
Peveril Terr. SK14 .... 113 F8
Pewfist Gn. BL5 .... 57 E6
Pewfist Spinney The. BL5 ... 57 D7
Pewfist The. BL5 .... 57 E7
Pewsey Rd. M22 .... 121 F3
Pexhill Ct. SK4 .... 168 A2
Pexwood. OL1 .... 47 E1
Pheasant Cl. M28 .... 78 B6
Pheasant Dr. M21 .... 109 D7
Pheasant Rise. WA14 .... 119 D1
Phelan Cl. M40 .... 156 C5
Phethean St. Bolton BL2 .... 148 A7
Phethean St. Farnworth BL4 . 42 C2
Philip Arnold Ct. 2 BL4 .... 60 C8
Philip Ave. M34 .... 100 E5
Philip Cl. 6 WN5 .... 54 D5
Philip Dr. M33 .... 108 B2
Philip Howard Rd. SK13 .... 116 C8
Philip St. Bolton BL3 .... 145 D5
Philip St. Eccles M30 .... 79 D1
Philip St. Oldham OL4 .... 67 C8
Philip St. R'dale OL11 .... 139 F5
Philips Ave. BL4 .... 60 D7
Philips Dr. M45 .... 62 D6
Philips High Sch. M45 .... 62 E8
Philips Park Rd. M'ster M11 160 F2
Philips Park Rd.
Whitefield M45 .... 62 D6
Phillimore St. OL4 .... 67 E5
Phillip Way. 1 SK14 .... 102 E1
Phillips Pl. M45 .... 62 F7
Phillips St. WN7 .... 75 E8
Phipps St. M28 .... 60 C4
Phoebe St. 5 Bolton BL3 .... 146 C4
Phoebe St. Salford M5 .... 161 B8
Phoenix Cl. OL10 .... 29 F1
Phoenix Park Ind Est. OL10 29 F1
Phoenix Pl. OL4 .... 67 F7
Phoenix St. Bolton BL1 ...... 148 A8
Phoenix St. Bury BL9 .... 140 E2
Phoenix St. Farnworth BL4 ... 60 D7
Phoenix St. Littleborough OL15 16 B6
Phoenix St. M'ster M60 ...... 159 A1
Phoenix St. Oldham OL4 .... 67 F7
Phoenix St. Oldham OL1 ..... 153 F6
Phoenix St. R'dale OL12 .... 14 C1
Phoenix Way. Eccles M41 ..... 95 E6
Phoenix Way. Radcliffe M26 .. 44 A2
Phyllis St. Middleton M24 ..... 65 C7
Phyllis St. R'dale OL11 & OL12 14 B1
Picadilly. WN5 .... 71 E5
Piccadilly.
M'ster M1 & M4 & M60 .... 159 B1
Piccadilly. Stockport SK1 ..... 169 F1
Piccadilly Gdns Sta. M1 ...... 159 A1
Piccadilly Plaza. M1 .... 159 A1
Piccadilly Sta. M1 .... 163 B8
Piccadilly Trad Est. M1 ...... 163 C8
Piccadilly Village. M1 .... 159 C1
Pickering Cl. Alt'ham WA15 120 A7
Pickering Cl. Bury BL8 .... 27 B5
Pickering Cl. Kearsley M26 ... 61 A8
Pickering Cl. Urmston M41 ... 95 B2
Pickford Ave. BL3 .... 43 C3
Pickford Ct. M16 .... 162 E5
Pickford La. SK16 .... 101 C8
Pickford Mews. SK16 .... 101 C8
Pickford St. M4 .... 159 B2
Pickford Wlk. OL2 .... 48 E3
Pickford's Brow. SK1 .... 169 F1
Pickhill La. OL3 .... 69 B8
Pickhill Mews. OL3 .... 69 B8
Pickley Gn. WN7 .... 57 E1
Pickmere Ave. M20 .... 110 B8
Pickmere Cl. 4
Droylsden M43 .... 84 B1
Pickmere Cl. Stockport SK3 123 C6
Pickmere Cl.
Wythenshawe M33 .... 108 F2
Pickmere Ct. 10 SK9 .... 131 D5
Pickmere Gdns. SK8 .... 122 F4
Pickmere Rd. SK9 .... 131 D5
Pickmere Terr. 2 SK16 ..... 166 B1
Picksley St. WN7 .... 76 B4
Pickthorn Cl. WN2 .... 56 B3
Pickup St. Ince-i-M WN2 ..... 151 F7
Pickup St. R'dale OL16 .... 31 A7
Pickwick Rd. SK12 .... 133 D3
Picton Cl. M3 .... 158 E2
Picton Dr. SK9 .... 131 E2
Picton Sch. M33 .... 107 F4
Picton Sq. 4 OL4 .... 67 A6
Picton St. Ashton-u-L OL7 .... 85 A6
Picton St. M'ster M7 .... 158 D3
Picton Wlk. 9 M16 .... 97 F3
Pierce St. OL1 .... 49 C1
Piercy Ave. M7 .... 158 D4
Piercy St. Failsworth M35 ..... 83 E7
Piercy St. M'ster M40 .... 160 D2
Pierpoint St. WA12 .... 90 A7
Piethorne Cl. OL16 .... 32 C4
Pigeon St. M1 & M60 .... 159 B1
Piggott St. BL4 .... 60 C7
Pigot St. 2 WN5 .... 54 B6
Pike Ave. Atherton M46 .... 58 A2
Pike Ave. Failsworth M35 ...... 84 C6
Pike Fold Golf Course. M9 . 64 D6
Pike Fold La. M9 .... 64 C3
Pike Fold Prim Sch. M9 .... 64 C3
Pike Nook Wkshp. BL3 ...... 145 D5
Pike Rd. BL3 .... 147 D4
Pike St. OL11 .... 139 F5
Pike View. BL6 .... 22 D4
Pike View Cl. OL4 .... 67 B5
Pike's La. SK13 .... 116 B8
Pikehouse Cotts. OL15 .... 16 D7
Pikes Lane Prim Sch. BL3 .. 145 D6
Pilgrim Dr. M11 .... 160 F1
Pilgrims Way. WN6 .... 37 A7
Pilkington Dr. M45 .... 45 B2
Pilkington Rd. Kearsley BL4 . 60 F6
Pilkington Rd. M'ster M9 ...... 65 A3
Pilkington Rd. Radcliffe M26 43 F4
Pilkington St. Bolton BL3 ... 145 E5
Pilkington St. Hindley WN2 ... 56 D6
Pilkington St. Middleton M24 47 C1
Pilkington St.
Ramsbottom BL0 .... 138 B5
Pilkington Way. M26 .... 44 A2
Pilling Field. BL7 .... 8 E1
Pilling St. Bury BL8 .... 27 C3
Pilling St. Denton M34 .... 100 F3
Pilling St. Leigh WN7 .... 75 D5
Pilling St. M'ster M10 & M40 157 F5
Pilling St. R'dale OL12 .... 139 D8
Pilling St. 3 Rawtenstall BB4 .. 2 F8
Pilling Wlk. OL9 .... 152 A6
Pilning St. BL3 .... 42 A4
Pilot Ind Est. BL3 .... 42 B4
Pilot St. BL9 .... 140 F1
Pilsley Cl. WN5 .... 36 A1
Pilsworth Cotts. BL9 .... 45 C5
Pilsworth Rd.
Heywood BL9 & OL10 .... 45 C7
Pilsworth Rd. Heywood OL10 46 A8
Pilsworth Way. BL9 .... 45 A6
Pimblett St. Golborne WA3 ... 90 A7
Pimblett St. M'ster M3 .... 158 F3
Pimbo La. WN8 .... 53 A4
Pimhole Rd. BL9 .... 141 A2
Pimlico Cl. M7 .... 155 D6
Pimlott Gr. Dukinfield SK14 . 101 D5
Pimlott Gr. Prestwich M25 .... 62 F2
Pimlott Rd. BL1 .... 25 B3
Pimmcroft Way. M23, M33 109 A3
Pin Mill Brow. M12 .... 164 D8
Pincher Wlk. 14 M11 .... 83 C1
Pinder Wlk. 7 M15 .... 162 F6
Pine Ave. Newton-l-W WA12 .. 89 D2
Pine Ave. Whitefield M45 ...... 62 F6
Pine Cl. Denton M34 .... 100 E6
Pine Cl. Marple SK6 .... 125 E4
Pine Ct. M'ster M20 .... 110 A4
Pine Ct. Stockport SK7 .... 123 D2
Pine Gr. Denton M34 .... 101 A3
Pine Gr. Eccles M30 .... 79 E4
Pine Gr. Farnworth BL4 .... 60 B8
Pine Gr. Golborne WA3 .... 90 C8
Pine Gr. M'ster M13 .... 98 E4
Pine Gr. Prestwich M45 .... 63 A6
Pine Gr. Royton OL2 .... 48 D6
Pine Gr. Sale M33 .... 107 D6
Pine Gr. Stalybridge SK16 ... 101 F8
Pine Gr. Swinton M27 .... 79 D7
Pine Gr. Westhoughton BL5 .. 57 E7
Pine Gr. Worsley M28 .... 78 E8
Pine Lodge. SK7 .... 132 F7
Pine Meadow. M26 .... 61 C6
Pine Rd. Bramhall SK7 .... 132 F8
Pine Rd. Dukinfield SK15 ..... 101 E8
Pine Rd. M'ster M20 .... 110 B4
Pine Rd. Poynton SK12 .... 133 F3
Pine Rd. Wigan WN5 .... 54 E6
Pine St. Ashton-u-L OL6 ..... 166 B4
Pine St. Bolton BL1 .... 143 F2
Pine St. Bury BL9 .... 141 B2
Pine St. Chadderton OL9 ..... 152 A8
Pine St. Dukinfield SK14 .... 101 D5
Pine St. Heywood OL10 .... 29 D2
Pine St. Littleborough OL15 .... 16 B6
Pine St. M'ster M60 .... 159 A1
Pine St. Middleton M24 .... 65 C7
Pine St. Newhey OL16 .... 32 B4
Pine St. R'dale OL16 .... 31 B7
Pine St. Radcliffe M26 .... 44 B4
Pine St. Romiley SK6 .... 113 B5
Pine St. Stockport SK3 .... 170 D8
Pine St. 5 Tyldesley M29 ...... 59 A1
Pine St S. BL9 .... 141 B3
Pine Tree Rd. OL8 .... 66 D1
Pine View. WN3 .... 54 B1
Pine Wlk. 1 M31 .... 105 E3
Pineapple St. SK7 .... 124 E2
Pinehurst Rd. M10 & M40 ... 157 E5
Pines The. WN7 .... 75 F3
Pinetop Cl. M21 .... 109 D7
Pinetree St. M18 .... 165 C5
Pinevale. WN6 .... 37 A7
Pineway. OL4 .... 67 F6
Pinewood. Alt'ham WA14 ..... 119 A2
Pinewood. Ashton-i-M WN4 ... 73 A2
Pinewood. Chadderton M24 .... 65 E7
Pinewood. Sale M33 .... 107 D4
Pinewood Cl. Abram WN2 ...... 74 C7
Pinewood Cl. 30 Bolton BL1 143 E2
Pinewood Cl.
Dukinfield SK16 .... 166 C1
Pinewood Cl. M'ster SK4 .... 168 A3
Pinewood Cres.
Ince-i-M WN2 .... 151 F6
Pinewood Cres. Orrell WN5 . 53 E6
Pinewood Cres.
Ramsbottom BL0 .... 11 B2
Pinewood Ct.
Alt'ham WA14 & WA15 .... 119 E1
Pinewood Ct. Sale M33 ...... 108 D5
Pinewood Rd. M'ster M21 .. 109 A7
Pinewood Rd. Wilmslow SK9 137 E8
Pinewoods The. SK6 .... 113 B5
Pinfold. Hadfield SK14 .... 171 E4
Pinfold. R'dale OL11 .... 139 E6
Pinfold Ave. M9 .... 65 A2
Pinfold Cl. Alt'ham WA15 .... 129 D7
Pinfold Cl. Westhoughton BL5 57 D5
Pinfold Ct. M32 .... 96 C1
Pinfold Cty Prim Sch. SK14 102 E1
Pinfold Dr. Cheadle SK8 ..... 123 A1
Pinfold Dr. Prestwich M25 ..... 62 F5
Pinfold La.
Alt'ham M90 & WA15 .... 129 F6
Pinfold La. Romiley SK6 ...... 113 E4
Pinfold La. Whitefield M45 .... 62 F8
Pinfold Rd. M28 .... 60 C1
Pinfold St. WN2 .... 56 A7
Pingate Dr. SK8 .... 132 A6
Pingate La. SK8 .... 132 A6
Pingate La S. SK8 .... 132 A6
Pingle La. OL3 .... 50 E5
Pingot. OL2 .... 32 D1
Pingot Ave. M23 .... 109 B1
Pingot Ct. 6 WN7 .... 75 D5
Pingot La. SK14 .... 103 B1
Pingot Rd. WN5 .... 71 E5
Pingot The. Irlam M44 .... 94 B3
Pingot The. Leigh WN7 .... 75 D5
Pingott La. 5 SK14 .... 104 A5
Pink Bank La. M12 & M18 ..... 99 A4
Pinnacle Dr. BL7 .... 8 E2
Pinner Pl. M19 .... 111 A6
Pinnington La. M32 .... 96 D2
Pinnington Rd. M18 .... 99 D6
Pinwood Ct. 13 SK9 .... 131 E1
Pioneer Rd. M27 .... 62 D2
Pioneer St. Droylsden M11 ... 83 B2
Pioneer St. Horwich BL6 .... 22 C4
Pioneer St. 4
Littleborough OL15 .... 16 B5
Pioneer St. Walsden OL14 .... 6 A7
Pioneers St. 4 OL11 .... 31 A6
Pioneers Villa. OL16 .... 32 E4
Piper Hill Sch. M23 .... 109 B2
Piperhill Ave. M22 .... 109 D2
Pipers The. WA3 .... 90 F8
Pipewell Ave. M18 .... 165 C5
Pipit Ave. WA12 .... 89 C3
Pipit Cl. M43 .... 84 C2
Pirie Wlk. 4 M40 .... 83 C6
Pit La. OL16 & OL2 .... 31 D1
Pit St. Denton M34 .... 100 F3
Pit St. Oldham OL9 .... 66 B4
Pitcairn House. 12 M30 .... 79 D1
Pitchcombe Rd. M22 .... 121 B2
Pitcombe Cl. BL1 .... 24 D7
Pitfield Gdns. M23 .... 120 F7
Pitfield La. BL2 .... 25 F4
Pitfield St. BL2 .... 148 B7
Pitman Cl. M11 .... 165 A8
Pitmore Wlk. 3 M40 .... 65 D2
Pits Farm Ave. OL11 .... 30 C7
Pitsford Rd. M10 & M40 ..... 157 E5
Pitshouse. OL12 .... 13 E2
Pitshouse La. OL11 & OL12 ... 13 E2
Pitt St. Denton M34 .... 100 F6
Pitt St. Heywood OL10 .... 29 C2
Pitt St. Hyde SK14 .... 167 D3
Pitt St. Ince-i-M WN3 .... 151 D6
Pitt St. Oldham OL4 .... 67 A5
Pitt St. R'dale OL12 .... 139 F8
Pitt St. Radcliffe M26 .... 43 E3
Pitt St. Stockport SK3 .... 170 D8
Pitt St. Wigan WN3 .... 150 B7
Pitt St E. OL4 .... 67 B5
Pittbrook St. M12 .... 164 D7
Pixmore Ave. BL1 .... 25 B4
Place Rd. WA14 .... 119 C6
Plain Pit St. SK14 .... 101 C5
Plainsfield Cl. M16 .... 97 F4
Plane Ave. WN5 .... 54 E7
Plane Ct. 4 M6 .... 81 A2
Plane Rd. M35 .... 83 F5
Plane St. OL4 .... 67 C7
Plane Tree Cl. SK6 .... 125 D5
Plane Tree Gr. WA11 .... 89 A7
Plane Tree Rd. M31 .... 105 D3
Planet Way. M34 .... 100 E5
Planetree Rd. WA15 .... 120 A2
Planetree Wlk. M23 .... 120 C8
Plank La. WN7 .... 75 B4
Plant Cl. M33 .... 108 A5
Plant Hill High Sch. M9 .... 64 C4
Plant Hill Rd. M9 .... 64 D4
Plant St. M60 .... 159 B1
Plantation Ave. M28 .... 60 C4
Plantation Gates. WN1 .... 37 E2
Plantation Ind Est. OL6 ..... 166 C2
Plantation Rd. BL7 .... 9 F7
Plantation St.
Ashton-u-L OL6 & SK16 .... 85 D2
Plantation St. Bacup OL13 ..... 3 C8
Plantation St. M'ster M18 ..... 99 E5
Plantation View. BL0 .... 11 C3
Plate St. OL1 .... 153 F7
Plato St. OL9 .... 153 D7
Platt Ave. OL6 .... 85 C6
Platt Croft. WN7 .... 76 C4
Platt Ct. M14 .... 98 C2
Platt Fold Rd. WN7 .... 76 A6
Platt Fold St. WN7 .... 76 A5
Platt Hall Art Gal & Mus.
M14 .... 98 C2
Platt Hill Ave. BL3 .... 146 A4
Platt La. Atherton BL5 .... 58 B7
Platt La. Hindley WN2 .... 56 D5
Platt La. M'ster M14 .... 98 B2
Platt La. Standish WN1 .... 20 B3
Platt La. Uppermill OL3 .... 50 F2
Platt La. Wigan WN1 .... 37 E1
Platt St. Cheadle SK8 .... 122 E6
Platt St. Dukinfield SK16 ..... 101 A7
Platt St. Hadfield SK14 .... 104 B5
Platt St. Leigh WN7 .... 75 F6
Platt St. 8 Oldham OL4 .... 67 F6
Platt St. Platt Bridge WN2 .... 56 A2
Platt Wlk. M34 .... 100 E1
Plattbrook Cl. M14 .... 98 B1
Platting Gr. Ashton-u-L OL7 ... 84 F5
Platting La. OL11 .... 31 A4
Platting Rd. OL4 .... 68 C7
Platts Dr. M44 .... 94 A2
Plattwood Wlk. 16 M15 ...... 162 D6
Play St. SK1 .... 170 F8
Playfair Cl. OL10 .... 46 E7
Playfair St. Bolton BL7 .... 24 F6
Playfair St. M'ster M14 .... 98 B4
Pleachway. SK4 .... 110 F2
Pleasance Way. WA12 .... 89 D4
Pleasant Ct. 5 OL11 .... 30 C2
Pleasant Gdns. BL1 .... 145 E8
Pleasant Rd. M30 .... 79 E1
Pleasant St. Bury BL8 .... 26 F4
Pleasant St. Heywood OL10 ... 29 C4
Pleasant St. M'ster M8, M9 .. 157 D7
Pleasant St. R'dale OL11 ...... 30 C2
Pleasant Terr. 6 SK16 .... 166 C1
Pleasant View. Bacup OL13 .... 3 C7
Pleasant View. Radcliffe M26 62 B8
Pleasant Way. SK7 & SK8 .. 132 C6
Pleasington Dr. Bury BL8 ...... 26 E2
Pleasington Dr.
Failsworth M40 .... 65 C2
Plevna St. BL2 .... 148 A7
Plodder La. BL4 & BL5 .... 59 D8
Plodder La Prim Sch. BL4 .... 60 B8
Plough Cl. M41 .... 94 C1
Plough St. 6 SK16 .... 101 D8
Ploughbank Dr. M21 .... 109 D7
Ploughfields. BL5 .... 39 E3
Plover Cl. Newton-l-W WA12 . 89 C3
Plover Cl. R'dale OL11 .... 29 F7
Plover Dr. Alt'ham WA14 ..... 119 B8
Plover Dr. Bury BL9 .... 141 B4
Plover Dr. Irlam M44 .... 94 A4
Plowden Ave. BL3 .... 146 C3
Plowden Rd. M22 .... 121 B2
Plowley Cl. M20 .... 110 B2
Plucksbridge Rd. SK6 .... 126 B3
Plum St. OL8 .... 153 D5
Plum Tree Ct. 2 M5 .... 81 A2
Plumbley Dr. M16 .... 97 C3
Plumbley St. 11 M18 .... 99 E7
Plumley Cl. SK3 .... 170 F5
Plumley Rd. SK9 .... 131 D5
Plummer Ave. M21 .... 109 B6
Plumpton Cl. OL1 & OL2 ...... 48 E1
Plumpton Dr. BL9 .... 27 E6
Plumpton Rd. OL11 .... 48 C8
Plumpton Wlk. 6 M13 .... 98 F4
Plunge Rd. BL0 .... 1 E3
Plymouth Ave. M13 .... 164 E5
Plymouth Cl. OL6 .... 85 C7
Plymouth Dr. Bramhall SK7 . 132 F7
Plymouth Dr. 1
Farnworth BL4 .... 59 F8
Plymouth Gr. M'ster M13 ... 164 D5
Plymouth Gr. Radcliffe M26 .. 43 D5
Plymouth Gr. Standish WN6 .. 37 A7
Plymouth Gr. Stockport SK3 123 B7
Plymouth Gr W. M13 .... 164 E5
Plymouth Grove Prim
Sch. M13 .... 164 E5
Plymouth Rd. M33 .... 107 D5
Plymouth St. OL8 .... 66 F4
Plymouth View. M13 .... 163 C6
Plymtree Cl. M8 .... 63 E2
Pobgreen La. OL3 .... 51 D1
Pochard Dr. Alt'ham WA14 . 119 B7
Pochard Dr. Poynton SK12 .. 133 A4
Pochin St. M10 & M40 .... 160 E3
Pocket Nook La. WA3 .... 91 B7
Pocket Nook Rd. BL6 .... 40 B3
Pocket Wkshp The. BL3 .... 144 C6
Pocklington Dr. M23 .... 120 F7
Podnor La. SK6 .... 127 A6
Podsmead Rd. M22 .... 121 B2
Poet's Nook. WN7 .... 75 E4
Poise Brook Dr. SK2 .... 124 F5

Poise Brook Rd.
Hazel Grove SK2 124 F5
Poise Cl. SK7 125 A3
Poke St. 1 WN5 54 B6
Poland St. Ashton-u-L M34 100 E8
Poland St. M'ster M4 159 C2
Poland Street Ind Est. M4 159 C2
Polden Wlk. 1 M9 64 F1
Polding St. WN3 55 E4
Pole La. Failsworth M35 83 F8
Pole La.
Whitefield BL9 & M25 & M45 45 C2
Pole La. Whitefield M45 45 D1
Pole Lane Ct. BL9 45 C3
Pole St. Ashton-u-L OL7 166 B4
Pole St. Bolton BL2 25 B1
Pole St. Standish WN6 19 E1
Poleacre La. SK6 113 C6
Polefield App. M25 63 B6
Polefield Circ. M25 63 B6
Polefield Gdns. M25 63 B6
Polefield Gr. M25 63 B6
Polefield Grange. M25 63 B6
Polefield Hall Rd. M25 63 B6
Polefield Rd. M'ster M9 64 E2
Polefield Rd. Prestwich M25 63 C6
Polegate Dr. WN2 57 D2
Polesworth Cl. M12 165 A6
Police St. 1 Alt'ham WA14 119 D5
Police St. Eccles M30 79 C2
Police St. M'ster M2 158 F1
Pollard Ct. 4 OL1 153 E8
Pollard House. BL3 146 B2
Pollard Sq. M31 106 A3
Pollard St. M'ster M4 160 D1
Pollard St E. M10 & M40 160 D2
Pollards La. BL9 11 C2
Pollen Cl. M33 108 D2
Pollen Rd. WA14 119 C6
Polletts Ave. SK5 112 C6
Pollit Croft. SK6 112 F1
Pollitt Ave. OL6 85 C5
Pollitt Cl. M12 164 F6
Pollitt St. M26 44 C3
Pollitts Cl. M30 79 B2
Polly Gn. OL12 14 F3
Polonia Ct. OL8 66 C3
Polperro Cl. OL2 49 A4
Polperro Wlk. SK14 102 D3
Polruan Rd. M21 97 A2
Polruan Wlk. SK14 102 E3
Polworth Rd. M9 64 E1
Polygon Ave. M13 163 C6
Polygon Rd. M8 63 F1
Polygon St. M13 163 C7
Polygon The. Eccles M30 80 A2
Polygon The. M'ster M7 81 C5
Pomfret St. M6 80 C5
Pomona Cres. M5 161 B7
Pomona St. OL11 139 F5
Pomona Strand.
Salford M15, M17, M5 161 B6
Pomona Strand.
Salford M15 161 C7
Pond St. WA3 91 A8
Ponds Cl. M21 97 B1
Pondwater Cl. M28 60 A3
Pondwood Wlk. 5 M16 97 E3
Ponsford Ave. M9 65 A3
Ponsonby Rd. M32 96 D3
Pontefract Cl. M27 80 B7
Pool Bank St. M24 64 B7
Pool Fold. M35 84 A6
Pool House Rd. SK12 134 D5
Pool Rd. WA3 105 A3
Pool St. Bolton BL1 145 F7
Pool St. Bolton BL1 145 E8
Pool St. Hindley WN2 56 D4
Pool St. Oldham OL8 66 F4
Pool St. Wigan WN3 150 B6
Pool Terr. BL1 142 A2
Poolcroft. M33 108 F3
Poole Cl. SK7 123 D1
Pooley Cl. M24 46 B1
Poolfield Cl. M26 43 E3
Poolstock. WN3 150 B6
Poolstock La. WN3 55 A4
Poolton Rd. M9 64 B4
Poorfield St. OL8 153 E5
Poot Hall. OL12 14 F3
Pope John Paul II RC
High Sch. M9 81 A5
Pope Way. 9 M34 113 A8
Poplar Ave. Alt'ham WA14 119 E6
Poplar Ave. Bolton BL1 24 F5
Poplar Ave. Bolton BL2 25 C6
Poplar Ave. Bury BL9 141 B3
Poplar Ave. Culcheth WA3 91 F3
Poplar Ave. Garswood WN4 72 D5
Poplar Ave. Horwich BL6 22 E1
Poplar Ave. M'ster M19 111 B7
Poplar Ave. New Mills SK12 127 D1
Poplar Ave.Newton-l-W WA12 89 D3
Poplar Ave. Oldham OL8 66 D2
Poplar Ave. 4 R'dale OL12 14 C1
Poplar Ave. Uppermill OL4 68 C4
Poplar Ave. Wigan WN5 54 E6
Poplar Ave. Wilmslow SK9 136 F5
Poplar Cl. SK8 122 B5
Poplar Ct. Dukinfield M34 100 F7
Poplar Ct. M'ster M14 98 D1
Poplar Dr. M25 63 A2
Poplar Gr. Ashton-u-L OL6 85 C5
Poplar Gr. Hindley WN2 57 B3
Poplar Gr. Irlam M44 105 D6
Poplar Gr. M'ster M18 99 D4
Poplar Gr. Ramsbottom BL0 11 D7
Poplar Gr. Sale M33 108 B3
Poplar Gr. Stockport SK2 124 C4
Poplar Gr. Tyldesley M29 77 A8
Poplar Gr. Urmston M41 95 E2
Poplar Gr. Westhoughton BL5 57 E8
Poplar Rd. Dukinfield SK16 101 F7
Poplar Rd. Eccles M30 79 E4
Poplar Rd. M'ster M19 110 D3
Poplar Rd. Stretford M32 108 C8
Poplar Rd. Swinton M27 79 D7
Poplar Rd. Walkden M28 60 E1
Poplar St. Dukinfield M34 100 F7
Poplar St. Failsworth M35 83 D6
Poplar St. Golborne WA3 74 B1
Poplar St. Leigh WN7 75 F4
Poplar St. M'ster SK4 110 F2
Poplar St. M'ster M11 164 E8
Poplar St. Middleton M24 65 D7
Poplar St. Tyldesley M29 59 A1
Poplar St Prim Sch. M34 100 E6
Poplar Way. SK6 135 A7
Poplar Wlk. Chadderton OL9 152 B8
Poplar Wlk. Partington M31 105 D3
Poplars Rd. SK15 86 D3
Poplars The. Adlington PR7 20 F6
Poplars The. Golborne WA3 74 B1
Poplars The. Golborne WN7 91 C8
Poplars The. Mossley OL5 68 E1
Poppy Cl. Chadderton M24 65 E7
Poppy Cl. Sale M33 108 E1
Poppythorn La. M25 63 A5
Porchester Dr. M26 43 C5
Porchfield Sq. M3 162 E8
Porlock Ave. Droylsden M34 100 C8
Porlock Ave.
Hattersley SK14 102 C2
Porlock Cl. Platt Bridge WN2 56 A1
Porlock Cl. Stockport SK1 124 C8
Porlock Rd. Urmston M41 107 B8
Porlock Rd.
Wythenshawe M23 121 B6
Porlock Wlk. SK14 102 C2
Porritt Cl. OL11 29 E6
Porritt St. Bury BL9 141 A4
Porritt St. Bury BL9 141 B4
Porritt Way. BL0 138 C7
Port Soderick Ave. M5 81 A1
Port St. M'ster M1 & M60 159 B1
Port St. Oldham OL8 66 F4
Port St. Stockport SK1 169 E2
Portal Ct. M24 65 C8
Portal Gr. M34 101 B1
Portal Wlk. 9 M9 157 D8
Porter Ave. WA12 89 C5
Porter St. Bury BL9 140 F4
Porter St. Oldham OL9 152 C5
Porters Wood Cl. WN5 54 B7
Portfield Wlk. 18 M40 83 A6
Portgate Wlk. M13 164 D5
Porthleven Cres. M29 77 C8
Porthleven Dr. M23 120 E6
Porthtowan Wlk. SK14 102 E3
Portinscale Cl. BL8 27 B3
Portland Cl.Hazel Grove SK7 124 B1
Portland Cl. Platt Bridge WN2 56 A1
Portland Cres. M13 164 D5
Portland Gr. SK4 168 B4
Portland House. 3
Ashton-u-L OL7 166 A2
Portland House. Eccles M6 80 A3
Portland House.Marple SK6 125 E5
Portland Ind Est. 10 BL9 141 A4
Portland Pl. OL7 166 A2
Portland Rd. Alt'ham WA14 119 D3
Portland Rd. Eccles M30 80 A4
Portland Rd. M'ster M13 98 F3
Portland Rd.New Mills SK12 127 D1
Portland Rd. Pendlebury M27 80 B7
Portland Rd. Stretford M32 96 E4
Portland Rd. Walkden M28 60 C5
Portland St. Bolton BL1 143 E2
Portland St. Bury BL9 141 A4
Portland St. 6 Leigh WN7 75 F5
Portland St. M'ster M1, M60 159 A1
Portland St. M'ster M1 163 A8
Portland St. R'dale OL16 139 F8
Portland St. Wigan WN5 54 E6
Portland St N. OL6 166 A3
Portland St S. OL7 166 A2
Portland Terr. OL7 166 A2
Portloe Rd. SK8 131 B7
Portman Cl. M16 97 E3
Portman Rd. M16 97 E3
Portman St. OL5 68 C1
Porton Wlk. 1 M22 121 B1
Portrea Cl. SK3 170 F5
Portree Cl. M30 79 B2
Portrush Rd. M22 121 E2
Portsdale Cl. M28 78 B5
Portslade Wlk.
Wythenshawe M23 120 F5
Portslade Wlk. 10
Wythenshawe M23 121 A5
Portsmouth Cl. M7 155 D5
Portsmouth St. M13 163 B5
Portstone Cl. 22 M16 97 E4
Portugal Rd. M25 63 A7
Portugal St. Ashton-u-L OL7 84 F1
Portugal St. Bolton BL2 148 B7
Portugal St. M'ster M40 159 C2
Portugal St. 12
M'ster M10 & M40 159 C3
Portugal St E. M1 163 C8
Portville Rd. M19 99 A2
Portway. M22 121 C1
Portwood Ind Est. SK1 112 B2
Portwood Pl. SK1 169 F2
Portwood Wlk. 9 M9 157 D7
Posnett St. SK3 123 C8
Post Office St. WA14 119 D5
Post St. SK14 104 B5
Postal St. M1 & M60 159 B1
Postbridge Cl. M13 163 C6
Pot Gn. BL0 11 A3
Pot Hill. OL6 166 C4
Pot Hill Sq. OL6 166 C4
Potato Wharf. M15, M3 162 D8
Pott St. M27 61 F2
Potter House. OL8 153 F5
Potter St. Bury BL9 141 A3
Potter St. Radcliffe M26 44 D4
Potterdale Cl. OL1 49 A1
Potters La. M9 157 F7
Pottery La. M11 & M12 165 A7
Pottery Rd. WN3 150 B7
Pottery Terr. WN3 150 B7
Pottinger St. Ashton-u-L OL7 84 F1
Pottinger St.
Dukinfield OL7 & SK16 100 F8
Poulton Ave. BL2 42 E7
Poulton Dr. 7 WN4 72 F5
Poulton St. M11 99 E7
Poundswick High Sch.M22 121 C3
Poundswick Inf Sch. M22 121 C2
Poundswick Jun Sch. M22 121 C2
Poundswick La. M22 121 D3
Powell Ave. SK14 167 E3
Powell Dr. WN5 71 D3
Powell St. Abram WN2 56 B1
Powell St. Bury BL8 27 B1
Powell St. Droylsden M11 83 D2
Powell St. M'ster M16 97 C4
Powell St. 10 Wigan WN1 37 C1
Powicke Dr. SK6 112 F1
Powicke Wlk. SK6 113 A1
Powis Rd. M41 94 C1
Pownall Ave. Bramhall SK7 132 F7
Pownall Ave. 4 M'ster M20 110 A8
Pownall Ct. SK9 136 E8
Pownall Green Cty Prim
Sch. SK7 132 E7
Pownall Hall Sch. SK9 136 F8
Pownall Rd. Alt'ham WA14 119 D3
Pownall Rd. Bramhall SK8 123 A1
Pownall Rd. Wilmslow SK9 136 F8
Pownall St. Hazel Grove SK7 124 D3
Pownall St. Leigh WN7 76 A5
Powys St. M46 58 E1
Poynings Dr. M22 121 C1
Poynt Chase. M28 78 B5
Poynter St. M40 65 C1
Poynter Wlk. OL1 49 D4
Poynton Cl. M15 162 F6
Poynton Cty High Sch.
SK12 133 F2
Poynton St. BL9 141 A1
Poynton Sta. SK12 133 C4
Poynton Worth Cty Prim
Sch. SK12 133 F2
Praed Rd. M17 96 C6
Pratt Wlk. 21 M11 160 F1
Precinct The. Cheadle SK8 123 A2
Precinct The. R'dale OL11 29 E7
Precinct The.
Ramsbottom BL8 10 F3
Precinct The. Stockport SK2 124 D6
Preece Cl. SK14 102 A4
Preesall Ave. SK8 131 B8
Preesall Cl. BL8 26 F1
Prefect Pl. WN5 54 C8
Premier Rd. M8 158 F4
Premier St. M16 97 D4
Prentice Wlk. M11 83 A1
Prenton St. M11 99 E8
Prenton Way. BL8 26 F5
Presall St. 2 BL2 148 C8
Presbyterian Fold. 3 WN2 56 D6
Prescot Ave. Atherton M46 58 E5
Prescot Ave. Tyldesley M29 59 D1
Prescot Cl. BL9 141 A1
Prescot Rd. Alt'ham WA15 119 F2
Prescot Rd. M'ster M8 & M9 157 D7
Prescott Ave. WA3 73 F2
Prescott La. WN5 54 B8
Prescott Rd. SK9 131 B1
Prescott St. Bolton BL3 146 C4
Prescott St. Golborne WA3 74 A1
Prescott St. Hindley WN2 56 D5
Prescott St. Leigh WN7 75 F6
Prescott St. R'dale OL16 15 C2
Prescott St. Walkden M28 60 B3
Prescott St. Wigan WN6 150 B8
Prescott Wlk. M34 101 B1
Press St. M18 99 D7
Prestage St. M'ster M16 97 D4
Prestage St. M'ster M18 99 B2
Prestbury Ave.
Alt'ham WA15 119 E6
Prestbury Ave. M'ster M14 97 F1
Prestbury Ave. Wigan WN3 54 E2
Prestbury Cl. Bury BL9 141 A1
Prestbury Cl. Stockport SK2 124 D4
Prestbury Dr. Bredbury SK6 112 E3
Prestbury Dr. Oldham OL1 48 D1
Prestbury Rd. Bolton BL1 25 A5
Prestbury Rd.
Wilmslow SK10 & SK9 137 E5
Prestfield Rd. M45 63 A7
Presto Gdns. BL3 146 B4
Presto St. Bolton BL3 146 B4
Presto St. Farnworth BL4 60 E8
Prestolee Prim Sch. M26 61 B8
Prestolee Rd. Kearsley M26 43 B1
Prestolee Rd. Little Lever BL3 43 A1
Preston Ave. Eccles M30 80 A3
Preston Ave. Irlam M44 105 F7
Preston Cl. M30 80 A3
Preston Rd. M'ster M19 111 A8
Preston Rd. Standish WN6 19 D5
Preston St. 2 Bolton BL3 42 B4
Preston St. M'ster M18 165 C6
Preston St. Middleton M24 65 A8
Preston St. Oldham OL4 67 A6
Preston St. 10 R'dale OL12 14 C1
Prestwich Ave. Culcheth WA3 91 E3
Prestwich Ave. Leigh WN7 76 B5
Prestwich Cl. SK2 124 B7
Prestwich High Sch. M25 63 B5
Prestwich Hills. M25 63 A2
Prestwich Hospl. M25 62 F5
Prestwich Ind Est. M46 58 B4
Prestwich Park Rd S. M25 63 A3
Prestwich Prep Sch. M25 63 C5
Prestwich St. Atherton M46 58 B3
Prestwich St. Denton M34 100 E4
Prestwich Sta. M25 63 A5
Prestwick Wlk. 1 M40 65 C2
Prestwood Cl. BL1 143 D1
Prestwood Dr. BL1 143 D1
Prestwood Rd.Farnworth BL4 42 A1
Prestwood Rd. Salford M6 80 C4
Pretoria Rd. Ashton-i-M WN4 73 B4
Pretoria Rd. Bolton BL2 42 E8
Pretoria Rd. Oldham OL8 66 C3
Pretoria St. 2 OL12 14 C1
Price St. Bury BL9 141 A1
Price St. Dukinfield SK16 101 C8
Price St. Farnworth BL4 42 D1
Price St. M'ster M4 160 D1
Prichard St. M32 96 D2
Prickshaw. OL12 14 B6
Prickshaw La. OL12 14 B6
Pridmouth Rd. M20 110 C6
Priest Ave. SK8 122 A4
Priest St. SK1 170 F7
Priestley Rd. M27 & M28 79 C8
Priestley Way. OL2 49 D7
Priestnall Ct. SK4 110 F3
Priestnall Rd. SK4 110 F3
Priestnall Rec Ctr. SK4 110 F3
Priestnall Sch. SK4 110 F3
Priestwood Ave. OL4 49 F4
Primley Wlk. 8 M9 157 E8
Primrose Ave. Farnworth BL4 42 A1
Primrose Ave. Hyde SK14 113 D8
Primrose Ave. Marple SK6 125 E6
Primrose Ave. Uppermill OL3 51 D1
Primrose Ave. Urmston M41 95 D2
Primrose Ave. Walkden M28 60 B2
Primrose Bank.
Alt'ham WA14 119 C1
Primrose Bank. 1 Bacup OL13 3 C8
Primrose Bank. Bury BL8 26 E7
Primrose Bank.Oldham OL8 153 E5
Primrose Bank.Uppermill OL3 69 B5
Primrose Bank.Walkden M28 60 B2
Primrose Cl. Bolton BL2 26 A4
Primrose Cl. Salford M6 154 F2
Primrose Cotts. WA14 119 C1
Primrose Cres.
Glossop SK13 116 B8
Primrose Cres. Hyde SK14 113 D8
Primrose Dr. Bury BL9 28 D4
Primrose Dr. Droylsden M43 84 C3
Primrose Gr. WN5 54 E7
Primrose Hill. SK13 116 B8
Primrose La. Glossop SK13 116 B8
Primrose La.
New Mills SK12 & SK6 127 A3
Primrose La. Standish WN6 19 D2
Primrose St. 9 Bacup OL13 3 C8
Primrose St. Bolton BL1 143 F4
Primrose St. Farnworth BL4 60 E7
Primrose St. 4 Leigh WN7 75 D5
Primrose St. M'ster M4 159 B2
Primrose St. Oldham OL8 153 E5
Primrose St. R'dale OL12 139 D8
Primrose St. Tyldesley M29 59 A1
Primrose St N. M29 59 A1
Primrose St S. M29 77 A8
Primrose Terr. M41 95 C6
Primrose View. WN4 73 C2
Primrose Wlk. Marple SK6 125 E6
Primrose Wlk. Oldham OL8 153 E5
Primula St. BL1 24 F5
Prince Albert Ave. 4 M19 99 A2
Prince Charlie St.
Oldham OL1 67 C8
Prince Edward Ave.
Denton M34 100 F2
Prince Edward Ave. 8
Oldham OL4 67 C7
Prince George St. 3
OL1 & OL4 49 C1
Prince of Wales Bsns Pk. 6
OL1 67 C8
Prince Rd. SK12 134 C5
Prince St. Ashton-i-M WN4 73 A5
Prince St. Bacup OL13 4 D7
Prince St. Bolton BL1 145 E8
Prince St. Heywood OL10 29 D2
Prince St. 6 Oldham OL1 67 A7
Prince St. R'dale OL11 & OL16 31 B5
Prince St. Ramsbottom BL0 138 C6
Prince Way. OL2 48 C6
Prince's Ave. Little Lever BL3 43 B4
Prince's Ave. M'ster M20 110 C4
Prince's Ave. Romiley SK6 113 A3
Prince's Ave. Tyldesley M29 77 B6
Prince's Bridge. M3 162 D8
Prince's Dr. SK6 125 E7
Prince's Pk. WN6 35 F4
Prince's Rd. SK6 113 A3
Prince's St. SK1 169 E2
Princedom St. M9 157 E8
Princes Ave. M44 94 C3
Princes Dr. M33 108 D3
Princes Gdns. WN7 76 C5
Princes Rd. Alt'ham WA14 119 D6
Princes Rd. M'ster SK4 168 A4
Princes Rd. Sale M33 108 D3
Princes St. WA12 89 B3
Princess Ave.Ashton-i-M WN4 73 C3
Princess Ave. Atherton M46 58 D5
Princess Ave. Cheadle SK8 123 A3
Princess Ave. Denton M34 100 E3
Princess Ave. Kearsley BL4 60 F6
Princess Ave. M'ster M25 63 C2
Princess Ave.
Newton-l-W WA12 89 A7
Princess Ave. R'dale OL12 15 C4
Princess Christian Coll.M14 98 C1
Princess Cl. Dukinfield SK16 101 D8
Princess Cl. Heywood OL10 29 D1
Princess Cl. Mossley OL5 86 E8
Princess Ct. M15 162 D6
Princess Dr. M24 64 E8
Princess Gr. BL4 60 D8
Princess Par. BL9 140 F2
Princess Parkway.
Wythenshawe M20,M22,M23 109 C2
Princess Parkway.
Wythenshawe M23 121 C7
Princess Prim Sch. M16 97 E4
Princess Rd. Adlington PR6 21 B8
Princess Rd. Ashton-i-M WN4 73 C3
Princess Rd. Bolton BL6 40 B8
Princess Rd. Failsworth OL9 65 E3
Princess Rd. M'ster M15 97 F4
Princess Rd.
M'ster M14, M20, M21, M15 109 E6
Princess Rd. Milnrow OL16 31 D7
Princess Rd. Prestwich M25 63 C4
Princess Rd. Shaw OL2 149 A6
Princess Rd. Urmston M41 95 B2
Princess Rd. Wigan WN6 36 C4
Princess Rd. Wilmslow SK9 136 F5
Princess St. Alt'ham WA14 119 C8
Princess St. Ashton-u-L OL6 85 D4
Princess St. Bolton BL1 145 F7
Princess St. Eccles M30 79 C2
Princess St. Failsworth M35 83 E7
Princess St. Glossop SK13 116 C8
Princess St. Hindley WN2 56 C5
Princess St. Hyde SK14 167 E2
Princess St. 5 Leigh WN7 76 A5
Princess St.M'ster M10, M40 160 E4
Princess St. M'ster M15 162 D6
Princess St.
M'ster M1, M60, M2 163 A8
Princess St. Oldham OL4 67 E6
Princess St. R'dale OL12 14 F1
Princess St. Radcliffe M26 43 E3
Princess St. Salford M6 81 A4
Princess St. Swinton M27 80 A7
Princess St. Whitworth OL12 14 C8
Princess St. Wigan WN3 150 C7
Princess Wlk. SK7 133 A7
Princethorpe Cl. BL6 40 D6
Prinknash Rd. M22 121 D1
Printer St. Droylsden M11 99 D8
Printer St. Oldham OL1 153 F6
Printers Fold. SK14 103 D5
Printers La. BL2 25 C6
Printers Pk. SK14 103 E5
Printon Ave. M9 64 B3
Printshop La. M46 58 E1
Printworks La. M19 99 C1
Printworks Rd. SK15 86 C3
Prior St. OL8 67 B5
Priory Ave. Leigh WN7 57 D1
Priory Ave. M'ster M7 81 C6
Priory Ave. M'ster M21 109 B8
Priory Cl. Dukinfield SK16 101 D6
Priory Cl. Oldham OL8 66 D3
Priory Cl. Sale M33 108 D6
Priory Cl. 1 Wigan WN5 54 B5
Priory Ct. SK5 111 E8
Priory Gr. M'ster M7 81 C6
Priory Gr. Oldham OL9 66 A4
Priory La. SK5 111 E8
Priory Nook. WN8 53 C7
Priory Pl. Bolton BL2 25 C2
Priory Pl. M'ster M7 81 C6
Priory Rd. Alt'ham WA14 128 B8
Priory Rd. Ashton-i-M WN4 72 F5
Priory Rd. Cheadle SK8 123 A5
Priory Rd. Orrell WN8 53 C7
Priory Rd. Sale M33 108 D5
Priory Rd. Swinton M27 79 E8
Priory Rd. Wilmslow SK9 136 E8
Priory Sch. M33 108 A4
Priory St. WA14 119 C1
Priory The. M7 81 C6
Pritchard St. M1 163 A7
Private La. BB4 1 C8
Privet St. OL4 49 D1
Proctor Cl. WN5 36 E1
Proctor St. BL8 27 C1
Proctor Way. M30 94 F7
Prodesse Ct. WN2 56 D6
Proe's Ct. WN1 150 B8
Progress Ave. M34 100 F6
Progress St. Ashton-u-L OL6 166 A3
Progress St. Bolton BL1 143 F1
Progress St. Hindley WN2 56 D5
Progress St. R'dale OL11 30 C1
Promenade St. OL10 29 E2
Propps Hall Dr. M35 83 E6
Propps Prim Sch. M35 83 E6
Prospect Ave. Farnworth BL4 60 C7
Prospect Ave. Irlam M44 105 E6
Prospect Cotts. WN2 38 A6
Prospect Ct. BL8 26 F7
Prospect Dr. Alt'ham WA15 129 D8
Prospect Dr. Failsworth M35 83 F5
Prospect Hill. BL2 25 F4
Prospect House. M9 157 E7
Prospect Pl. Ashton-u-L OL6 85 D5
Prospect Pl. Farnworth BL4 60 C7
Prospect Pl. Heywood OL10 29 D3
Prospect Rd. Ashton-u-L OL6 85 E5
Prospect Rd.Dukinfield SK16 101 D8
Prospect Rd. Irlam M44 105 E6
Prospect Rd. Oldham OL9 152 C7
Prospect Rd. Standish WN6 36 E7
Prospect St. Bolton BL1 143 F1
Prospect St. Heywood OL10 46 E8
Prospect St. Hindley WN2 56 D5
Prospect St.
Littleborough OL15 16 B6
Prospect St. R'dale OL11 30 E4
Prospect St. Tyldesley M29 58 F1
Prospect Terr. Bacup OL13 3 E7
Prospect Terr. Bury BL8 140 D4
Prospect Vale. SK8 122 B1
Prospect Vale Prim Sch.
SK8 122 B1
Prospect View. M27 80 A7
Prospect Villas. 3 M9 64 F1
Prosperity. M29 77 D8
Prosser Ave. M46 58 A2
Prout St. M12 99 A3
Providence St. 4
Ashton-u-L OL6 85 D4
Providence St. Bolton BL3 145 F5
Providence St.
Dukinfield M34 100 F7
Providence St. M'ster M4 160 D1
Providence St.
Walsden OL14 6 A7
Provident Ave. M19 99 C1
Provident St. OL2 149 B7
Provident Way. WA15 120 A7
Provis Rd. M21 109 B7
Prubella Ave. M34 100 E5
Pryce Ave. WN2 151 F7
Pryce St. BL1 143 D1
Pryme St. M15 162 E7
Pudding La. SK14 102 C3
Puffin Ave. SK12 133 B4
Pugin Wlk. M9 157 D6
Pulborough Cl. BL8 27 B7
Pulford Ave. M21 109 D4
Pulford Rd. M33 108 D2
Pullman Cl. M19 111 B8
Pullman Dr. M32 95 F3
Pullman St. OL11 139 F5
Pulman Ct. BL3 148 A5
Pump House (Mus) The.
M3 158 E1
Pump St. 10 Hindley WN2 56 D5
Pump St.
M'ster M10, M11, M40 160 E2
Pump St. Oldham OL9 66 B2
Punch La. BL3 40 D2
Punch St. BL3 145 D6
Pungle The. BL5 57 D5
Purbeck Cl. M22 121 C1
Purbeck Dr. Bury BL8 27 C6
Purbeck Dr. Horwich BL6 39 F8
Purbeck Way. M29 77 B7
Purcell Cl. BL1 143 D1
Purcell St. M12 99 A3
Purdon St. BL9 27 F6
Purdy House. OL8 153 E5
Puritan Wlk. 7 M40 156 C5
Purley Ave. M23 109 B1
Purley Dr. M44 105 C5
Purple St. BL1 145 F7
Purslow Cl. M12 160 E1
Purton Wlk. 9 M9 157 E7
Putney Cl. OL1 48 E1
Puzzletree Ct. SK2 124 C7
Pye Cl. WA11 89 B8
Pyegreave Cl. M15 162 D7
Pyegrove. SK13 104 F1
Pyegrove Rd. SK13 104 E1
Pyke St. WN1 37 D1
Pym St. Eccles M30 79 D2
Pym St. Heywood OL10 29 D1
Pym St. M'ster M40 & M9 157 F8
Pymgate Dr. SK8 122 A2
Pymgate La. SK8 122 A2
Pyramid Ct. M7 155 D6
Pyrus Cl. M30 94 F8
Pytha Fold Rd. M20 110 D5

Quadrant The.Droylsden M43 83 F1
Quadrant The. M'ster M9 65 A3
Quadrant The. Romiley SK6 113 A2
Quadrant The.Stockport SK1 112 B4
Quail Dr. M44 94 A3
Quail St. OL4 67 C6
Quainton House. 5 M5 154 F1
Quakerfields. BL5 57 D7
Quakers Field. BL8 26 F8
Quakers' Pl. WN6 19 E1
Quakers Terr. WN6 19 D3
Quantock Cl. 12 M'ster M16 97 E4
Quantock Cl. Stockport SK4 169 E2
Quantock Cl. Wigan WN3 54 C2
Quarlton Dr. BL8 10 B3
Quarmby Rd. M18 99 F4
Quarry Bank Rd. SK9 130 F3
Quarry Cl. SK13 104 D1
Quarry Clough. SK15 102 D8
Quarry Hill. OL12 14 E3
Quarry Pl. WN1 151 E8
Quarry Pond Rd. M28 59 F3
Quarry Rd. Kearsley BL4 61 A7
Quarry Rd. New Mills SK12 127 F2
Quarry Rd. Romiley SK6 113 B2
Quarry Rise. SK15 101 F8
Quarry St. R'dale OL12 14 E1
Quarry St. Radcliffe M26 44 B3
Quarry St. Ramsbottom BL0 11 D6
Quarry St. Romiley SK6 113 B5
Quarry St. Stalybridge SK15 85 F1
Quarry St. Whitworth OL12 4 E6
Quarry Wlk. 17 M11 160 F1
Quay Cl. Heywood OL10 29 E1
Quay St. M'ster M2 158 E1
Quay St. M'ster M3 158 E1
Quay View. M5 161 A8
Quays The. M5 96 E7
Quayside Cl. M28 78 B5
Quebec Pl. BL3 145 D5
Quebec St. Bolton BL3 145 D5
Quebec St. Denton M34 100 E4
Quebec St. Leigh WN2 & WN7 74 E5
Quebec St. Oldham OL9 153 D8
Queen Alexandra Cl. M5 161 C8
Queen Ann Cl. BL9 45 C4
Queen Ann Dr. M28 78 B7
Queen Elizabeth Sch The.
M24 46 F4
Queen Sq. OL6 85 D4
Queen St. Ashton-u-L OL6 166 C3
Queen St. 5 Bacup OL13 3 C8
Queen St. Bolton BL1 145 E7
Queen St. Bury BL8 27 A5
Queen St. Bury BL9 141 A2
Queen St. Cheadle SK8 122 F6
Queen St. Denton M34 100 E4
Queen St. Denton M34 100 F6
Queen St. Dukinfield SK16 166 B1
Queen St. Eccles M30 79 F1
Queen St. Failsworth M35 83 E7
Queen St. Farnworth BL4 60 D8
Queen St. Glossop SK13 116 B8
Queen St. Golborne WA3 90 B8
Queen St. Hadfield SK14 104 A4
Queen St. Heywood OL10 29 D2
Queen St. 2 Hindley WN2 56 D6
Queen St. Horwich BL6 22 B3
Queen St. Hyde SK14 167 E2
Queen St. Leigh WN7 76 A5
Queen St. Littleborough OL15 16 B5
Queen St. M'ster M3 158 E2
Queen St. M'ster M2 158 F1
Queen St. Marple SK6 126 A6
Queen St. Middleton M24 65 C8
Queen St. Mossley OL5 68 C1
Queen St. Newton-l-W WA12 89 B3
Queen St. 10 Oldham OL4 67 F6
Queen St. Oldham OL1 153 F6
Queen St. Platt Bridge WN2 56 A2
Queen St. R'dale OL12 139 F8
Queen St. Radcliffe M26 44 C2
Queen St. Ramsbottom BL0 138 B6
Queen St. Royton OL2 48 D4
Queen St. Salford M6 80 D5
Queen St. Shaw OL2 149 B6
Queen St. Stalybridge SK15 86 A2

Queen St. Stockport SK1 ... 112 A2
Queen St. Walkden M38 ... 60 B3
Queen St. Westhoughton BL5 . 57 E8
Queen St. Wigan WN5 ... 54 B6
Queen St. Wigan WN5 ... 54 D5
Queen St. Wigan WN3 ... 150 C7
Queen St Prim Sch. BL4 ... 60 D8
Queen St W. M20 ... 110 B7
Queen Victoria St.
Eccles M30 ... 79 C2
Queen Victoria St.
R'dale OL11 ... 31 A4
Queen's Ave. Ashton-i-M WN4 73 B3
Queen's Ave. Atherton M46 ... 58 C5
Queen's Ave. Bolton BL7 ... 25 A7
Queen's Ave. Glazebury WA3 92 C7
Queen's Ave. Little Lever BL3 43 A4
Queen's Ave. Romiley SK6 .. 113 A3
Queen's Cl. M28 ... 60 D3
Queen's Ct. 3 M'ster M21 ... 97 B2
Queen's Ct. M'ster M20 ... 110 A4
Queen's Dr. Glossop SK13 ... 104 F1
Queen's Dr. M'ster M25 ... 63 C2
Queen's Dr. M'ster SK4 ... 168 A2
Queen's Gdns. SK8 ... 122 E6
Queen's Gr. M12 ... 99 A4
Queen's Park Rd. OL10 ... 29 D3
Queen's Rd. Alt'ham WA15 .. 119 F3
Queen's Rd. Ashton-i-M WN4 73 B4
Queen's Rd. Ashton-u-L OL6 .. 85 D5
Queen's Rd. Cheadle SK8 ... 122 F4
Queen's Rd. Cheadle SK8 ... 123 A3
Queen's Rd. Hazel Grove SK7 124 E3
Queen's Rd. 12
Littleborough OL15 ... 16 B5
Queen's Rd. Romiley SK6 ... 113 A3
Queen's Rd. Urmston M41 ... 95 D1
Queen's Rd. Wilmslow SK9 . 137 A6
Queen's Terr. 3 Bacup OL13 .. 3 E8
Queen's Terr. 7
Dukinfield SK16 ... 166 B1
Queenhill Dr. SK14 ... 102 A5
Queenhill Rd. M22 ... 109 E1
Queens Ave.
M'ster M12 & M18 ... 165 B5
Queens Ave. R'dale OL12 ... 15 C4
Queens Cl. Boothstown M28 .. 77 F7
Queens Cl. Hyde SK14 ... 113 E7
Queens Cl. M'ster SK4 ... 168 A2
Queens Ct. M'ster M40 ... 157 D5
Queens Ct. M'ster SK4 ... 168 A3
Queens Ct. Urmston M41 ... 94 E2
Queens Dr. Cheadle SK8 ... 123 A2
Queens Dr. Golborne WA3 ... 90 C8
Queens Dr. Hyde SK14 ... 113 F7
Queens Dr. Newton-l-W WA12 89 C5
Queens Dr. R'dale OL11 ... 30 E3
Queens Gdns. WN7 ... 76 C5
Queens Park Fst Sch. M40 157 D5
Queens Pl. BL9 ... 11 C2
Queens Rd. Bolton BL3 ... 146 B4
Queens Rd. Chadderton OL9 152 A7
Queens Rd. M'ster M7 & M8 156 A5
Queens Rd. M'ster
M10, M40, M7, M8, M9 ... 156 C6
Queens Rd.M'ster M40, M9 . 157 D5
Queens Rd.M'ster M10, M40 160 E4
Queens Rd.Newton-l-W WA11 89 A7
Queens Rd. Oldham OL8 ... 67 A5
Queens Rd. Orrell WN5 ... 53 C5
Queens Rd. Sale M33 ... 107 F5
Queens Road Prim Sch.
SK8 ... 123 A3
Queens Terr. SK9 ... 131 D3
Queens View. OL15 ... 16 A3
Queens Wlk. M43 ... 84 A1
Queensbrook. BL1 ... 145 E7
Queensbury Ct. M40 ... 160 E3
Queensferry St. M40 ... 83 C6
Queensgate. Bolton BL1 ... 144 C8
Queensgate. Bramhall SK7 . 132 E5
Queensgate Dr. OL2 ... 48 C6
Queensgate Prim Sch.
SK7 ... 132 E4
Queensland Rd. M12, M18 . 165 B5
Queenston Rd. M20 ... 110 A4
Queensway. Dukinfield SK16 101 F7
Queensway. Gatley SK8 ... 131 C8
Queensway. Ince-i-M WN2 ... 56 A8
Queensway. Irlam M44 ... 93 F2
Queensway. Kearsley BL4 ... 60 F5
Queensway. Leigh WN7 ... 76 D6
Queensway. M'ster M19 ... 110 D2
Queensway. Mossley OL5 ... 86 D8
Queensway. Poynton SK12 .. 133 D3
Queensway. R'dale OL11 ... 30 E3
Queensway. Shevington WN6 35 F4
Queensway. Swinton M27 ... 62 A2
Queensway. Uppermill OL3 ... 69 B6
Queensway. Urmston M41 ... 95 E4
Queensway. Walkden M28 ... 78 C8
Queensway. Wigan WN1 ... 37 B2
Queensway Prim Sch. OL11 30 F3
Quenby St . M15 ... 162 D7
Quendon Ave. M7 ... 158 E4
Quick Edge La. OL4 ... 68 B4
Quick Rd. OL4 & OL5 ... 68 D4
Quick View. OL5 ... 68 E3
Quickedge Rd. OL4 & OL5 ... 68 C3
Quickwood. OL5 ... 68 D4
Quilter Gr. M9 ... 64 C2
Quinn St. M11 ... 83 A1
Quinney Cres. M16 ... 97 F4
Quinton. 10 OL12 ... 139 E8
Quinton Wlk. M13 ... 163 B6

Rabbit La. SK14 ... 103 A6
Raby St. M'ster M16 ... 97 E4
Raby St. M'ster M14 ... 97 F4
Race The. SK9 ... 131 D2
Racecourse Pk. SK9 ... 136 F6
Racecourse Rd. SK9 ... 136 E6
Racecourse Wlk. M26 ... 44 F4
Racefield Hamlet. OL2 ... 48 A4
Racefield Rd. WA14 ... 119 C4
Rachel Rosing Wlk. M8 ... 155 F8
Rachel St. M12 ... 163 C8
Rackhouse Rd. M23 ... 109 B1
Radbourne Cl. M12 ... 165 A6
Radcliffe Ave. WA3 ... 91 E3
Radcliffe Cty Inf Sch. M26 43 E4
Radcliffe Cty Jun Sch. M26 43 E4
Radcliffe Gr. WN7 ... 75 F7
Radcliffe Hall CE/Meth
Prim Sch. M26 ... 44 D4
Radcliffe High Sch. M26 ... 44 A3
Radcliffe Moor Rd.
BL2, BL3, M26 ... 43 C5
Radcliffe New Rd.
M45 & M26 ... 44 D2
Radcliffe Park Cres. M6 ... 80 C5
Radcliffe Park Rd. M6 ... 80 C5
Radcliffe Rd. Bolton BL2, BL3 42 D5
Radcliffe Rd. Bolton BL2 ... 148 B7
Radcliffe Rd. Bury BL9 ... 44 E7
Radcliffe Rd. Oldham OL4 ... 49 D2
Radcliffe St. Oldham OL4 ... 68 A6
Radcliffe St. Oldham OL1 ... 153 F7
Radcliffe St. Oldham OL1 ... 153 F8
Radcliffe St. Royton OL2 ... 48 E4
Radcliffe Sta. M26 ... 44 B3
Radcliffe View. M5 ... 161 B7
Radclyffe Prim Sch. M5 ... 161 A7
Radclyffe Sch The.
Chadderton OL9 ... 65 F7
Radclyffe Sch The.
Oldham OL9 ... 152 A6
Radclyffe St. Middleton M24 . 47 A2
Radclyffe St. Oldham OL9 ... 152 C8
Radclyffe Terr. M24 ... 47 A2
Radelan Gr. M26 ... 43 D4
Radford Cl. SK2 ... 124 E7
Radford Dr. Irlam M44 ... 94 A3
Radford Dr. 2 M'ster M9 .. 157 E8
Radford House. SK2 ... 124 E7
Radford St. M7 ... 81 C8
Radium St. M4 ... 159 C2
Radlet Dr. WA15 ... 120 A8
Radlett Wlk. 9 M13 ... 163 C5
Radley Cl. BL1 ... 142 A1
Radley St. M43 ... 99 E8
Radley Wlk. 12 M16 ... 97 F3
Radnor Ave. M34 ... 100 B3
Radnor Cl. WN2 ... 57 A3
Radnor Dr. WN7 ... 75 C5
Radnor St. M'ster M15 ... 97 F4
Radnor St. M'ster M18 ... 99 C4
Radnor St. Oldham OL9 ... 152 C5
Radnor St. Stretford M32 ... 96 D1
Radnormere Dr. SK8 ... 123 A4
Radstock Rd. M32 ... 96 C2
Radstock Cl. M'ster M14 ... 98 B1
Radstock Rd. M32 ... 96 C2
Radway. M29 ... 59 C1
Rae St. SK3 ... 123 C8
Raeburn Dr. SK6 ... 126 B8
Raglan Ave.
Prestwich M25 & M45 ... 63 B7
Raglan Ave. Swinton M27 ... 62 B2
Raglan Cl. M11 ... 160 F1
Raglan Dr. WA14 ... 119 E8
Raglan Rd. Sale M33 ... 108 A3
Raglan Rd. Stretford M32 ... 96 B3
Raglan St. Bolton BL1 ... 143 D2
Raglan St. Denton SK14 ... 101 C2
Raglan St. R'dale OL11 ... 30 C3
Raglan Wlk. 8 M15 ... 162 F6
Ragley Cl. SK12 ... 133 F4
Raikes Clough Ind Est. BL3 42 C4
Raikes La. BL3 ... 42 B4
Raikes Rd. BL3 ... 42 D5
Railgate. OL13 ... 4 C8
Railside Terr. M30 ... 80 A2
Railton Ave. M16 ... 97 D3
Railton Terr. M9 ... 157 F7
Railway App. 4 OL11 ... 30 C2
Railway Bank. SK14 ... 101 C2
Railway Brow. OL11 ... 30 C1
Railway Cotts.Bredbury SK6 112 F4
Railway Cotts.
Hollinfare WA3 ... 105 B5
Railway Rd. Adlington PR6 ... 21 A7
Railway Rd. Golborne WA3 ... 74 B1
Railway Rd. Leigh WN7 ... 75 E5
Railway Rd. Oldham OL9 ... 66 A2
Railway Rd. Oldham OL9 ... 153 D6
Railway Rd.
Stockport SK1 & SK3 ... 170 E8
Railway Rd.
Stretford M16, M17, M32 ... 96 F5
Railway Rd. Urmston M41 ... 95 E2
Railway St. Alt'ham WA14 ... 119 D4
Railway St. Atherton M46 ... 58 B4
Railway St. Bacup OL13 ... 3 B8
Railway St. Dukinfield SK16 166 B1
Railway St. Farnworth BL4 ... 42 E1
Railway St. Glossop SK13 ... 104 C1
Railway St. Hadfield SK14 ... 104 A5
Railway St. Heywood OL10 ... 29 E1
Railway St. Hindley WN2 ... 56 E7
Railway St.Littleborough OL15 16 B5
Railway St. M'ster M18 ... 99 D6
Railway St. Newhey OL16 ... 32 B4
Railway St. Newton-l-W WA12 89 B3
Railway St. R'dale OL16 ... 31 A6
Railway St. Radcliffe M26 ... 44 A3
Railway St.
Ramsbottom BL0 & BL9 ... 11 C2
Railway St. Ramsbottom BL0 138 C6
Railway St. Stockport SK4 ... 169 E2
Railway St. Wigan WN6 ... 37 A1
Railway St Ind Est. M18 ... 99 D6
Railway Terr. Bury BL8 ... 27 C1
Railway Terr. Disley SK12 .. 135 D6
Railway Terr. Edgworth BL7 ... 9 B8
Railway Terr. 5 M'ster M21 97 B2
Railway View. 3 Oldham OL4 67 F6
Railway View. Shaw OL2 ... 149 C8
Raimond St. BL1 ... 142 C3
Rainbow Cl. M21 ... 109 B7
Rainbow Dr. M46 ... 58 D5
Raincliff Ave. M13 ... 98 F2
Raines Crest. OL16 ... 32 A6
Rainford Ave.Alt'ham WA15 120 A6
Rainford Ave. M'ster M20 .. 110 A8
Rainford House. 2 BL1 ... 145 F8
Rainford Rd. WA11 & WN5 ... 71 C5
Rainford St. BL2 ... 25 C6
Rainforth St. M13 ... 98 F3
Rainham Dr. Bolton BL1 ... 143 E1
Rainham Dr. M'ster M8 ... 156 A7
Rainham Gr. 2 BL1 ... 143 E1
Rainham Way.
Brinnington SK5 ... 112 B6
Rainham Way. Oldham OL9 152 B6
Rainhill Wlk. M40 ... 83 D4
Rainow Ave. M43 ... 83 E1
Rainow Rd. SK3 ... 123 C6
Rainow Way. 10 SK9 ... 131 E1
Rainshaw St. Bolton BL1 ... 143 F4
Rainshaw St. 1 Oldham OL4 67 D8
Rainshaw St. Royton OL2 ... 48 D4
Rainsough Ave. M25 ... 63 A1
Rainsough Brow. M25 ... 62 F1
Rainsough Cl. M25 ... 63 A1
Rainton Wlk. 2 M40 ... 65 D2
Rainwood. OL9 ... 65 E8
Raithby Dr. WN3 ... 55 A3
Raja Cl. M8 ... 156 B7
Rake. OL11 ... 29 D8
Rake Fold. BL0 ... 138 A6
Rake Head Barn La. OL14 ... 6 A8
Rake La. M27 ... 62 B2
Rake St. BL9 ... 140 F4
Rake Terr. OL15 ... 16 C6
Rakehead La. OL13 ... 3 B8
Rakehead Wlk. M15 ... 162 F5
Rakewood Dr. OL4 ... 49 E4
Rakewood Rd. OL15 ... 16 C2
Raleigh Cl. M'ster M20 ... 110 A5
Raleigh Cl. Oldham OL1 ... 153 F8
Raleigh Gdns. OL15 ... 6 C1
Raleigh St. Reddish SK5 ... 169 E4
Raleigh St. Stretford M32 ... 96 E2
Ralli Courts. M3 ... 158 E1
Ralph Ave. SK14 ... 113 E7
Ralph Green St. OL9 ... 66 B3
Ralph Sherwin Ct. OL12 ... 15 D4
Ralph St. Bolton BL1 ... 143 D2
Ralph St. Droylsden M11 ... 83 D1
Ralph St. R'dale OL12 ... 15 A1
Ralphs La. SK16 ... 101 C7
Ralston Cl. M7 ... 155 F8
Ralstone Ave. OL8 ... 66 F4
Ram St. M38 ... 59 F5
Ramage Wlk. M11 ... 160 E1
Ramillies Ave. SK8 ... 123 C1
Ramillies Hall Sch. SK8 ... 123 C2
Ramp Rd E. M90 ... 130 C7
Ramp Rd S. M90 ... 130 C7
Ramp Rd W. M90 ... 130 B7
Ramsay Ave. BL4 ... 60 B7
Ramsay Pl. OL16 ... 31 A8
Ramsay St. Bolton BL1 ... 143 E4
Ramsay St. R'dale OL16 ... 31 A8
Ramsay Terr. 19 OL16 ... 31 A8
Ramsbottom Cottage
Hospl. BL0 ... 138 C5
Ramsbottom La. BL0 ... 138 C7
Ramsbottom Rd.Horwich BL6 22 C3
Ramsbottom Rd.
Ramsbottom BL8 & BL7 ... 10 A3
Ramsbottom St. BB4 ... 2 E8
Ramsbottom Sta. BL0 ... 138 C6
Ramsbury Dr.
M10 & M40 & M9 ... 65 D2
Ramsdale Rd. SK7 ... 132 E8
Ramsdale St. OL9 ... 152 A7
Ramsden Cl. Glossop SK13 . 104 D2
Ramsden Cl. Oldham OL1 ... 153 E7
Ramsden Cl. Wigan WN3 ... 150 A5
Ramsden Cres. OL1 ... 153 E8
Ramsden Fold. M27 ... 61 F2
Ramsden La. OL14 ... 5 F7
Ramsden Rd. OL12 ... 15 C6
Ramsden St.Ashton-u-L OL6 166 B4
Ramsden St. Bolton BL3 ... 42 D5
Ramsden St. Oldham OL1 ... 153 E7
Ramsden St. Walsden OL14 ... 6 A7
Ramsden Wood Rd. OL14 ... 6 A7
Ramsey Ave. SK5 ... 99 D1
Ramsey Cl. Ashton-i-M WN4 . 73 B2
Ramsey Cl. Atherton M46 ... 58 E2
Ramsey Gr. BL8 ... 27 B2
Ramsey St. Failsworth M40 ... 83 B7
Ramsey St. 3 Leigh WN7 ... 76 A4
Ramsey St. Oldham OL1 ... 67 B8
Ramsey St. Oldham OL9 ... 152 B5
Ramsgate Rd.Failsworth M40 83 C4
Ramsgate Rd. Reddish SK5 . 111 F7
Ramsgate St. M7 & M8 ... 155 E5
Ramsgill Cl. M23 ... 108 F1
Ramsgreave Cl. BL9 ... 44 D7
Ramwell Gdns. BL3 ... 145 D5
Ramwells Brow. BL7 ... 25 A8
Ranby Ave. M9 ... 64 F4
Rand St. 6 OL1 ... 49 D1
Randal St. BL3 ... 146 C4
Randale Dr. BL9 ... 45 A2
Randall Ave. WN6 ... 36 A5
Randall Wlk. 22 M11 ... 160 F1
Randerson St. M12 ... 163 C7
Randle St. WN2 ... 56 D6
Randlesham St. M25 ... 63 C4
Randolph Pl. SK3 ... 170 E7
Randolph Rd. BL4 ... 60 F7
Randolph St. Bolton BL3 ... 145 D6
Randolph St.M'ster M12,M19 99 B2
Randolph St. Oldham OL8 ... 66 C2
Rands Clough Dr. M28 ... 78 B6
Ranelagh Rd. M27 ... 80 C7
Ranelagh St. M11 ... 83 B2
Raneley Gr. OL11 ... 31 A2
Ranford Rd. M19 ... 111 A8
Range Dr. SK6 ... 113 C6
Range La. OL3 ... 33 D1
Range Rd. Dukinfield SK16 ... 102 B7
Range Rd. M'ster M16 ... 97 E3
Range Rd. Stalybridge SK15 102 B8
Range Rd. Stockport SK3 ... 170 E7
Range St. Bolton BL3 ... 147 D4
Range St. M'ster M11 ... 165 C8
Rangemore Ave. M22 ... 121 D8
Ranicar Steet. WN2 ... 57 C3
Rankine Terr. BL3 ... 145 D5
Ranmore Ave. WN4 ... 72 D4
Rannoch Rd. BL2 ... 43 A7
Ransfield Rd. M21 ... 97 B1
Ranulph Ct. 1 M6 ... 80 D5
Ranworth Ave. SK4 ... 110 F2
Ranworth Cl. Bolton BL1 ... 25 A6
Ranworth Cl. M'ster M11 ... 165 A8
Raper St. OL4 ... 67 C8
Rapes Highway. OL15 & OL3 33 F5
Raphael St. BL1 ... 143 D2
Rappax Rd. WA15 ... 129 A8
Rasbottom St. BL3 ... 145 E5
Raspberry La. M44 ... 94 A5
Rassbottom Brow. 5 SK15 ... 85 F2
Rassbottom Ind Est. SK15 ... 85 F2
Rassbottom St. SK15 ... 85 F2
Rassey Cl. WN6 ... 37 A7
Rastell Wlk. 23 M9 ... 64 E3
Ratcliffe Ave. M44 ... 94 A2
Ratcliffe Rd. WN2 ... 38 C6
Ratcliffe St. Leigh WN7 ... 75 F6
Ratcliffe St. M'ster M19 ... 99 B1
Ratcliffe St. 6 Stockport SK1 170 F8
Ratcliffe St. Tyldesley M29 ... 59 B1
Ratcliffe St. Wigan WN6 ... 37 A1
Ratcliffe Terr. OL5 ... 86 C8
Rath Wlk. 14 M40 ... 83 C5
Rathan Rd. M41 ... 95 C4
Rathbone St. OL16 ... 31 C7
Rathbourne Ave. M9 ... 64 D4
Rathen Ave. WN2 ... 56 A8
Rathen Rd. M20 ... 110 C5
Rathmel Rd. M23 ... 108 F2
Rathmell Cl. WA3 ... 91 E3
Rathmore Ave. M10 & M40 157 E5
Rathvale Dr. M22 ... 130 C8
Rattenbury Ct. M6 ... 80 C5
Raveden Cl. BL1 ... 142 C3
Raveley Ave. M14 ... 110 D8
Ravelston Dr. M9 ... 157 D7
Raven Ave. Haslingden BB4 ... 1 A7
Raven Ave. Oldham OL9 ... 152 A5
Raven Cl. M43 ... 84 C3
Raven Croft. BB4 ... 1 B8
Raven Ct. M16 ... 162 E5
Raven Dr. M44 ... 94 A3
Raven House. M6 ... 81 A5
Raven Pk. BB4 ... 1 B8
Raven Rd. Bolton BL3 ... 146 A4
Raven Rd. Sale M33 ... 108 B1
Raven St. Bury BL9 ... 140 F4
Raven St. M'ster M12 ... 163 C8
Raven St. R'dale OL11 ... 13 E1
Raven Terr. 1 SK16 ... 166 C1
Raven Way. 5 M6 ... 81 A3
Ravendale Cl. OL12 ... 14 A1
Ravenfield Gr. 10 BL1 ... 145 D8
Ravenhead Cl. 13 M14 ... 110 D8
Ravenhead Dr. WN8 ... 53 A7
Ravenhead Sq. SK15 ... 86 E5
Ravenhurst. 4 M7 ... 63 E1
Ravenhurst Dr. BL1 ... 40 D6
Ravenna Ave. M23 ... 120 D7
Ravenoak Ave. M19 ... 111 C8
Ravenoak Dr. M35 ... 84 A8
Ravenoak Park Rd. SK8 ... 132 B8
Ravenoak Rd. Cheadle SK8 . 132 B8
Ravenoak Rd. Stockport SK2 124 A4
Ravens Cl. M25 & M8 ... 63 E2
Ravens Wood. BL1 ... 40 E7
Ravensbury Cty Prim Sch.
M11 ... 83 B2
Ravensbury St. M11 ... 83 B2
Ravenscar Cres. M22 ... 130 D8
Ravenscar Wlk. BL4 ... 60 D7
Ravenscraig Rd. M38 ... 60 B6
Ravensdale Gdns. M30 ... 79 E3
Ravensdale Rd. BL1 & BL6 ... 40 D7
Ravensdale St. M14 ... 98 C3
Ravenside Pk. OL9 ... 152 A5
Ravenstone Dr. Diggle OL3 ... 51 C3
Ravenstone Dr. Sale M33 ... 108 E5
Ravenstonedale Dr. OL2 ... 48 E5
Ravensway. M25 & M8 ... 63 D2
Ravenswood. M20 ... 109 F4
Ravenswood Ave.
Stockport SK4 ... 168 A1
Ravenswood Ave.
Wigan WN3 ... 54 D3
Ravenswood Ct. 3 SK3 ... 123 F4
Ravenswood Dr. Bolton BL1 . 40 E7
Ravenswood Dr.
Cheadle SK8 ... 132 B8
Ravenswood Dr.Hindley WN2 56 E7
Ravenswood Dr. M'ster M9 .. 64 E3
Ravenswood Rd.
Stretford M16 & M32 ... 96 F4
Ravenswood Rd.
Wilmslow SK9 ... 136 E4
Ravenwood. M24 ... 65 D8
Ravenwood Dr.
Alt'ham WA15 ... 129 D7
Ravenwood Dr.Denton M34 100 E6
Ravine Ave. M9 ... 157 F7
Rawcliffe Ave. BL2 ... 42 F7
Rawcliffe St. M14 ... 98 B3
Rawdon Cl. 9 M19 ... 99 B1
Rawkin Cl. M15 ... 162 E5
Rawlinson St. 13 BL6 ... 22 B4
Rawlyn Rd. BL1 ... 142 A2
Rawpool Gdns. M23 ... 121 A7
Rawson Ave. BL4 ... 42 E1
Rawson Rd. BL1 ... 142 C1
Rawson St. BL4 ... 42 E1
Rawsons Rake. BL0 & BL8 .. 138 A6
Rawsthorne Ave. BL0 ... 1 D2
Rawsthorne St. Bolton BL1 ... 143 E2
Rawsthorne St.Tyldesley M29 77 D8
Rawstron St. OL12 ... 4 C1
Rawthey Pl. WN2 ... 55 F2
Rayburn Way. M8 ... 156 A5
Raycroft Ave. M9 ... 65 A2
Raydale Cl. WA3 ... 74 E1
Rayden Cres. BL5 ... 57 E6
Raydon Ave. M40 & M9 ... 157 D5
Rayleigh Ave. M18 ... 99 F7
Raymond Ave. Bury BL9 ... 27 F5
Raymond Ave. Oldham OL9 ... 66 B4
Raymond Rd. M23 ... 109 B2
Raymond St. M27 ... 61 F1
Rayner Ave. WN2 ... 56 E3
Rayner La. M34 & OL7 ... 84 E2
Rayner St. SK1 ... 124 B8
Raynham Ave. M20 ... 110 B3
Raynham St. OL6 ... 166 C3
Rayson St. M9 ... 64 C2
Reabrook Ave. M12 ... 164 F6
Reach The. M28 ... 60 E2
Read Cl. BL9 ... 44 D7
Read St. SK14 ... 101 C3
Read St W. SK14 ... 101 C3
Reade Ave. M41 ... 94 F1
Reade House. M41 ... 94 F1
Reading Cl. M11 ... 165 C8
Reading Dr. M33 ... 107 D4
Reading St. M6 ... 81 B5
Reading Wlk. 1 M34 ... 100 F1
Readitt Wlk. M11 ... 83 B2
Reaney Wlk. M12 ... 165 A6
Reather Wlk. M10 & M40 ... 159 C3
Rebecca St. M8 ... 156 A8
Recreation Ave. WN4 ... 73 D4
Recreation Dr. WN5 ... 71 E5
Recreation Rd. M35 ... 66 B1
Recreation St. Bolton BL2 ... 25 E5
Recreation St. Bolton BL3 ... 147 E4
Recreation St.Prestwich M25 63 C4
Rectory Ave. Golborne WA3 .. 90 C8
Rectory Ave. M'ster M8 ... 64 A1
Rectory Ave. Prestwich M25 .. 63 B4
Rectory CE Prim Sch. WN4 72 D5
Rectory Cl. Denton M34 ... 101 A2
Rectory Cl. Radcliffe M26 ... 44 D4
Rectory Ct. 3 SK6 ... 125 F5
Rectory Fields. SK1 ... 112 A1
Rectory Gdns. Prestwich M25 63 B4
Rectory Gdns.
Westhoughton BL5 ... 57 E5
Rectory Gn. Prestwich M25 ... 63 B4
Rectory Gn. Stockport SK1 .. 112 A1
Rectory Gr. M25 ... 63 B3
Rectory La. Bury BL9 ... 28 D4
Rectory La. Prestwich M25 ... 63 A4
Rectory La. Radcliffe M26 ... 44 B3
Rectory La.
Standish WN1 & WN6 ... 20 A1
Rectory Rd. Garswood WN4 .. 72 D5
Rectory Rd. M'ster M8 ... 63 F1
Rectory St. M24 ... 46 F1
Red Bank. M4 & M8 ... 159 A3
Red Bank Ave. WA12 ... 89 F1
Red Bank Rd. M26 ... 43 F5
Red Barn Rd. WN5 ... 71 C6
Red Bridge. BL2 ... 26 A1
Red Brook St. OL11 ... 139 D7
Red Gables. OL7 ... 166 A4
Red Hall St. OL4 ... 67 C6
Red Hill Way. WN2 ... 56 D6
Red House La. WA14 ... 118 C8
Red La. Bolton BL2 ... 25 E1
Red La. Disley SK12 ... 135 C5
Red La. R'dale OL12 ... 15 B2
Red Lane Cty Prim Sch. BL2 25 F1
Red Lion St. M4 & M60 ... 159 A2
Red Lumb St. OL12 ... 13 A3
Red Pike Wlk. 2 OL1 ... 67 A8
Red Rock Brow. WN1 ... 37 E8
Red Rock La. Kearsley M26 ... 61 E6
Red Rock La.
Standish WN1 & WN2 ... 37 D8
Red Rose Cres. M19 ... 111 C7
Red Rose Ct. M33 ... 108 B6
Red Rose Gdns. M28 ... 60 A4
Red Rose Ret Pk. M5 ... 161 B8
Red Row. SK7 ... 134 B8
Red St. M46 ... 58 E3
Red Waters. WN7 ... 76 A6
Redacre. SK12 ... 133 F6
Redacre Rd. M18 ... 99 E5
Redbarn Cl. SK6 ... 112 F4
Redbourne Dr. M41 ... 94 F4
Redbrick Ct. 8 OL7 ... 166 A1
Redbridge Gr. M21 ... 109 A8
Redbrook Ave. M10 & M40 157 E5
Redbrook Cl. 6 BL4 ... 42 E1
Redbrook Gr. 2 SK9 ... 131 D1
Redbrook Rd.Alt'ham WA15 120 D5
Redbrook Rd.
Partington M31 ... 105 E2
Redburn Cl. WN3 ... 150 B6
Redburn Rd. M23 ... 121 B7
Redby St. M11 ... 165 B7
Redcar Ave. M'ster M20 ... 110 B6
Redcar Ave. Urmston M41 ... 95 A4
Redcar Cl. SK7 ... 125 A1
Redcar Rd. Bolton BL1 ... 142 B4
Redcar Rd. Little Lever BL3 ... 43 A3
Redcar Rd. Pendlebury M27 ... 80 C7
Redcar St. OL12 ... 139 E8
Redcliffe Ct. M25 ... 63 B2
Redclyffe Ave. M14 ... 98 C3
Redclyffe Rd. Eccles M41 ... 95 D7
Redclyffe Rd. M'ster M20 ... 110 A5
Redcot Ct. M45 ... 62 C7
Redcote St. M40 ... 83 A8
Redcourt Ave. M20 ... 110 B4
Redcroft Gdns. 2 M19 ... 110 E4
Redcroft Rd. M33 ... 107 E6
Redcross St. R'dale OL12 ... 14 F1
Redcross St. R'dale OL12 ... 139 F8
Redcross St N. OL12 ... 14 F1
Reddaway Cl. M6 ... 81 A5
Reddish Cl. BL2 ... 25 E6
Reddish La. Lymm WA13 ... 117 A5
Reddish La.
Reddish M18 & M34 ... 99 E4
Reddish North Sta. SK5 ... 99 F2
Reddish Rd. SK5 ... 111 F6
Reddish South Sta. SK5 ... 111 F7
Reddish Vale Rd. SK5 ... 112 A7
Reddish Vale Sch. SK5 ... 111 F7
Reddy La. WA14 ... 118 B1
Reddyshore Scout Gate.
OL14 ... 6 C5
Redesmere Cl.
Alt'ham WA15 ... 120 D6
Redesmere Cl.Droylsden M43 84 B1
Redesmere Dr.
Alderley Edge SK9 ... 137 A1
Redesmere Dr. Cheadle SK8 122 F4
Redesmere Pk. M41 ... 107 B8
Redesmere Rd. SK9 ... 131 D5
Redfearn Wood. OL12 ... 14 B2
Redfern Ave. M33 ... 108 E3
Redfern Cotts. OL11 ... 13 D1
Redfern House. SK6 ... 113 A2
Redfern St. M4 & M60 ... 159 A2
Redfern Way. OL11 ... 13 D1
Redfield Cl. M11 ... 160 F1
Redford Cl. WN7 ... 76 A5
Redford Dr. SK7 ... 124 A2
Redford Rd. M9 ... 63 F4
Redford St. BL8 ... 27 C3
Redgate. Glossop SK14 ... 104 C4
Redgate. Hyde SK14 ... 113 D8
Redgate La. M'ster M12 ... 99 A4
Redgate La. M'ster M12 ... 164 F5
Redgate Rd. WN4 ... 73 B6
Redgate Way. BL4 ... 147 F1
Redgrave Pas. OL4 ... 67 D8
Redgrave Rise. WN3 ... 54 D3
Redgrave St. OL4 ... 67 D8
Redgrave Wlk. M19 ... 99 C1
Redhill Dr. SK6 ... 112 E3
Redhill Gr. BL1 ... 143 E1
Redhill St. M4 ... 159 C2
Redhouse La. Disley SK12 .. 135 E7
Redhouse La. Romiley SK6 . 113 A4
Redington Cl. M28 ... 78 A5
Redisher Cl. BL8 ... 10 F3
Redisher La. BL8 ... 10 E3
Redland Ave. SK5 ... 111 F5
Redland Cl. OL15 ... 16 B6
Redland Cres. M21 ... 109 B6
Redland Ct. WN2 ... 73 E7
Redlynch Wlk. M8 ... 156 A7
Redmain Gr. WA3 ... 90 E8
Redmayne Cl. WA12 ... 89 B4
Redmere Gr. M14 ... 110 C8
Redmire Mews. SK16 ... 101 F7
Redmires Ct. 7 M5 ... 81 A1
Redmond Cl. M34 ... 100 E7
Redmoor Sq. 3 M13 ... 163 B7
Rednal Wlk. WN3 ... 150 B6
Redpol Ave. WN7 ... 76 B5
Redpoll Cl. M28 ... 78 B7
Redruth St. M14 ... 98 B2
Redscar Wlk. M24 ... 46 E1
Redshank Cl. WA12 ... 89 C4
Redshank Gr. WN7 ... 76 A6
Redshaw Cl. M14 ... 98 D1
Redstock Cl. BL5 ... 40 B1
Redstone Rd. M19 ... 110 D3
Redthorn Ave. 2 M19 ... 110 F7
Redvale Wlk. M7 ... 155 E6
Redvales Rd. BL9 ... 44 E7
Redvers St. M'ster M11 ... 164 E8
Redvers St. Oldham OL1 ... 153 D8
Redwater Cl. M28 ... 78 A5
Redwing Rd. BL8 ... 10 F2
Redwood. Chadderton M24 ... 65 D7
Redwood. Sale M33 ... 107 C4
Redwood. Shevington WN6 ... 36 B6
Redwood. Westhoughton BL5 57 D6
Redwood Ave. Wigan WN6 ... 36 F3
Redwood Ave. Wigan WN5 ... 54 A6
Redwood Cl. OL12 ... 14 B3
Redwood Dr. Bredbury SK6 . 112 F3
Redwood Dr. Denton M34 .. 100 E6
Redwood Dr. M'ster M8 ... 156 B5
Redwood Dr. Rawtenstall BB4 . 1 F8
Redwood House. M22 ... 109 E1
Redwood La. OL4 ... 67 E7
Redwood Park Gr. OL16 ... 31 D7
Redwood Rd. OL3 ... 69 C7
Redwood St. M6 ... 81 A4
Reece Ct. 4 SK16 ... 101 D8
Reed Cres. WN3 ... 55 A4
Reed Ct. 2 OL1 ... 153 E8
Reed Hill. OL16 ... 139 F8
Reed St. M'ster M18 ... 99 D6
Reed St. 9 Oldham OL1 ... 67 A7
Reedbank. M26 ... 62 A8
Reedham Cl. BL1 ... 144 C8
Reedham Wlk. M'ster M40 160 D4
Reedham Wlk. Oldham OL9 .. 66 C4
Reedley Dr. M28 ... 78 C8
Reedmace Cl. M28 ... 60 E1
Reedshaw Bank. SK2 ... 124 D5
Reedsmere Cl. WN5 ... 54 F6
Reeman Cl. SK6 ... 113 A4
Reeman Ct. SK9 ... 131 B2
Reepham Cl. WN3 ... 54 D3
Reeve Cl. SK2 ... 124 F5
Reeve St. WA3 ... 91 B8
Reeves Ct. M5 ... 80 A2
Reeves Rd. M21 ... 109 B7
Reeves St. WN7 ... 75 F6
Reevey Ave. SK7 ... 124 C2
Reform St. OL12 ... 14 F1
Reform Wlk. M11 ... 165 B8
Refuge St. OL2 ... 149 B6
Regaby Gr. WN2 ... 57 A5
Regal Cl. M45 ... 63 B8
Regal Wlk. 11 M40 ... 83 C6
Regan Ave. M21 ... 109 D7
Regan St. Bolton BL1 ... 143 D3
Regan St. 5 Radcliffe M26 ... 44 B2
Regatta St. M6 ... 80 F6
Regency Cl. Glossop SK13 .. 104 D1
Regency Cl. M'ster M40 ... 157 D5
Regency Cl. Oldham OL8 ... 66 D4
Regency Ct. Cheadle SK8 .. 123 A2
Regency Ct. Wigan WN1 ... 151 D8
Regency Lodge. M25 ... 63 A3
Regency Pk. SK9 ... 136 F5
Regency Wharf. WN7 ... 76 C4
Regent Ave. Ashton-i-M WN4 72 F5
Regent Ave. M'ster M14 ... 98 A2
Regent Ave. Walkden M38 ... 60 C4
Regent Bank. SK9 ... 136 F5
Regent Cl. Bramhall SK7 ... 132 D4
Regent Cl. Cheadle SK8 ... 123 C4
Regent Cl. Wilmslow SK9 ... 136 F5
Regent Cres. Failsworth M35 83 E6
Regent Cres.Oldham OL1,OL2 48 D2

Regent Ct. Alt'ham WA14 .... 119 D4
Regent Ct. M'ster M7 .... 63 D1
Regent Ct. M'ster SK4 .... 111 C5
Regent Dr. Bolton BL6 .... 40 B6
Regent Dr. Denton M34 .... 100 D1
Regent Dr. Leigh WN7 .... 76 D7
Regent House. M14 .... 98 D3
Regent Pl. M14 .... 98 C4
Regent Rd. Alt'ham WA14 .... 119 D4
Regent Rd. Bolton BL6 .... 40 B6
Regent Rd. Platt Bridge WN2 . 56 A3
Regent Rd. Salford M5 .... 81 A1
Regent Rd. Salford M15, M5 161 C8
Regent Rd. Stockport SK2 .... 124 A6
Regent Road Ind Est. M5 .. 162 D8
Regent Sq. M16 .... 161 B8
Regent St. Bury BL9 .... 140 F4
Regent St. Eccles M30 .... 79 F2
Regent St. Failsworth M40 ..... 83 D5
Regent St. Glossop SK13 ...... 104 D1
Regent St. Hadfield SK14 ..... 104 B5
Regent St. Heywood OL10 ...... 29 B2
Regent St. 3 Hindley WN2 .... 56 D5
Regent St. Littleborough OL15 16 B5
Regent St. Middleton M24 ...... 46 F2
Regent St. Newton-l-W WA12 89 A3
Regent St. Oldham OL1 .... 67 A7
Regent St. R'dale OL12, OL16 . 15 A1
Regent St. 2 R'dale OL16 ...... 31 A8
Regent St. Ramsbottom BL0 ... 11 A4
Regent St. Shaw OL2 .... 149 B7
Regent St. Tyldesley M46 ...... 58 E2
Regent Trad Est. M3 .... 158 D1
Regent Wlk. BL4 .... 60 D8
Regents Dr. OL5 .... 86 D8
Regina Ave. SK15 .... 86 A2
Regina Cres. WN7 .... 76 E6
Regina Ct. M6 .... 80 A3
Reginald Latham Ct. M40 . 160 D3
Reginald St. Bolton BL3 ...... 146 A2
Reginald St 2 Droylsden M11 99 F7
Reginald St. Eccles M30 .... 95 A8
Reginald St. Swinton M27 ...... 61 D1
Reid Cl. M34 .... 113 A8
Reigate Cl. BL8 .... 27 B1
Reigate Rd. M31 & M41 ...... 106 E8
Reins Lee Ave. OL8 .... 67 A2
Reins Lee Rd. OL7 .... 85 A6
Reliance St. M40 .... 83 C6
Reliance Street Ent Pk. 1
M40 .... 83 C6
Reliance Street Trad Est.
M35 & M40 .... 83 C6
Rembrandt Wlk. OL1 .... 49 D4
Rena Cl. SK4 .... 169 D3
Rena Ct. SK4 .... 169 D3
Rendel Cl. Newton-l-W WA12 89 D2
Rendel Cl. Stretford M32 ...... 96 D2
Renfrew Cl. WN3 .... 55 A3
Renfrew Dr. BL3 .... 40 F3
Renfrew Rd. WN2 .... 38 D5
Rennie Cl. M32 .... 96 E2
Renshaw Ave. M30 .... 79 D1
Renshaw Dr. BL9 .... 44 F8
Renshaw St. Alt'ham WA14 ... 119 E5
Renshaw St. Eccles M30 .... 79 D1
Renton Rd. Bolton BL3 .... 146 B3
Renton Rd. Stretford M32 ...... 96 E3
Renton Rd.
Wythenshawe M22 .... 121 D4
Renwick Gr. BL3 .... 146 C3
Renwick Sq. WN4 .... 72 F3
Repton Ave. Droylsden M43 .. 83 D3
Repton Ave. Failsworth M40 .. 65 E1
Repton Ave. Hyde SK14 .... 167 E3
Repton Ave. Ince-i-M WN2 .... 55 F4
Repton Ave. Oldham OL8 .... 66 D3
Repton Ave. Reddish M34 .... 100 A3
Repton Ave. Urmston M41 ...... 94 D2
Reservoir Rd. SK3 .... 170 D7
Reservoir St. Aspull WN2 ...... 38 F3
Reservoir St. Ince-i-M WN2 ... 56 A8
Reservoir St. M'ster M3 ...... 158 E3
Reservoir St. R'dale OL16 ...... 15 C1
Reservoir St. Salford M6 ...... 154 F2
Restormel Ave. WN2 .... 38 D5
Retford Ave. OL16 .... 31 B4
Retford Cl. BL8 .... 27 E5
Retford St. OL4 & OL8 .... 67 B5
Retiro St. OL1 .... 153 F6
Retreat The. SK6 .... 113 C1
Reuben St. SK4 .... 169 E4
Revers St. BL8 .... 140 D3
Reveton Gn. SK7 .... 124 A2
Rex Bldgs. SK9 .... 137 B6
Reynard Rd. M21 .... 109 B7
Reynard St. SK14 .... 167 D3
Reynell Rd. M13 .... 98 F2
Reyner St. Ashton-u-L OL6 ..... 85 E2
Reyner St. M'ster M1 .... 163 A8
Reynold St. SK14 .... 167 D2
Reynolds Cl. Atherton BL5 ..... 58 F6
Reynolds Dr. Atherton BL5 .... 58 F7
Reynolds Dr. M'ster M18 .... 99 D6
Reynolds Dr. Marple SK6 ..... 126 B8
Reynolds Mews. SK9 .... 137 E8
Reynolds Rd. M16 .... 97 C4
Rhine Cl. BL8 .... 26 F7
Rhiwlas Dr. BL9 .... 44 F8
Rhode Houses. SK6 .... 125 F3
Rhode St. BL8 .... 26 F6
Rhodes Ave. Haslingden BB4 ... 1 A7
Rhodes Ave. Oldham OL4 .... 67 F5
Rhodes Ave. Uppermill OL3 ... 51 C1
Rhodes Bank. OL1 .... 67 A6
Rhodes Cres. OL11 .... 30 F3
Rhodes Dr. BL9 .... 45 A2
Rhodes Hill. OL4 .... 67 F5
Rhodes St. Dukinfield SK14 . 101 C3
Rhodes St. Glossop SK14 ..... 104 B5
Rhodes St. M'ster M10, M40 160 E4
Rhodes St. Oldham OL1 .... 67 A7
Rhodes St. Oldham OL4 .... 67 F7
Rhodes St. R'dale OL12 .... 15 B3
Rhodes St. Royton OL2 .... 49 A3
Rhodes St N. SK14 .... 101 C3
Rhodeswood Dr. SK14 .... 104 A6
Rhos Ave. Cheadle SK8 .... 122 E1
Rhos Ave. M'ster M14 .... 110 E8
Rhos Ave. Middleton M24 .... 65 A7
Rhos Dr. SK7 .... 124 D1
Rhosleigh Ave. BL1 .... 143 E4
Rialto Gdns. M7 .... 155 E6
Ribbesford Rd. WN3 .... 54 C4
Ribble Ave. Bolton BL2 .... 42 E7
Ribble Ave. Chadderton OL9 .. 47 F1
Ribble Ave. Littleborough OL15 15 F6
Ribble Cl. Culcheth WA3 .... 91 F2
Ribble Cres. WN5 .... 71 C3
Ribble Dr. Boothstown M28 .... 77 F6
Ribble Dr. Bury BL9 .... 27 F8
Ribble Dr. Kearsley BL4 .... 61 B5
Ribble Dr. Whitefield M45 ..... 45 A1
Ribble Dr. Wigan WN5 .... 54 C7
Ribble Drive Cty Prim Sch.
M45 .... 45 A1
Ribble Gr. Heywood OL10 ...... 29 A3
Ribble Gr. Leigh WN7 .... 75 C5
Ribble Rd. Oldham OL8 .... 66 C3
Ribble Rd. Platt Bridge WN2 .. 56 A2
Ribble Rd.
Shevington Moor WN6 .... 19 B2
Ribble St. Bacup OL13 .... 4 A8
Ribble St. R'dale OL11 .... 30 E4
Ribble Wlk. M43 .... 100 A8
Ribblesdale Cl. OL10 .... 46 E7
Ribblesdale Dr. M40 .... 156 C5
Ribblesdale Rd. BL3 .... 147 D4
Ribbleton Cl. BL8 .... 26 F1
Ribchester Dr. BL9 .... 44 D7
Ribchester Gdns. WA3 .... 92 A3
Ribchester Gr. BL2 .... 25 E1
Ribchester Wlk. M15 .... 162 F6
Riber Bank. SK13 .... 171 E1
Riber Cl. 25 SK13 .... 171 E1
Riber Fold. 27 SK13 .... 171 E1
Riber Gn. 26 SK13 .... 171 E1
Rice St. M3 .... 162 E8
Richard Burch St. 3 BL9 .. 140 F3
Richard Gwyn Cl. BL5 .... 57 D6
Richard Reynolds Ct. M44 105 E6
Richard St. Failsworth M35 .... 83 F7
Richard St. Ince-i-M WN3 .. 151 D6
Richard St. R'dale OL11 ...... 139 F6
Richard St. Radcliffe M26 ...... 43 F3
Richard St. Ramsbottom BL0 . 11 E7
Richard St. Stockport SK1 ... 169 F2
Richards Rd. WN6 .... 19 B3
Richardson Cl. M45 .... 44 F1
Richardson Rd. M30 .... 79 E2
Richardson St. 8 M'ster M18 99 E7
Richardson St.
Stockport SK1 .... 124 A7
Richbell Cl. M44 .... 105 F7
Richborough Cl. M7 & M8 . 155 E5
Richelieu St. BL3 .... 42 A4
Richmond Ave.
Handforth SK9 .... 131 D4
Richmond Ave. M'ster M25 .. 63 C1
Richmond Ave. Oldham OL9 .. 66 A4
Richmond Ave. Royton OL2 .. 48 D4
Richmond Ave. Urmston M41 95 E2
Richmond Cl. Bury BL8 .... 26 F6
Richmond Cl. Culcheth WA3 . 91 D4
Richmond Cl.
Dukinfield SK16 .... 101 D6
Richmond Cl. Hadfield SK14 104 A5
Richmond Cl. Lymm WA13 . 117 B4
Richmond Cl. Mossley OL5 ..... 86 E8
Richmond Cl. Sale M33 .... 108 F3
Richmond Cl. Shaw OL2 ..... 149 B5
Richmond Cl.
Stalybridge SK15 .... 86 A1
Richmond Cl. Standish WN1 . 37 B7
Richmond Cl. Whitefield M45 62 D7
Richmond Cres. OL5 .... 86 E8
Richmond Ct.Alt'ham WA14 119 B2
Richmond Ct. Cheadle SK8 . 122 C5
Richmond Ct. Stockport SK2 124 D5
Richmond Cty Inf Sch.
OL9 .... 153 D6
Richmond Cty Jun Sch.
OL9 .... 153 D6
Richmond Dr. Leigh WN7 ...... 76 D7
Richmond Dr. Lymm WA13 ... 117 B4
Richmond Dr. Swinton M28 .. 79 C8
Richmond Gdns. Bolton BL3 . 42 B3
Richmond Gdns.
Newton-l-W WA12 .... 89 C2
Richmond Gn. WA14 .... 119 B2
Richmond Gr. Cheadle SK8 . 122 F1
Richmond Gr. Eccles M30 ..... 79 E3
Richmond Gr. Farnworth BL4 42 A1
Richmond Gr. Leigh WN7 ...... 76 E6
Richmond Gr. M'ster M13 ..... 98 E4
Richmond Gr E. M12 .... 164 E5
Richmond Hill. Hyde SK14 .. 167 F1
Richmond Hill. Wigan WN5 .. 54 C6
Richmond Hill Rd. SK8 ...... 122 C6
Richmond House. 1
M'ster M13 .... 98 E4
Richmond House. 7
Stalybridge SK15 .... 86 A1
Richmond Rd.
Alt'ham WA14 .... 119 C2
Richmond Rd.
Alt'ham WA14 .... 119 D5
Richmond Rd.
Ashton-i-M WN4 .... 72 F5
Richmond Rd.
Boothstown M28 .... 77 E7
Richmond Rd.
Dukinfield SK16 .... 101 D6
Richmond Rd. Eccles M17 ..... 96 A7
Richmond Rd.Failsworth M35 84 B8
Richmond Rd. Hindley WN2 .. 57 A3
Richmond Rd. M'ster M14 . 110 D8
Richmond Rd. M'ster SK4 .. 110 F2
Richmond Rd. Reddish M34 100 A3
Richmond Rd. Romiley SK6 113 C3
Richmond St. Ashton-u-L OL7 84 F3
Richmond St. Atherton M46 .. 58 C2
Richmond St. Bury BL9 .... 44 E8
Richmond St. Denton M34 .. 100 F6
Richmond St. Droylsden M43 84 C2
Richmond St. Horwich BL6 .... 22 B3
Richmond St. Hyde SK14 .... 167 E2
Richmond St. M'ster M3 .... 158 E3
Richmond St. M'ster M1 .... 163 A8
Richmond St.
Stalybridge SK15 .... 86 C2
Richmond St. Wigan WN3 .. 150 B5
Richmond St. Wigan WN1 .. 150 B8
Richmond Terr. SK6 .... 126 B1
Richmond Wlk. Oldham OL9 153 D6
Richmond Wlk.Radcliffe M26 43 E6
Ricroft Rd. SK6 .... 114 B3
Ridding Ave. M22 .... 121 E3
Ridding Cl. SK2 .... 124 D6
Riddings Ct. WA15 .... 119 F8
Riddings Rd. Alt'ham WA15 . 119 F2
Riddings Rd.Sale M33,WA15 108 A1
Riddings Rd. Sale WA15 ..... 120 A8
Riddle Ct. M5 .... 80 C2
Ridge Ave. Alt'ham WA15 ... 129 D6
Ridge Ave. Marple SK6 .... 126 A4
Ridge Ave. Standish WN1 ...... 37 B7
Ridge Cl. Hadfield SK14 ..... 171 E3
Ridge Cl. Romiley SK6 .... 113 F2
Ridge Cres. Marple SK6 ..... 126 A3
Ridge Cres. Whitefield M45 ... 63 B8
Ridge Danyers. Marple SK6 125 E5
Ridge Danyers. Marple SK6 125 F5
Ridge End Fold. SK6 .... 126 A2
Ridge Gr. M45 .... 63 B8
Ridge Hill La.
Stalybridge SK15 .... 86 A3
Ridge La. OL3 .... 51 D5
Ridge Pk. SK7 .... 132 D6
Ridge Rd. SK6 .... 126 A3
Ridge The. SK6 .... 126 A3
Ridge Wlk. M9 .... 64 D3
Ridgecroft. OL6 & OL7 .... 85 B6
Ridgedale Ctr. 3 SK6 .... 125 F6
Ridgefield. M2 .... 158 F1
Ridgefield St. M35 .... 83 E6
Ridgemont Ave. SK4 .... 168 B2
Ridgemont Wlk. M23 .... 108 F2
Ridgeway. Golborne WA3 ..... 90 E7
Ridgeway. Swinton M27 .... 62 B2
Ridgeway. Wilmslow SK9 ..... 137 F7
Ridgeway Gates. 3 BL1 ..... 145 F7
Ridgeway Rd. WA15 .... 120 C5
Ridgeway St. M10 & M40 .. 160 D2
Ridgeway The. SK12 .... 135 C6
Ridgewell Ave. WA3 .... 90 D8
Ridgewood. OL9 .... 65 E8
Ridgewood Ave.
M10, M40, M9 .... 157 D5
Ridgmont Cl. BL6 .... 22 F3
Ridgmont Dr.Boothstown M28 77 F6
Ridgmont Dr. Horwich BL6 .... 22 F3
Ridgmont Rd. SK7 .... 132 E5
Ridgway. BL6 .... 21 C2
Ridgway The. SK6 .... 113 A1
Riding Cl. M29 .... 77 D7
Riding Fold La. M28 .... 79 A5
Riding Gate. BL2 .... 25 E6
Riding Gate Mews. BL2 .... 25 E6
Riding Head La. BL0 .... 11 F8
Riding La. WN4 .... 73 F5
Riding St. M3 .... 158 E1
Ridings Ct. OL3 .... 51 A2
Ridings Rd. SK14 .... 103 F5
Ridings St. M'ster M10, M40 157 E5
Ridings St. M'ster M11 ...... 165 B8
Ridley Dr. WA14 .... 107 E1
Ridley Gr. M33 .... 108 F3
Ridley St. OL4 .... 67 A6
Ridley Wlk. M15 .... 163 A5
Ridling La. SK14 .... 167 E2
Ridsdale Ave. M20 .... 110 A6
Ridsdale Way. M6 .... 81 A5
Ridyard St. Platt Bridge WN2 . 56 B3
Ridyard St.Walkden M28, M38 60 C4
Ridyard St. Wigan WN5 .... 54 E7
Rifield. BL1 .... 142 B3
Rifle Rd. M21 & M33 .... 108 F5
Rifle St. OL1 .... 153 F8
Riga Rd. M14 .... 98 C1
Riga St. M4 & M60 .... 159 A2
Rigby Ave. Blackrod BL6 .... 21 C2
Rigby Ave. Radcliffe M26 ...... 44 C5
Rigby Ct. Bolton BL3 .... 147 F4
Rigby Ct. R'dale OL12 .... 13 E2
Rigby Gr. M38 .... 59 E4
Rigby La. Bolton BL2 .... 25 C5
Rigby St. Alt'ham WA14 ..... 119 D3
Rigby St. Ashton-i-M WN4 .... 73 A3
Rigby St. Bolton BL3 .... 147 F4
Rigby St. Golborne WA3 .... 90 A8
Rigby St. Hindley WN2 .... 56 E6
Rigby St. M'ster M7 .... 155 D6
Rigby Wlk. M7 .... 155 E6
Rigby's Yd. 6 WN5 .... 54 B6
Rigel Pl. M7 .... 81 C3
Rigel St. M10 & M40 .... 160 C3
Rigton Cl. M12 .... 165 A5
Riley Cl. M33 .... 107 B1
Riley Ct. 3 BL1 .... 143 F1
Riley La. WN2 .... 38 B7
Riley Sq. Wigan WN1 .... 37 D1
Riley Sq. Wigan WN1 .... 151 D8
Riley St. M46 .... 58 A1
Riley Wood Cl. SK6 .... 112 F1
Rilston Ave. WA3 .... 91 D3
Rimington Ave. WA3 .... 74 C1
Rimington Cl. WA3 .... 91 E3
Rimmer Cl. M11 .... 160 E1
Rimmington Cl. M9 .... 65 A2
Rimsdale Cl. SK8 .... 122 A3
Rimsdale Wlk. BL3 .... 40 E5
Rimworth Dr. M10 & M40 .. 159 C4
Rindle Rd. M29 .... 93 C8
Ring Lows La. OL12 .... 15 A4
Ring-o-Bells La. SK12 .... 135 D6
Ringcroft Gdns. M40 .... 65 B1
Ringfield Cl. M16 .... 97 E4
Ringford Wlk. M40 .... 157 E5
Ringley Ave. WA3 .... 73 F1
Ringley Chase. M45 .... 62 E8
Ringley Cl. M45 .... 62 D8
Ringley Dr. M45 .... 62 D7
Ringley Gr. BL1 .... 24 E5
Ringley Hey. M45 .... 62 D8
Ringley Meadows. M26 .... 61 C7
Ringley Old Brow. M26 .... 61 C7
Ringley Pk. M45 .... 62 D8
Ringley Rd. Kearsley M26 ..... 61 C8
Ringley Rd. Kearsley M26 ..... 61 D8
Ringley Rd.
Whitefield M45 & M26 .... 62 C7
Ringley Rd W. M26 .... 61 E8
Ringley St. M9 .... 157 D8
Ringlow Ave. M27 .... 79 C7
Ringlow Park Rd. M27, M28 79 C7
Ringmer Dr. 4 M22 .... 121 C1
Ringmere Ct. 7 OL1 .... 153 E8
Ringmore Rd. SK7 .... 124 A2
Rings Cl. M35 .... 83 F6
Ringstead Cl. SK9 .... 131 D1
Ringstead Dr. M10 & M40 .. 159 C3
Ringstone. M25 .... 63 A3
Ringway Ave. WN7 .... 75 F8
Ringway Golf Cse. WA15 .. 120 C1
Ringway Gr. M33 .... 108 E2
Ringway Rd. M22 & M90 ..... 130 D7
Ringway Rd W. M22 & M90 130 D8
Ringway Trad Est. M22 ..... 130 E8
Ringwood Ave.
Droylsden M34 .... 84 C1
Ringwood Ave.
Hazel Grove SK7 .... 124 B1
Ringwood Ave. Hyde SK14 . 102 A1
Ringwood Ave.
M'ster M12 & M18 .... 99 B3
Ringwood Ave. Radcliffe M26 44 B1
Ringwood Ave.
Ramsbottom BL0 .... 11 A4
Ringwood Way. OL9 .... 152 C8
Rink St. M14 & M20 .... 110 D7
Ripley Ave. Bramhall SK8 ... 132 B5
Ripley Ave. Stockport SK2 .. 124 B4
Ripley Cl. Hazel Grove SK7 .. 133 E8
Ripley Cl. M'ster M4 .... 164 D8
Ripley Cres. M41 .... 94 F5
Ripley Dr. Leigh WN7 .... 75 F6
Ripley Dr. Wigan WN3 & WN5 54 C4
Ripley St. BL1 & BL2 .... 25 B4
Ripley Way. M34 .... 112 F8
Ripon Ave. Bolton BL1 .... 23 F1
Ripon Ave. Golborne WA3 ..... 90 D8
Ripon Ave. 1 Wigan WN6 ..... 37 B3
Ripon Cl. Alt'ham WA15 ..... 120 C1
Ripon Cl. Little Lever BL3 ..... 42 F3
Ripon Cl. Newton-l-W WA12 .. 89 C5
Ripon Cl. Oldham OL9 .... 152 B6
Ripon Cl. Radcliffe BL9 .... 44 D5
Ripon Cl. 5 Whitefield M45 .. 44 F2
Ripon Cres. M32 .... 95 F3
Ripon Dr. Ashton-i-M WN4 .... 73 D2
Ripon Dr. Bolton BL1 .... 23 F1
Ripon Gr. M33 .... 107 F6
Ripon Hall Ave. BL0 .... 11 B4
Ripon Rd. M32 .... 95 F3
Ripon St. Ashton-u-L OL6 .... 166 C3
Ripon St. M'ster M15 .... 163 A5
Ripon St. Oldham OL1 .... 153 D8
Ripon Wlk. SK6 .... 113 A1
Rippenden Ave. M21 .... 97 A2
Rippingham Rd. M20 .... 110 B7
Rippleton Rd. M22 .... 121 E4
Ripponden Rd. Denshaw OL3 33 D3
Ripponden Rd.
Oldham OL1 & OL4 .... 49 E3
Ripponden St. 11
OL1 & OL4 .... 49 C1
Ripton Wlk. M9 .... 64 B4
Risbury Wlk. 5 M40 .... 83 C6
Rise The. Oldham OL4 .... 67 F7
Rise The. Wigan WN6 .... 36 C3
Rises The. SK14 .... 103 F5
Rishton Ave. BL3 .... 147 F2
Rishton La. BL3 .... 147 F3
Rishworth Cl. SK2 .... 124 D5
Rishworth Dr. M40 .... 83 E8
Rishworth Rise. OL2 .... 32 A1
Rising La. OL8 .... 66 E2
Rising Lane Cl. OL8 .... 66 E2
Risley Ave. M9 .... 64 D1
Risley St. OL1 .... 153 F8
Rita Ave. 4 M14 .... 98 B3
Ritson Cl. M18 .... 165 B6
Riva Rd. M19 .... 110 D2
River La. M31 .... 105 F4
River Pl. Milnrow OL16 .... 31 F6
River Pl. M'ster M15 .... 162 E7
River St. Bolton BL2 .... 148 A6
River St. Heywood OL10 .... 29 D3
River St. M'ster M12 .... 162 F7
River St. M'ster M12 .... 163 C8
River St. R'dale OL16 .... 139 F7
River St. Radcliffe M26 .... 44 B2
River St. Ramsbottom BL0 ... 138 C6
River St. Stockport SK1 ..... 112 B3
River St. Wilmslow SK9 ...... 137 B8
River View. SK5 .... 112 A7
River View Cl. M25 .... 62 F2
River Way. WN1 .... 150 C8
Riverbank Dr. BL8 .... 140 D3
Riverbank Lawns. M3 .... 158 E3
Riverbank The. M26 .... 61 A8
Riverbank Tower. M3 .... 158 E3
Riverbank Way. SK13 .... 116 F7
Riverbank Wlk. M20 .... 109 E4
Riverdale Cl. WN6 .... 36 D4
Riverdale Rd. M9 .... 64 B3
Rivermead. OL16 .... 32 B3
Rivermead Ave. WA15 .... 129 C7
Rivermead Cl. M34 .... 113 A7
Rivermead Rd. M34 .... 113 B7
Riverpark Rd. M11 & M40 ..... 83 A3
Rivers La. M41 .... 95 C5
Rivers St. WN5 .... 53 E6
Riversdale Dr. OL8 .... 67 A1
Riversdale Rd. SK8 .... 122 C5
Riversdale View. SK6 .... 113 A5
Riversdole Ct. M25 .... 63 A3
Rivershill. M33 .... 108 A6
Rivershill Dr. OL10 .... 29 B1
Rivershill Gdns. WA15 .... 129 D6
Riverside. Bolton BL1 .... 25 A2
Riverside. Chadderton OL1 ..... 47 E1
Riverside. Dukinfield SK16 .. 166 C1
Riverside. M'ster M7 .... 158 D3
Riverside Ave. Irlam M44 ...... 94 B1
Riverside Ave. M'ster M21 . 109 D3
Riverside Ave. Wigan WN1 .... 37 D1
Riverside Bsns Pk. SK9 ..... 137 B7
Riverside Cl. SK13 .... 104 D1
Riverside Ct. M'ster M20 .... 109 F3
Riverside Ct. Whitworth OL12 . 4 D4
Riverside Dr. Kearsley M26 ... 61 B8
Riverside Dr.Ramsbottom BL0 11 B2
Riverside Dr. Urmston M41 .. 107 B8
Riverside Rd. M26 .... 44 D4
Riversleigh Cl. BL1 .... 23 F3
Riversmeade. Bolton BL2 ...... 25 C7
Riversmeade. Leigh WN7 ...... 76 A6
Riverstone Dr. M23 .... 120 D7
Riverton Rd. M20 .... 122 B8
Riverview Cotts. SK13 .... 116 C7
Riverview Ct. M7 .... 81 C8
Riviera Ct. OL11 .... 13 C2
Rivington. M6 .... 80 C5
Rivington Ave. Adlington PR6 21 B7
Rivington Ave. Golborne WA3 74 C1
Rivington Ave.
Pendlebury M27 .... 80 C8
Rivington Ave.
Platt Bridge WN2 .... 56 B3
Rivington Ave. Wigan WN1 .... 37 B2
Rivington & Blackrod
High Sch. BL6 .... 22 B6
Rivington & Blackrod High
Sch (Annexe). BL6 .... 22 B4
Rivington Cres. M27 .... 80 C7
Rivington Ct. M45 .... 62 C7
Rivington Dr. Bury BL8 .... 27 A1
Rivington Dr. Leigh WN2 ...... 74 F8
Rivington Dr. Orrell WN8 ...... 53 C7
Rivington Dr. Shaw OL2 .... 49 D7
Rivington Gr.
Droylsden M34 .... 100 C8
Rivington Gr. Irlam M44 ...... 105 D6
Rivington La. Adlington PR6 .. 21 D6
Rivington La. Horwich BL6 .... 22 A7
Rivington Pl. PR7 .... 19 D6
Rivington Rd. Alt'ham WA15 119 F2
Rivington Rd. Oldham OL4 .... 48 F2
Rivington Rd. Salford M6 ...... 80 C4
Rivington Service Area.
PR6 .... 21 E4
Rivington St. Atherton M46 ... 58 B2
Rivington St. Blackrod BL6 .... 21 D2
Rivington St. Oldham OL1 ..... 48 F1
Rivington St. R'dale OL12 ...... 14 F1
Rivington Way. WN6 .... 36 F8
Rivington Wlk. M12 .... 164 F5
Rix St. BL1 .... 143 E2
Rixson St. OL4 .... 49 D2
Rixton Ct. M16 .... 97 B3
Rixton Dr. M29 .... 77 B8
RL Hughes Prim Sch. WN4 . 73 A3
Roach Ct. M40 .... 159 C4
Roach Gn. WN1 .... 37 E1
Roach Pl. OL16 .... 31 A8
Roach St. Bury BL9 .... 44 F4
Roach St. Bury BL9 .... 141 C2
Roaches Mews. OL5 .... 68 D3
Roaches Way. OL5 .... 68 E3
Roachill Cl. WA14 .... 119 B5
Roachwood Cl. OL9 .... 65 E7
Road La. OL12 .... 14 D4
Roading Brook Rd. BL2 .... 26 B3
Roads Ford Ave. OL16 .... 31 F7
Roadside Ct. WA3 .... 90 C8
Roaring Gate La. WA15 .... 120 E2
Rob La. WA12 .... 89 E5
Robe Wlk. 5 M18 .... 99 D6
Robert Hall St. M5 .... 161 B8
Robert Lawrence Ct. M41 ..... 95 A1
Robert Malcolm Cl. M40 .. 157 D5
Robert Owen Gdns. M22 .. 121 D8
Robert Owen St. M43 .... 84 C2
Robert Saville Ct. OL11 .... 30 C6
Robert St. Bolton BL2 .... 25 E5
Robert St. Bury BL8 .... 27 C3
Robert St. Dukinfield SK16 .. 101 B8
Robert St. Dukinfield SK14 .. 101 C3
Robert St. 6 Failsworth M35 66 A1
Robert St. Heywood OL10 ..... 46 E8
Robert St. M'ster M10, M40 . 157 F5
Robert St. M'ster M3 .... 158 F3
Robert St. Oldham OL8 .... 66 B3
Robert St. Platt Bridge WN2 .. 56 A3
Robert St. Prestwich M25 ...... 63 C4
Robert St. 15 R'dale OL16 ..... 31 A8
Robert St. Radcliffe M26 ...... 44 A4
Robert St. Ramsbottom BL0 ..... 1 C1
Robert St. Sale M33 .... 108 E4
Robert St. Tyldesley M46 ..... 58 E1
Roberts Ave. M14 .... 98 B4
Roberts St. M30 .... 79 D1
Robertscroft Cl. M22 .... 121 C3
Robertshaw Ave. M21 .... 109 B6
Robertshaw St. WN7 .... 75 E7
Robertson St. M26 .... 44 A4
Robin Cl. BL4 .... 59 F7
Robin Croft. SK6 .... 112 D3
Robin Dr. M44 .... 94 A3
Robin Hill Dr. WN6 .... 19 B2
Robin Hill La. WN6 .... 19 C3
Robin Hood La. WN6 .... 18 B3
Robin Hood St. M7 .... 155 F8
Robin Park Rd. Wigan WN5 .. 54 F7
Robin Park Rd. Wigan WN5 150 A7
Robin Rd. BL0 .... 11 B3
Robin St. OL1 .... 153 E8
Robin's La. Billinge WA11 ..... 71 A8
Robin's La. Bramhall SK7 ... 132 D7
Robinia Cl. M30 .... 94 F8
Robins Cl. Bramhall SK7 .... 132 E7
Robins Cl. Droylsden M43 .... 84 C3
Robins La. WA3 .... 91 D2
Robinsbay Rd. M22 .... 130 E8
Robinson La. OL7 .... 84 F3
Robinson St.Ashton-u-L OL6 166 B4
Robinson St.Dukinfield SK15 101 E8
Robinson St. 15 Horwich BL6 22 B4
Robinson St. Hyde SK14 ..... 167 F3
Robinson St. Leigh WN7 .... 76 A4
Robinson St. Oldham OL9 .... 152 B6
Robinson St. R'dale OL16 ...... 31 A7
Robinson St. Stockport SK3 170 D7
Robinson St. 14
Tyldesley M29 .... 59 A1
Robinsway. WA14 .... 119 C1
Robinswood Rd. M22 .... 121 D2
Robinwood Lodge. SK13 ... 171 E1
Robson Ave. M41 .... 95 E7
Robson Pl. Abram WN2 .... 74 B8
Robson St. Oldham OL1 .... 67 A6
Robson St. Oldham OL1 ...... 153 F6
Roby Mill. WN8 .... 35 B3
Roby Mill CE Prim Sch.WN8 35 B3
Roby Rd. M30 .... 95 C8
Roby St. M1 .... 159 B1
Roby Well Way. WN5 .... 71 D5
Roch Ave. OL10 .... 29 A2
Roch Cl. M45 .... 45 B1
Roch Cres. M45 .... 45 C1
Roch Mills Cres. OL11 .... 30 C5
Roch Mills Gdns. OL11 ...... 139 D5
Roch Pl. WN2 .... 55 F2
Roch St. OL16 .... 15 B1
Roch Valley Way. OL11 .... 30 C5
Roch Way. M45 .... 45 B1
Roch Wlk. M45 .... 45 B1
Rochbury Cl. OL11 .... 29 F6
Rochdale Golf Cse. OL11 ..... 30 A8
Rochdale Ind Ctr. OL11 ..... 139 D6
Rochdale Infmy. OL12 .... 14 F1
Rochdale La. Heywood OL10 . 29 D2
Rochdale La. Royton OL2 ..... 48 D5
Rochdale Old Rd. BL9 .... 28 D4
Rochdale Rd. Bacup OL13 ...... 4 B8
Rochdale Rd. Bury BL9 ...... 141 B2
Rochdale Rd.
Denshaw OL2 & OL3 .... 33 C3
Rochdale Rd. Edenfield BL0 ..... 1 F2
Rochdale Rd. Heywood OL10 29 D2
Rochdale Rd.
Littleborough HX6 & OL15 .... 7 E1
Rochdale Rd. M'ster M9 ...... 64 D3
Rochdale Rd.
M'ster M40, M8, M9 .... 157 D6
Rochdale Rd.
Middleton M24 &OL11 .... 47 C4
Rochdale Rd. Milnrow OL16 .. 31 E7
Rochdale Rd. Oldham OL1 ..... 48 E1
Rochdale Rd.
Oldham OL1 & OL9 .... 153 E8
Rochdale Rd.
Ramsbottom BL0 & BL9 .... 12 B7
Rochdale Rd. Royton OL2 ..... 48 D6
Rochdale Rd.
Shaw OL2 & OL16 .... 48 F8
Rochdale Rd. Shaw OL2 ..... 149 B7
Rochdale Rd.
Walsden OL14 & OL15 .... 6 B6
Rochdale Rd E. OL10 & OL11 29 F3
Rochdale Sta. OL11 .... 139 F6
Roche Gdns. SK8 .... 132 B6
Roche Rd. OL3 .... 50 E5
Rochester Ave. Bolton BL2 ..... 25 E1
Rochester Ave. M'ster M25 .. 63 C2
Rochester Ave. Walkden M28 60 C1
Rochester Cl. Ashton-u-L OL6 85 C7
Rochester Cl.
Dukinfield SK16 .... 102 A7
Rochester Cl. Golborne WA3 . 90 A8
Rochester Dr. WA14 .... 107 E1
Rochester Gr. SK7 .... 124 E3
Rochester Rd. M41 .... 95 D4
Rochester Way. OL9 .... 152 B6
Rochford Ave.Whitefield M45 62 D7
Rochford Ave.
Wythenshawe M22 .... 130 D8
Rochford Cl. M45 .... 62 D7
Rochford House. M34 .... 100 E6
Rochford Rd. M30 .... 94 F8
Rock Ave. BL1 .... 142 C2
Rock Fold. BL7 .... 8 F1
Rock Gdns. SK14 .... 113 E7
Rock House Prim Sch.
M23 .... 109 A1
Rock Nook. OL15 .... 6 D1
Rock Rd. Boothstown M28 ..... 78 B2
Rock Rd. Urmston M41 .... 95 F2
Rock St. Ashton-u-L OL7 ...... 85 A5
Rock St. Droylsden M11 .... 99 E8
Rock St. Golborne WA3 .... 74 A2
Rock St. 3 Heywood OL10 ..... 29 E1
Rock St. Horwich BL6 .... 22 B3
Rock St. Hyde SK14 .... 113 E7
Rock St. M'ster M7 .... 155 D6
Rock St. Oldham OL1 .... 153 F7
Rock St. Radcliffe M26 .... 44 B2
Rock St. Ramsbottom BL0 ...... 11 E7
Rock Terr. Bolton BL7 .... 8 D3
Rock Terr. Mossley OL5 .... 68 D3
Rock The. Bury BL9 .... 140 E2
Rock The. Bury BL9 .... 140 F3
Rockall Wlk. M11 .... 160 F1
Rockbourne Cl. WN2 .... 56 D4
Rockcliffe Villas. OL13 .... 3 E8
Rockdove Ave. M15 .... 162 F7
Rockfield Dr. 5 M9 .... 157 E8
Rockhampton St. M18 .... 99 E5
Rockhaven Ave. BL6 .... 22 C4
Rockhouse Cl. M30 .... 95 C8
Rockingham Cl.M'ster M12 164 D6
Rockingham Cl. Shaw OL2 .... 48 E8
Rockland Wlk. 6 M40 .... 65 C2
Rockley Gdns. M6 .... 81 B4
Rocklyn Ave. M40 .... 65 C2
Rocklynes. SK6 .... 113 B2
Rockmead Dr. M9 .... 64 E3
Rocky Bank Terr. WN3 .... 151 E5
Rocky La. M27 & M30 .... 79 D4
Roda St. M9 .... 157 F7
Rodborough Rd. M23 .... 121 A3
Rodeheath Cl. SK9 .... 137 D7
Rodenhurst Dr. 14 M40 .... 83 A7
Rodepool Cl. SK9 .... 131 D2
Rodgers Cl. BL5 .... 57 E6
Rodgers Way. BL5 .... 57 E6
Rodmell Ave. M10 & M40 ... 157 D5
Rodmell Cl. BL7 .... 24 F7
Rodmill Ct. M14 .... 98 C1

Rodmill Dr. SK8 122 A4
Rodney Ct. 10 M40 159 C3
Rodney Dr. SK6 113 A5
Rodney St. Ashton-u-L OL6 85 D4
Rodney St. Atherton M46 58 C2
Rodney St. M'ster M3 158 D1
Rodney St. M'ster M40 159 C2
Rodney St. R'dale OL11 30 B2
Rodney St. Wigan WN1 150 C7
Roe Cross Gn. SK14 102 F5
Roe Cross Ind Est. SK14 103 A5
Roe Cross Rd.
Stalybridge SK14 102 F5
Roe Gn. M28 79 A8
Roe Green Ave. M28 79 A8
Roe La. OL4 67 D5
Roe St. M'ster M4 159 C3
Roe St. R'dale OL12 14 C1
Roeacre St. OL10 29 E2
Roebuck La. Oldham OL4 50 A3
Roebuck La. Sale M33 108 A4
Roebuck St. WN2 57 C3
Roeburn Wlk.
Platt Bridge WN2 55 F2
Roeburn Wlk. Whitefield M45 63 C8
Roecliffe Cl. WN3 150 B6
Roedean Gdns. M41 94 D2
Roefield Terr. OL11 & OL12 30 C8
Rogate Dr. M23 121 A5
Roger Byrne Cl. M40 83 B5
Roger Cl. SK6 112 F2
Roger Hay. SK8 123 A2
Roger St. M8 159 A3
Rogerstead. BL3 144 C6
Rogerton Cl. WN7 76 B4
Rokeby Ave. Golborne WA3 74 D1
Rokeby Ave. Stretford M32 96 D1
Rokeden. WA12 89 D4
Roker Ave. M13 98 F2
Roker Ind Est. OL1 67 B7
Roker Park Ave. M34 100 D7
Roland Rd. 2 Bolton BL3 146 C4
Roland Rd. Reddish SK5 111 F7
Rolla St. M3 158 E2
Rollesby Cl. BL8 27 D5
Rolleston Ave. M10 & M40 160 D2
Rollins La. SK6 114 A1
Rolls Cres. M15 162 E5
Rollswood Dr. M40 83 A6
Roman Cl. Newton-l-W WA12 89 C2
Roman Cl. Wigan WN3 54 F4
Roman Ct. M7 155 D5
Roman Rd. Ashton-i-M WN4 73 A5
Roman Rd. M'ster M25 63 A1
Roman Rd.Oldham M35 & OL8 66 B1
Roman Rd. Royton OL2 48 E3
Roman Rd. Stockport SK4 169 E2
Roman St. M'ster M4 & M60 159 A2
Roman St. Mossley OL5 68 D3
Roman St. Radcliffe M26 43 E3
Rome Rd. M40 159 C3
Romer Ave. M40 65 E1
Romer St. BL2 148 C7
Romford Ave.
Dukinfield M34 101 A4
Romford Ave. Leigh WN7 75 F6
Romford Cl. OL8 153 E5
Romford Pl. WN2 56 E5
Romford Rd. M33 107 E6
Romford St. WN2 56 E5
Romford Wlk. M9 64 A3
Romiley Cres. BL2 42 D8
Romiley Dr. Bolton BL2 42 D8
Romiley dr. Bolton BL2 148 B8
Romiley Golf Course. SK6 113 F4
Romiley Prec. SK6 113 C2
Romiley Prim Sch. SK6 113 C2
Romiley Sq. WN6 36 E8
Romiley St. Salford M6 80 B5
Romiley St. Stockport SK1 112 B3
Romiley Sta. SK6 113 C2
Romley Rd. M41 95 D4
Romney Ave. OL11 30 F2
Romney Rd. BL1 23 E2
Romney St. Ashton-u-L OL6 166 C3
Romney St. M'ster M40 83 A8
Romney St. Salford M6 81 B5
Romney Towers. SK5 112 B6
Romney Way.
Brinnington SK5 112 B6
Romney Way. Wigan WN1 37 B3
Romney Wlk. OL9 152 B6
Romsey. 9 OL12 139 E8
Romsey Ave. M24 46 F3
Romsey Dr. SK8 132 C6
Romsey Gdns. M23 121 A6
Romsey Gr. WN3 54 D2
Romsley Cl. M12 165 A6
Romsley Dr. BL3 146 C3
Rona Wlk. M12 164 E5
Ronald St. Droylsden M43 83 D1
Ronald St. Oldham OL4 67 C7
Ronald St. R'dale OL11 30 C1
Ronaldsay Gdns. M5 & M6 154 E1
Rondin Cl. M12 164 E7
Rondin Rd. M12 164 E8
Ronnis Mount. OL7 85 A7
Ronton Wlk. M8 156 C8
Roocroft Ct. BL1 143 D4
Roocroft Sq. BL6 21 C2
Rooden Ct. M25 63 C4
Roods La. OL11 13 C1
Rook Hill Rd. 2 OL13 3 B8
Rook St. Oldham OL4 67 C6
Rook St. Ramsbottom BL0 138 C6
Rooke St. M30 95 A8
Rookery Ave.
Appley Bridge WN6 35 E8
Rookery Ave.Ashton-i-M WN4 73 B2
Rookery Ave. Droylsden M18 99 F6
Rookery Cl. SK15 102 E7
Rookery The. WA12 89 D4
Rookerypool Cl. SK9 131 D2
Rookfield. M33 108 C5
Rookfield Ave. M33 108 C5
Rookley Wlk. 11 M14 98 C3
Rookswood Dr. OL11 30 B3
Rookway. Middleton M24 65 A7
Rookwood. OL1 & OL9 47 E1
Rookwood Ave. M23 120 F7
Rookwood Hill. SK7 123 E1
Rooley Moor Rd.
Bacup OL12 & OL13 3 C4
Rooley Moor Rd.R'dale OL12 14 A3
Rooley Moor Rd.R'dale OL12 14 C1
Rooley St. OL11 & OL12 14 C1
Roosevelt Rd. BL4 60 F7
Rooth St. SK4 169 D2
Rope St. OL12 139 F8
Rope Wlk. M3 158 E3
Ropewalk The. WN7 75 E4
Ropley Wlk. 4 M9 64 F1
Rosa Gr. M7 155 D6
Rosalind Ct. M5 161 C8
Rosamond Dr. M3 158 D2
Rosamond St. BL3 146 C4
Rosamond St W. M15 163 A6
Rosary Rd. OL8 67 A1
Roscoe Ave. WA12 89 E3
Roscoe Ct. BL5 57 F7
Roscoe Lowe Brow. PR6 21 D7
Roscoe Pk Est. WA14 119 E8
Roscoe Rd. Irlam M44 93 E1
Roscoe Rd. Irlam M44 105 F8
Roscoe St. Oldham OL1 67 A6
Roscoe St. Stockport SK3 170 D8
Roscoe St. Wigan WN1 151 E7
Roscow Ave. BL2 42 E8
Roscow Fold Prim Sch. BL2 42 E8
Roscow Rd. BL4 61 A7
Rose Acre. M28 78 B7
Rose Ave. Abram WN2 74 B7
Rose Ave. Farnworth BL4 42 C1
Rose Ave. Irlam M44 93 F1
Rose Ave. Littleborough OL15 15 F3
Rose Ave. R'dale OL11 13 D2
Rose Ave. Wigan WN6 37 A4
Rose Bank Cl.
Hollingworth SK14 103 D5
Rose Bank Cl. Wigan WN1 37 B4
Rose Bridge High Sch.
WN1 151 F8
Rose Cottage Rd. M14 110 B8
Rose Cotts. 11 M14 110 D8
Rose Cres. M44 93 F1
Rose Gr. Bury BL8 27 A2
Rose Gr. Kearsley BL4 60 F7
Rose Hey La. M35 & M40 83 E4
Rose Hill. Bolton BL2 & BL3 148 A5
Rose Hill. Delph OL3 50 F4
Rose Hill. Denton M34 100 E3
Rose Hill. Ramsbottom BL0 138 B6
Rose Hill. Stalybridge SK15 102 A8
Rose Hill Ave.Failsworth M40 83 B4
Rose Hill Ave. Wigan WN5 54 C6
Rose Hill Cl. Ashton-u-L OL6 85 F5
Rose Hill Cl. Bolton BL7 25 A7
Rose Hill Cres. OL6 85 F5
Rose Hill Dr. BL7 25 A7
Rose Hill Rd. OL6 85 F5
Rose Hill St. OL10 29 B2
Rose Hill Sta. SK6 125 E6
Rose Hill View. WN4 72 F7
Rose La. SK6 125 E6
Rose Lea. BL2 25 E4
Rose Leigh. M41 95 D2
Rose Mount. M24 46 F2
Rose St. Bolton BL2 & BL3 148 A5
Rose St. Hindley WN2 56 D5
Rose St. Middleton M24 65 C8
Rose St. Oldham OL9 66 A3
Rose St. Stockport SK5 169 F3
Rose St. Wigan WN1 151 F8
Rose Terr. SK15 86 A1
Rose Thorns Cl. M24 46 F4
Rose Vale. SK8 122 B1
Rose Wlk. Marple SK6 125 E6
Rose Wlk. 5 Partington M31 105 E3
Rose Wood. M34 100 D3
Roseacre Cl. BL2 148 C8
Roseacre Dr. SK8 122 C1
Rosebank. BL6 40 C7
Rosebank Cl. BL2 26 C1
Rosebank Rd. Failsworth M40 83 B4
Rosebank Rd. Irlam M44 105 C4
Roseberry Ave. 4 OL1 49 B1
Roseberry Cl. BL0 11 C3
Roseberry Rd. WN4 73 A5
Roseberry St. Bolton BL3 146 C4
Roseberry St. Oldham OL8 153 D6
Rosebery St. M'ster M14 97 F3
Rosebery St. Stockport SK2 124 D4
Rosebury St.
Westhoughton BL5 57 F8
Rosebury Ave. WN7 76 B5
Rosebury Gr. WN7 76 B6
Rosecroft Cl. SK3 123 E4
Rosecroft Prep Sch. M20 110 B3
Rosecroft Sch. M20 110 B2
Rosedale Ave. Atherton M46 58 D3
Rosedale Ave. Bolton BL1 24 E5
Rosedale Ave. Golborne WA3 90 C7
Rosedale Cl. OL1 49 B1
Rosedale Ct. M34 100 E3
Rosedale Dr. WN7 76 C5
Rosedale Rd. M'ster M14 98 A2
Rosedale Rd. Reddish SK4 169 D4
Rosedale Way. SK16 101 C6
Rosefield Cres. OL16 31 C7
Rosegarth Ave. M20 109 D4
Rosegate Cl. M16 97 F3
Rosehay Ave. M34 100 F2
Rosehill Cl. M6 154 F2
Rosehill Ct. Oldham OL4 67 E8
Rosehill Ct. Salford M6 154 F2
Rosehill Rd. M27 61 F2
Rosehill Sch. WN4 72 F7
Roseland Ave. M20 110 B4
Roseland Dr. M25 63 C6
Roselands Ave. M33 107 F2
Roseleigh Ave. M19 110 F7
Rosemary Cres. WN1 37 D2
Rosemary Dr. Hyde SK14 113 D7
Rosemary Dr.
Littleborough OL15 15 F6
Rosemary Dr.
Newton-l-W WA12 89 F3
Rosemary Gr. M7 81 C5
Rosemary La. Atherton BL5 59 B6
Rosemary La. Stockport SK1 112 A1
Rosemary Wlk. M31 105 F2
Rosemead Ct. 5 SK5 111 F6
Rosemount. SK14 101 D5
Rosemount Cres. SK14 101 D5
Rosen Sq. OL9 152 B7
Roseneath Ave. M19 99 C1
Roseneath Gr. BL3 147 D3
Roseneath Rd. Bolton BL3 147 D3
Roseneath Rd. Urmston M41 95 C2
Rosette Wlk. 3 M27 79 F7
Rosevale Ave. M19 110 E5
Roseway. SK7 123 F2
Rosewell Cl. M10 & M40 160 D4
Rosewood. R'dale OL11 13 E1
Rosewood.Westhoughton BL5 57 D6
Rosewood Ave.
Droylsden M43 84 C3
Rosewood Ave.
Stockport SK4 168 A1
Rosewood Cl. Abram WN2 74 B7
Rosewood Cl.
Dukinfield SK16 101 D6
Rosewood Cres. OL9 48 B1
Rosewood Wlk. M23 120 C8
Rosford Ave. M14 98 B2
Rosgill Cl. SK4 110 E2
Rosgill Wlk. M18 165 C5
Rosina Cl. WN4 72 F6
Rosina St. M11 & M18 99 F7
Rosley Rd. WN3 55 B3
Roslin Gdns. BL1 142 C3
Roslin St. M11 83 D2
Roslyn Ave. M41 94 E1
Roslyn Rd. SK3 170 E5
Ross Ave. M'ster M19 98 F1
Ross Ave. Oldham OL9 65 F4
Ross Ave. Stockport SK3 170 E5
Ross Ave. Whitefield M45 62 F6
Ross Cl. Billinge WN5 71 E6
Ross Cl. Wigan WN2 37 F2
Ross Dr. M27 61 E4
Ross Gr. M41 95 C2
Ross Lave La. Denton M34 100 C1
Ross St. OL8 153 D5
Rossall Ave. 5 Radcliffe M26 44 C3
Rossall Ave. Stretford M32 96 C3
Rossall Cl. BL2 148 C8
Rossall Cres. WN7 76 A3
Rossall Dr. SK7 132 E6
Rossall Rd. Bolton BL2 148 C8
Rossall Rd. R'dale OL12 15 A2
Rossall St. 1 BL2 148 C8
Rossall Way. M6 81 A3
Rossdale Gr. WN6 37 A2
Rossenclough Rd. SK9 131 D1
Rossendale Ave. 6 M9 64 F1
Rossendale Cl. OL2 49 D7
Rossendale Golf Cse. BB4 1 B7
Rossendale Rd. SK8 131 C8
Rossendale Sch. BL0 12 A7
Rossendale Way. OL2 149 B8
Rossett Ave. Sale WA15 120 A8
Rossett Ave. 1
Wythenshawe M22 130 D8
Rossett Cl. WN3 54 D2
Rossett Dr. M41 95 A4
Rossetti Wlk. 2 M34 113 A7
Rosshill Wlk. 26 M15 162 D6
Rossington St. M40 83 D5
Rossini St. BL1 143 D3
Rosslare Rd. M22 121 E2
Rosslove Wlk. SK5 112 C7
Rosslyn Gr. WA15 120 A6
Rosslyn Rd. Cheadle SK8 122 D1
Rosslyn Rd. M'ster M40 65 A1
Rosslyn Rd. M'ster M16 97 A2
Rossmere Ave. OL11 30 C6
Rossmill La. WA15 129 B7
Rostherne Ave.
Golborne WA3 90 D8
Rostherne Ave.
High Lane SK6 134 E8
Rostherne Ave. M'ster M16 97 C3
Rostherne Ave. M'ster M14 98 A1
Rostherne Ct. WA14 119 D3
Rostherne Gdns. BL3 146 B4
Rostherne Rd. Sale M33 108 F3
Rostherne Rd.Stockport SK3 170 E5
Rostherne Rd.Wilmslow SK9 136 F4
Rostherne St. 1
Alt'ham WA14 119 D3
Rostherne St. 1 Salford M6 154 E1
Rosthernmere Rd. SK8 122 F4
Rosthwaite Cl.Middleton M24 46 C1
Rosthwaite Cl. Wigan WN3 55 A2
Rosthwaite Gr. WA11 71 B1
Roston Ct. M7 155 E8
Roston Rd. M7 155 E8
Rostrevor Rd. SK3 170 E5
Rostron Ave. M12 164 E6
Rostron Rd. BL0 138 B6
Rostron St. 6 M19 99 B1
Rothay Cl. BL2 25 F1
Rothay Dr. Middleton M24 46 E3
Rothay Dr. Reddish SK5 111 F8
Rothay St. WN7 76 B4
Rothbury Ave. OL7 84 E5
Rothbury Cl. BL8 26 F2
Rothbury Ct. BL3 146 B3
Rotherby Rd. M22 121 E5
Rotherdale Ave. WA15 120 D5
Rothermere Wlk. 5 M23 120 F7
Rotherwood Ave. M32 96 E3
Rotherwood Rd. SK9 136 D6
Rothesay Ave. SK16 101 C7
Rothesay Cres. M33 107 C2
Rothesay Rd. Bolton BL3 146 B3
Rothesay Rd. M'ster M8 63 E2
Rothesay Rd. Oldham OL1 49 C1
Rothesay Rd.Pendlebury M27 80 D7
Rothesay Terr. OL16 31 C4
Rothiemay Rd. M41 94 E2
Rothley Ave. M22 121 D5
Rothman Cl. M40 83 C6
Rothwell Cres. M38 59 E5
Rothwell La. M38 59 E5
Rothwell Rd. Adlington PR6 21 B7
Rothwell Rd. Golborne WA3 74 C1
Rothwell St. Bolton BL3 145 E5
Rothwell St. Failsworth M40 83 C6
Rothwell St. Failsworth M35 83 F7
Rothwell St. R'dale OL12 15 B1
Rothwell St.
Ramsbottom BL0 138 B6
Rothwell St. Royton OL2 48 D3
Rothwell St. Walkden M28 60 F3
Rottingdene Dr. 3 M22 121 C1
Rough Hill La. BL9 28 E4
Roughey Gdns. M22 121 D4
Roughlea Ave. WA3 91 D4
Roughlee Ave. M27 79 D7
Roughtown Rd. OL5 68 D2
Round Hey. OL5 86 C8
Round Hill Cl. SK13 171 F3
Round House Ave. WN1 37 E1
Round Thorn Rd. M24 65 B7
Roundcroft. SK6 113 E3
Roundham Wlk. 27 M9 157 E8
Roundhey. SK8 131 C8
Roundhill Way. OL4 49 E1
Roundmoor Rd. WN6 37 A7
Roundthorn Bsns Pk. M23 120 E5
Roundthorn Ct. M23 120 F7
Roundthorn Ind Est. M23 120 E6
Roundthorn La. BL5 57 E7
Roundthorn Prim Sch. OL4 67 C5
Roundthorn Rd.
Oldham OL4 & OL8 67 C5
Roundthorn Rd.
Wythenshawe M23 120 F6
Roundthorn Wlk. 9 M23 120 F6
Roundway. SK7 132 D6
Roundwood Rd. M22 121 D7
Roundwood Upper Sch.
M22 121 D7
Rousdon Cl. M40 157 D5
Rouse Cl. M11 160 F1
Rouse St. OL11 30 C4
Routledge Wlk. M9 157 E8
Rowan Ave. Golborne WA3 90 F7
Rowan Ave. 2 Horwich BL6 22 E1
Rowan Ave. M'ster M16 97 D3
Rowan Ave. Sale M33 108 C2
Rowan Ave. Urmston M41 95 D3
Rowan Ave. Wigan WN6 36 F3
Rowan Cl. Failsworth M35 83 F6
Rowan Cl. R'dale OL12 14 B3
Rowan Cl. 6 Salford M6 81 A2
Rowan Cres. SK16 101 F7
Rowan Ct. SK14 167 E1
Rowan Dr. SK8 132 C8
Rowan Lodge. SK7 132 F7
Rowan Pl. M25 63 B3
Rowan St. SK14 167 F1
Rowan Tree Dr. M33 108 B1
Rowan Tree Rd. OL8 66 D1
Rowan Wlk. Hadfield SK14 171 E4
Rowan Wlk. Partington M31 105 E2
Rowanhill. WN1 37 D1
Rowans St. BL8 27 C4
Rowans The. Bolton BL1 40 F7
Rowans The. Mossley OL5 68 D1
Rowanside Dr. SK9 137 E8
Rowanswood Dr. SK14 102 A3
Rowanwood. M24 & OL9 65 E7
Rowany Cl. M25 63 A2
Rowarth Ave. Denton M34 113 A8
Rowarth Ave. 10
Gamesley SK13 171 D2
Rowarth Bank. 5 SK13 171 D2
Rowarth Cl. 6 SK13 171 D2
Rowarth Fold. 9 SK13 171 D2
Rowarth Rd.
Wythenshawe M23 120 F2
Rowarth Rd.
Wythenshawe M22 & M23 121 A2
Rowarth Way. 8 SK13 171 D2
Rowbotham St. SK14 113 E8
Rowbottom Sq. WN1 150 C8
Rowbottom Wlk. OL8 153 E5
Rowcon Cl. M34 100 E6
Rowdell Wlk. M23 109 B2
Rowden Rd. OL4 67 E4
Rowe Gn. M34 100 F2
Rowe St. M29 77 B8
Rowell Sq. M3 158 D2
Rowell St. M3 158 D2
Rowena St. BL3 42 C2
Rowendale St. M1 162 F8
Rowfield Dr. M23 120 F3
Rowland Ave. M41 95 E3
Rowland Ct. 17 OL16 31 B6
Rowland St. Atherton M46 58 D2
Rowland St. Atherton M46 58 D3
Rowland St. 18 R'dale OL16 31 B6
Rowland St. Salford M5 161 A8
Rowland Way. OL4 67 E7
Rowlands Rd. BL9 11 D2
Rowlandsway. M22 121 D2
Rowley Rd. SK7 133 E8
Rowley St. OL6 85 D6
Rowood Ave. M'ster M8 156 B6
Rowood Ave. Reddish SK5 99 F2
Rowrah Cres. M24 46 C1
Rowsley Ave. Bolton BL1 142 A1
Rowsley Ave. M'ster M20 109 E4
Rowsley Cl. 27 SK13 171 E2
Rowsley Gn. 29 SK13 171 E2
Rowsley Gr. 30
Gamesley SK13 171 E2
Rowsley Gr. Reddish SK5 111 E7
Rowsley Mews. SK13 171 E2
Rowsley Rd. Eccles M30 95 C8
Rowsley Rd. Stretford M32 96 A3
Rowsley St. M'ster M11 160 F1
Rowsley St. Salford M6 81 B5
Rowsley Wlk. 28 SK13 171 E2
Rowson Dr. M44 105 D6
Rowton Rise. WN1 37 B8
Rowton St. BL2 25 B3
Roxalina St. BL3 147 E4
Roxburgh St. 5 M18 99 D5
Roxbury Ave. OL4 67 D5
Roxby Cl. M28 60 B3
Roxby Dr. 18 M40 65 D2
Roxholme Wlk. M22 130 C8
Roxton Cl. BL6 22 B5
Roxton Rd. SK4 111 C6
Roxwell Wlk. 8 M9 157 D8
Roy Grainger Ct. 10 M16 97 E3
Roy House. OL2 48 D6
Roy St. Bolton BL3 146 B4
Roy St. Royton OL2 48 D4
Royal Arc. 5 WN1 150 C8
Royal Ave. Bury BL9 27 F5
Royal Ave. Droylsden M43 84 B2
Royal Ave. Heywood OL10 29 D1
Royal Ave. M'ster M21 109 A8
Royal Ave. Urmston M41 95 D2
Royal Dr. WN7 76 E6
Royal Eye Hospl. M13 163 B5
Royal George Cotts. OL3 68 E5
Royal George St. SK1 & SK3 170 F8
Royal Manchester
Children's Hospl. M27 80 C7
Royal Northern Coll of
Music. M15 163 A6
Royal Oak Prim Sch. M23 121 A7
Royal Oak Rd. M23 121 A7
Royal Oak Yd. SK1 169 F1
Royal Oldham Hospl The.
OL1 48 D1
Royal Rd. SK12 135 D5
Royal School for the
Deaf The. SK8 131 D6
Royal St. OL16 15 C3
Royalthorn Ave. M22 121 D6
Royalthorn Dr. M22 121 C6
Royalthorn Rd. M22 121 D6
Royce Ave. WA15 119 E5
Royce Ct. 22 M15 162 D6
Royce Prim Sch. M15 162 E5
Royce Rd. M15 162 E6
Royce Trad Est. M17 95 F7
Royd St. OL8 66 C4
Roydale St. M10 & M40 160 E3
Royden Ave. Irlam M44 105 F8
Royden Ave. M'ster M9 64 D5
Royden Ave. Wigan WN3 55 A2
Royden Cres. WN5 71 E5
Royden Rd. WN5 71 E5
Roydes St. M24 47 B2
Royds Cl. M12 & M13 164 D5
Royds Pl. 16 OL16 31 A5
Royds Rd. OL13 3 A7
Royds St. Bury BL8 26 F7
Royds St. Bury BL9 28 D4
Royds St. Littleborough OL15 16 C5
Royds St. Milnrow OL16 32 A5
Royds St. R'dale OL16 31 B5
Royds St W. OL11 & OL16 31 A5
Royland Ave. BL3 42 A3
Royland Ct. BL3 147 F3
Royle Ave. SK13 104 D1
Royle Barn Rd. OL11 30 C3
Royle Cl. Oldham OL8 66 F3
Royle Cl. Stockport SK2 124 A5
Royle Green Rd. M22 121 E8
Royle Pennine Trad Est.
OL11 30 D3
Royle Rd. OL11 30 D3
Royle St. Denton M34 100 F5
Royle St. M'ster M14 110 D7
Royle St. Salford M6 154 F1
Royle St. Stockport SK1 170 F8
Royle St. Walkden M28 60 D2
Roylelands Bglws. OL11 30 C3
Royley. OL2 48 C3
Royley Carr Flats. SK6 113 A3
Royley Cres. OL2 48 C3
Royley House. OL2 48 C3
Royley Rd. OL8 66 E4
Royley Way. OL2 48 C3
Roynton Rd. BL6 22 B7
Royon Dr. SK3 123 B7
Royston Ave. Bolton BL2 148 C8
Royston Ave. M'ster M16 97 D3
Royston Ave. Reddish M34 100 A3
Royston Cl. Golborne WA3 90 E8
Royston Cl. Ramsbottom BL8 10 F1
Royston Ct. 5 M16 97 D3
Royston Rd. M'ster M16 97 D3
Royston Rd. Urmston M41 95 E3
Royton Ave. M33 108 E2
Royton & Crompton Sch.
OL2 49 A4
Royton Hall Wlk. OL2 48 E4
Royton Junction Sta. OL1 49 A1
Rozel Sq. M3 162 E8
Ruabon Cres. Hindley WN2 57 A4
Ruabon Rd. M20 110 C2
Rubens Cl. SK6 126 C8
Rubens Rd. SK6 126 C8
Ruby Gr. WN7 75 E4
Ruby St. Bolton BL1 143 F3
Ruby St. Denton M34 100 E3
Ruby St. Ramsbottom BL0, BL9 11 C3
Rudcroft Cl. M13 163 B6
Rudd St. M40 83 A7
Rudding St. OL1 & OL2 49 A2
Ruddpark Rd. M22 121 D1
Rudford Ave. M11 99 E8
Rudford Gdns. BL1 147 F4
Rudgwick Dr. BL8 27 C7
Rudheath Ave. M20 110 A7
Rudman Dr. M5 161 C8
Rudman St. OL12 14 E2
Rudolph St. BL3 147 F3
Rudston Ave. M40 65 B2
Rudyard Ave. Middleton M24 47 C3
Rudyard Ave. Standish WN6 19 E2
Rudyard Gr. R'dale OL11 30 F2
Rudyard Gr. Reddish SK4 111 D6
Rudyard Gr. Sale M33 107 E2
Rudyard Rd. M6 80 C5
Rudyard St. M7 155 D6
Rufford Ave. Hyde SK14 167 F2
Rufford Ave. R'dale OL11 30 D4
Rufford Cl. Ashton-u-L OL6 85 C7
Rufford Cl. Shaw OL2 48 F7
Rufford Cl.
Whitefield BL9 & M45 45 A2
Rufford Dr. Bolton BL3 147 D2
Rufford Dr. Whitefield M45 44 F2
Rufford Gr. BL3 147 D2
Rufford Pl. Reddish M18 99 F4
Rufford Pl. Tyldesley M29 76 F4
Rufford Rd. M16 97 D3
Rufford St. 4 WN4 72 F5
Rufus St. M14 110 E7
Rugby Dr. Orrell WN5 53 F8
Rugby Dr. Sale M33 108 A2
Rugby Rd. Eccles M6 80 A3
Rugby Rd. Leigh WN7 75 F3
Rugby Rd. R'dale OL12, OL16 15 A1
Rugby Rd Ind Est. OL16 15 A1
Rugby St. M7 & M8 158 E4
Rugeley St. M6 81 B5
Ruins La. BL2 25 E4
Ruislip Ave. M10, M40, M9 157 E5
Ruislip Cl. OL8 67 B4
Rumbles La. OL3 50 B3
Rumbold St. 6 M'ster M18 99 E6
Rumbold St. R'dale OL11 139 F5
Rumford St. M13 163 B5
Rumworth Rd. BL6 40 C6
Rumworth St. BL3 147 D4
Runcorn St. M15 161 C7
Runger La. M22, M90, WA15 129 F8
Runhall Cl. M12 165 A6
Running Hill Farm. OL3 51 D2
Running Hill Gate. OL3 51 D1
Running Hill La. OL3 51 D2
Runnymeade. M6 80 B5
Runnymede Cl. SK3 123 C6
Runnymede Ct. Bolton BL3 145 D5
Runnymede Ct. Royton OL2 48 E4
Runnymede Ct.
Stockport SK3 123 C6
Runshaw Ave. WN6 35 E8
Rupert St. Bolton BL3 147 F3
Rupert St. Failsworth M40 83 E4
Rupert St. R'dale OL12 14 C1
Rupert St. Radcliffe M26 44 B1
Rupert St. Reddish SK5 111 E7
Rupert St. Wigan WN1 151 E7
Rupert Terr. 5 SK5 111 E7
Rush Acre Cl. M26 43 E3
Rush Bank. OL2 48 F8
Rush Gr. OL3 69 B7
Rush Hill Rd. OL3 69 B7
Rush Mount. Shaw OL2 48 F8
Rush Mount. Shaw OL2 149 A8
Rush St. SK16 101 F8
Rushall Wlk. WA15 120 F2
Rushbrooke Ave. 1 M11 83 C2
Rushbury Dr. OL2 49 A4
Rushcroft Ct. M9 65 A2
Rushcroft Prim Sch. OL2 149 B8
Rushcroft Rd. OL2 48 F8
Rushden Rd. M19 99 B2
Rushdene. WN3 55 B4
Rushen St. 4 M11 83 C1
Rushes The. SK14 171 F4
Rushey Ave. M22 121 C6
Rushey Cl. WA15 129 D7
Rushey Field. BL7 24 F8
Rushey Fold Ct. 24 BL1 143 D2
Rushey Fold La. BL1 143 D2
Rushey Rd. M22 121 C6
Rushfield Dr. M13 98 F3
Rushfield Rd. SK8 132 A6
Rushford Ave. M19 99 A2
Rushford Ct. 1 M19 99 A2
Rushford Gr. BL1 143 F4
Rushford St. M12 99 A3
Rushgreen Rd. WA13 117 A4
Rushill Terr. OL3 69 B7
Rushlake Dr. BL1 143 E1
Rushley Ave. M7 81 B7
Rushmere. OL6 85 E6
Rushmere Ave. M19 99 B1
Rushmere Dr. BL8 27 C5
Rushmere Wlk. M16 162 D5
Rushmoor Ave. WN4 73 E4
Rushmoor Cl. M44 94 A2
Rusholme Gdns. 3 M14 98 C2
Rusholme Gr. M14 98 C3
Rusholme Pl. M14 98 C4
Rushside Rd. SK8 132 A6
Rushton Ave. Leigh WN7 75 D8
Rushton Ave.
Newton-l-W WA12 89 B4
Rushton Cl. SK6 126 A5
Rushton Dr. Marple SK6 125 F5
Rushton Dr. Romiley SK6 113 C3
Rushton Dr. Stockport SK7 123 D3
Rushton Gdns. SK7 123 D2
Rushton Gr. M'ster M18 99 E7
Rushton Gr. Oldham OL4 49 E3
Rushton Rd. Bolton BL1 142 B1
Rushton Rd. Cheadle SK8 132 A6
Rushton Rd. Stockport SK3 123 B7
Rushton St. 5 Bacup OL13 3 E8
Rushton St. M'ster M20 110 B2
Rushton St. Walkden M28 60 D2
Rushwick Ave.
M10, M40, M9 157 E5
Rushworth Bldgs. OL13 3 C8
Rushworth Ct. SK4 111 C5
Rushy Hill View. OL12 14 C1
Rushycroft. SK14 103 A4
Rushyfield Cres. SK6 113 D3
Ruskin Ave. Denton M34 100 E1
Ruskin Ave. Droylsden M34 100 C7
Ruskin Ave. Kearsley BL4 60 F7
Ruskin Ave. M'ster M14 98 B4
Ruskin Ave.Newton-l-W WA12 89 C4
Ruskin Ave. Oldham OL9 65 F3
Ruskin Ave. Wigan WN3 54 F3
Ruskin Cres. Abram WN2 56 B1
Ruskin Cres. Prestwich M25 62 F3
Ruskin Gdns. SK6 113 A3
Ruskin Gr. SK6 113 A3
Ruskin Rd. Droylsden M43 84 A2
Ruskin Rd. Little Lever BL3 43 B4
Ruskin Rd. M'ster M16 97 C3
Ruskin Rd. Prestwich M25 62 F3
Ruskin Rd. R'dale OL11 30 F2
Ruskin Rd. Reddish SK5 99 E1
Ruskin St. Oldham OL1 153 D8
Ruskin St. Radcliffe M26 44 C4

Ruskington Dr. M9 ... 157 D7
Rusland Ct. M'ster M9 ... 65 A3
Rusland Ct. Sale M33 ... 108 A5
Rusland Dr. BL2 ... 25 E2
Rusland Wlk. 6 M22 ... 121 C2
Russel St. OL11 ... 139 E5
Russeldene Rd. WN3 ... 54 E3
Russell Ave. High Lane SK6 . 134 E7
Russell Ave. M'ster M16 ... 97 D2
Russell Ave. Sale M33 ... 108 D5
Russell Cl. BL1 ... 144 C8
Russell Ct. Farnworth BL4 ... 60 E7
Russell Ct. M'ster M16 ... 97 C3
Russell Ct. Walkden M38 ... 60 C3
Russell Dr. M44 ... 94 A2
Russell Gdns. SK4 ... 168 B1
Russell House. 2 WN1 ... 151 D8
Russell Rd. M'ster M16 ... 97 D3
Russell Rd. Partington M31 . 106 A3
Russell Rd. Pendlebury M6 ... 80 B5
Russell Scott Prim Sch. M34 ... 100 E4
Russell St. 6 Ashton-u-L OL6 85 D4
Russell St. Atherton M46 ... 58 C3
Russell St. Bolton BL1 ... 145 D8
Russell St. 5 Bury BL9 ... 140 F4
Russell St. Denton M34 ... 100 F3
Russell St. Dukinfield SK16 .. 101 C8
Russell St. Eccles M30 ... 79 F2
Russell St. Farnworth BL4 ... 60 E8
Russell St. Heywood OL10 ... 29 E1
Russell St. Hindley WN2 ... 57 C2
Russell St. Hyde SK14 ... 167 D3
Russell St. Ince-i-M WN2 ... 56 A8
Russell St. M'ster M16 ... 97 F3
Russell St. M'ster M8 ... 158 F4
Russell St. Mossley OL5 ... 68 C1
Russell St. Oldham OL9 ... 152 B7
Russell St. Prestwich M25 ... 63 C4
Russell St. Stockport SK2 ... 124 A6
Russell St. Walkden M38 ... 60 C3
Russet Rd. M9 ... 64 D1
Russet Wlk. BL1 ... 143 E4
Rustons Wlk. 2 M40 ... 65 E1
Ruth Ave. M40 ... 65 E1
Ruth St. Bolton BL1 ... 145 E8
Ruth St. 10 Bury BL9 ... 140 F4
Ruth St. Edenfield BL0 ... 1 D2
Ruth St. M'ster M18 ... 99 D3
Ruth St. Oldham OL1 ... 153 F8
Ruth St. Whitworth OL12 ... 4 D1
Ruthen La. M16 ... 97 B4
Rutherford Ave. 2 M14 ... 98 B3
Rutherford Cl. SK14 ... 167 D2
Rutherford Dr. BL5 ... 58 F7
Rutherford Way. SK14 ... 167 D2
Rutherglade Cl. M40 ... 156 C6
Rutherglen Dr. BL3 ... 40 F6
Rutherglen Wlk. M40 ... 157 E5
Ruthin Ave. Cheadle SK8 ... 122 E2
Ruthin Ave. M'ster M9 ... 64 C5
Ruthin Ave. Middleton M24 ... 65 A6
Ruthin Cl. Oldham OL8 ... 66 B2
Ruthin Cl. Salford M6 ... 81 A2
Ruthin Ct. M6 ... 81 A2
Rutland. OL11 ... 139 E6
Rutland Ave. Atherton M46 ... 58 F5
Rutland Ave. Denton M34 ... 101 B2
Rutland Ave. Golborne WA3 . 90 D7
Rutland Ave. M'ster M16 ... 97 A3
Rutland Ave. M'ster M20 ... 110 A6
Rutland Ave. Swinton M27 ... 61 F2
Rutland Ave. Urmston M41 ... 95 E3
Rutland Cl. 5 Ashton-u-L OL6 85 D2
Rutland Cl. Gatley SK8 ... 122 B6
Rutland Cl. Little Lever BL3 ... 43 B4
Rutland Cres. SK5 ... 112 D6
Rutland Ct. M'ster M20 ... 110 B3
Rutland Ct. Stockport SK2 ... 124 A5
Rutland Dr. Ashton-i-M WN4 . 73 C4
Rutland Dr. Bury BL9 ... 45 A8
Rutland Dr. M'ster M7 ... 63 D1
Rutland Gr. Bolton BL1 ... 142 C1
Rutland Gr. Farnworth BL4 ... 60 C7
Rutland La. M33 ... 108 F4
Rutland Rd. Alt'ham WA14 . 119 D6
Rutland Rd. Droylsden M43 ... 83 E2
Rutland Rd. Eccles M30 ... 79 F3
Rutland Rd. Hazel Grove SK7 133 E8
Rutland Rd. Hindley WN2 ... 56 F6
Rutland Rd. Irlam M44 ... 105 D5
Rutland Rd. Partington M31 105 E2
Rutland Rd. Tyldesley M29 ... 58 F2
Rutland Rd. Walkden M28 ... 60 D1
Rutland St. Ashton-u-L OL6 ... 85 D2
Rutland St. Bolton BL3 ... 147 D4
Rutland St. Droylsden M34 . 100 B8
Rutland St. Dukinfield SK14 101 D5
Rutland St. Failsworth M35 ... 83 F8
Rutland St. Heywood OL10 ... 29 D3
Rutland St. Leigh M46 & WN7 76 E4
Rutland St. 4 M'ster M18 ... 99 E6
Rutland St. Oldham OL9 ... 152 C5
Rutland St. Swinton M27 ... 61 E1
Rutland Way. OL2 ... 149 C7
Rutland Wlk. BB4 ... 1 A8
Rutter's La. SK7 ... 124 C2
Ryall Ave. M5 ... 161 B8
Ryall Ave S. M5 ... 161 B8
Ryan St. M11 ... 99 E7
Ryburn Sq. OL11 ... 29 E6
Rydal Ave. Chadderton OL9 ... 47 F1
Rydal Ave. Droylsden M43 ... 83 E1
Rydal Ave. Dukinfield SK14 .. 101 C5
Rydal Ave. Hazel Grove SK7 124 C3
Rydal Ave. High Lane SK6 ... 134 E8
Rydal Ave. Hindley WN2 ... 56 E5
Rydal Ave. Middleton M24 ... 64 F6
Rydal Ave. Orrell WN5 ... 53 F7
Rydal Ave. Royton OL2 ... 48 C8
Rydal Ave. Sale M33 ... 107 F5
Rydal Ave. Swinton M28 ... 79 B4
Rydal Ave. Urmston M41 ... 107 A8
Rydal Cl. Ashton-i-M WN4 ... 73 C4
Rydal Cl. Blackrod BL6 ... 21 C3
Rydal Cl. Bury BL9 ... 44 E7
Rydal Cl. Gatley SK8 ... 122 B4
Rydal Cl. Reddish M34 ... 100 B2
Rydal Cl. Tyldesley M29 ... 77 A7
Rydal Cres. Swinton M27 ... 79 F7
Rydal Cres. Walkden M28 ... 60 E1
Rydal Dr. WA15 ... 129 D8
Rydal Gr. Ashton-u-L OL7 ... 166 A4
Rydal Gr. Farnworth BL4 ... 59 F7
Rydal Gr. Heywood OL10 ... 46 D8
Rydal Gr. Whitefield M45 ... 63 A8
Rydal House. 4 M28 ... 60 E2
Rydal Mount. SK5 ... 99 F2
Rydal Pl. Abram WN2 ... 74 B8
Rydal Pl. Ince-i-M WN2 ... 56 B8
Rydal Rd. Bolton BL1 ... 144 A8
Rydal Rd. Haslingden BB4 ... 1 C8
Rydal Rd. Little Lever BL3 ... 43 A3
Rydal Rd. Stretford M32 ... 96 D3
Rydal St. Leigh WN7 ... 75 E5
Rydal St. Newton-l-W WA12 ... 89 C3
Rydal Wlk. Stalybridge SK15 .. 86 A3
Rydal Wlk. Wigan WN5 ... 54 C7
Ryde Ave. Denton M34 ... 113 B8
Ryde Ave. M'ster SK4 ... 168 B2
Ryde St. Bolton BL3 ... 146 A4
Ryde St. Wigan WN5 ... 54 E6
Ryder Ave. WA14 ... 119 E7
Ryder Brow. M18 ... 99 D4
Ryder Brow Sta. M18 ... 99 D4
Ryder Gr. WN7 ... 76 C2
Ryder St. Bolton BL1 ... 142 C2
Ryder St. Heywood OL10 ... 29 D2
Ryder St. M'ster M10 & M40 160 D4
Ryderbrow Rd. M18 ... 99 D4
Rydings La. OL12 ... 15 A5
Rydings Rd. OL12 ... 15 B4
Rydings Sch. OL12 ... 15 B4
Rydley St. BL2 ... 148 B6
Rye Bank Rd. M16 ... 97 B3
Rye Croft. M45 ... 62 C7
Rye Croft Ave. M6 ... 80 C3
Rye Hill. BL5 ... 57 F8
Rye St. OL10 ... 29 E3
Rye Walk. OL9 ... 152 A6
Rye Wlk. M13 ... 163 C5
Ryebank Gr. OL6 ... 85 D5
Ryebank Mews. M21 ... 96 F1
Ryebank Rd. M21 ... 96 F1
Ryeburn Ave. M22 ... 121 D3
Ryeburn Dr. BL2 ... 25 B5
Ryeburn Wlk. M41 ... 94 F4
Ryeburne St. OL4 ... 67 C7
Ryecroft Ave. Bury BL8 ... 26 F6
Ryecroft Ave. Golborne WA3 . 74 E1
Ryecroft Ave. Heywood OL10 29 E2
Ryecroft Cl. OL9 ... 65 F3
Ryecroft Dr. BL5 ... 39 D3
Ryecroft Gr. M23 ... 121 A7
Ryecroft House. 2 OL7 ... 166 A1
Ryecroft La. Dukinfield M34 . 100 F7
Ryecroft La. Worsley M28 ... 78 F4
Ryecroft Rd. M32 ... 96 C1
Ryecroft St. OL7 ... 84 F1
Ryecroft View. M34 ... 100 C8
Ryedale Ave. M10 & M40 ... 157 D5
Ryedale Cl. SK4 ... 168 B3
Ryefield. M6 ... 80 D6
Ryefield Cl. WA15 ... 120 C5
Ryefield Rd. M33 ... 107 C2
Ryefield St. BL1 ... 25 A1
Ryefields. OL12 ... 15 D4
Ryefields Dr. OL3 ... 51 B1
Ryeford Cl. WN3 ... 151 F6
Ryeland Cl. OL16 ... 31 B4
Ryelands. BL5 ... 57 F8
Ryelands Ct. BL5 ... 57 F8
Rygate Wlk. 3 M8 ... 155 F6
Ryhope Wlk. M8 ... 155 E5
Rylance St. M11 ... 164 E8
Ryland Cl. SK5 ... 99 F1
Rylands Ave. WN6 ... 37 A2
Rylands Ct. 8 M15 ... 162 D6
Rylands House. 7 M14 ... 110 D8
Rylands St. M18 ... 99 E6
Rylane Wlk. M40 ... 157 D5
Rylatt Ct. M33 ... 107 F5
Ryley Ave. BL3 ... 144 B5
Ryley St. 4 BL3 ... 144 C6
Ryleys La. SK9 ... 136 F1
Ryleys Sch The. SK9 ... 136 F1
Rylstone Ave. M21 ... 109 D3
Ryther Gr. M9 ... 64 B5
Ryton Ave. M18 ... 99 C3
Ryton Cl. WN3 ... 150 B6

Sabden Cl. Bury BL9 ... 27 F7
Sabden Cl. Heywood OL10 ... 29 A2
Sabden Cl. M'ster M10, M40 160 E3
Sabden Rd. BL1 ... 23 E2
Sabrina St. M7 ... 81 C8
Sack St. 4 SK14 ... 101 D5
Sackville Cl. OL2 ... 32 A1
Sackville St. Ashton-u-L OL6 166 B3
Sackville St. 2 Bolton BL2 . 148 C7
Sackville St. Bury BL9 ... 141 A3
Sackville St. M'ster M3 ... 158 E2
Sackville St. M'ster M1 ... 163 A8
Sackville St. 6 R'dale OL11 .. 30 C2
Sacred Heart RC Inf Sch. M18 ... 99 D4
Sacred Heart RC Jun Sch. M18 ... 99 C4
Sacred Heart RC Prim Sch. Hindley WN2 ... 57 B3
Sacred Heart RC Prim Sch. Leigh WN7 ... 75 E5
Sacred Heart RC Prim Sch. Oldham OL1 ... 49 C2
Sacred Heart RC Prim Sch. R'dale OL16 ... 31 C6
Sacred Heart RC Prim Sch. Tyldesley M46 ... 58 E1
Sacred Heart RC Prim Sch. Westhoughton BL5 ... 39 F1
Sacred Heart RC Prim Sch. Wythenshawe M23 ... 120 F6
Saddle Ct. 6 WN5 ... 54 F6
Saddle Gr. M43 ... 84 D3
Saddle St. BL2 ... 25 B2
Saddleback Cl. M28 ... 78 B6
Saddleback Cres. WN5 ... 54 B6
Saddleback Rd. WN5 ... 54 B7
Saddlewood Ave. M19, M20 110 D2
Saddleworth Prep Sch. OL4 68 C8
Saddleworth Sch. OL3 ... 51 B1
Sadie Ave. M32 ... 96 A4
Sadler St. Bolton BL3 ... 42 A4
Sadler St. Middleton M24 ... 46 F1
Sadler St. 2 Middleton M24 ... 47 A1
Saffron Dr. OL4 ... 49 D2
Saffron Wlk. Partington M31 105 F2
Saffron Wlk. 8 Wythenshawe M22 ... 121 D1
Sagar St. M8 ... 158 F4
Sagars Rd. SK9 ... 131 C3
SS Aidan & Oswald's RC Prim Sch. OL2 ... 48 E3
SS Peter & John RC Prim Sch. M3 ... 158 D2
SS Simon & Jude's CE Prim Sch. BL3 ... 42 A3
St Aelred's RC High Sch. WA12 ... 89 D4
St Agnes CE Prim Sch. M13 98 F3
St Agnes Rd. M13 ... 98 F2
St Agnes St. M34 ... 99 F3
St Agnes's CE Prim Sch. OL4 ... 68 A4
St Aidan's Cl. Billinge WN5 ... 71 E6
St Aidan's Cl. R'dale OL11 ... 139 D5
St Aidan's Gr. M7 ... 81 B6
St Aidan's Rc Prim Sch. WN3 ... 54 D2
St Aidans RC Prim Sch. M23 ... 109 B1
St Aiden's Cl. Radcliffe M26 ... 44 A1
St Alban's Ave. SK4 ... 111 C5
St Alban's Ct. OL11 ... 139 E6
St Alban's St. OL16 ... 139 E6
St Alban's Terr. M'ster M7 & M8 ... 155 F5
St Alban's Terr. R'dale OL11 139 E6
St Albans Ave. Ashton-u-L OL6 ... 85 C7
St Albans Ave. Failsworth M40 ... 83 B5
St Albans Cl. Newton-l-W WA11 ... 89 A7
St Albans Cl. Oldham OL8 ... 66 F4
St Albans Cres. WA14 ... 119 C8
St Albans RC High Sch. M18 ... 99 D2
St Aldates. SK6 ... 112 F2
St Aldwyn's Rd. M20 ... 110 B5
St Alphonsus RC Prim Sch. M16 ... 162 D5
St Ambrose Barlow RC High Sch. M27 ... 79 F7
St Ambrose Barlow RC Prim Sch. M29 ... 77 A5
St Ambrose Coll. WA15 ... 129 B8
St Ambrose Gdns. M6 ... 154 F2
St Ambrose RC Prim Sch. M'ster M21 ... 109 D4
St Ambrose RC Prim Sch. Stockport SK3 ... 170 E5
St Ambrose Rd. Oldham OL1 . 49 C1
St Ambrose Rd. Tyldesley M29 ... 77 A5
St Andrew's Ave. Alt'ham WA15 ... 119 F7
St Andrew's Ave. Droylsden M43 ... 83 E1
St Andrew's (Boothstown) CE Prim Sch. M28 ... 78 A6
St Andrew's C E Prim Sch. BL0 ... 138 B5
St Andrew's CE Prim Sch. Eccles M30 ... 79 E1
St Andrew's CE Prim Sch. M'ster M19 ... 111 B8
St Andrew's CE Prim Sch. Radcliffe M26 ... 43 F6
St Andrew's CE Prim Sch. Shevington WN6 ... 36 F2
St Andrew's Cl. Ramsbottom BL0 ... 138 C5
St Andrew's Cl. Romiley SK6 113 B1
St Andrew's Cres. WN2 ... 56 D5
St Andrew's Dr. Heywood OL10 ... 29 D1
St Andrew's Dr. Shevington WN6 ... 36 F2
St Andrew's RC Prim Sch. BL2 ... 42 E8
St Andrew's Rd.Radcliffe M26 43 F6
St Andrew's Rd. Stretford M32 ... 96 B2
St Andrew's Sq. M1 ... 163 C8
St Andrew's St. M'ster M1 .. 163 C8
St Andrew's St. Radcliffe M26 43 F6
St Andrew's View. M26 ... 43 F6
St Andrews Ave. M30 ... 79 E1
St Andrews Cl. M'ster SK4 . 168 B4
St Andrews Cl. Sale M33 ... 107 C1
St Andrews Ct. Alt'ham WA15 ... 119 F3
St Andrews Ct. Stockport SK1 ... 112 A1
St Andrews Dr. Heywood OL10 ... 46 D8
St Andrews Dr. Leigh WN7 ... 76 C5
St Andrews Meth Prim Sch. M28 ... 60 B3
St Andrews Over Hulton CE Prim Sch. BL5 ... 59 A8
St Andrews Rd. Bolton BL6 ... 40 B7
St Andrews Rd. Gatley SK8 . 122 C1
St Andrews Rd. M'ster SK4 . 168 B4
St Ann St. Bolton BL1 ... 143 E1
St Ann St. M'ster M2 ... 158 F1
St Ann's Pas. M2 ... 158 F1
St Ann's RC Inf Sch. M32 ... 96 D2
St Ann's RC Jun Sch. M32 .. 96 D2
St Ann's RC Prim Sch. OL6 166 A3
St Ann's Rd.Hazel Grove SK7 124 C1
St Ann's Rd. Prestwich M25 ... 63 A3
St Ann's Rd. R'dale OL16 ... 31 D8
St Ann's Rd N. SK8 ... 122 B2
St Ann's Rd S. SK8 ... 131 C8
St Ann's Sq. Gatley SK8 ... 131 C8
St Ann's Sq. M'ster M2 ... 158 F1
St Ann's St. M27 ... 79 E8
St Anne's Ave. Oldham OL2 ... 48 E3
St Anne's Ave. Salford M6 ... 154 E3
St Anne's Ave. Tyldesley M46 58 E1
St Anne's CE Prim Sch. Oldham OL2 ... 48 E3
St Anne's CE Prim Sch. Sale M33 ... 108 D4
St Anne's CE Prim Sch. Wigan WN6 ... 36 D3
St Anne's Cres. OL4 ... 68 D5
St Anne's Ct. Denton M34 ... 100 E6
St Anne's Ct. Sale M33 ... 108 C4
St Anne's Ct. Shevington WN6 35 F5
St Anne's Cty Prim Sch. M34 ... 101 A4
St Anne's Dr. Dukinfield M34 101 A4
St Anne's Dr. Shevington WN6 36 A5
St Anne's Gdns. OL10 ... 29 F2
St Anne's Hospl. WA14 ... 119 C3
St Anne's RC Prim Sch. Droylsden M34 ... 100 A7
St Anne's RC Prim Sch. M'ster M8 ... 156 A8
St Anne's RC Prim Sch. M'ster M4 ... 160 D1
St Anne's RC Prim Sch. Oldham OL4 ... 67 C7
St Anne's Rd. M34 ... 101 A4
St Anne's St. Bury BL9 ... 140 F4
St Anne's St. M'ster M10 & M40 ... 157 F5
St Annes RC High Sch. SK4 ... 169 D4
St Annes Rd. Denton M34 ... 100 F6
St Annes Rd. Horwich BL6 ... 22 C4
St Annes Rd. M'ster M21 ... 109 B7
St Annes Sq. OL3 ... 50 F4
St Annes St. SK14 ... 115 A8
St Anns Cl. M25 ... 63 A3
St Anns St. M33 ... 108 F3
St Anselm's RC Prim Sch. OL12 ... 4 D2
St Anthony's RC Prim Sch. M22 ... 121 D1
St Antony's RC High Sch. M41 ... 95 F2
St Asaph's Dr. M7 ... 155 F8
St Asaphs Dr. OL6 ... 85 B6
St Aubin's Rd. BL2 ... 148 B6
St Aubyn's Rd. WN1 ... 37 C4
St Augustine of Canterbury RC Sch. OL8 ... 66 D3
St Augustine St. Bolton BL1 143 D2
St Augustine St. M'ster M10 & M40 ... 157 E5
St Augustine's CE Prim Sch. M'ster M40 ... 157 E5
St Augustine's CE Prim Sch. Pendlebury M27 ... 80 B8
St Augustine's Rd. SK3 ... 123 B8
St Augustine's Sch. M15 ... 163 A7
St Austell Ave. M29 ... 77 C8
St Austell Dr. Gatley SK8 ... 131 B8
St Austell Dr.Ramsbottom BL8 10 F2
St Austell House. M21 ... 97 E1
St Austell Rd. M21 ... 97 E1
St Austell's Dr. M27 ... 80 C7
St Austells Dr. M25 ... 63 B5
St Barnabas Sq. M11 ... 165 B8
St Barnabas's Dr. OL15 ... 16 A6
St Bartholomew St. 4 BL3 .. 42 A4
St Bartholomew's CE Prim Sch. OL12 ... 14 C8
St Bartholomew's Dr. M5 . 161 C8
St Bede CE (VA) Prim Sch. BL3 ... 146 C2
St Bede's Ave. BL3 ... 146 B2
St Bede's Coll. M16 ... 97 E3
St Bees Cl. Gatley SK8 ... 122 B3
St Bees Cl. M'ster M14 ... 98 A4
St Bees Rd. BL2 ... 25 C2
St Bees Wlk. 9 M24 ... 46 E2
St Benedict's RC Prim Sch. SK9 ... 131 E3
St Benedict's Sq. M12 ... 164 F6
St Benedicts RC Prim Sch. WN2 ... 56 C6
St Bernadett's RC Prim Sch. WN6 ... 36 A6
St Bernadette's RC Prim Sch. Brinnington SK5 ... 112 B4
St Bernadette's RC Prim Sch. Whitefield M45 ... 44 F2
St Bernard's Ave. 1 M6, M7 . 81 C5
St Bernard's Cl. M6 ... 81 B5
St Bernard's RC Prim Sch. Bolton BL3 ... 40 E5
St Bernard's RC Prim Sch. M'ster M19 ... 110 F6
St Boniface RC Prim Sch. M7 ... 81 C6
St Boniface Rd. M7 ... 81 C4
St Brannock's Rd. M21 ... 97 C1
St Brannocks Rd. SK8 ... 132 B7
St Brelades Dr. M7 ... 155 F8
St Brendan's RC Prim Sch. BL2 ... 25 F4
St Brendan's Rd. M20 ... 110 B7
St Brendan's Rd N. M20 ... 110 B7
St Bride St. M16 ... 162 D5
St Brides Cl. BL6 ... 22 A4
St Brides Way. M16 ... 162 D5
St Brigid's RC Prim Sch (Jun & Inf). M11 ... 165 A8
St Catherine's CE Prim Sch. Horwich BL6 ... 22 B3
St Catherine's CE Prim Sch. Wigan WN1 ... 151 E8
St Catherine's RC Prim Sch. Golborne WA3 ... 90 E7
St Catherine's RC Prim Sch. M'ster M20 ... 110 C3
St Catherine's Rd. M20 ... 110 B3
St Catherines Prep Sch. SK6 ... 126 B7
St Chad's Ave. SK6 ... 113 C2
St Chad's CE Prim Sch. OL3 51 C1
St Chad's Cl. OL16 ... 139 F7
St Chad's Ct. OL16 ... 139 F7
St Chad's Gr. SK6 ... 113 C2
St Chad's Jun Sch. BL9 ... 44 F8
St Chad's Rd. M14 & M20 ... 110 D7
St Chad's St. M8 ... 159 A4
St Chads Cres. Oldham OL8 .. 66 D1
St Chads Cres. Uppermill OL3 69 C8
St Chads RC Prim Sch. M8 156 A5
St Charles Cl. SK14 ... 103 F5
St Charles's RC Prim Sch. M27 ... 79 D8
St Christopher's Ave. OL6 ... 85 E6
St Christopher's Dr. SK6 ... 113 A2
St Christopher's RC Prim Sch. Ashton-u-L OL6 ... 85 E6
St Christopher's RC Prim Sch. Romiley SK6 ... 113 A2
St Christopher's Rd. OL6 ... 85 E6
St Chrysostoms CE Prim Sch. M13 ... 164 D5
St Clair Rd. BL8 ... 10 F3
St Clare Terr. BL6 ... 39 F8
St Clare's RC Inf Sch. M9 ... 64 C5
St Clare's RC Jun Sch. M9 ... 64 C5
St Clement (Egerton) CE Prim Sch. M5 ... 161 B7
St Clement's CE Prim Sch. M18 ... 99 E7
St Clement's Ct. Irlam M44 ... 94 B3
St Clement's Ct. Oldham OL8 ... 153 F5
St Clement's Ct. Prestwich M25 ... 63 C4
St Clement's Ct. Wigan WN3 ... 150 A5
St Clement's Dr. M5 ... 161 B7
St Clement's Rd. M'ster M21 ... 109 A8
St Clement's Rd. Wigan WN1 37 C4
St Clement's St. WN2 ... 55 F4
St Columbo's RC Prim Sch. BL2 ... 25 B4
St Cuthbert's RC High Sch. OL16 ... 31 B1
St Cuthbert's RC Inf Sch. WN5 ... 54 D6
St Cuthbert's RC Jun Sch. WN5 ... 54 D6
St Cuthbert's RC Prim Sch. M20 ... 110 C6
St Damian's RC High Sch. OL6 ... 85 E7
St David's Ave. SK6 ... 113 B2
St David's Cl. OL6 ... 85 D7
St David's Cres. WN2 ... 38 B5
St David's Lodge. M8 ... 156 A5
St David's Rd. SK7 ... 124 C1
St David's Wlk. M32 ... 96 A2
St Davids Cl. M33 ... 108 A3
St Domingo St. OL9 ... 153 E6
St Dominics Mews. BL3 ... 146 C3
St Dominics Way. M24 ... 65 A7
St Dunstan's RC Prim Sch. M40 ... 83 A8
St Dunston Wlk. 14 M40 ... 83 A6
St Edmund Arrowsmith RC High Sch. WN4 ... 73 A2
St Edmund Hall Cl. BL0 ... 11 C4
St Edmund St. BL1 ... 145 E7
St Edmund's RC Sch. M38 ... 60 B4
St Edmund's Rd. M40 & M9 157 E6
St Edmunds RC Prim Sch. M40 ... 157 E6
St Edward's RC Prim Sch. Oldham OL4 ... 67 E7
St Edward's RC Prim Sch. Wigan WN5 ... 54 F7
St Edward's RC Sch. M14 ... 98 B2
St Edwards RC Prim Sch. OL11 ... 30 C2
St Elisabeth's CE Prim Sch. SK5 ... 111 E8
St Elisabeth's Way. SK5 ... 111 E8
St Elizabeth's RC Prim Sch. M22 ... 121 E2
St Elizabeth's Rd. WN2 ... 38 B5
St Elmo Ave. SK2 ... 124 D7
St Elmo Pk. SK12 ... 134 C4
St Ethelbert's Ave. BL3 ... 144 B5
St Ethelbert's RC Prim Sch. BL3 ... 144 B5
St Francis' RC Prim Sch. M12 ... 165 B6
St Gabriel Cl. WN8 ... 35 C3
St Gabriel's CE Prim Sch. M24 ... 65 D7
St Gabriel's Cl. OL11 ... 30 D1
St Gabriel's RC High Sch. BL9 ... 140 D1
St Gabriel's RC Prim Sch. Leigh WN7 ... 76 E7
St Gabriel's RC Prim Sch. R'dale OL11 ... 30 D1
St George's Ave. M'ster M15 ... 162 D7
St George's Ave. Sale WA15 ... 120 A8
St George's Ave. Westhoughton BL5 ... 57 E6
St George's CE Inf Sch. Atherton M46 ... 58 B4
St George's CE Inf Sch. Stockport SK2 ... 170 F6
St George's CE Jun Sch. SK2 ... 170 F6
St George's CE Prim Sch. Salford M6 ... 81 A5
St George's CE Prim Sch. Tyldesley M29 ... 76 F8
St George's CE (VA) Prim Sch. SK14 ... 167 D1
St George's Cres. Eccles M6 . 80 A3
St George's Cres. Sale WA15 ... 120 B8
St George's Cres. Walkden M28 ... 60 D2
St George's Ct. Alt'ham WA14 ... 119 B7
St George's Ct. 16 Bolton BL1 ... 145 E8
St George's Ct. 8 Bolton BL1 ... 145 F8
St George's Ct. Eccles M30 ... 79 F1
St George's Ct. Stretford M32 96 C1
St George's Ct. Whitefield BL9 45 C3
St George's Dr. M40 ... 83 B7
St George's Gdns. M34 ... 101 A1
St George's Pl. Atherton M46 58 B4
St George's Pl. Salford M6 ... 81 A5
St George's Prim Sch. OL2 . 49 D7
St George's RC High Sch. M28 ... 60 C2
St George's Rd. Bolton BL1 . 145 E8
St George's Rd. Carrington M31 ... 106 D6
St George's Rd. Droylsden M43 ... 83 F3
St George's Rd. M'ster M14 110 E7
St George's Rd. R'dale OL11 .. 29 F8
St George's Sq. 7 Bolton BL1 ... 145 F8
St George's Sq. Failsworth OL9 ... 65 E3
St George's St. Bolton BL1 ... 145 F8
St George's St. Stalybridge SK15 ... 86 A3
St George's St. Tyldesley M29 76 F8
St George's Terr. BB4 ... 3 A6
St George's Way. M6 ... 81 A4
St Georges CE Prim Sch. BL5 ... 57 D7
St Georges Ct. Hyde SK14 ... 167 E2
St Georges Ct. M'ster M15 .. 162 D7
St Georges Dr. SK14 ... 167 D1
St Georges Rd. Stretford M32 96 C1
St Georges Rd. Whitefield BL9 45 C4
St Germain St. BL4 ... 60 C8
St Gilbert's RC Prim Sch. M30 ... 79 B2
St Giles Dr. SK14 ... 167 F2
St Gregory's High Sch. M11 99 E8
St Gregory's RC Prim Sch. BL4 ... 60 E8
St Gregorys Cl. BL4 ... 60 C8
St Gregorys RC High Sch. M11 ... 160 E1
St Helen's Coll Newton Campus. WA12 ... 89 B4
St Helena Rd. BL1 ... 145 E7
St Helens CE Prim Sch. WA3 ... 105 B2
St Helens Cl. WA3 ... 105 B3
St Helens Rd. Bolton BL3 & BL5 ... 146 B3
St Helens Rd. Golborne WN7 . 75 C1
St Helens Rd. Leigh WN7 ... 75 E2
St Helier's Dr. M7 & M8 ... 155 F8
St Heliers St. BL3 ... 147 D4
St Herberts Ct. OL9 ... 152 B7
St Herberts RC Prim Sch. OL9 ... 152 A7
St Hilary's Sch. SK9 ... 137 A1
St Hilda's CE Prim Sch. M'ster M16 ... 97 B2
St Hilda's CE Prim Sch. Oldham OL1 ... 153 D8
St Hilda's CE Prim Sch. Prestwich M25 ... 63 C4
St Hilda's Cl. M22 ... 109 E1
St Hilda's Dr. OL1 ... 153 D8
St Hilda's Rd. Denton M34 ... 100 F6
St Hilda's Rd. M'ster M16 ... 161 C5
St Hilda's Rd. Wythenshawe M22 ... 109 D1
St Hilda's View. M34 ... 100 E5
St Hugh of Lincoln RC Prim Sch. M32 ... 95 F3
St Hugh's CE Prim Sch. OL4 67 E3
St Hugh's Cl. WA14 ... 119 E8
St Hugh's RC Prim Sch. WA15 ... 119 F8
St Ignatius Prim Sch. M13 163 C6
St Ignatius Wlk. M5 ... 161 B8
St Ives Ave. SK8 ... 123 A6
St Ives Cres. M33 ... 108 A1
St Ives Rd. M14 ... 98 B2
St Jame's Cl. OL16 & OL12 ... 48 C8
St James Ave. Bolton BL2 ... 42 E7
St James' Ave. Bury BL8 ... 27 B4
St James' CE Prim Sch. Ashton-u-L OL6 ... 166 C3
St James CE Prim Sch. Farnworth BL4 ... 60 C7
St James CE Prim Sch. Littleborough OL12 ... 15 C6
St James CE Prim Sch. M'ster M14 ... 98 D2
St James' CE Prim Sch. M'ster M18 ... 99 D5
St James CE Prim Sch. Shaw OL2 ... 149 B7
St James' CE Prim Sch. Wigan WN3 ... 54 F5
St James Cl. Glossop SK13 .. 116 C7
St James Cl. Salford M6 ... 80 B3
St James Cres. Leigh WN2 ... 74 F8
St James Ct. Alt'ham WA15 . 119 E4
St James Ct. Cheadle SK8 ... 131 F6
St James' Ct. Eccles M6 ... 80 B3
St James Ct. M'ster M20 ... 122 B8
St James Ct. 4 Oldham OL4 .. 67 C8
St James Dr. Sale M33 ... 108 A3
St James' Dr. Wilmslow SK9 137 A6
St James' Gr. 8 Heywood OL10 ... 29 C2
St James Gr. Wigan WN3 ... 150 B6
St James Lodge. SK3 ... 124 A4
St James' RC High Sch. SK8 ... 131 F6
St James' RC Prim Sch. Hattersley SK14 ... 102 D2
St James' RC Prim Sch. Orrell WN5 ... 53 D4
St James Rd. M'ster SK4 ... 111 B5

Thistlewood Dr. SK9 .... 137 D8
Thomas Cl. M34 .... 101 A4
Thomas Cl. M15 .... 162 D7
Thomas Dr. BL3 .... 145 D5
Thomas Garnet Ct. 1 BL4 ... 60 C8
Thomas Gibbon Cl. M32 ...... 96 C1
Thomas Henshaw Ct. OL11 .. 30 C4
Thomas Holden St. BL1 ..... 145 E8
Thomas House. 1 OL2 .... 48 E4
Thomas Regan Ct. 4 M18 .. 99 D6
Thomas St. Alt'ham WA15 ... 119 E4
Thomas St. Aspull WN2 .... 38 B6
Thomas St. Atherton M46 .... 58 D3
Thomas St. Bolton BL3 .... 145 D5
Thomas St. Farnworth BL4 ...... 60 E7
Thomas St. Farnworth BL4 ...... 60 E8
Thomas St. Glossop SK13 .... 104 E1
Thomas St. Golborne WA3 ...... 90 A8
Thomas St. Hindley WN2 .... 57 B3
Thomas St. Littleborough OL15 15 E4
Thomas St. M'ster M7 & M8 . 155 F8
Thomas St. M'ster M4 & M60 159 A2
Thomas St. Oldham OL4 .... 67 E5
Thomas St. 8 R'dale OL16 ...... 31 A8
Thomas St. Radcliffe M26 ...... 44 B3
Thomas St. Romiley SK6 ...... 113 A3
Thomas St. Romiley SK6 ...... 114 B2
Thomas St. Royton OL2 .... 49 A3
Thomas St. Shaw OL2 .... 149 C6
Thomas St. Stockport SK1 ..... 170 F7
Thomas St. Stretford M32 ...... 96 D3
Thomas St. Westhoughton BL5 39 E3
Thomas St. Whitworth OL12 ...... 4 D2
Thomas St W. SK1 & SK2 ...... 170 F7
Thomas Telford Basin. 14 M1 .... 159 C1
Thomason Fold. BL7 .... 9 D6
Thomasson Cl. 7 BL1 .... 143 E1
Thomasson Memorial Sch. BL1 .... 144 B7
Thompson Ave. Ainsworth BL2 .... 26 D1
Thompson Ave. Culcheth WA3 91 E3
Thompson Ave. Whitefield M45 .... 63 A7
Thompson Cl. Newton-l-W WA12 .... 89 B1
Thompson Cl. Reddish M34 100 B3
Thompson Ct. M34 .... 100 B3
Thompson Dr. BL9 .... 141 C3
Thompson House. M46 .... 58 C3
Thompson La. OL9 .... 66 A4
Thompson Rd. Bolton BL1 .... 142 B1
Thompson Rd. Eccles M17 ...... 95 E8
Thompson Rd. Reddish M34 100 B3
Thompson St. Ashton-I-M WN4 .... 73 D4
Thompson St. Bolton BL3 ..... 145 F5
Thompson St. Horwich BL6 .... 22 A3
Thompson St. Leigh WN7 ...... 75 B5
Thompson St. M'ster M10 & M40 .... 157 F5
Thompson St. M'ster M3 ...... 158 F3
Thompson St. M'ster M4 ...... 159 B2
Thompson St. Oldham OL9 .. 153 D7
Thompson St. Wigan WN1 ..... 37 E1
Thompson St. Wigan WN3 ...... 55 A4
Thomson Rd. M18 .... 99 C4
Thomson St. M'ster M13 ...... 163 C6
Thomson St. Stockport SK3 . 170 E8
Thor Gr. M5 .... 161 C8
Thoralby Cl. M12 .... 165 A5
Thorburn Dr. OL12 .... 14 B7
Thorburn Hse. WN5 .... 54 C7
Thorburn La. WN5 .... 54 D8
Thorburn Rd. WN5 .... 54 D6
Thoresby Cl. Little Lever M26 . 43 C5
Thoresby Cl. Wigan WN3 ...... 54 E3
Thoresway Rd. M'ster M13 .... 98 E3
Thoresway Rd. Wilmslow SK9 .... 136 F5
Thorgill Wlk. 10 M40 .... 83 A7
Thoriby Rd. WA3 .... 91 F3
Thorley Cl. OL9 .... 65 E2
Thorley Dr. Alt'ham WA15 .... 120 B5
Thorley Dr. Urmston M41 ...... 95 D2
Thorley La. Alt'ham WA15 .... 120 B4
Thorley La. Wythenshawe M22 & WA15 . 121 A1
Thorley Mews. SK7 .... 132 F7
Thorley St. M35 .... 83 F8
Thorn Ave. M35 .... 83 F6
Thorn Cl. OL10 .... 29 B3
Thorn Ct. 2 M6 .... 81 B2
Thorn Dr. M22 .... 131 A8
Thorn Gr. Alt'ham WA15 ...... 119 E3
Thorn Gr. Bramhall SK8 ...... 132 A7
Thorn Gr. M'ster M14 .... 110 D8
Thorn Gr. Sale M33 .... 108 B4
Thorn Grove Prim Sch. SK8 .... 132 A7
Thorn Lea. M46 .... 58 E2
Thorn Lea Cl. BL1 .... 40 F7
Thorn Rd. Bramhall SK7 ...... 132 E5
Thorn Rd. Oldham OL8 .... 67 C3
Thorn Rd. Swinton M27 ...... 79 E6
Thorn St. Bolton BL1 .... 143 F2
Thorn St. Hindley WN2 .... 56 D4
Thorn St. Ramsbottom BL0 ...... 11 C3
Thorn View. BL9 .... 141 C3
Thorn Well. BL5 .... 57 E7
Thorn Wlk. M31 .... 105 E2
Thornaby Wlk. M9 .... 157 D6
Thornage Dr. M10 & M40 .... 159 C4
Thornbank. BL3 .... 144 C6
Thornbank Cl. OL10 .... 46 E7
Thornbeck Dr. BL1 .... 23 F1
Thornbeck Rd. BL1 .... 23 F1
Thornbridge Ave. M21 .... 109 B8
Thornbury. 9 OL11 .... 139 E6
Thornbury Ave. Golborne WA3 .... 90 E7
Thornbury Ave. Hattersley SK14 .... 102 E2
Thornbury Cl. 3 Bolton BL1 143 E2
Thornbury Cl. Bramhall SK8 123 C1
Thornbury Rd. M32 .... 96 E4
Thornbury Way. M18 .... 165 C5
Thornbush Cl. WA3 .... 74 E1
Thornbush Way. OL16 .... 31 C8
Thornby Wlk. 8 M23 .... 121 A5
Thorncliff Ave. OL8 .... 66 E3
Thorncliffe Ave. Dukinfield SK16 .... 101 C7
Thorncliffe Ave. Royton OL2 .. 48 C6
Thorncliffe Gr. M19 .... 99 C1
Thorncliffe Pk. OL2 .... 48 C6
Thorncliffe Rd. Bolton BL1 ..... 24 E5
Thorncliffe Rd. Hadfield SK14 .... 171 F4
Thorncombe Cl. 1 M16 ...... 97 E3
Thorncross Cl. M15 .... 161 C7
Thorndale Cl. OL2 .... 48 E5
Thorndale Gr. WA15 .... 120 A5
Thornden Rd. M10 & M40 .... 160 D4
Thorne Ave. M41 .... 95 A3
Thorne House. M14 .... 98 D2
Thorne St. BL4 .... 42 C1
Thornecliffewood. SK14 ...... 103 D5
Thorneside. M34 .... 100 F5
Thorney Dr. SK7 & SK8 ...... 132 C6
Thorney Hill Cl. 10 OL4 ...... 67 A6
Thorneycroft. WN7 .... 76 C5
Thorneycroft Ave. M21 ...... 109 C5
Thorneycroft Cl. WA15 ...... 120 B5
Thorneycroft Rd. WA15 ...... 120 B5
Thorneyholme Cl. BL6 .... 40 C6
Thorneylea. OL12 .... 4 D1
Thornfield Ave. 8 BB4 .... 2 F8
Thornfield Cl. WA3 .... 90 C8
Thornfield Cres. M38 .... 59 F5
Thornfield Dr. 4 M27 .... 79 E7
Thornfield Gr. Cheadle SK8 . 123 A2
Thornfield Gr. Walkden M38 .. 59 F5
Thornfield Hey. SK9 .... 137 E8
Thornfield Rd. Bury BL8 ...... 26 E7
Thornfield Rd. M'ster M19 .. 110 E5
Thornfield Rd. M'ster SK4 .. 168 A3
Thornfield Sch. SK4 .... 168 A3
Thornfield St. M5 .... 154 D1
Thornford Wlk. 14 M40 .... 65 D2
Thorngrove Ave. 1 M23 .... 120 D7
Thorngrove Dr. SK9 .... 137 C6
Thorngrove Hill. SK9 .... 137 C6
Thorngrove House. 4 M23 .... 120 D7
Thorngrove Rd. SK9 .... 137 C6
Thornham Cl. BL8 .... 27 C6
Thornham Ct. OL16 .... 48 C8
Thornham Dr. BL1 .... 25 A6
Thornham La. Middleton M24 & OL11 & OL2 .. 47 E6
Thornham La. Royton OL16 & OL2 .... 48 C8
Thornham New Rd. OL11 & OL16 .... 47 E8
Thornham Old Rd. OL2 .... 48 B7
Thornham Rd. Sale M33 ...... 107 F3
Thornham Rd. Shaw OL2 ...... 48 E8
Thornham St James CE (VC) Prim Sch. OL2 .... 48 C8
Thornhill Cl. Bolton BL1 ...... 142 C3
Thornhill Cl. Reddish M34 ... 100 A2
Thornhill Dr. Walkden M28 .... 60 E1
Thornhill Rd. Droylsden M43 . 84 B2
Thornhill Rd. Garswood WN4 72 C4
Thornhill Rd. M'ster SK4 ...... 110 F2
Thornhill Rd. Ramsbottom BL0 11 A1
Thornholme Cl. M18 .... 99 B3
Thornholme Rd. Marple SK6 125 F4
Thornley Brow. M4 & M60 . 159 A2
Thornlea Ave. Oldham OL8 ...... 66 C1
Thornlea Ave. Swinton M27 .. 79 D6
Thornlea Dr. OL12 .... 14 B2
Thornlee Ct. OL4 .... 68 B5
Thornleigh Rd. M14 .... 98 B1
Thornleigh Salesian Coll. BL1 .... 143 F4
Thornley Ave. BL1 .... 142 C2
Thornley Cl. OL4 .... 68 A5
Thornley Cres. Oldham OL4 .... 68 A5
Thornley Cres. Romiley SK6 113 A4
Thornley La. OL4 .... 68 A5
Thornley La N. M34 .... 99 F3
Thornley La S. M34 & SK5 .... 100 A2
Thornley Park Rd. OL4 .... 68 A5
Thornley Rd. Dukinfield M34 101 A4
Thornley Rd. Prestwich M25 .. 63 C7
Thornley St. Hyde SK14 ...... 167 E1
Thornley St. Middleton M24 .... 47 B1
Thornley St. Radcliffe M26 ...... 44 B2
Thornmere Cl. M27 .... 61 C2
Thorns Ave. BL1 .... 143 D3
Thorns Cl. BL1 .... 143 D3
Thorns Clough. OL3 .... 51 C5
Thorns Rd. BL1 .... 143 D3
Thorns The. M21 .... 109 B7
Thorns Villa Gdns. M28 ...... 78 A5
Thornsett. SK12 .... 127 E2
Thornsett Cl. 11 M9 .... 157 E8
Thornsett Cty Prim Sch. SK12 .... 127 E3
Thornsgreen Rd. M22 .... 130 D8
Thornton Ave. Bolton BL1 ...... 23 F1
Thornton Ave. Droylsden M34 .... 100 C8
Thornton Ave. Urmston M41 .. 95 A2
Thornton Cl. Ashton-i-M WN4 72 F4
Thornton Cl. Boothstown M28 77 E7
Thornton Cl. Farnworth BL4 .... 60 B7
Thornton Cl. Golborne WA3 .... 75 A1
Thornton Cl. Leigh WN7 .... 75 F1
Thornton Cl. Little Lever BL3 .. 43 C3
Thornton Cres. M25 .... 62 F5
Thornton Ct. M16 .... 161 C5
Thornton Dr. SK9 .... 131 D3
Thornton Gate. M22 & SK8 . 122 A6
Thornton Pl. SK4 .... 168 B4
Thornton Rd. Boothstown M28 .... 77 E7
Thornton Rd. Gatley SK8 ...... 131 C8
Thornton Rd. M'ster M14 ...... 98 A2
Thornton St. 1 Bolton BL2 .. 148 A7
Thornton St. M'ster M40 ...... 160 D4
Thornton St. Oldham OL4 & OL8 .... 153 F5
Thornton St. R'dale OL11 ...... 139 F5
Thornton St N. M40 .... 157 D5
Thorntree Cl. M9 .... 157 E7
Thorntree Pl. 2 OL12 .... 139 E8
Thornvale. Abram WN2 .... 74 C7
Thornvale. Boothstown M28 .... 78 A8
Thornway. Bramhall SK7 & SK8 .... 132 C7
Thornway. High Lane SK6 ...... 134 F7
Thornwood Ave. M18 .... 99 E4
Thornydyke Ave. BL1 .... 24 E5
Thorold Gr. M33 .... 108 E4
Thorp Ave. BL9 .... 44 D5
Thorp Prim Sch. OL2 .... 48 C5
Thorp Rd. Failsworth M40 ...... 83 A6
Thorp Rd. Royton OL2 .... 48 D4
Thorp St. Eccles M30 .... 95 B8
Thorp St. Whitefield M45 ...... 44 E1
Thorp View. OL2 .... 48 C6
Thorpe Ave. M27 .... 61 E1
Thorpe Cl. Denton M34 ...... 100 F4
Thorpe Cl. Oldham OL4 .... 68 A8
Thorpe Gr. SK4 .... 111 D6
Thorpe Hall Gr. SK14 ...... 101 F6
Thorpe La. Denton M34 ...... 100 F5
Thorpe La. Oldham OL4 .... 68 A8
Thorpe St. Bolton BL1 .... 143 D2
Thorpe St. Glossop SK13 .... 104 E2
Thorpe St. M'ster M16 .... 97 C4
Thorpe St. Middleton M24 .... 64 C7
Thorpe St. Ramsbottom BL0 . 138 B3
Thorpe St. Walkden M28 ...... 60 D4
Thorpe View. M5 .... 161 C7
Thorpebrook Rd. M40 .... 83 A6
Thorpeness Sq. M18 .... 99 D6
Thorsby Ave. SK14 .... 167 F2
Thorsby Cl. Bolton BL7 ...... 24 F8
Thorsby Cl. Droylsden M18 .... 99 E5
Thorsby Rd. WA15 .... 119 E5
Thorsby Way. 16 M34 .... 101 A1
Thorverton Sq. M40 .... 83 C8
Thrapston Ave. M34 .... 84 D1
Threaphurst La. SK7 .... 125 C1
Threapwood Rd. M22 .... 121 E1
Three Acre Ave. OL2 .... 49 A4
Three Lane Ends. BL9 & OL10 .... 45 F7
Three Sisters Rd. WN4 .... 73 B7
Three Sisters Recn Area. WN4 .... 73 C7
Threlkeld Cl. M24 .... 46 C1
Threlkeld Rd. Bolton BL1 ...... 24 D6
Threlkeld Rd. Middleton M24 . 46 C1
Thresher Cl. 3 M33 .... 108 F3
Threshfield Cl. BL9 .... 27 F7
Threshfield Dr. WA15 .... 120 C7
Throstle Bank St. SK14 ...... 101 C4
Throstle Ct. 3 OL2 .... 48 D4
Throstle Gr. Bury BL8 .... 27 C5
Throstle Gr. Marple SK6 ...... 125 E5
Throstle Hall Ct. 1 M24 ...... 46 F1
Throstle Nest Ave. WN6 ...... 37 A2
Throstle St. OL14 .... 6 B6
Throstles Cl. M43 .... 84 C3
Thrum Fold. OL12 .... 14 D3
Thrum Hall La. R'dale OL12 .. 14 D3
Thrum Hall La. R'dale OL12 .. 14 E3
Thrush Ave. BL4 .... 59 F8
Thrush Dr. BL9 .... 141 B4
Thrush House. M6 .... 81 A5
Thrush St. OL12 .... 14 C1
Thruxton Cl. 4 M16 .... 97 E3
Thurland Rd. OL4 .... 67 C6
Thurland St. OL9 .... 65 E8
Thurlby Ave. M9 .... 64 E5
Thurlby Cl. WN4 .... 73 D4
Thurlby St. M13 .... 98 D4
Thurleigh Rd. M20 .... 110 B4
Thurlestone Ave. BL2 .... 26 D1
Thurlestone Dr. Stockport SK7 .... 124 B2
Thurlestone Dr. 3 Urmston M41 .... 95 C3
Thurlestone Rd. WA14 .... 119 B6
Thurloe St. M14 .... 98 C3
Thurlow. WA3 .... 90 E7
Thurlow St. Salford M5 .... 154 F1
Thurlow St. Stretford M5 ...... 96 F8
Thurlston Cres. M8 .... 156 B7
Thurlwood Ave. M20 .... 110 A7
Thurnham St. BL3 .... 146 C3
Thurnley Wlk. M8 .... 155 F5
Thursby Ave. M20 .... 110 A6
Thursby House. WN5 .... 54 C7
Thursby Wlk. M24 .... 46 C2
Thursfield St. M6 .... 81 B5
Thursford Gr. BL6 .... 21 D1
Thurstan St. WN2 .... 55 E4
Thurstane St. BL1 .... 142 C2
Thurston Ave. WN3 .... 55 B3
Thurston Cl. BL9 .... 45 A2
Thurston Clough Rd. OL3 & OL4 .... 50 D2
Thurston Gn. SK9 .... 137 A1
Thurstons. OL3 .... 51 D6
Thynne St. Bolton BL3 ...... 145 F5
Thynne St. Farnworth BL4 .... 42 C2
Tib La. M2 .... 158 F1
Tib St. Denton SK14 .... 101 A2
Tib St. M'ster M1 & M4 & M60 159 A2
Tib St. Ramsbottom BL0 ...... 138 B5
Tiber Ave. OL8 .... 66 C1
Tidebrook Wlk. M40 .... 157 D5
Tideswell Ave. M'ster M10 & M40 .... 160 D3
Tideswell Ave. Wigan WN5 .... 36 A1
Tideswell Bank. 8 SK13 ...... 171 E1
Tideswell Cl. SK8 .... 131 D8
Tideswell Rd. Droylsden M43 . 83 E3
Tideswell Rd. Hazel Grove SK7 .... 133 E8
Tideswell Way. M34 .... 113 A8
Tideswell Wlk. 7 SK13 ...... 171 E1
Tidworth Ave. M4 .... 160 D2
Tiefield Wlk. M21 .... 109 E6
Tiflis St. OL12 .... 139 E8
Tig Fold Rd. BL4 .... 59 E8
Tilbury Gr. WN6 .... 35 D7
Tilbury St. OL1 .... 153 E8
Tilbury Wlk. M40 .... 160 D3
Tilby Cl. M41 .... 94 E2
Tildsley St. BL3 .... 147 E4
Tile St. BL9 .... 140 F3
Tilehurst Dr. M7 .... 81 B7
Tilgate Wlk. 17 M9 .... 64 E3
Tillard Ave. SK3 .... 123 B8
Tillhey Rd. M22 .... 121 D2
Tillington Cl. BL1 .... 143 E3
Tilney Ave. M32 .... 96 E1
Tilshead Wlk. M13 .... 163 C6
Tilson Rd. M23 .... 120 F5
Tilstock Wlk. M23 .... 120 E8
Tilston Wlk. 5 SK9 .... 131 E1
Tilton St. OL1 .... 49 C1
Timberbottom. BL2 .... 25 C4
Timbercliffe. OL15 .... 6 D1
Timberhurst. BL9 .... 28 D2
Timbersbrook Gr. 5 SK9 .. 131 D2
Times St. M24 .... 65 B8
Timothy Cl. M6 .... 80 B3
Timperley Cl. OL8 .... 67 B2
Timperley Fold. OL6 .... 85 C6
Timperley Heyes Lane Prim Sch. WA15 .... 120 B8
Timperley La. WN7 .... 76 B2
Timperley Rd. OL6 .... 85 C6
Timperley St. M11 .... 165 C8
Timperley Sta. WA15 .... 119 F8
Timpson Rd. M23 .... 120 E7
Timsbury Cl. BL2 .... 42 F5
Timson St. 2 Failsworth M35 83 F7
Timwood Wlk. 16 M16 .... 97 E4
Tin St. Bolton BL3 .... 145 E5
Tin St. Oldham OL9 .... 153 D8
Tindall St. Eccles M30 .... 95 B8
Tindall St. Reddish M34 & SK5 99 F3
Tindle St. M28 .... 60 F3
Tinkersfield. WN7 .... 75 D7
Tinline St. BL9 .... 141 A2
Tinningham Cl. 7 M11 & M18 .... 99 E7
Tinsdale Wlk. M24 .... 46 C1
Tinshill Cl. M12 .... 165 A5
Tinsley Cl. M10 & M40 .... 160 E2
Tinsley Gr. BL2 .... 148 B8
Tintagel Cres. M26 .... 43 C5
Tintagel Ct. SK15 .... 85 F2
Tintagel Rd. WN2 .... 57 A4
Tintagel Wlk. SK14 .... 102 E3
Tintern Ave. Ashton-i-M WN4 73 D3
Tintern Ave. Bolton BL2 ...... 25 B2
Tintern Ave. Heywood OL10 .... 29 C4
Tintern Ave. Littleborough OL15 .... 16 A7
Tintern Ave. M'ster M20 ...... 109 F5
Tintern Ave. R'dale OL12 ...... 14 E2
Tintern Ave. Tyldesley M29 .... 77 C7
Tintern Ave. Urmston M41 .... 107 A8
Tintern Ave. Whitefield M45 .. 44 F1
Tintern Cl. SK12 .... 133 D5
Tintern Dr. WA15 .... 120 C2
Tintern Gr. SK1 .... 112 B1
Tintern Pl. OL10 .... 29 C4
Tintern Rd. Bramhall SK8 ...... 132 B6
Tintern Rd. Middleton M24 .... 47 A4
Tintern St. M14 .... 98 B2
Tintwistle CE (VA) Sch. SK14 .... 104 A7
Tinwald Pl. WN1 .... 37 F1
Tipperary St. SK15 .... 86 E5
Tipping St. Alt'ham WA14 .... 119 D3
Tipping St. Wigan WN3 .... 150 B6
Tipton Cl. Cheadle SK8 ...... 123 B4
Tipton Cl. Radcliffe M26 ...... 43 D5
Tipton Dr. M23 .... 109 B2
Tiptree Wlk. 13 M9 .... 157 E8
Tiree Cl. SK7 .... 124 F1
Tirza Ave. M19 .... 110 F8
Tissington Bank. 15 SK13 .. 171 D1
Tissington Terr. 16 SK13 ... 171 D1
Titanian Rise. OL1 .... 49 D5
Titchfield Rd. OL8 .... 67 C4
Tithe Barn Cl. OL12 & OL16 .... 15 D4
Tithe Barn Cres. BL1 .... 25 B4
Tithe Barn Ct. SK4 .... 110 F4
Tithe Barn Prim Sch. SK4 . 168 A3
Tithe Barn Rd. Garswood WN4 .... 72 C2
Tithe Barn Rd. M'ster SK4 .... 110 F4
Tithe Barn St. 6 BL5 .... 39 E1
Tithebarn Rd. Alt'ham WA15 129 C8
Tithebarn Rd. Garswood WN4 72 D2
Tithebarn St. 3 Bury BL9 .... 140 F2
Tithebarn St. Orrell WN8 ...... 53 B7
Tithebarn St. Radcliffe M26 .... 44 D4
Titherington Cl. SK5 .... 99 D1
Titherington Dr. SK5 .... 99 D1
Titian Rise. OL1 .... 49 D3
Titterington Ave. M21 .... 97 B2
Tiverton Ave. Hindley WN7 .... 57 D2
Tiverton Ave. Sale M33 ...... 107 F3
Tiverton Cl. Little Lever M26 ... 43 C5
Tiverton Cl. Tyldesley M29 .... 77 D7
Tiverton Dr. M33 .... 107 F3
Tiverton House. M6 .... 80 A3
Tiverton Pl. OL7 .... 85 A5
Tiverton Rd. M41 .... 95 E3
Tiverton Wlk. BL1 .... 142 C1
Tiviot Dale. SK1 .... 169 F2
Tiviot Way. SK1 & SK4 & SK5 169 F3
Tivoli St. M3 .... 158 E1
Tixall Wlk. 3 M8 .... 63 E2
Toad La. OL12 .... 139 F8
Tobermory Cl. M11 .... 83 D1
Tobermory Rd. SK8 .... 122 C1
Todd St. Bury BL9 .... 140 F4
Todd St. Heywood OL10 ...... 29 A2
Todd St. M'ster M7 .... 155 D6
Todd St. M'ster M4 & M60 .... 159 A2
Todd St. R'dale OL16 .... 31 A7
Todd's Pl. M9 .... 64 C1
Toddbrook Cl. M15 .... 162 E7
Toddington La. WN2 .... 38 B8
Todmorden Rd. OL15 .... 16 C7
Toft Way. SK9 .... 131 E4
Togford Cl. M16 .... 97 D4
Toledo St. M11 .... 83 D1
Toll Bar Bsns Pk. OL13 .... 3 C8
Toll Bar St. M12 .... 164 E6
Toll Gate Cl. M13 .... 98 E4
Toll Green Cl. WN2 .... 56 D7
Toll St. Platt Bridge WN2 ...... 56 A1
Toll St. Radcliffe M26 .... 43 D4
Tolland La. WA15 .... 128 F8
Tollard Ave. M10 & M40 ...... 157 D5
Tollard Cl. SK8 .... 132 B6
Tollbar St. SK1 .... 170 F8
Tollemache Cl. SK14 .... 103 A5
Tollemache Rd. SK14 .... 103 A5
Tollesbury Cl. M40 .... 160 D4
Tollgate Way. OL16 .... 31 C8
Tolworth Dr. M8 .... 156 B7
Tom Lomas Wlk. M11 .... 83 B2
Tom Shepley St. SK14 ...... 167 E2
Tomcroft La. M34 .... 100 D2
Tomlin Sq. 7 BL2 .... 148 C7
Tomlinson Cl. OL8 .... 153 E5
Tomlinson St. Horwich BL6 .... 22 B3
Tomlinson St. M'ster M40 ...... 65 C3
Tomlinson St. R'dale OL11 .... 30 C4
Tommy Browell Cl. 9 M14 .. 98 A3
Tommy Johnson Wlk. 7 M14 .... 98 A3
Tommy Taylor Cl. 1 M40 .... 83 C5
Tonacliffe Cty Prim Sch. OL12 .... 14 C6
Tonacliffe Rd. OL12 .... 14 C6
Tonacliffe Terr. OL12 .... 14 C7
Tonacliffe Way. OL12 .... 14 C6
Tonbridge Cl. BL8 .... 27 C7
Tonbridge Pl. 5 BL2 .... 25 B1
Tonbridge Rd. M'ster M19 .. 111 B8
Tonbridge Rd. Reddish SK5 . 111 F8
Tong End. OL12 .... 4 C2
Tong Head Ave. BL1 .... 25 B4
Tong La. Bacup OL13 .... 4 C8
Tong La. Whitworth OL12 ...... 4 D1
Tong Rd. BL3 .... 43 A5
Tong St. BL4 .... 61 C5
Tonge Bridge Way. BL2 ...... 148 B8
Tonge Cl. M45 .... 45 B1
Tonge Clough. BL7 .... 24 F8
Tonge Ct. M24 .... 65 B8
Tonge Fold Rd. BL2 .... 148 C7
Tonge Gn. SK15 .... 102 E6
Tonge Hall Cl. M24 .... 65 B8
Tonge Moor Prim Sch. BL2 . 25 B1
Tonge Moor Rd. BL2 .... 25 B2
Tonge Old Rd. BL2 .... 148 C7
Tonge Park Ave. BL2 .... 25 C1
Tonge Roughs. M24 .... 65 D8
Tonge St. Heywood OL10 ...... 29 D2
Tonge St. M'ster M12 .... 164 D7
Tonge St. Oldham M24 .... 65 E6
Tonge St. R'dale OL11 & OL16 . 31 A6
Tongfields. BL7 .... 24 F8
Tongley Wlk. 15 M40 .... 65 D2
Tonman St. M3 .... 162 E8
Tontine. WN5 .... 53 C5
Tontine Rd. WN5 & WN8 ...... 53 C6
Toogood La. WN6 .... 18 D6
Tooley House. M30 .... 95 D8
Toon Cres. BL8 .... 27 C6
Total Dr. M5 & M6 .... 80 C3
Total Drive Prim Sch. M6 .. 80 C3
Total Gr. M5 .... 80 C2
Total Rd. M5 .... 154 D2
Toothill Cl. WN4 .... 73 B5
Top o' th' Brow Prim Sch. BL2 .... 25 E2
Top o' th' Gn. OL9 .... 66 C4
Top o' th' Gorses. BL2 & BL3 .... 148 D5
Top o' th' La. BL2 .... 42 D5
Top o' th' Meadows La. OL4 .... 50 A1
Top o' th' Close Rd. OL14 ...... 6 C6
Top of Heap. OL10 .... 28 F2
Top of Wallsuches. BL6 ...... 22 F4
Top Schwabe St. M24 .... 64 C8
Top St. Middleton M24 .... 46 F1
Top St. Oldham OL4 .... 67 D8
Top St. Walsden OL14 .... 5 F7
Topaz St. M11 .... 160 F1
Topcliffe St. WN2 .... 56 F6
Topcroft Cl. M22 .... 121 E8
Topfield Rd. M22 .... 121 C4
Topham St. Bury BL9 .... 45 A8
Topham St. Bury BL9 .... 141 A1
Topley St. M40 .... 157 D6
Topp St. BL4 .... 60 E7
Topp Way. BL1 .... 145 E8
Topping Fold Rd. BL9 .... 141 C3
Topping St. Bolton BL1 .... 143 E1
Topping St. Bury BL9 .... 141 A3
Toppings Gn. BL7 .... 25 A7
Toppings The. SK6 .... 113 A3
Topsham Wlk. M40 .... 83 D5
Tor Ave. BL8 .... 10 F2
Tor End Rd. BB4 .... 1 A6
Tor View Sch Valley Site. BB4 .... 1 D8
Torah St. M8 .... 159 A4
Torbay Cl. 1 BL3 .... 144 C5
Torbay Dr. SK2 .... 124 B7
Torbay Rd. M'ster M21 .... 109 C8
Torbay Rd. Urmston M41 ...... 95 E1
Torcross Rd. M9 .... 64 B5
Torkington Ave. M27 .... 61 F1
Torkington La. SK6 & SK7 .. 125 E3
Torkington Prim Sch. SK7 125 A2
Torkington Rd. Gatley SK8 .. 122 B5
Torkington Rd. Hazel Grove SK7 .... 124 F2
Torkington Rd. Hazel Grove SK7 .... 125 B3
Torkington Rd. Wilmslow SK9 .... 137 D6
Torkington St. SK3 .... 170 D8
Torksey Wlk. M9 .... 64 C5
Torness Wlk. M11 .... 83 B1
Toronto Ave. M90 .... 130 B7
Toronto Rd. SK2 .... 124 A6
Toronto St. BL2 .... 42 E8
Torpoint Wlk. M40 .... 65 C1
Torquay Cl. 2 M13 .... 163 C5
Torquay Dr. WN5 .... 71 E8
Torquay Gr. SK2 .... 124 B4
Torra Barn Cl. BL7 .... 8 E3
Torrax Cl. M6 .... 80 B6
Torre Cl. M24 .... 47 A3
Torre Wlk. OL8 .... 67 C3
Torrens St. M6 .... 80 D5
Torridon Cl. WN6 .... 37 B7
Torridon Rd. BL2 .... 42 F7
Torridon Wlk. 1 M22 .... 121 C1
Torrin Cl. SK3 .... 170 F5
Torrington Ave. Bolton BL1 143 E3
Torrington Ave. M'ster M9 .... 65 A2
Torrington Dr. SK14 .... 102 E2
Torrington Rd. M27 .... 80 B6
Torrington St. OL10 .... 46 E8
Torrisdale Cl. BL3 .... 144 B5
Torside Way. SK14 .... 104 A5
Torver Cl. WN3 .... 55 A2
Torver Dr. Bolton BL2 .... 42 F8
Torver Dr. Middleton M24 ...... 46 D2
Torver Wlk. M22 .... 121 B2
Torwood Dr. OL9 .... 47 E1
Totland Cl. M18 .... 99 B3
Totley Ave. 35 SK13 .... 171 D1
Totley Cl. 32 SK13 .... 171 D1
Totley Gdns. 30 SK13 .... 171 D1
Totley Gn. 33 SK13 .... 171 D1
Totley Lanes. 34 SK13 .... 171 D1
Totley Mews. SK13 .... 171 D1
Totley Pl. 31 SK13 .... 171 D1
Totnes Ave. Chadderton OL9 .. 47 F1
Totnes Ave. Stockport SK7 .... 124 A2
Totnes Rd. M'ster M21 .... 109 C8
Totnes Rd. Sale M33 .... 107 D5
Totridge Cl. SK2 .... 124 D5
Tottenham Dr. M23 .... 120 E7
Tottington Ave. Oldham OL4 .. 67 F7
Tottington High Sch. BL8 ...... 26 F6
Tottington La. M25 .... 62 F5
Tottington Rd. Bolton BL7 & BL8 .... 9 F2
Tottington Rd. Bolton BL2 & BL8 .... 25 E6
Tottington Rd. Bury BL8 ...... 27 C4
Tottington South Cty Prim Sch. BL8 .... 26 F5
Tottington St. 18 M11 .... 83 C2
Totton House. BL1 .... 144 C7
Totton Rd. M35 .... 83 F7
Touchet Hall Rd. M24 .... 47 D4
Tours Ave. M23 .... 109 A2
Towcester Cl. M4 .... 160 D1
Tower Ave. BL0 .... 138 A5
Tower Ct. BL7 .... 9 C4
Tower Gr. WN7 .... 76 D6
Tower Grange. M7 .... 155 D8
Tower Hill Rd. WN8 .... 53 B6
Tower Nook. WN8 .... 53 A5
Tower Sq. M13 .... 163 C6
Tower St. Edgworth BL7 .... 9 C4
Tower St. Heywood OL10 ...... 29 C2
Tower St. Hyde SK14 .... 167 D1
Tower St. Radcliffe M26 .... 44 D4
Tower St. Stalybridge SK16 .... 85 D1
Tower View. BL6 .... 21 C3
Towers Ave. BL3 .... 146 A4
Towers Cl. SK12 .... 133 F5
Towers Rd. Poynton SK12 .... 133 F5
Towers St. 2 OL4 .... 49 D1
Towey Cl. M18 .... 99 D6
Town Fold. SK6 .... 126 B7
Town Gate Dr. M41 .... 94 C2
Town Hall La. 14 M2 .... 158 F1
Town Hall Sq. OL16 .... 139 F7
Town House Rd. OL15 .... 16 B6
Town La. Charlesworth SK14 115 D6
Town La. Coppull PR7 .... 19 B8
Town La. Denton M34 .... 100 E2
Town La. Dukinfield SK16 ...... 101 C8
Town Mill Brow. OL12 .... 139 E7
Town Sq. M33 .... 108 B4
Town Sq Sh Ctr. OL1 .... 153 F6
Town St. SK6 .... 126 B7
Town's View. SK15 .... 86 B1
Towncliffe Wlk. 18 M15 ...... 162 D6
Towncroft. M34 .... 101 A4
Towncroft Ave. M24 .... 46 F2
Towncroft La. BL1 .... 40 E8
Townend St. SK14 .... 167 E2
Townfield. M41 .... 95 B1
Townfield Ave. WN4 .... 73 B2
Townfield Gdns. WA14 .... 119 D5
Townfield La. WA13 .... 117 B7
Townfield Rd. WA14 .... 119 D5
Townfield St. 9 OL4 .... 67 B7
Townfield Wlk. 10 M15 .... 162 D6
Townfields. WN4 .... 73 A3
Townley Fold. SK14 .... 102 B6
Townley Rd. OL16 .... 32 A6
Townley St. M'ster M7 & M8 155 F5
Townley St. M'ster M11 .... 164 F8
Townley St. Middleton M24 .... 65 A8
Townrow St. OL10 .... 29 E2
Townscliffe La. SK6 .... 126 C6
Townsend Rd. M27 .... 61 F1
Townsend St. BB4 .... 2 F8
Townsfield Rd. BL5 .... 57 F7
Townside Row. BL9 .... 140 F1
Townsley Gr. OL6 .... 85 E5
Towns on Dr. WN7 .... 75 F1
Towton St. M9 .... 157 E8
Toxhead Cl. BL6 .... 22 A3
Toxteth St. M11 .... 99 F7
Tracey St. M8 .... 64 A1
Tracks La. WN5 .... 53 D3
Tracy Dr. WA12 .... 89 E3
Traders Ave. M41 .... 95 E6
Trafalgar Ave. Denton M34 . 100 C7
Trafalgar Ave. Poynton SK12 134 A3
Trafalgar Bsns Pk. M7, M8 158 E4
Trafalgar Cl. SK12 .... 134 A3
Trafalgar Ct. M16 .... 97 E2
Trafalgar Gr. M7 .... 155 D5
Trafalgar Pl. M20 .... 110 A4
Trafalgar Rd. Eccles M6 .... 80 A3
Trafalgar Rd. Hindley WN2 .... 56 D5
Trafalgar Rd. Sale M33 .... 108 C6
Trafalgar Rd. Wigan WN1 ...... 37 C1

Vavasour Ct. 5 OL16 31 B6
Vavasour St. OL16 31 B6
Vawdrey Dr. M23 108 F2
Vaynor. 15 OL12 139 E8
Vega St. M8 158 E4
Vela Wlk. M6 81 C3
Velmere Ave. M9 64 A5
Velvet Ct. M1 163 A8
Vendale Ave. M27 79 D6
Venesta Ave. M6 80 B4
Venetia St. M40 83 C5
Venice St. Bolton BL3 146 C4
Venice St. M'ster M1 163 A8
Venlow Gdns. SK8 123 B1
Ventnor Ave. Bolton BL1 143 F3
Ventnor Ave. Reddish M19 111 C8
Ventnor Ave. Sale M33 108 B6
Ventnor Ave. Whitefield BL9 45 A3
Ventnor Cl. M34 113 B8
Ventnor Rd. M'ster M20 110 C3
Ventnor Rd. M'ster SK4 168 A2
Ventnor St. M'ster M9 157 E8
Ventnor St. R'dale OL11 139 F5
Ventnor St. Salford M6 81 B4
Ventor St. M9 157 D8
Ventura Cl. M14 98 A1
Ventura Ct. SK12 127 D1
Venwood Rd. M25 62 F2
Verbena Ave. BL4 42 A1
Verbena Cl. M31 105 F3
Verda St. Abram WN2 74 B8
Verdant La. Eccles M30 94 F8
Verdant La. Eccles M30 95 A8
Verdon St. M4 159 A3
Verdun Ave. M6 80 B3
Verdun Cres. OL11 30 C8
Verdun Rd. M28 79 B4
Verdure Ave. Bolton BL1 40 E8
Verdure Ave. Sale M33 108 C1
Verdure Cl. M35 84 B7
Vere St. M5 154 F1
Verity Cl. M'ster M20 110 C6
Verity Cl. Royton OL2 48 D3
Verity Wlk. M9 64 B3
Vermont St. BL1 145 D8
Verne Ave. M27 79 E8
Verne Dr. OL1 49 E5
Verney Rd. OL2 48 E2
Vernham Wlk. BL3 147 E4
Vernon Ave. Eccles M30 79 F2
Vernon Ave. Stockport SK1 112 B2
Vernon Ave. Stretford M32 96 D1
Vernon Cl. Cheadle SK8 122 E1
Vernon Cl. Poynton SK12 133 D2
Vernon Cty Inf Sch The. SK12 133 E3
Vernon Cty Jun Sch The. SK12 133 E3
Vernon Dr. Marple SK6 125 D7
Vernon Dr. Prestwich M25 63 A2
Vernon Gr. M33 108 E3
Vernon Park Prim Sch. SK1 112 A1
Vernon Pk. WA15 120 A7
Vernon Rd. Bredbury SK6 113 A1
Vernon Rd. Droylsden M43 83 E2
Vernon Rd. M'ster M7 63 C1
Vernon Rd. Poynton SK12 133 E2
Vernon Rd. Ramsbottom BL8 11 A1
Vernon St. Ashton-u-L OL6 166 C4
Vernon St. Bolton BL1 145 E8
Vernon St. Bury BL9 140 F4
Vernon St. Farnworth BL4 42 E1
Vernon St. Hazel Grove SK7 124 D3
Vernon St. Hyde SK14 167 E2
Vernon St. Leigh WN7 75 F5
Vernon St. M'ster M7 155 D5
Vernon St. M'ster M9 157 E7
Vernon St. M'ster M16 162 D5
Vernon St. Mossley OL5 68 C2
Vernon St. Stockport SK1 169 F2
Vernon View. SK5 112 C7
Vernon Wlk. 5 Bolton BL1 145 E8
Vernon Wlk. Stockport SK1 169 E1
Verona Dr. M40 83 C4
Veronica Rd. M20 110 C3
Verrill Ave. M23 109 C1
Verwood Wlk. 9 M23 121 A5
Vesper St. M35 84 A8
Vesta St. M'ster M4 159 C1
Vesta St. Ramsbottom BL0 138 B6
Vestris Dr. M6 80 B3
Vetch Cl. WA3 105 B5
Viaduct Rd. WA14 119 D7
Viaduct St. M'ster M3 158 F2
Viaduct St. M'ster M12 164 E8
Viaduct St. Newton-l-W WA12 89 A3
Viaduct St. Stockport SK3 169 E1
Vicar's Dr. OL11 & OL16 139 F6
Vicar's Gate. OL16 139 F7
Vicarage Ave. SK8 132 B7
Vicarage Cl. Adlington PR6 21 A8
Vicarage Cl. Dukinfield SK16 101 E8
Vicarage Cl. Oldham OL4 67 F7
Vicarage Cl. Platt Bridge WN2 56 A2
Vicarage Cl. Salford M6 80 B3
Vicarage Cres. OL6 85 D5
Vicarage Dr. Dukinfield SK16 101 E8
Vicarage Dr. Littleborough OL12 & OL16 15 C3
Vicarage Gdns. SK14 167 F2
Vicarage Gr. M30 79 F2
Vicarage La. Alt'ham WA14 119 C1
Vicarage La. Middleton M24 65 D7
Vicarage La. Poynton SK12 133 E5
Vicarage La. Shevington WN6 36 A5
Vicarage Rd. Abram WN2 56 B1
Vicarage Rd. Ashton-i-M WN4 73 B2
Vicarage Rd. Ashton-u-L OL7 85 B5
Vicarage Rd. Blackrod BL6 21 D2
Vicarage Rd. Irlam M44 94 A2
Vicarage Rd. Orrell WN5 53 D4
Vicarage Rd. Stockport SK3 170 E6
Vicarage Rd. Swinton M27 79 E8
Vicarage Rd. Urmston M41 95 B4
Vicarage Rd. Walkden M28 60 C4
Vicarage Rd N. OL11 30 D1
Vicarage Rd S. OL11 30 C1
Vicarage Rd W. BL6 21 C2
Vicarage Sq. WN7 75 F5
Vicarage St. Bolton BL3 145 D5
Vicarage St. Oldham OL8 66 C3
Vicarage St. 1 Radcliffe M26 44 A3
Vicarage St. Shaw OL2 149 B7
Vicarage View. OL11 30 D1
Vicarage Way. OL2 149 A6
Vicars Hall Gdns. M28 77 F5
Vicars Hall La. M28 77 F4
Vicars Rd. M21 109 A8
Vicars St. M30 79 F2
Viceroy Ct. M20 110 B2
Vicker Cl. M27 61 F2
Vicker Gr. M20 109 F5
Vickerman St. BL1 143 D2
Vickers Row. BL4 60 B8
Vickers St. Bolton BL3 145 E5
Vickers St. M'ster M10, M40 160 E4
Victor Ave. BL9 140 E4
Victor Cl. WN5 54 D8
Victor Mann St. M11 100 A7
Victor St. Heywood OL10 46 E8
Victor St. M'ster M3 158 D2
Victor St. M'ster M40 159 C4
Victor St. Oldham OL8 66 B1
Victoria Ave. Alt'ham WA15 119 F7
Victoria Ave. Bredbury SK6 112 F3
Victoria Ave. Cheadle SK8 123 A2
Victoria Ave. Eccles M30 79 F3
Victoria Ave. Hadfield SK14 104 A5
Victoria Ave. Hazel Grove SK7 124 E3
Victoria Ave. Leigh WN2 56 E1
Victoria Ave. M'ster M9 64 C5
Victoria Ave. M'ster M20 110 A3
Victoria Ave. M'ster M19 111 A8
Victoria Ave. Swinton M27 80 A8
Victoria Ave. Whitefield M45 63 A8
Victoria Ave. Wigan WN6 37 A1
Victoria Ave E. M24, M40, M9 65 B4
Victoria Avenue Cty Prim Sch. M9 64 D5
Victoria Bridge St. M3 158 F2
Victoria Cl. Aspull WN2 38 B6
Victoria Cl. Boothstown M28 78 A6
Victoria Cl. Bramhall SK7 132 D6
Victoria Cl. Stockport SK3 170 E7
Victoria Cres. Eccles M30 79 F3
Victoria Cres. Standish WN6 36 E8
Victoria Ct. 5 Ashton-u-L OL7 166 A1
Victoria Ct. Farnworth BL4 42 C2
Victoria Ct. Horwich BL6 22 C3
Victoria Ct. M'ster M11 165 C8
Victoria Ct. Stretford M32 96 C2
Victoria Dr. M33 108 D3
Victoria Gdns. Hyde SK14 167 F4
Victoria Gdns. Shaw OL2 149 B7
Victoria Gr. Bolton BL1 142 C1
Victoria Gr. M'ster M14 110 C7
Victoria Gr. Reddish SK4 111 D5
Victoria Grange. M20 110 A4
Victoria House. Eccles M30 80 A4
Victoria House. M'ster M11 165 C8
Victoria Ind Est. WN6 37 B7
Victoria Ind Est The. M4 160 D1
Victoria La. Swinton M27 79 D8
Victoria La. Whitefield M45 62 F7
Victoria Lodge. M7 81 C5
Victoria Mews. 1 Dukinfield SK16 101 C6
Victoria Mews. Whitefield M45 & BL9 45 B2
Victoria Mkt. SK15 86 A1
Victoria Par. Rawtenstall BB4 2 E8
Victoria Par. Urmston M41 95 D2
Victoria Park Jun Sch. M32 96 D2
Victoria Pk. SK1 124 B8
Victoria Rd. Alt'ham WA15 119 D3
Victoria Rd. Alt'ham WA15 120 A6
Victoria Rd. Bolton BL1 40 D8
Victoria Rd. Dukinfield SK14 & SK16 101 C6
Victoria Rd. Eccles M30 79 E3
Victoria Rd. Eccles M6 80 A4
Victoria Rd. Garswood WN4 72 D4
Victoria Rd. Horwich BL6 22 C2
Victoria Rd. Irlam M44 93 F1
Victoria Rd. Kearsley BL4 61 A6
Victoria Rd. M'ster M16 97 D2
Victoria Rd. M'ster M19 98 F1
Victoria Rd. M'ster M14 110 B8
Victoria Rd. Newton-l-W WA12 89 C3
Victoria Rd. Platt Bridge WN2 56 A2
Victoria Rd. Sale M33 108 D3
Victoria Rd. Stockport SK1 112 B1
Victoria Rd. Stretford M32 96 D2
Victoria Rd. Urmston M41 95 B2
Victoria Rd. Wilmslow SK9 137 B8
Victoria Rd. Wythenshawe M22 121 D8
Victoria Sq. Bolton BL1 145 F7
Victoria Sq. M'ster M4 159 B2
Victoria Sq. Walkden M28 60 D3
Victoria St. Alt'ham WA14 119 D5
Victoria St. Ashton-u-L OL7 166 A1
Victoria St. Bacup OL13 3 D8
Victoria St. Blackrod BL6 21 D2
Victoria St. Boothstown M28 78 A6
Victoria St. Bury BL8 26 E7
Victoria St. Bury BL8 140 D2
Victoria St. Bury BL8 140 D3
Victoria St. Denton M34 100 F3
Victoria St. Dukinfield SK16 101 D8
Victoria St. Dukinfield SK14 102 A5
Victoria St. Failsworth M35 83 D6
Victoria St. 4 Farnworth BL4 42 B2
Victoria St. Glossop SK13 116 C8
Victoria St. Heywood OL10 29 E1
Victoria St. Leigh WN7 75 E6
Victoria St. Littleborough OL15 16 B5
Victoria St. M'ster M3 158 F2
Victoria St. M'ster M11 165 C8
Victoria St. Middleton M24 65 A8
Victoria St. Oldham OL4 67 A6
Victoria St. Oldham OL4 67 E6
Victoria St. Oldham OL8 84 F8
Victoria St. Oldham OL9 152 C8
Victoria St. Platt Bridge WN2 56 A2
Victoria St. 22 R'dale OL12 14 F1
Victoria St. 1 Radcliffe M26 44 A3
Victoria St. Ramsbottom BL0 138 B6
Victoria St. Rawtenstall BB4 2 E8
Victoria St. Shaw OL2 149 B7
Victoria St. 1 Stalybridge SK15 85 F2
Victoria St. Stalybridge SK15 86 D4
Victoria St. Westhoughton BL5 57 F8
Victoria St. Whitworth OL12 14 C8
Victoria St. Wigan WN5 54 F6
Victoria St E. OL7 166 A2
Victoria Sta. M3 159 A3
Victoria Station App. M'ster M3 & M4 159 A2
Victoria Terr. Heywood OL10 29 C4
Victoria Terr. Leigh WN2 74 F8
Victoria Terr. M'ster M12 98 F4
Victoria Terr. Milnrow OL16 32 A5
Victoria Way. Bramhall SK7 132 D6
Victoria Way. Leigh WN7 75 E7
Victoria Way. Royton OL2 48 C6
Victoria Wlk. OL9 48 C1
Victory Gr. M34 100 C7
Victory Rd. Irlam M44 105 C4
Victory Rd. Little Lever BL3 43 B4
Victory St. Bolton BL1 144 C8
Victory St. M'ster M14 98 C3
Victory Trad Est. BL3 148 A5
Vienna Rd. SK3 170 D6
Vienna Rd E. SK3 170 E6
View Cl. OL3 51 C5
View St. BL3 145 D5
Viewfield Wlk. 16 M9 157 E7
Viewlands Dr. SK9 131 D2
Vigo Ave. BL3 146 B3
Vigo St. Heywood OL10 29 E1
Vigo St. Oldham OL4 67 D5
Vigo St. 1 Wigan WN2 37 F2
Viking Cl. M11 160 F1
Viking St. Bolton BL3 42 A4
Viking St. R'dale OL11 30 C8
Villa Ave. WN6 37 A4
Villa Rd. OL8 66 F4
Village Circ. M17 96 D6
Village Ct. SK9 131 D1
Village Gn. OL3 69 B8
Village St. M7 81 C5
Village The. M31 & M41 106 F8
Village View. 2 WN7 76 B4
Village Way. SK9 131 D1
Village Wlk. 13 M11 83 C1
Villdale Ave. SK2 124 C7
Villiers Ct. M45 63 A6
Villiers Dr. OL8 153 E5
Villiers St. Ashton-u-L OL6 85 D2
Villiers St. Bury BL9 141 A3
Villiers St. Hyde SK14 167 F2
Villiers St. Salford M6 154 F4
Vinca Gr. M7 155 D6
Vincent Ave. Eccles M30 79 D4
Vincent Ave. M'ster M21 97 A1
Vincent Ave. Oldham OL4 67 C8
Vincent Ct. BL3 147 E3
Vincent St. Bolton BL1 145 D6
Vincent St. Hyde SK14 113 F8
Vincent St. Littleborough OL15 16 A6
Vincent St. M'ster M7 155 F7
Vincent St. M'ster M11 165 C8
Vincent St. Middleton M24 47 A2
Vincent St. 18 R'dale OL16 31 A5
Vincent Way. WN5 54 D8
Vine Ave. M27 80 B8
Vine Cl. Sale M33 107 C5
Vine Cl. Shaw OL2 149 B7
Vine Ct. R'dale OL16 31 B6
Vine Ct. Stretford M32 96 D1
Vine Fold. M40 65 F1
Vine Gr. Stockport SK2 124 C6
Vine Gr. Wigan WN3 150 C7
Vine Pl. OL11 139 F5
Vine St. Ashton-u-L OL6 166 C4
Vine St. Eccles M30 79 C1
Vine St. Hazel Grove SK7 124 E3
Vine St. Hindley WN2 56 D6
Vine St. M'ster M7 81 C8
Vine St. M'ster M11 & M18 99 E6
Vine St. Oldham OL9 66 B3
Vine St. Prestwich M25 63 C5
Vine St. Ramsbottom BL0 11 A4
Vine St. Wigan WN1 37 D1
Vinery Gr. M34 100 E3
Vineyard Cl. OL12 15 C7
Vineyard St. OL4 67 B7
Viola Cl. WN6 19 D2
Viola St. Bolton BL1 143 E3
Viola St. Droylsden M11 83 D2
Violet Ave. BL4 42 A1
Violet Ct. M22 121 D3
Violet Hill Ct. OL4 67 E8
Violet St. Ashton-i-M WN4 73 B2
Violet St. Droylsden M18 99 F6
Violet St. Ince-i-M WN3 151 E6
Violet St. Stockport SK2 170 F6
Violet Way. M24 65 D7
Vip Centre Ind Est. OL1 49 C1
Virgil St. M15 162 D6
Virginia Chase. SK8 131 F8
Virginia Cl. M23 120 D7
Virginia St. Bolton BL3 146 B4
Virginia St. R'dale OL11 30 E4
Virginia Way. WN5 54 C8
Viscount Dr. Alt'ham M90 & WA15 129 F7
Viscount Dr. Gatley SK8 131 D7
Viscount Rd. WN5 54 D8
Viscount St. M14 98 C3
Vista Ave. WA12 89 A4
Vista Rd. WA11 & WA12 89 A6
Vista The. M44 105 C4
Vivian St. OL11 139 E5
Vixen Cl. M21 109 E7
Voewood House. SK1 124 B8
Voltaire Ave. M6 80 B3
Vulcan Cl. WA12 89 C1
Vulcan Dr. WN1 151 D7
Vulcan Ind Est. WA12 89 D1
Vulcan Rd. WN5 54 D8
Vulcan St. OL1 & OL4 49 B1
Vyner Gr. M33 107 F6
Wadcroft Wlk. 19 M9 157 E8
Waddicor Ave. OL6 85 E6
Waddington Cl. Bury BL8 26 E2
Waddington Cl. Golborne WA3 90 F8
Waddington Fold. OL16 31 C2
Waddington Rd. BL1 142 A1
Waddington St. OL9 152 C8
Wade Bank. BL5 57 F8
Wade Hill La. OL3 & OL4 68 E8
Wade House. 8 M30 79 D1
Wade Row. OL3 69 B8
Wade St. 7 Bolton BL3 147 F3
Wade St. Middleton M24 65 D6
Wade Wlk. M11 165 A8
Wadebridge Ave. M23 120 D7
Wadebrook Gr. 4 SK9 131 D1
Wadeford Cl. M40 159 C3
Wadesmill Wlk. M13 163 B7
Wadeson Rd. M13 163 C7
Wadham Gdns. SK6 113 C5
Wadham Way. WA15 119 F1
Wadhurst Wlk. 4 M13 163 C5
Wadridge Ct. 3 BL1 25 B1
Wadsworth Cl. SK9 131 E3
Wadsworth Mews. M43 83 F1
Waggon Rd. Bolton BL2 42 D8
Waggon Rd. Mossley OL5 86 C8
Waggoners Ct. 2 M27 & M28 79 F7
Wagner St. BL1 143 D3
Wagstaffe Dr. M35 83 F7
Wagstaffe St. M24 47 A2
Wain Cl. M30 79 B2
Wain Stones Gn. SK2 124 E6
Waincliffe Ave. M20 & M21 109 D4
Wainfleet Cl. WN3 54 E2
Waingap Cres. OL12 14 D8
Waingap Rise. R'dale OL12 14 F4
Waingap Rise. Whitworth OL12 14 D7
Wainman St. M6 & M7 81 B5
Wainwright Ave. M34 99 F3
Wainwright Cl. Oldham OL4 68 A7
Wainwright Cl. Stockport SK2 124 A7
Wainwright Rd. WA14 119 C5
Wainwright St. Oldham OL8 153 E5
Wainwright St. Stalybridge SK16 85 D1
Waithlands Rd. OL16 31 B6
Wakefield Cres. Romiley SK6 113 A1
Wakefield Cres. Standish WN6 37 A6
Wakefield Dr. Kearsley M27 61 D4
Wakefield Dr. Oldham OL1 48 C1
Wakefield Rd. SK15 86 B3
Wakefield St. Golborne WA3 90 A7
Wakefield St. 2 M'ster M1 163 A7
Wakefield Wlk. M34 101 A1
Wakeling Rd. M34 112 E8
Walcot Pl. WN3 54 F2
Walcott Cl. M13 164 E5
Wald Ave. M14 110 E7
Waldeck St. 1 BL1 145 D8
Waldeck Wlk. 24 M9 64 E3
Walden Ave. OL4 49 D2
Walden Cl. M14 110 A8
Walden Cres. SK7 124 C3
Waldon Ave. SK8 122 D5
Waldon Cl. BL3 146 C4
Waldorf Cl. WN3 54 D2
Wales St. OL1 & OL4 49 C1
Walford Cl. M16 97 E4
Walford Rd. WN4 73 C3
Walk Mill Cl. OL12 15 D4
Walk The. Atherton M46 58 D3
Walk The. R'dale OL16 139 F7
Walkden Ave. WN1 & WN6 37 B2
Walkden Ave E. WN1 37 C2
Walkden High Sch. M28 60 E1
Walkden Market Pl. M28 60 D3
Walkden Rd. Walkden M27 & M28 60 D1
Walkden Rd. Worsley M28 78 E7
Walkden Sta. M28 60 D2
Walkdene Dr. M28 60 B3
Walkdens Ave. M46 58 A2
Walker Ave. Bolton BL3 147 F3
Walker Ave. Failsworth M35 84 B6
Walker Ave. Prestwich M25 & M45 63 A6
Walker Ave. Stalybridge SK15 86 C2
Walker Cl. Hyde SK14 167 F2
Walker Cl. Kearsley BL4 61 A6
Walker Fold. SK14 167 F2
Walker Fold Rd. BL1 23 D4
Walker Gn. M28 79 B5
Walker House. 9 M30 79 D1
Walker La. SK14 167 F2
Walker Rd. Failsworth OL9 65 F2
Walker Rd. Irlam M44 93 F1
Walker Rd. M'ster M9 64 E4
Walker Rd. Worsley M28 79 A4
Walker St. Bolton BL1 145 D6
Walker St. 3 Bury BL9 44 E8
Walker St. Denton M34 100 E4
Walker St. Hadfield SK14 104 A4
Walker St. Heywood OL10 29 C1
Walker St. Middleton M24 64 C7
Walker St. Oldham OL8 153 D6
Walker St. R'dale OL16 31 A7
Walker St. 4 Radcliffe M26 44 C1
Walker St. Stockport SK1 169 E1
Walker St. Westhoughton BL5 57 E8
Walker's Croft. M3 158 F2
Walker's La. OL4 68 A6
Walker's Rd. OL8 66 C2
Walkers Cl. OL3 69 B8
Walkers Ct. Farnworth BL4 60 D8
Walkers Ct. Oldham OL4 67 A6
Walkerwood Dr. SK15 86 D2
Walkway The. BL3 40 F5
Wall Hill Rd. OL3 & OL4 50 E2
Wall St. Oldham OL8 153 F5
Wall St. Salford M5 & M6 154 F2
Wall St. Shevington WN6 36 F1
Wallace Ave. M14 98 D3
Wallace La. WN1 37 E1
Wallace St. 2 OL8 66 F4
Wallasey Ave. M14 98 A1
Wallbank Dr. OL12 14 C7
Wallbank Rd. SK7 124 A1
Wallbrook Ave. WN5 53 D1
Wallbrook Cres. M38 60 B6
Wallbrook Gr. BL4 42 B2
Waller Ave. M14 110 C8
Walley St. BL1 143 E3
Wallgarth Cl. WN3 54 E2
Wallgate. WN3 & WN1 & wn6 150 B7
Wallgate Sta. WN1 150 C8
Wallingford Rd. Handforth SK9 131 C5
Wallingford Rd. Urmston M41 95 F3
Wallis St. Failsworth M40 83 C5
Wallis St. Oldham OL9 66 A4
Wallness La. M6 81 C3
Walls St. WN2 57 C2
Wallshaw Pl. OL1 67 A7
Wallshaw St. OL1 67 A7
Wallsuches. BL6 22 F4
Wallwork Cl. OL11 13 E1
Wallwork Rd. M29 77 D6
Wallwork St. Droylsden M11 99 E8
Wallwork St. Radcliffe M26 44 A4
Wallwork St. Reddish SK5 99 F2
Wallworth Ave. M18 99 D5
Wallworth Terr. SK9 136 E8
Wally Sq. M7 155 E6
Walmer Dr. SK7 124 A1
Walmer Rd. WN2 57 A5
Walmer St. M'ster M14 98 C3
Walmer St. M'ster M18 99 E6
Walmer St E. M14 98 C3
Walmersley Ct. 6 SK6 125 F6
Walmersley Golf Course. BL9 28 B8
Walmersley Old Rd. Bury BL9 27 F7
Walmersley Rd. Bury BL9 27 F6
Walmersley Rd. Failsworth M40 65 E1
Walmesley Ave. WN3 150 C6
Walmesley Dr. WN2 56 B7
Walmesley Rd. WN7 75 E5
Walmesley St. WN1 151 D7
Walmley Gr. BL3 146 C3
Walmsley Ave. OL15 15 F3
Walmsley CE Prim Sch. BL7 8 E1
Walmsley Gr. M41 95 D2
Walmsley St. 1 Bury BL8 27 B4
Walmsley St. Newton-l-W WA12 89 D4
Walmsley St. Stalybridge SK15 102 A8
Walmsley St. Stockport SK5 169 F3
Walney Rd. Wigan WN3 54 D2
Walney Rd. Wythenshawe M22 121 D4
Walnut Ave. Bury BL9 141 C3
Walnut Ave. Oldham OL4 67 D8
Walnut Ave. Wigan WN1 37 D2
Walnut Cl. Hyde SK14 102 A2
Walnut Cl. Kearsley M27 61 D4
Walnut Cl. Wilmslow SK9 137 E8
Walnut Gr. Leigh WN7 75 F8
Walnut Gr. Sale M33 108 A4
Walnut Rd. Partington M31 105 D3
Walnut Rd. Worsley M28 79 A4
Walnut St. Bolton BL1 143 F2
Walnut St. 2 M'ster M18 99 D5
Walnut Tree Rd. SK3 123 A8
Walnut Wlk. M32 96 C1
Walpole Ave. WN3 54 F3
Walpole St. OL16 31 A7
Walsall St. M6 81 A5
Walsden Est. OL14 6 B7
Walsden St. M11 83 C2
Walsh Ave. M9 64 D2
Walsh Cl. WA12 89 C5
Walsh Fold. BL7 9 D2
Walsh House. M46 58 D4
Walsh St. Horwich BL6 22 B4
Walsh St. Oldham OL9 152 B6
Walshaw Brook Cl. BL8 26 F4
Walshaw Dr. M27 79 F7
Walshaw La. BL8 26 E4
Walshaw Rd. BL8 27 B4
Walshaw Wlk. BL8 26 F5
Walshe St. BL9 140 D2
Walsingham Ave. M'ster M20 109 F4
Walsingham Ave. Middleton M24 65 A5
Walter Scott Ave. WN1 37 B5
Walter Scott St. 3 OL1 67 B8
Walter St. Ashton-i-M WN4 73 D4
Walter St. Droylsden M18 99 E6
Walter St. Leigh WN7 75 B5
Walter St. M'ster M16 97 C4
Walter St. M'ster M9 157 D8
Walter St. 3 Oldham OL1 153 F6
Walter St. Prestwich M25 62 F4
Walter St. Radcliffe M26 43 F6
Walter St. Walkden M28 60 D2
Walter St. Wigan WN5 54 D6
Waltham Ave. Glazebury WA3 92 C7
Waltham Ave. Shevington WN6 36 F2
Waltham Dr. SK8 132 B6
Waltham Gdns. M26 43 E5
Waltham Rd. M16 97 E1
Waltham St. OL4 & OL8 67 C4
Walthew House La. WN5 36 C2
Walthew La. Platt Bridge WN2 56 A2
Walton Cl. Heywood OL10 46 D8
Walton Cl. Middleton M24 46 C1
Walton Ct. BL3 147 F4
Walton Dr. Bury BL9 27 E8
Walton Dr. Marple SK6 125 D7
Walton Hall. SK5 99 D2
Walton Hall Dr. SK5 99 D1
Walton House. M35 83 F8
Walton Pl. BL4 60 E7
Walton Rd. Alt'ham WA14 119 B5
Walton Rd. Culcheth WA3 91 F3
Walton Rd. M'ster M9 64 D5
Walton Rd. Sale M33 107 F2
Walton St. Adlington PR7 21 A6
Walton St. Ashton-u-L OL7 84 F5
Walton St. Atherton M46 58 E4
Walton St. Heywood OL10 29 D1
Walton St. 1 Middleton M24 47 A2
Walton St. Stockport SK1 170 F7
Walton Way. M34 101 B1
Walworth Cl. M26 61 C7
Walwyn Cl. M32 96 E1
Wanborough Cl. WN7 75 F7
Wandsworth Ave. M11 83 D2
Wanley Wlk. 12 M9 64 E3
Wansbeck Cl. M32 96 E1
Wansbeck Lodge. M32 96 E1
Wansfell Wlk. M40 160 D2
Wansford St. M14 98 A3
Wanstead Ave. M9 65 B3
Wapping St. BL1 143 D2
War Office Rd. OL11 29 E6
Warbeck Cl. Hindley WN2 56 E3
Warbeck Cl. Reddish SK5 100 A2
Warbeck Rd. M40 65 D2
Warbreck Gr. M33 108 D3
Warburton Bridge Rd. WA13 & WA3 105 A1
Warburton Cl. Alt'ham WA15 129 D6
Warburton Cl. Lymm WA13 117 A4
Warburton Cl. Romiley SK6 113 A1
Warburton Dr. WA15 129 D6
Warburton La. Partington M31 & WA13 105 E2
Warburton La. Partington M31 105 F4
Warburton Pl. 12 M46 58 D3
Warburton Rd. SK9 131 D4
Warburton St. Bolton BL1 143 F2
Warburton St. Eccles M30 79 E1
Warburton St. 3 M'ster M20 110 B3
Warburton St. Salford M5 161 B6
Warburton View. WA3 105 A2
Warcock Rd. OL4 67 C7
Ward La. Diggle OL3 51 D3
Ward La. Disley SK12 135 F4
Ward Rd. M43 84 B1
Ward St. Bredbury SK6 112 F3
Ward St. Hindley WN2 56 E7
Ward St. Hyde SK14 167 E2
Ward St. M'ster M9 64 C2
Ward St. 1 M'ster M20 110 B3
Ward St. M'ster M40 & M9 157 F8
Ward St. Oldham OL9 152 C7
Ward St. Oldham OL1 153 D8
Ward St. Stockport SK1 124 A7
Warden La. M40 83 B6
Warden St. M40 83 B6
Wardend Cl. M38 60 A6
Wardens Bank. BL5 57 E5
Wardle Brook Ave. SK14 102 D3
Wardle Brook Wlk. SK14 102 D3
Wardle Cl. Radcliffe M26 43 E5
Wardle Cl. Stretford M32 96 E2
Wardle Ct. M33 108 C4
Wardle Edge. OL12 15 B4
Wardle Fold. OL12 15 C7
Wardle Gdns. OL12 15 C3
Wardle High Sch. OL12 15 D5
Wardle Rd. R'dale OL12 15 C4
Wardle Rd. Sale M33 108 C4
Wardle St. Bacup OL13 3 D8
Wardle St. Bolton BL2 148 C5
Wardle St. Littleborough OL15 16 A6
Wardle St. M'ster M10 & M40 160 E3
Wardley Ave. M'ster M21 97 E1
Wardley Ave. M'ster M16 & M21 109 E8
Wardley Ave. Walkden M28 60 B3
Wardley CE (VC) Prim Sch. M27 61 E2
Wardley Hall La. M28 79 A8
Wardley Hall Rd. M27 & M28 61 B1
Wardley House. M6 80 C4
Wardley Ind Est. Swinton M27 61 C1
Wardley Ind Est. Swinton M28 79 C8
Wardley Rd. M29 77 D8
Wardley Sq. M29 77 D8
Wardley St. Swinton M27 79 F8
Wardley St. Wigan WN5 54 B6
Wardlow Ave. 25 Gamesley SK13 171 D1
Wardlow Ave. Wigan WN5 36 A1
Wardlow Fold. 28 SK13 171 D1
Wardlow Gdns. 27 SK13 171 D1
Wardlow Gr. 29 SK13 171 D1
Wardlow Mews. SK13 171 D1
Wardlow St. BL3 146 B4
Wardlow Wlk. 26 SK13 171 D1
Wardour St. Atherton M46 58 C2
Wardour St. Atherton M46 58 D2
Wards Pl. 3 WN7 76 B4
Wardsend Wlk. 13 M15 162 D6
Wareham Gr. M30 79 C3
Wareham St. M8 64 B1
Wareing St. M29 76 F8
Wareing Way. BL3 145 E6
Wareings Yd. 5 OL11 31 A4
Warfield Wlk. 30 M9 64 E3
Warford Ave. SK12 134 A2
Warford La. WA16 136 B1
Warford St. M40 159 B3
Warford Terr. WA16 136 B2
Wargrave CE Prim Sch. WA12 89 C1
Wargrave House Sch. WA12 89 D1
Wargrave Mews. WA12 89 C1
Wargrave Rd. WA12 89 C2
Warham St. SK9 137 B7
Warke The. M28 78 F6
Warlands End Gate. OL14 6 F5
Warley Cl. SK8 122 E6
Warley Gr. SK16 101 C8

Win – Woo 239

Windsor Ave. Irlam M44 .... 94 B3
Windsor Ave. Little Lever BL3 43 A3
Windsor Ave. M'ster SK4 ...... 168 A3
Windsor Ave.
Newton-l-W WA12 .... 89 D2
Windsor Ave. Oldham OL9 .... 66 A4
Windsor Ave. Sale M33 .... 108 B6
Windsor Ave. Swinton M27 ... 62 A2
Windsor Ave. Tyldesley M29 .. 77 A6
Windsor Ave. Urmston M41 .... 94 F2
Windsor Ave. Walkden M38 ... 60 B5
Windsor Ave. Whitefield M45 . 63 A7
Windsor Ave. Wilmslow SK9 136 F7
Windsor Cl. Poynton SK12 .. 133 D4
Windsor Cl. Ramsbottom BL8 . 11 A1
Windsor Comm High Sch
The. M5 .... 81 A2
Windsor Cres. Aspull WN2 .... 38 D5
Windsor Cres.
M'ster M25 & M8 .... 63 E3
Windsor Ct. Bolton BL3 .... 147 D2
Windsor Ct. Sale M33 .... 107 F5
Windsor Dr. Ashton-u-L OL7 ... 84 F4
Windsor Dr. Bury BL8 .... 44 B8
Windsor Dr. Droylsden M34 ... 84 D1
Windsor Dr. Dukinfield SK16 101 F7
Windsor Dr. Horwich BL6 .... 22 E2
Windsor Dr. Marple SK6 ...... 125 E5
Windsor Dr.
Newton-l-W WA11 .... 89 A7
Windsor Dr. Sale WA14 .... 119 F8
Windsor Dr. Stalybridge SK15 86 A3
Windsor Gr. Ashton-u-L OL6 ... 85 C7
Windsor Gr. Bolton BL1 .... 142 C1
Windsor Gr. Cheadle SK8 ..... 131 F8
Windsor Gr. Hindley WN2 ...... 57 B3
Windsor Gr. Kearsley M26 ..... 61 B7
Windsor Gr. Romiley SK6 ..... 113 E2
Windsor Rd. Ashton-i-M WN4 . 73 C1
Windsor Rd. Billinge WN5 ...... 71 F5
Windsor Rd. Bolton BL7 .... 25 A7
Windsor Rd. Bredbury SK6 .. 112 C3
Windsor Rd. Droylsden M43 ... 83 E1
Windsor Rd. Failsworth M40 .. 83 E4
Windsor Rd. Golborne WA3 .... 90 C8
Windsor Rd. Hazel Grove SK7 124 F2
Windsor Rd. Hyde SK14 .... 113 E7
Windsor Rd. Leigh WN7 .... 76 E6
Windsor Rd. M'ster M25 .... 63 E3
Windsor Rd. M'ster M19 .... 99 A1
Windsor Rd. M'ster M9 .... 157 E7
Windsor Rd. Oldham OL8 .... 66 D4
Windsor Rd. Orrell WN8 .... 53 A8
Windsor Rd. Reddish M34 ... 100 A3
Windsor St. Failsworth M40 ... 83 E4
Windsor St. Failsworth M35 ... 84 A8
Windsor St. M'ster M18 .... 99 C4
Windsor St. R'dale OL11 .... 31 A5
Windsor St. Salford M5 .... 81 B1
Windsor St. Stockport SK2 .. 124 A6
Windsor St. Tyldesley M46 ..... 58 E2
Windsor St. Wigan WN1 .... 37 D1
Windsor Terr. Milnrow OL16 .. 31 E6
Windsor Terr. R'dale OL16 ..... 31 C7
Windsor Wlk. SK2 .... 170 F6
Windy Bank Ave. WA3 .... 90 E8
Windy Harbour La. BL7 .... 25 B8
Windybank. M9 .... 64 C5
Winfell Dr. M10 & M40 .... 160 D3
Winfield Ave. M20 .... 110 D6
Winfield Dr. M18 .... 99 D6
Winfield Gr. SK6 .... 114 B1
Winfield St. SK14 .... 167 F2
Winford St. M9 .... 157 E8
Wingate Ave. BL8 .... 27 B2
Wingate Dr. Alt'ham WA15 .. 120 B5
Wingate Dr. M'ster M20 ...... 110 C2
Wingate Dr. Whitefield M45 ... 44 E1
Wingate Rd. M'ster SK4 ..... 168 C4
Wingate Rd. Walkden M38 ..... 60 B4
Wingate St. OL11 .... 13 E1
Wingates Gr. BL5 .... 39 D3
Wingates Ind Est. BL5 .... 39 D2
Wingates La. BL5 & BL6 .... 39 E5
Wingates Rd. WN1 .... 37 C4
Wingates Sq. BL5 .... 39 E3
Wingates St John's CE
Prim Sch. BL5 .... 39 E3
Wingfield Ave. SK9 .... 136 E6
Wingfield Dr. Pendlebury M27 80 A6
Wingfield Dr. Wilmslow SK9 136 E6
Wingfield Gr. SK13 .... 116 F7
Wingfield St. M32 .... 96 D4
Wingfield Villas. OL15 .... 16 C7
Wingrove House. 3 M6 ..... 154 F2
Wings Gr. OL10 .... 46 D7
Winhill Rd. SK12 .... 127 C1
Winifred Ave. BL9 .... 28 F4
Winifred Rd. Failsworth M40 .. 83 B7
Winifred Rd. Farnworth BL4 ... 42 A1
Winifred Rd. M'ster M20 ...... 110 B3
Winifred Rd. Stockport SK2 . 124 A6
Winifred Rd. Urmston M41 .... 95 D2
Winifred St. 2 Eccles M30 ..... 79 B1
Winifred St. Hyde SK14 .... 113 E7
Winifred St. Ince-i-M WN3 .. 151 E6
Winifred St. R'dale OL12 .... 14 B1
Winifred St.
Ramsbottom BL0 .... 138 B5
Winmarith Dr. WA15 .... 129 D7
Winmarleigh Cl. BL8 .... 26 F1
Winmarleigh Gdns. WN7 .... 75 E3
Winnall Wlk. 3 M40 .... 83 C6
Winnard St. WA3 .... 74 B2
Winnats Cl. SK13 .... 116 F8
Winnie St. M40 .... 83 A8
Winnington Gn. SK2 .... 124 D6
Winnington Rd. Marple SK6 125 F7
Winnipeg Quay. M5 .... 99 F8
Winnows The. M34 .... 100 D3
Winscombe Dr. M40 .... 159 C4
Winser St. M1 .... 163 A8
Winsfield Rd. SK7 .... 133 E8
Winsford Dr. OL11 .... 29 F5
Winsford Gr. BL3 .... 40 F5
Winsford Rd. M'ster M14 ...... 98 A1
Winsford Wlk. M33 .... 108 E3
Winskill Rd. M44 .... 106 A8
Winslade Cl. SK7 .... 124 A2
Winsley Rd. M23 .... 108 F2
Winslow Ave. SK14 .... 103 A2
Winslow Pl. M19 .... 110 F6
Winslow Rd. BL3 .... 40 D3
Winslow St. M11 .... 165 A8
Winson Cl. BL3 .... 147 E4
Winstanley Cl. 6 M6 .... 80 D5
Winstanley Coll. WN5 .... 53 F3
Winstanley Pl. WN3 .... 151 E6
Winstanley Prim Sch. WN3 . 54 C2
Winstanley Rd.
Ashton-i-M WN2 .... 73 F8
Winstanley Rd.
Garswood WN4 &WN5 .... 72 B6
Winstanley Rd.
M'ster M10 & M40 .... 160 D3
Winstanley Rd. Orrell WN5 .... 53 F3
Winstanley Rd. Sale M33 .... 108 C5
Winstanley St. WN5 .... 54 F6
Winster Ave. M'ster M7 .... 81 B6
Winster Ave. M'ster M20 ..... 109 E4
Winster Ave. Stretford M32 ... 96 A3
Winster Cl. Bolton BL2 .... 25 F1
Winster Cl. Whitefield M45 .... 63 B8
Winster Dr. Bolton BL2 .... 25 F1
Winster Dr. 3 Middleton M24 46 E2
Winster Dr. Platt Bridge WN2 . 55 F2
Winster Gn. M30 .... 95 B8
Winster Gr. SK2 .... 124 A6
Winster Mews. 17 SK13 ...... 171 E2
Winster Rd. M30 .... 95 B8
Winston Ave. Little Lever BL3 . 43 C3
Winston Ave.
Newton-l-W WA12 .... 89 C3
Winston Ave. R'dale OL11 ..... 29 E6
Winston Cl. Marple SK6 ...... 125 D7
Winston Cl. Radcliffe M26 ..... 43 E5
Winston Rd. M'ster M9 .... 64 F1
Winston Rd. M'ster M40, M9 157 F8
Winston Rd. Sale M33 .... 107 F5
Winswell Cl. M11 .... 83 B2
Winter Hey La. BL6 .... 22 B3
Winter St. BL1 .... 143 D3
Winterbottom Gr. SK14 ...... 102 F2
Winterbottom St. OL9 .... 153 D7
Winterbottom Wlk. 4
SK14 .... 102 F2
Winterburn Ave. M21 .... 109 D4
Winterburn Gn. SK2 .... 124 E5
Winterbutlee Gr. OL14 .... 6 A8
Winterdyne St. M9 .... 157 E7
Winterfield Dr. BL3 .... 146 A3
Winterford Ave. M13 .... 164 D5
Winterford Rd.
M'ster M7 & M8 .... 155 F7
Winterford Rd. Mossley OL5 .. 68 E1
Wintergreen Wlk. 3 M31 .. 105 F3
Wintermans Rd. M21 .... 109 E7
Wintersmlow Ave. M23 .... 108 D1
Winterton Cl. BL5 .... 40 A1
Winterton Rd. SK5 .... 100 A1
Winthrop Ave. M40 & M9 .... 157 D5
Winton Ave. Denton M34 ... 100 D7
Winton Ave. Failsworth M40 .. 65 D1
Winton Ave. Wigan WN5 .... 54 D5
Winton Cl. SK7 .... 123 D1
Winton Ct. WA14 .... 119 C2
Winton Gn. Horwich BL6 ...... 22 F1
Winton Gr. BL3 .... 40 E4
Winton Rd. Alt'ham WA14 ... 119 C2
Winton Rd. Golborne WA3 ..... 90 E6
Winton Rd. Salford M6 .... 80 D5
Winton St. Ashton-u-L OL6 .. 166 B3
Winton St. Littleborough OL15 16 B5
Winton St. 2
Stalybridge SK15 .... 86 B1
Winward St. Bolton BL3 ...... 146 A4
Winward St. Leigh WN7 .... 75 B5
Winward St. 13
Westhoughton BL5 .... 39 E1
Winwick La. WA3 .... 90 E3
Winwick Rd. WA12 .... 89 F1
Winwood Dr. M24 .... 47 B1
Winwood Fold. M24 .... 46 F4
Winwood Rd. M20 .... 122 C8
Wirral Cl. Culcheth WA3 .... 91 E4
Wirral Cl. Swinton M27 .... 62 A2
Wirral Cres. SK3 .... 123 A8
Wirral Dr. WN3 .... 54 C2
Wisbech Dr. M23 .... 108 F1
Wisbeck Rd. BL2 .... 148 C8
Wiseley St. M11 .... 164 E8
Wiseman Terr. M25 .... 63 C4
Wishaw Sq. M21 .... 109 A7
Wisley Cl. SK5 .... 112 A8
Wistaria Rd. M18 .... 99 D5
Withall House. 3 WN1 .... 151 D8
Witham Ave. M22 .... 121 E5
Witham Cl. Heywood OL10 ..... 29 A4
Witham Cl. Standish WN6 ...... 19 D1
Witham St. OL6 .... 85 E4
Withenfield Rd. M23 .... 120 F8
Withens Gn. SK2 .... 124 E6
Withington Ave. WA3 .... 92 A4
Withington Dr. M29 .... 77 C7
Withington Girls Sch. M14 110 C8
Withington Gn. M24 .... 47 A6
Withington Golf Course.
M20 .... 109 F2
Withington Hospl. M20 .... 109 F6
Withington La. WN2 .... 38 C2
Withington Rd.
M'ster M16 & M21 .... 97 D2
Withington Rd.
M'ster M16 & M21 .... 109 D8
Withington St. Heywood OL10 46 E8
Withington St. Salford M6 ...... 81 A5
Withins Ave. M26 .... 44 C5
Withins Cl. BL2 .... 42 E8
Withins Dr. BL2 .... 42 E8
Withins Gr. BL2 .... 42 E8
Withins La. Bolton BL2 .... 42 E8
Withins La. Radcliffe M26 ...... 44 C5
Withins Rd. Culcheth WA3 ..... 91 D3
Withins Rd. Oldham OL8 .... 66 B2
Withins Sch. BL2 .... 25 E2
Withins Sports Ctr. BL2 .... 25 E2
Withins St. M26 .... 44 C4
Withnell Dr. BL8 .... 27 A1
Withnell Rd. M19 .... 110 D3
Withy Gr. M4 & M60 .... 159 A2
Withy Tree Gr. 1 M34 .... 101 A2
Withycombe Pl. M6 .... 81 A5
Withypool Dr. SK2 .... 124 C5
Witley Dr. M33 .... 107 D6
Witley Rd. OL16 .... 31 B7
Witney Cl. 15 BL1 .... 143 E2
Wittenbury Rd. SK4 .... 168 B2
Witterage Cl. M12 .... 164 F6
Witton Wlk. M7 .... 155 F6
Woburn Ave. Bolton BL2 .... 25 C3
Woburn Ave. Leigh WN7 .... 57 D1
Woburn Ave.
Newton-l-W WA12 .... 89 D2
Woburn Cl. M'ster M16 .... 97 F3
Woburn Cl. Milnrow OL16 ...... 31 E6
Woburn Ct. SK12 .... 133 F4
Woburn Dr. Alt'ham WA15 ... 120 B2
Woburn Dr. Bury BL9 .... 44 F5
Woburn Rd. M16 .... 97 A2
Woden St. M5 .... 161 C7
Woden's Ave. M5 .... 161 C7
Woking Rd. SK8 .... 132 A7
Woking Terr. BL1 .... 143 E1
Wolfenden Gn. BB4 .... 2 F8
Wolfenden Prim Sch. BL1 . 143 E2
Wolfenden St. BL1 .... 143 E2
Wolfenden Terr. 26 BL1 ...... 143 E2
Wolford Dr. M29 .... 59 C1
Wolfreton Cres. M27 .... 62 A3
Wolfson Sq. WN4 .... 72 F4
Wollaton Wlk. M34 .... 100 E1
Wolmer St. WN4 .... 73 A4
Wolseley House. M33 .... 108 C6
Wolseley Pl. M20 .... 110 B5
Wolseley Rd. M33 .... 108 C6
Wolseley St. 1 Bury BL8 .... 27 B1
Wolseley St. Newhey OL16 .... 32 B4
Wolsey Cl. Ashton-i-M WN4 .. 73 A5
Wolsey Cl. Radcliffe M26 ...... 44 A3
Wolsey Dr. WA14 .... 119 A1
Wolsey St. Heywood OL10 ..... 29 C1
Wolsey St. Radcliffe M26 .... 44 A3
Wolstenholme Ave. BL9 .... 27 F6
Wolstenholme Coalpit La.
OL11 .... 13 B2
Wolstenholme La. OL11 .... 13 C2
Wolstenvale Cl. M24 .... 47 B1
Wolver Cl. M38 .... 60 B6
Wolverton Ave. OL8 .... 66 D3
Wolverton Dr. SK9 .... 131 D1
Wolvesey. OL11 .... 139 E6
Wolveton St. M12 .... 164 F7
Wood Bank Rd. OL15 .... 16 A3
Wood Bank Terr. OL5 .... 68 D2
Wood Brook La. OL4 .... 68 B7
Wood Brook Rd. OL4 .... 68 B7
Wood Cottage Cl. 4 M28 ...... 59 F3
Wood Cotts. SK6 .... 113 A6
Wood Cres. OL4 .... 67 E3
Wood End. SK7 .... 123 D2
Wood Fold. BL7 .... 25 C6
Wood Fold Prim Sch. WN6 . 36 D8
Wood Gdns. SK9 .... 137 B2
Wood Gr. Denton M34 .... 100 F4
Wood Gr. Romiley SK6 .... 113 A5
Wood Gr. Whitefield M45 ...... 44 F3
Wood Hey Cl. M26 .... 43 D3
Wood Hey Gr. 2
Denton M34 .... 101 A2
Wood Hey Gr. R'dale OL12 .... 14 F4
Wood La. Alt'ham WA15 ...... 120 B5
Wood La.
Ashton-u-L OL6 & OL7 .... 85 B5
Wood La. Marple SK6 .... 125 E5
Wood La. Middleton M24 .... 65 B7
Wood La. Mobberley WA16 .. 129 B1
Wood La. Mobberley WA16 .. 129 D1
Wood La. Partington M31 ... 105 D3
Wood La.
Wrightington Bar WN6 .... 18 E8
Wood La N. SK10 .... 134 B1
Wood La W. SK10 .... 133 F1
Wood Lea Bank. 9 BB4 .... 2 F8
Wood Lea Rd. BB4 .... 2 F8
Wood Mount. WA15 .... 120 B5
Wood Rd. M'ster M16 .... 97 D3
Wood Rd. Sale M33 .... 108 B1
Wood Rd N. M16 .... 97 C3
Wood Road La. Bury BL8 .... 27 B8
Wood Road La.
Ramsbottom BL8 & BL9 .... 11 C1
Wood Sq. Droylsden M43 .... 100 A8
Wood Sq. Uppermill OL3 .... 69 B6
Wood St. Alt'ham WA14 ...... 119 D4
Wood St. Ashton-u-L OL6 ... 166 B2
Wood St. Atherton M46 .... 58 B4
Wood St. Bolton BL1 .... 145 F7
Wood St. Bury BL8 .... 27 C3
Wood St. Cheadle SK8 .... 122 D6
Wood St. Denton M34 .... 100 F4
Wood St. Dukinfield SK16 .... 101 C6
Wood St. Eccles M30 .... 79 F1
Wood St. Glossop SK13 .... 116 C8
Wood St. Golborne WA3 .... 90 B8
Wood St. Heywood OL10 .... 29 D2
Wood St. Hindley WN2 .... 57 B3
Wood St. Hollingworth SK14 . 103 D5
Wood St. Horwich BL6 .... 22 C3
Wood St. Hyde SK14 .... 167 E2
Wood St. Littleborough OL15 .. 16 B5
Wood St. M'ster M3 .... 158 E2
Wood St. M'ster M3 .... 158 F1
Wood St. M'ster M11 .... 165 B8
Wood St. Middleton M24 .... 64 F8
Wood St. Newhey OL16 .... 32 C4
Wood St. Oldham OL1 .... 67 B8
Wood St. R'dale OL11 & OL16 . 31 A6
Wood St. Radcliffe M26 .... 61 E8
Wood St. Ramsbottom BL0 ... 138 B5
Wood St. Shaw OL2 .... 48 F8
Wood St. 6 Stalybridge SK15 85 F2
Wood St. Stockport SK3 ...... 169 E1
Wood St. Tyldesley M29 .... 77 B8
Wood St. Westhoughton BL5 .. 57 E8
Wood St. Wigan WN5 .... 54 F7
Wood St. Wigan WN3 .... 150 C7
Wood Terr. BL2 .... 26 D1
Wood Top Ave. OL11 .... 29 F5
Wood View. Heywood OL10 .... 29 C4
Wood View. Shevington WN6 . 36 B5
Wood View.
Wythenshawe M22 .... 109 D1
Wood's Hospl. SK13 .... 104 C3
Wood's La. WN4 .... 73 C5
Wood's St. WN3 .... 150 C7
Woodacres Ct. SK9 .... 136 F6
Woodall Cl. M33 .... 108 D4
Woodark Cl. OL4 .... 67 F5
Woodbank. SK1 .... 112 B1
Woodbank Ave.
Bredbury SK6 .... 112 E3
Woodbank Ave.
Stockport SK1 .... 124 C8
Woodbank Ct. M41 .... 95 B3
Woodbank Dr. BL8 .... 27 C4
Woodbank Works Ind Est.
SK1 .... 112 B1
Woodbine Ave. M44 .... 105 D4
Woodbine Cres. SK2 .... 170 F7
Woodbine Rd. Bolton BL3 ... 146 C3
Woodbine Rd. Lymm WA13 . 117 B4
Woodbine St. OL11 & OL16 .. 31 A5
Woodbine St E. OL16 .... 31 B5
Woodbourne Ct. M33 .... 108 B2
Woodbourne Rd.
M'ster SK4 .... 111 C6
Woodbourne Rd. Sale M33 108 A2
Woodbray Ave. M19 .... 110 E5
Woodbridge Ave. M34 .... 100 E7
Woodbridge Gdns. OL12 .... 14 C2
Woodbridge Gr. M23 .... 109 A1
Woodbridge Rd. M41 .... 94 D3
Woodbrook Ave. Hyde SK14 167 F2
Woodbrook Ave. Oldham OL4 68 B7
Woodbrook Dr. WN3 .... 54 D4
Woodbrook Rd. SK9 .... 137 C1
Woodburn Dr. BL1 .... 142 B3
Woodburn Rd. M22 .... 121 D8
Woodbury Cres. SK16 .... 101 B7
Woodbury Rd. SK3 .... 123 B7
Woodchurch. WN1 .... 37 F1
Woodchurch Cl. 3 BL1 ...... 143 E1
Woodchurch Wlk. OL9 .... 152 B6
Woodcock Cl. Droylsden M43 84 C3
Woodcock Cl. R'dale OL11 ..... 29 F7
Woodcock Dr. WN2 .... 56 B2
Woodcock Gr. SK13 .... 104 E1
Woodcock House. WN1 .... 151 D8
Woodcock Sq. M'ster M15 ... 162 F6
Woodcock Sq. 10
Wigan WN1 .... 150 C8
Woodcote Ave. SK7 .... 123 C2
Woodcote Rd. Sale M33 ..... 107 A3
Woodcote Rd. Sale WA14 ... 107 D1
Woodcote View. SK9 .... 131 F1
Woodcote Wlk. M8 .... 156 C8
Woodcott Gr. 3 SK9 .... 131 E1
Woodcourt. WN3 .... 150 B6
Woodcroft.
Appley Bridge WN6 .... 35 E6
Woodcroft. Stockport SK2 ... 124 D6
Woodcroft Ave. M19 .... 110 E4
Wooddagger Cl. WN2 .... 56 F5
Woodeaton Cl. OL2 .... 49 A4
Wooded Cl. BL9 .... 27 F5
Woodedge. WN4 .... 73 A3
Woodend. OL2 .... 149 C8
Woodend Ctr Ind Pk. OL5 ..... 68 D2
Woodend Dr. SK15 .... 102 D6
Woodend La. Alt'ham WA16 129 E1
Woodend La. Hyde SK14 ..... 167 D1
Woodend La.
Littleborough OL12 .... 15 D6
Woodend La.
Stalybridge SK15 .... 102 D6
Woodend Mills. OL4 .... 67 F5
Woodend Rd. Stockport SK3 123 F4
Woodend Rd.
Wythenshawe M22 .... 121 D4
Woodend St. Oldham OL1 ...... 48 E1
Woodend St. Oldham OL4 ...... 67 F5
Woodend View. OL5 .... 68 D2
Woodfield. M22 .... 121 D3
Woodfield Ave. Hyde SK14 .. 113 D8
Woodfield Ave. R'dale OL12 .. 14 E2
Woodfield Ave. Romiley SK6 113 A4
Woodfield Cl.
Hollingworth SK14 .... 103 F5
Woodfield Cl. Oldham OL8 .... 66 C4
Woodfield Cres.
Ashton-i-M WN4 .... 73 A2
Woodfield Cres.
Bredbury SK6 .... 112 F2
Woodfield Ct. SK2 .... 124 A4
Woodfield Dr. M28 .... 78 B6
Woodfield Gr. Eccles M30 ..... 79 C1
Woodfield Gr. Farnworth BL4 60 C6
Woodfield Gr. Sale M33 ..... 108 A6
Woodfield Mews. SK14 ...... 113 D8
Woodfield Prim Sch. WN1 ... 37 C4
Woodfield Rd.
Alt'ham WA14 .... 119 C6
Woodfield Rd. Bramhall SK8 132 B7
Woodfield Rd. M'ster M8 ...... 64 A1
Woodfield Rd. M'ster M24 ..... 64 E6
Woodfield Rd. Salford M6 .... 154 D4
Woodfield St. Bolton BL3 ...... 42 A3
Woodfield St. Wigan WN2 ..... 38 A3
Woodfield Terr. OL10 .... 29 E3
Woodfold Ave. M19 .... 99 A2
Woodfold Rd. M35 .... 84 A7
Woodford Ave.
Dukinfield M34 .... 101 A4
Woodford Ave. Eccles M30 ... 79 B2
Woodford Ave. Golborne WA3 90 D7
Woodford Ave. Shaw OL2 ...... 49 D7
Woodford Ct. Droylsden M34 100 B8
Woodford Ct. 3 Hindley WN2 56 E6
Woodford Dr. M27 .... 61 E2
Woodford Gdns. M20 .... 110 A2
Woodford Gr. BL3 .... 146 C4
Woodford Rd. Bramhall SK7 132 E4
Woodford Rd.
Bramhall SK12 .... 133 B6
Woodford St. 4 Hindley WN2 56 E6
Woodford St. 8 Wigan WN5 54 B6
Woodgarth. WN7 .... 75 C5
Woodgarth Ave. M40 .... 83 D5
Woodgarth Dr. M27 .... 79 E6
Woodgarth La. M28 .... 78 F5
Woodgate Ave. Bury BL9 ...... 28 D4
Woodgate Ave. R'dale OL11 .. 30 A6
Woodgate Cl. SK6 .... 112 F3
Woodgate Dr. M25 .... 63 C6
Woodgate Hill Rd. Bury BL9 28 D4
Woodgate Hill Rd. Bury BL9 141 C4
Woodgate Rd. M16 .... 97 E1
Woodgate St. BL3 .... 42 A3
Woodgrange Cl. 2 M6 ...... 154 E2
Woodgreen Cl. 1 WN2 .... 56 D4
Woodgreen Dr. M26 .... 62 A8
Woodhall Ave. M'ster M20 .. 110 A7
Woodhall Ave. Whitefield M45 62 D6
Woodhall Cl. Bolton BL2 .... 25 C3
Woodhall Cl. Bury BL8 .... 27 D5
Woodhall Cl. Woodford SK7 132 E3
Woodhall Cres. SK5 .... 112 A4
Woodhall Rd. SK5 .... 169 F4
Woodhall St. M35 .... 83 F8
Woodhalt Rd. M8 .... 156 A8
Woodham Rd. M23 .... 108 F1
Woodham Wlk. BL1 .... 145 D5
Woodhead Cl. 11
M'ster M16 .... 97 E4
Woodhead Cl. Oldham OL4 .... 67 E8
Woodhead Cl.
Ramsbottom BL0 .... 11 C4
Woodhead Dr. WA15 .... 119 F1
Woodhead Gr. WN3 .... 55 B2
Woodhead Rd.
Alt'ham WA15 .... 119 F1
Woodhead Rd.
Glossop SK14 .... 104 D4
Woodhead Rd.
Tintwistle SK14 .... 104 B8
Woodhey Ct. M33 .... 107 E1
Woodhey High Sch. BL0 .... 11 A3
Woodhey Rd. BL0 .... 11 A3
Woodheys. SK4 .... 110 F3
Woodheys Dr. M33 .... 107 D1
Woodheys Prim Sch. M33 . 107 E2
Woodheys Rd. OL15 .... 16 A2
Woodheys St. 1 M6 .... 154 F1
Woodhill. M24 .... 46 F2
Woodhill Cl. M'ster M18 .... 99 B4
Woodhill Cl. Middleton M24 ... 46 F2
Woodhill Dr. M25 .... 63 B3
Woodhill Fold. BL8 .... 140 D3
Woodhill Gr. M25 .... 63 B3
Woodhill House. 3 M6 ...... 154 F3
Woodhill Rd. Bury BL8 .... 140 D3
Woodhill Rd. Bury BL8 .... 140 D4
Woodhill St. BL8 .... 140 D4
Woodhouse Ct. M41 .... 95 A4
Woodhouse Dr. WN6 .... 36 E2
Woodhouse Knowl. OL3 .... 50 F4
Woodhouse La.
Partington WA14 .... 118 C4
Woodhouse La. R'dale OL12 .. 13 E3
Woodhouse La. Sale M33 ..... 107 C2
Woodhouse La. Sale M33 ..... 107 D2
Woodhouse La. Wigan WN6 .. 36 E3
Woodhouse La. Wigan WN6 .. 36 F2
Woodhouse La.
Wythenshawe M22 .... 121 D4
Woodhouse La.
Wythenshawe M90 .... 130 D7
Woodhouse La.
Wythenshawe M22 .... 130 D8
Woodhouse La E.
M33 & WA15 .... 108 A1
Woodhouse Park Prim Sch.
M22 .... 130 D8
Woodhouse Prim Sch. M41 . 95 A4
Woodhouse Rd. Shaw OL2 .... 32 C1
Woodhouse Rd. Urmston M41 94 F4
Woodhouse Rd. Urmston M41 95 A4
Woodhouse Rd.
Wythenshawe M22 .... 130 D8
Woodhouse St. Atherton M46 58 D2
Woodhouse St. M'ster M18 .... 99 E5
Woodhouse St.
M'ster M10 & M40 .... 157 F5
Woodhouses CE & Free
Church Prim Sch. M35 .... 84 C6
Woodhurst Dr. WN6 .... 19 D1
Wooding Cl. M31 .... 106 A4
Woodlake Ave. M21 .... 109 C4
Woodland Ave. Bolton BL3 ..... 42 B2
Woodland Ave.
Hazel Grove SK7 .... 124 E1
Woodland Ave. Hindley WN2 .. 57 A3
Woodland Ave. Lymm WA13 117 A2
Woodland Ave.
Newton-l-W WA12 .... 89 F3
Woodland Ave. Reddish M18 . 99 E4
Woodland Cres. M25 .... 63 B2
Woodland Dr.
Ashton-i-M WN4 .... 73 B5
Woodland Dr. Lymm WA13 .. 117 A2
Woodland Dr. Standish WN6 . 19 E2
Woodland Gr. Bolton BL7 .... 8 D2
Woodland Gr. Wigan WN1 ...... 37 D2
Woodland Pk. OL2 .... 48 B6
Woodland Rd. Heywood OL10 29 D3
Woodland Rd. M'ster M19 .. 111 A7
Woodland Rd. R'dale OL12 .... 14 C2
Woodland Rd. Reddish M18 ... 99 E6
Woodland Rd. Tyldesley M29 . 77 B7
Woodland St. Heywood OL10 29 D2
Woodland St. M'ster M12 .... 165 B5
Woodland St. R'dale OL12 ..... 15 A2
Woodland View. BL7 .... 25 B8
Woodland Way. M24 .... 64 F6
Woodlands. Bolton BL2 .... 25 D2
Woodlands. Failsworth M35 ... 83 E4
Woodlands. 5 Urmston M41 . 95 C3
Woodlands Ave.
Cheadle SK8 .... 123 A2
Woodlands Ave. Eccles M30 ... 95 A8
Woodlands Ave.
Ince-i-M WN3 .... 151 F6
Woodlands Ave. Irlam M44 .... 94 A3
Woodlands Ave. Leigh WN7 .. 75 F3
Woodlands Ave. R'dale OL11 . 30 A6
Woodlands Ave.
Romiley SK6 .... 113 A5
Woodlands Ave.
Stretford M32 .... 96 D2
Woodlands Ave. Swinton M27 79 D6
Woodlands Ave.
Urmston M41 .... 94 C2
Woodlands Ave.
Whitefield M45 .... 44 E1
Woodlands Cl.
Hollingworth SK14 .... 103 F6
Woodlands Cl.
Mottram-i-L SK14 .... 102 F1
Woodlands Cl.
Stalybridge SK15 .... 102 D7
Woodlands Cl. Worsley M28 .. 78 E7
Woodlands Ct.
Alt'ham WA15 .... 119 E5
Woodlands Ct.
Stockport SK2 .... 124 D8
Woodlands Dr. Atherton M46 58 F5
Woodlands Dr. Romiley SK6 113 A5
Woodlands Dr.
Sale M23 & M33 .... 108 C1
Woodlands Dr.
Shevington WN6 .... 35 F4
Woodlands Dr.
Stockport SK2 .... 124 D8
Woodlands Gr. Bury BL8 .... 27 B3
Woodlands Gr.
Mottram-i-L SK14 .... 102 F1
Woodlands Hospl. M38 .... 59 F4
Woodlands Ind Est. WA12 .... 89 C6
Woodlands Inf Sch. M31 .... 105 D3
Woodlands La. WA15 .... 119 E5
Woodlands Park Rd. SK2 .. 124 D8
Woodlands Parkway.
WA15 .... 119 E6
Woodlands Rd.
Alt'ham WA14 & WA15 .... 119 E5
Woodlands Rd.
Ashton-u-L OL6 .... 85 E6
Woodlands Rd. Edenfield BL0 .. 1 D2
Woodlands Rd.
Handforth SK9 .... 131 E3
Woodlands Rd.
High Lane SK12 .... 135 A6
Woodlands Rd.
M'ster M16 & M21 .... 97 E1
Woodlands Rd. M'ster SK4 . 110 E2
Woodlands Rd. M'ster M8 ... 156 B7
Woodlands Rd. Milnrow OL16 31 F5
Woodlands Rd. Sale M33 .... 108 C4
Woodlands Rd.
Stalybridge SK15 .... 102 D7
Woodlands Rd.
Wilmslow SK9 .... 130 F1
Woodlands Rd. Worsley M28 78 F7
Woodlands Road Sta. M8 . 156 B7
Woodlands Sch. SK2 .... 124 D8
Woodlands St. M8 .... 156 A8
Woodlands The. Bolton BL6 .. 40 C8
Woodlands The. Bury BL8 .. 140 D4
Woodlands The.
Heywood OL10 .... 46 E8
Woodlands The. Wigan WN1 37 D3
Woodlands View. BL0 .... 138 C6
Woodlark Cl. M3 .... 158 D1
Woodlawn Ct. M16 .... 97 C3
Woodlea. M24 .... 65 D7
Woodlea Ave. M19 .... 110 E6
Woodlea Gr. M28 .... 78 E8
Woodleigh Ct. SK9 .... 137 A2
Woodleigh Dr. M35 & M43 .... 84 C4
Woodleigh Rd. OL4 .... 68 A7
Woodleigh St. M9 .... 64 F1
Woodley Ave. M26 .... 44 B1
Woodley Cl. SK2 .... 124 D7
Woodley Gr. WN7 .... 75 D5
Woodley Inf Sch. SK6 .... 113 C5
Woodley Jun Sch. SK6 .... 113 C5
Woodley Prec. SK6 .... 113 A5
Woodley St. BL9 .... 44 F8
Woodley Sta. SK6 .... 113 B6
Woodliffe St. M16 .... 161 C5
Woodlinn Wlk. M9 .... 157 D7
Woodman Dr. BL9 .... 27 E6
Woodman St. SK1 .... 169 E2
Woodmeadow Ct. 9 OL5 ...... 68 C2
Woodmere Dr. M9 .... 64 E3
Woodmount Cl. SK6 .... 113 F2
Woodnook Rd. WN6 .... 35 E8
Woodpark Cl. OL8 .... 67 A3
Woodridge Dr. BL2 .... 25 B1
Woodridings. WA14 .... 119 B3
Woodrow Way. M44 .... 105 F8
Woodrow Wlk. M12 .... 164 F6
Woodroyd Cl. SK7 .... 123 D1
Woodroyd Dr. BL9 .... 141 C3
Woodruff Wlk. 7 M31 .... 105 F3
Woodruffe Gdns. SK6 .... 125 A8
Woodrush Rd. WN6 .... 36 D3
Woods Ct. Middleton M24 ...... 64 C7
Woods Ct.
Newton-l-W WA12 .... 89 A3
Woods Gr. SK8 .... 132 B7
Woods La. Bramhall SK8 ..... 132 B7
Woods La. Uppermill OL3 .... 51 A2
Woods Lea. BL1 .... 40 F7
Woods Moor La. SK2 & SK3 124 A4
Woods Rd. M44 .... 105 F8
Woods The. Alt'ham WA14 ... 119 E6
Woods The. Oldham OL4 .... 68 B6
Woods The. R'dale OL11 .... 30 C3
Woodseats La. SK14 .... 115 B6
Woodsend Circ. M41 .... 94 D3
Woodsend Crescent Rd.
M41 .... 94 D2
Woodsend Gn. M41 .... 94 D3
Woodsend Prim Sch. M41 .. 94 D3
Woodsend Rd. M41 .... 94 E3
Woodsend Rd S. M41 .... 94 E1
Woodshaw Gr. M28 .... 78 C8
Woodside. M'ster SK4 .... 110 F1
Woodside. Newhey OL16 .... 32 C5
Woodside. Shaw OL2 .... 49 D8

Also available in various formats

- Berkshire
- Bristol and Avon
- Buckinghamshire
- Cardiff, Swansea and Glamorgan
- Cheshire
- Derbyshire
- Durham
- Edinburgh & East Central Scotland
- East Essex

- West Essex
- Glasgow & West Central Scotland
- North Hampshire
- South Hampshire
- Hertfordshire
- East Kent
- West Kent
- Lancashire
- Merseyside
- Nottinghamshire

- Oxfordshire
- Staffordshire
- Surrey
- East Sussex
- West Sussex
- Tyne and Wear
- Warwickshire
- South Yorkshire
- West Yorkshire

◆ Colour editions (Hardback, Spiral, Pocket) ◆ Black and white editions (Hardback, Softback, Pocket)

◆ Spiral

◆ Pocket

◆ Hardback

⌂ Ordnance Survey
STREET ATLASES on CD-ROM

The Interactive Street Atlases are CD-ROM versions of the Ordnance Survey/Philip's Street Atlases. They have a wide range of software features, additional levels of mapping, and are remarkably easy to use.

Searches can be carried out for street names and buildings, towns and villages, National Grid references, Postcode districts and sectors, and for page-grid references from the printed Atlases.

You can move around the mapping with no breaks at page boundaries, and scale bars, keys and locator maps can be displayed or hidden. You can measure distances along complex routes, add bookmarks, draw over the mapping with a range of tools, and create hotspots connected to database tables. You can print sections of mapping, and the price includes a licence to make 1,500 prints.

The Interactive Street Atlases can be used effectively together with the printed atlases – for example, you can always see on which page of the printed Atlas a section of electronic mapping appears.

Available now:
- **Berkshire** (£150 + VAT)
- **Hertfordshire** (£150 + VAT)

More titles coming soon!

Network licences and discounts for bulk purchases are available. Prices subject to change without notice.

You can obtain the Atlases by mail order direct from the publisher:

Mapping includes:
- **General Map for orientation**
- **County Map showing major routes**
- **Road Map showing the majority of roads and streets, and highlighting through routes**
- **Street Map, the full mapping from the printed Street Atlases, which forms a "seamless" map of the whole region and can be magnified**

Tel: 01733 371999
Fax: 01733 370585

Reed Books Direct,
43 Stapledon Road, Orton Southgate,
Peterborough PE2 6TD

⌂ Ordnance Survey
MOTORING ATLAS
Updated annually
Britain

The best-selling *OS Motoring Atlas Britain* uses unrivalled and up-to-date mapping from the Ordnance Survey digital database. The exceptionally clear mapping is at a large scale of 3 miles to 1 inch (Orkney/Shetland Islands at 5 miles to 1 inch).

A special feature of the atlas is its wealth of tourist and leisure information. It includes a comprehensive directory of National Trust properties in England, Wales and Scotland, and a useful diary of British Tourist Authority Events listing over 300 days out around Britain during the year. From autumn 1997, it features a new section detailing historic English Heritage properties throughout the country.

Available from all good bookshops or, direct from the publisher:
Tel: 01733 371999

The atlas includes:
- **112 pages of fully updated mapping**
- **45 city and town plans**
- **8 extra-detailed city approach maps**
- **route-planning maps**
- **restricted motorway junctions**
- **local radio information**
- **distances chart**
- **a county boundaries map**
- **multi-language legend**